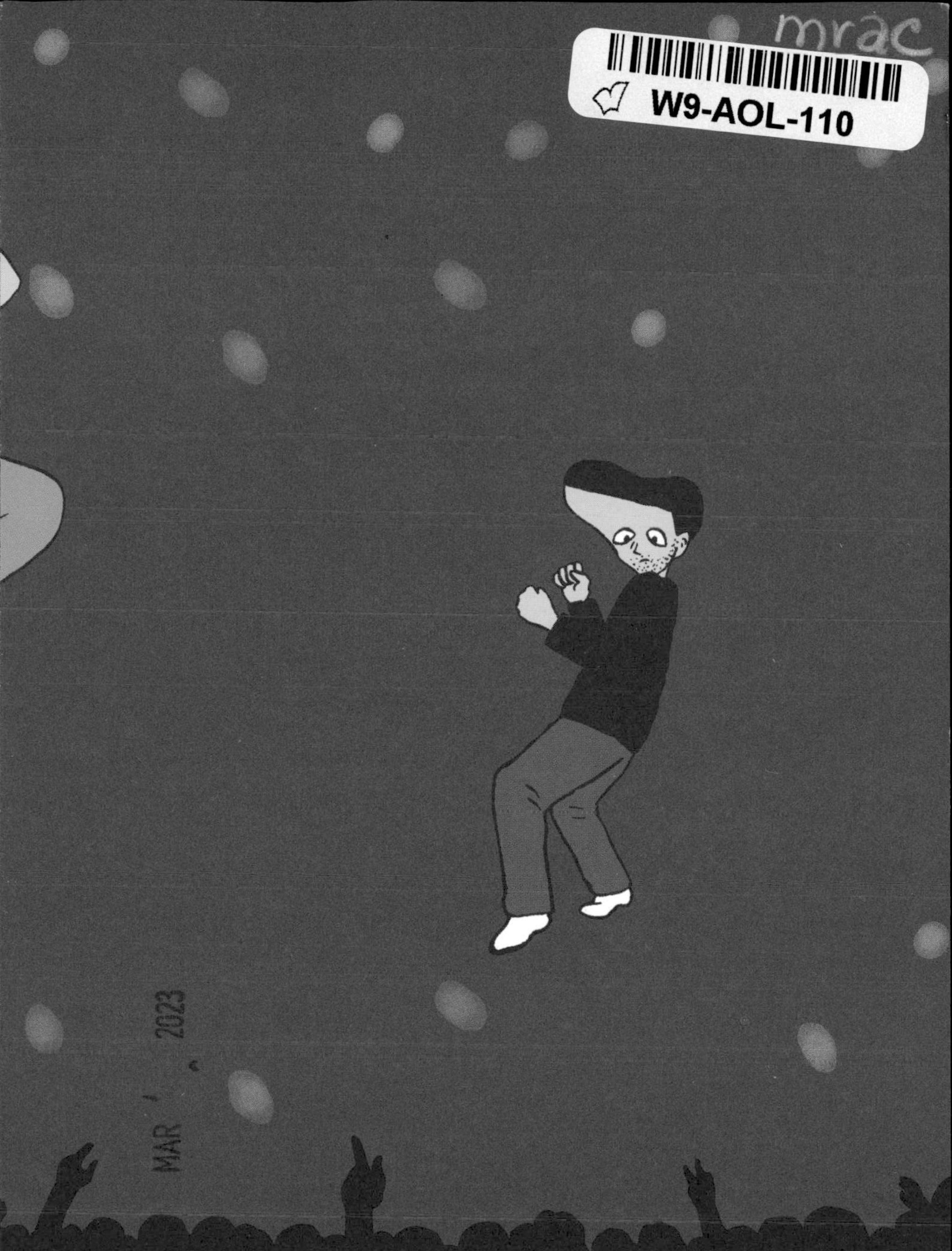

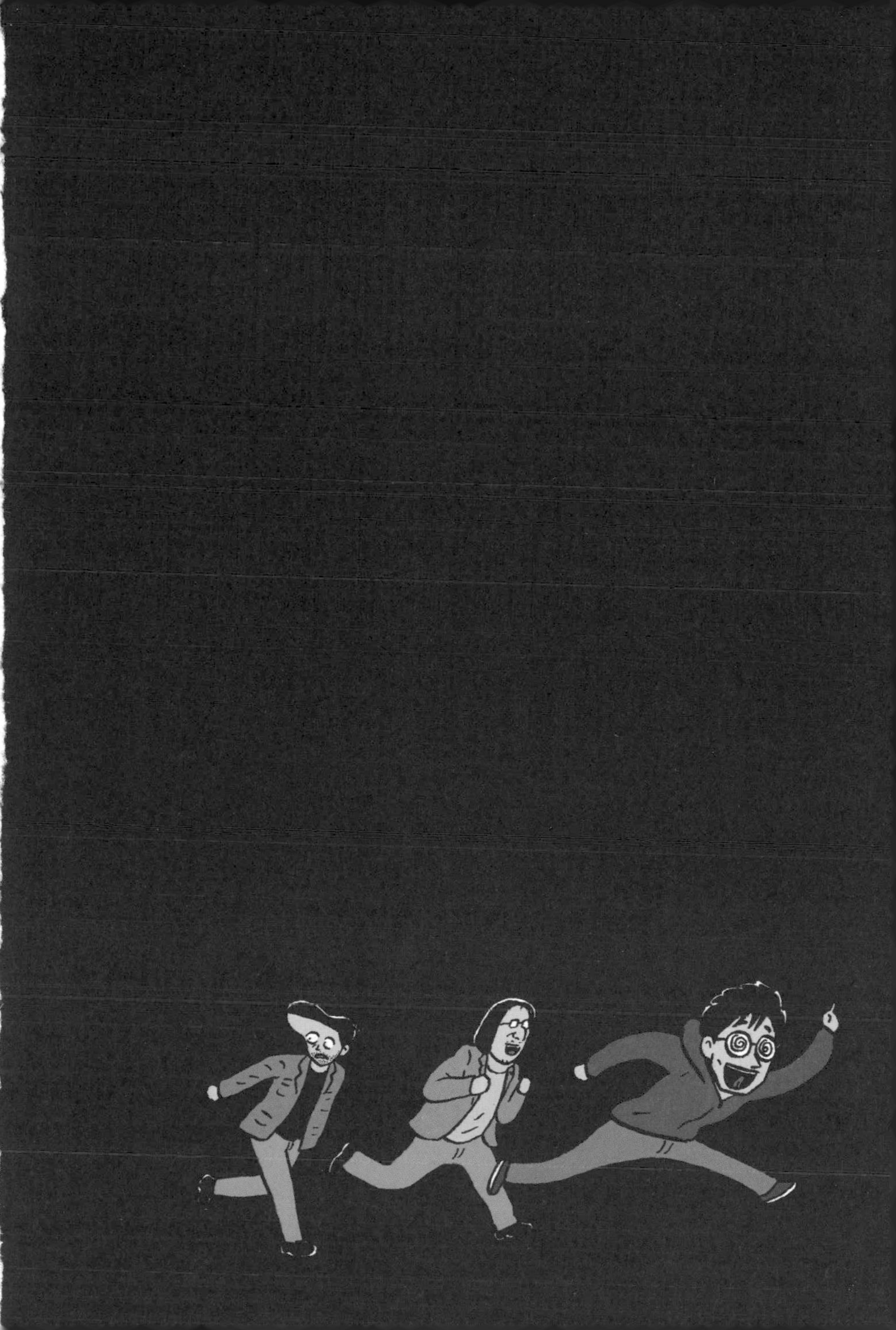

ARTIST

yeong-shin ma

drawn & quarterly

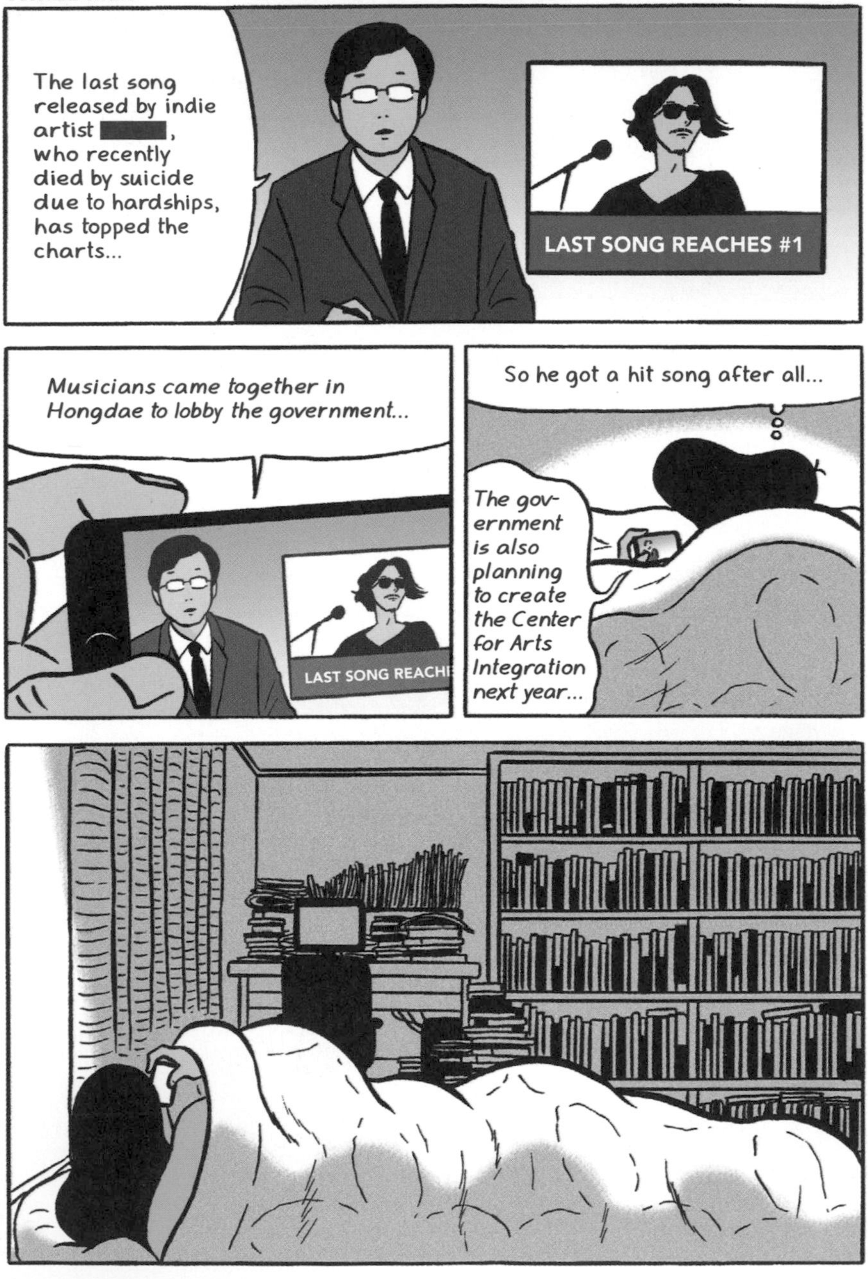

The last song released by indie artist [redacted], who recently died by suicide due to hardships, has topped the charts...
LAST SONG REACHES #1
Musicians came together in Hongdae to lobby the government...
So he got a hit song after all...
The government is also planning to create the Center for Arts Integration next year...

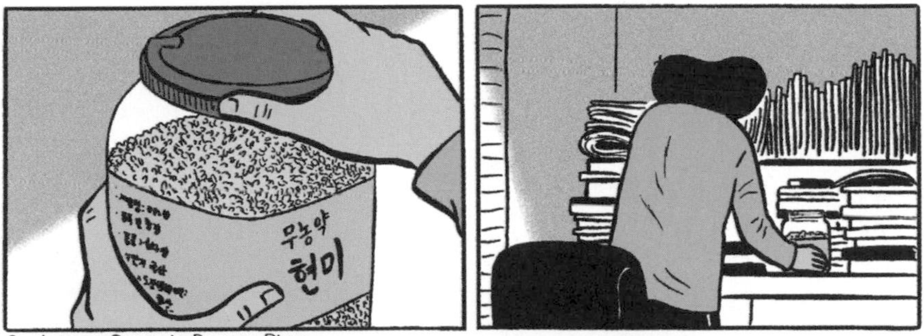
무농약
현미

Container: Organic Brown Rice

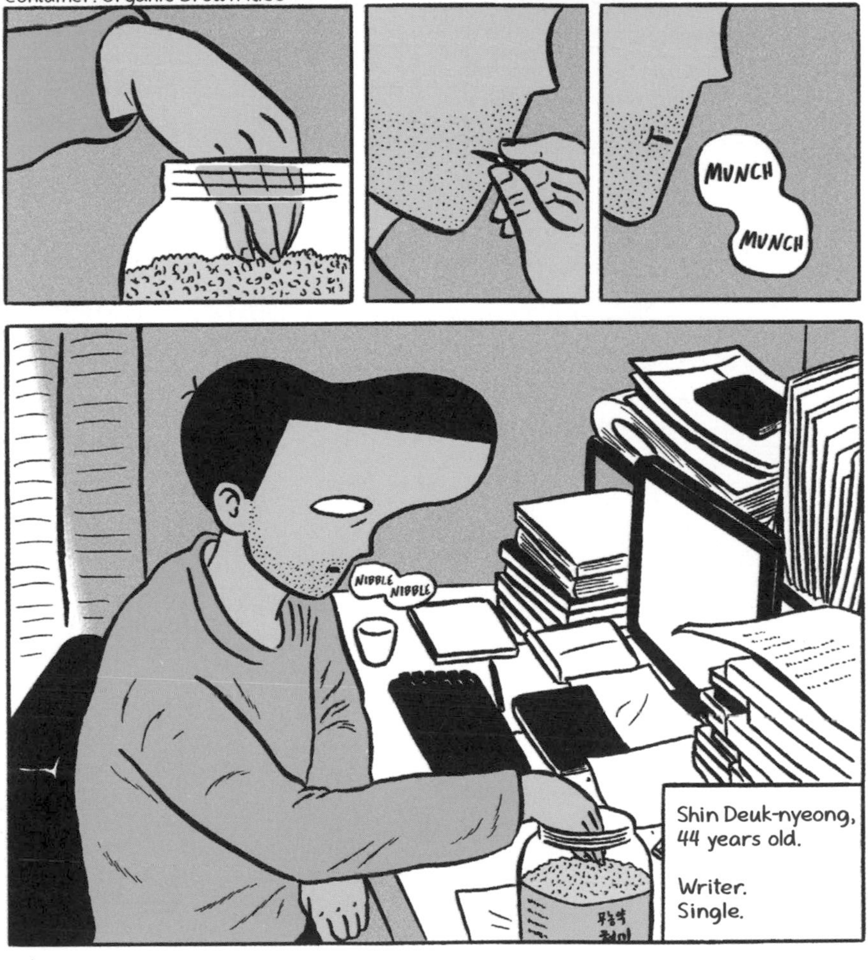
MUNCH
MUNCH
NIBBLE
NIBBLE
Shin Deuk-nyeong,
44 years old.
Writer.
Single.
무농약
현미

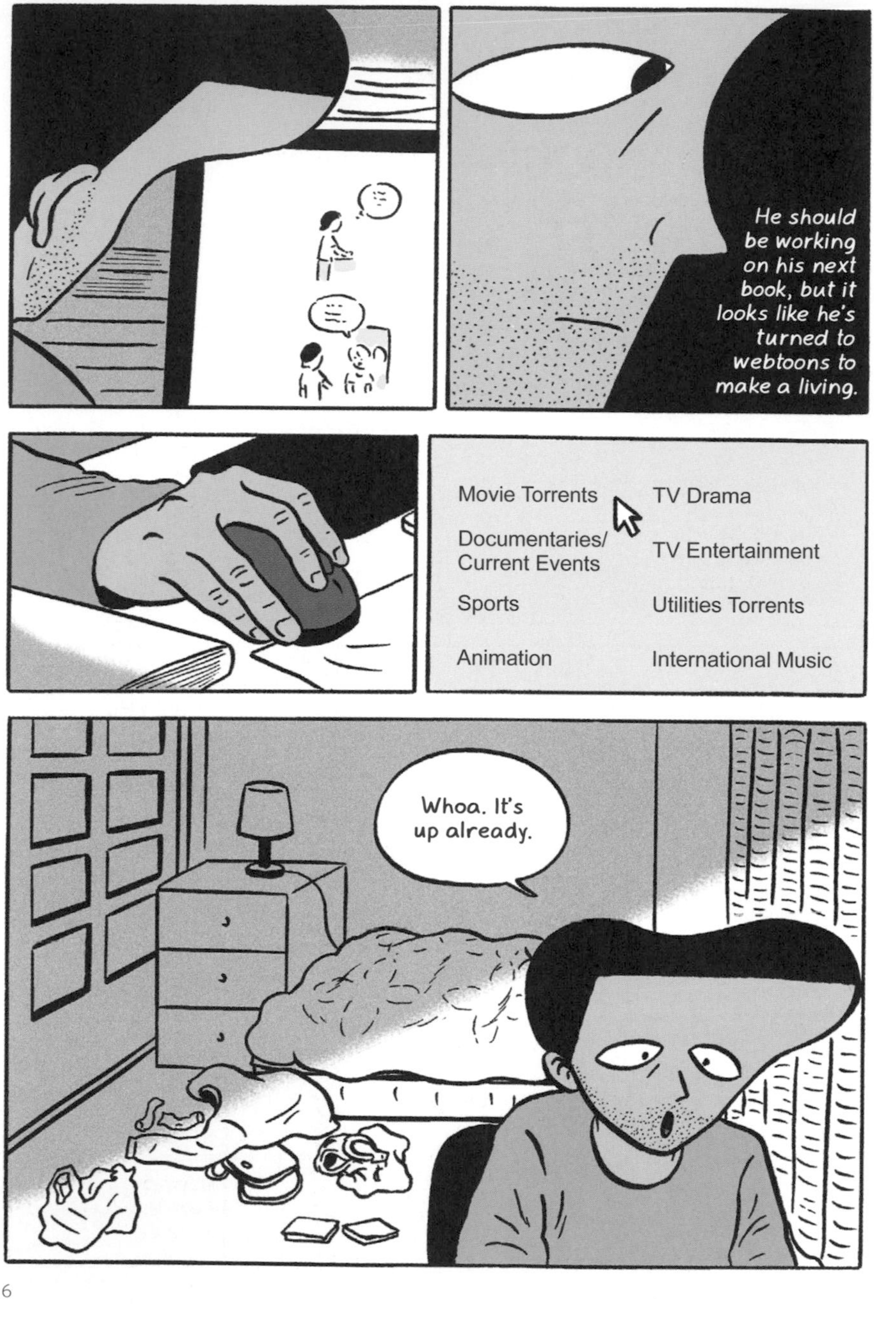
He should be working on his next book, but it looks like he's turned to webtoons to make a living.
Movie Torrents
TV Drama
Documentaries/ Current Events
TV Entertainment
Sports
Utilities Torrents
Animation
International Music
Whoa. It's up already.

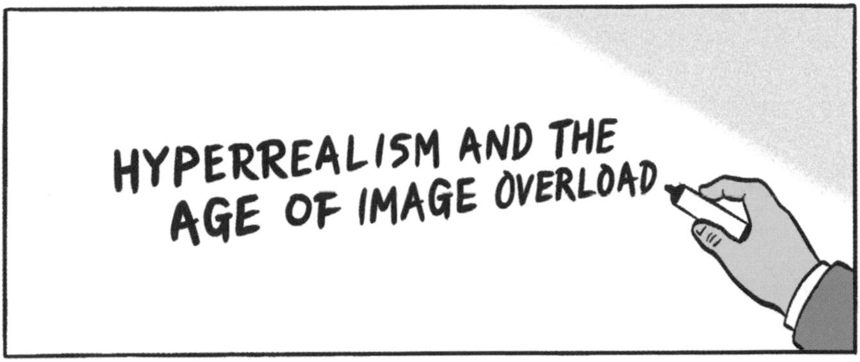
HYPERREALISM AND THE AGE OF IMAGE OVERLOAD

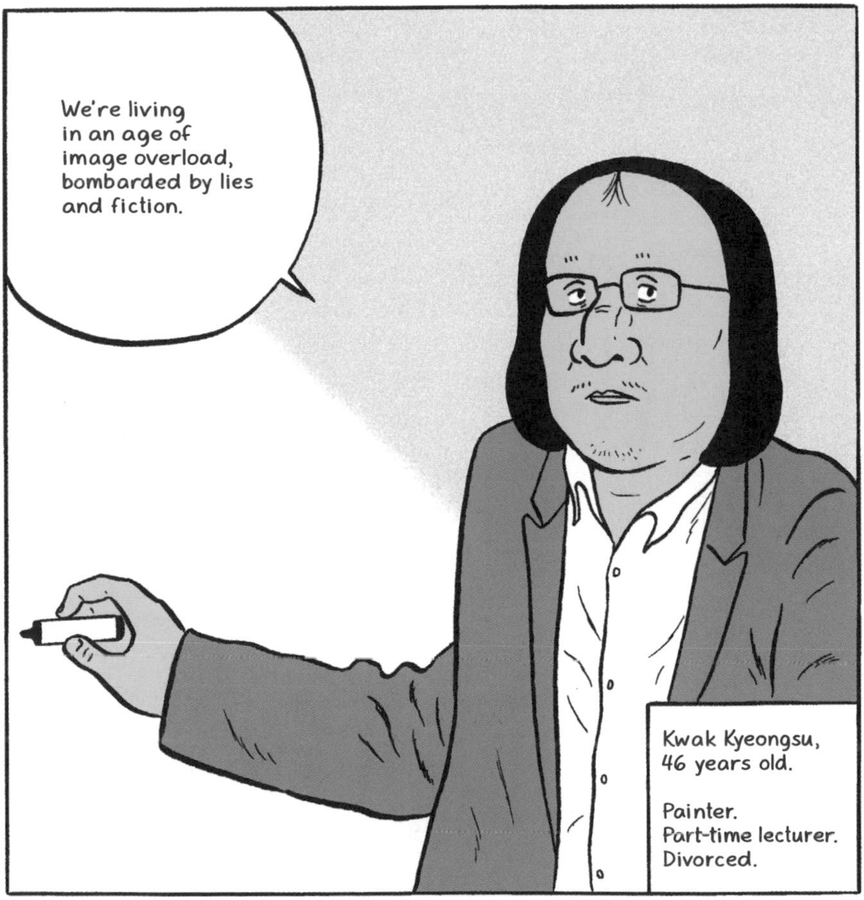
We're living in an age of image overload, bombarded by lies and fiction.
Kwak Kyeongsu, 46 years old.
Painter. Part-time lecturer. Divorced.

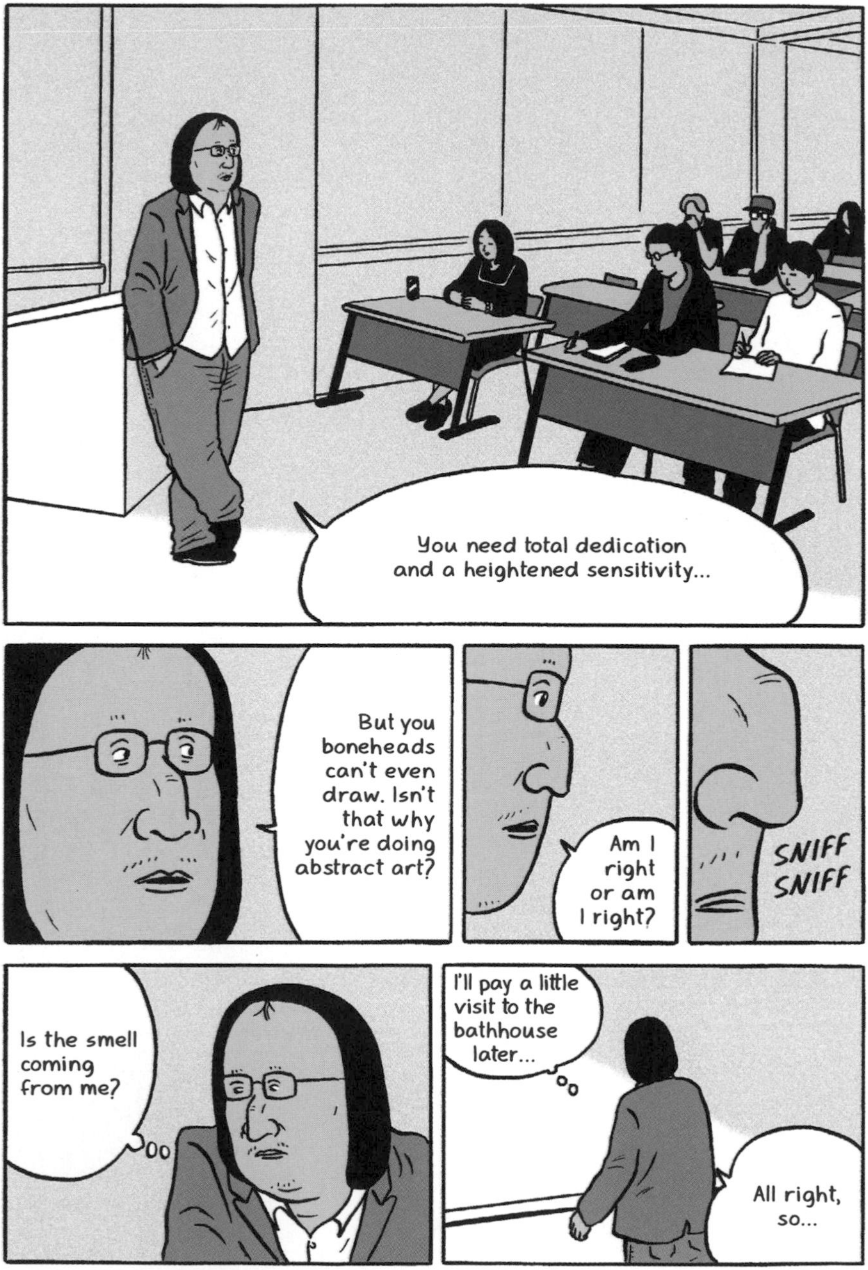
You need total dedication and a heightened sensitivity...
But you boneheads can't even draw. Isn't that why you're doing abstract art?
Am I right or am I right?
SNIFF SNIFF
Is the smell coming from me?
I'll pay a little visit to the bathhouse later...
All right, so...

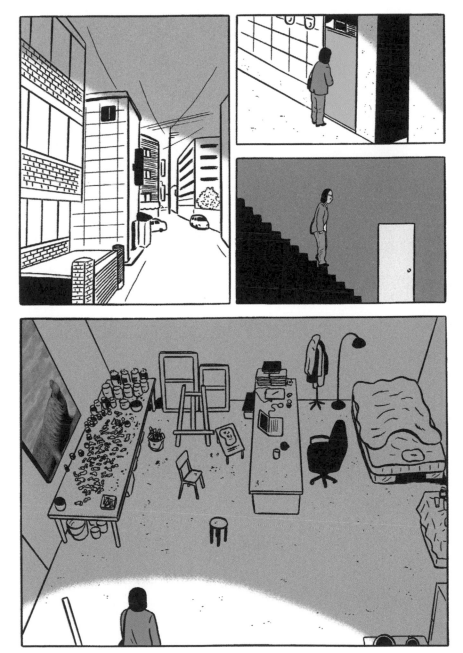

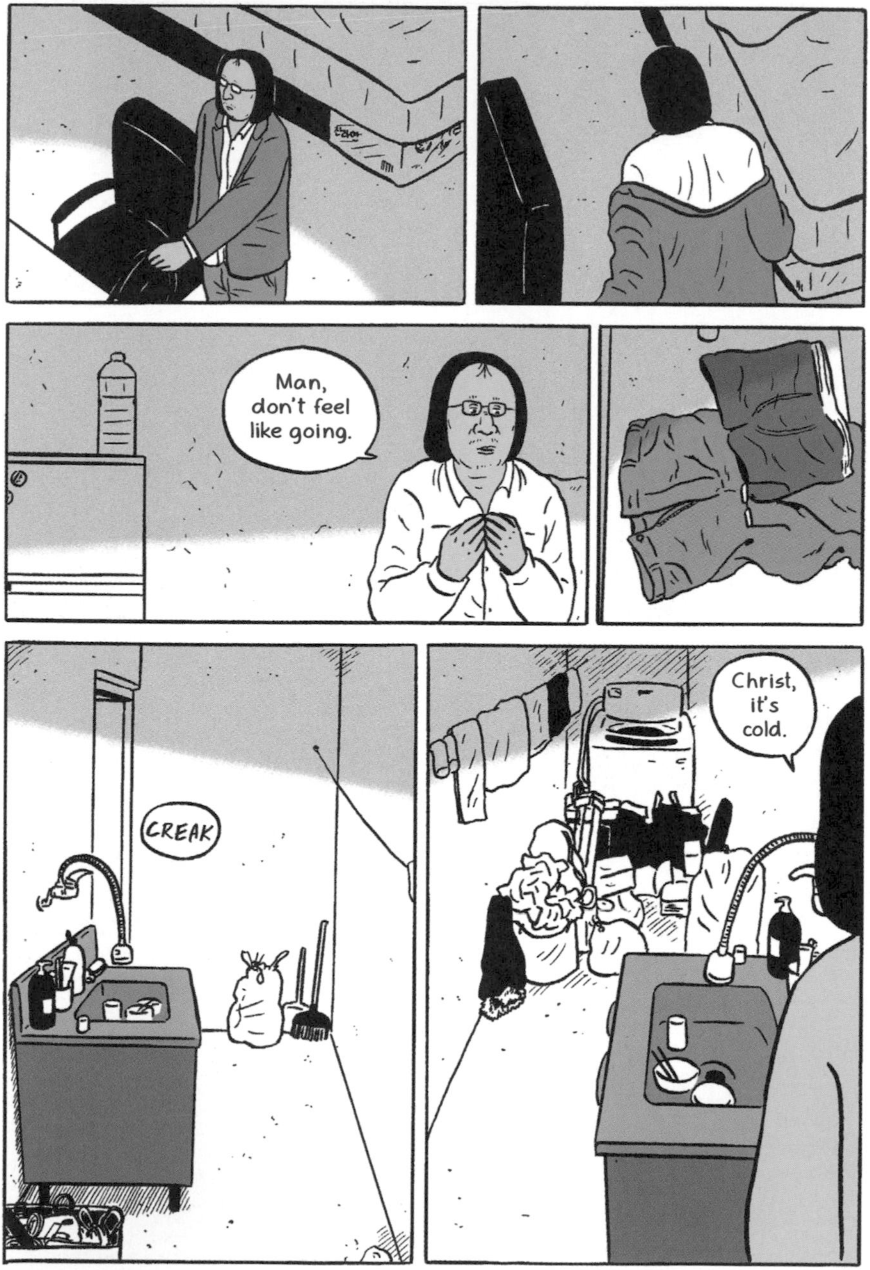
Man, don't feel like going.
CREAK
Christ, it's cold.

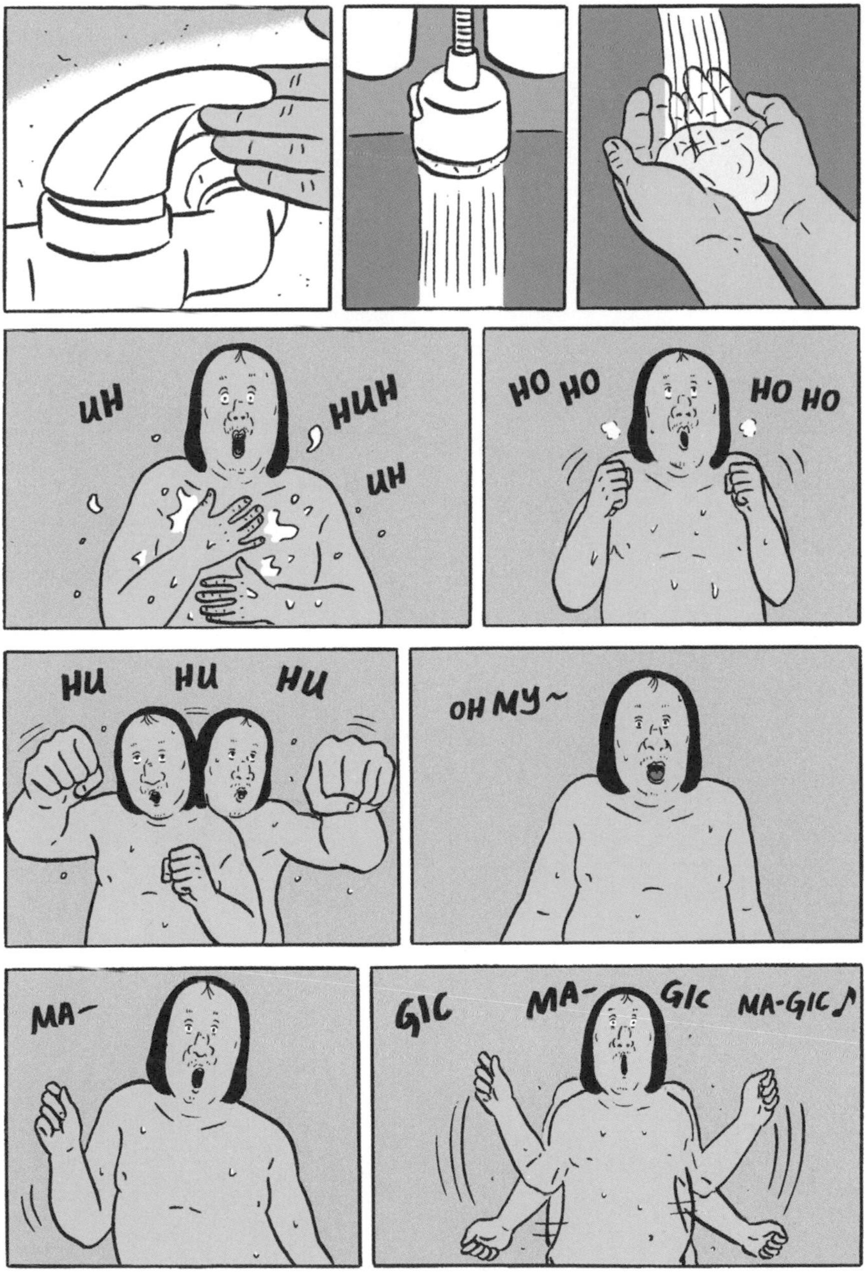
UH
HUH
UH
HO HO
HO HO
HU HU HU
OH MY~
MA-
GIC
MA-
GIC
MA-GIC♪

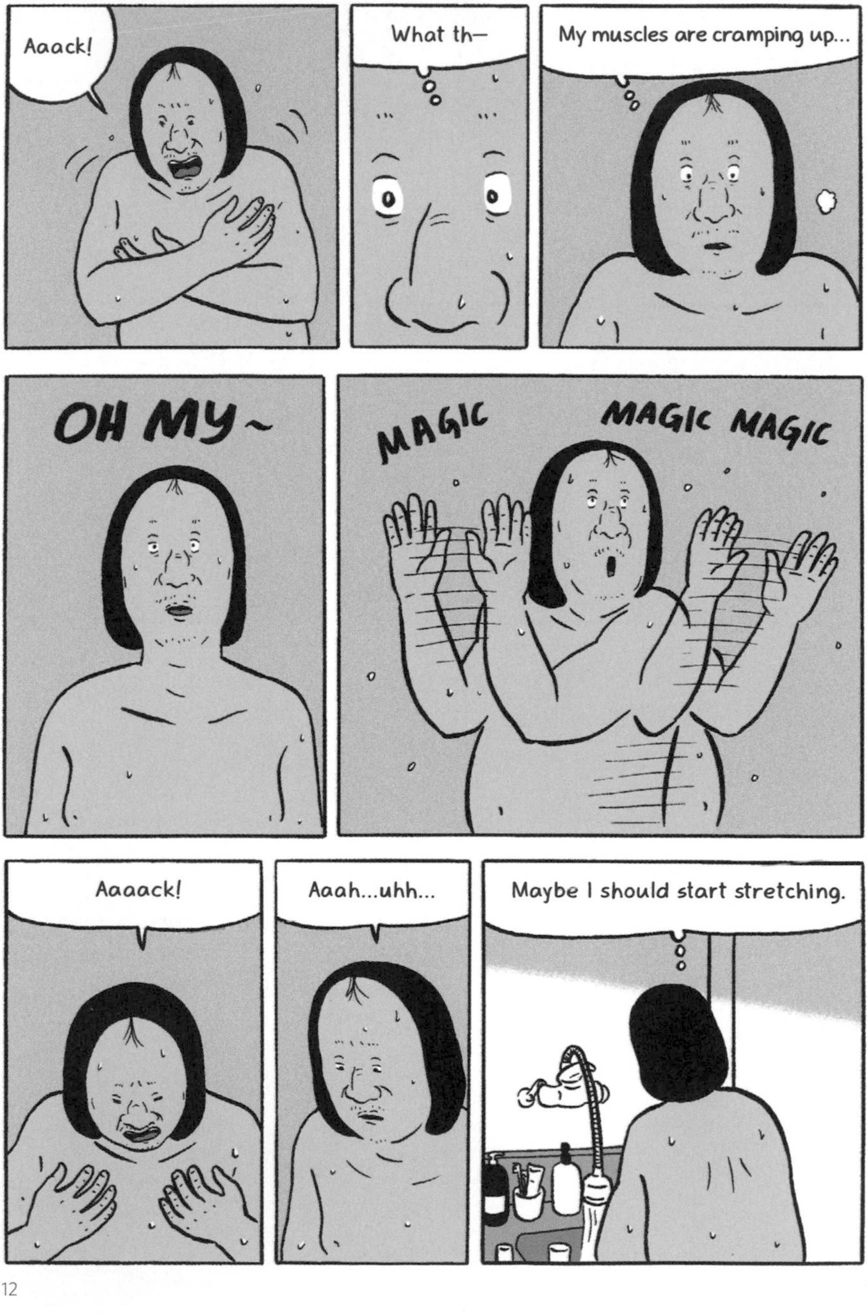
Aaack!
What th–
My muscles are cramping up...
OH MY~
MAGIC
MAGIC MAGIC
Aaaack!
Aaah...uhh...
Maybe I should start stretching.

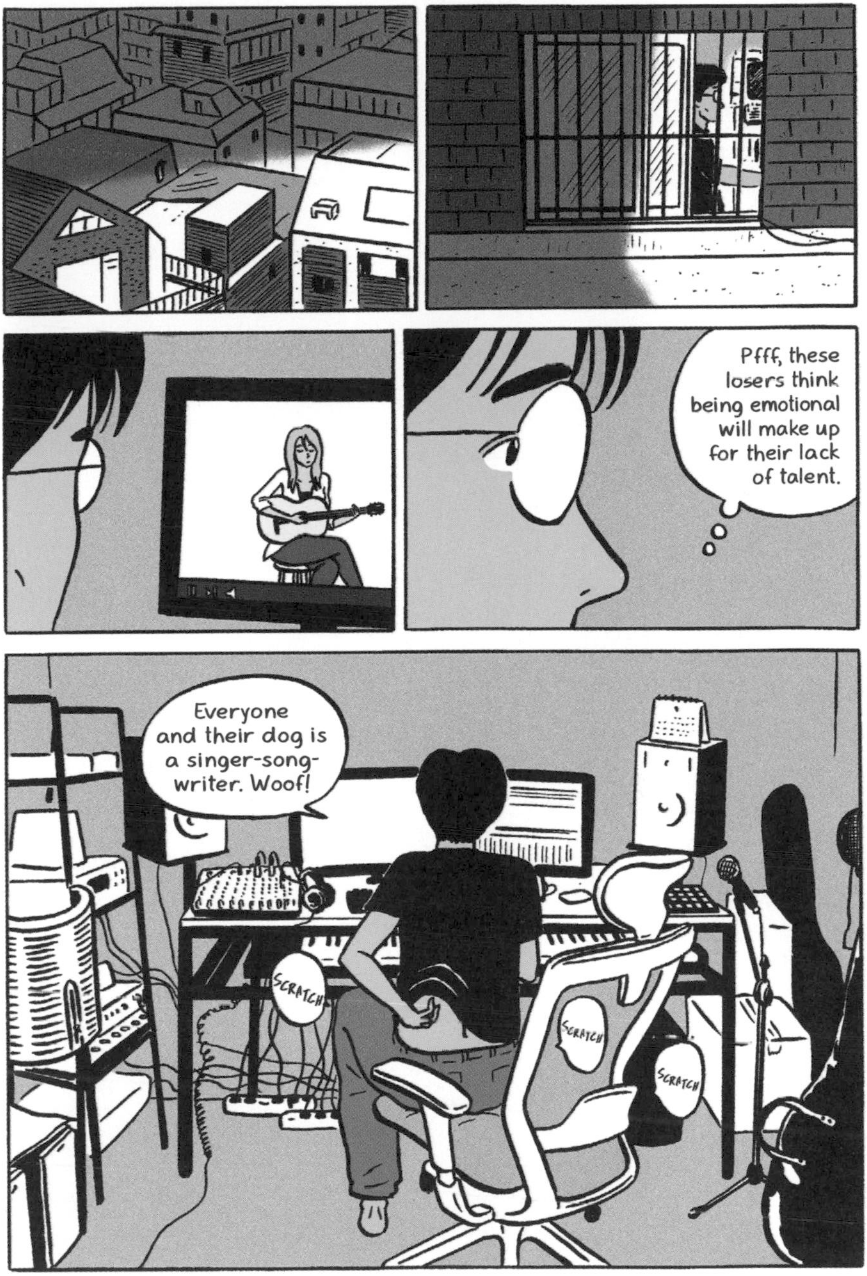
Pfff, these losers think being emotional will make up for their lack of talent.
Everyone and their dog is a singer-song-writer. Woof!
SCRATCH
SCRATCH
SCRATCH

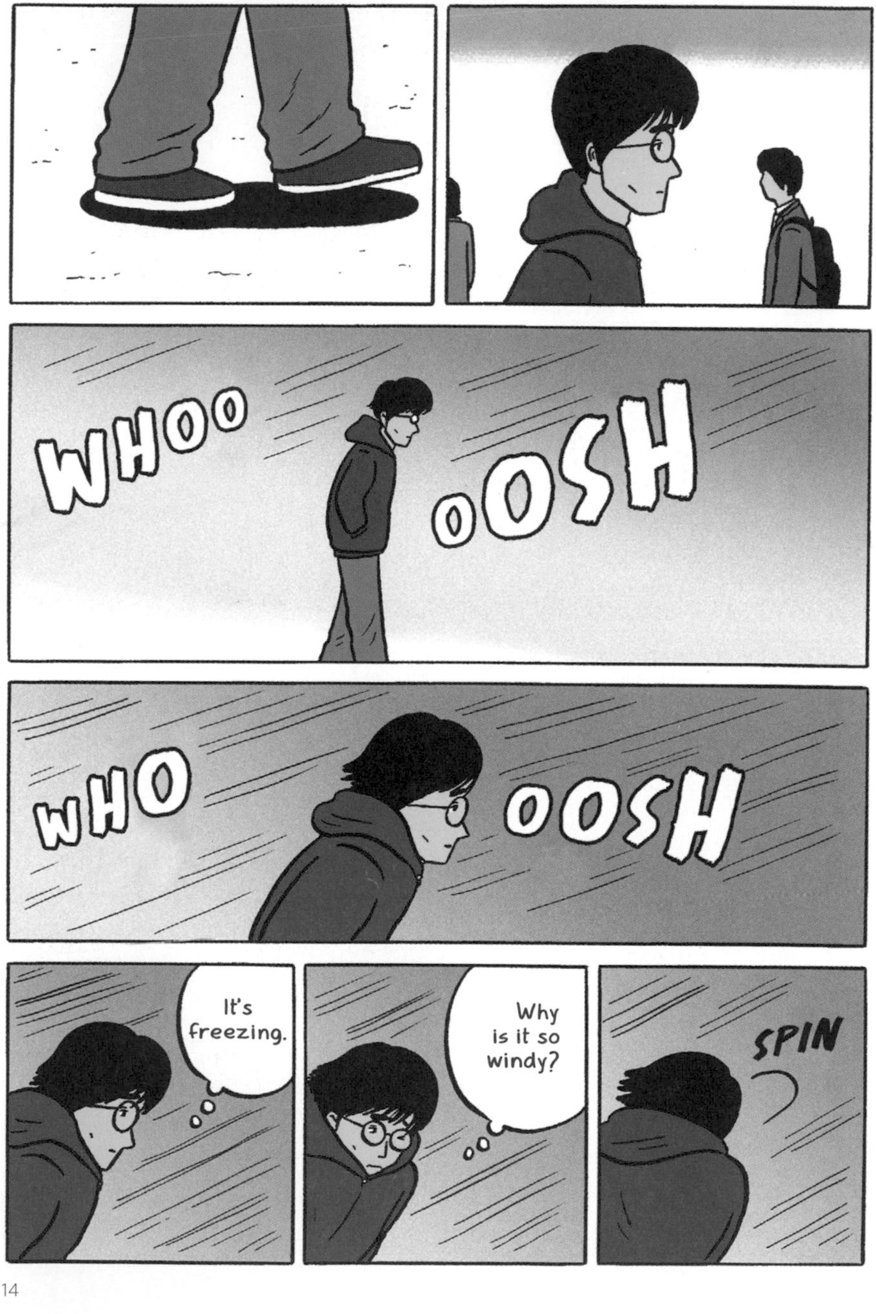
WHOO
OOSH
WHO
OOSH
It's freezing.
Why is it so windy?
SPIN

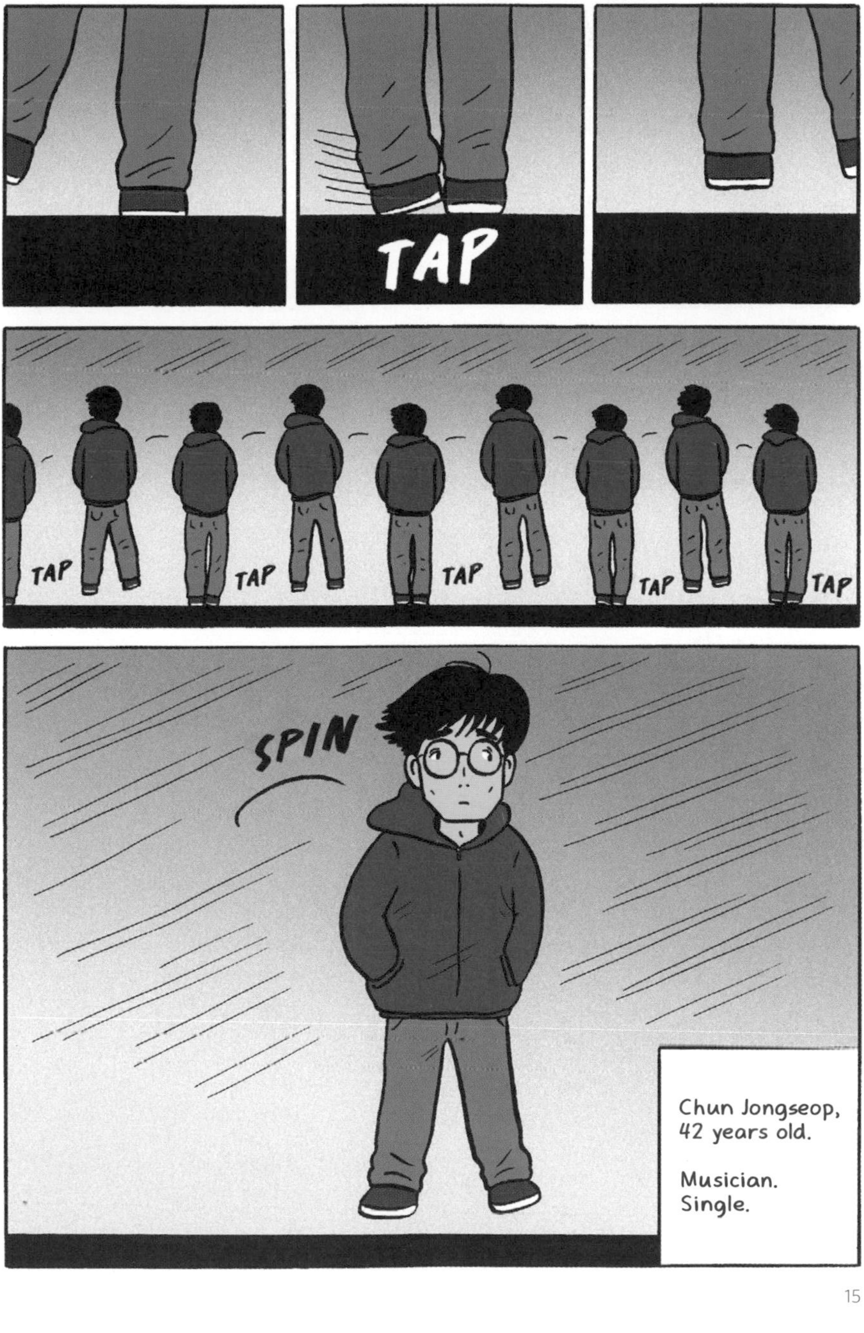
TAP
TAP
TAP
TAP
TAP
TAP
SPIN
Chun Jongseop,
42 years old.
Musician.
Single.

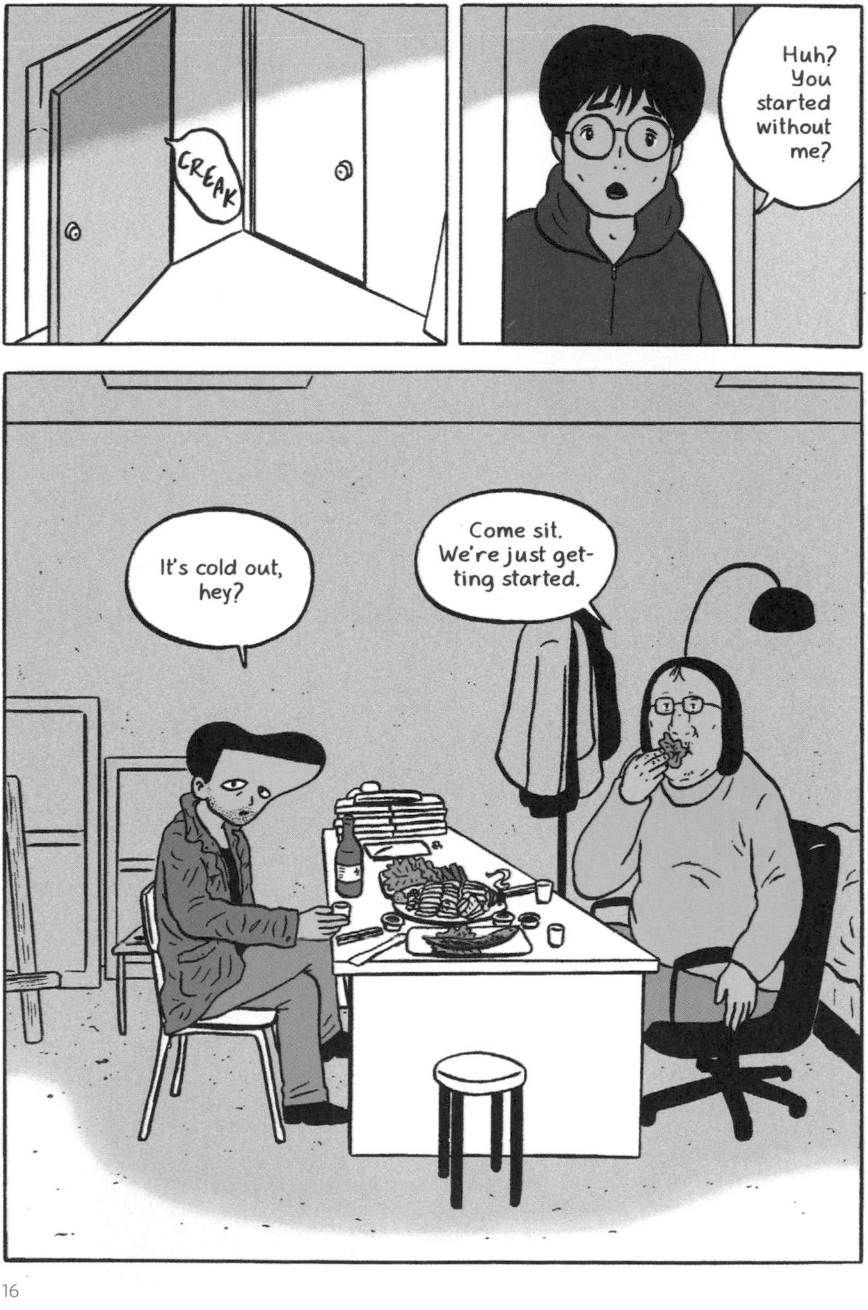
CREAK
Huh? You started without me?
It's cold out, hey?
Come sit. We're just getting started.

DRINKING PARTY

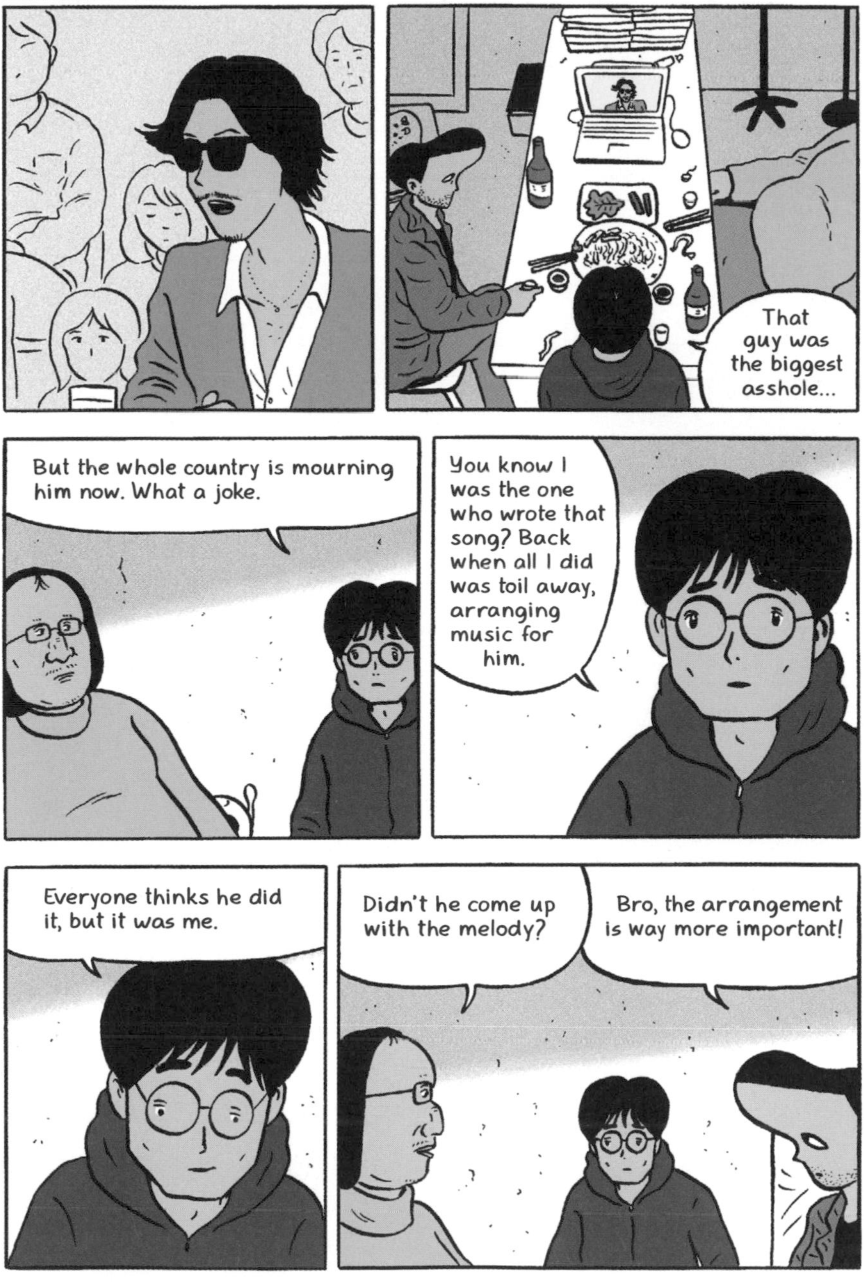
That guy was the biggest asshole...
But the whole country is mourning him now. What a joke.
You know I was the one who wrote that song? Back when all I did was toil away, arranging music for him.
Everyone thinks he did it, but it was me.
Didn't he come up with the melody?
Bro, the arrangement is way more important!

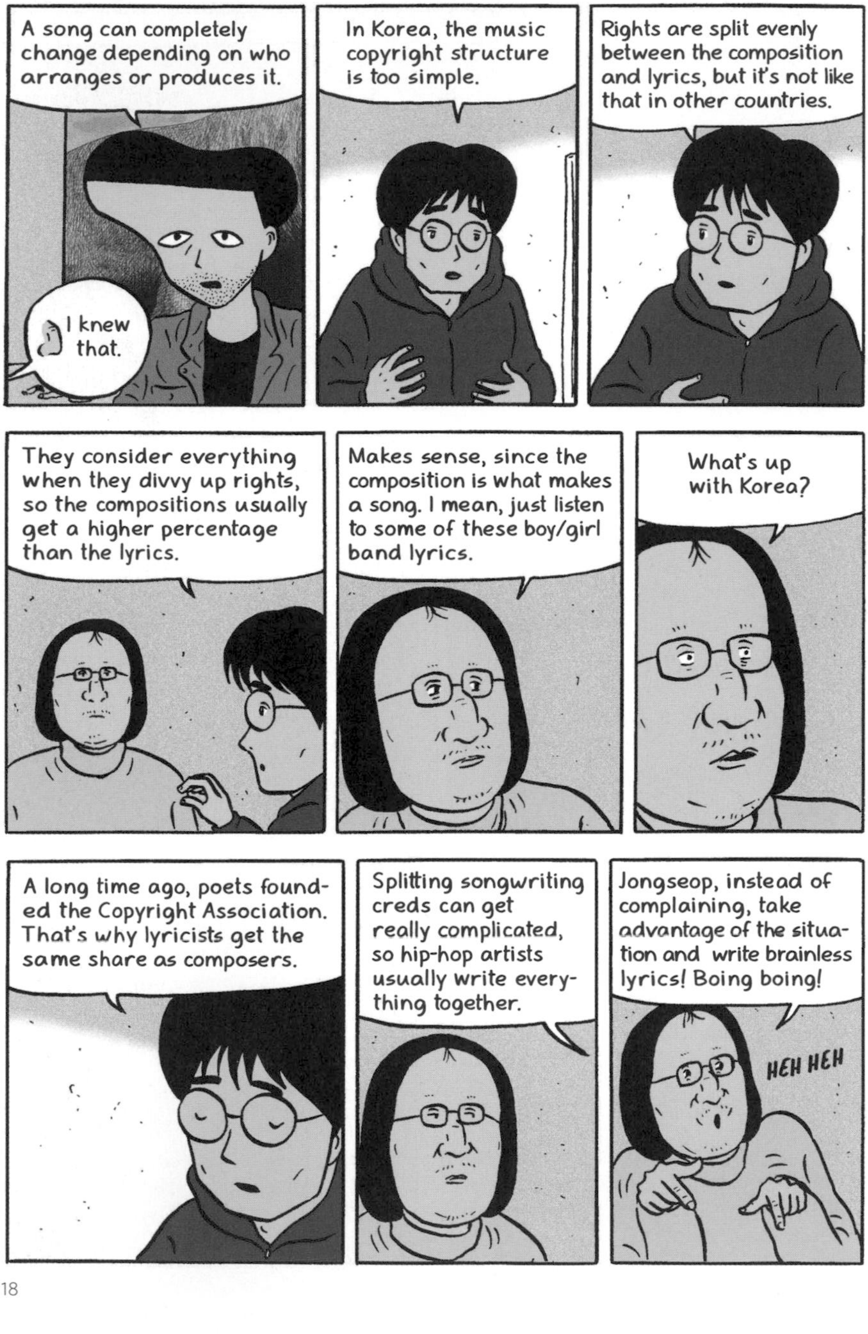
A song can completely change depending on who arranges or produces it.
I knew that.
In Korea, the music copyright structure is too simple.
Rights are split evenly between the composition and lyrics, but it's not like that in other countries.
They consider everything when they divvy up rights, so the compositions usually get a higher percentage than the lyrics.
Makes sense, since the composition is what makes a song. I mean, just listen to some of these boy/girl band lyrics.
What's up with Korea?
A long time ago, poets founded the Copyright Association. That's why lyricists get the same share as composers.
Splitting songwriting creds can get really complicated, so hip-hop artists usually write everything together.
Jongseop, instead of complaining, take advantage of the situation and write brainless lyrics! Boing boing!
HEH HEH

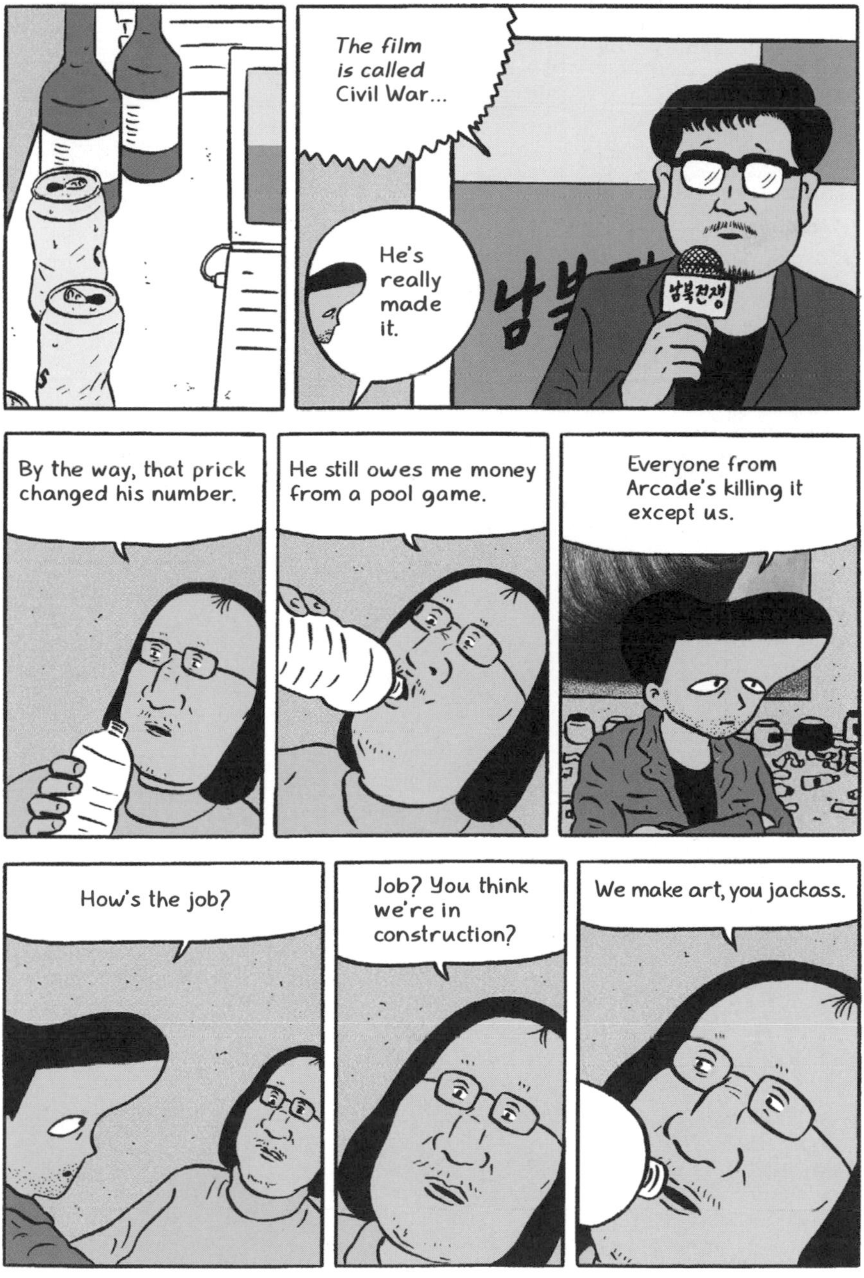
The film is called Civil War...
He's really made it.
남북
남북전쟁
By the way, that prick changed his number.
He still owes me money from a pool game.
Everyone from Arcade's killing it except us.
How's the job?
Job? You think we're in construction?
We make art, you jackass.

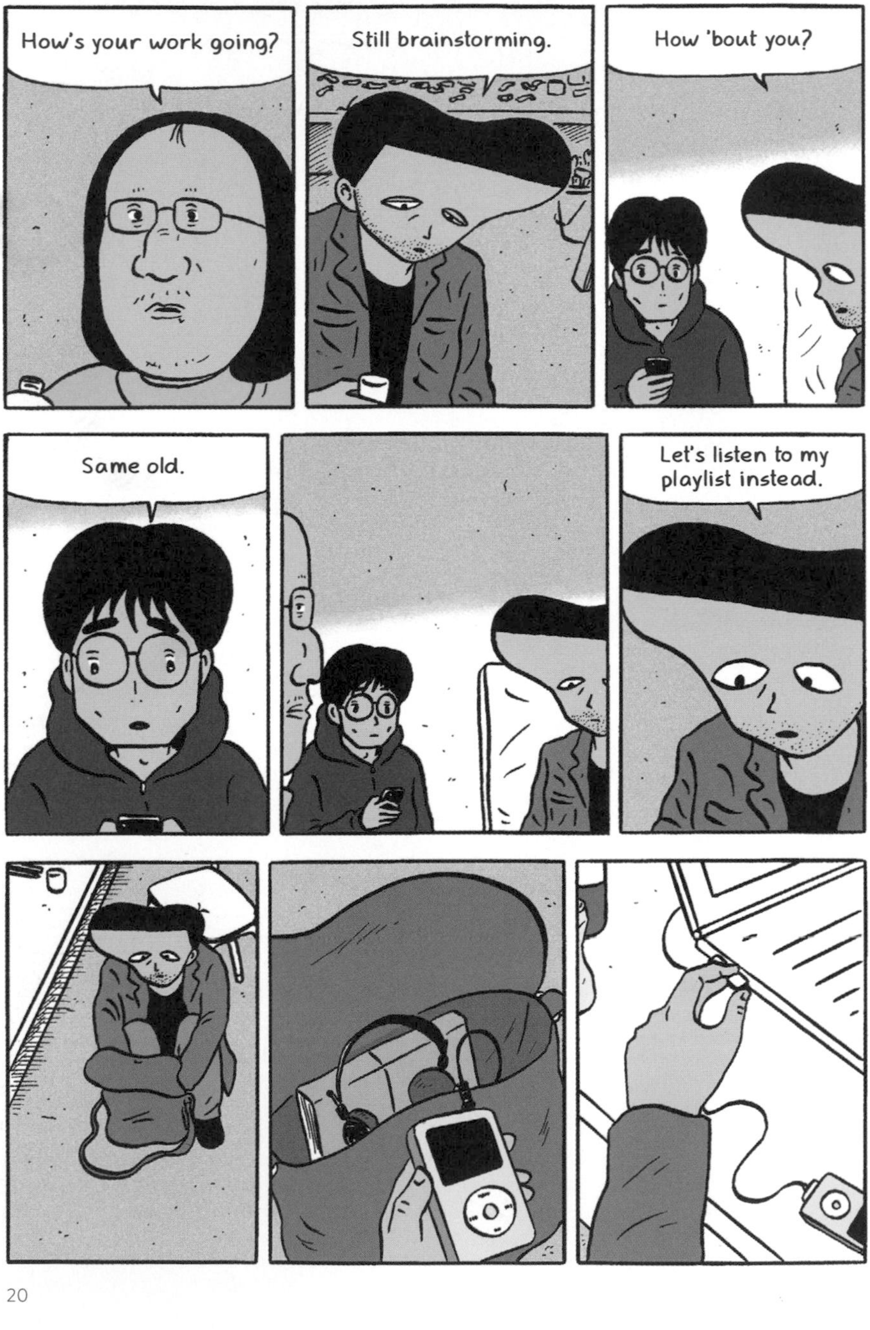
How's your work going?
Still brainstorming.
How 'bout you?
Same old.
Let's listen to my playlist instead.

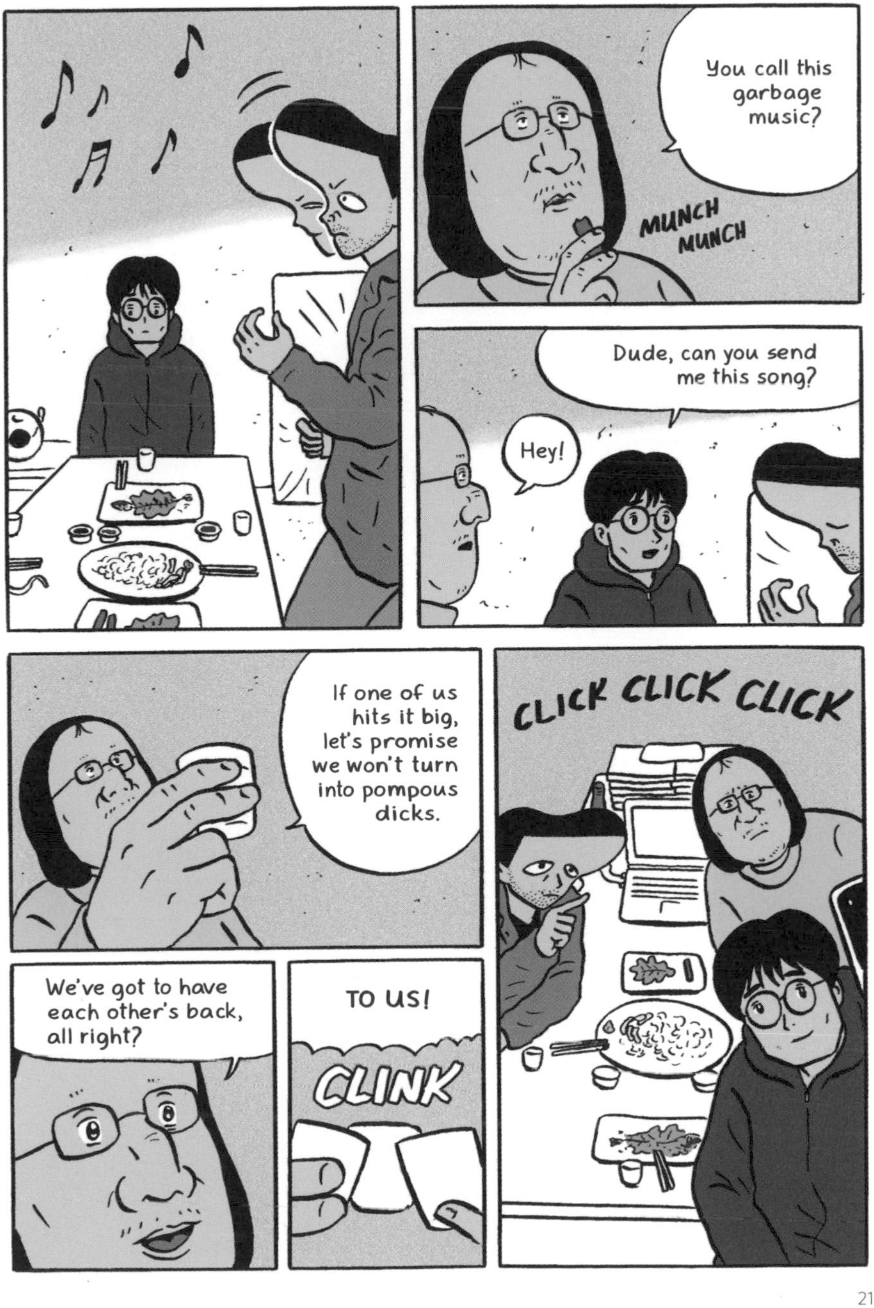
You call this garbage music?
MUNCH MUNCH
Dude, can you send me this song?
Hey!
If one of us hits it big, let's promise we won't turn into pompous dicks.
CLICK CLICK CLICK
We've got to have each other's back, all right?
TO US!
CLINK

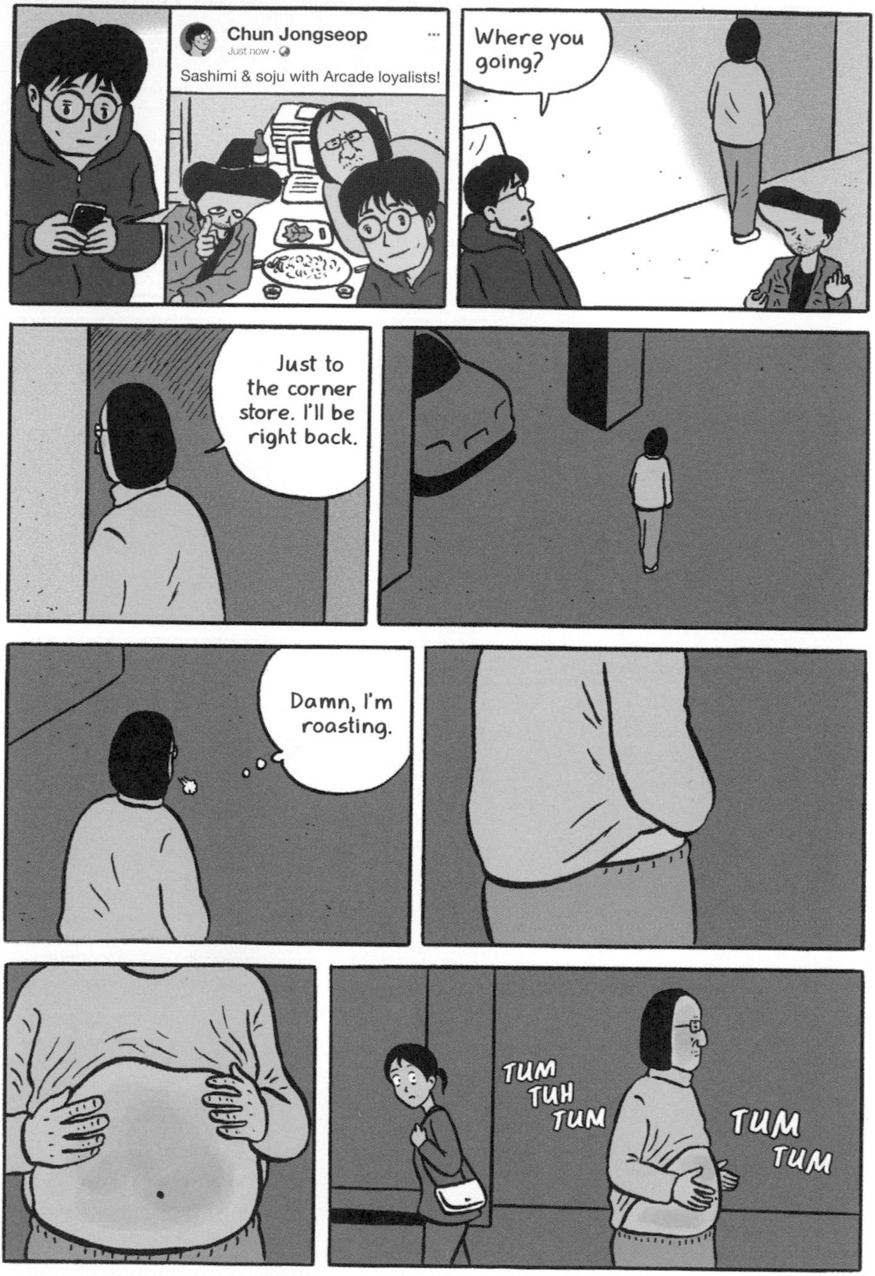
Chun Jongseop
Just now ·
Sashimi & soju with Arcade loyalists!
Where you going?
Just to the corner store. I'll be right back.
Damn, I'm roasting.
TUM TUH TUM
TUM TUM

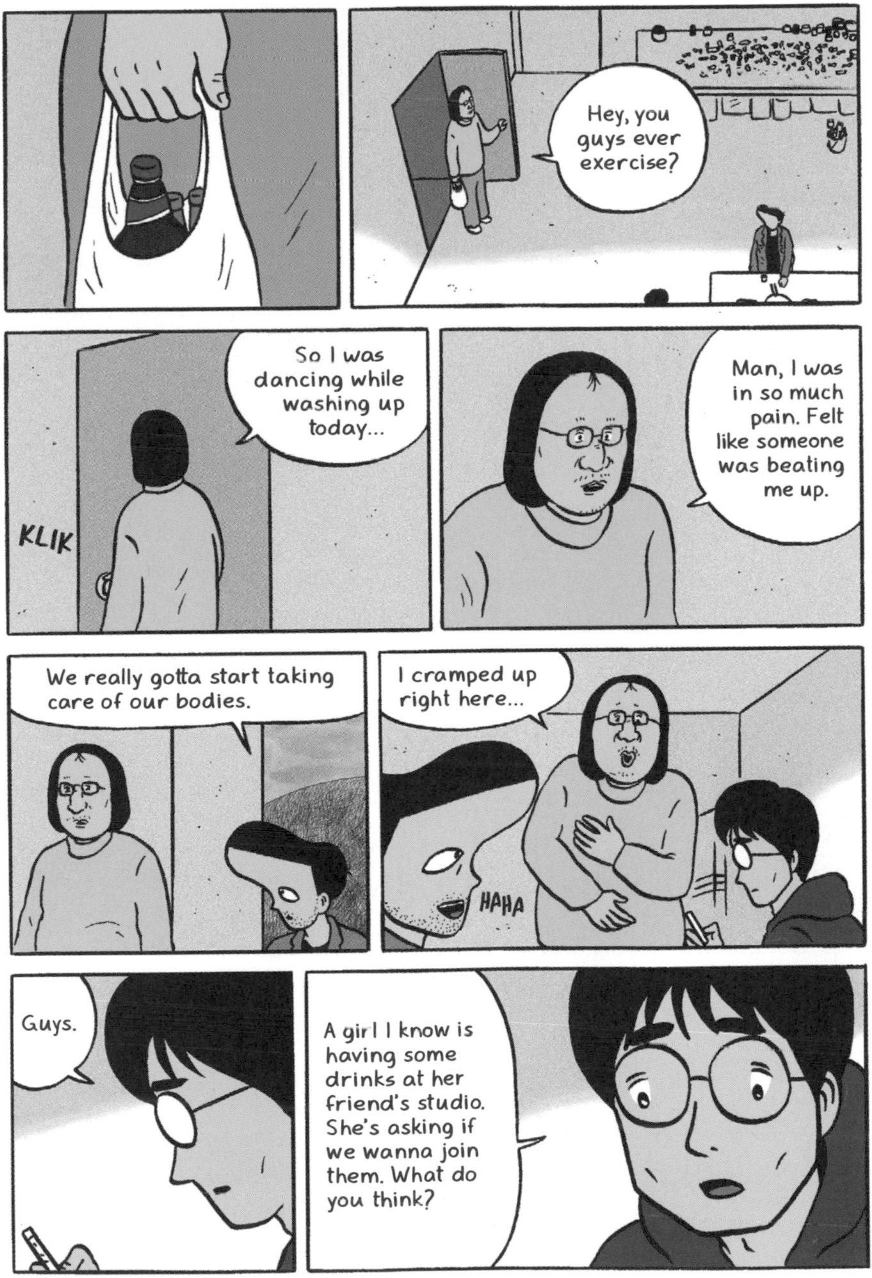
Hey, you guys ever exercise?
So I was dancing while washing up today...
KLIK
Man, I was in so much pain. Felt like someone was beating me up.
We really gotta start taking care of our bodies.
I cramped up right here...
HAHA
Guys.
A girl I know is having some drinks at her friend's studio. She's asking if we wanna join them. What do you think?

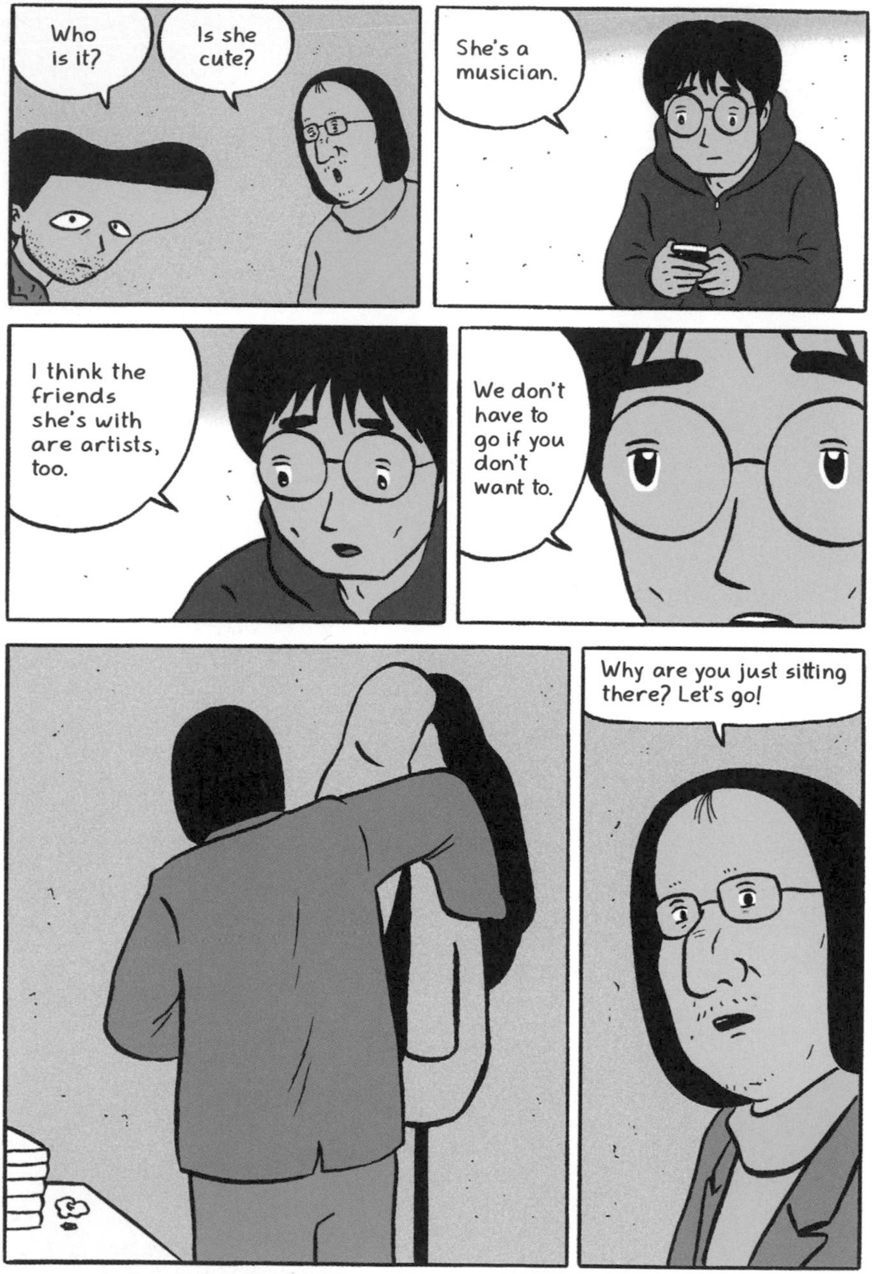
Who is it?
Is she cute?
She's a musician.
I think the friends she's with are artists, too.
We don't have to go if you don't want to.
Why are you just sitting there? Let's go!

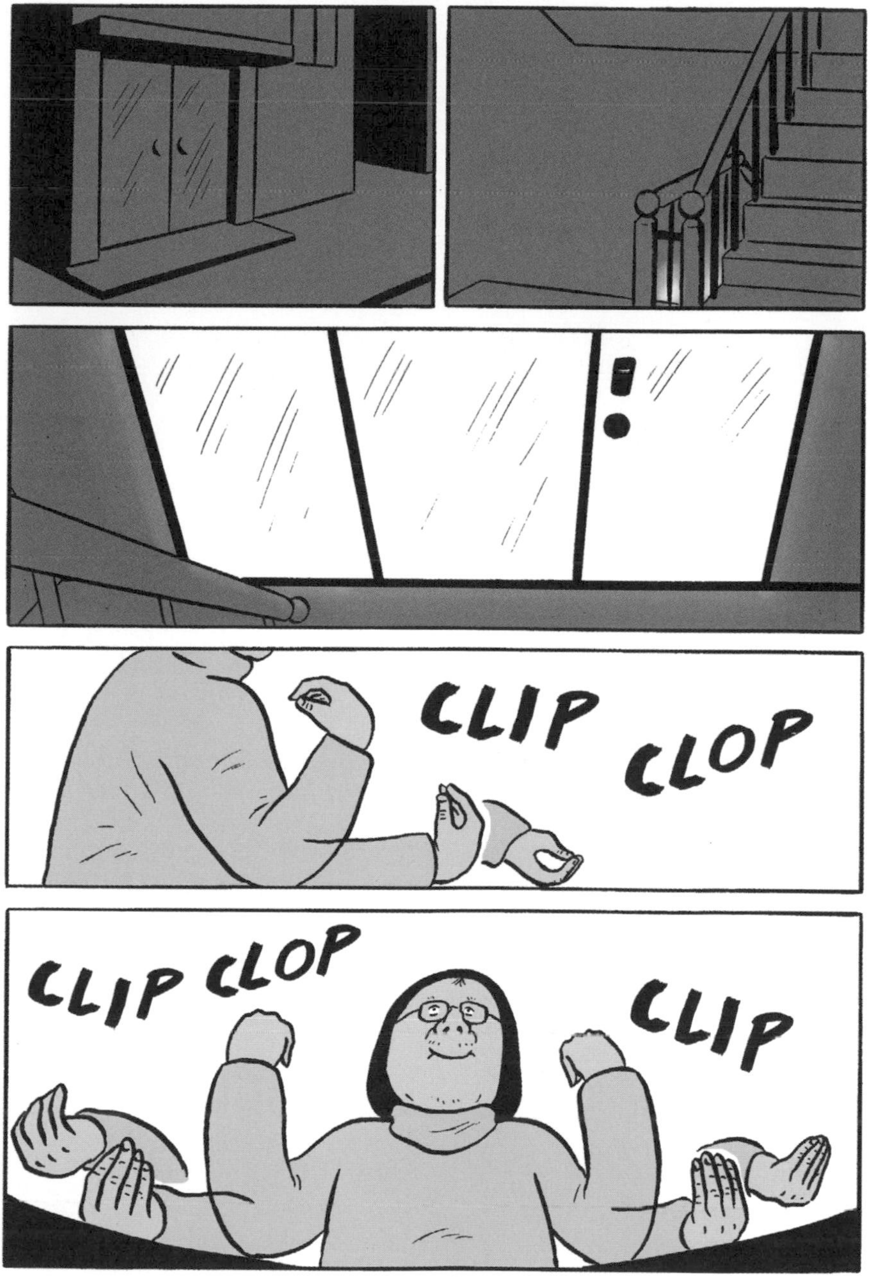
CLIP
CLOP
CLIP CLOP
CLIP

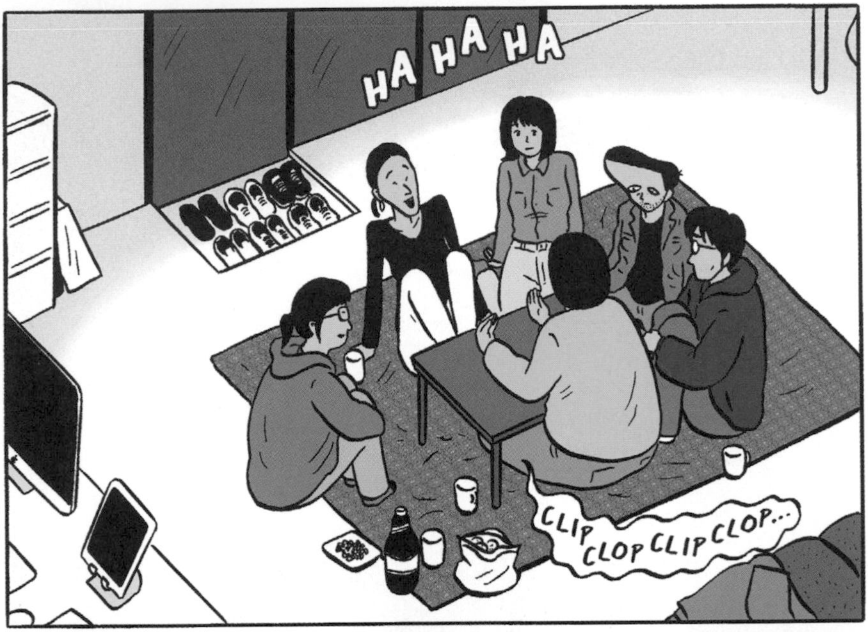
HA HA HA HA
CLIP CLOP CLIP CLOP...

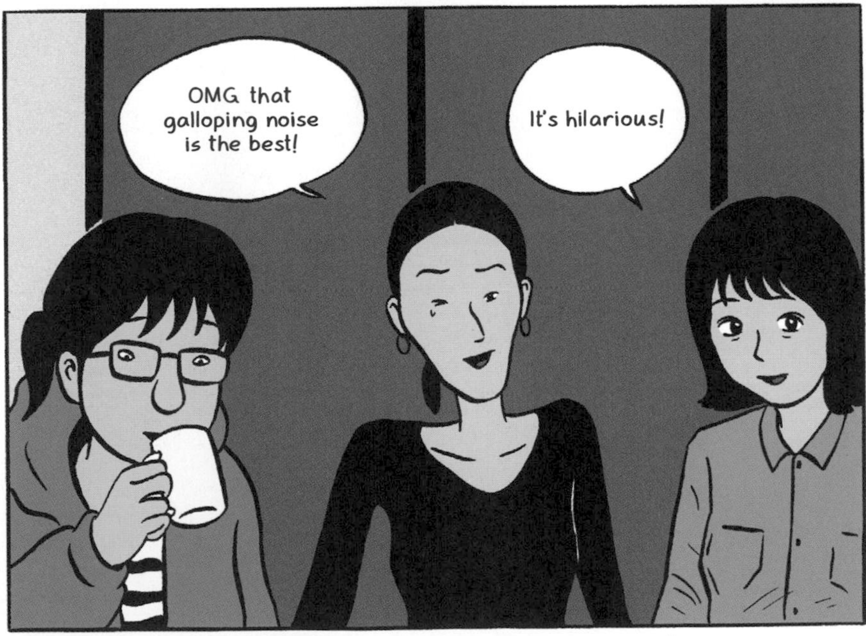
OMG that galloping noise is the best!
It's hilarious!

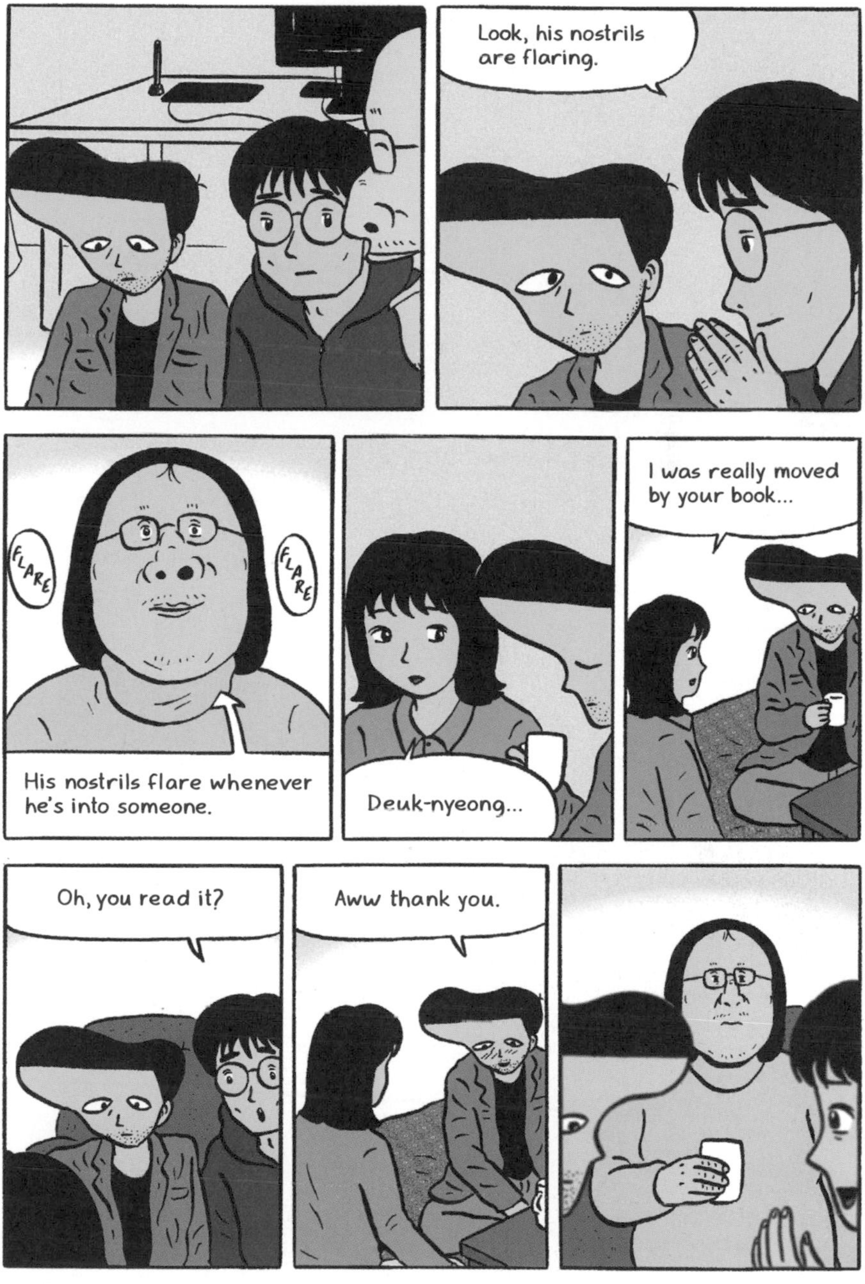
Look, his nostrils are flaring.
FLARE
FLARE
His nostrils flare whenever he's into someone.
Deuk-nyeong...
I was really moved by your book...
Oh, you read it?
Aww thank you.

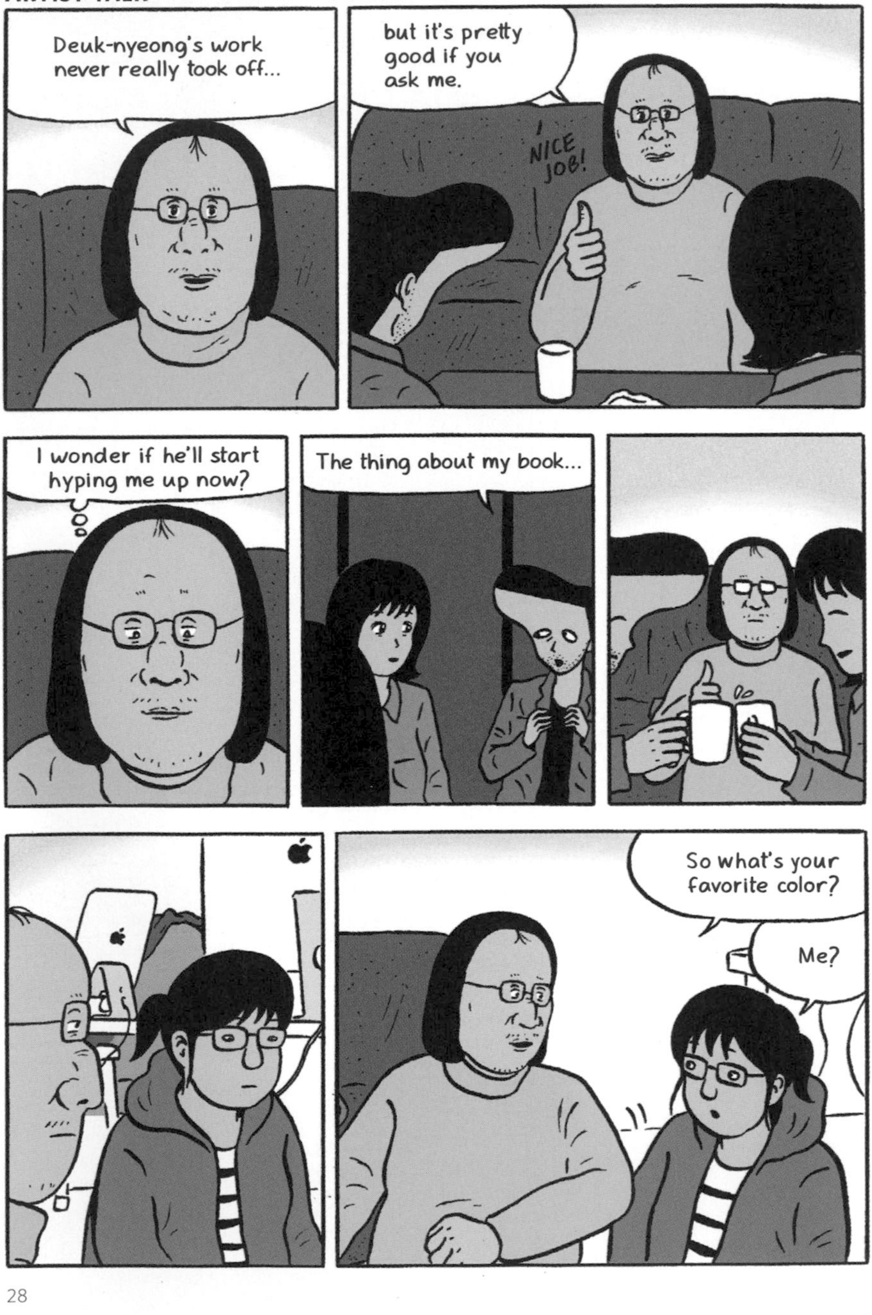
Deuk-nyeong's work never really took off...
but it's pretty good if you ask me.
NICE JOB!
I wonder if he'll start hyping me up now?
The thing about my book...
So what's your favorite color?
Me?

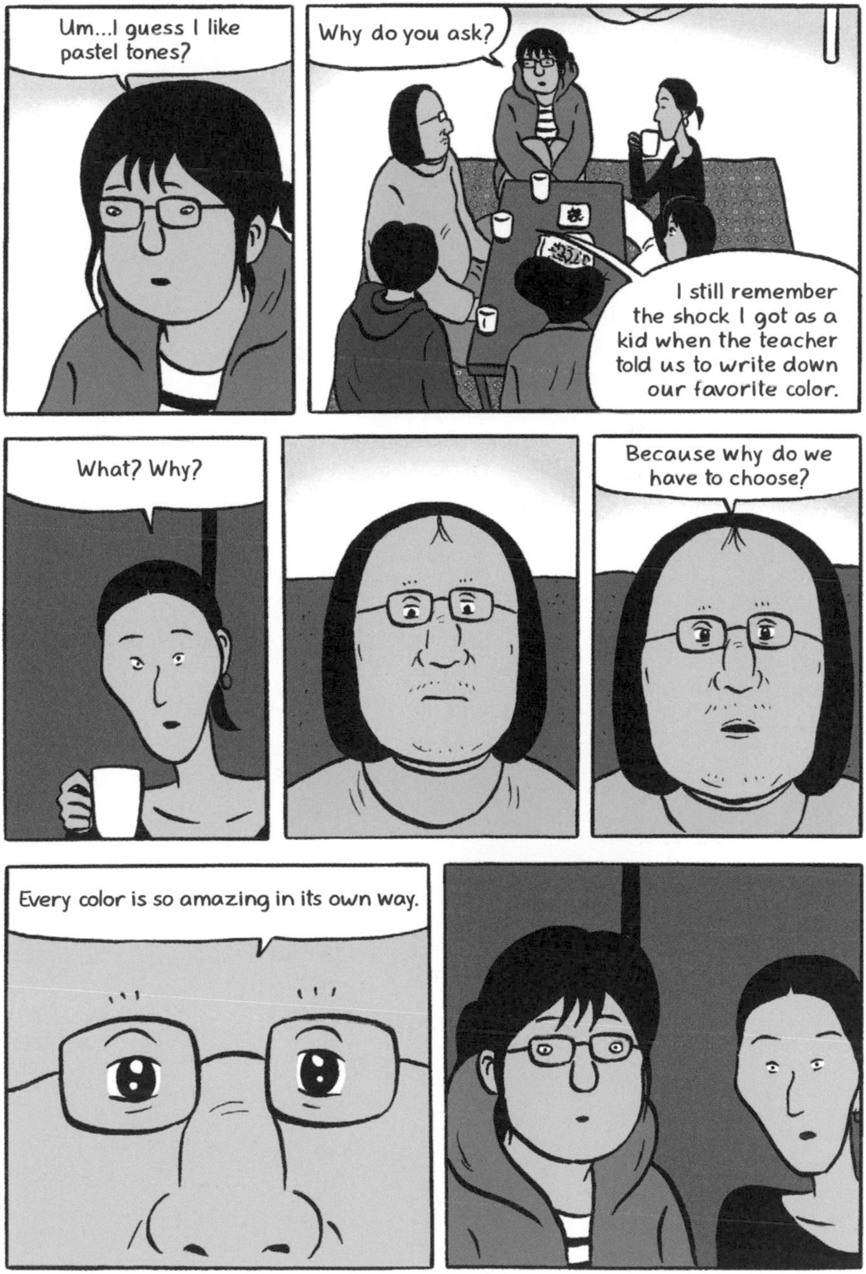
Um...I guess I like pastel tones?
Why do you ask?
I still remember the shock I got as a kid when the teacher told us to write down our favorite color.
What? Why?
Because why do we have to choose?
Every color is so amazing in its own way.

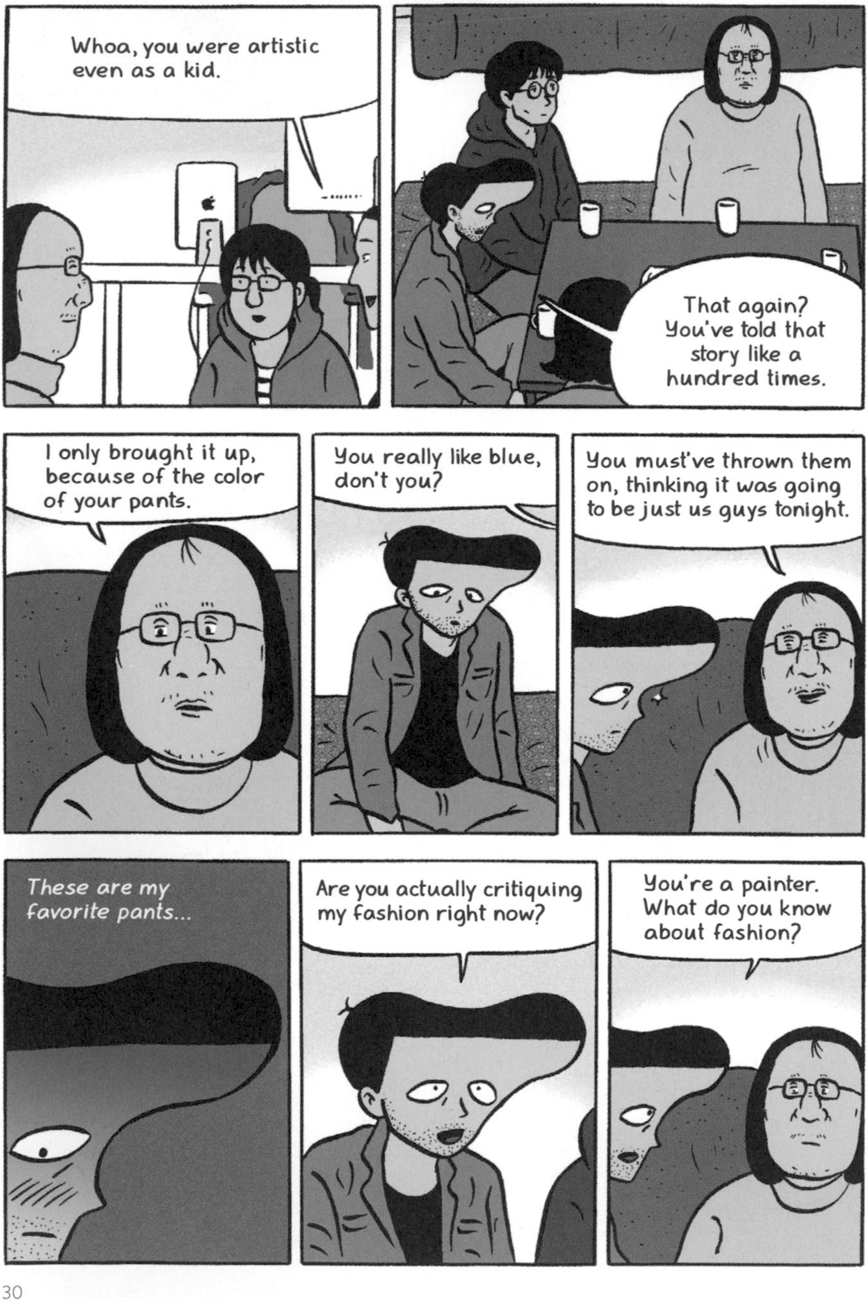
Whoa, you were artistic even as a kid.
That again? You've told that story like a hundred times.
I only brought it up, because of the color of your pants.
You really like blue, don't you?
You must've thrown them on, thinking it was going to be just us guys tonight.
These are my favorite pants...
Are you actually critiquing my fashion right now?
You're a painter. What do you know about fashion?

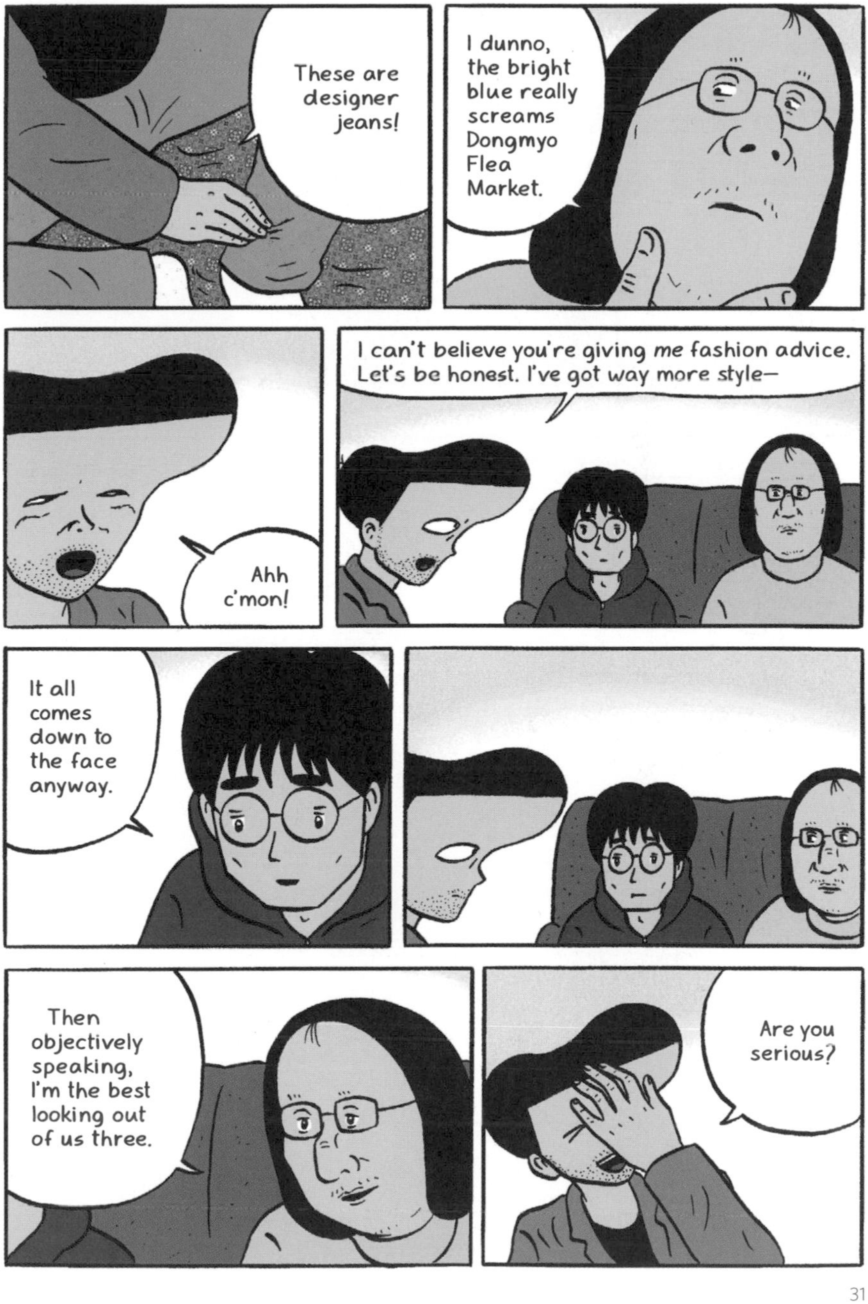
These are designer jeans!
I dunno, the bright blue really screams Dongmyo Flea Market.
Ahh c'mon!
I can't believe you're giving *me* fashion advice. Let's be honest. I've got way more style—
It all comes down to the face anyway.
Then objectively speaking, I'm the best looking out of us three.
Are you serious?

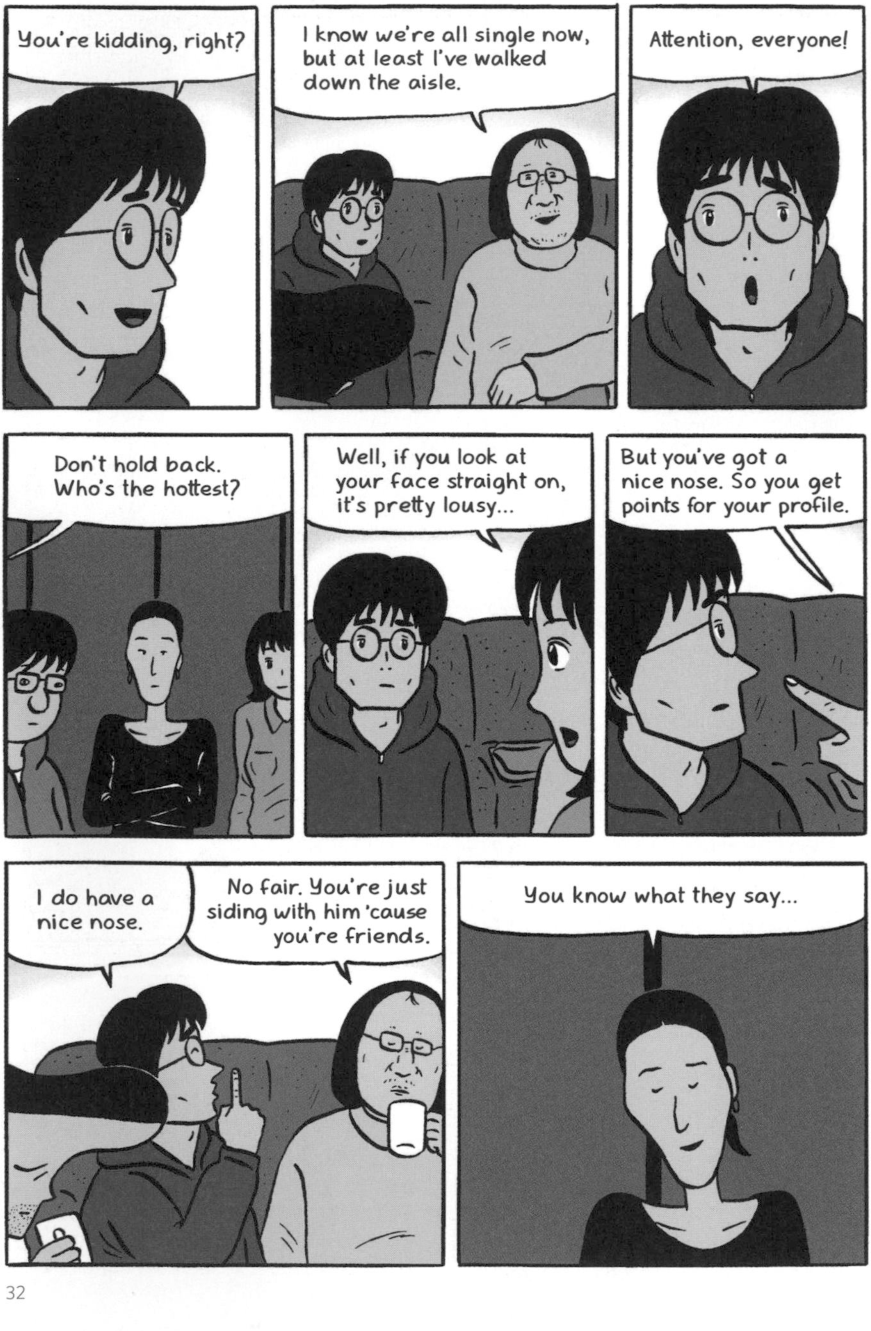
You're kidding, right?
I know we're all single now, but at least I've walked down the aisle.
Attention, everyone!
Don't hold back. Who's the hottest?
Well, if you look at your face straight on, it's pretty lousy...
But you've got a nice nose. So you get points for your profile.
I do have a nice nose.
No fair. You're just siding with him 'cause you're friends.
You know what they say...

Your face is the face of your lover from a previous life.

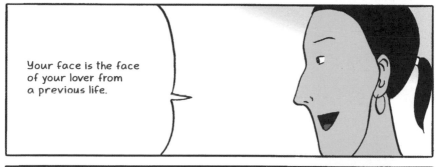

Aaaand she finishes us off with one blow.

They say true genius is written all over a face.

Why?

Because a beauti-ful face needs no explana-tion.

Ha! You're a riot. Are your films this funny too?

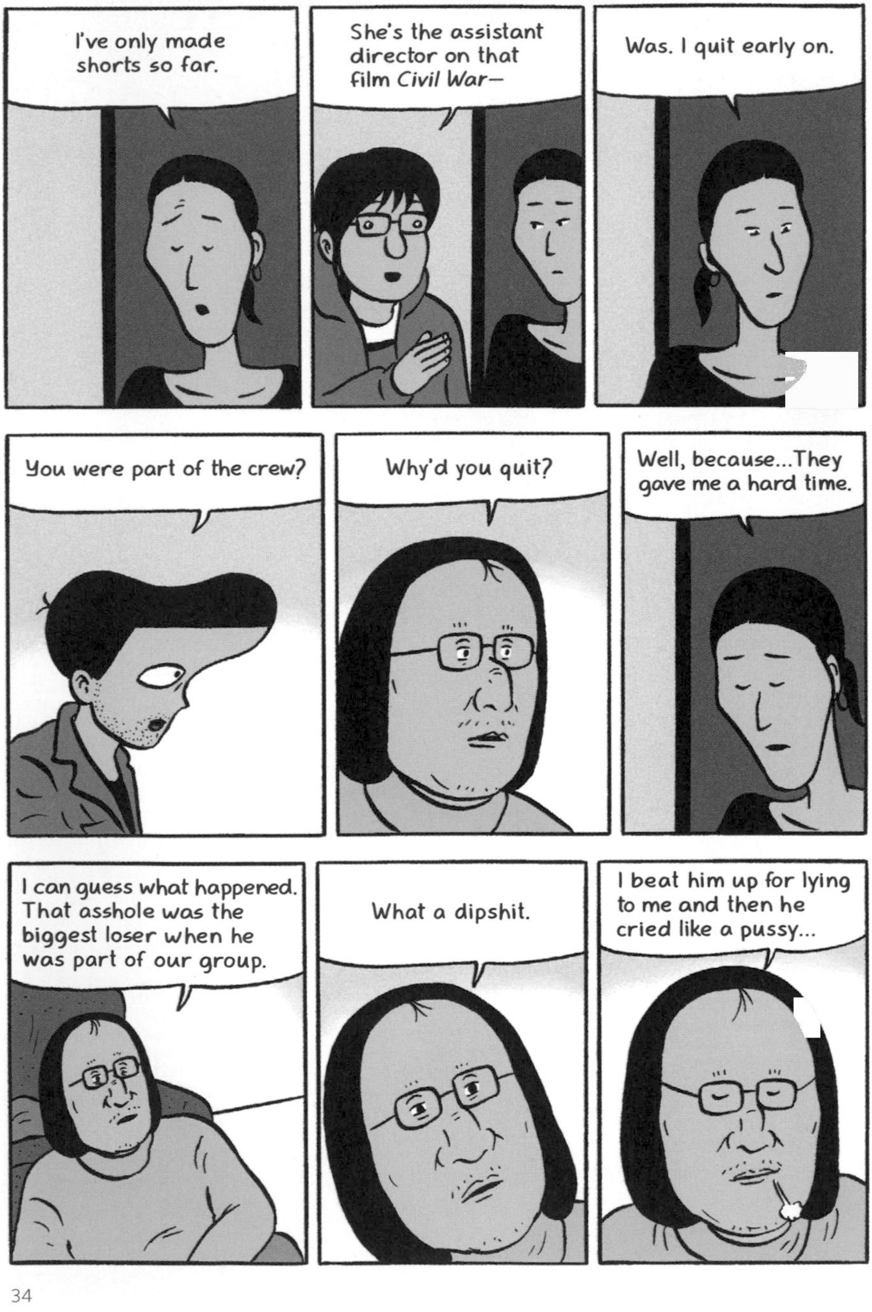

I've only made shorts so far.
She's the assistant director on that film *Civil War*—
Was. I quit early on.
You were part of the crew?
Why'd you quit?
Well, because...They gave me a hard time.
I can guess what happened. That asshole was the biggest loser when he was part of our group.
What a dipshit.
I beat him up for lying to me and then he cried like a pussy...

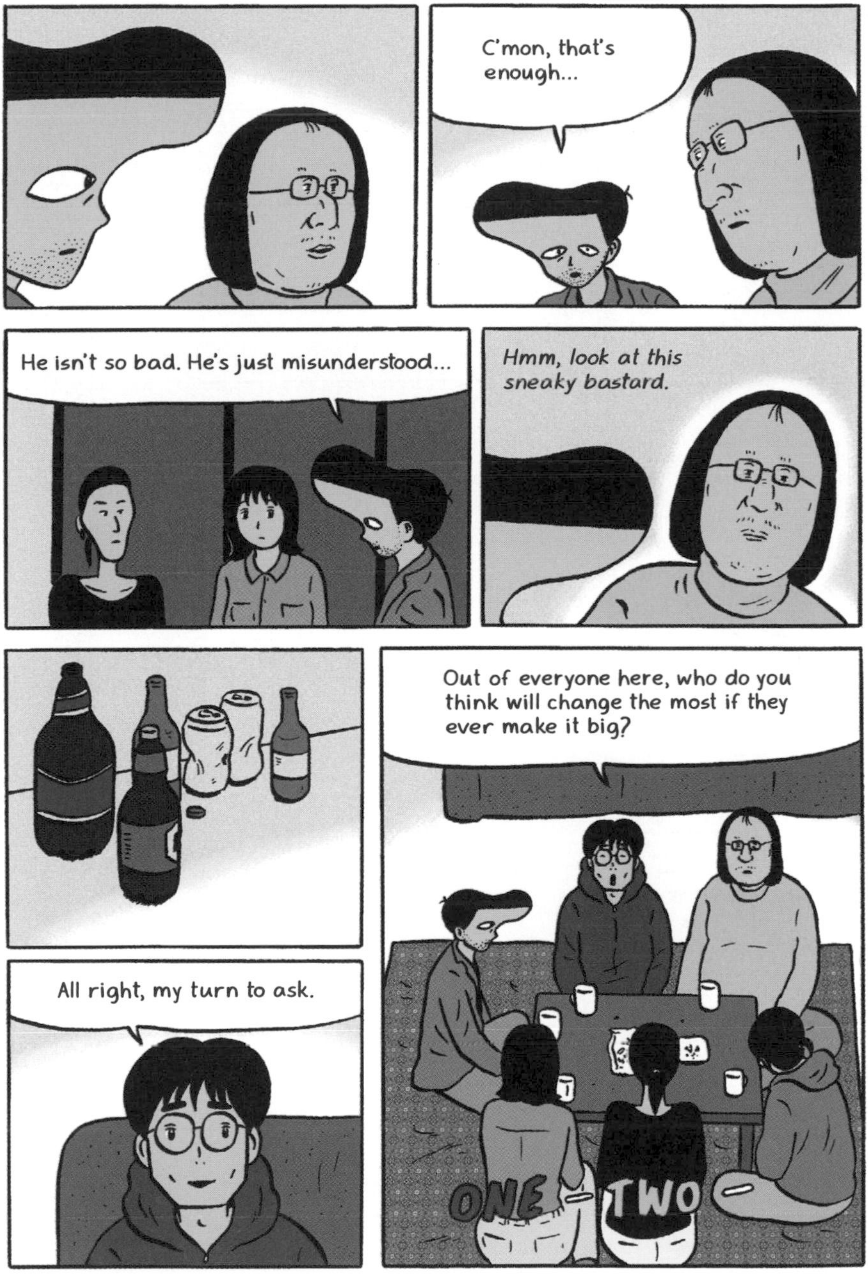
C'mon, that's enough...
He isn't so bad. He's just misunderstood...
Hmm, look at this sneaky bastard.
All right, my turn to ask.
Out of everyone here, who do you think will change the most if they ever make it big?
ONE
TWO

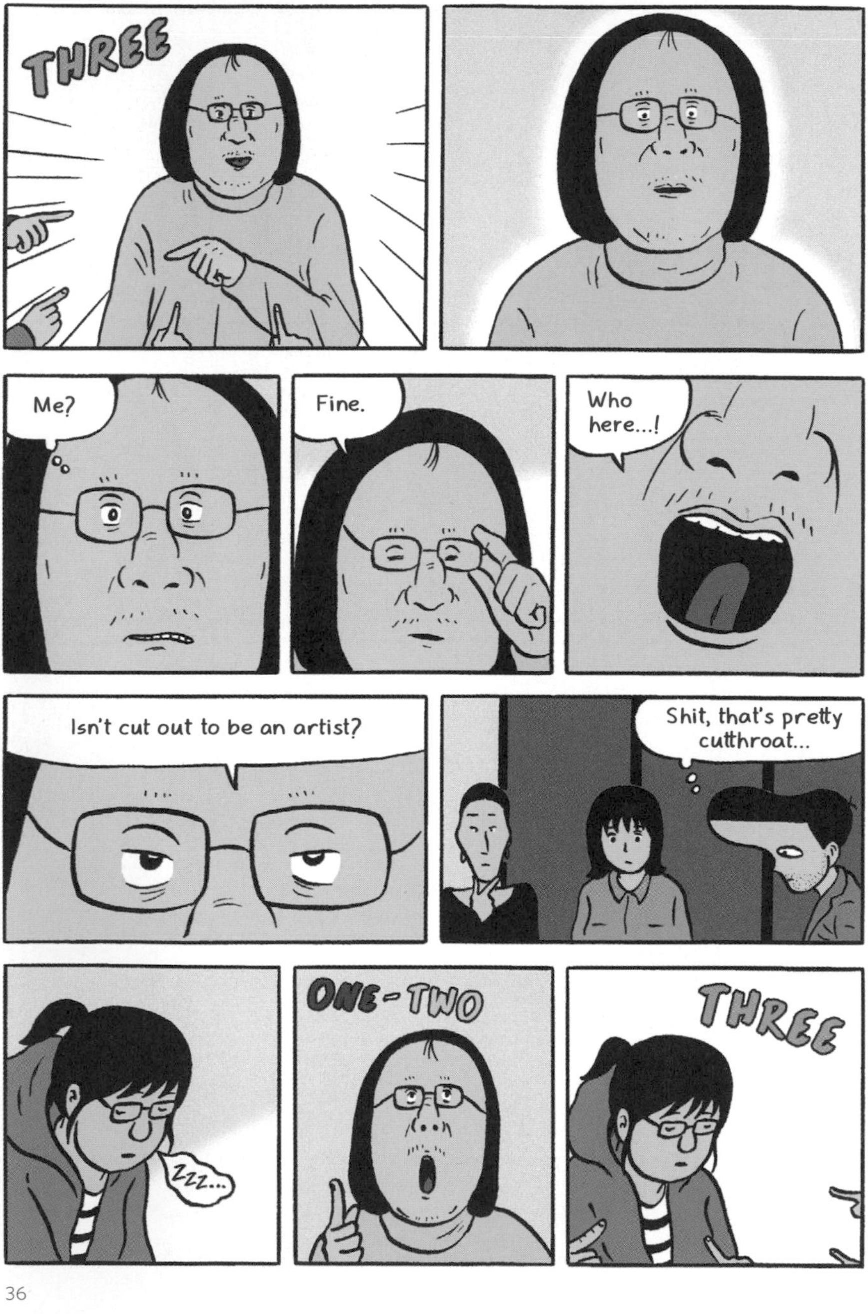
THREE
Me?
Fine.
Who here...!
Isn't cut out to be an artist?
Shit, that's pretty cutthroat...
ZZZ...
ONE-TWO
THREE

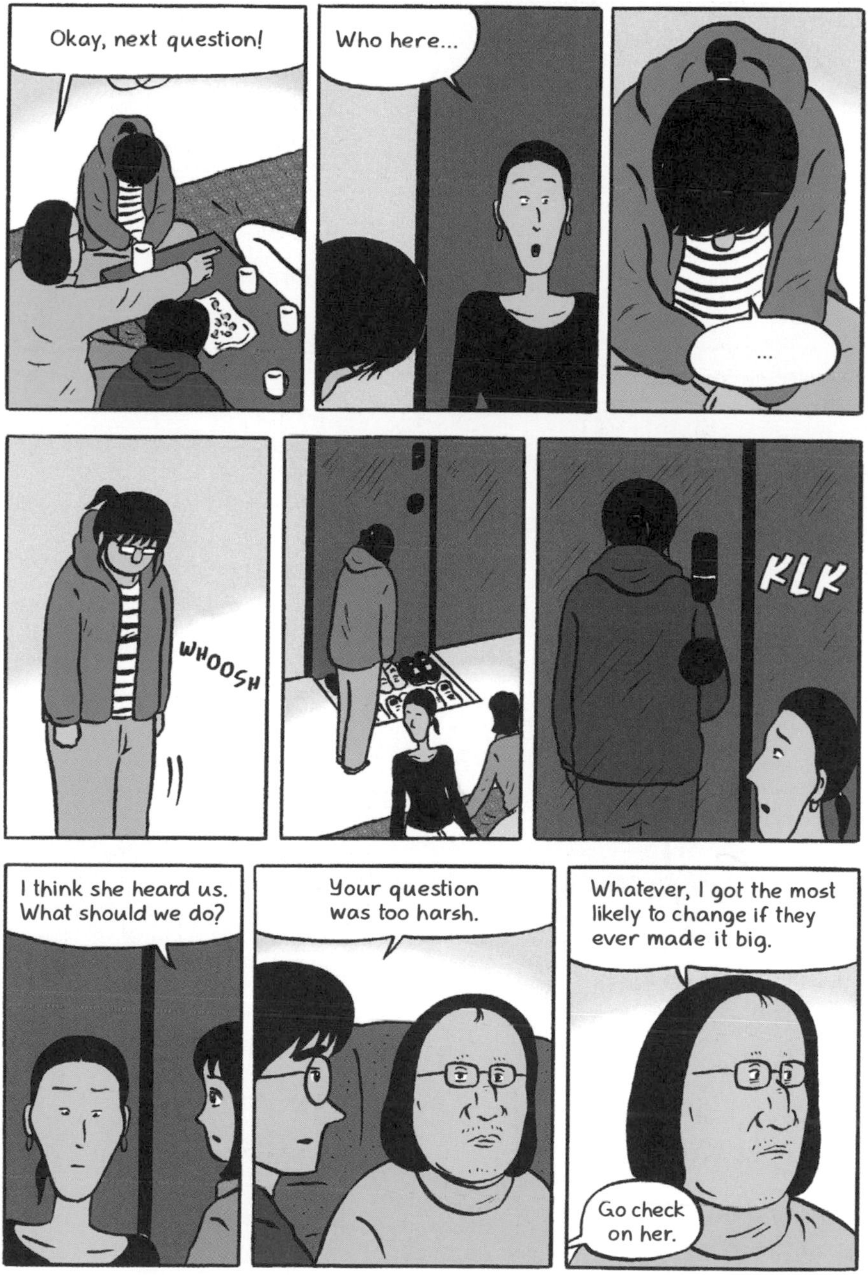
Okay, next question!
Who here...
...
WHOOSH
KLK
I think she heard us. What should we do?
Your question was too harsh.
Whatever, I got the most likely to change if they ever made it big.
Go check on her.

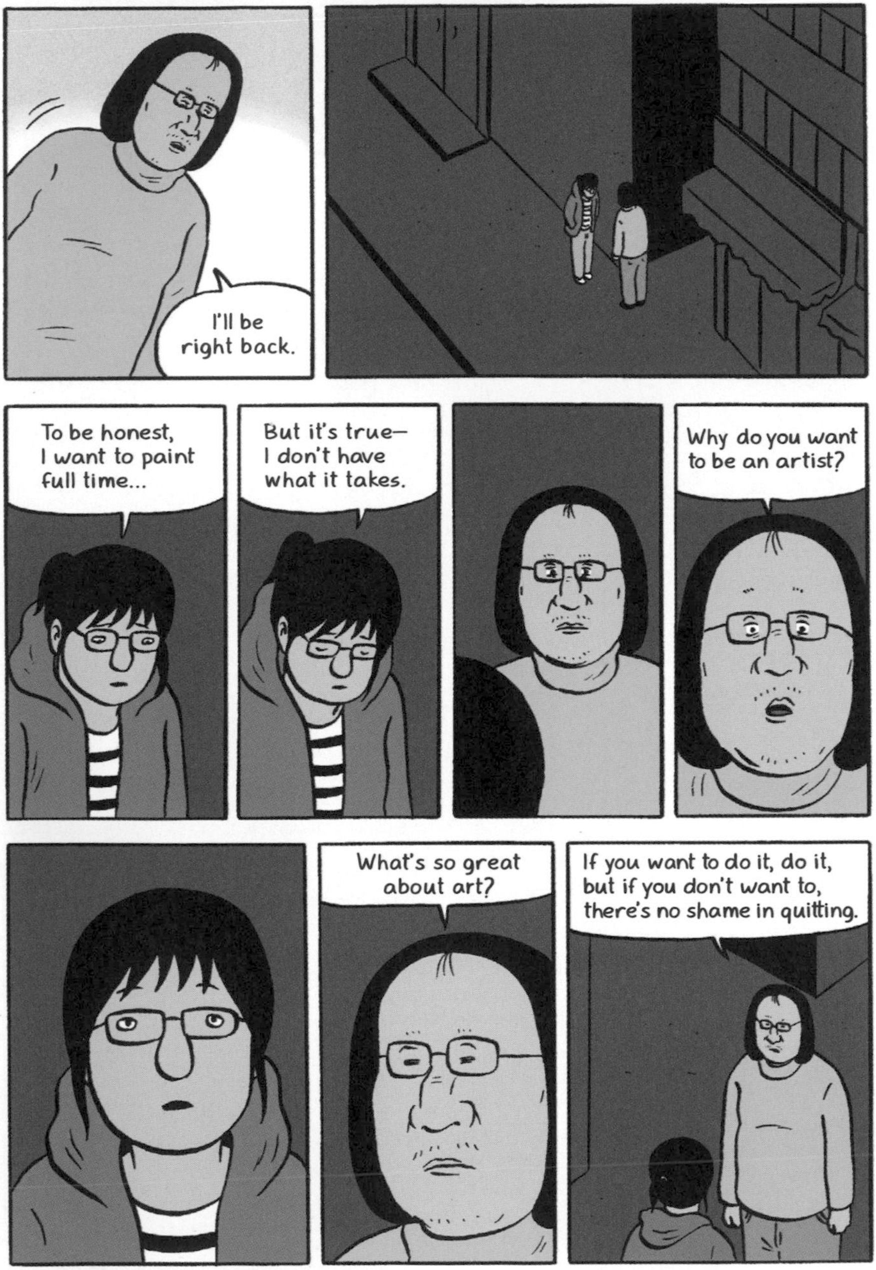
I'll be right back.
To be honest, I want to paint full time...
But it's true— I don't have what it takes.
Why do you want to be an artist?
What's so great about art?
If you want to do it, do it, but if you don't want to, there's no shame in quitting.

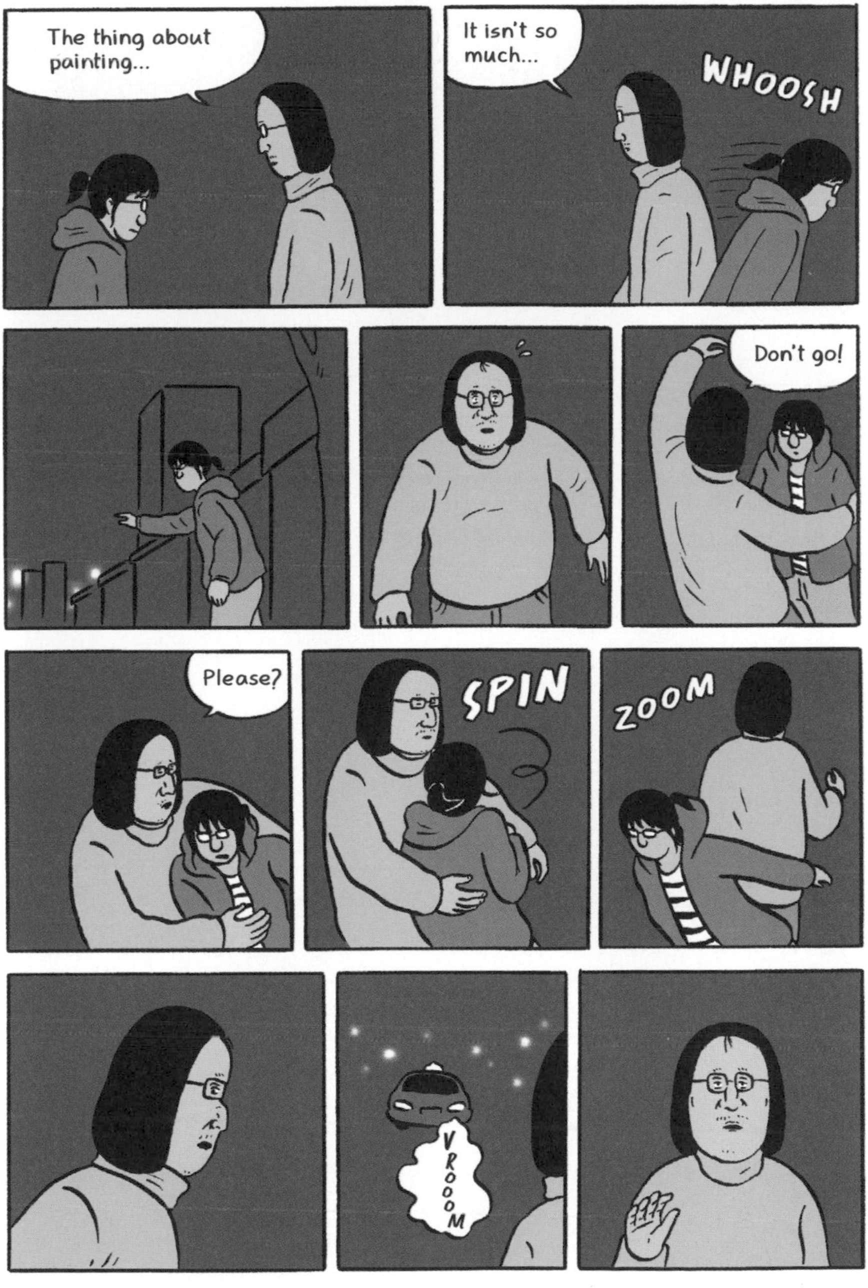

The thing about painting...
It isn't so much...
WHOOSH
Don't go!
Please?
SPIN
ZOOM
VROOOM

HANGOVER SOUP

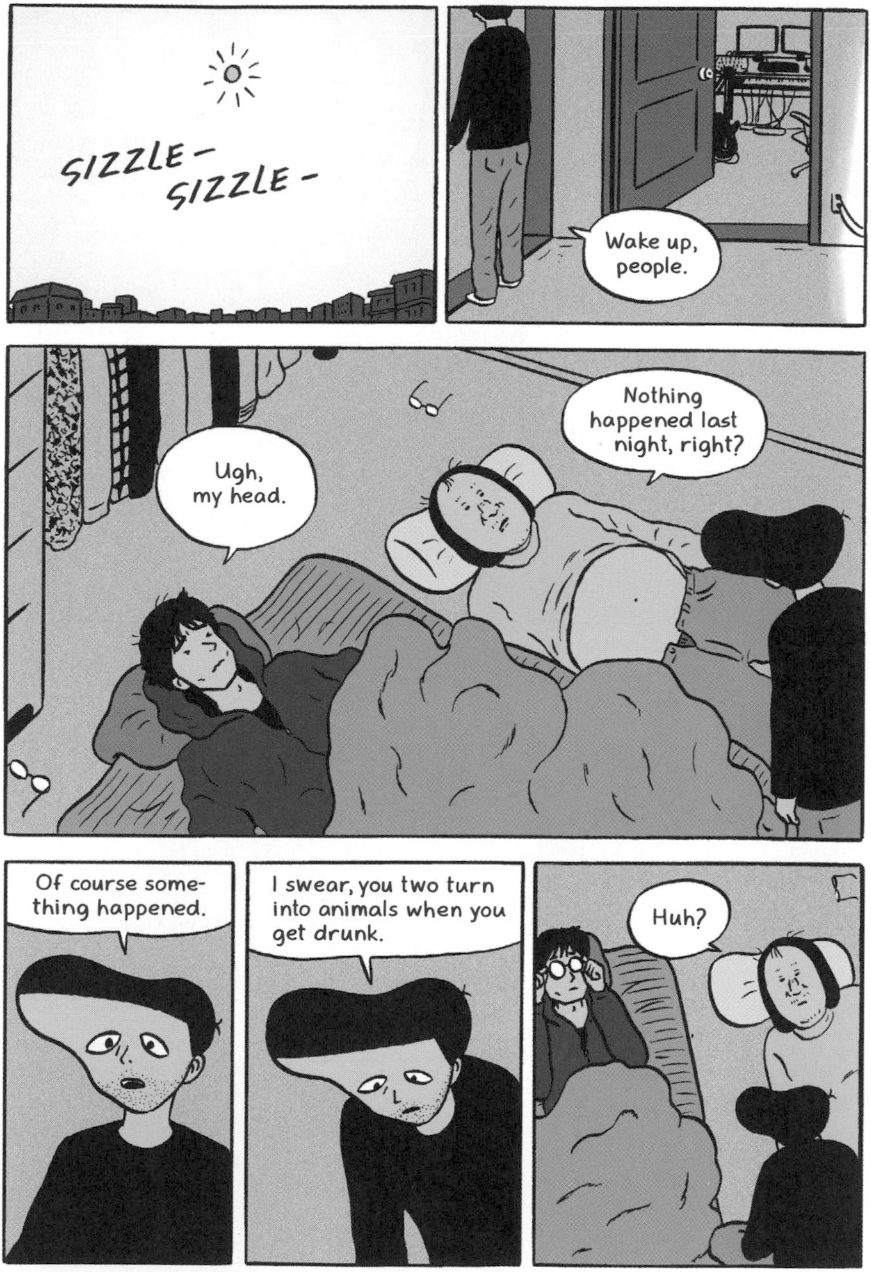
SIZZLE-
SIZZLE-
Wake up, people.
Ugh, my head.
Nothing happened last night, right?
Of course some-thing happened.
I swear, you two turn into animals when you get drunk.
Huh?

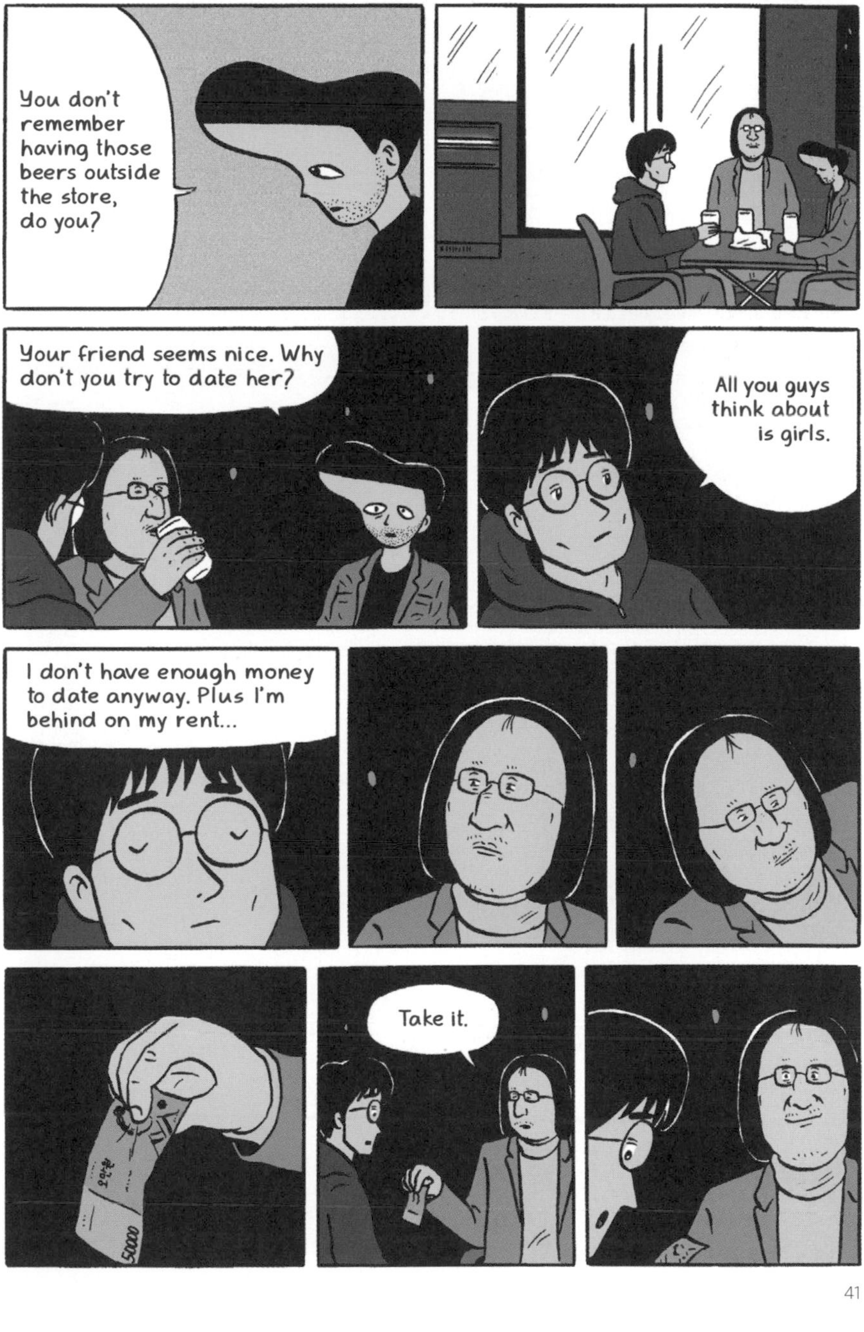
You don't remember having those beers outside the store, do you?
Your friend seems nice. Why don't you try to date her?
All you guys think about is girls.
I don't have enough money to date anyway. Plus I'm behind on my rent...
Take it.

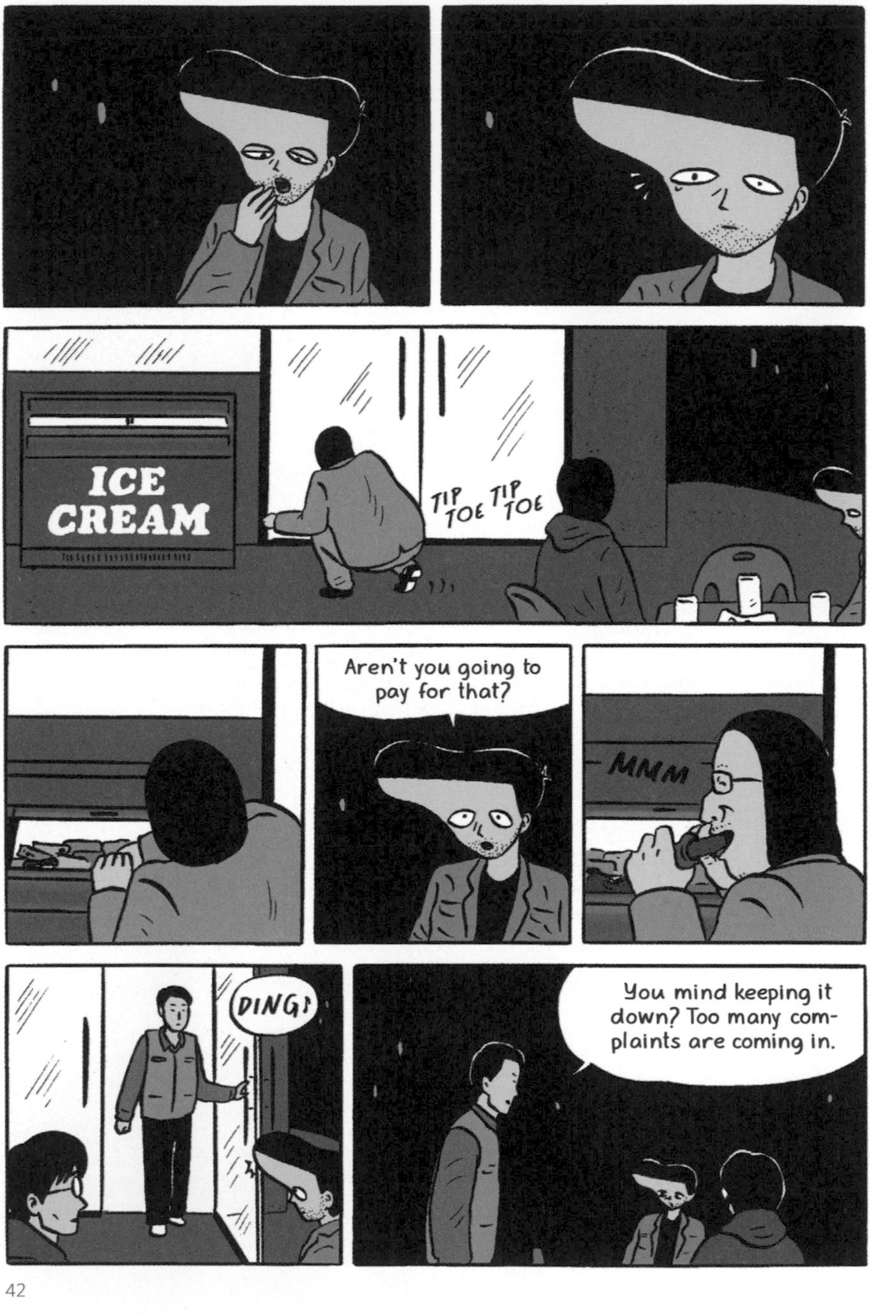
ICE CREAM
TIP TOE TIP TOE
Aren't you going to pay for that?
MMM
DING!
You mind keeping it down? Too many complaints are coming in.

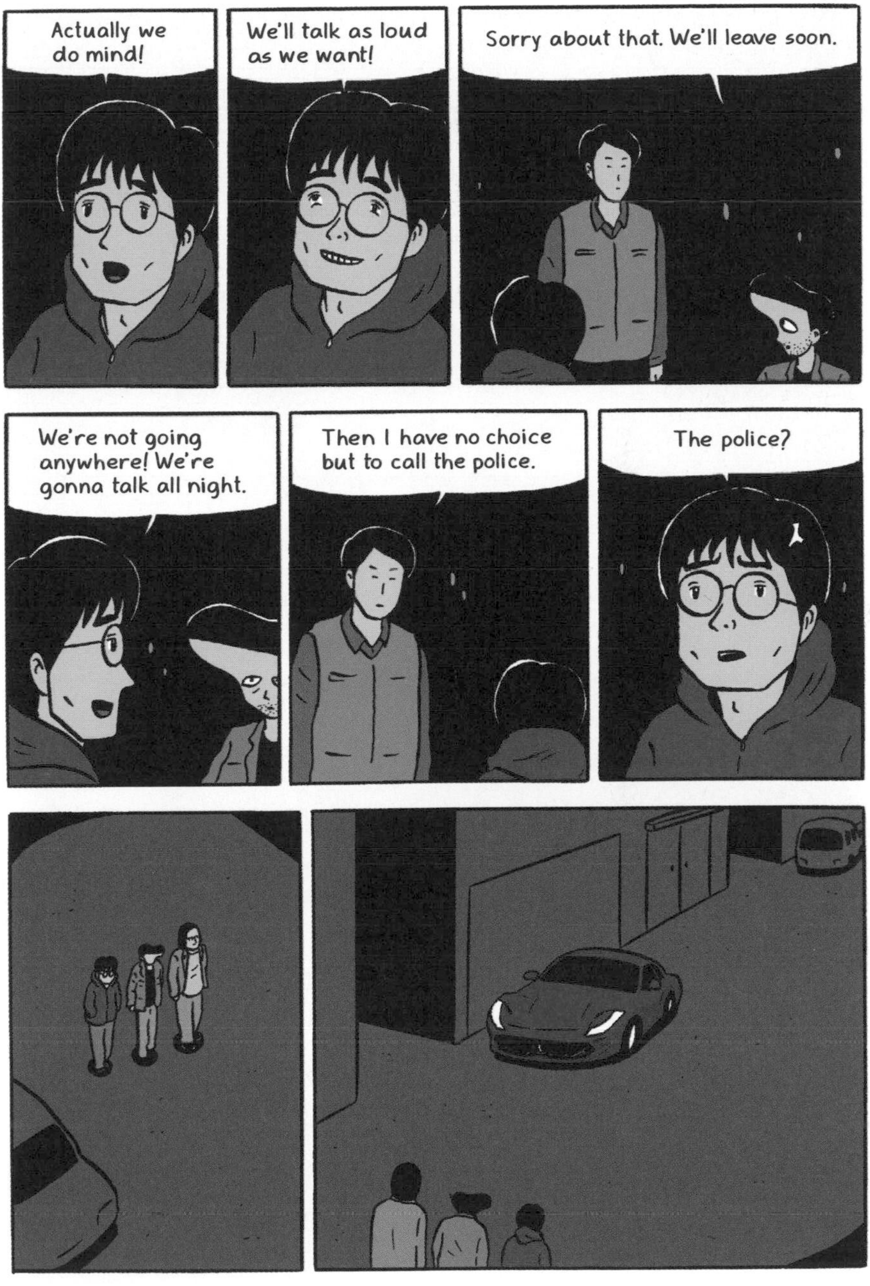
Actually we do mind!
We'll talk as loud as we want!
Sorry about that. We'll leave soon.
We're not going anywhere! We're gonna talk all night.
Then I have no choice but to call the police.
The police?

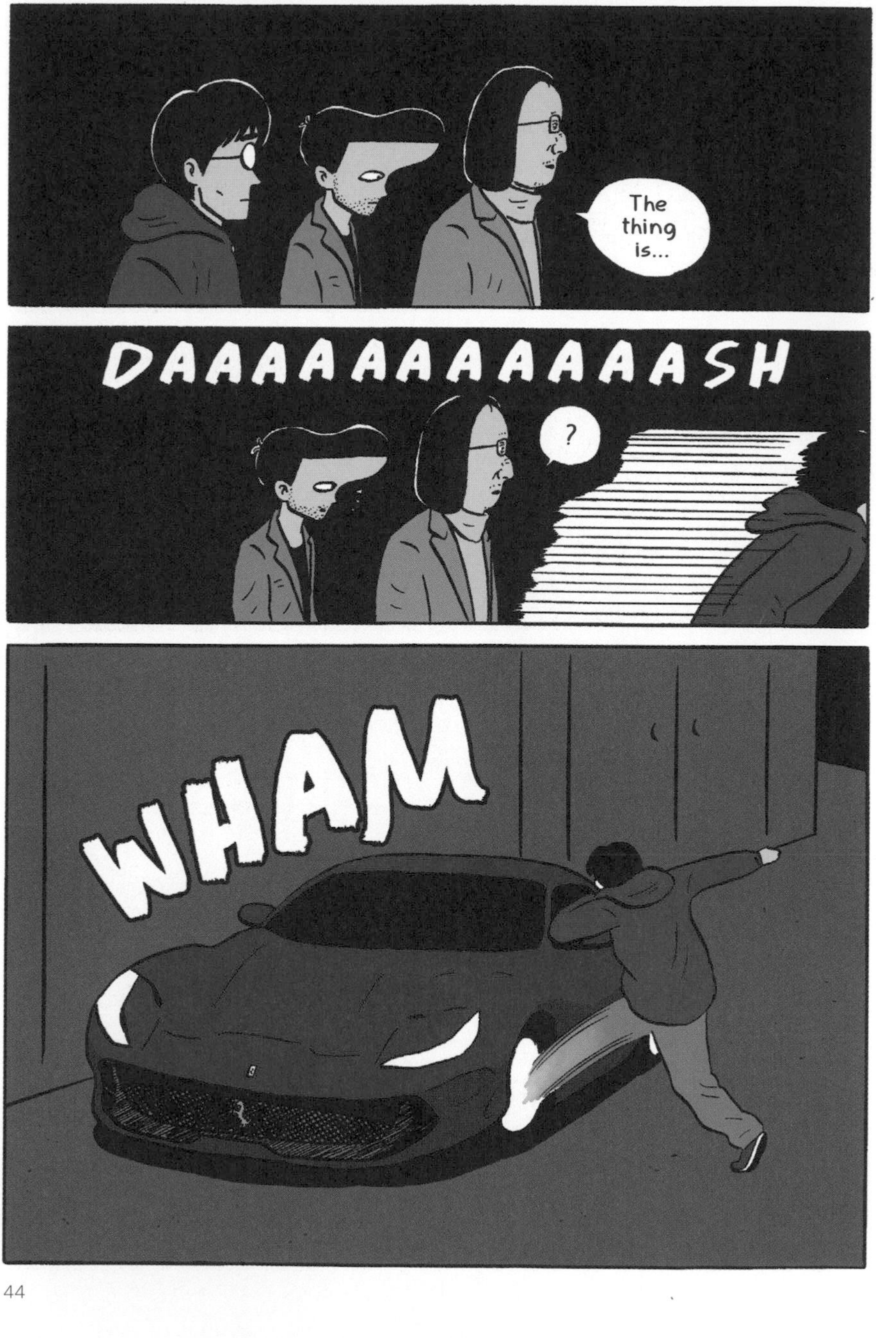

The thing is...
DAAAAAAAAAAASH
?
WHAM

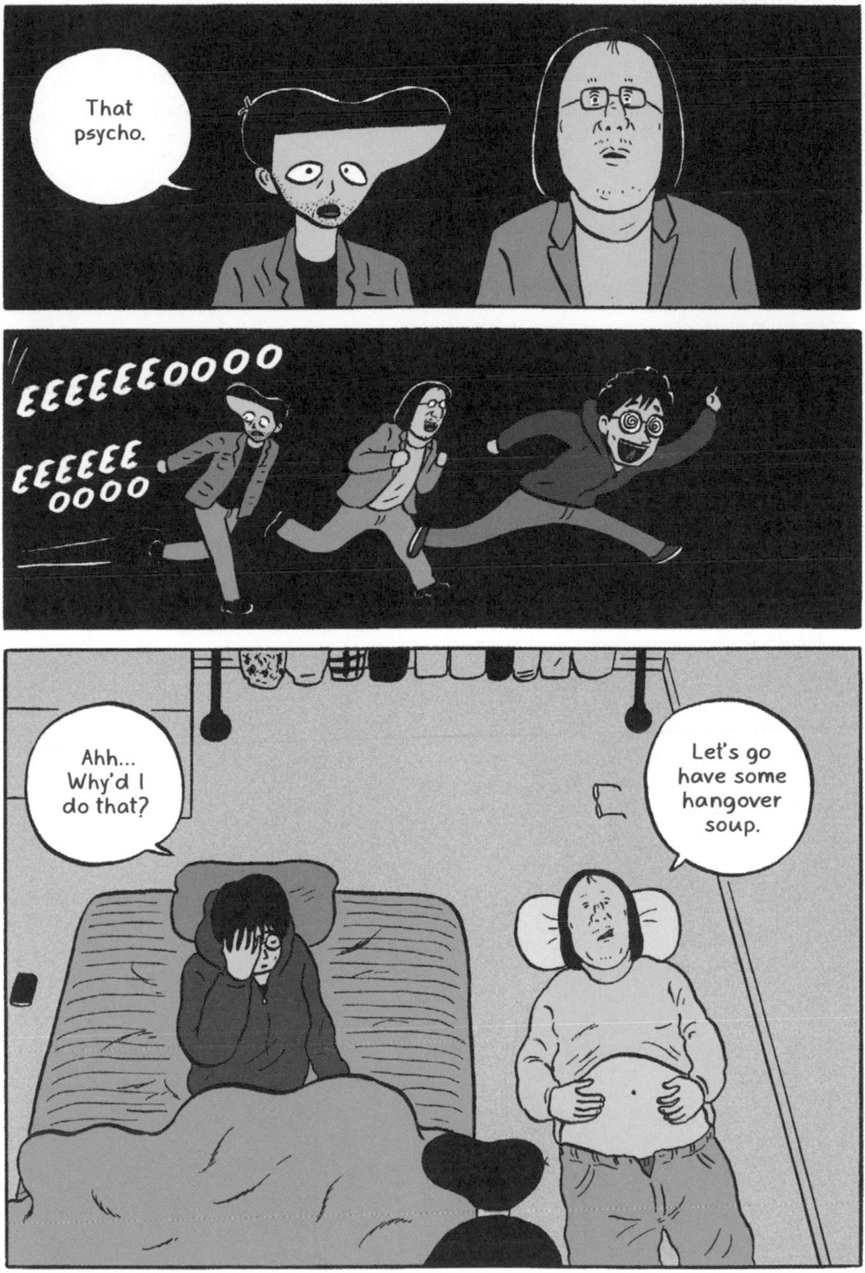
That psycho.
EEEEEEOOOO
EEEEEE OOOO
Ahh... Why'd I do that?
Let's go have some hangover soup.

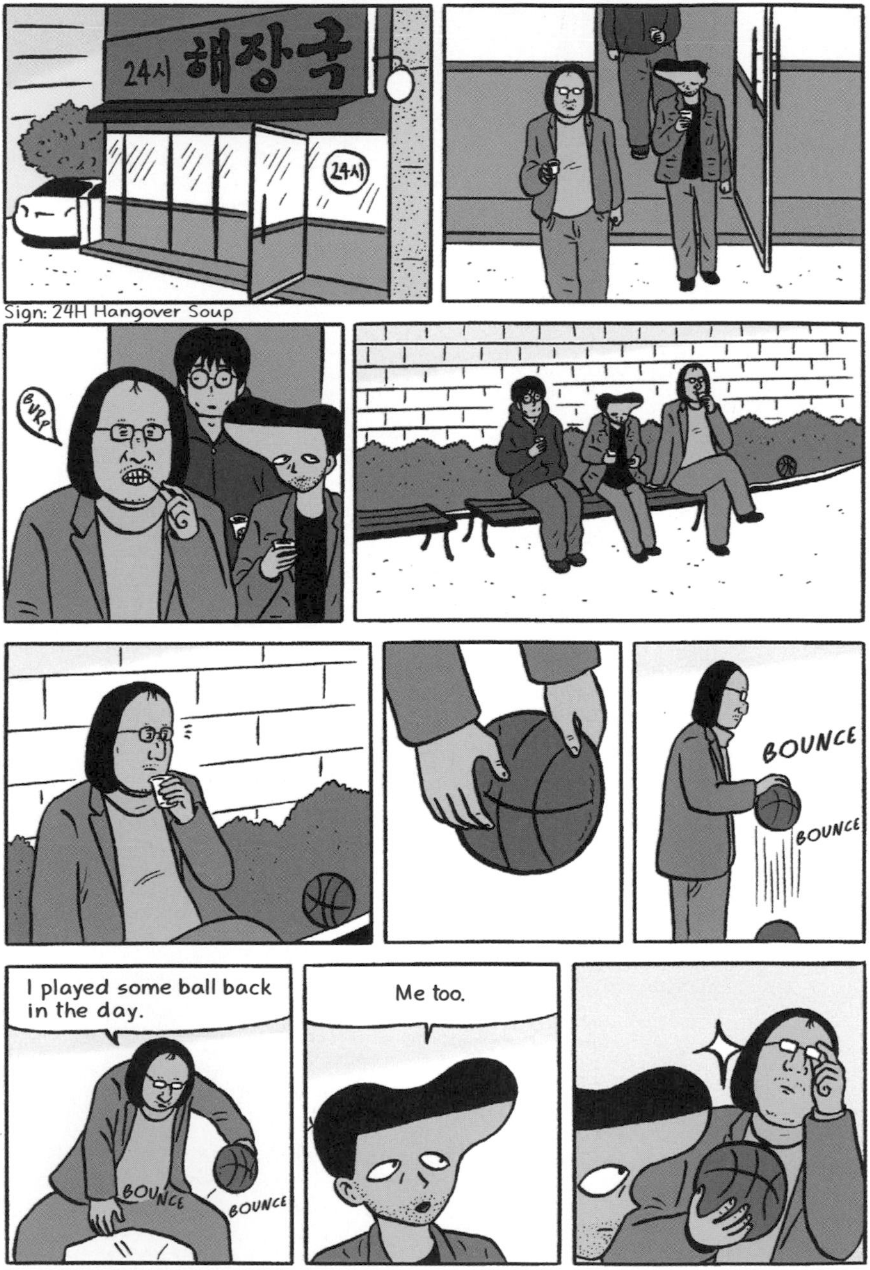

24시 해장국
24시
Sign: 24H Hangover Soup
BURP
BOUNCE
BOUNCE
I played some ball back in the day.
BOUNCE
BOUNCE
Me too.

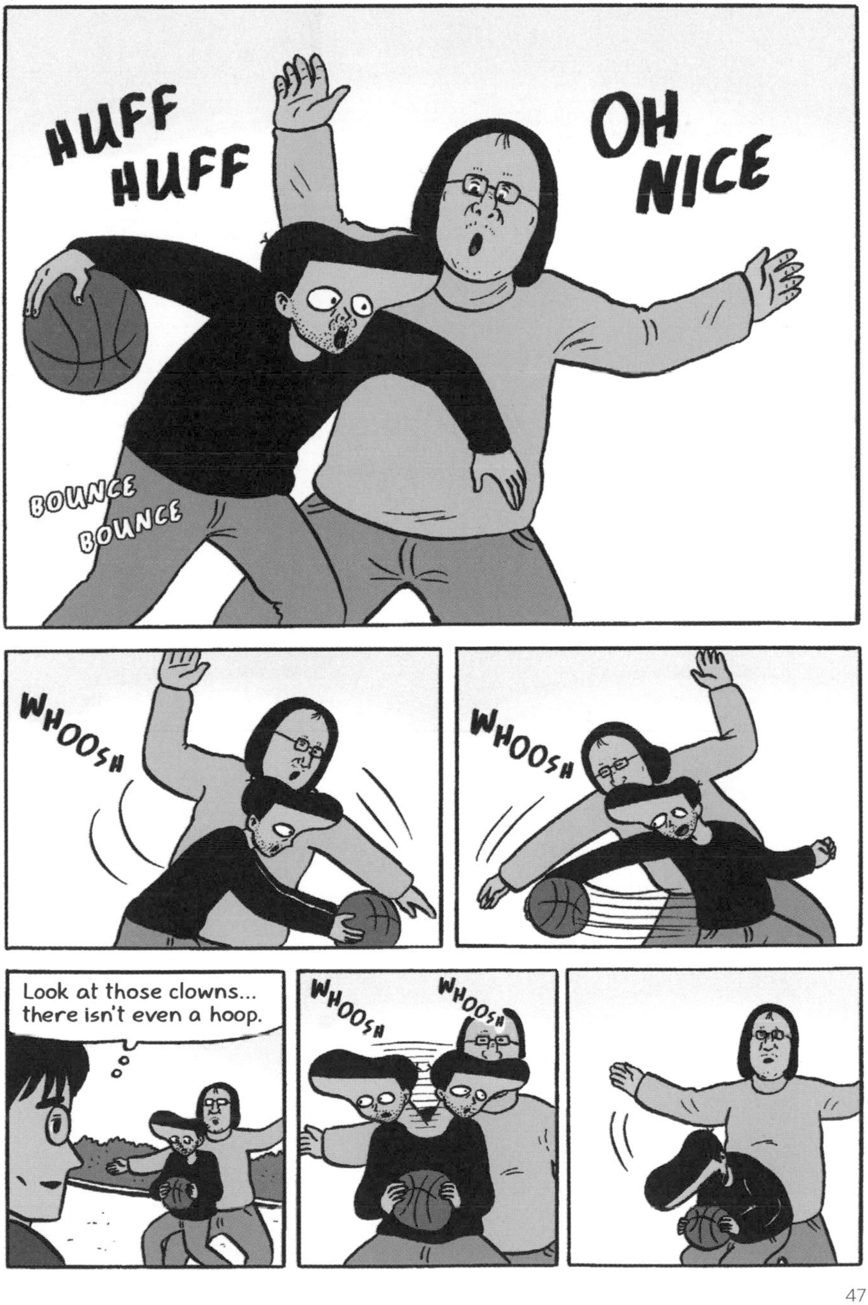
HUFF
HUFF
OH
NICE
BOUNCE
BOUNCE
WHOOSH
WHOOSH
Look at those clowns...
there isn't even a hoop.
WHOOSH
WHOOSH

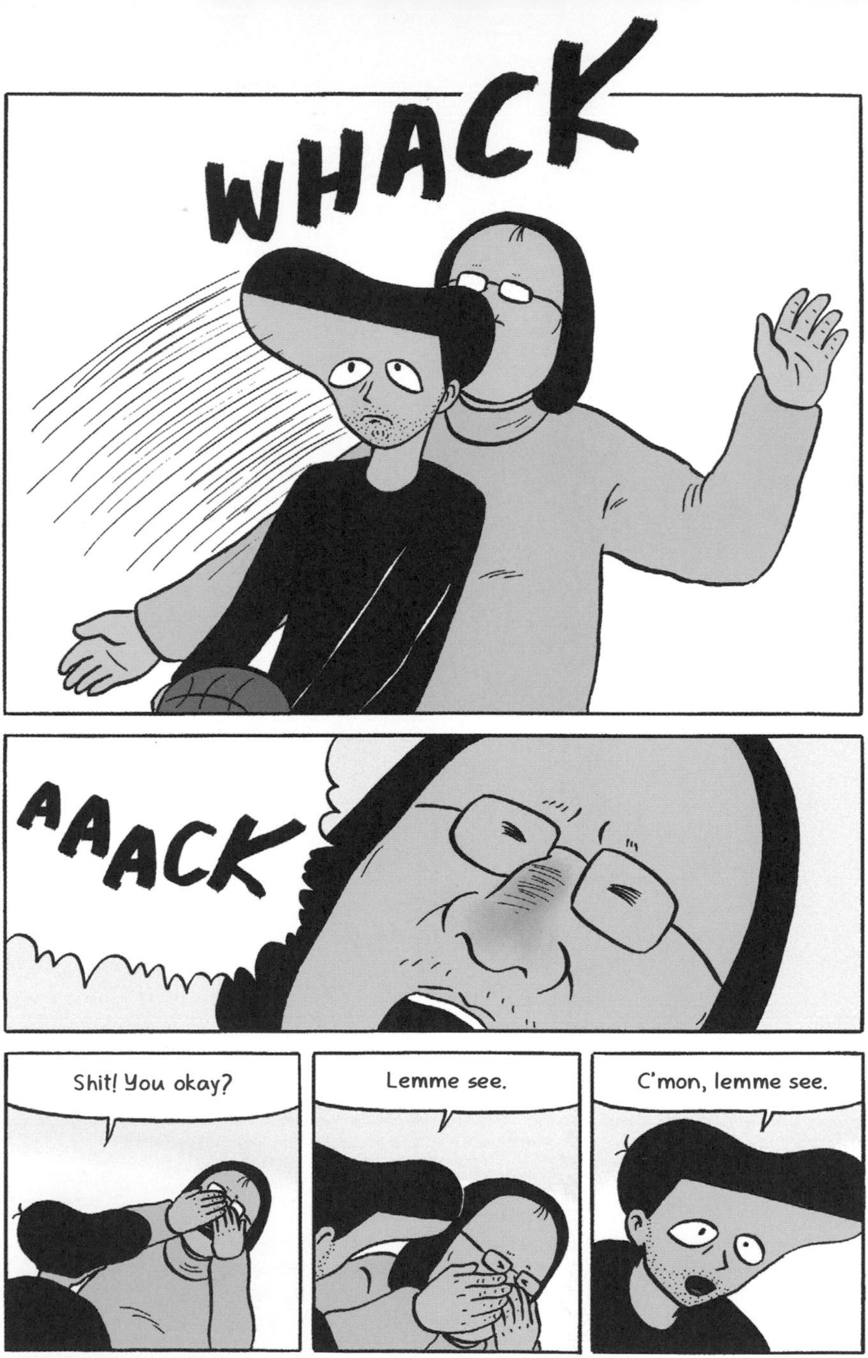
WHACK
AAACK
Shit! You okay?
Lemme see.
C'mon, lemme see.

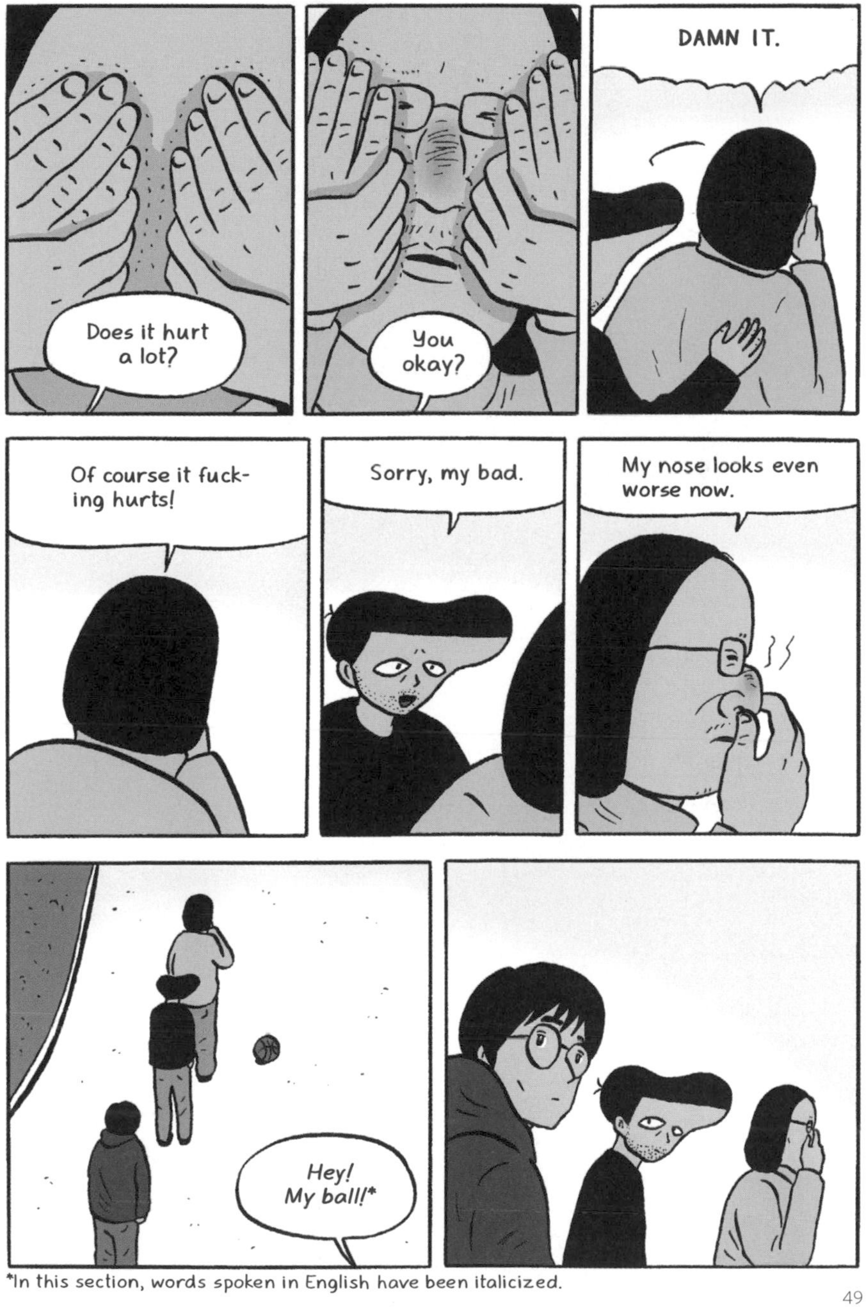
Does it hurt a lot?
You okay?
DAMN IT.
Of course it fucking hurts!
Sorry, my bad.
My nose looks even worse now.
*Hey! My ball!**

*In this section, words spoken in English have been italicized.

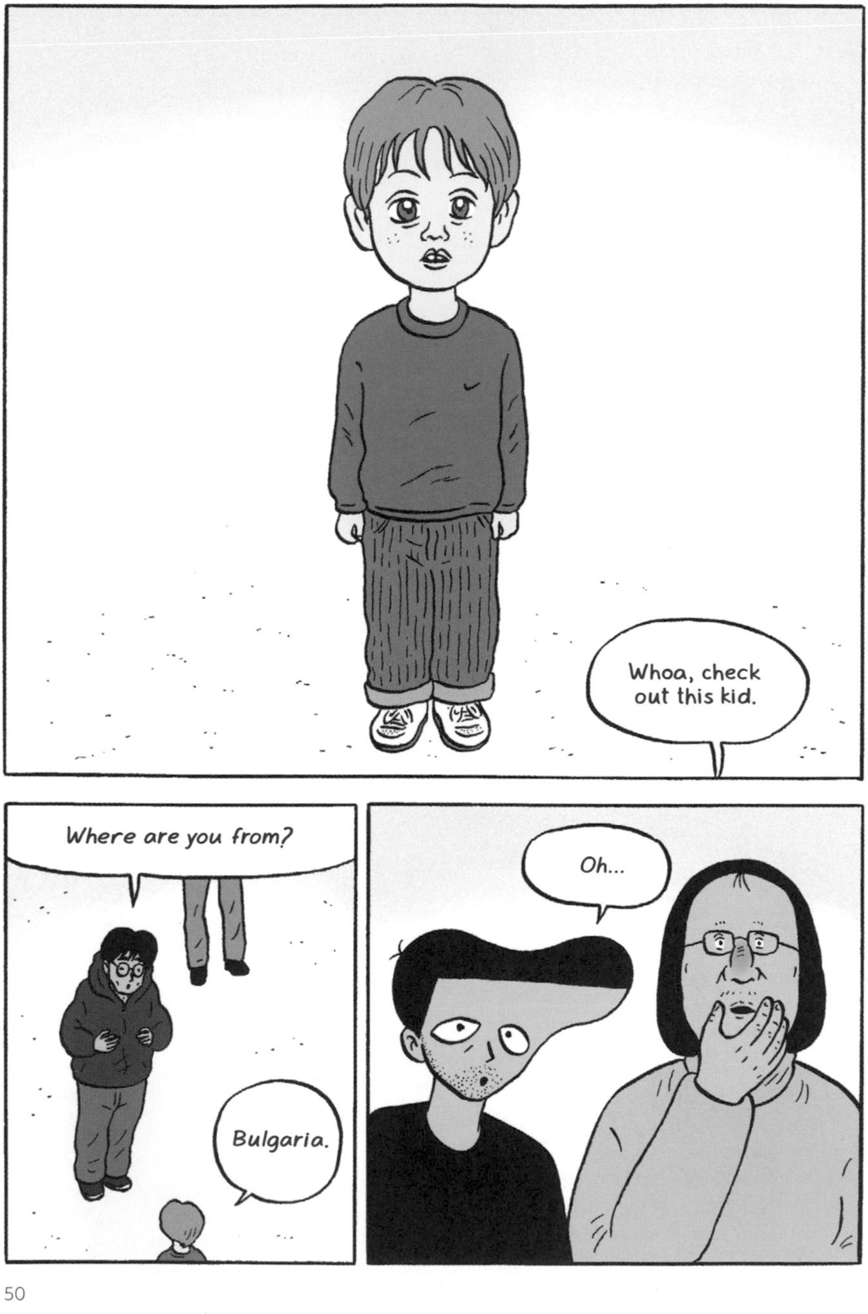
Whoa, check out this kid.
Where are you from?
Bulgaria.
Oh...

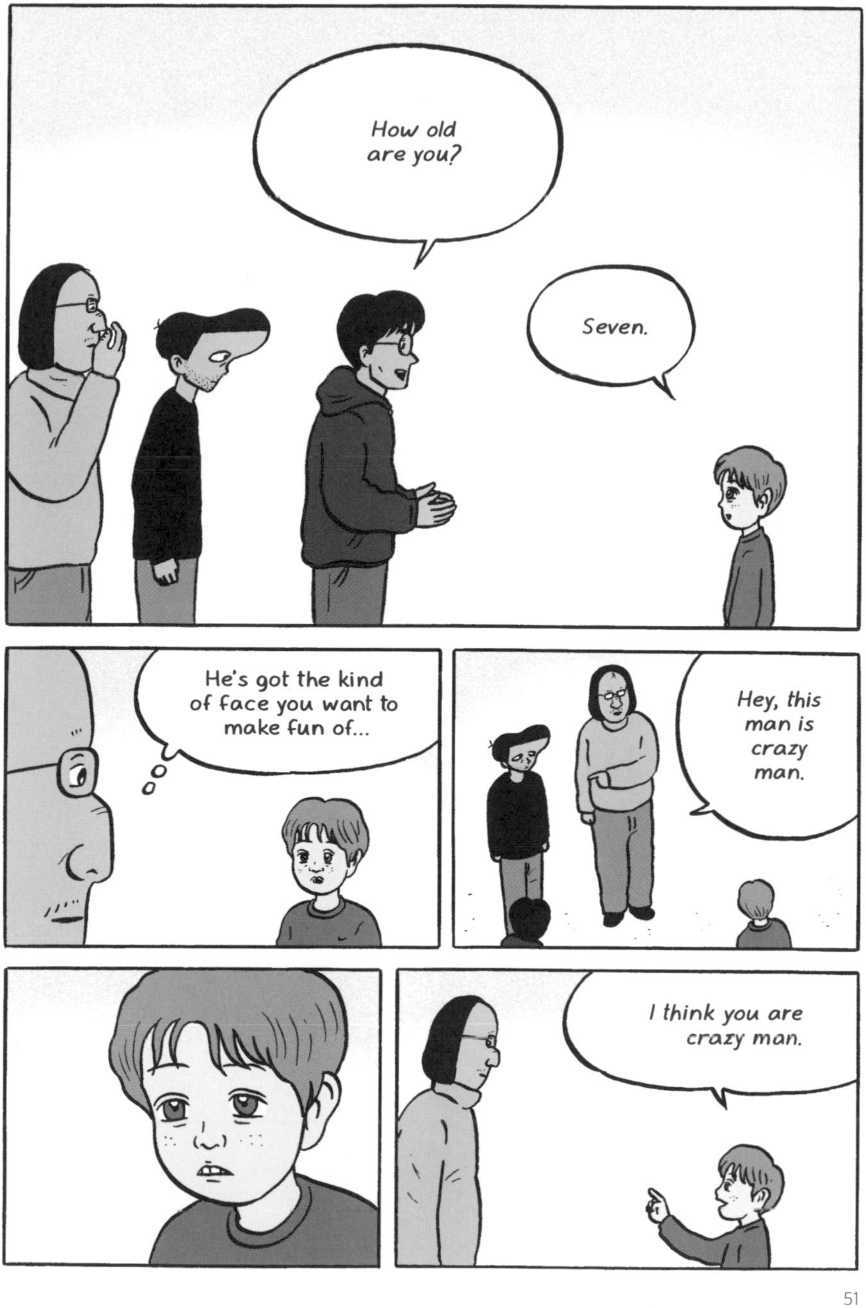
How old are you?
Seven.
He's got the kind of face you want to make fun of...
Hey, this man is crazy man.
I think you are crazy man.

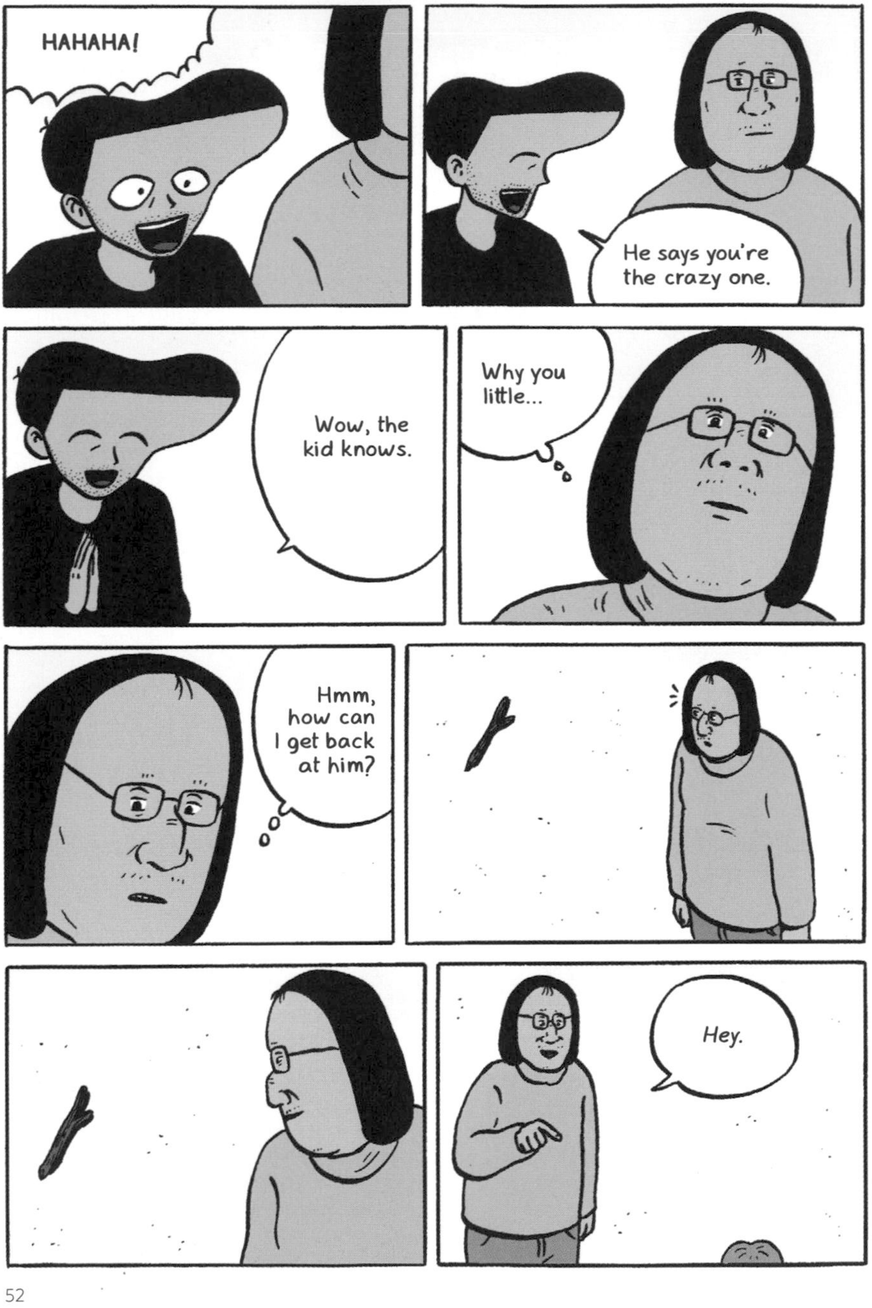
HAHAHA!
He says you're the crazy one.
Wow, the kid knows.
Why you little...
Hmm, how can I get back at him?
Hey.

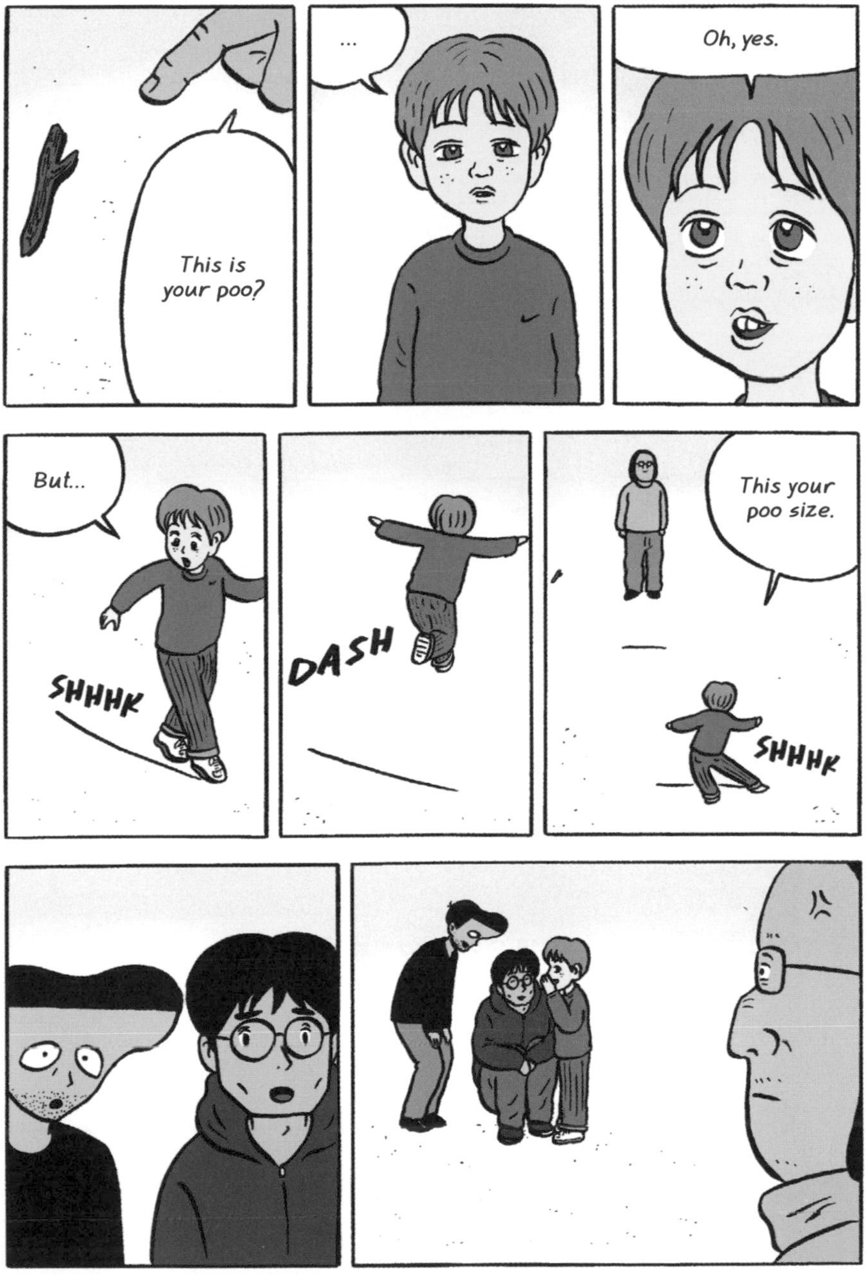
This is your poo?
...
Oh, yes.
But...
SHHHK
DASH
This your poo size.
SHHHK

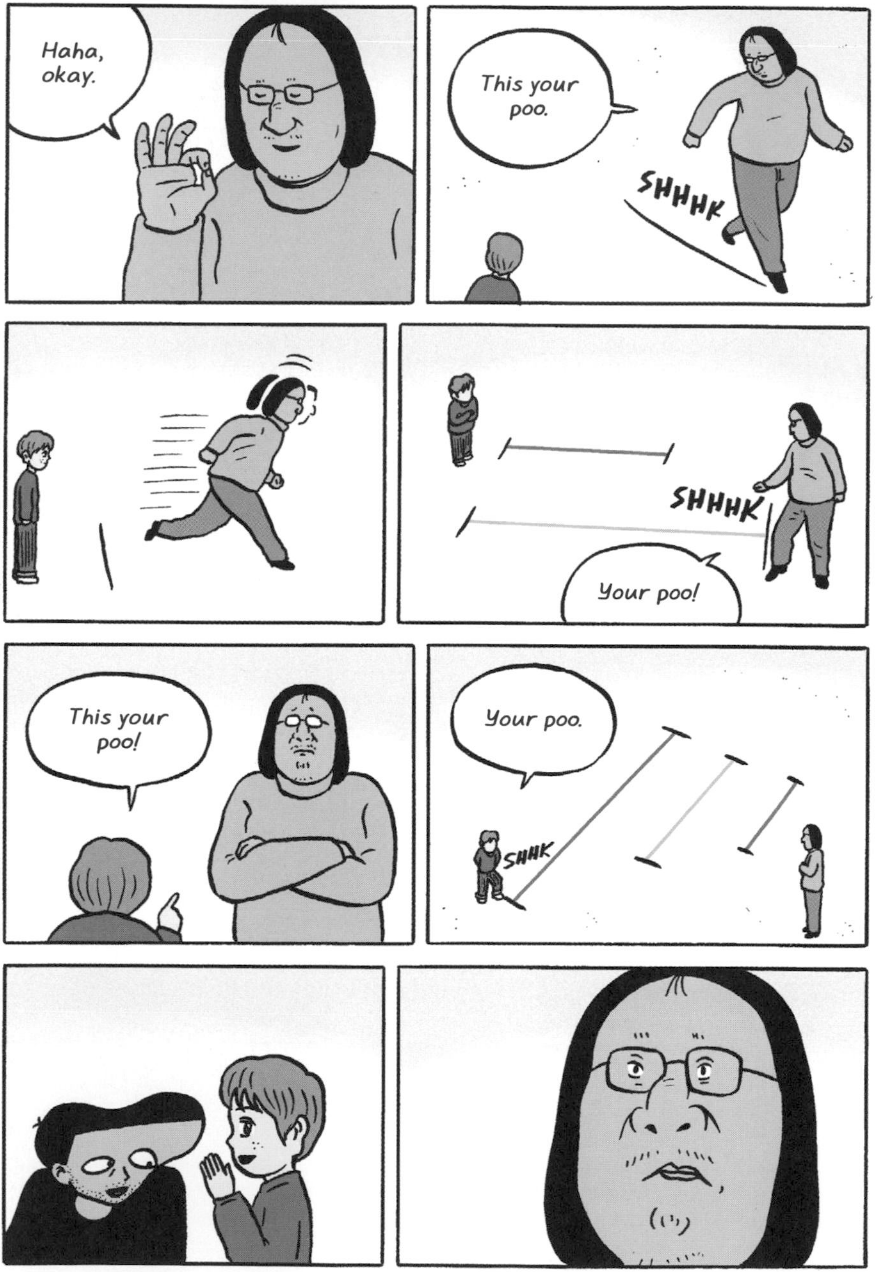

Haha, okay.
This your poo.
SHHHK
SHHHK
Your poo!
This your poo!
Your poo.
SHHK

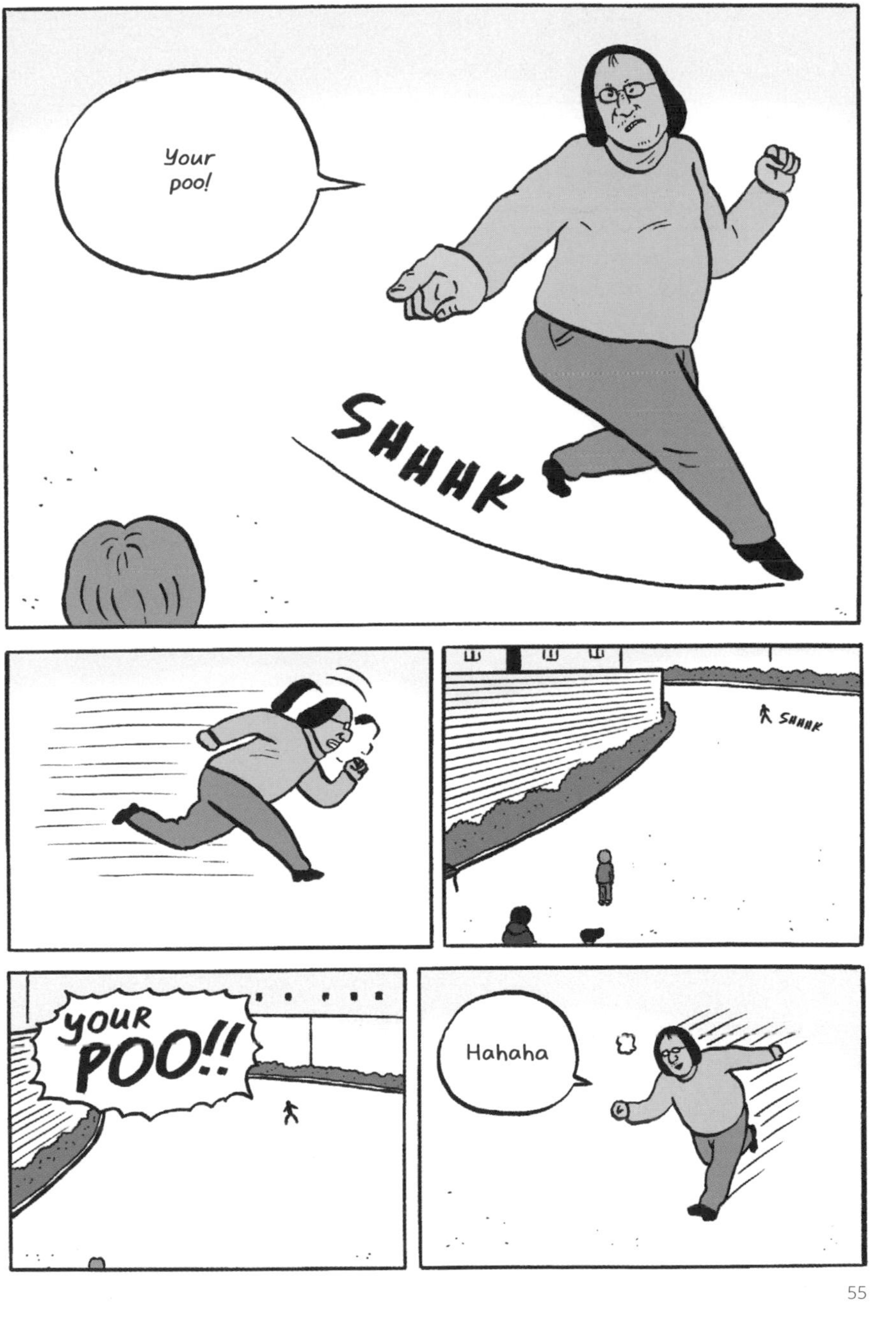
Your poo!
SHHHK
SHHHK
YOUR POO!!
Hahaha

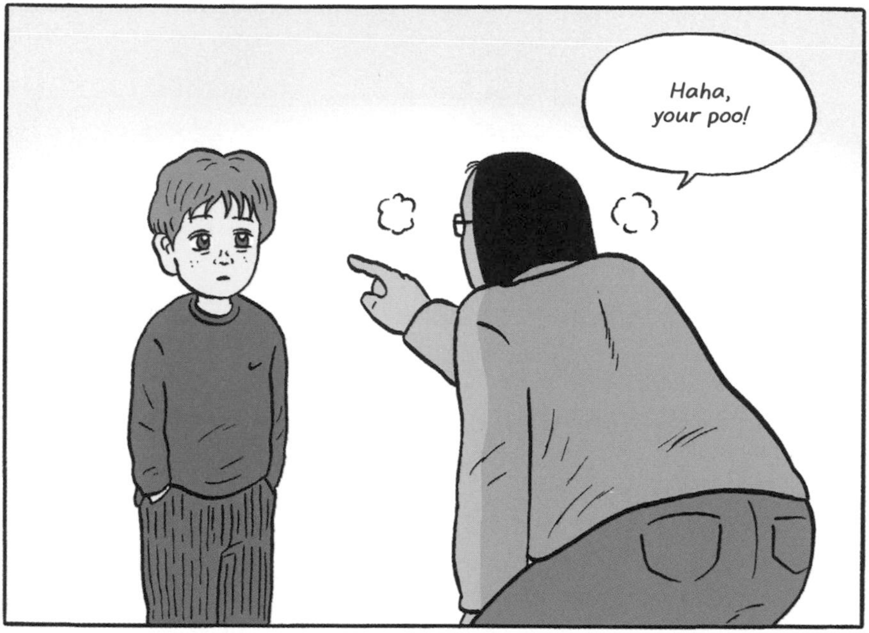
Haha, your poo!

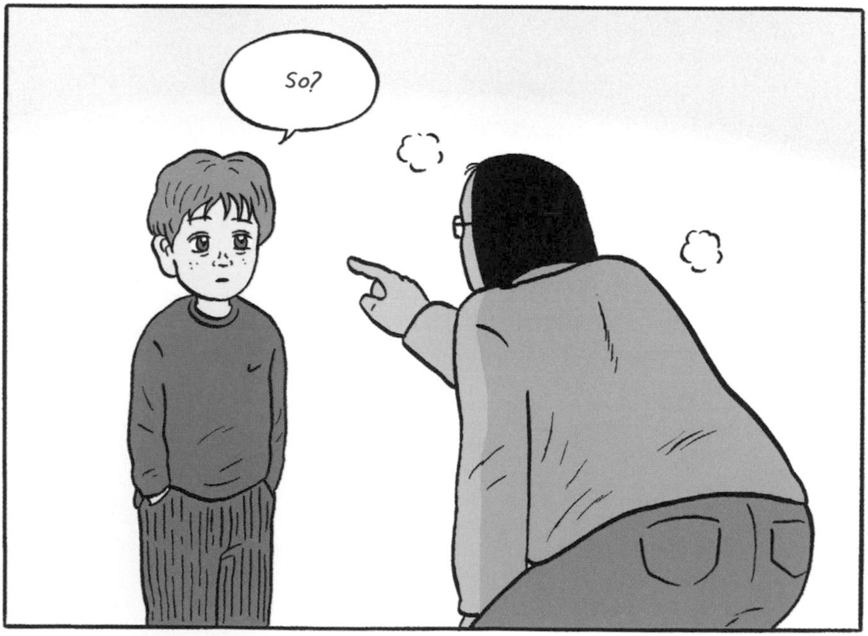
So?

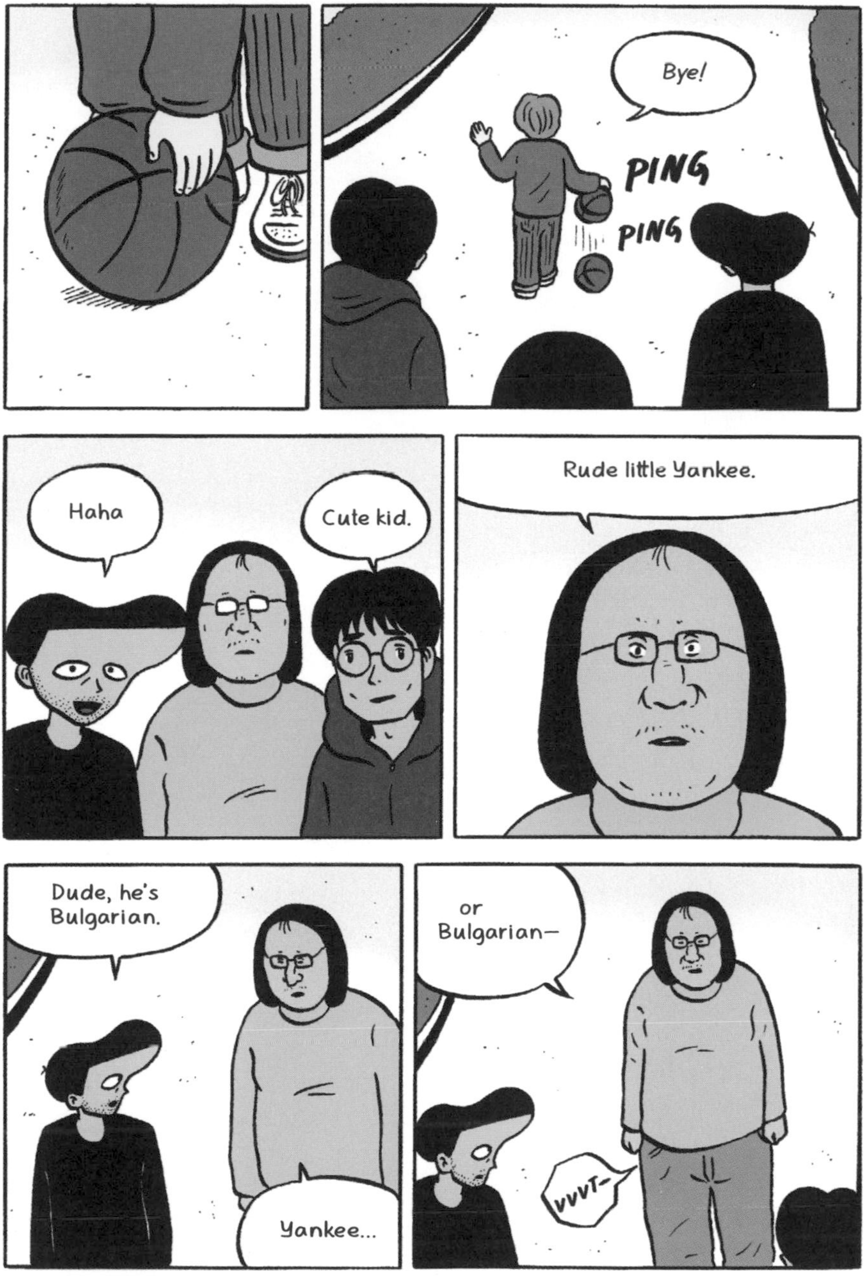
Bye!
PING
PING
Haha
Cute kid.
Rude little Yankee.
Dude, he's Bulgarian.
Yankee...
or Bulgarian—
VVVT-

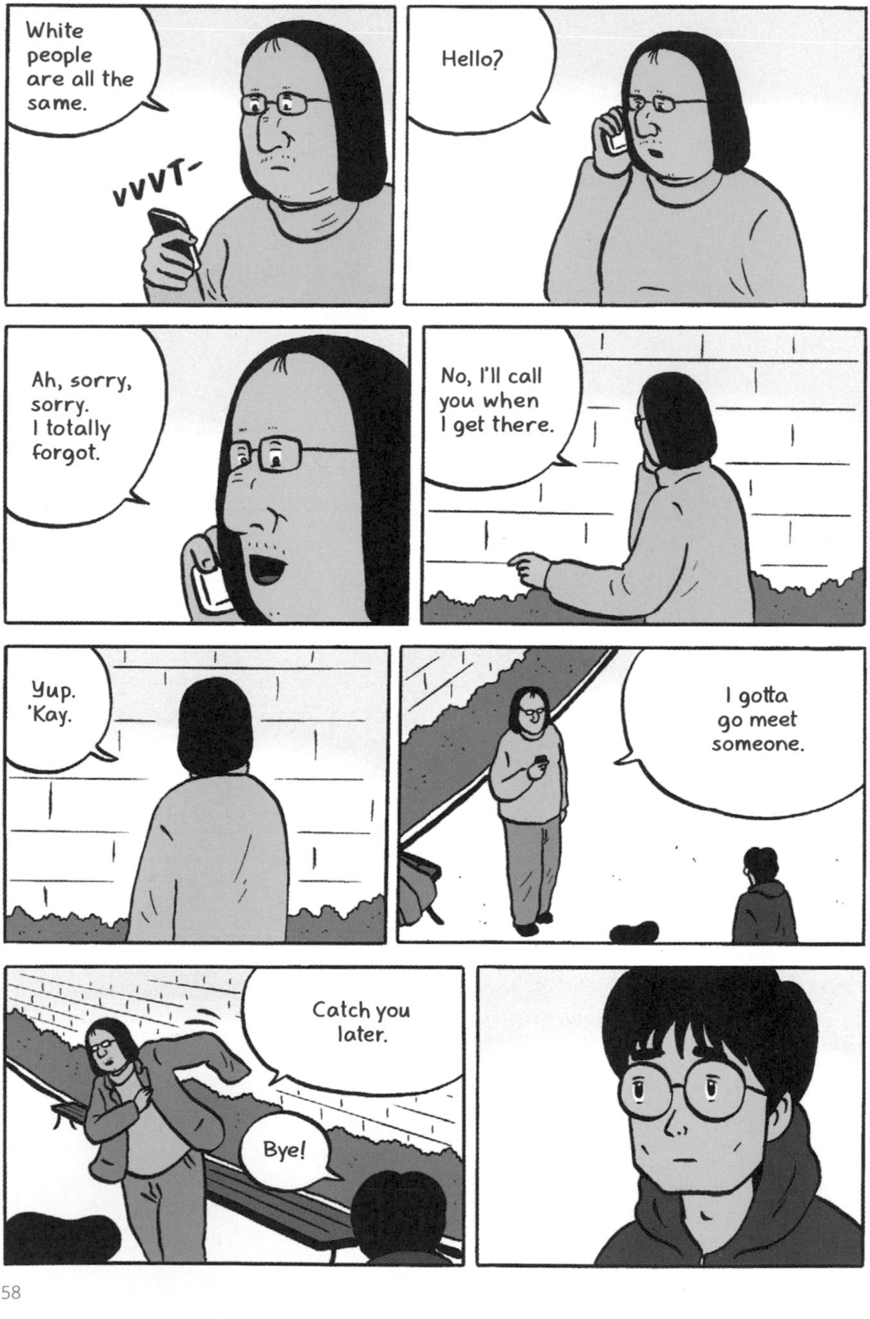
White people are all the same.
VVVT-
Hello?
Ah, sorry, sorry. I totally forgot.
No, I'll call you when I get there.
Yup. 'Kay.
I gotta go meet someone.
Catch you later.
Bye!

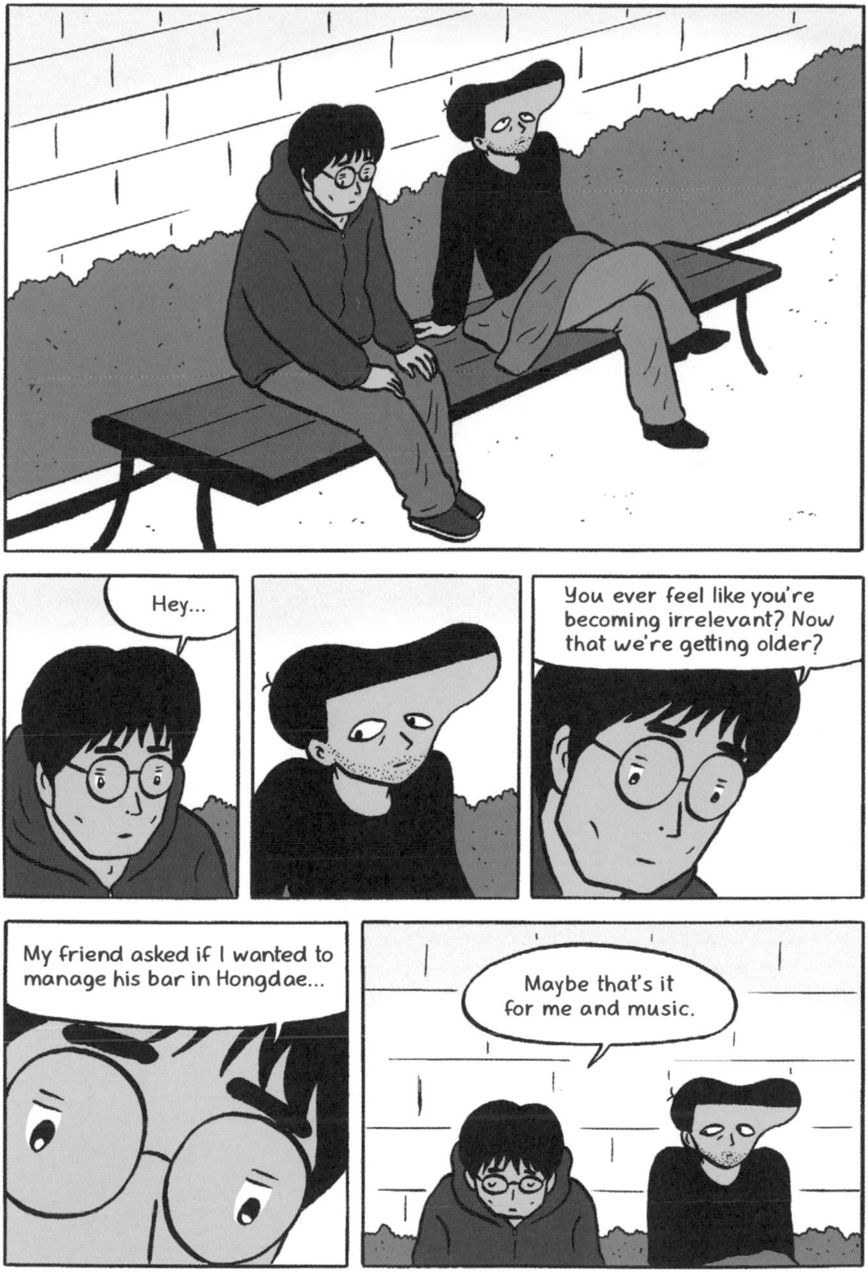
Hey...
You ever feel like you're becoming irrelevant? Now that we're getting older?
My friend asked if I wanted to manage his bar in Hongdae...
Maybe that's it for me and music.

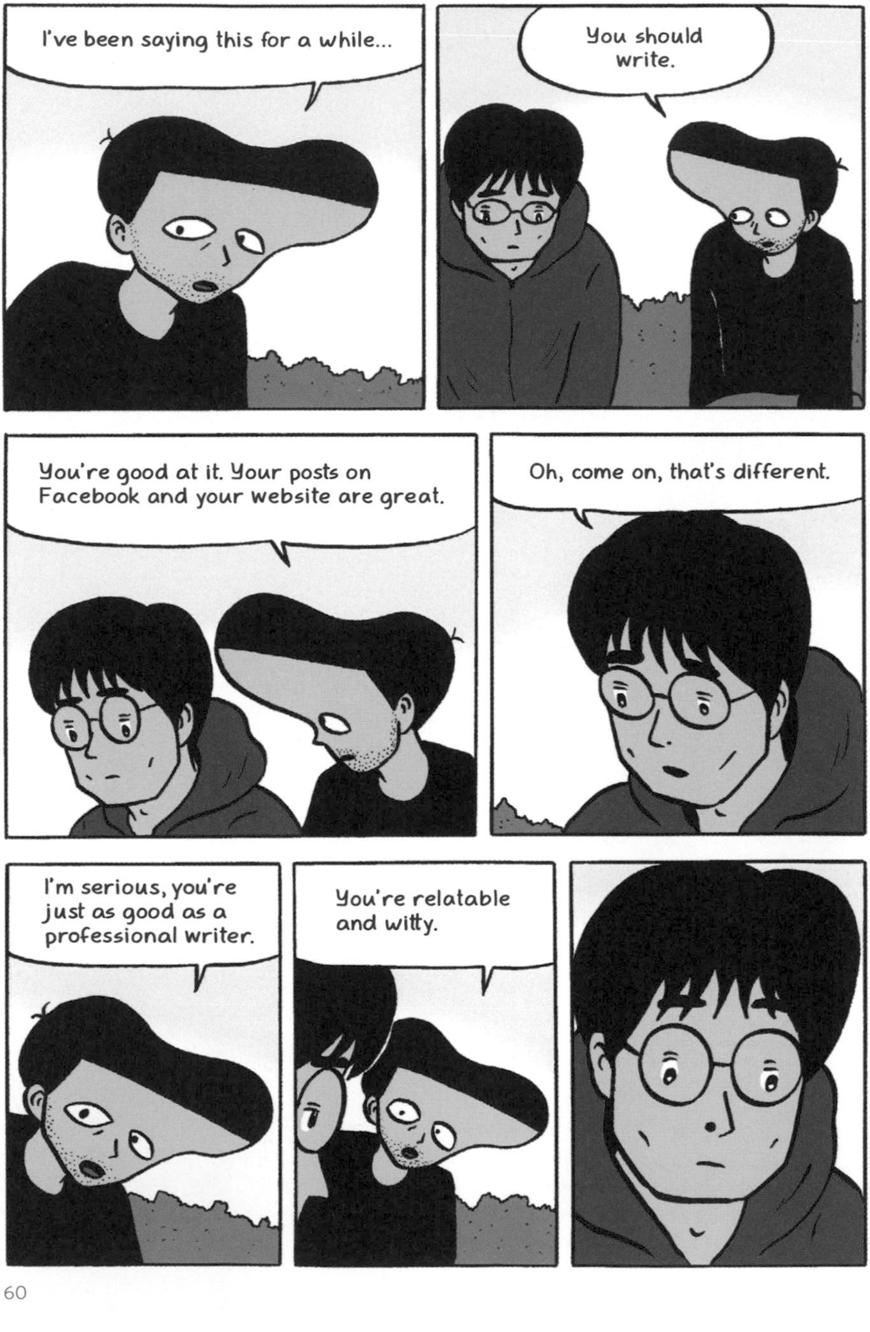
I've been saying this for a while...
You should write.
You're good at it. Your posts on Facebook and your website are great.
Oh, come on, that's different.
I'm serious, you're just as good as a professional writer.
You're relatable and witty.

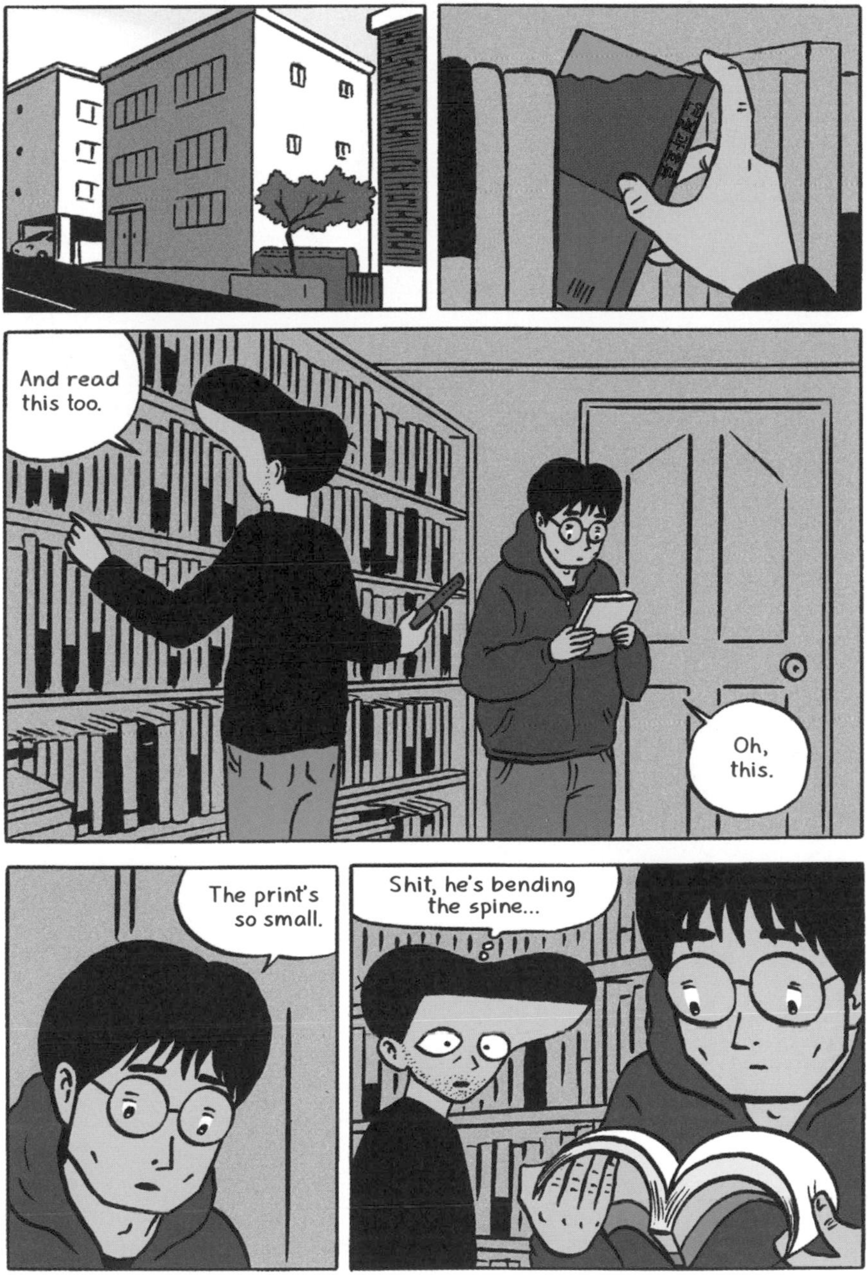
And read this too.
Oh, this.
The print's so small.
Shit, he's bending the spine...

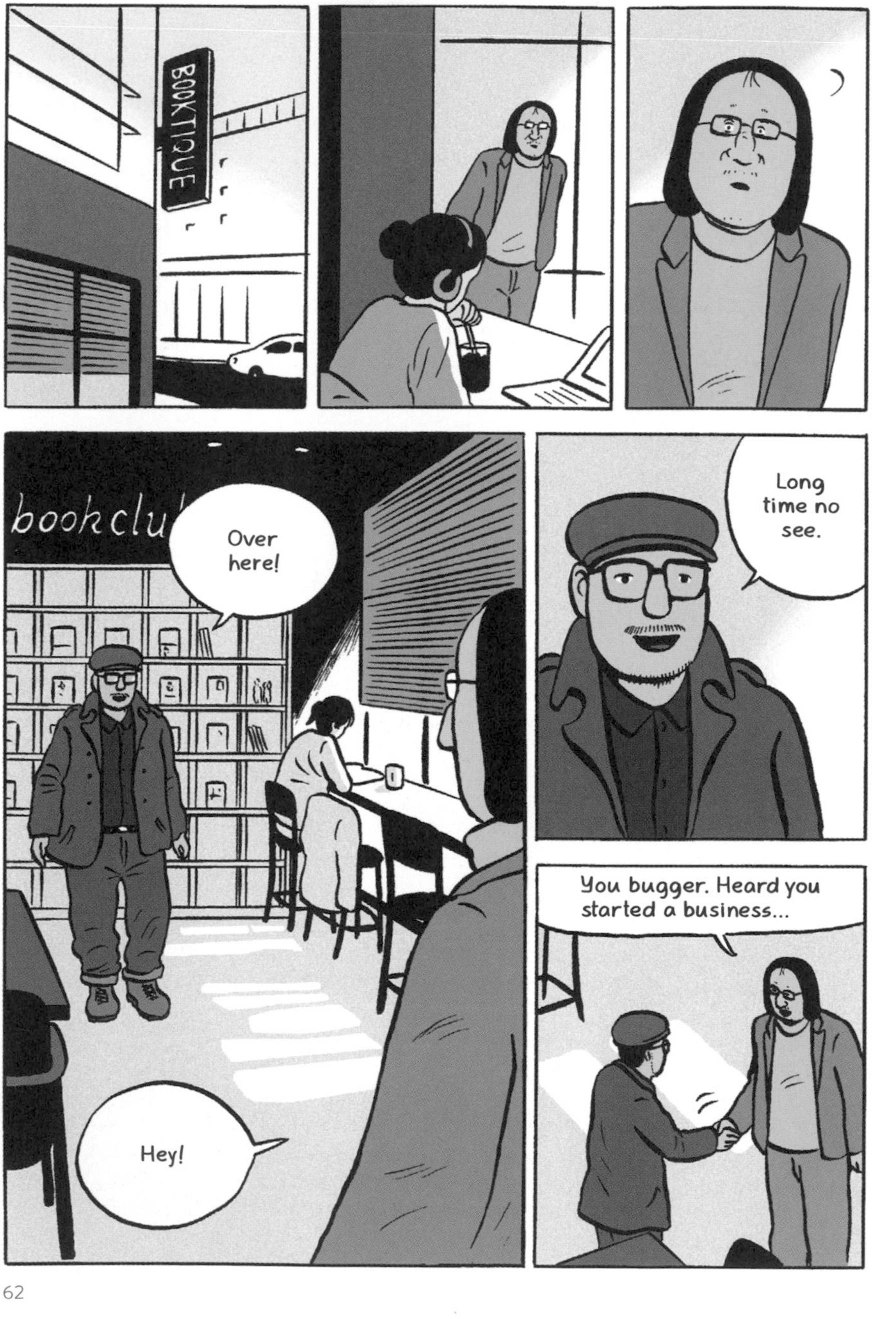
BOOKTIQUE
bookclu
Over here!
Hey!
Long time no see.
You bugger. Heard you started a business...

BUSINESS MEETING

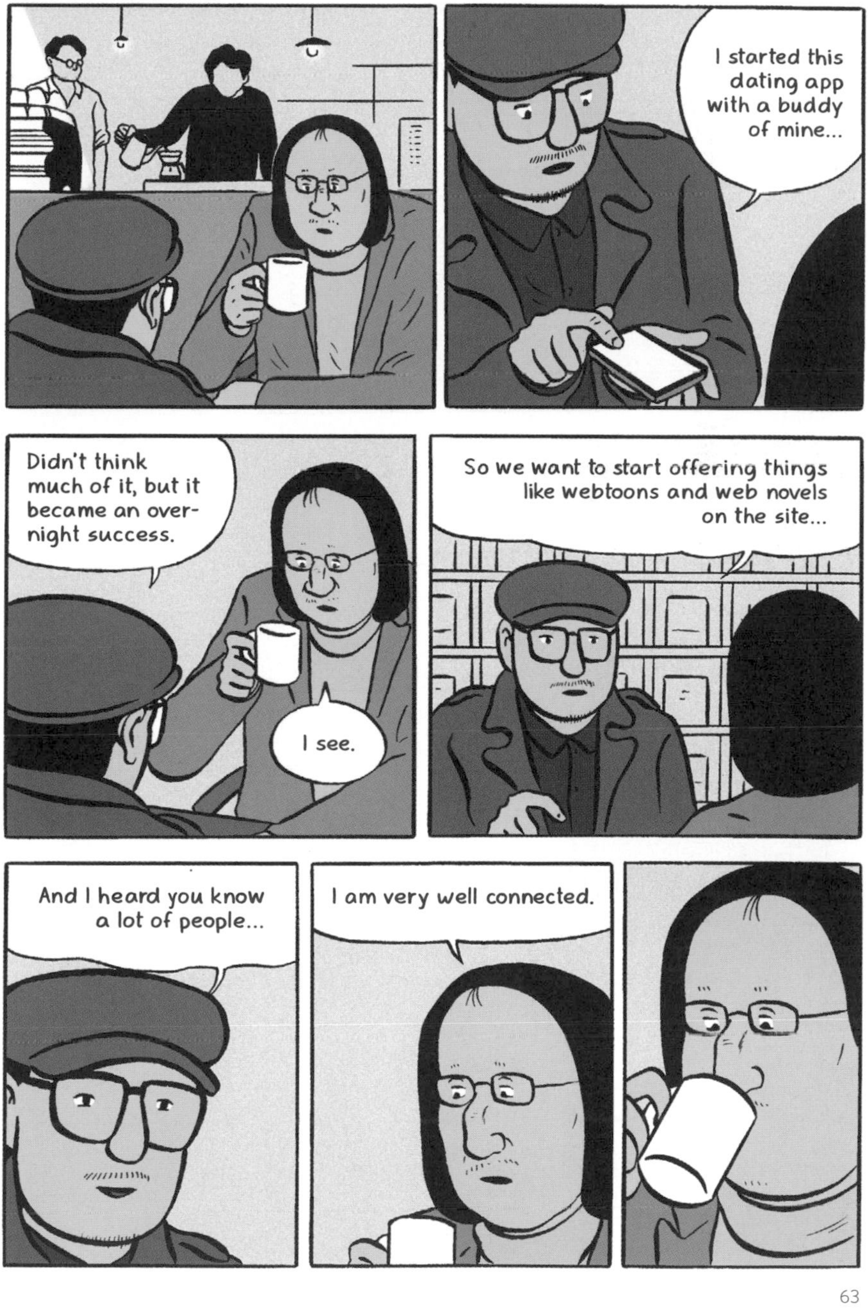
I started this dating app with a buddy of mine...
Didn't think much of it, but it became an over-night success.
I see.
So we want to start offering things like webtoons and web novels on the site...
And I heard you know a lot of people...
I am very well connected.

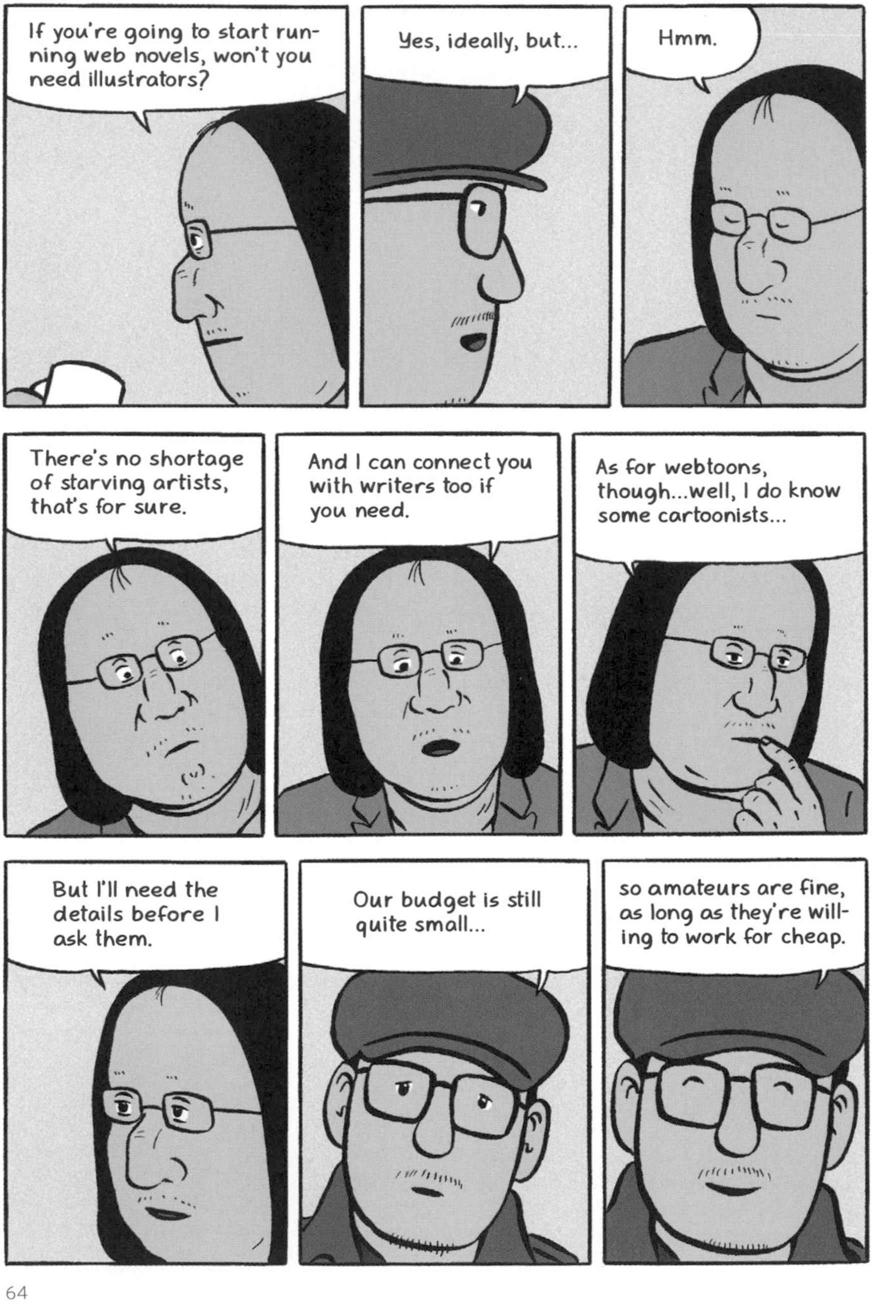
If you're going to start running web novels, won't you need illustrators?
Yes, ideally, but...
Hmm.
There's no shortage of starving artists, that's for sure.
And I can connect you with writers too if you need.
As for webtoons, though...well, I do know some cartoonists...
But I'll need the details before I ask them.
Our budget is still quite small...
so amateurs are fine, as long as they're willing to work for cheap.

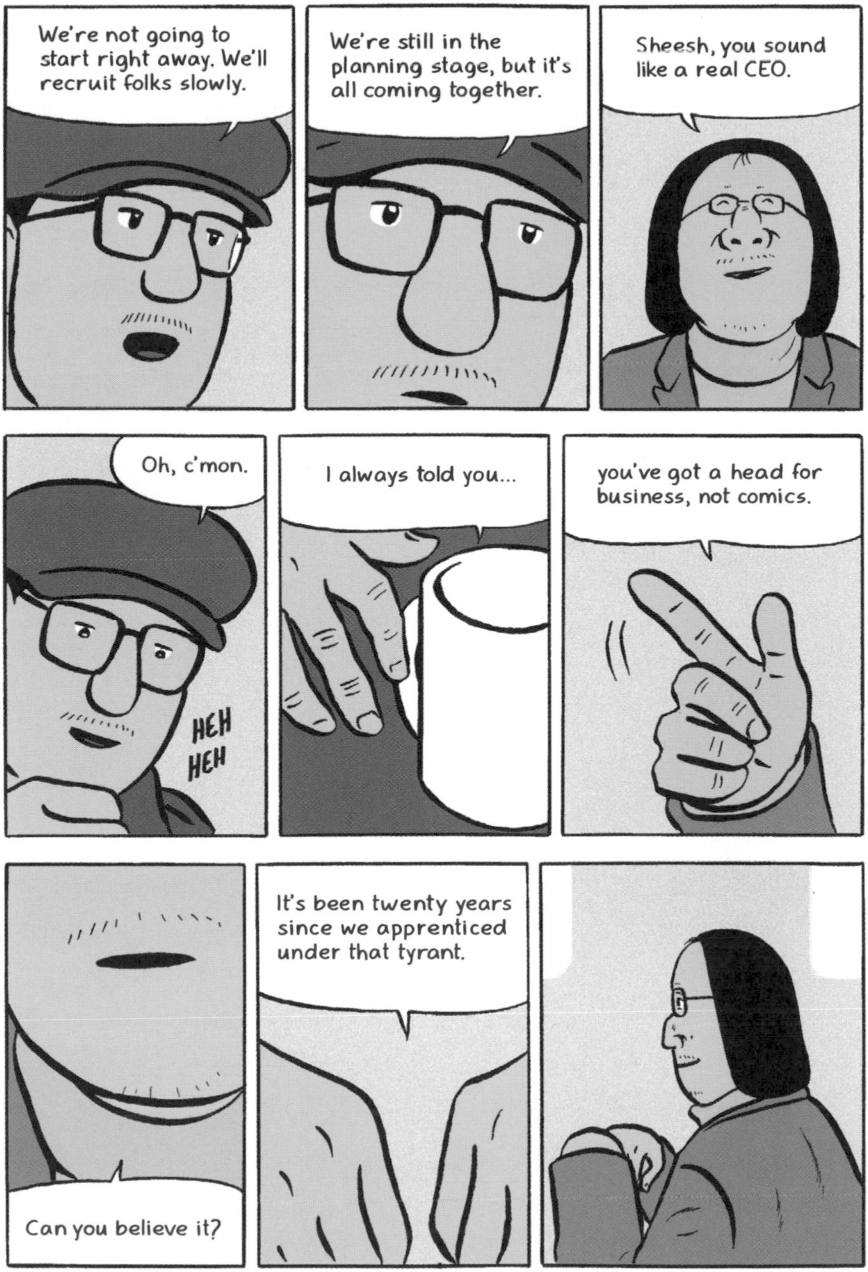
We're not going to start right away. We'll recruit folks slowly.
We're still in the planning stage, but it's all coming together.
Sheesh, you sound like a real CEO.
Oh, c'mon.
HEH HEH
I always told you...
you've got a head for business, not comics.
Can you believe it?
It's been twenty years since we apprenticed under that tyrant.

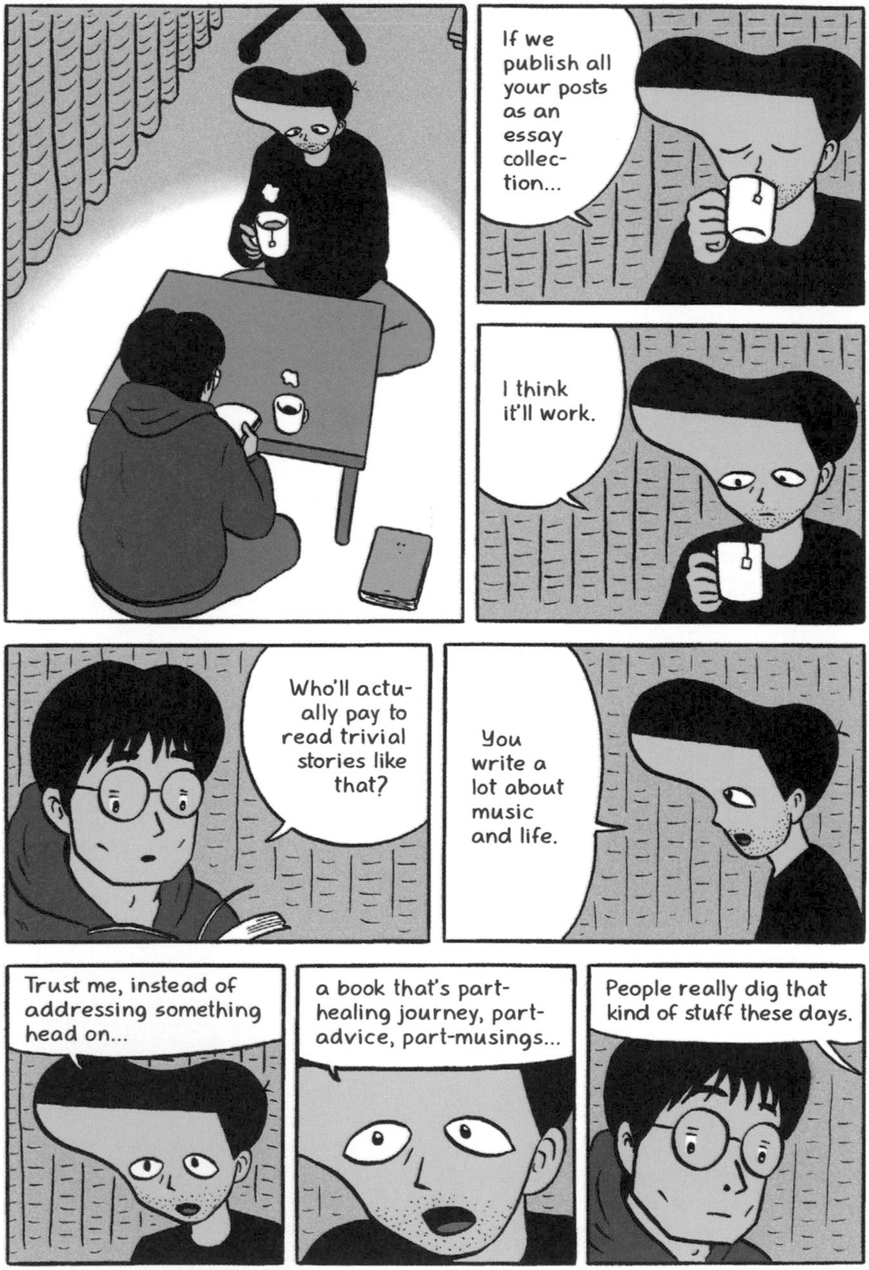
If we publish all your posts as an essay collec-tion...
I think it'll work.
Who'll actu-ally pay to read trivial stories like that?
You write a lot about music and life.
Trust me, instead of addressing something head on...
a book that's part-healing journey, part-advice, part-musings...
People really dig that kind of stuff these days.

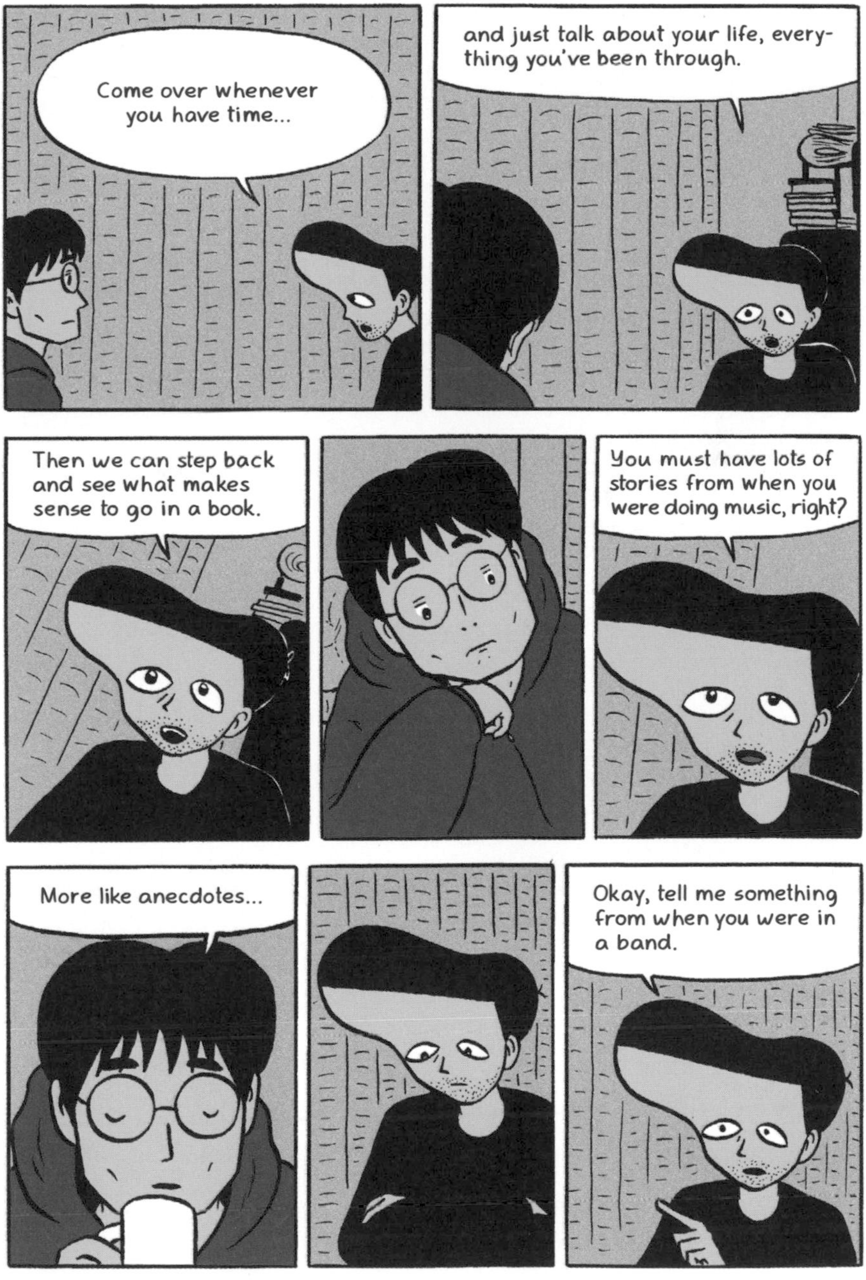
Come over whenever you have time...
and just talk about your life, everything you've been through.
Then we can step back and see what makes sense to go in a book.
You must have lots of stories from when you were doing music, right?
More like anecdotes...
Okay, tell me something from when you were in a band.

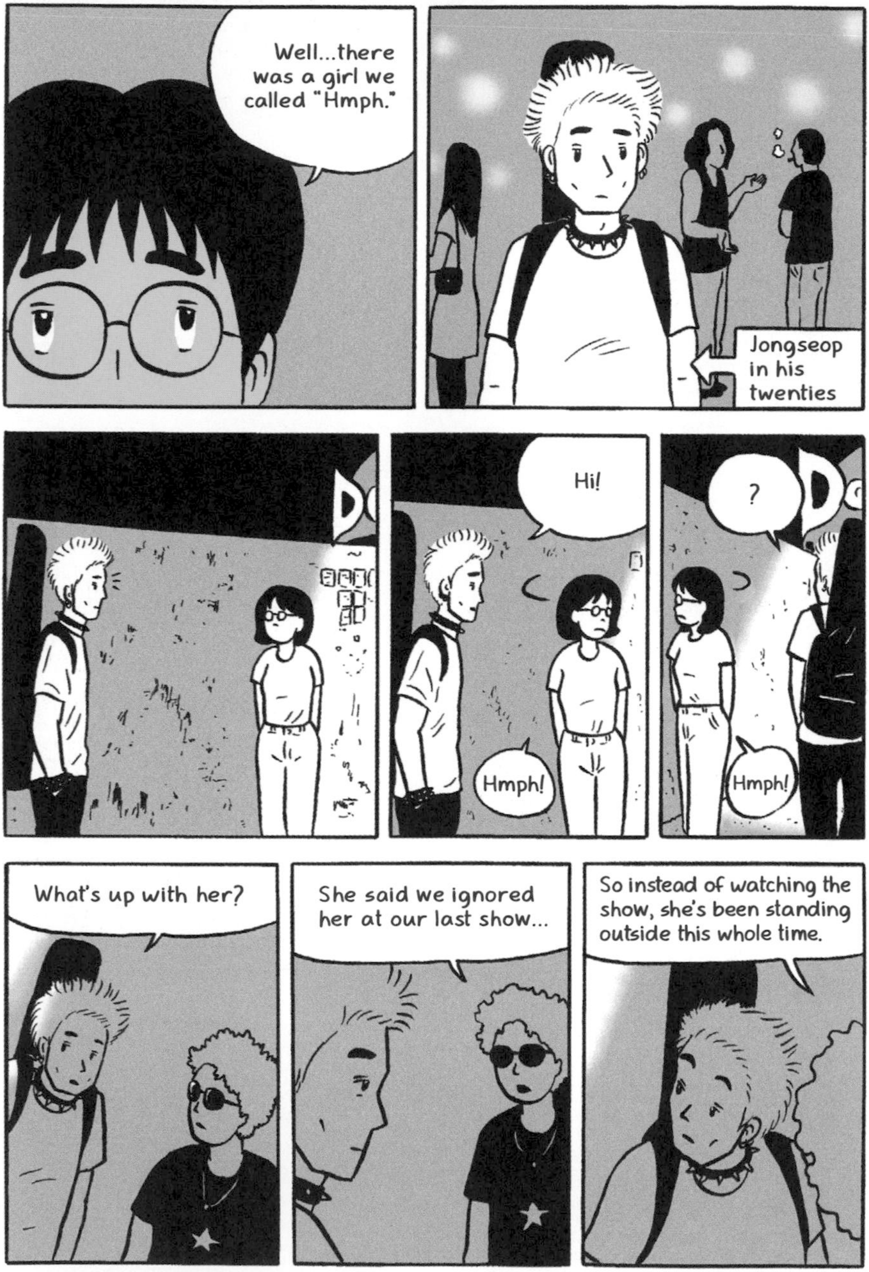
Well...there was a girl we called "Hmph."
Jongseop in his twenties
Hi!
Hmph!
?
Hmph!
What's up with her?
She said we ignored her at our last show...
So instead of watching the show, she's been standing outside this whole time.

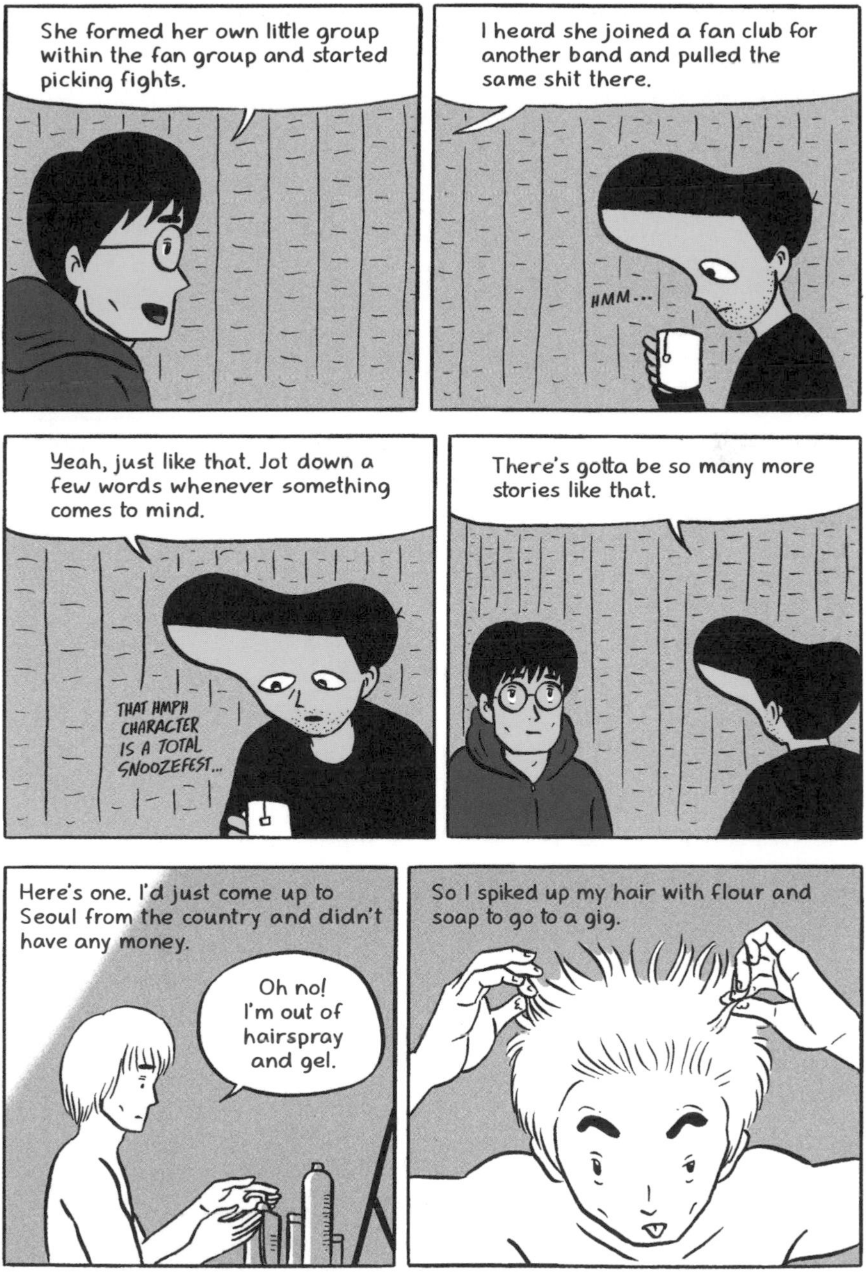
She formed her own little group within the fan group and started picking fights.
I heard she joined a fan club for another band and pulled the same shit there.
HMM...
Yeah, just like that. Jot down a few words whenever something comes to mind.
THAT HMPH CHARACTER IS A TOTAL SNOOZEFEST...
There's gotta be so many more stories like that.
Here's one. I'd just come up to Seoul from the country and didn't have any money.
Oh no! I'm out of hairspray and gel.
So I spiked up my hair with flour and soap to go to a gig.

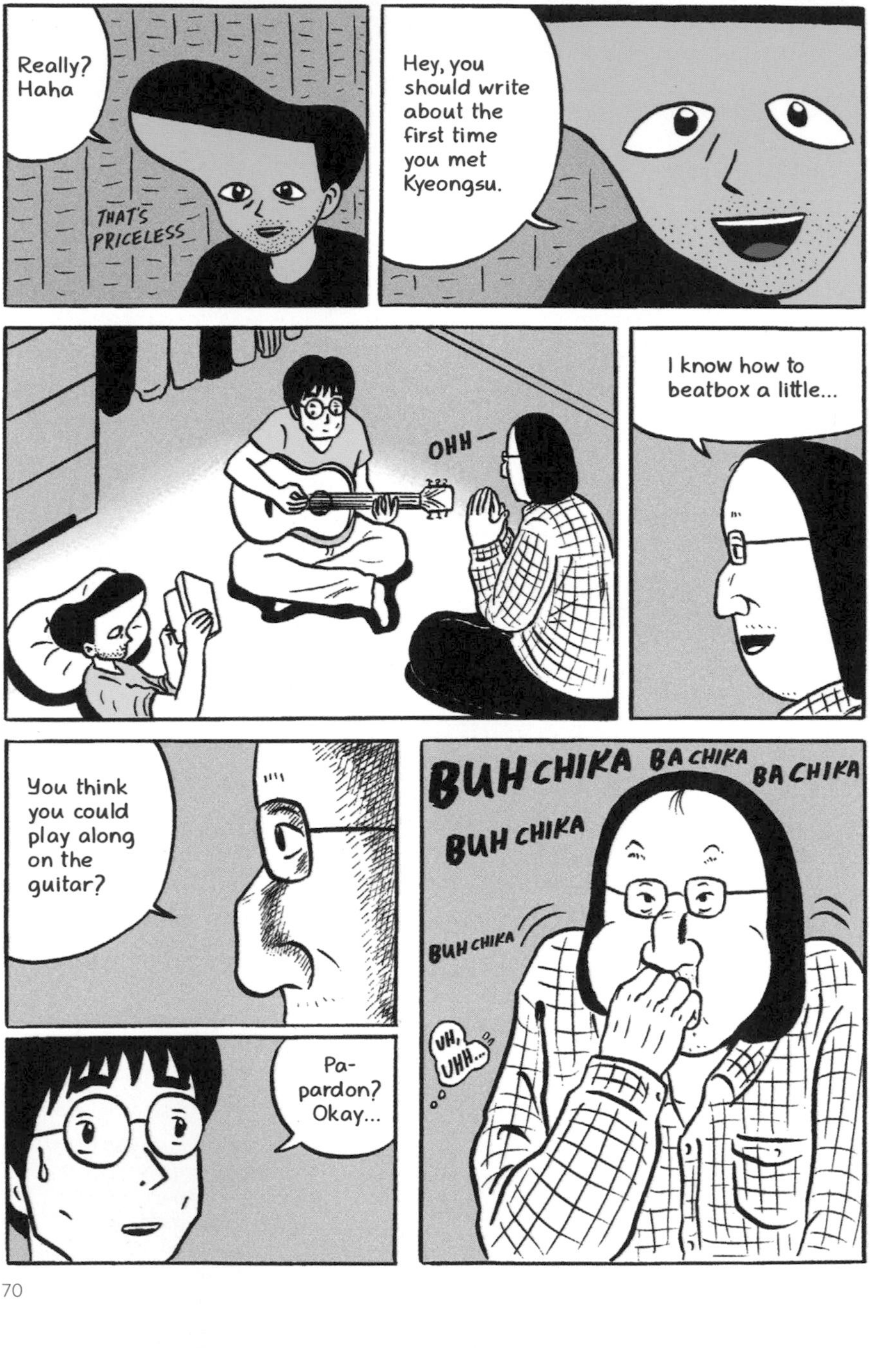

Really? Haha
THAT'S PRICELESS
Hey, you should write about the first time you met Kyeongsu.
OHH—
I know how to beatbox a little...
You think you could play along on the guitar?
Pa- pardon? Okay...
BUH CHIKA BA CHIKA BA CHIKA
BUH CHIKA
BUH CHIKA
UH, UHH...

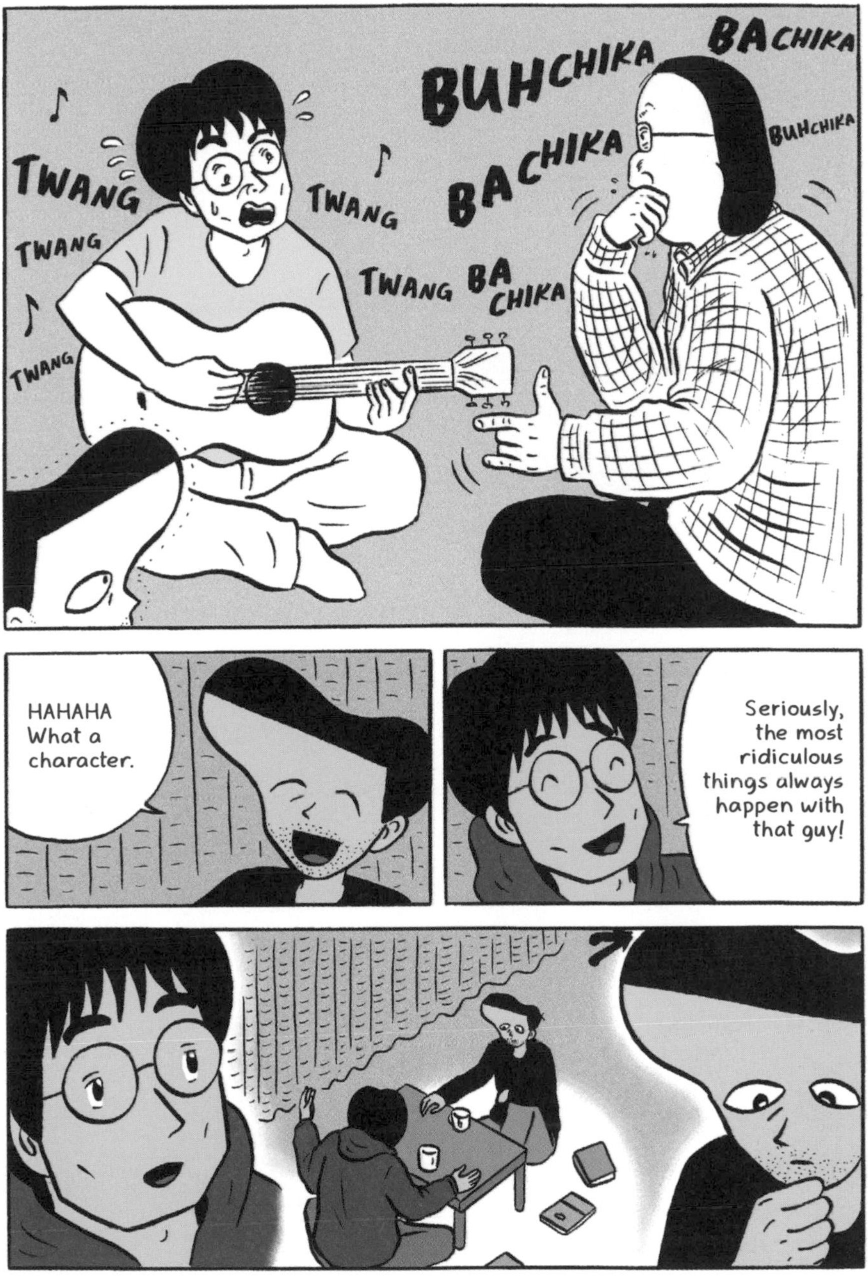
TWANG
TWANG
TWANG
TWANG
TWANG
BUHCHIKA
BACHIKA
BACHIKA
BUHCHIKA
BACHIKA
BA CHIKA
HAHAHA What a character.
Seriously, the most ridiculous things always happen with that guy!

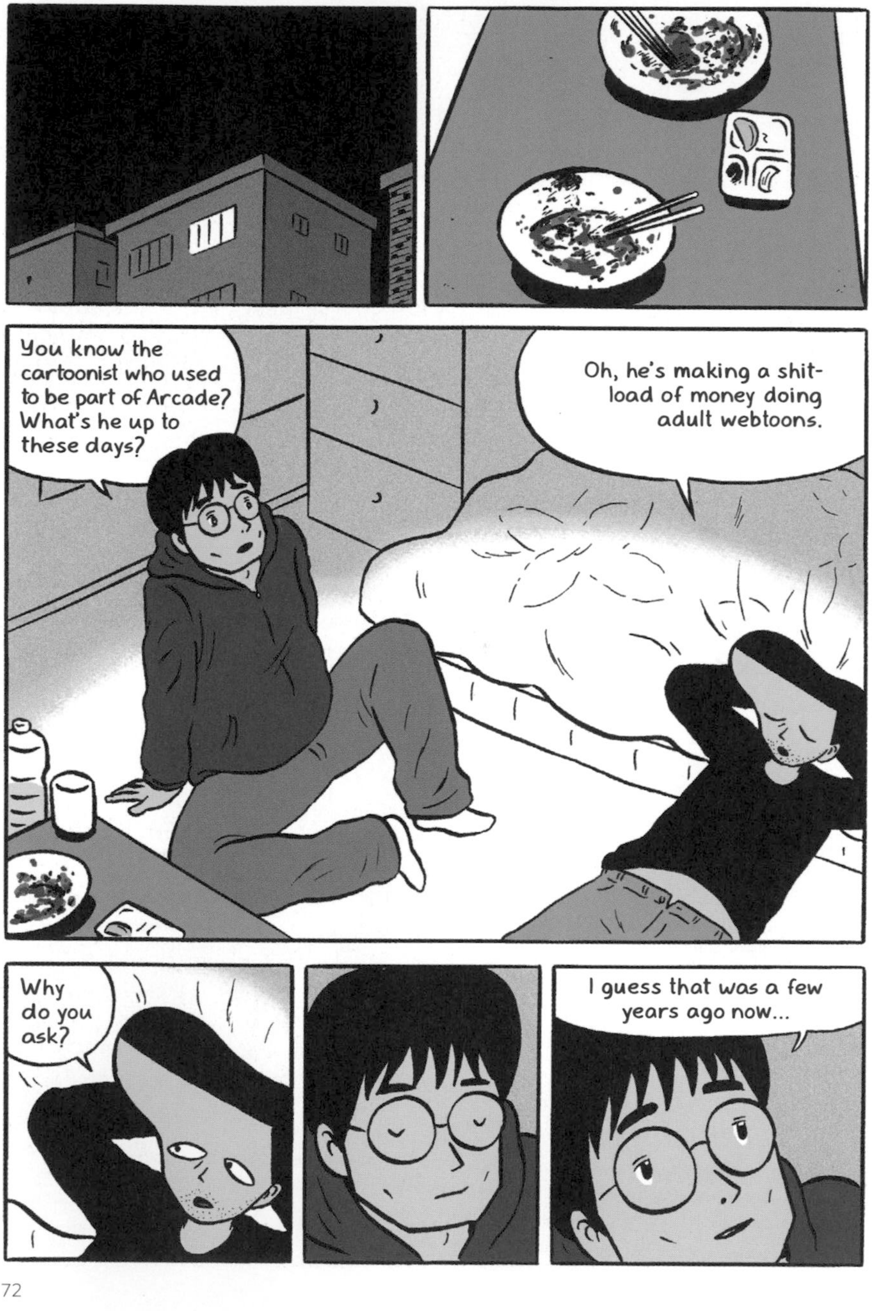
You know the cartoonist who used to be part of Arcade? What's he up to these days?
Oh, he's making a shit-load of money doing adult webtoons.
Why do you ask?
I guess that was a few years ago now...

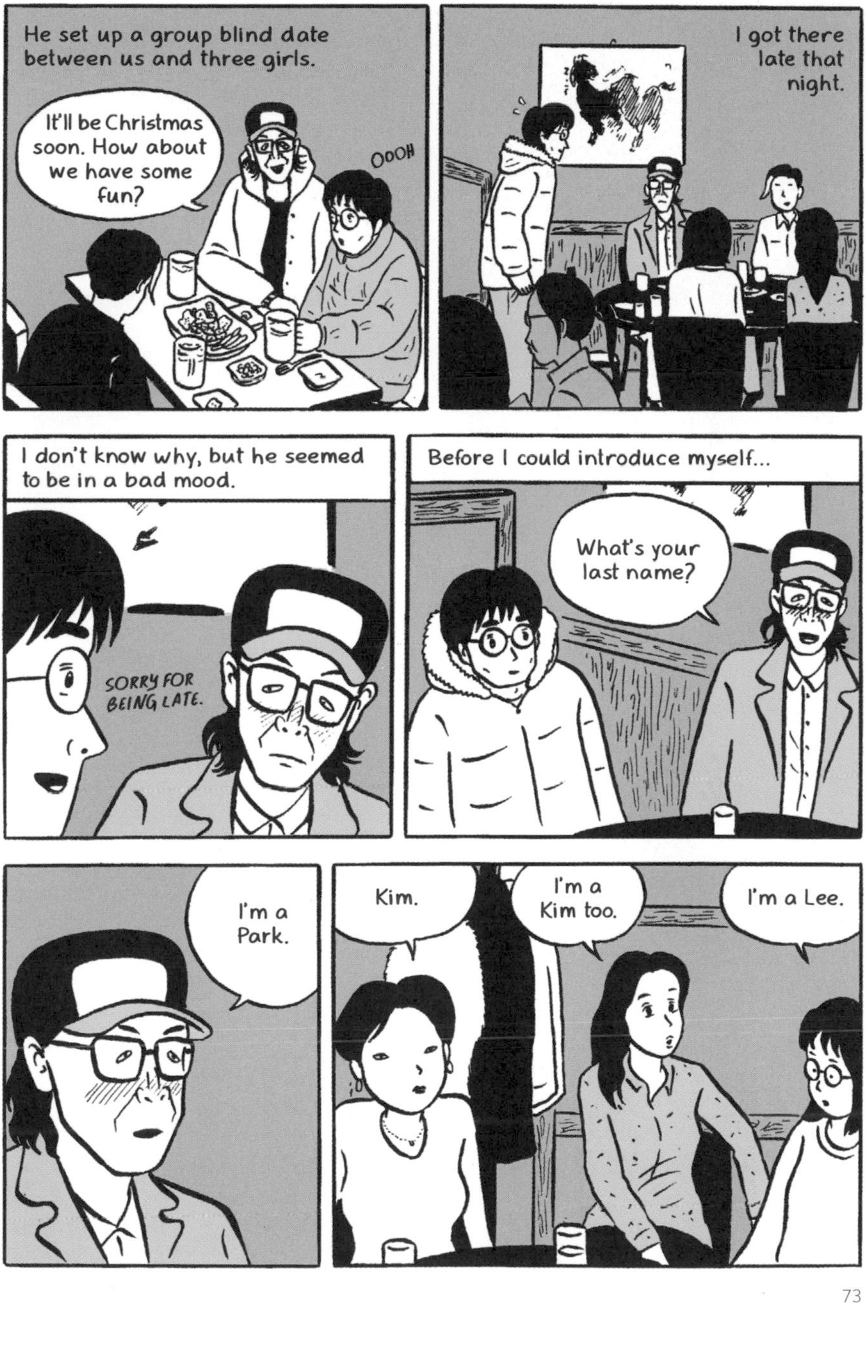
He set up a group blind date between us and three girls.
It'll be Christmas soon. How about we have some fun?
OOOH
I got there late that night.
I don't know why, but he seemed to be in a bad mood.
SORRY FOR BEING LATE.
Before I could introduce myself...
What's your last name?
I'm a Park.
Kim.
I'm a Kim too.
I'm a Lee.

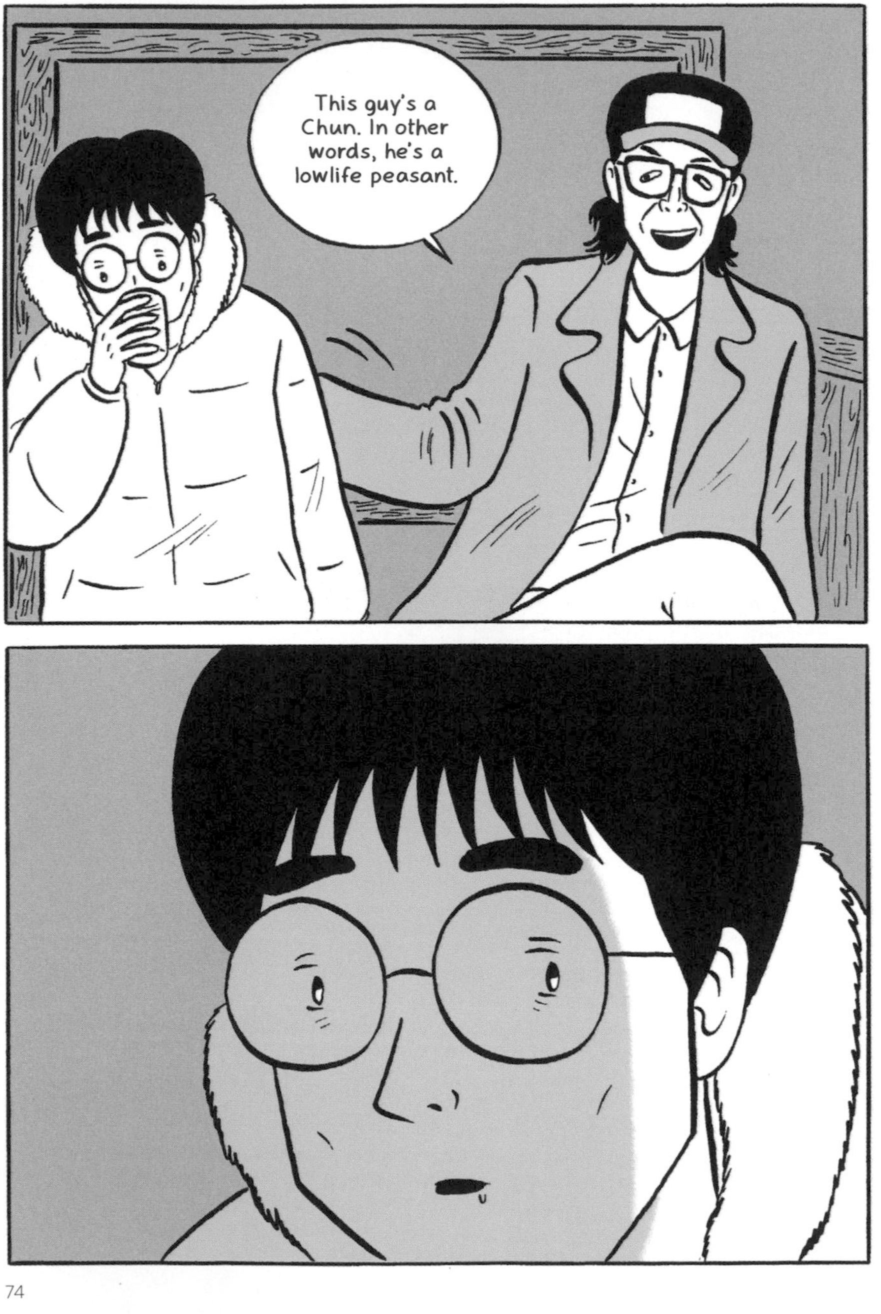
This guy's a Chun. In other words, he's a lowlife peasant.

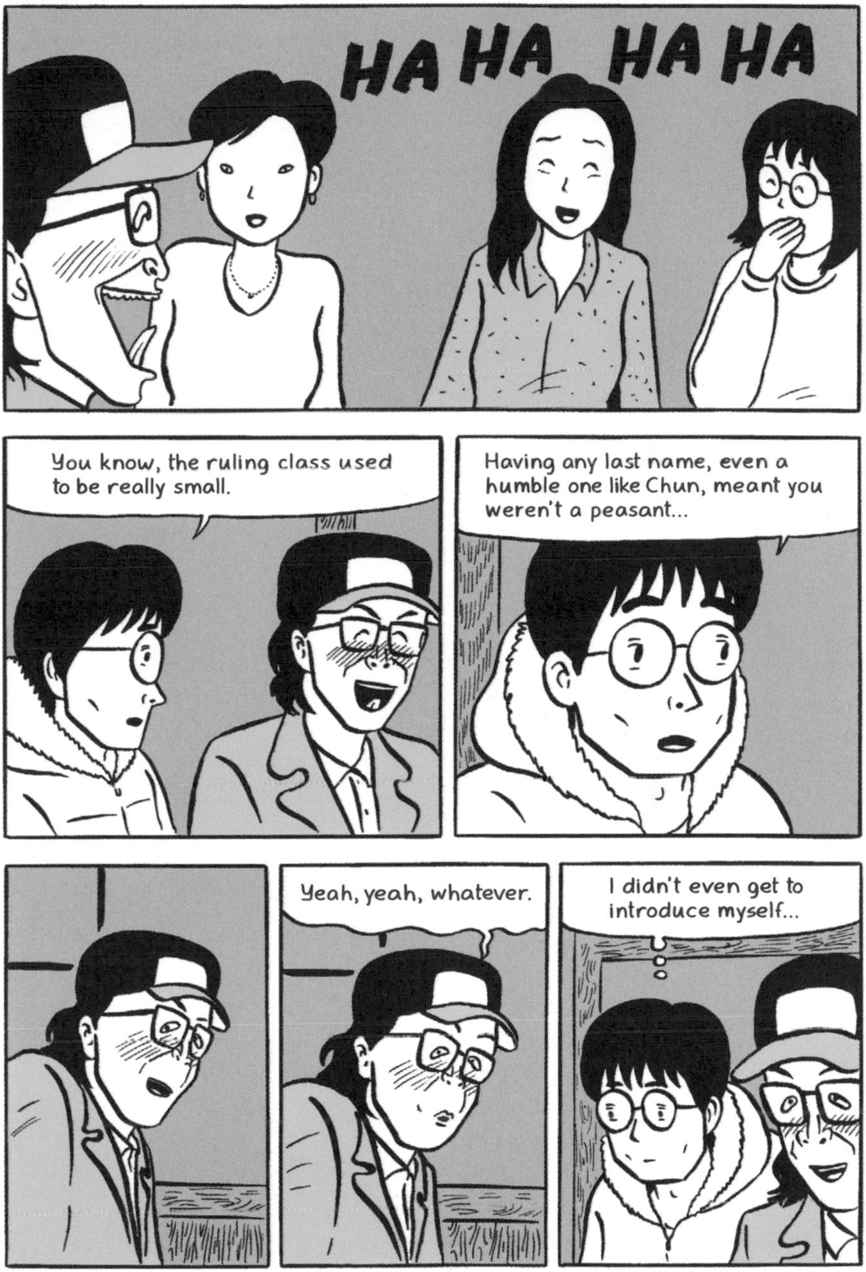
HA HA HA HA
You know, the ruling class used to be really small.
Having any last name, even a humble one like Chun, meant you weren't a peasant...
Yeah, yeah, whatever.
I didn't even get to introduce myself...

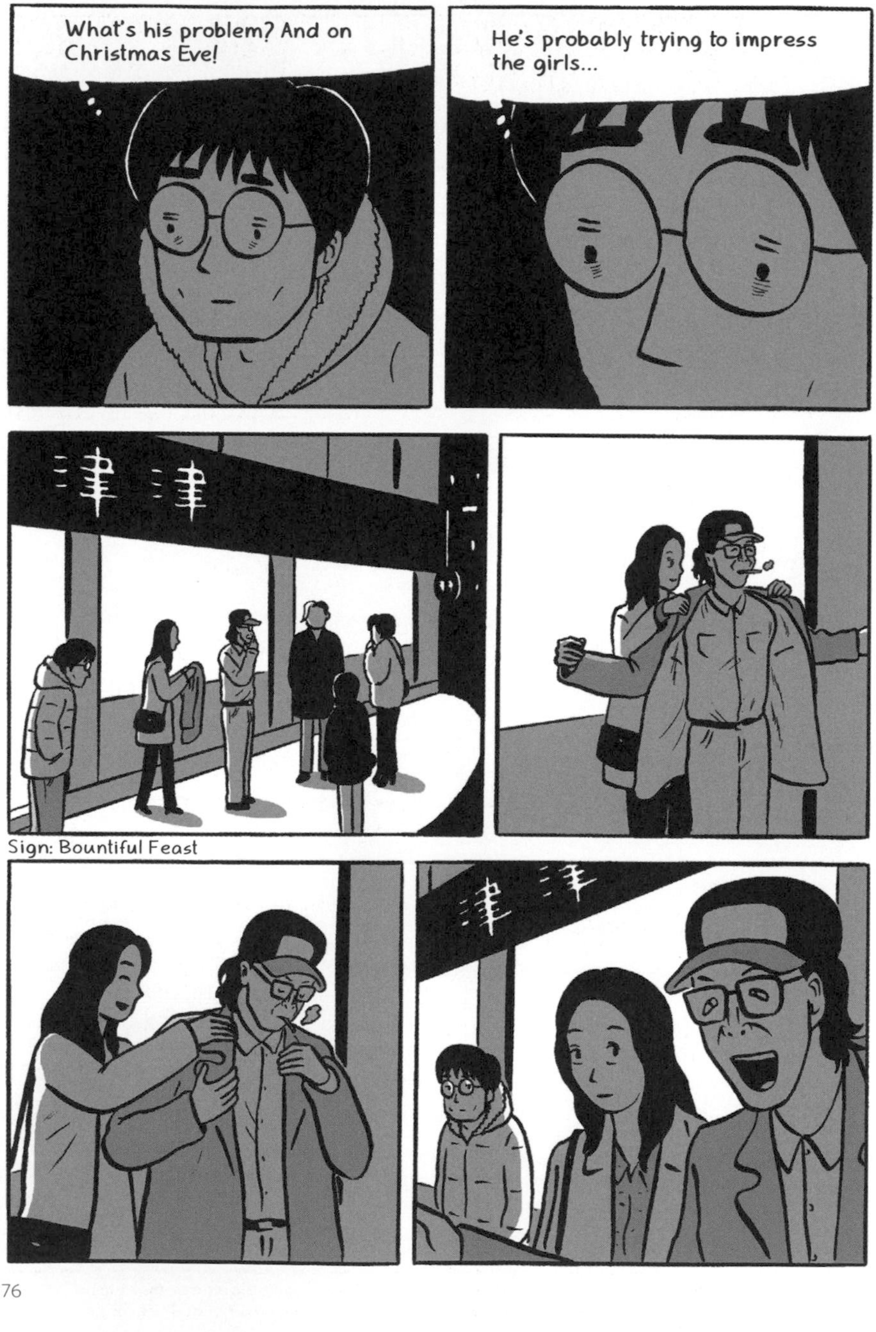
What's his problem? And on Christmas Eve!
He's probably trying to impress the girls...
Sign: Bountiful Feast

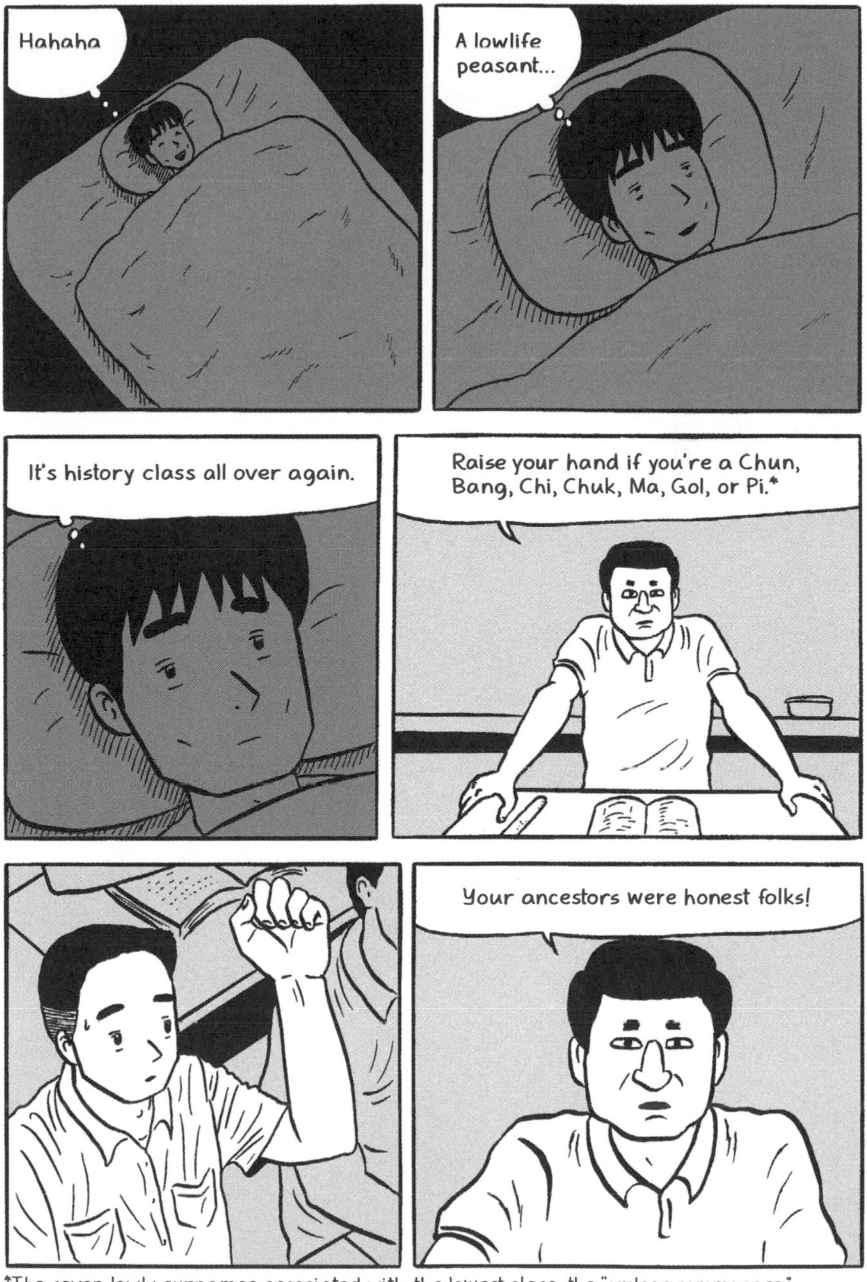
Hahaha
A lowlife peasant...
It's history class all over again.
Raise your hand if you're a Chun, Bang, Chi, Chuk, Ma, Gol, or Pi.*
Your ancestors were honest folks!

*The seven lowly surnames associated with the lowest class, the "vulgar commoners." However, this is understood to be an urban legend, since there are no such records.

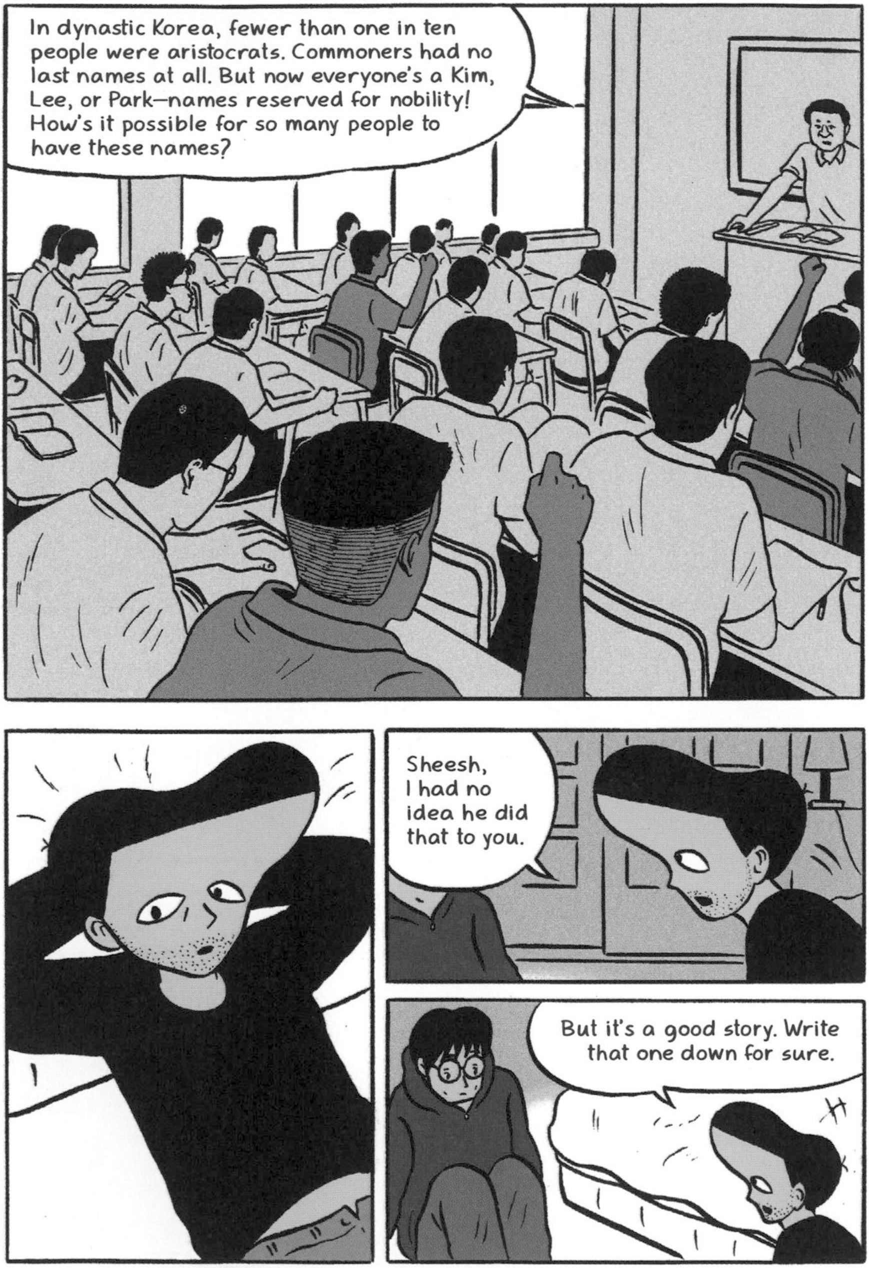
In dynastic Korea, fewer than one in ten people were aristocrats. Commoners had no last names at all. But now everyone's a Kim, Lee, or Park—names reserved for nobility! How's it possible for so many people to have these names?
Sheesh, I had no idea he did that to you.
But it's a good story. Write that one down for sure.

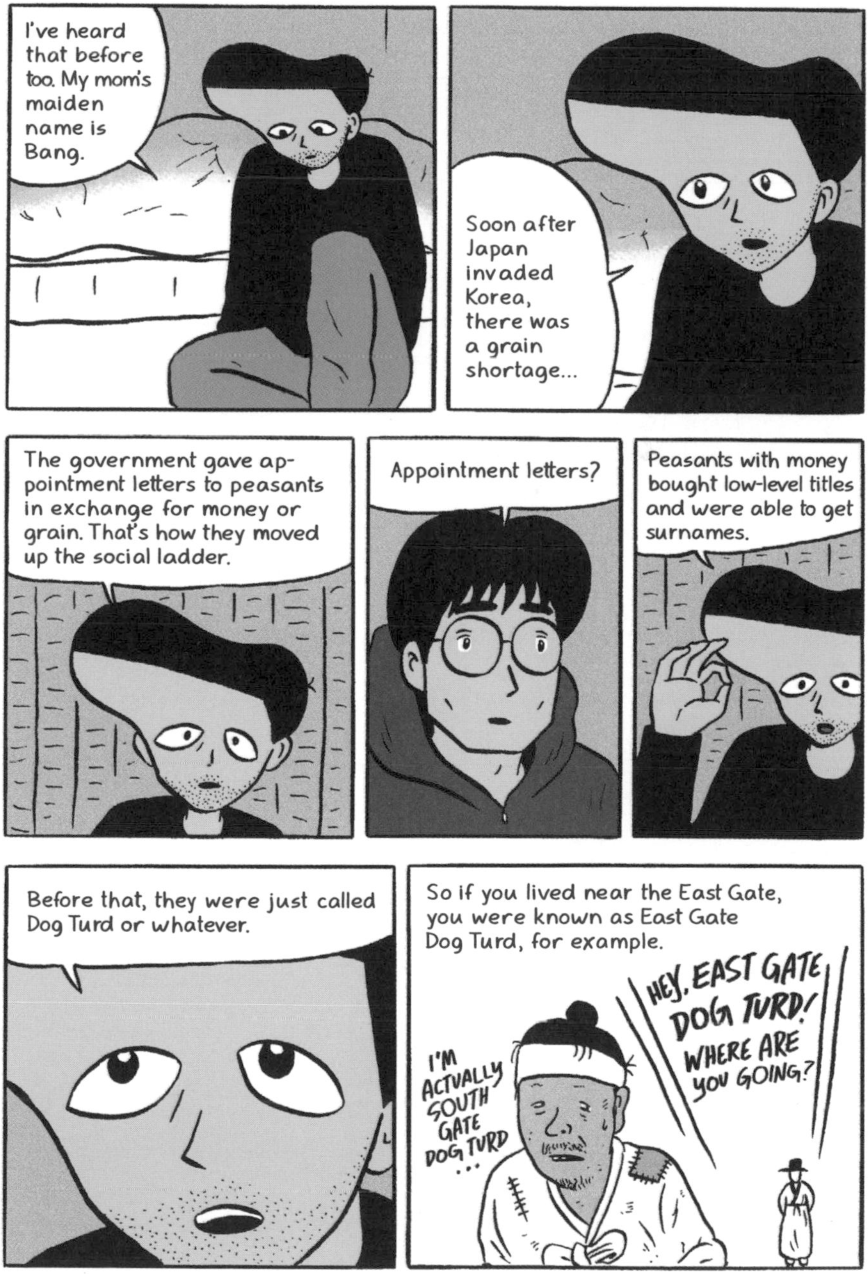

I've heard that before too. My mom's maiden name is Bang.
Soon after Japan invaded Korea, there was a grain shortage...
The government gave appointment letters to peasants in exchange for money or grain. That's how they moved up the social ladder.
Appointment letters?
Peasants with money bought low-level titles and were able to get surnames.
Before that, they were just called Dog Turd or whatever.
So if you lived near the East Gate, you were known as East Gate Dog Turd, for example.
HEY, EAST GATE DOG TURD! WHERE ARE YOU GOING?
I'M ACTUALLY SOUTH GATE DOG TURD...

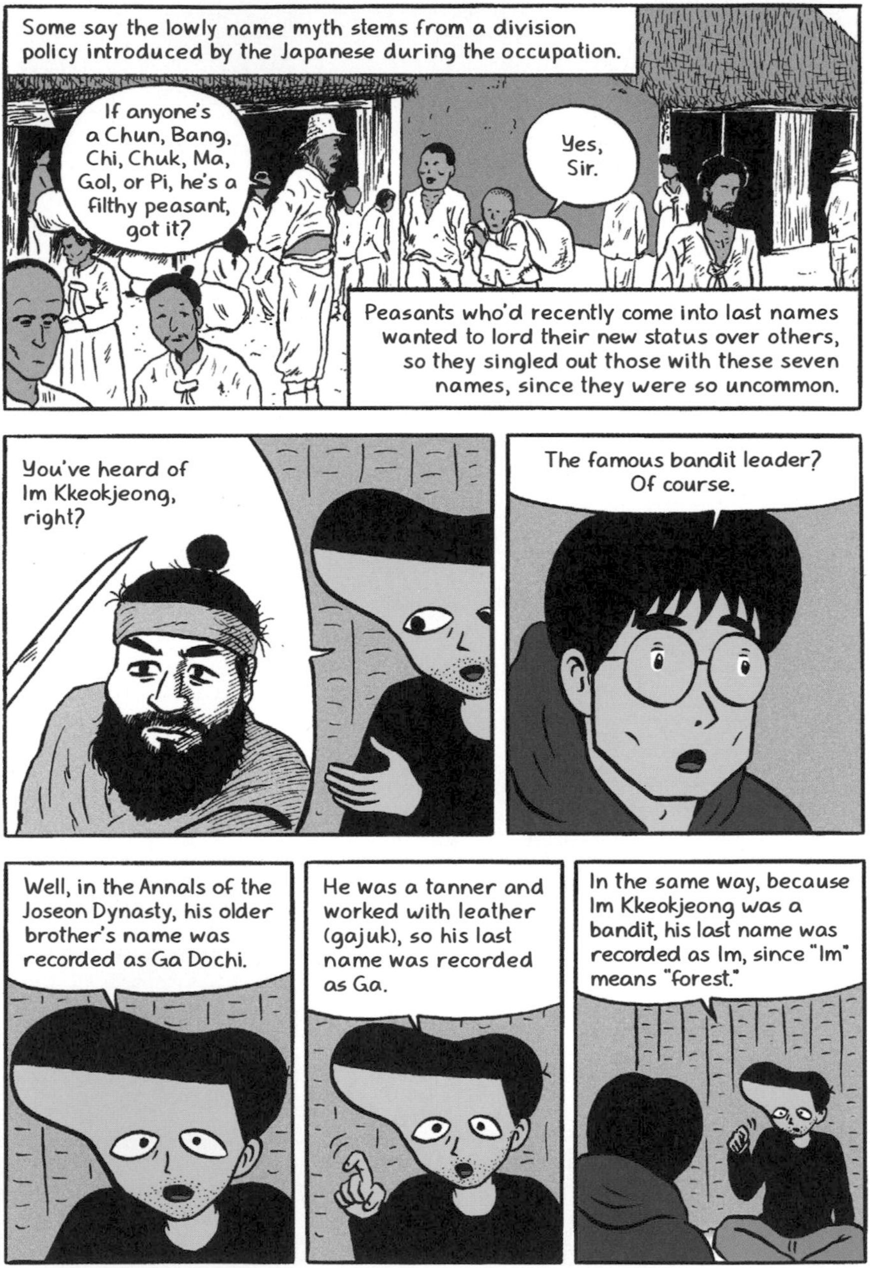
Some say the lowly name myth stems from a division policy introduced by the Japanese during the occupation.
If anyone's a Chun, Bang, Chi, Chuk, Ma, Gol, or Pi, he's a filthy peasant, got it?
Yes, Sir.
Peasants who'd recently come into last names wanted to lord their new status over others, so they singled out those with these seven names, since they were so uncommon.
You've heard of Im Kkeokjeong, right?
The famous bandit leader? Of course.
Well, in the Annals of the Joseon Dynasty, his older brother's name was recorded as Ga Dochi.
He was a tanner and worked with leather (gajuk), so his last name was recorded as Ga.
In the same way, because Im Kkeokjeong was a bandit, his last name was recorded as Im, since "Im" means "forest."

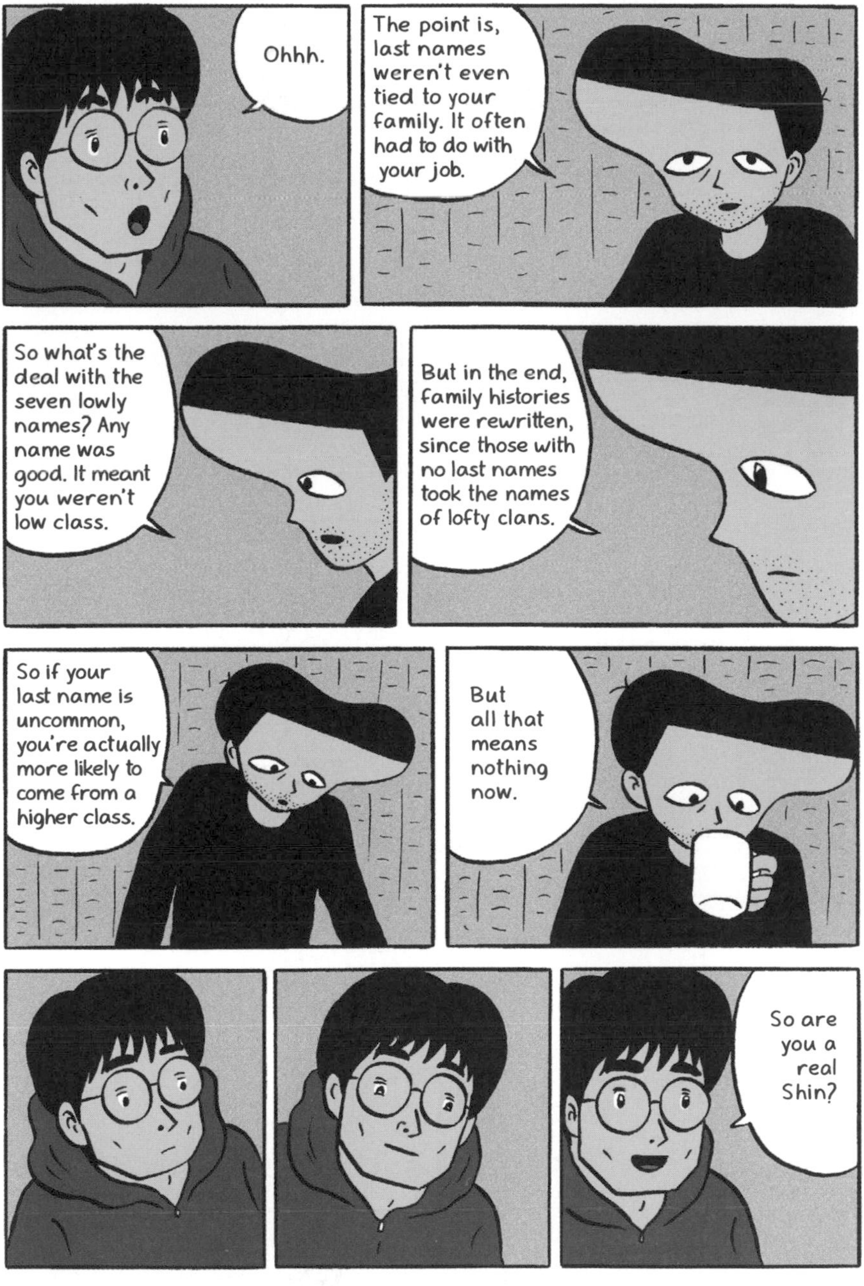
Ohhh.
The point is, last names weren't even tied to your family. It often had to do with your job.
So what's the deal with the seven lowly names? Any name was good. It meant you weren't low class.
But in the end, family histories were rewritten, since those with no last names took the names of lofty clans.
So if your last name is uncommon, you're actually more likely to come from a higher class.
But all that means nothing now.
So are you a real Shin?

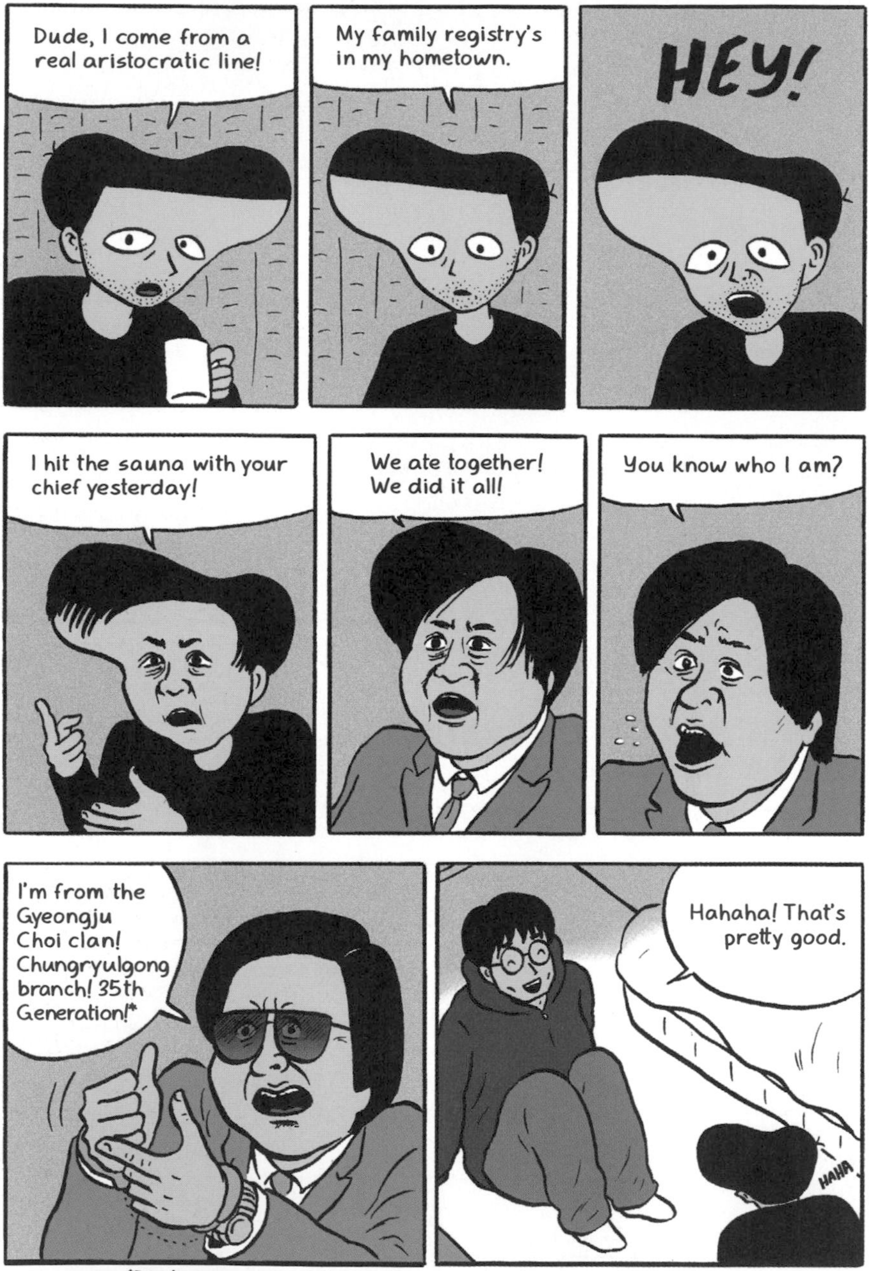
Dude, I come from a real aristocratic line!
My family registry's in my hometown.
HEY!
I hit the sauna with your chief yesterday!
We ate together! We did it all!
You know who I am?
I'm from the Gyeongju Choi clan! Chungryulgong branch! 35th Generation!*
Hahaha! That's pretty good.
HAHA

*Deuk-nyeong is imitating actor Choi Min-sik's character in a famous scene from *Nameless Gangster: Rules of the Time*, where a significant plot point is the central character's name and family connections.

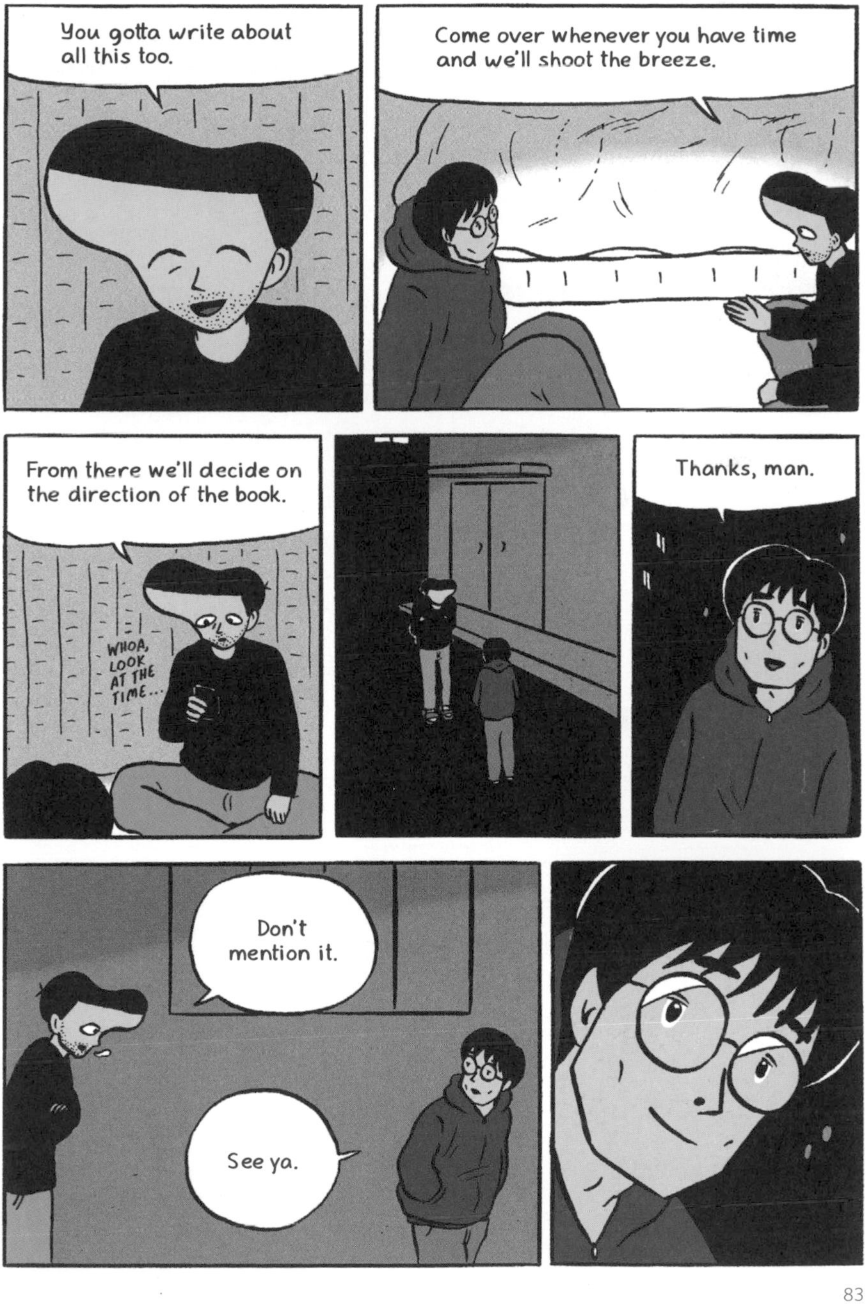
You gotta write about all this too.
Come over whenever you have time and we'll shoot the breeze.
From there we'll decide on the direction of the book.
WHOA, LOOK AT THE TIME...
Thanks, man.
Don't mention it.
See ya.

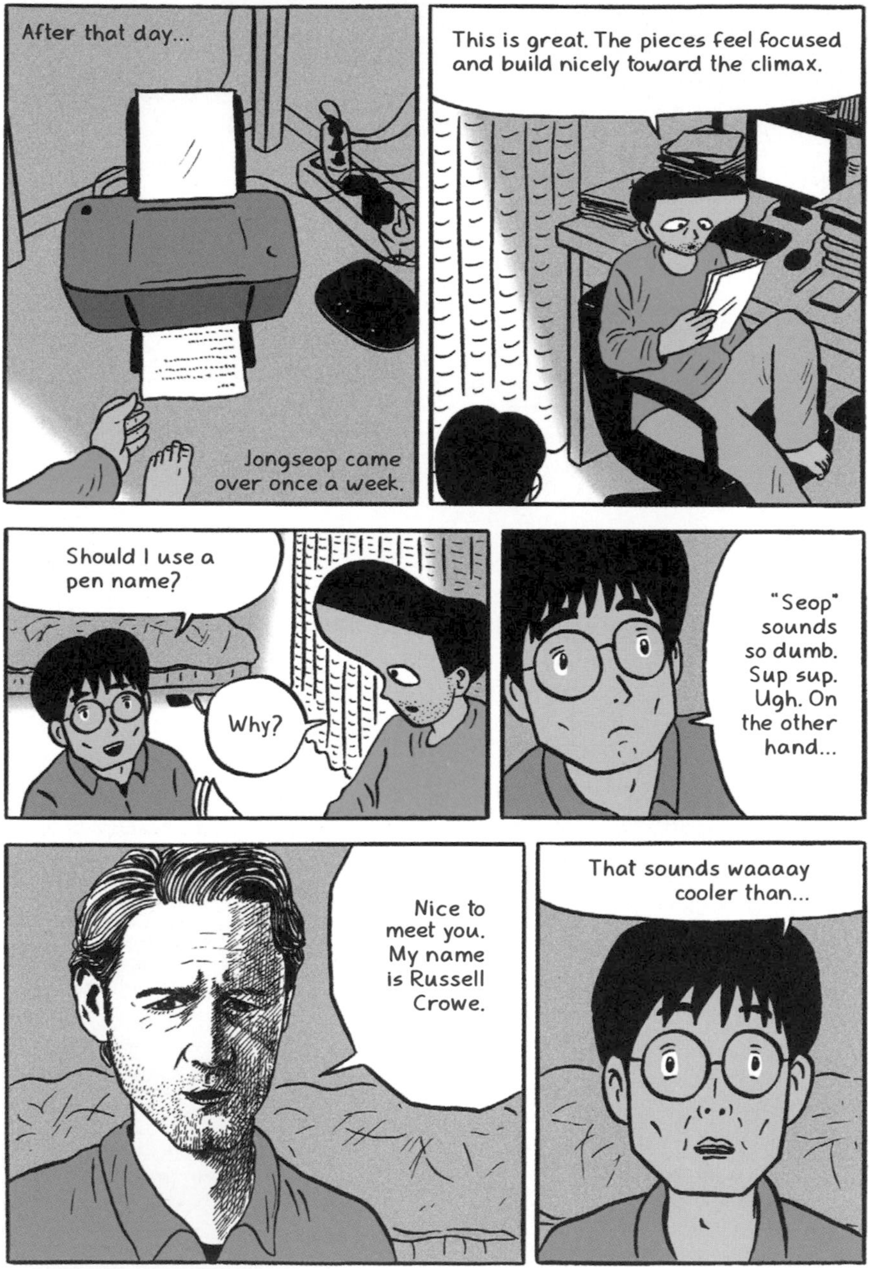
After that day...
Jongseop came over once a week.
This is great. The pieces feel focused and build nicely toward the climax.
Should I use a pen name?
Why?
"Seop" sounds so dumb. Sup sup. Ugh. On the other hand...
Nice to meet you. My name is Russell Crowe.
That sounds waaaay cooler than...

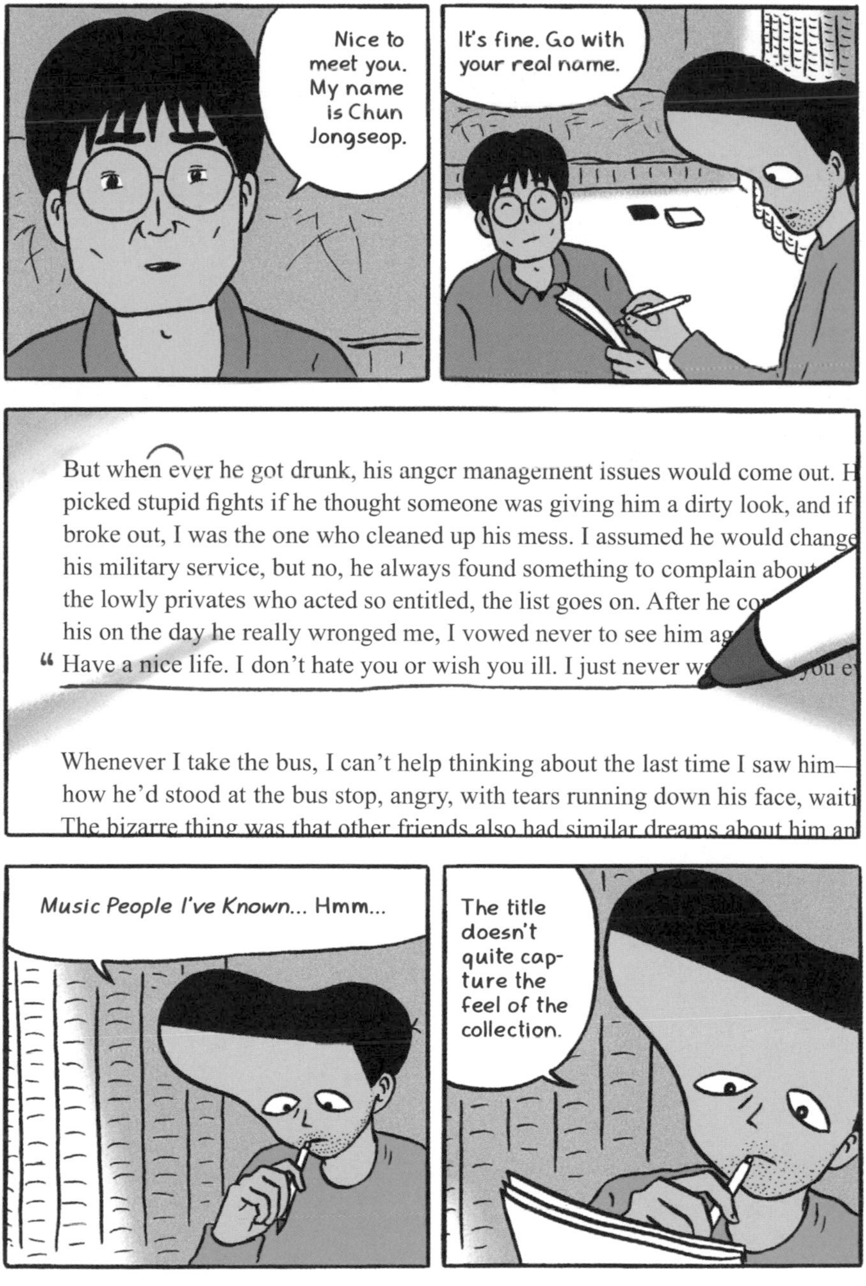
Nice to meet you. My name is Chun Jongseop.
It's fine. Go with your real name.
But when ever he got drunk, his anger management issues would come out.
picked stupid fights if he thought someone was giving him a dirty look, and if
broke out, I was the one who cleaned up his mess. I assumed he would
his military service, but no, he always found something to complain
the lowly privates who acted so entitled, the list goes on. After he
his on the day he really wronged me, I vowed never to see him
" Have a nice life. I don't hate you or wish you ill. I just never
Whenever I take the bus, I can't help thinking about the last time I saw him—
how he'd stood at the bus stop, angry, with tears running down his face,
The bizarre thing was that other friends also had similar dreams about him
Music People I've Known... Hmm...
The title doesn't quite capture the feel of the collection.

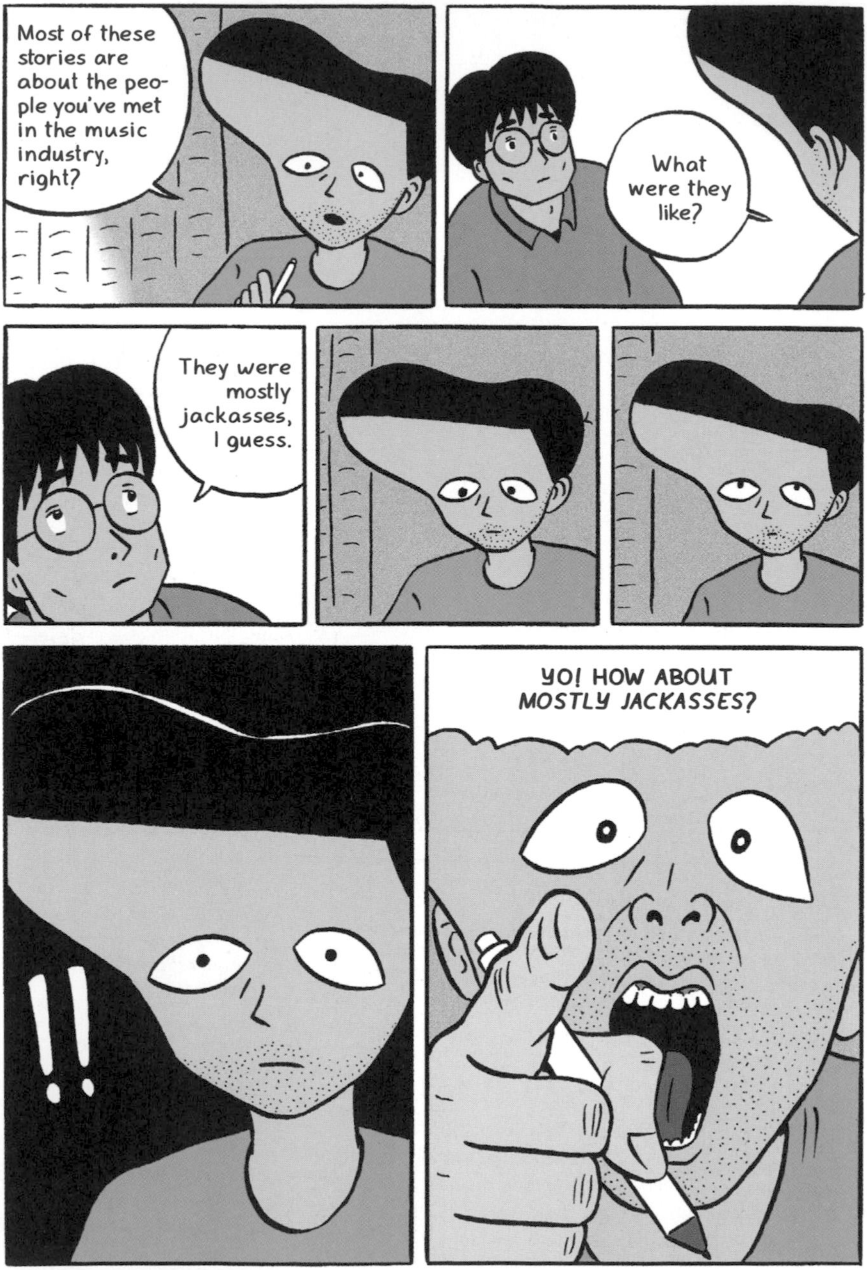
Most of these stories are about the people you've met in the music industry, right?
What were they like?
They were mostly jackasses, I guess.
!!
YO! HOW ABOUT MOSTLY JACKASSES?

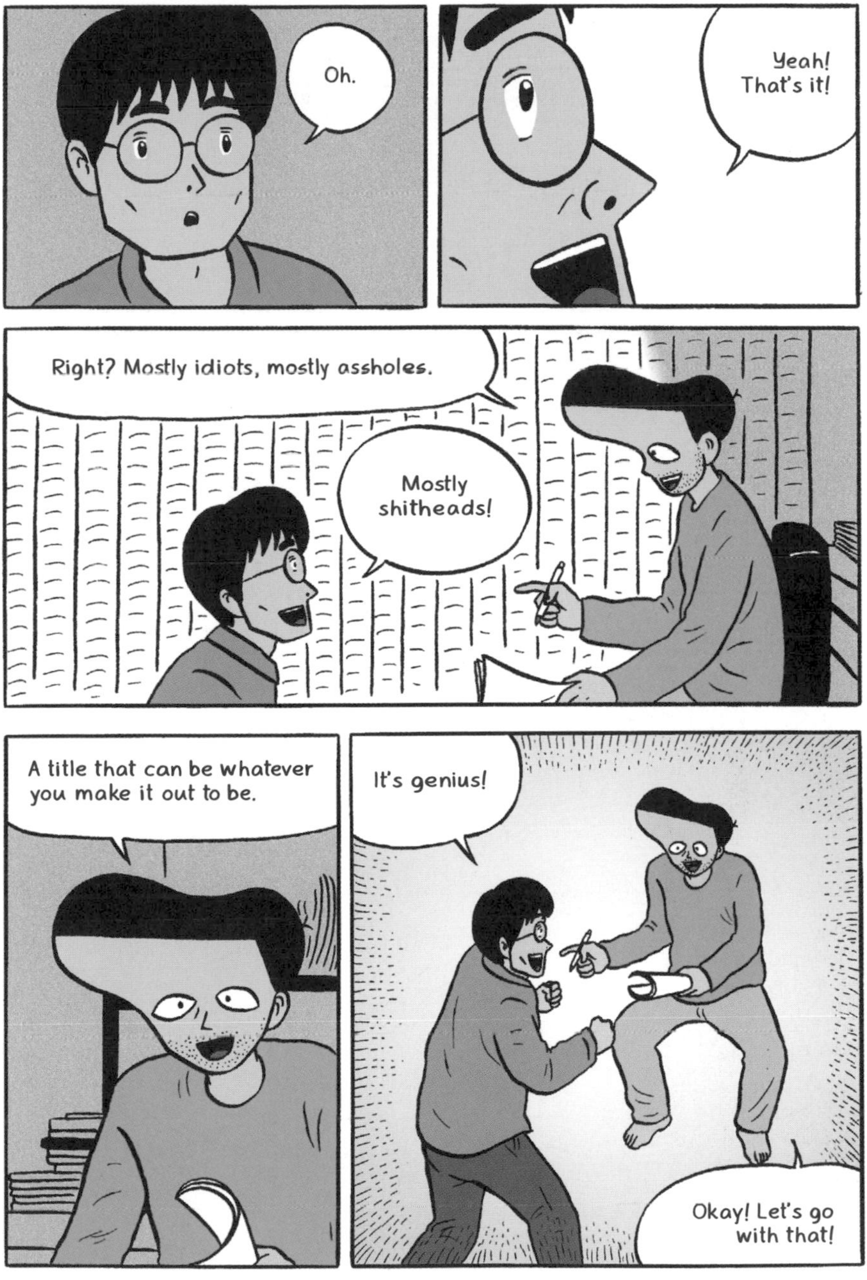
Oh.
Yeah! That's it!
Right? Mostly idiots, mostly assholes.
Mostly shitheads!
A title that can be whatever you make it out to be.
It's genius!
Okay! Let's go with that!

CONTRACT

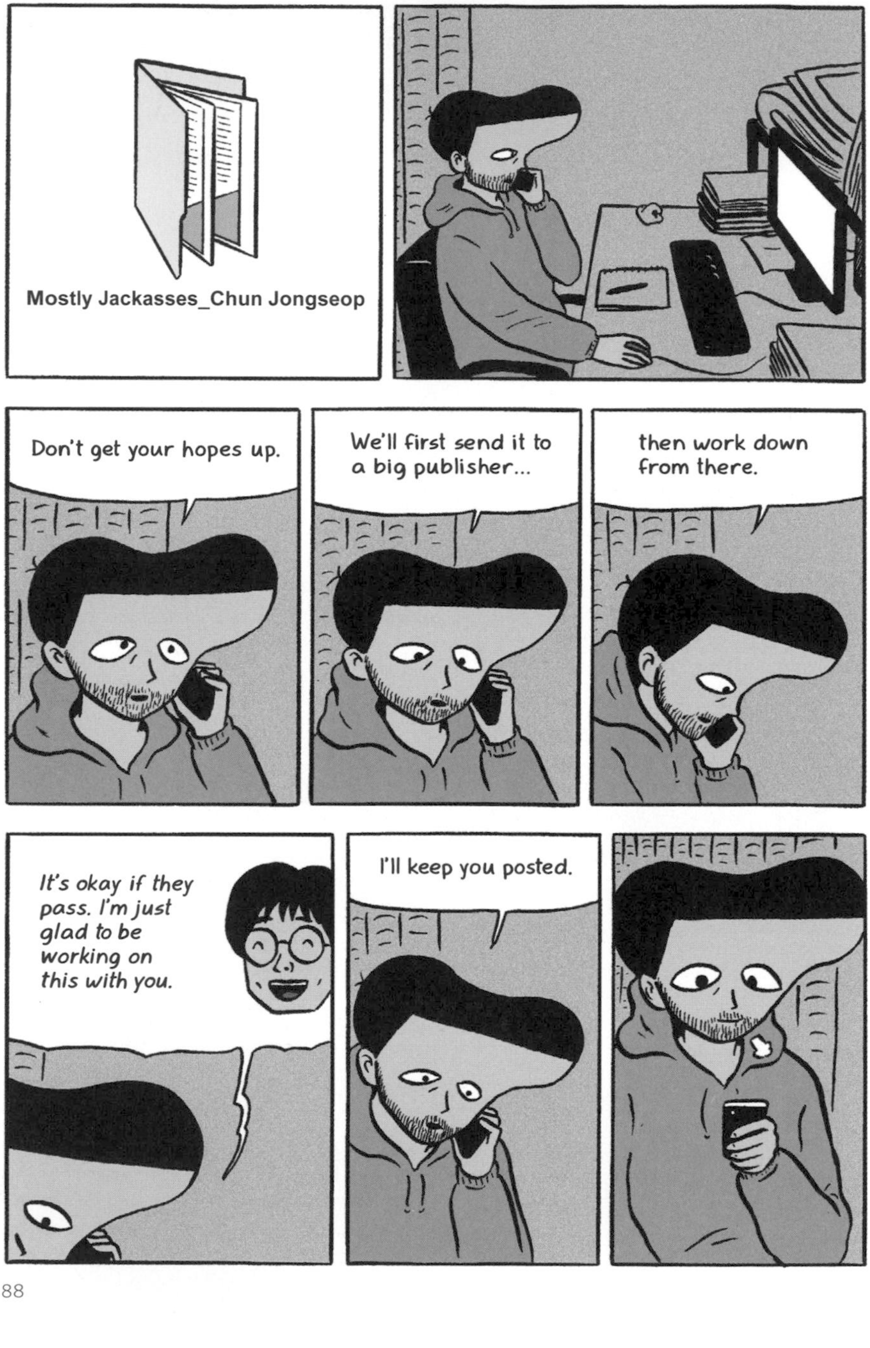
Mostly Jackasses_Chun Jongseop
Don't get your hopes up.
We'll first send it to a big publisher...
then work down from there.
It's okay if they pass. I'm just glad to be working on this with you.
I'll keep you posted.

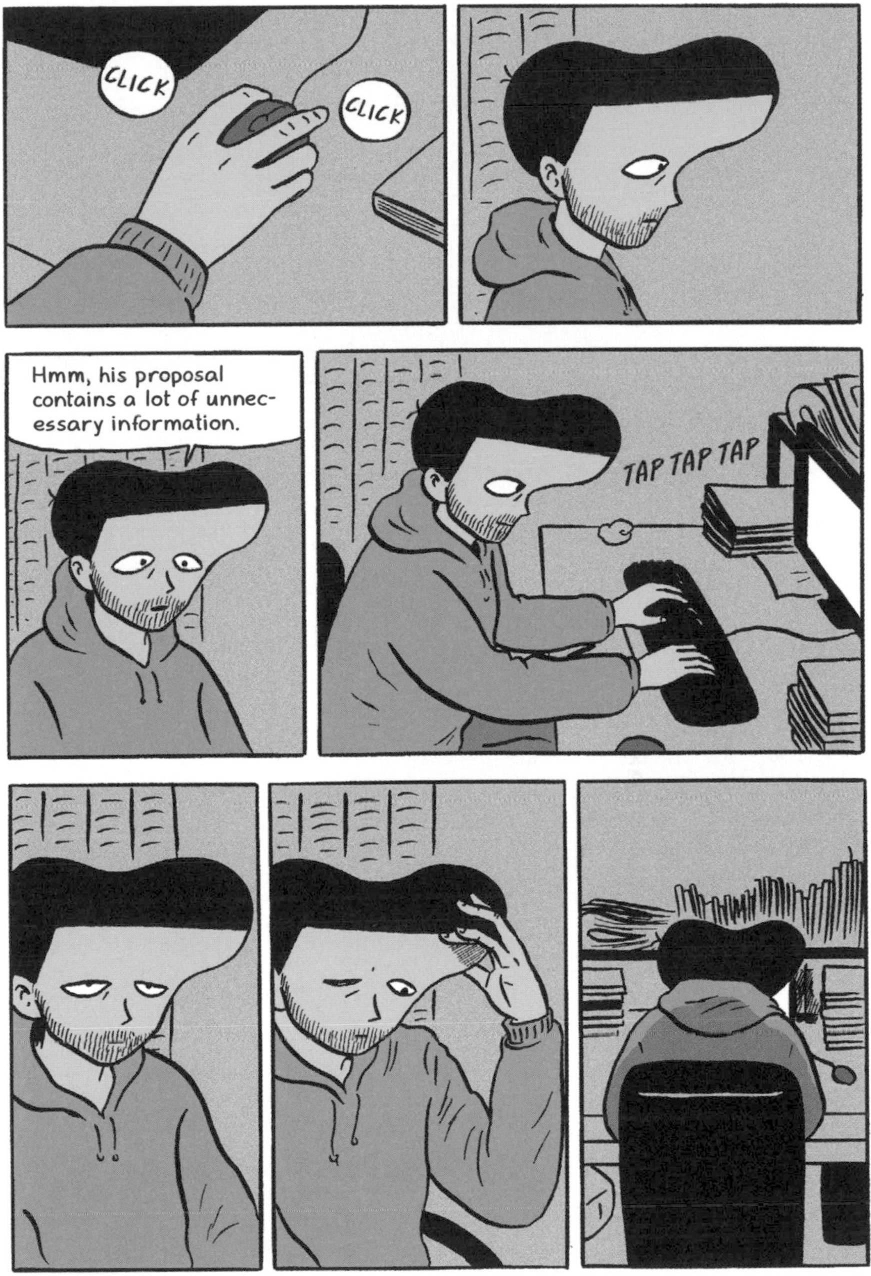
CLICK
CLICK
Hmm, his proposal contains a lot of unnecessary information.
TAP TAP TAP

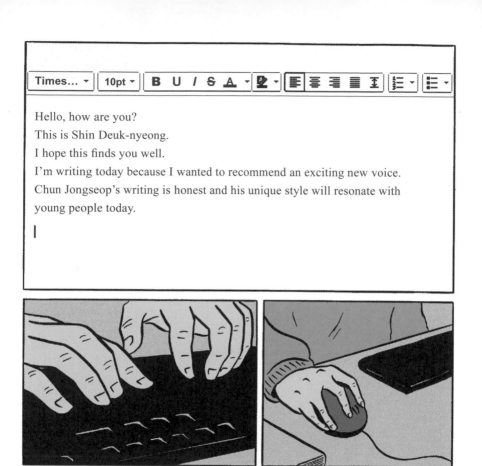

Hello, how are you?
This is Shin Deuk-nyeong.
I hope this finds you well.
I'm writing today because I wanted to recommend an exciting new voice.
Chun Jongseop's writing is honest and his unique style will resonate with
young people today.

Your email has been
successfully sent.

Inbox   Compose

Whew.

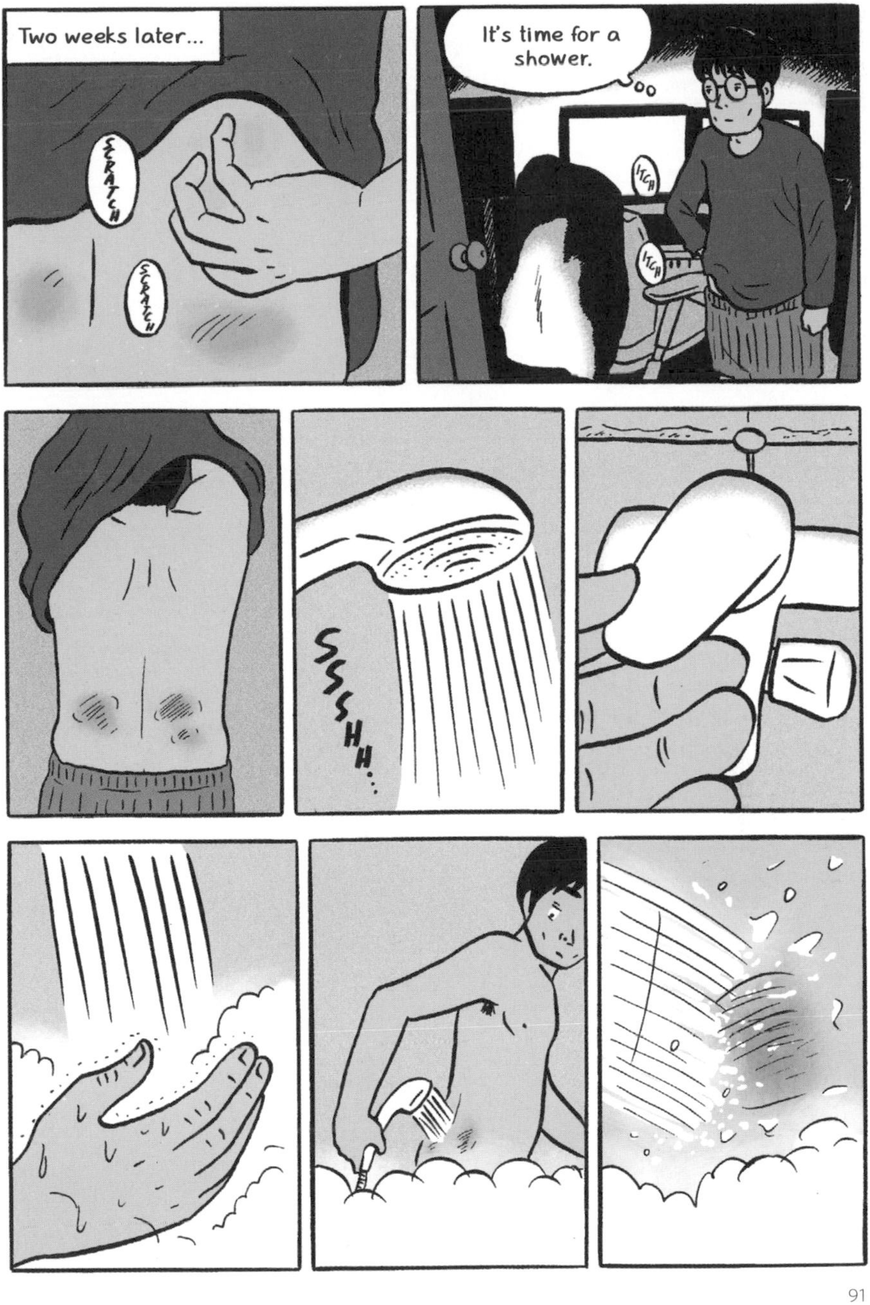
Two weeks later...
SCRATCH
SCRATCH
It's time for a shower.
ITCH
ITCH
SSSHH...

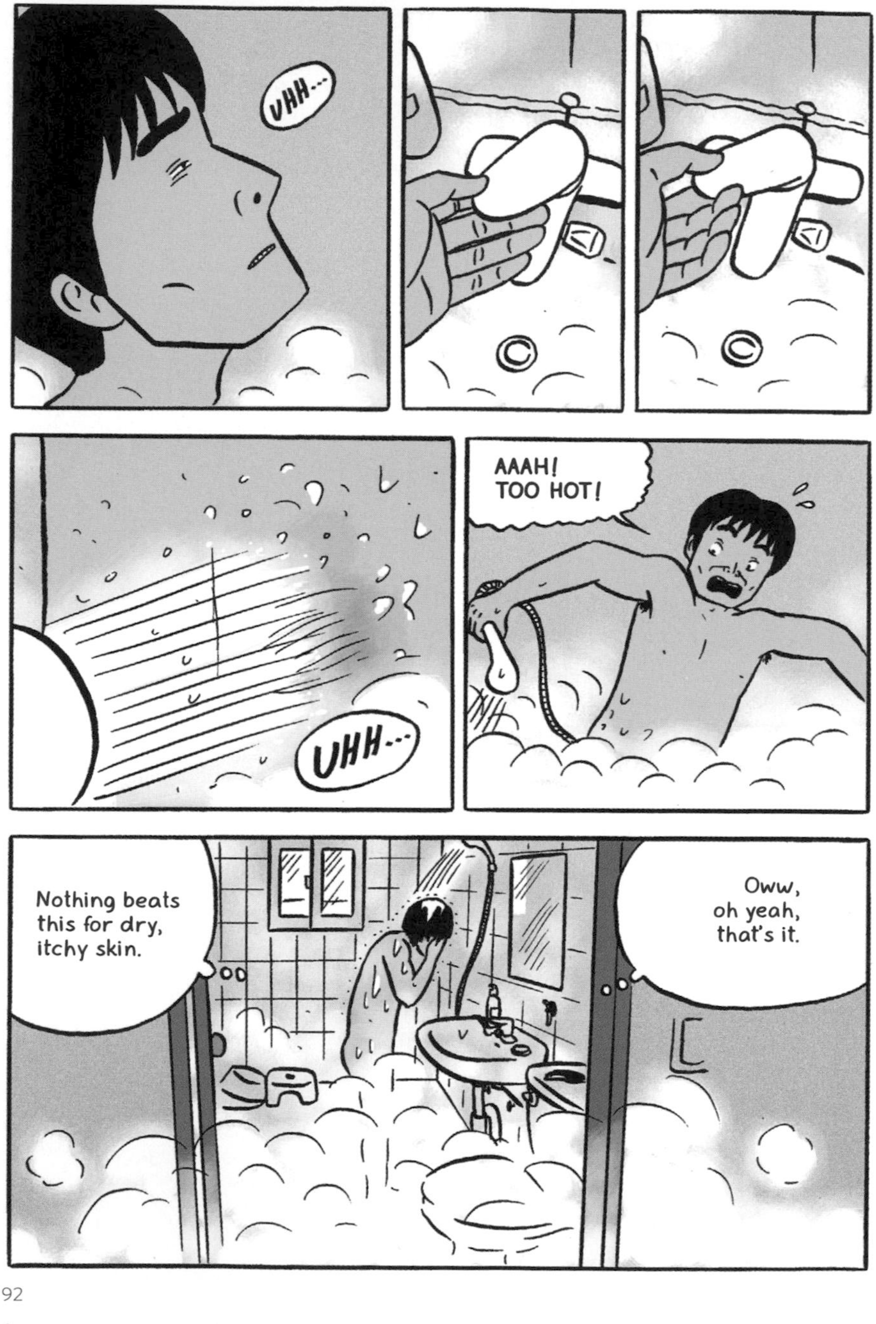
UHH...
UHH...
AAAH! TOO HOT!
Nothing beats this for dry, itchy skin.
Oww, oh yeah, that's it.

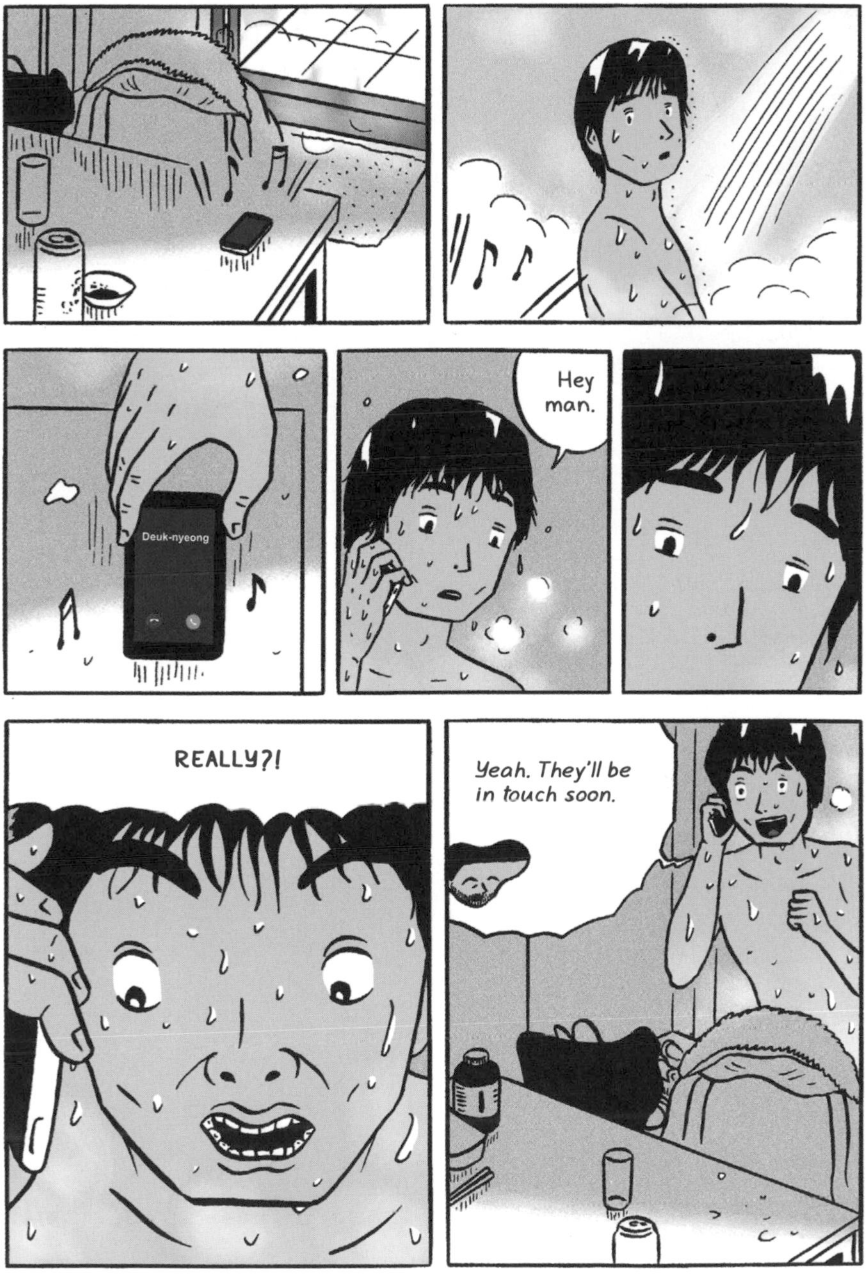
Deuk-nyeong
Hey man.
REALLY?!
Yeah. They'll be in touch soon.

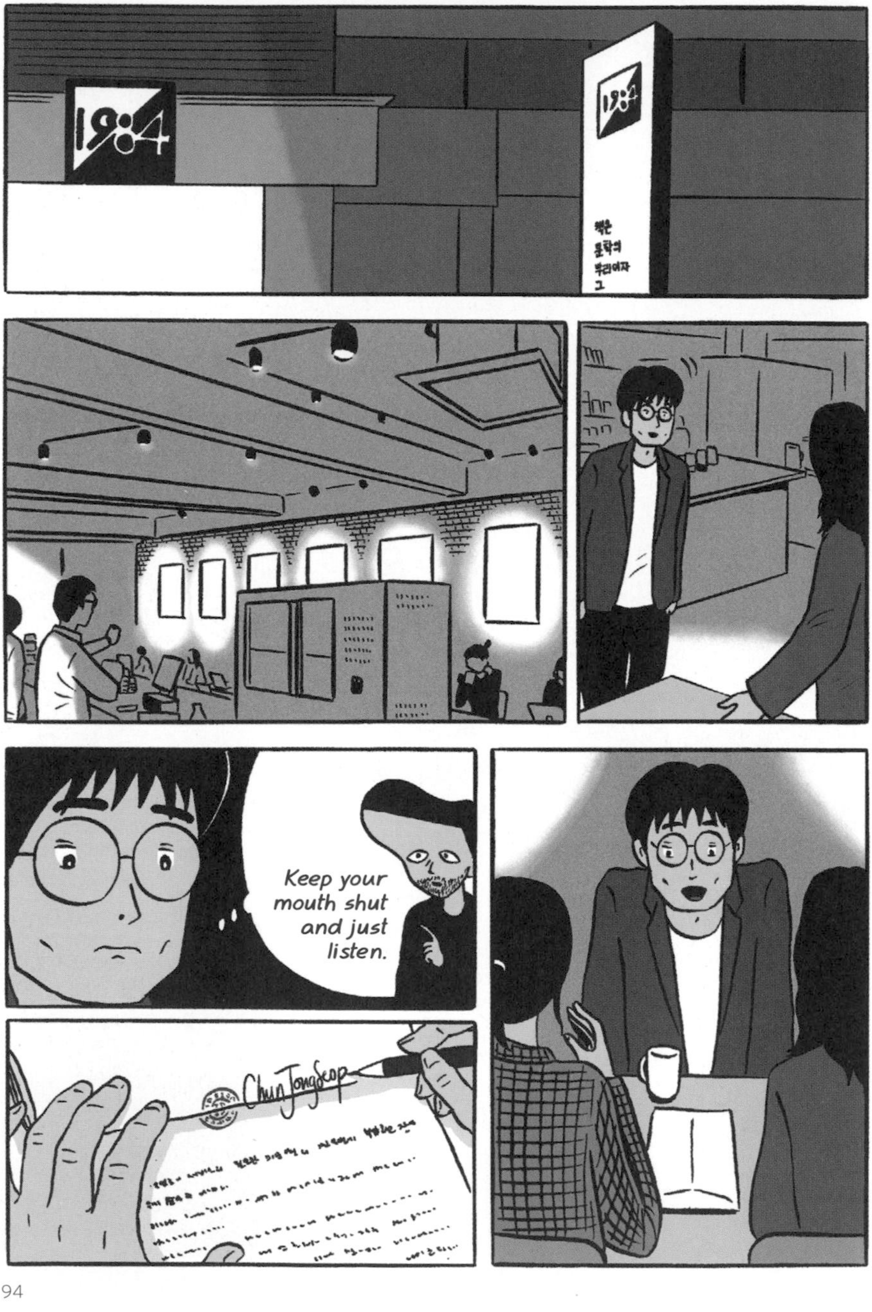
1984
1984
책은
문학의
뿌리이자
그
Keep your mouth shut and just listen.
Chun JongSeop

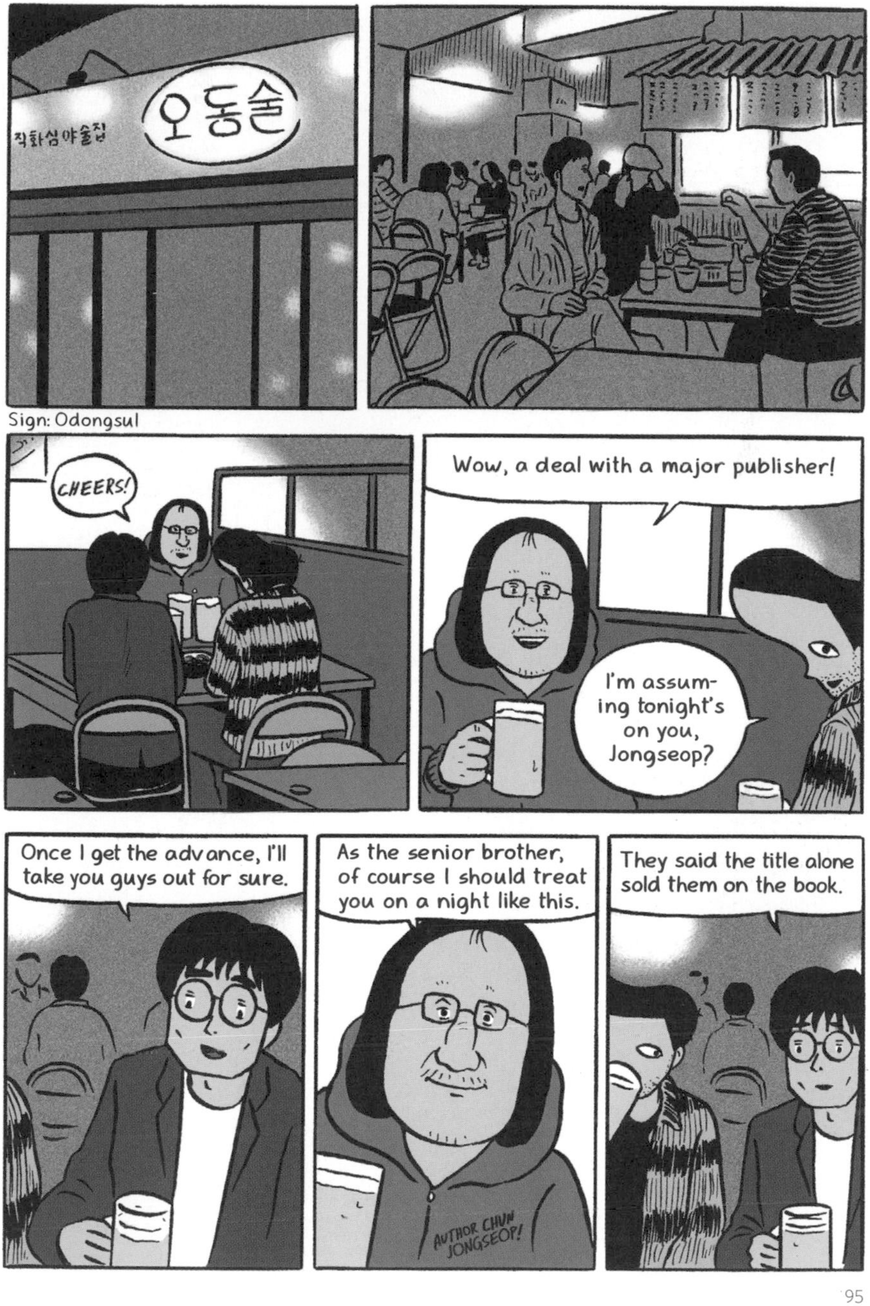
작화심야술집
오동술
Sign: Odongsul
CHEERS!
Wow, a deal with a major publisher!
I'm assuming tonight's on you, Jongseop?
Once I get the advance, I'll take you guys out for sure.
As the senior brother, of course I should treat you on a night like this.
AUTHOR CHUN JONGSEOP!
They said the title alone sold them on the book.

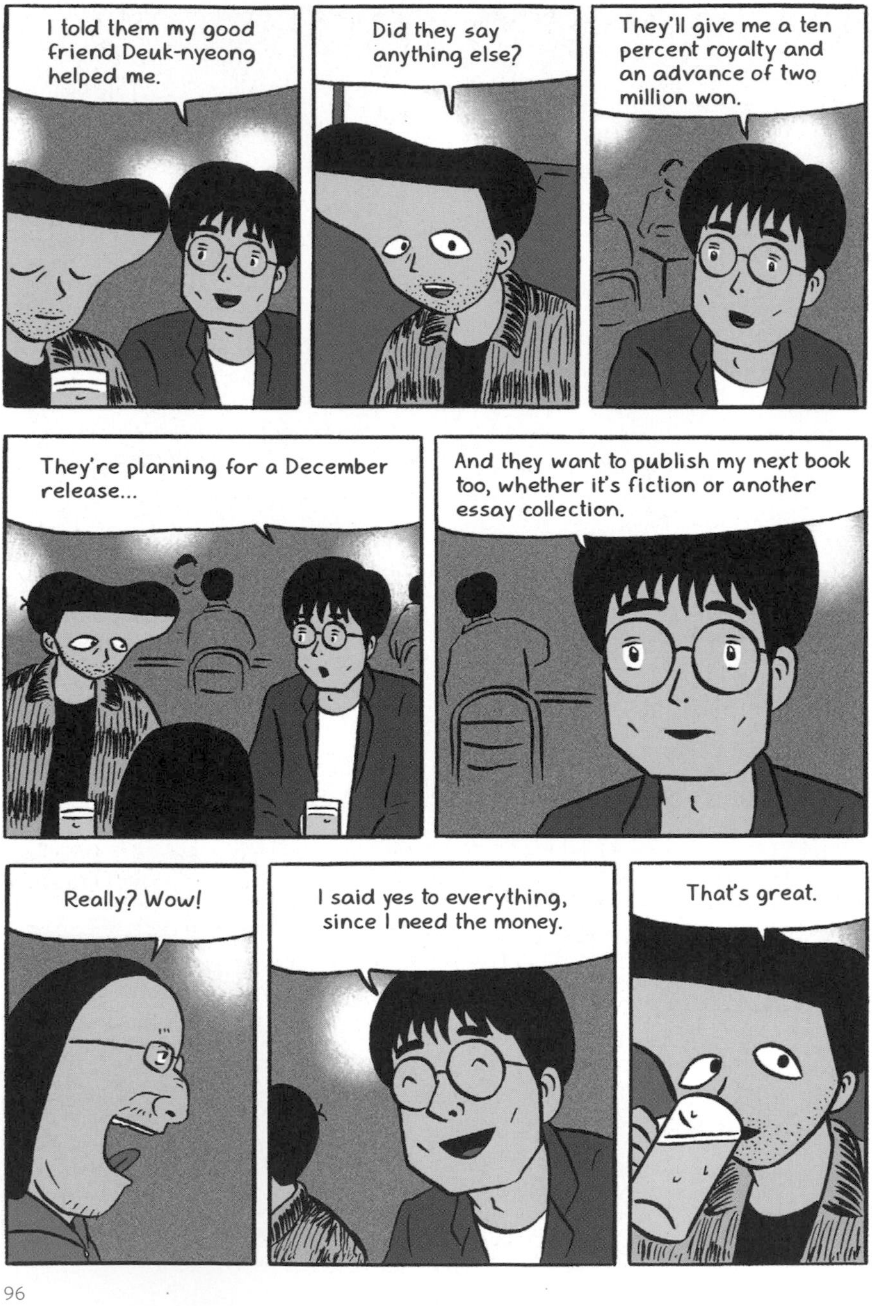
I told them my good friend Deuk-nyeong helped me.
Did they say anything else?
They'll give me a ten percent royalty and an advance of two million won.
They're planning for a December release...
And they want to publish my next book too, whether it's fiction or another essay collection.
Really? Wow!
I said yes to everything, since I need the money.
That's great.

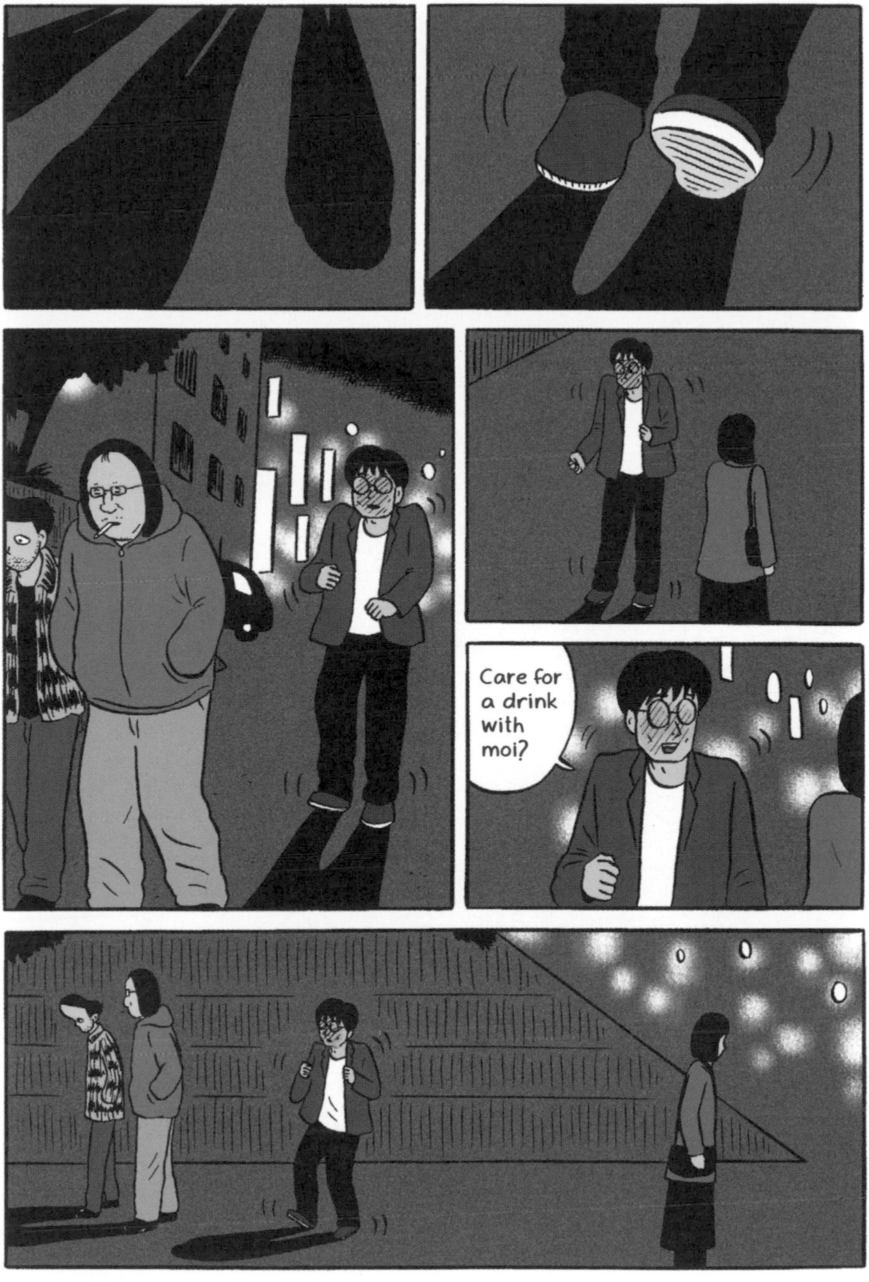
Care for a drink with moi?

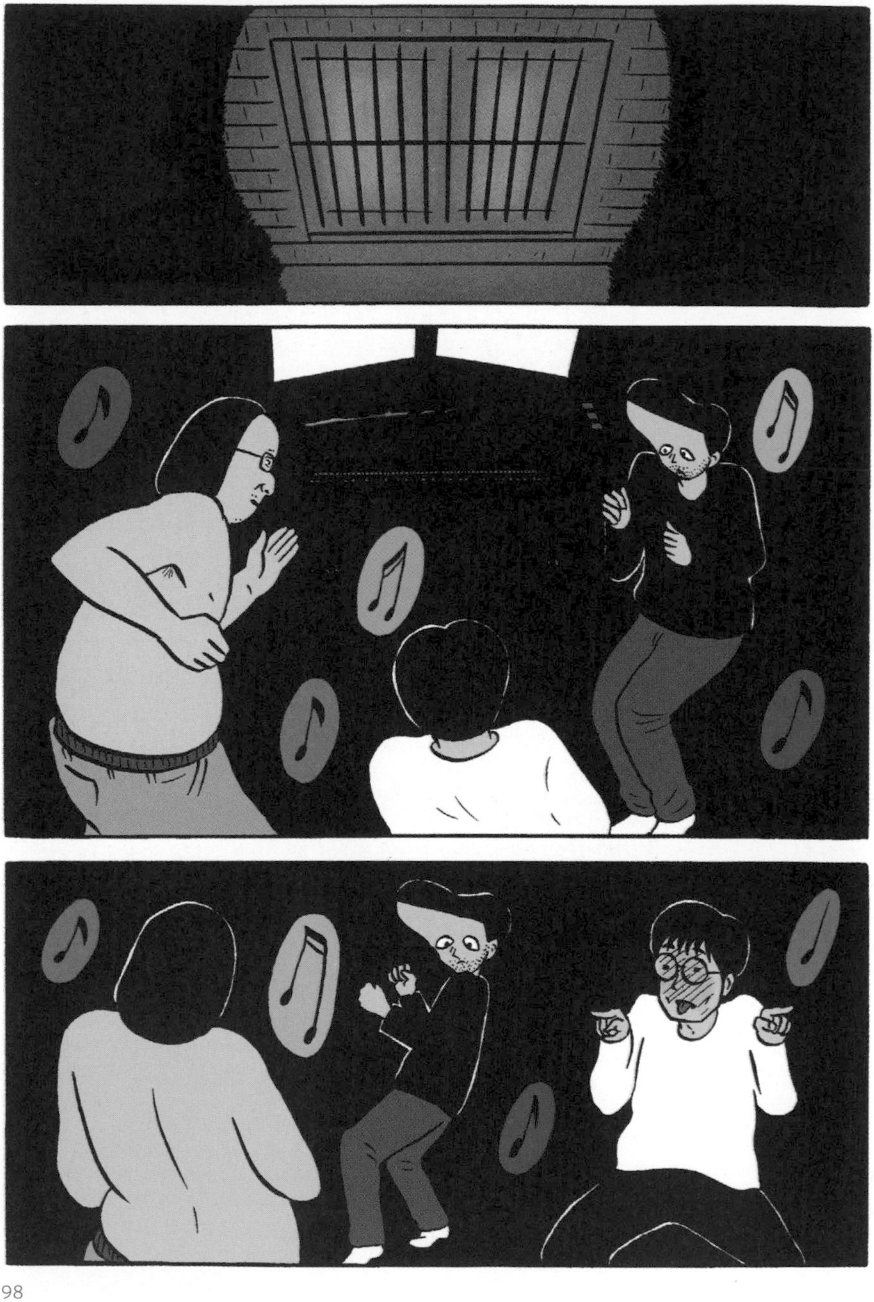

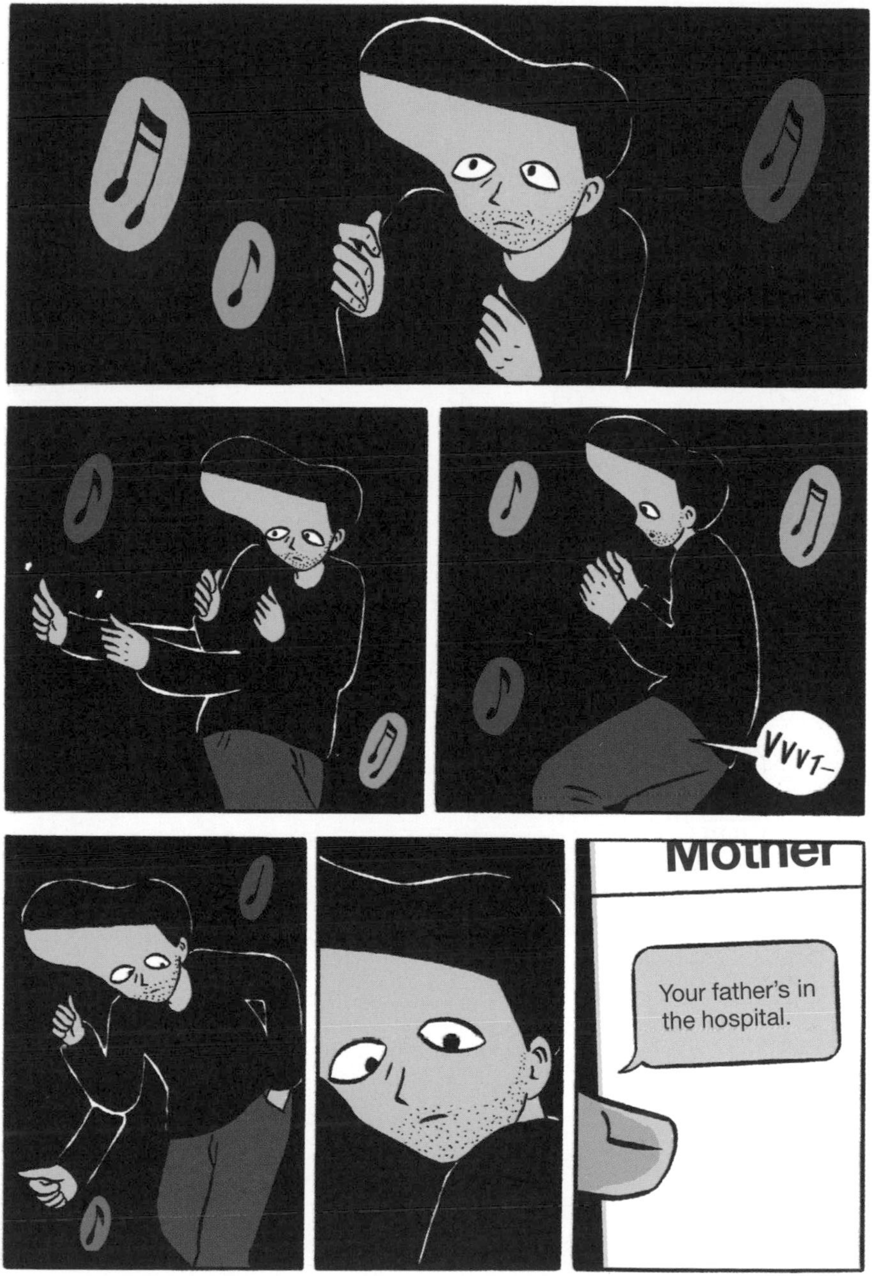
VVV1-
Mother
Your father's in the hospital.

CHARACTER DEVELOPMENT

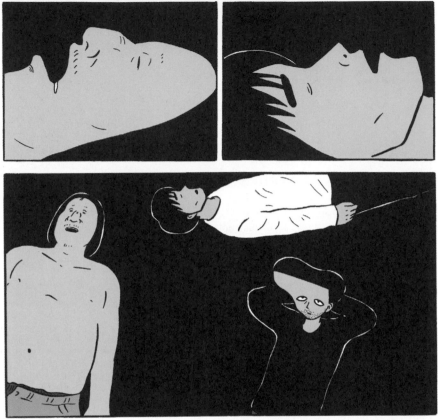

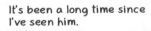

It's been a long time since I've seen him.

I was thirty-four when my first book came out. It was around the time my grandmother passed away.

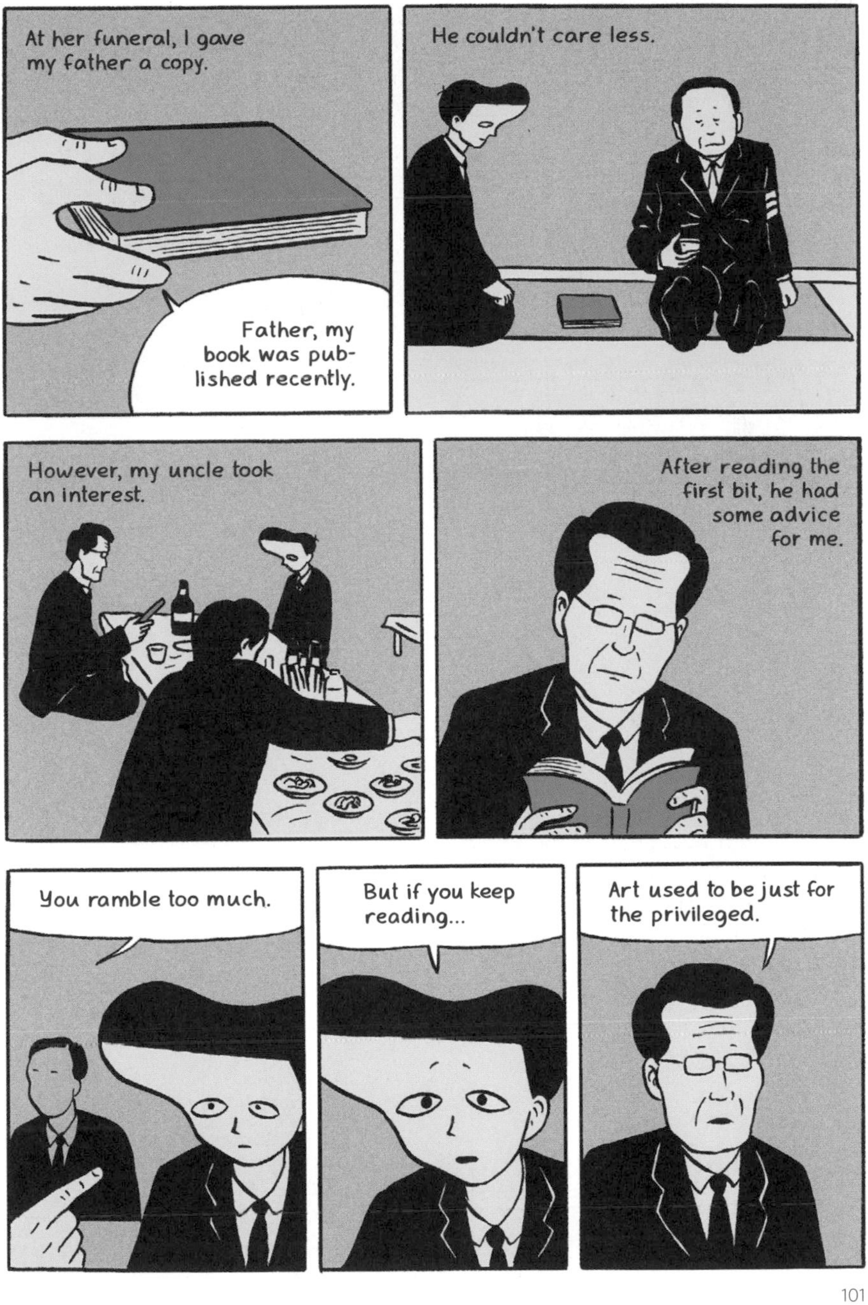
At her funeral, I gave my father a copy.
Father, my book was published recently.
He couldn't care less.
However, my uncle took an interest.
After reading the first bit, he had some advice for me.
You ramble too much.
But if you keep reading...
Art used to be just for the privileged.

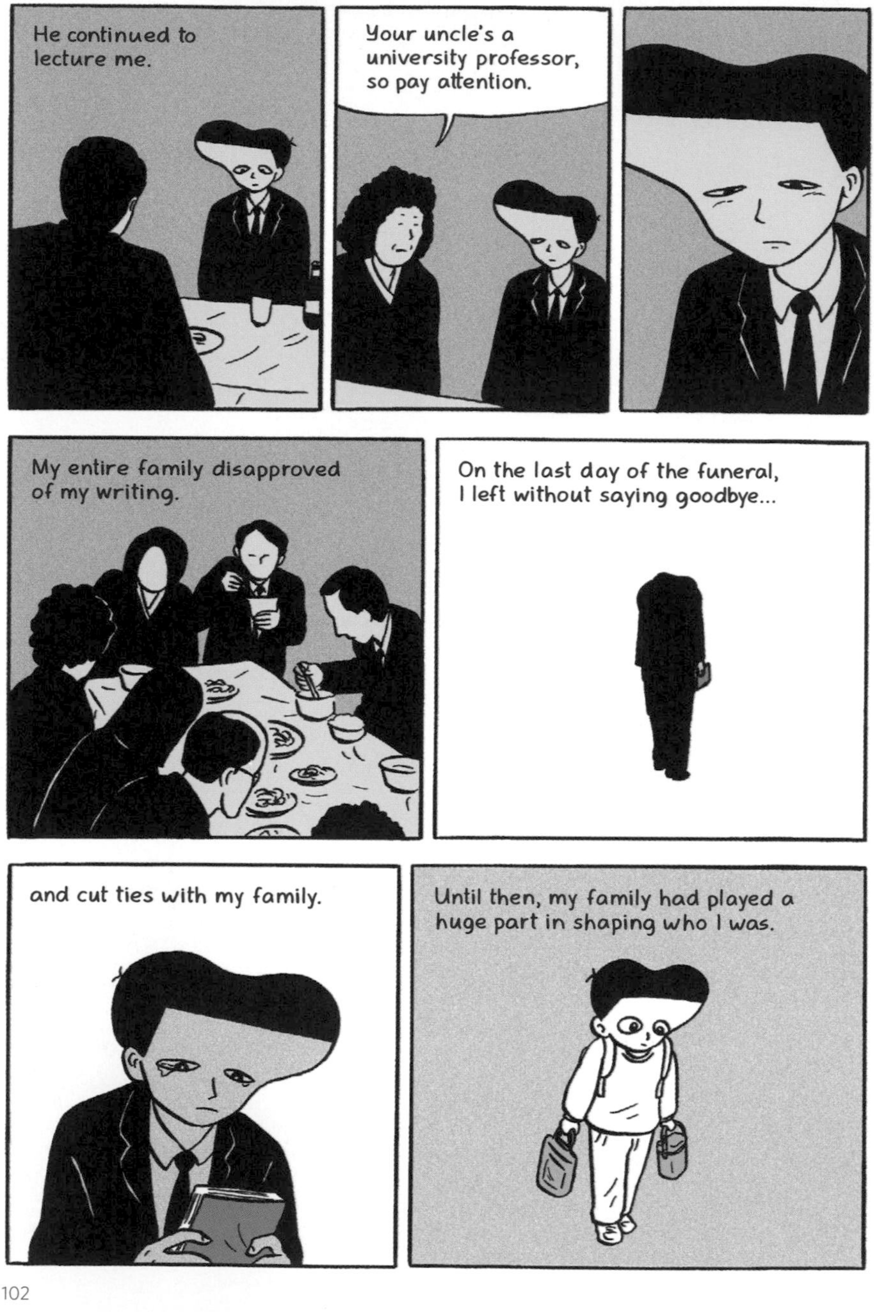
He continued to lecture me.
Your uncle's a university professor, so pay attention.
My entire family disapproved of my writing.
On the last day of the funeral, I left without saying goodbye...
and cut ties with my family.
Until then, my family had played a huge part in shaping who I was.

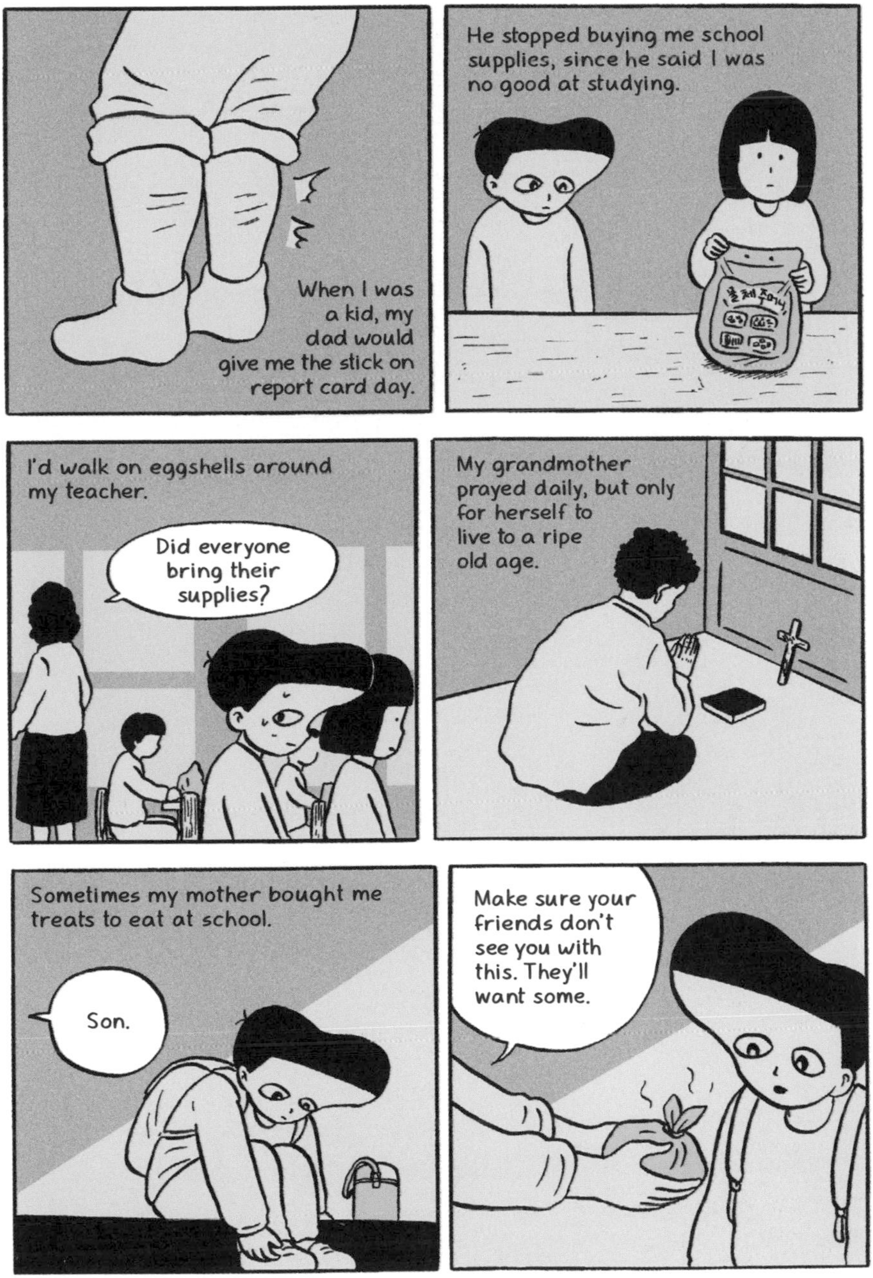
When I was a kid, my dad would give me the stick on report card day.
He stopped buying me school supplies, since he said I was no good at studying.
I'd walk on eggshells around my teacher.
Did everyone bring their supplies?
My grandmother prayed daily, but only for herself to live to a ripe old age.
Sometimes my mother bought me treats to eat at school.
Son.
Make sure your friends don't see you with this. They'll want some.

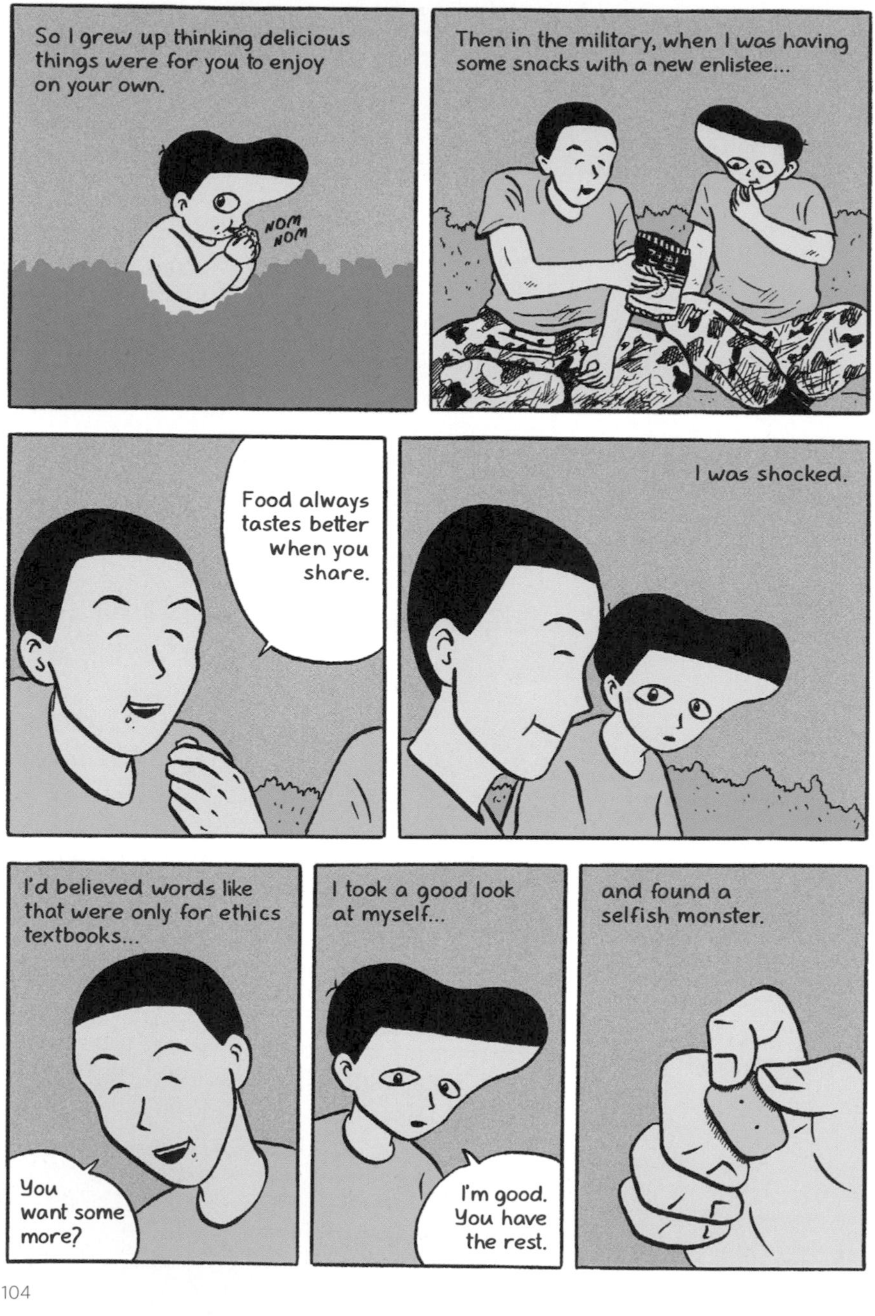
So I grew up thinking delicious things were for you to enjoy on your own.
NOM NOM
Then in the military, when I was having some snacks with a new enlistee...
Food always tastes better when you share.
I was shocked.
I'd believed words like that were only for ethics textbooks...
You want some more?
I took a good look at myself...
I'm good. You have the rest.
and found a selfish monster.

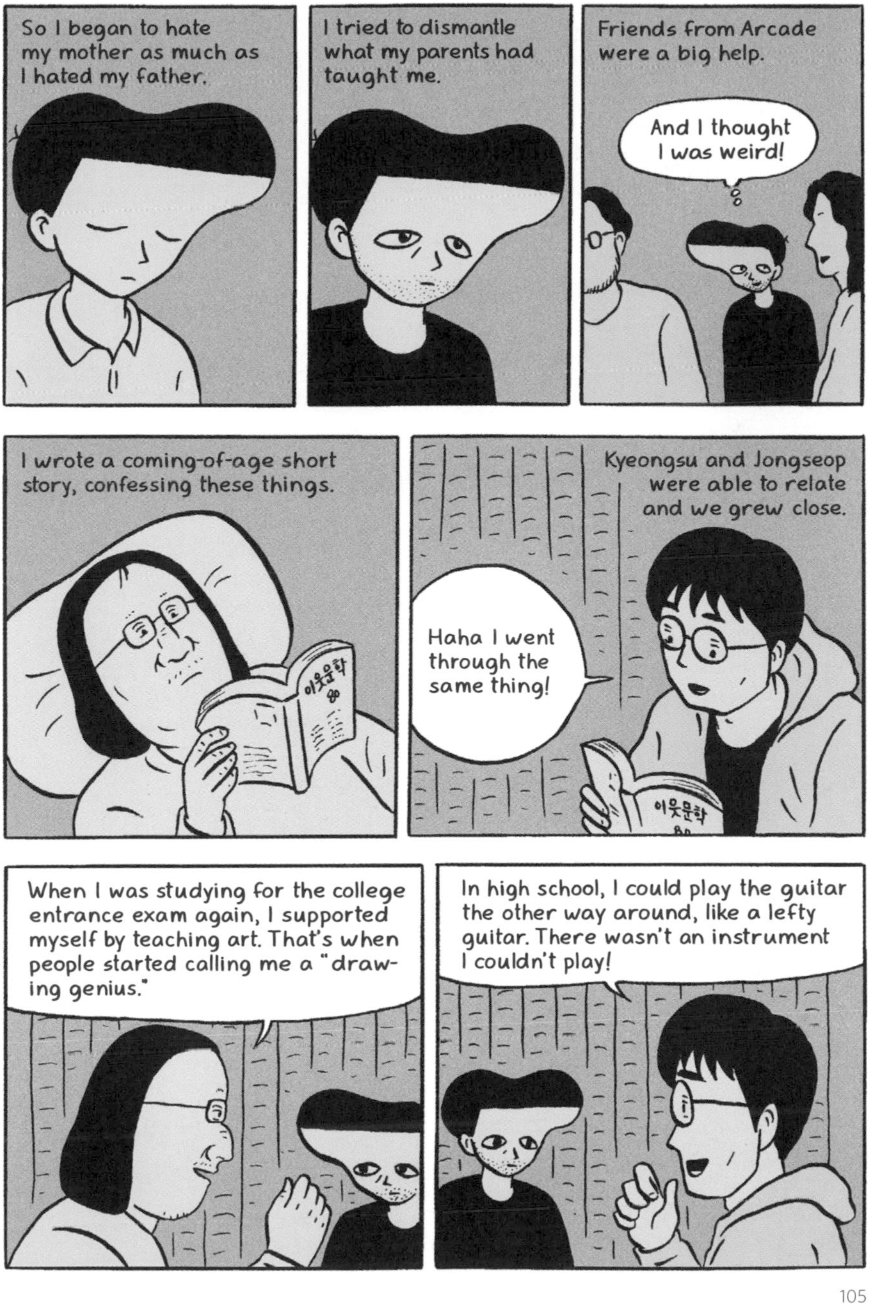

So I began to hate my mother as much as I hated my father.
I tried to dismantle what my parents had taught me.
Friends from Arcade were a big help.
And I thought I was weird!
I wrote a coming-of-age short story, confessing these things.
이웃문학 80
Kyeongsu and Jongseop were able to relate and we grew close.
Haha I went through the same thing!
이웃문학
When I was studying for the college entrance exam again, I supported myself by teaching art. That's when people started calling me a "drawing genius."
In high school, I could play the guitar the other way around, like a lefty guitar. There wasn't an instrument I couldn't play!

Our journeys were the same, even our families' disapproval of our decision to become artists.

My father was right.

That's why we've been able to lean on each other.

Art's something only lucky, rich bastards do.

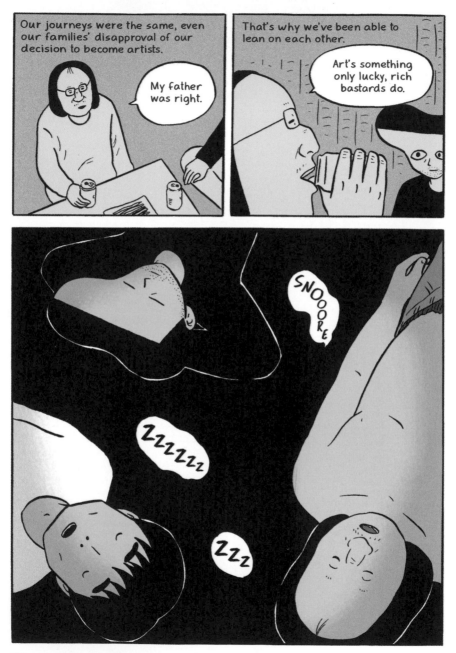

SNOOORE

ZZZZZz

ZZZ

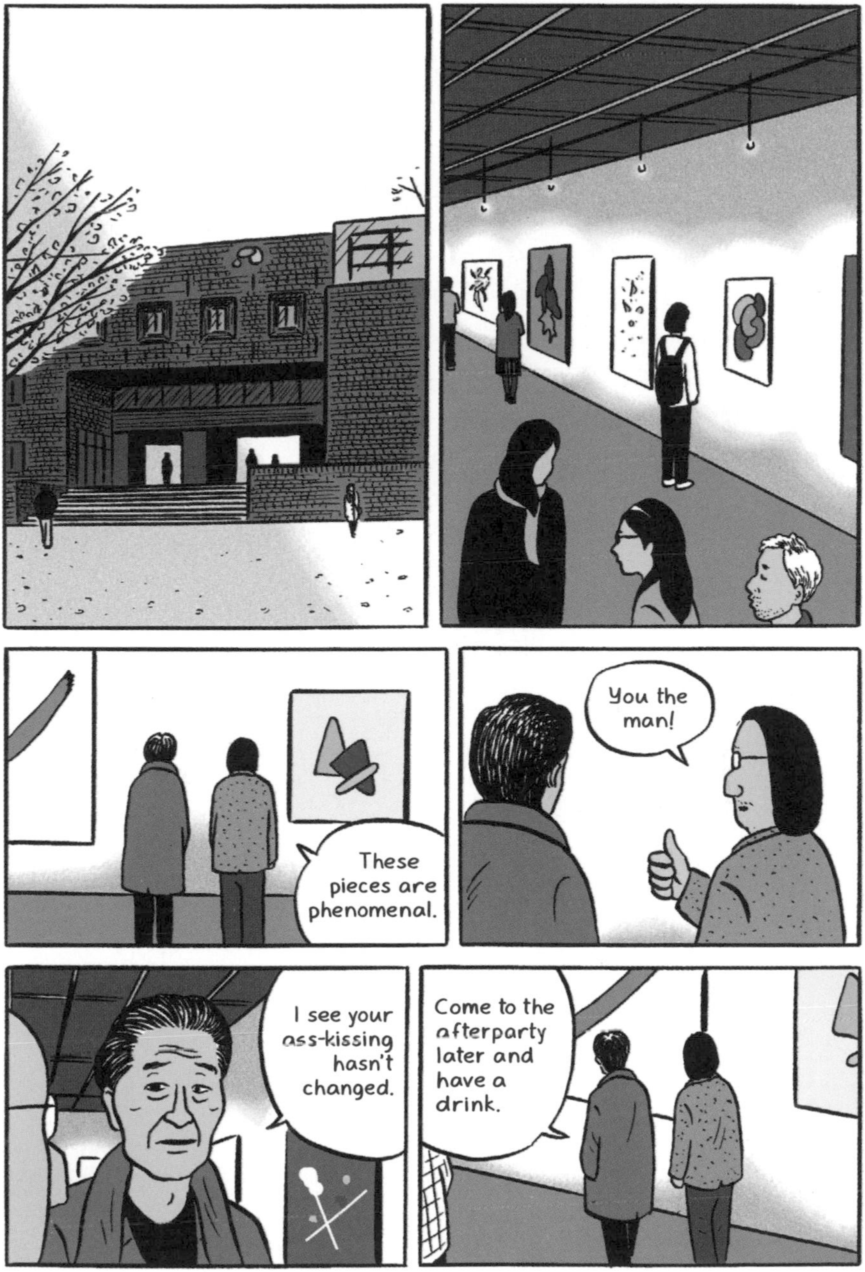
These pieces are phenomenal.
You the man!
I see your ass-kissing hasn't changed.
Come to the afterparty later and have a drink.

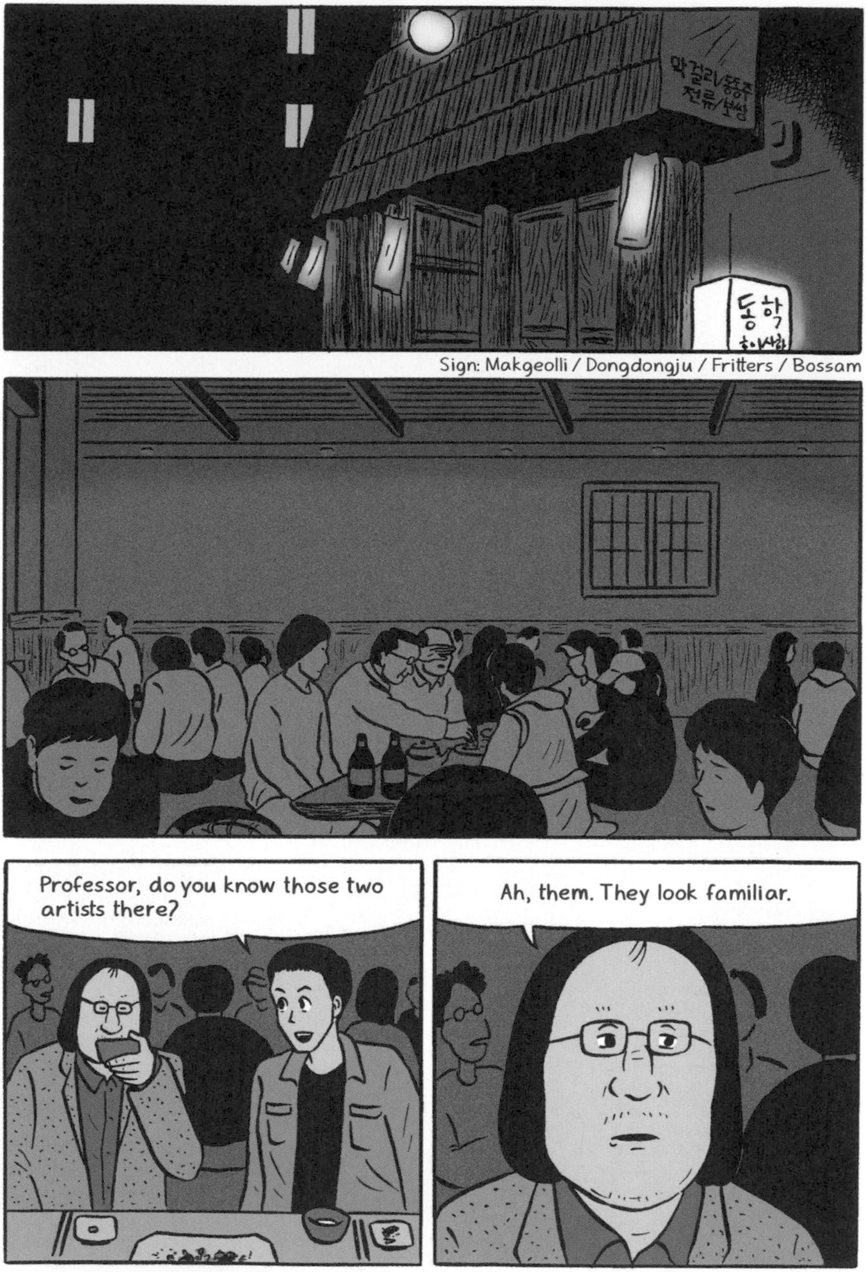
막걸리/동동주
전류/보쌈
동학
Sign: Makgeolli / Dongdongju / Fritters / Bossam
Professor, do you know those two artists there?
Ah, them. They look familiar.

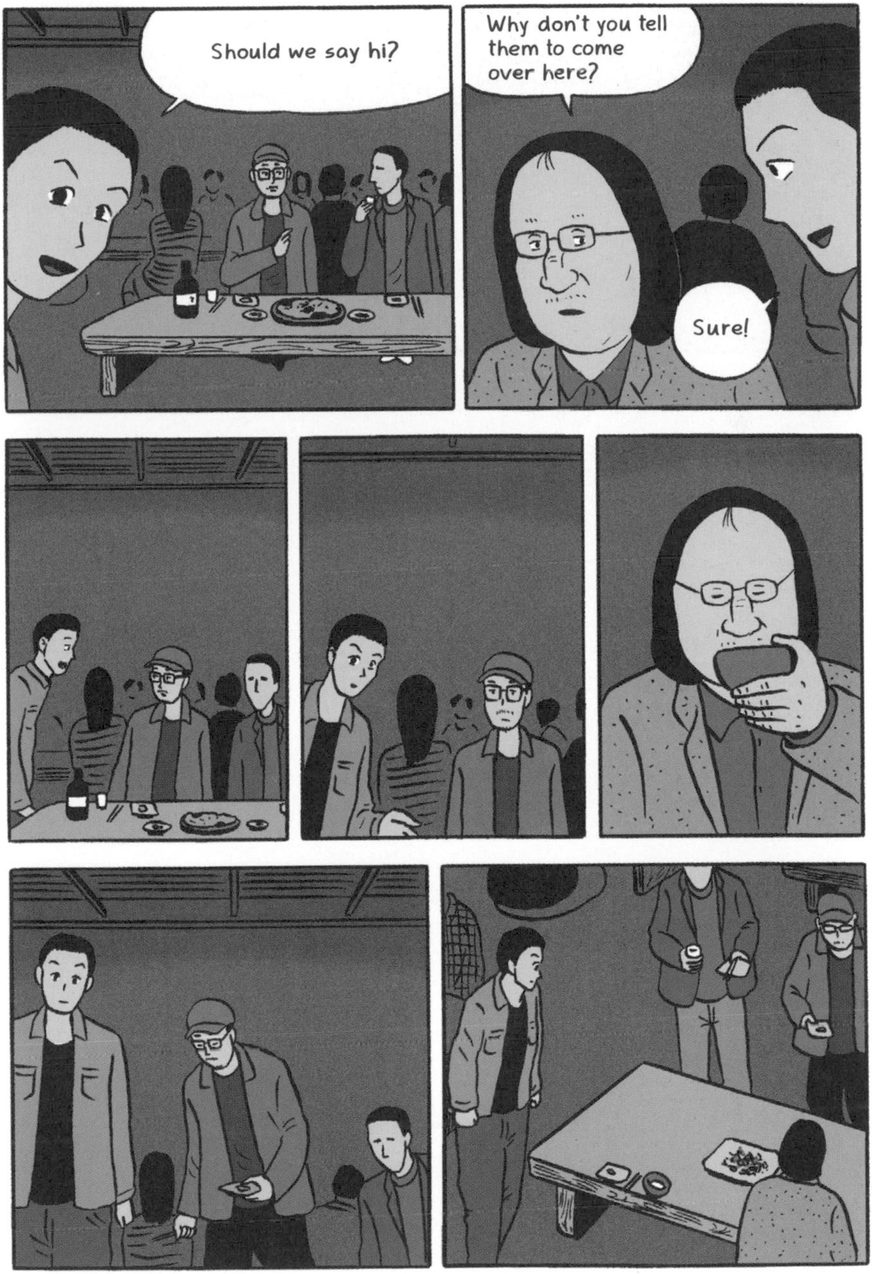
Should we say hi?
Why don't you tell them to come over here?
Sure!

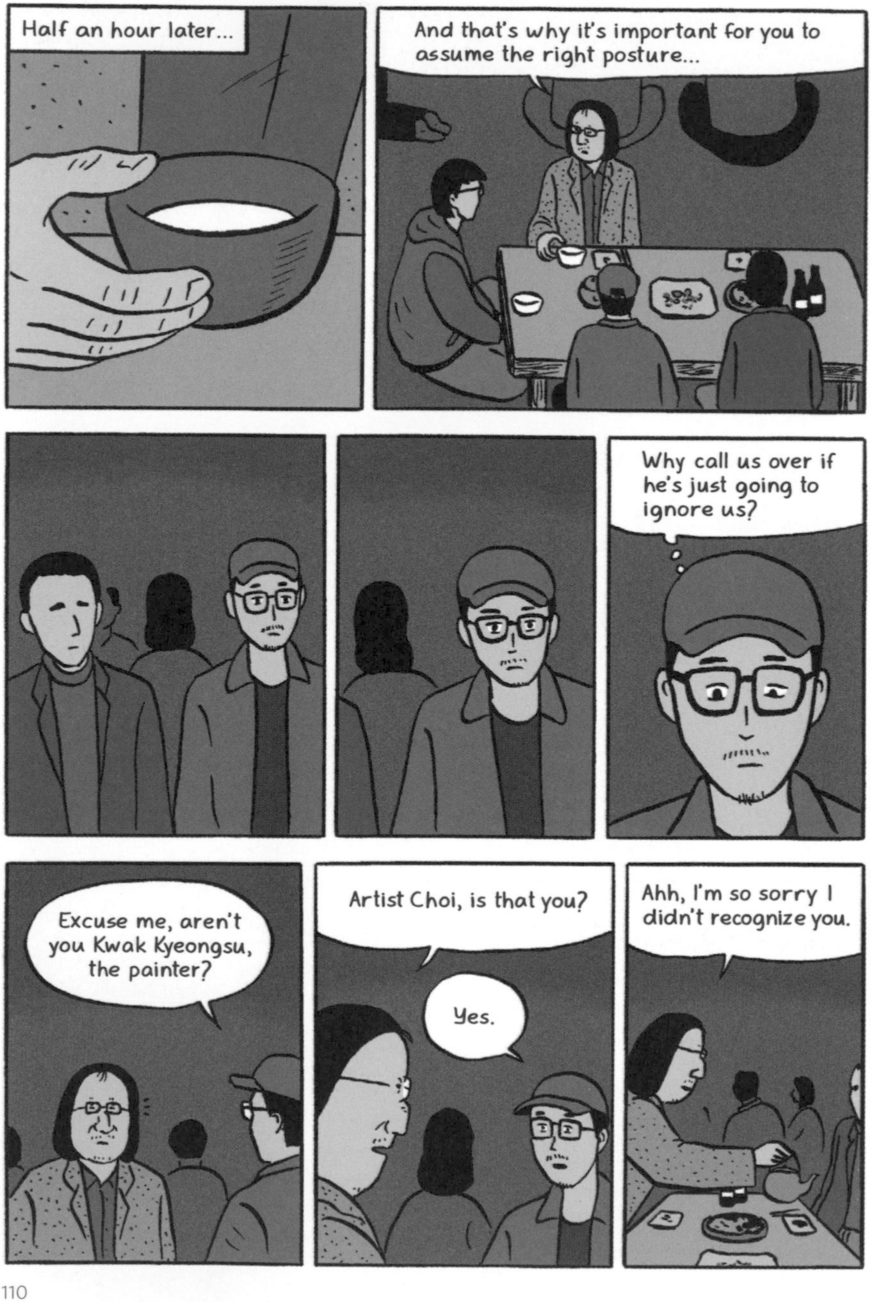
Half an hour later...
And that's why it's important for you to assume the right posture...
Why call us over if he's just going to ignore us?
Excuse me, aren't you Kwak Kyeongsu, the painter?
Artist Choi, is that you?
Yes.
Ahh, I'm so sorry I didn't recognize you.

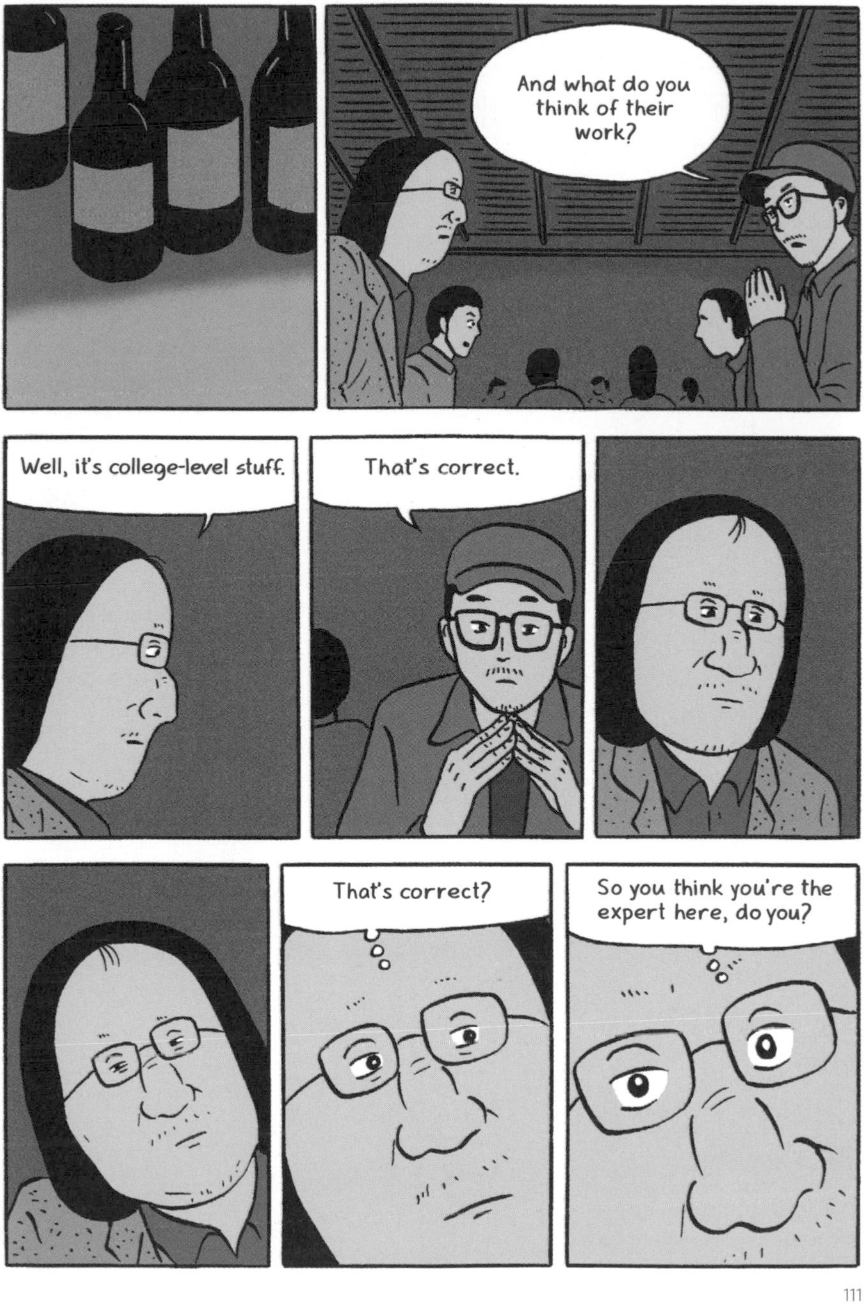
And what do you think of their work?
Well, it's college-level stuff.
That's correct.
That's correct?
So you think you're the expert here, do you?

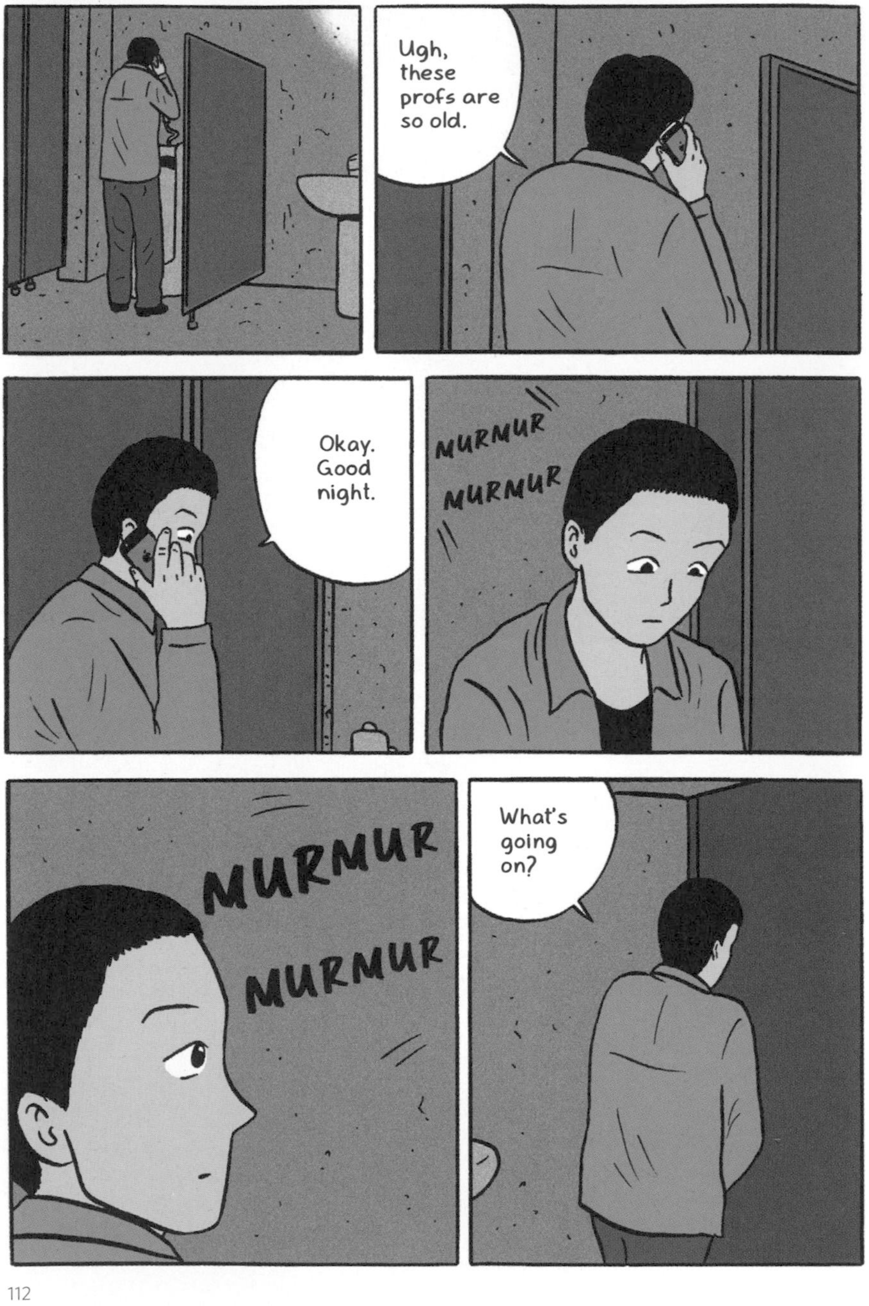
Ugh, these profs are so old.
Okay. Good night.
MURMUR
MURMUR
MURMUR
MURMUR
What's going on?

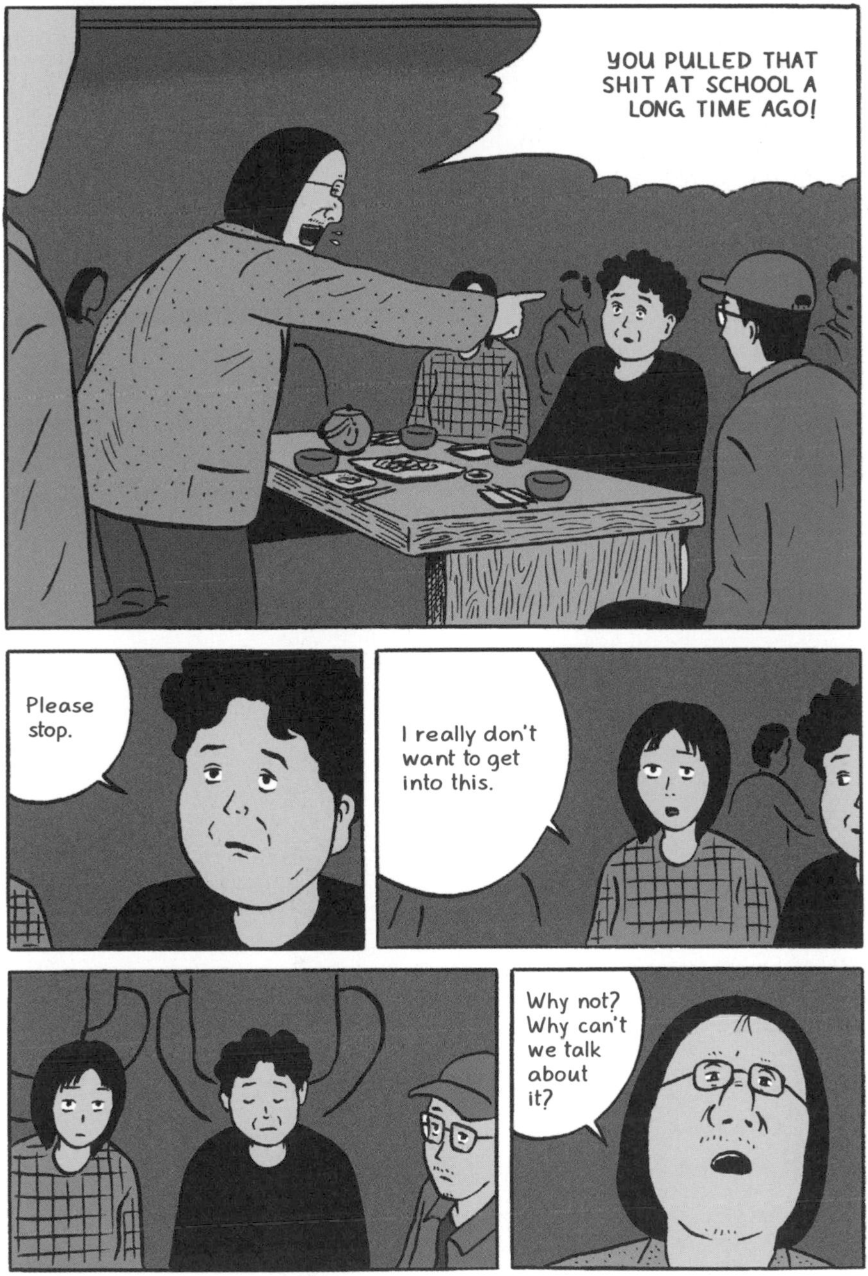
YOU PULLED THAT SHIT AT SCHOOL A LONG TIME AGO!
Please stop.
I really don't want to get into this.
Why not? Why can't we talk about it?

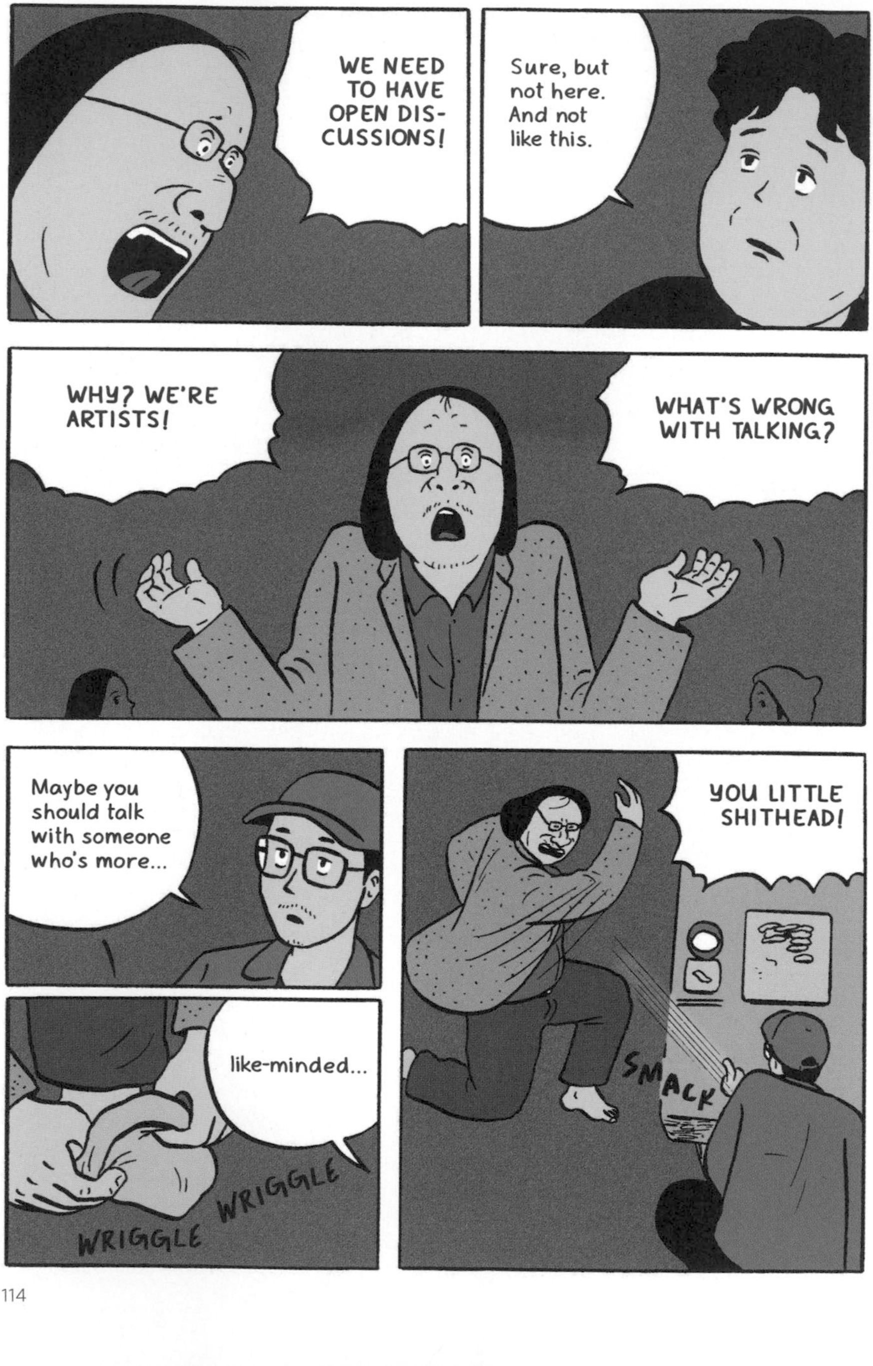
WE NEED TO HAVE OPEN DIS-CUSSIONS!
Sure, but not here. And not like this.
WHY? WE'RE ARTISTS!
WHAT'S WRONG WITH TALKING?
Maybe you should talk with someone who's more...
like-minded...
WRIGGLE
WRIGGLE
YOU LITTLE SHITHEAD!
SMACK

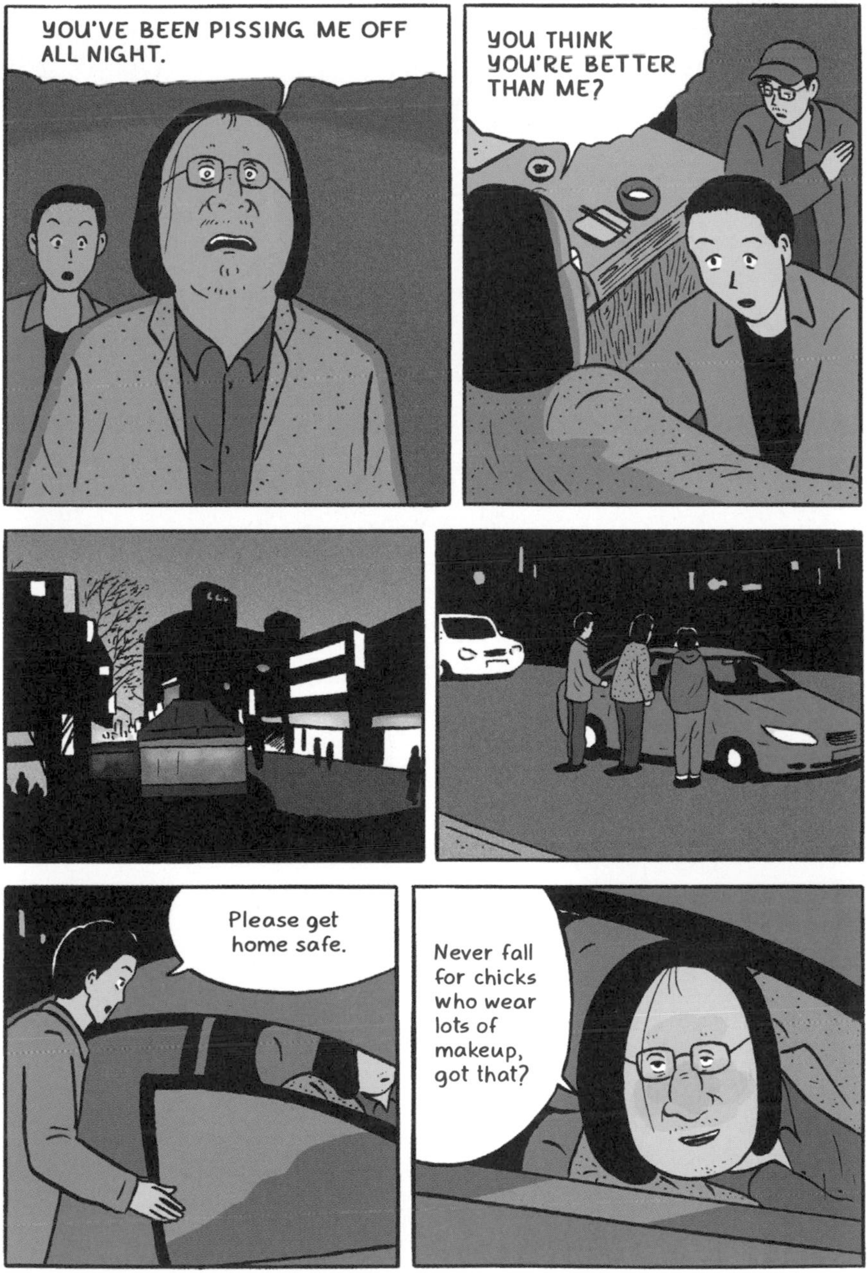
YOU'VE BEEN PISSING ME OFF ALL NIGHT.
YOU THINK YOU'RE BETTER THAN ME?
Please get home safe.
Never fall for chicks who wear lots of makeup, got that?

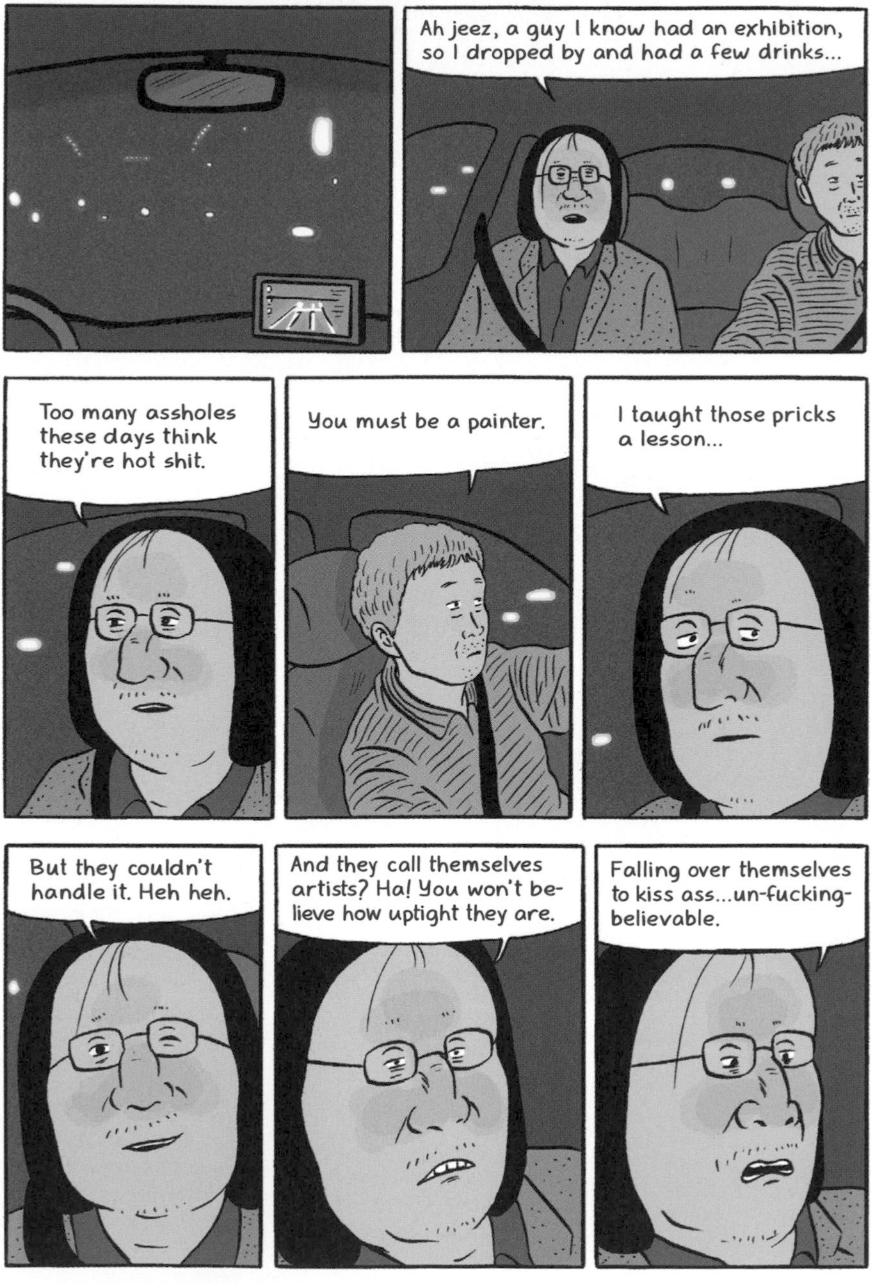
Ah jeez, a guy I know had an exhibition, so I dropped by and had a few drinks...
Too many assholes these days think they're hot shit.
You must be a painter.
I taught those pricks a lesson...
But they couldn't handle it. Heh heh.
And they call themselves artists? Ha! You won't believe how uptight they are.
Falling over themselves to kiss ass...un-fucking-believable.

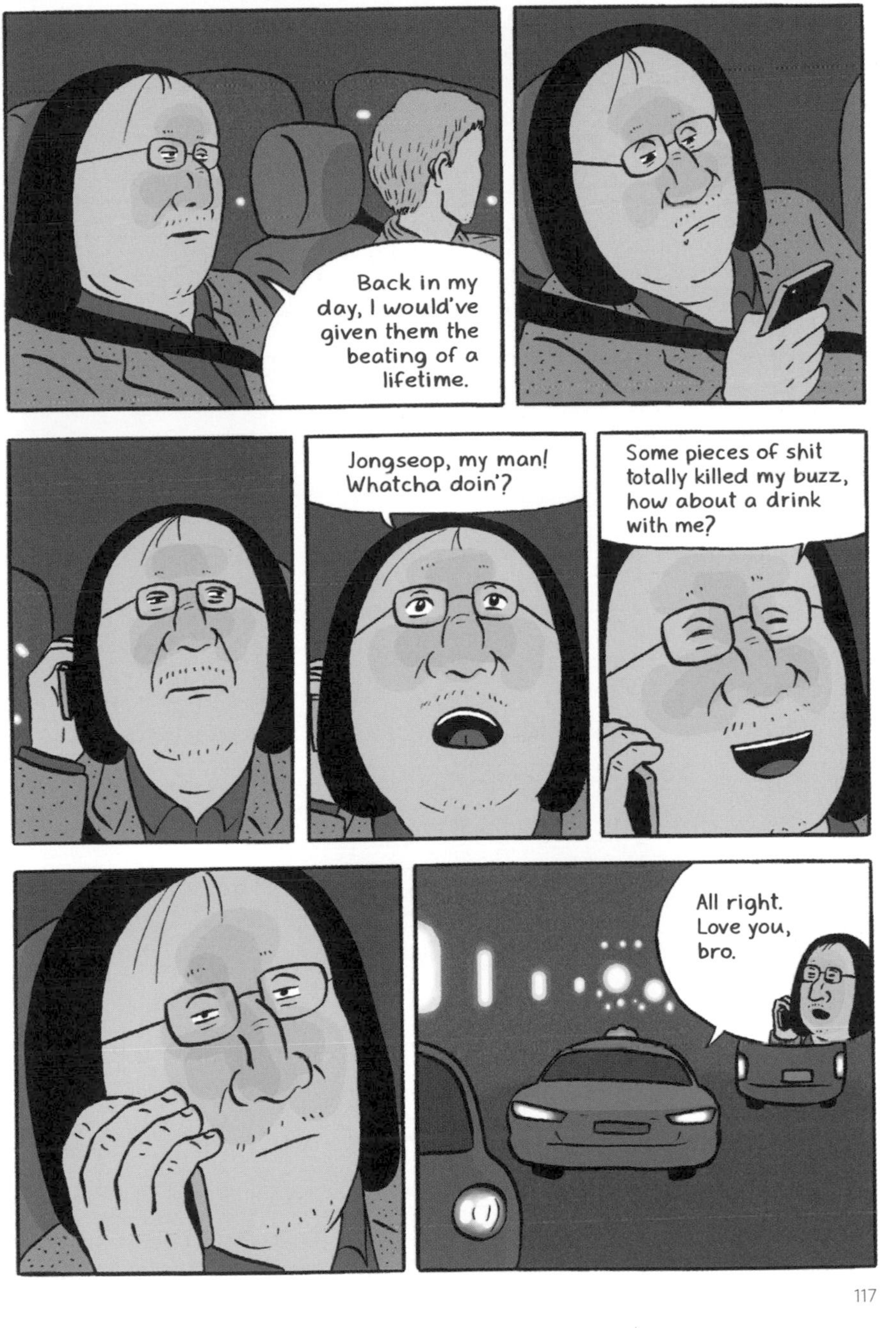
Back in my day, I would've given them the beating of a lifetime.
Jongseop, my man! Whatcha doin'?
Some pieces of shit totally killed my buzz, how about a drink with me?
All right. Love you, bro.

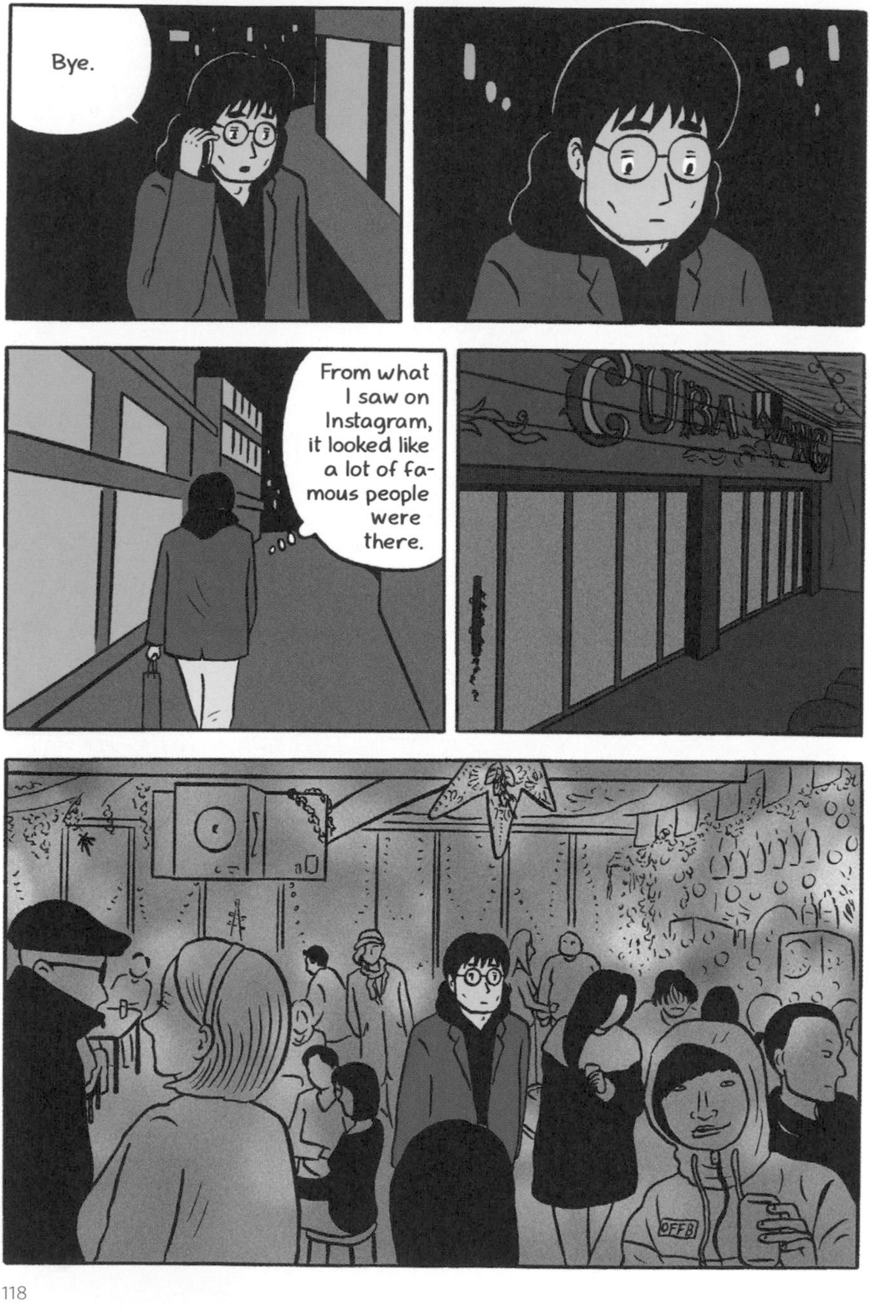
Bye.
From what I saw on Instagram, it looked like a lot of famous people were there.
OFFB

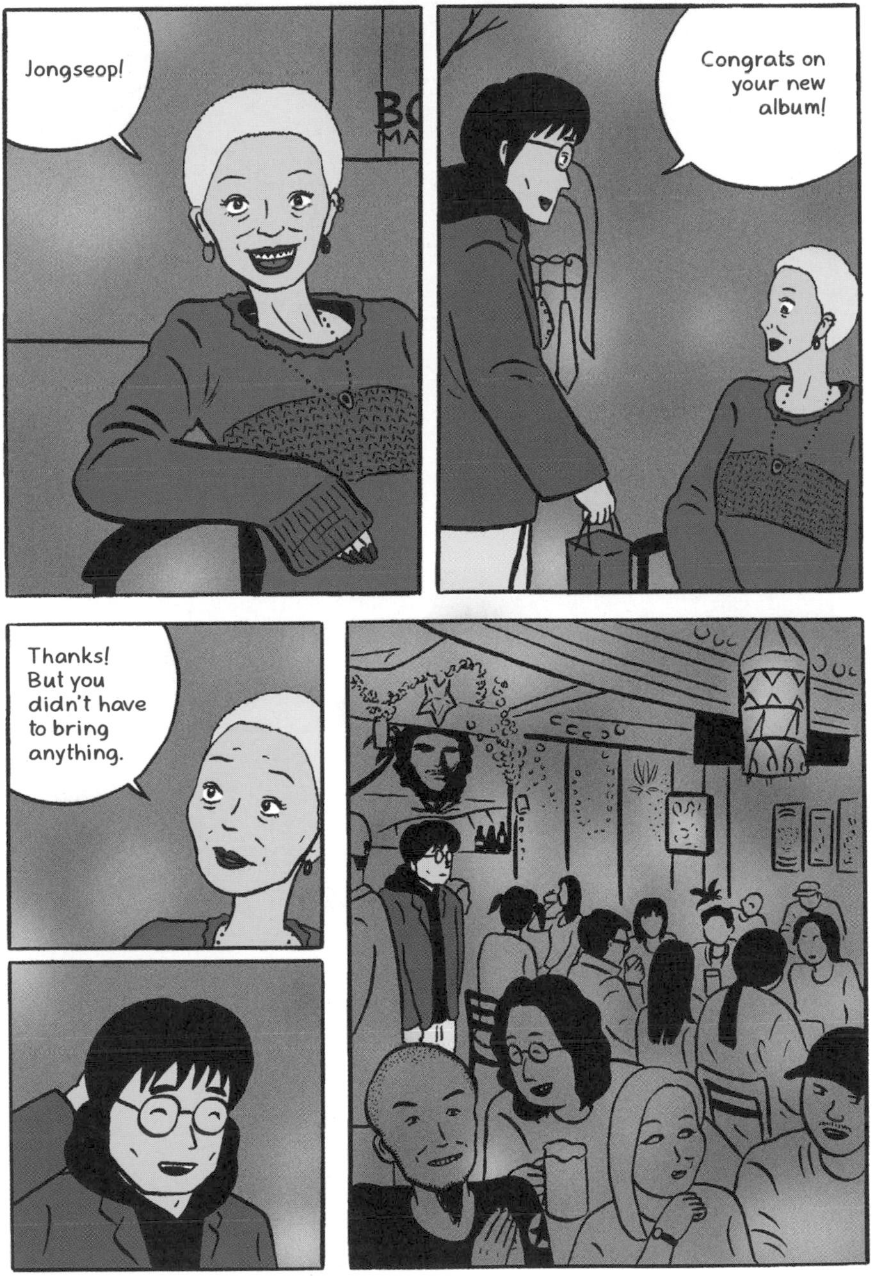
Jongseop!
Congrats on your new album!
Thanks! But you didn't have to bring anything.
BO
MA

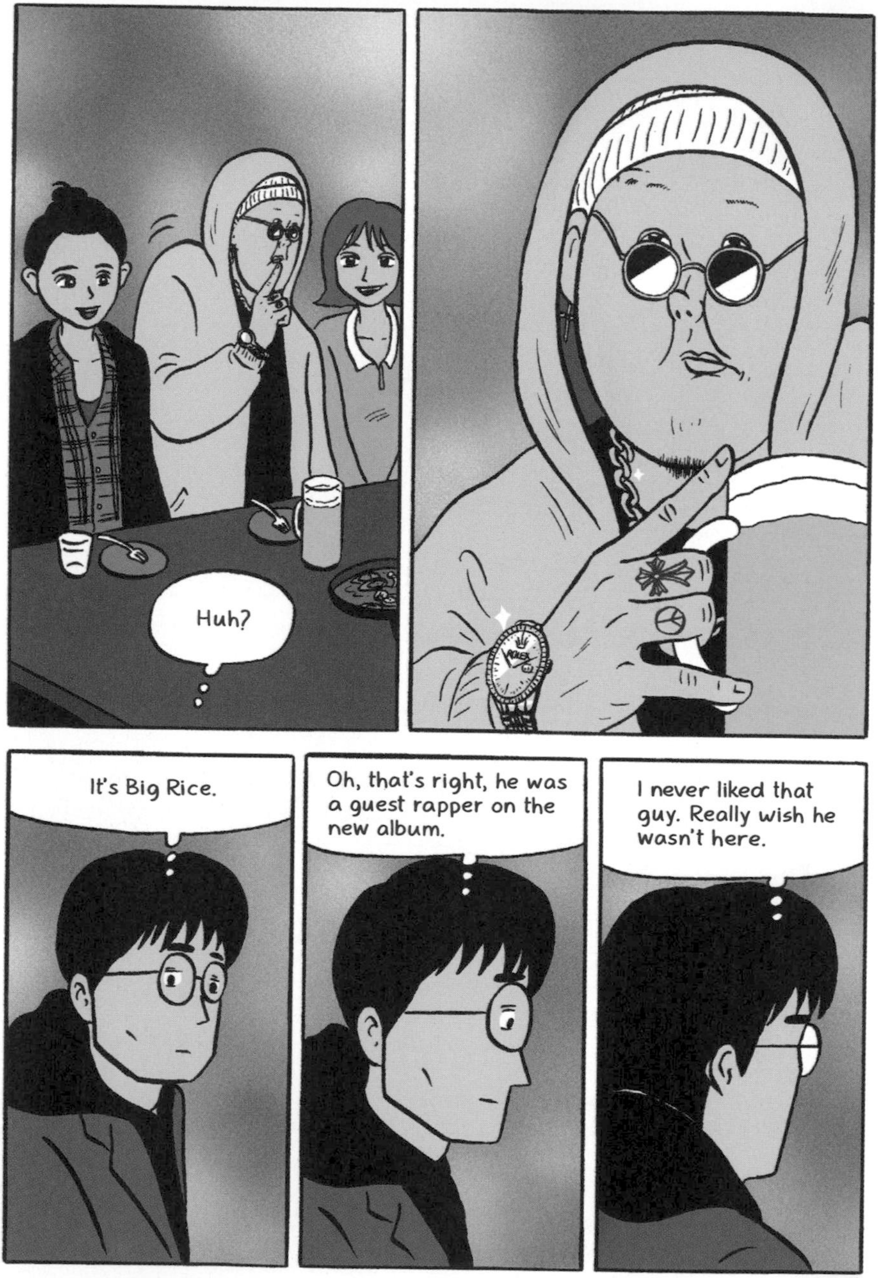
Huh?
ROLEX
It's Big Rice.
Oh, that's right, he was a guest rapper on the new album.
I never liked that guy. Really wish he wasn't here.

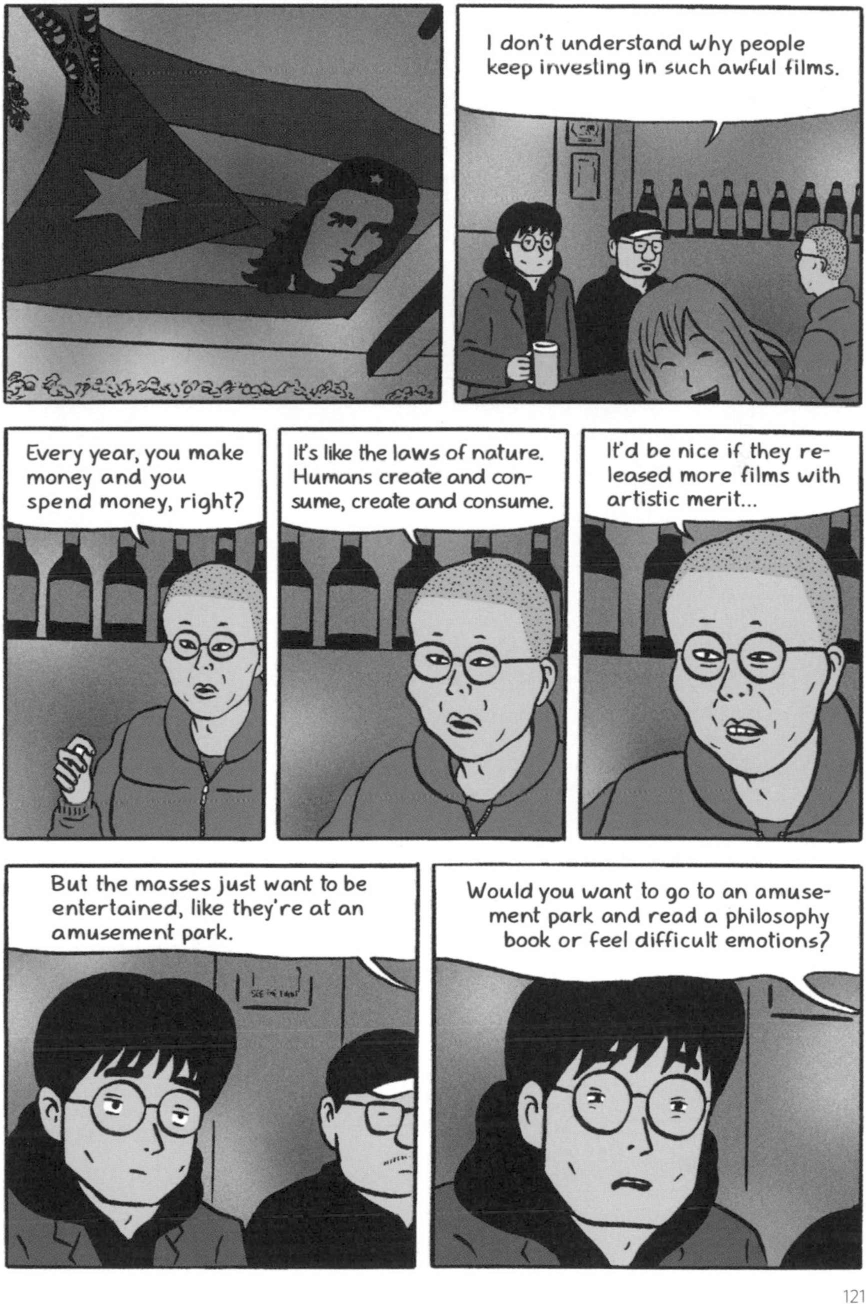

I don't understand why people keep investing in such awful films.
Every year, you make money and you spend money, right?
It's like the laws of nature. Humans create and consume, create and consume.
It'd be nice if they released more films with artistic merit...
But the masses just want to be entertained, like they're at an amusement park.
Would you want to go to an amusement park and read a philosophy book or feel difficult emotions?

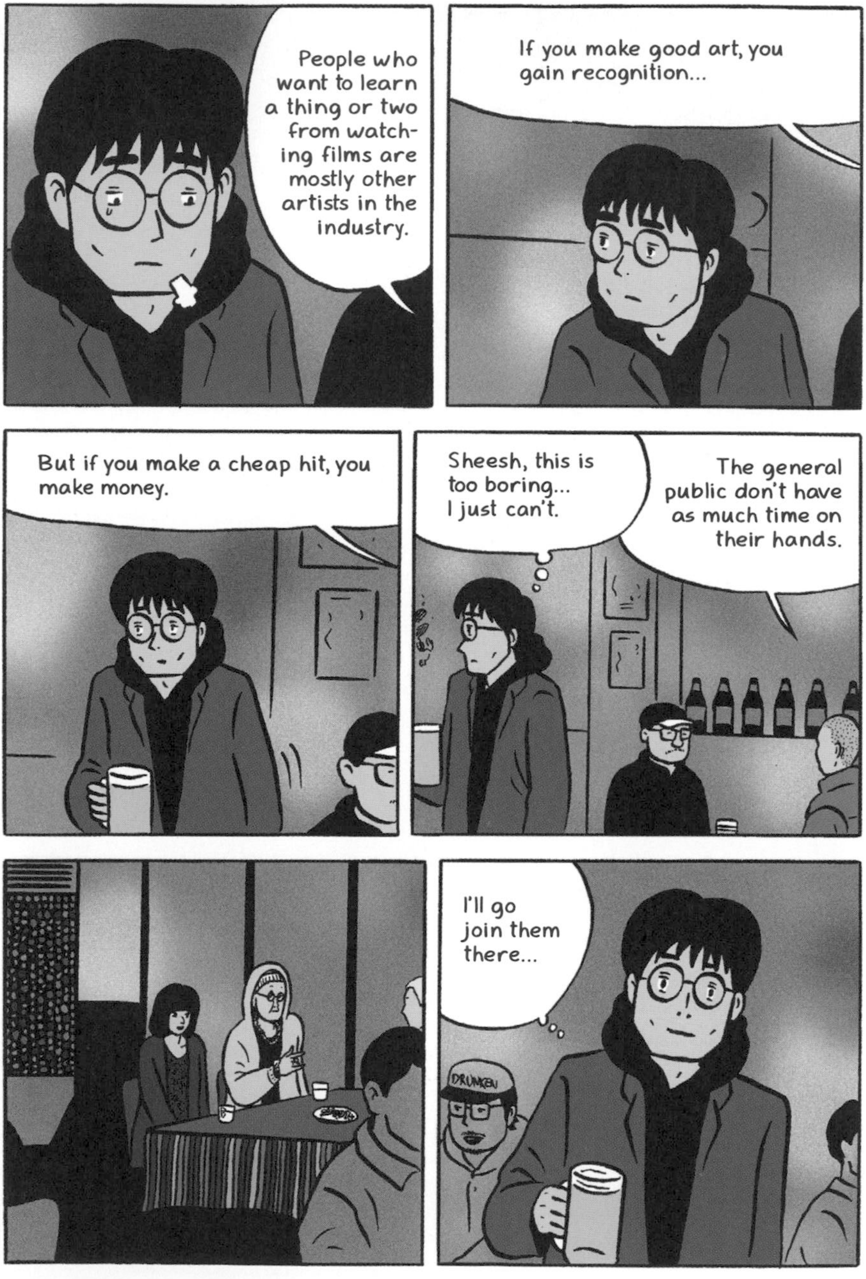
People who want to learn a thing or two from watching films are mostly other artists in the industry.
If you make good art, you gain recognition...
But if you make a cheap hit, you make money.
Sheesh, this is too boring... I just can't.
The general public don't have as much time on their hands.
I'll go join them there...
DRUNKEN

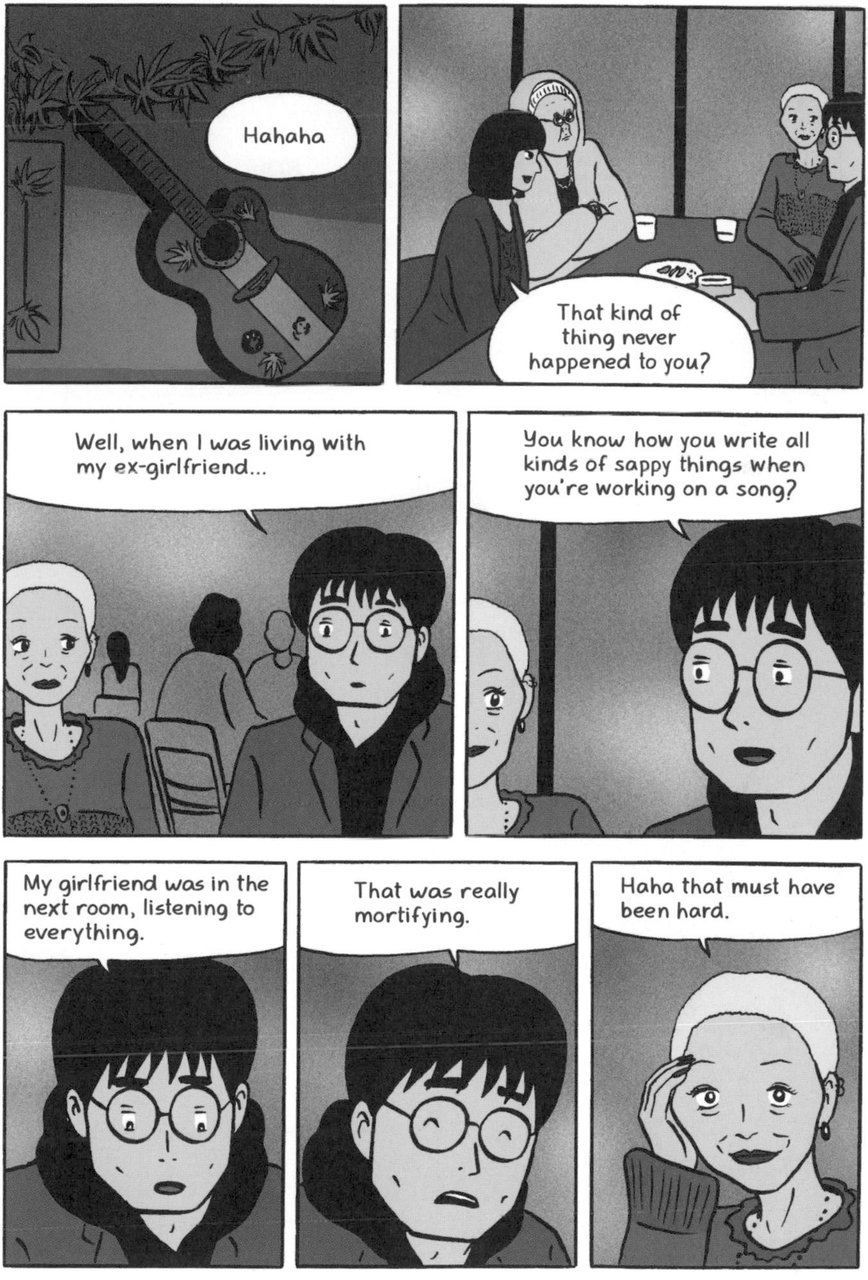
Hahaha
That kind of thing never happened to you?
Well, when I was living with my ex-girlfriend...
You know how you write all kinds of sappy things when you're working on a song?
My girlfriend was in the next room, listening to everything.
That was really mortifying.
Haha that must have been hard.

Sappy things, huh?
Pfff.
Did you just laugh at me?
How dare you?
You hip-hop piece of shit.

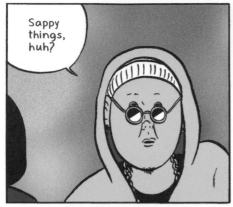

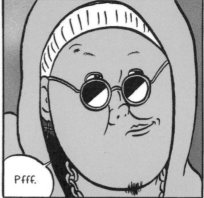

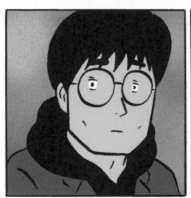

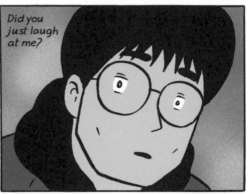

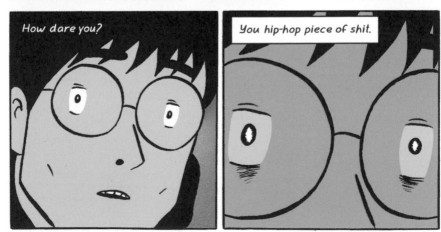

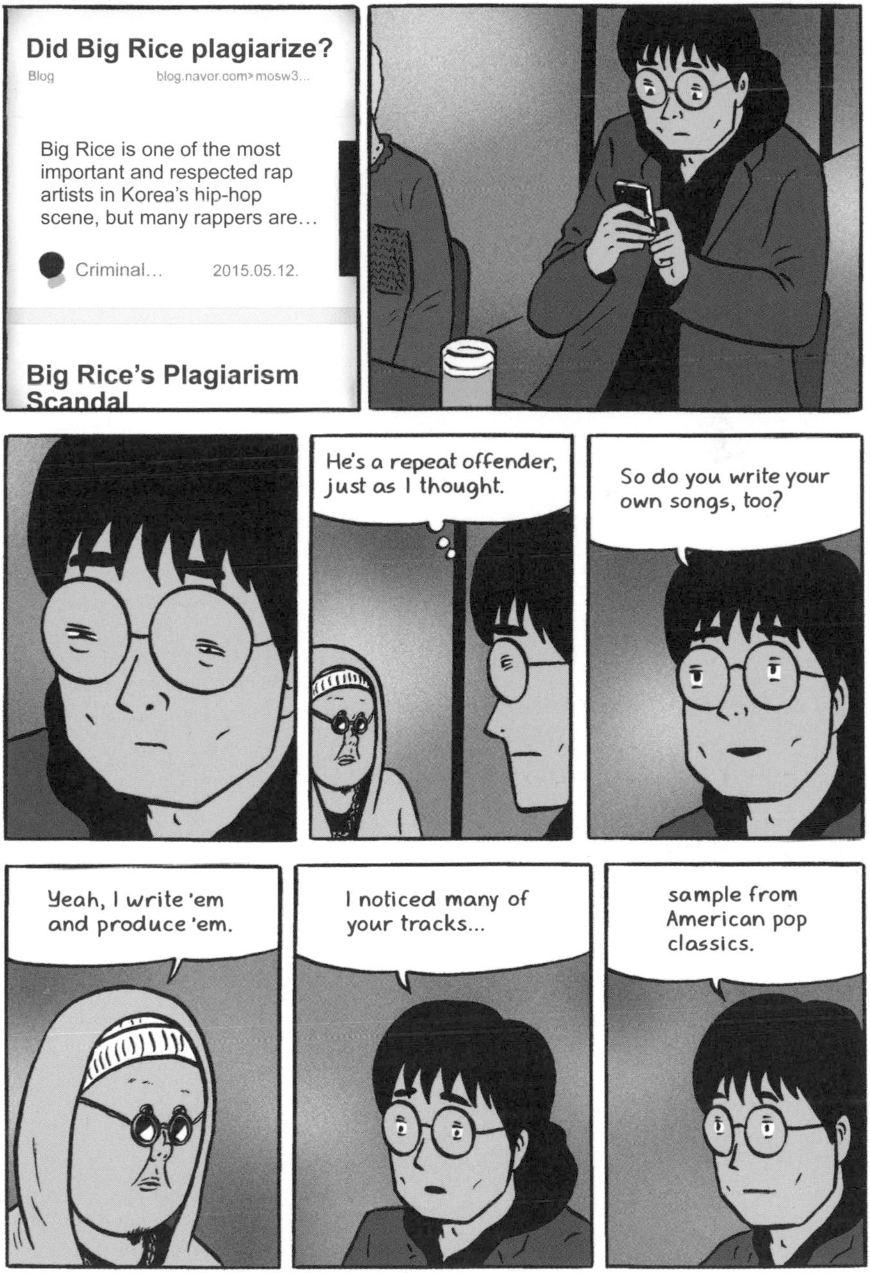
Did Big Rice plagiarize?
Blog
blog.navor.com> mosw3...
Big Rice is one of the most important and respected rap artists in Korea's hip-hop scene, but many rappers are...
Criminal...
2015.05.12.
Big Rice's Plagiarism Scandal
He's a repeat offender, just as I thought.
So do you write your own songs, too?
Yeah, I write 'em and produce 'em.
I noticed many of your tracks...
sample from American pop classics.

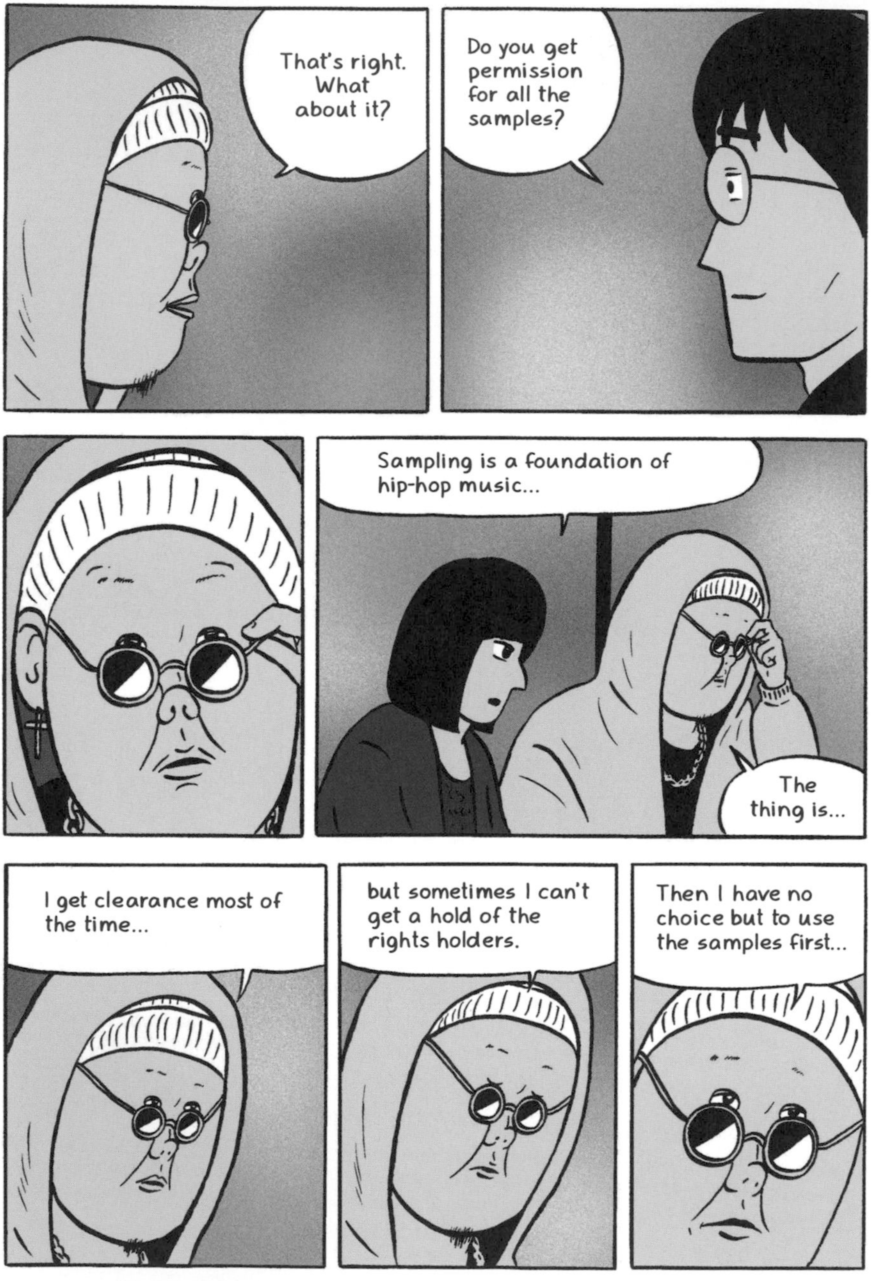
That's right. What about it?
Do you get permission for all the samples?
Sampling is a foundation of hip-hop music...
The thing is...
I get clearance most of the time...
but sometimes I can't get a hold of the rights holders.
Then I have no choice but to use the samples first...

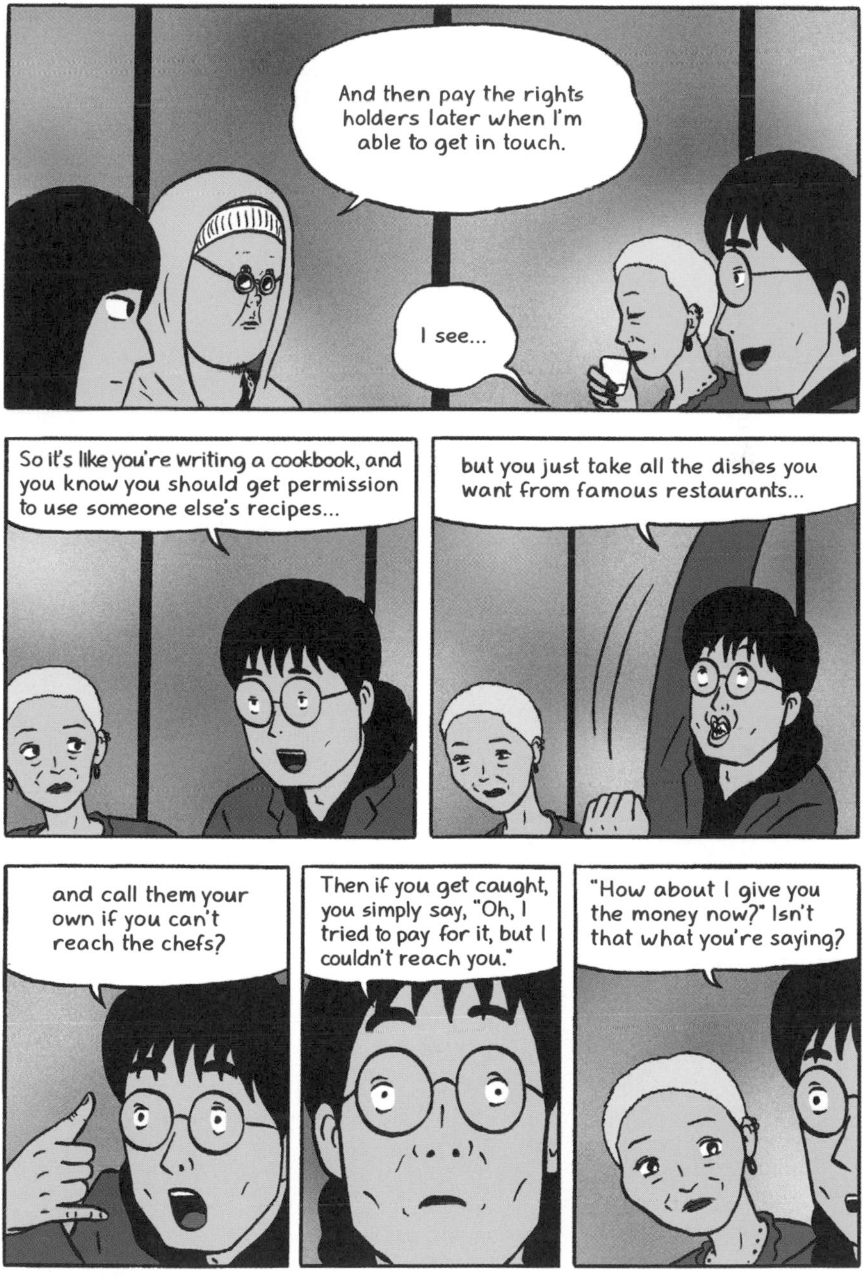
And then pay the rights holders later when I'm able to get in touch.
I see...
So it's like you're writing a cookbook, and you know you should get permission to use someone else's recipes...
but you just take all the dishes you want from famous restaurants...
and call them your own if you can't reach the chefs?
Then if you get caught, you simply say, "Oh, I tried to pay for it, but I couldn't reach you."
"How about I give you the money now?" Isn't that what you're saying?

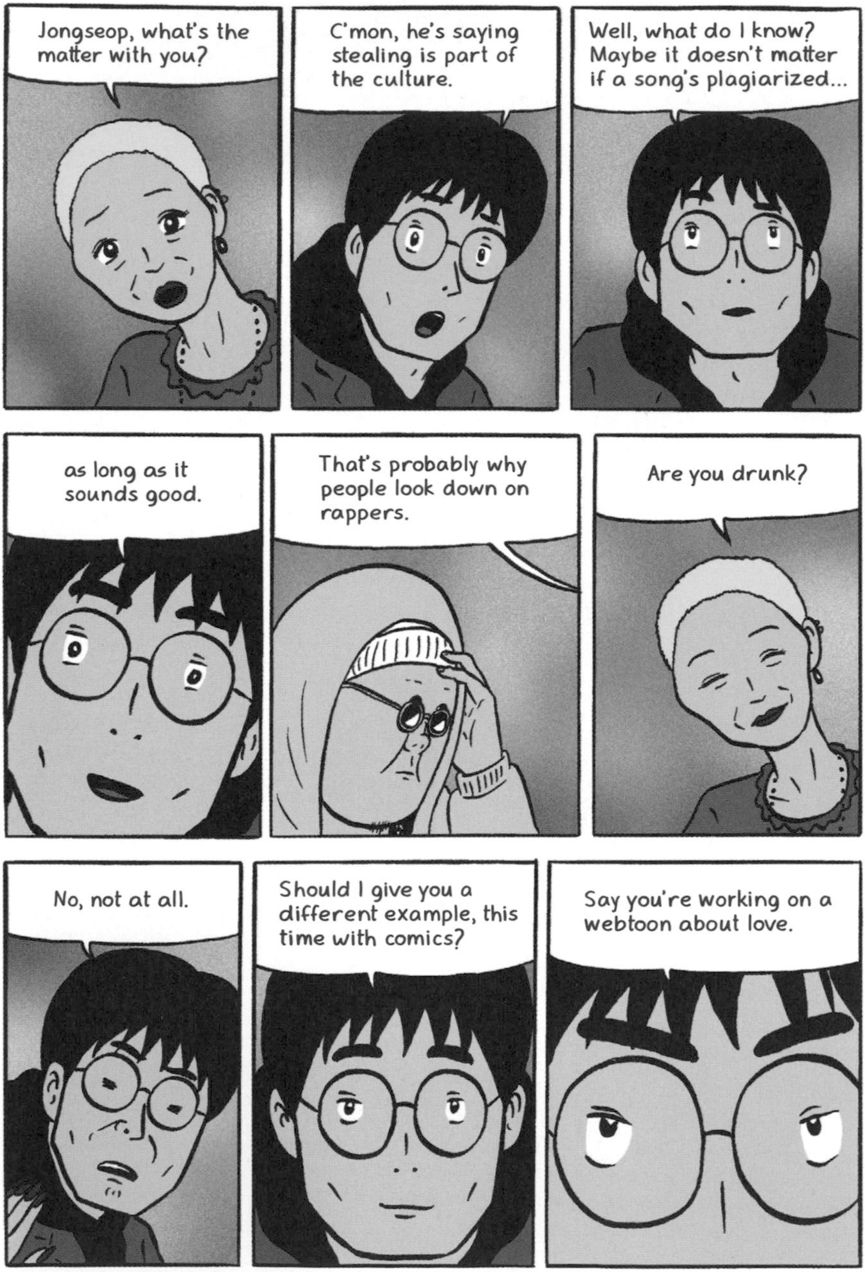

Jongseop, what's the matter with you?
C'mon, he's saying stealing is part of the culture.
Well, what do I know? Maybe it doesn't matter if a song's plagiarized...
as long as it sounds good.
That's probably why people look down on rappers.
Are you drunk?
No, not at all.
Should I give you a different example, this time with comics?
Say you're working on a webtoon about love.

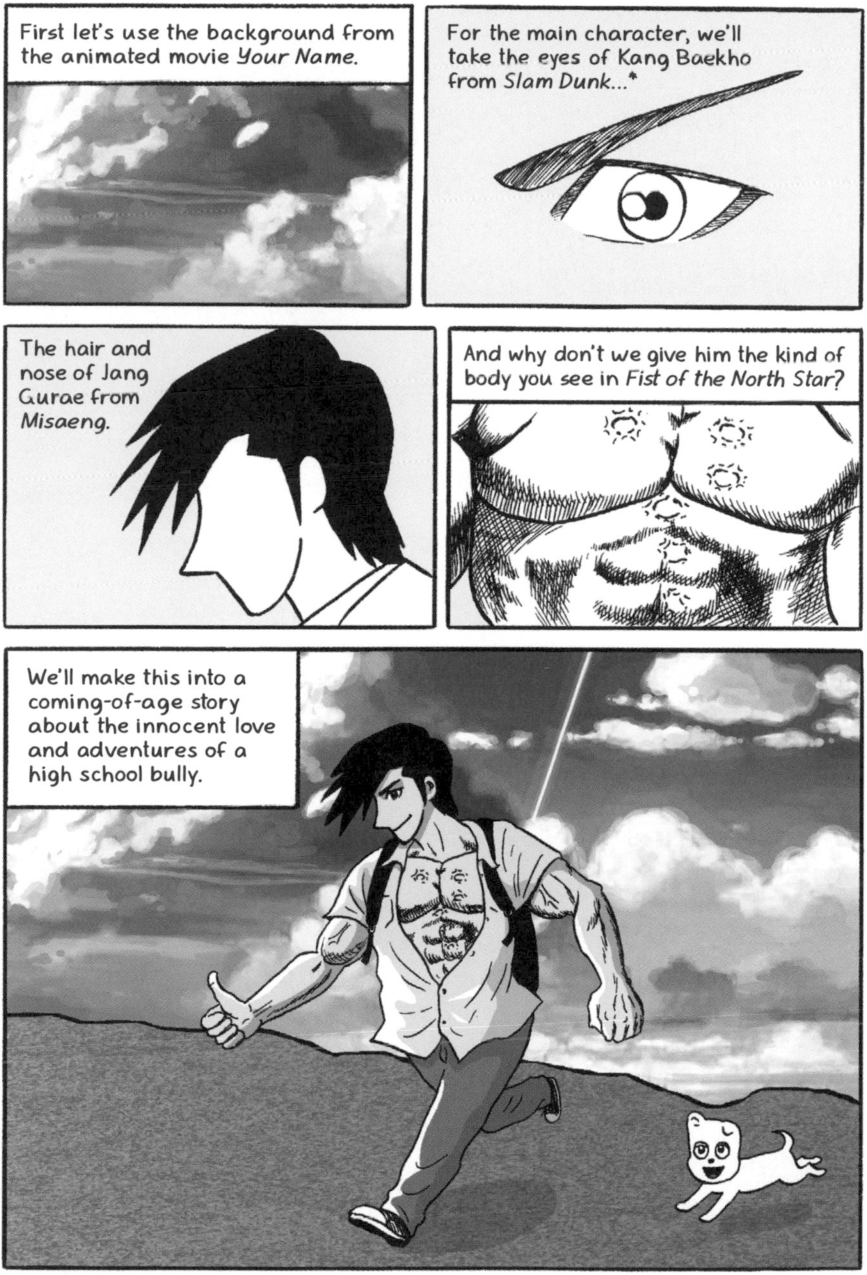
First let's use the background from the animated movie *Your Name*.
For the main character, we'll take the eyes of Kang Baekho from *Slam Dunk*...*
The hair and nose of Jang Gurae from *Misaeng*.
And why don't we give him the kind of body you see in *Fist of the North Star*?
We'll make this into a coming-of-age story about the innocent love and adventures of a high school bully.

* Kang Baekho is the name used for the main character in the Korean translation of the Japanese manga *Slam Dunk*.

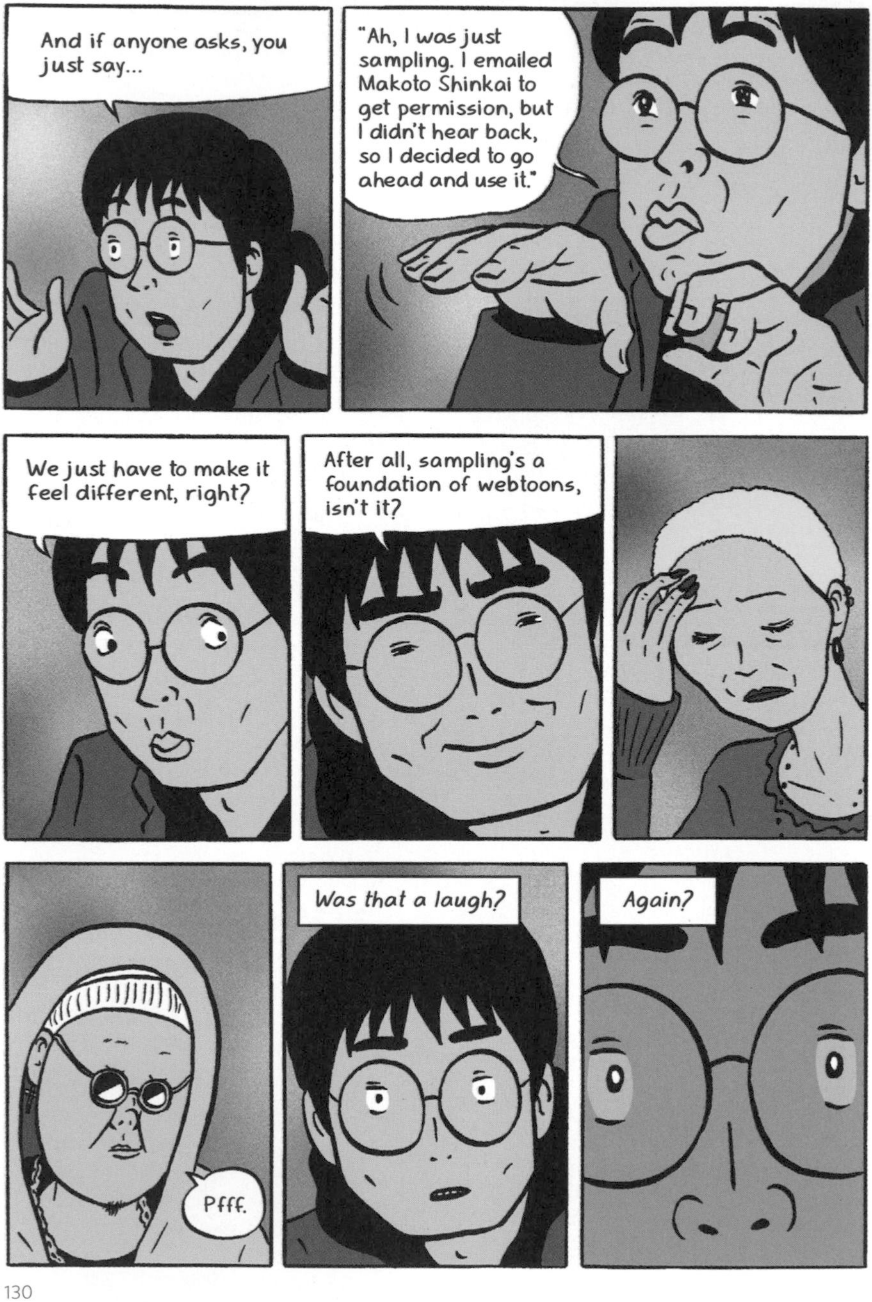
And if anyone asks, you just say...
"Ah, I was just sampling. I emailed Makoto Shinkai to get permission, but I didn't hear back, so I decided to go ahead and use it."
We just have to make it feel different, right?
After all, sampling's a foundation of webtoons, isn't it?
Pfff.
Was that a laugh?
Again?

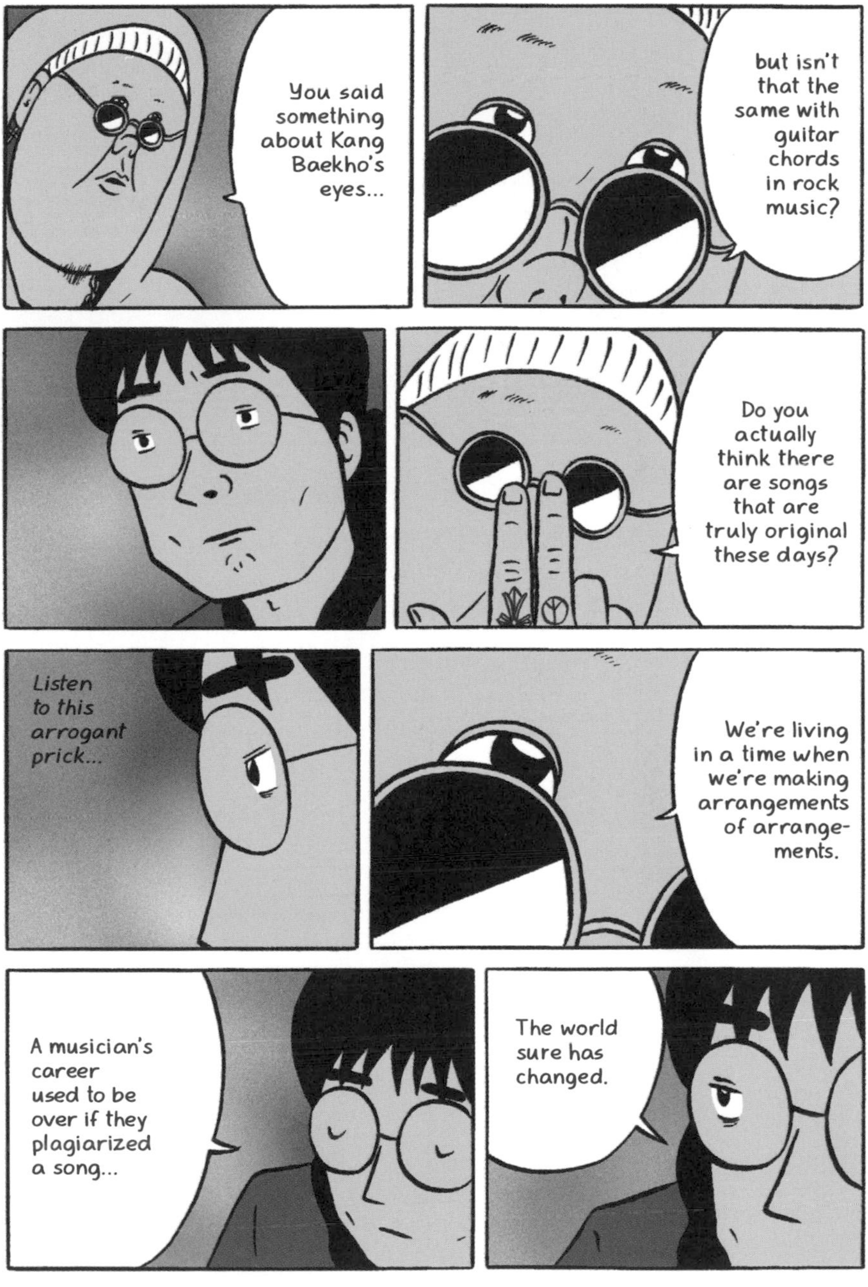
You said something about Kang Baekho's eyes...
but isn't that the same with guitar chords in rock music?
Do you actually think there are songs that are truly original these days?
Listen to this arrogant prick...
We're living in a time when we're making arrangements of arrange-ments.
A musician's career used to be over if they plagiarized a song...
The world sure has changed.

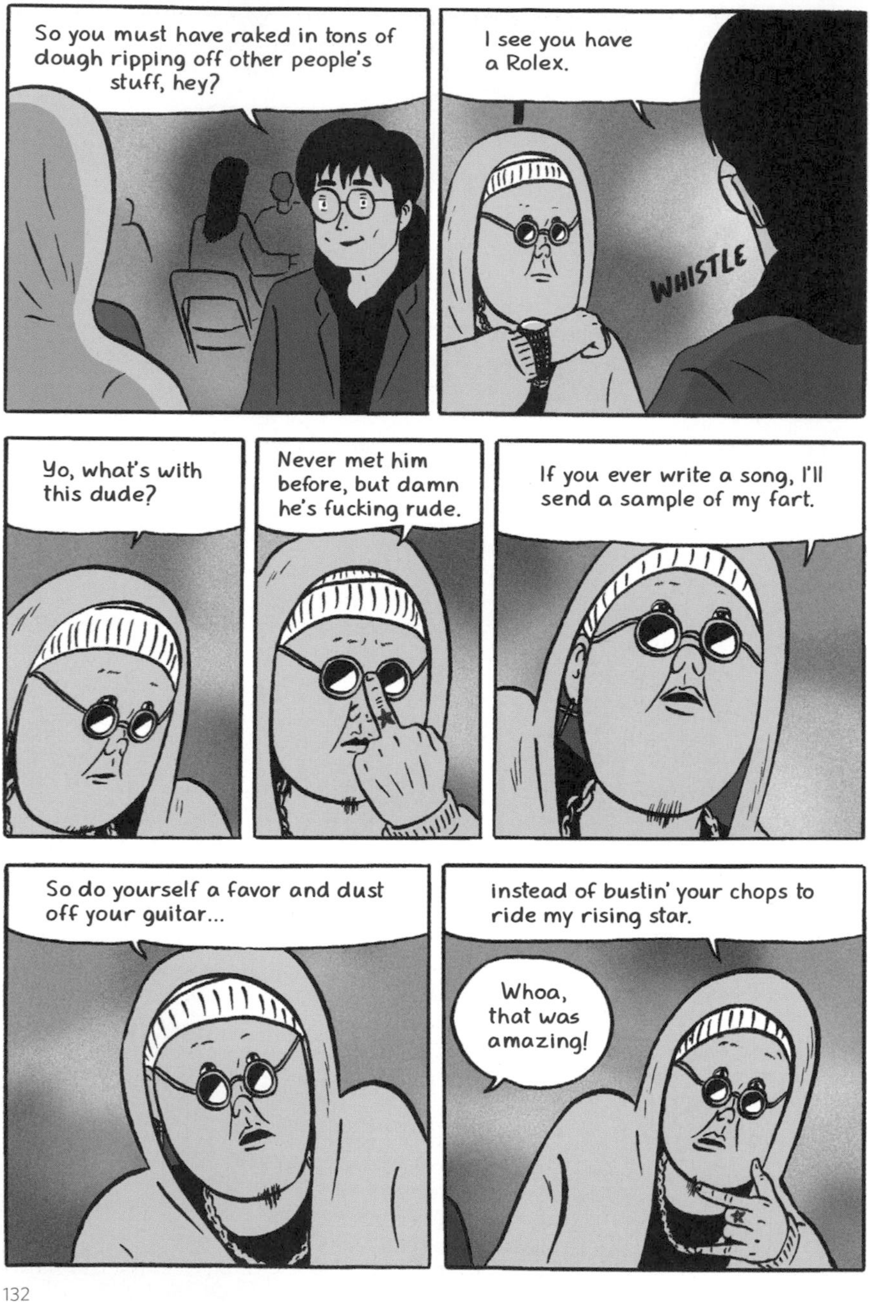
So you must have raked in tons of dough ripping off other people's stuff, hey?
I see you have a Rolex.
WHISTLE
Yo, what's with this dude?
Never met him before, but damn he's fucking rude.
If you ever write a song, I'll send a sample of my fart.
So do yourself a favor and dust off your guitar...
instead of bustin' your chops to ride my rising star.
Whoa, that was amazing!

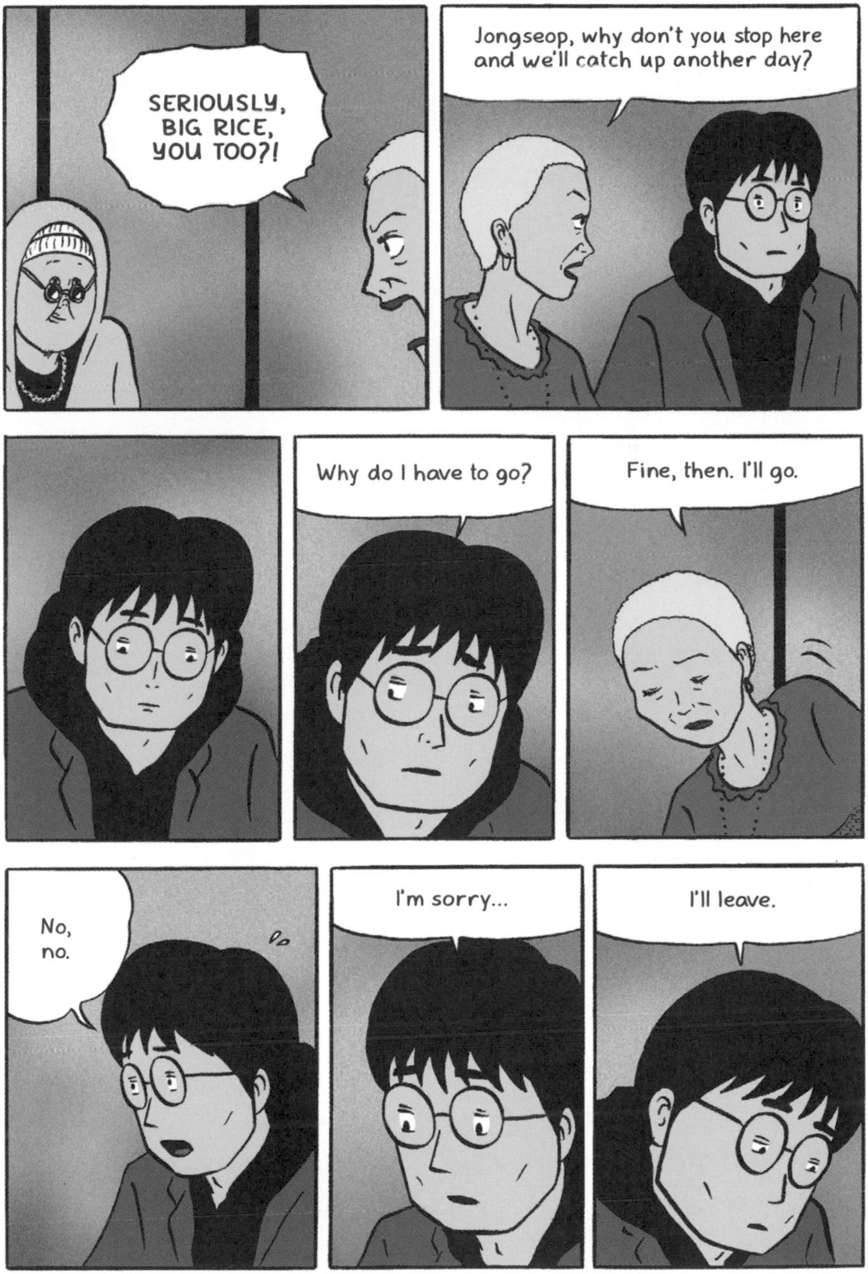
SERIOUSLY, BIG RICE, YOU TOO?!
Jongseop, why don't you stop here and we'll catch up another day?
Why do I have to go?
Fine, then. I'll go.
No, no.
I'm sorry...
I'll leave.

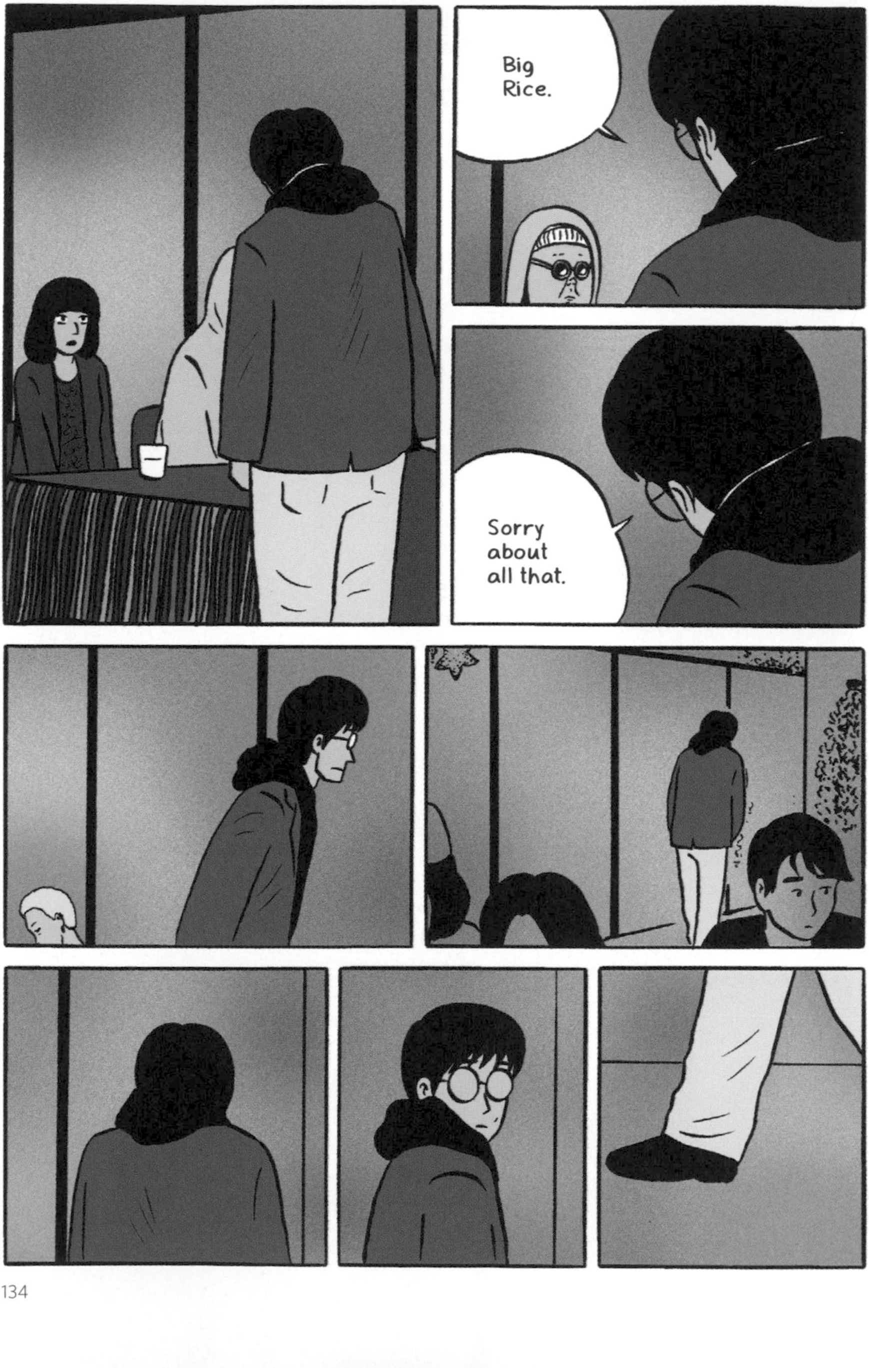
Big Rice.
Sorry about all that.

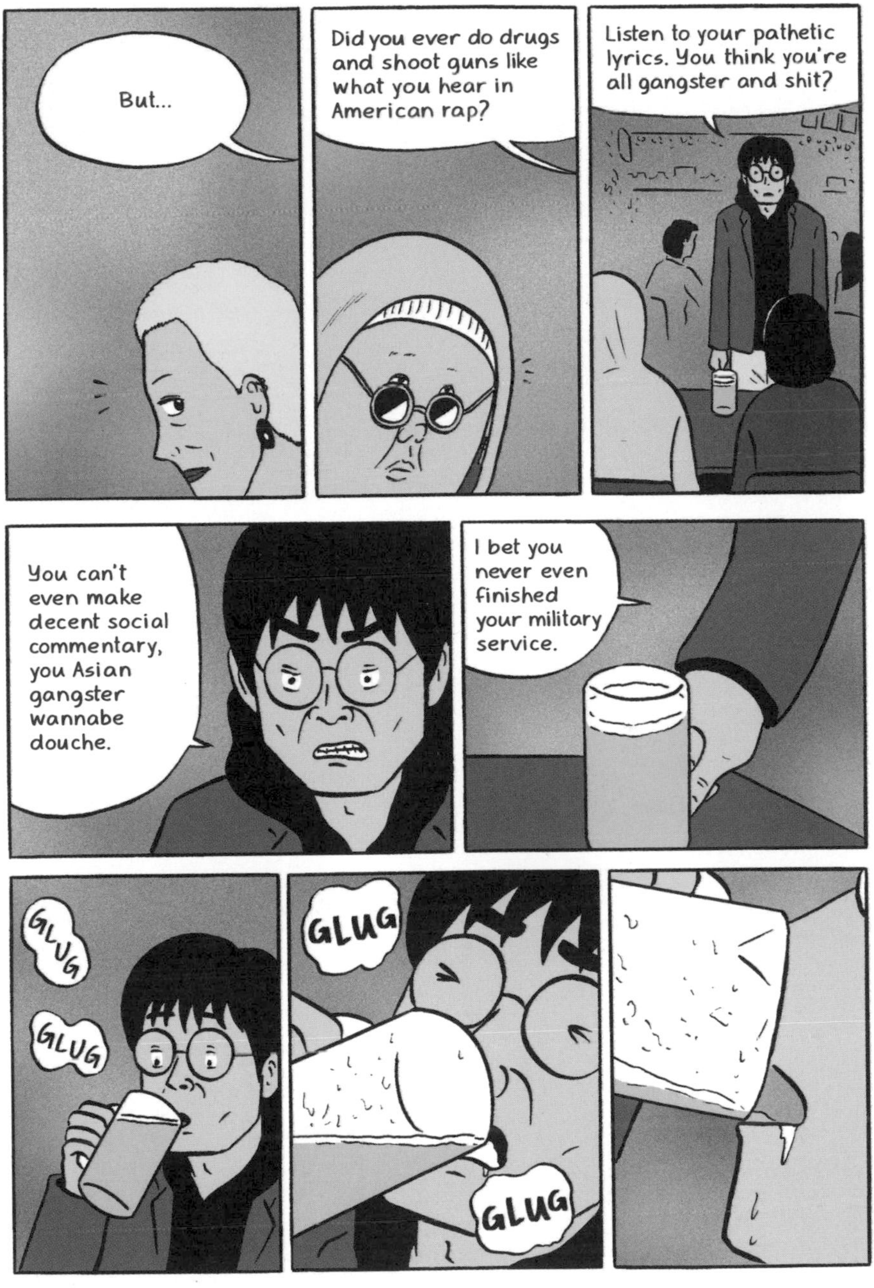
But...
Did you ever do drugs and shoot guns like what you hear in American rap?
Listen to your pathetic lyrics. You think you're all gangster and shit?
You can't even make decent social commentary, you Asian gangster wannabe douche.
I bet you never even finished your military service.
GLUG
GLUG
GLUG
GLUG

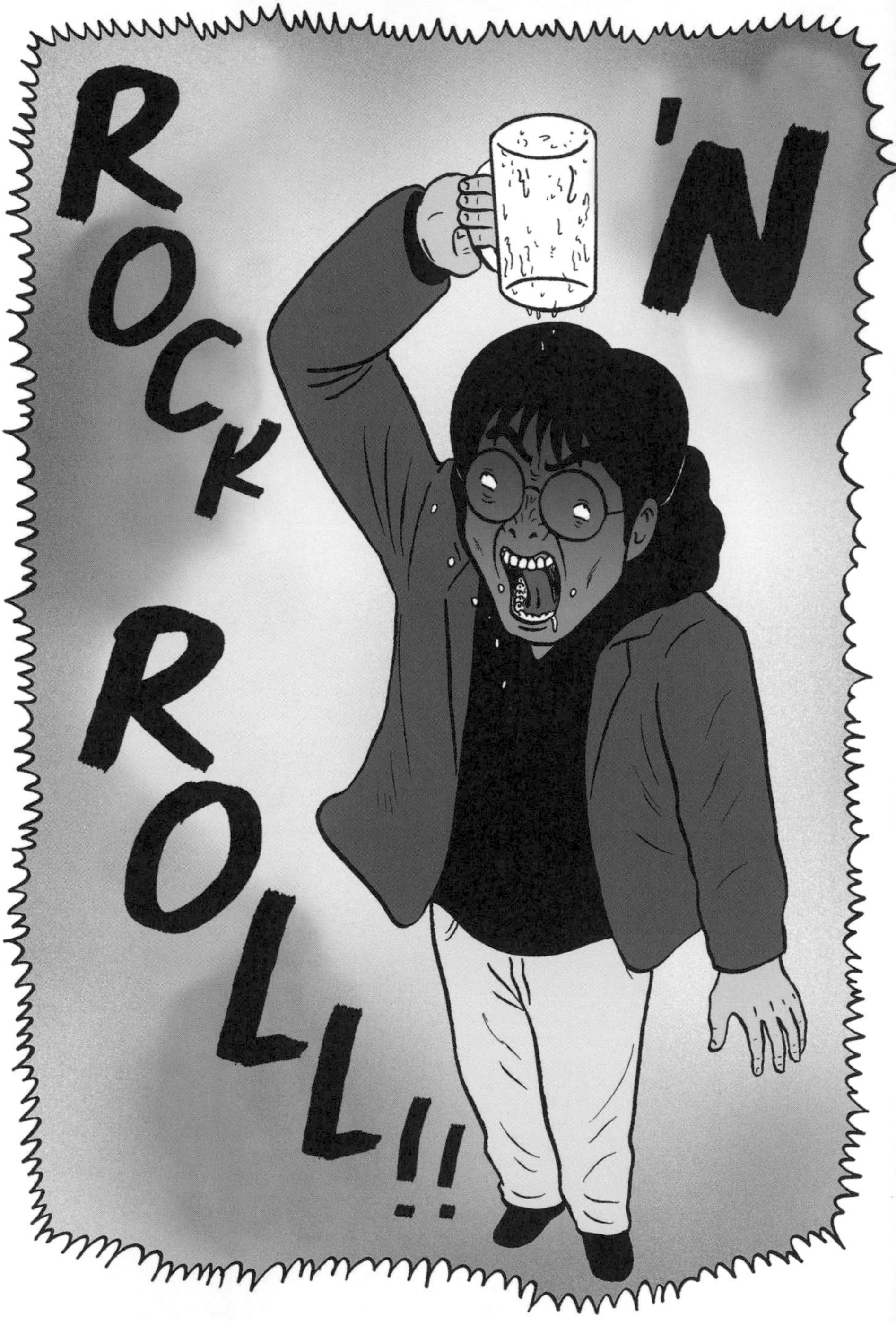
ROCK 'N ROLL!!

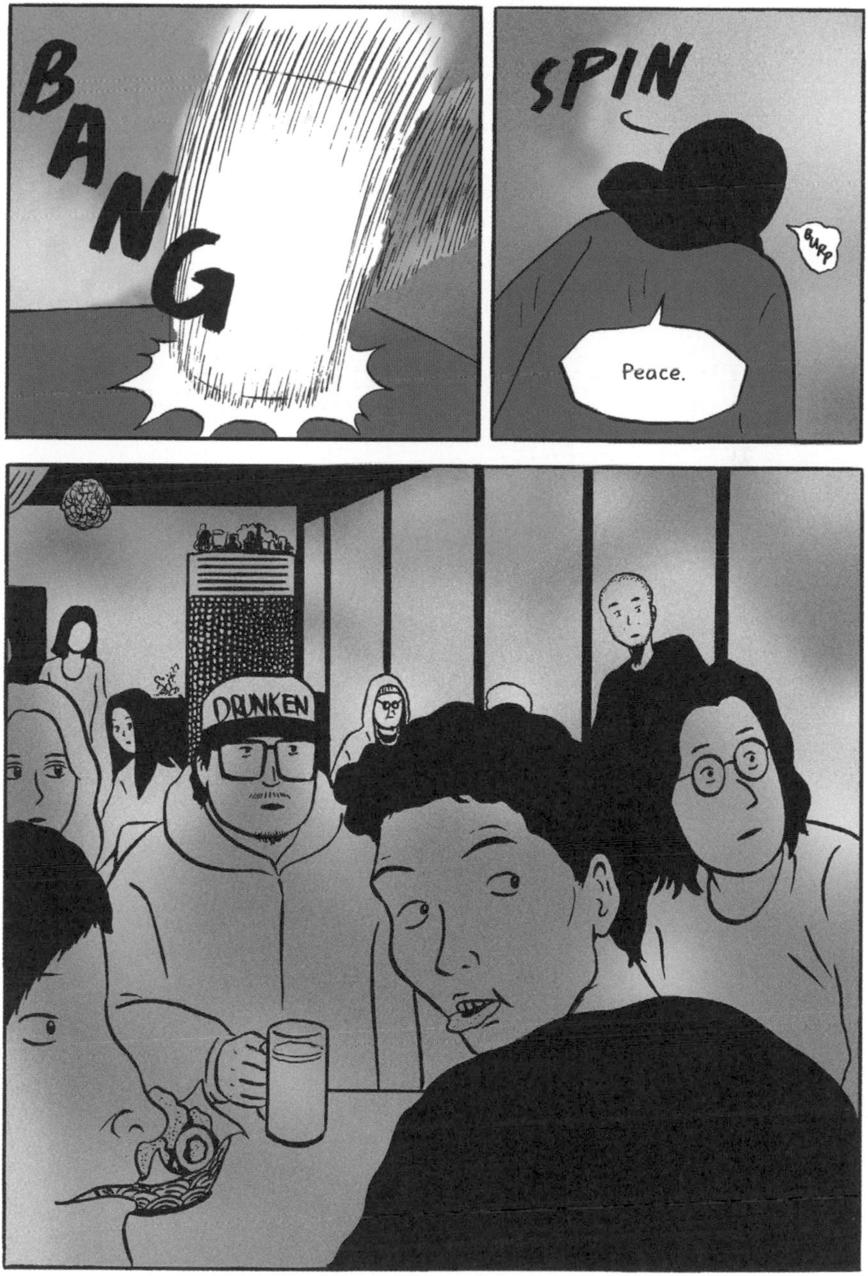
BANG
SPIN
BURP
Peace.
DRUNKEN

BOOK LAUNCH

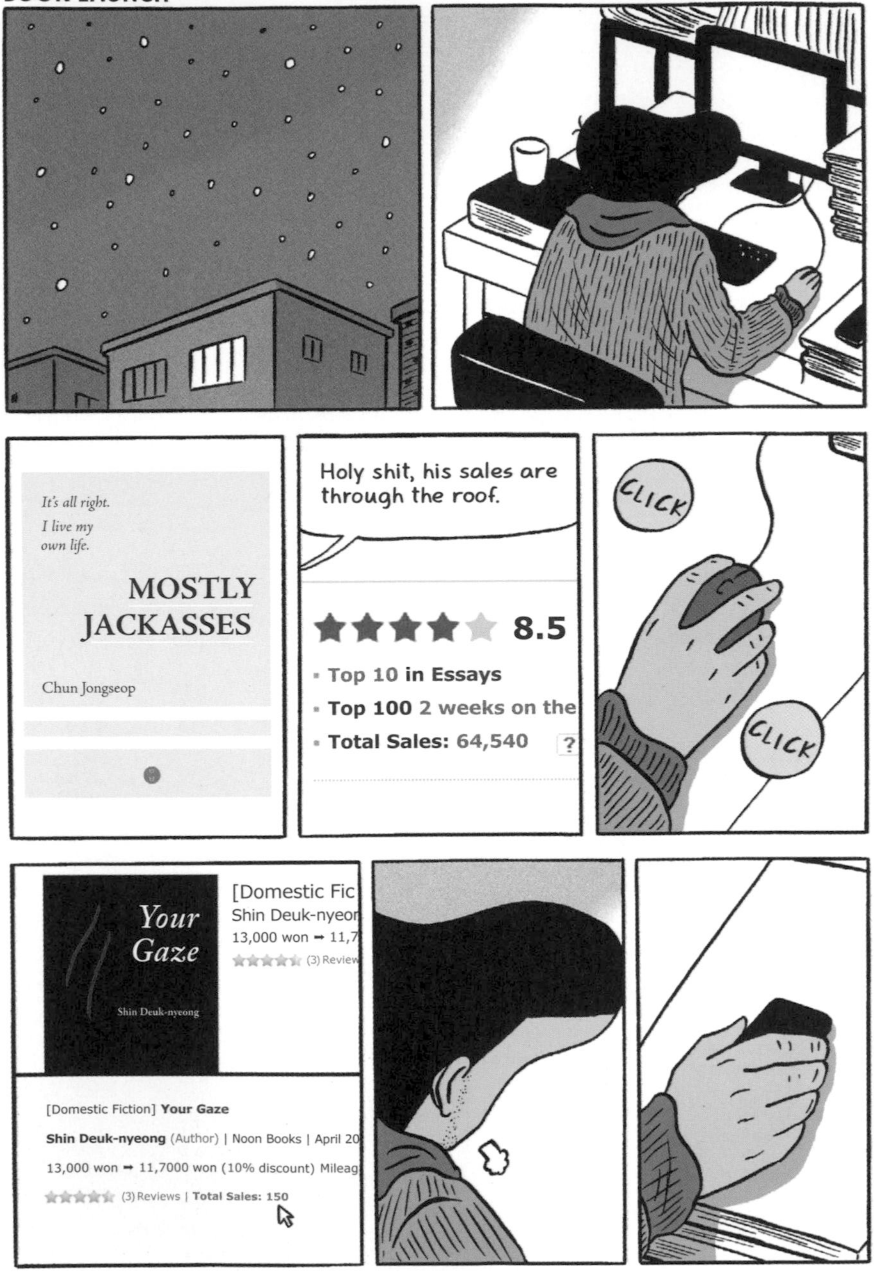
It's all right.
I live my
own life.
MOSTLY
JACKASSES
Chun Jongseop
Holy shit, his sales are through the roof.
8.5
Top 10 in Essays
Top 100 2 weeks on the
Total Sales: 64,540
?
CLICK
CLICK
Your
Gaze
Shin Deuk-nyeong
[Domestic Fic
Shin Deuk-nyeor
13,000 won ➡ 11,7
(3) Review
[Domestic Fiction] Your Gaze
Shin Deuk-nyeong (Author) | Noon Books | April 20
13,000 won ➡ 11,7000 won (10% discount) Mileag
(3) Reviews | Total Sales: 150

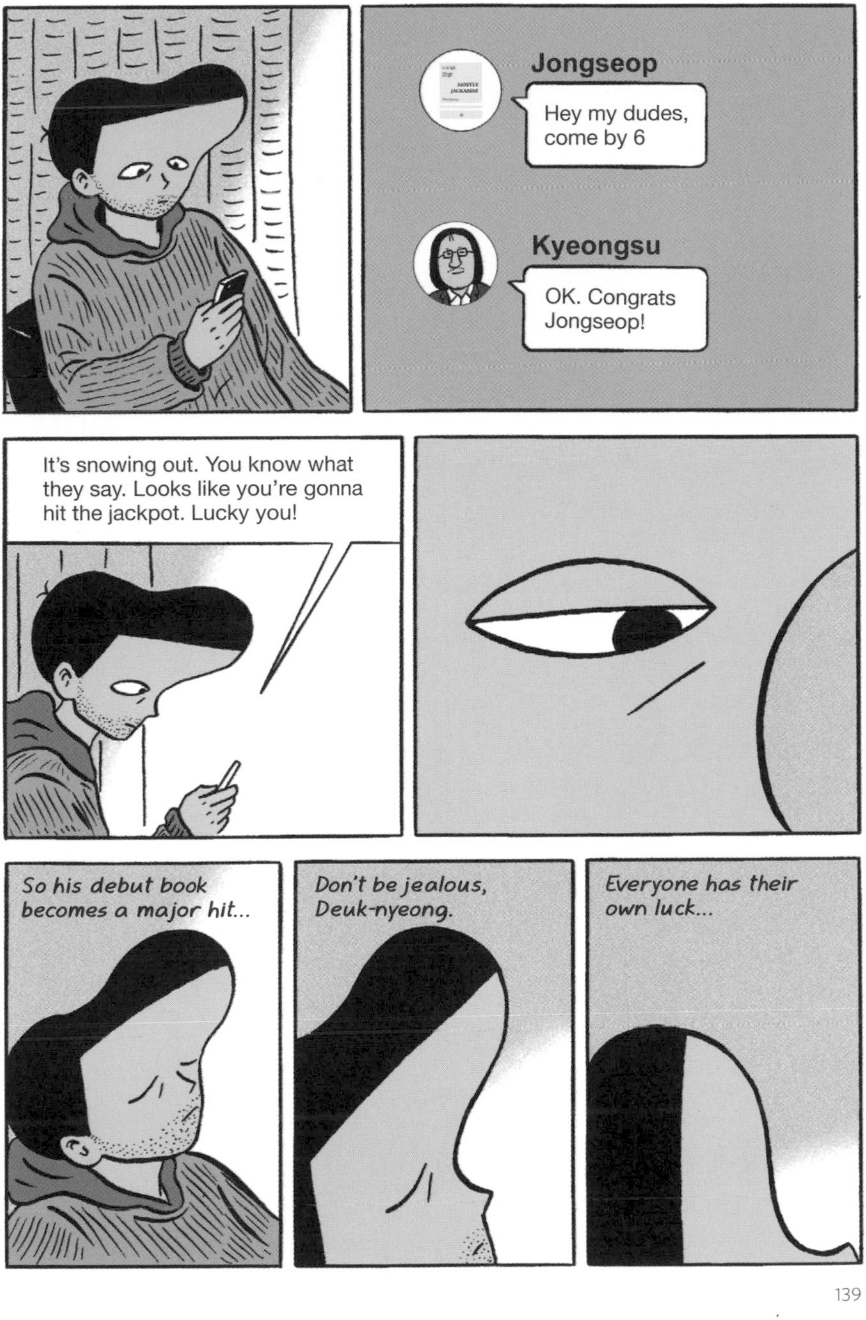
Jongseop
Hey my dudes, come by 6
Kyeongsu
OK. Congrats Jongseop!
It's snowing out. You know what they say. Looks like you're gonna hit the jackpot. Lucky you!
So his debut book becomes a major hit...
Don't be jealous, Deuk-nyeong.
Everyone has their own luck...

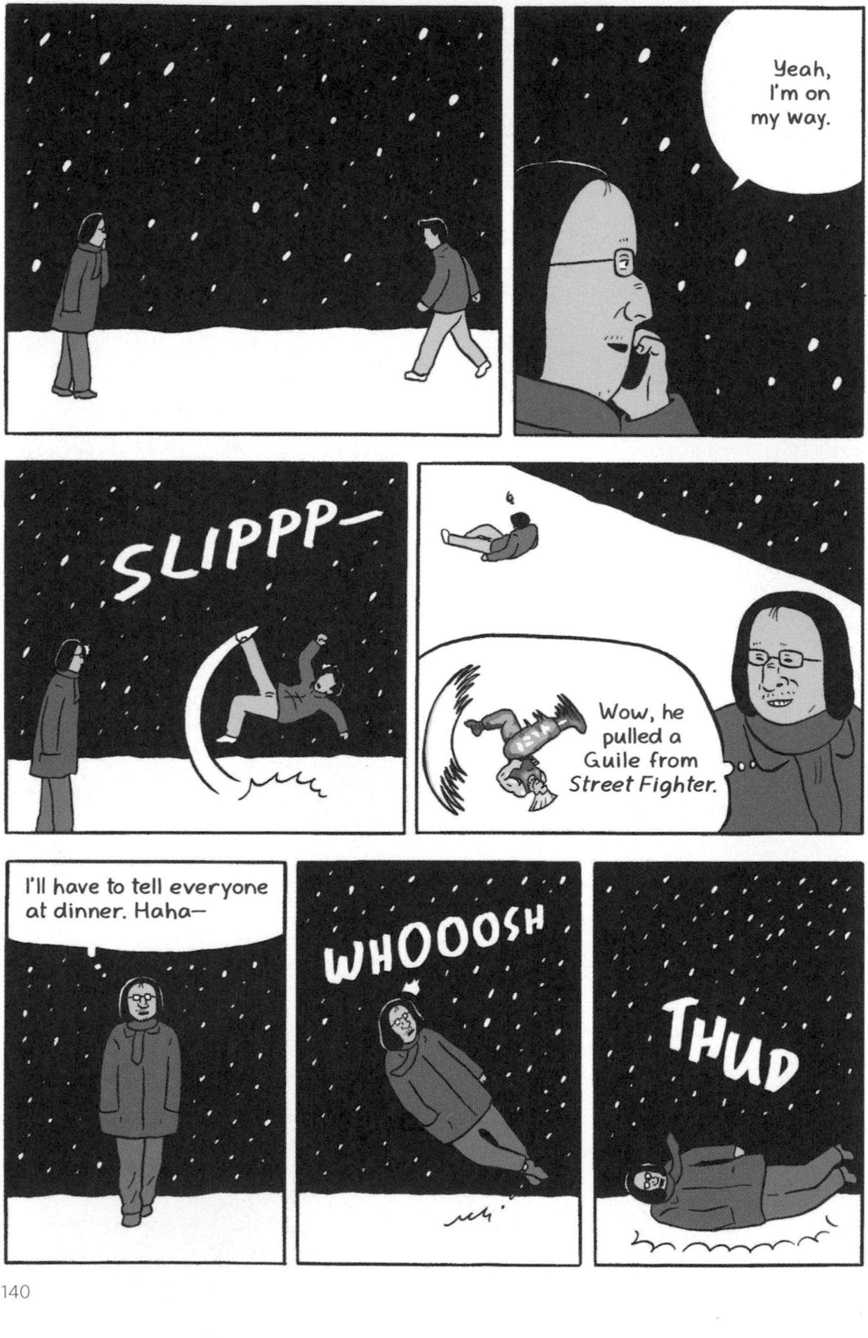
Yeah, I'm on my way.
SLIPPP—
Wow, he pulled a Guile from *Street Fighter.*
I'll have to tell everyone at dinner. Haha—
WHOOOSH
THUD

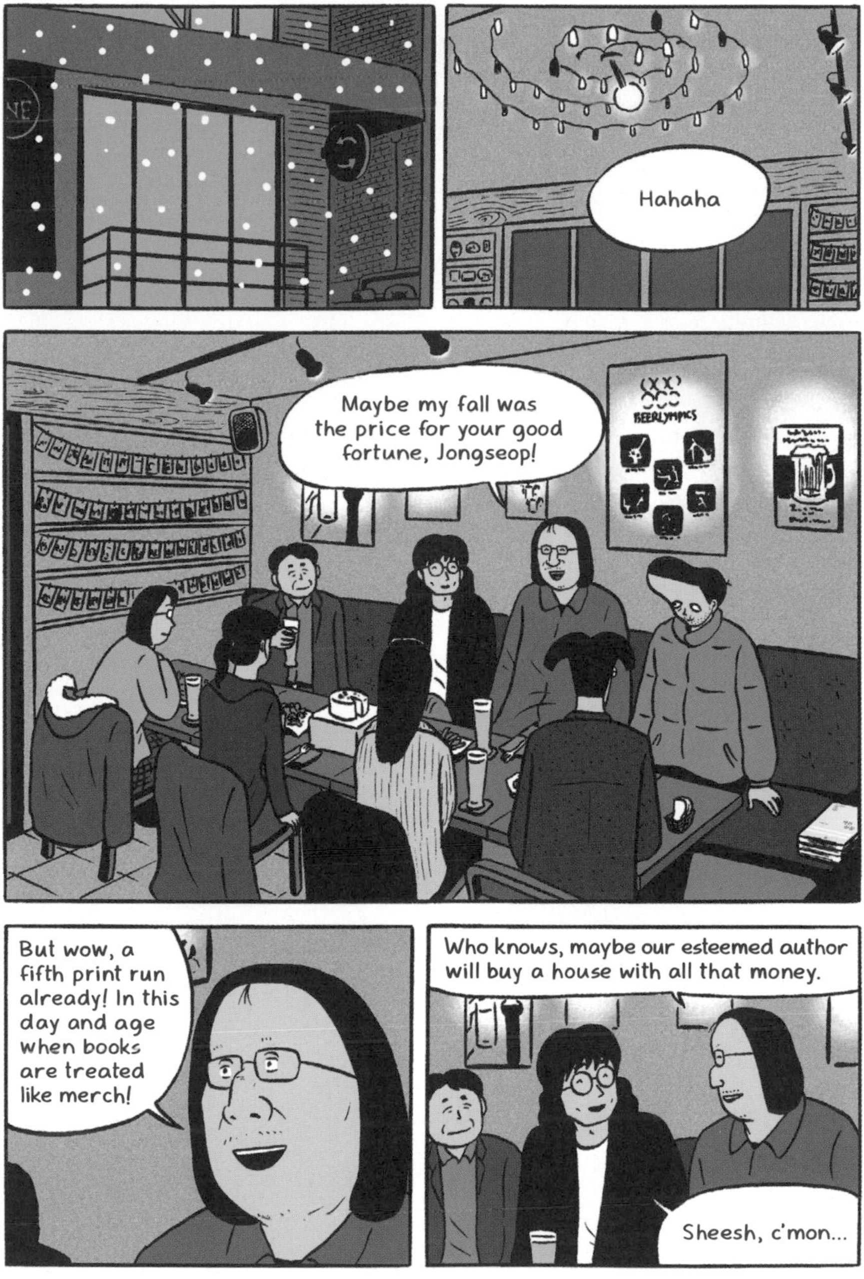
Hahaha
Maybe my fall was the price for your good fortune, Jongseop!
BEERLYMPICS
But wow, a fifth print run already! In this day and age when books are treated like merch!
Who knows, maybe our esteemed author will buy a house with all that money.
Sheesh, c'mon...

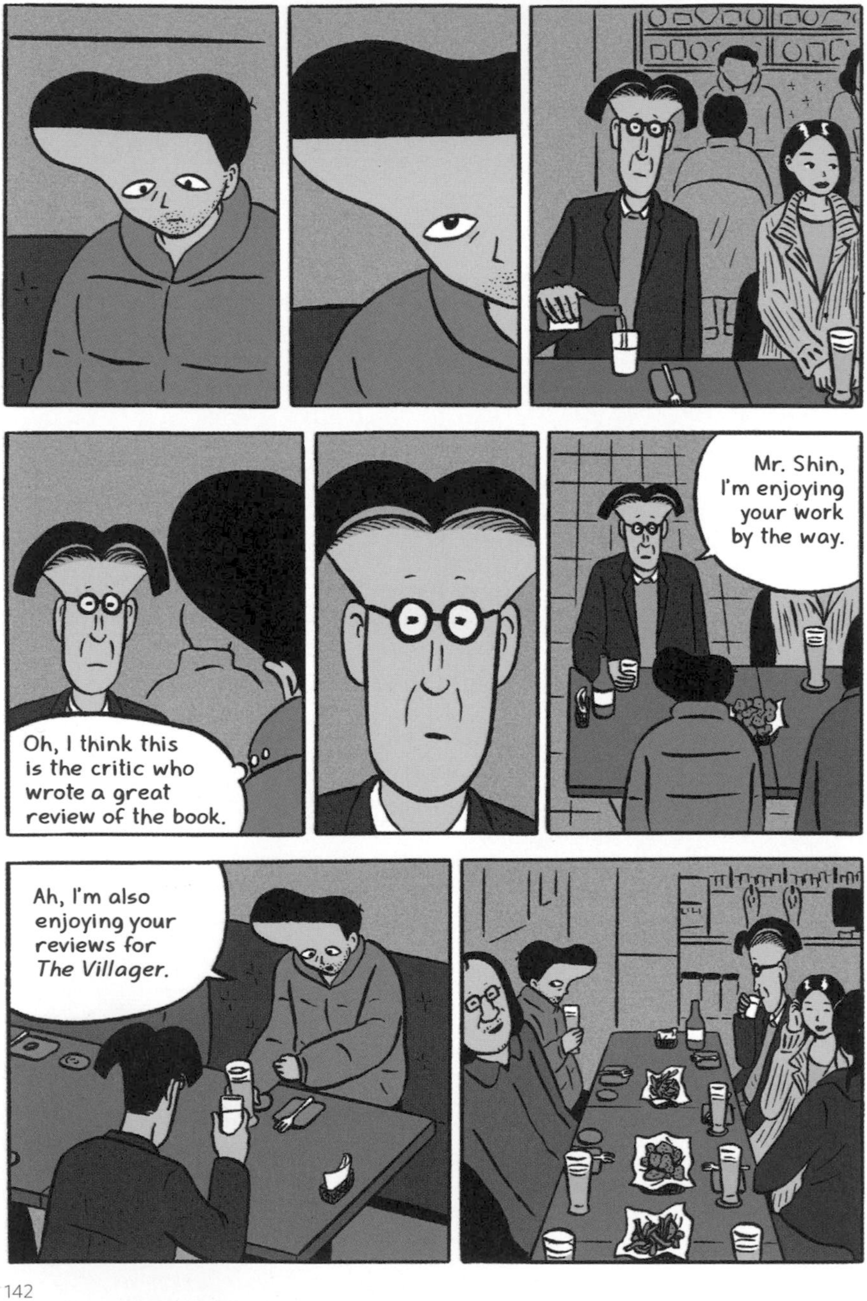
Oh, I think this is the critic who wrote a great review of the book.
Mr. Shin, I'm enjoying your work by the way.
Ah, I'm also enjoying your reviews for *The Villager*.

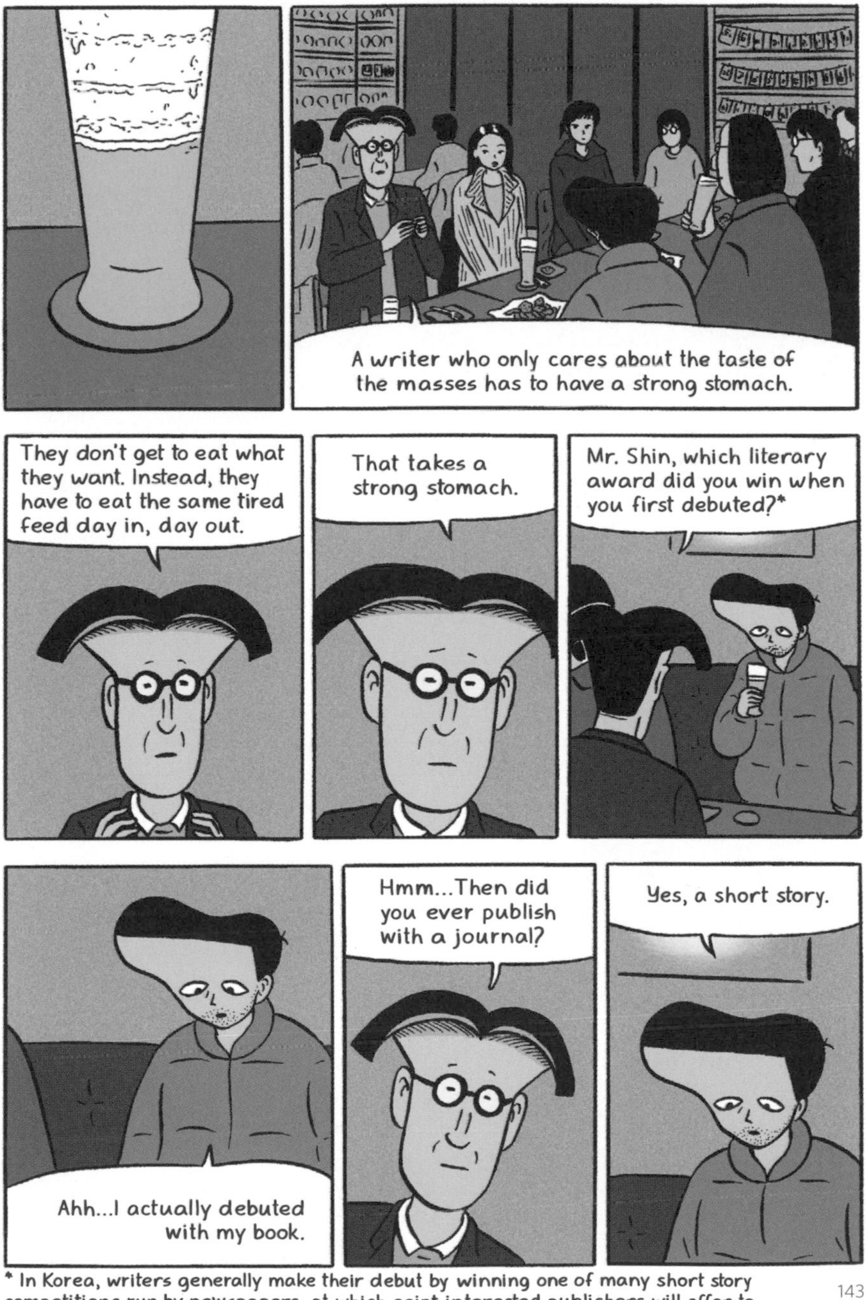

A writer who only cares about the taste of the masses has to have a strong stomach.
They don't get to eat what they want. Instead, they have to eat the same tired feed day in, day out.
That takes a strong stomach.
Mr. Shin, which literary award did you win when you first debuted?*
Ahh...I actually debuted with my book.
Hmm...Then did you ever publish with a journal?
Yes, a short story.

* In Korea, writers generally make their debut by winning one of many short story competitions run by newspapers, at which point interested publishers will offer to publish their first full-length work.

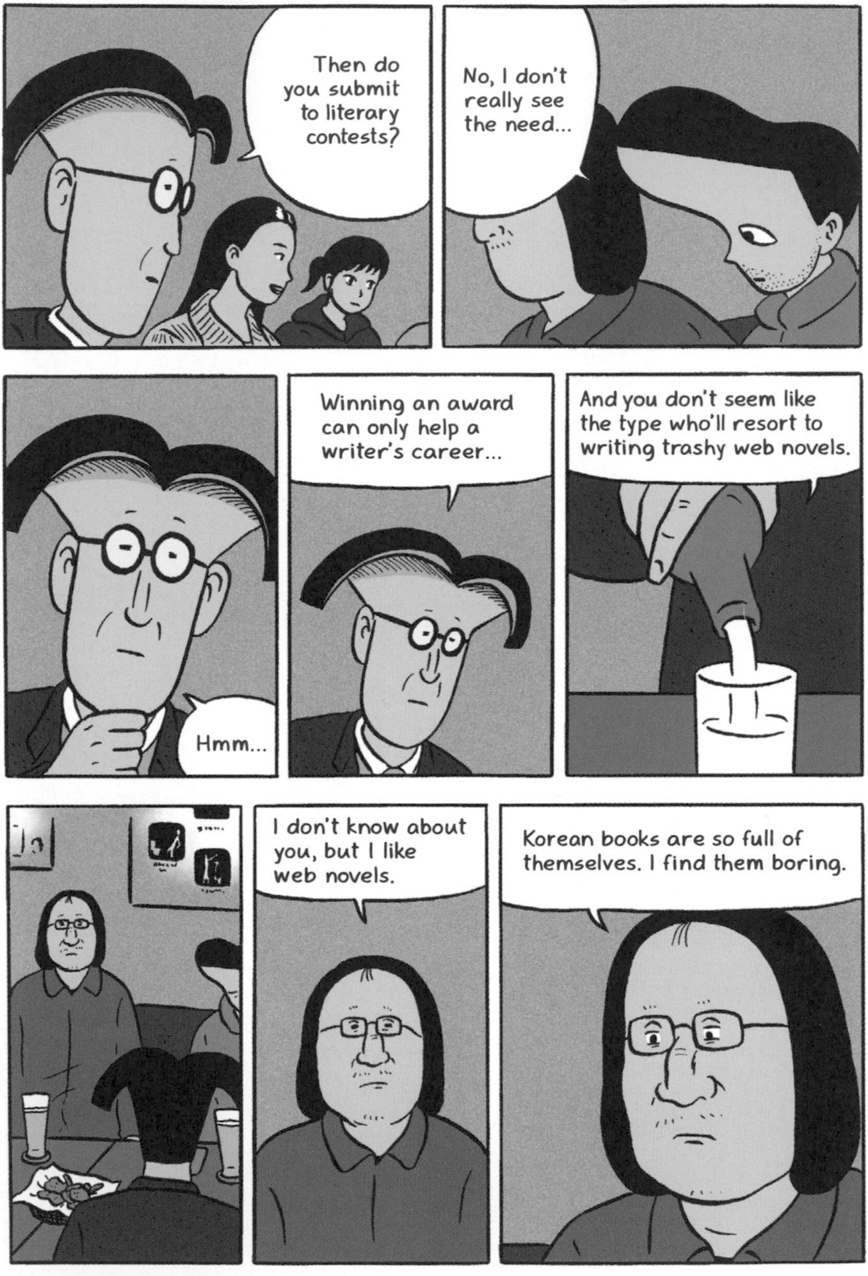
Then do you submit to literary contests?
No, I don't really see the need...
Hmm...
Winning an award can only help a writer's career...
And you don't seem like the type who'll resort to writing trashy web novels.
I don't know about you, but I like web novels.
Korean books are so full of themselves. I find them boring.

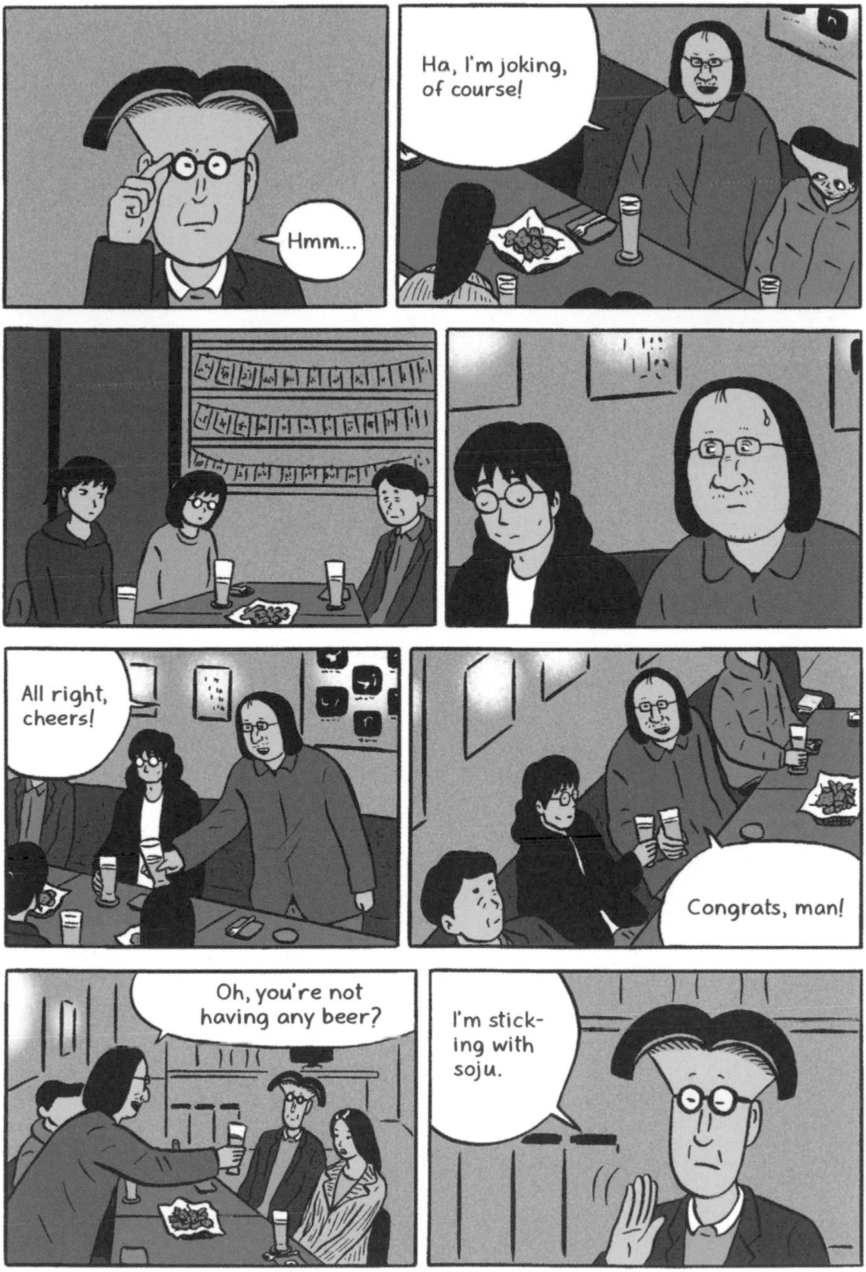
Hmm...
Ha, I'm joking, of course!
All right, cheers!
Congrats, man!
Oh, you're not having any beer?
I'm stick-ing with soju.

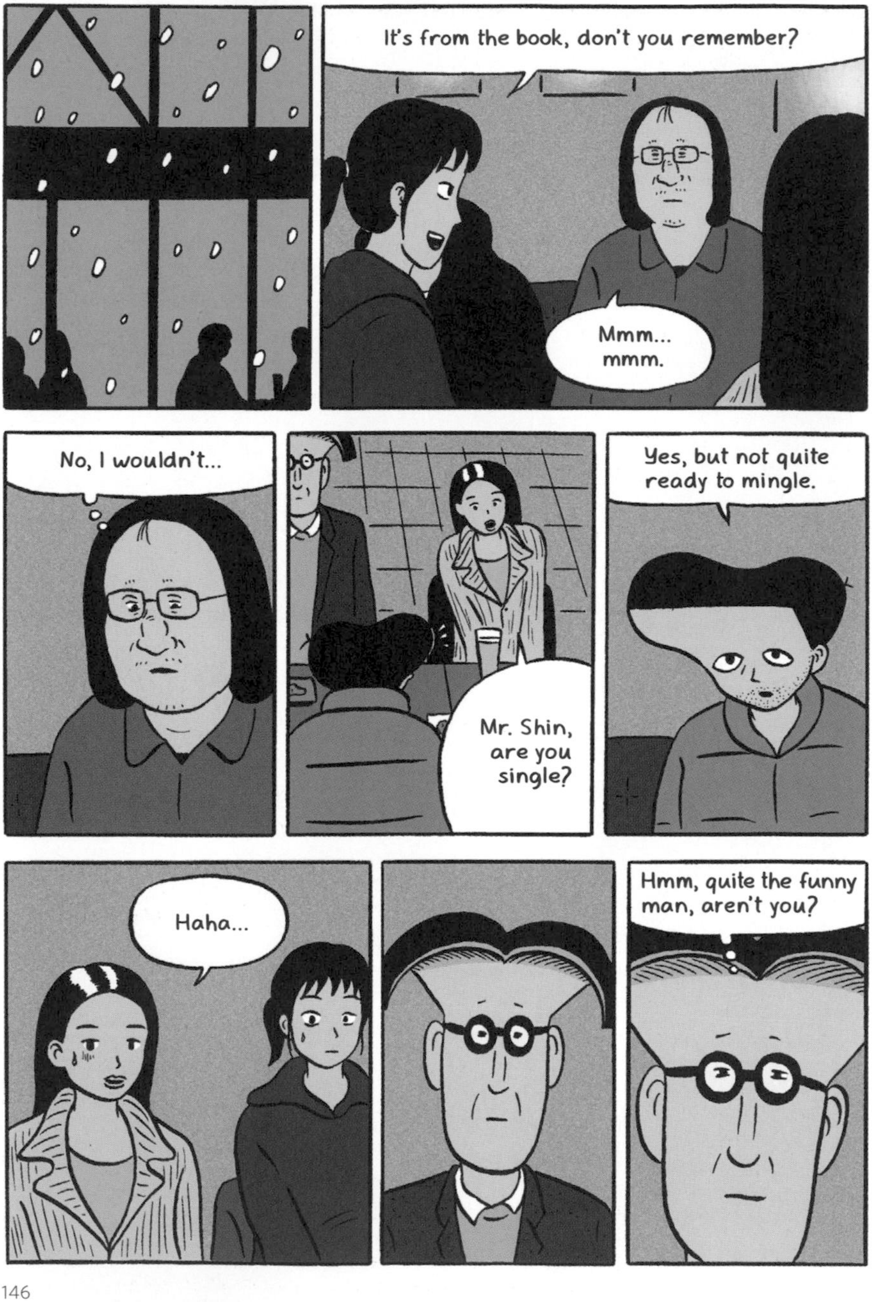
It's from the book, don't you remember?
Mmm... mmm.
No, I wouldn't...
Mr. Shin, are you single?
Yes, but not quite ready to mingle.
Haha...
Hmm, quite the funny man, aren't you?

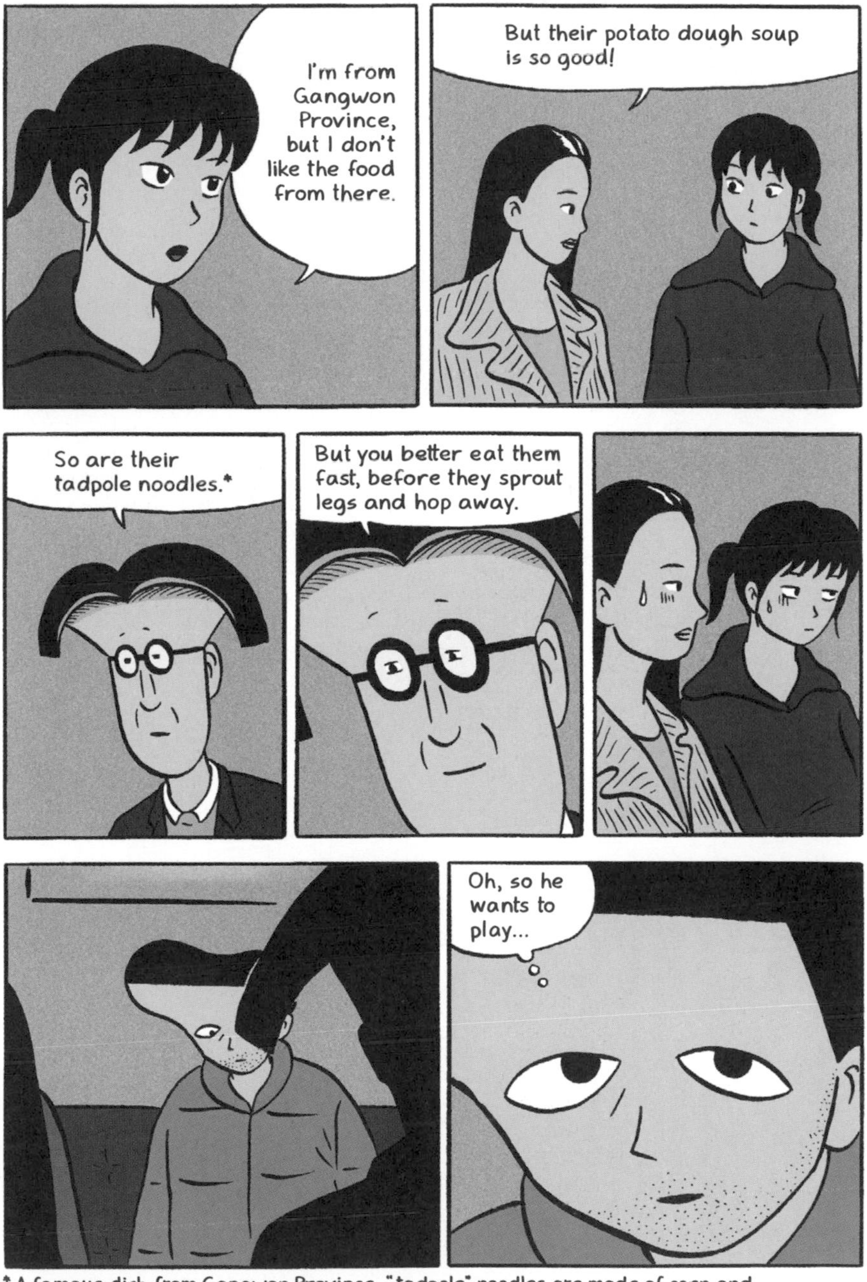
I'm from Gangwon Province, but I don't like the food from there.
But their potato dough soup is so good!
So are their tadpole noodles.*
But you better eat them fast, before they sprout legs and hop away.
Oh, so he wants to play...

* A famous dish from Gangwon Province, "tadpole" noodles are made of corn and named for their particular shape.

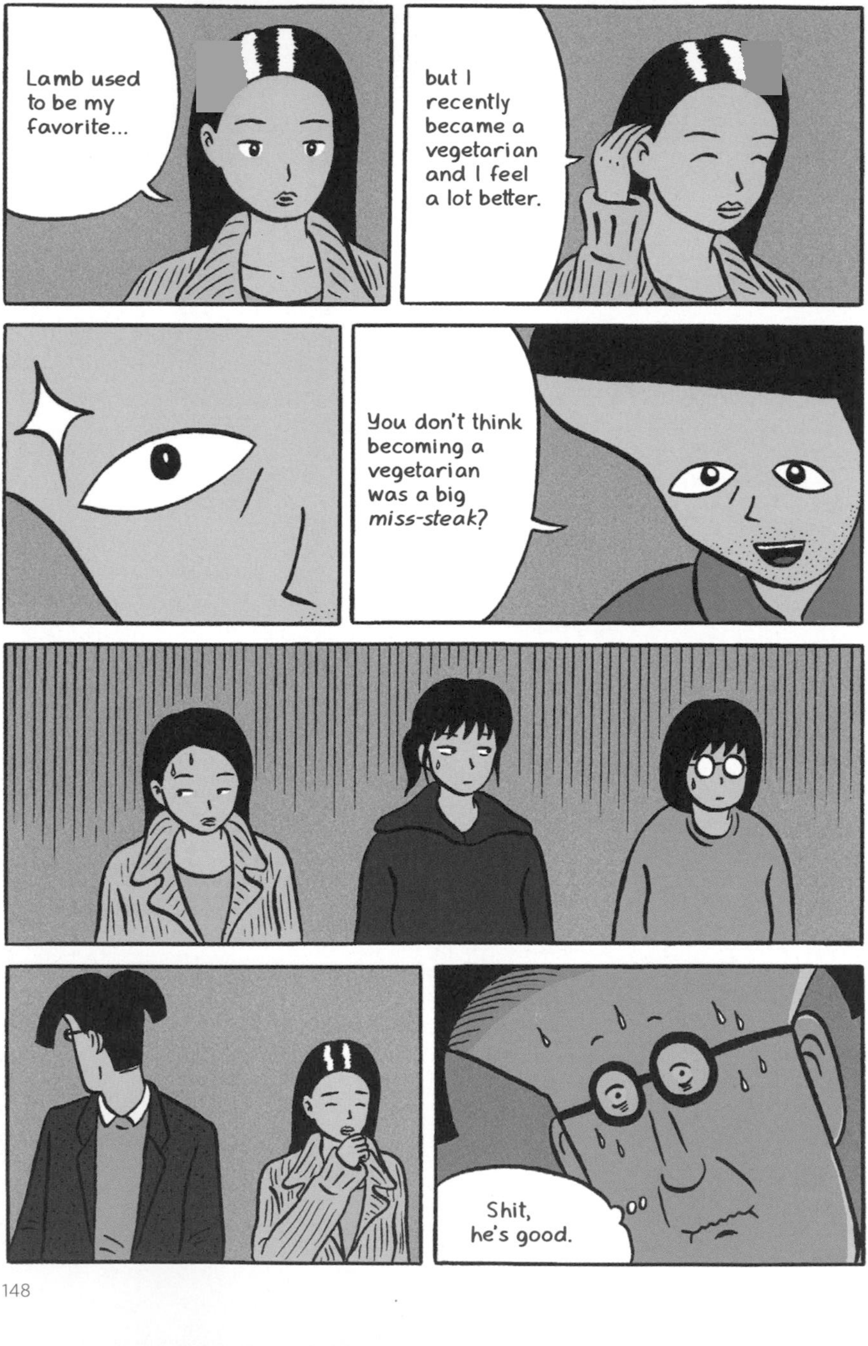
Lamb used to be my favorite...
but I recently became a vegetarian and I feel a lot better.
You don't think becoming a vegetarian was a big *miss-steak*?
Shit, he's good.

NICE TO MEET YOU

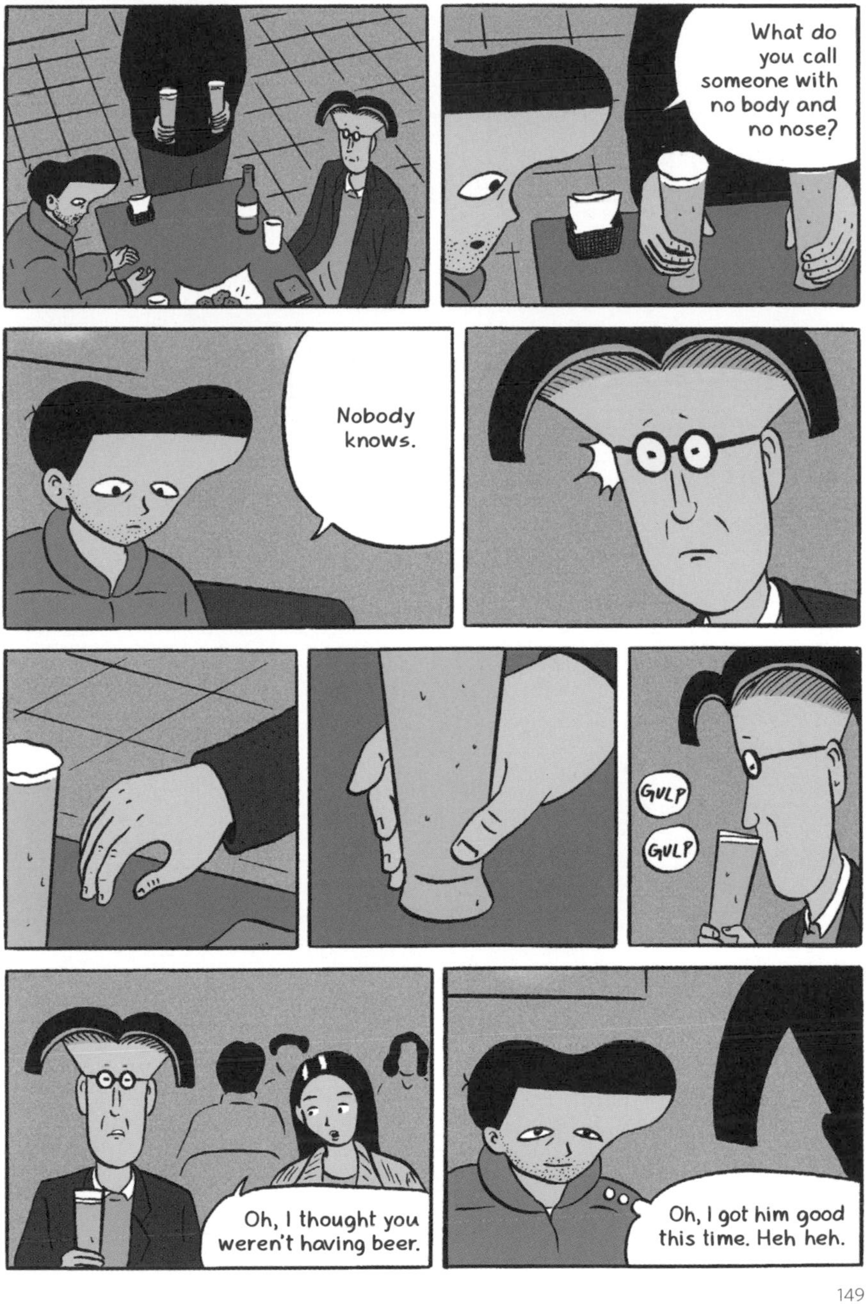

What do you call someone with no body and no nose?
Nobody knows.
GULP
GULP
Oh, I thought you weren't having beer.
Oh, I got him good this time. Heh heh.

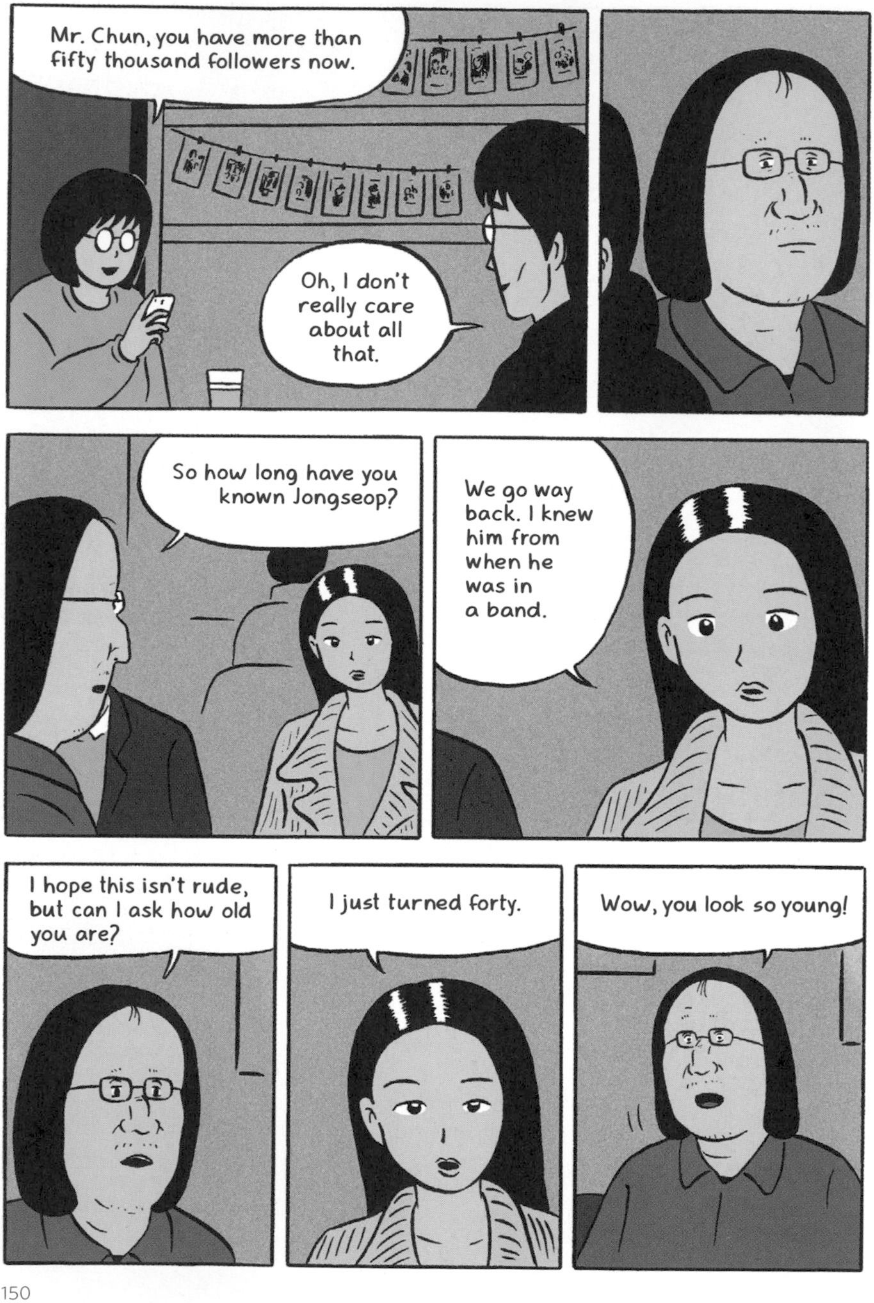
Mr. Chun, you have more than fifty thousand followers now.
Oh, I don't really care about all that.
So how long have you known Jongseop?
We go way back. I knew him from when he was in a band.
I hope this isn't rude, but can I ask how old you are?
I just turned forty.
Wow, you look so young!

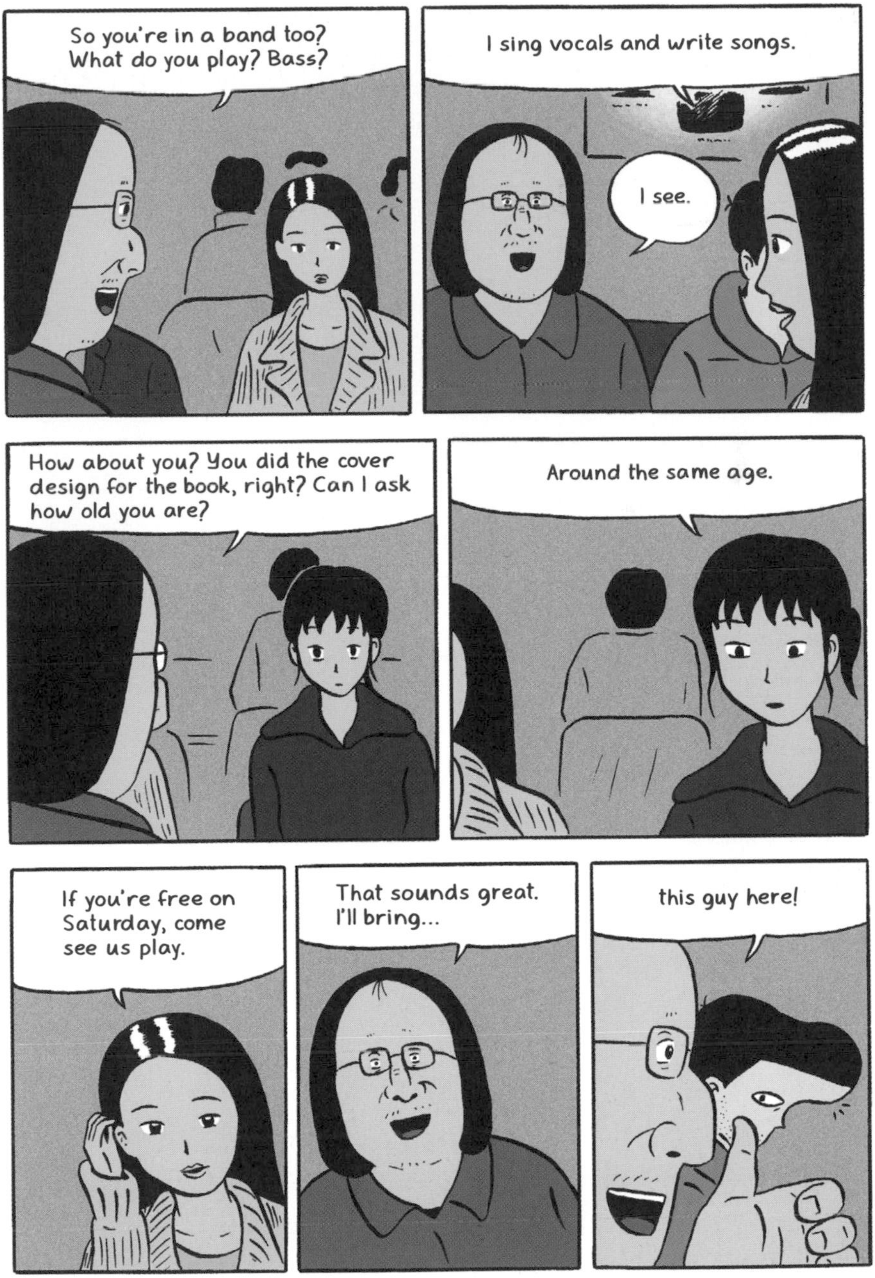
So you're in a band too? What do you play? Bass?
I sing vocals and write songs.
I see.
How about you? You did the cover design for the book, right? Can I ask how old you are?
Around the same age.
If you're free on Saturday, come see us play.
That sounds great. I'll bring...
this guy here!

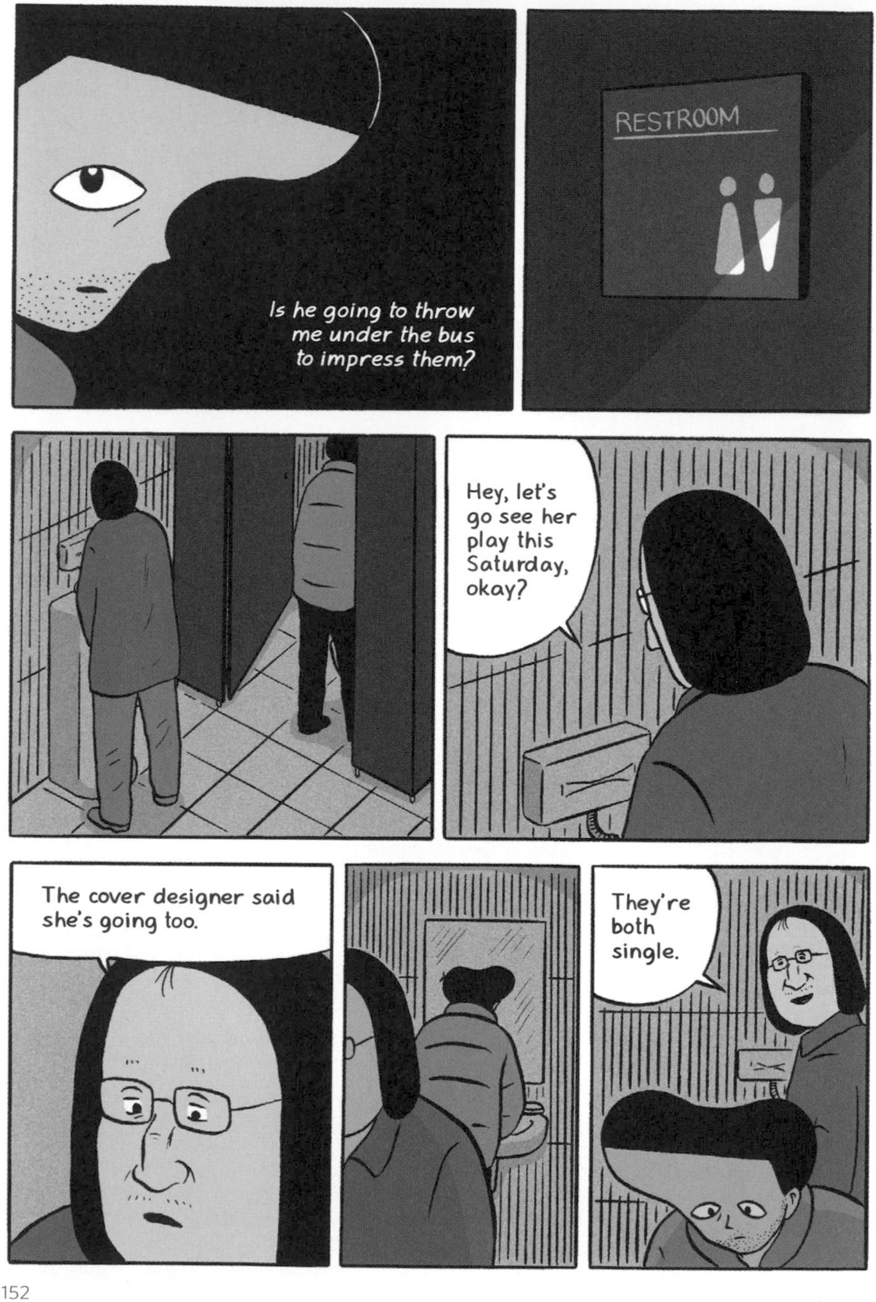
Is he going to throw me under the bus to impress them?
RESTROOM
Hey, let's go see her play this Saturday, okay?
The cover designer said she's going too.
They're both single.

VVVT_

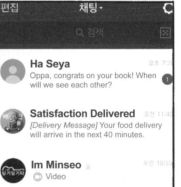

Ha Seya
오후 7:2
Oppa, congrats on your book! When will we see each other?

Satisfaction Delivered
오전 11:4
[Delivery Message] Your food delivery will arrive in the next 40 minutes.

Im Minseo
오전 10:5
Video

Jeez, what does she want now?

Ha Seya
I'm having a drink with a friend. Wanna join us?

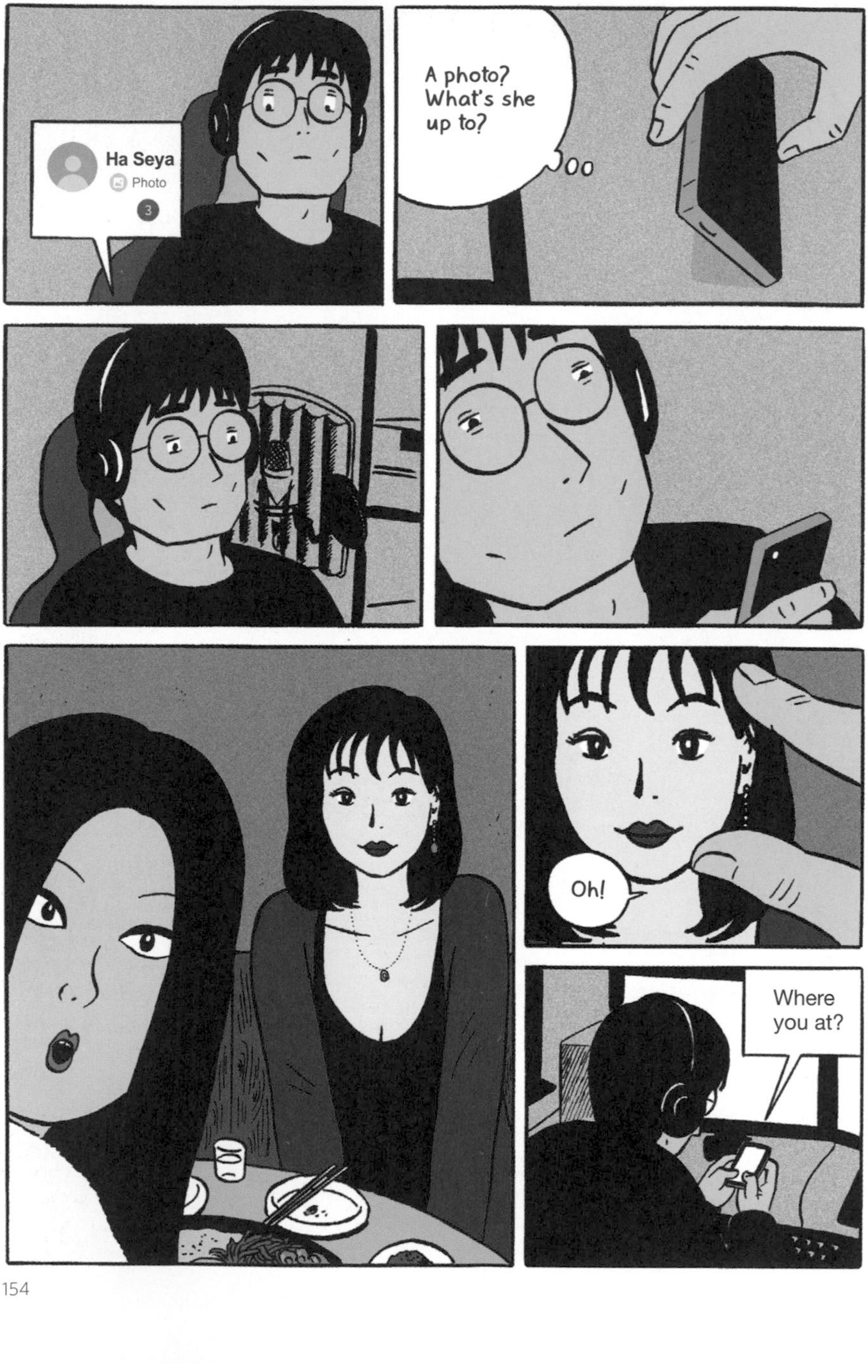
Ha Seya
Photo
3
A photo? What's she up to?
Oh!
Where you at?

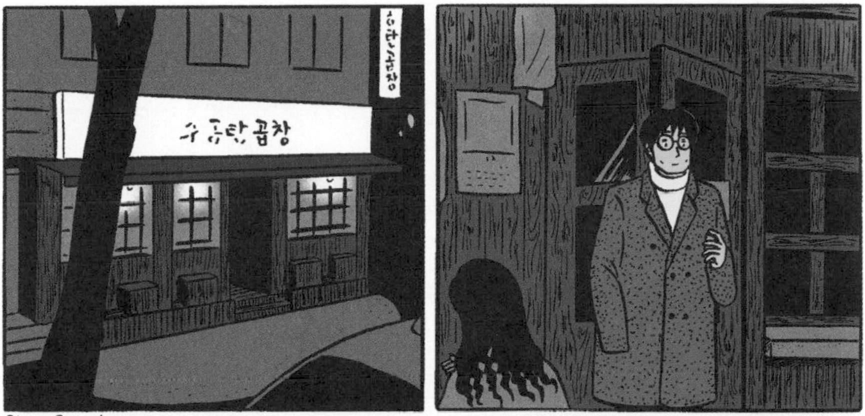
Sign: Gopchang

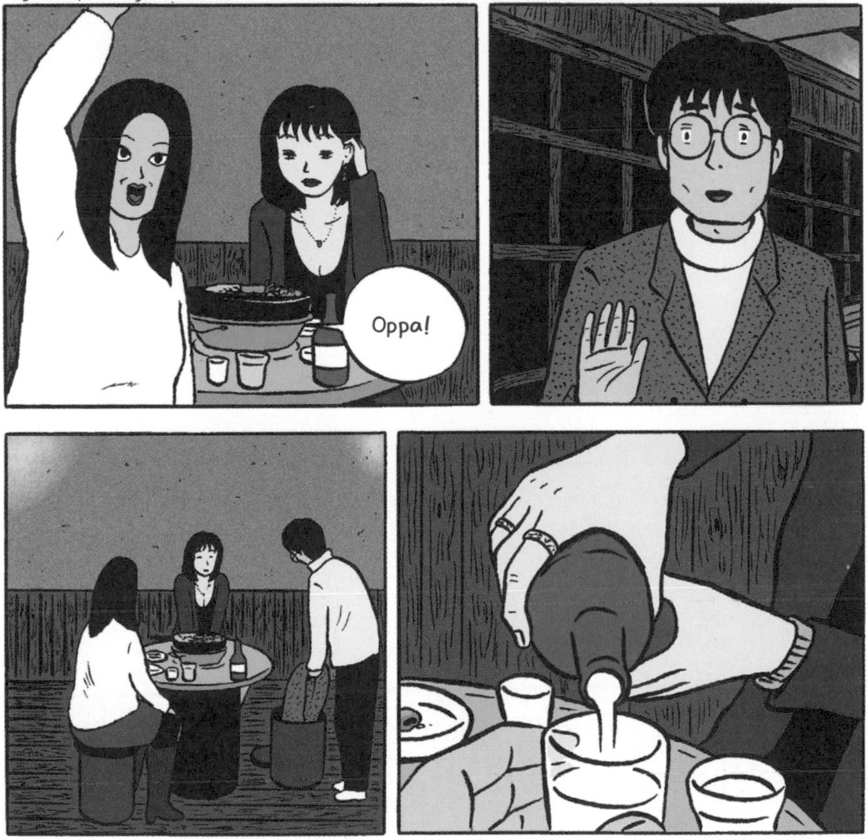
Oppa!

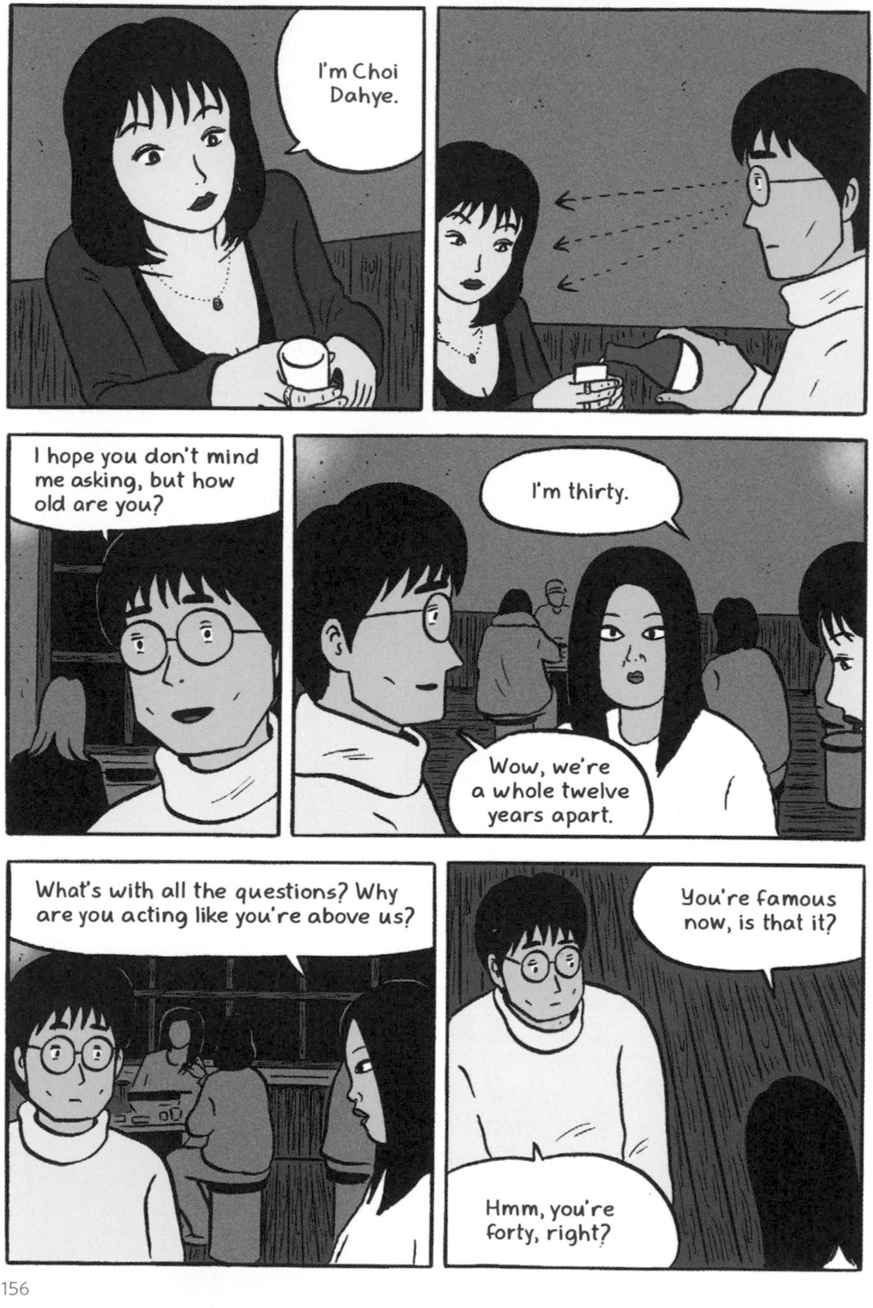
I'm Choi Dahye.
I hope you don't mind me asking, but how old are you?
I'm thirty.
Wow, we're a whole twelve years apart.
What's with all the questions? Why are you acting like you're above us?
You're famous now, is that it?
Hmm, you're forty, right?

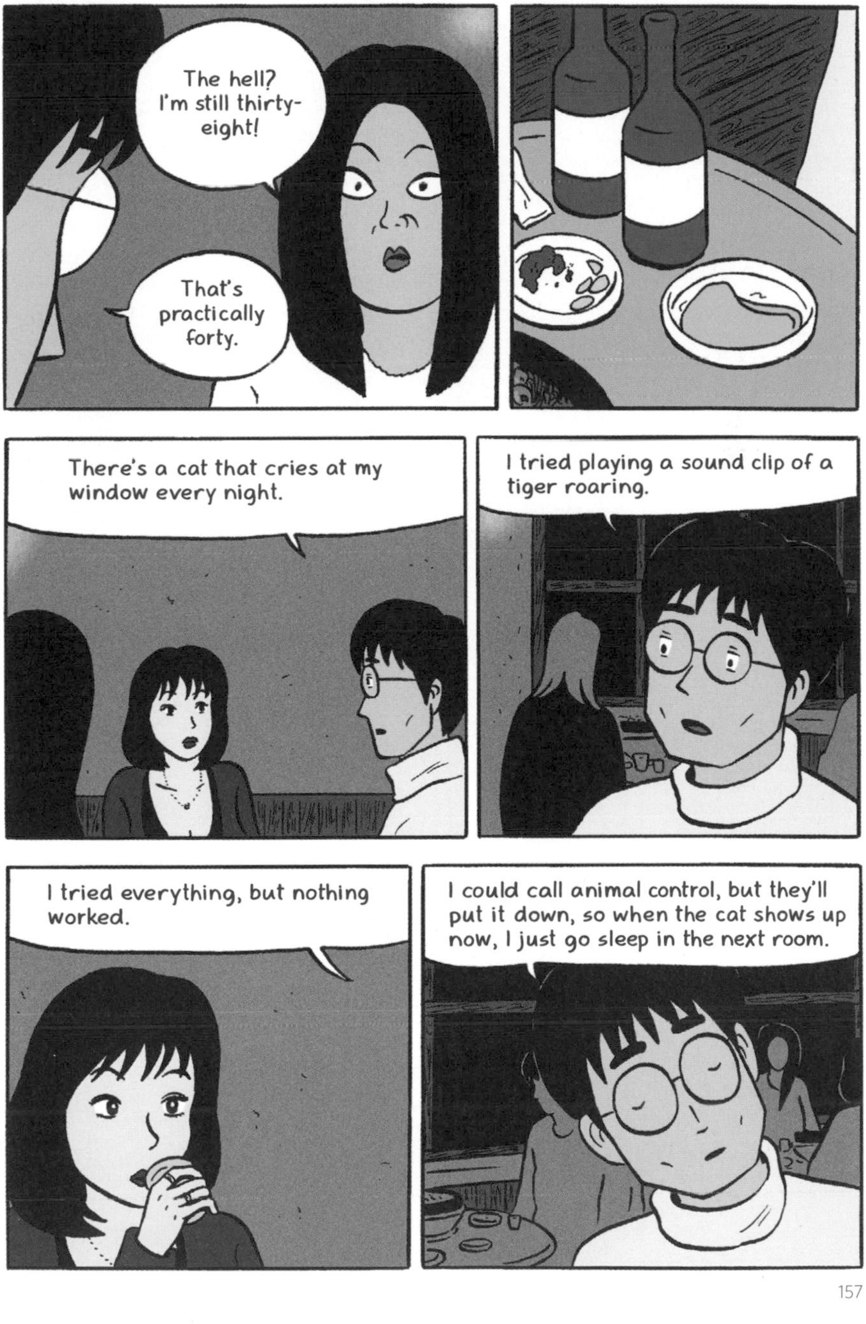
The hell? I'm still thirty-eight!
That's practically forty.
There's a cat that cries at my window every night.
I tried playing a sound clip of a tiger roaring.
I tried everything, but nothing worked.
I could call animal control, but they'll put it down, so when the cat shows up now, I just go sleep in the next room.

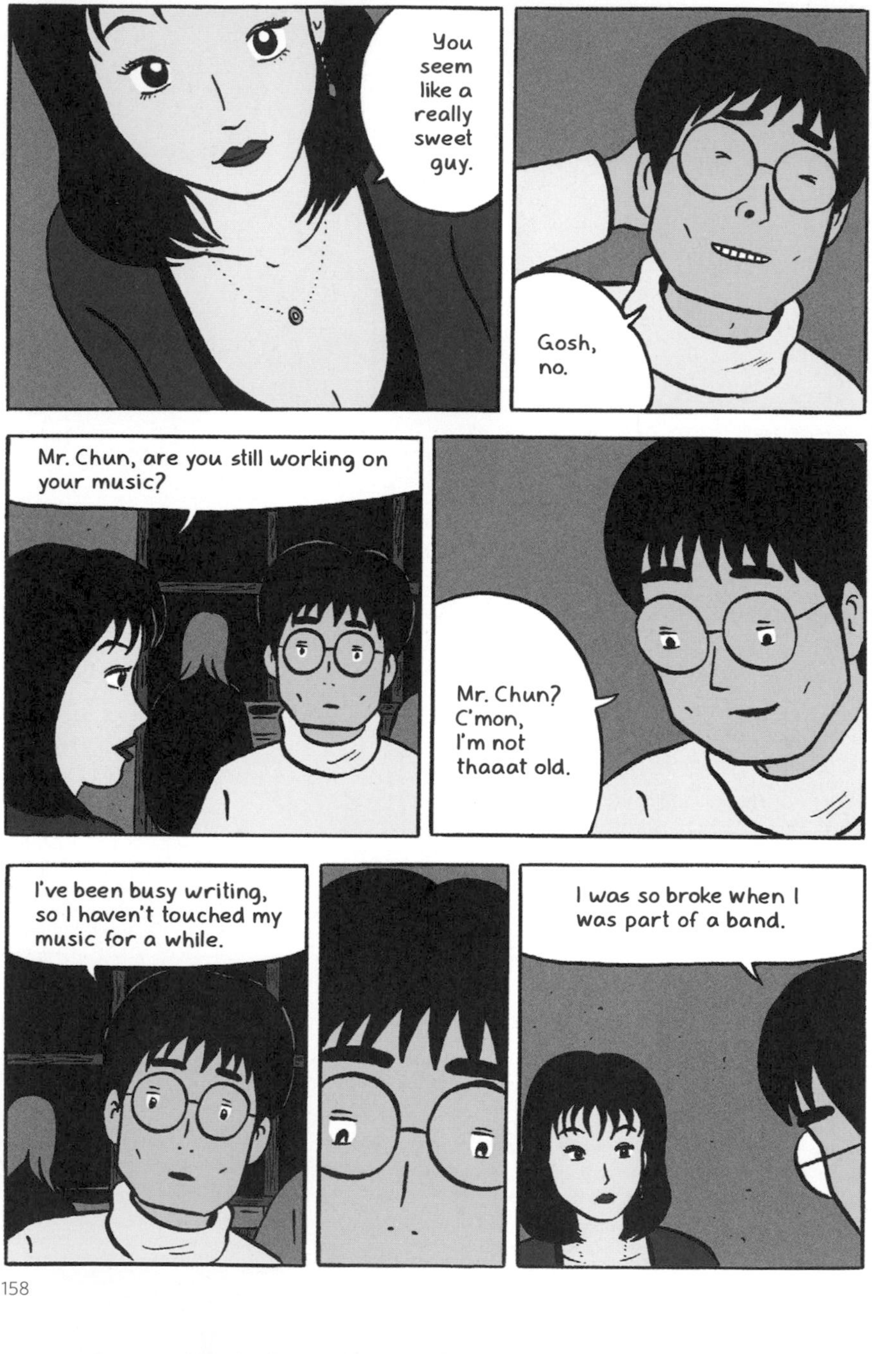
You seem like a really sweet guy.
Gosh, no.
Mr. Chun, are you still working on your music?
Mr. Chun? C'mon, I'm not thaaat old.
I've been busy writing, so I haven't touched my music for a while.
I was so broke when I was part of a band.

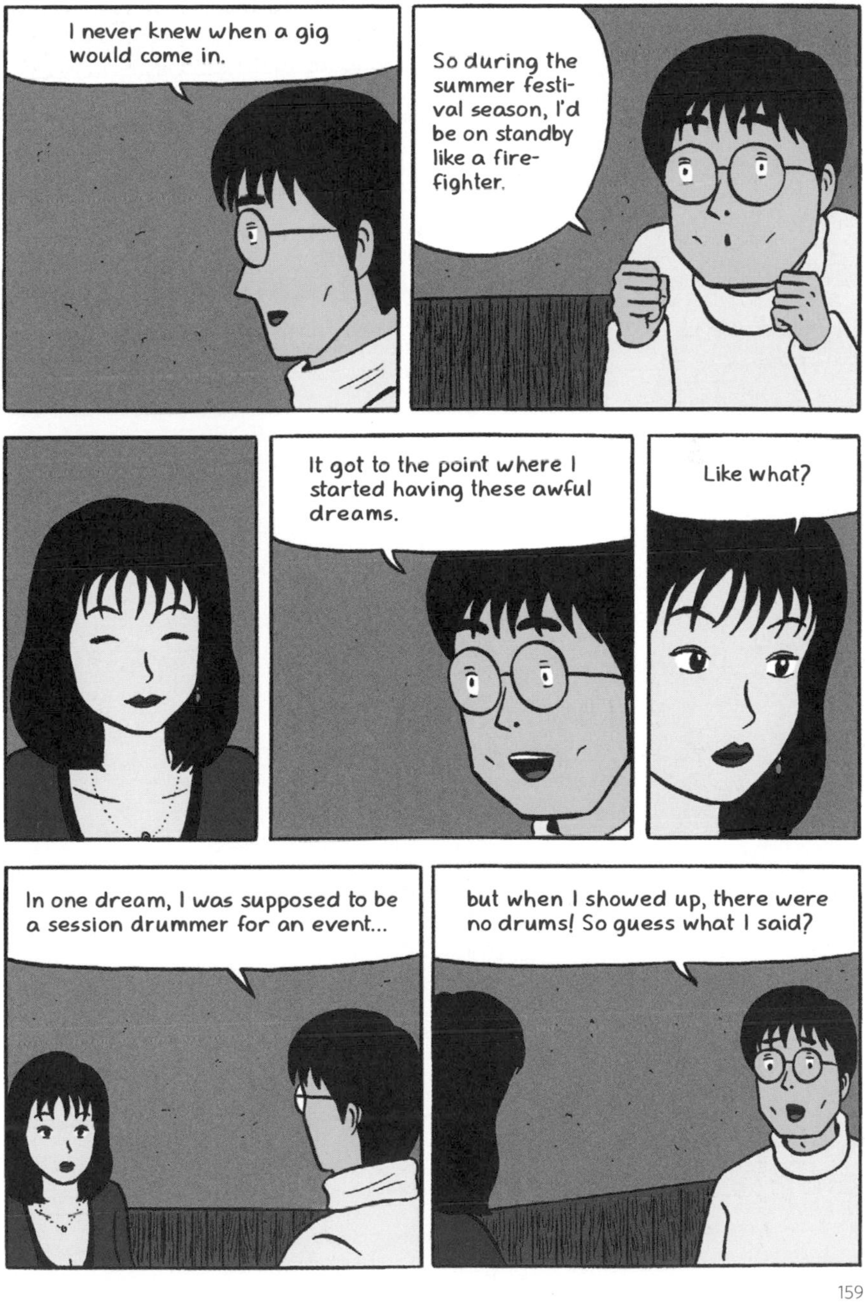
I never knew when a gig would come in.
So during the summer festival season, I'd be on standby like a firefighter.
It got to the point where I started having these awful dreams.
Like what?
In one dream, I was supposed to be a session drummer for an event...
but when I showed up, there were no drums! So guess what I said?

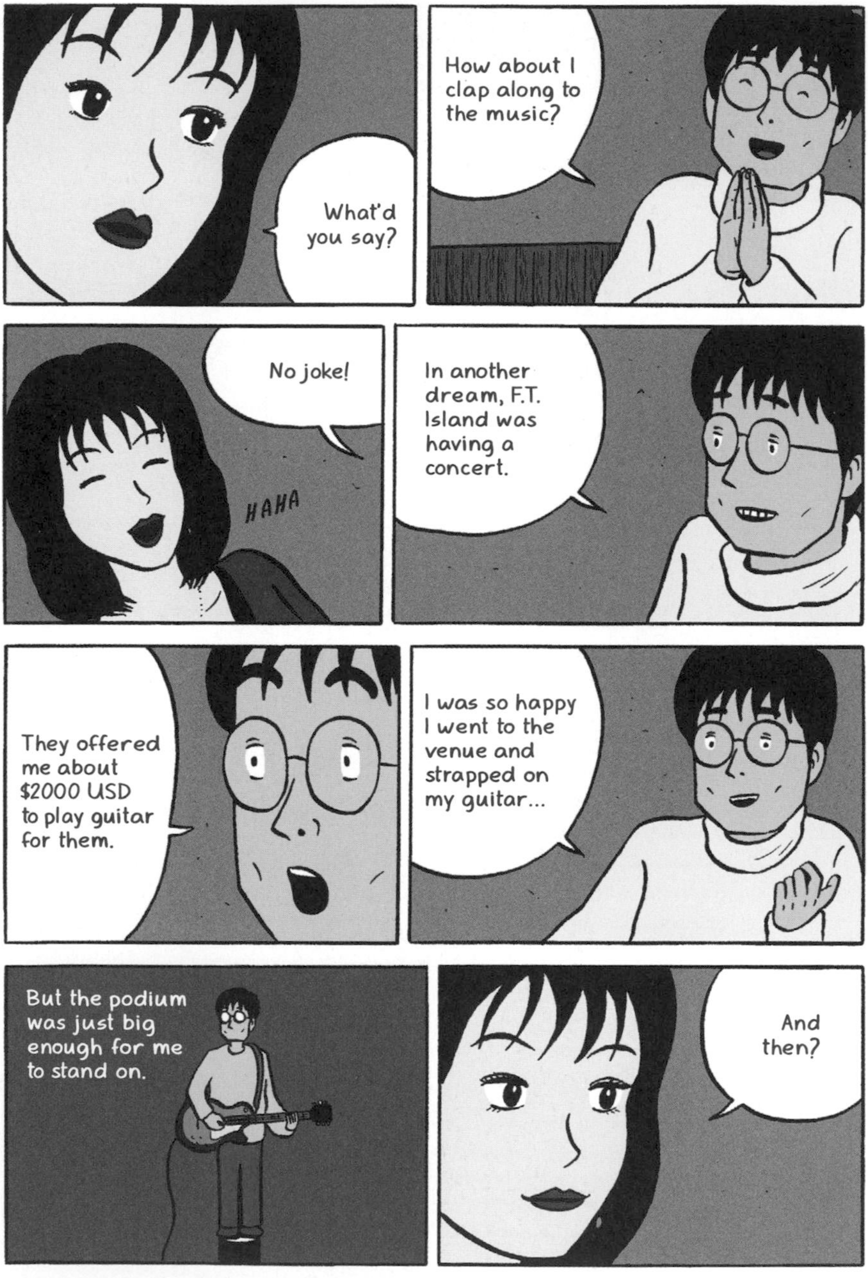
What'd you say?
How about I clap along to the music?
No joke!
HAHA
In another dream, F.T. Island was having a concert.
They offered me about $2000 USD to play guitar for them.
I was so happy I went to the venue and strapped on my guitar...
But the podium was just big enough for me to stand on.
And then?

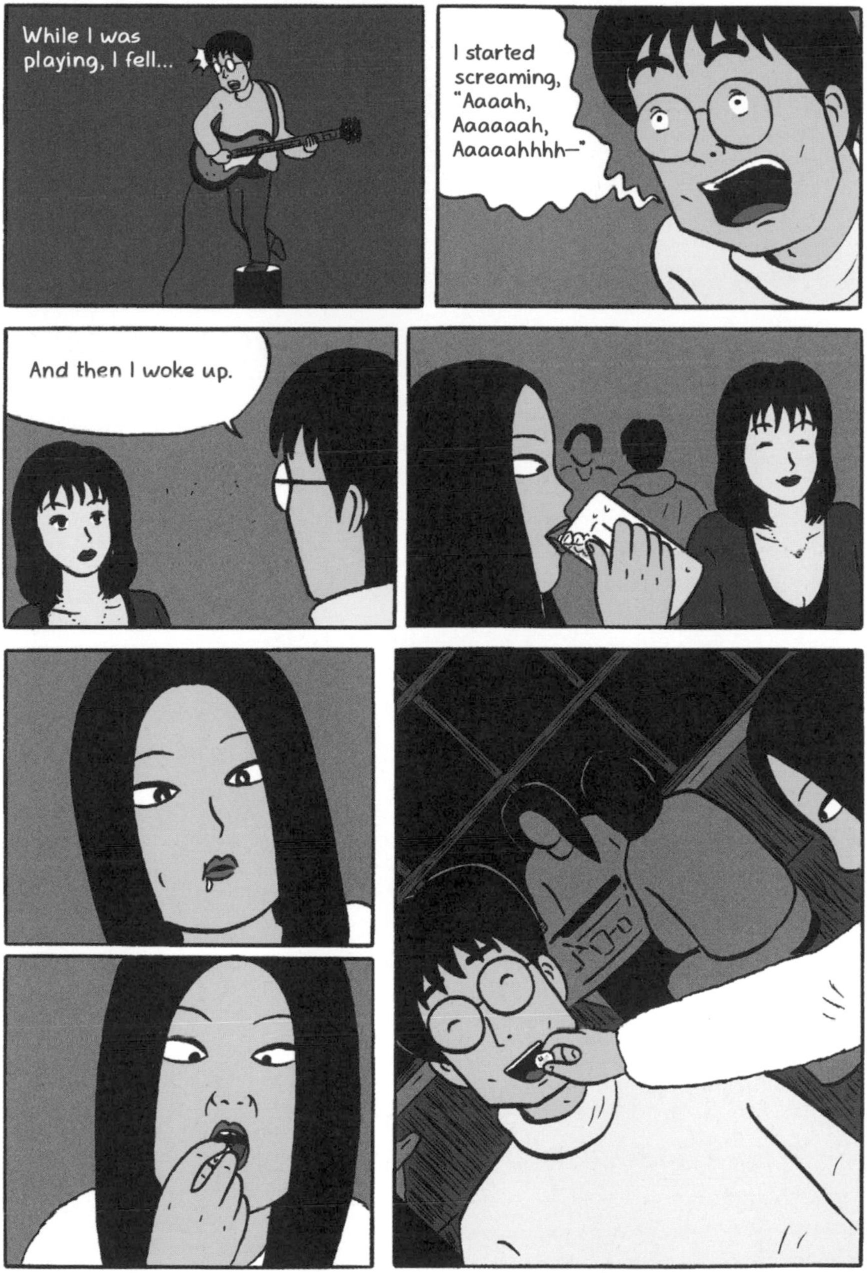
While I was playing, I fell...
I started screaming, "Aaaah, Aaaaaah, Aaaaahhhh–"
And then I woke up.

AT THE CONCERT

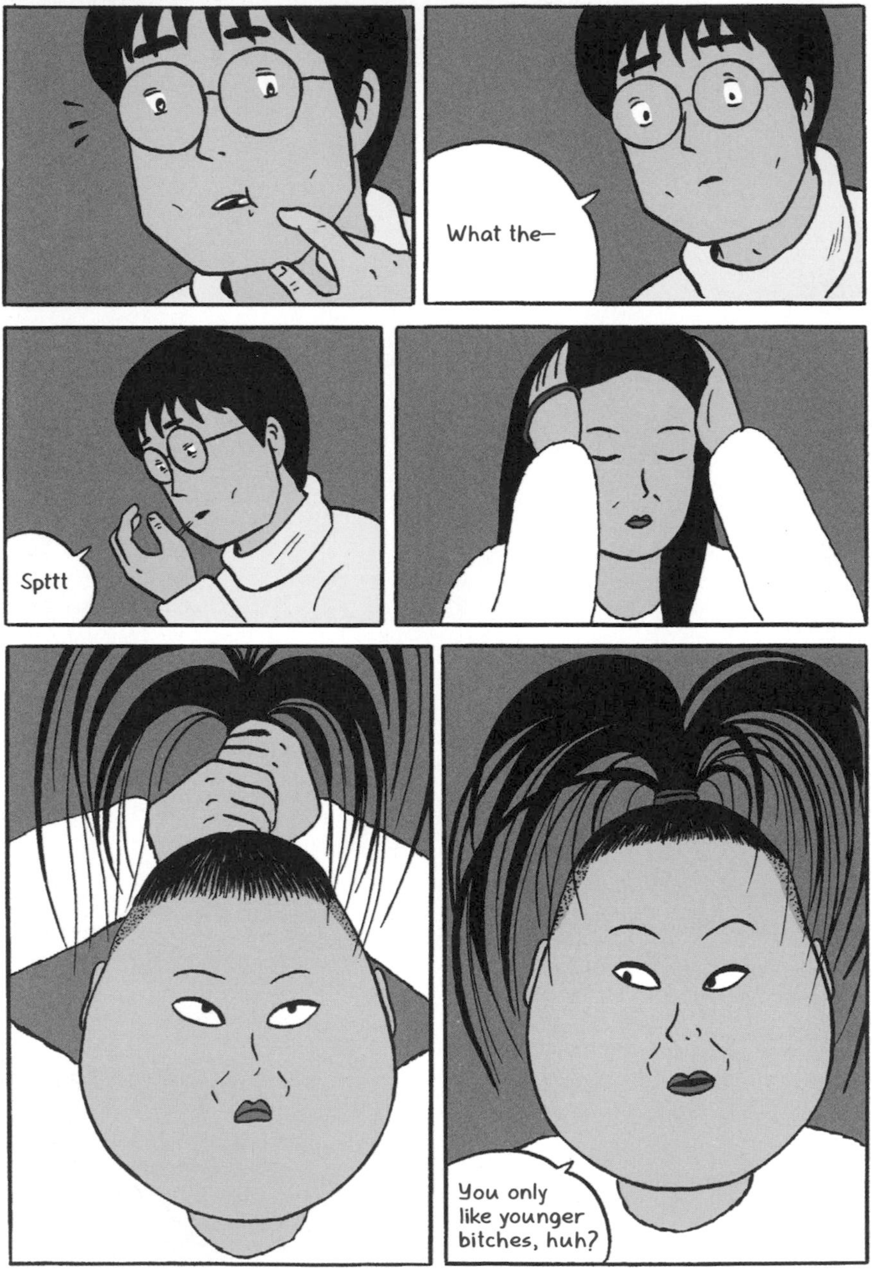
What the—
Spttt
You only like younger bitches, huh?

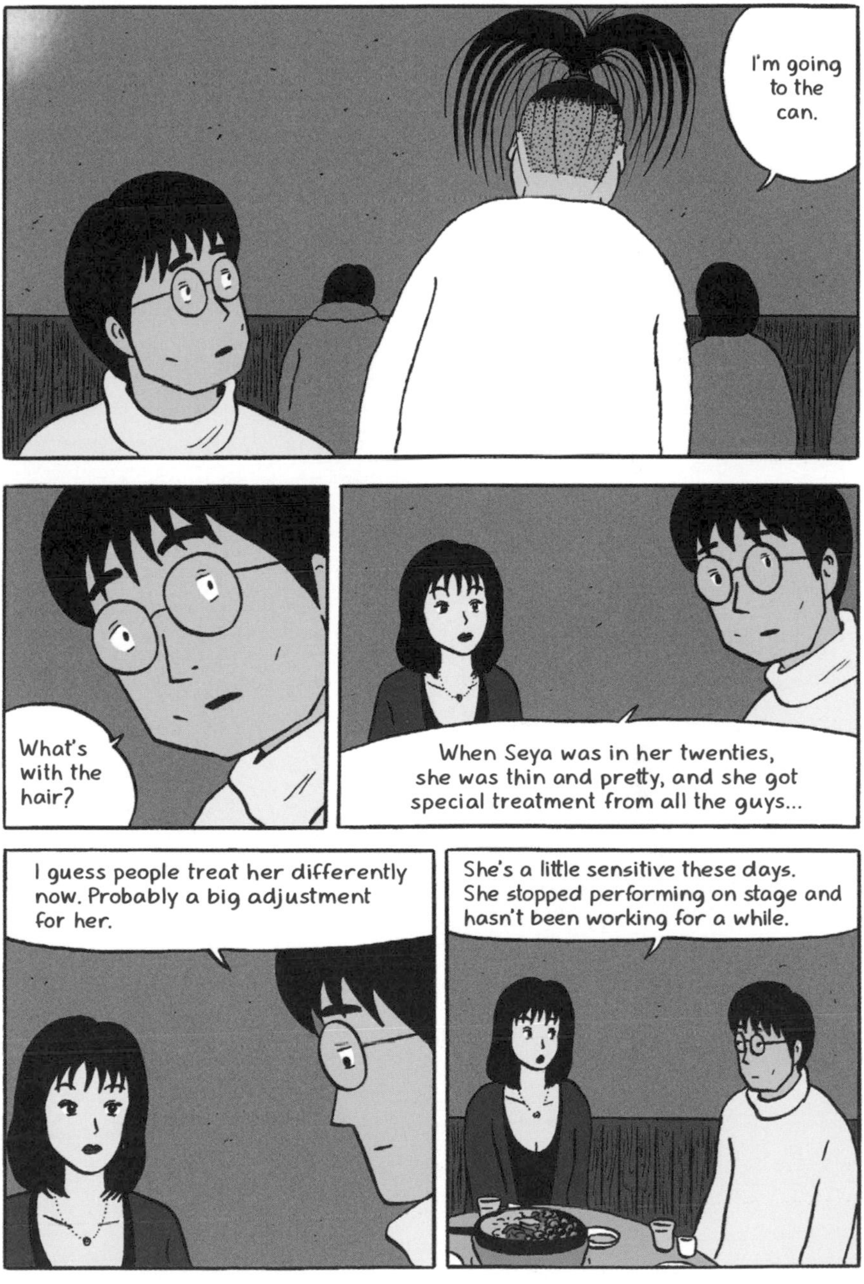
I'm going to the can.
What's with the hair?
When Seya was in her twenties, she was thin and pretty, and she got special treatment from all the guys...
I guess people treat her differently now. Probably a big adjustment for her.
She's a little sensitive these days. She stopped performing on stage and hasn't been working for a while.

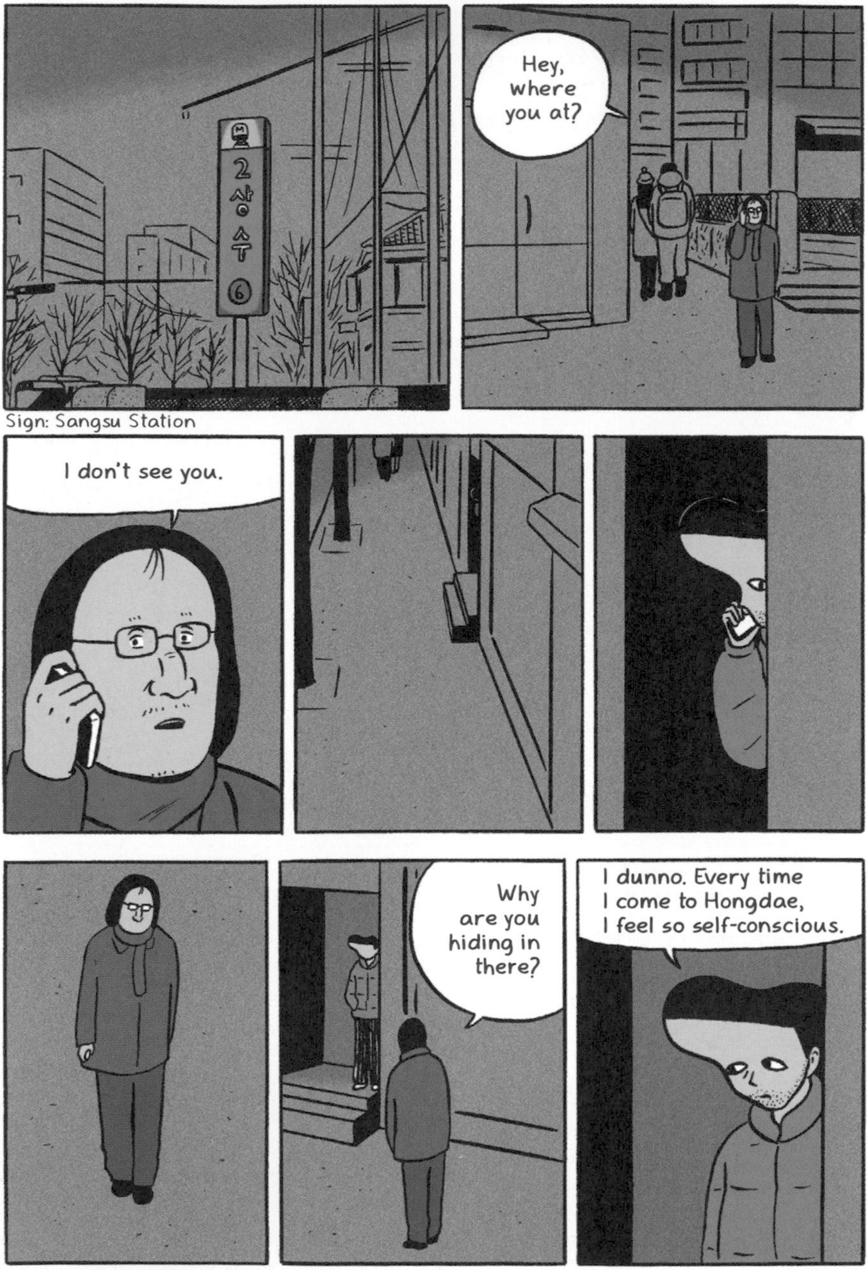
상수
Sign: Sangsu Station
Hey, where you at?
I don't see you.
Why are you hiding in there?
I dunno. Every time I come to Hongdae, I feel so self-conscious.

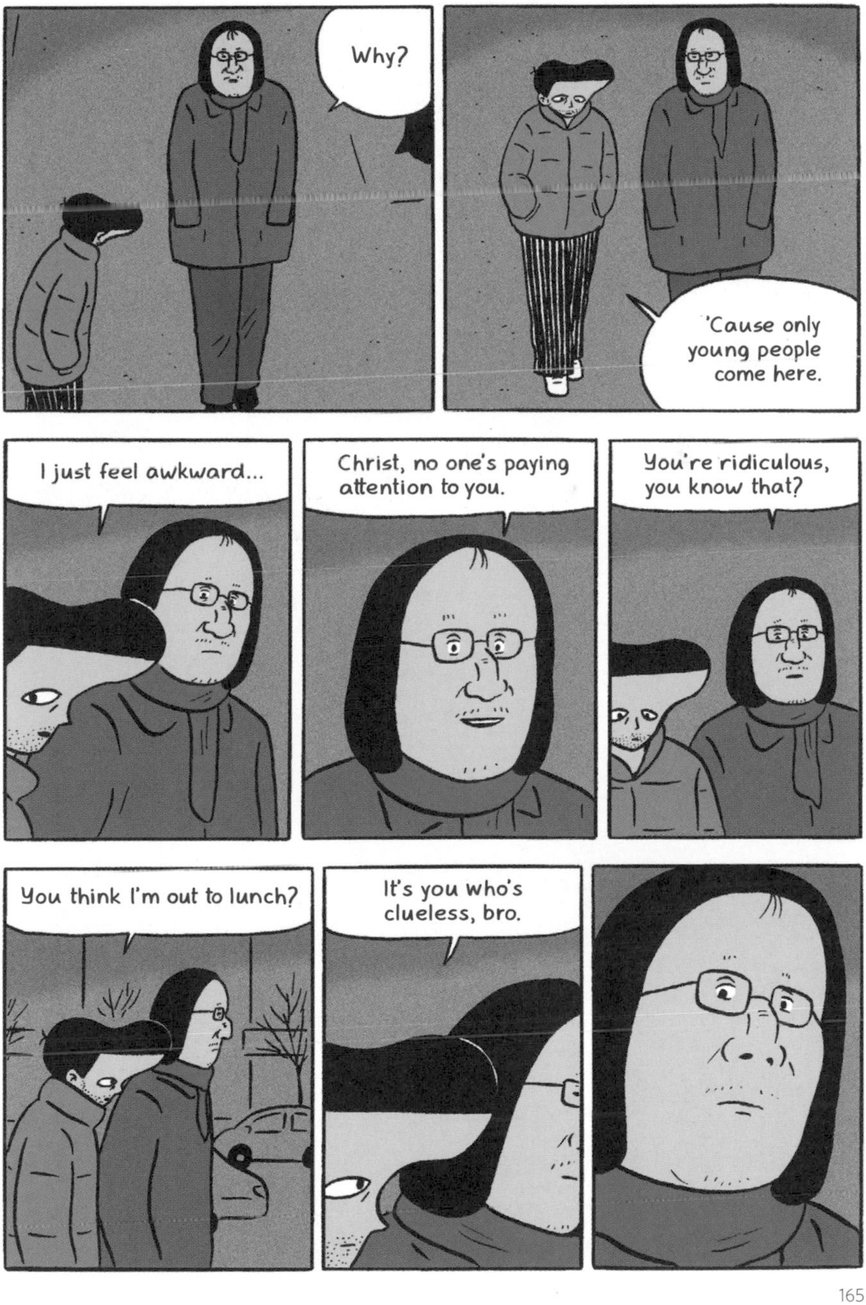
Why?
'Cause only young people come here.
I just feel awkward...
Christ, no one's paying attention to you.
You're ridiculous, you know that?
You think I'm out to lunch?
It's you who's clueless, bro.

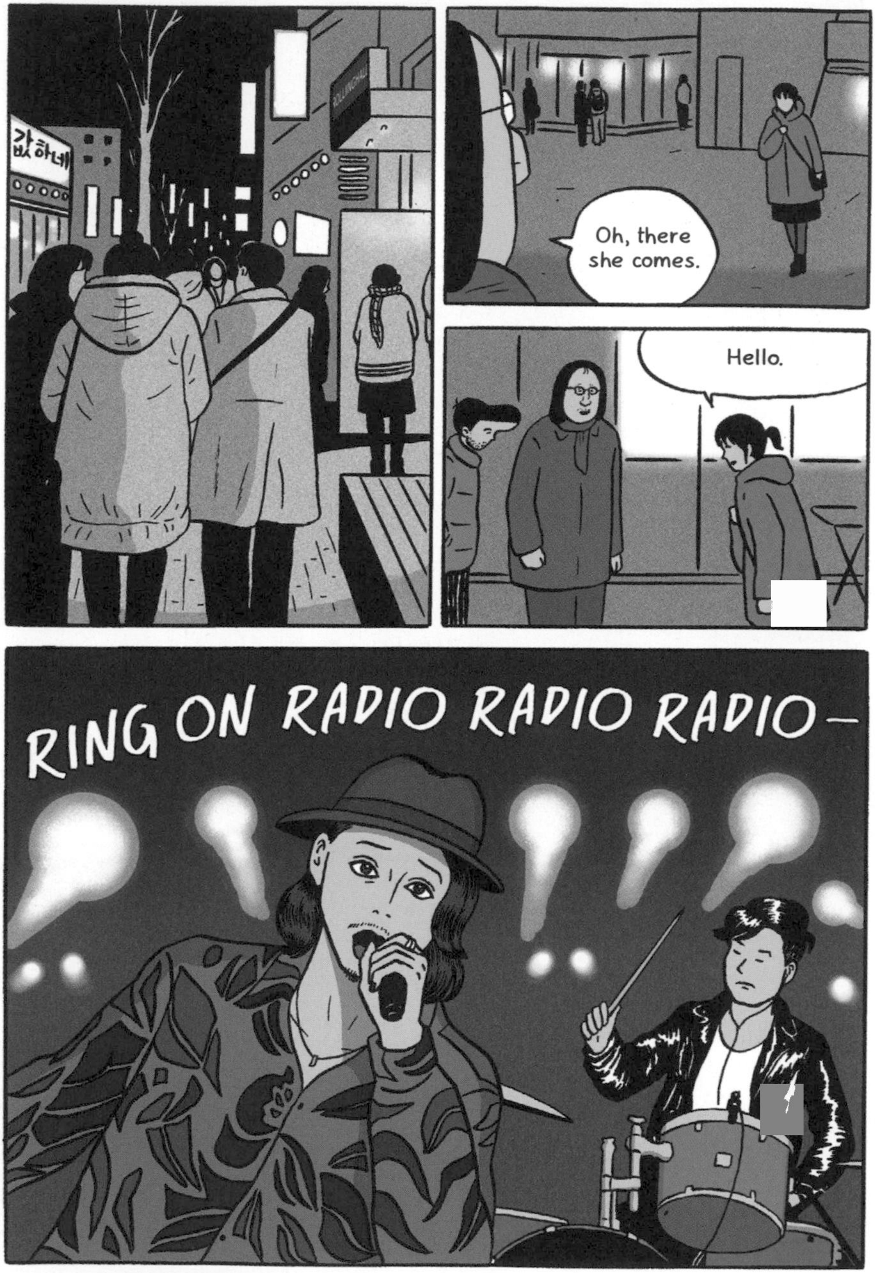
Oh, there she comes.
Hello.
RING ON RADIO RADIO RADIO—

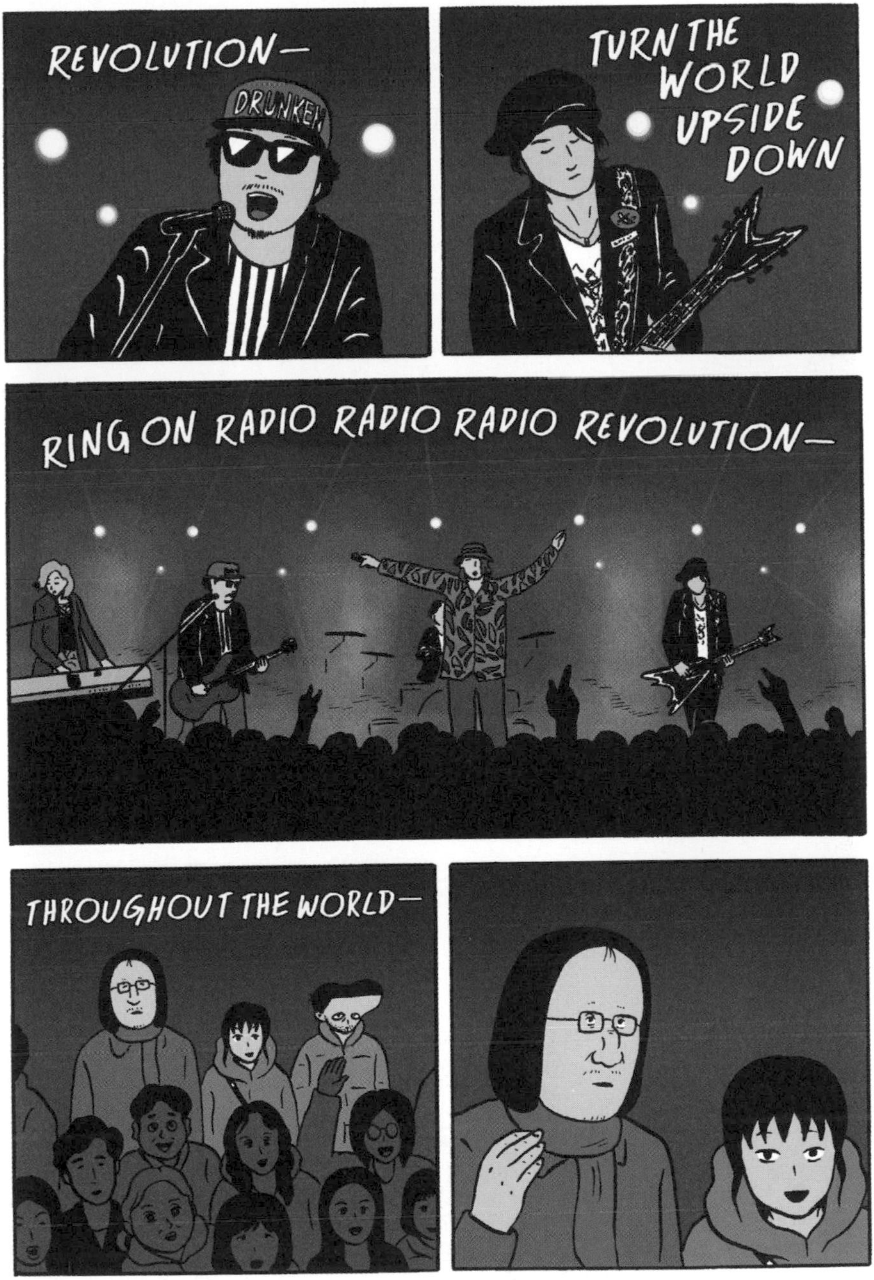
REVOLUTION—
DRUNKEN
TURN THE WORLD UPSIDE DOWN
RING ON RADIO RADIO RADIO REVOLUTION—
THROUGHOUT THE WORLD—

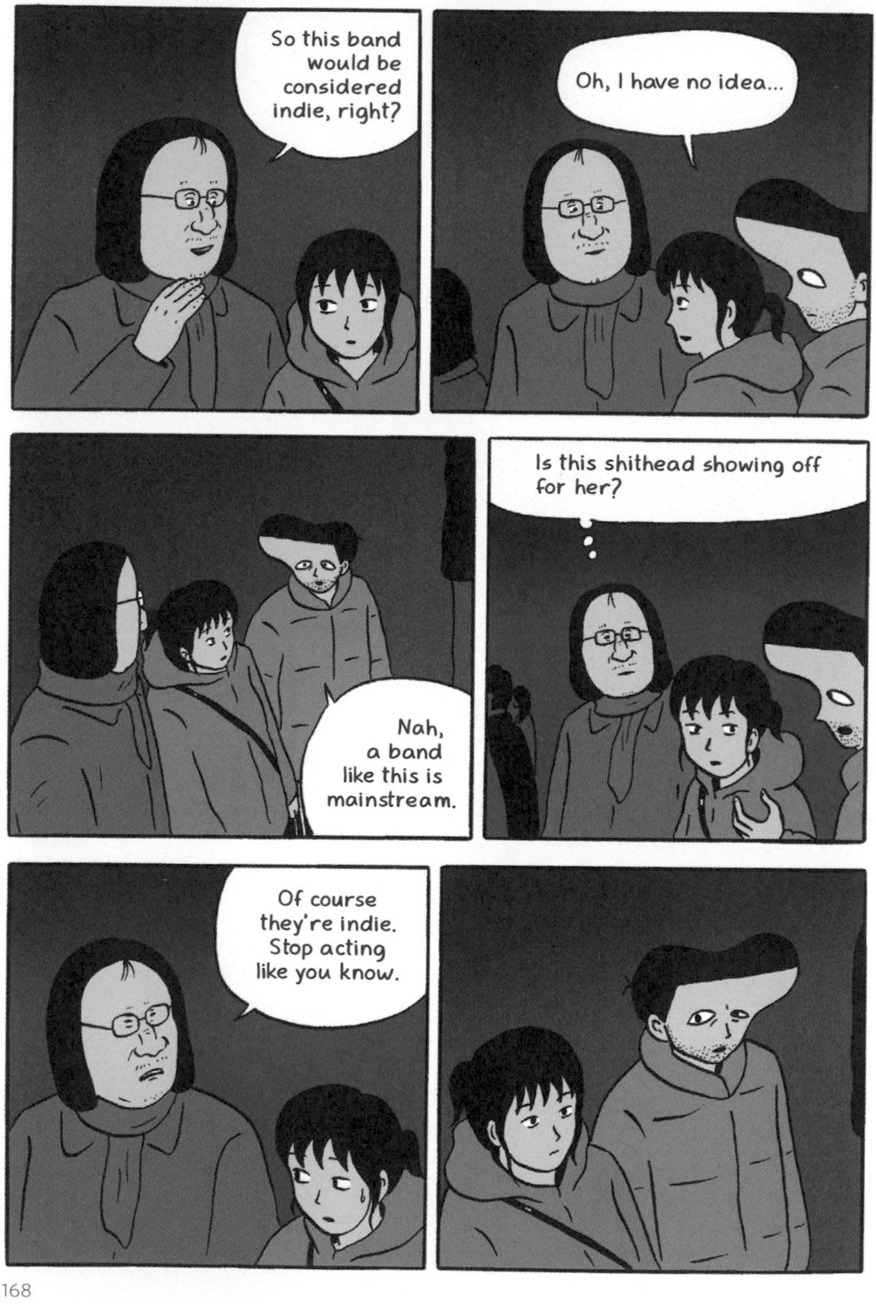
So this band would be considered indie, right?
Oh, I have no idea...
Nah, a band like this is mainstream.
Is this shithead showing off for her?
Of course they're indie. Stop acting like you know.

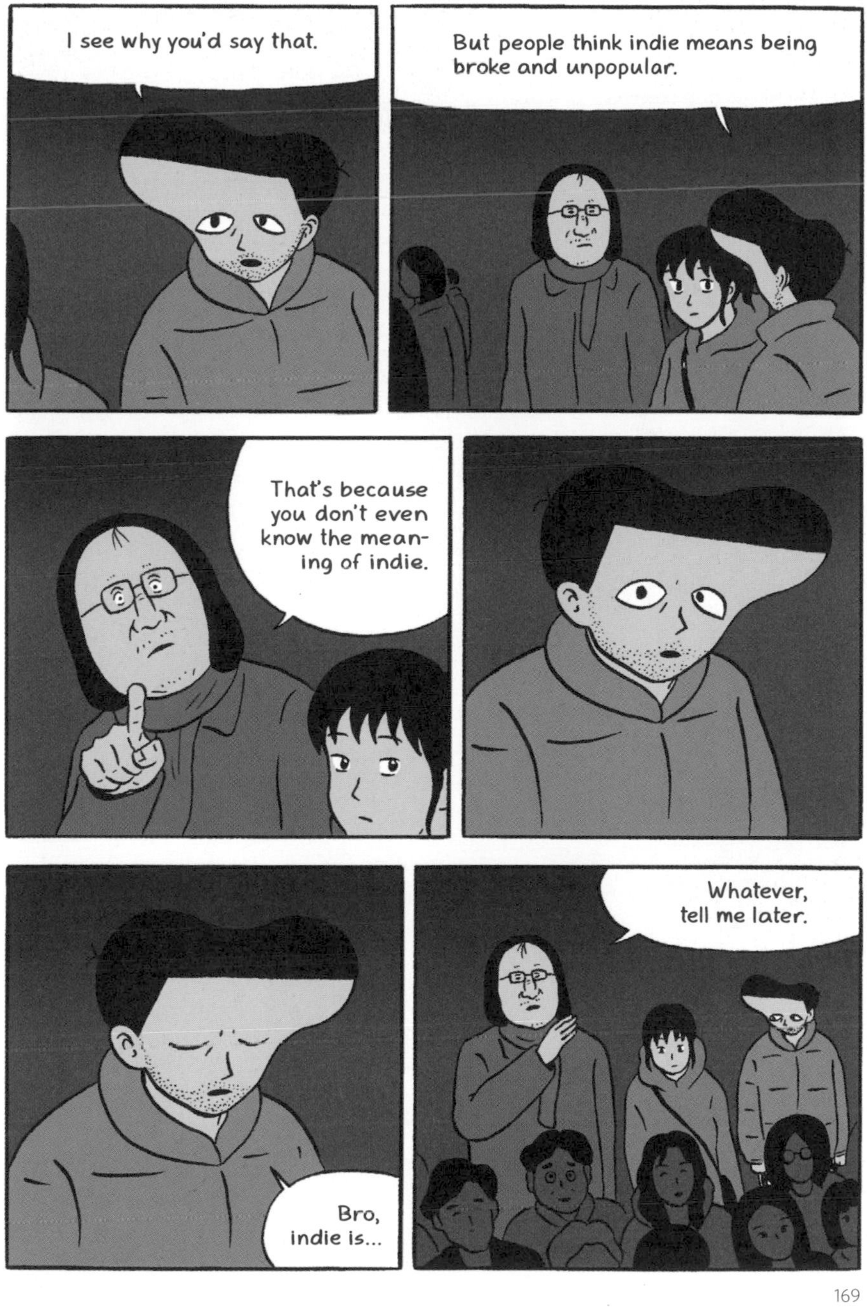
I see why you'd say that.
But people think indie means being broke and unpopular.
That's because you don't even know the meaning of indie.
Bro, indie is...
Whatever, tell me later.

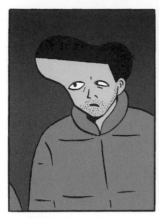

How could anyone call this mainstream? This is definitely indie.

Don't you
agree?

It does sound
like it, I guess.

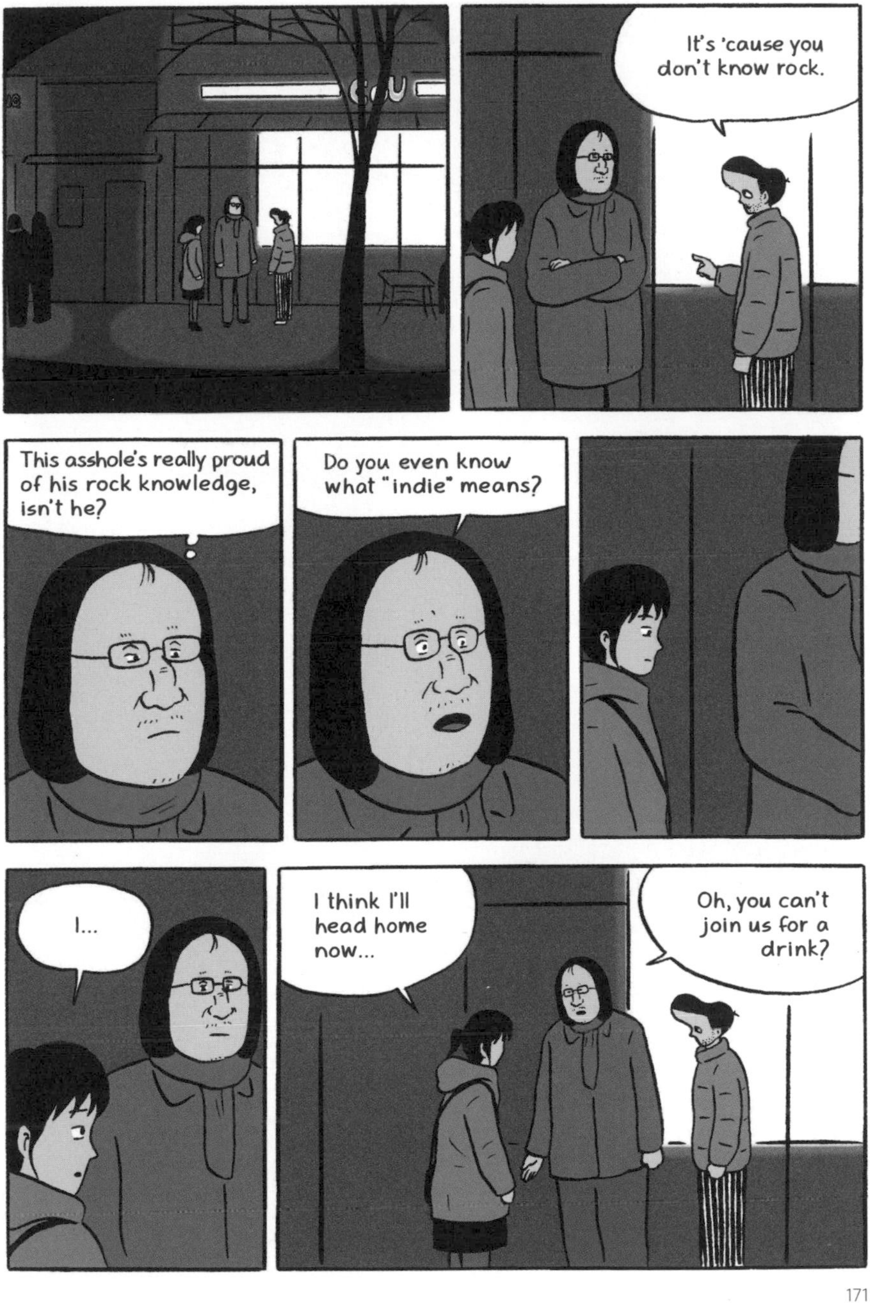
It's 'cause you don't know rock.
This asshole's really proud of his rock knowledge, isn't he?
Do you even know what "indie" means?
I...
I think I'll head home now...
Oh, you can't join us for a drink?

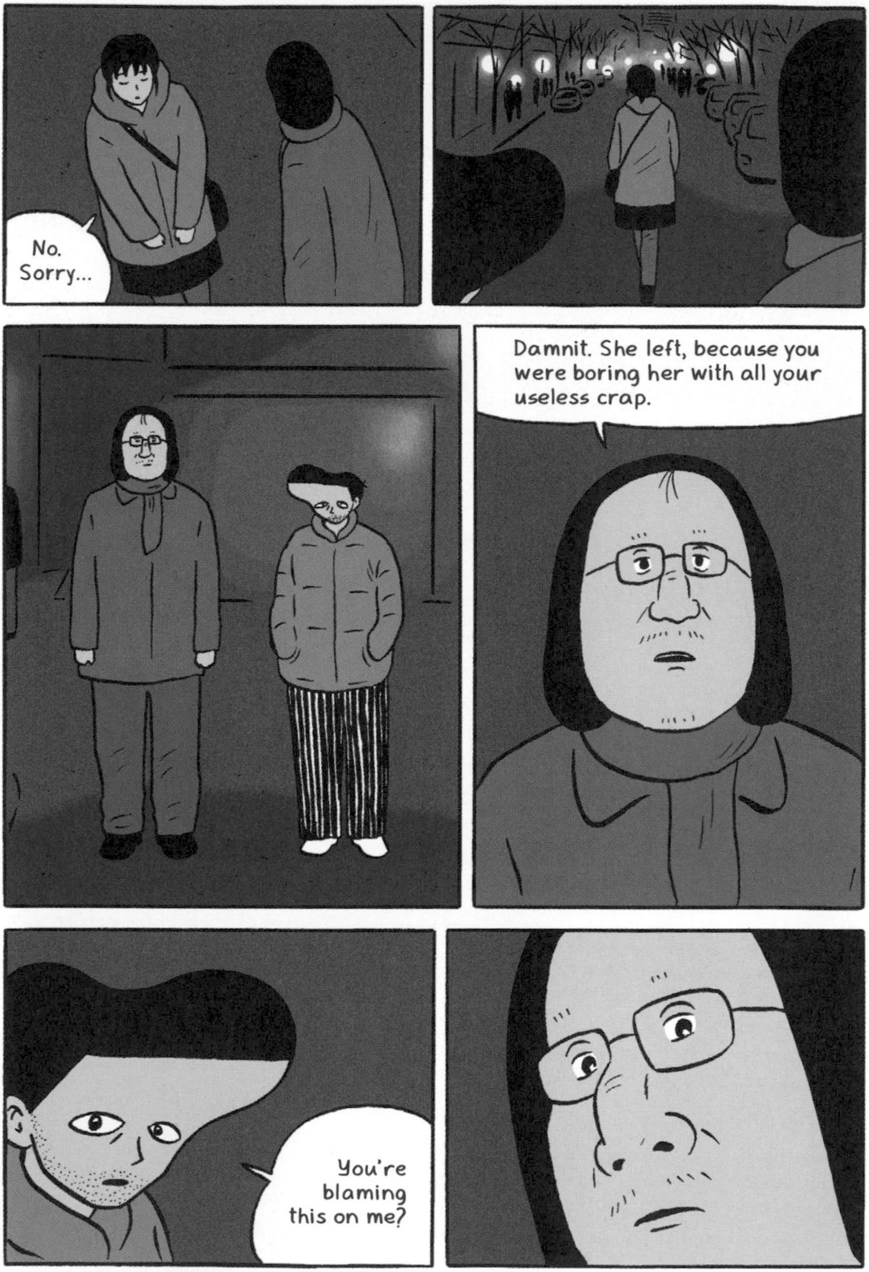
No.
Sorry...
Damnit. She left, because you were boring her with all your useless crap.
You're blaming this on me?

WHAT IS INDIE?

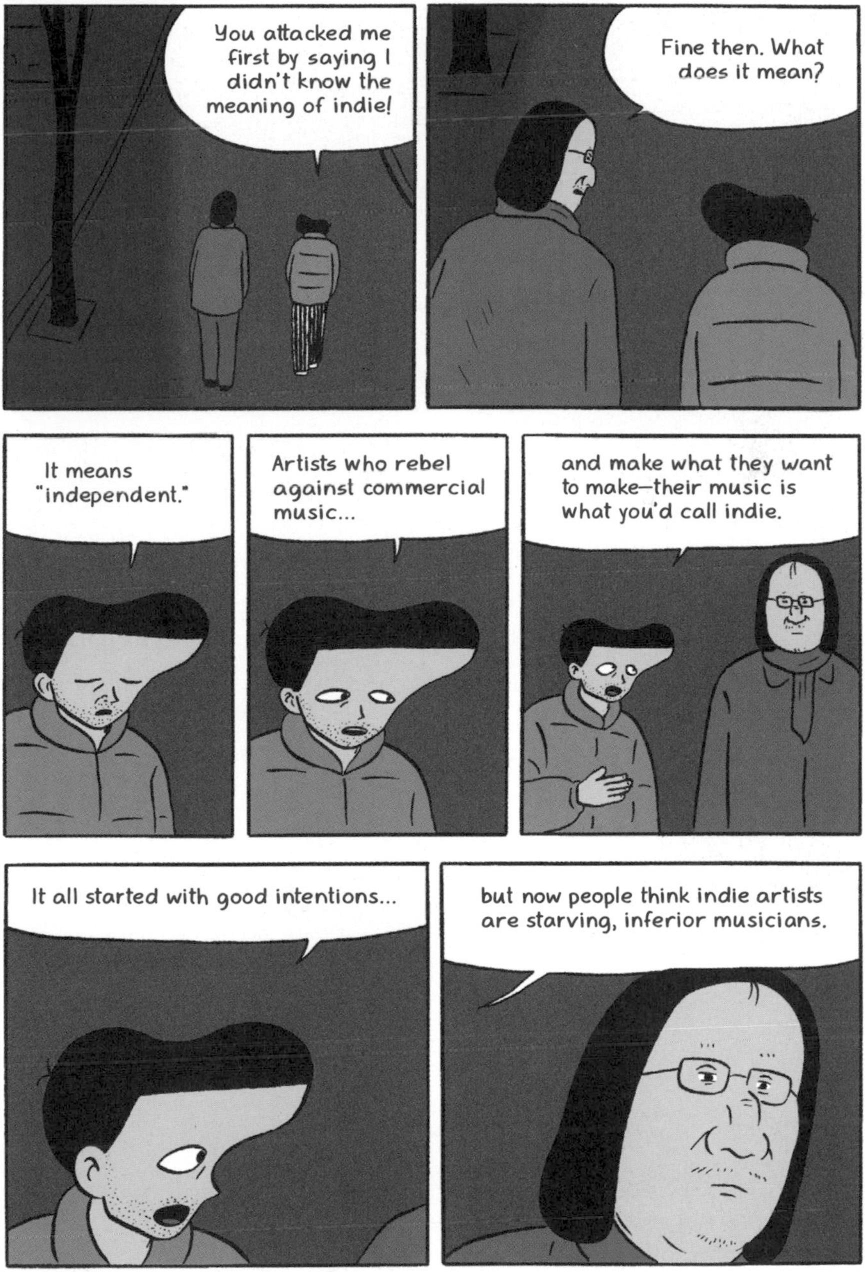
You attacked me first by saying I didn't know the meaning of indie!
Fine then. What does it mean?
It means "independent."
Artists who rebel against commercial music...
and make what they want to make—their music is what you'd call indie.
It all started with good intentions...
but now people think indie artists are starving, inferior musicians.

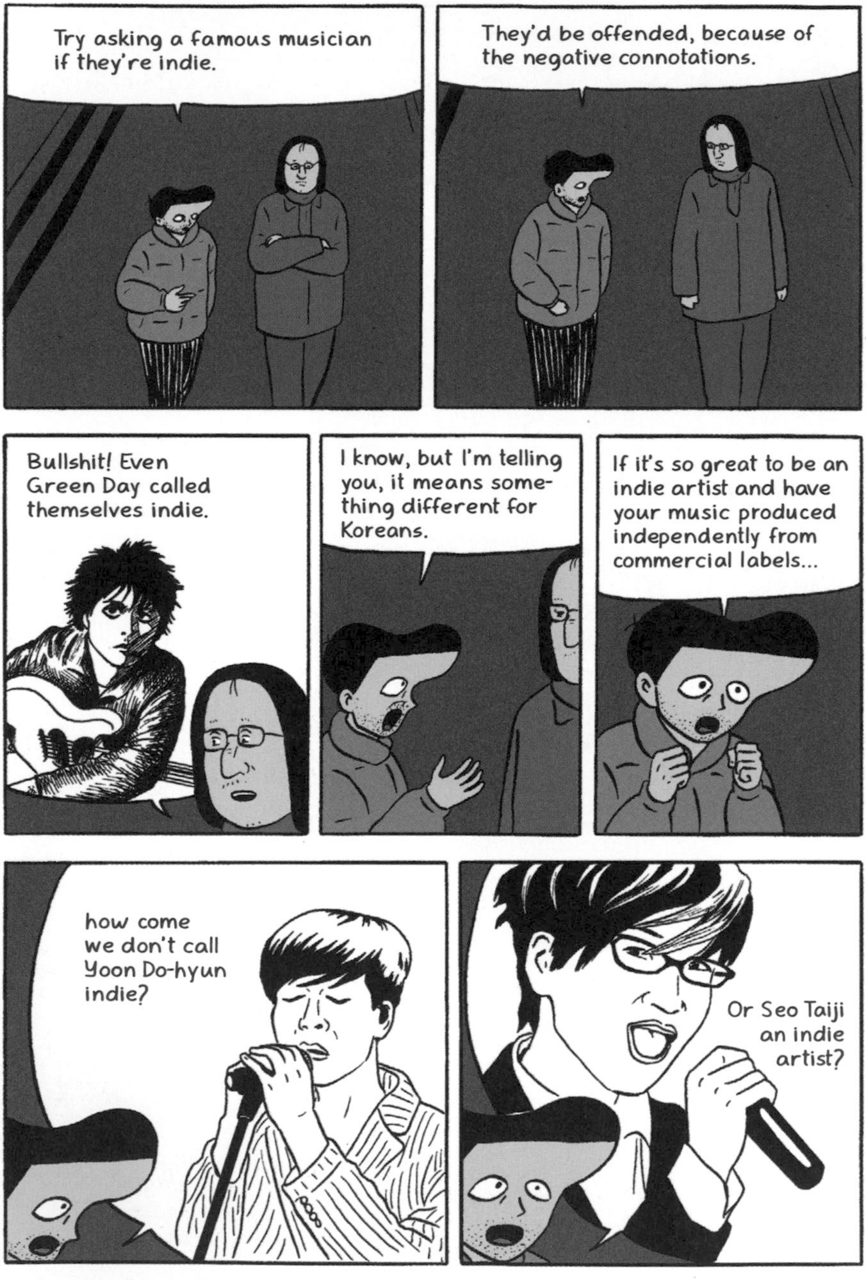
Try asking a famous musician if they're indie.
They'd be offended, because of the negative connotations.
Bullshit! Even Green Day called themselves indie.
I know, but I'm telling you, it means something different for Koreans.
If it's so great to be an indie artist and have your music produced independently from commercial labels...
how come we don't call Yoon Do-hyun indie?
Or Seo Taiji an indie artist?

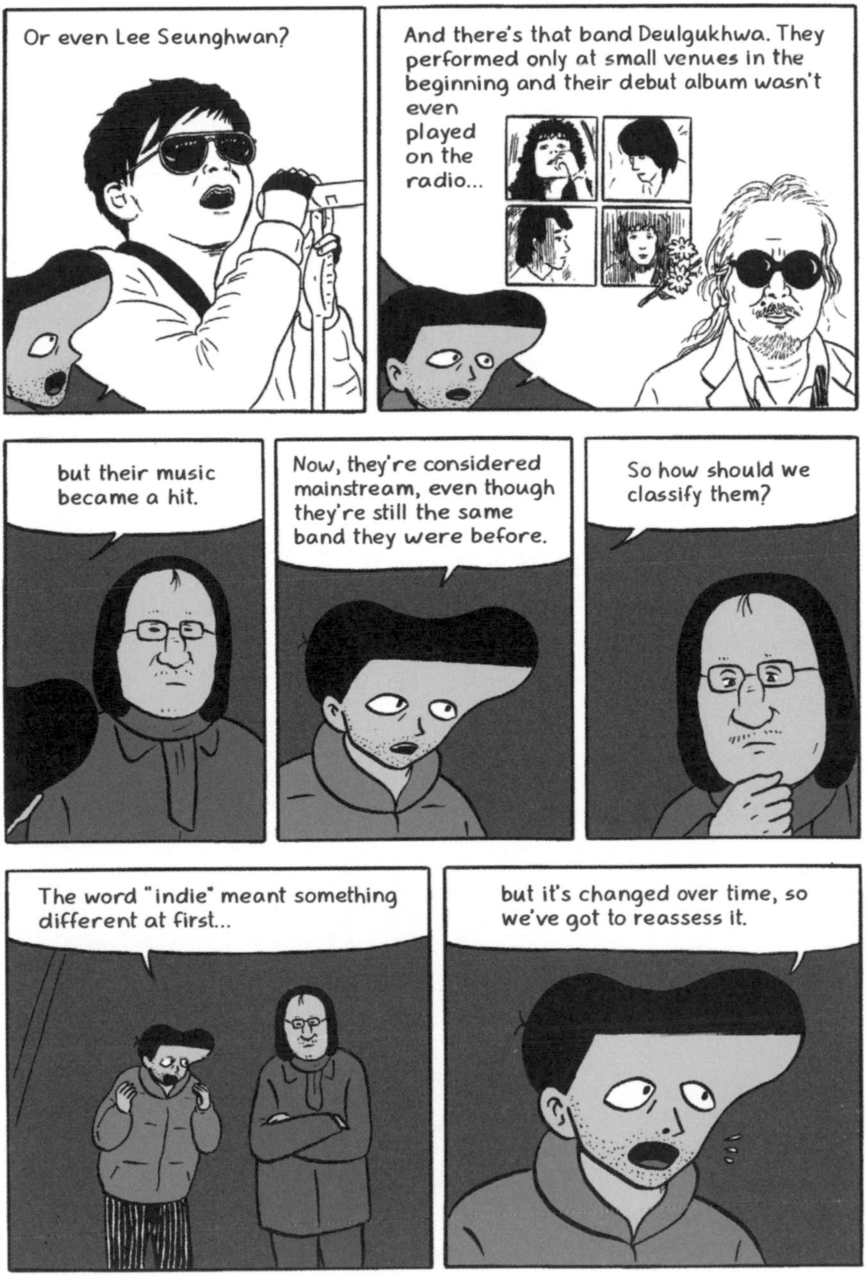
Or even Lee Seunghwan?
And there's that band Deulgukhwa. They performed only at small venues in the beginning and their debut album wasn't even played on the radio...
but their music became a hit.
Now, they're considered mainstream, even though they're still the same band they were before.
So how should we classify them?
The word "indie" meant something different at first...
but it's changed over time, so we've got to reassess it.

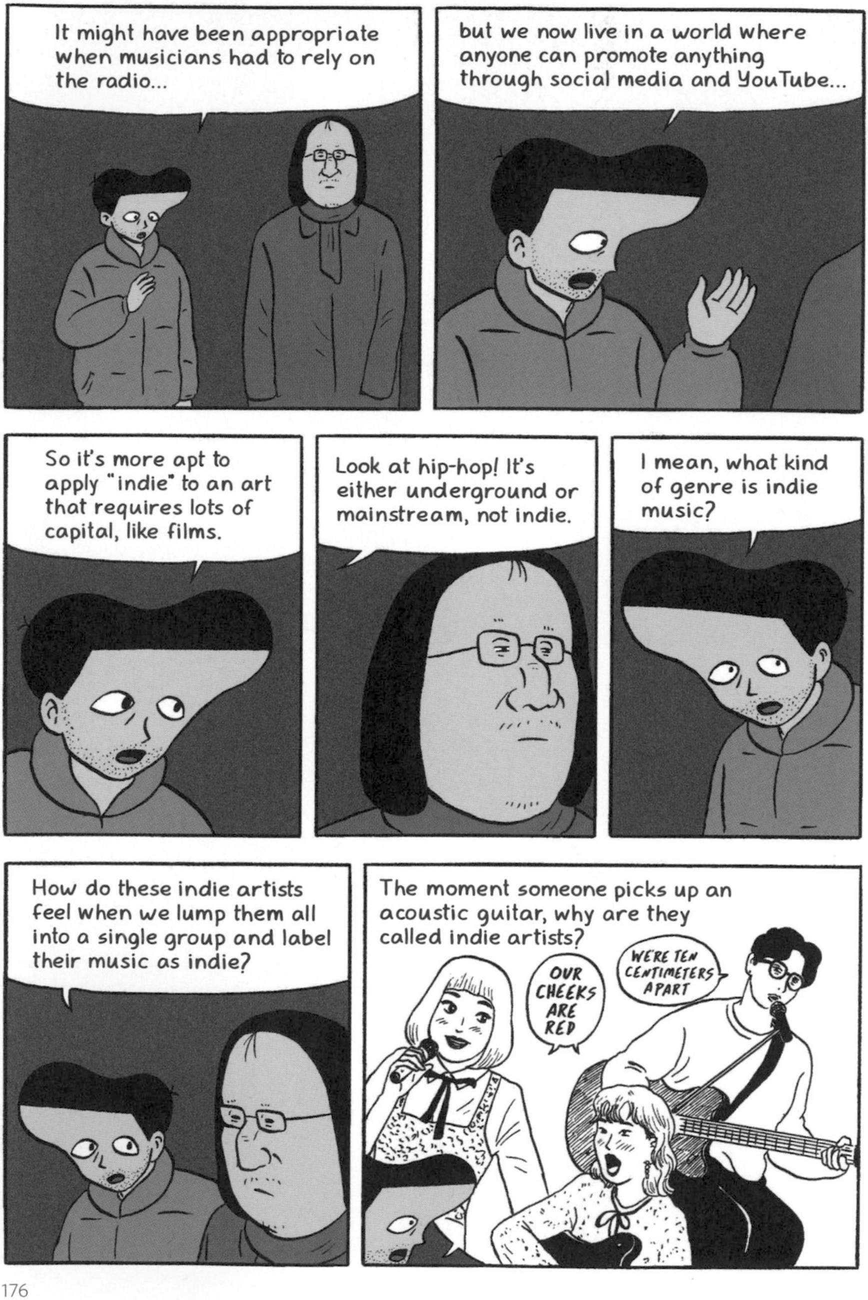
It might have been appropriate when musicians had to rely on the radio...
but we now live in a world where anyone can promote anything through social media and YouTube...
So it's more apt to apply "indie" to an art that requires lots of capital, like films.
Look at hip-hop! It's either underground or mainstream, not indie.
I mean, what kind of genre is indie music?
How do these indie artists feel when we lump them all into a single group and label their music as indie?
The moment someone picks up an acoustic guitar, why are they called indie artists?
OUR CHEEKS ARE RED
WE'RE TEN CENTIMETERS APART

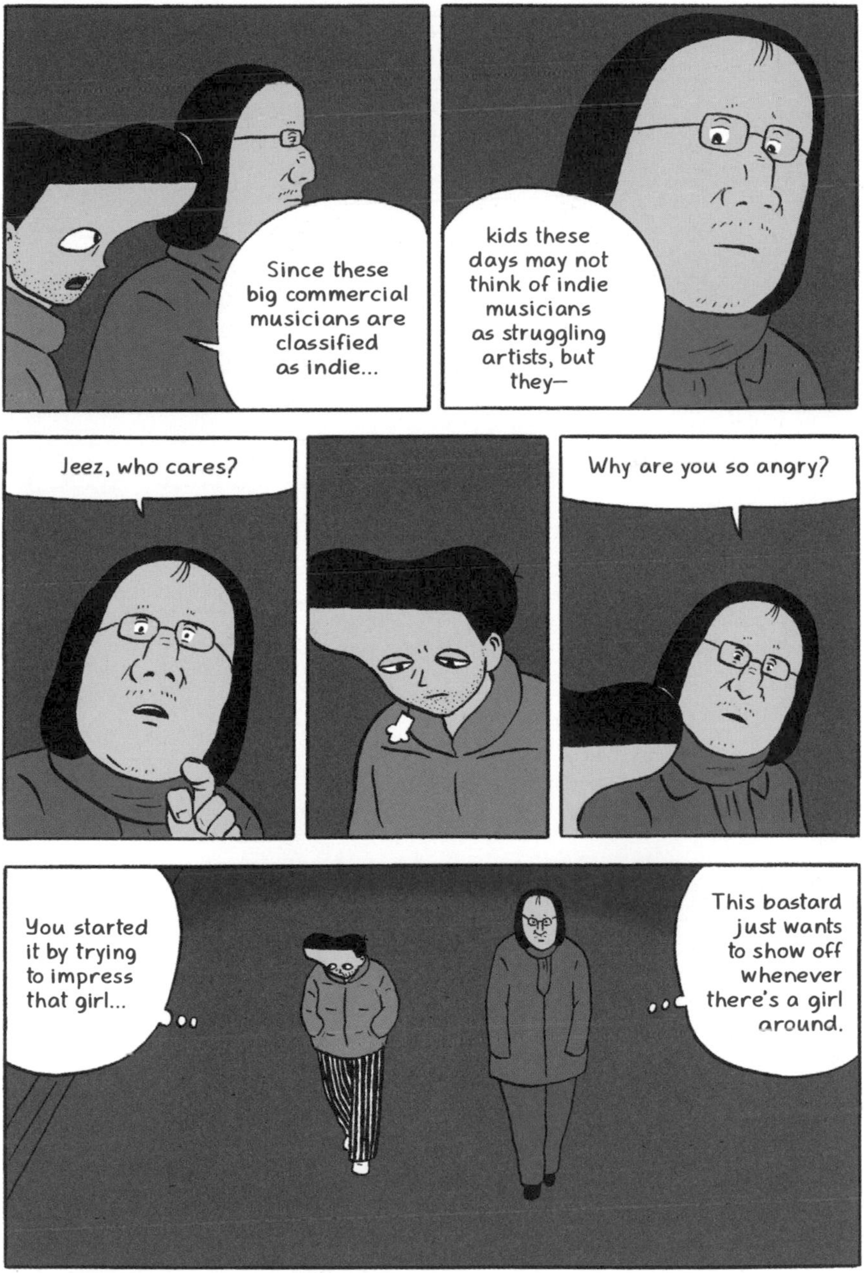
Since these big commercial musicians are classified as indie...
kids these days may not think of indie musicians as struggling artists, but they—
Jeez, who cares?
Why are you so angry?
You started it by trying to impress that girl...
This bastard just wants to show off whenever there's a girl around.

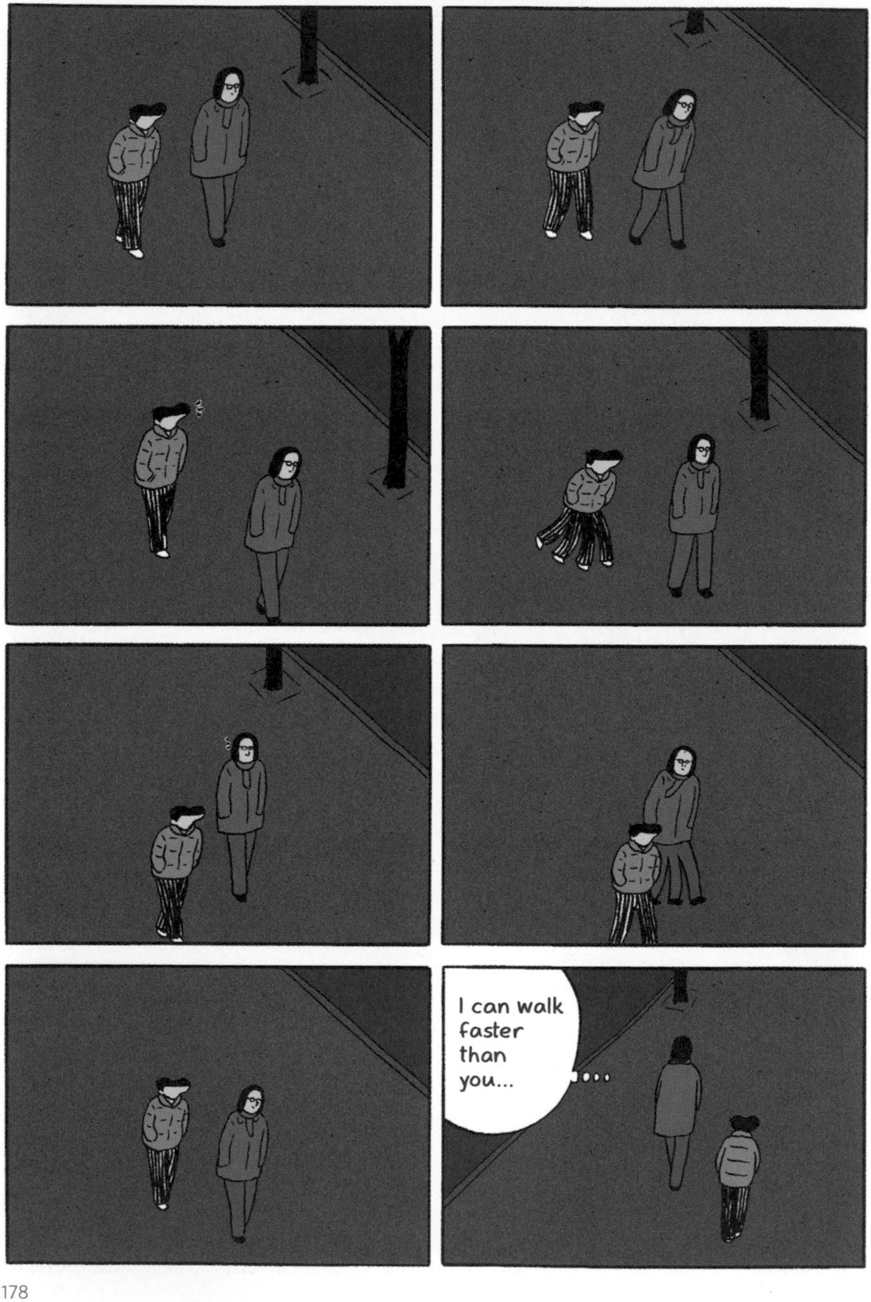
I can walk faster than you...

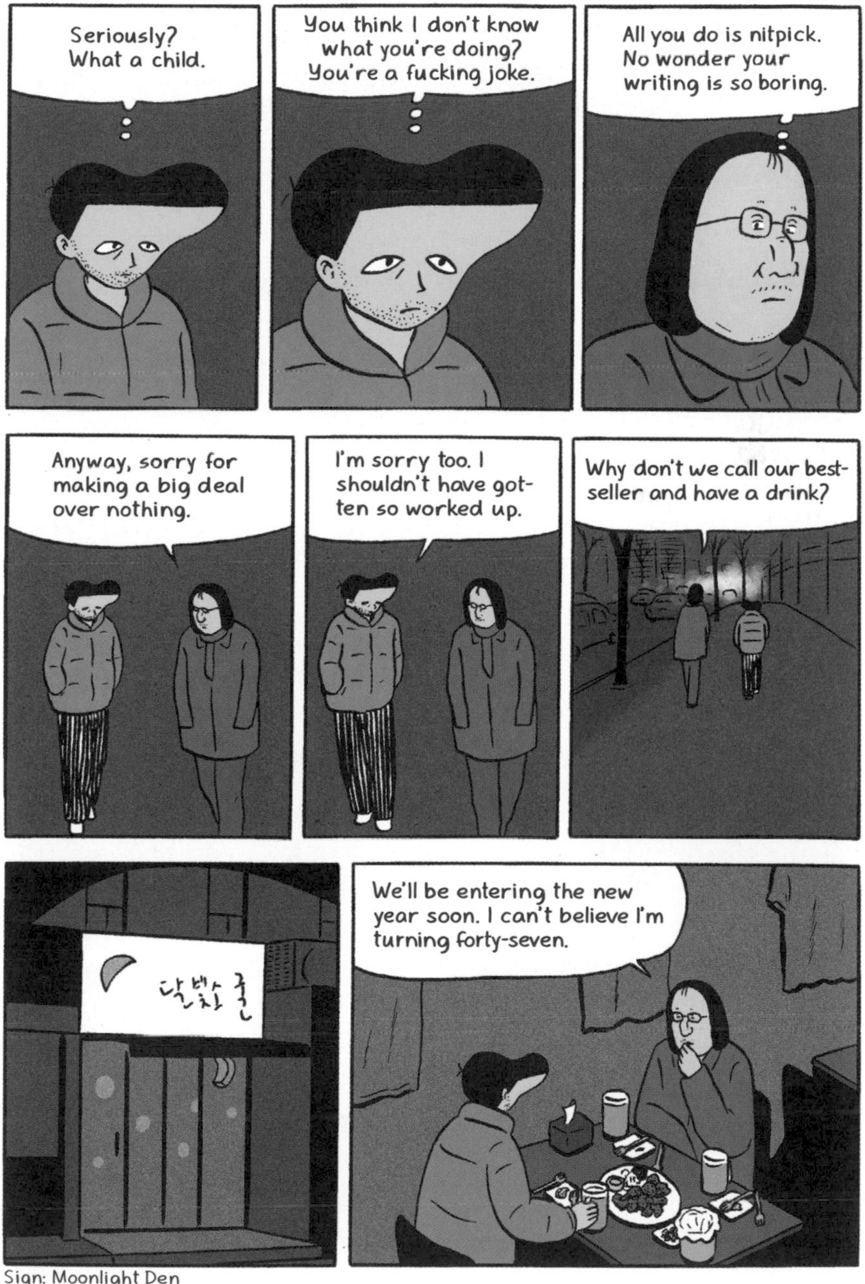
Seriously? What a child.
You think I don't know what you're doing? You're a fucking joke.
All you do is nitpick. No wonder your writing is so boring.
Anyway, sorry for making a big deal over nothing.
I'm sorry too. I shouldn't have got-ten so worked up.
Why don't we call our best-seller and have a drink?
달빛소굴
We'll be entering the new year soon. I can't believe I'm turning forty-seven.
Sign: Moonlight Den

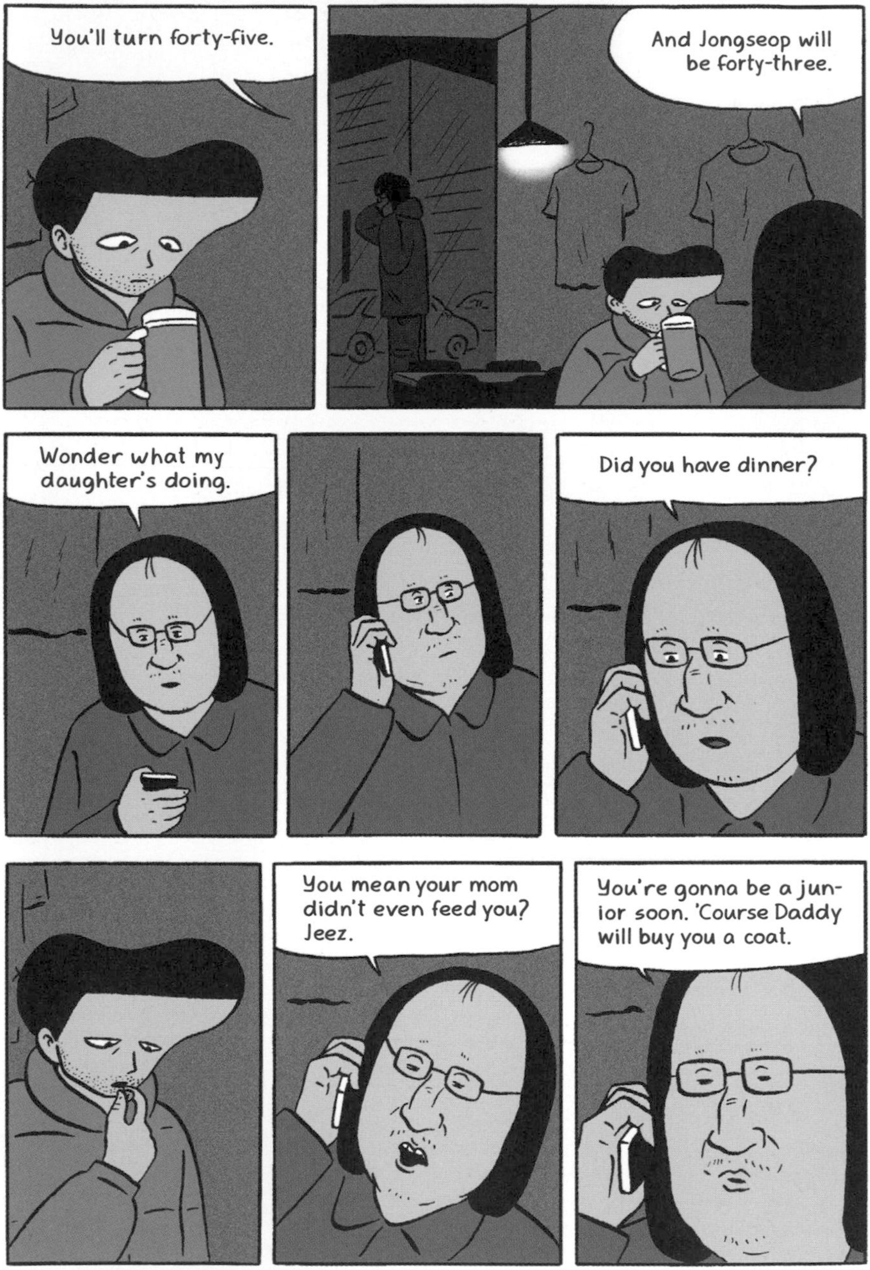
You'll turn forty-five.
And Jongseop will be forty-three.
Wonder what my daughter's doing.
Did you have dinner?
You mean your mom didn't even feed you? Jeez.
You're gonna be a junior soon. 'Course Daddy will buy you a coat.

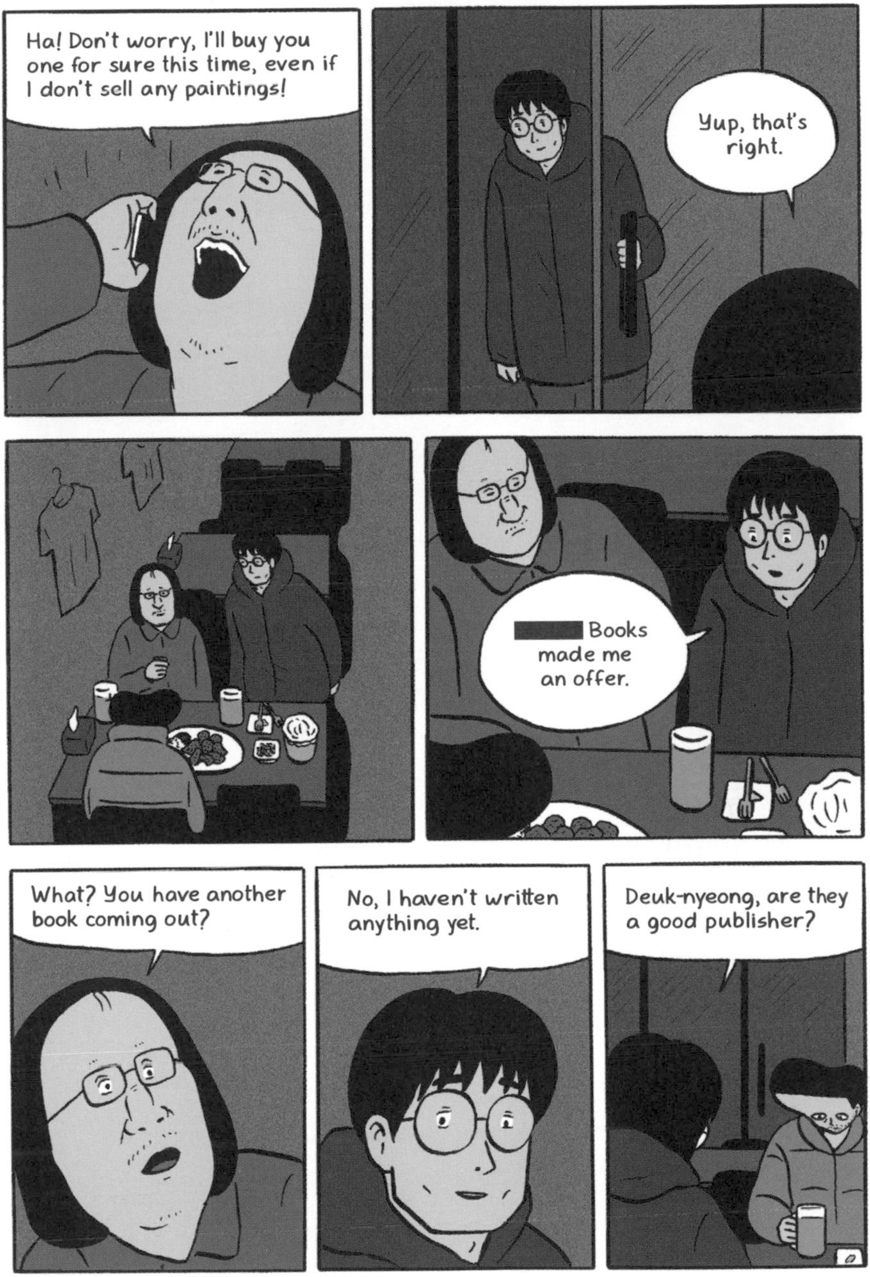
Ha! Don't worry, I'll buy you one for sure this time, even if I don't sell any paintings!
Yup, that's right.
[redacted] Books made me an offer.
What? You have another book coming out?
No, I haven't written anything yet.
Deuk-nyeong, are they a good publisher?

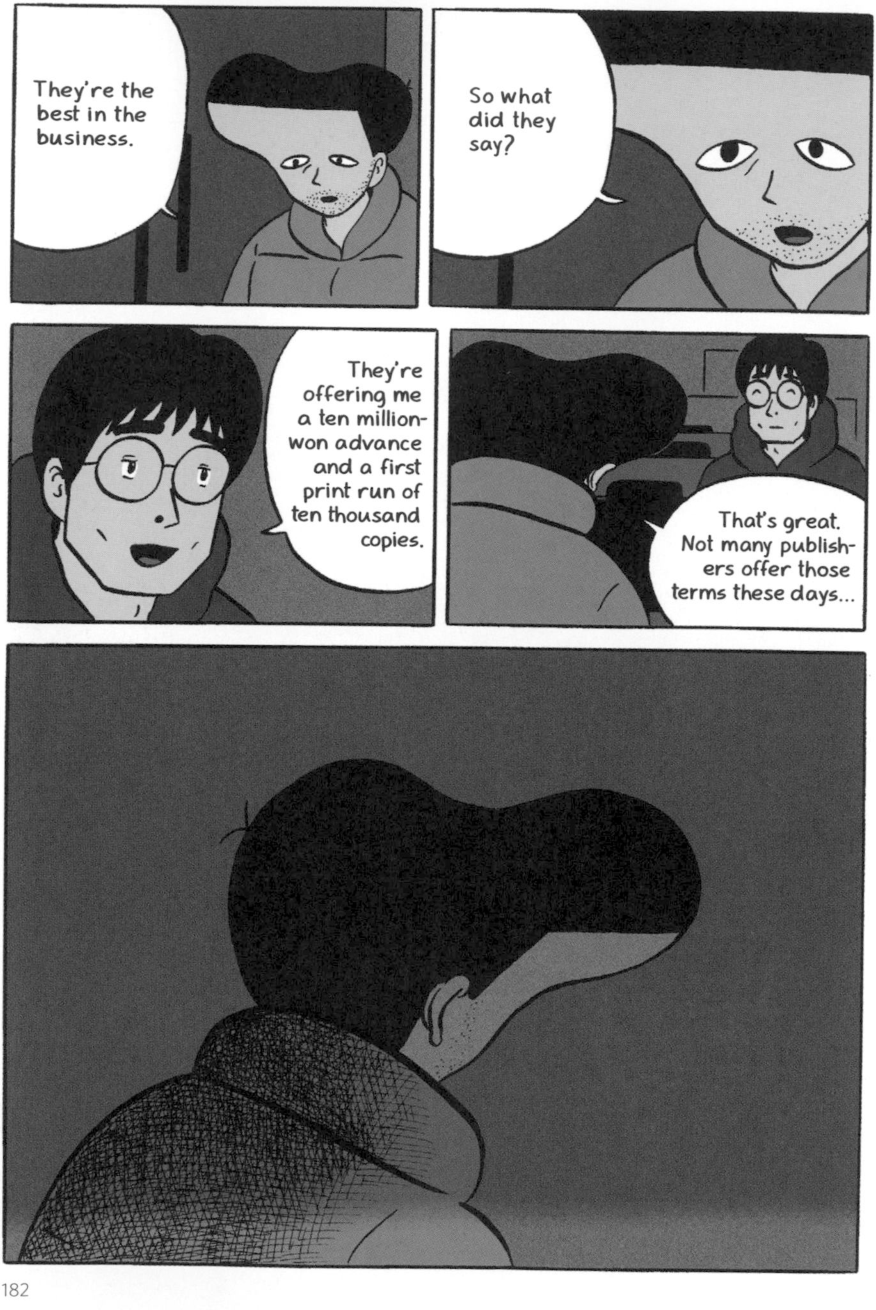
They're the best in the business.
So what did they say?
They're offering me a ten million-won advance and a first print run of ten thousand copies.
That's great. Not many publishers offer those terms these days...

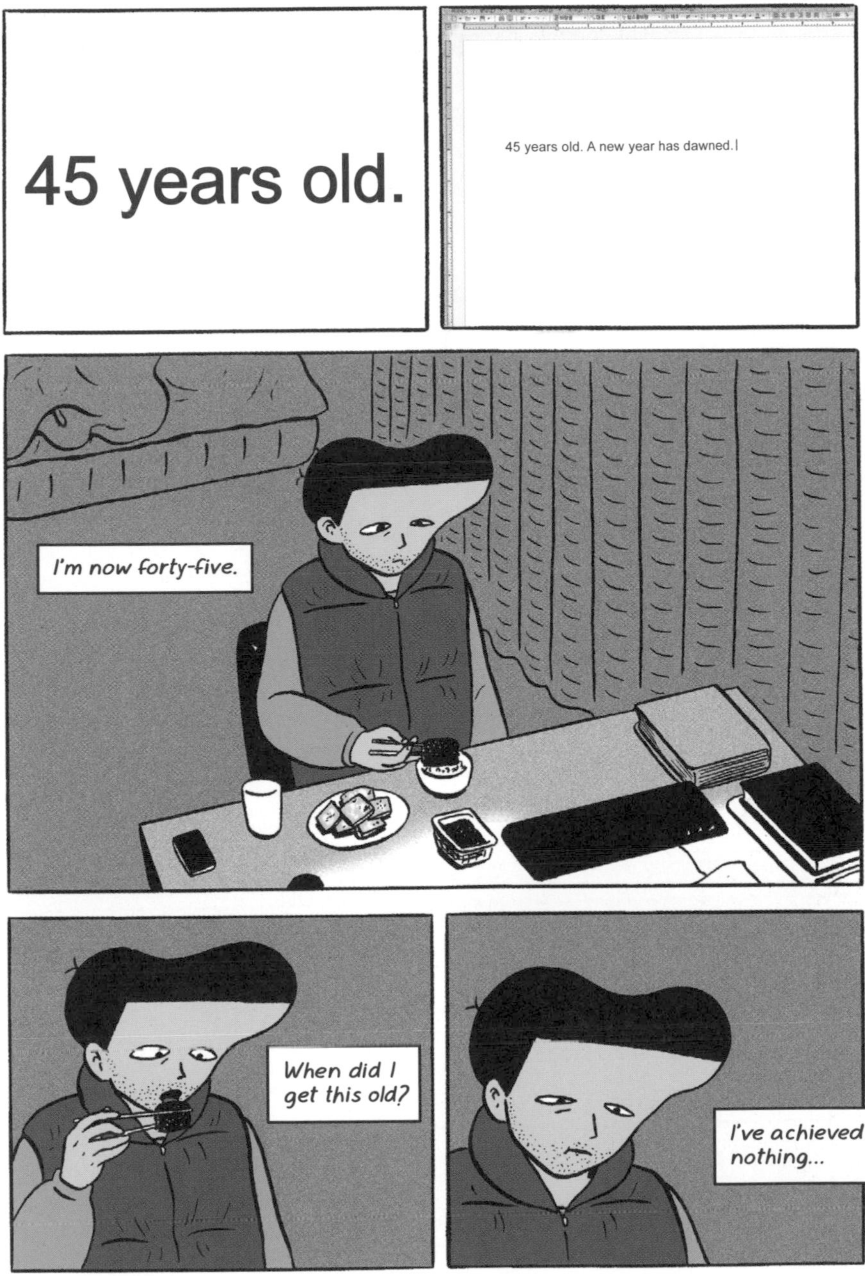
45 years old.
45 years old. A new year has dawned.
I'm now forty-five.
When did I get this old?
I've achieved nothing...

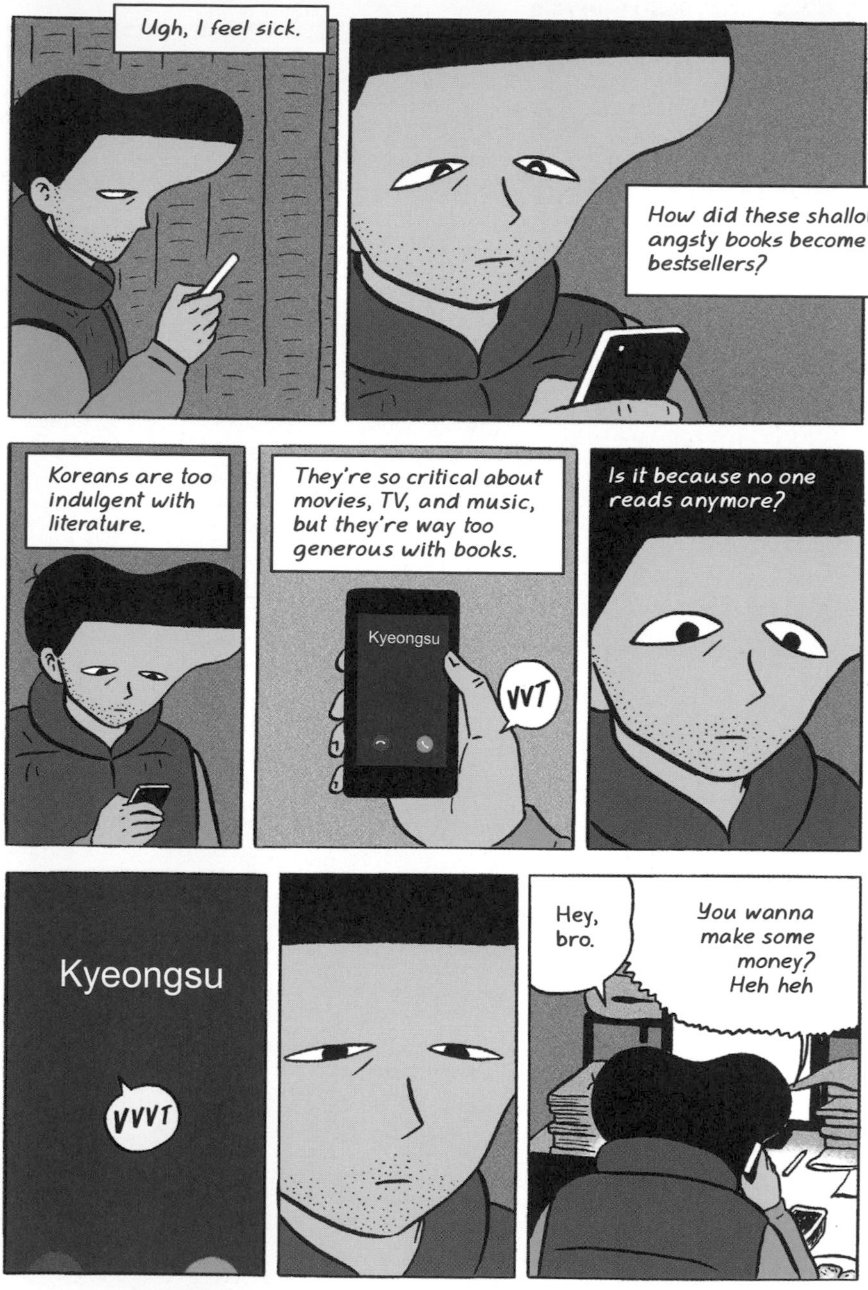
Ugh, I feel sick.
How did these shallow, angsty books become bestsellers?
Koreans are too indulgent with literature.
They're so critical about movies, TV, and music, but they're way too generous with books.
Kyeongsu
VVT
Is it because no one reads anymore?
Kyeongsu
VVVT
Hey, bro.
You wanna make some money? Heh heh

THE PATH TO A SMALL POWER

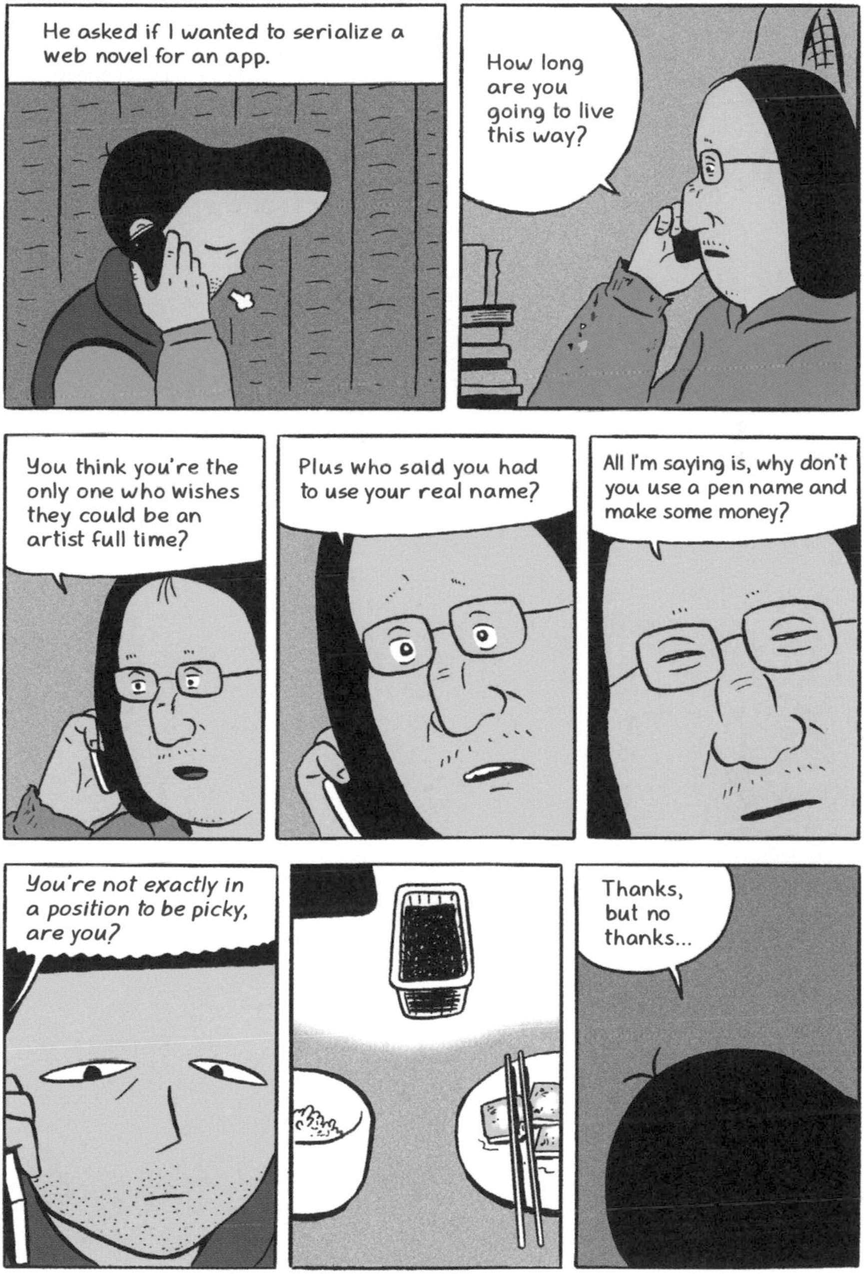
He asked if I wanted to serialize a web novel for an app.
How long are you going to live this way?
You think you're the only one who wishes they could be an artist full time?
Plus who said you had to use your real name?
All I'm saying is, why don't you use a pen name and make some money?
You're not exactly in a position to be picky, are you?
Thanks, but no thanks...

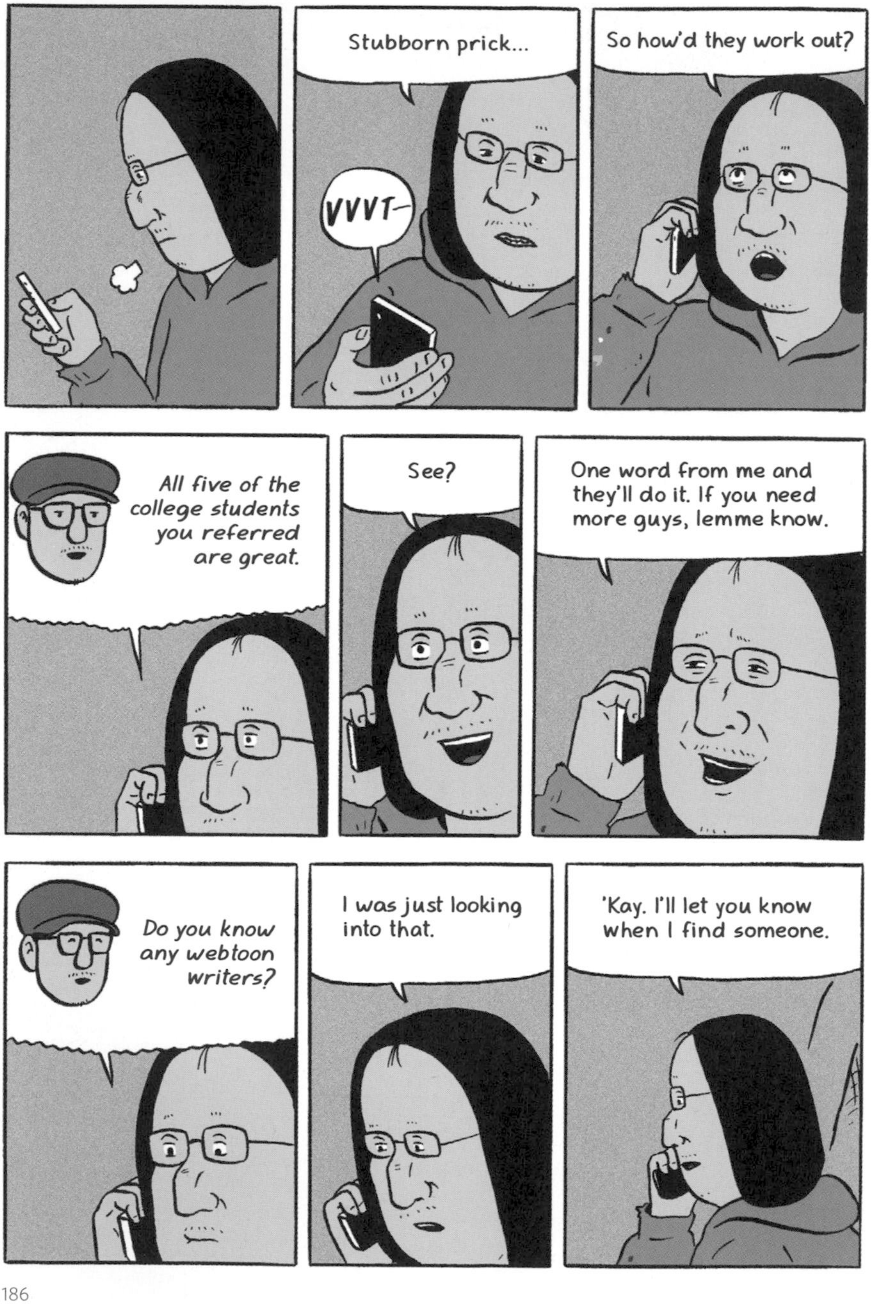
Stubborn prick...
VVVT-
So how'd they work out?
All five of the college students you referred are great.
See?
One word from me and they'll do it. If you need more guys, lemme know.
Do you know any webtoon writers?
I was just looking into that.
'Kay. I'll let you know when I find someone.

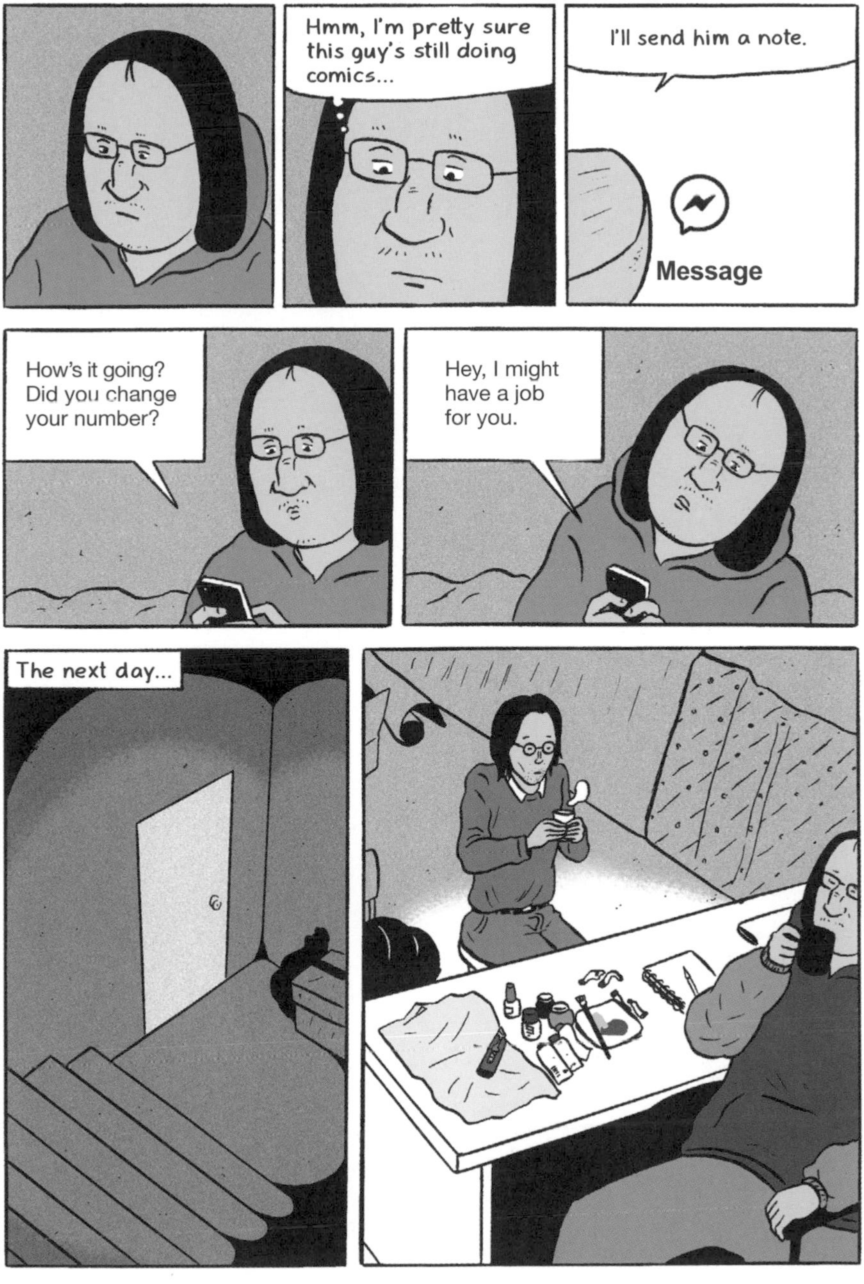
Hmm, I'm pretty sure this guy's still doing comics...
I'll send him a note.
Message
How's it going? Did you change your number?
Hey, I might have a job for you.
The next day...

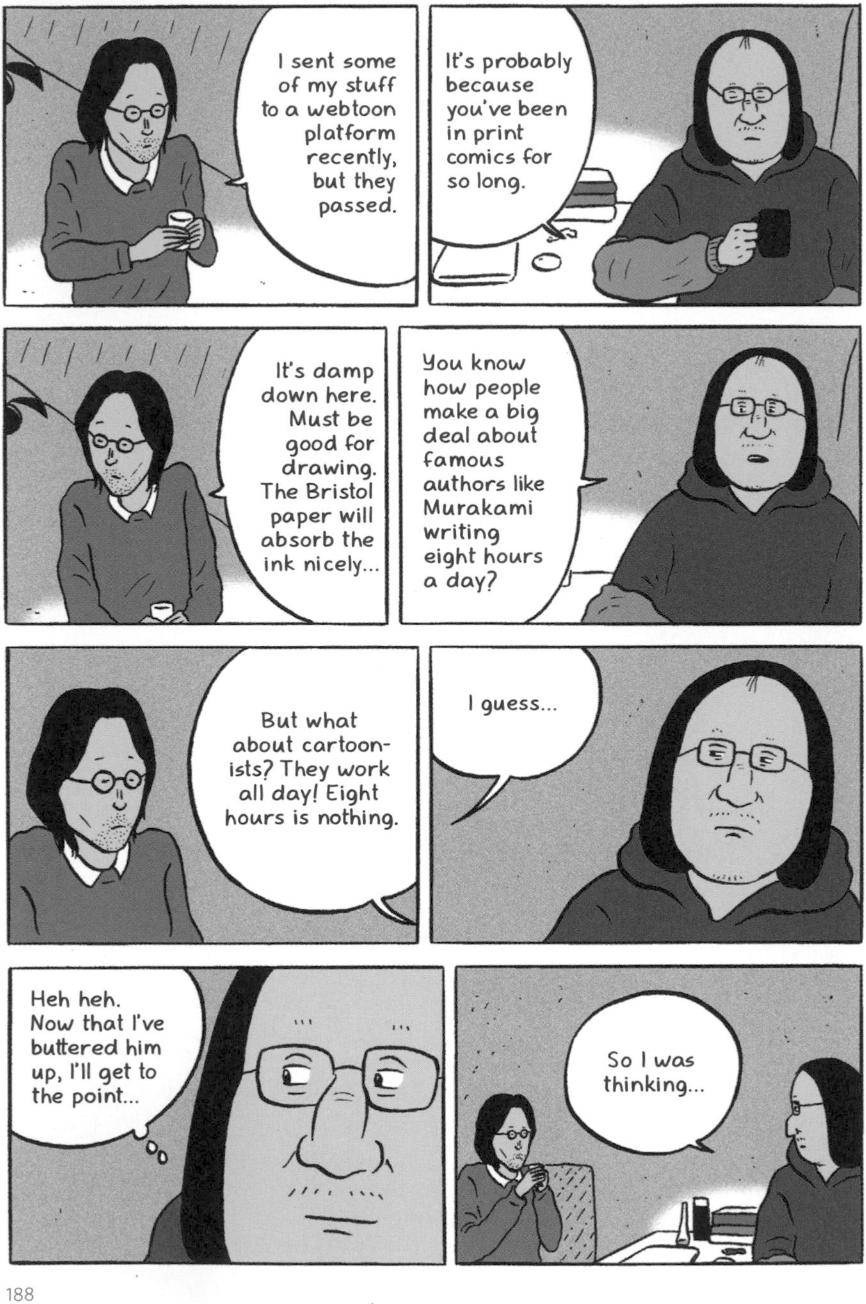
I sent some of my stuff to a webtoon platform recently, but they passed.
It's probably because you've been in print comics for so long.
It's damp down here. Must be good for drawing. The Bristol paper will absorb the ink nicely...
You know how people make a big deal about famous authors like Murakami writing eight hours a day?
But what about cartoonists? They work all day! Eight hours is nothing.
I guess...
Heh heh. Now that I've buttered him up, I'll get to the point...
So I was thinking...

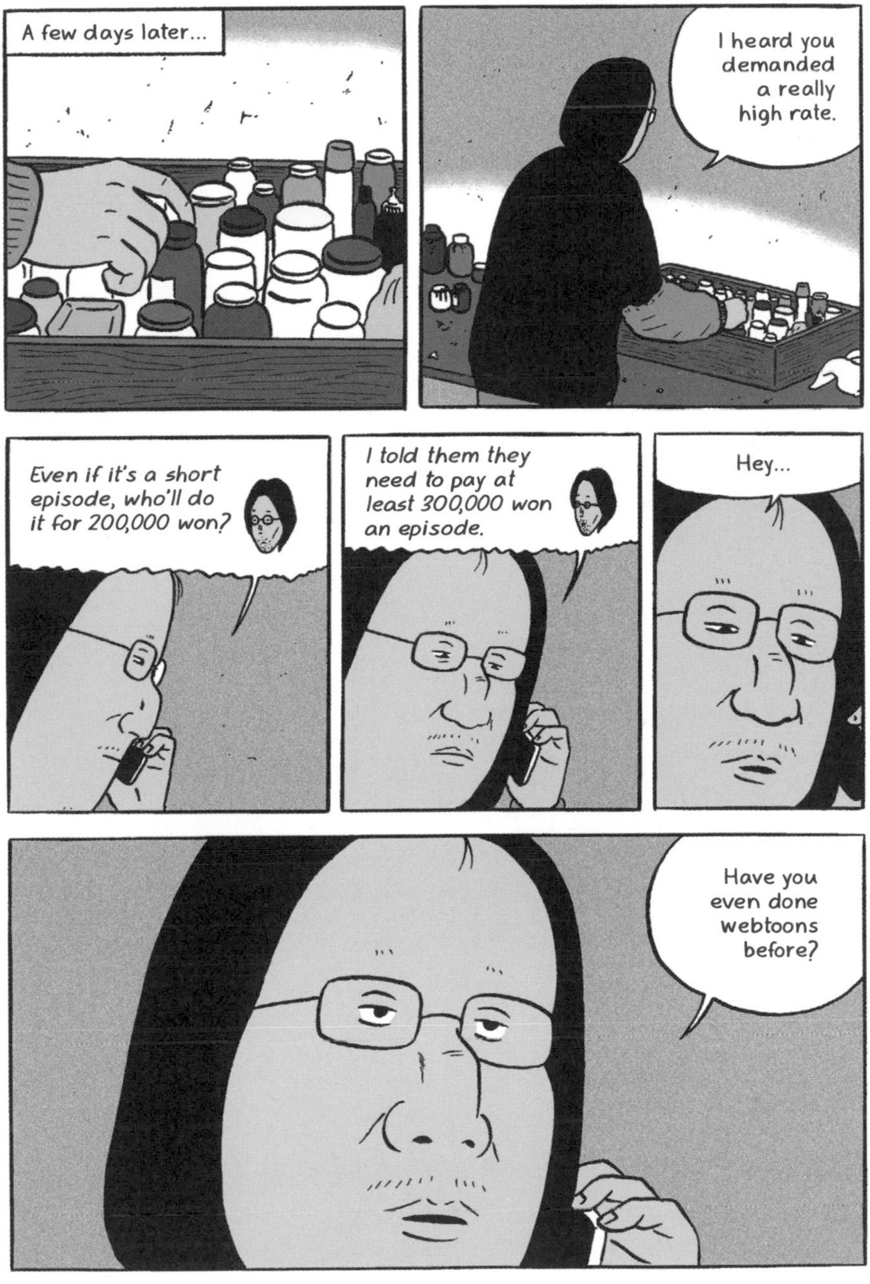
A few days later...
I heard you demanded a really high rate.
Even if it's a short episode, who'll do it for 200,000 won?
I told them they need to pay at least 300,000 won an episode.
Hey...
Have you even done webtoons before?

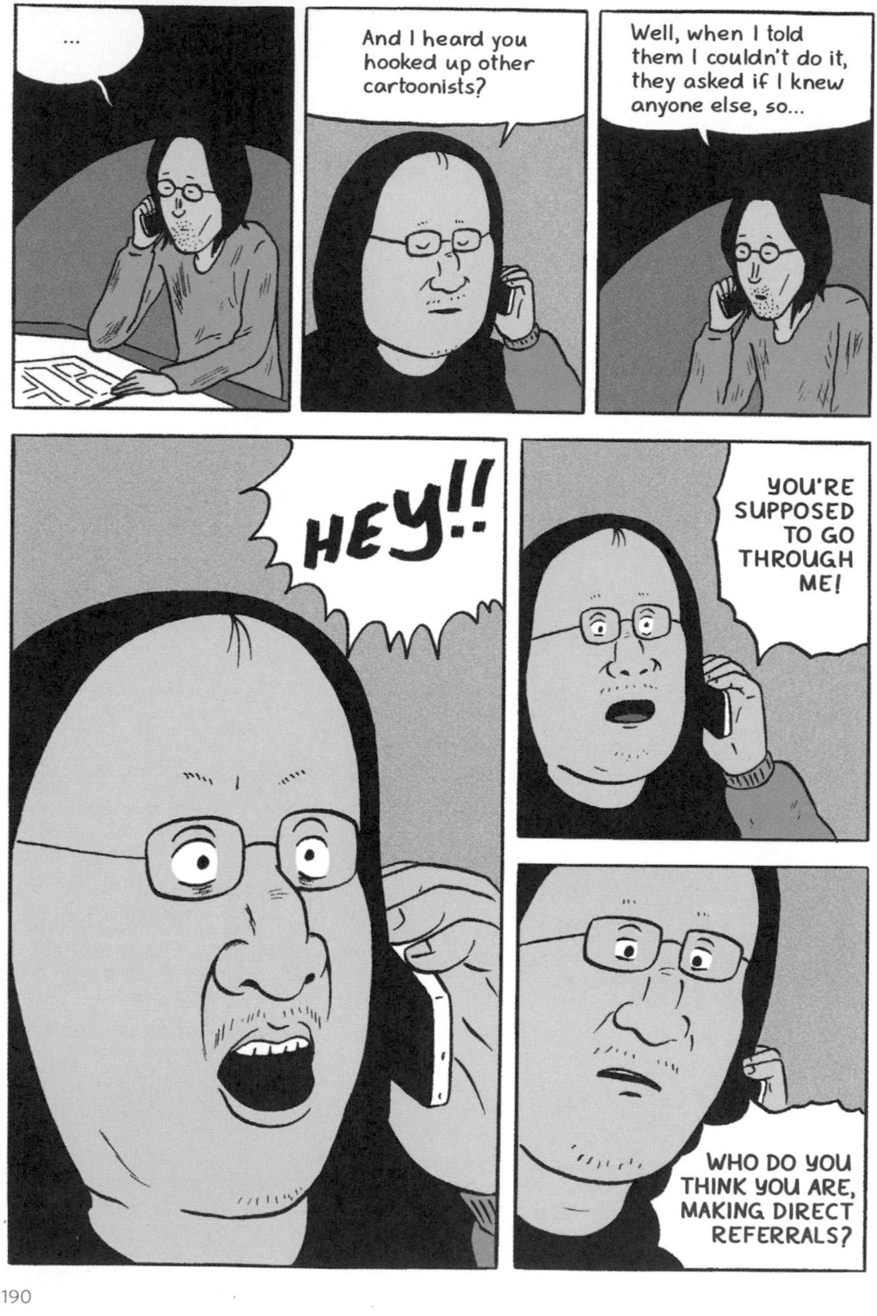
...
And I heard you hooked up other cartoonists?
Well, when I told them I couldn't do it, they asked if I knew anyone else, so...
HEY!!
YOU'RE SUPPOSED TO GO THROUGH ME!
WHO DO YOU THINK YOU ARE, MAKING DIRECT REFERRALS?

What's the big deal? It's not like it's your app.
Are you saying I'm running some kind of scam here?
I'm not getting a single won out of this.
Fine. Bye.
Damnit, these shitheads always stick their noses in and ruin everything.
Professor, thank you for referring me for the illustration job…

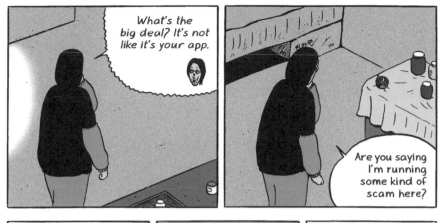

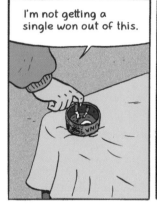

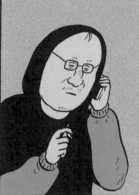

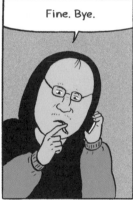

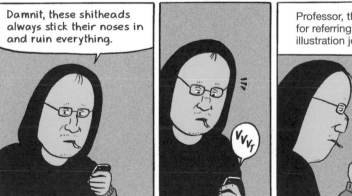

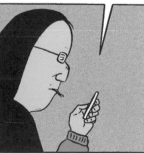

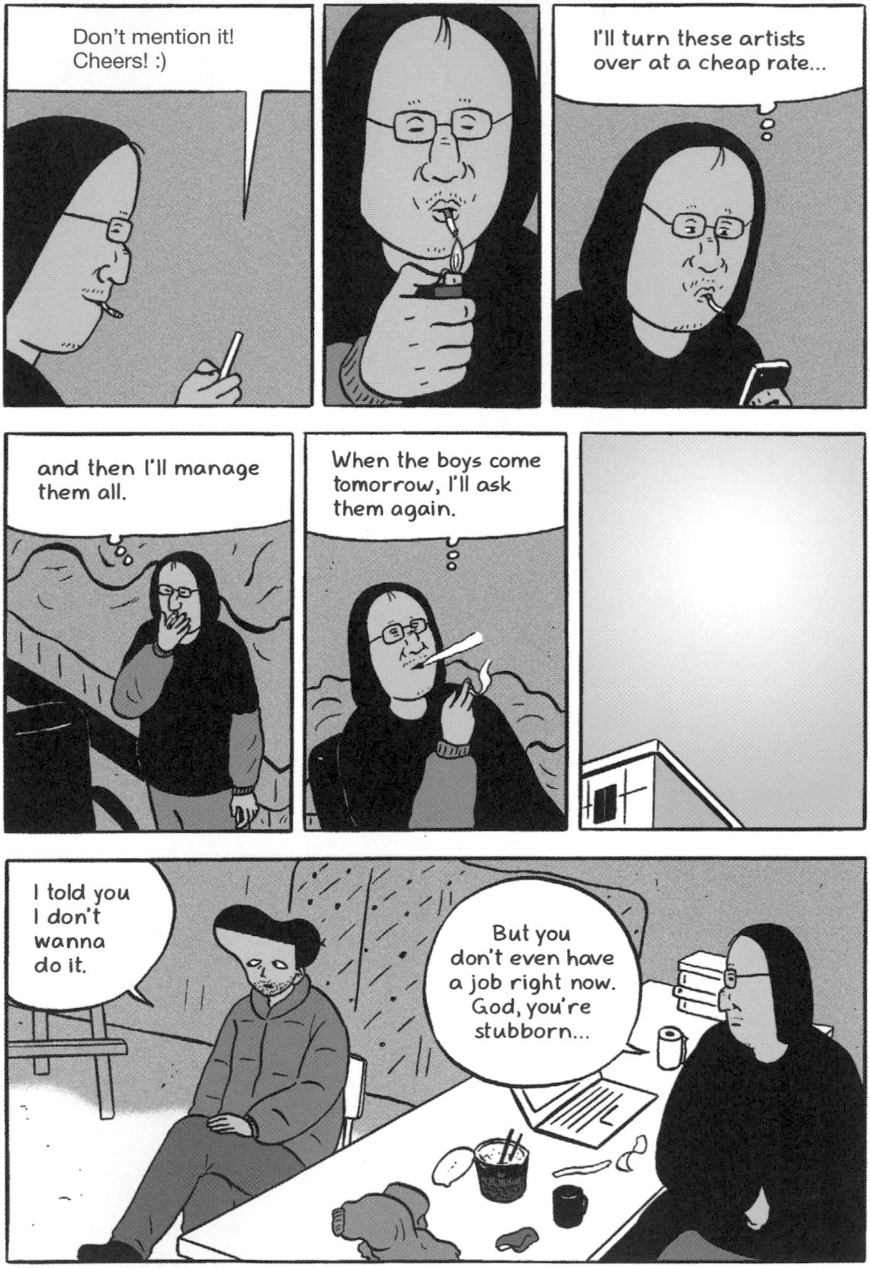
Don't mention it!
Cheers! :)
I'll turn these artists over at a cheap rate...
and then I'll manage them all.
When the boys come tomorrow, I'll ask them again.
I told you I don't wanna do it.
But you don't even have a job right now. God, you're stubborn...

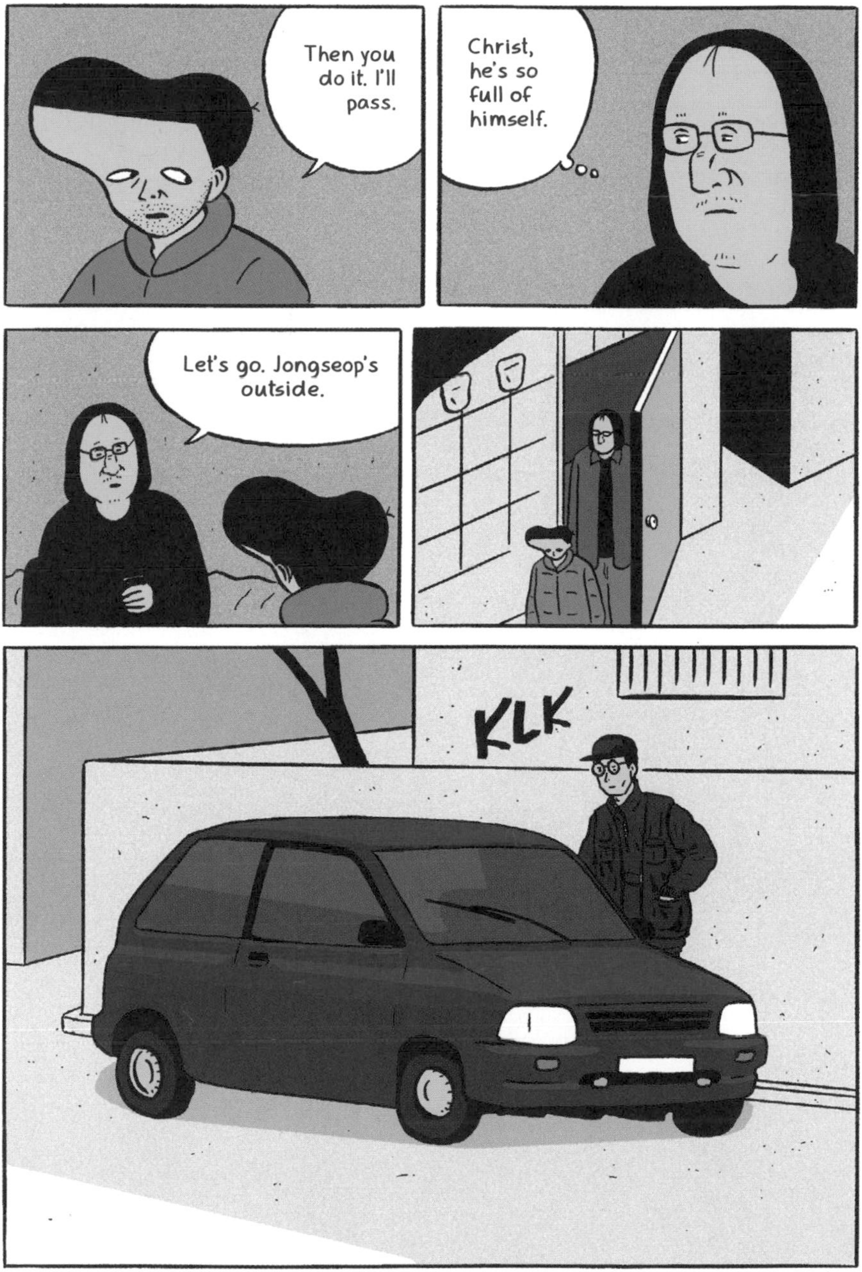

Then you do it. I'll pass.
Christ, he's so full of himself.
Let's go. Jongseop's outside.
KLK

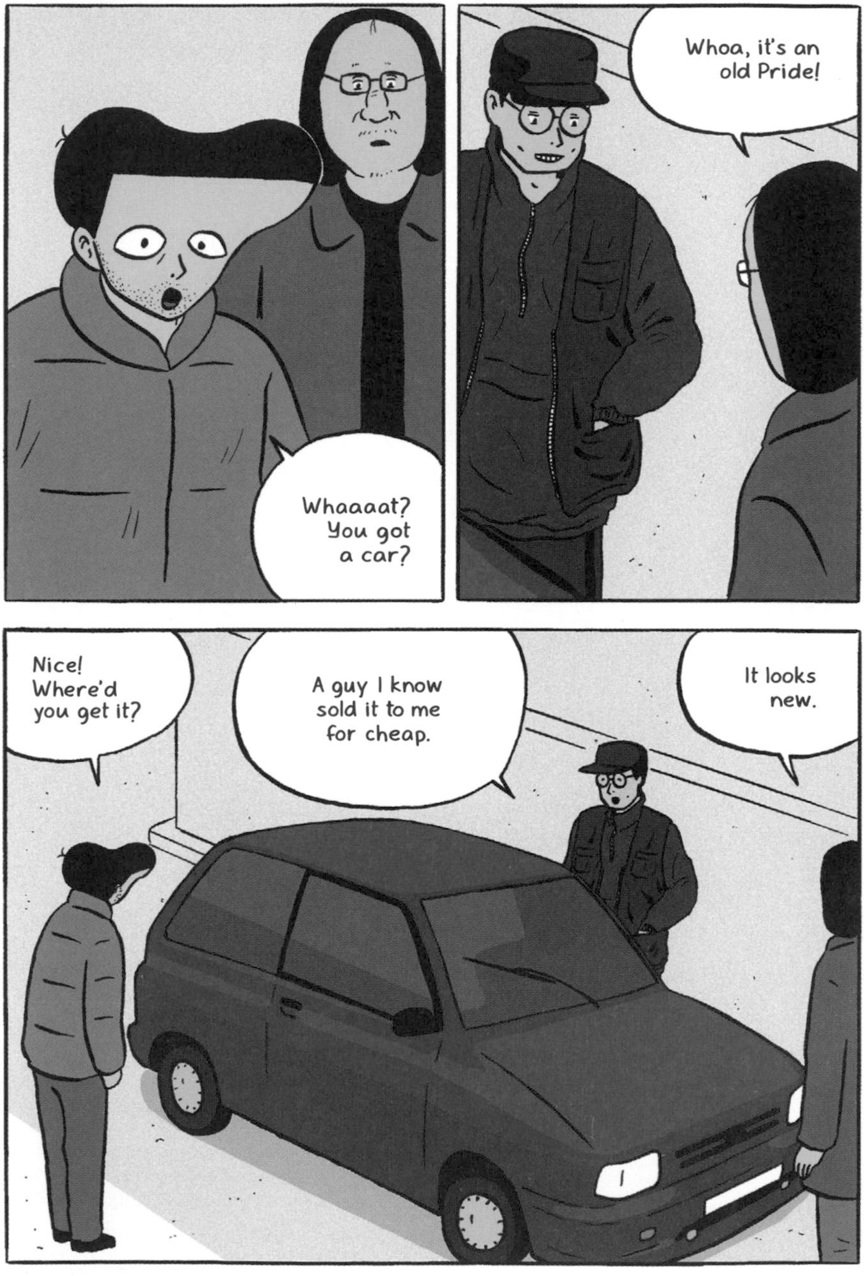
Whaaaat? You got a car?
Whoa, it's an old Pride!
Nice! Where'd you get it?
A guy I know sold it to me for cheap.
It looks new.

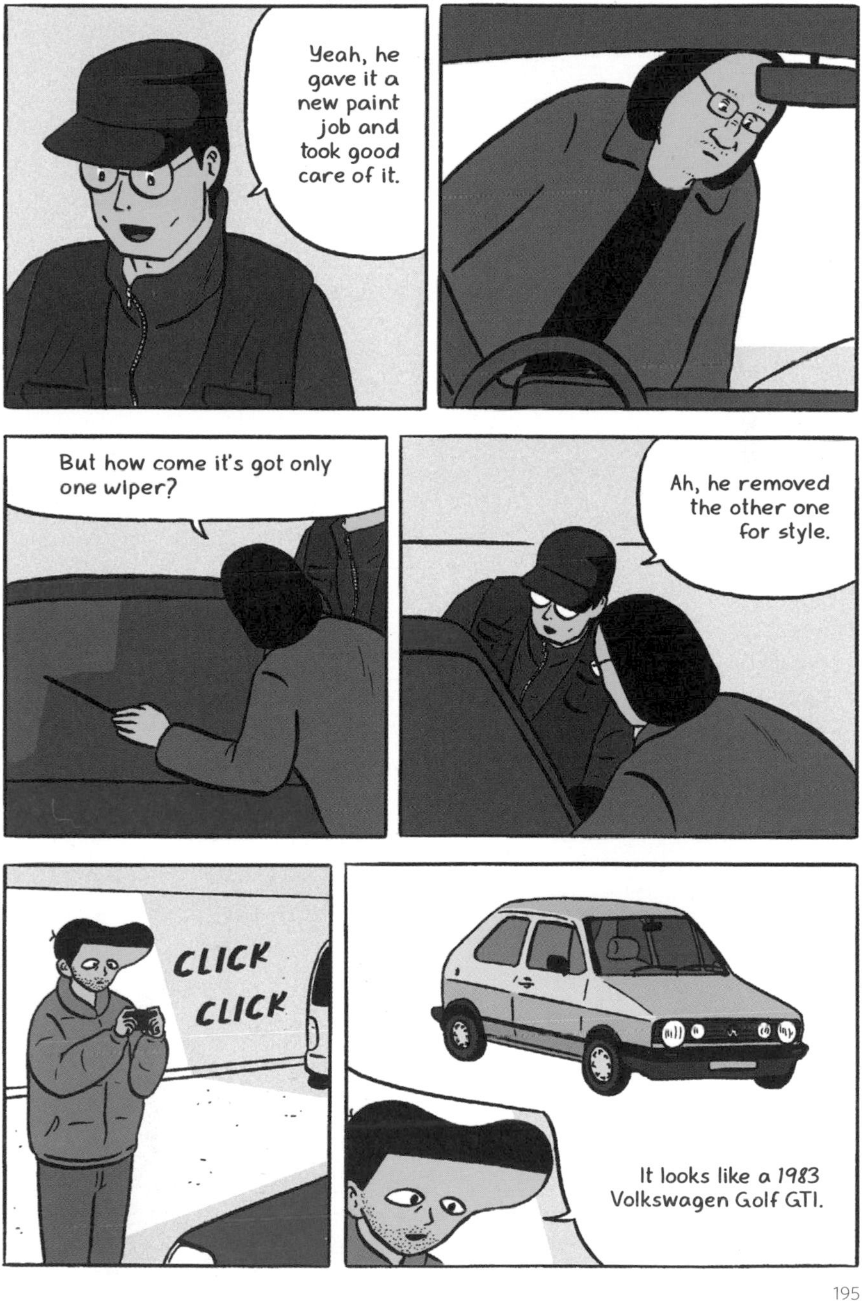
Yeah, he gave it a new paint job and took good care of it.
But how come it's got only one wiper?
Ah, he removed the other one for style.
CLICK
CLICK
It looks like a 1983 Volkswagen Golf GTI.

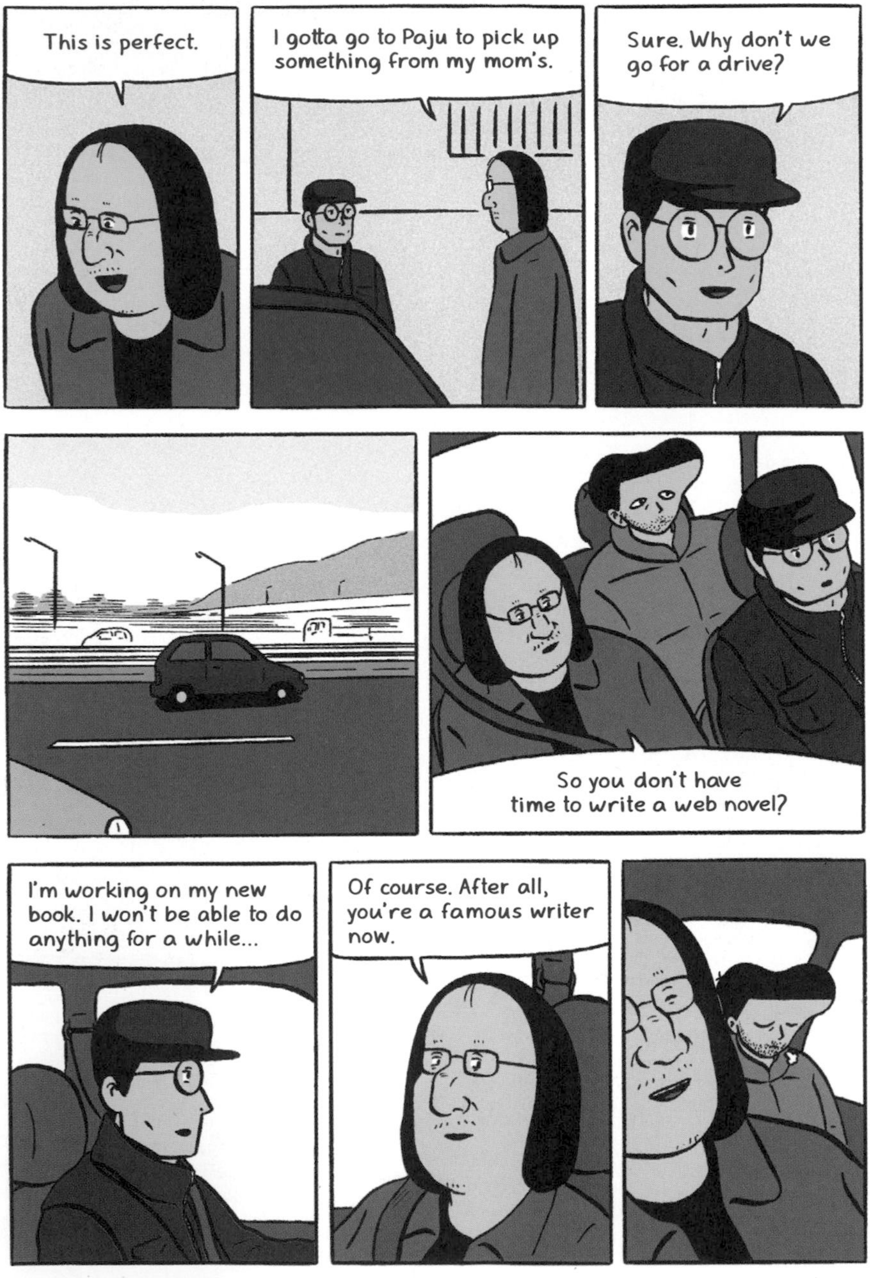
This is perfect.
I gotta go to Paju to pick up something from my mom's.
Sure. Why don't we go for a drive?
So you don't have time to write a web novel?
I'm working on my new book. I won't be able to do anything for a while...
Of course. After all, you're a famous writer now.

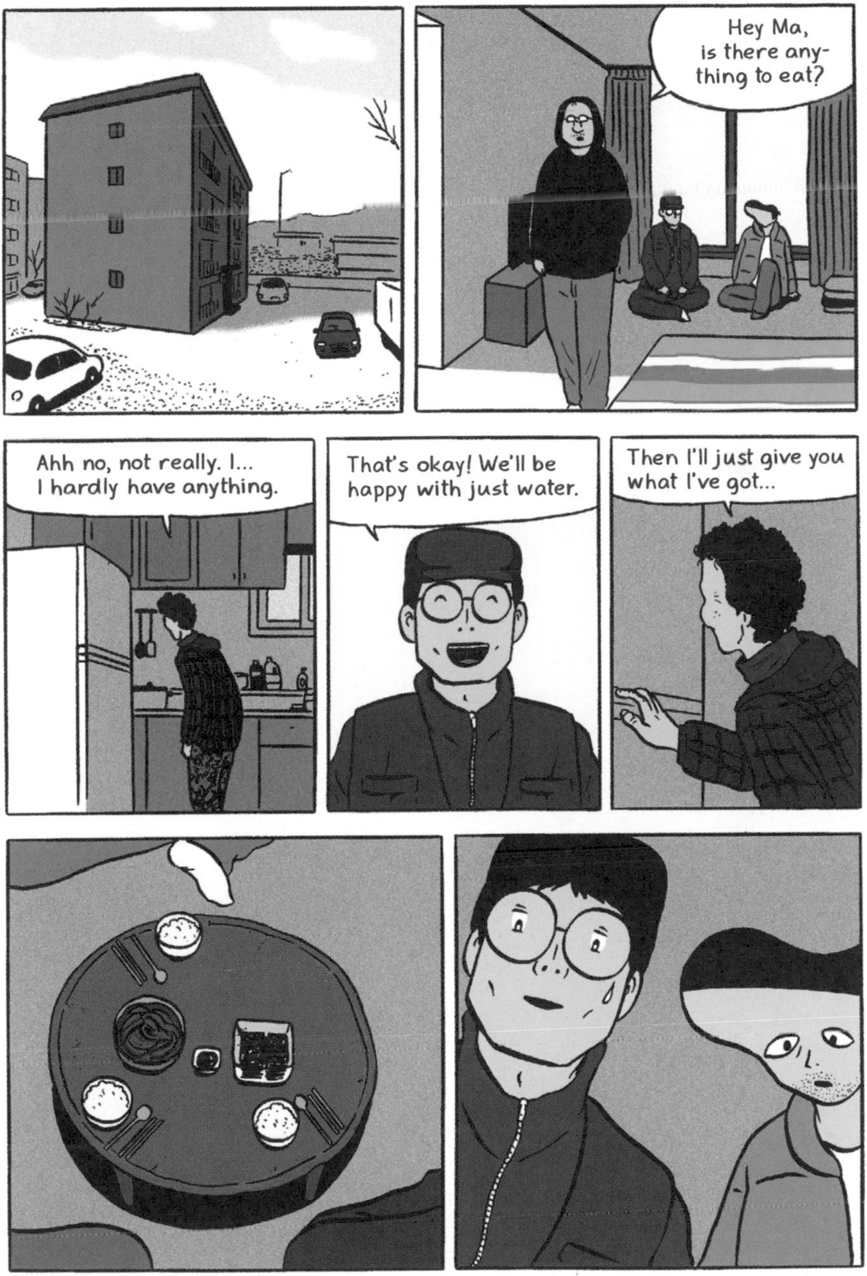
Hey Ma, is there anything to eat?
Ahh no, not really. I... I hardly have anything.
That's okay! We'll be happy with just water.
Then I'll just give you what I've got...

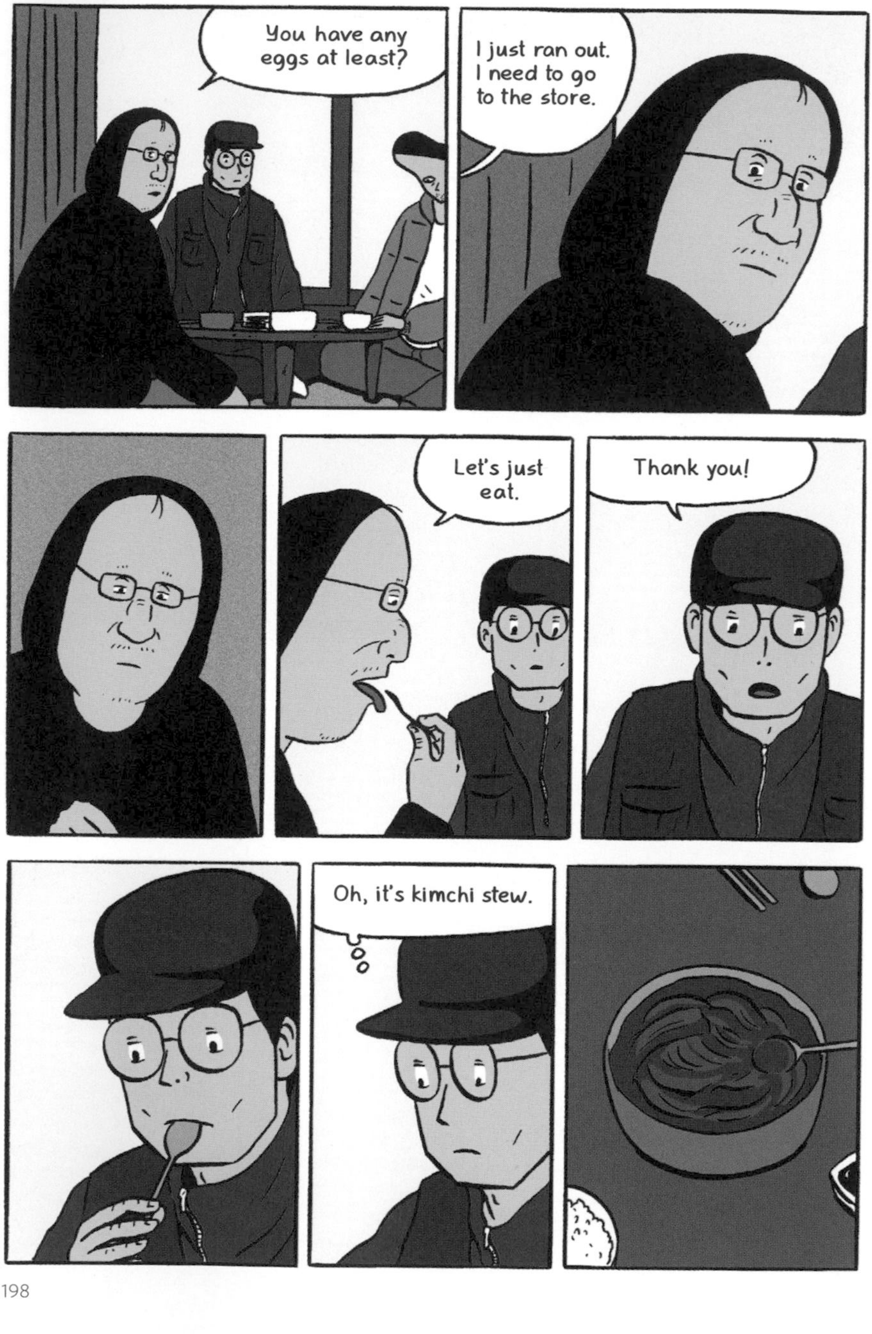
You have any eggs at least?
I just ran out. I need to go to the store.
Let's just eat.
Thank you!
Oh, it's kimchi stew.

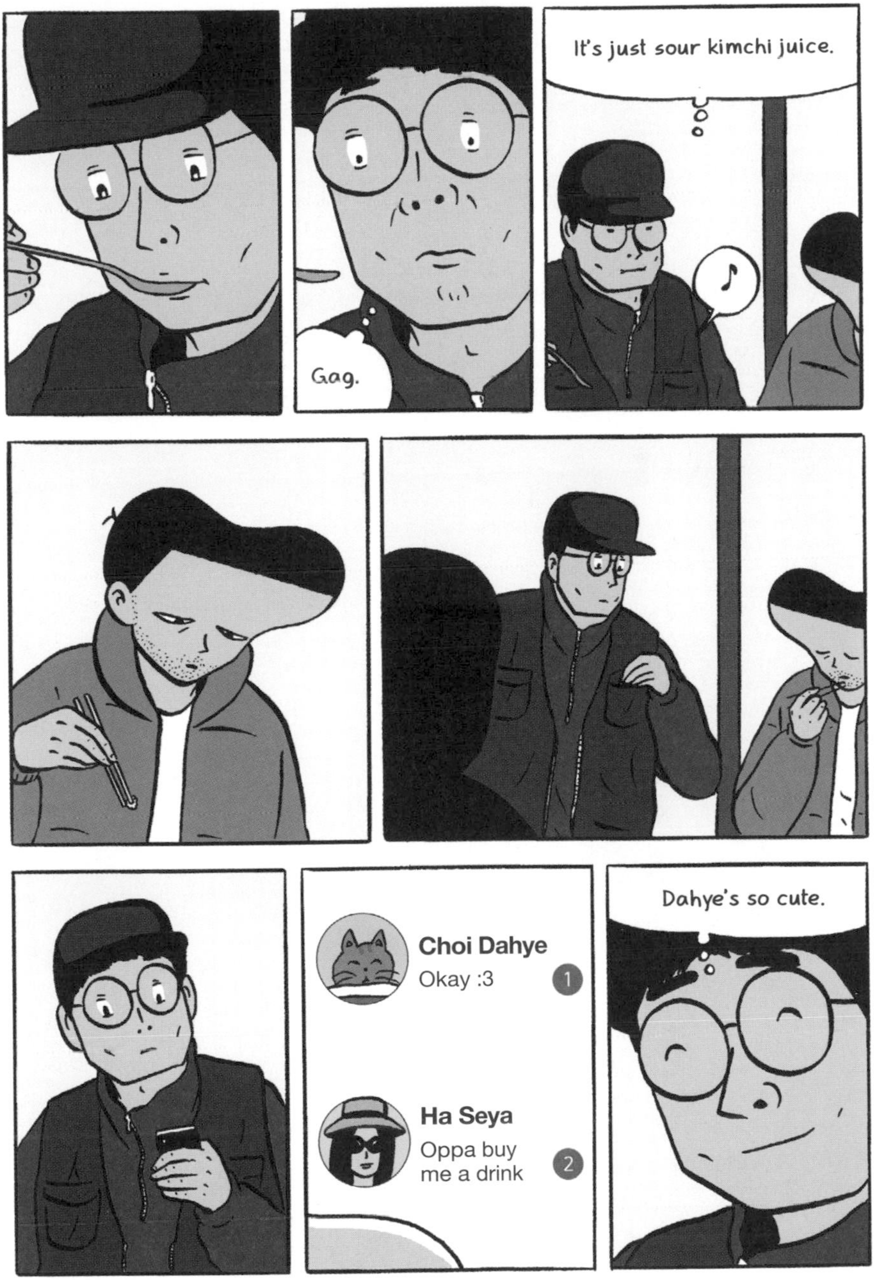
Gag.
It's just sour kimchi juice.
♪
Choi Dahye
Okay :3
1
Ha Seya
Oppa buy me a drink
2
Dahye's so cute.

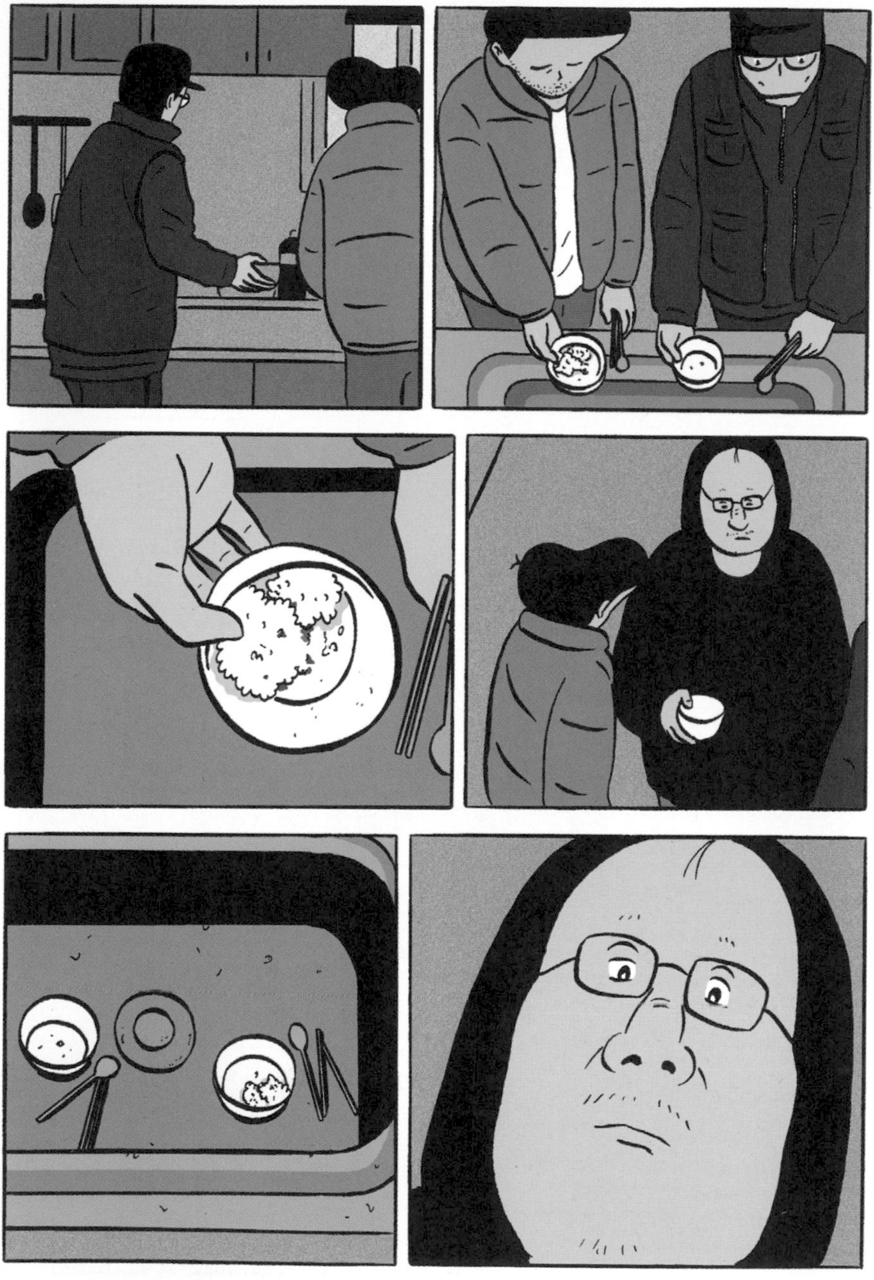

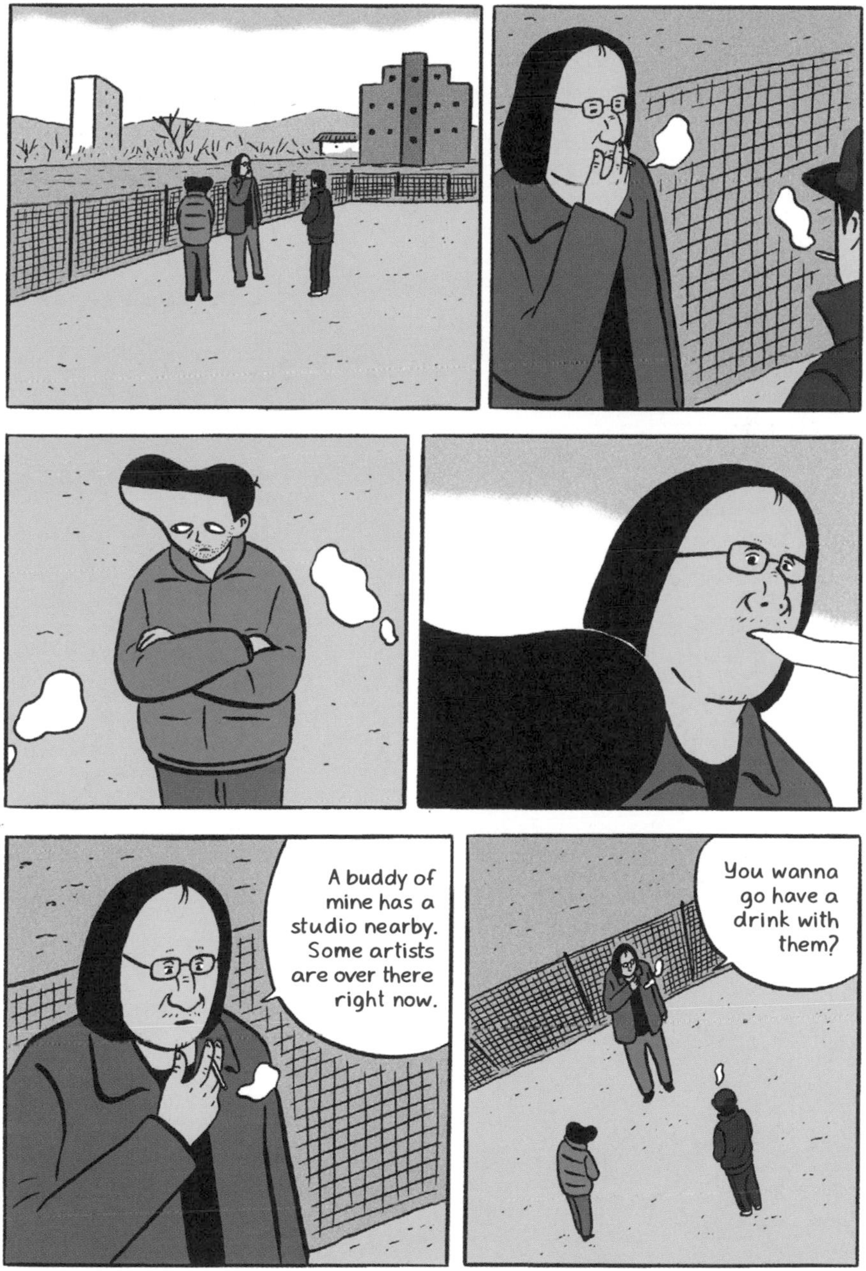
A buddy of mine has a studio nearby. Some artists are over there right now.
You wanna go have a drink with them?

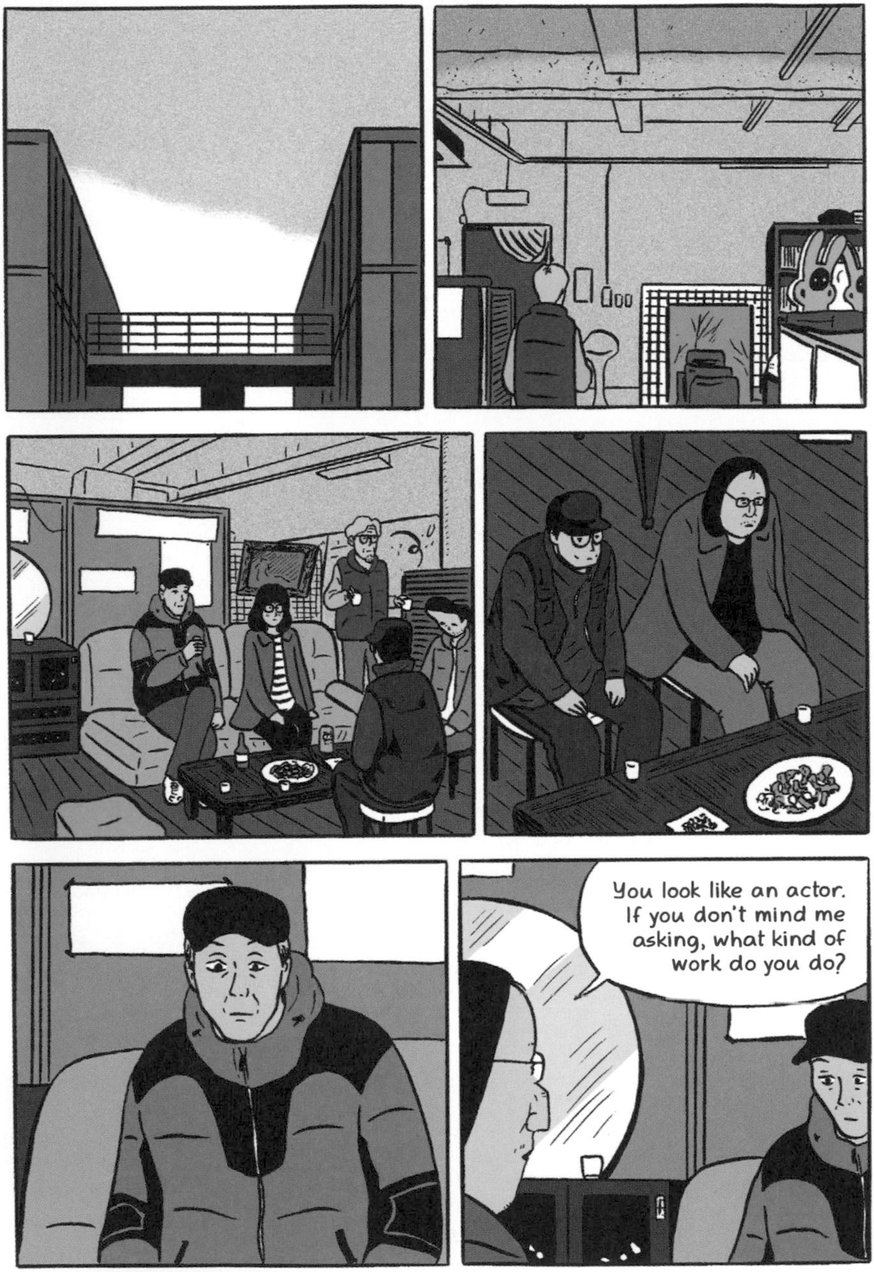
You look like an actor. If you don't mind me asking, what kind of work do you do?

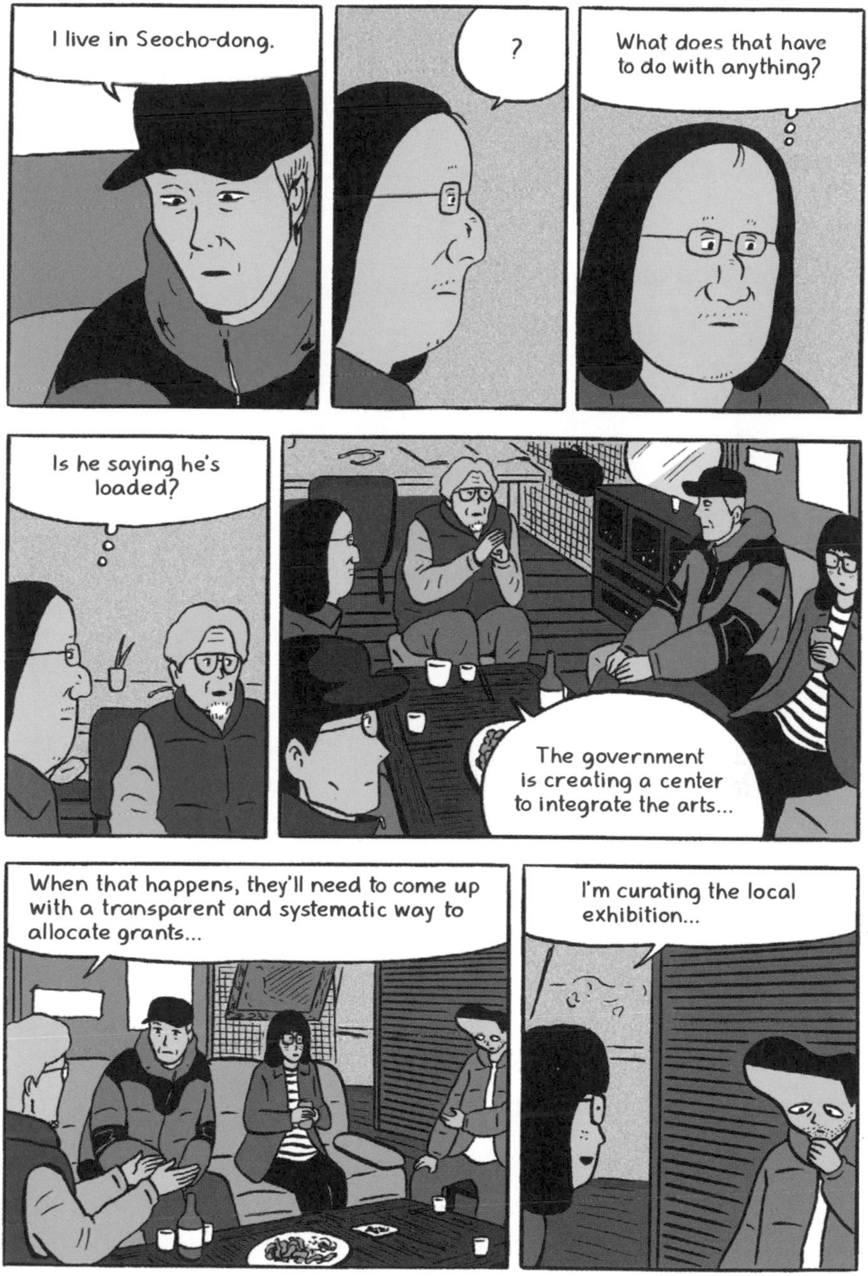
I live in Seocho-dong.
?
What does that have to do with anything?
Is he saying he's loaded?
The government is creating a center to integrate the arts...
When that happens, they'll need to come up with a transparent and systematic way to allocate grants...
I'm curating the local exhibition...

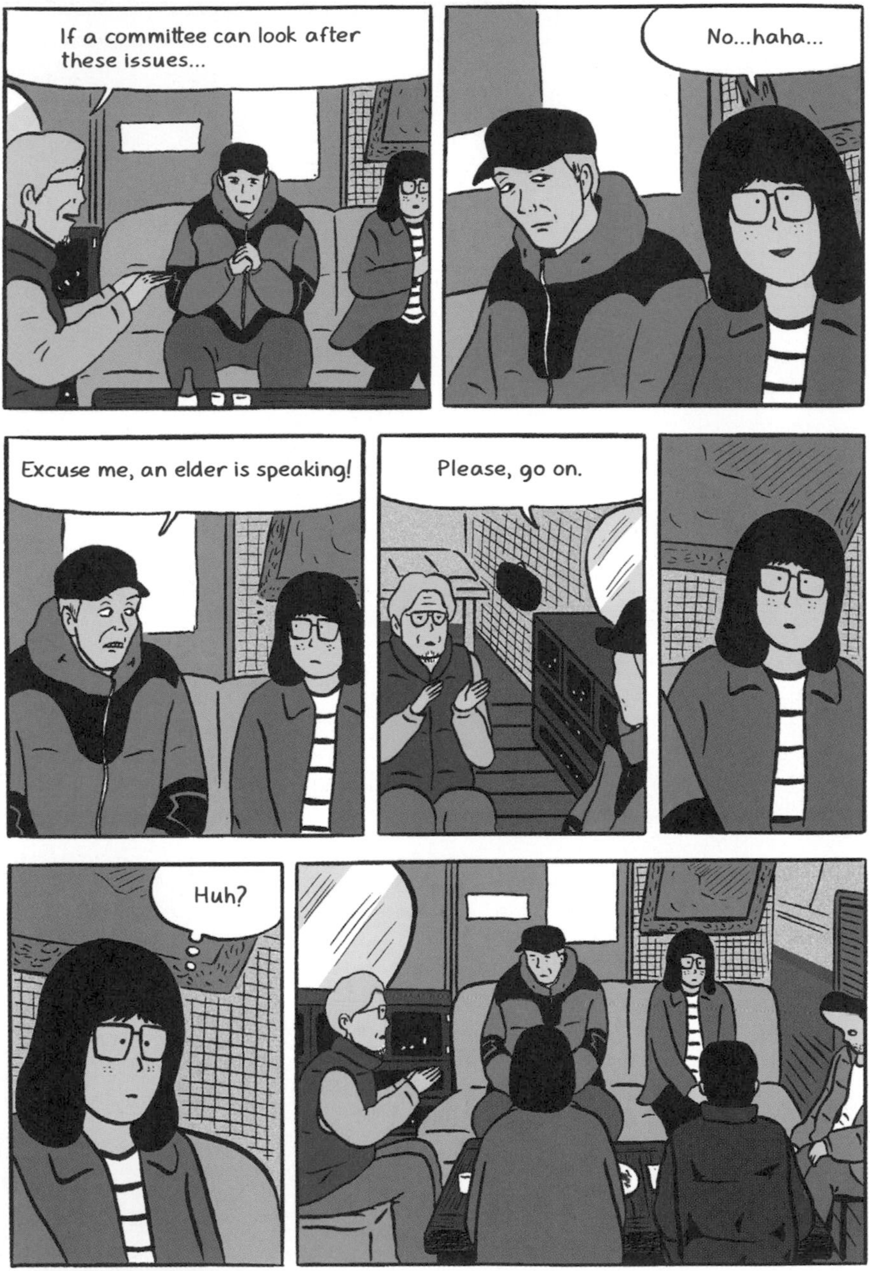
If a committee can look after these issues...
No...haha...
Excuse me, an elder is speaking!
Please, go on.
Huh?

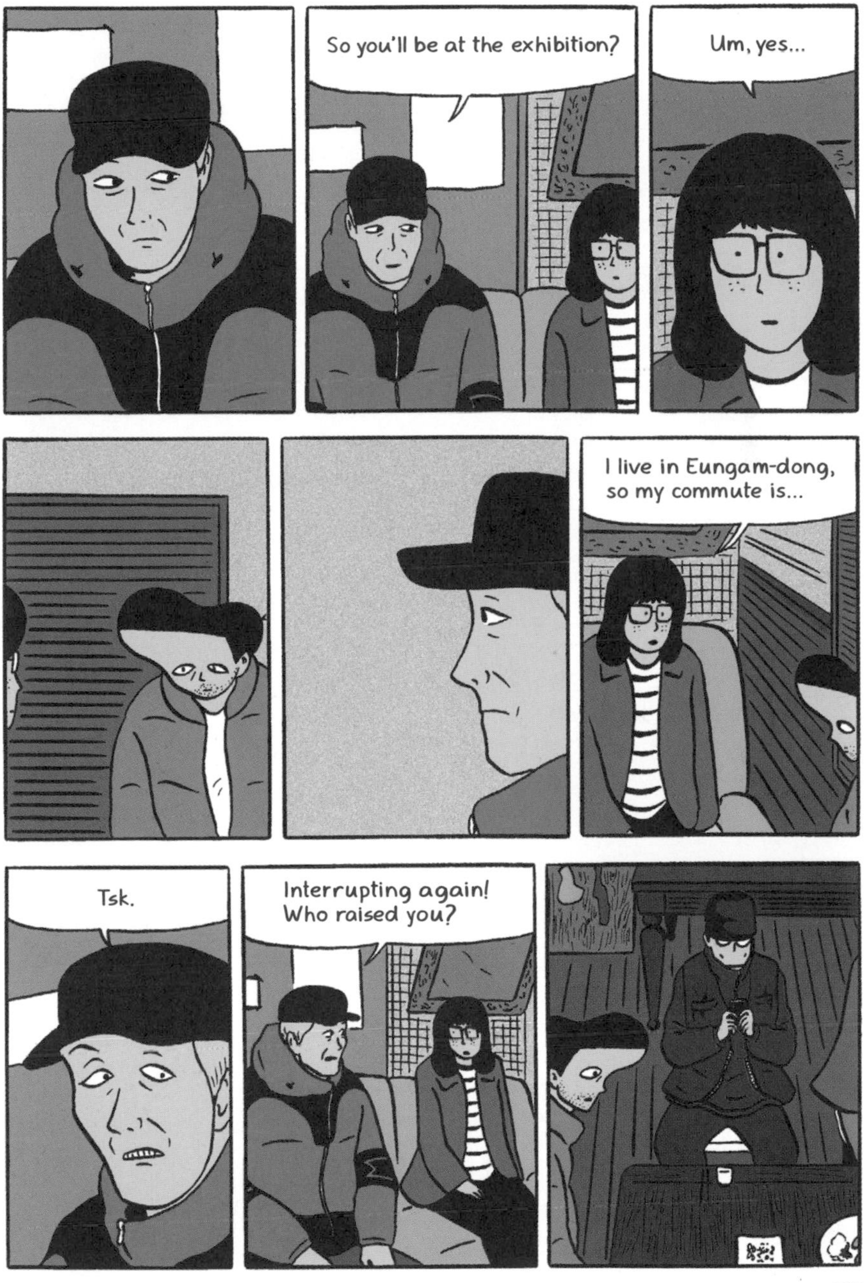
So you'll be at the exhibition?
Um, yes...
I live in Eungam-dong, so my commute is...
Tsk.
Interrupting again! Who raised you?

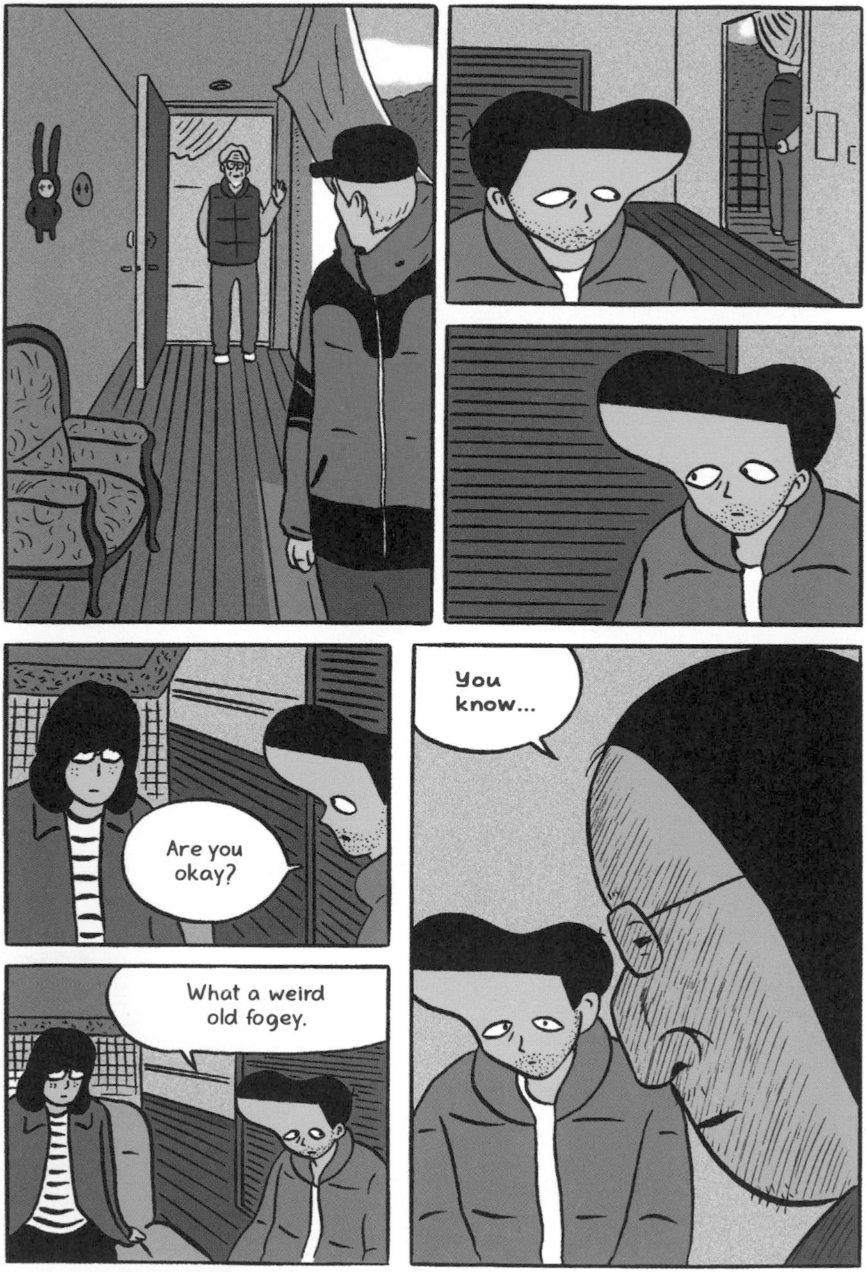
Are you okay?
What a weird old fogey.
You know...

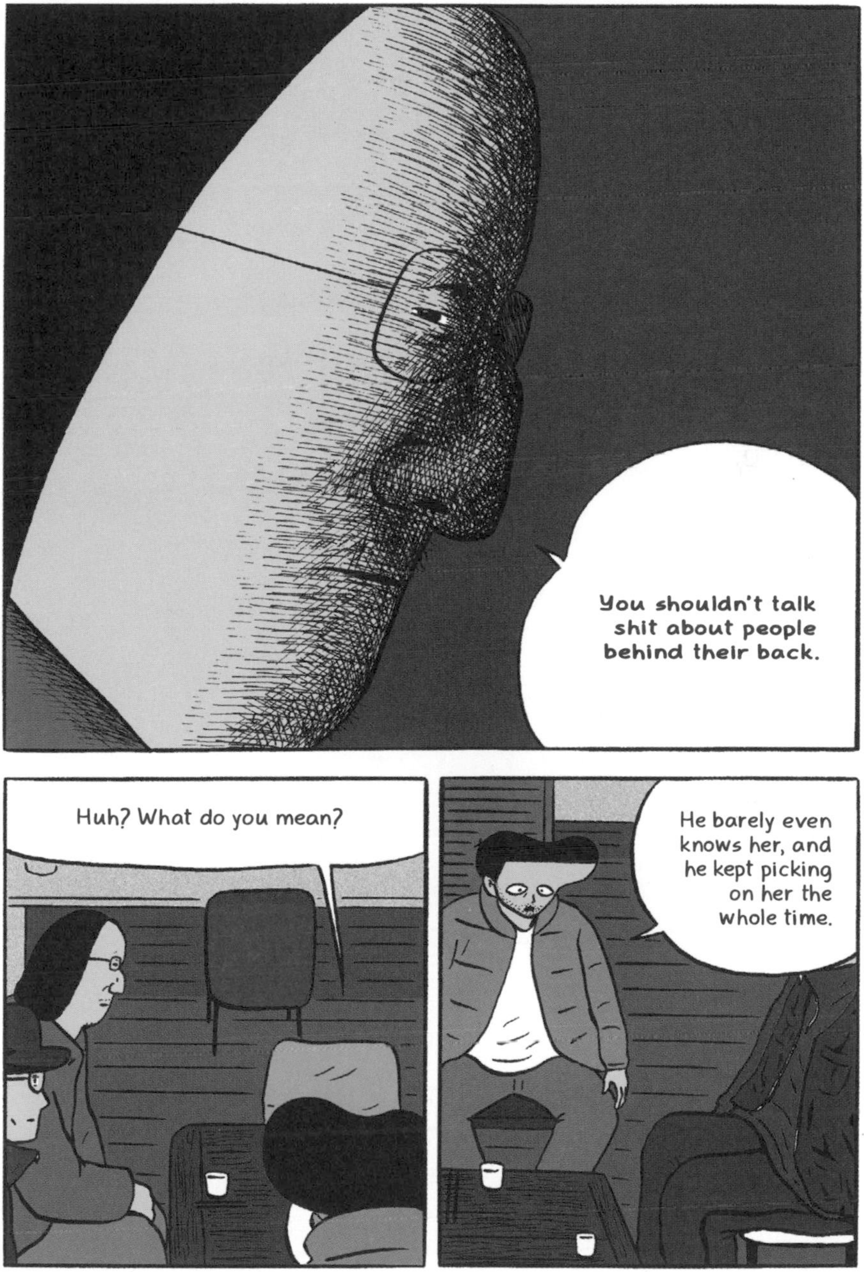
You shouldn't talk shit about people behind their back.
Huh? What do you mean?
He barely even knows her, and he kept picking on her the whole time.

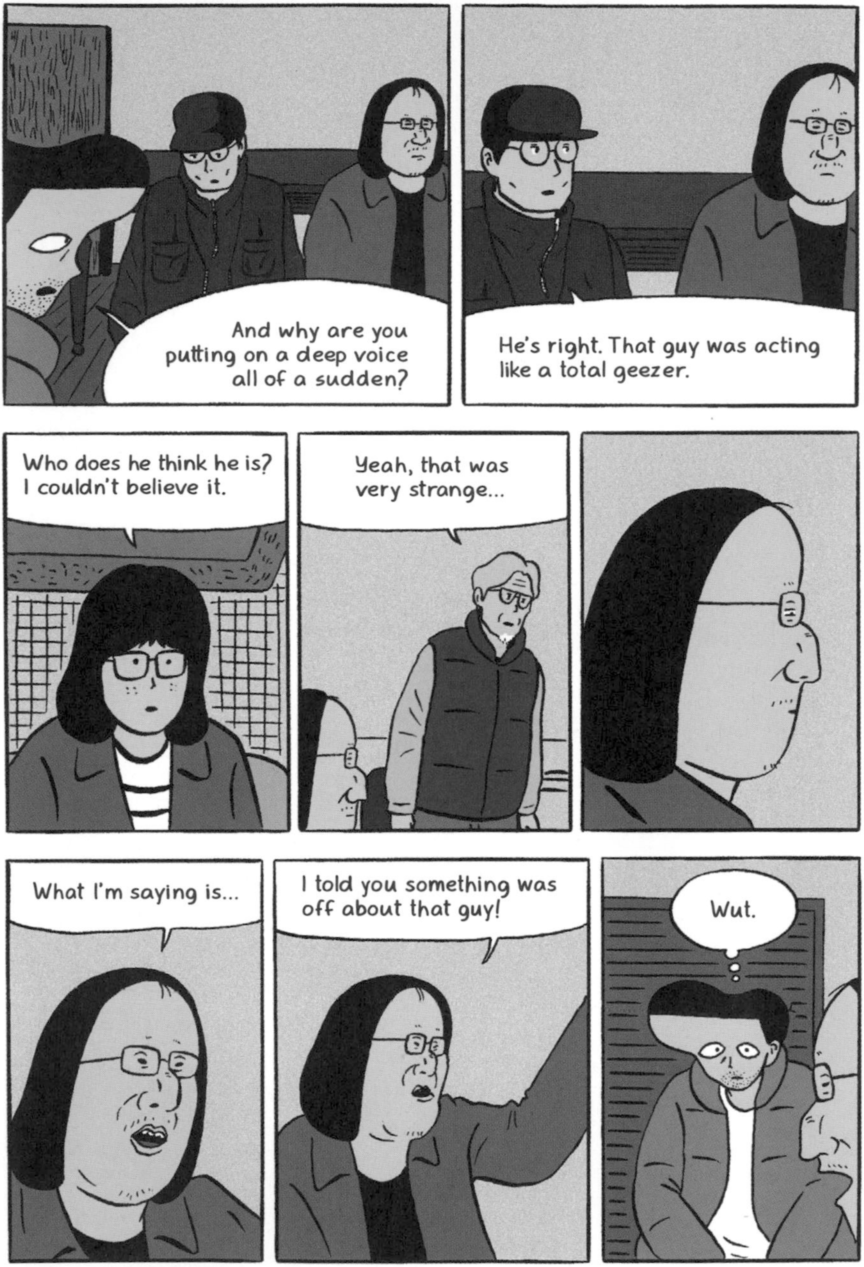
And why are you putting on a deep voice all of a sudden?
He's right. That guy was acting like a total geezer.
Who does he think he is? I couldn't believe it.
Yeah, that was very strange...
What I'm saying is...
I told you something was off about that guy!
Wut.

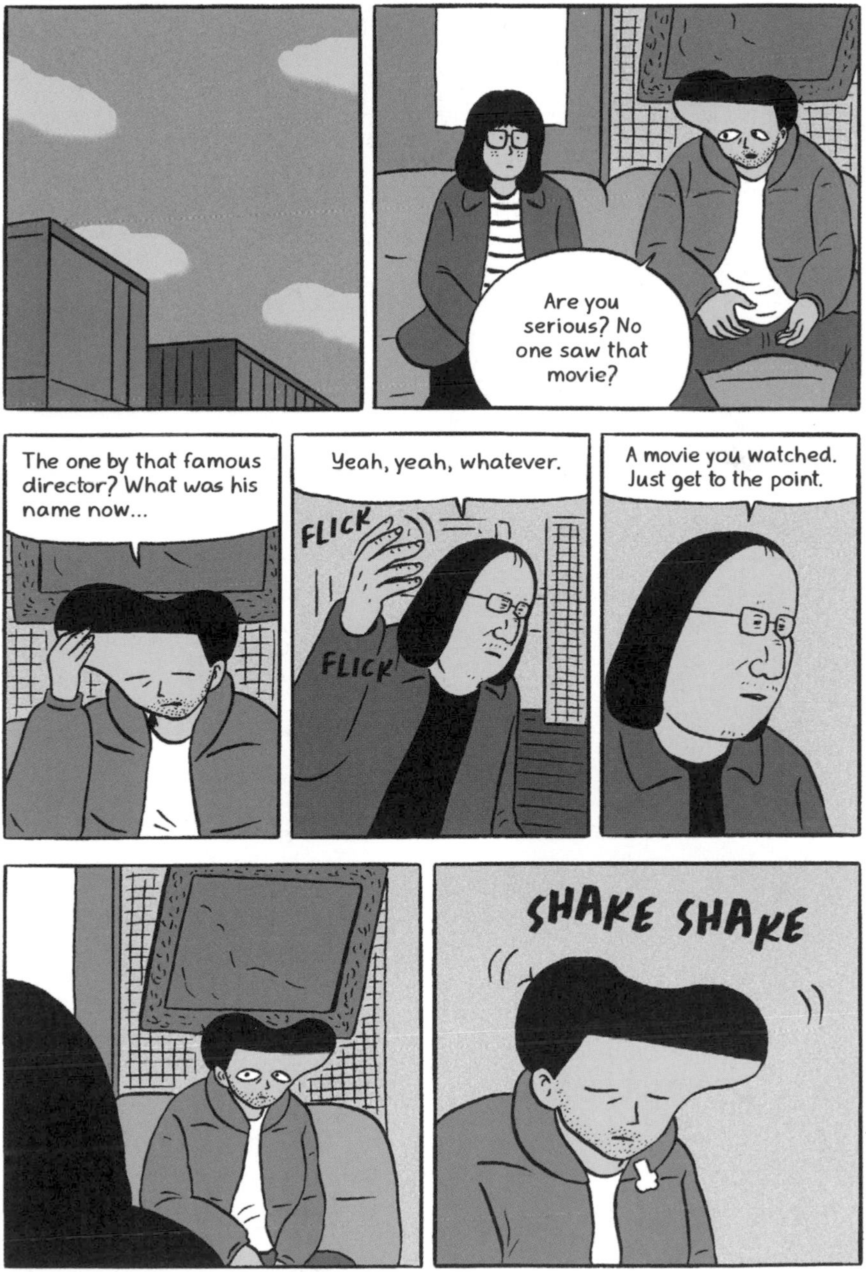
Are you serious? No one saw that movie?
The one by that famous director? What was his name now...
Yeah, yeah, whatever.
FLICK
FLICK
A movie you watched. Just get to the point.
SHAKE SHAKE

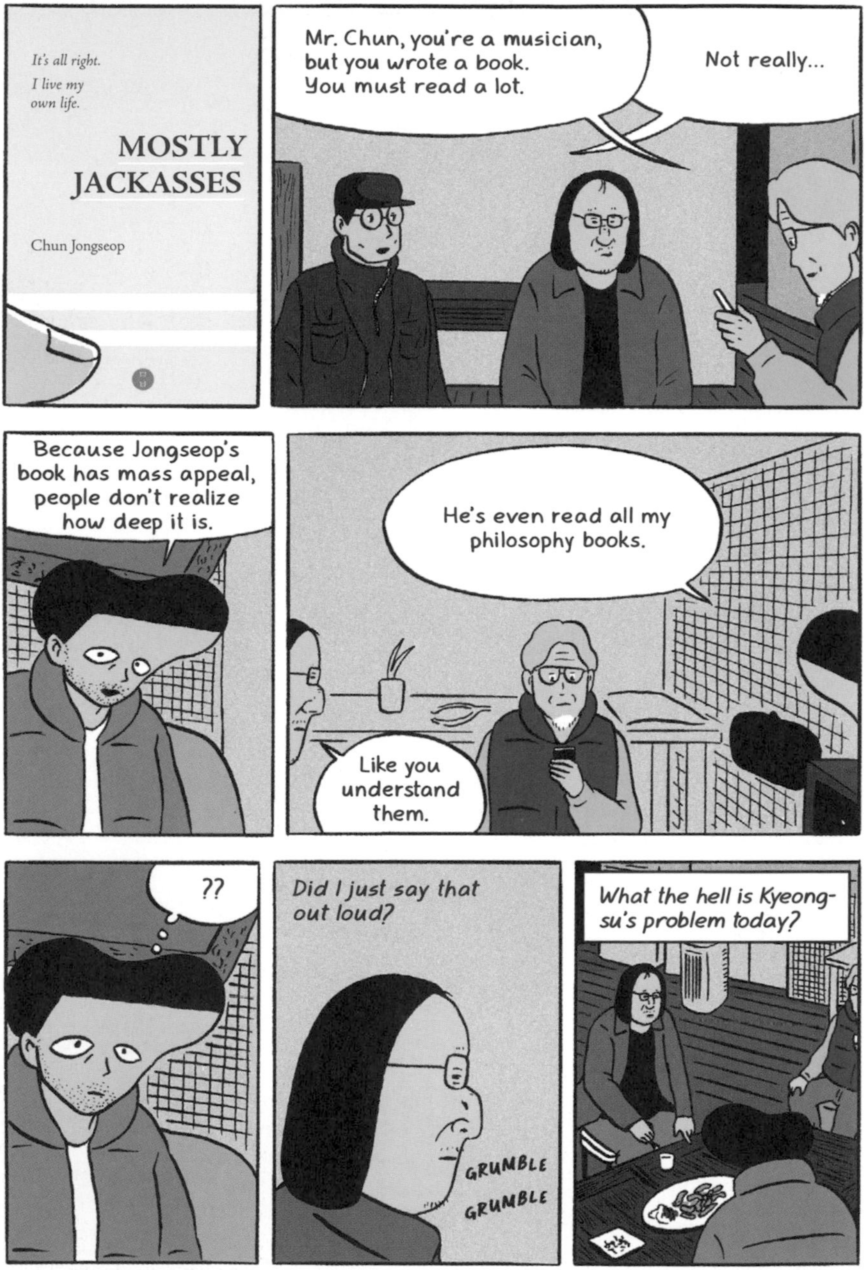
It's all right.
I live my
own life.
MOSTLY
JACKASSES
Chun Jongseop
Mr. Chun, you're a musician, but you wrote a book. You must read a lot.
Not really...
Because Jongseop's book has mass appeal, people don't realize how deep it is.
He's even read all my philosophy books.
Like you understand them.
??
Did I just say that out loud?
GRUMBLE
GRUMBLE
What the hell is Kyeong-su's problem today?

IT'S SPRINGTIME FOR JONGSEOP

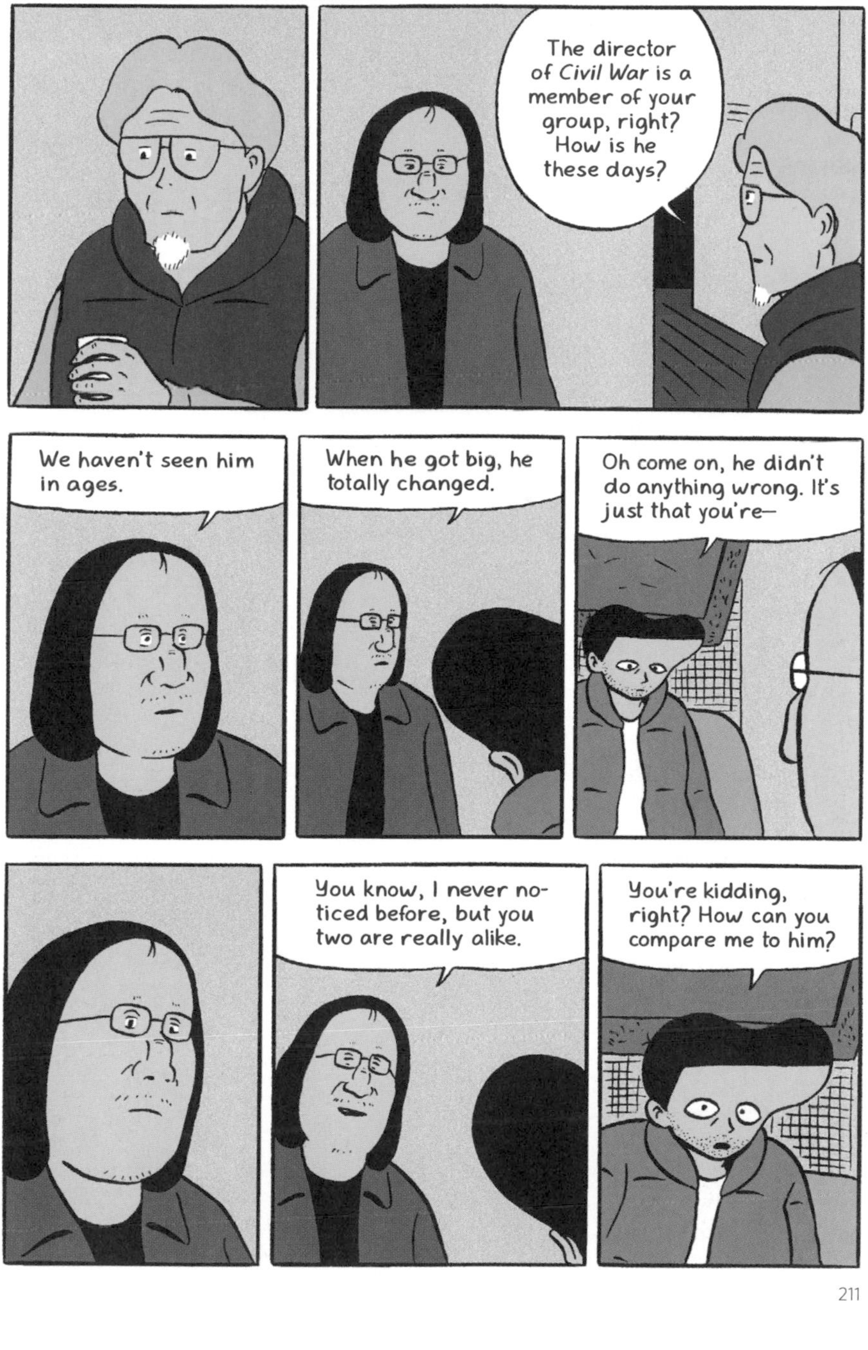

The director of *Civil War* is a member of your group, right? How is he these days?
We haven't seen him in ages.
When he got big, he totally changed.
Oh come on, he didn't do anything wrong. It's just that you're—
You know, I never noticed before, but you two are really alike.
You're kidding, right? How can you compare me to him?

What the fuck?

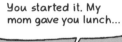

What's your problem?

You started it. My mom gave you lunch...

but you didn't even finish it, you arrogant little jerk!

Especially when Jongseop said he was happy with just water!

Jeez, when are they going to grow up?

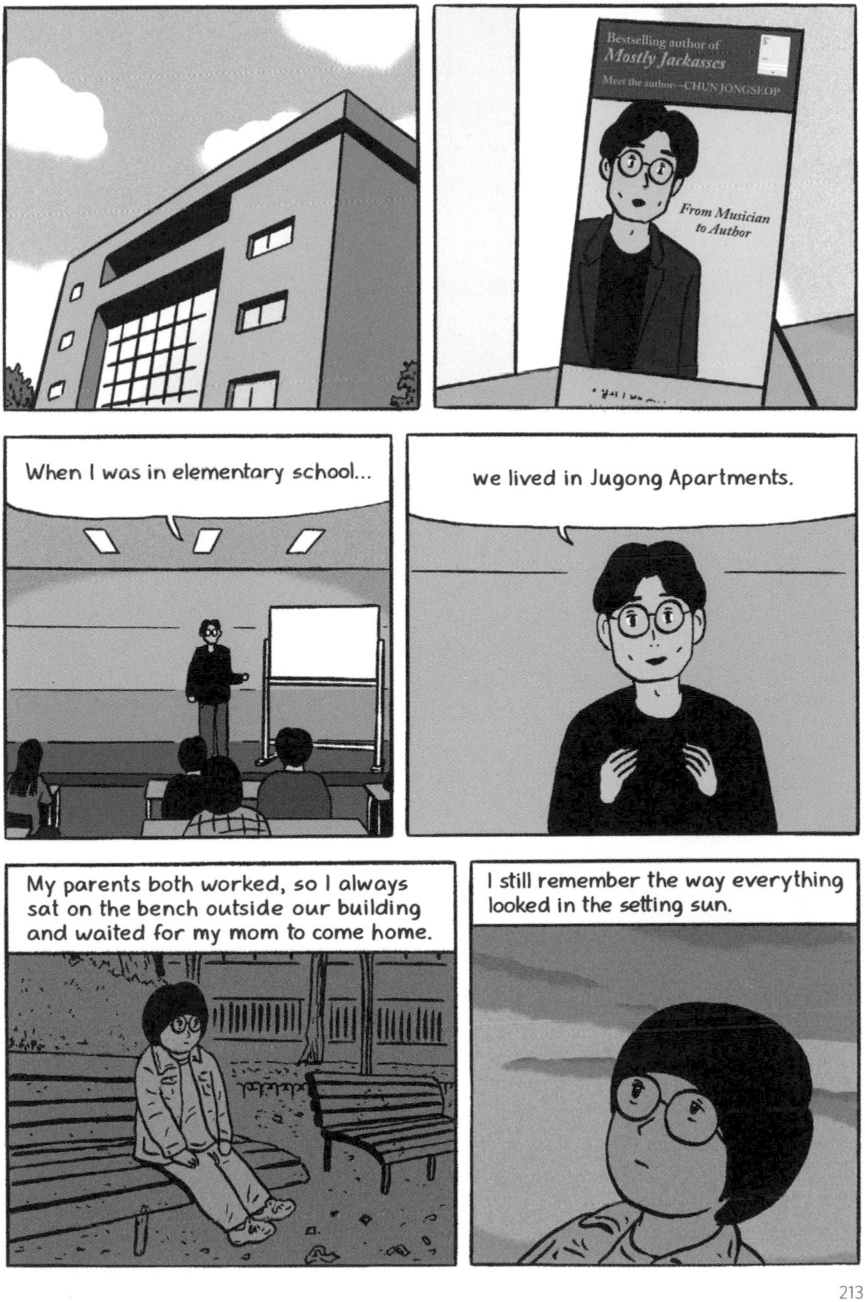
Bestselling author of
Mostly Jackasses
Meet the author—CHUN JONGSEOP
From Musician to Author
When I was in elementary school...
we lived in Jugong Apartments.
My parents both worked, so I always sat on the bench outside our building and waited for my mom to come home.
I still remember the way everything looked in the setting sun.

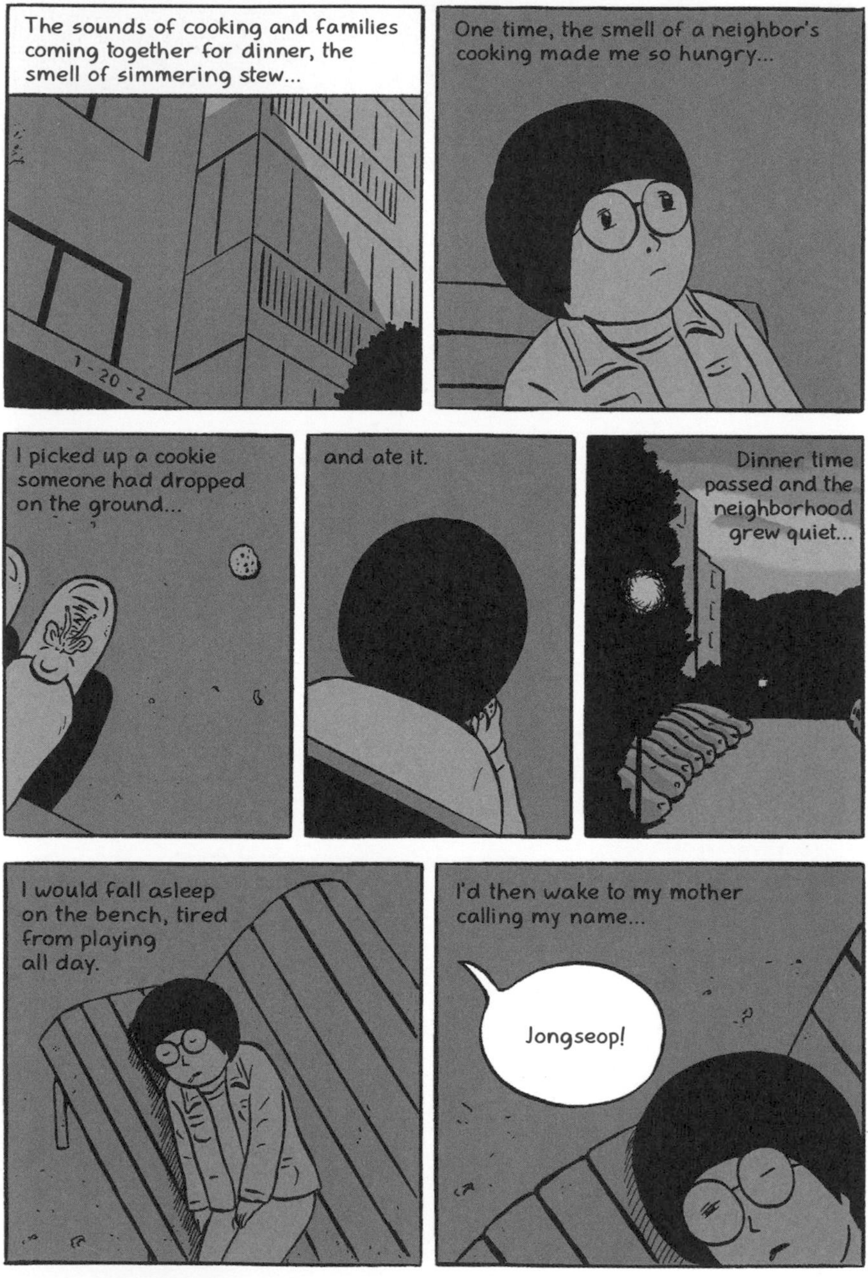
The sounds of cooking and families coming together for dinner, the smell of simmering stew...
1-20-2
One time, the smell of a neighbor's cooking made me so hungry...
I picked up a cookie someone had dropped on the ground...
and ate it.
Dinner time passed and the neighborhood grew quiet...
I would fall asleep on the bench, tired from playing all day.
I'd then wake to my mother calling my name...
Jongseop!

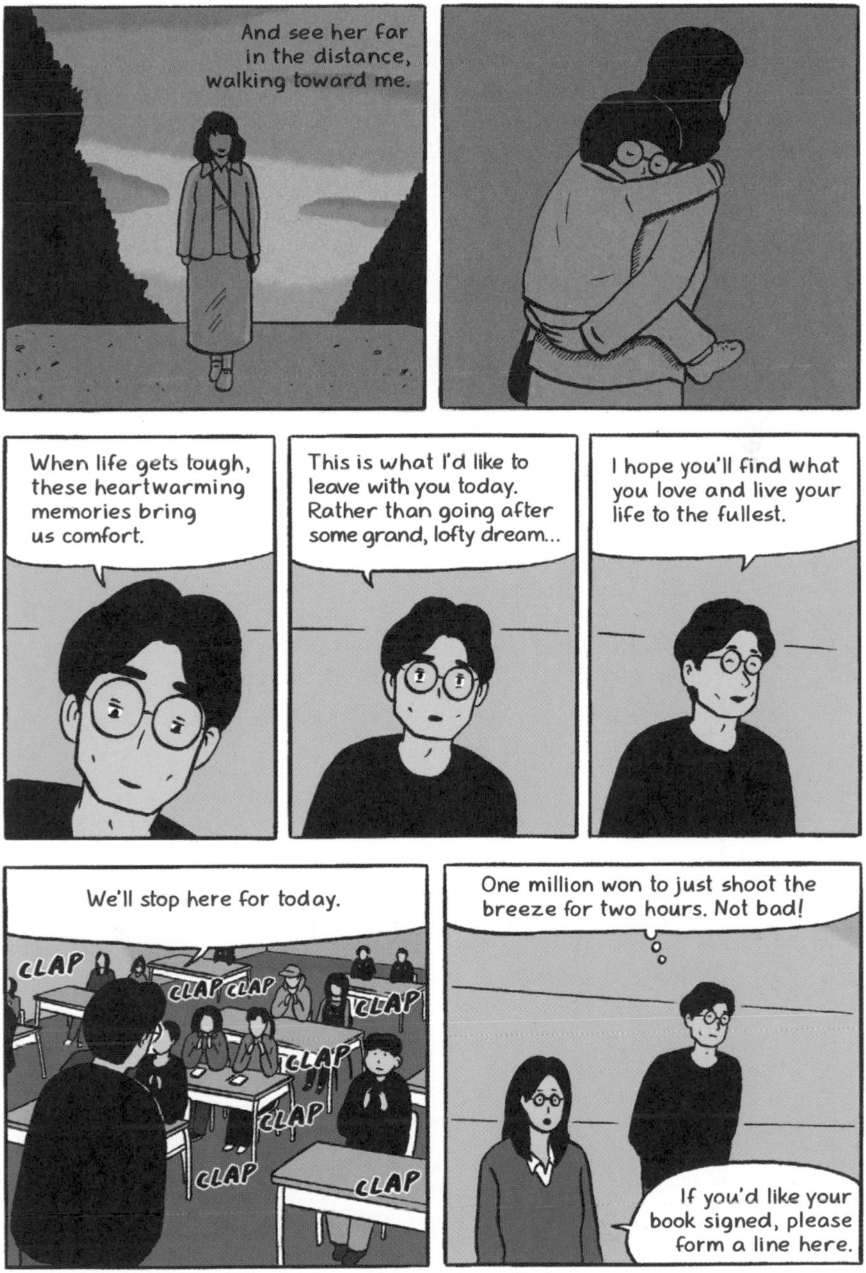
And see her far in the distance, walking toward me.
When life gets tough, these heartwarming memories bring us comfort.
This is what I'd like to leave with you today. Rather than going after some grand, lofty dream...
I hope you'll find what you love and live your life to the fullest.
We'll stop here for today.
CLAP
CLAP CLAP
CLAP
CLAP
CLAP
CLAP
CLAP
One million won to just shoot the breeze for two hours. Not bad!
If you'd like your book signed, please form a line here.

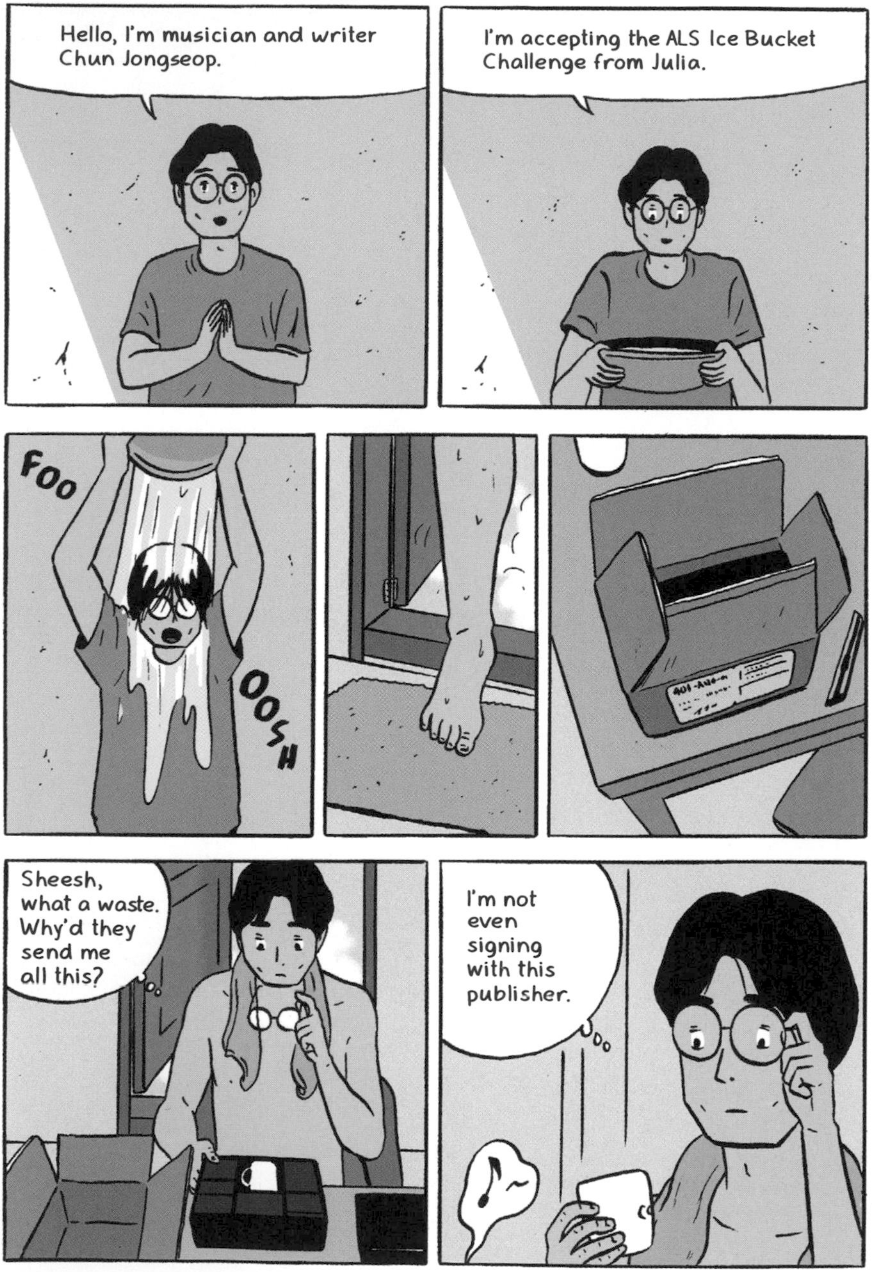
Hello, I'm musician and writer Chun Jongseop.
I'm accepting the ALS Ice Bucket Challenge from Julia.
FOO
OOSH
Sheesh, what a waste. Why'd they send me all this?
I'm not even signing with this publisher.

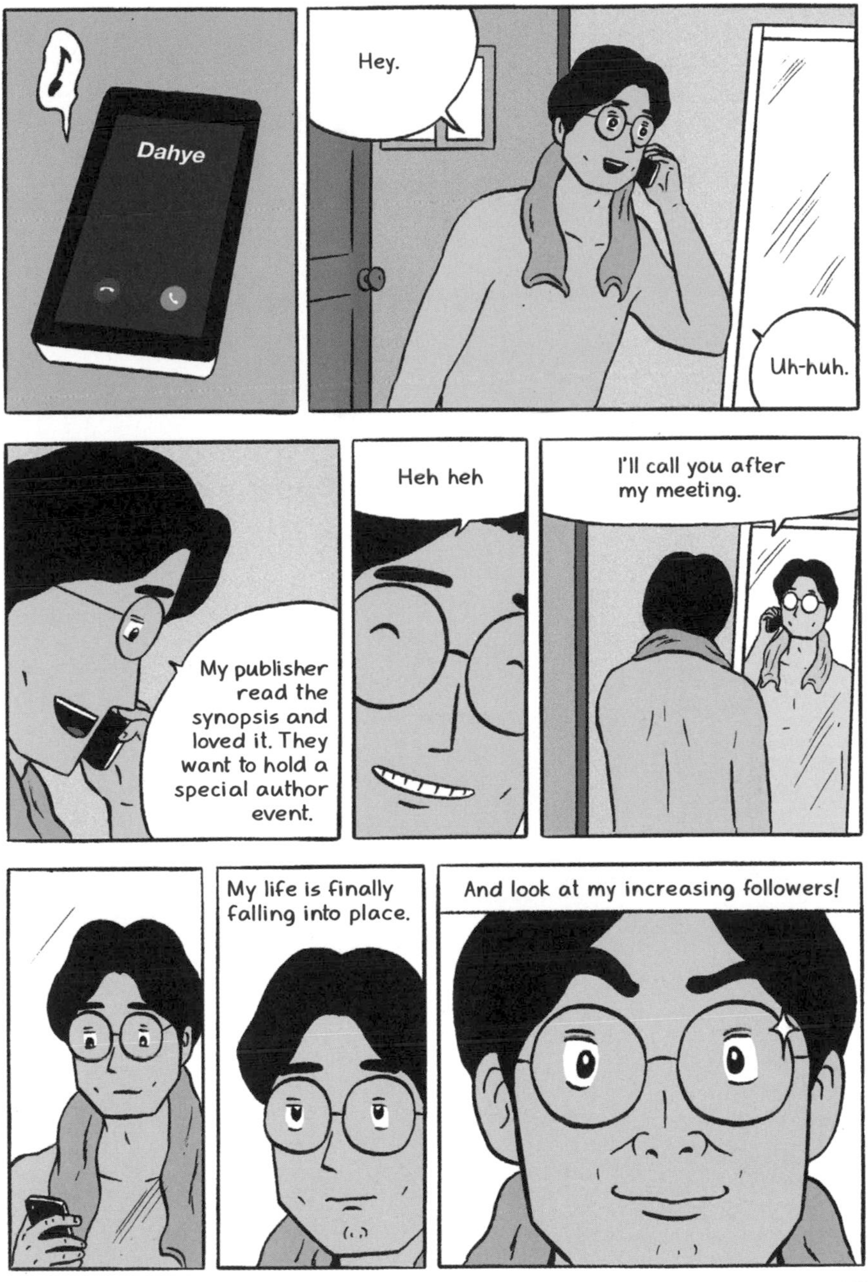
Dahye
Hey.
Uh-huh.
My publisher read the synopsis and loved it. They want to hold a special author event.
Heh heh
I'll call you after my meeting.
My life is finally falling into place.
And look at my increasing followers!

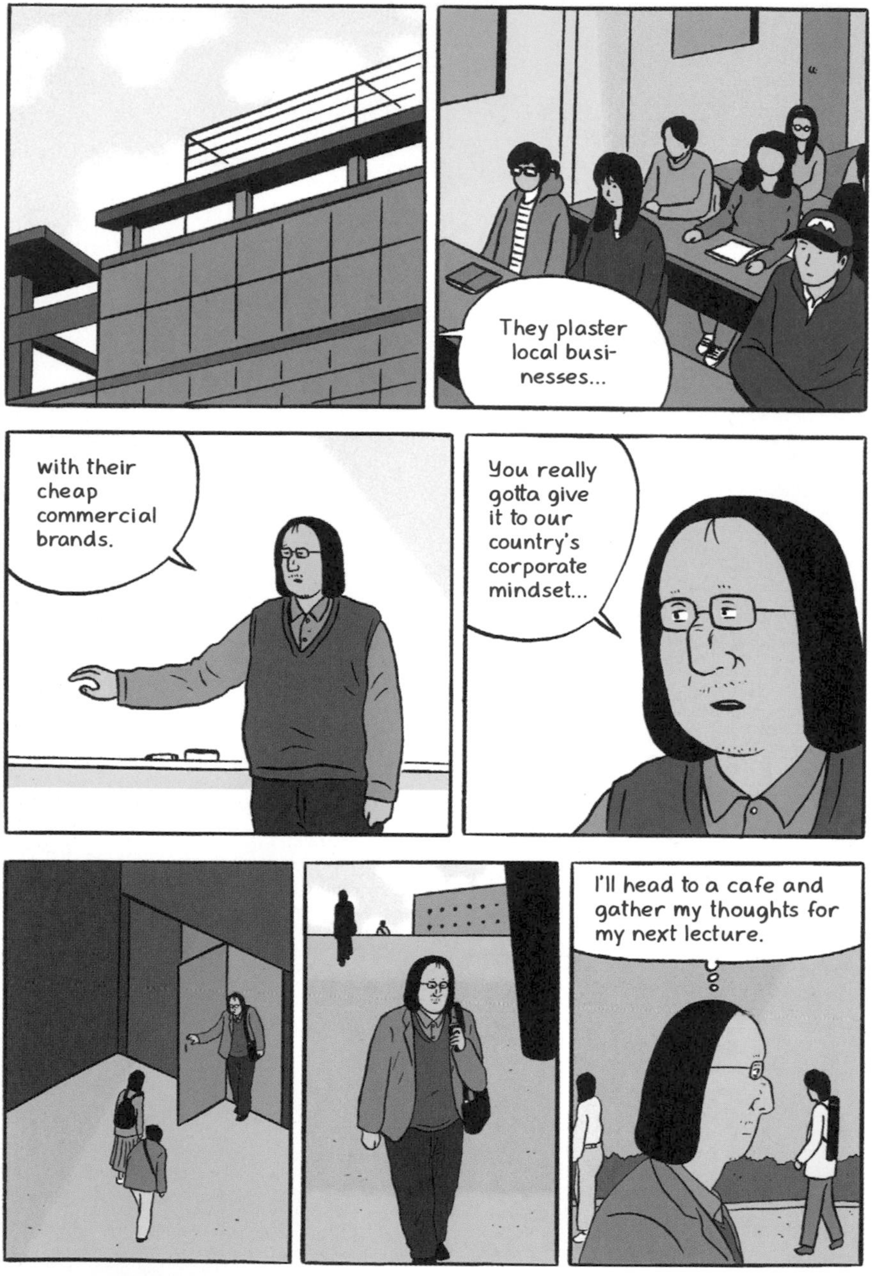
They plaster local businesses...
with their cheap commercial brands.
You really gotta give it to our country's corporate mindset...
I'll head to a cafe and gather my thoughts for my next lecture.

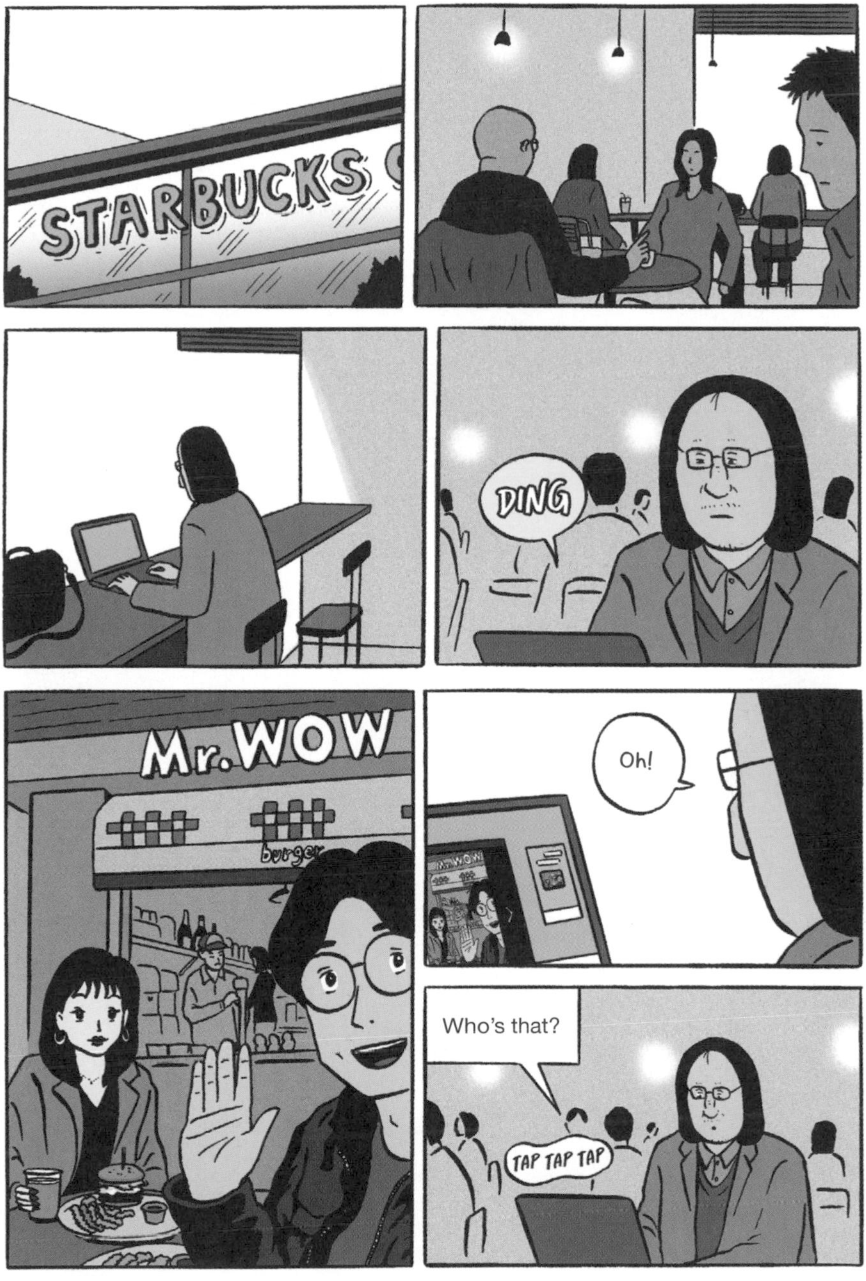
STARBUCKS
DING
Mr.WOW
burger
Oh!
Who's that?
TAP TAP TAP

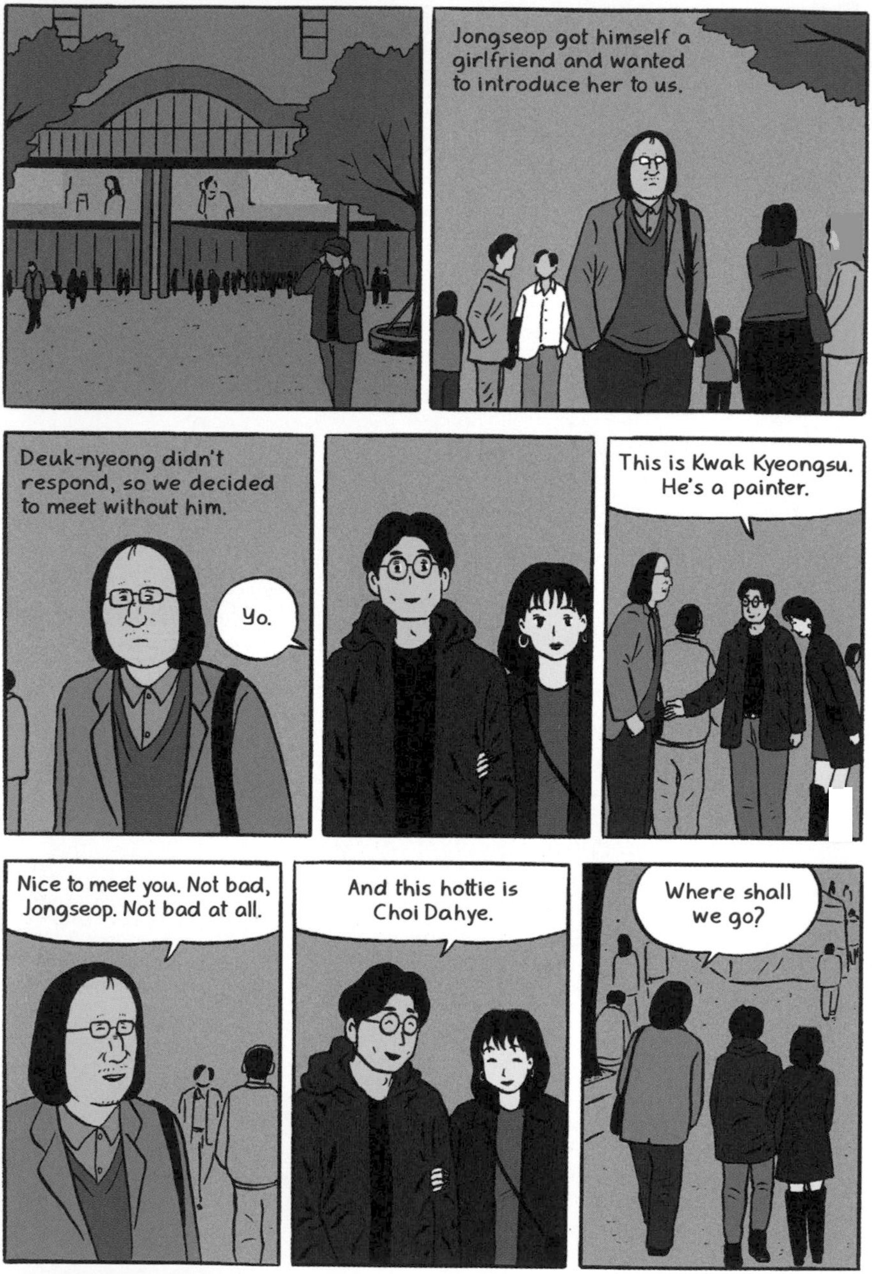
Jongseop got himself a girlfriend and wanted to introduce her to us.
Deuk-nyeong didn't respond, so we decided to meet without him.
Yo.
This is Kwak Kyeongsu. He's a painter.
Nice to meet you. Not bad, Jongseop. Not bad at all.
And this hottie is Choi Dahye.
Where shall we go?

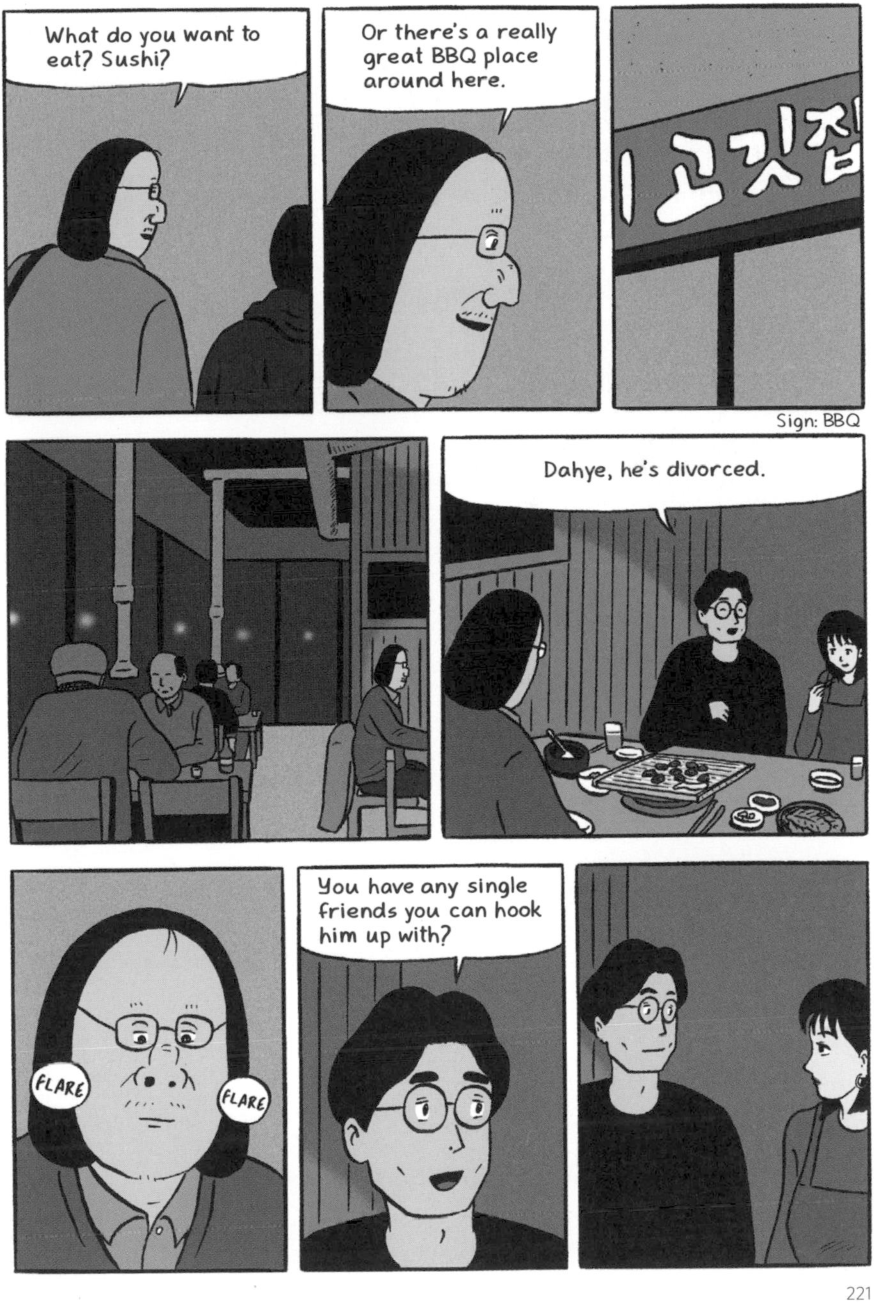

What do you want to eat? Sushi?
Or there's a really great BBQ place around here.
고깃집
Sign: BBQ
Dahye, he's divorced.
FLARE
FLARE
You have any single friends you can hook him up with?

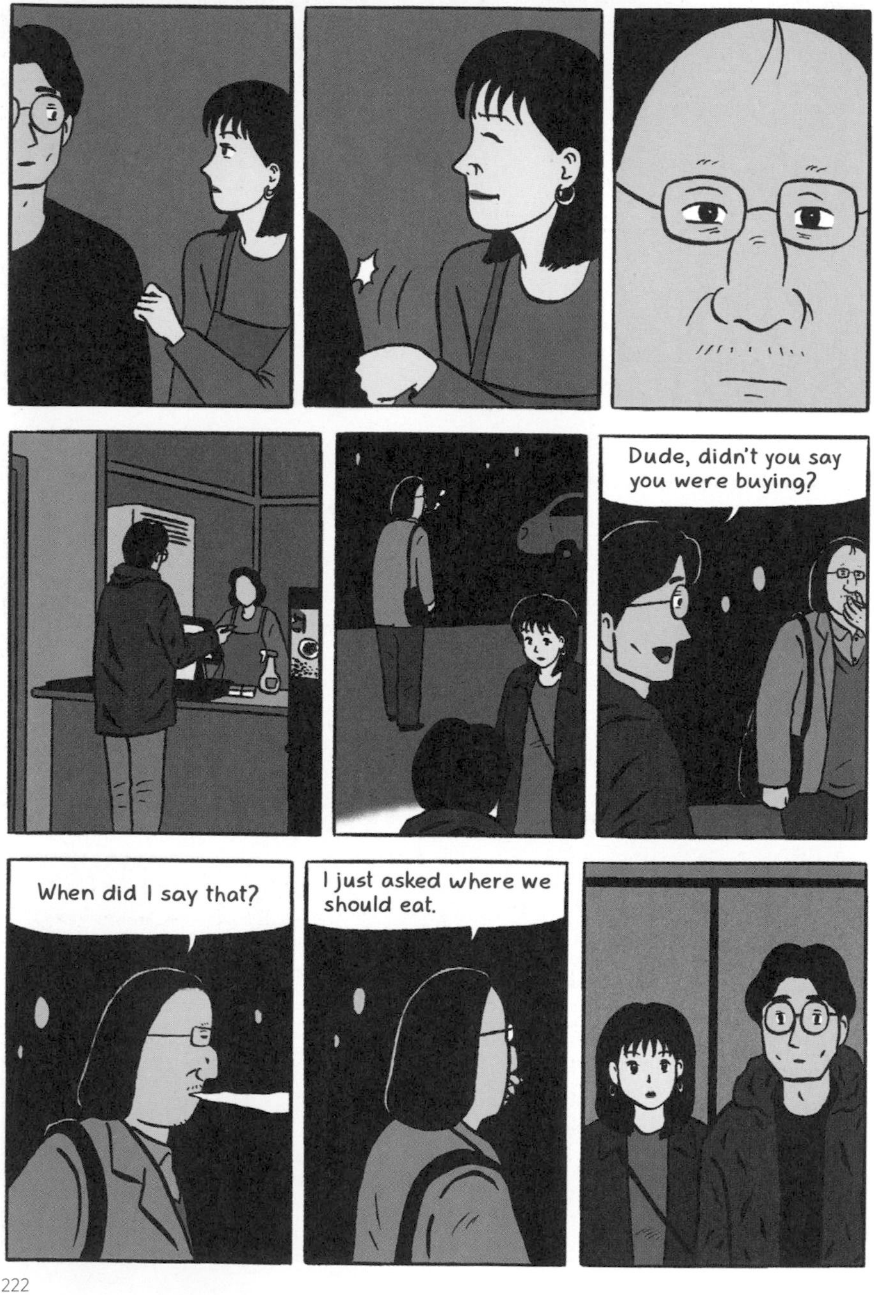
Dude, didn't you say
you were buying?
When did I say that?
I just asked where we
should eat.

SENSITIVE

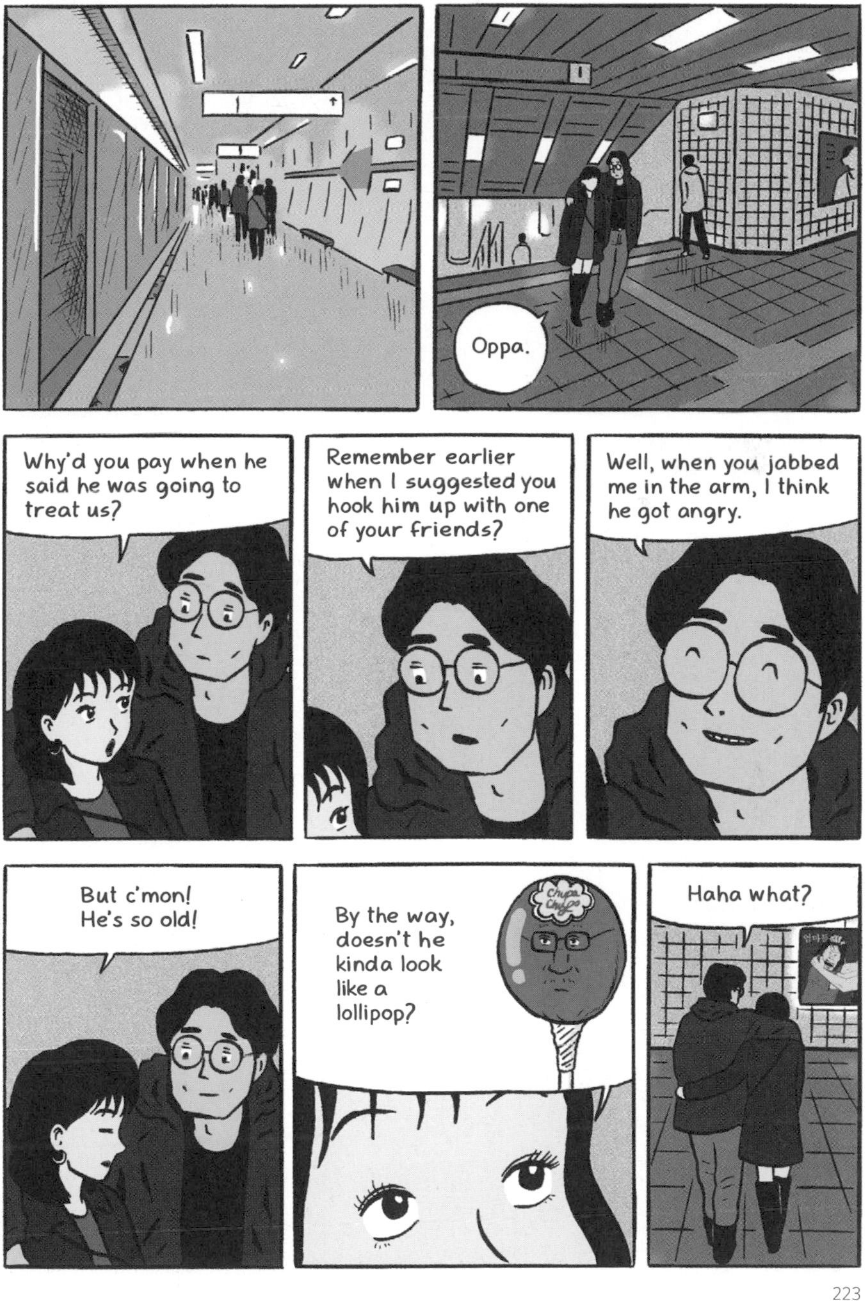
Oppa.
Why'd you pay when he said he was going to treat us?
Remember earlier when I suggested you hook him up with one of your friends?
Well, when you jabbed me in the arm, I think he got angry.
But c'mon! He's so old!
By the way, doesn't he kinda look like a lollipop?
Chupa Chups
Haha what?

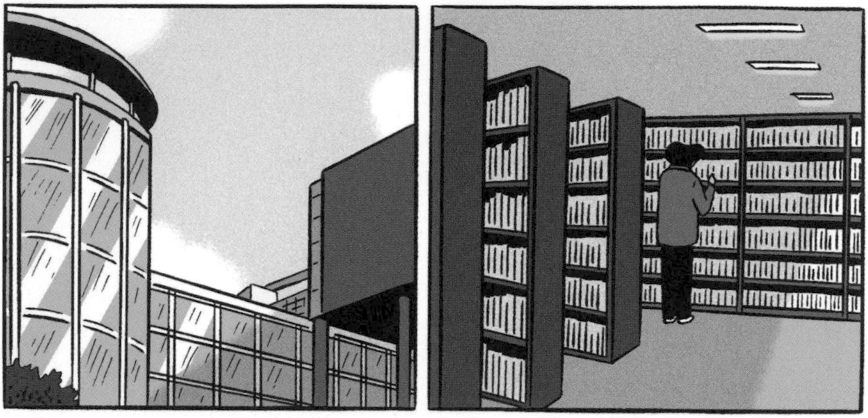

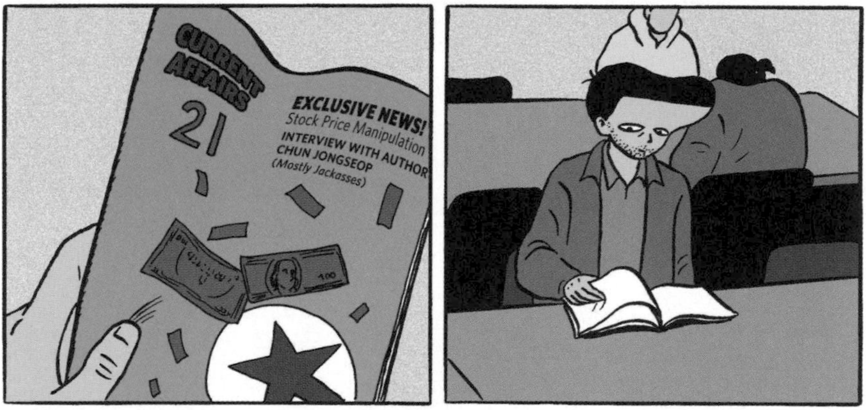
CURRENT AFFAIRS
21
EXCLUSIVE NEWS!
Stock Price Manipulation
INTERVIEW WITH AUTHOR
CHUN JONGSEOP
(Mostly Jackasses)

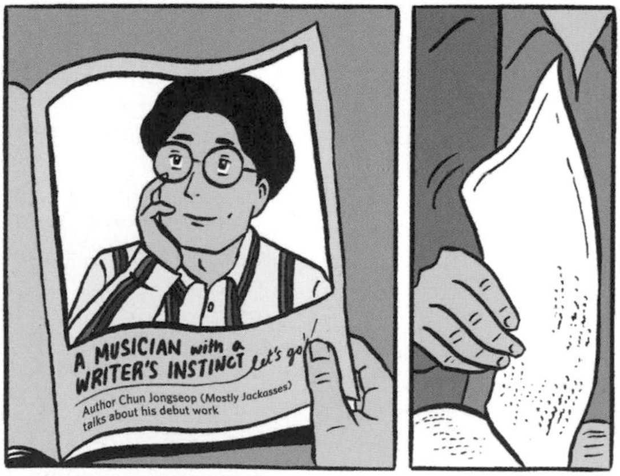
A MUSICIAN with a
WRITER'S INSTINCT
let's go
Author Chun Jongseop (Mostly Jackasses)
talks about his debut work

How did this book come to be published?

I've always made posts online, so when the writer Shin Deuk-nyeong suggested I try my hand at a book, I started writing one on my own.

Who came up with the idea?

Everything fell naturally into place since these stories are based on my life experiences. In other words, it just happened.

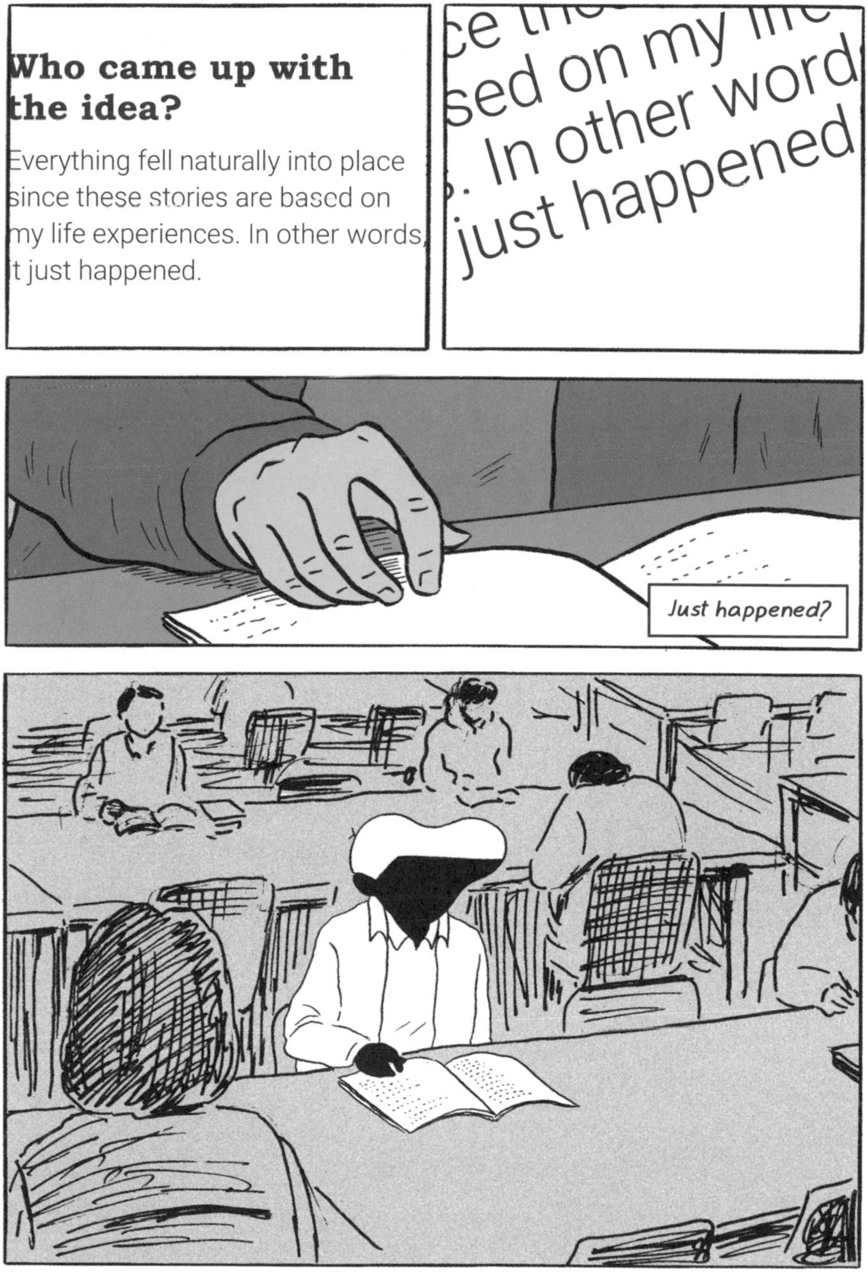
Who came up with the idea?
Everything fell naturally into place since these stories are based on my life experiences. In other words, it just happened.
sed on my
. In other word
just happened
Just happened?

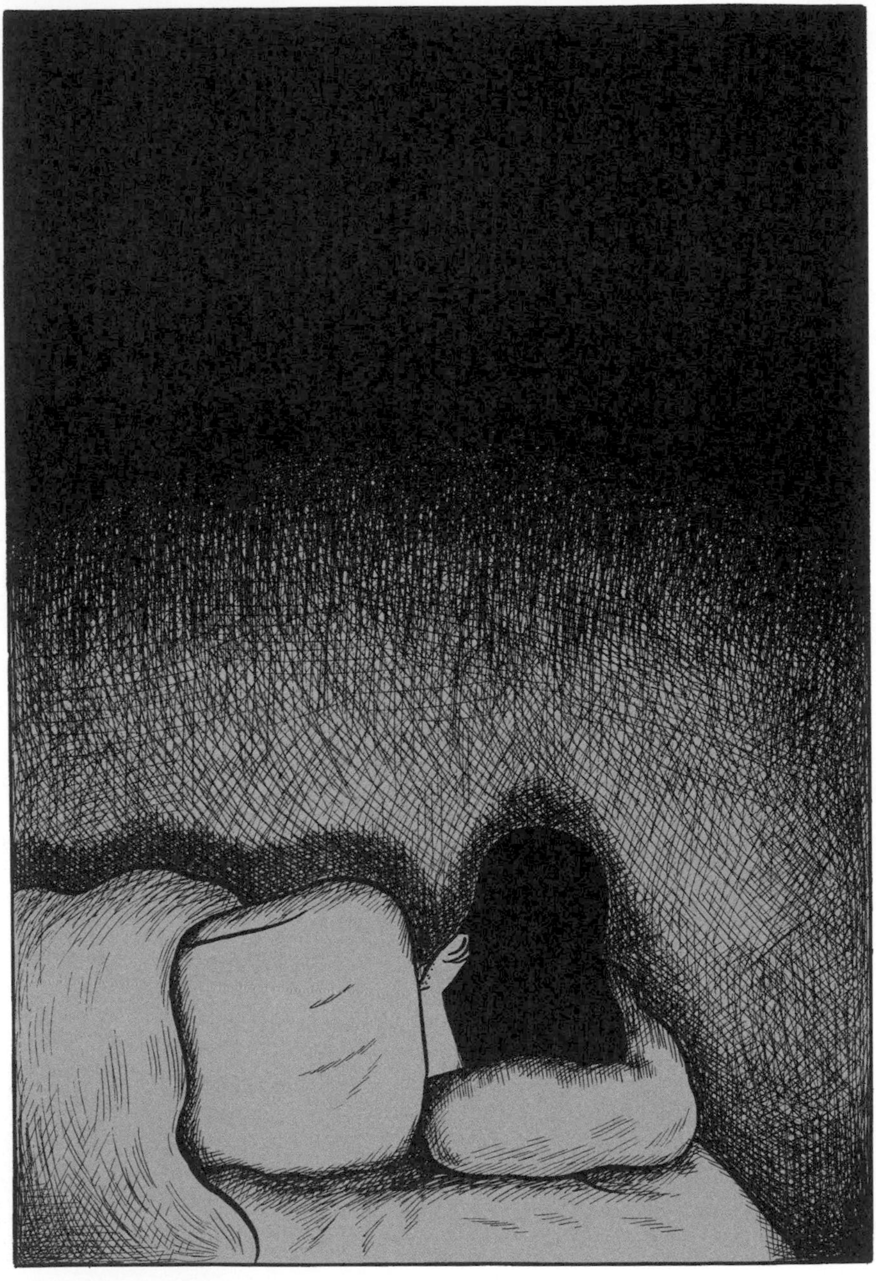

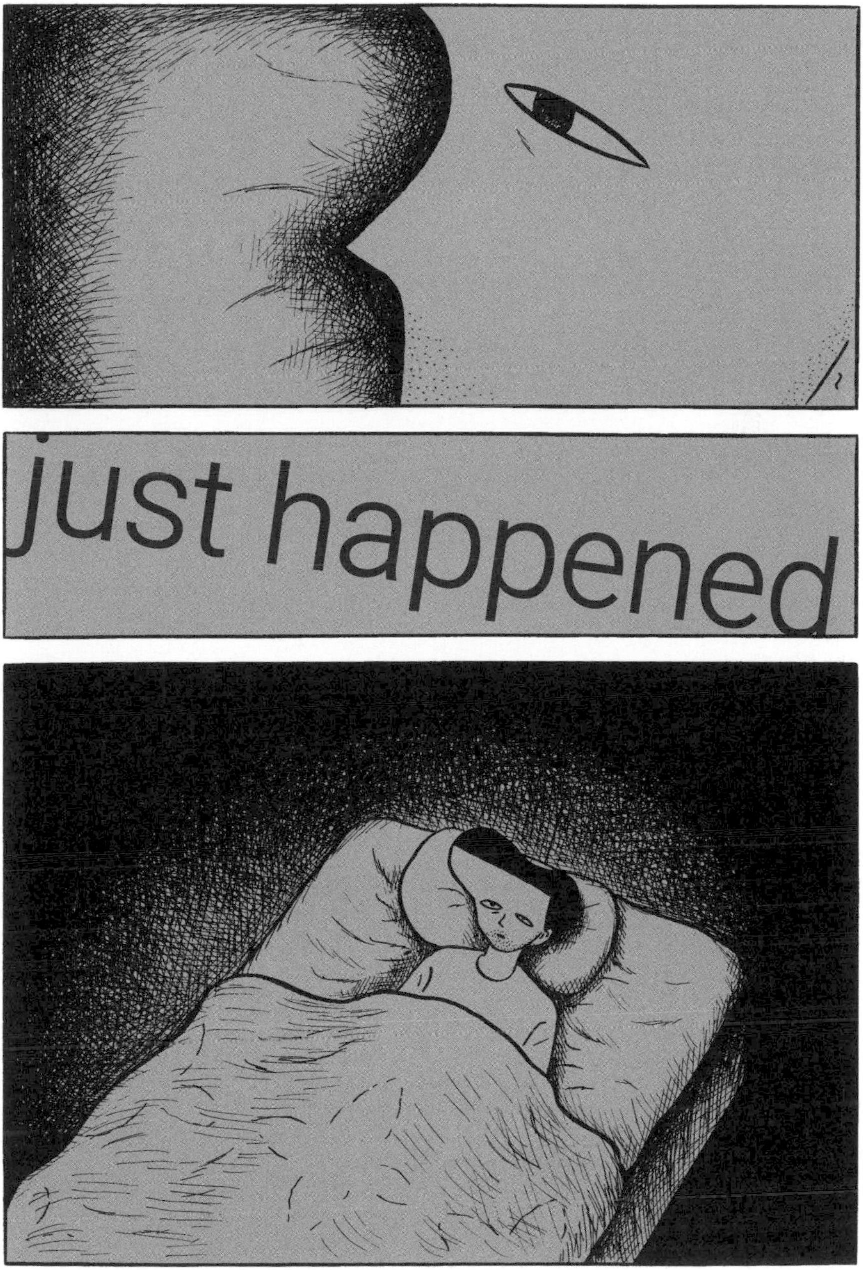
just happened

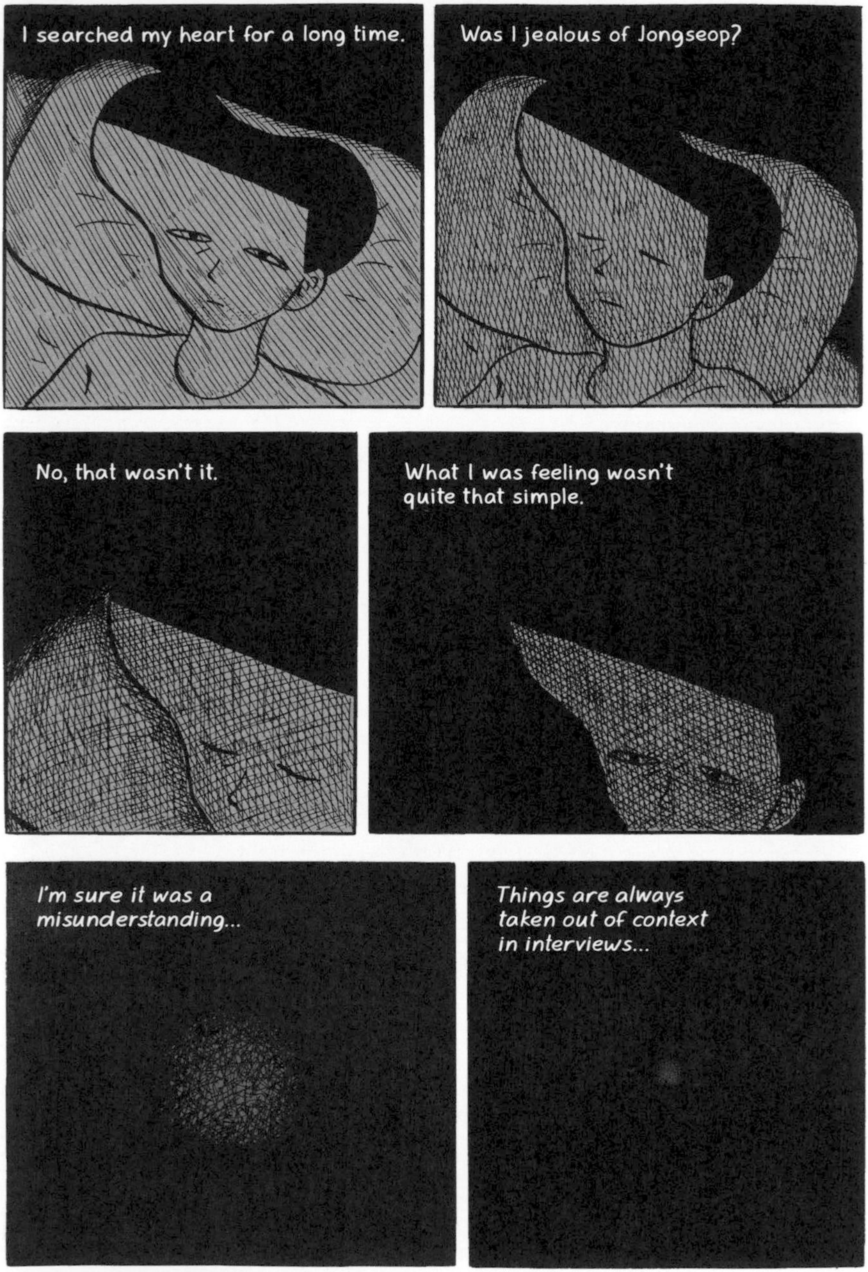
I searched my heart for a long time.
Was I jealous of Jongseop?
No, that wasn't it.
What I was feeling wasn't quite that simple.
I'm sure it was a misunderstanding...
Things are always taken out of context in interviews...

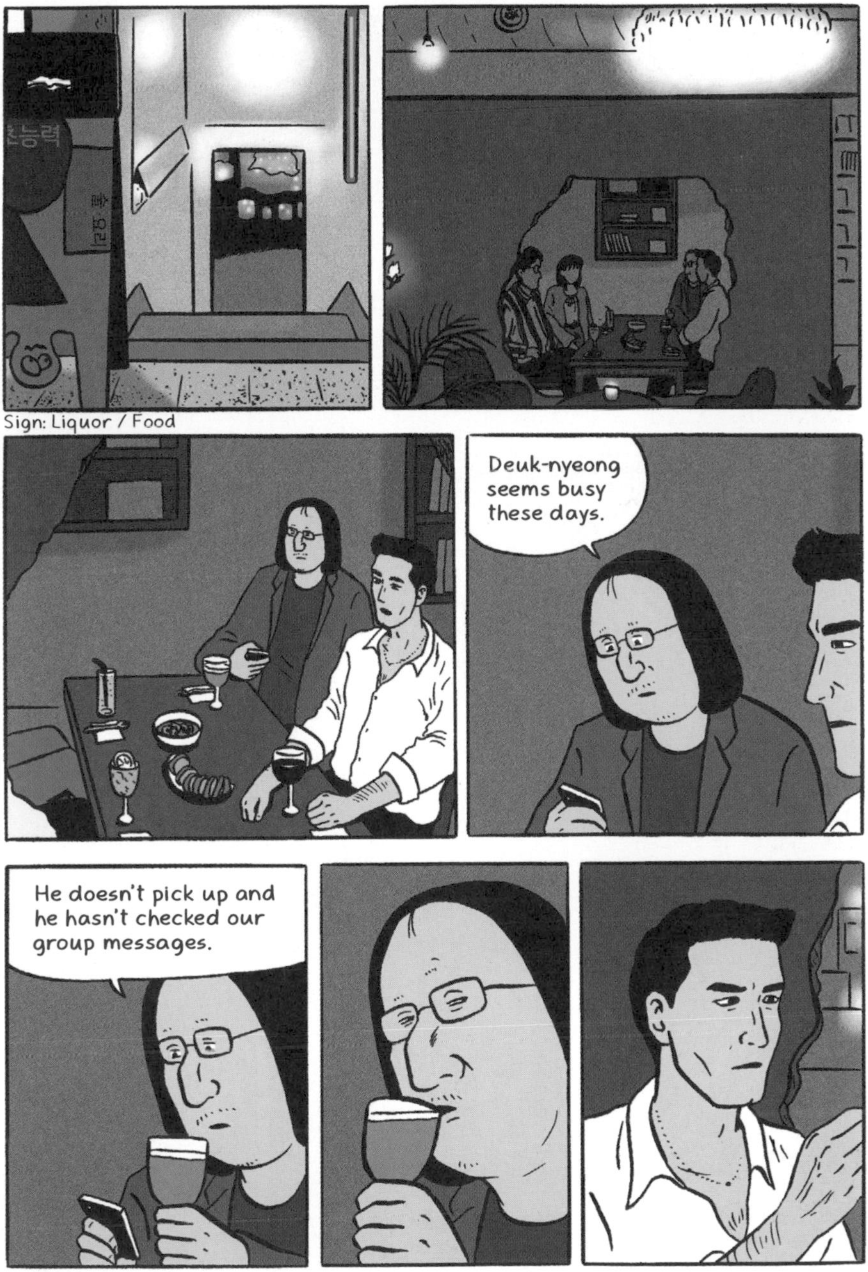
Sign: Liquor / Food
Deuk-nyeong seems busy these days.
He doesn't pick up and he hasn't checked our group messages.

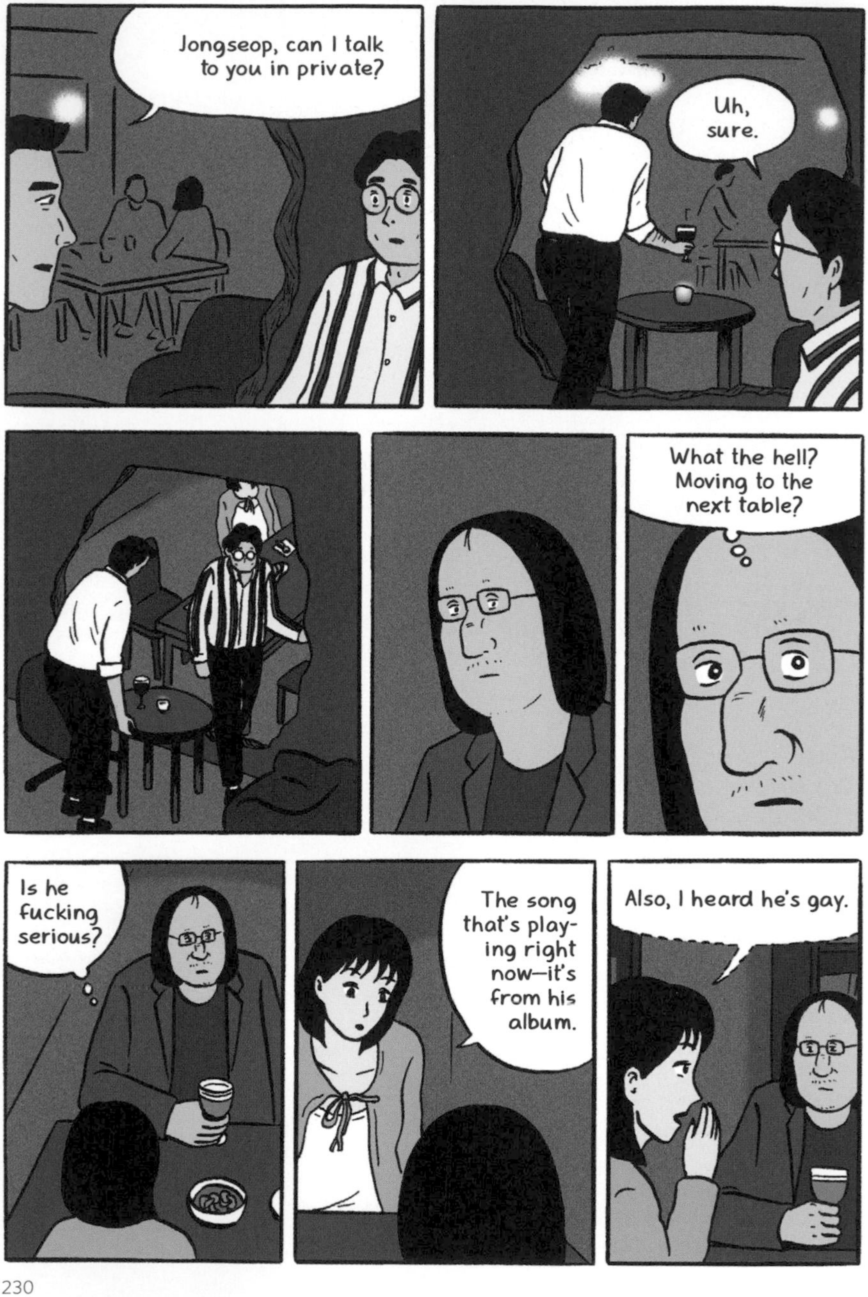
Jongseop, can I talk to you in private?
Uh, sure.
What the hell? Moving to the next table?
Is he fucking serious?
The song that's playing right now—it's from his album.
Also, I heard he's gay.

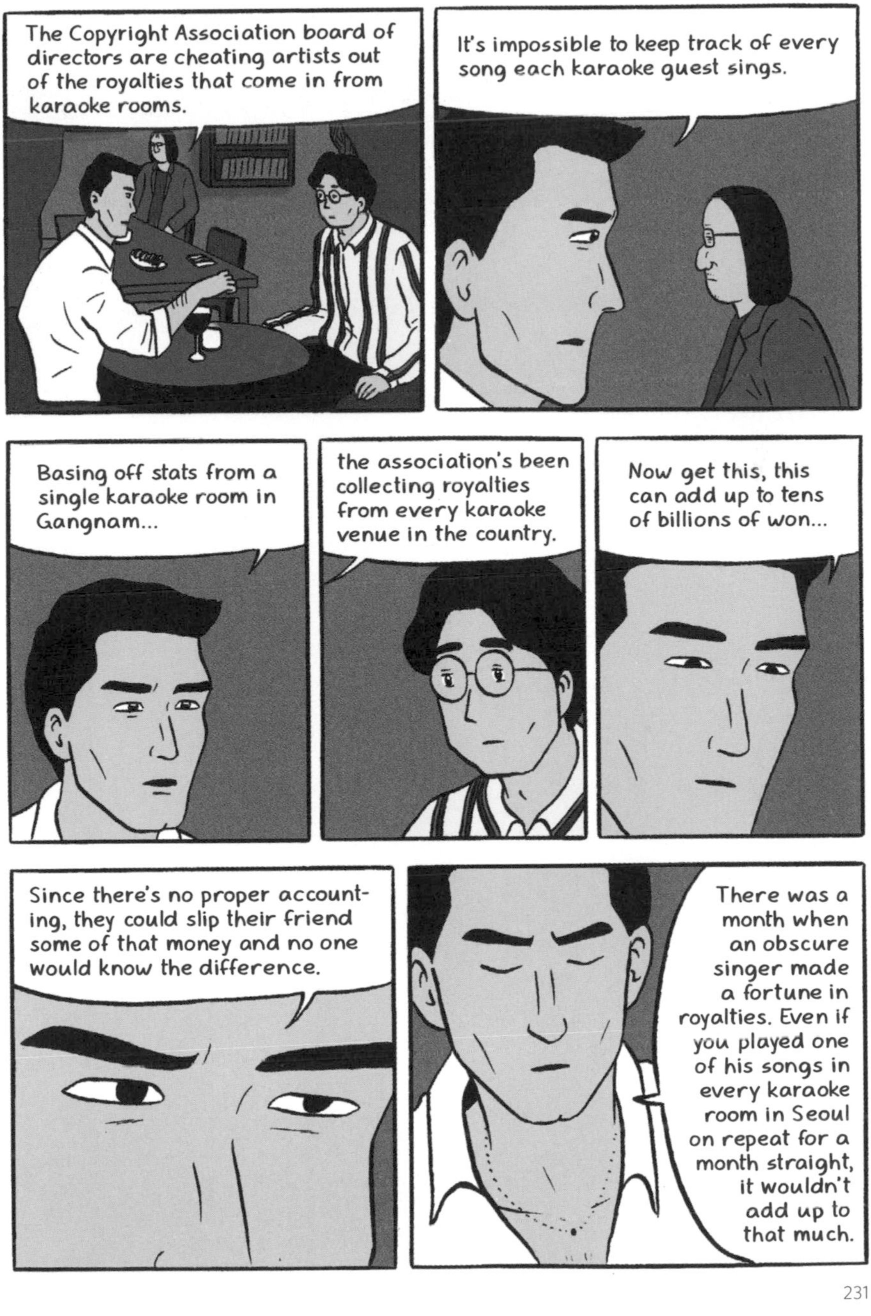
The Copyright Association board of directors are cheating artists out of the royalties that come in from karaoke rooms.
It's impossible to keep track of every song each karaoke guest sings.
Basing off stats from a single karaoke room in Gangnam...
the association's been collecting royalties from every karaoke venue in the country.
Now get this, this can add up to tens of billions of won...
Since there's no proper accounting, they could slip their friend some of that money and no one would know the difference.
There was a month when an obscure singer made a fortune in royalties. Even if you played one of his songs in every karaoke room in Seoul on repeat for a month straight, it wouldn't add up to that much.

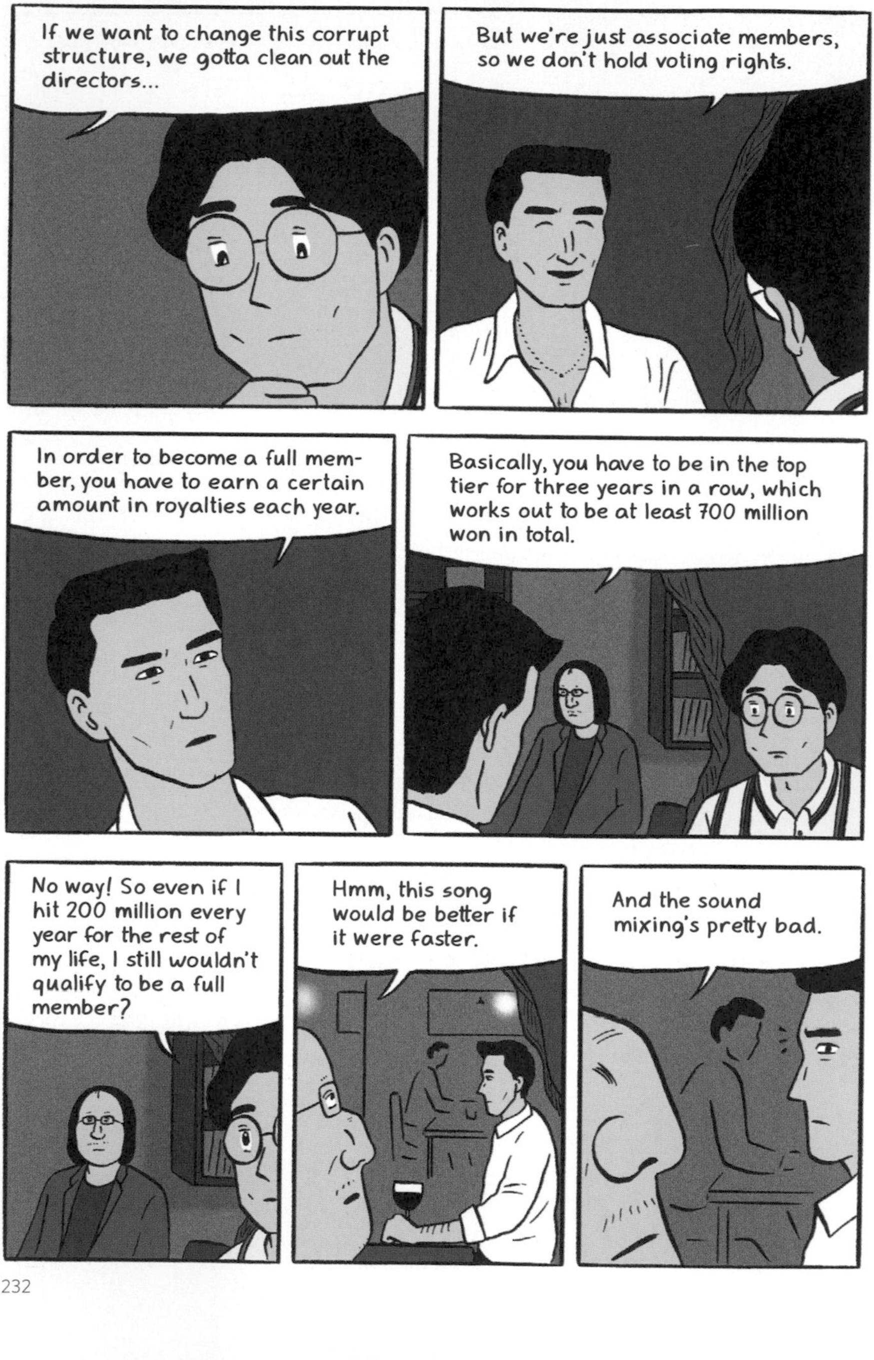
If we want to change this corrupt structure, we gotta clean out the directors...
But we're just associate members, so we don't hold voting rights.
In order to become a full member, you have to earn a certain amount in royalties each year.
Basically, you have to be in the top tier for three years in a row, which works out to be at least 700 million won in total.
No way! So even if I hit 200 million every year for the rest of my life, I still wouldn't qualify to be a full member?
Hmm, this song would be better if it were faster.
And the sound mixing's pretty bad.

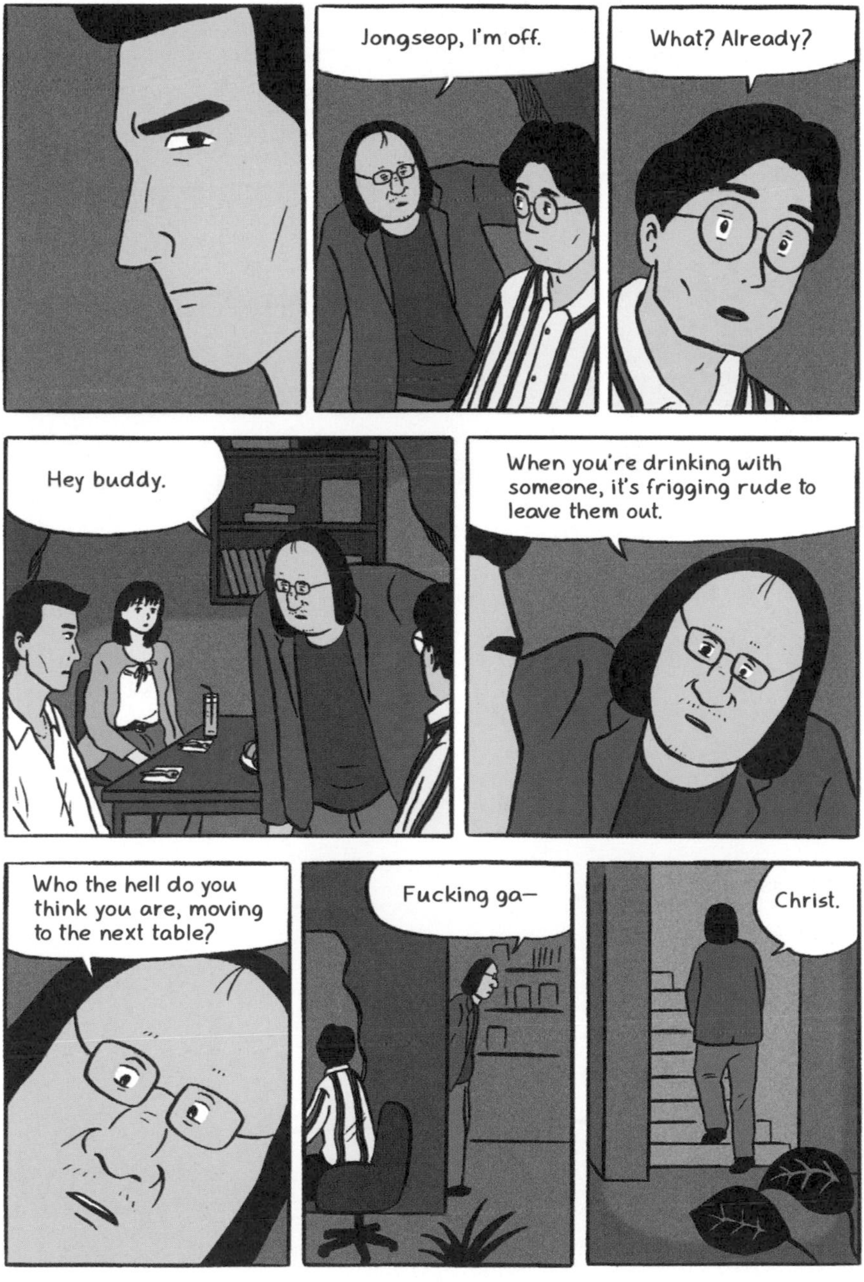
Jongseop, I'm off.
What? Already?
Hey buddy.
When you're drinking with someone, it's frigging rude to leave them out.
Who the hell do you think you are, moving to the next table?
Fucking ga—
Christ.

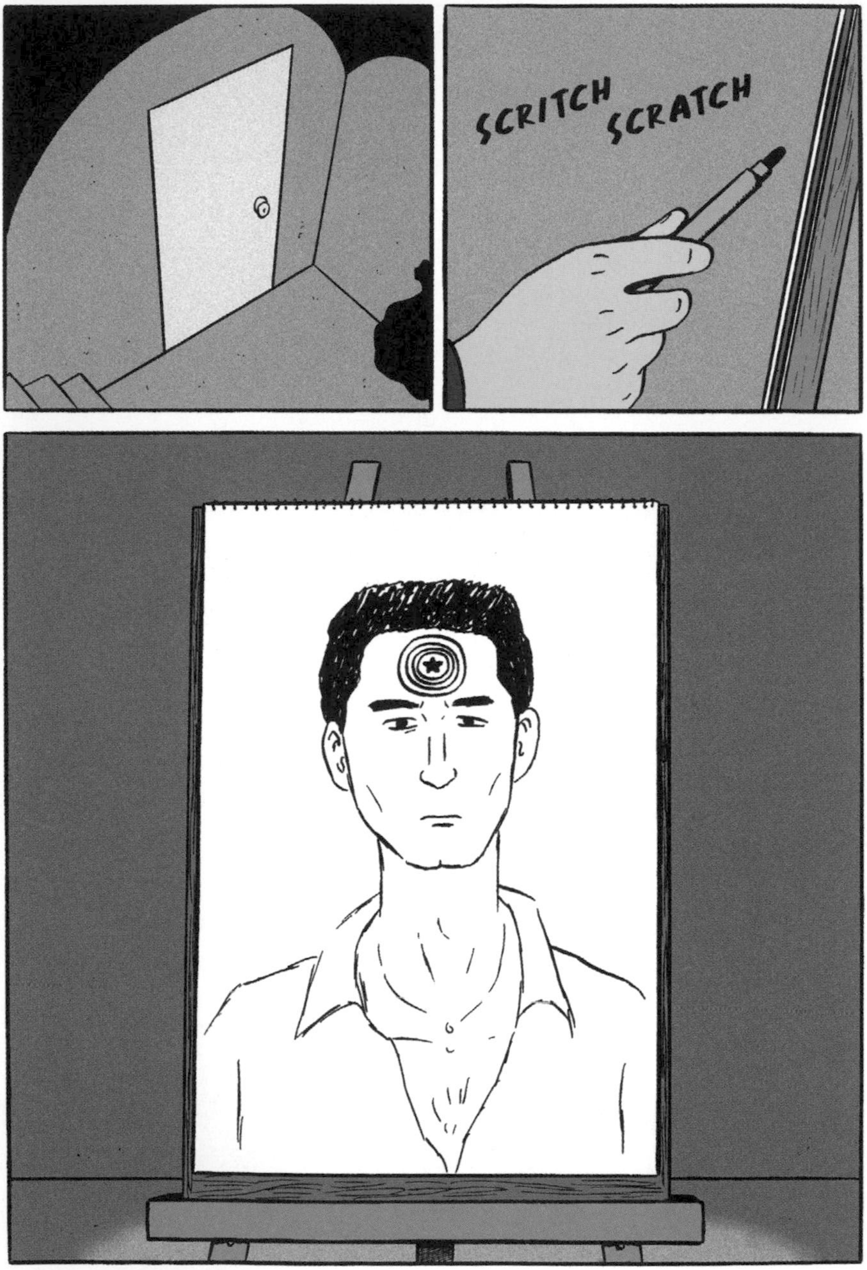
SCRITCH
SCRATCH

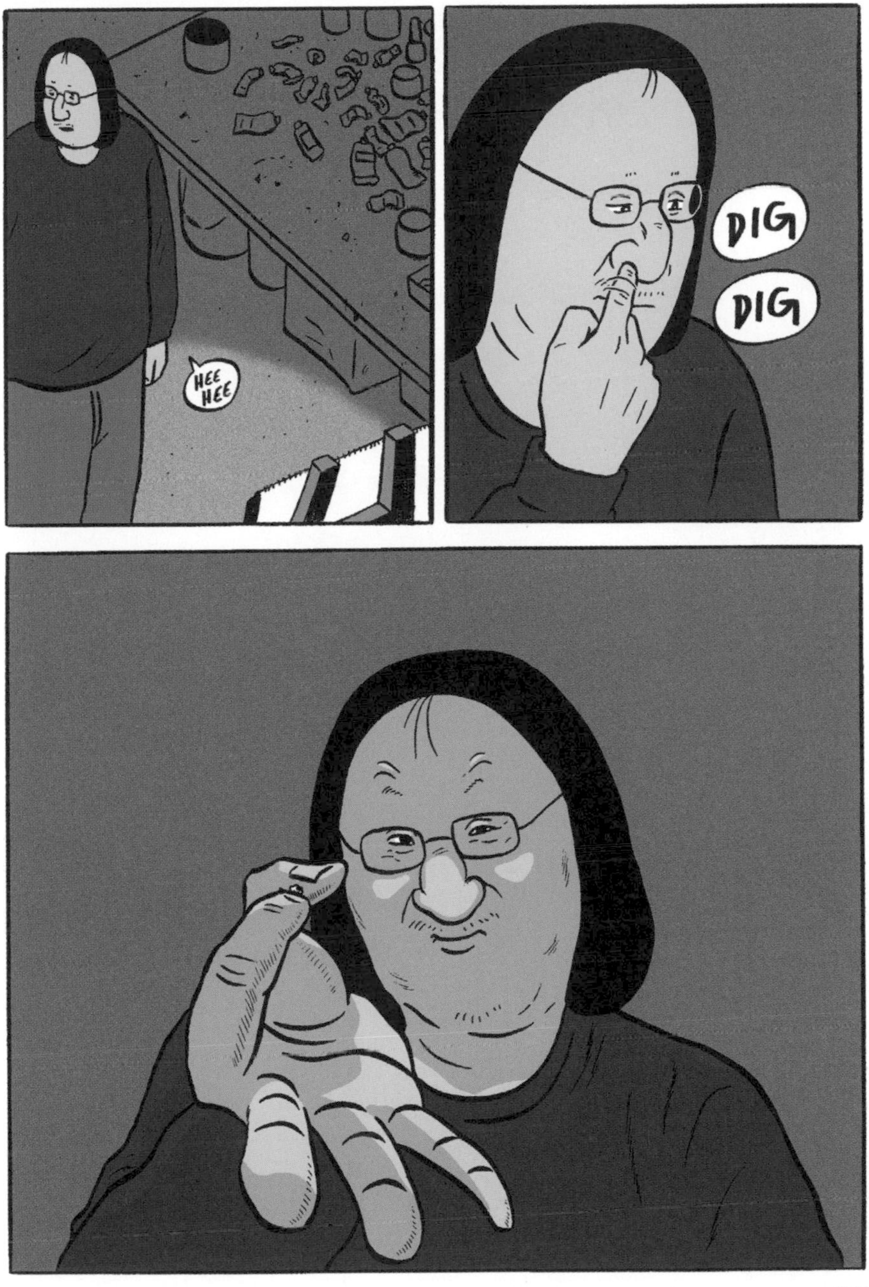
HEE HEE
DIG
DIG

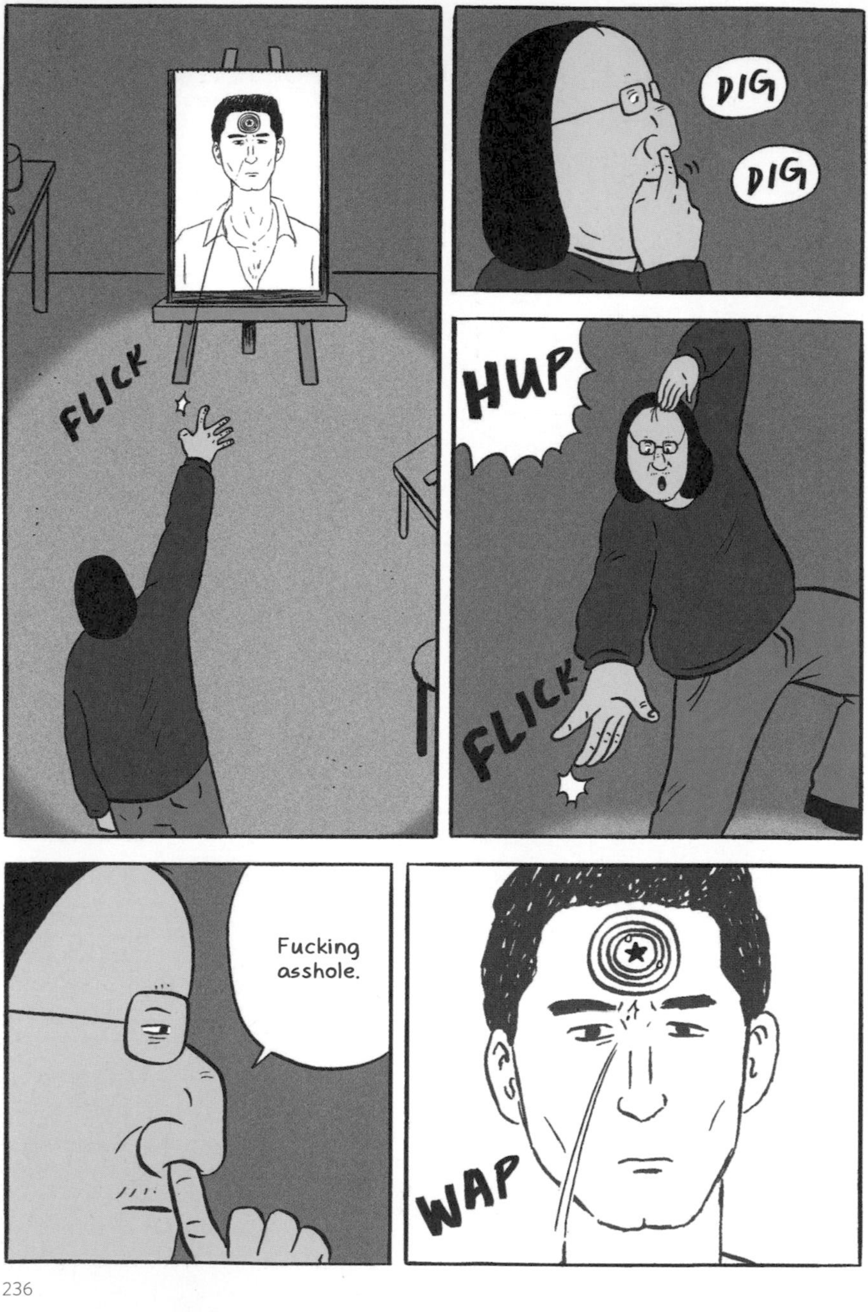
FLICK
DIG
DIG
HUP
FLICK
Fucking asshole.
WAP

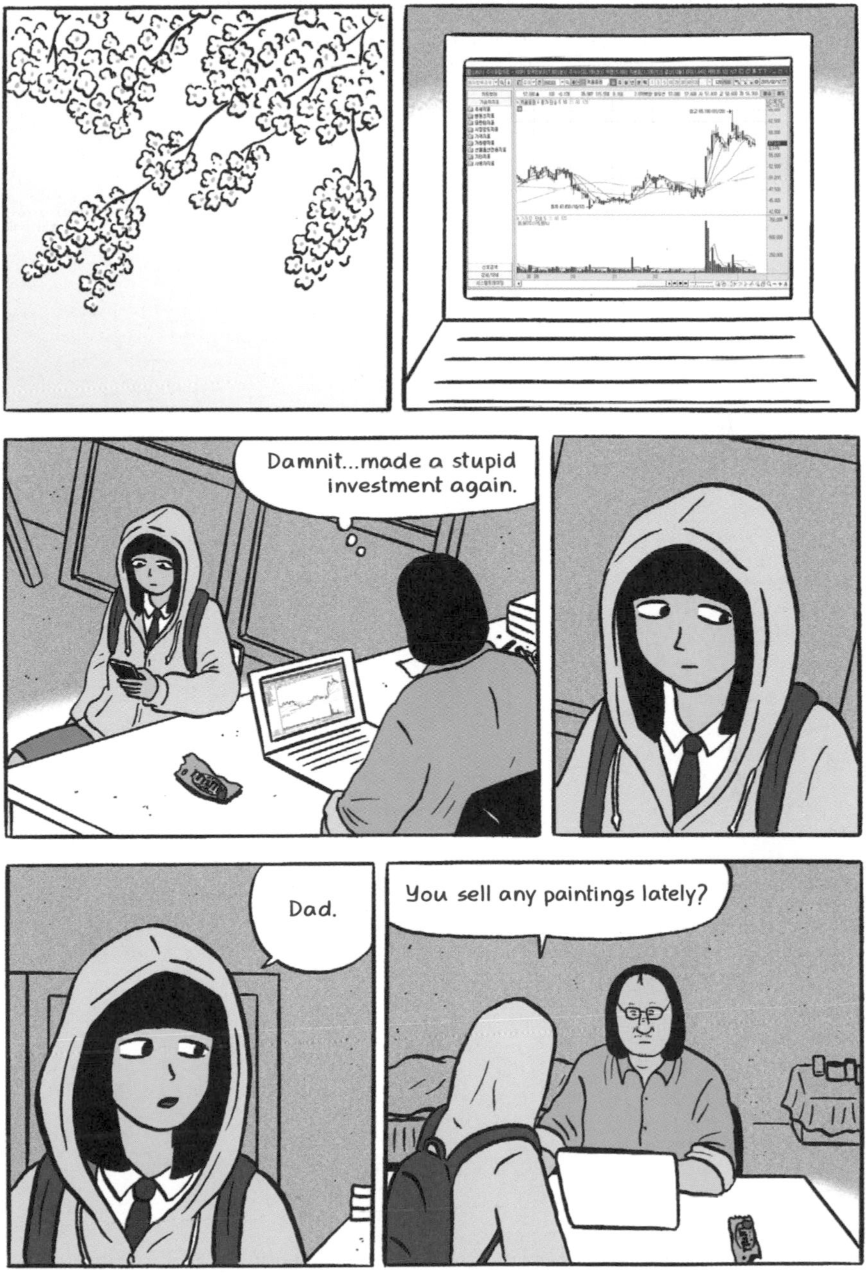
Damnit...made a stupid investment again.
Dad.
You sell any paintings lately?

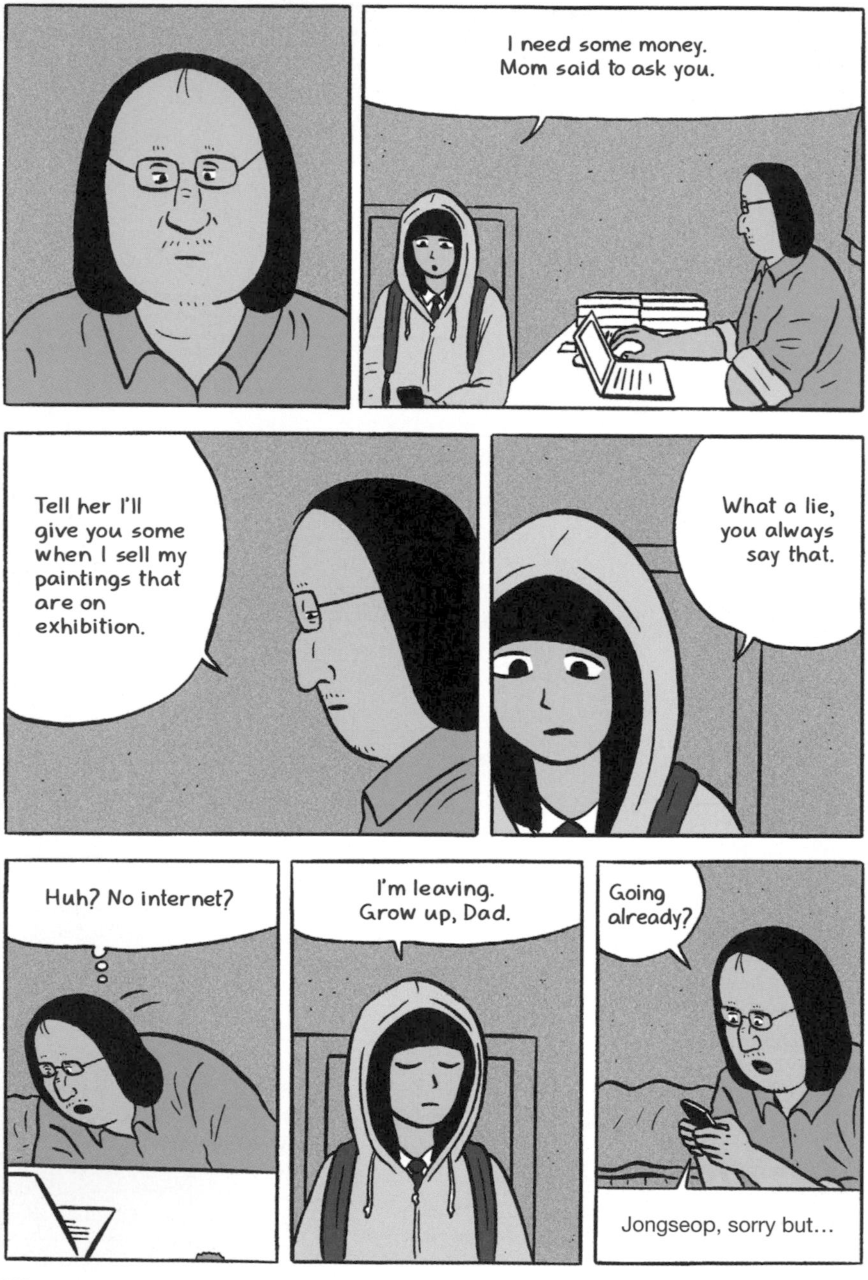
I need some money.
Mom said to ask you.
Tell her I'll give you some when I sell my paintings that are on exhibition.
What a lie, you always say that.
Huh? No internet?
I'm leaving.
Grow up, Dad.
Going already?
Jongseop, sorry but…

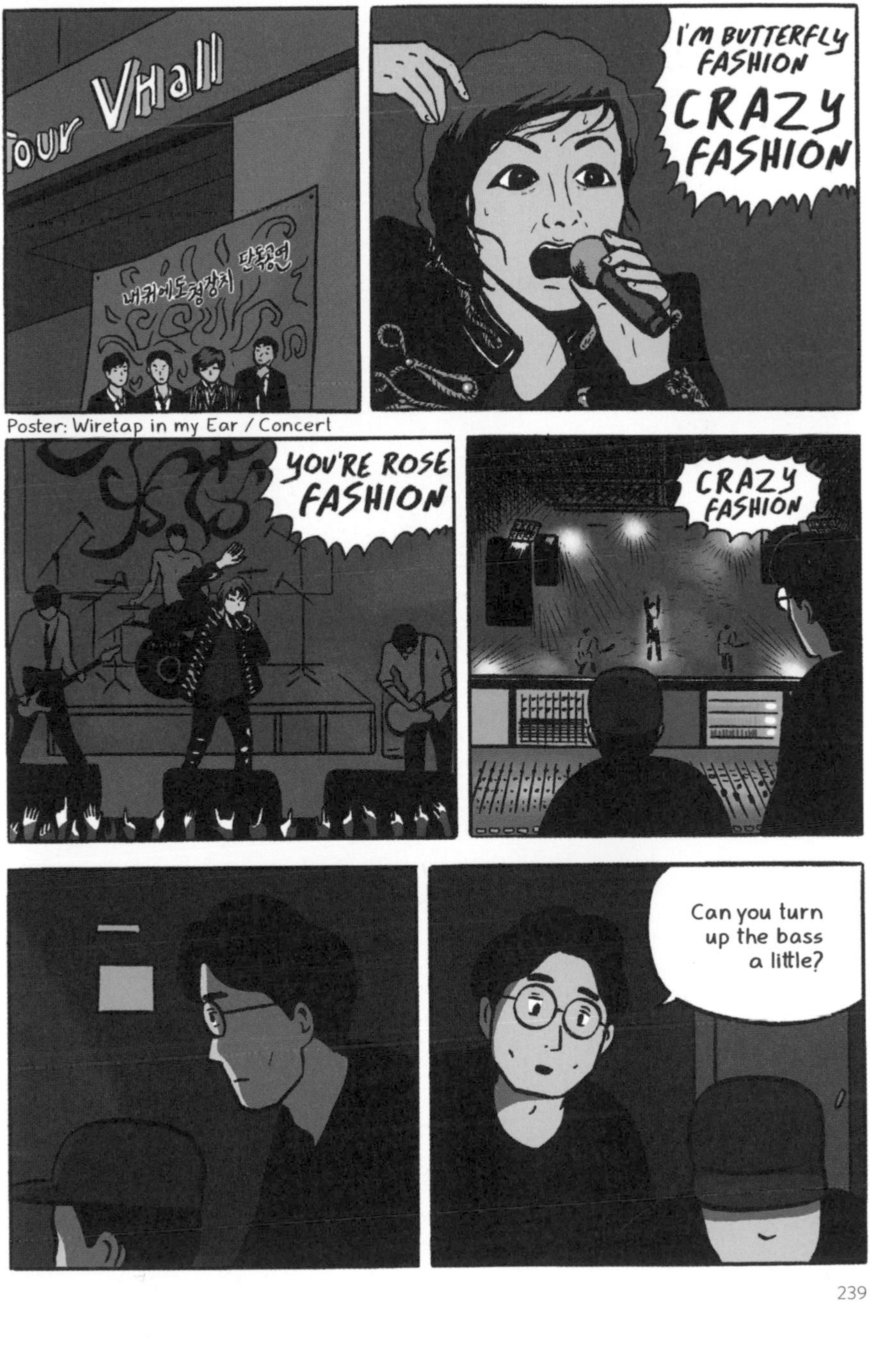

Tour VHall
내귀에도청장치 단독공연
Poster: Wiretap in my Ear / Concert
I'M BUTTERFLY FASHION
CRAZY FASHION
YOU'RE ROSE FASHION
CRAZY FASHION
Can you turn up the bass a little?

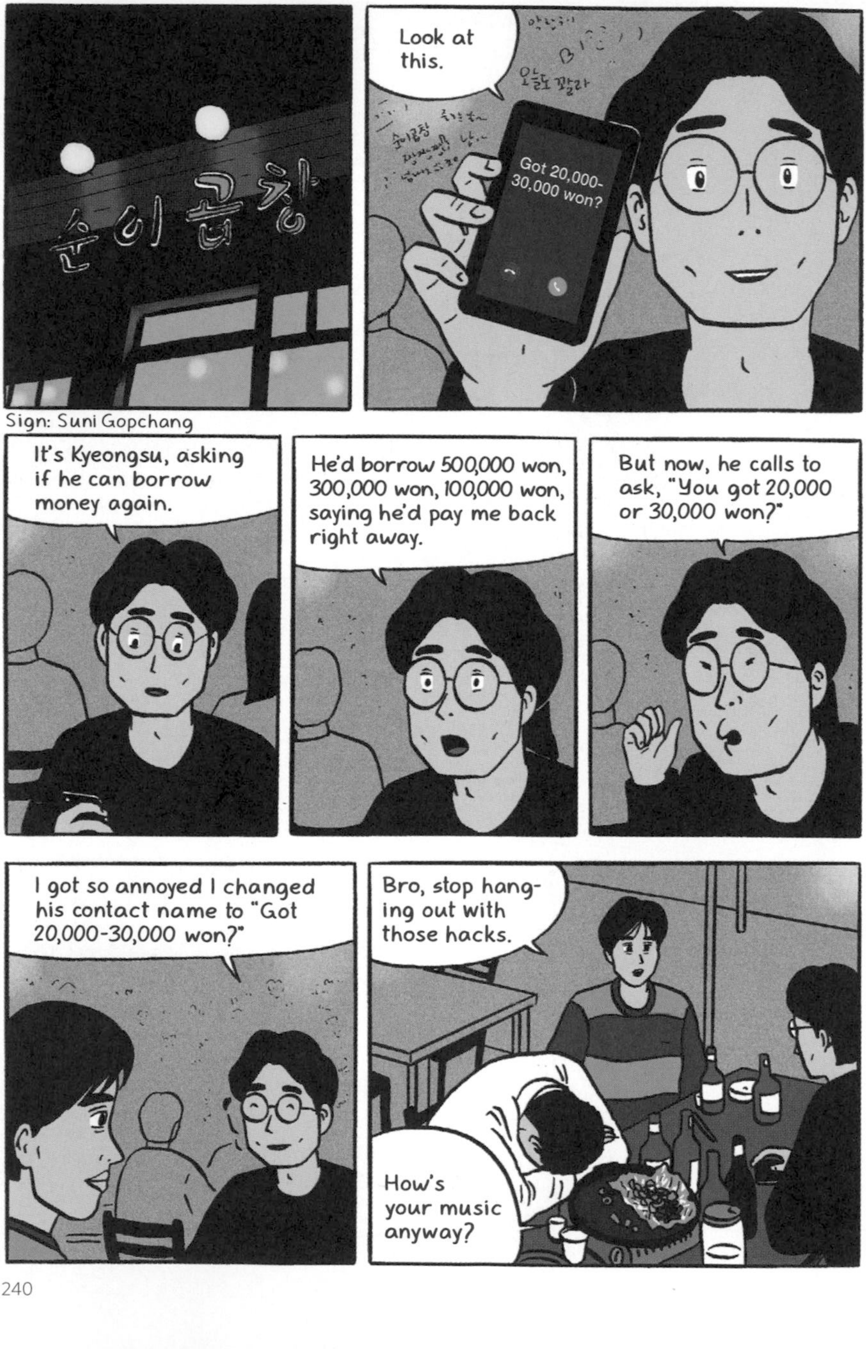
순이곱창
Look at this.
Got 20,000-30,000 won?
It's Kyeongsu, asking if he can borrow money again.
He'd borrow 500,000 won, 300,000 won, 100,000 won, saying he'd pay me back right away.
But now, he calls to ask, "You got 20,000 or 30,000 won?"
I got so annoyed I changed his contact name to "Got 20,000-30,000 won?"
Bro, stop hanging out with those hacks.
How's your music anyway?
Sign: Suni Gopchang

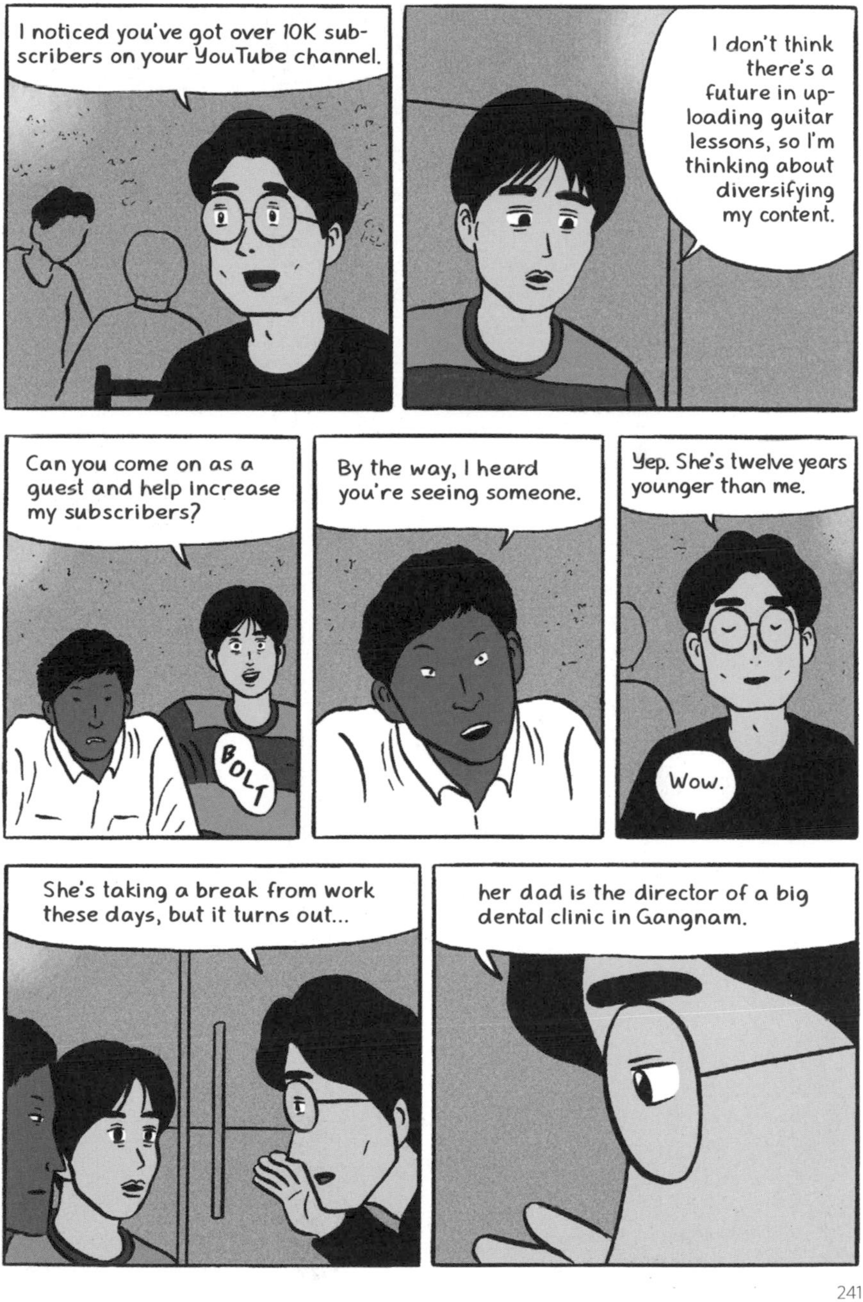
I noticed you've got over 10K subscribers on your YouTube channel.
I don't think there's a future in uploading guitar lessons, so I'm thinking about diversifying my content.
Can you come on as a guest and help increase my subscribers?
BOLT
By the way, I heard you're seeing someone.
Yep. She's twelve years younger than me.
Wow.
She's taking a break from work these days, but it turns out...
her dad is the director of a big dental clinic in Gangnam.

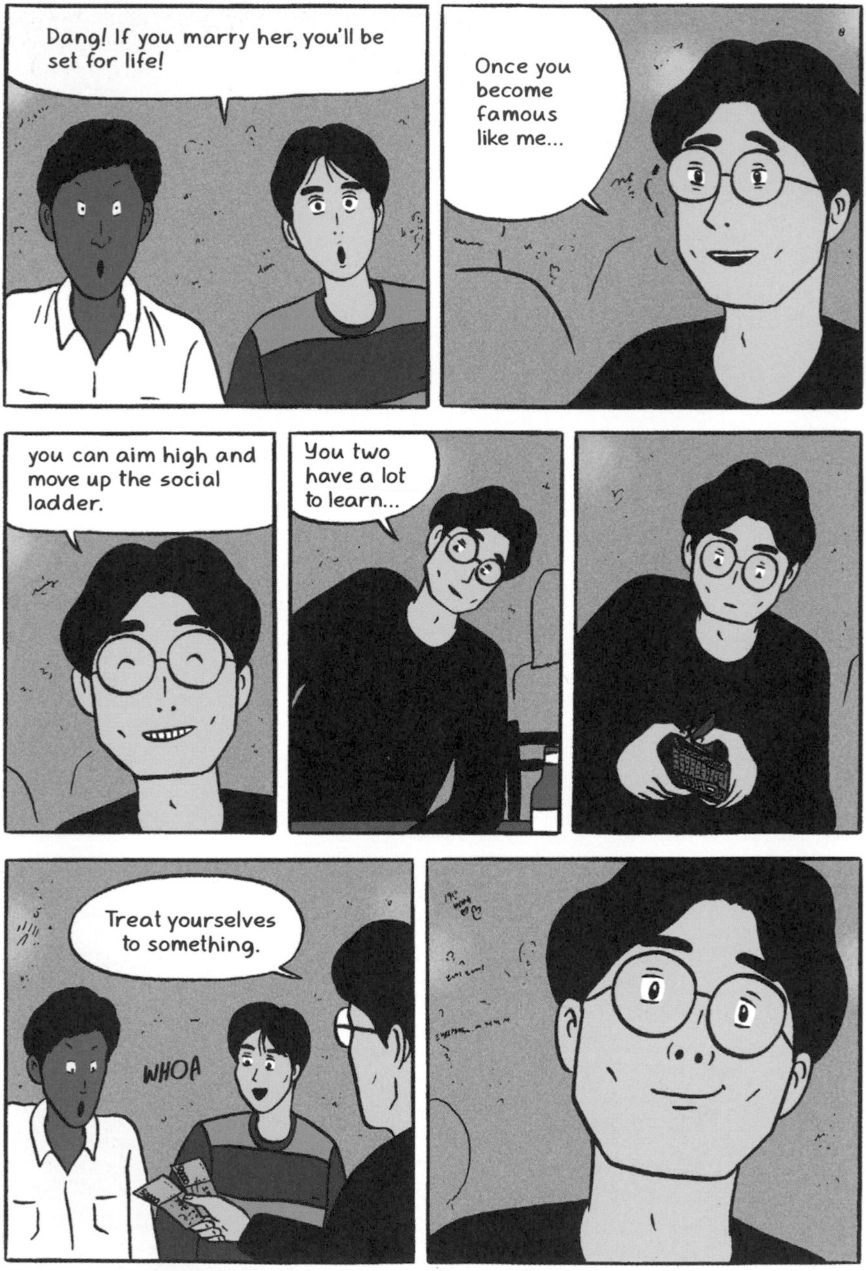
Dang! If you marry her, you'll be set for life!
Once you become famous like me...
you can aim high and move up the social ladder.
You two have a lot to learn...
Treat yourselves to something.
WHOA

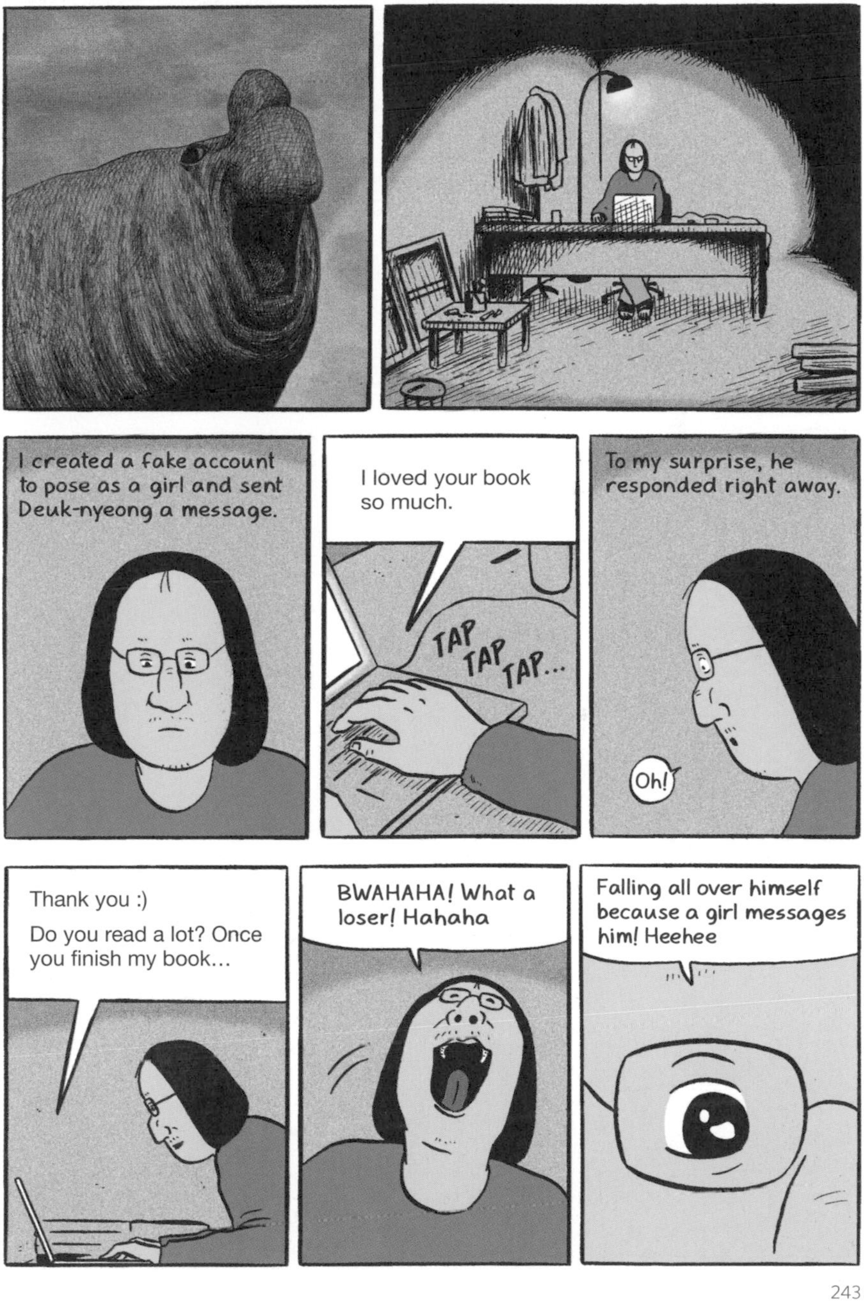
I created a fake account to pose as a girl and sent Deuk-nyeong a message.
I loved your book so much.
TAP TAP TAP...
To my surprise, he responded right away.
Oh!
Thank you :)
Do you read a lot? Once you finish my book...
BWAHAHA! What a loser! Hahaha
Falling all over himself because a girl messages him! Heehee

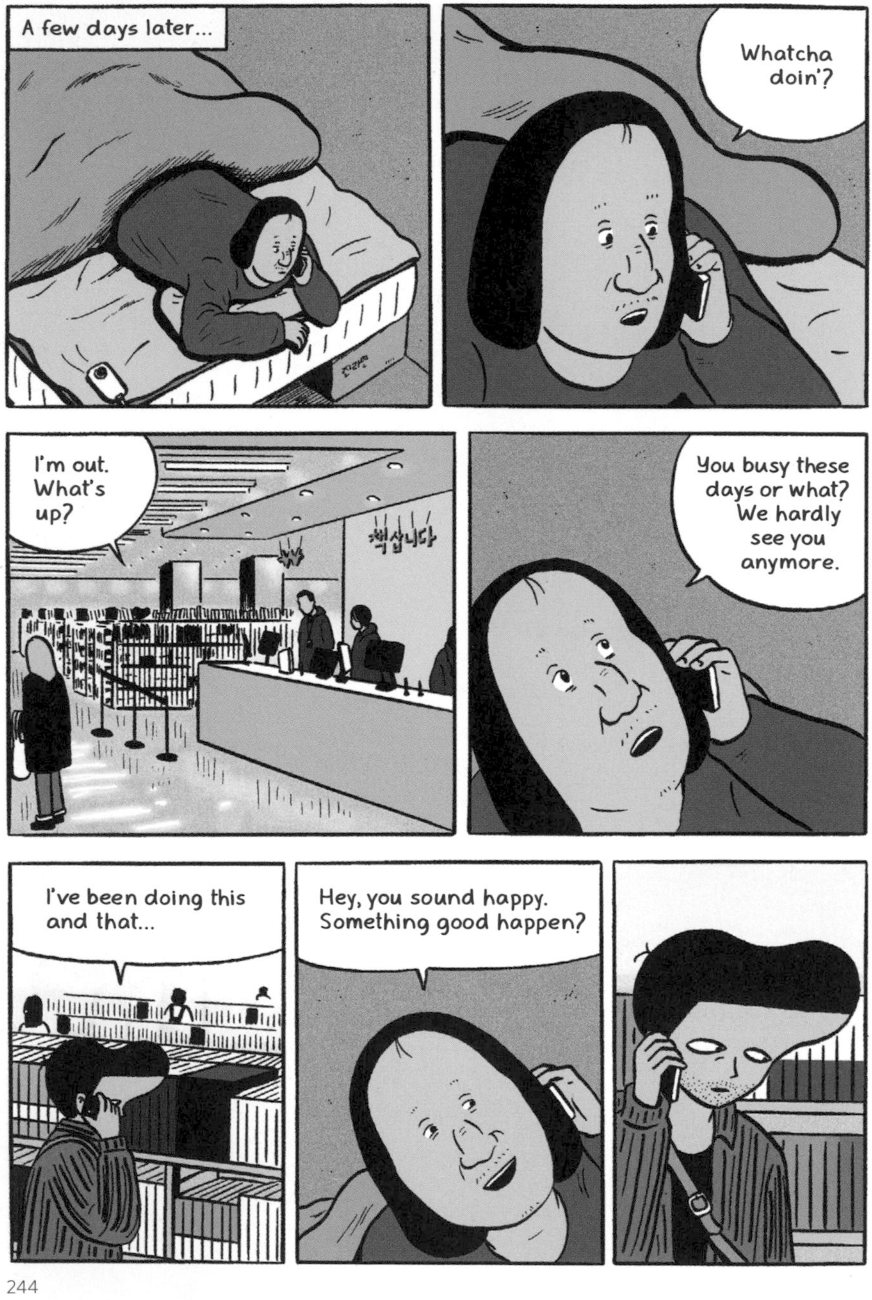
A few days later...
Whatcha doin'?
I'm out. What's up?
책삽니다
You busy these days or what? We hardly see you anymore.
I've been doing this and that...
Hey, you sound happy. Something good happen?

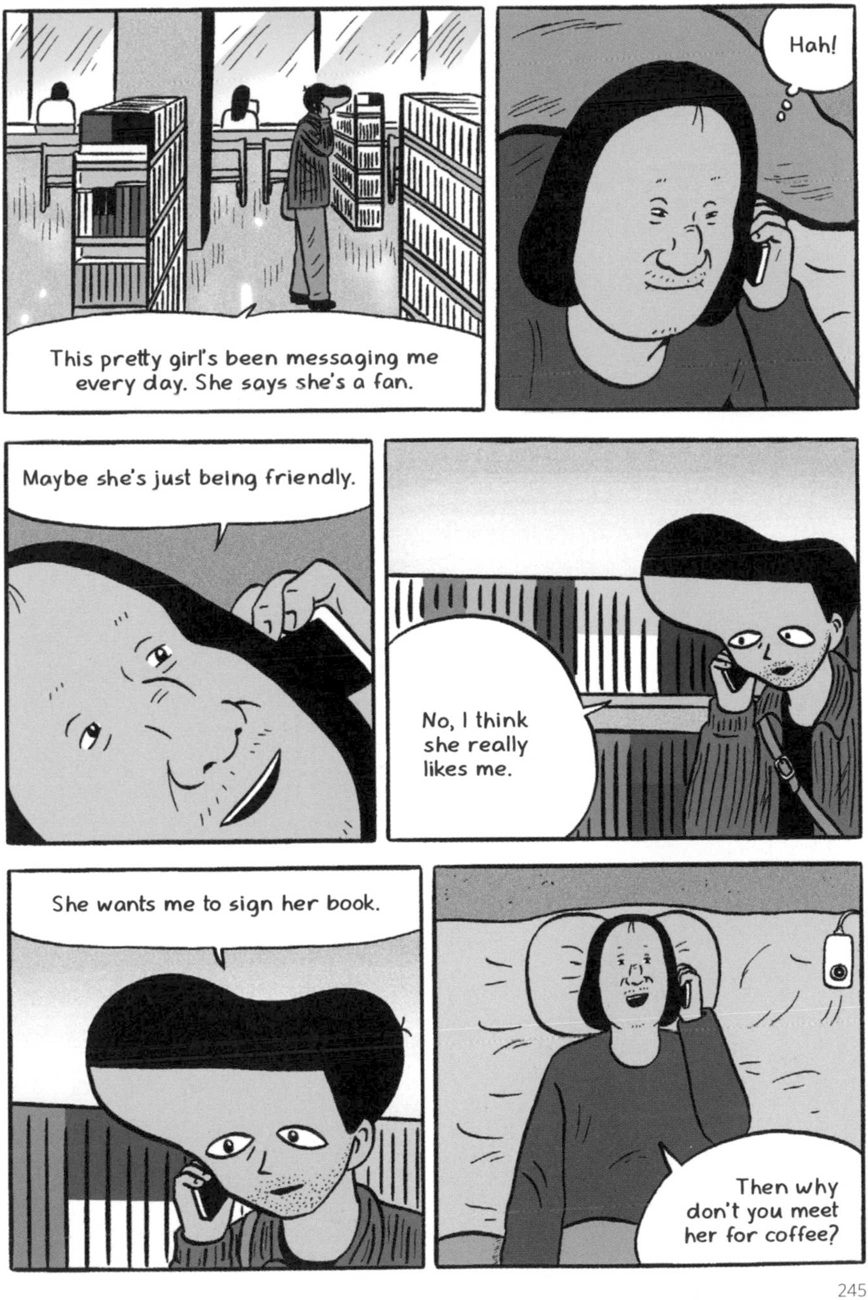
This pretty girl's been messaging me every day. She says she's a fan.
Hah!
Maybe she's just being friendly.
No, I think she really likes me.
She wants me to sign her book.
Then why don't you meet her for coffee?

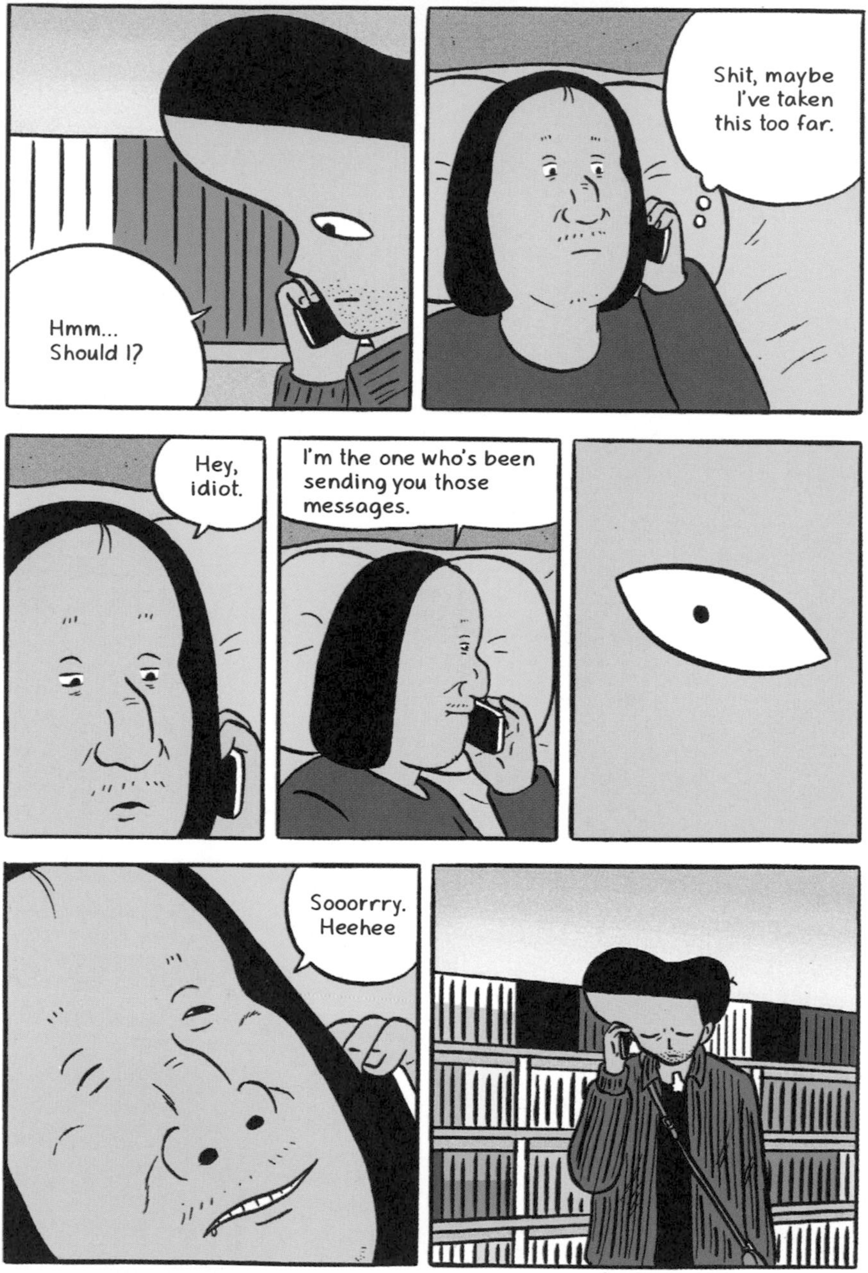
Hmm...
Should I?
Shit, maybe I've taken this too far.
Hey, idiot.
I'm the one who's been sending you those messages.
Sooorrry.
Heehee

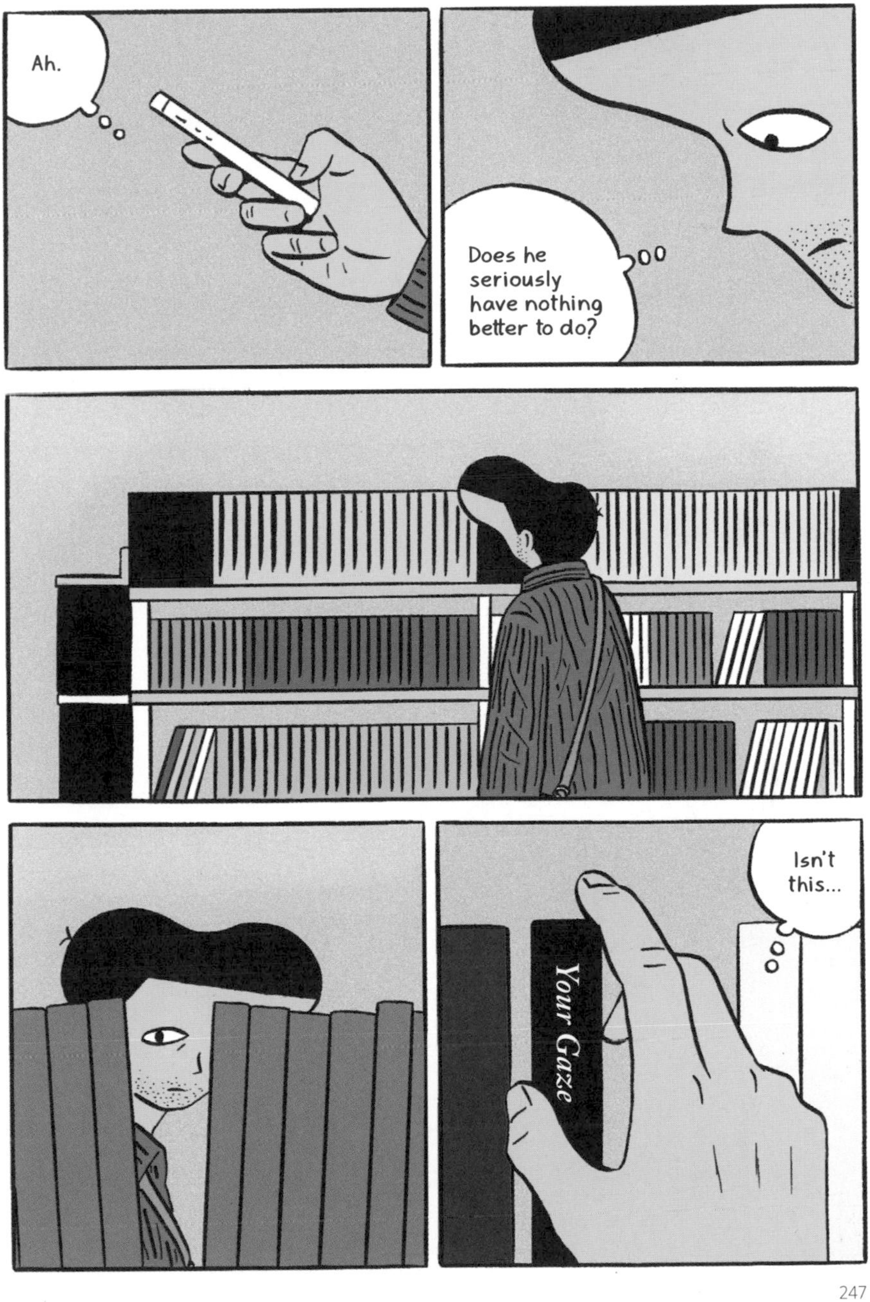
Ah.
Does he seriously have nothing better to do?
Isn't this...
Your Gaze

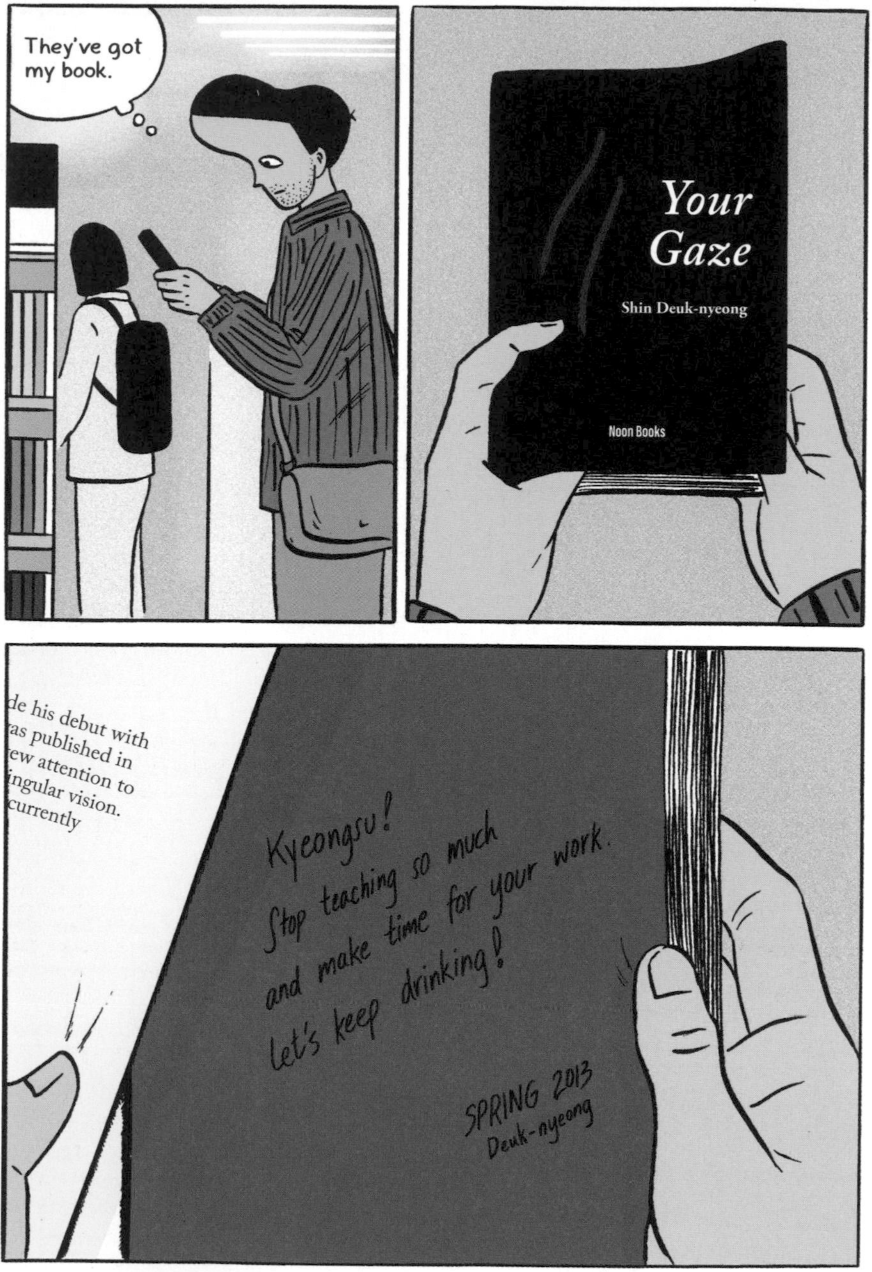
They've got my book.
Your Gaze
Shin Deuk-nyeong
Noon Books
de his debut with
as published in
ew attention to
ingular vision.
currently
Kyeongsu!
Stop teaching so much
and make time for your work.
Let's keep drinking!
SPRING 2013
Deuk-nyeong

THE BEGINNING OF THE END

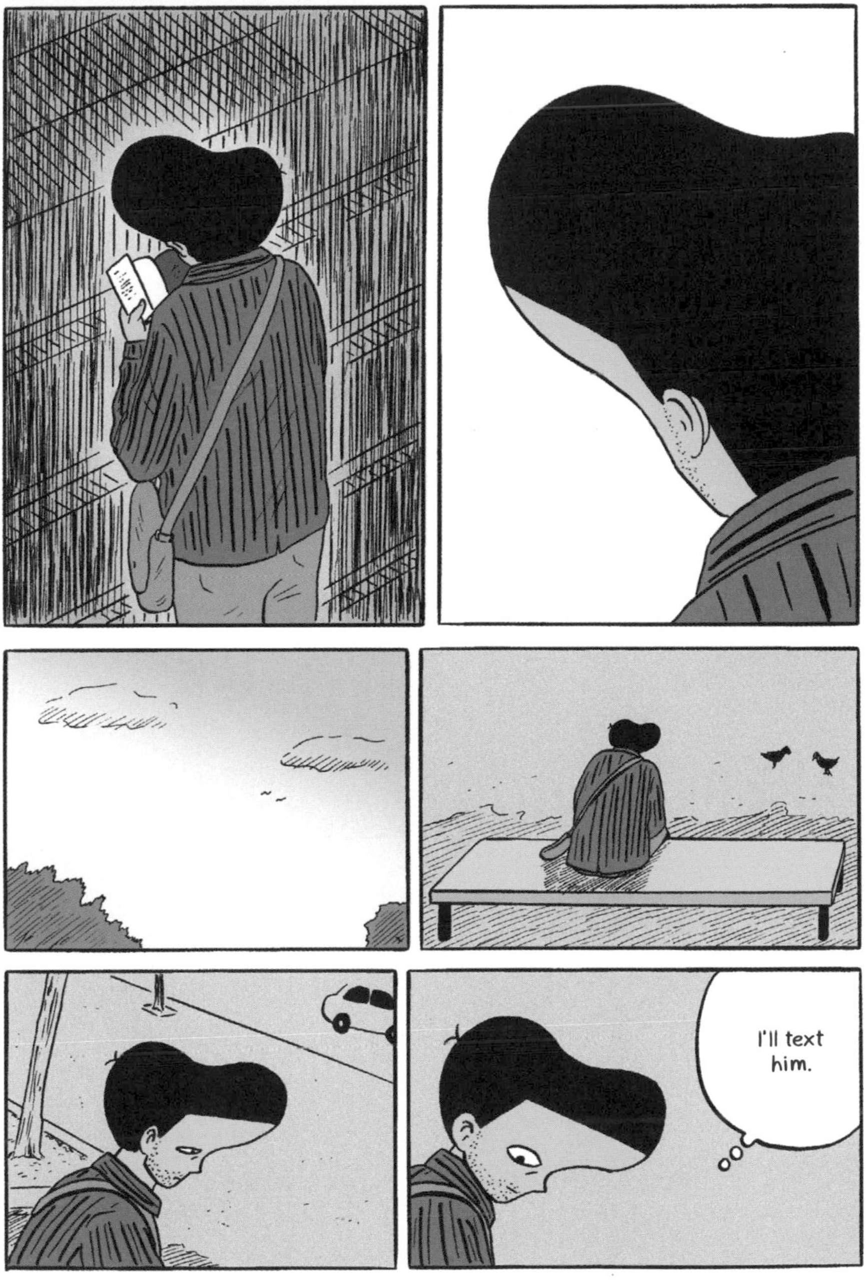
I'll text
him.

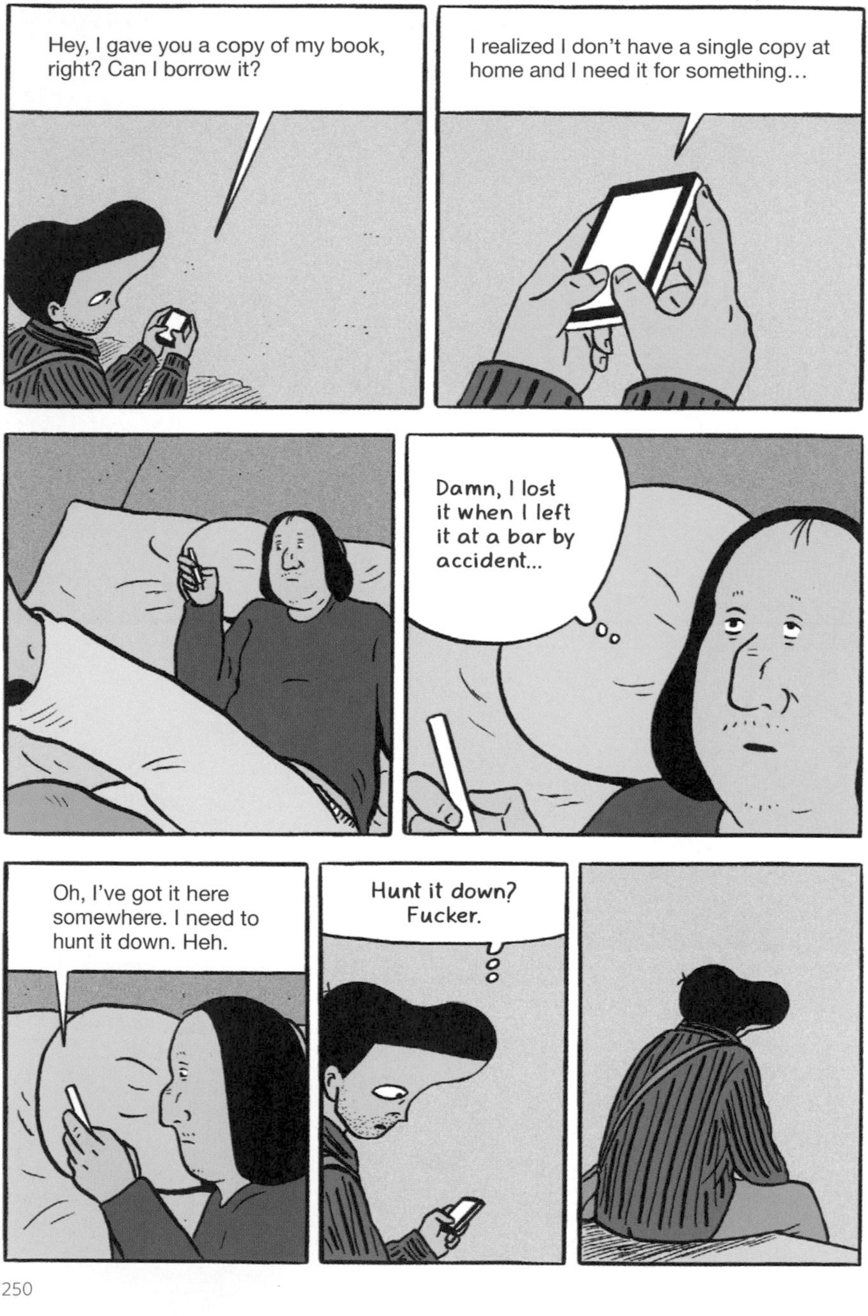
Hey, I gave you a copy of my book, right? Can I borrow it?
I realized I don't have a single copy at home and I need it for something…
Damn, I lost it when I left it at a bar by accident...
Oh, I've got it here somewhere. I need to hunt it down. Heh.
Hunt it down? Fucker.

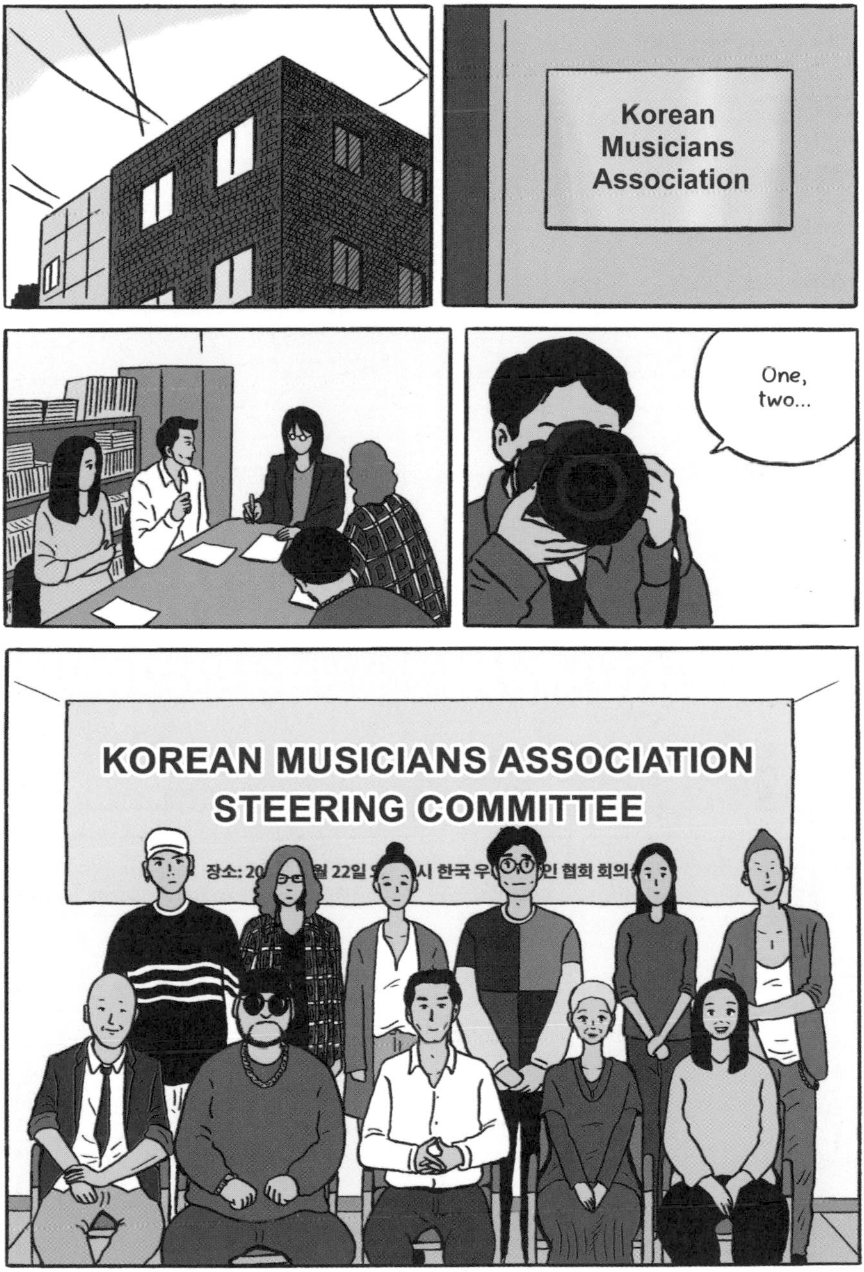
Korean Musicians Association
One, two...
KOREAN MUSICIANS ASSOCIATION STEERING COMMITTEE

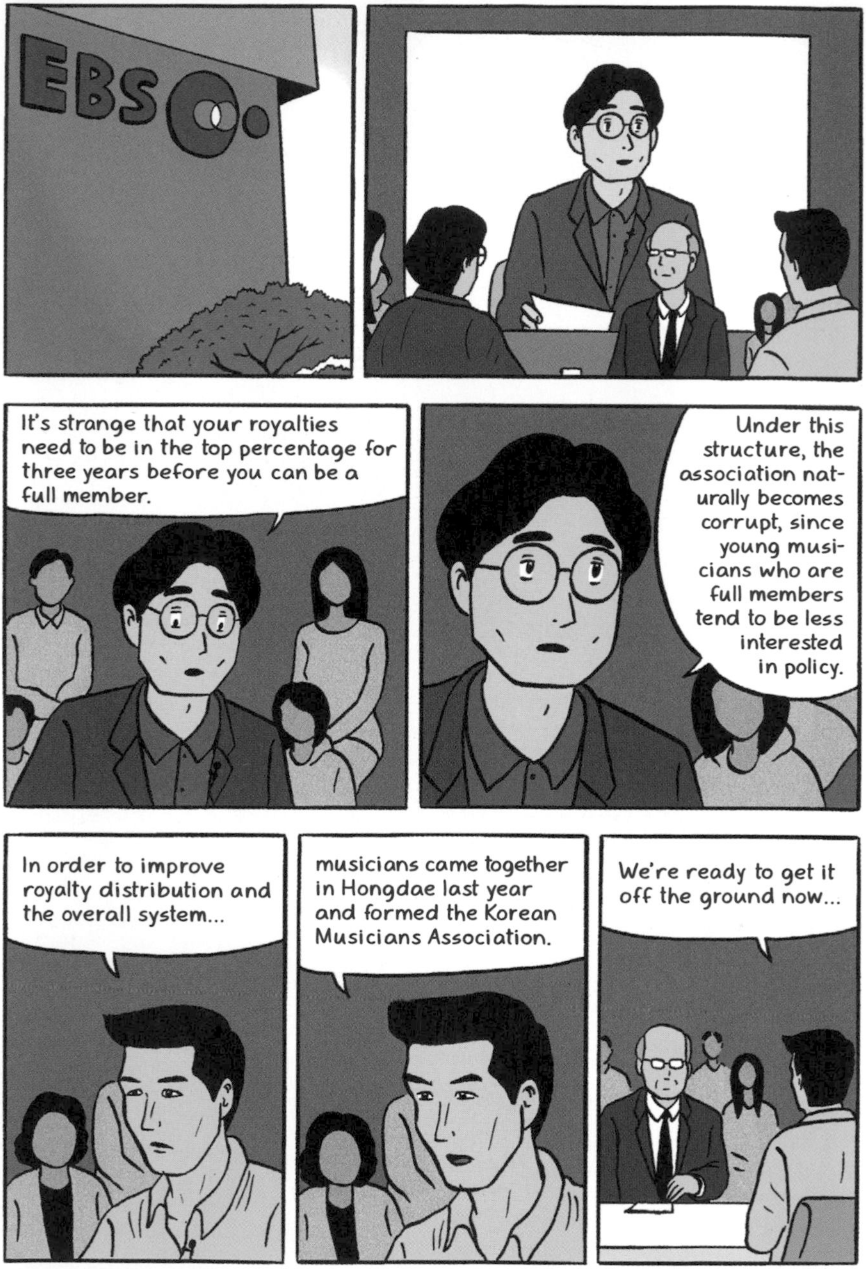
EBS
It's strange that your royalties need to be in the top percentage for three years before you can be a full member.
Under this structure, the association naturally becomes corrupt, since young musicians who are full members tend to be less interested in policy.
In order to improve royalty distribution and the overall system...
musicians came together in Hongdae last year and formed the Korean Musicians Association.
We're ready to get it off the ground now...

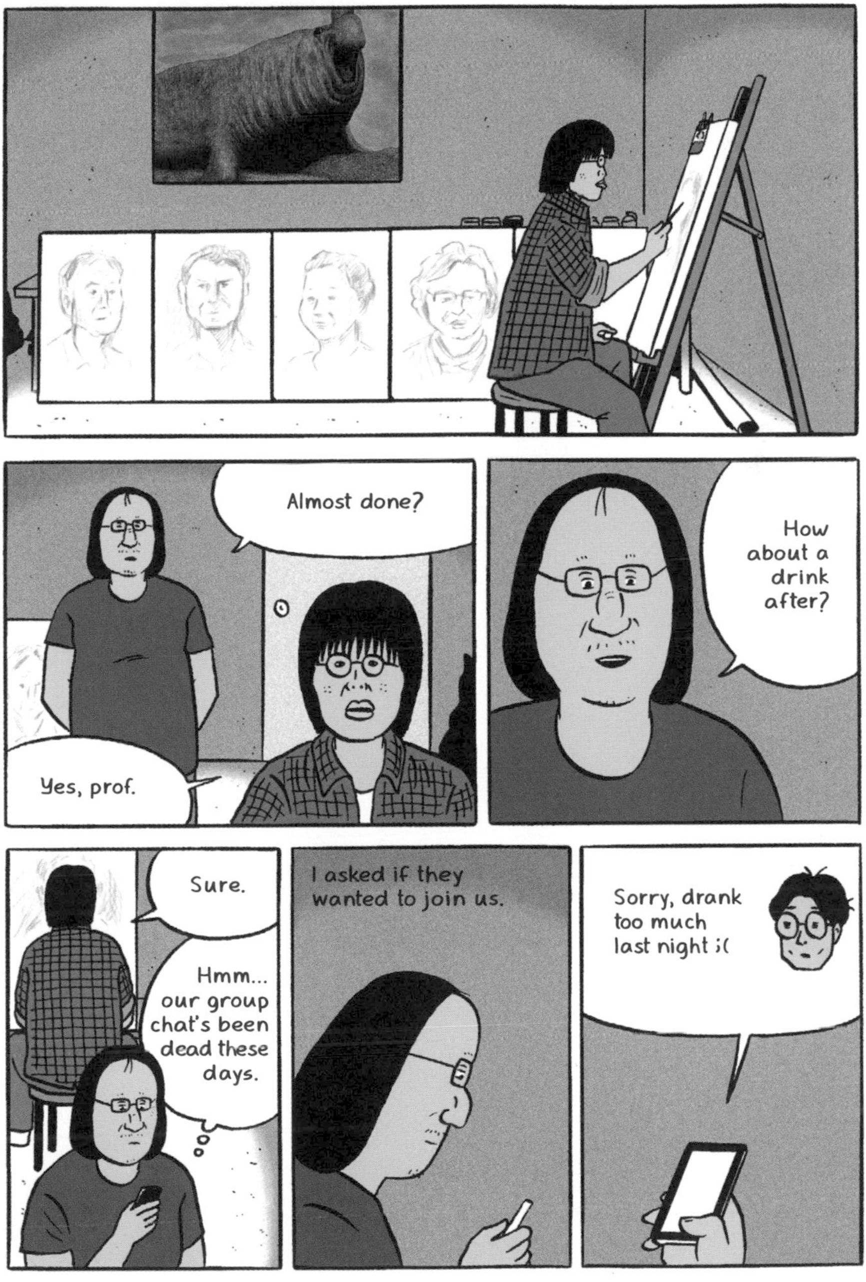
Almost done?
Yes, prof.
How about a drink after?
Sure.
Hmm... our group chat's been dead these days.
I asked if they wanted to join us.
Sorry, drank too much last night ;(

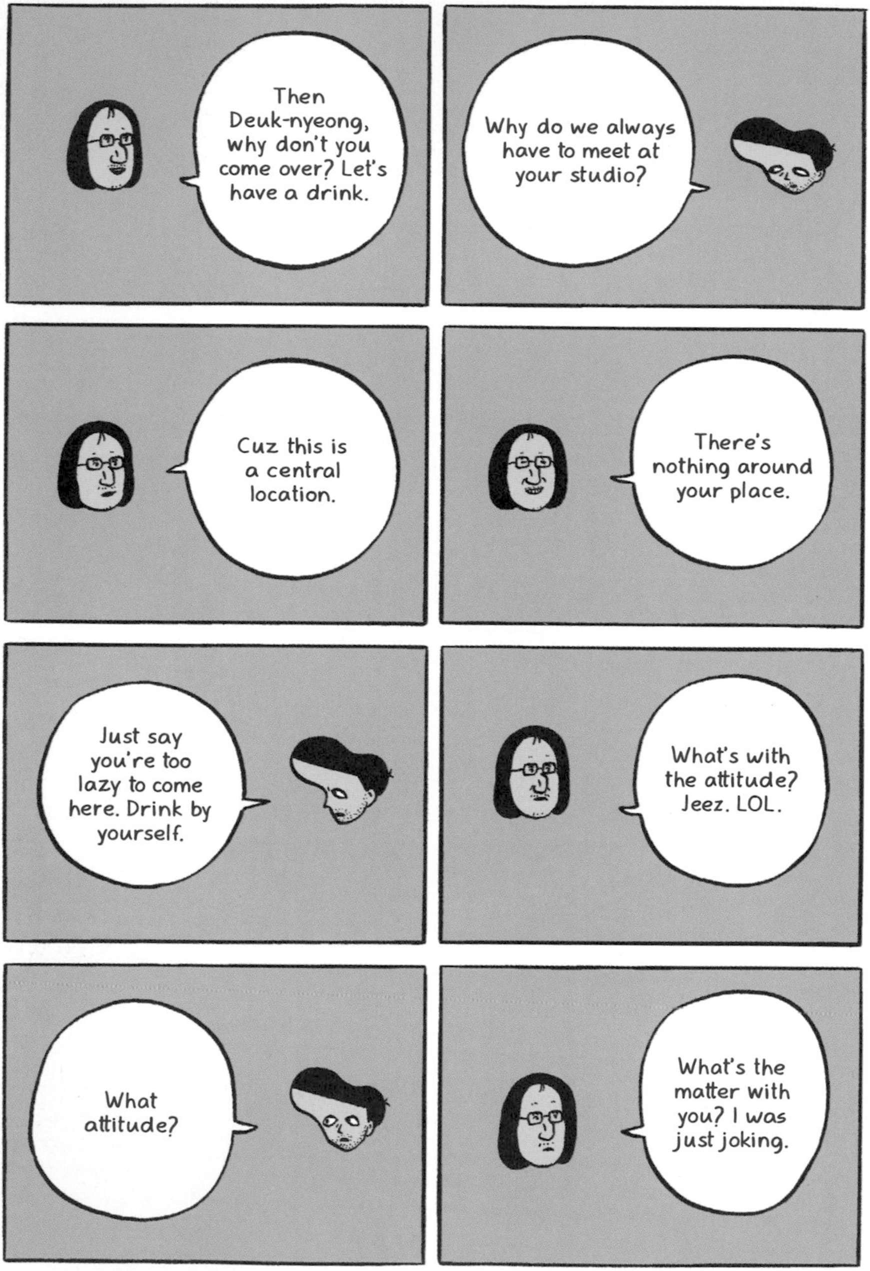
Then Deuk-nyeong, why don't you come over? Let's have a drink.
Why do we always have to meet at your studio?
Cuz this is a central location.
There's nothing around your place.
Just say you're too lazy to come here. Drink by yourself.
What's with the attitude? Jeez. LOL.
What attitude?
What's the matter with you? I was just joking.

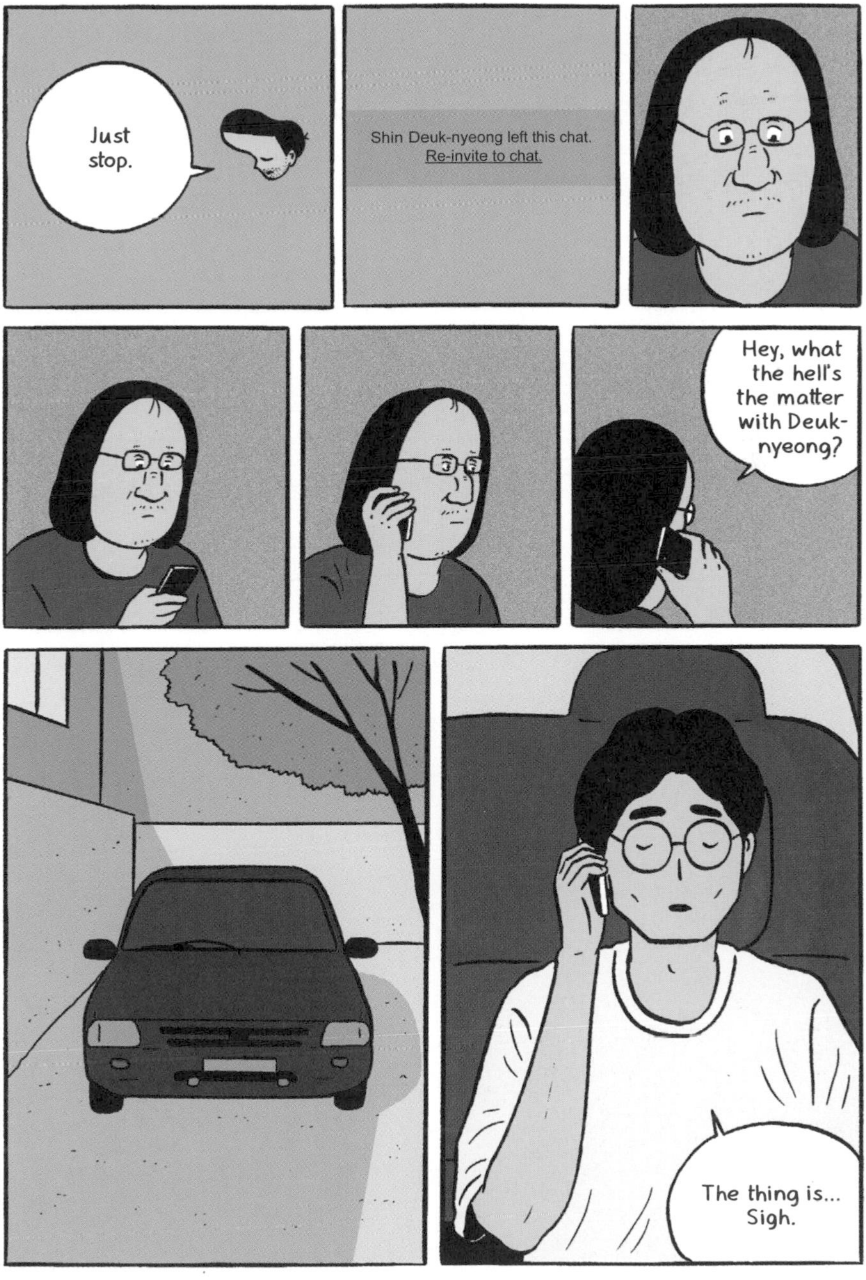
Just stop.
Shin Deuk-nyeong left this chat.
Re-invite to chat.
Hey, what the hell's the matter with Deuk-nyeong?
The thing is... Sigh.

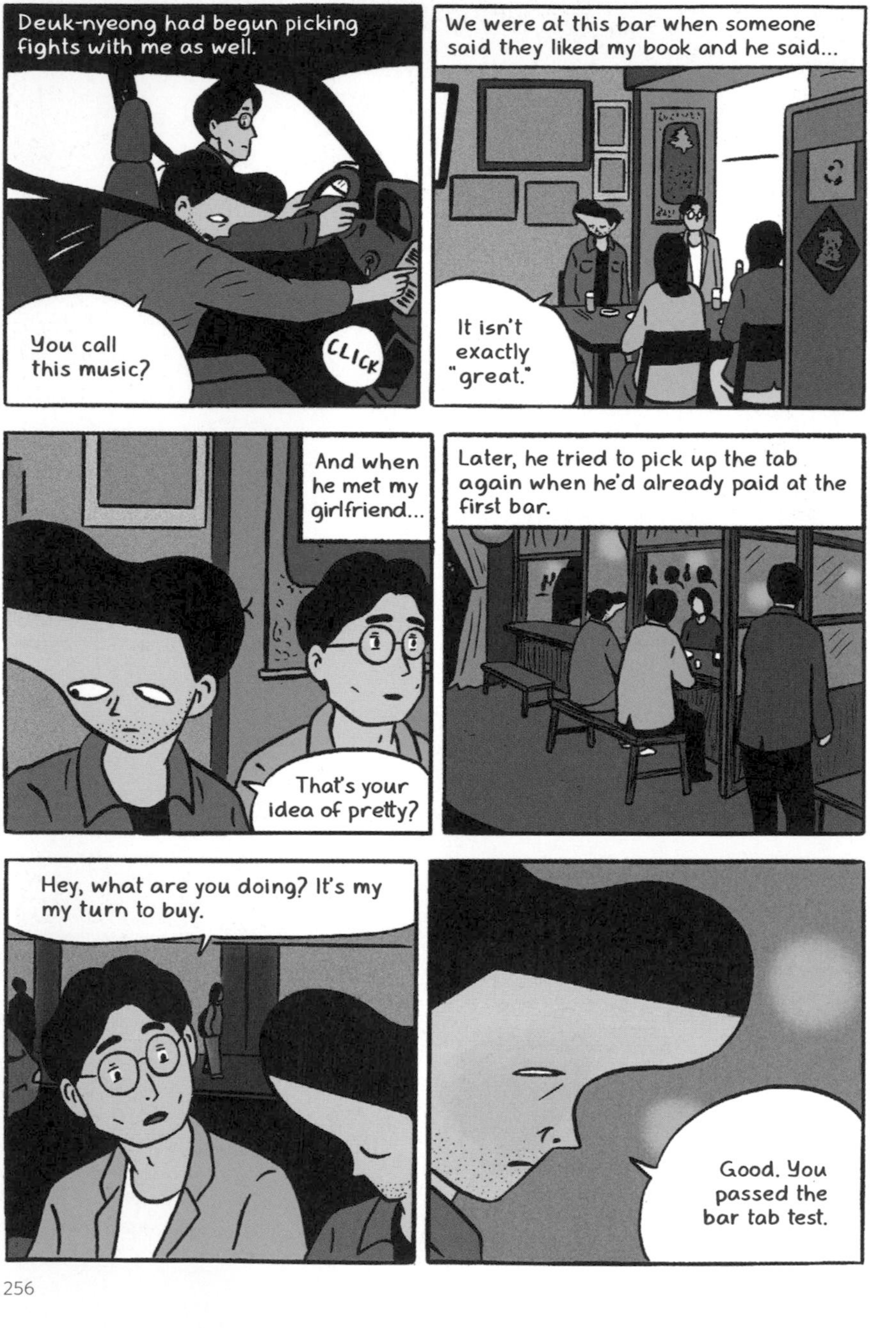
Deuk-nyeong had begun picking fights with me as well.
You call this music?
CLICK
We were at this bar when someone said they liked my book and he said...
It isn't exactly "great."
And when he met my girlfriend...
That's your idea of pretty?
Later, he tried to pick up the tab again when he'd already paid at the first bar.
Hey, what are you doing? It's my my turn to buy.
Good. You passed the bar tab test.

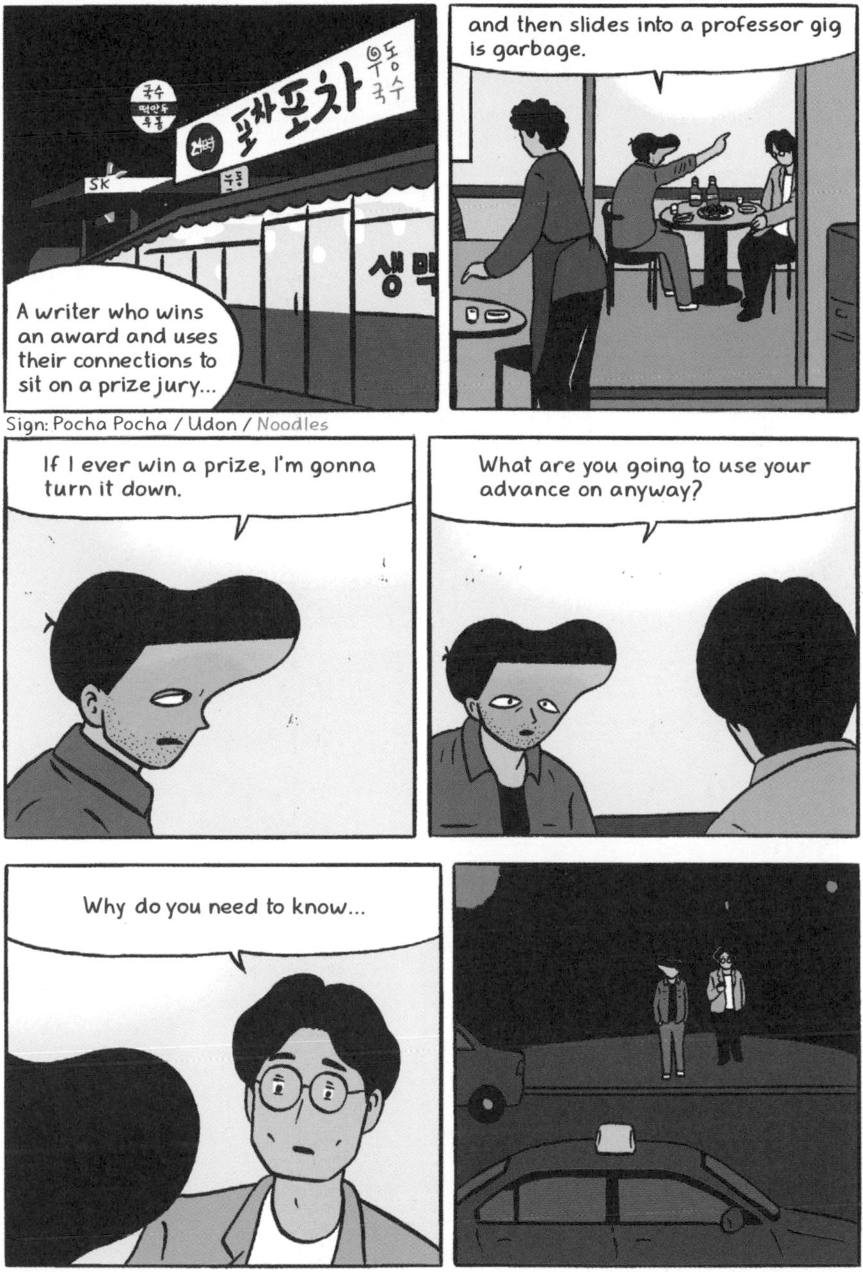

포차포차
우동
국수
A writer who wins an award and uses their connections to sit on a prize jury...
Sign: Pocha Pocha / Udon / Noodles
and then slides into a professor gig is garbage.
If I ever win a prize, I'm gonna turn it down.
What are you going to use your advance on anyway?
Why do you need to know...

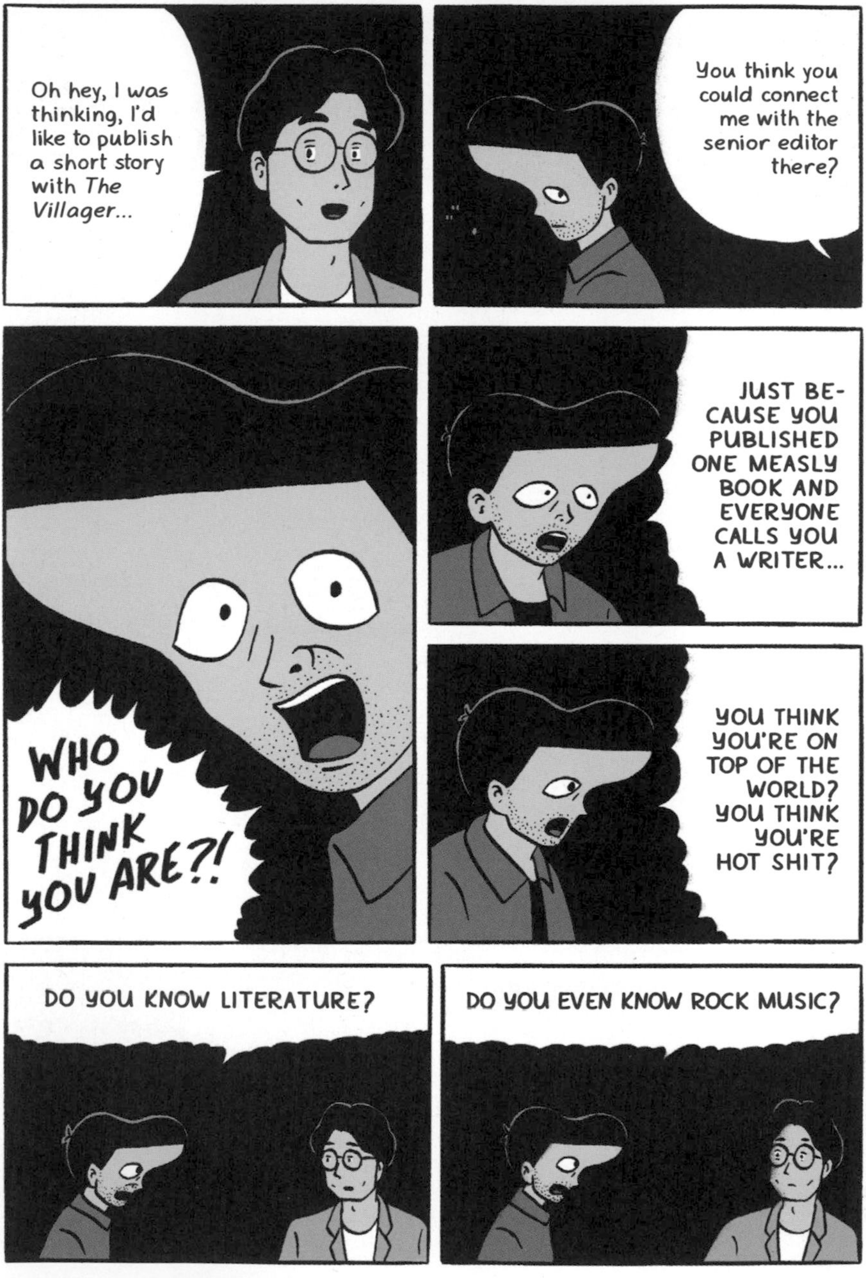

Oh hey, I was thinking, I'd like to publish a short story with *The Villager*...
You think you could connect me with the senior editor there?
WHO DO YOU THINK YOU ARE?!
JUST BE-CAUSE YOU PUBLISHED ONE MEASLY BOOK AND EVERYONE CALLS YOU A WRITER...
YOU THINK YOU'RE ON TOP OF THE WORLD? YOU THINK YOU'RE HOT SHIT?
DO YOU KNOW LITERATURE?
DO YOU EVEN KNOW ROCK MUSIC?

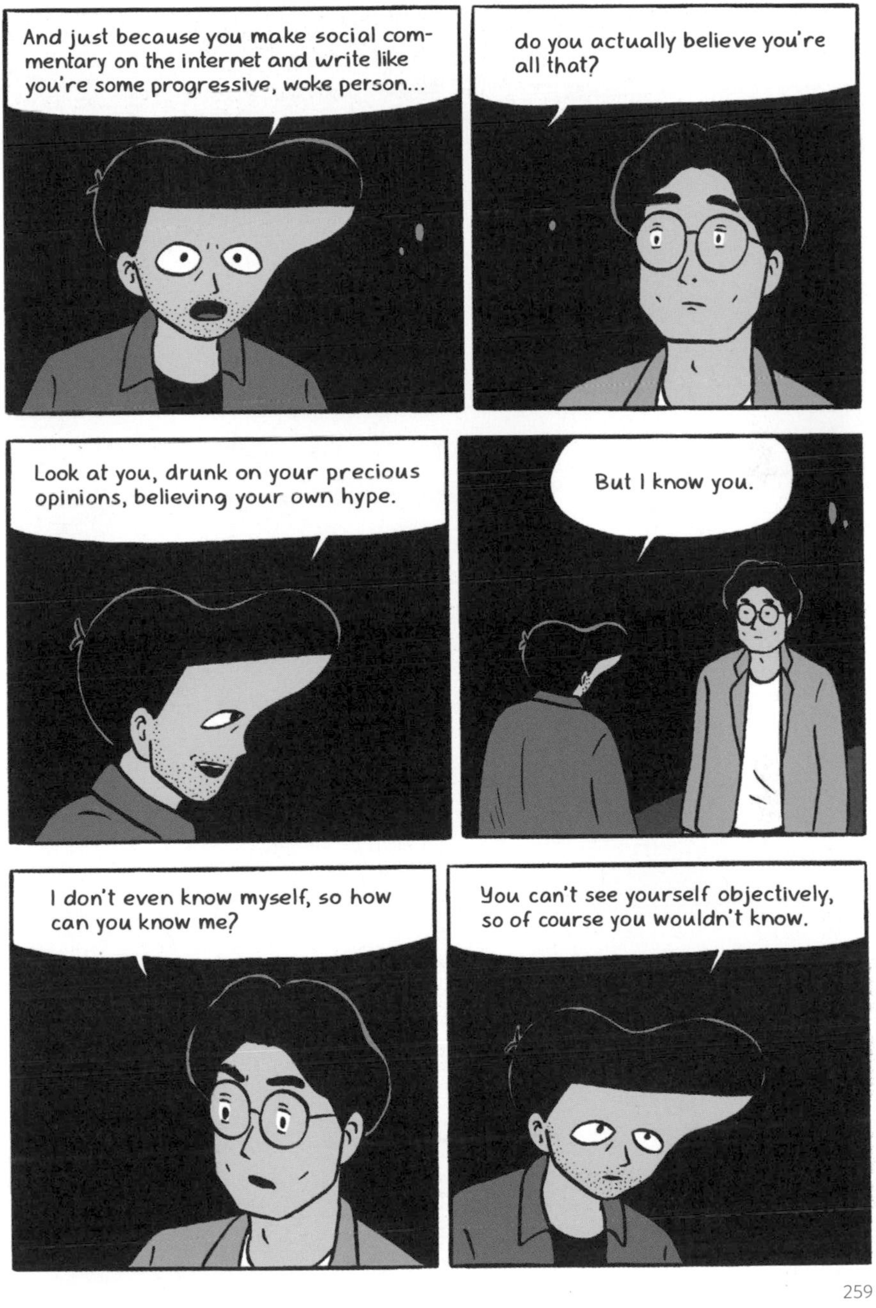
And just because you make social commentary on the internet and write like you're some progressive, woke person...
do you actually believe you're all that?
Look at you, drunk on your precious opinions, believing your own hype.
But I know you.
I don't even know myself, so how can you know me?
You can't see yourself objectively, so of course you wouldn't know.

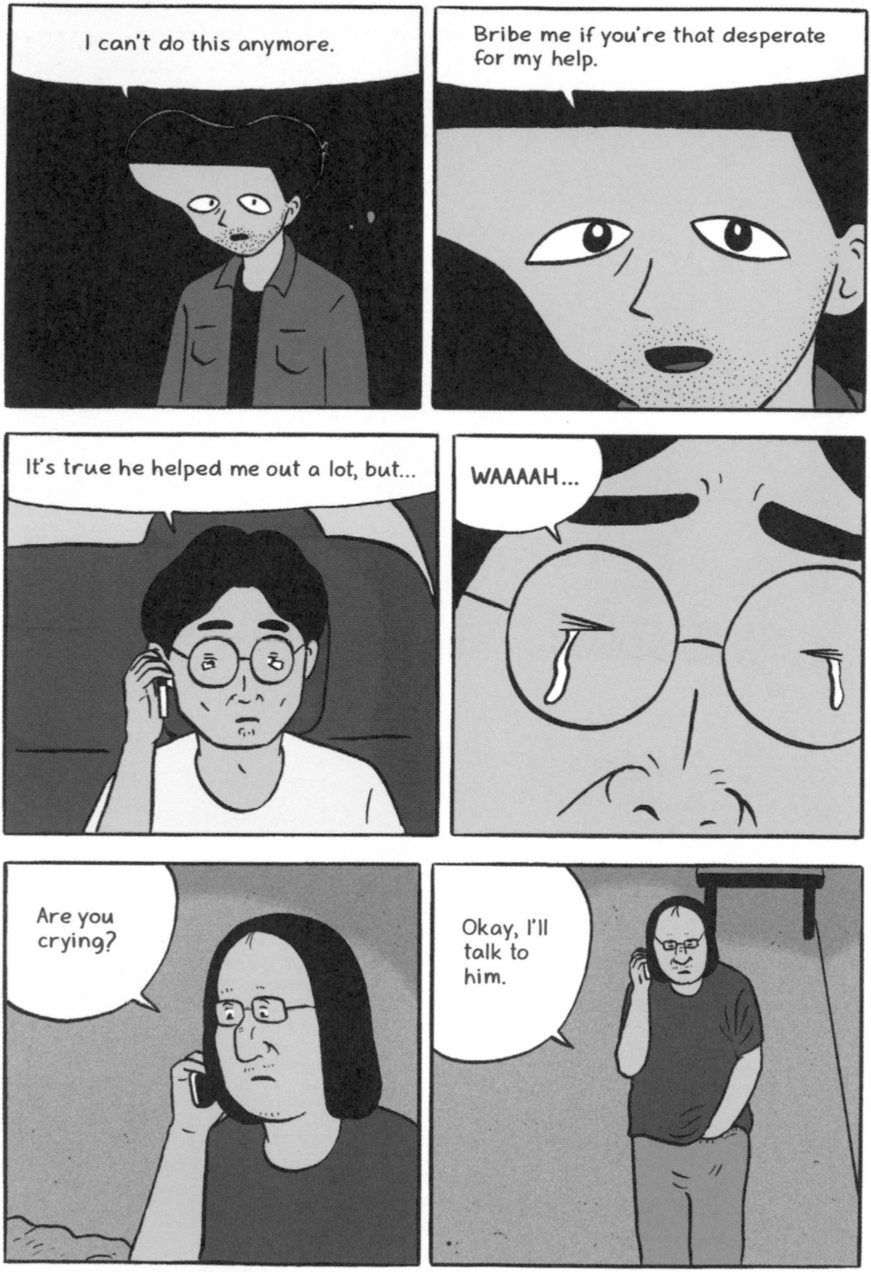
I can't do this anymore.
Bribe me if you're that desperate for my help.
It's true he helped me out a lot, but...
WAAAAH...
Are you crying?
Okay, I'll talk to him.

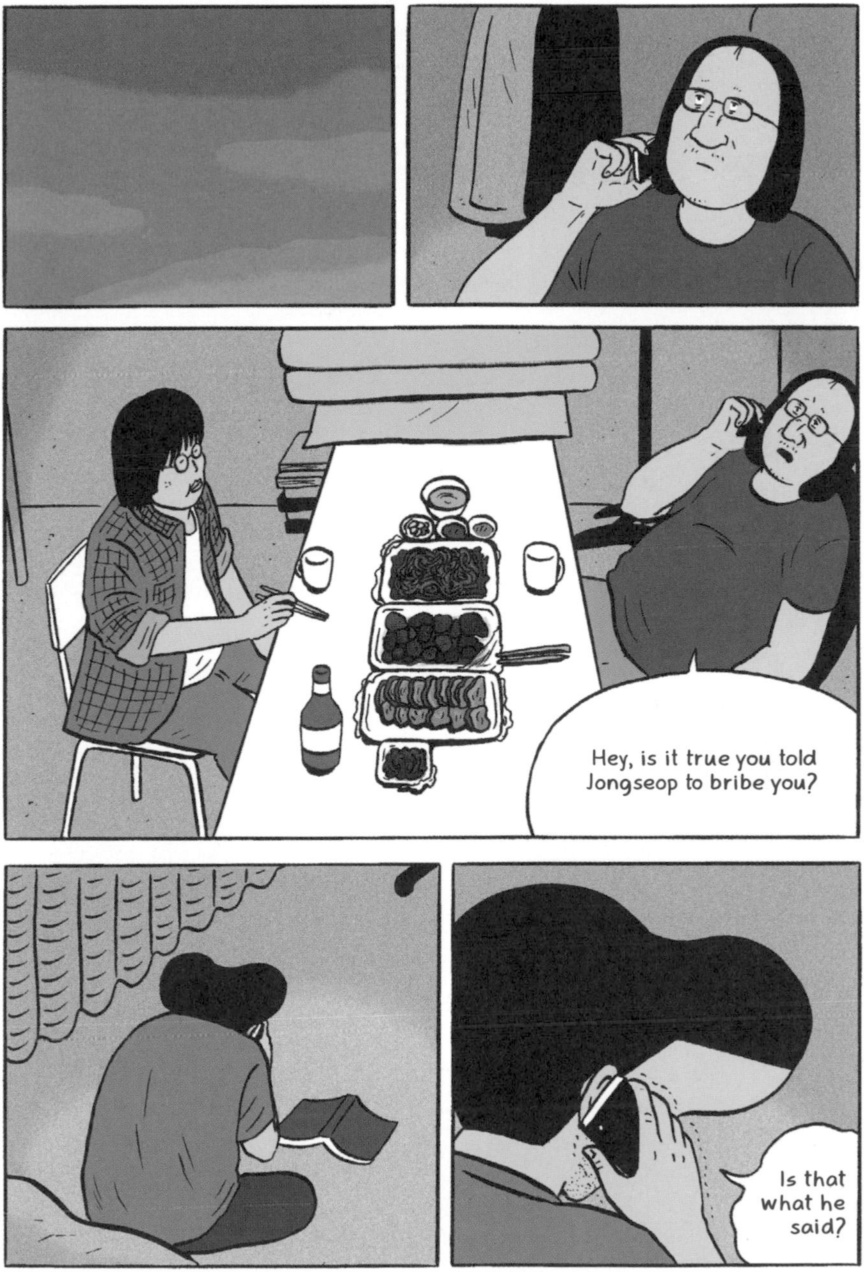
Hey, is it true you told
Jongseop to bribe you?
Is that what he said?

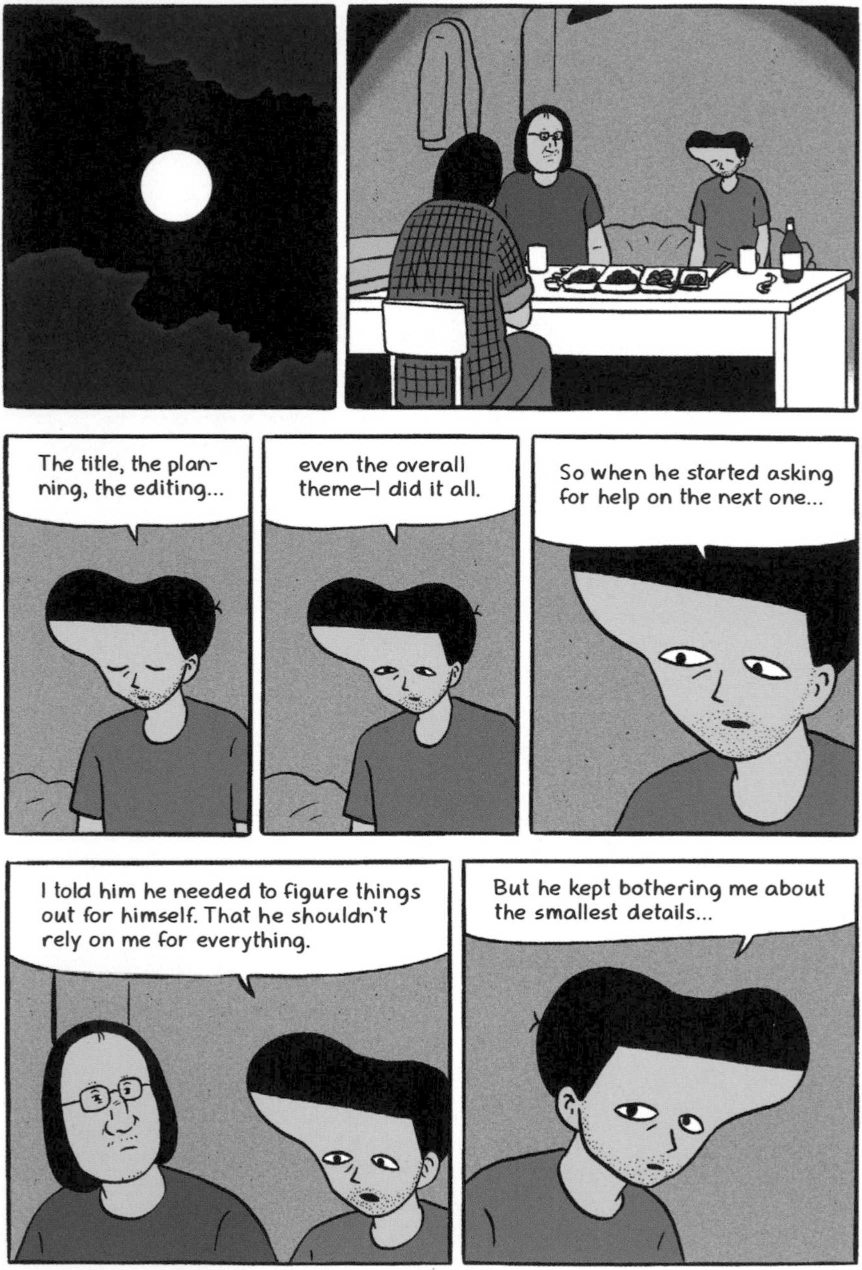
The title, the planning, the editing...
even the overall theme—I did it all.
So when he started asking for help on the next one...
I told him he needed to figure things out for himself. That he shouldn't rely on me for everything.
But he kept bothering me about the smallest details...

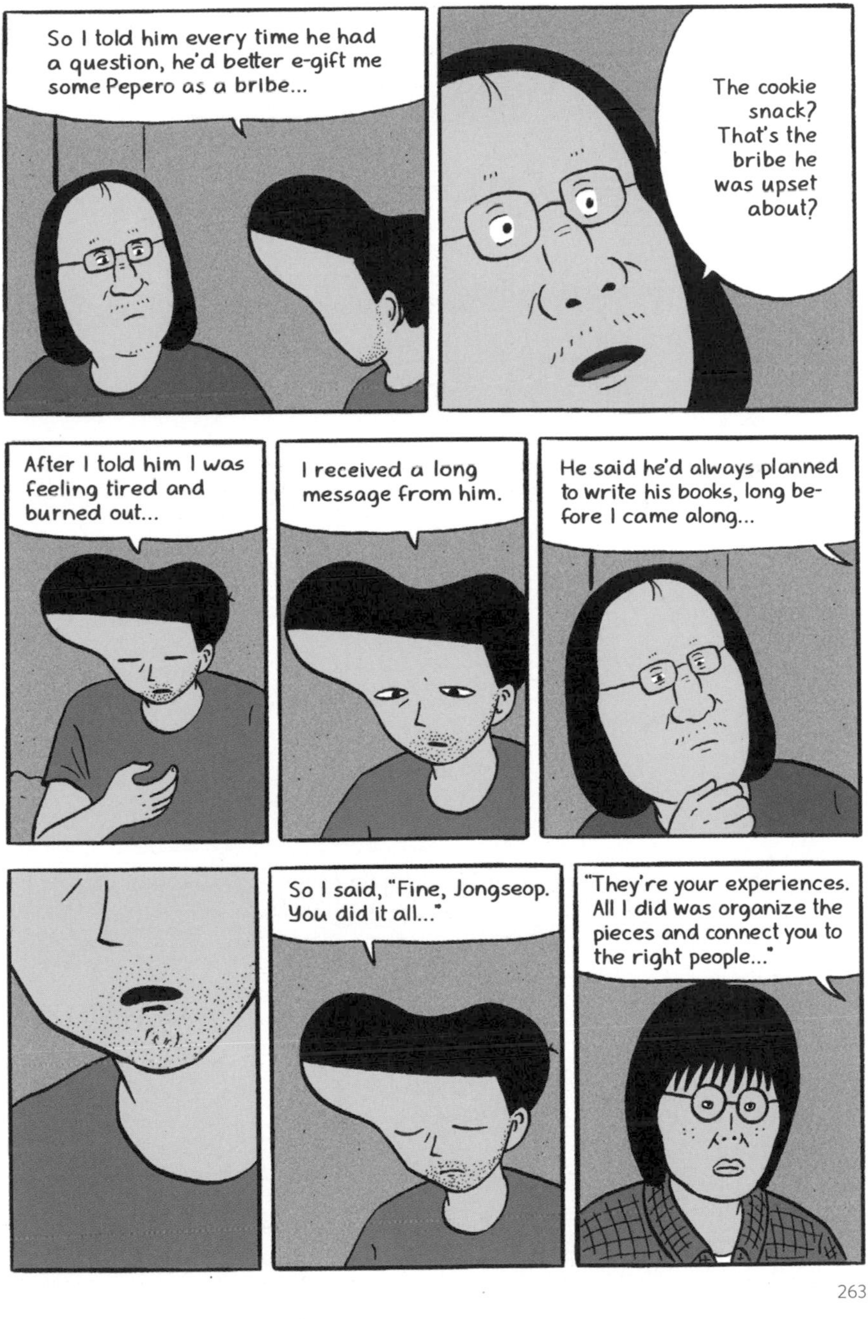

So I told him every time he had a question, he'd better e-gift me some Pepero as a bribe...
The cookie snack? That's the bribe he was upset about?
After I told him I was feeling tired and burned out...
I received a long message from him.
He said he'd always planned to write his books, long before I came along...
So I said, "Fine, Jongseop. You did it all..."
"They're your experiences. All I did was organize the pieces and connect you to the right people..."

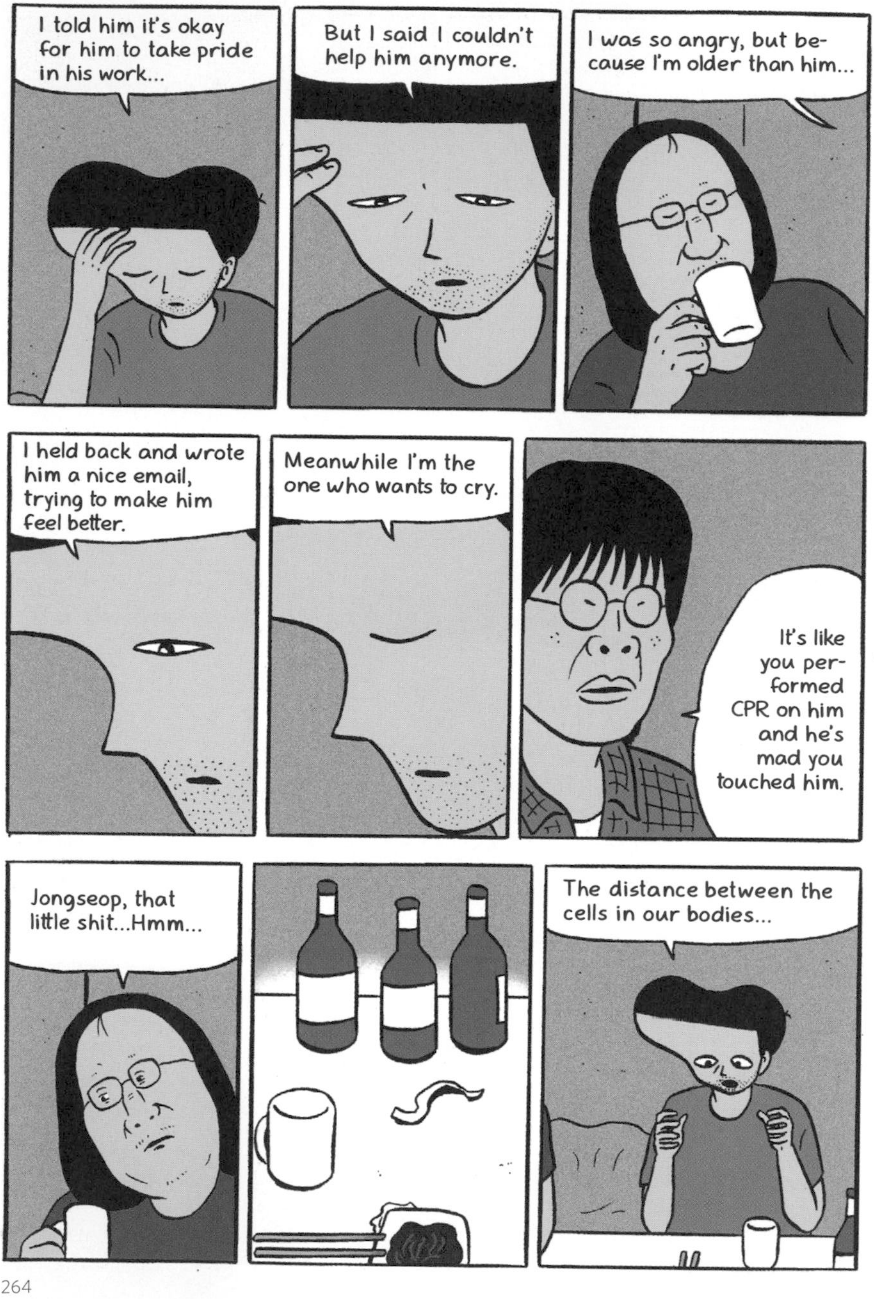
I told him it's okay for him to take pride in his work...
But I said I couldn't help him anymore.
I was so angry, but be-cause I'm older than him...
I held back and wrote him a nice email, trying to make him feel better.
Meanwhile I'm the one who wants to cry.
It's like you per-formed CPR on him and he's mad you touched him.
Jongseop, that little shit...Hmm...
The distance between the cells in our bodies...

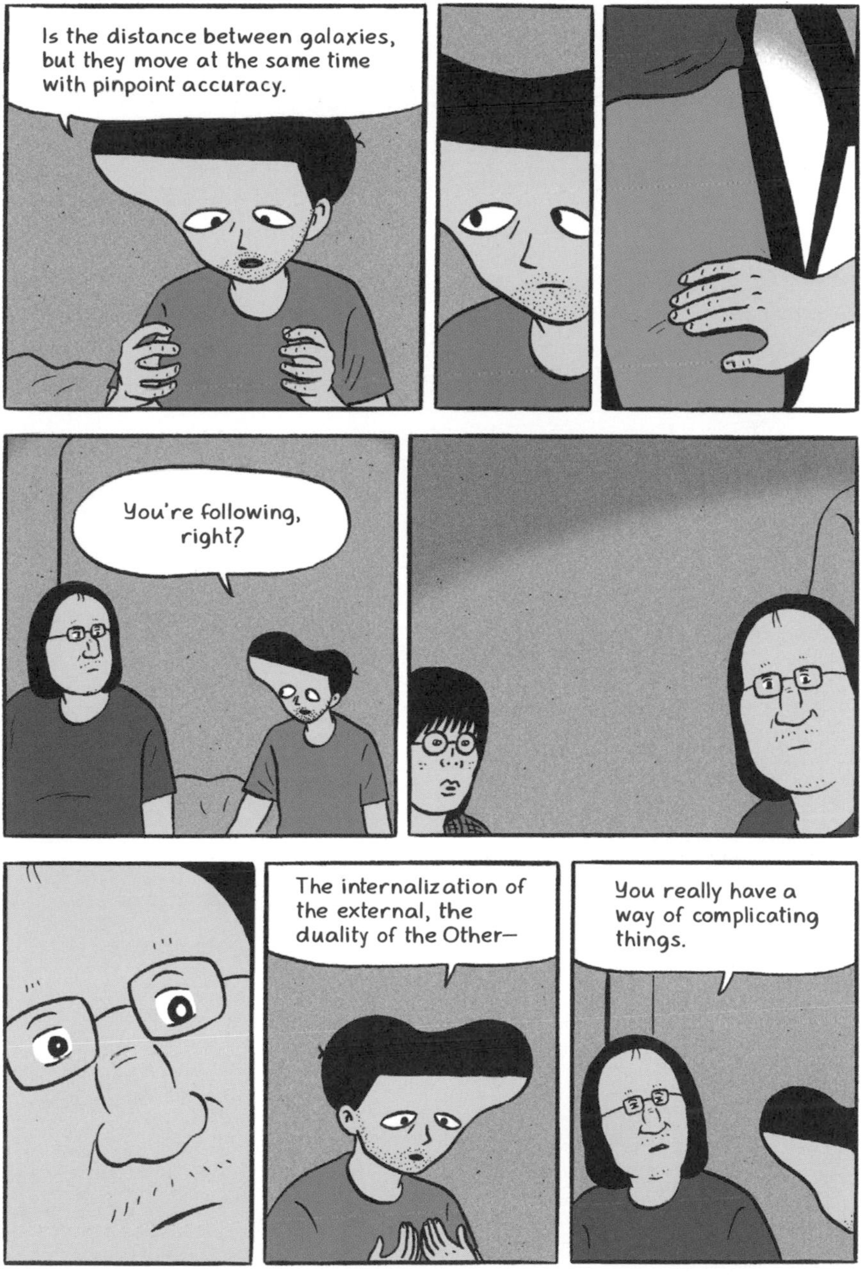
Is the distance between galaxies, but they move at the same time with pinpoint accuracy.
You're following, right?
The internalization of the external, the duality of the Other—
You really have a way of complicating things.

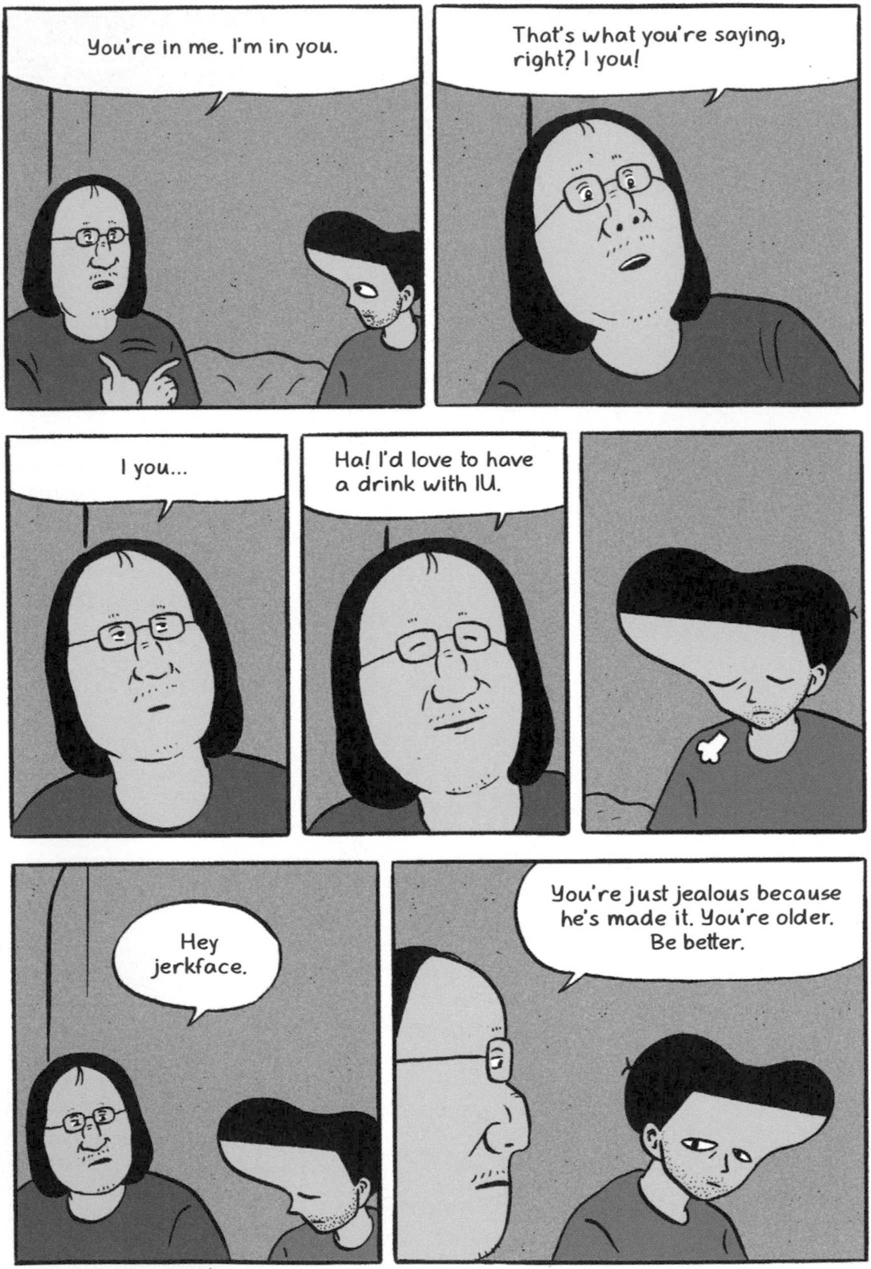
You're in me. I'm in you.
That's what you're saying, right? I you!
I you...
Ha! I'd love to have a drink with IU.
Hey jerkface.
You're just jealous because he's made it. You're older. Be better.

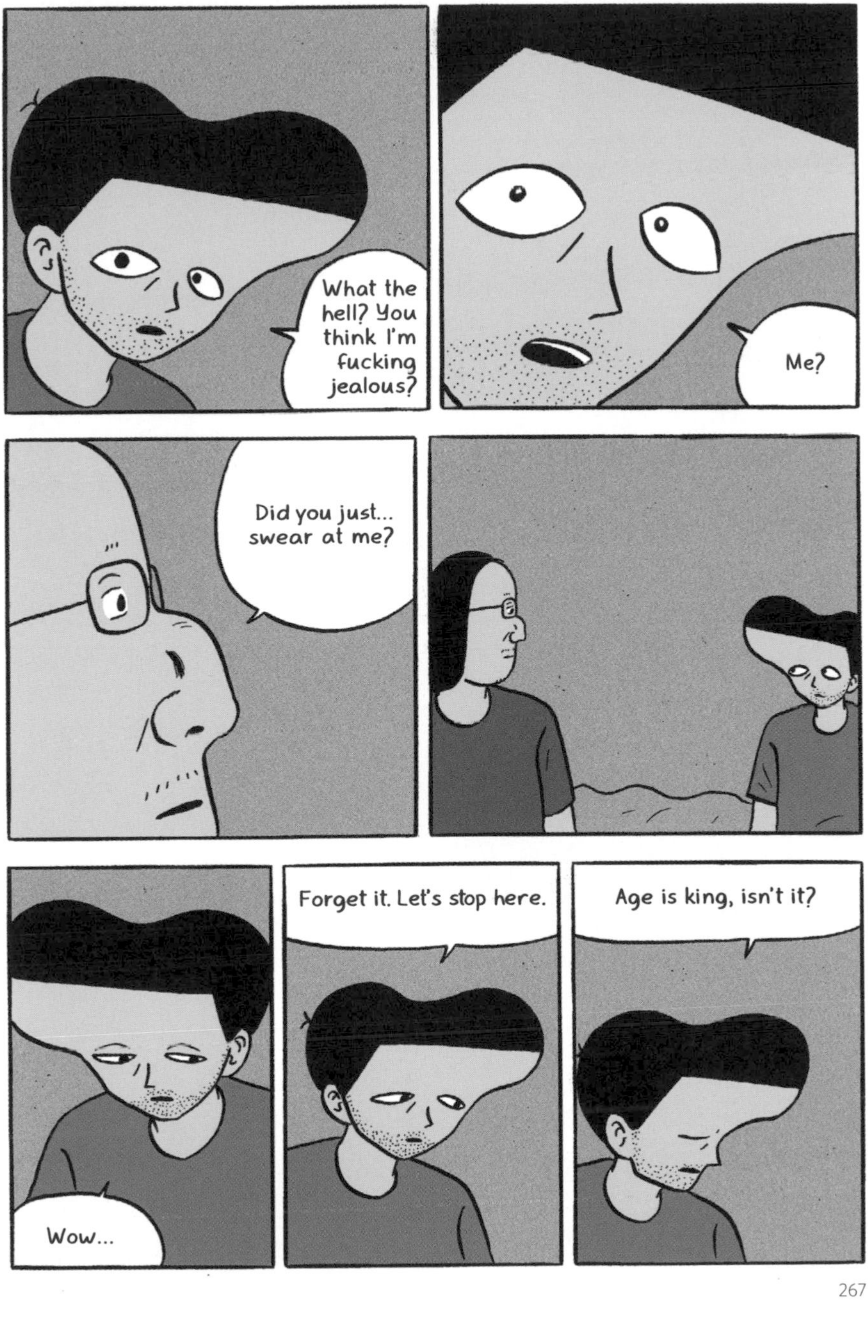
What the hell? You think I'm fucking jealous?
Me?
Did you just... swear at me?
Wow...
Forget it. Let's stop here.
Age is king, isn't it?

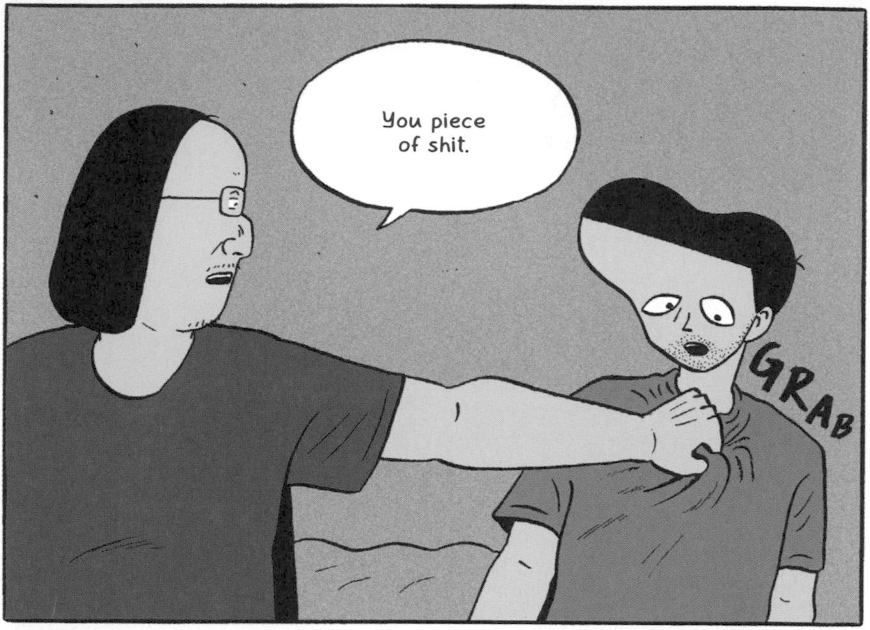
You piece of shit.
GRAB

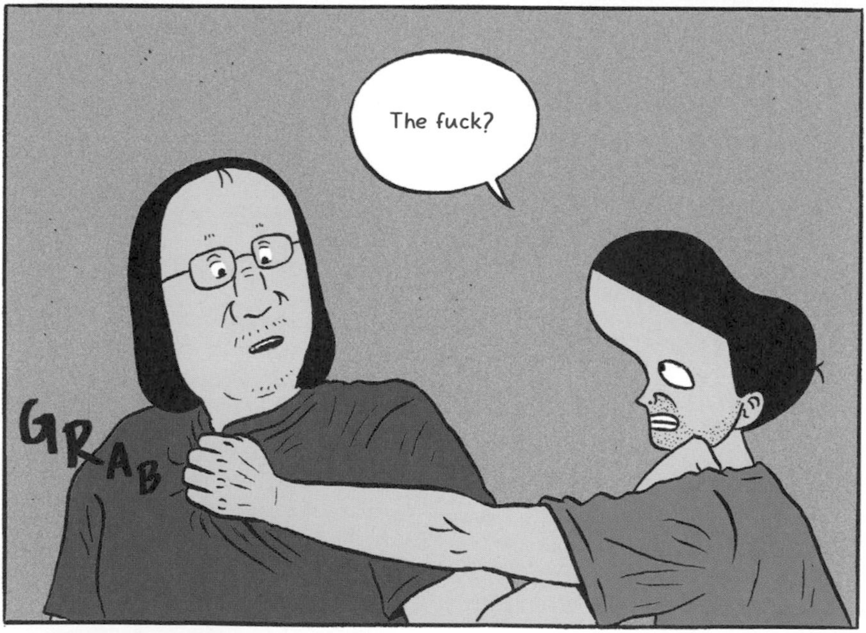
The fuck?
GRAB

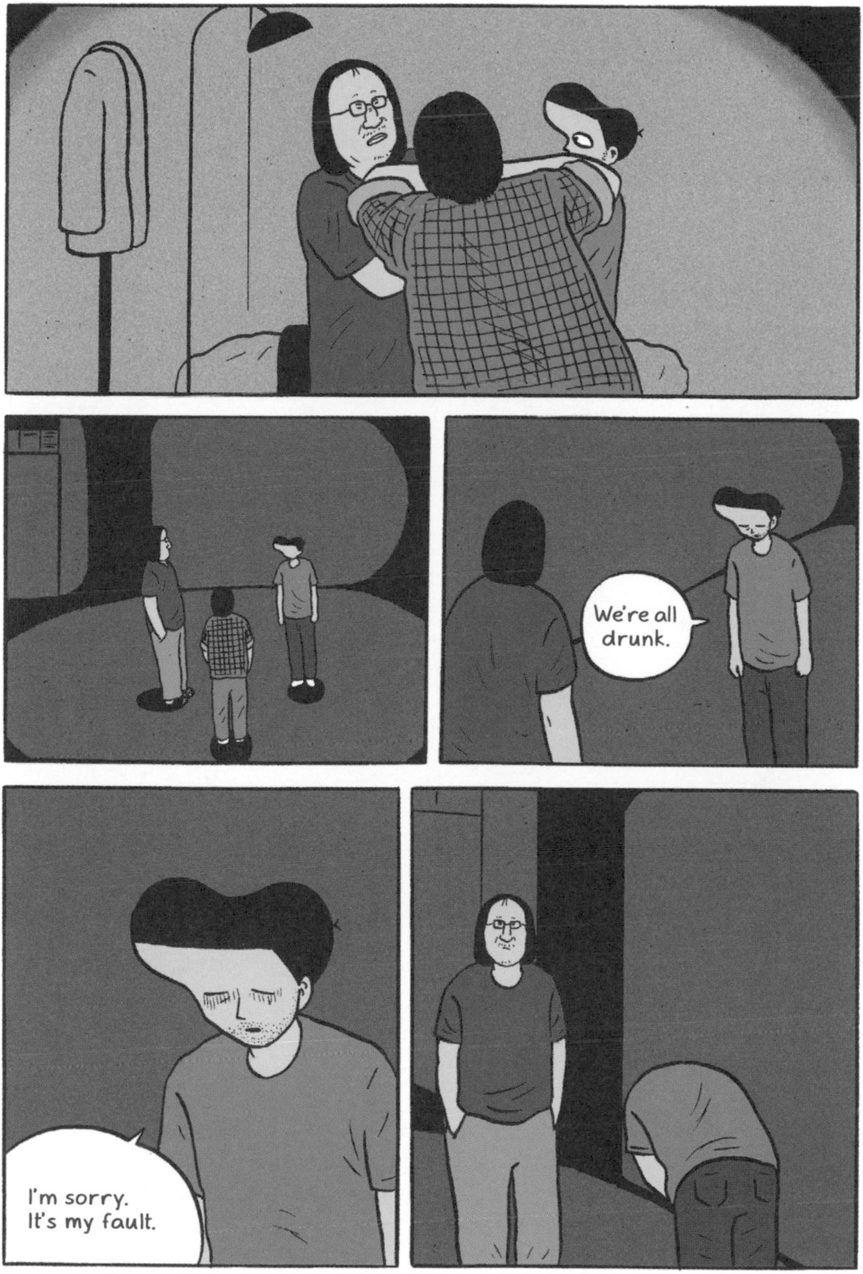
We're all drunk.
I'm sorry. It's my fault.

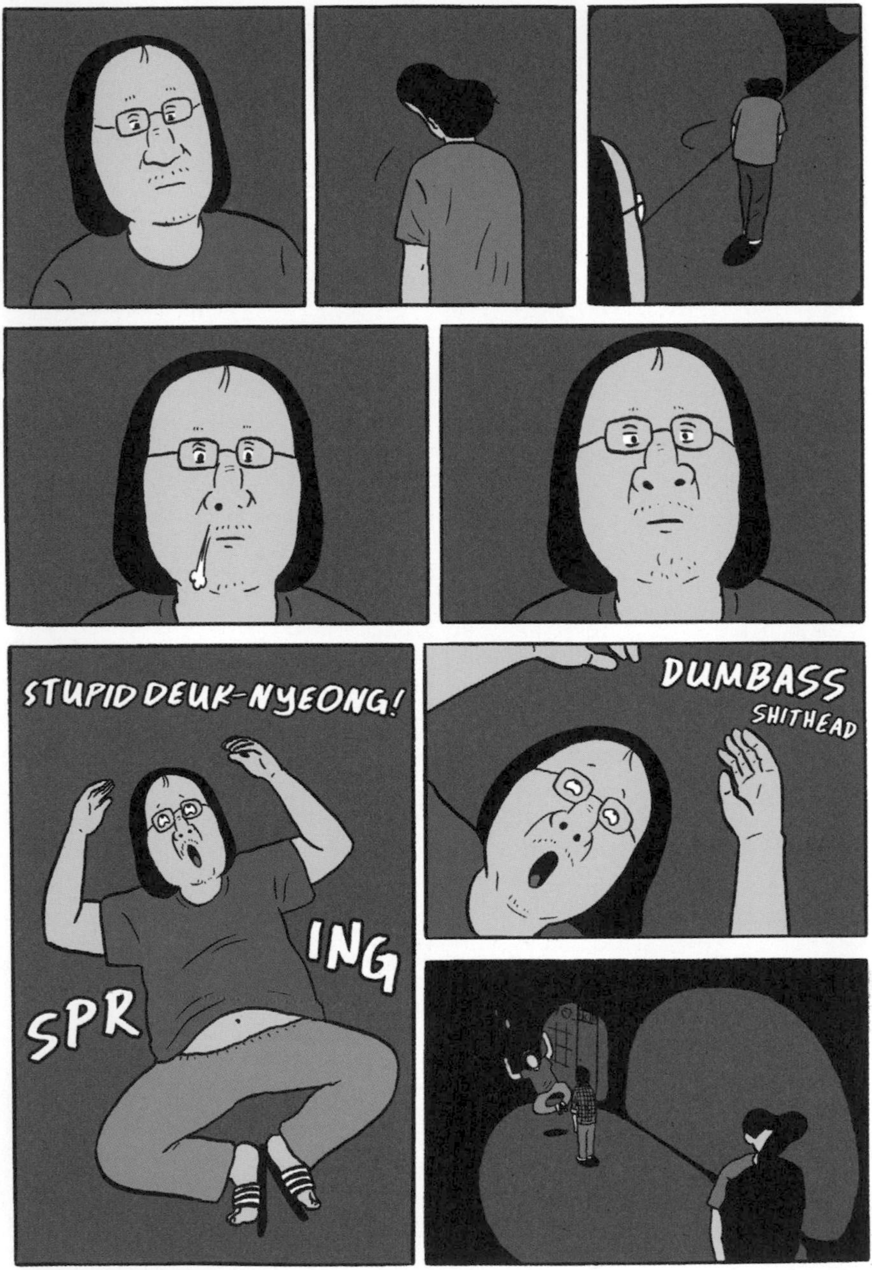
STUPID DEUK-NYEONG!
SPR
ING
DUMBASS
SHITHEAD

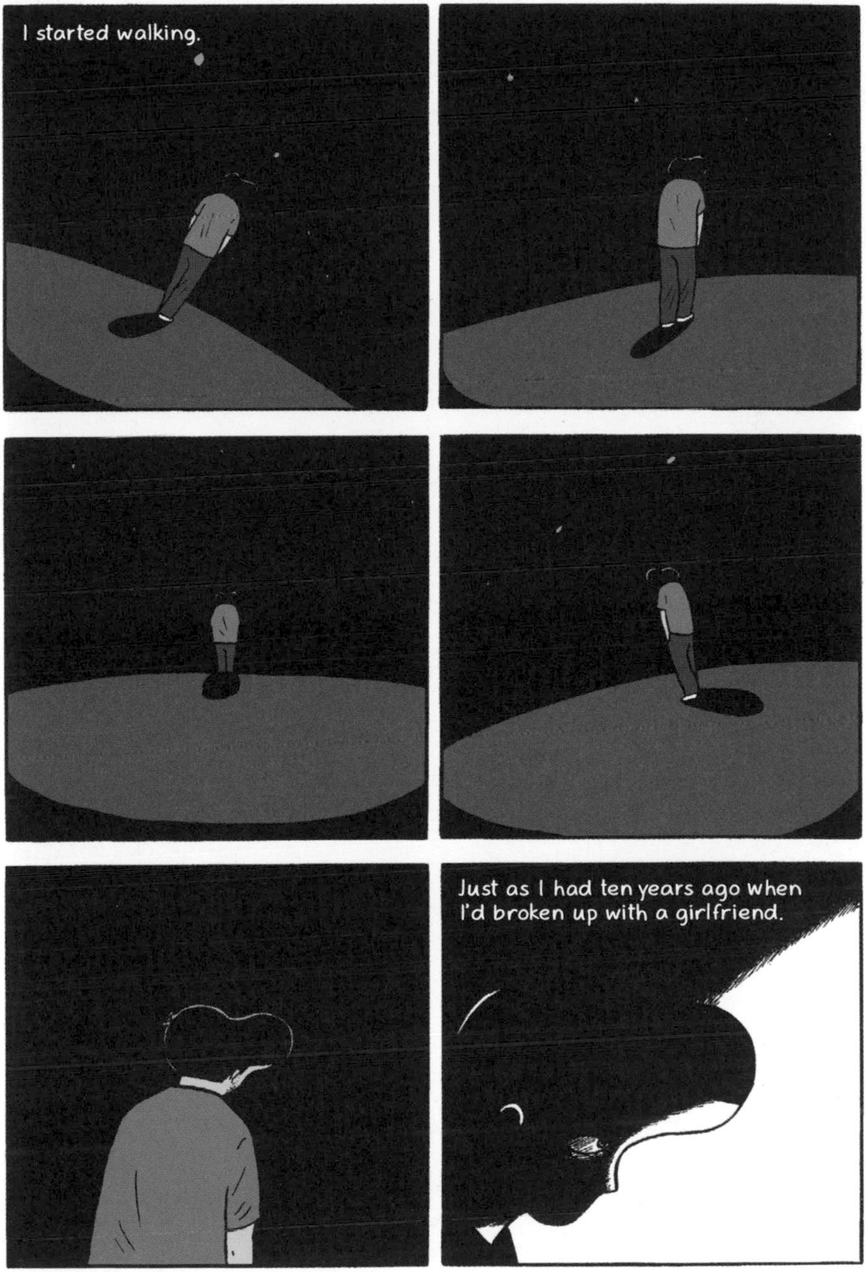
I started walking.
Just as I had ten years ago when I'd broken up with a girlfriend.

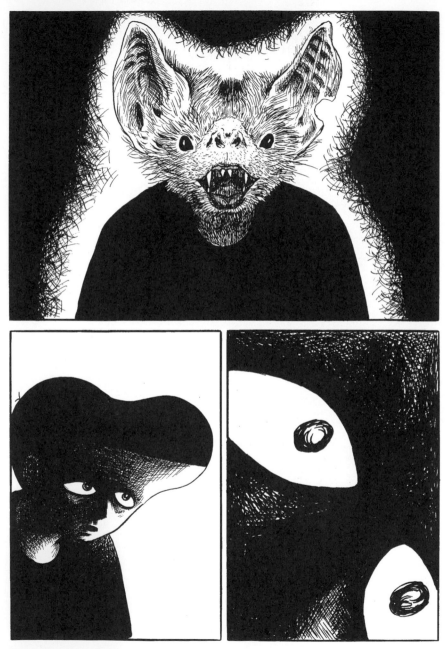

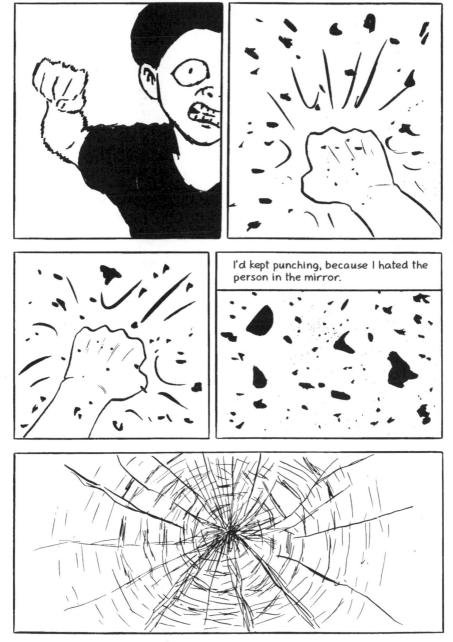

I'd kept punching, because I hated the person in the mirror.

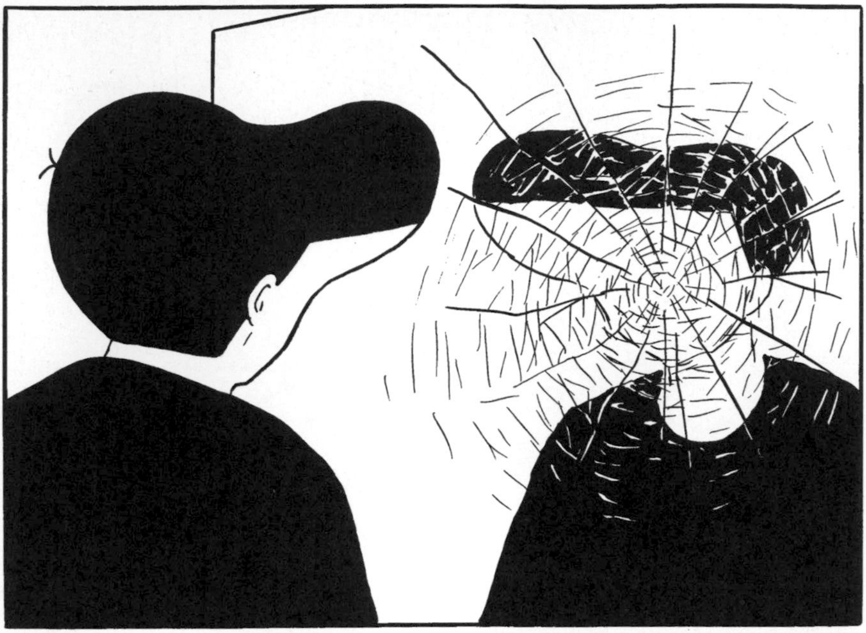

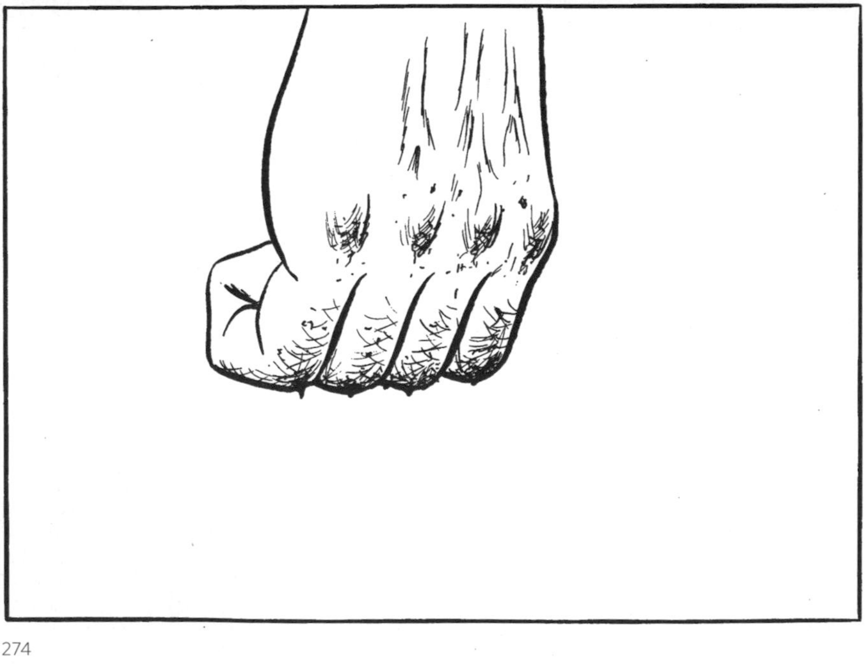

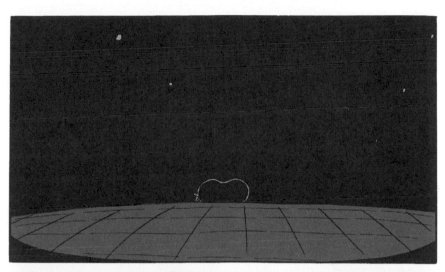

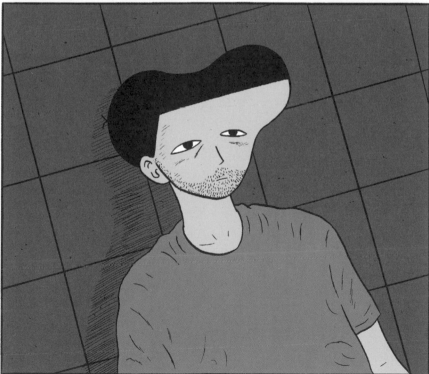

OPPORTUNITY

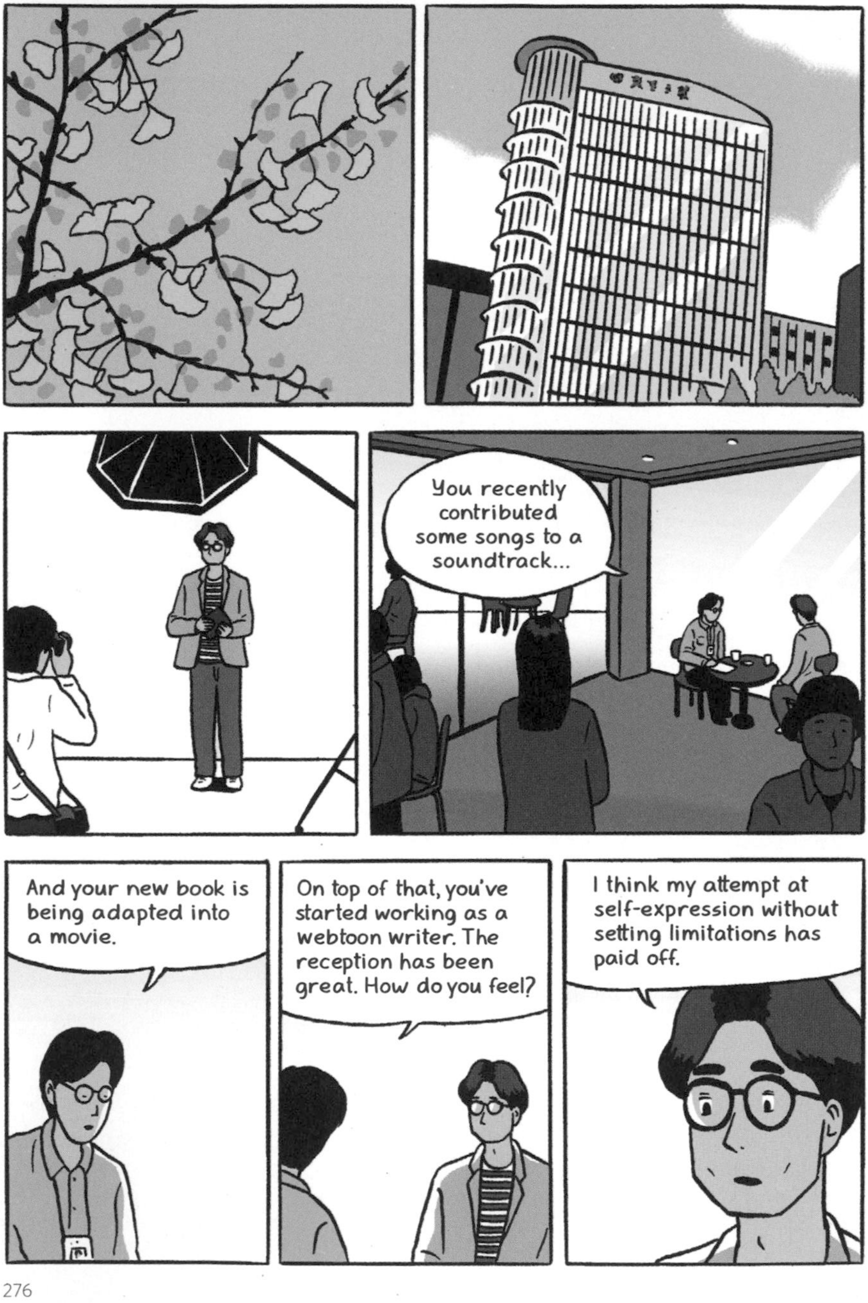
You recently contributed some songs to a soundtrack...
And your new book is being adapted into a movie.
On top of that, you've started working as a webtoon writer. The reception has been great. How do you feel?
I think my attempt at self-expression without setting limitations has paid off.

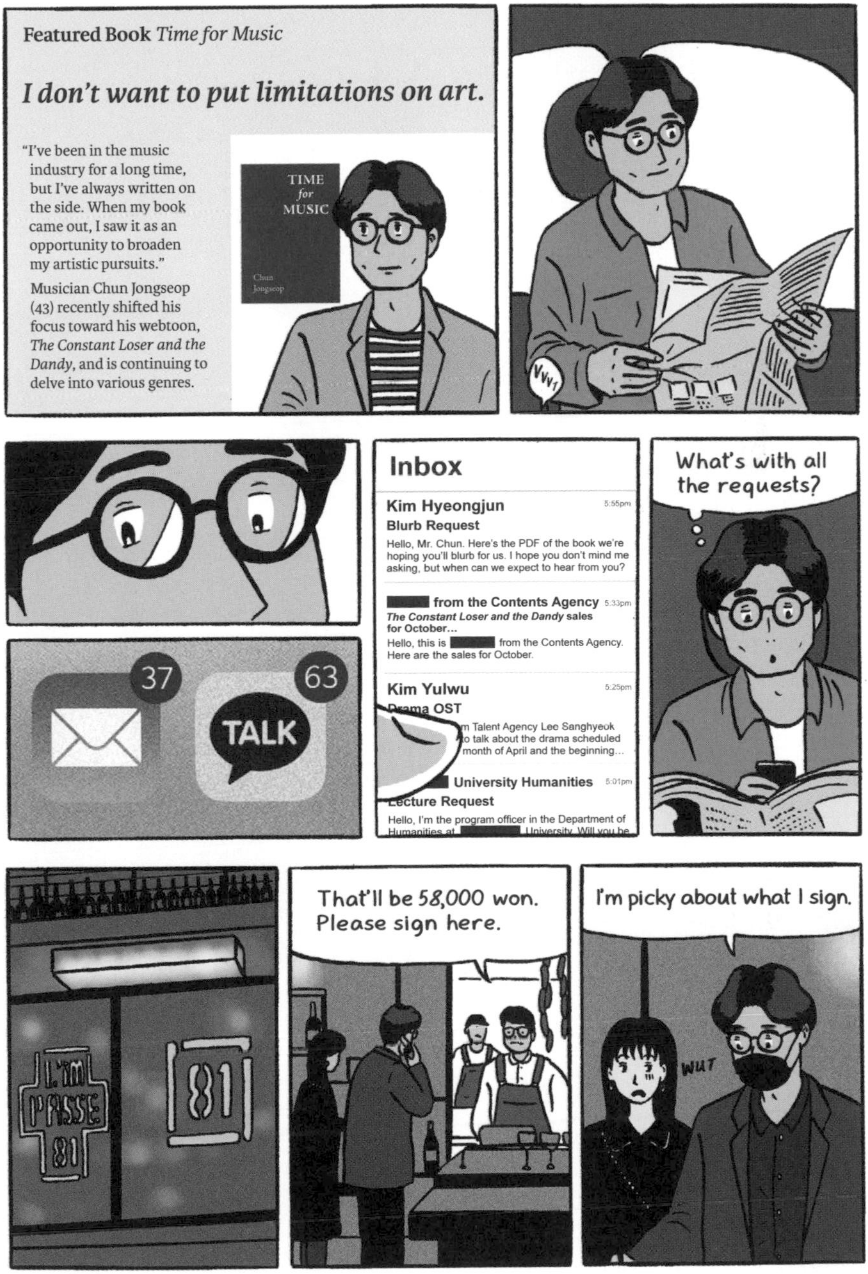
Featured Book Time for Music
I don't want to put limitations on art.
"I've been in the music industry for a long time, but I've always written on the side. When my book came out, I saw it as an opportunity to broaden my artistic pursuits."
Musician Chun Jongseop (43) recently shifted his focus toward his webtoon, The Constant Loser and the Dandy, and is continuing to delve into various genres.
TIME for MUSIC
Chun Jongseop
37
63
TALK
Inbox
Kim Hyeongjun 5:55pm
Blurb Request
Hello, Mr. Chun. Here's the PDF of the book we're hoping you'll blurb for us. I hope you don't mind me asking, but when can we expect to hear from you?
[redacted] from the Contents Agency 5:33pm
The Constant Loser and the Dandy sales for October...
Hello, this is [redacted] from the Contents Agency. Here are the sales for October.
Kim Yulwu 5:25pm
rama OST
m Talent Agency Lee Sanghyeok
o talk about the drama scheduled
month of April and the beginning…
[redacted] University Humanities 5:01pm
ecture Request
Hello, I'm the program officer in the Department of Humanities at [redacted] University. Will you be
What's with all the requests?
L'IM PASSE 81
81
That'll be 58,000 won. Please sign here.
I'm picky about what I sign.
WUT

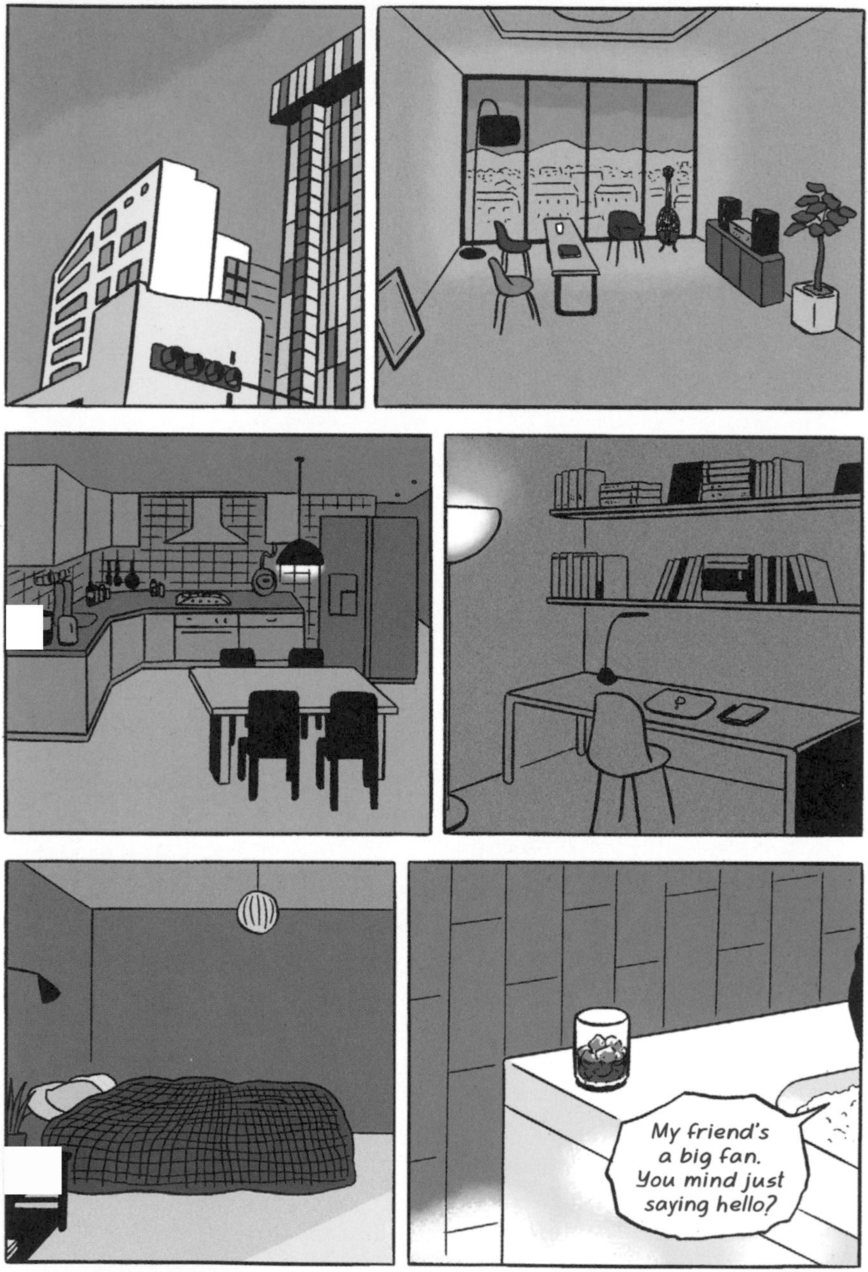
My friend's a big fan. You mind just saying hello?

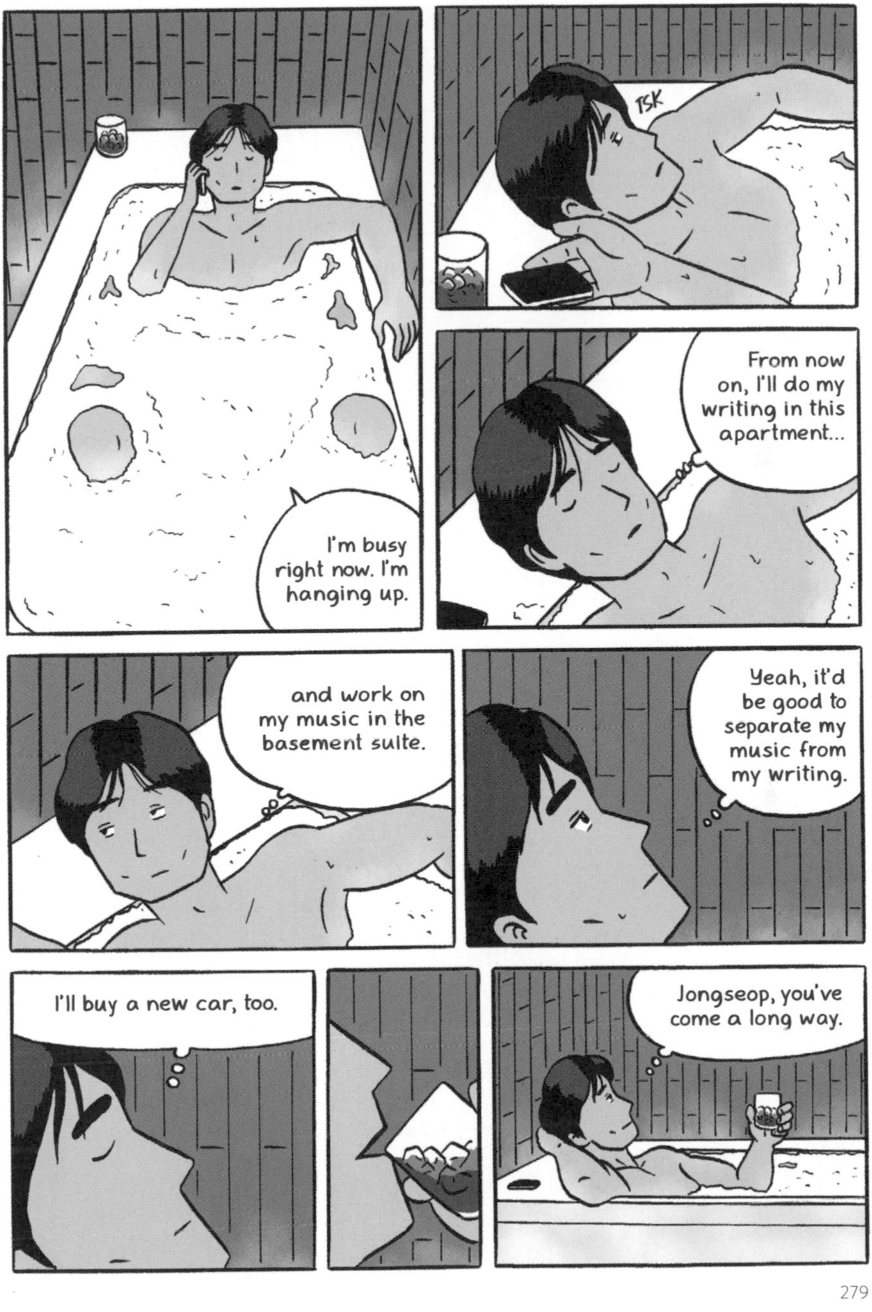
TSK
I'm busy right now. I'm hanging up.
From now on, I'll do my writing in this apartment...
and work on my music in the basement suite.
Yeah, it'd be good to separate my music from my writing.
I'll buy a new car, too.
Jongseop, you've come a long way.

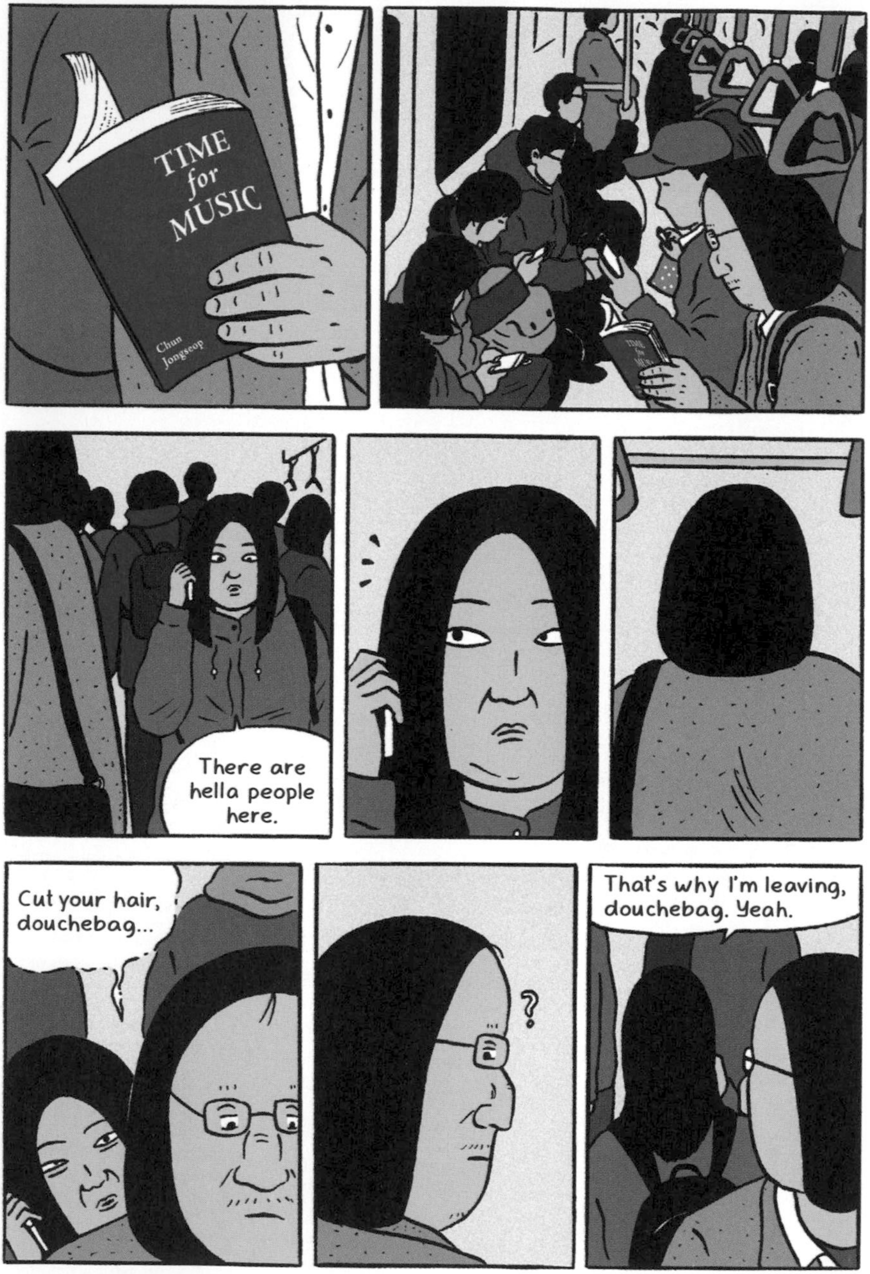
TIME for MUSIC
Chun Jongseop
There are hella people here.
Cut your hair, douchebag...
?
That's why I'm leaving, douchebag. Yeah.

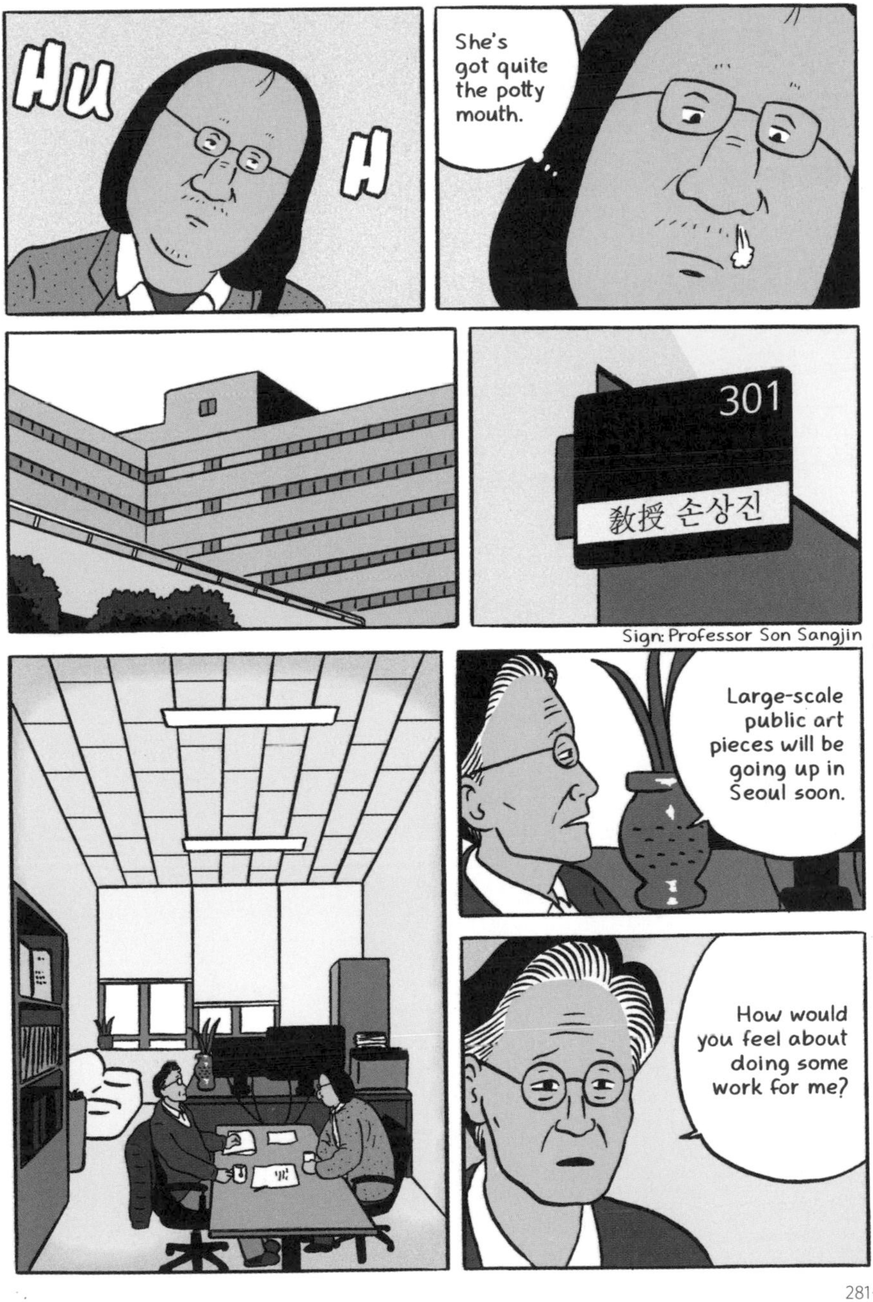
HU
H
She's got quite the potty mouth.
301
教授 손상진
Sign: Professor Son Sangjin
Large-scale public art pieces will be going up in Seoul soon.
How would you feel about doing some work for me?

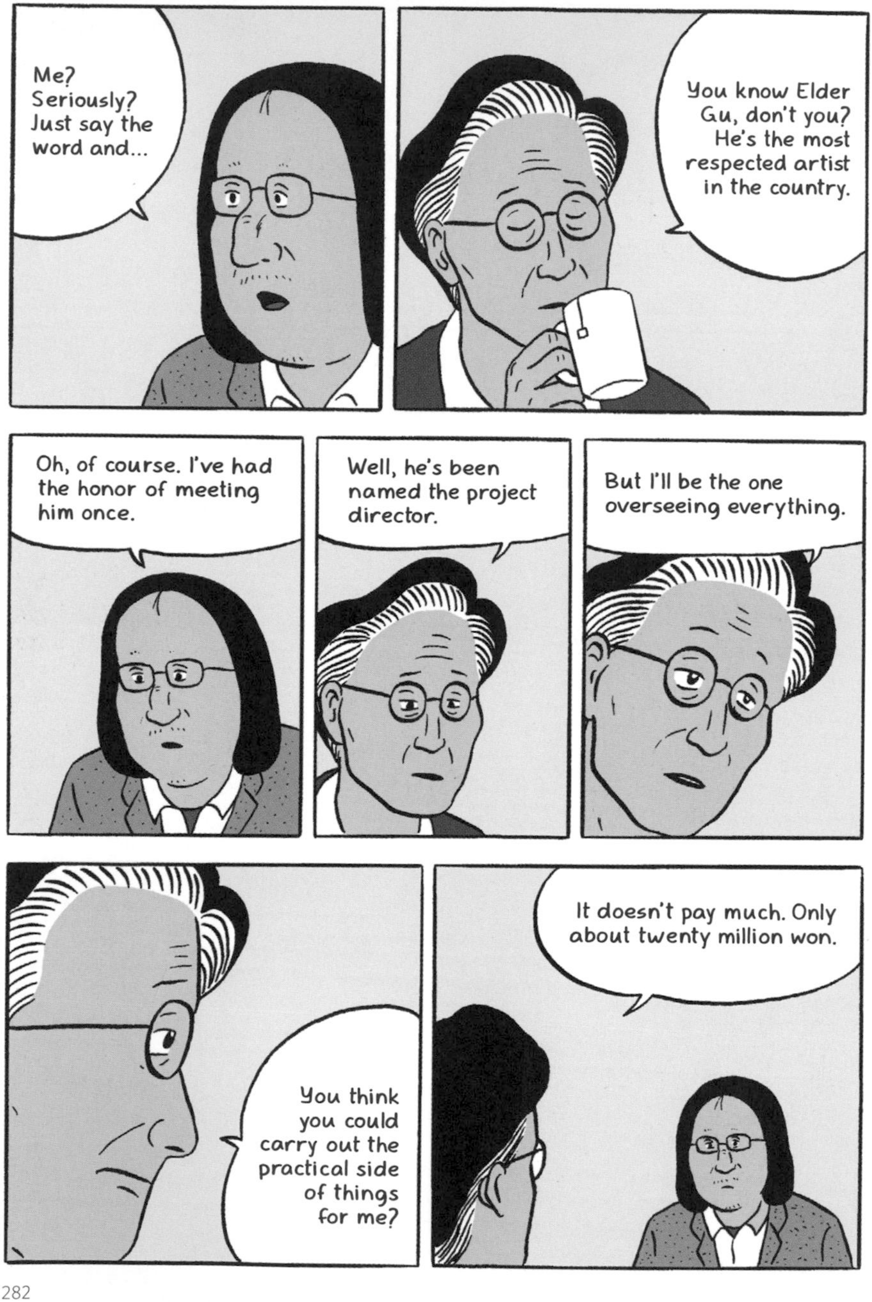

Me? Seriously? Just say the word and...
You know Elder Gu, don't you? He's the most respected artist in the country.
Oh, of course. I've had the honor of meeting him once.
Well, he's been named the project director.
But I'll be the one overseeing everything.
You think you could carry out the practical side of things for me?
It doesn't pay much. Only about twenty million won.

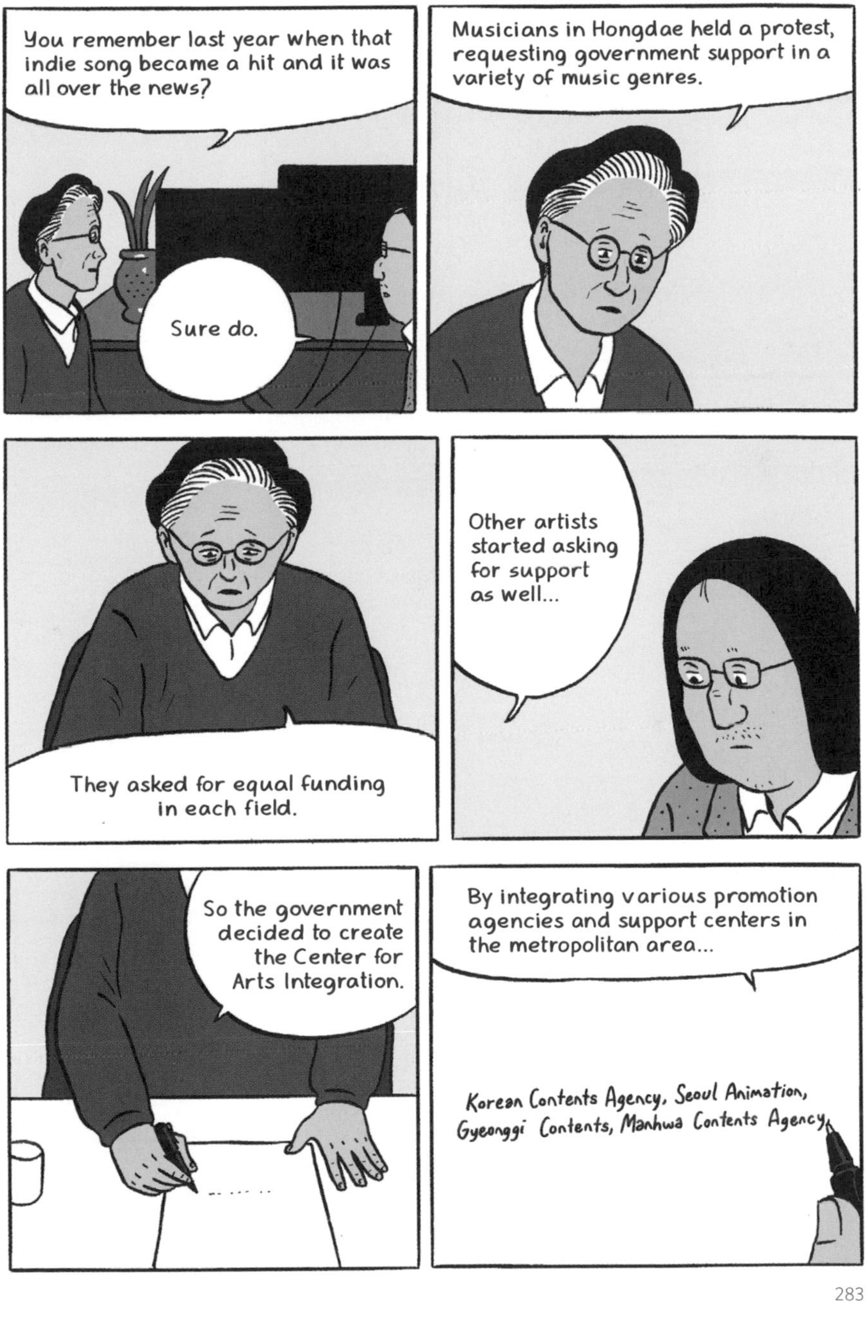
You remember last year when that indie song became a hit and it was all over the news?
Sure do.
Musicians in Hongdae held a protest, requesting government support in a variety of music genres.
They asked for equal funding in each field.
Other artists started asking for support as well...
So the government decided to create the Center for Arts Integration.
By integrating various promotion agencies and support centers in the metropolitan area...
Korean Contents Agency, Seoul Animation, Gyeonggi Contents, Manhwa Contents Agency,

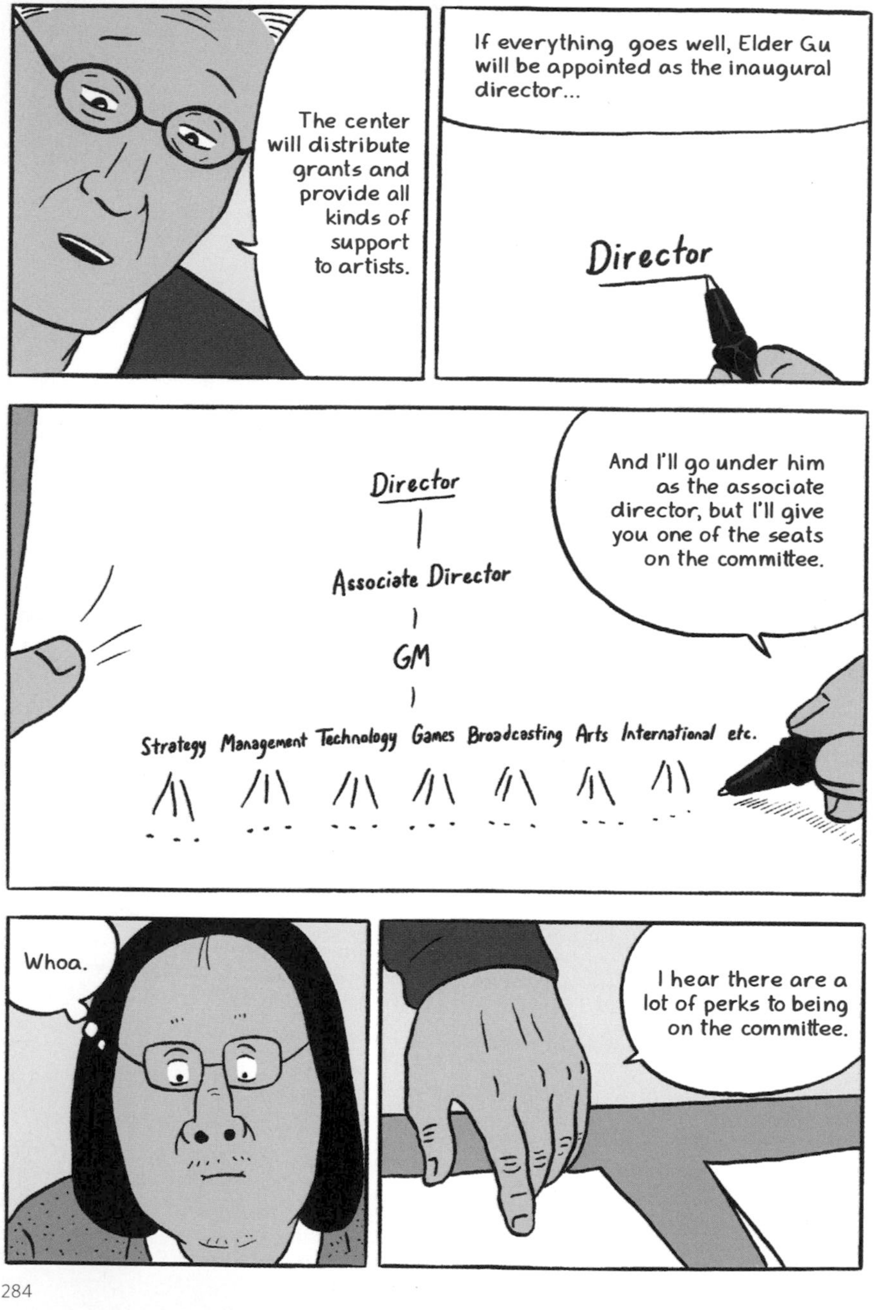
The center will distribute grants and provide all kinds of support to artists.
If everything goes well, Elder Gu will be appointed as the inaugural director...
Director
Director
Associate Director
GM
Strategy Management Technology Games Broadcasting Arts International etc.
And I'll go under him as the associate director, but I'll give you one of the seats on the committee.
Whoa.
I hear there are a lot of perks to being on the committee.

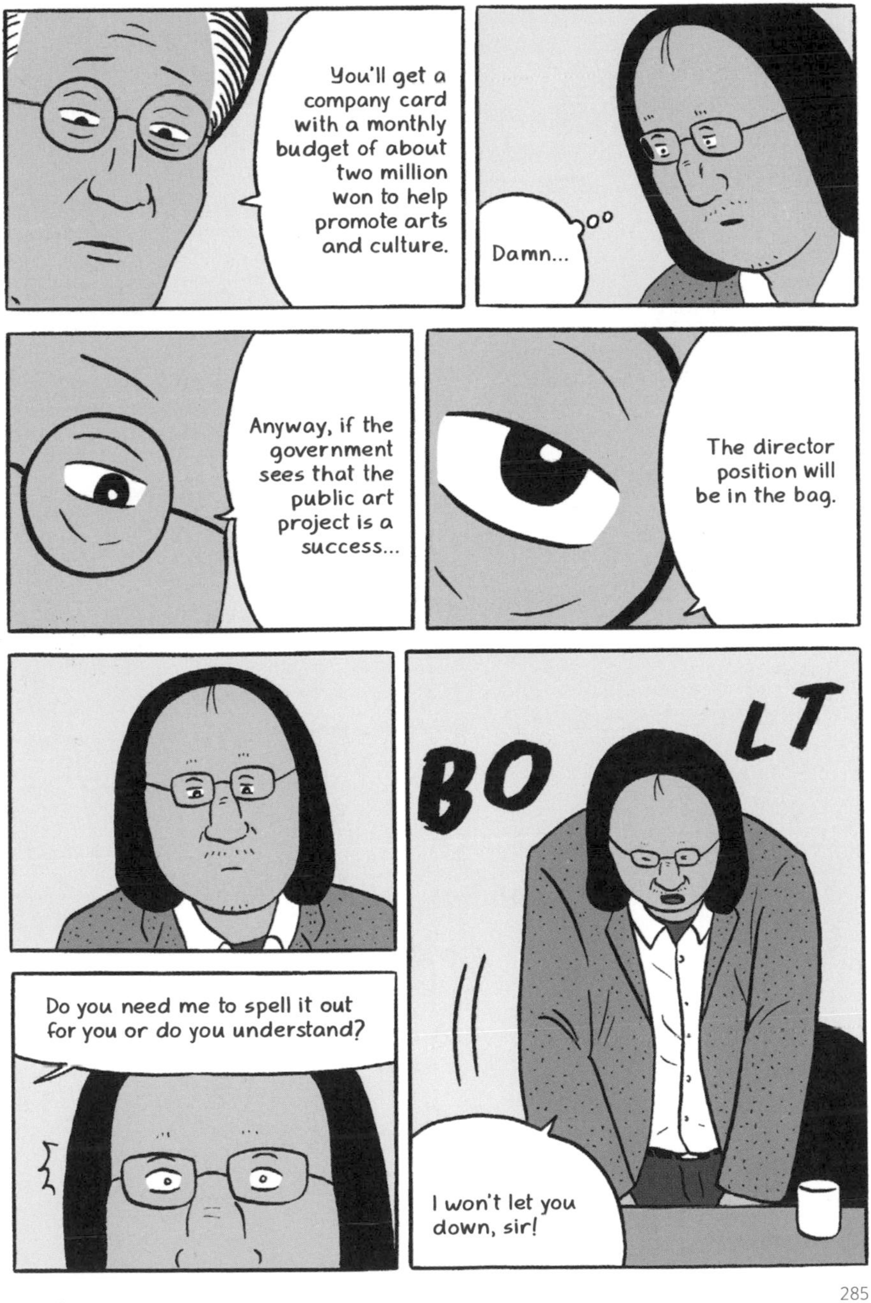
You'll get a company card with a monthly budget of about two million won to help promote arts and culture.
Damn...
Anyway, if the government sees that the public art project is a success...
The director position will be in the bag.
BOLT
Do you need me to spell it out for you or do you understand?
I won't let you down, sir!

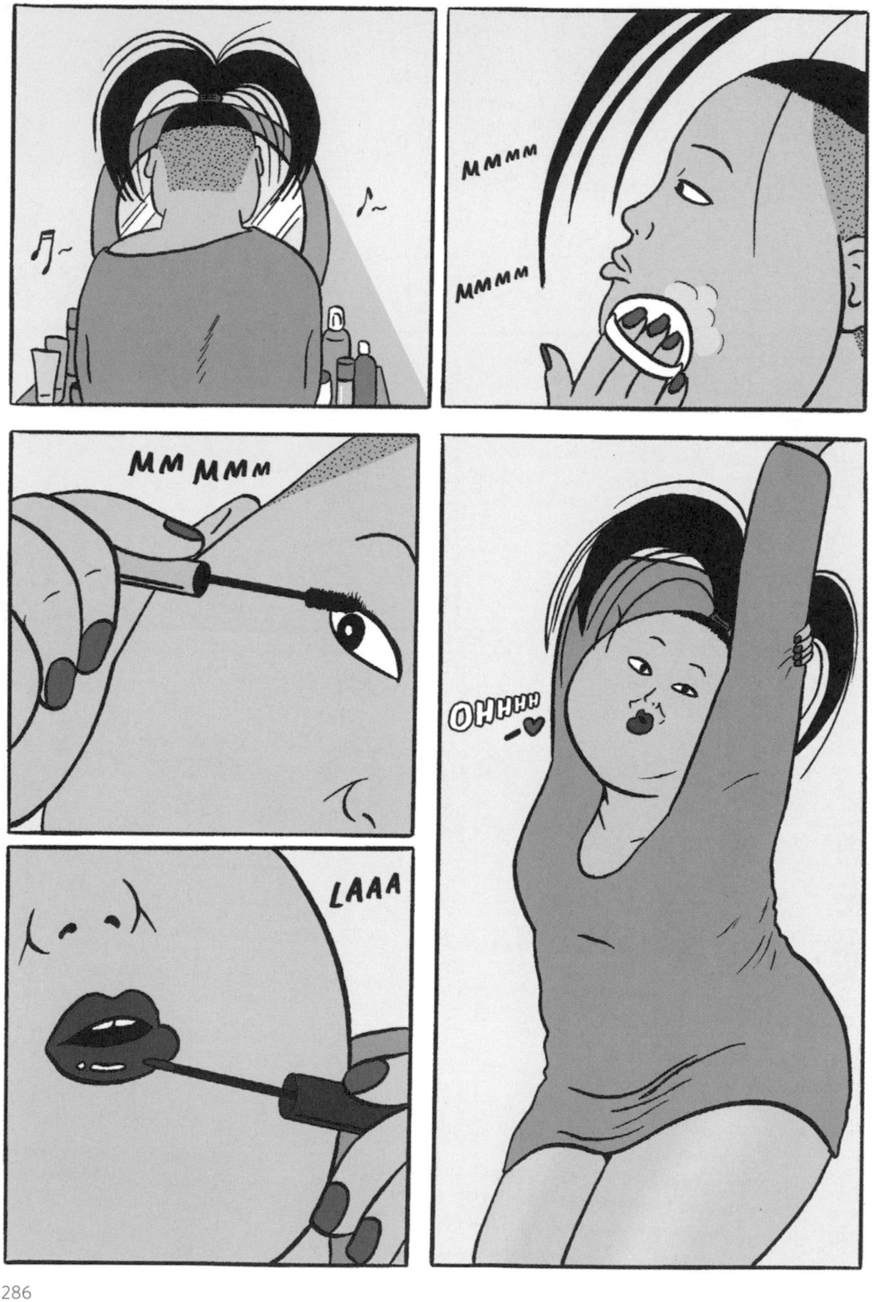
MMMM
MMMM
MM MMM
OHHHH
LAAA

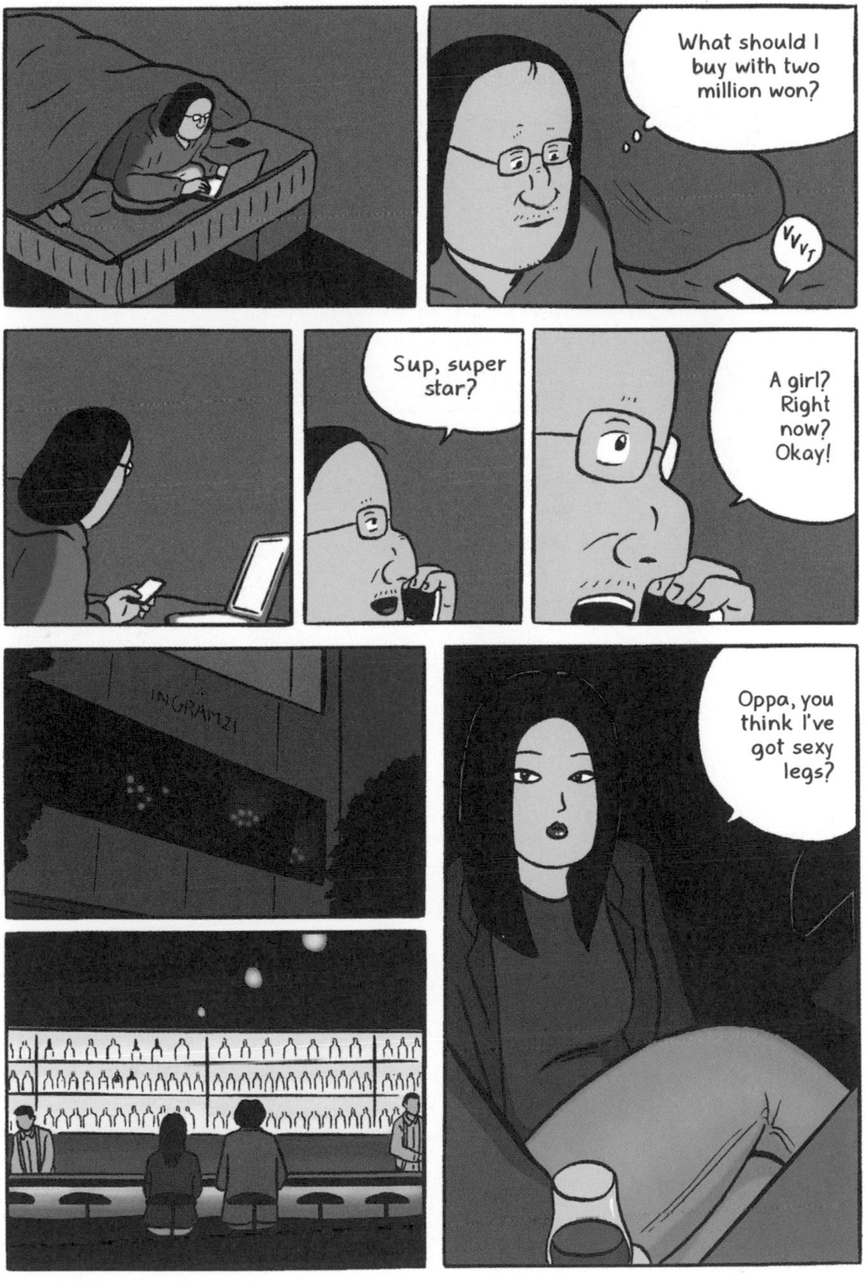
What should I buy with two million won?
VVVT
Sup, super star?
A girl? Right now? Okay!
INGRAM21
Oppa, you think I've got sexy legs?

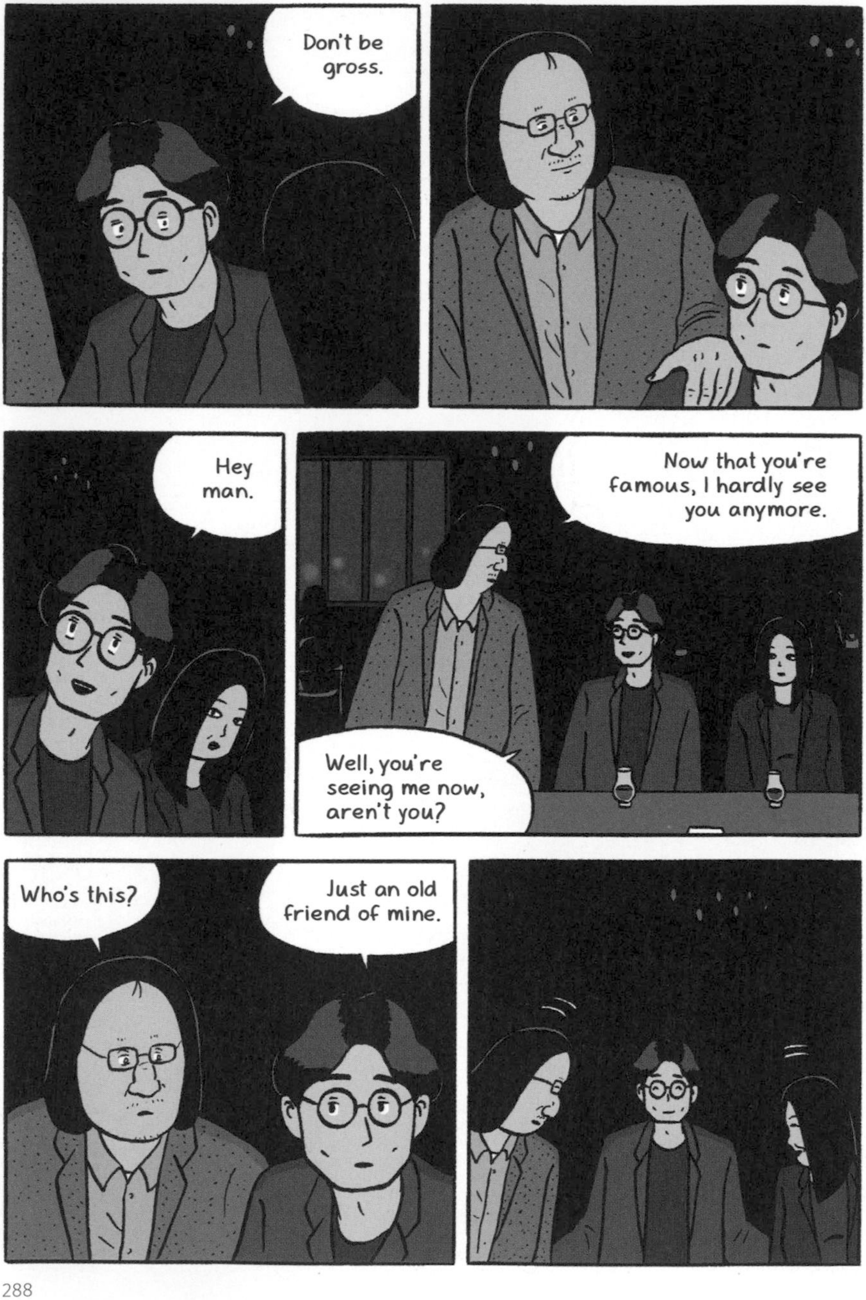
Don't be gross.
Hey man.
Now that you're famous, I hardly see you anymore.
Well, you're seeing me now, aren't you?
Who's this?
Just an old friend of mine.

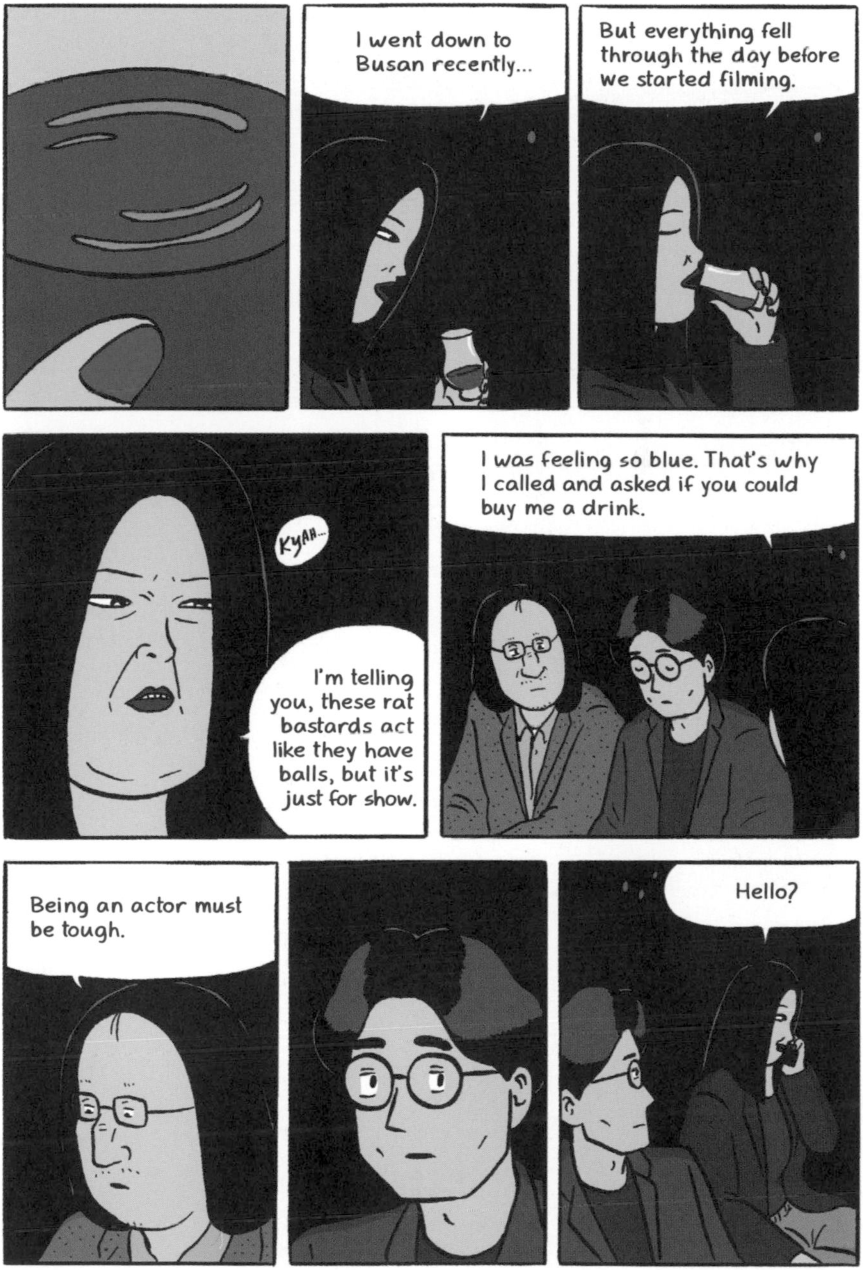
I went down to Busan recently...
But everything fell through the day before we started filming.
KYAH...
I'm telling you, these rat bastards act like they have balls, but it's just for show.
I was feeling so blue. That's why I called and asked if you could buy me a drink.
Being an actor must be tough.
Hello?

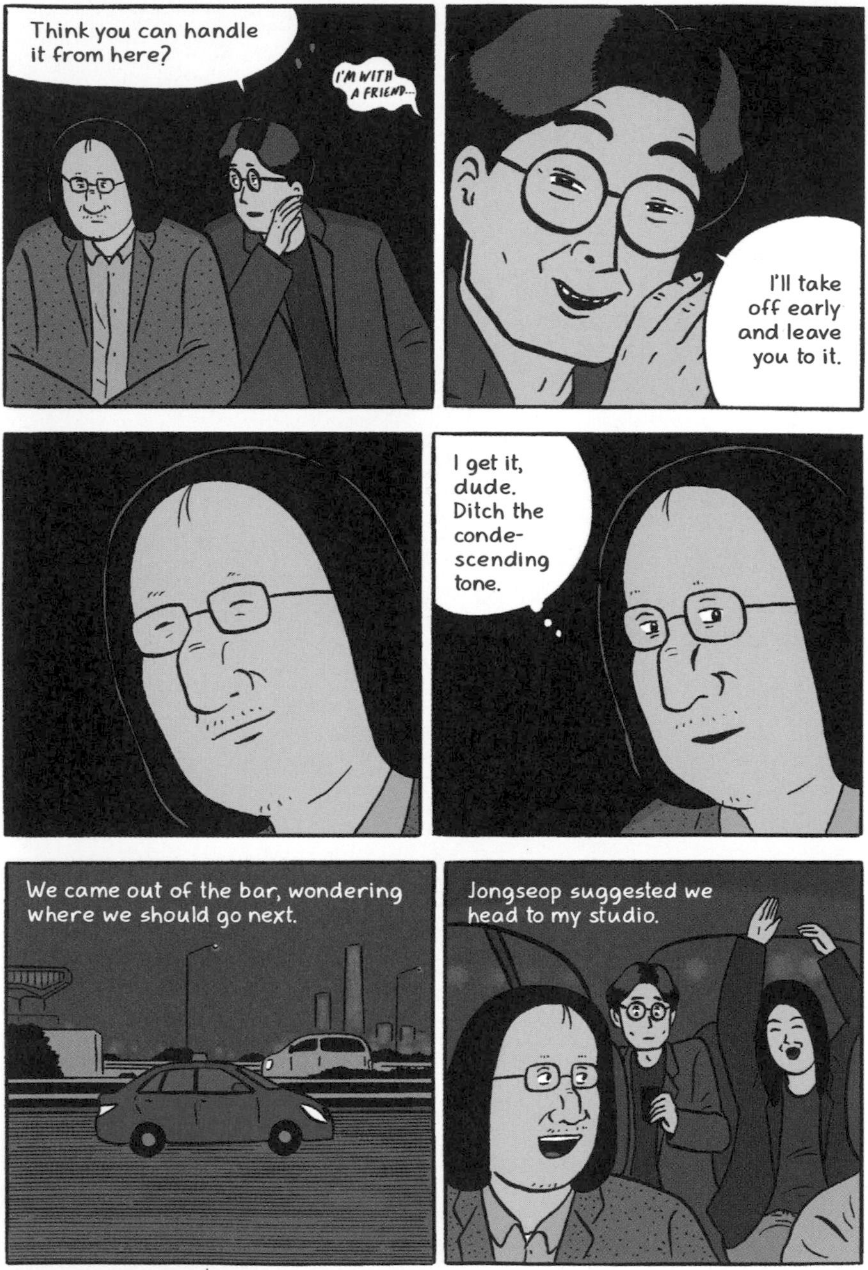
Think you can handle it from here?
I'M WITH A FRIEND...
I'll take off early and leave you to it.
I get it, dude. Ditch the conde-scending tone.
We came out of the bar, wondering where we should go next.
Jongseop suggested we head to my studio.

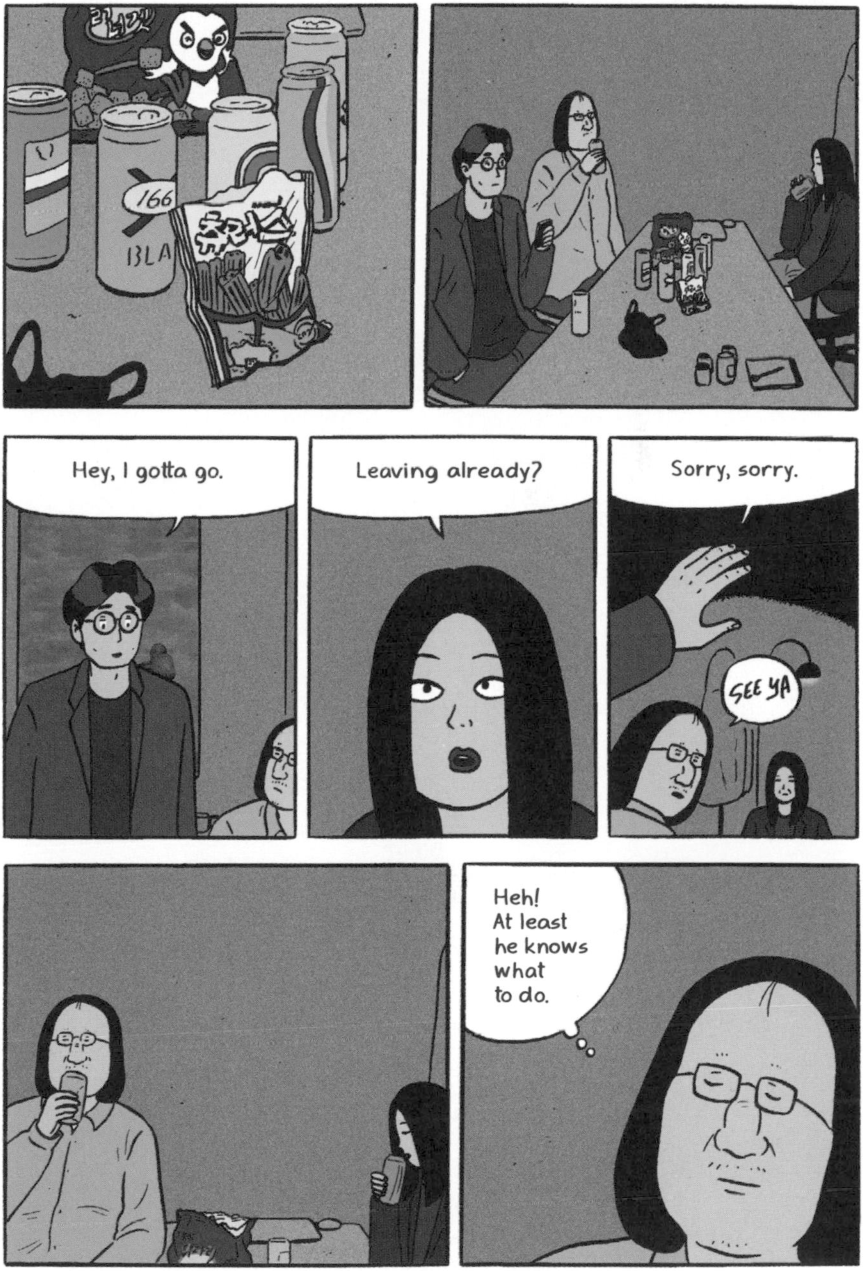
166
BLA
Hey, I gotta go.
Leaving already?
Sorry, sorry.
SEE YA
Heh!
At least
he knows
what
to do.

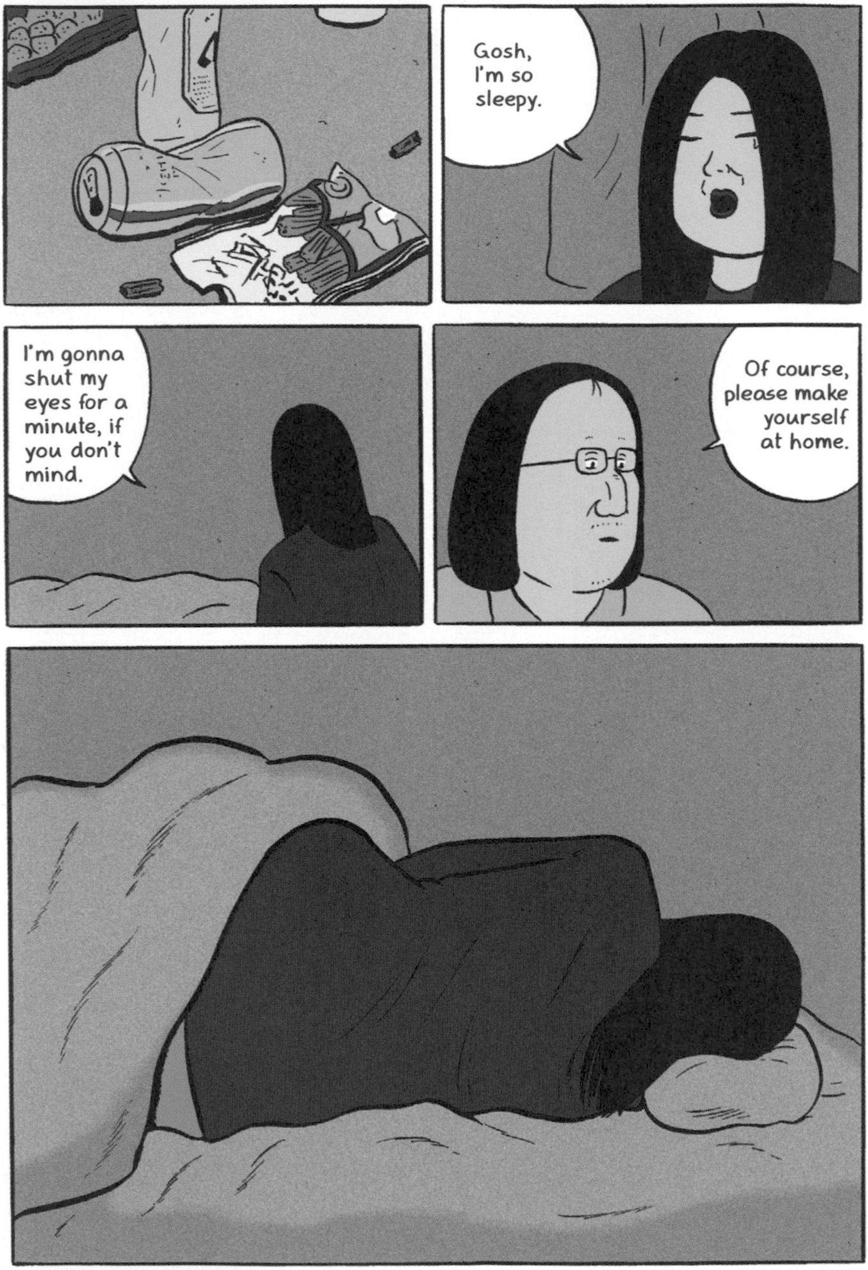
Gosh, I'm so sleepy.
I'm gonna shut my eyes for a minute, if you don't mind.
Of course, please make yourself at home.

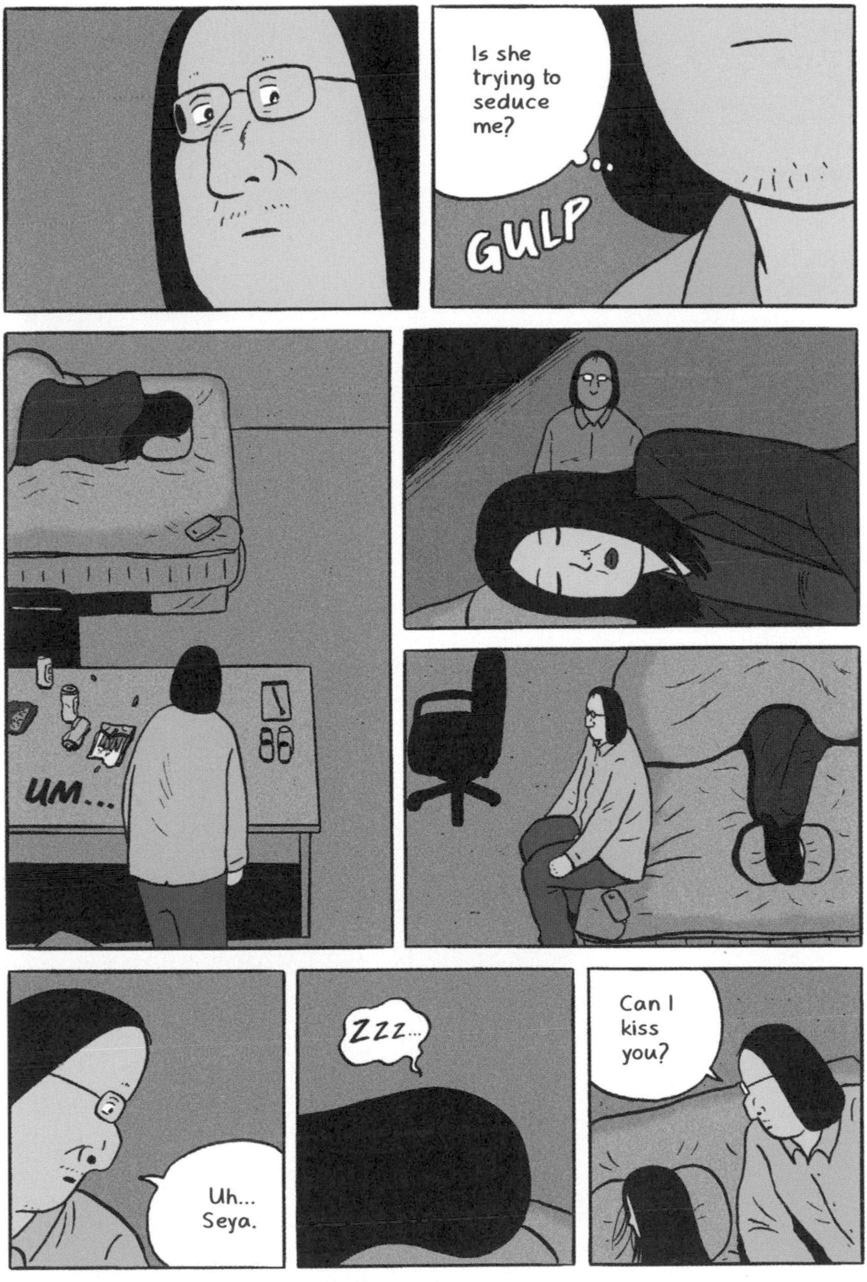
Is she trying to seduce me?
GULP
UM...
Uh... Seya.
ZZZ...
Can I kiss you?

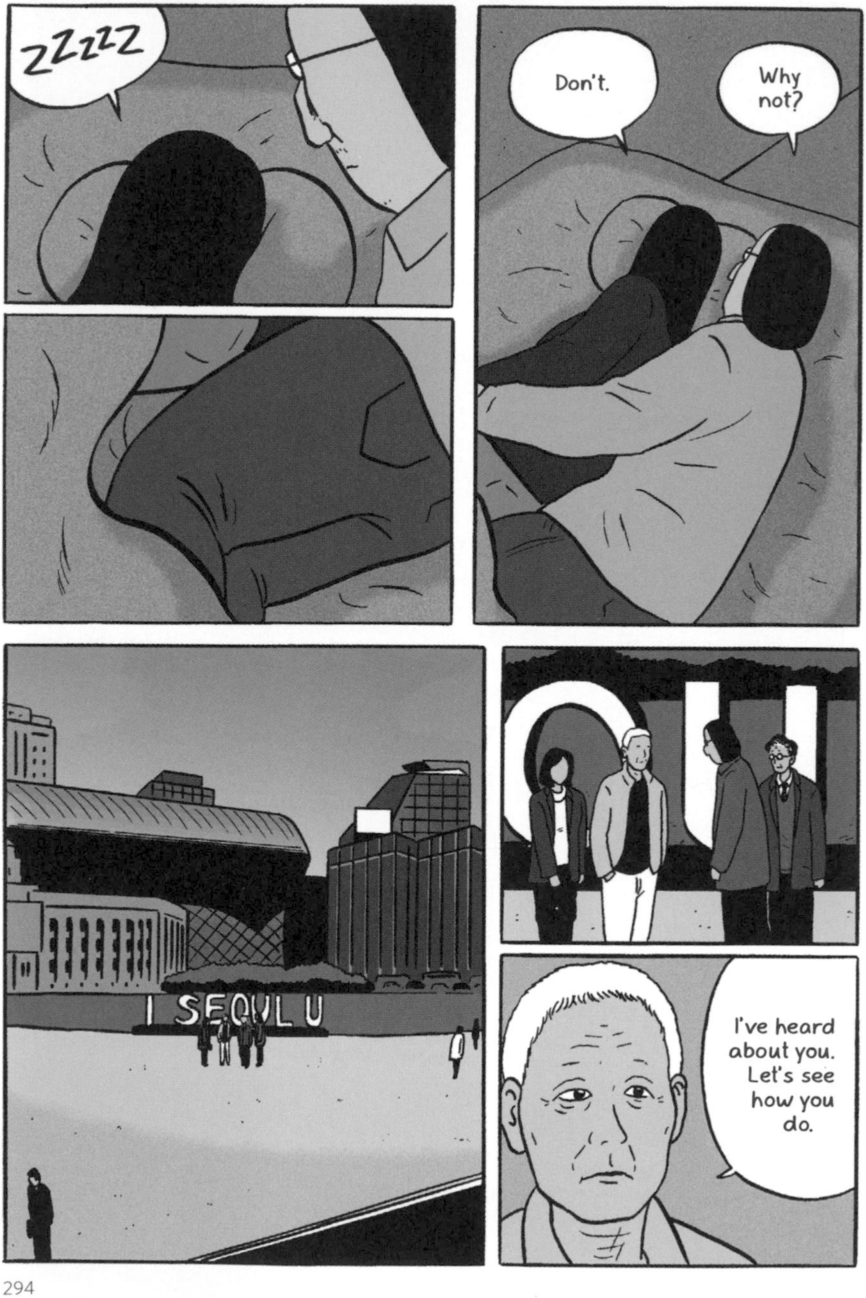
ZZZZZ
Don't.
Why not?
I SEOUL U
I've heard about you. Let's see how you do.

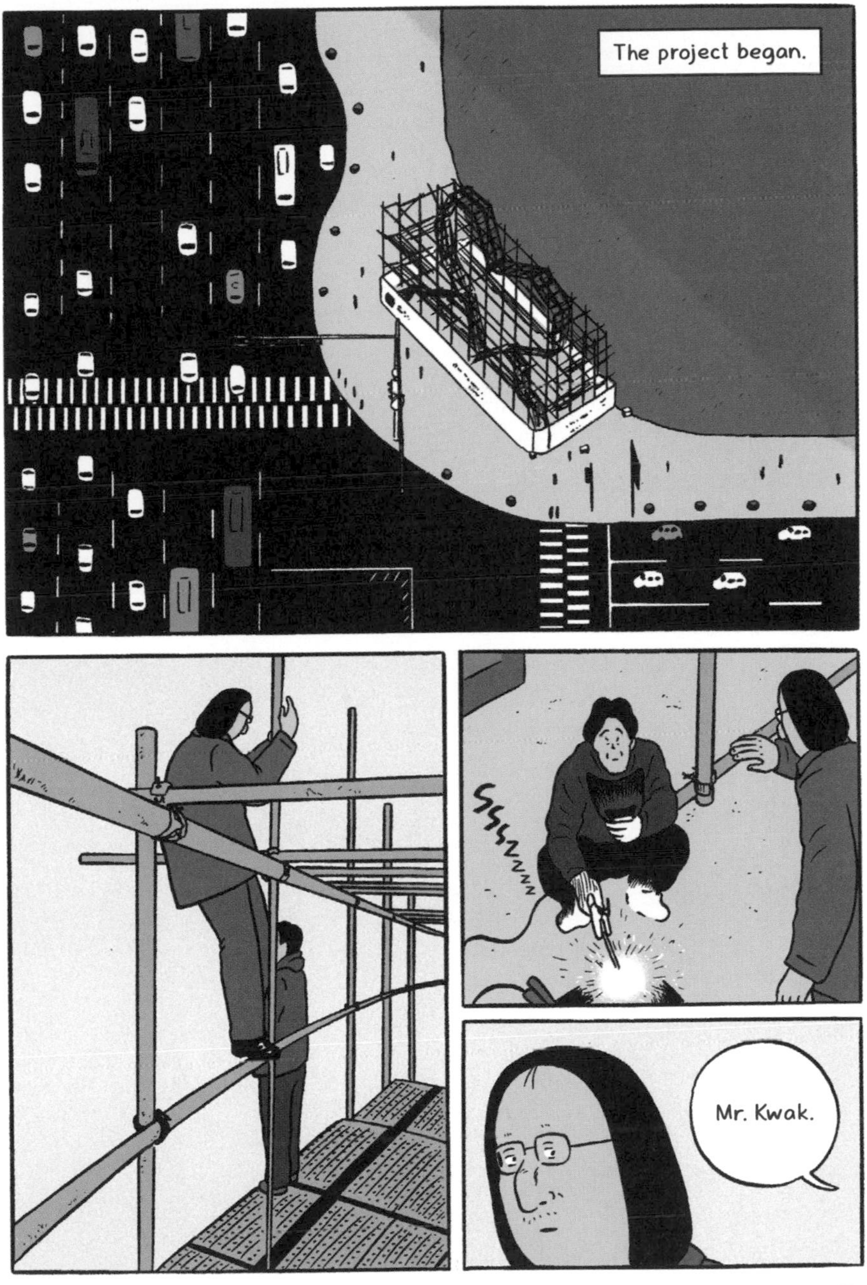
The project began.
SSSZZZZ
Mr. Kwak.

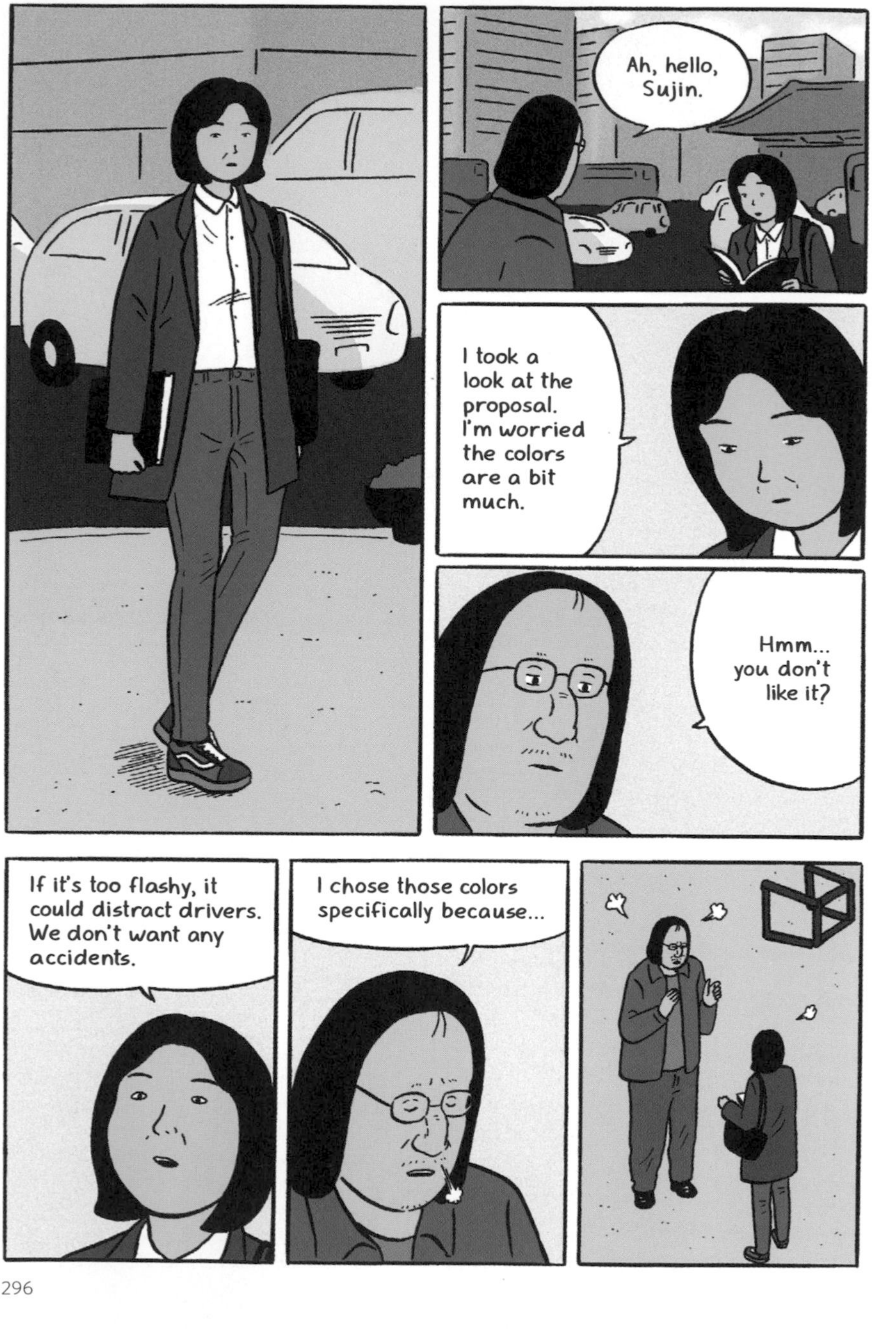
Ah, hello, Sujin.
I took a look at the proposal. I'm worried the colors are a bit much.
Hmm... you don't like it?
If it's too flashy, it could distract drivers. We don't want any accidents.
I chose those colors specifically because...

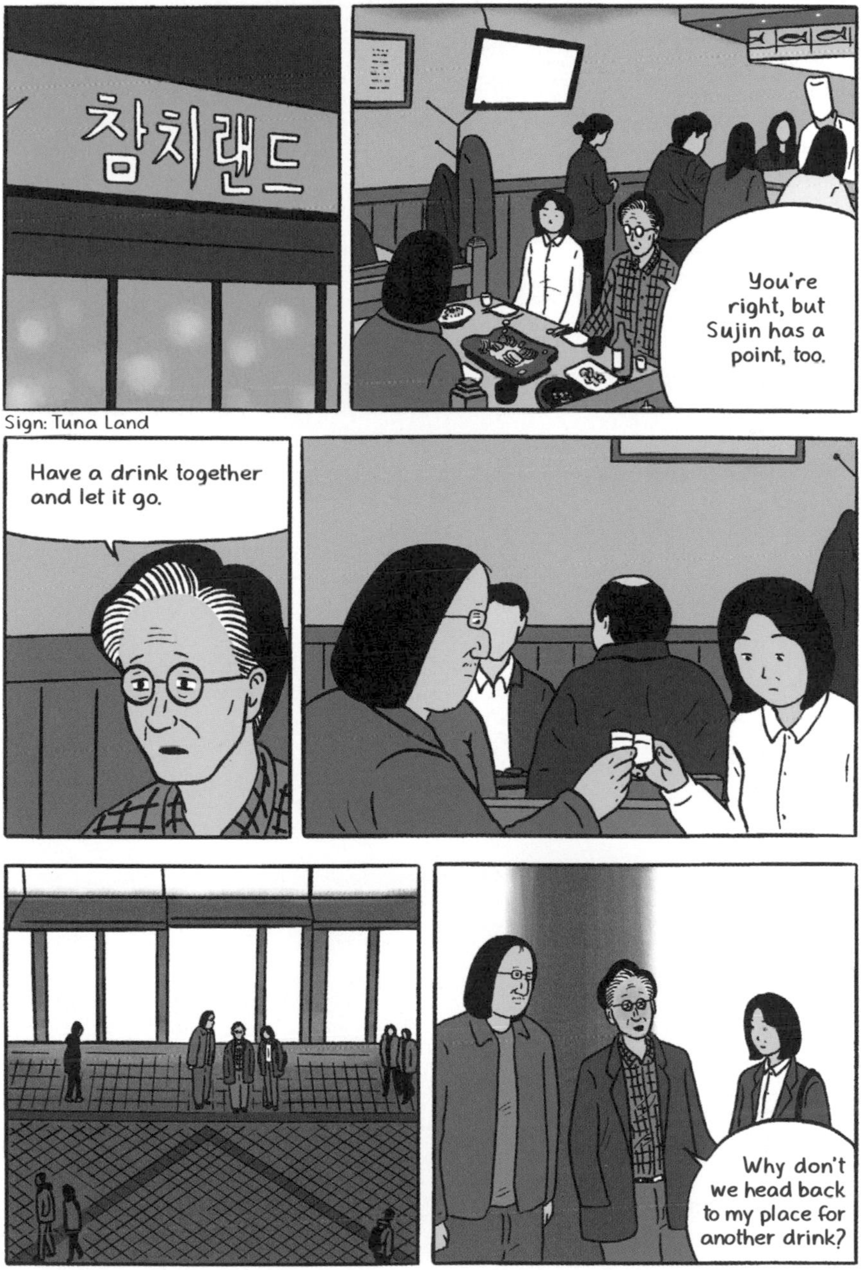

참치랜드
You're right, but Sujin has a point, too.
Have a drink together and let it go.
Why don't we head back to my place for another drink?

Sign: Tuna Land

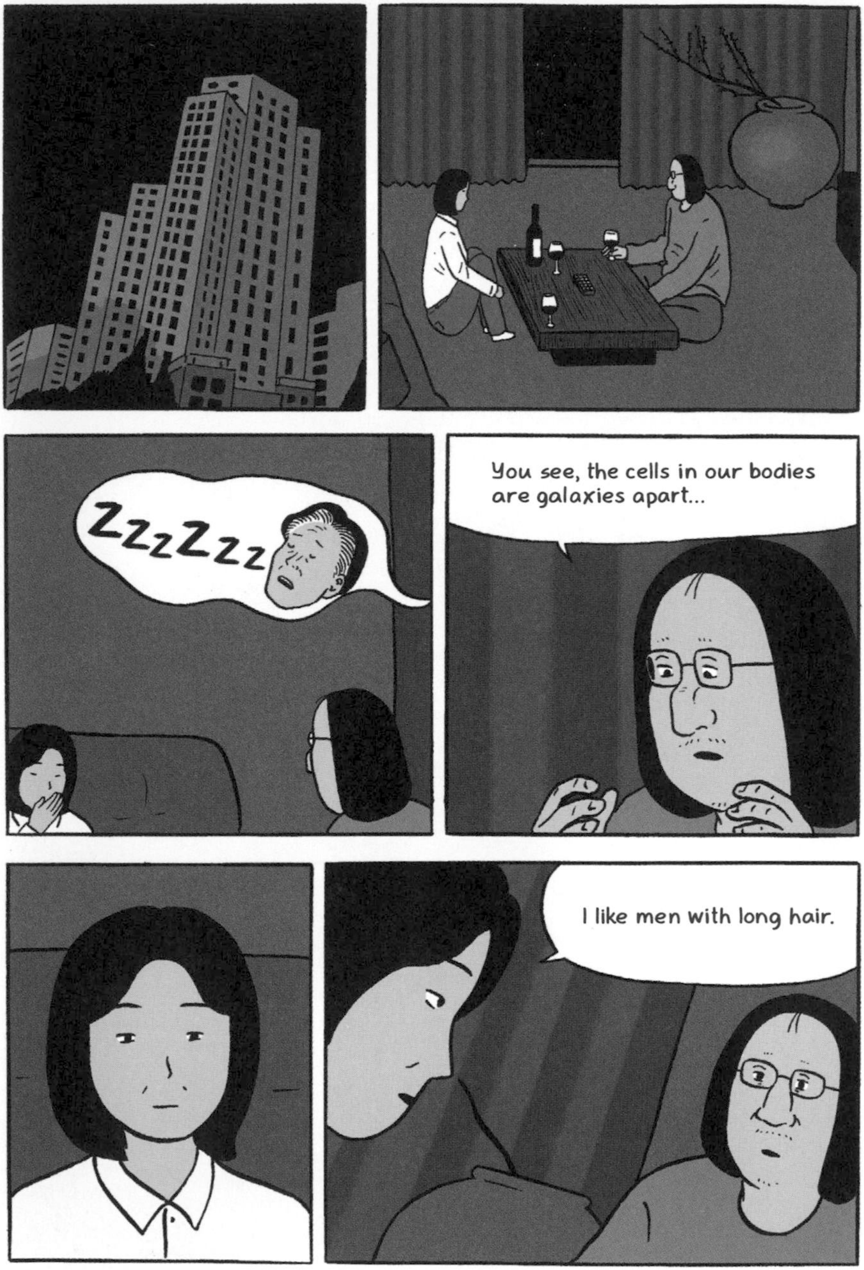
ZzzZzz
You see, the cells in our bodies are galaxies apart...
I like men with long hair.

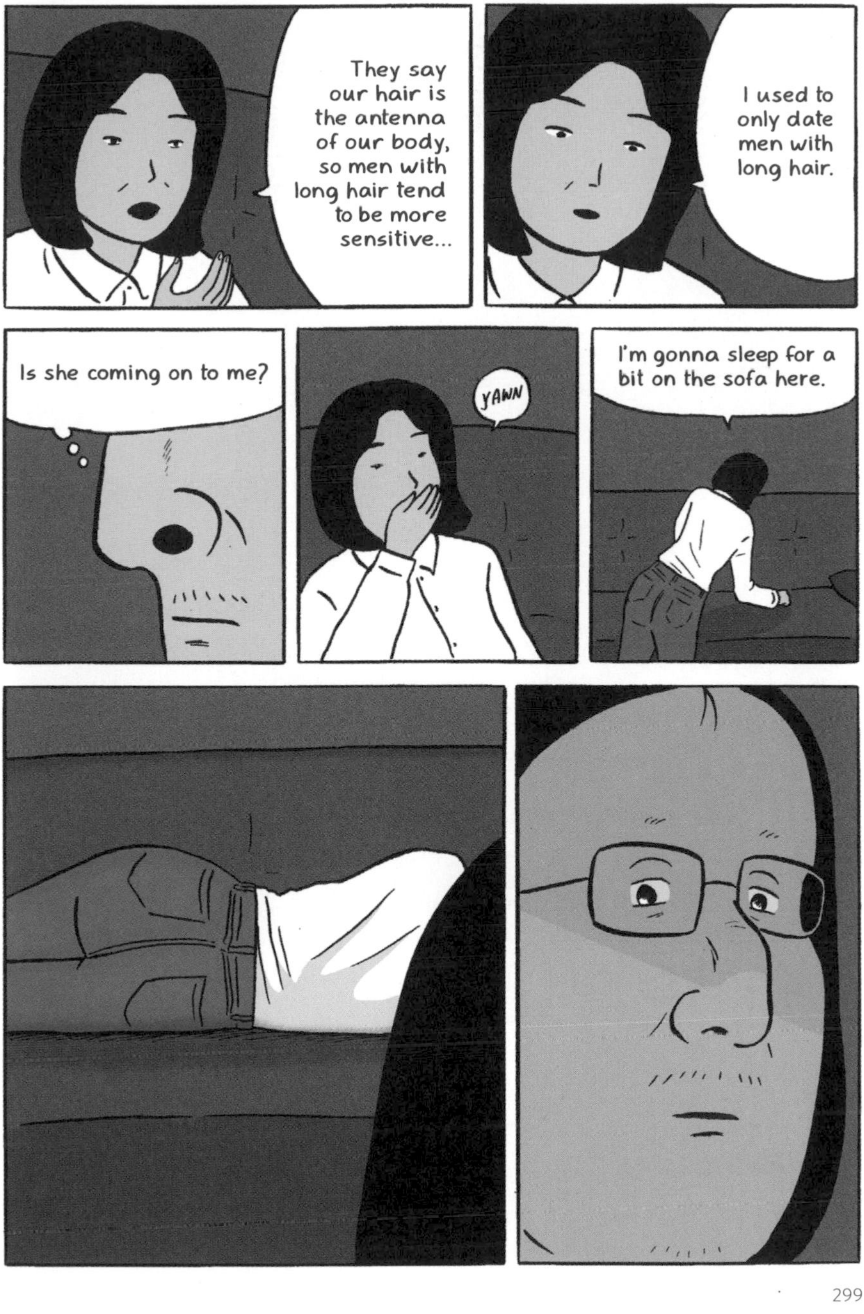
They say our hair is the antenna of our body, so men with long hair tend to be more sensitive...
I used to only date men with long hair.
Is she coming on to me?
YAWN
I'm gonna sleep for a bit on the sofa here.

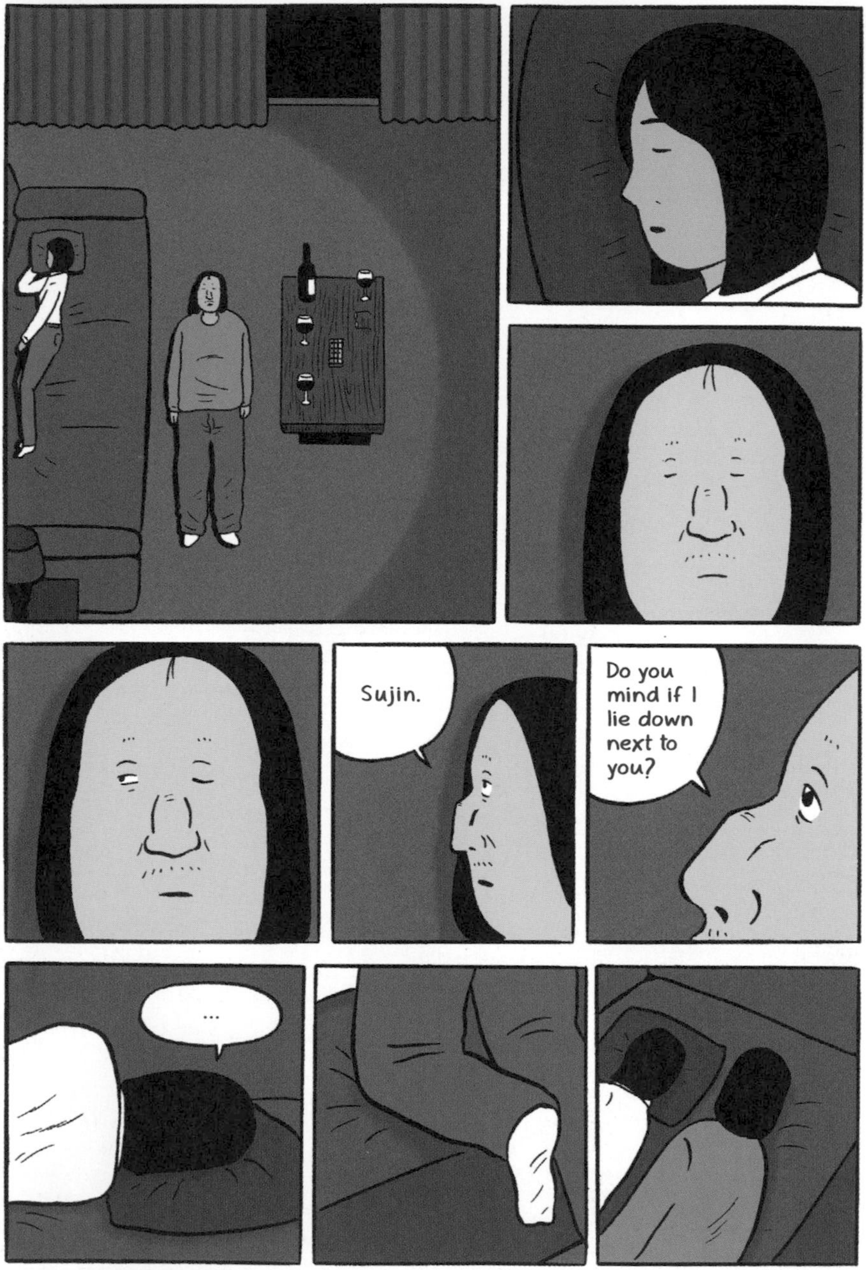
Sujin.
Do you mind if I lie down next to you?
...

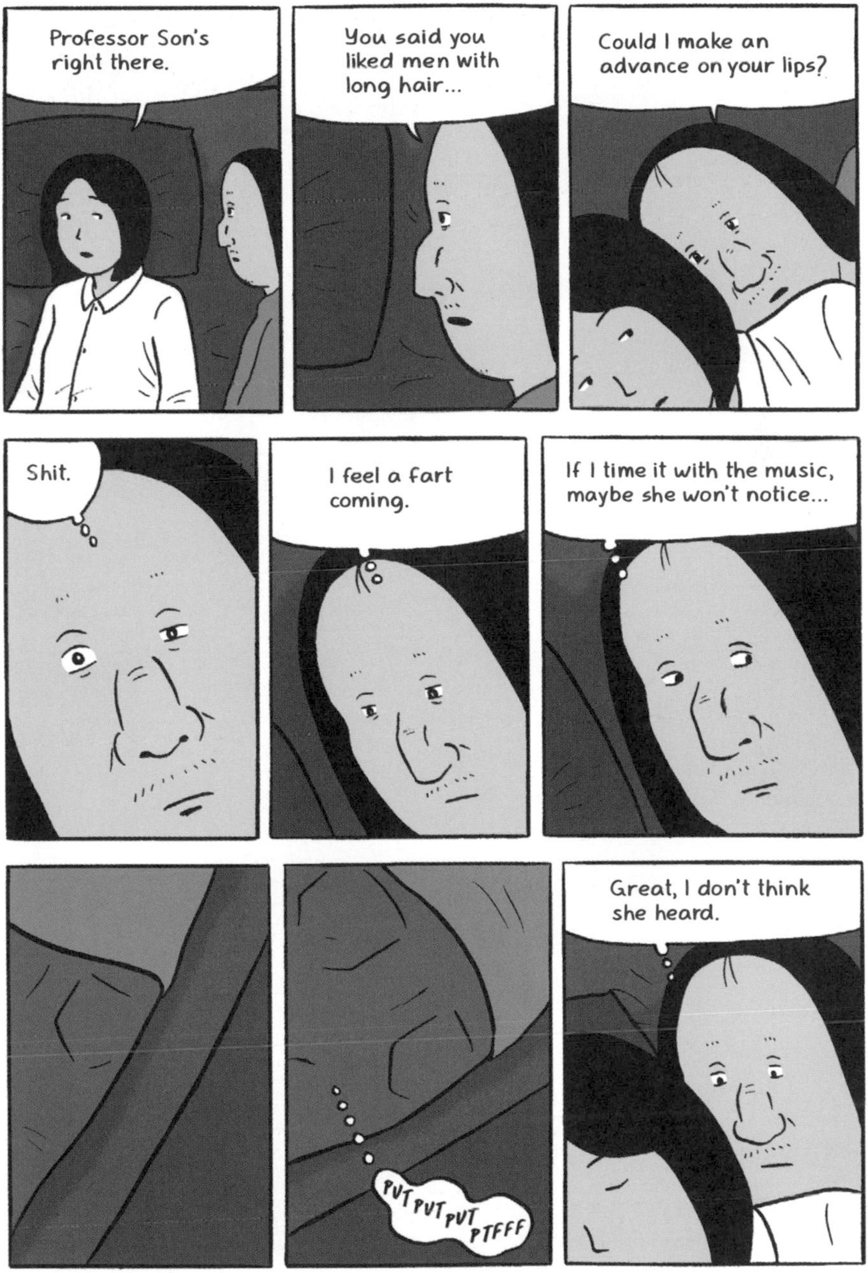
Professor Son's right there.
You said you liked men with long hair...
Could I make an advance on your lips?
Shit.
I feel a fart coming.
If I time it with the music, maybe she won't notice...
PUT PUT PUT PTFFF
Great, I don't think she heard.

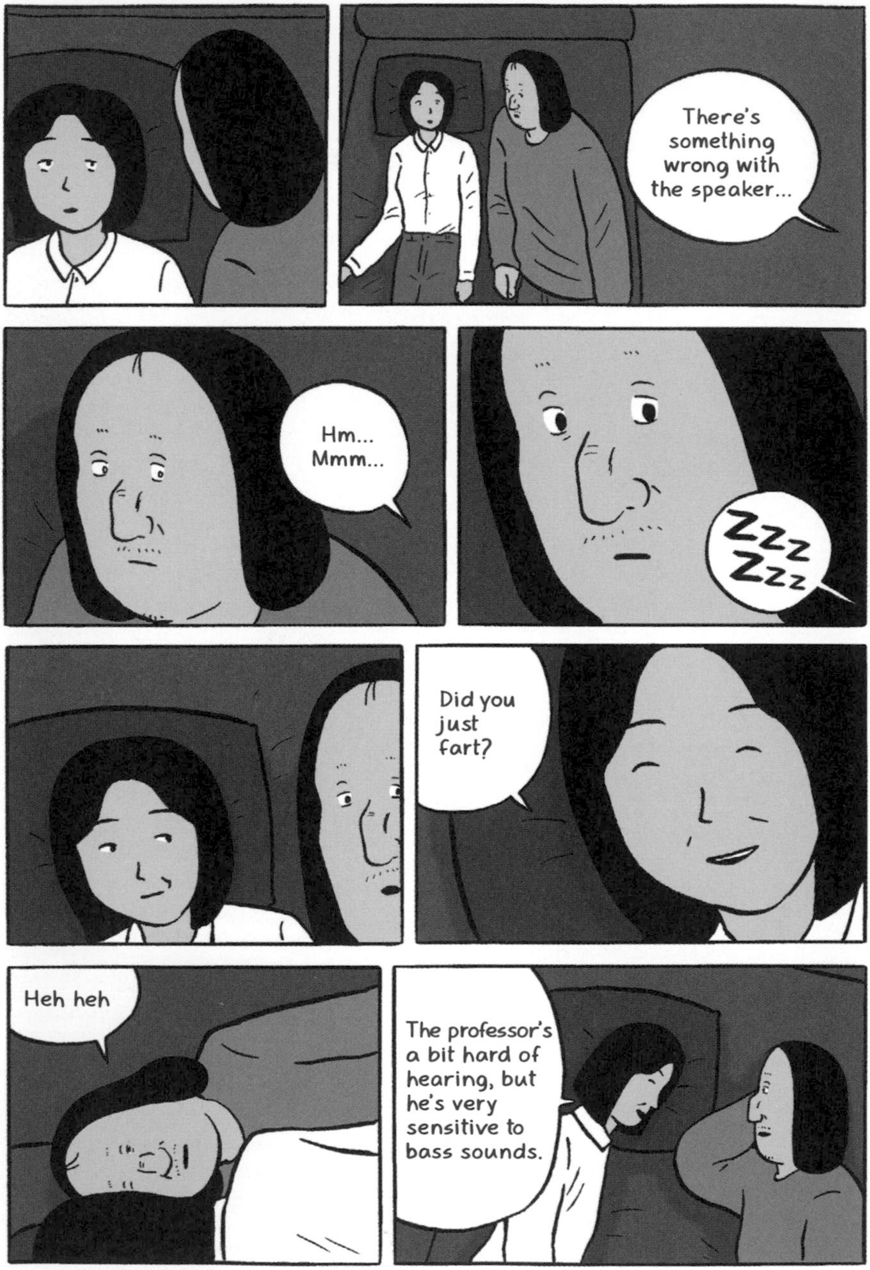
There's something wrong with the speaker...
Hm... Mmm...
Zzz Zzz
Did you just fart?
Heh heh
The professor's a bit hard of hearing, but he's very sensitive to bass sounds.

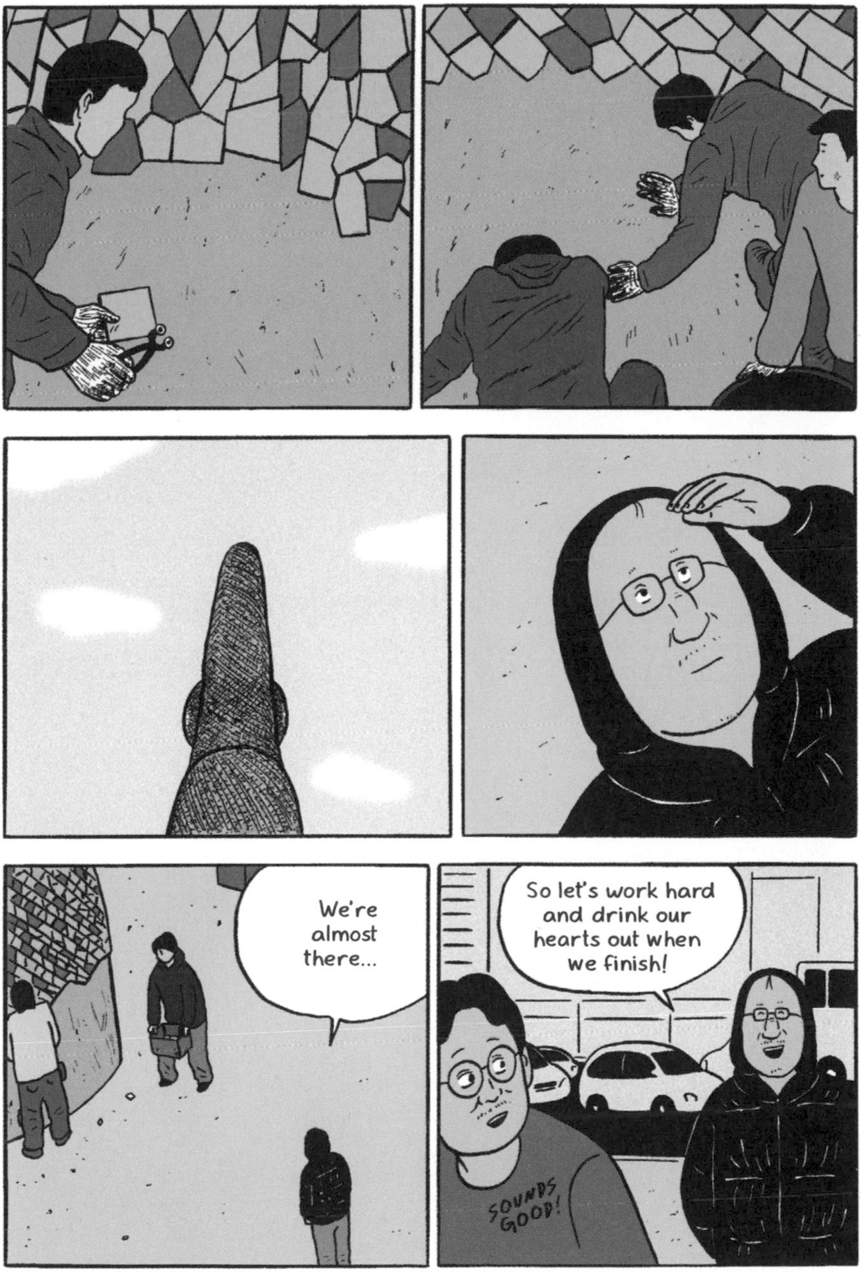

We're almost there...
So let's work hard and drink our hearts out when we finish!
SOUNDS GOOD!

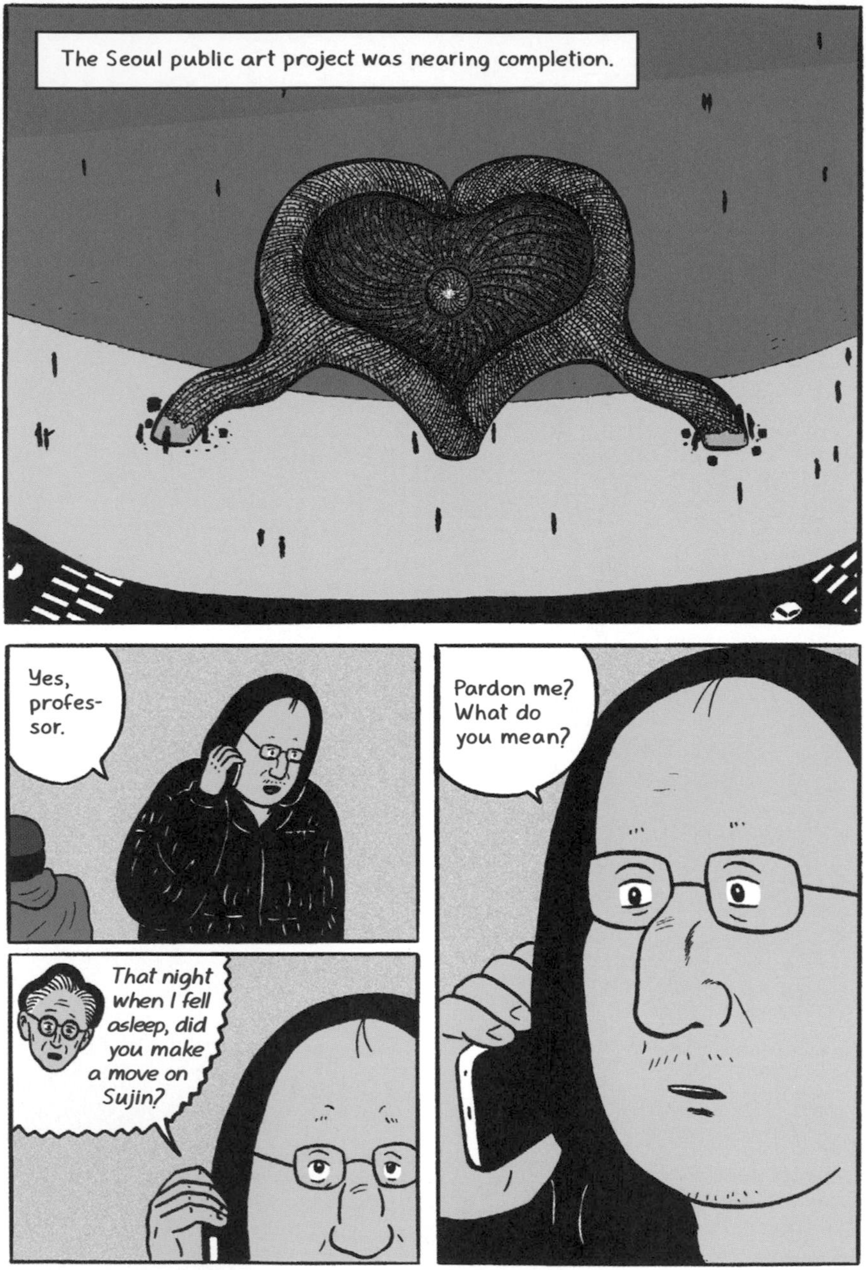

The Seoul public art project was nearing completion.
Yes, profes-sor.
Pardon me? What do you mean?
That night when I fell asleep, did you make a move on Sujin?

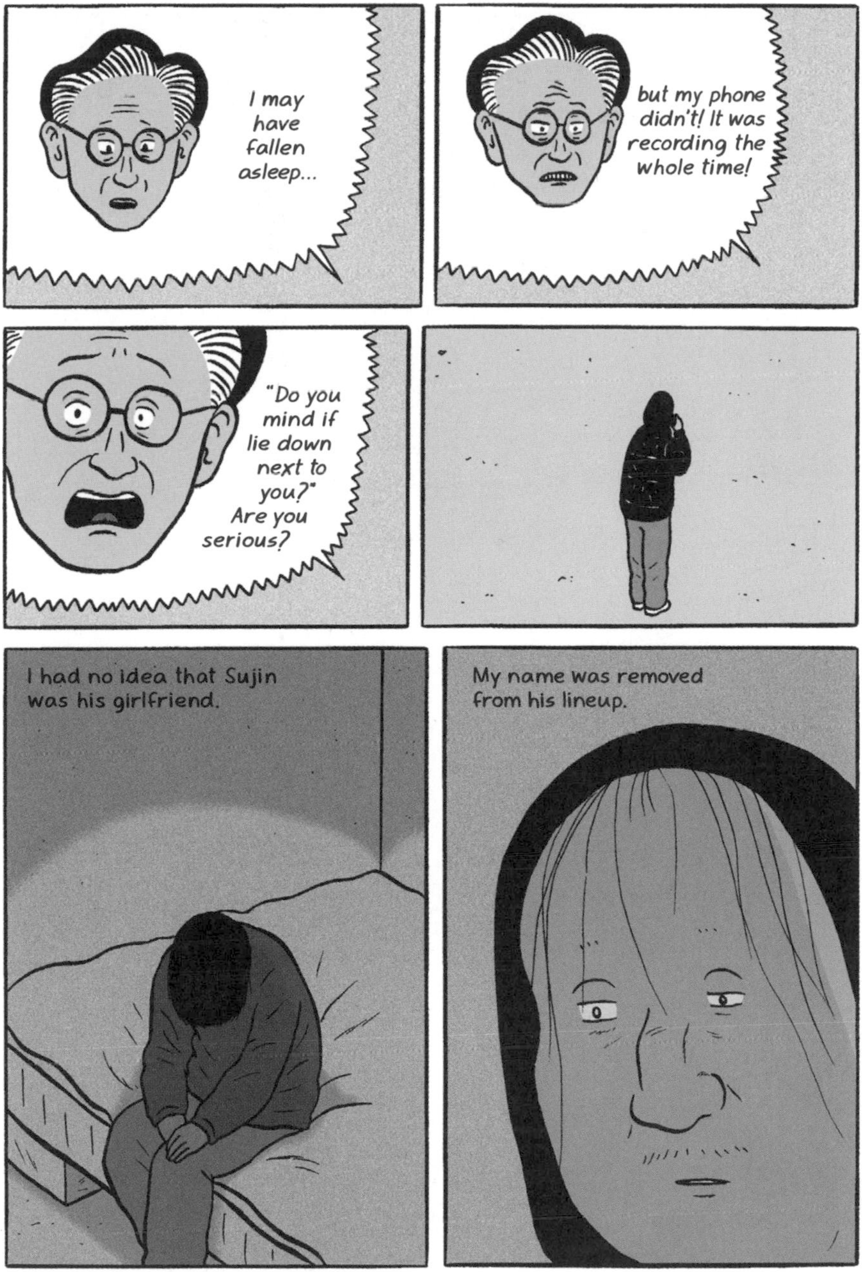
I may have fallen asleep...
but my phone didn't! It was recording the whole time!
"Do you mind if lie down next to you?" Are you serious?
I had no idea that Sujin was his girlfriend.
My name was removed from his lineup.

WAA
AAA
AH

WAA
AAAH

SNIFF...

I want to bawl my eyes out, but the tears won't come.

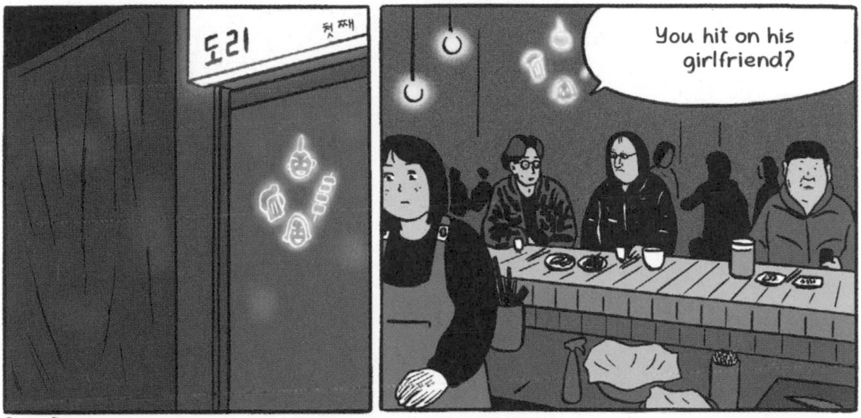
도리
You hit on his girlfriend?

Sign: Dori

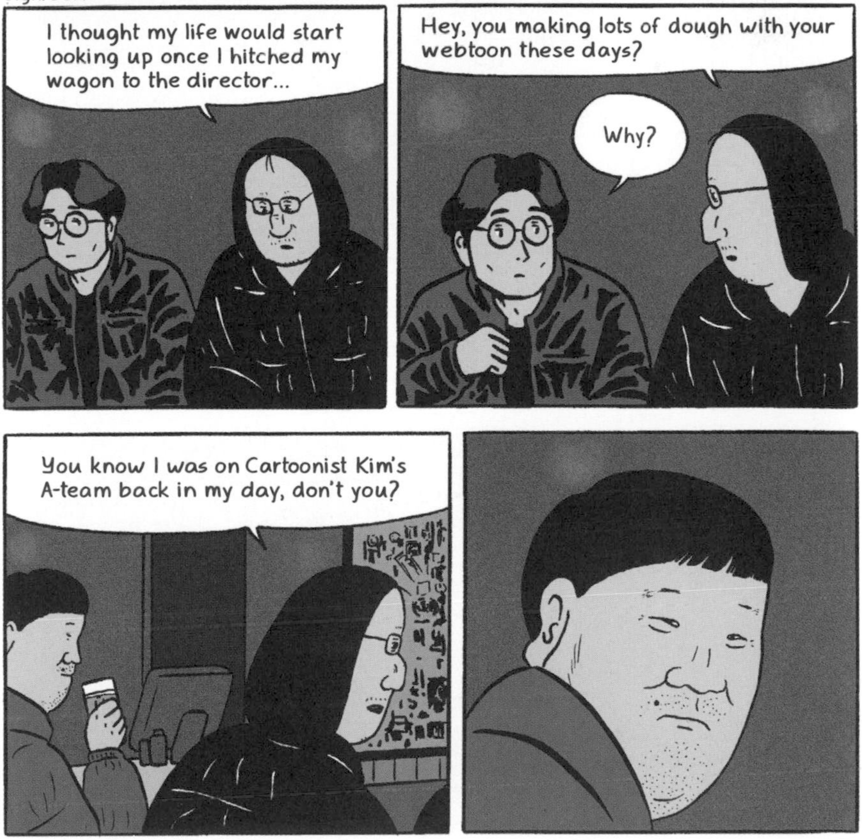
I thought my life would start looking up once I hitched my wagon to the director...
Hey, you making lots of dough with your webtoon these days?
Why?
You know I was on Cartoonist Kim's A-team back in my day, don't you?

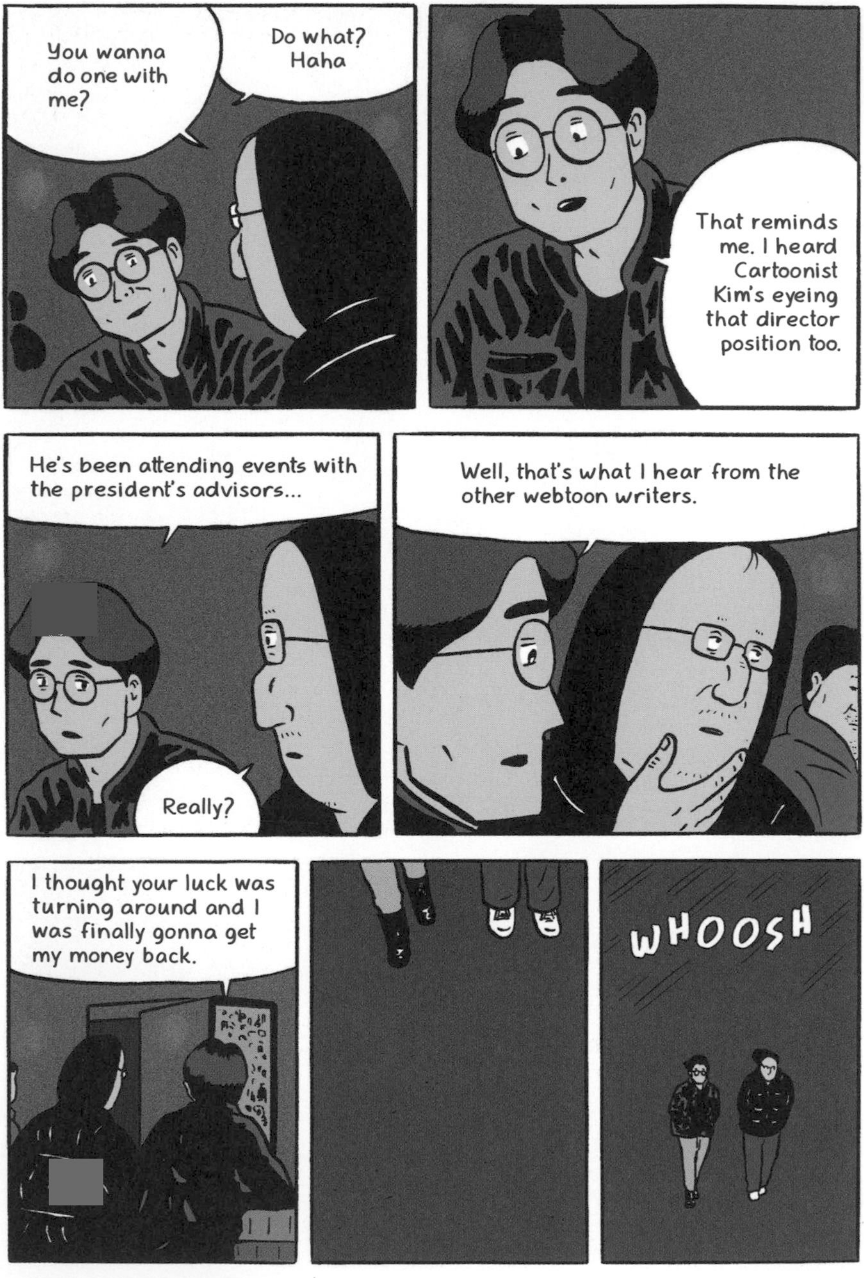
You wanna do one with me?
Do what? Haha
That reminds me. I heard Cartoonist Kim's eyeing that director position too.
He's been attending events with the president's advisors...
Really?
Well, that's what I hear from the other webtoon writers.
I thought your luck was turning around and I was finally gonna get my money back.
WHOOSH

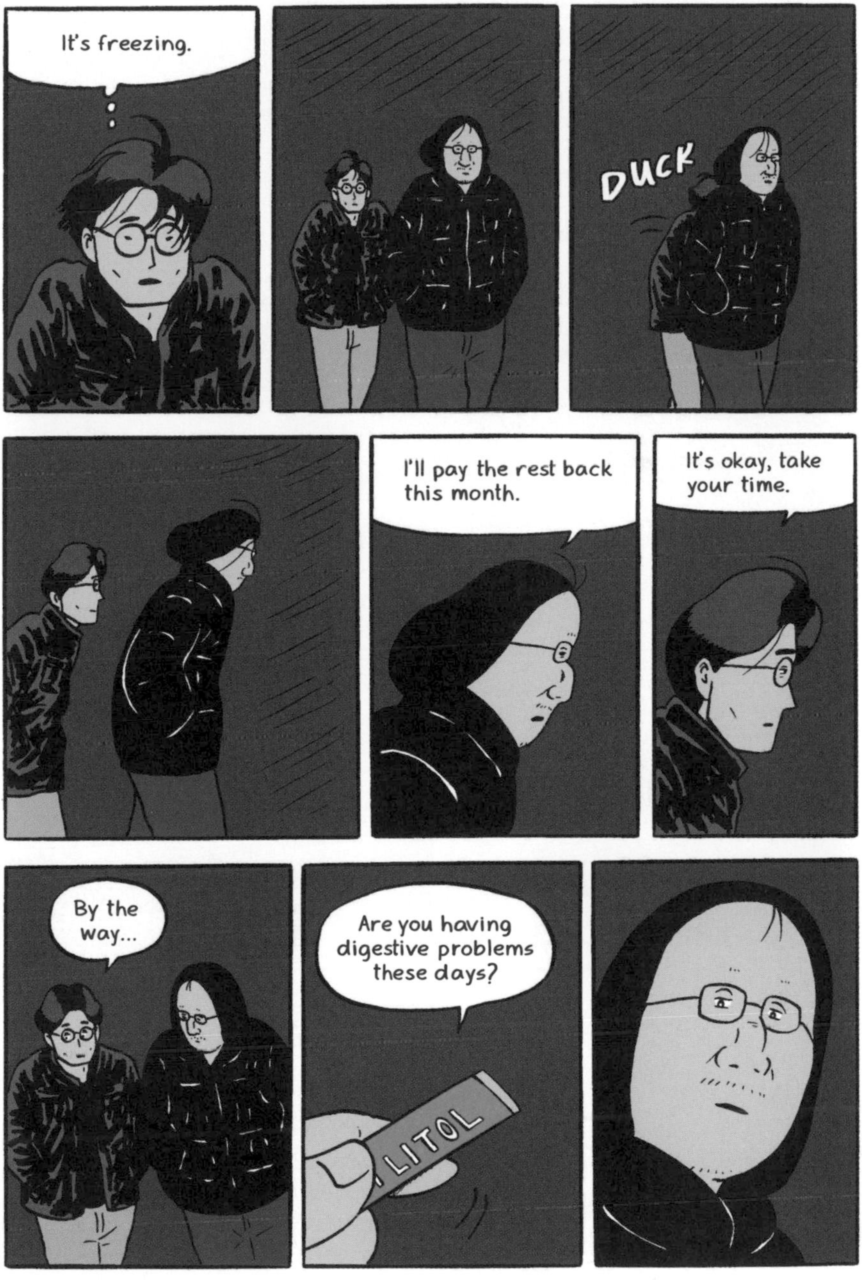
It's freezing.
DUCK
I'll pay the rest back this month.
It's okay, take your time.
By the way...
Are you having digestive problems these days?
LITOL

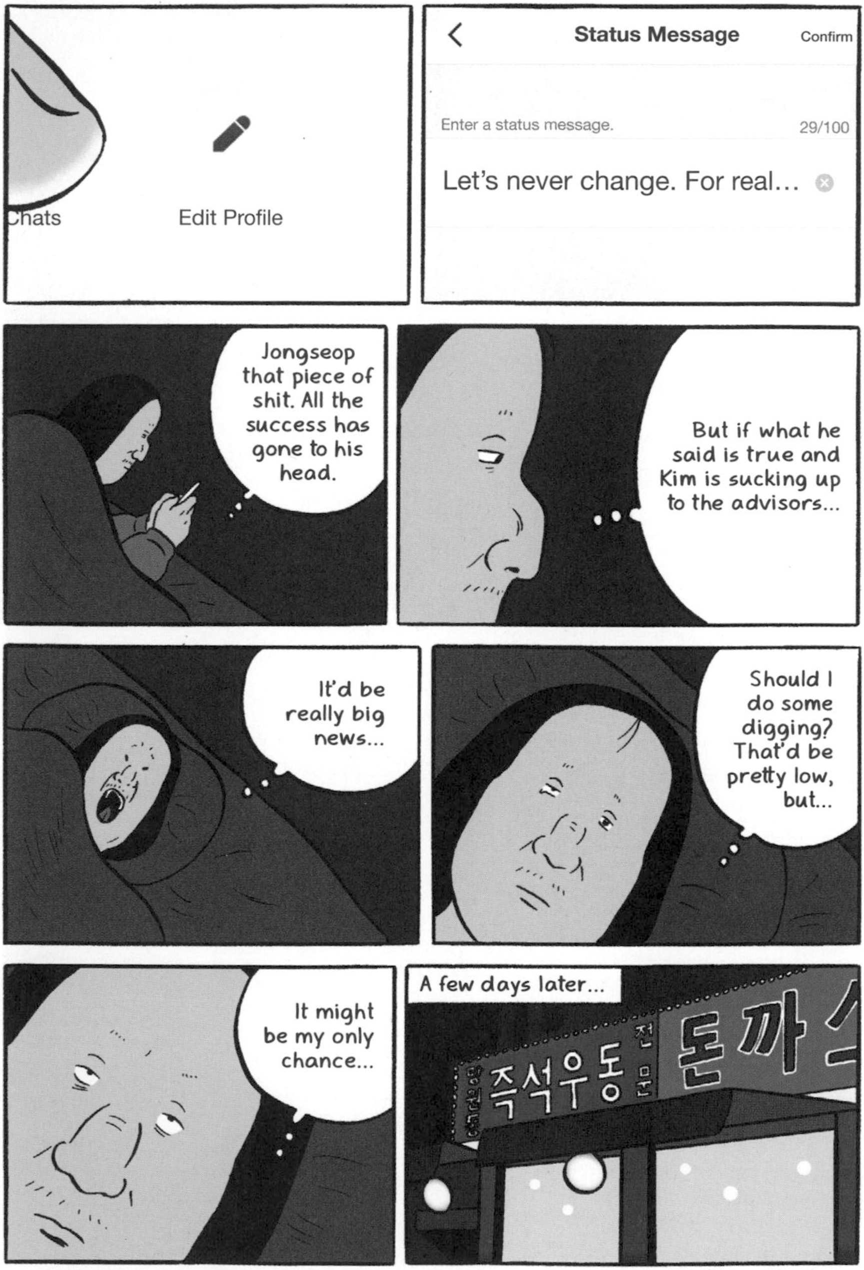
Chats
Edit Profile
Status Message
Confirm
Enter a status message.
29/100
Let's never change. For real...
Jongseop that piece of shit. All the success has gone to his head.
But if what he said is true and Kim is sucking up to the advisors...
It'd be really big news...
Should I do some digging? That'd be pretty low, but...
It might be my only chance...
A few days later...
즉석우동
전문
돈까

Signs: Instant Udon / Donkatsu

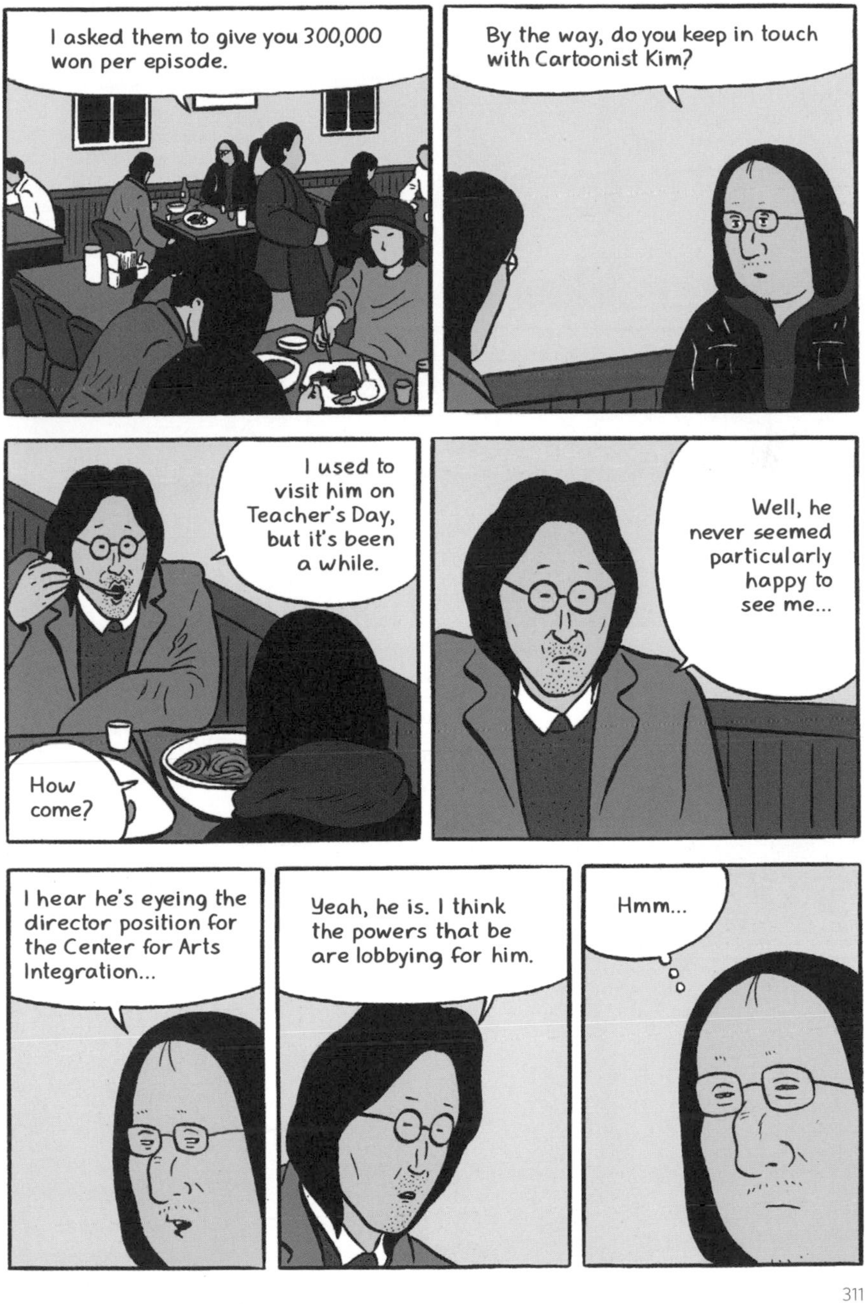
I asked them to give you 300,000 won per episode.
By the way, do you keep in touch with Cartoonist Kim?
I used to visit him on Teacher's Day, but it's been a while.
How come?
Well, he never seemed particularly happy to see me...
I hear he's eyeing the director position for the Center for Arts Integration...
Yeah, he is. I think the powers that be are lobbying for him.
Hmm...

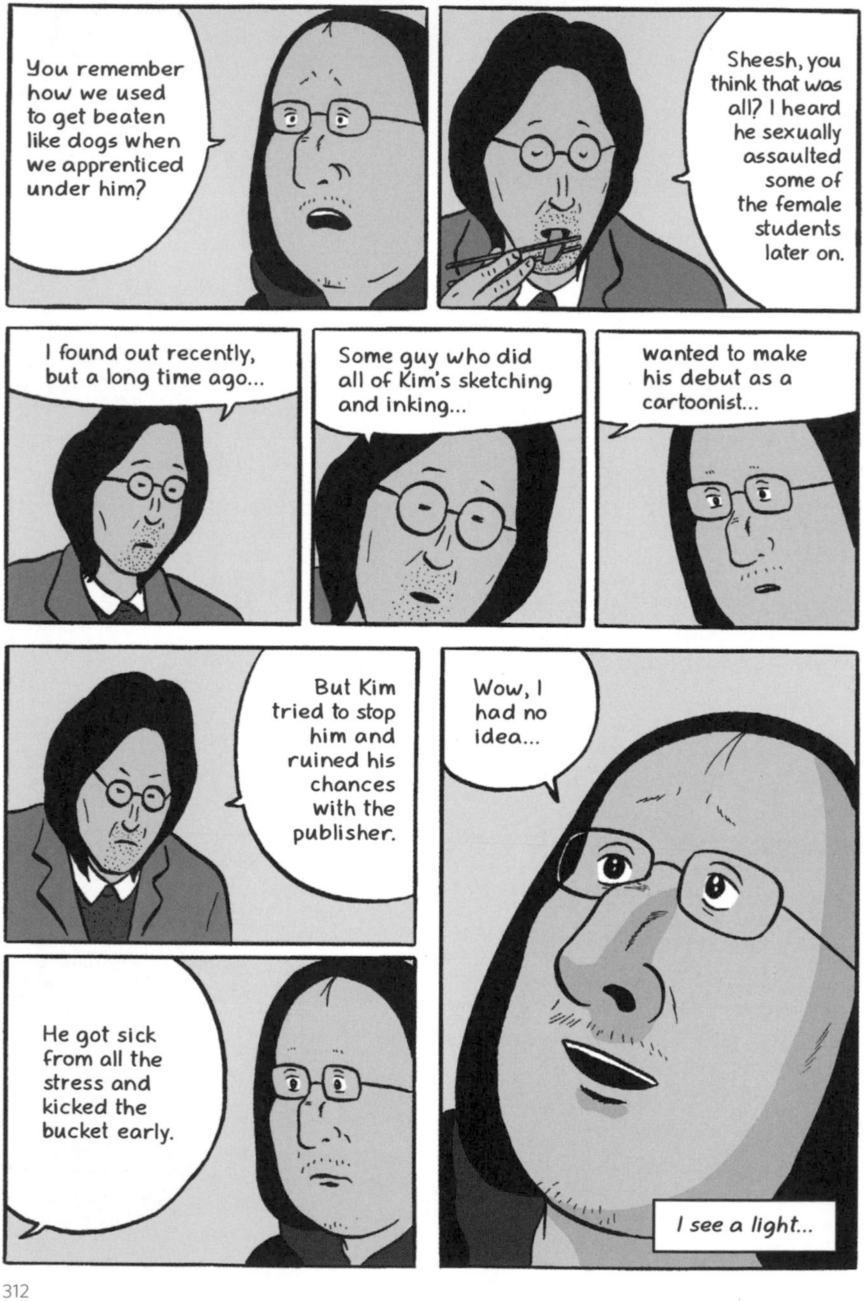
You remember how we used to get beaten like dogs when we apprenticed under him?
Sheesh, you think that was all? I heard he sexually assaulted some of the female students later on.
I found out recently, but a long time ago...
Some guy who did all of Kim's sketching and inking...
wanted to make his debut as a cartoonist...
But Kim tried to stop him and ruined his chances with the publisher.
He got sick from all the stress and kicked the bucket early.
Wow, I had no idea...
I see a light...

LAST LIFELINE

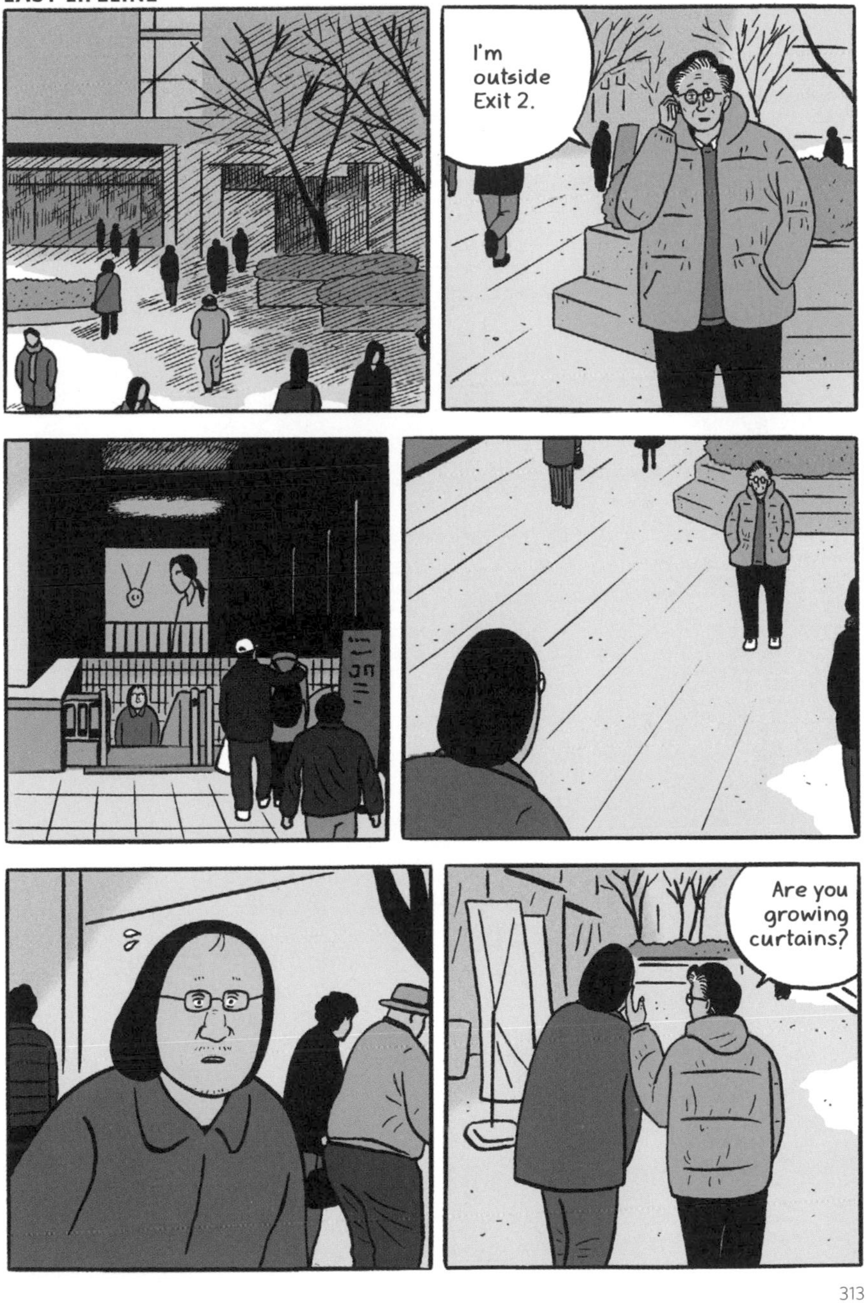
I'm outside Exit 2.
Are you growing curtains?

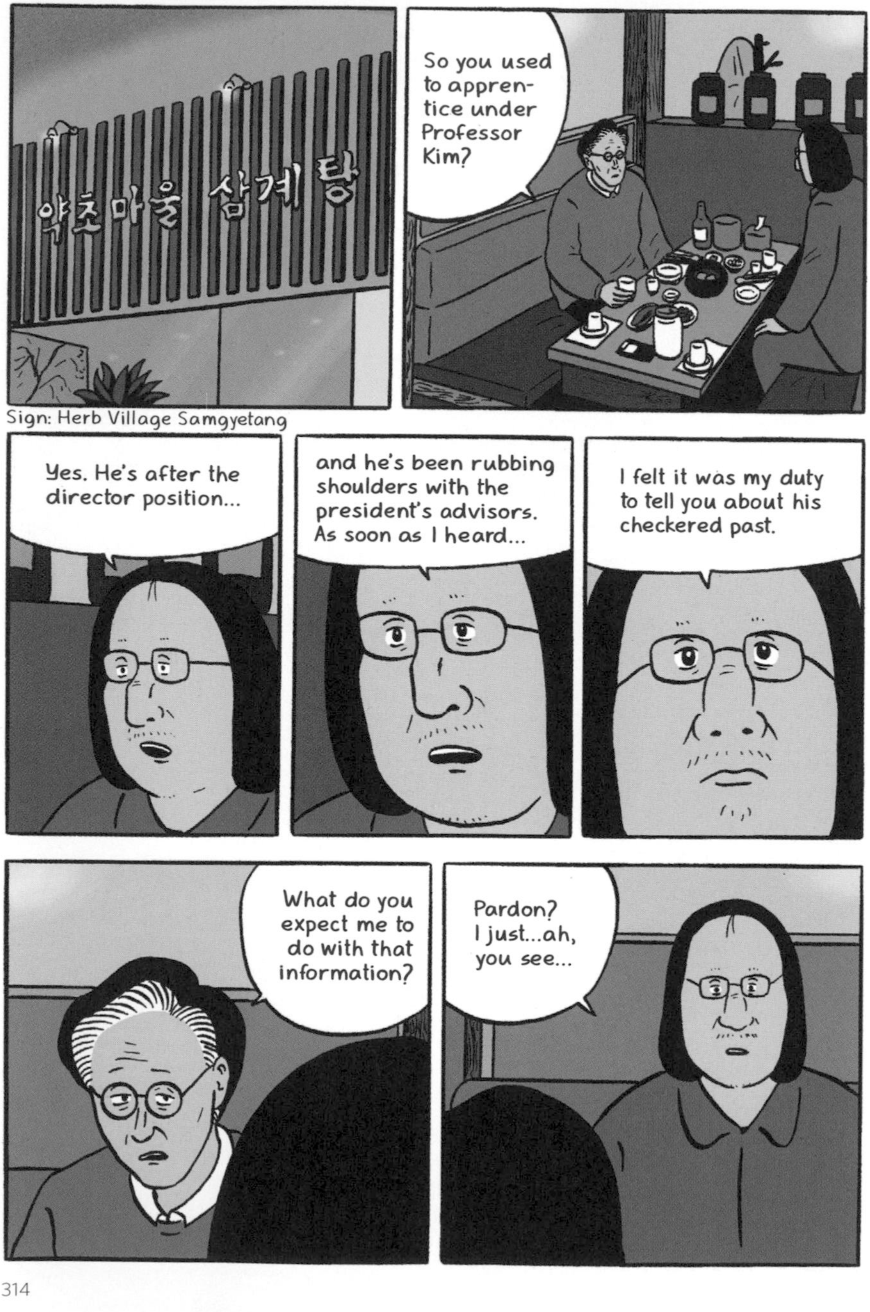
약초마을 삼계탕
So you used to apprentice under Professor Kim?
Yes. He's after the director position...
and he's been rubbing shoulders with the president's advisors. As soon as I heard...
I felt it was my duty to tell you about his checkered past.
What do you expect me to do with that information?
Pardon? I just...ah, you see...

Sign: Herb Village Samgyetang

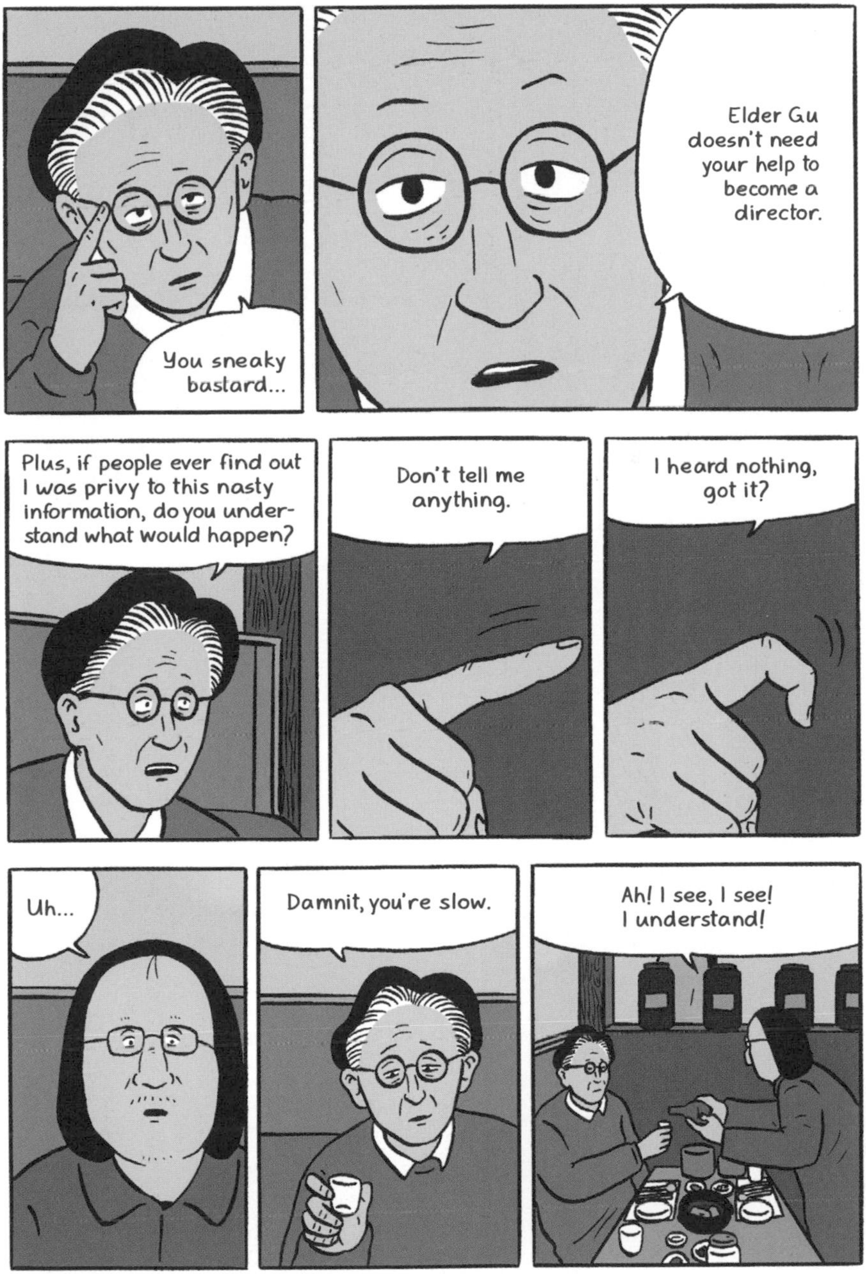
You sneaky bastard...
Elder Gu doesn't need your help to become a director.
Plus, if people ever find out I was privy to this nasty information, do you understand what would happen?
Don't tell me anything.
I heard nothing, got it?
Uh...
Damnit, you're slow.
Ah! I see, I see! I understand!

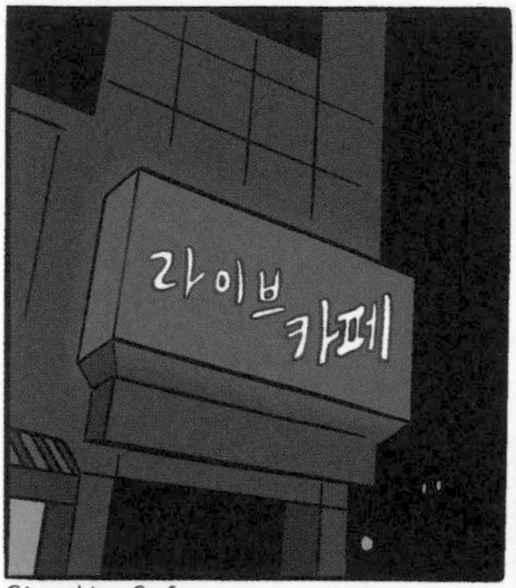
라이브 카페

Sign: Live Cafe

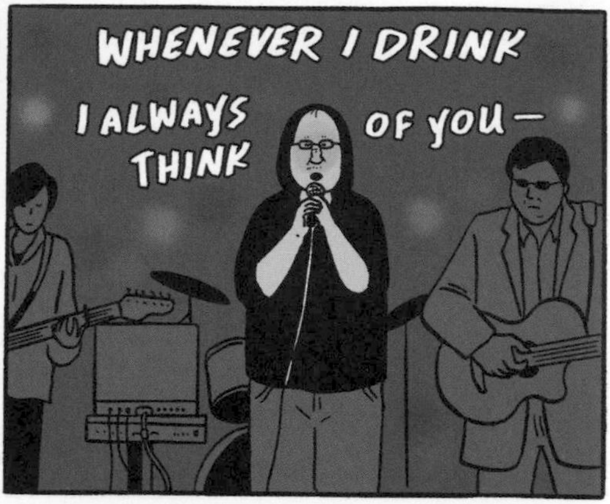
WHENEVER I DRINK
I ALWAYS THINK
OF YOU—

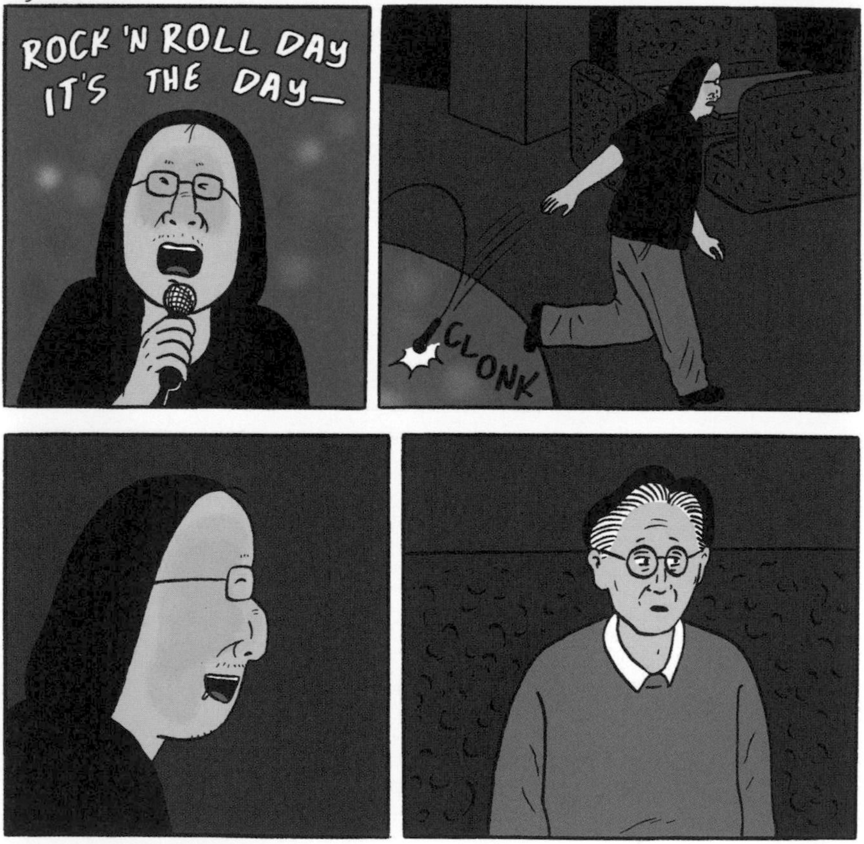
ROCK 'N ROLL DAY
IT'S THE DAY—
CLONK

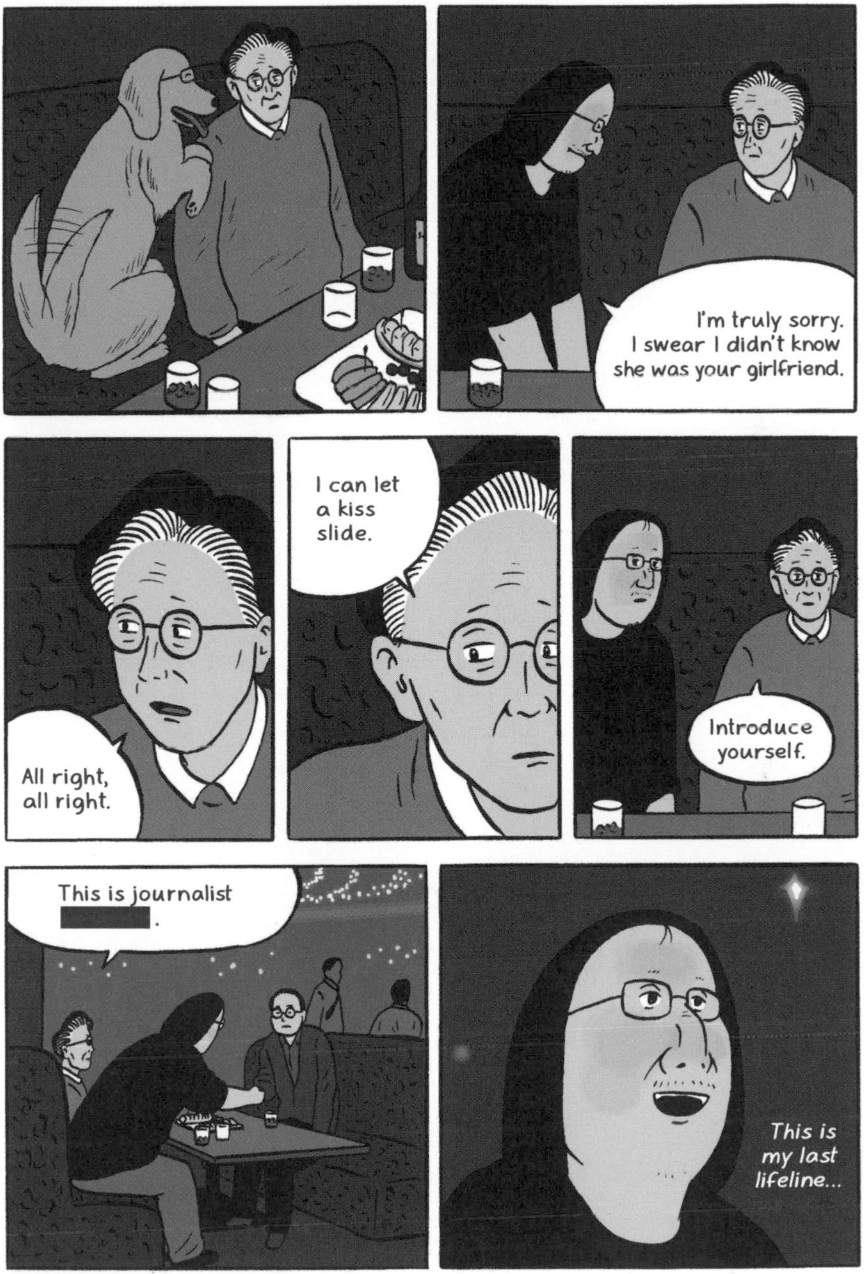
I'm truly sorry.
I swear I didn't know
she was your girlfriend.
All right,
all right.
I can let
a kiss
slide.
Introduce
yourself.
This is journalist
[redacted].
This is
my last
lifeline...

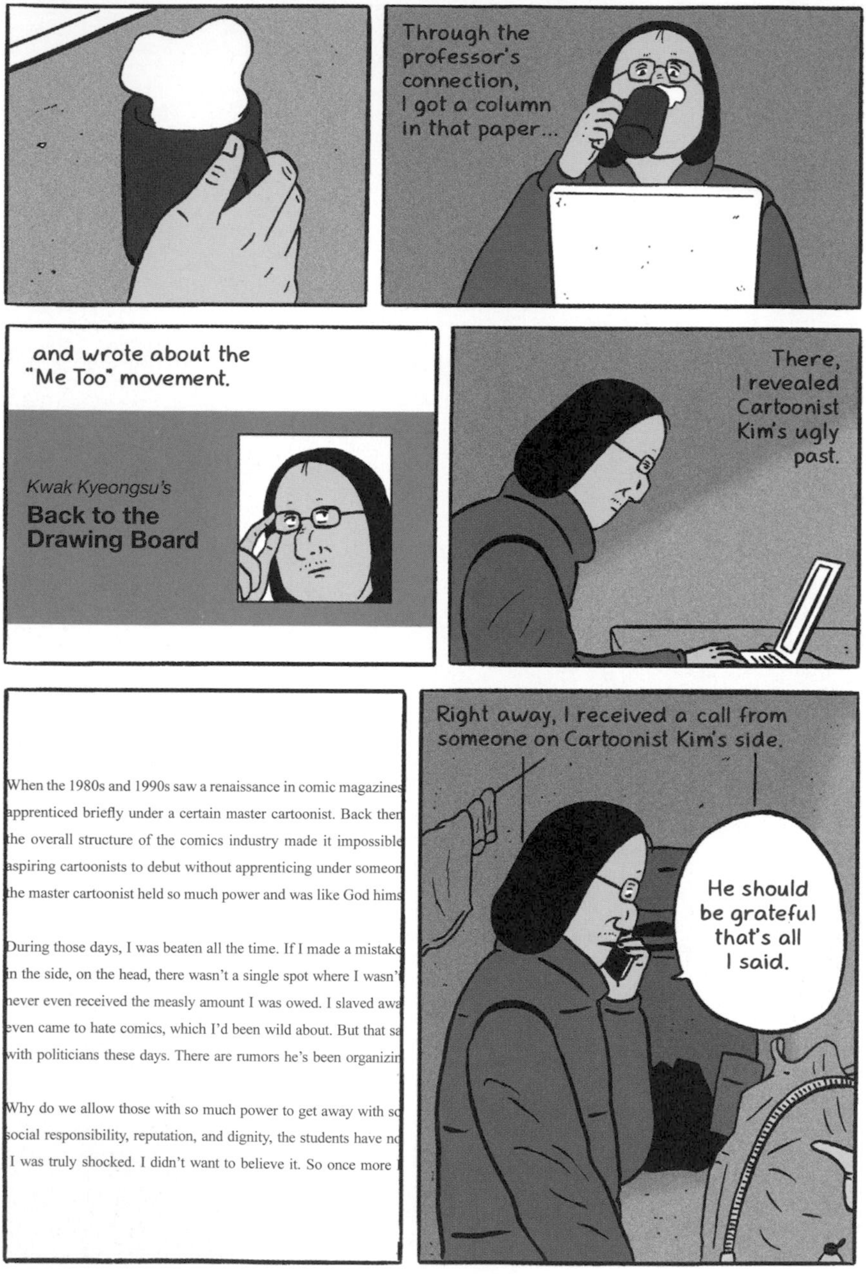
Through the professor's connection, I got a column in that paper...
and wrote about the "Me Too" movement.
Kwak Kyeongsu's
Back to the Drawing Board
There, I revealed Cartoonist Kim's ugly past.
When the 1980s and 1990s saw a renaissance in comic magazines
apprenticed briefly under a certain master cartoonist. Back then
the overall structure of the comics industry made it impossible
aspiring cartoonists to debut without apprenticing under someon
the master cartoonist held so much power and was like God hims
During those days, I was beaten all the time. If I made a mistake
in the side, on the head, there wasn't a single spot where I wasn'
never even received the measly amount I was owed. I slaved awa
even came to hate comics, which I'd been wild about. But that sa
with politicians these days. There are rumors he's been organizin
Why do we allow those with so much power to get away with so
social responsibility, reputation, and dignity, the students have no
I was truly shocked. I didn't want to believe it. So once more I
Right away, I received a call from someone on Cartoonist Kim's side.
He should be grateful that's all I said.

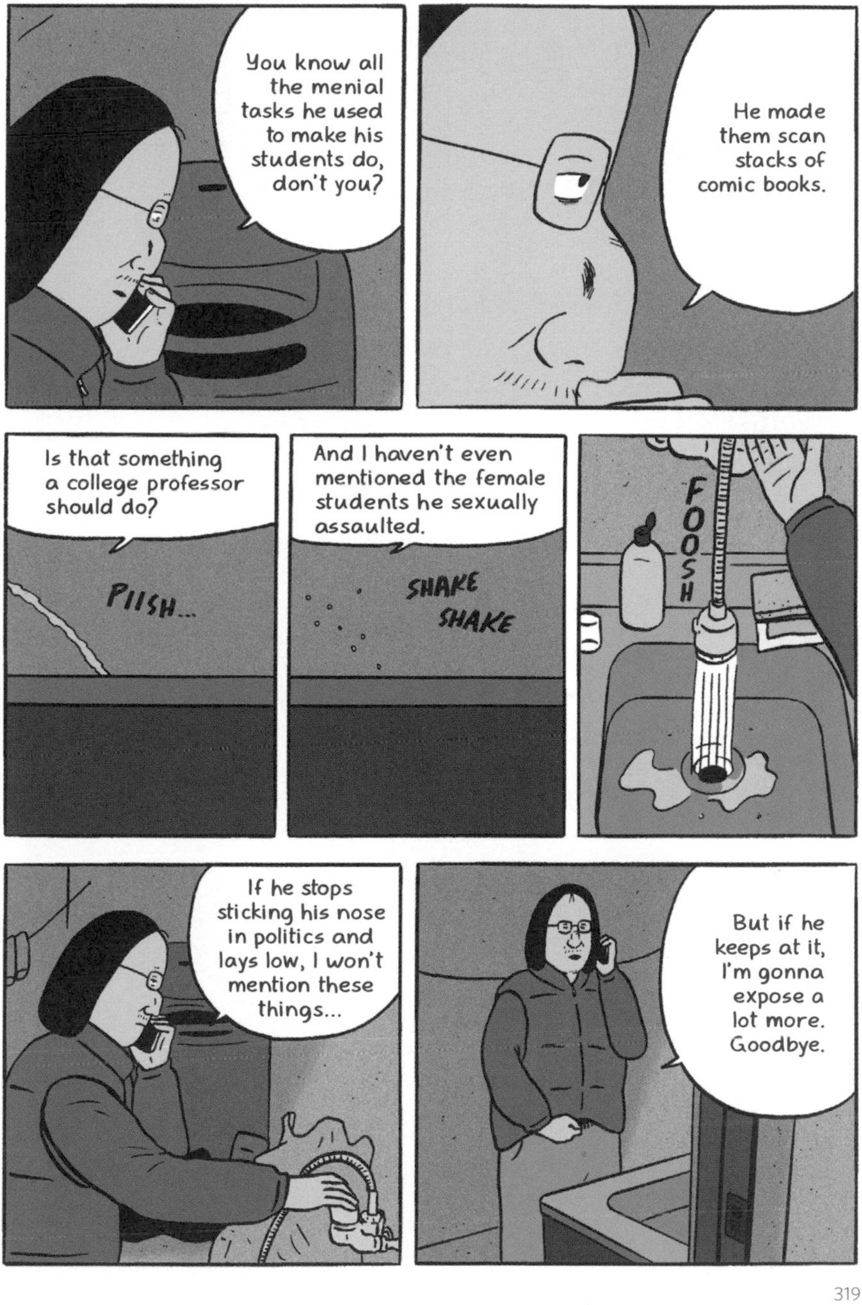
You know all the menial tasks he used to make his students do, don't you?
He made them scan stacks of comic books.
Is that something a college professor should do?
PIISH...
And I haven't even mentioned the female students he sexually assaulted.
SHAKE SHAKE
FOOOSH
If he stops sticking his nose in politics and lays low, I won't mention these things...
But if he keeps at it, I'm gonna expose a lot more. Goodbye.

Look, I'm a poet, but you know I do other things for money, right?

You can do that too. Do something else while you write.

Or how about submitting something for a screen-writing competition?

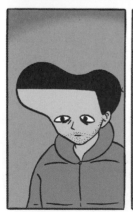

Drinking and getting old are the only two things I'm good at.

Here, take a look.

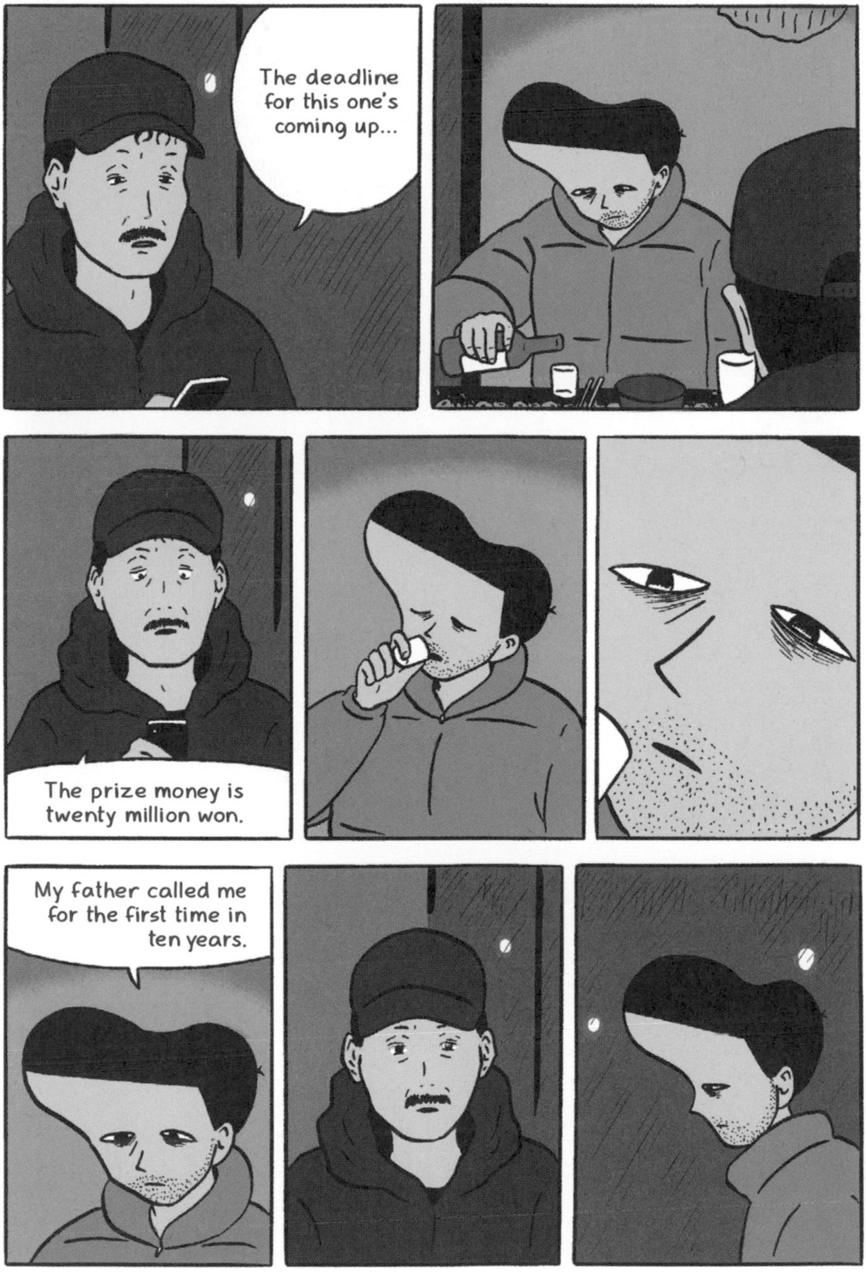
The deadline for this one's coming up...
The prize money is twenty million won.
My father called me for the first time in ten years.

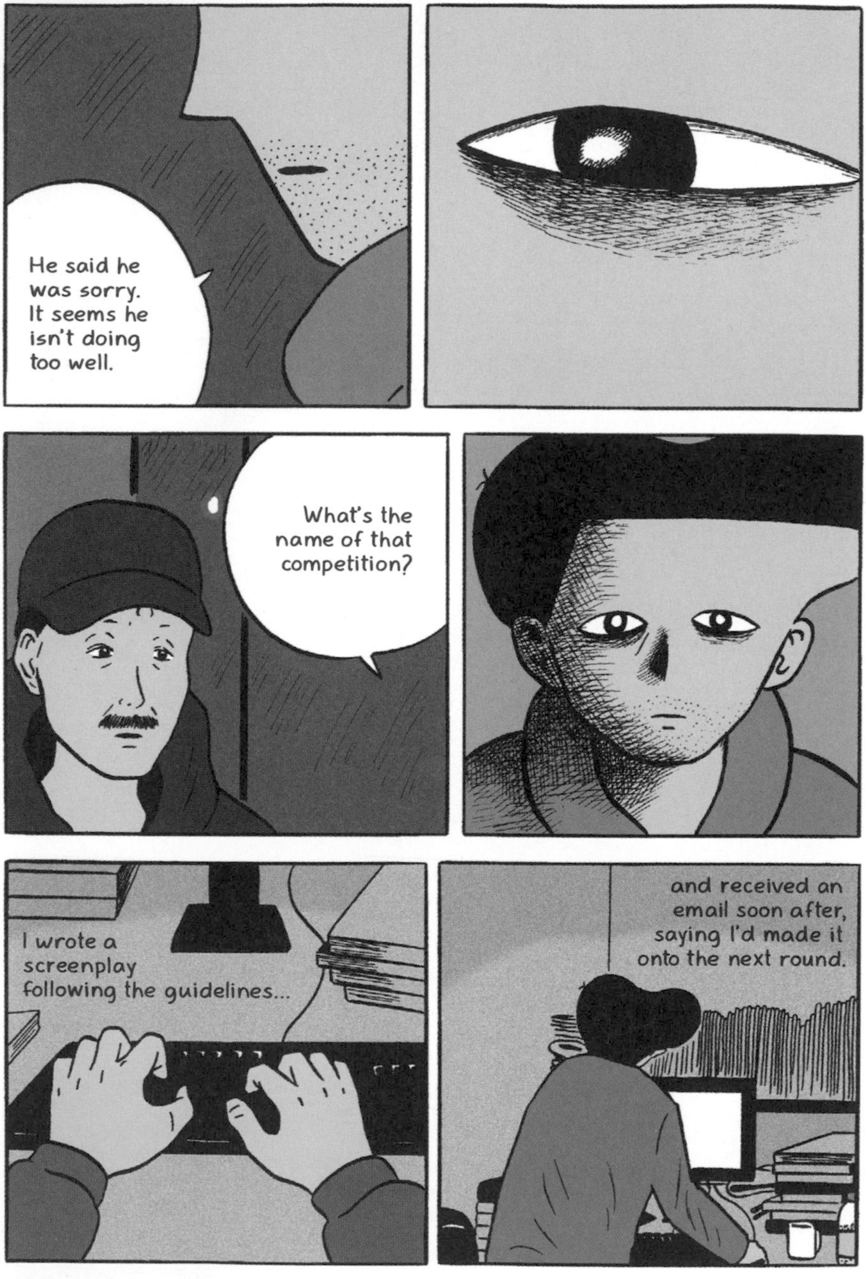
He said he was sorry. It seems he isn't doing too well.
What's the name of that competition?
I wrote a screenplay following the guidelines...
and received an email soon after, saying I'd made it onto the next round.

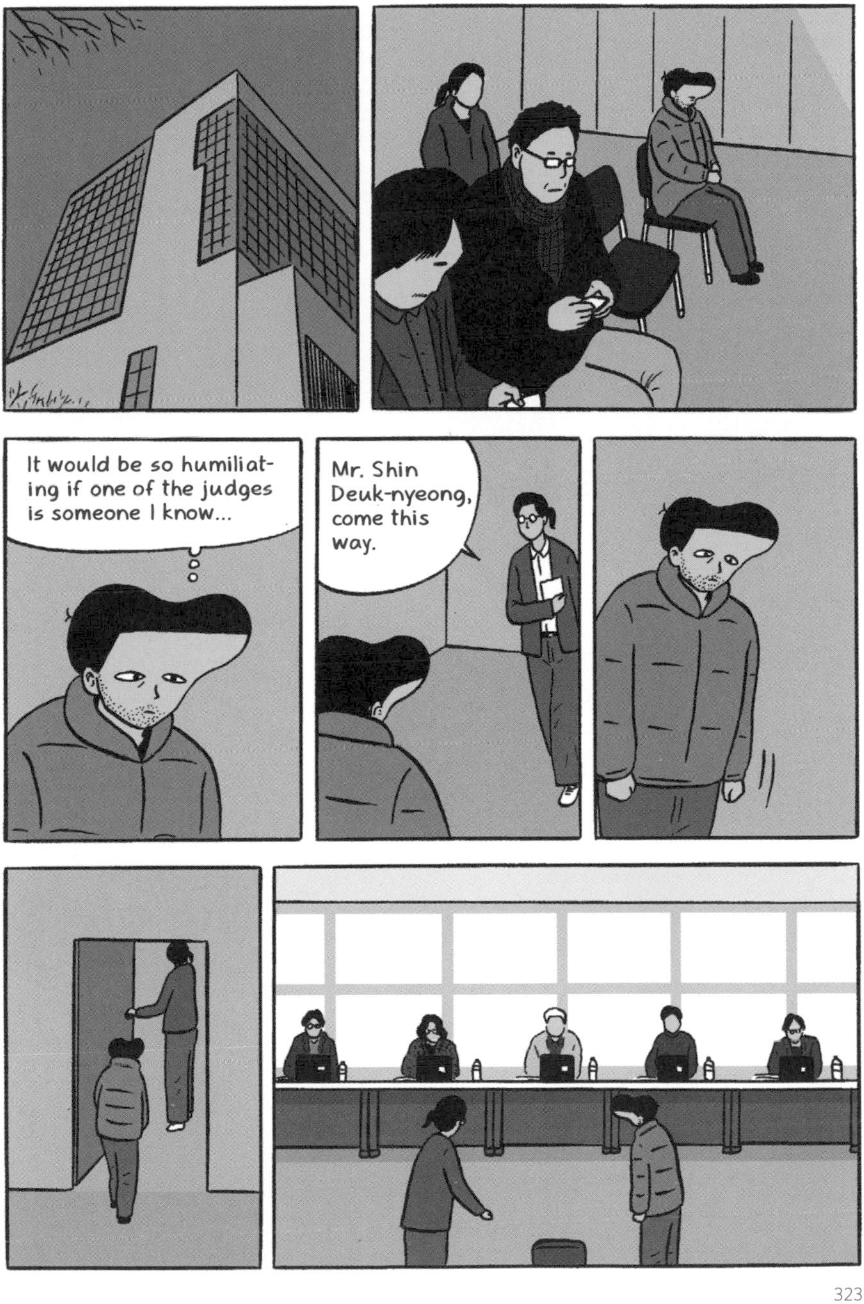
It would be so humiliating if one of the judges is someone I know...
Mr. Shin Deuk-nyeong, come this way.

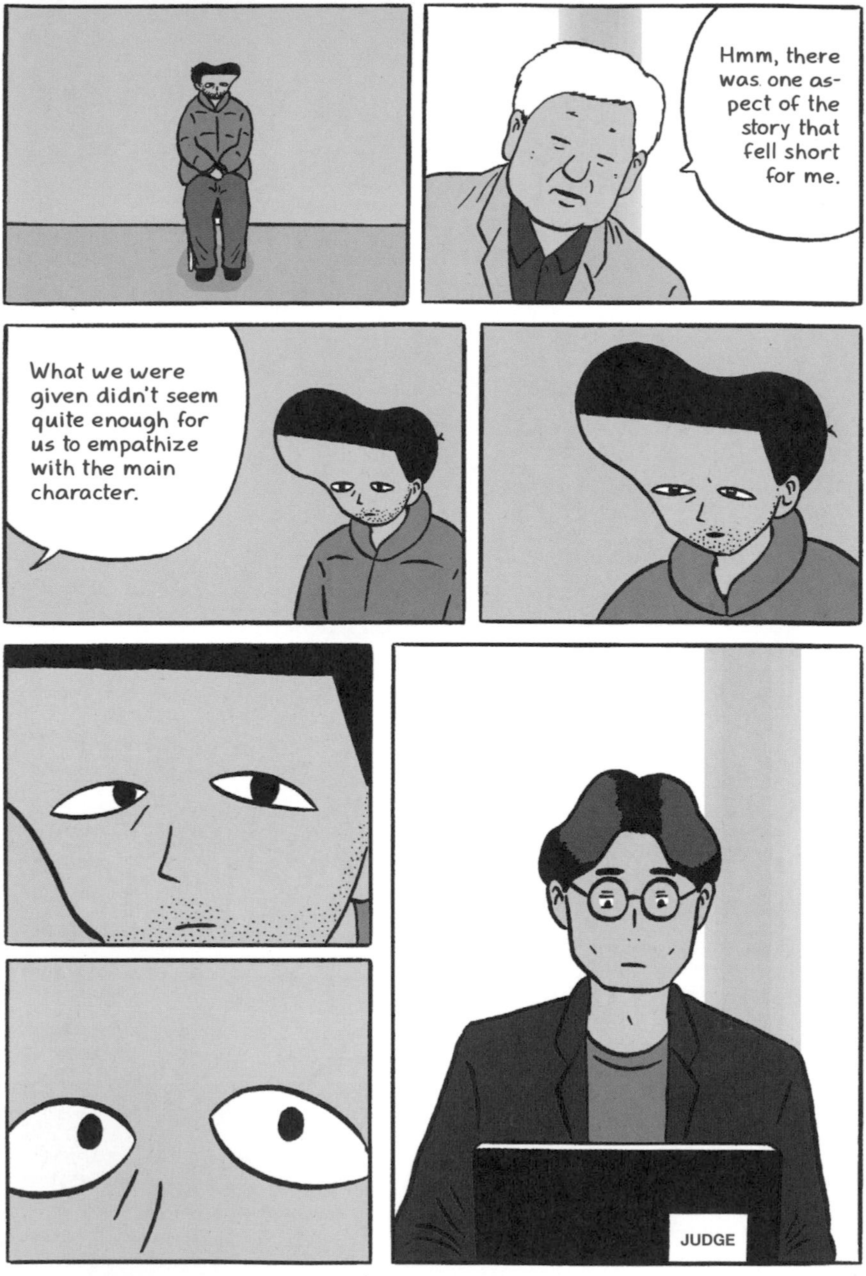
Hmm, there was one aspect of the story that fell short for me.
What we were given didn't seem quite enough for us to empathize with the main character.
JUDGE

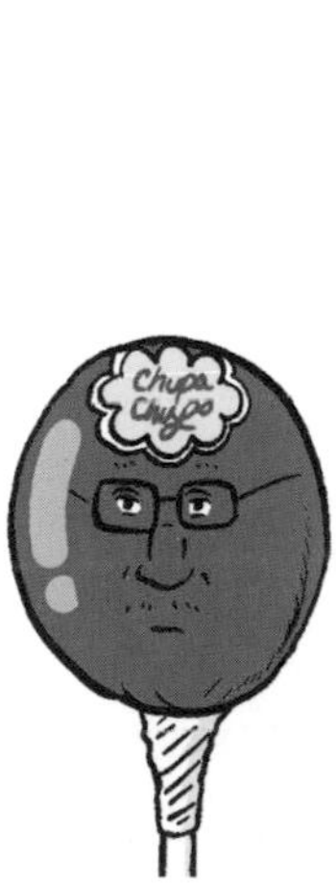
Chupa

PROFESSOR

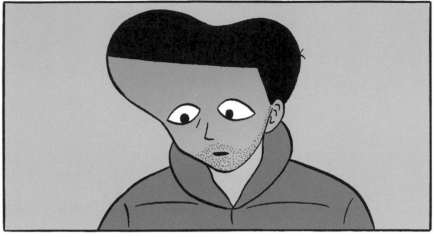

I really enjoyed your story, but...

As I was blasted with questions, my mind went blank.

I lost the competition.

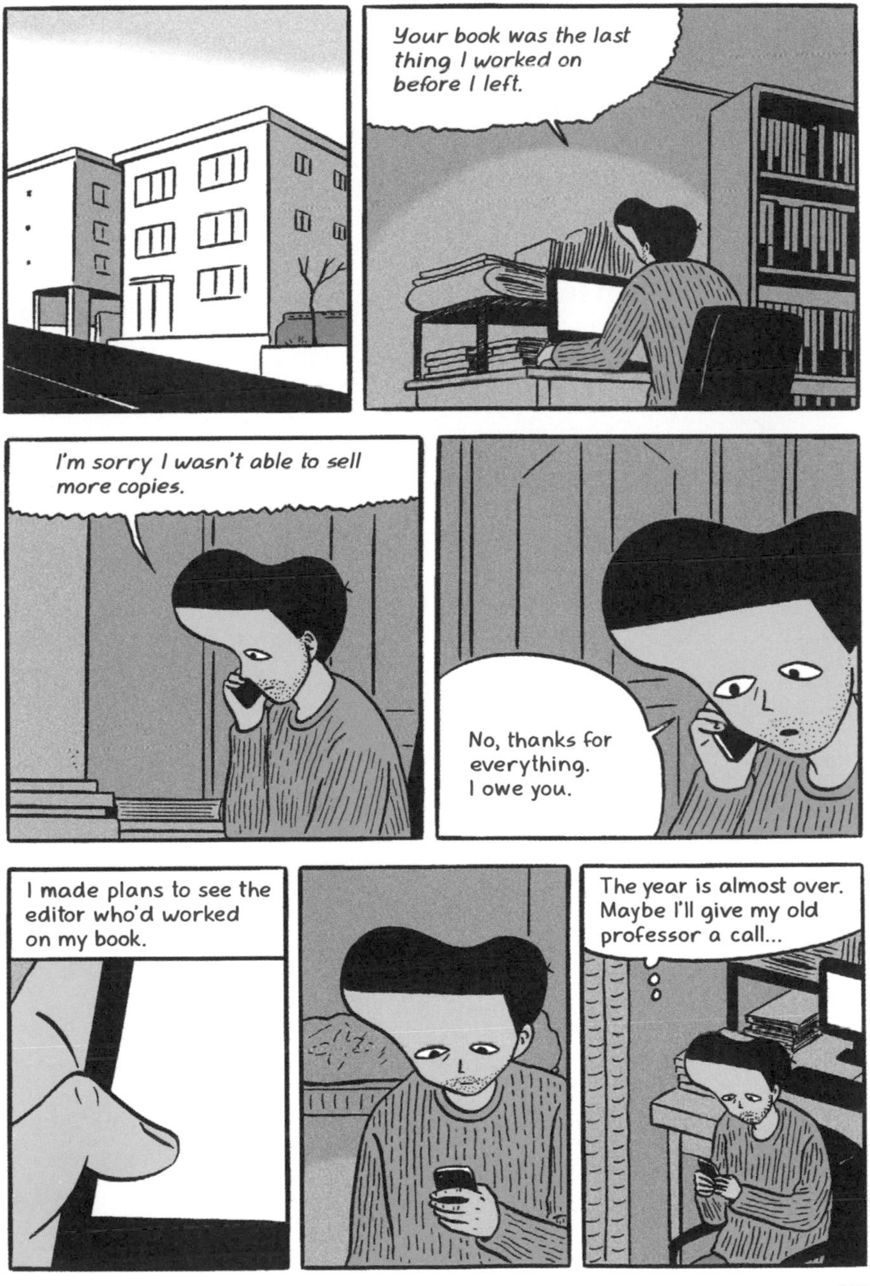
Your book was the last thing I worked on before I left.
I'm sorry I wasn't able to sell more copies.
No, thanks for everything. I owe you.
I made plans to see the editor who'd worked on my book.
The year is almost over. Maybe I'll give my old professor a call...

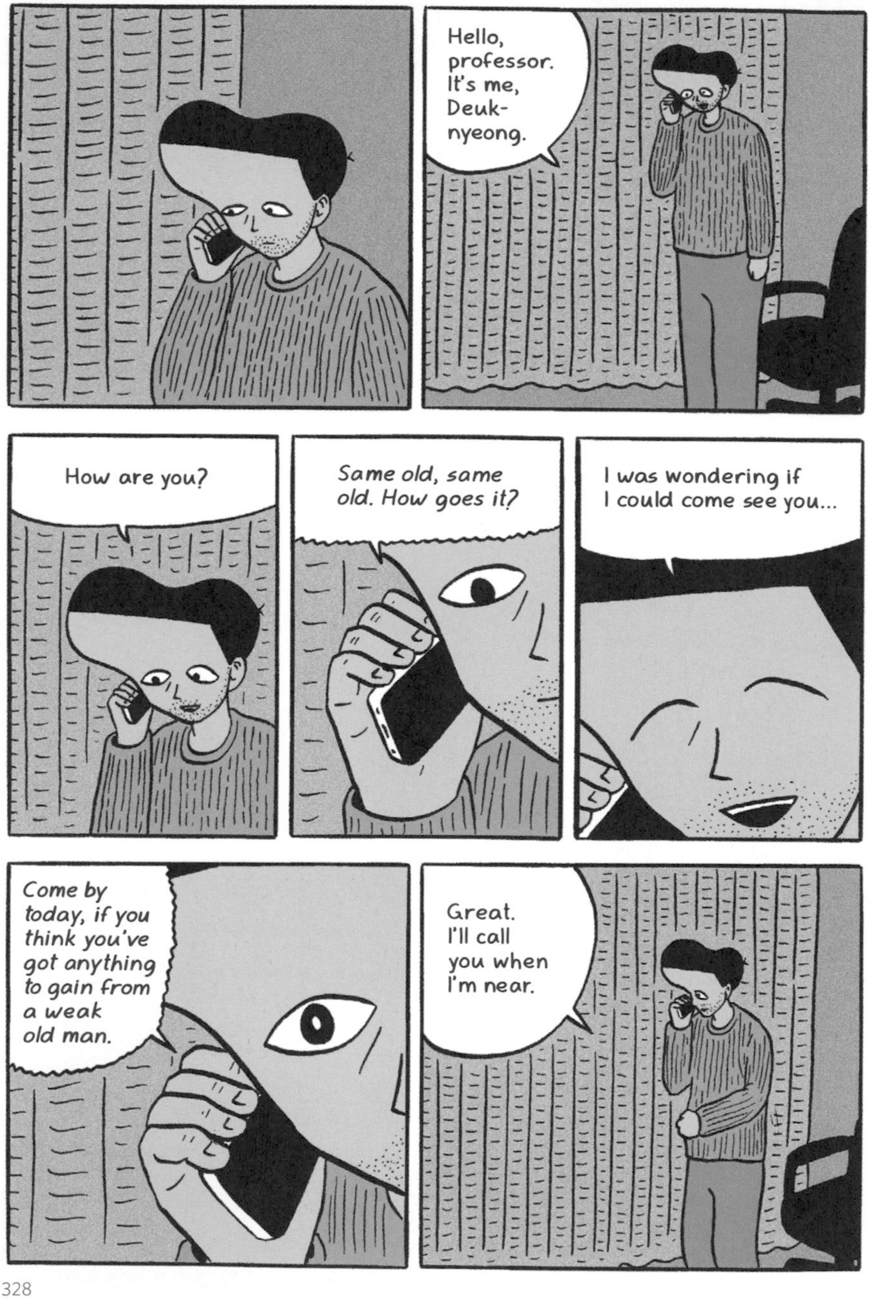

Hello, professor. It's me, Deuk-nyeong.
How are you?
Same old, same old. How goes it?
I was wondering if I could come see you...
Come by today, if you think you've got anything to gain from a weak old man.
Great. I'll call you when I'm near.

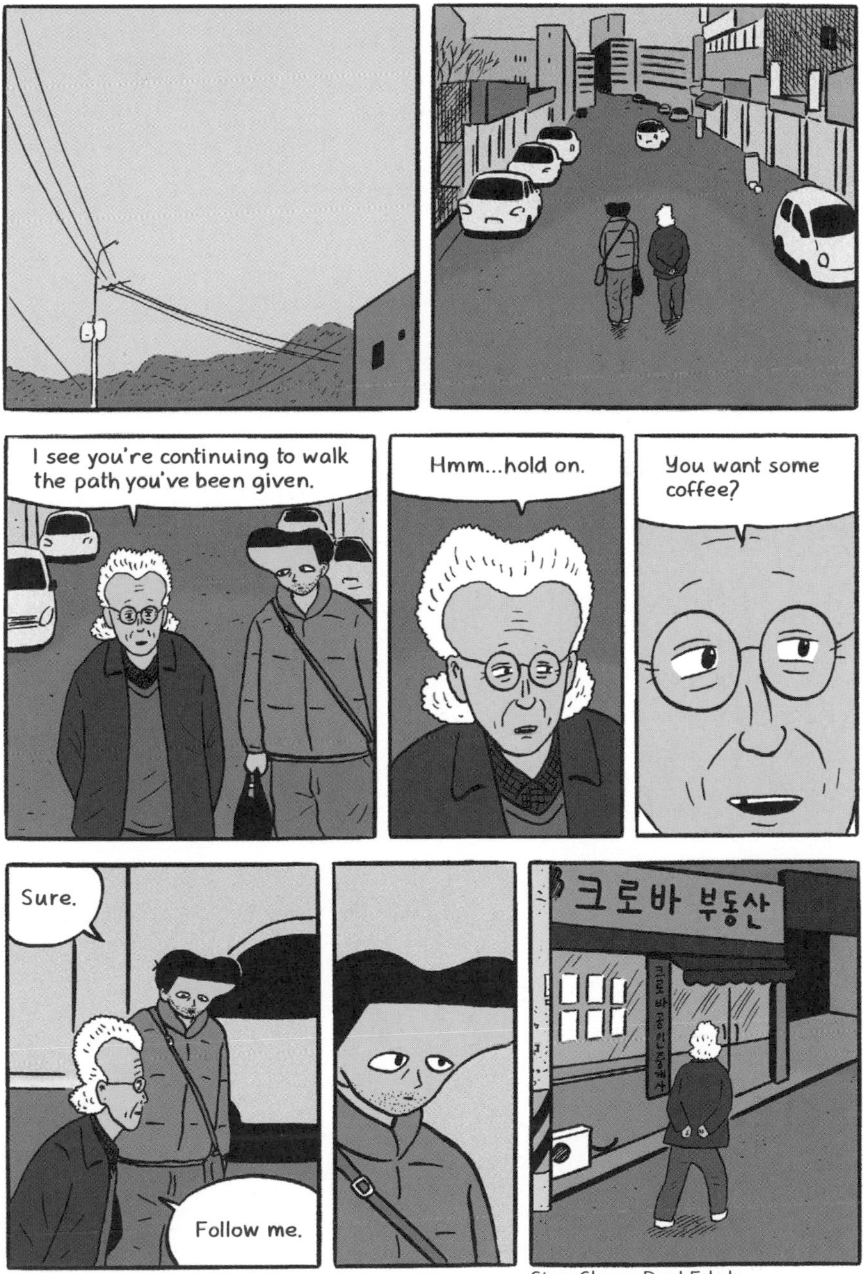
I see you're continuing to walk the path you've been given.
Hmm...hold on.
You want some coffee?
Sure.
Follow me.
크로바 부동산
Sign: Clover Real Estate

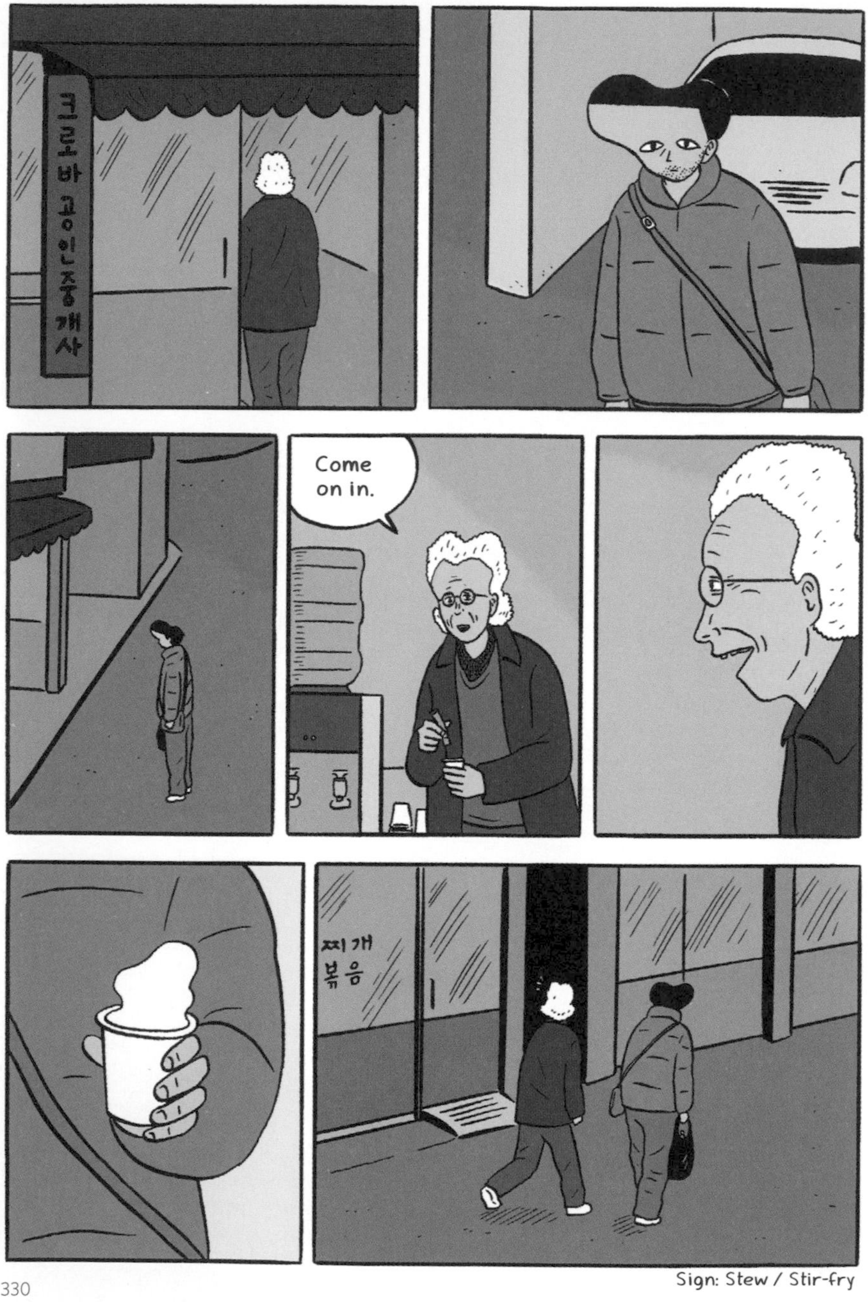
크로바 공인중개사
Come on in.
찌개
볶음

Sign: Stew / Stir-fry

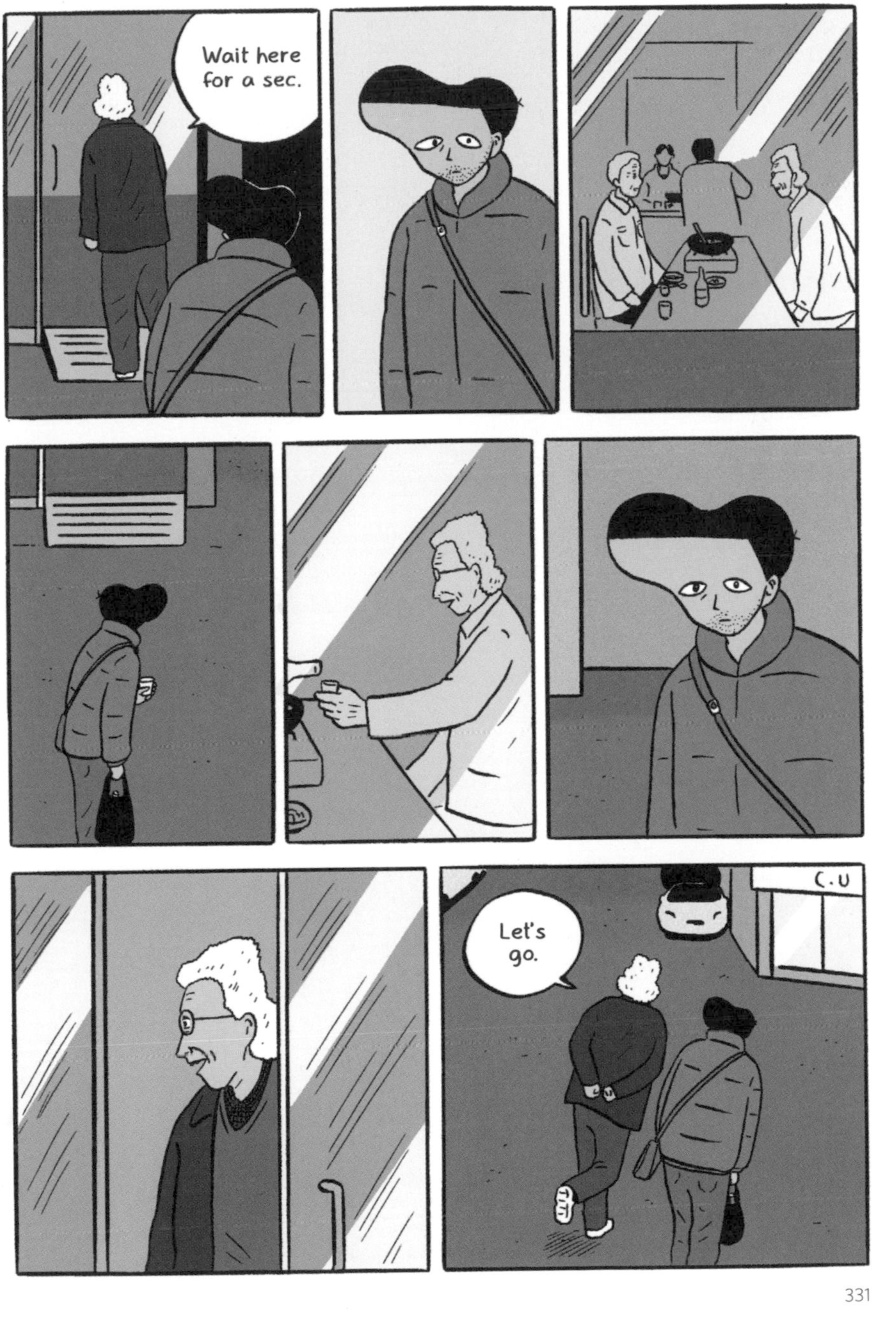
Wait here for a sec.
C.U
Let's go.

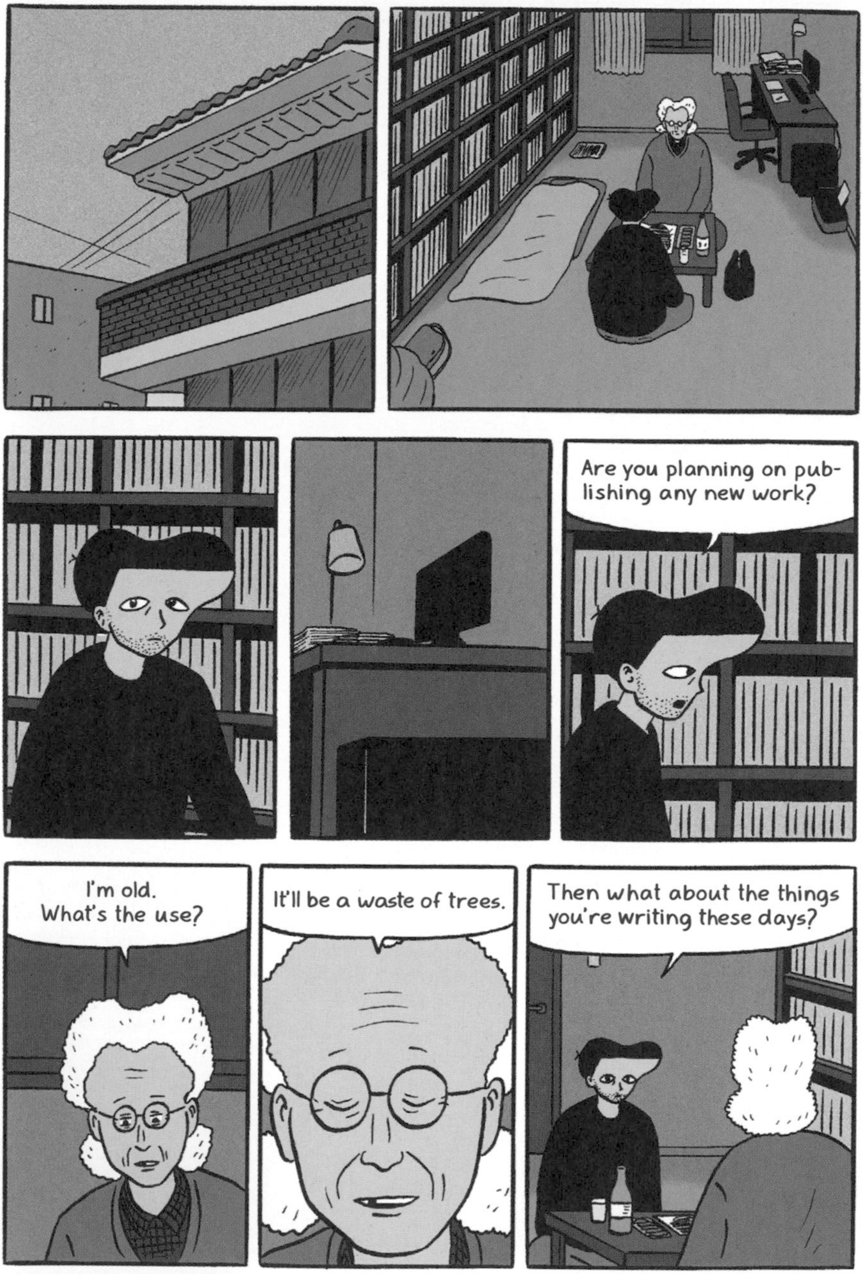
Are you planning on publishing any new work?
I'm old.
What's the use?
It'll be a waste of trees.
Then what about the things you're writing these days?

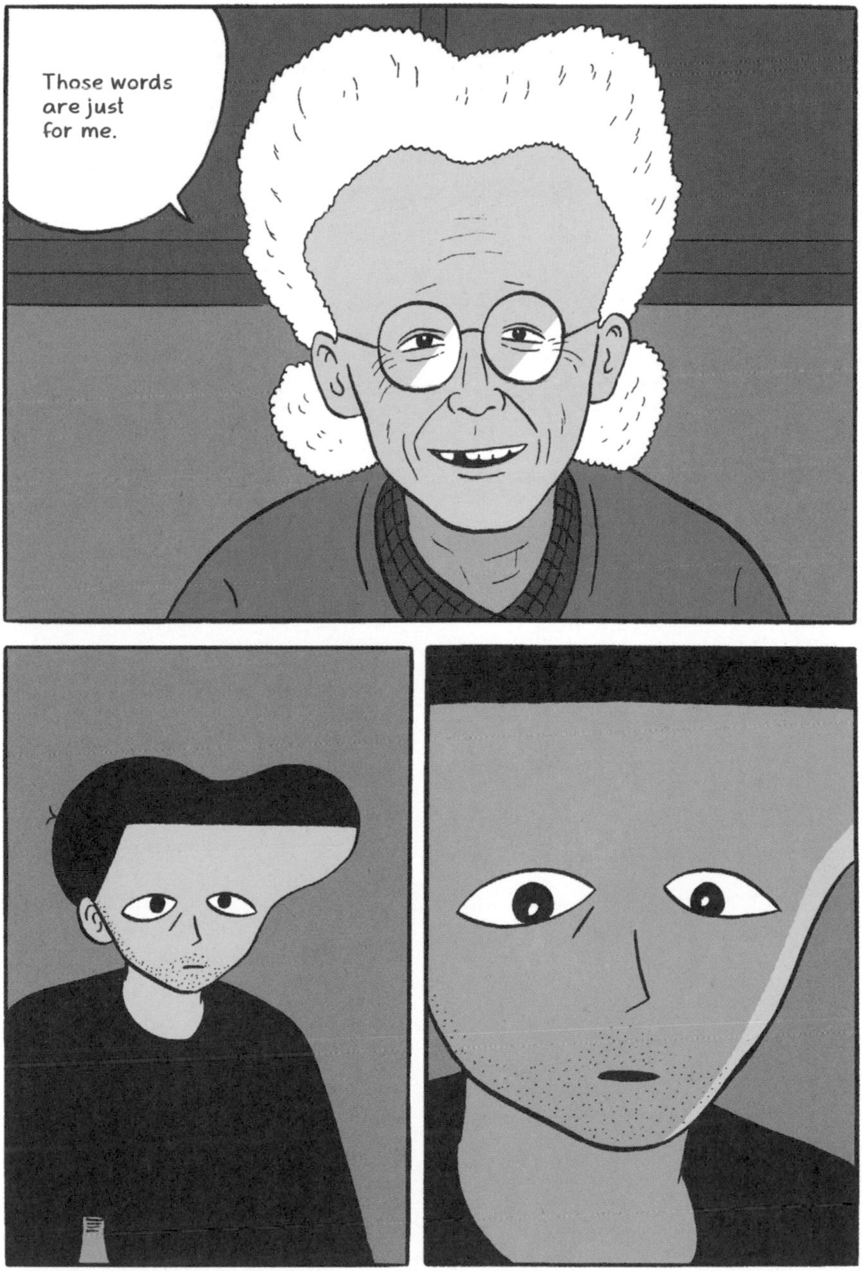
Those words are just for me.

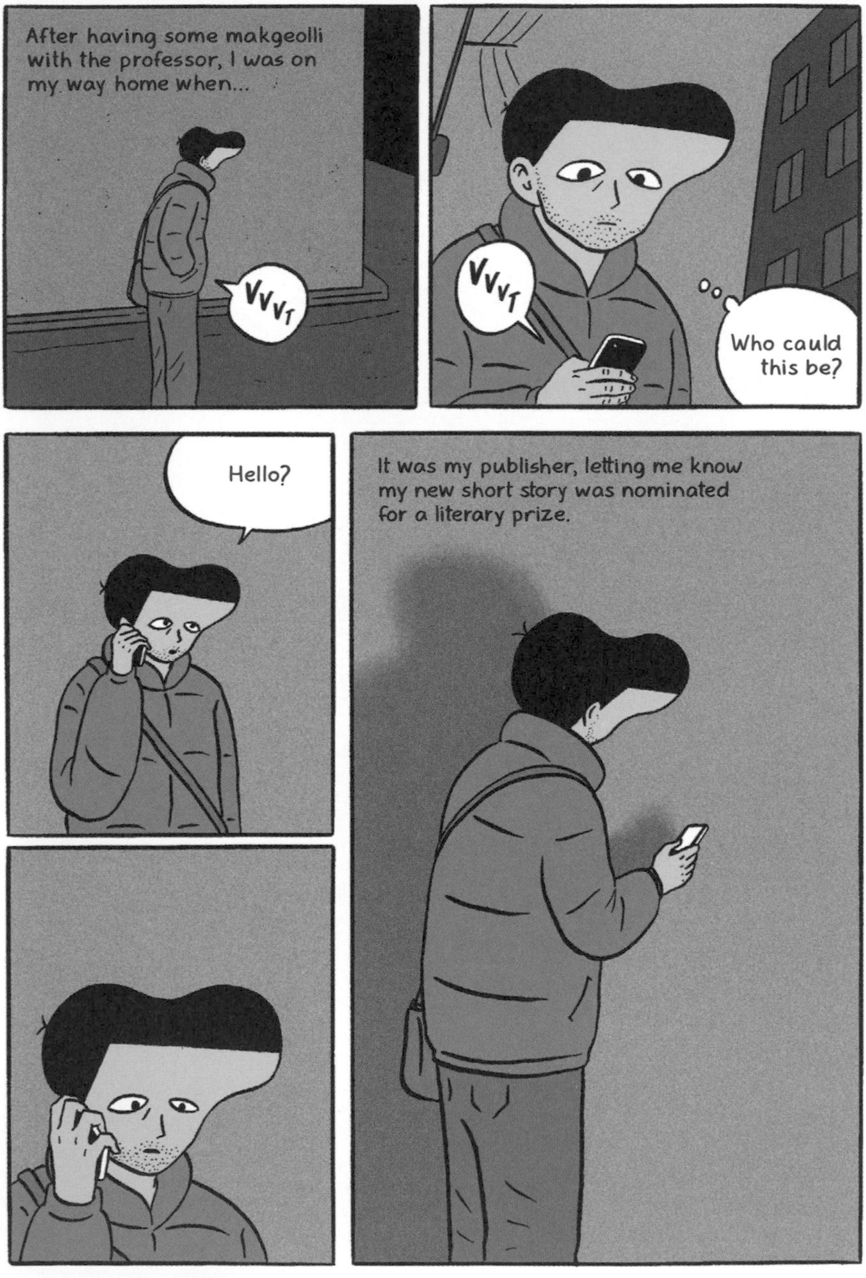
After having some makgeolli with the professor, I was on my way home when...
Vvvt
Vvvt
Who cauld this be?
Hello?
It was my publisher, letting me know my new short story was nominated for a literary prize.

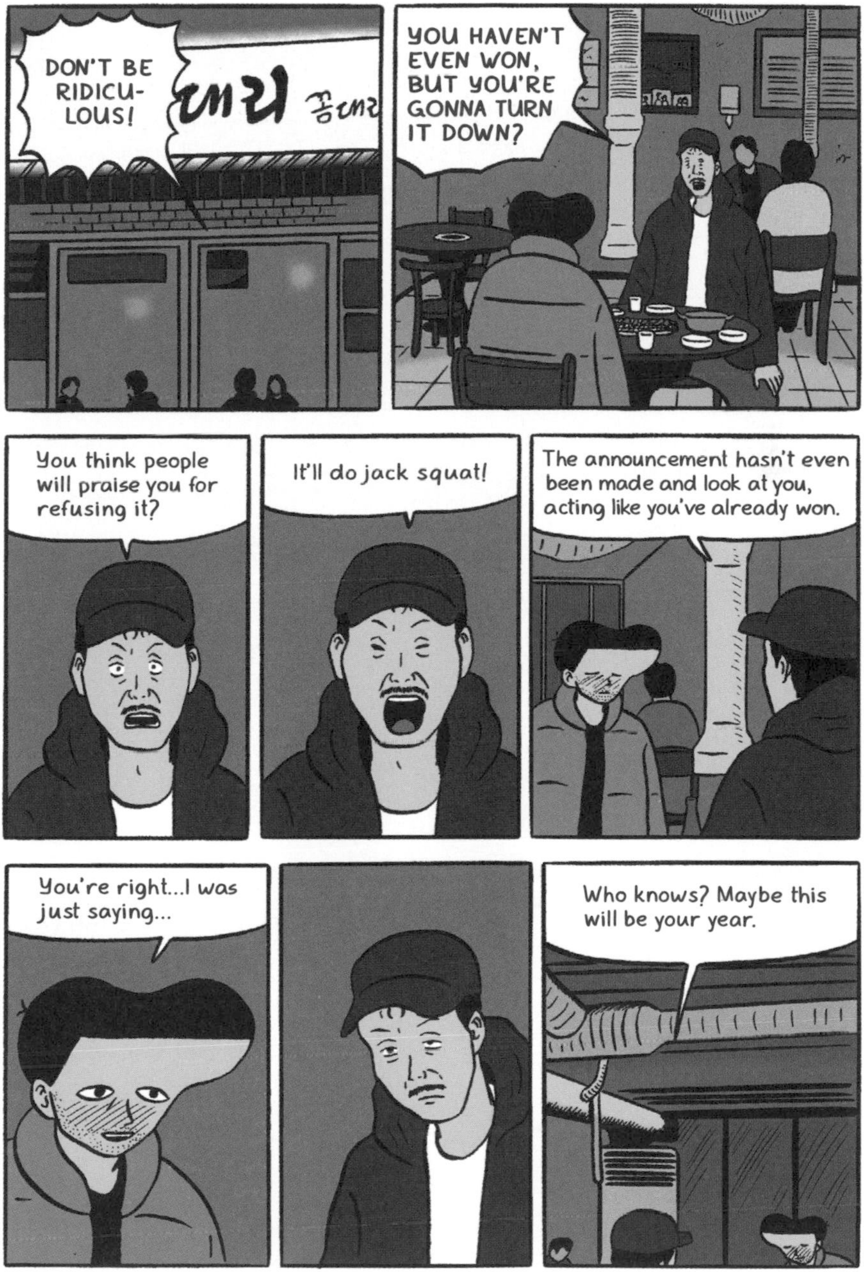
DON'T BE RIDICU-LOUS!
대리
YOU HAVEN'T EVEN WON, BUT YOU'RE GONNA TURN IT DOWN?
You think people will praise you for refusing it?
It'll do jack squat!
The announcement hasn't even been made and look at you, acting like you've already won.
You're right...I was just saying...
Who knows? Maybe this will be your year.

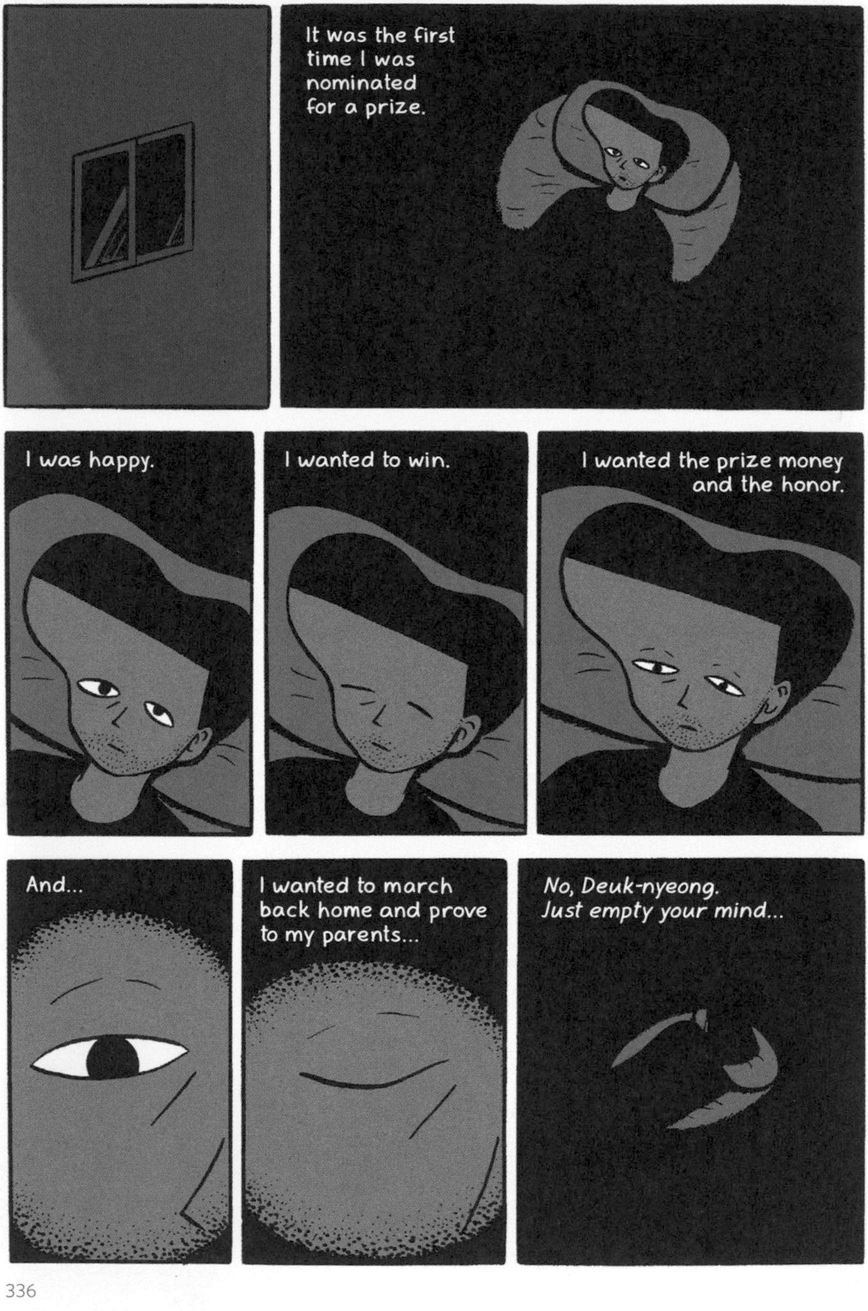
It was the first time I was nominated for a prize.
I was happy.
I wanted to win.
I wanted the prize money and the honor.
And...
I wanted to march back home and prove to my parents...
No, Deuk-nyeong. Just empty your mind...

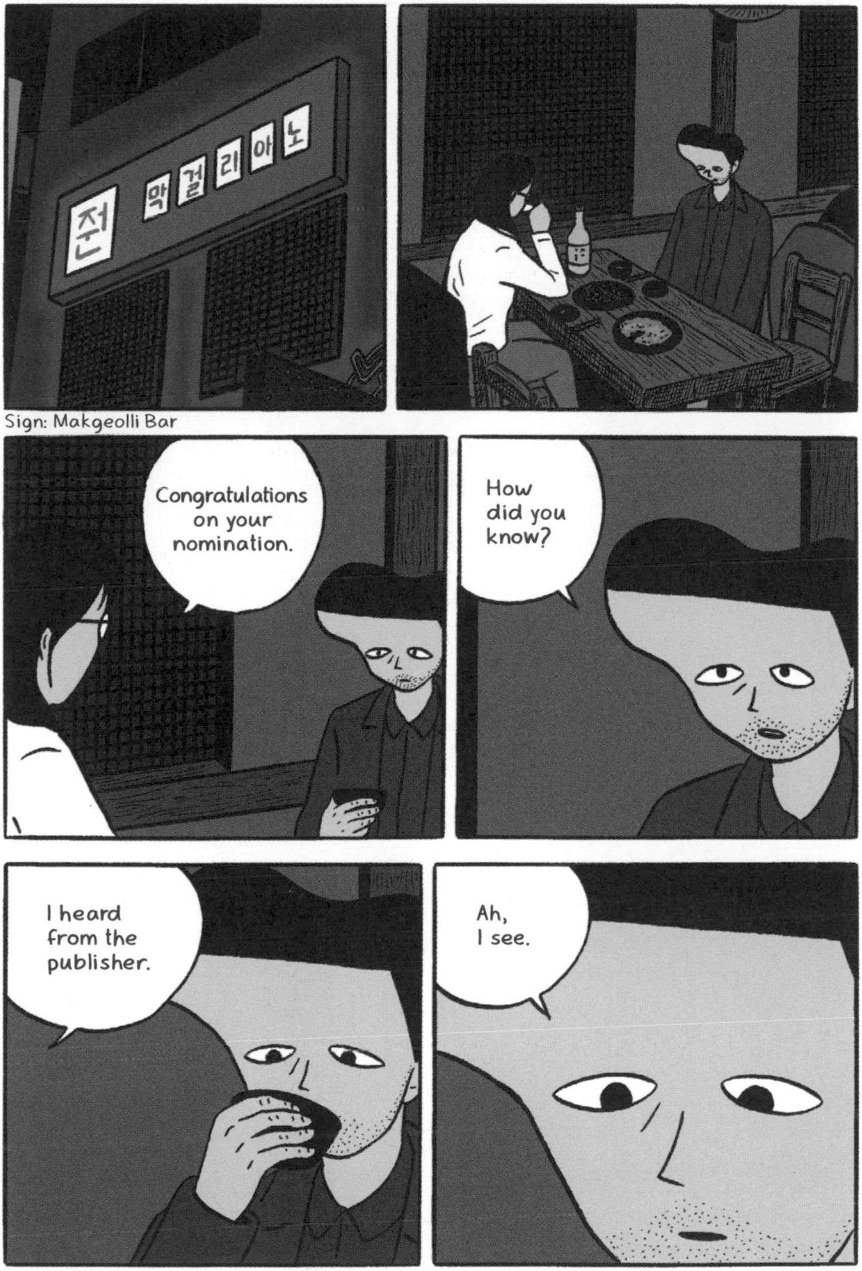
막걸리아노
Congratulations on your nomination.
How did you know?
I heard from the publisher.
Ah, I see.
Sign: Makgeolli Bar

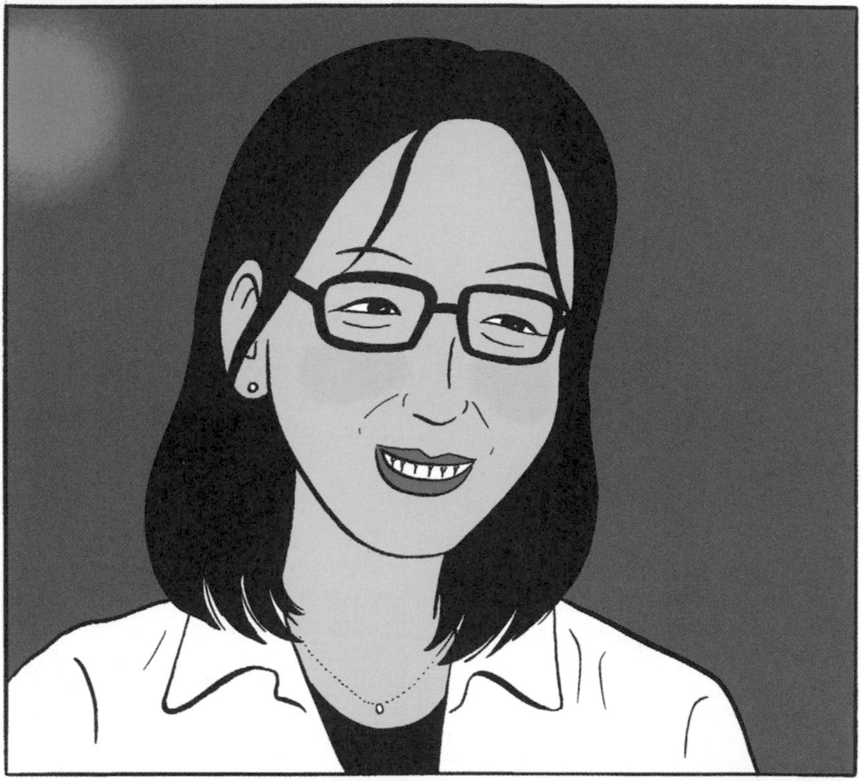

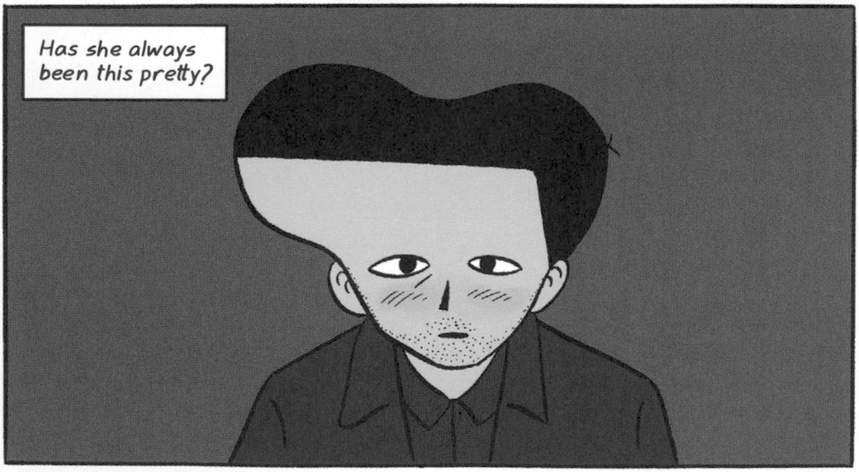
Has she always been this pretty?

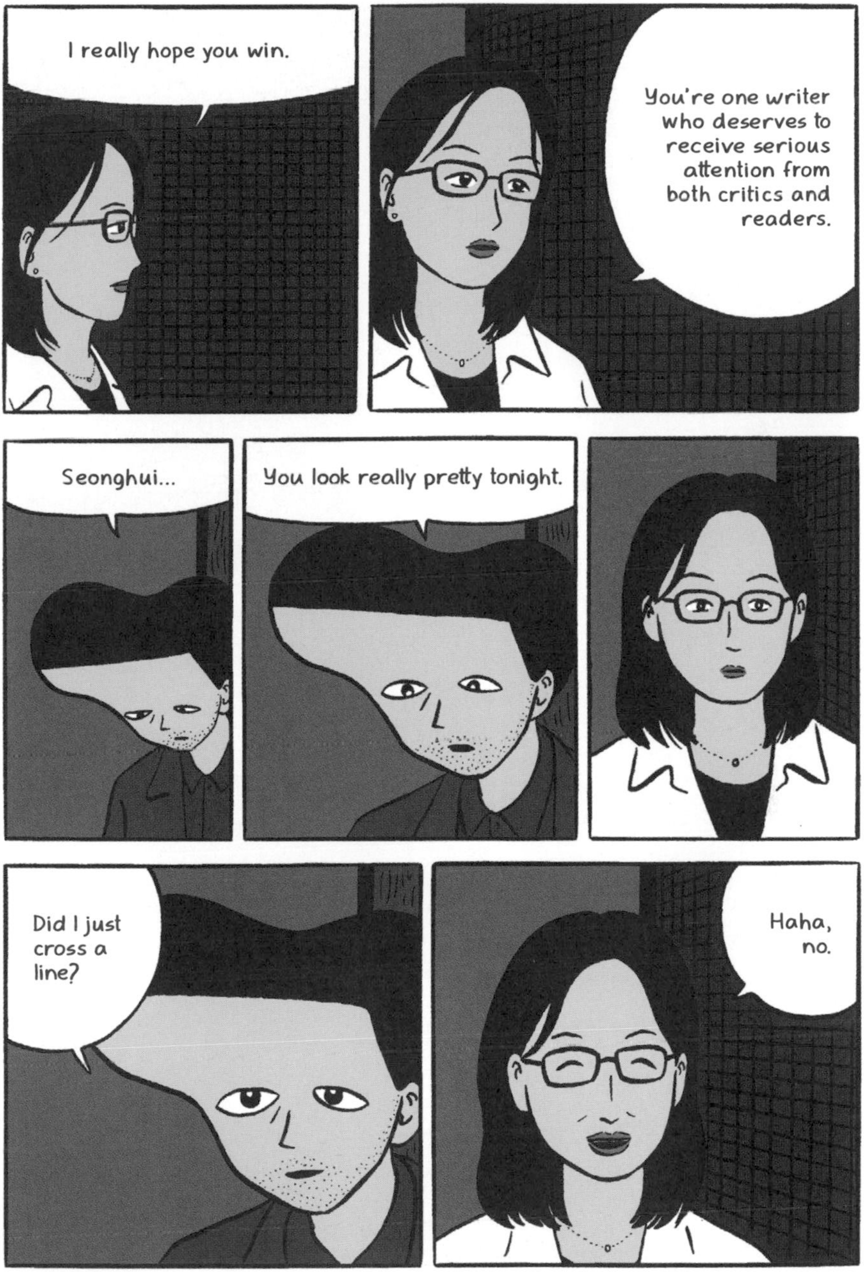
I really hope you win.
You're one writer who deserves to receive serious attention from both critics and readers.
Seonghui...
You look really pretty tonight.
Did I just cross a line?
Haha, no.

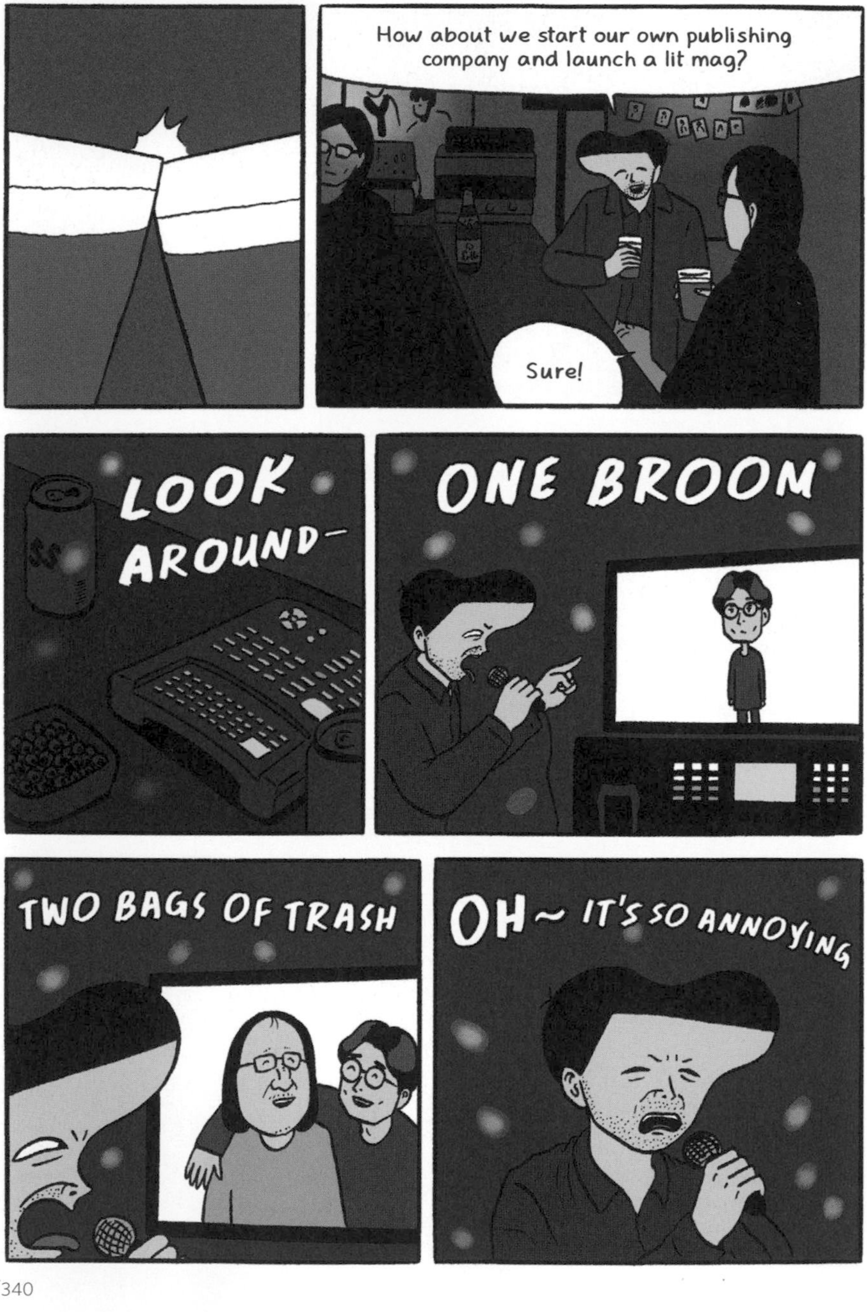
How about we start our own publishing company and launch a lit mag?
Sure!
LOOK AROUND-
ONE BROOM
TWO BAGS OF TRASH
OH~ IT'S SO ANNOYING

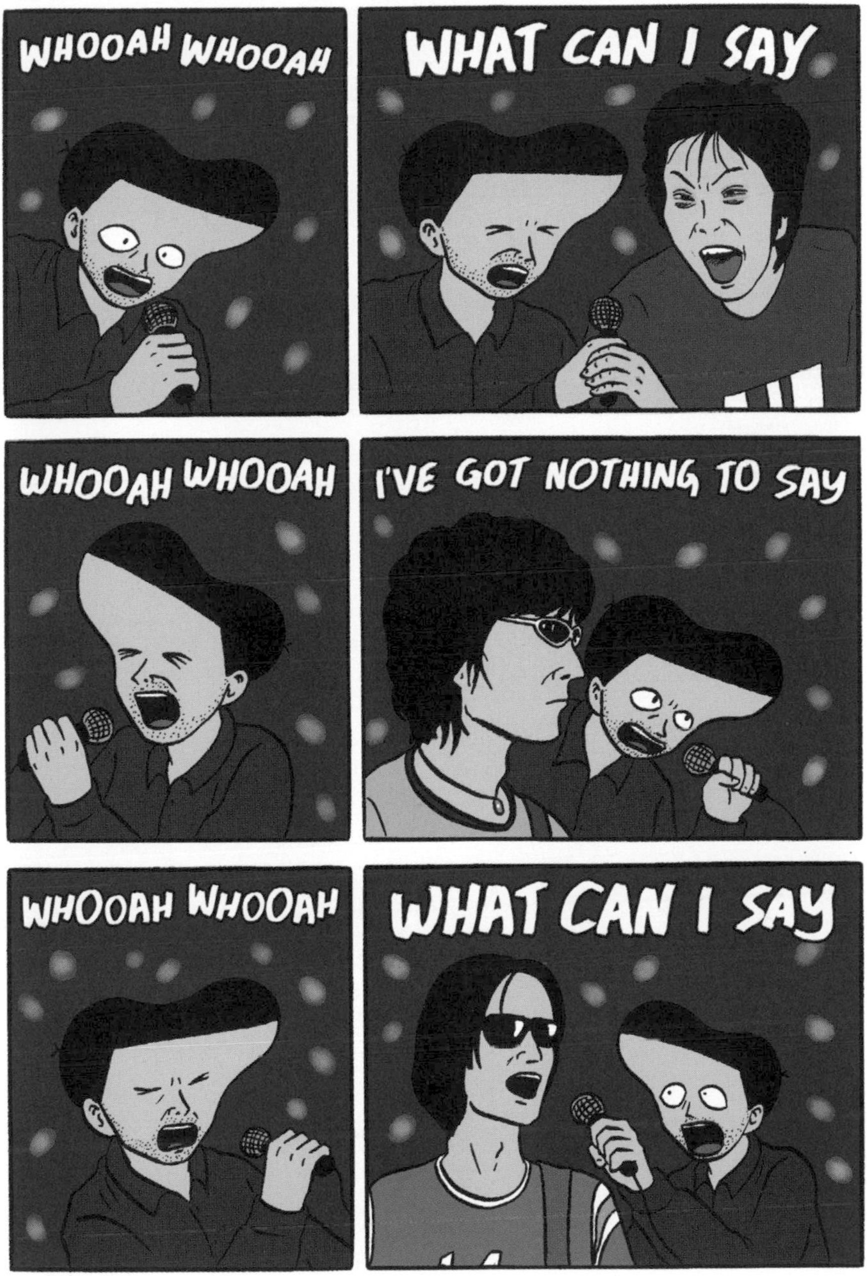
WHOOAH WHOOAH
WHAT CAN I SAY
WHOOAH WHOOAH
I'VE GOT NOTHING TO SAY
WHOOAH WHOOAH
WHAT CAN I SAY

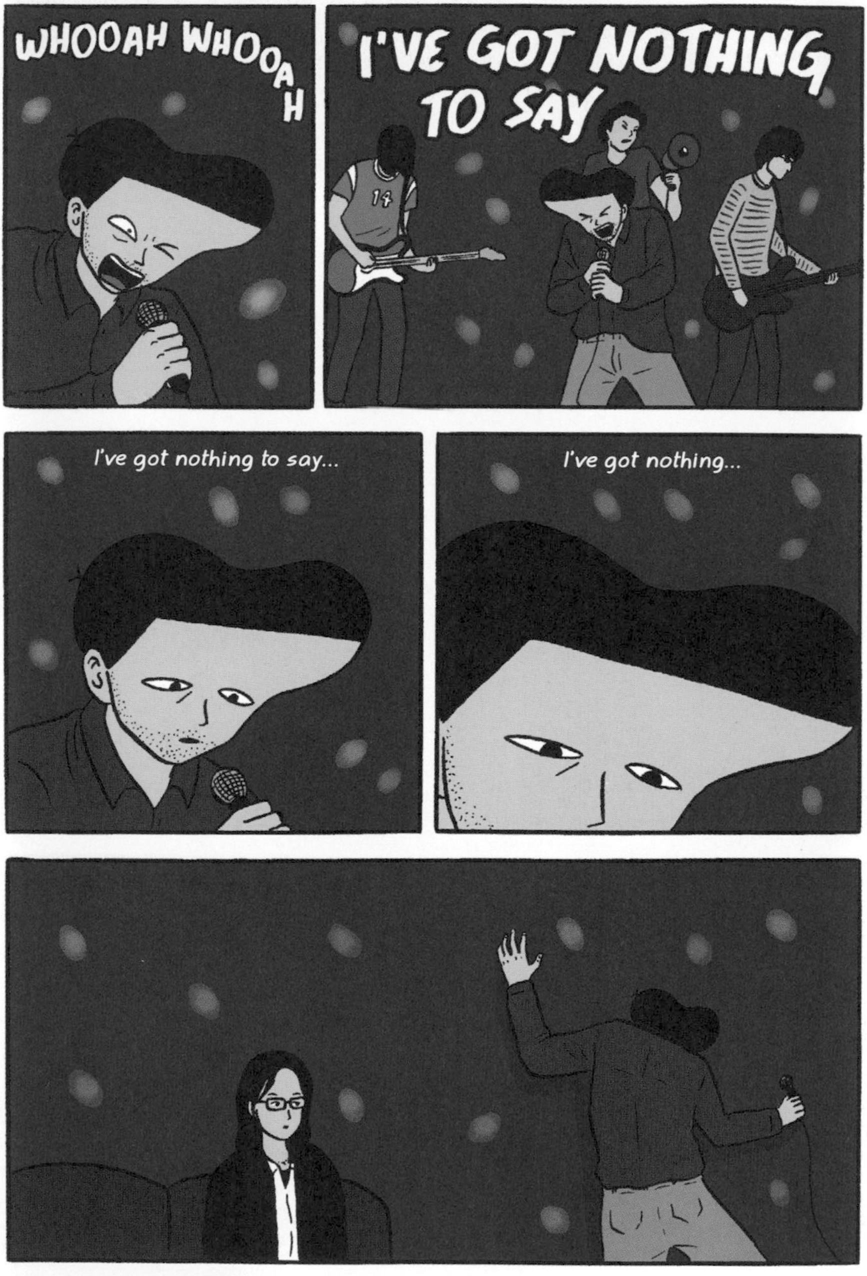
WHOOAH WHOOAH
I'VE GOT NOTHING TO SAY
14
I've got nothing to say...
I've got nothing...

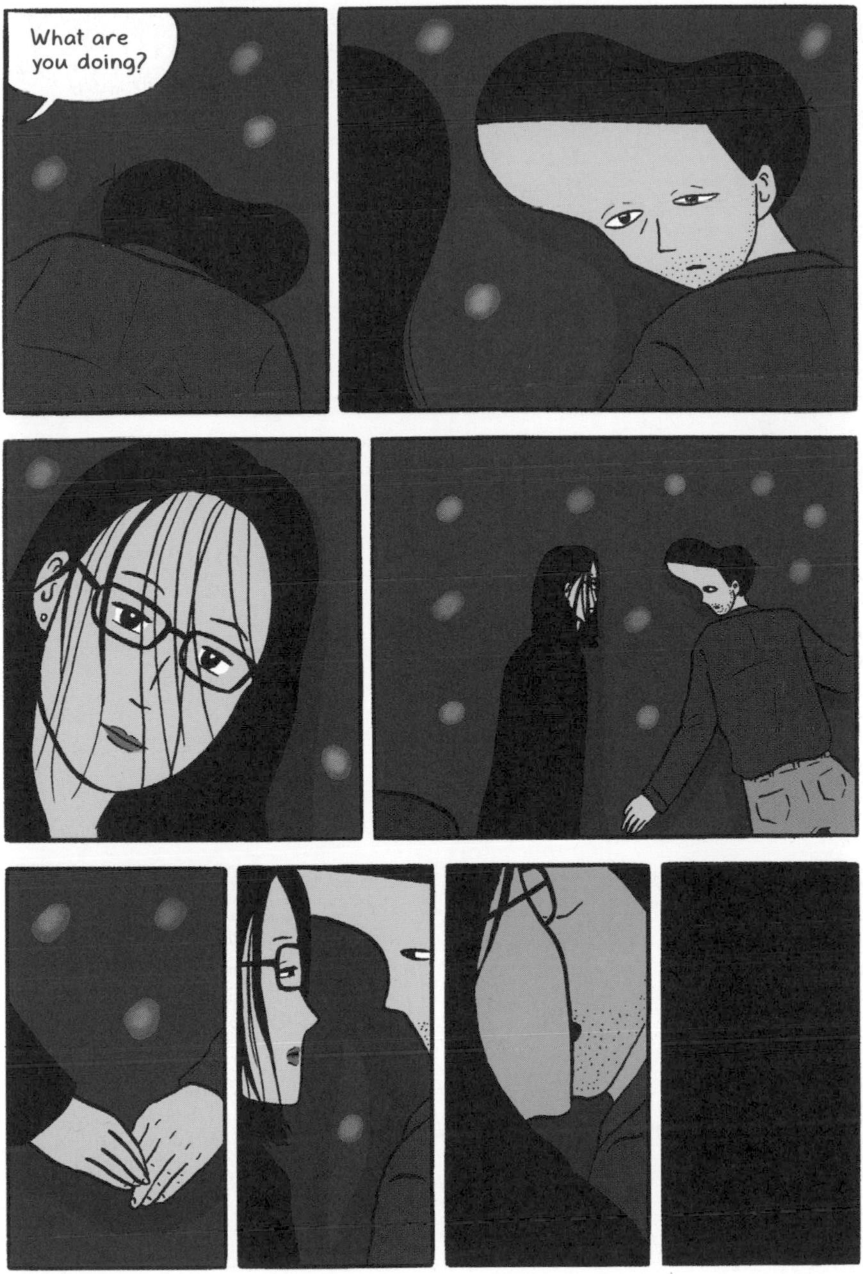
What are you doing?

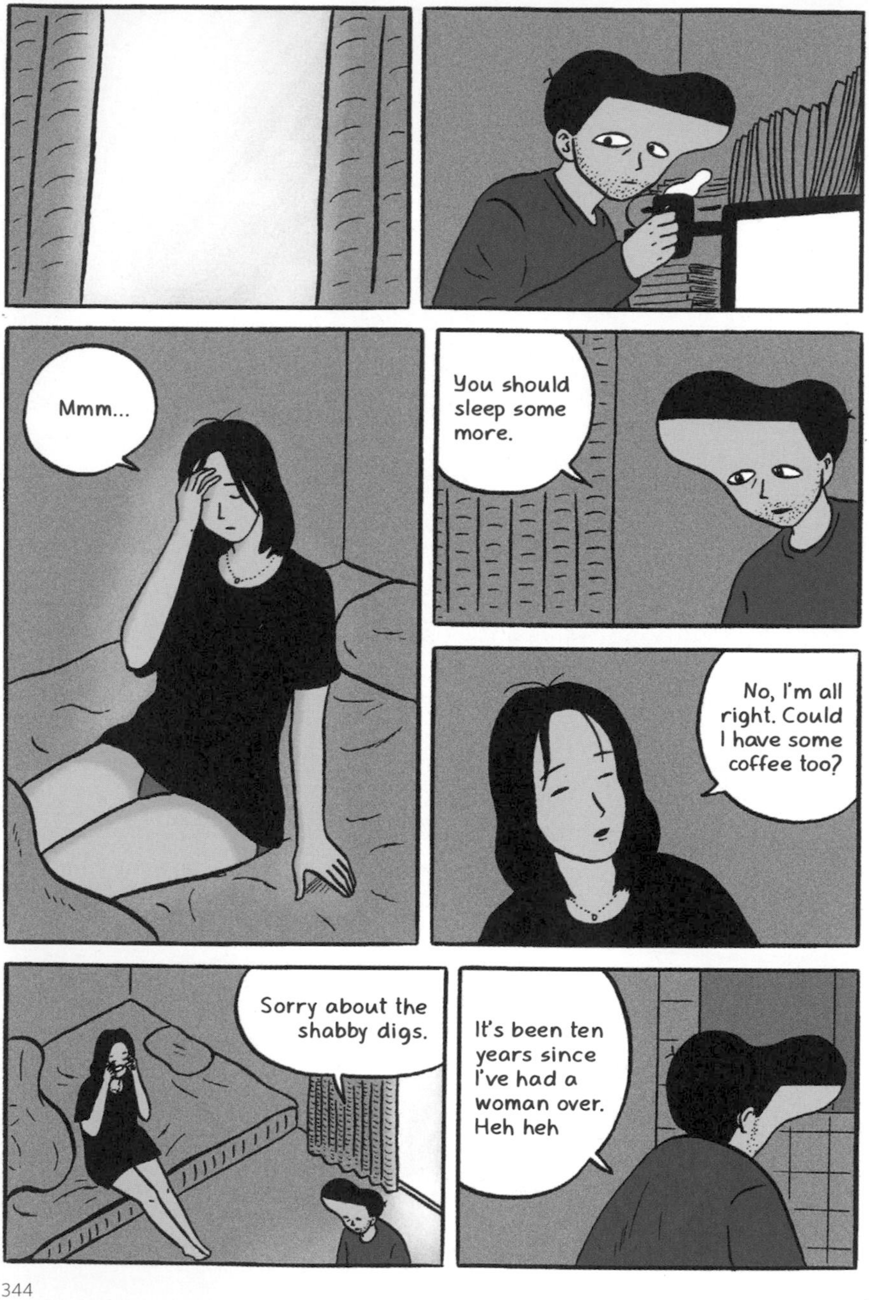
Mmm...
You should sleep some more.
No, I'm all right. Could I have some coffee too?
Sorry about the shabby digs.
It's been ten years since I've had a woman over. Heh heh

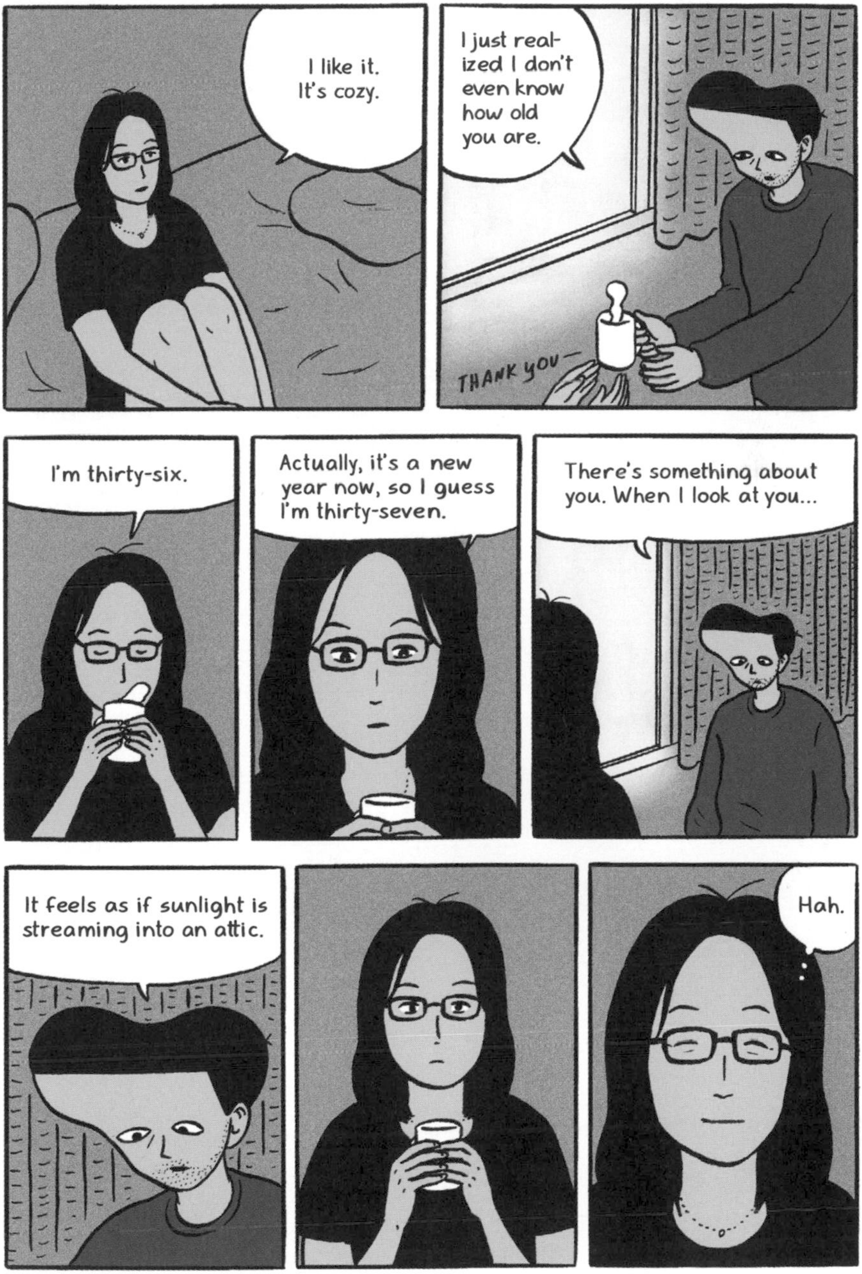
I like it. It's cozy.
I just realized I don't even know how old you are.
THANK YOU—
I'm thirty-six.
Actually, it's a new year now, so I guess I'm thirty-seven.
There's something about you. When I look at you...
It feels as if sunlight is streaming into an attic.
Hah.

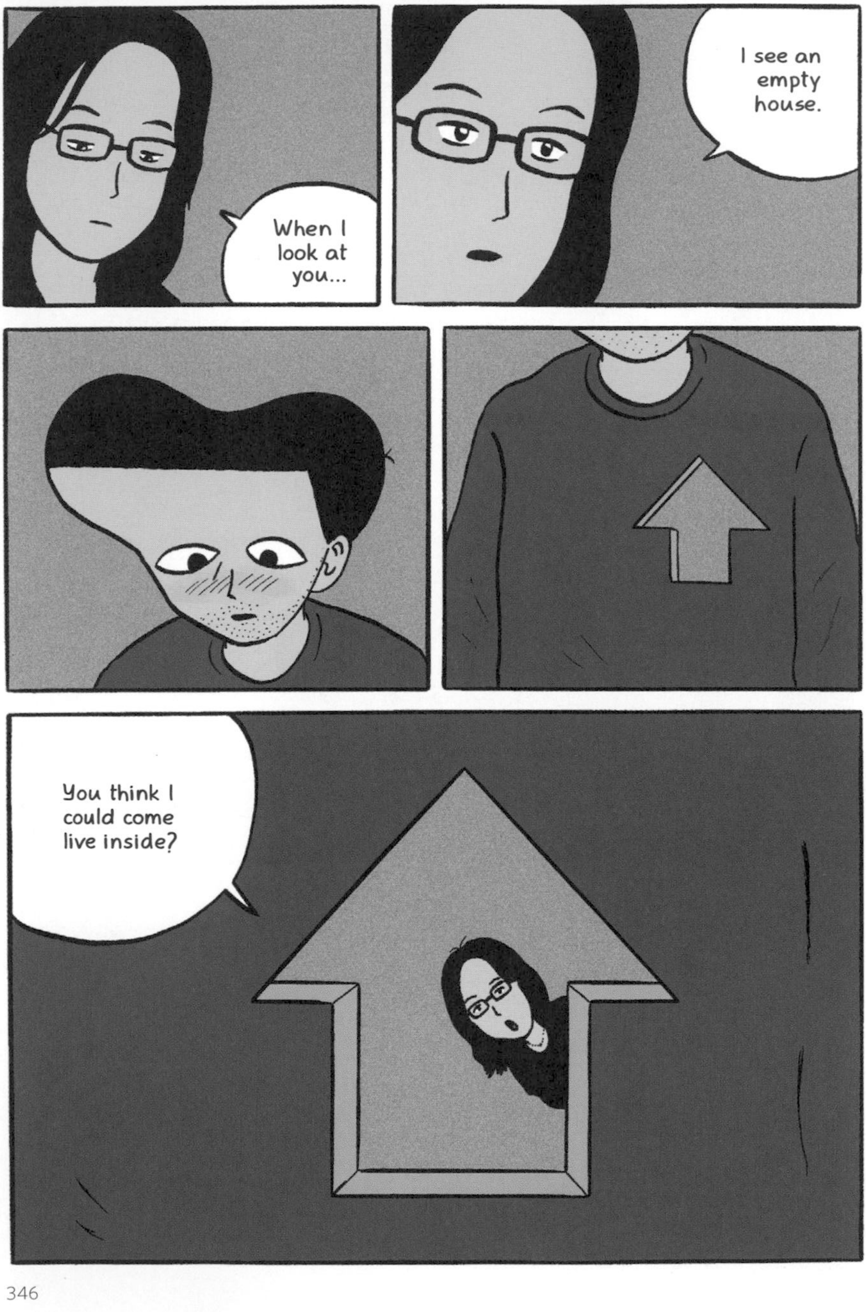
When I look at you...
I see an empty house.
You think I could come live inside?

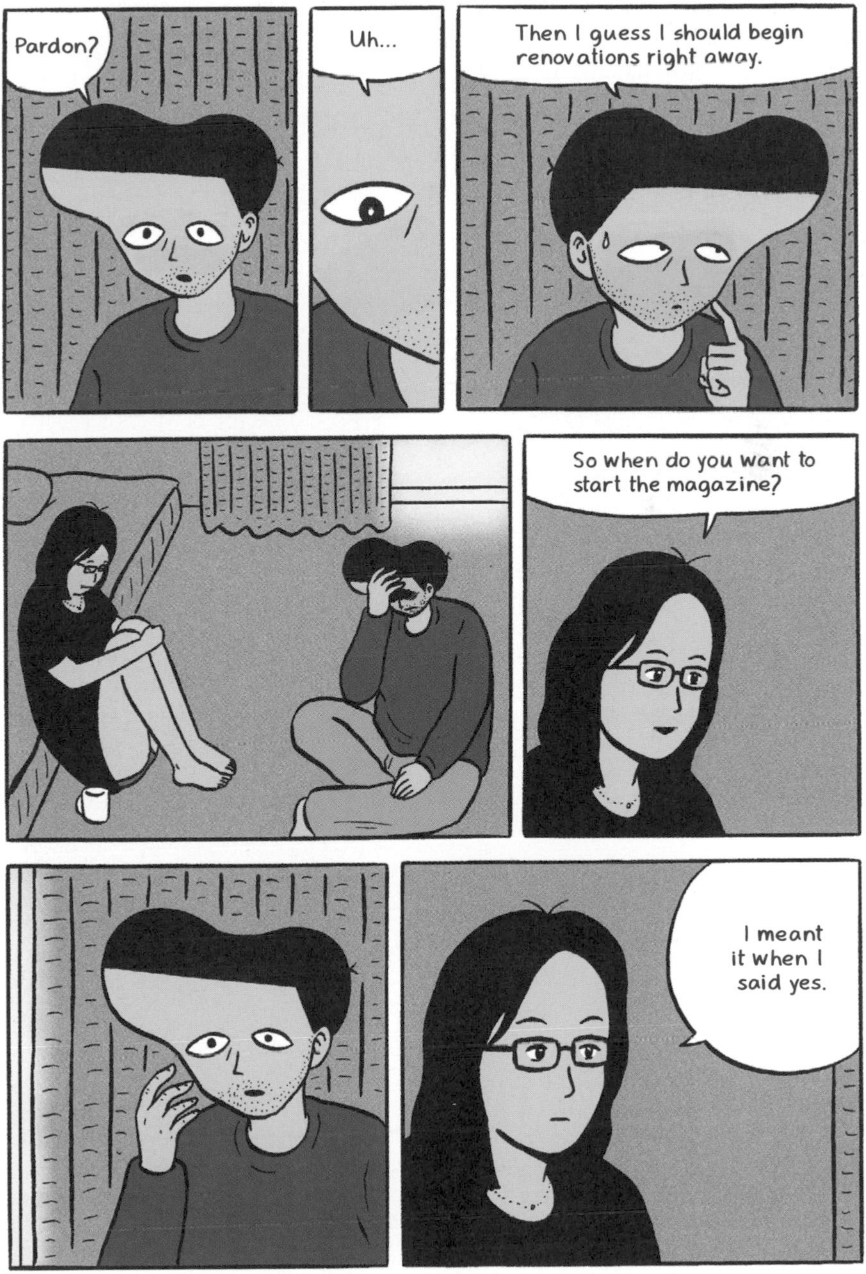
Pardon?
Uh...
Then I guess I should begin renovations right away.
So when do you want to start the magazine?
I meant it when I said yes.

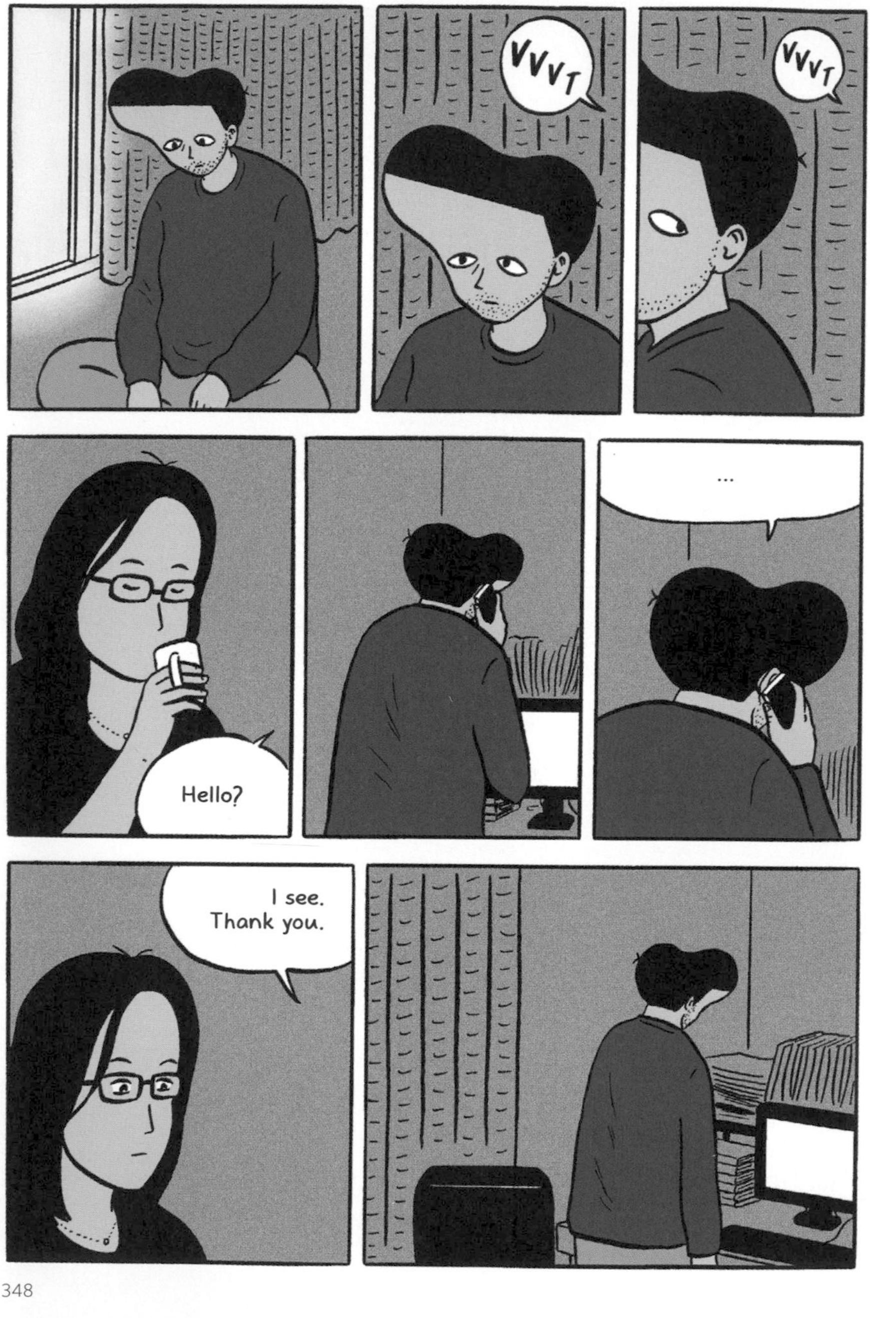
VVVT
VVVT
Hello?
...
I see. Thank you.

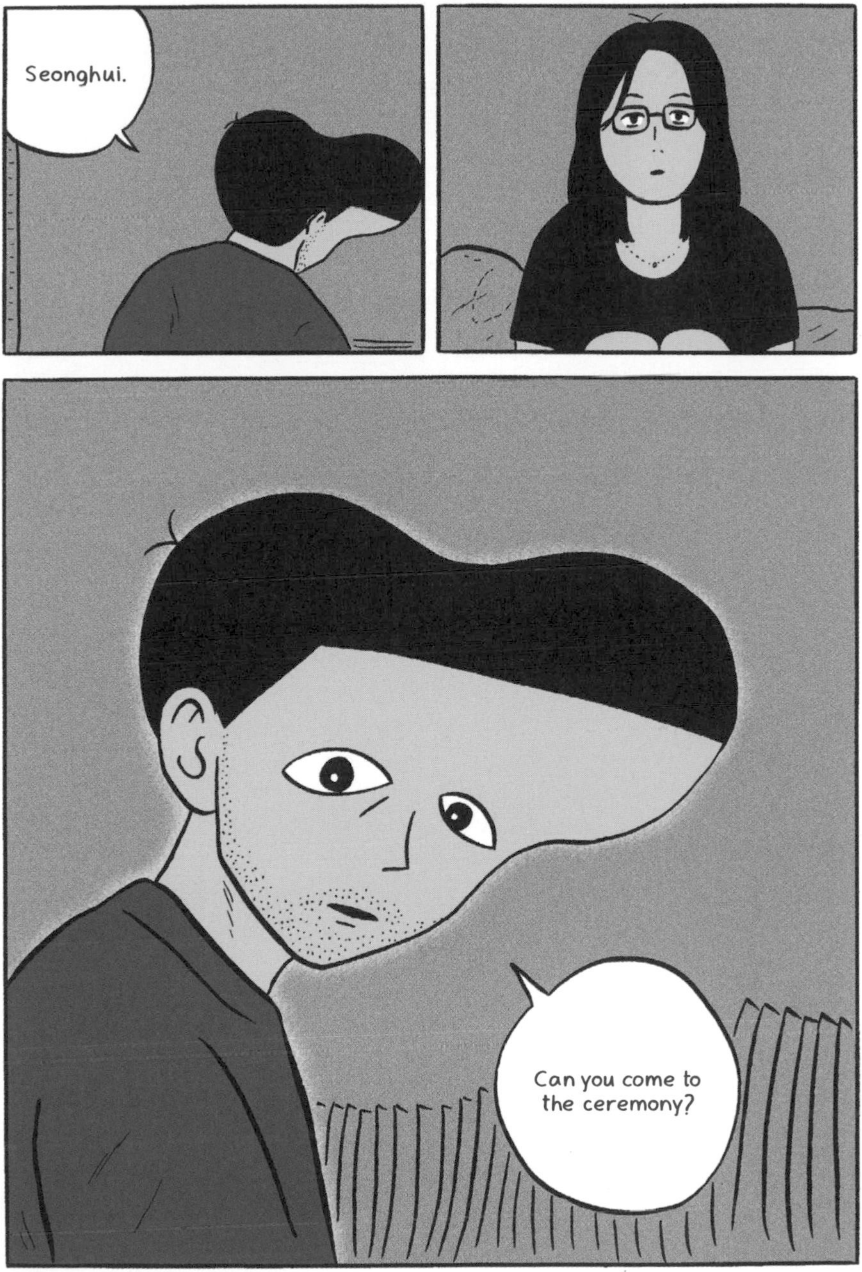
Seonghui.
Can you come to the ceremony?

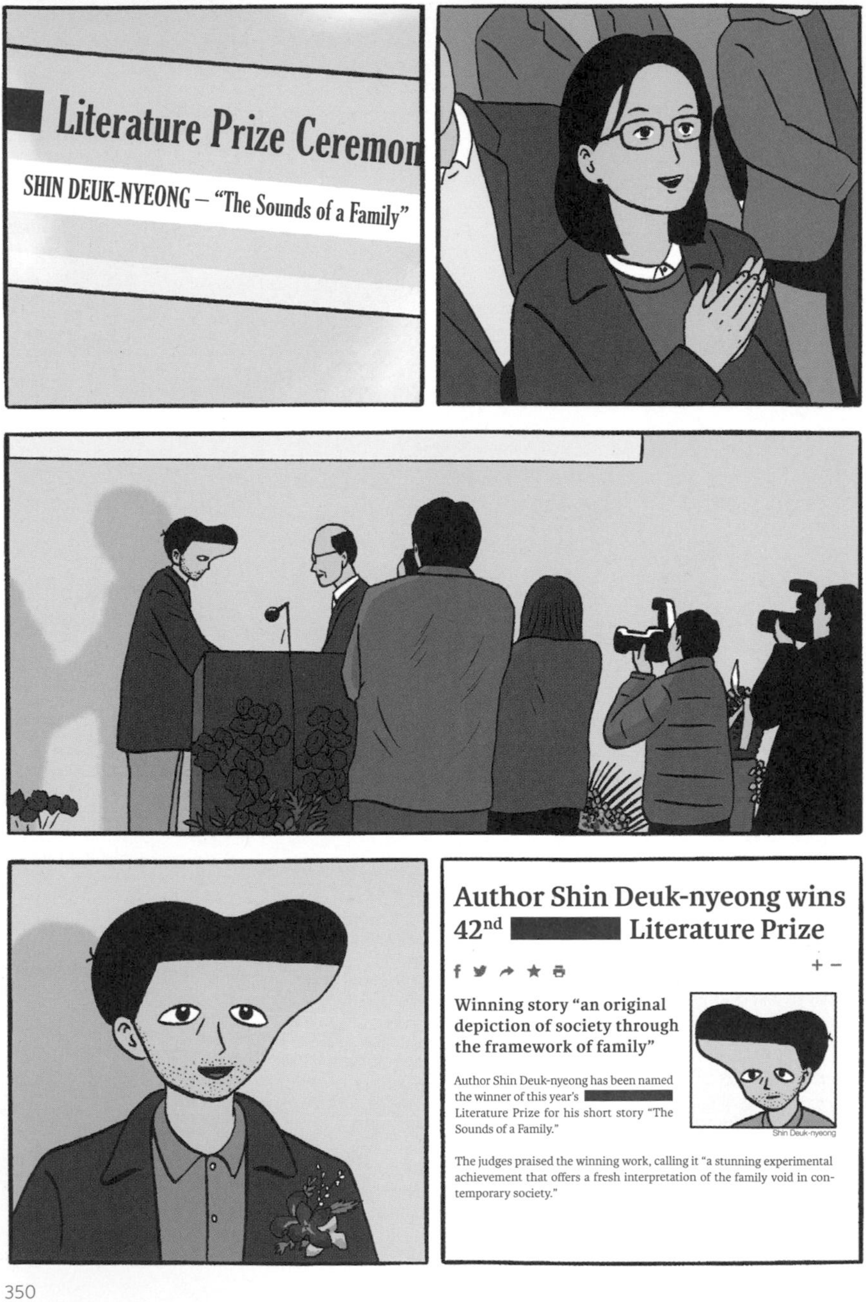
[redacted] Literature Prize Ceremon
SHIN DEUK-NYEONG – "The Sounds of a Family"
Author Shin Deuk-nyeong wins 42nd [redacted] Literature Prize
+ –
Winning story "an original depiction of society through the framework of family"
Author Shin Deuk-nyeong has been named the winner of this year's [redacted] Literature Prize for his short story "The Sounds of a Family."
Shin Deuk-nyeong
The judges praised the winning work, calling it "a stunning experimental achievement that offers a fresh interpretation of the family void in contemporary society."

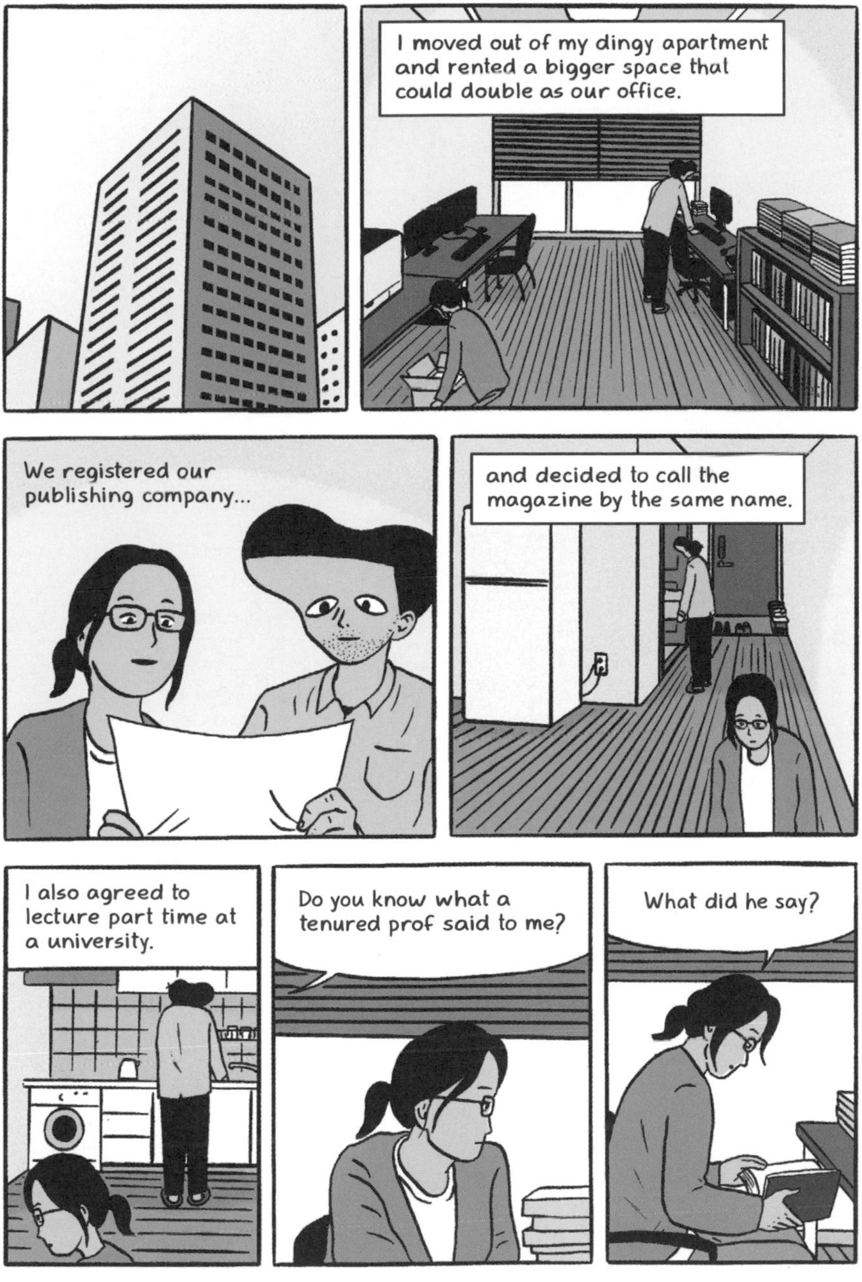
I moved out of my dingy apartment and rented a bigger space that could double as our office.
We registered our publishing company...
and decided to call the magazine by the same name.
I also agreed to lecture part time at a university.
Do you know what a tenured prof said to me?
What did he say?

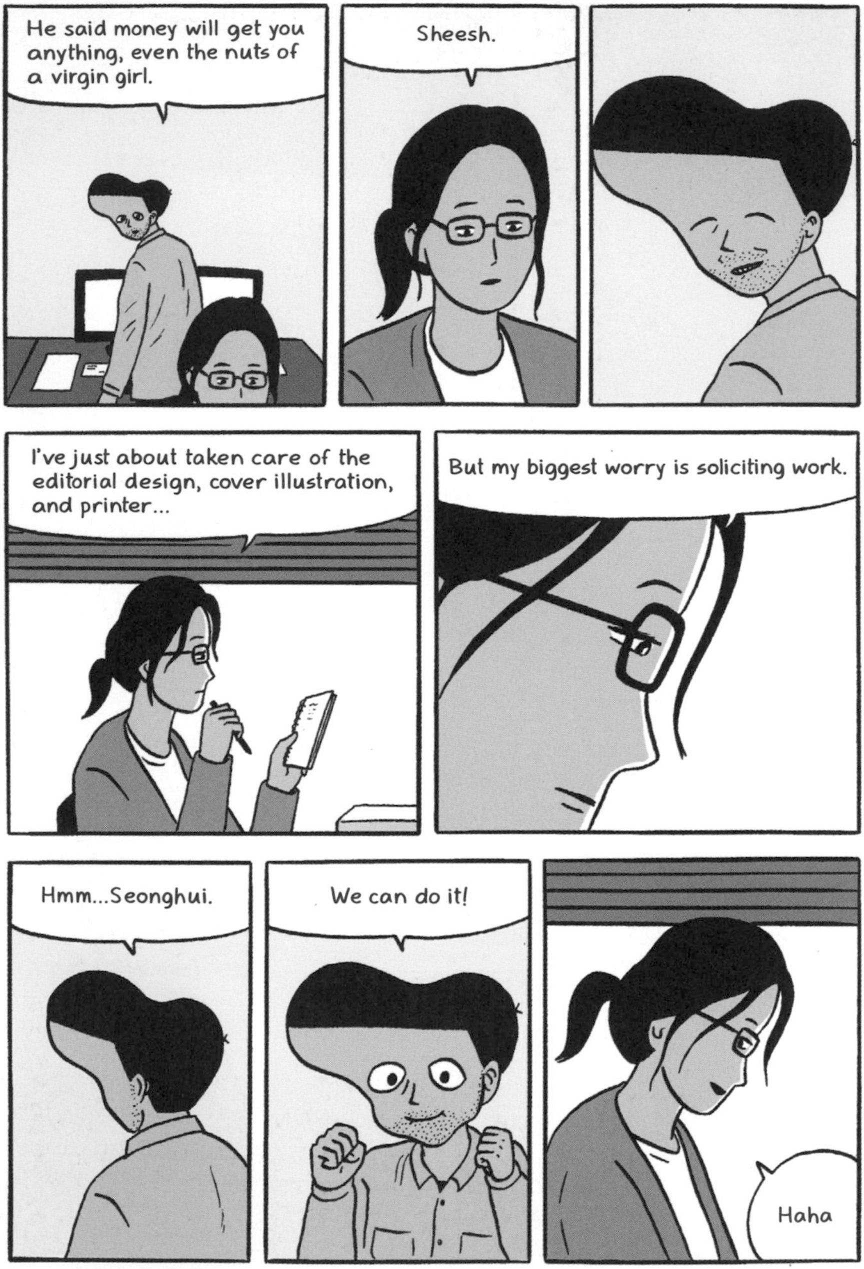
He said money will get you anything, even the nuts of a virgin girl.
Sheesh.
I've just about taken care of the editorial design, cover illustration, and printer...
But my biggest worry is soliciting work.
Hmm...Seonghui.
We can do it!
Haha

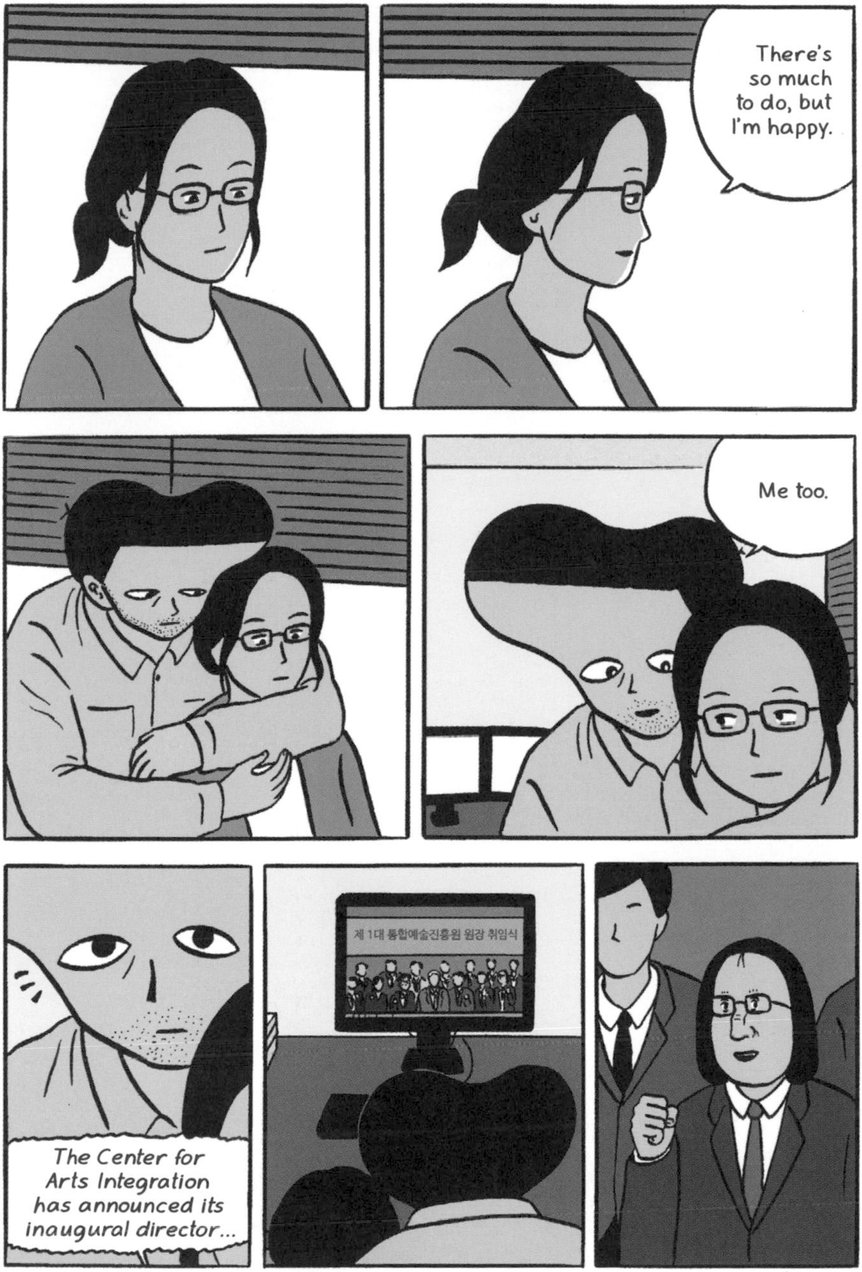
There's so much to do, but I'm happy.
Me too.
The Center for Arts Integration has announced its inaugural director...
제 1대 통합예술진흥원 원장 취임식

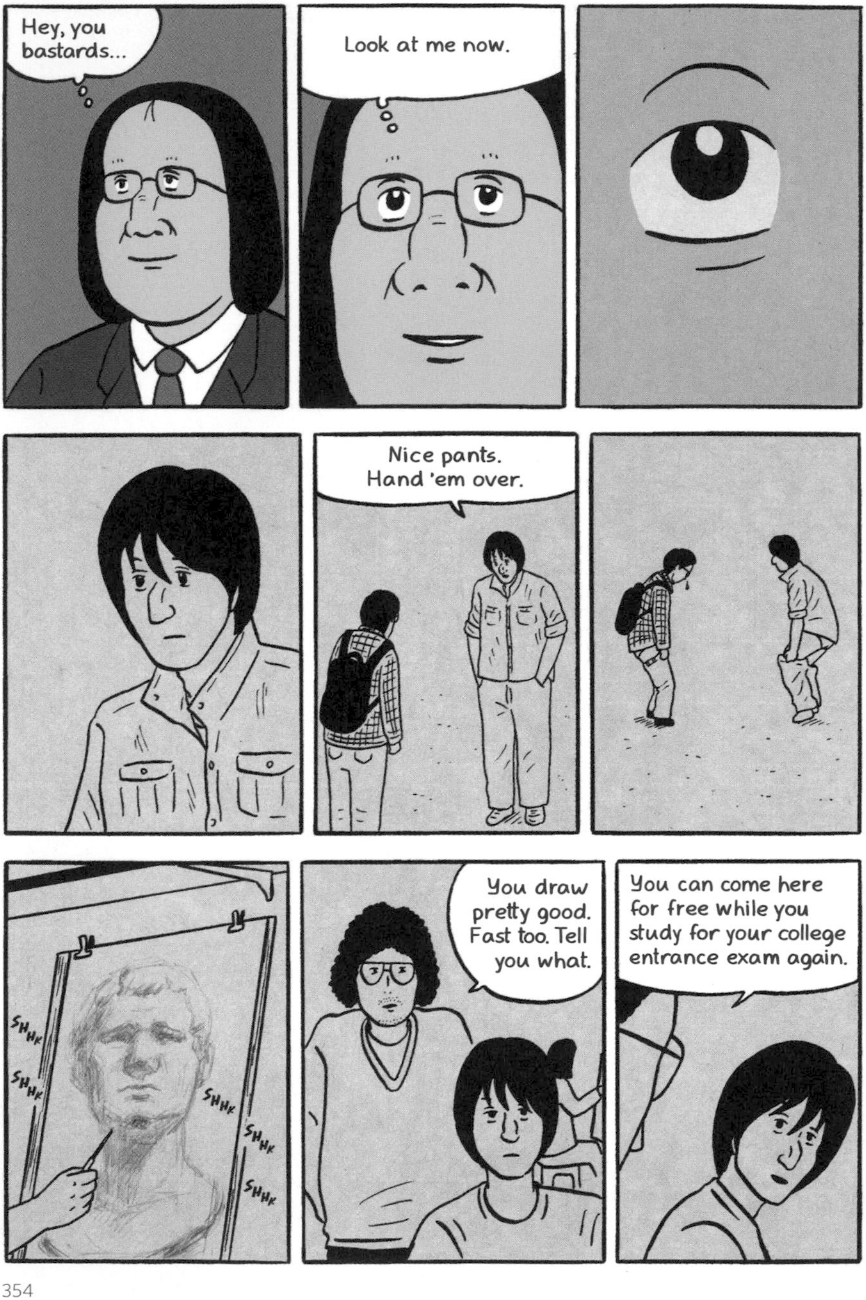
Hey, you bastards...
Look at me now.
Nice pants. Hand 'em over.
SHHK
SHHK
SHHK
SHHK
SHHK
You draw pretty good. Fast too. Tell you what.
You can come here for free while you study for your college entrance exam again.

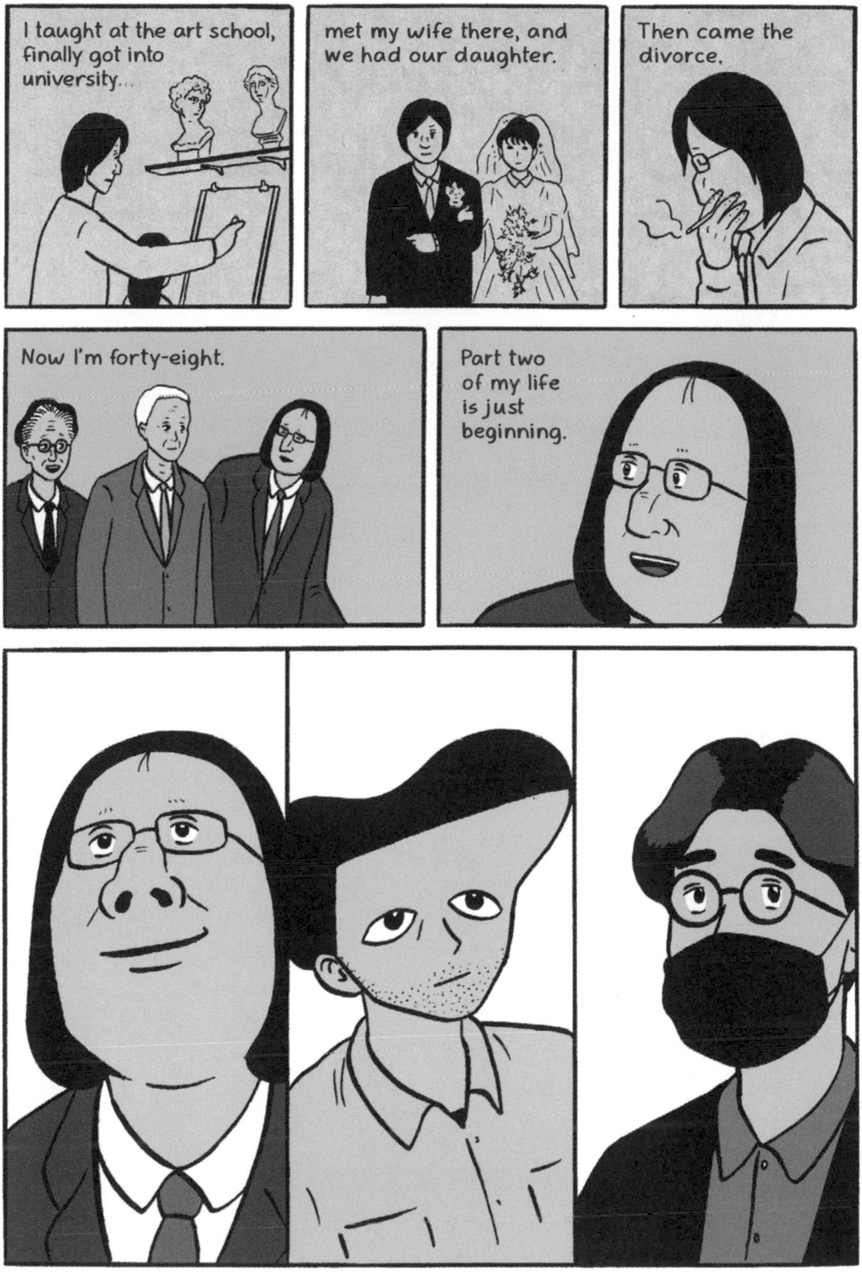
I taught at the art school, finally got into university...
met my wife there, and we had our daughter.
Then came the divorce.
Now I'm forty-eight.
Part two of my life is just beginning.

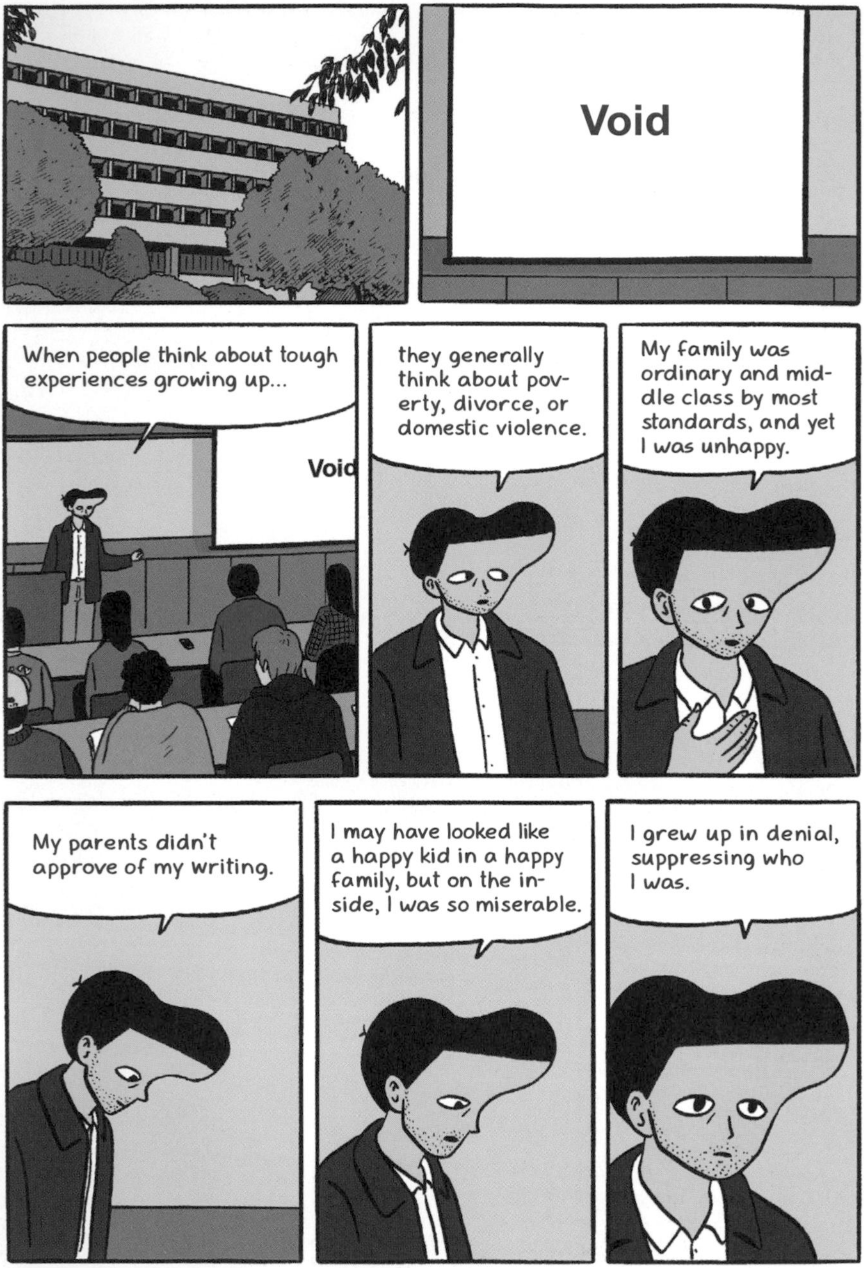
Void
When people think about tough experiences growing up...
Void
they generally think about pov-erty, divorce, or domestic violence.
My family was ordinary and mid-dle class by most standards, and yet I was unhappy.
My parents didn't approve of my writing.
I may have looked like a happy kid in a happy family, but on the in-side, I was so miserable.
I grew up in denial, suppressing who I was.

You were all raised in different environments, so naturally your thoughts and opinions will be just as different.

But today's society, despite being comprised of different people, sees the Other as violent.

And unlike the past, times are rapidly changing, with new opinions popping up every day.

Unable to keep up...

we have no choice but to accept what the media portrays.

You might be asking, "So what? What's the big deal?"

Well, this creates problems with our perception of the Other.

Let me give you a few examples.

Mother
Democratization
Generation
Liberals
Conservatives

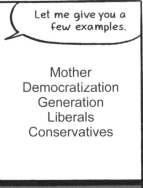

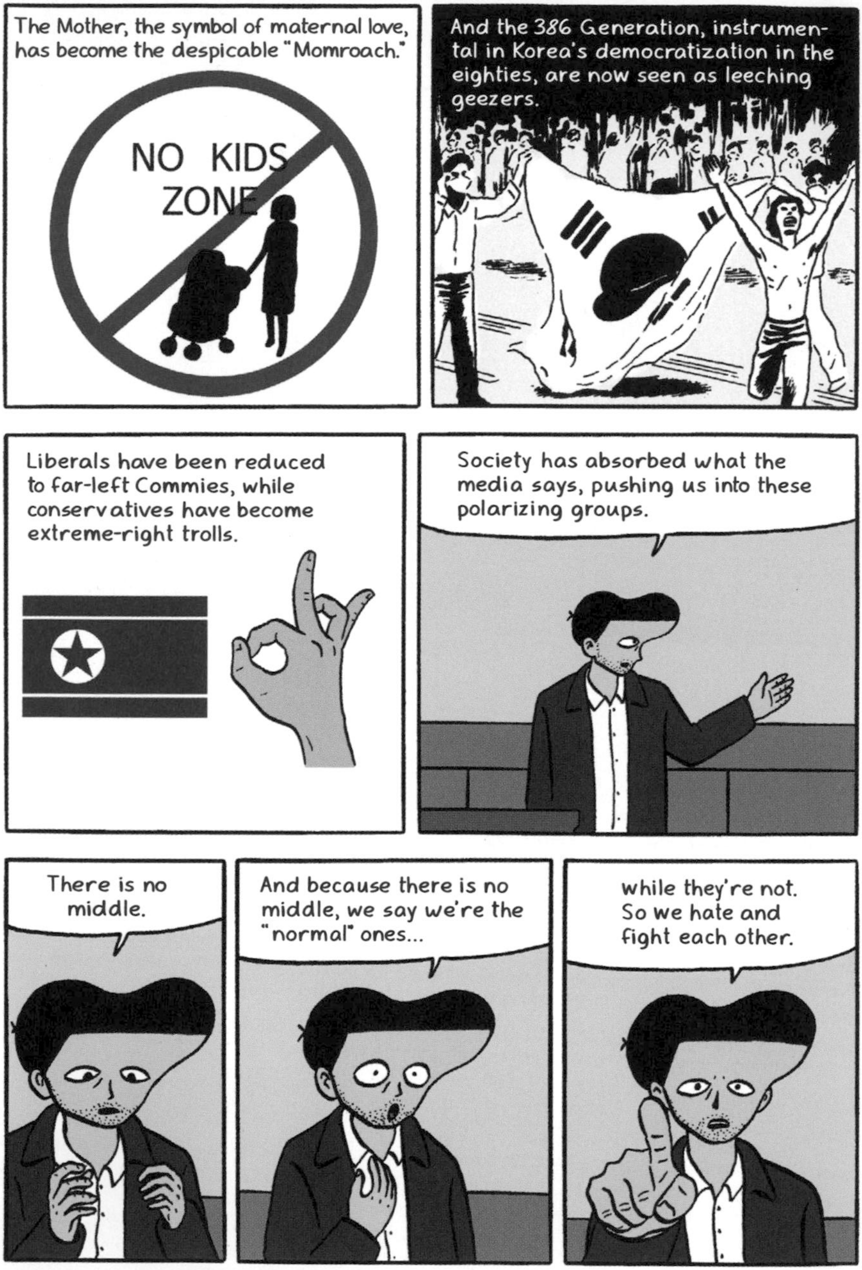
The Mother, the symbol of maternal love, has become the despicable "Momroach."
NO KIDS ZONE
And the 386 Generation, instrumental in Korea's democratization in the eighties, are now seen as leeching geezers.
Liberals have been reduced to far-left Commies, while conservatives have become extreme-right trolls.
Society has absorbed what the media says, pushing us into these polarizing groups.
There is no middle.
And because there is no middle, we say we're the "normal" ones...
while they're not. So we hate and fight each other.

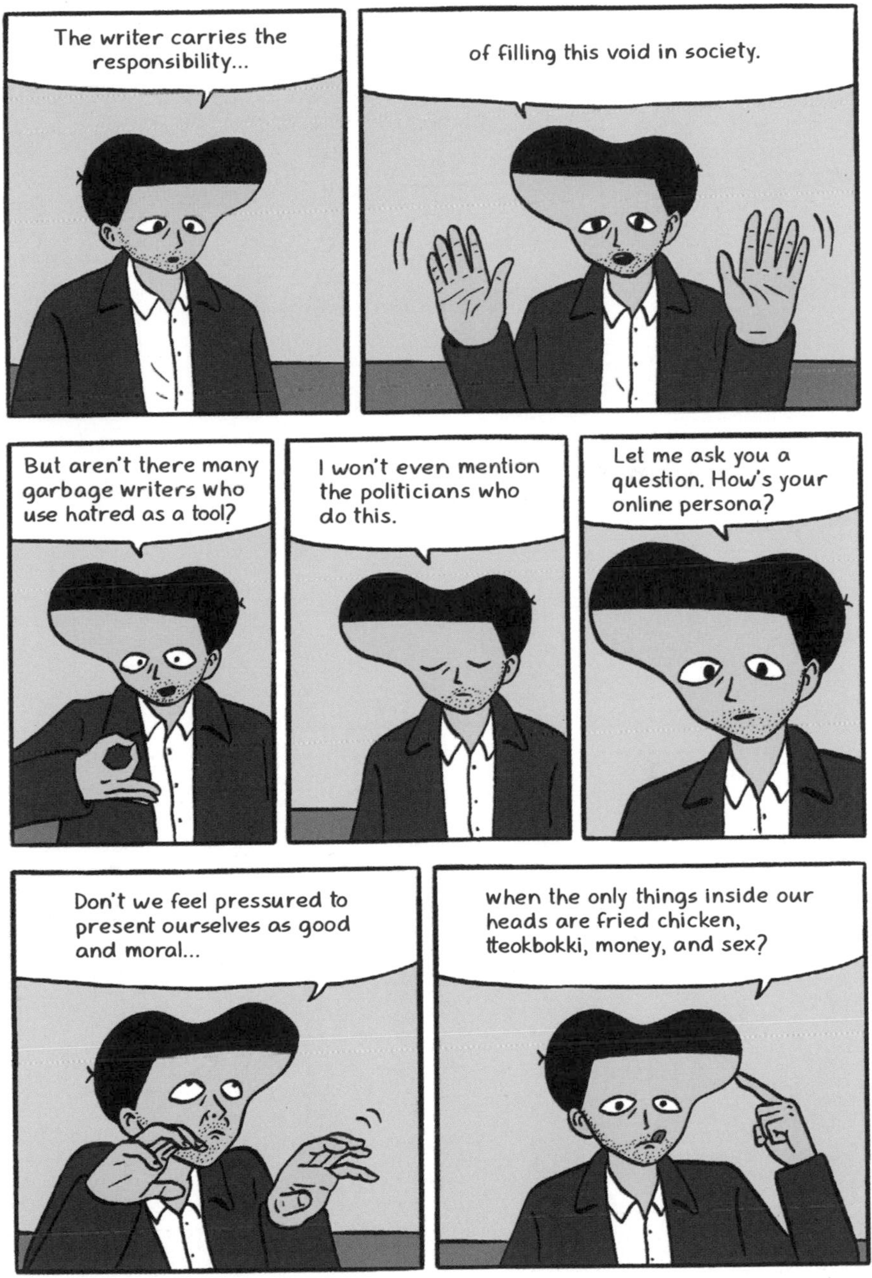
The writer carries the responsibility...
of filling this void in society.
But aren't there many garbage writers who use hatred as a tool?
I won't even mention the politicians who do this.
Let me ask you a question. How's your online persona?
Don't we feel pressured to present ourselves as good and moral...
when the only things inside our heads are fried chicken, tteokbokki, money, and sex?

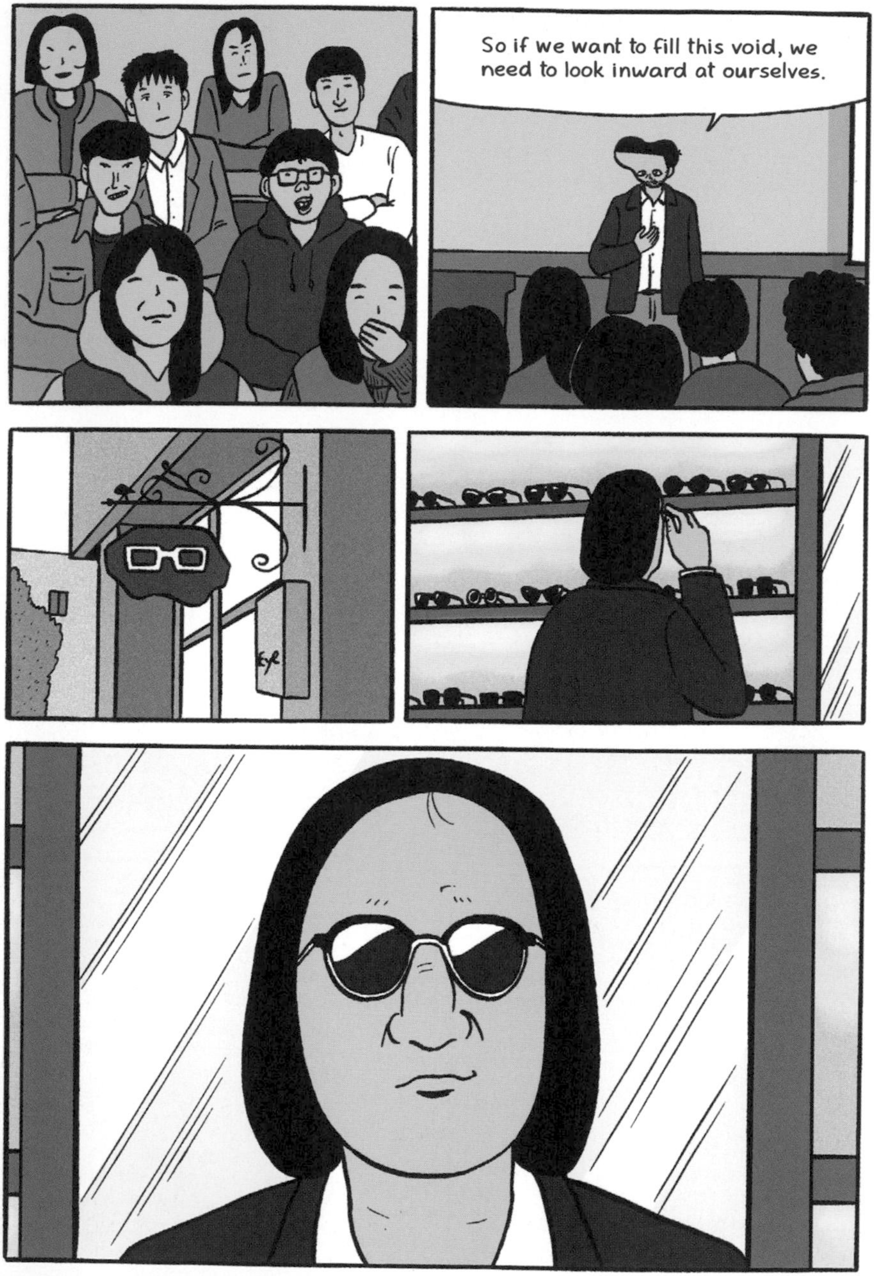
So if we want to fill this void, we need to look inward at ourselves.

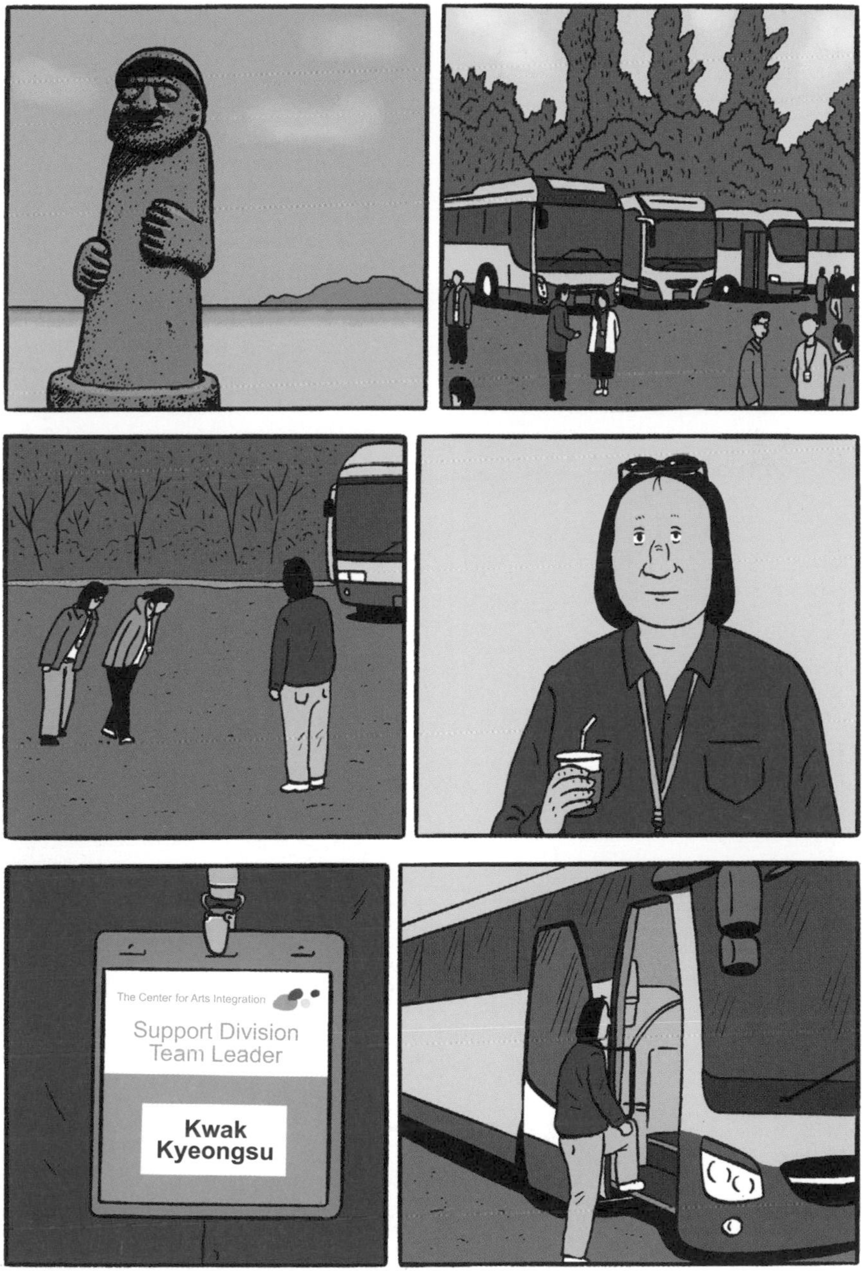
The Center for Arts Integration
Support Division
Team Leader
Kwak
Kyeongsu

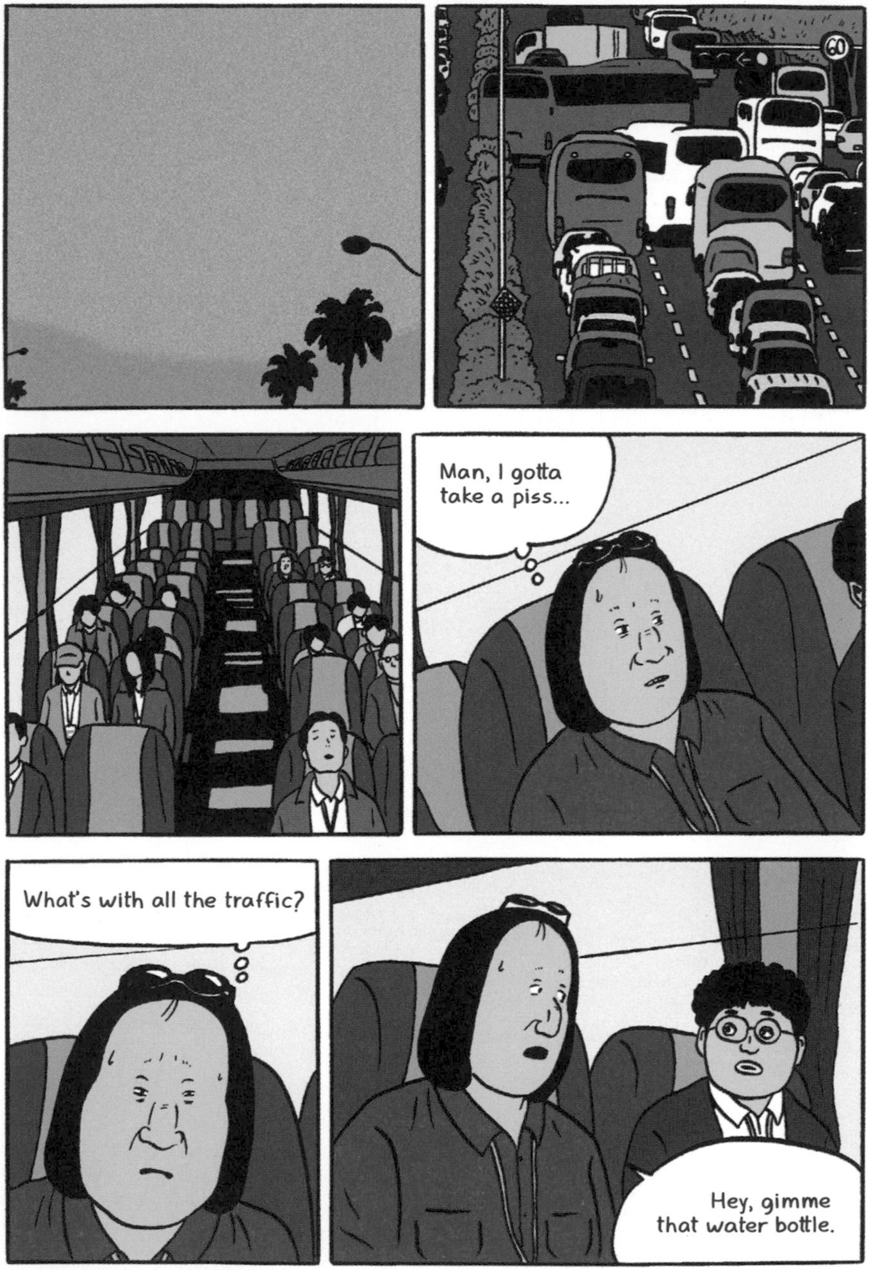
Man, I gotta take a piss...
What's with all the traffic?
Hey, gimme that water bottle.

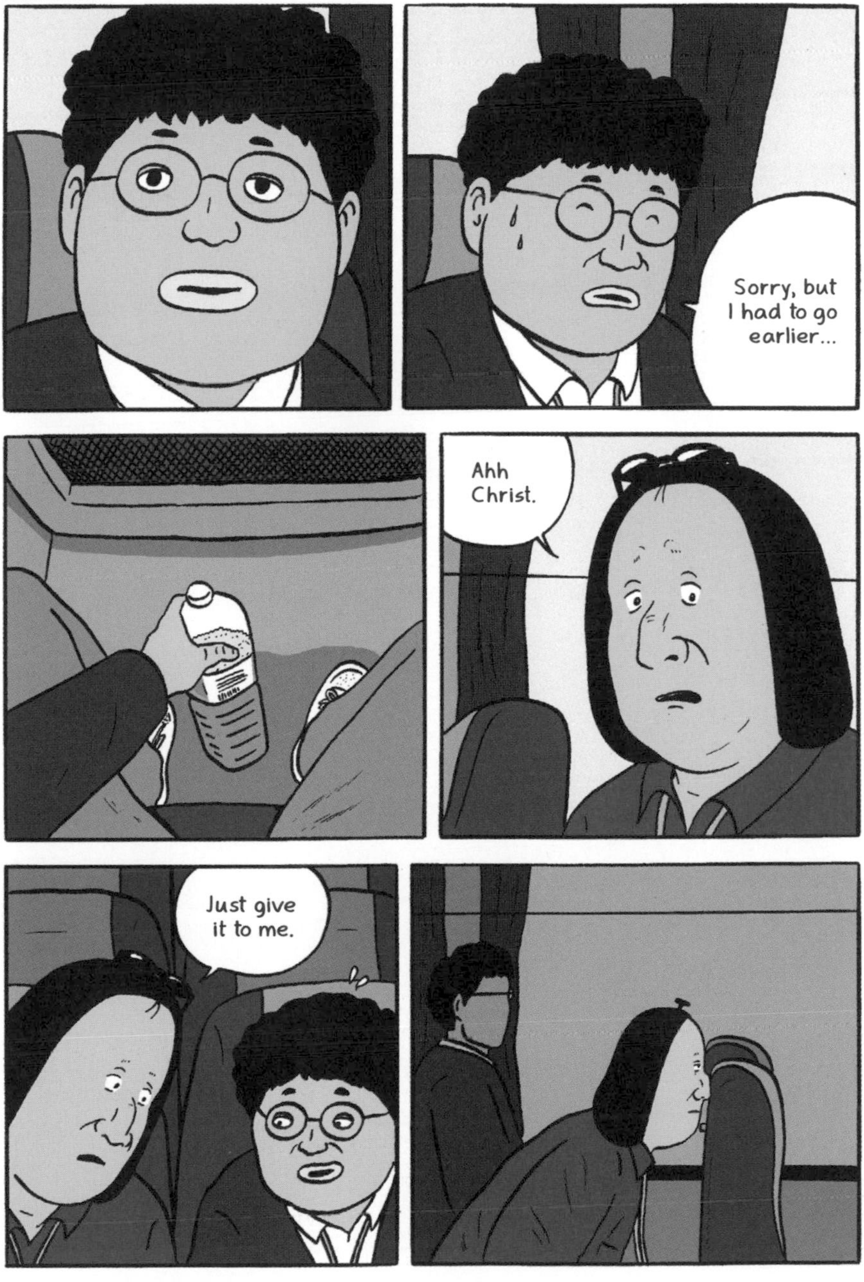
Sorry, but I had to go earlier...
Ahh Christ.
Just give it to me.

Sign: The Center for Arts Integration Workshop

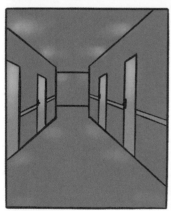

Now for the penalty!

Uh...I'll perform a special skill.

A... YOGA... POSE...

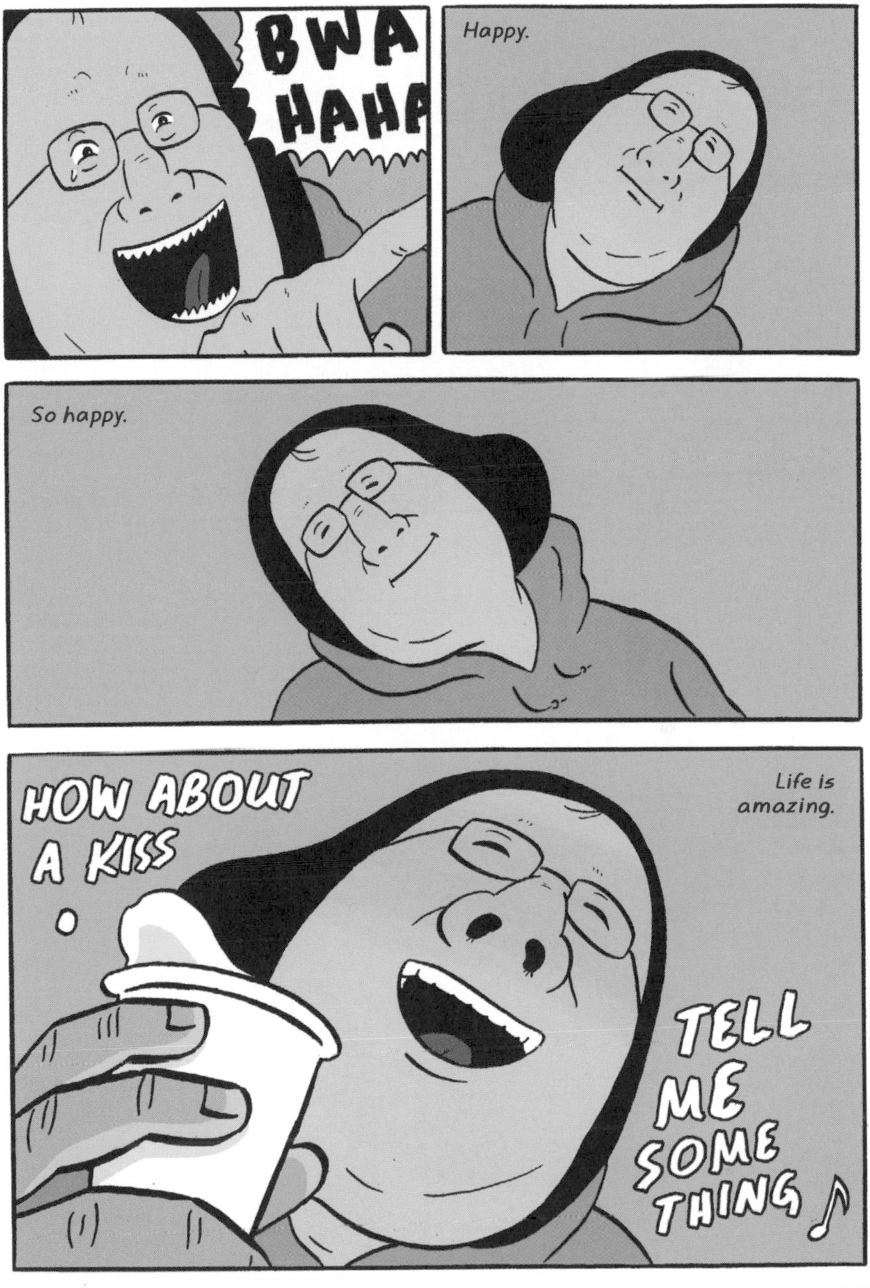
BWA HAHA
Happy.
So happy.
HOW ABOUT A KISS
Life is amazing.
TELL ME SOME THING ♪

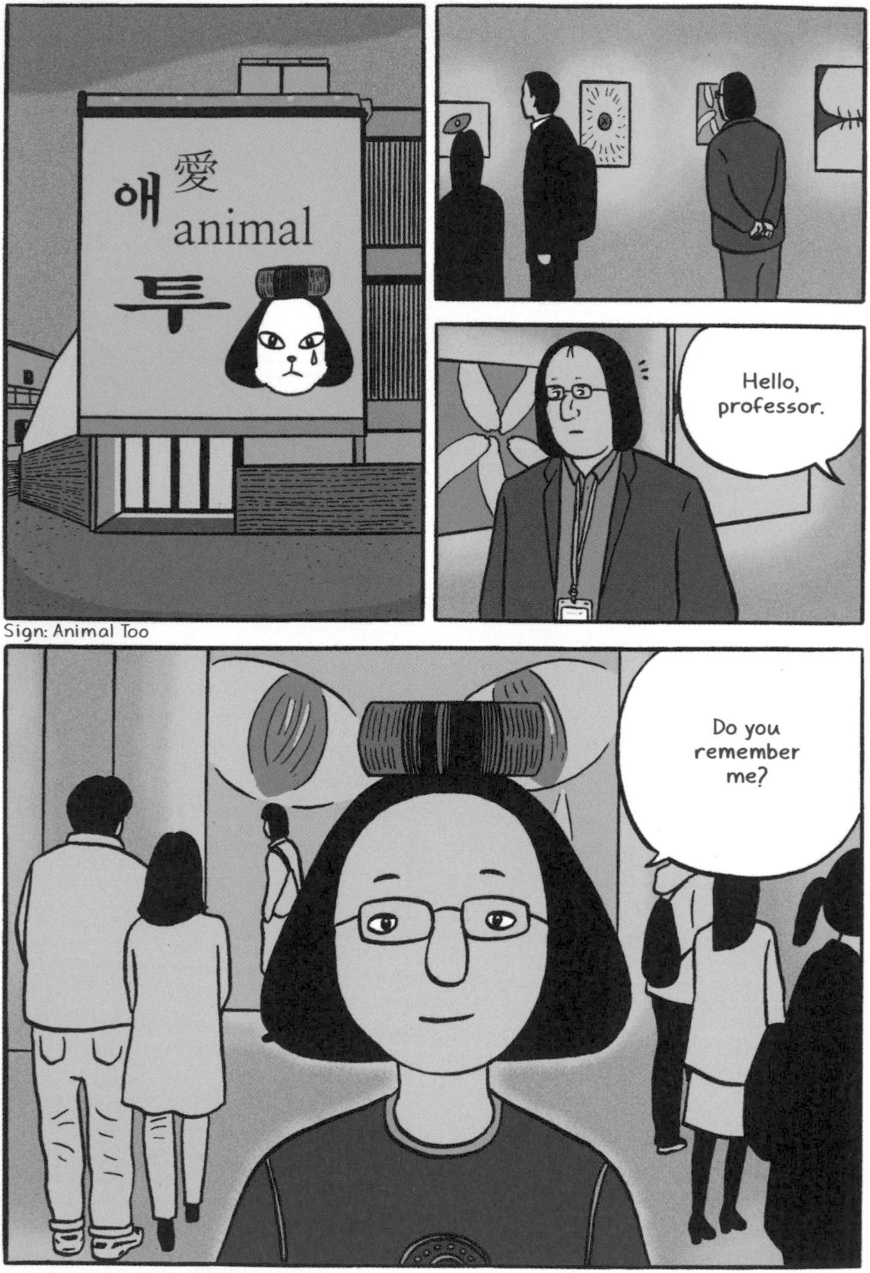
애
愛
animal
투
Hello, professor.
Do you remember me?
Sign: Animal Too

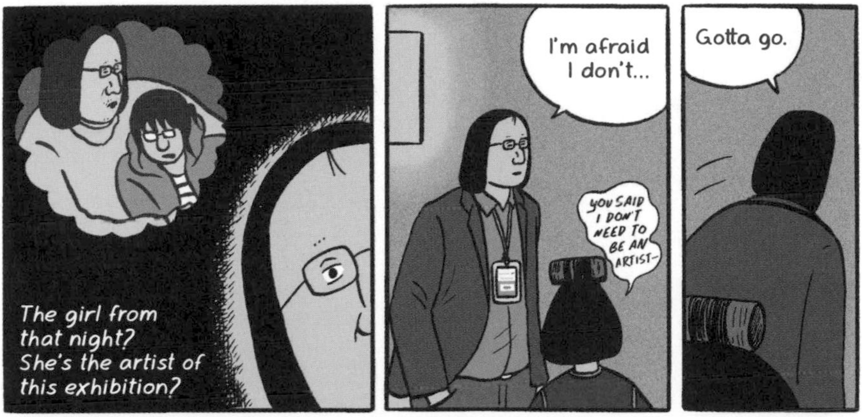
The girl from that night? She's the artist of this exhibition?
I'm afraid I don't...
YOU SAID I DON'T NEED TO BE AN ARTIST—
Gotta go.

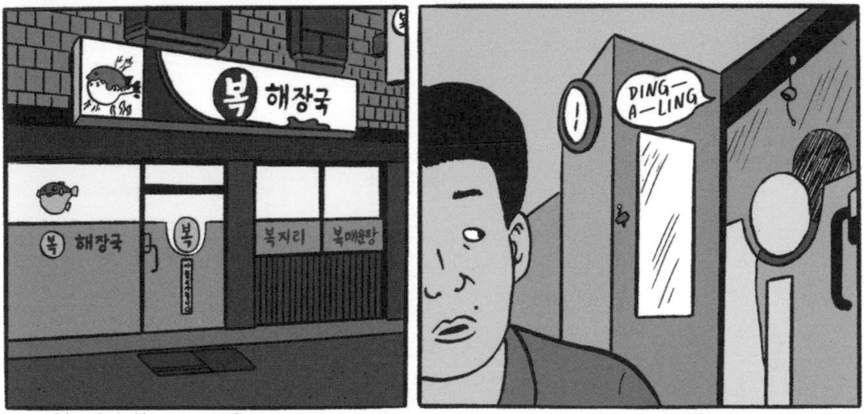
복 해장국
복 해장국
복
복지리
복매운탕
DING—A—LING

Sign: Blowfish Hangover Soup

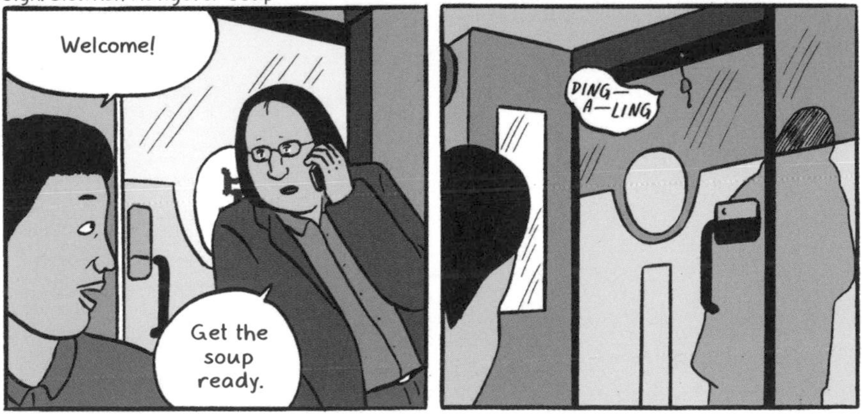
Welcome!
Get the soup ready.
DING—A—LING

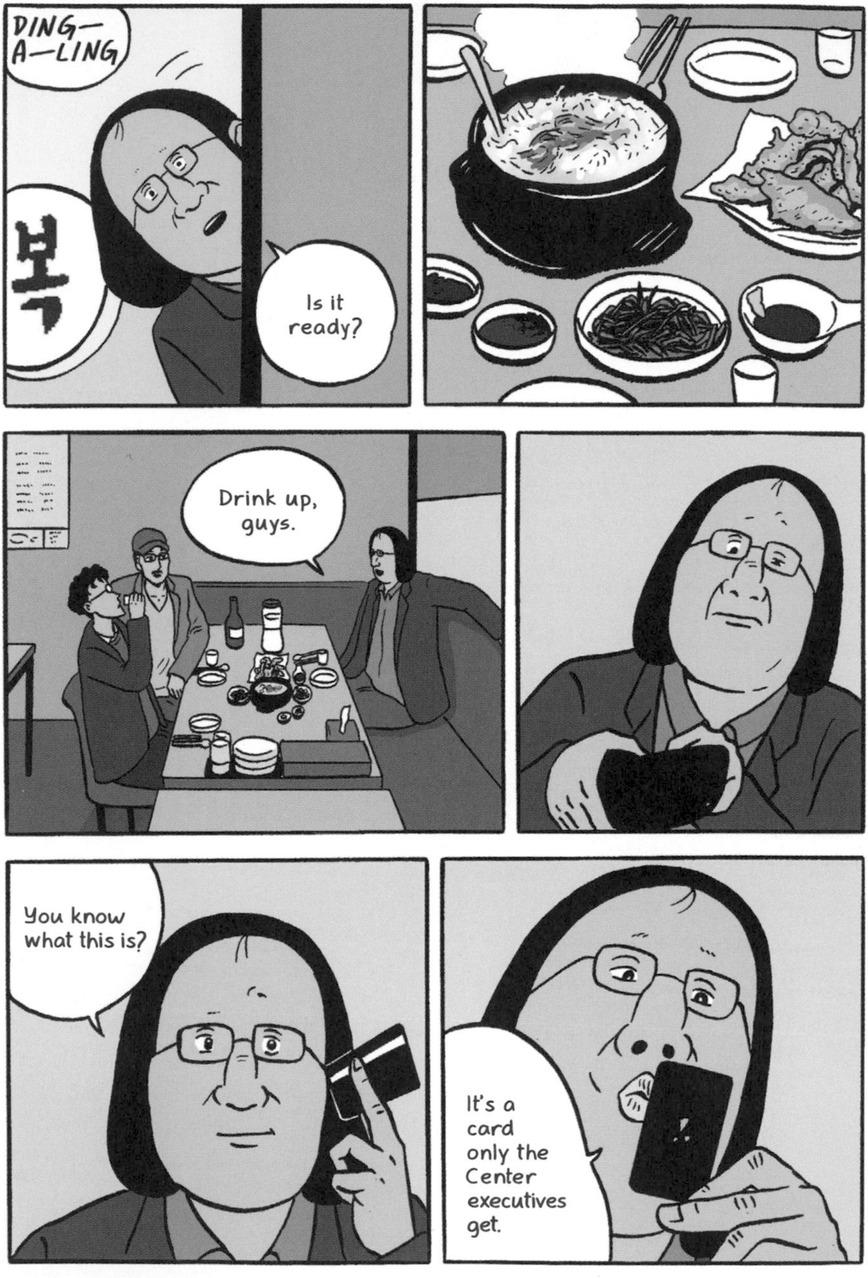
DING—
A—LING
보
Is it ready?
Drink up, guys.
You know what this is?
It's a card only the Center executives get.

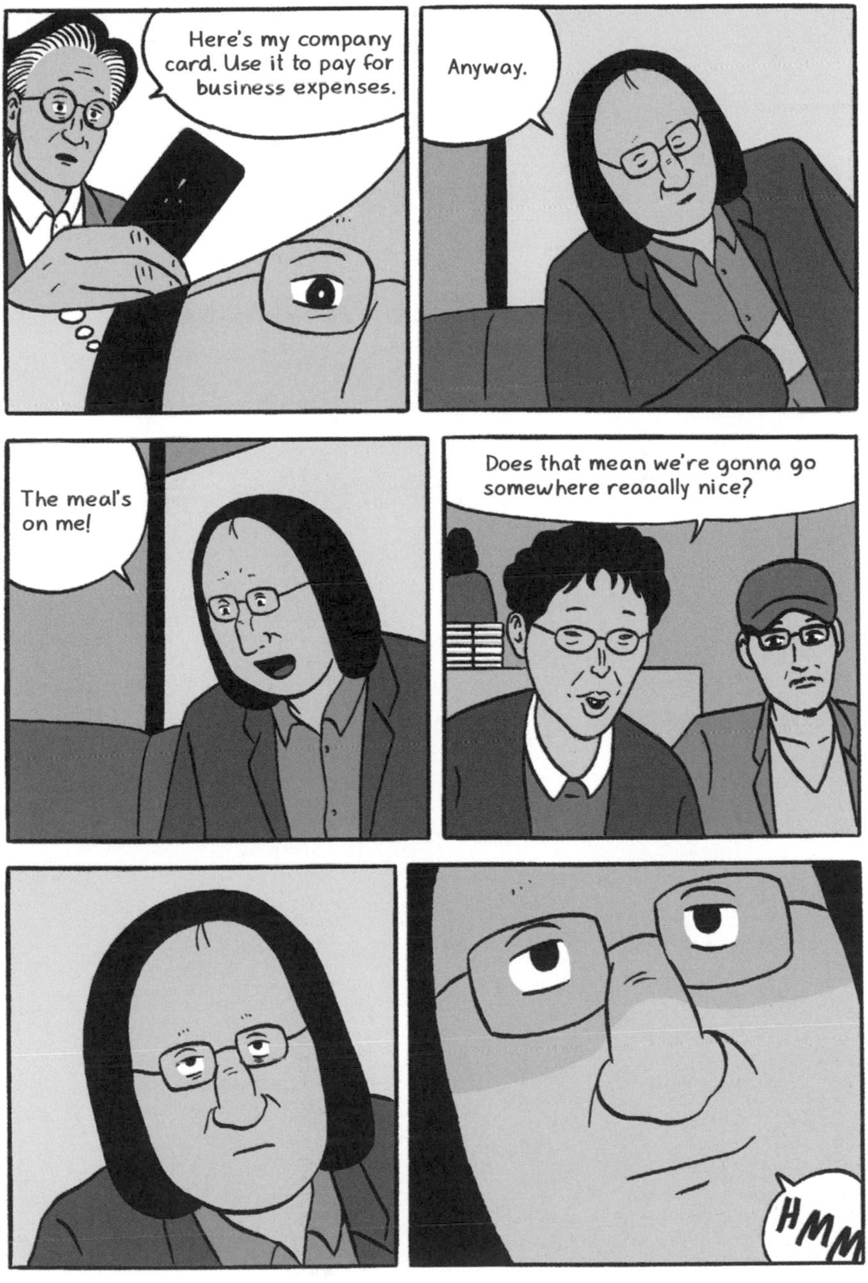

Here's my company card. Use it to pay for business expenses.
Anyway.
The meal's on me!
Does that mean we're gonna go somewhere reaaally nice?
HMM

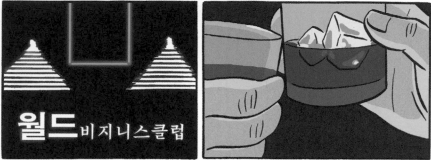

Sign: World Business Club

Please come again.

370

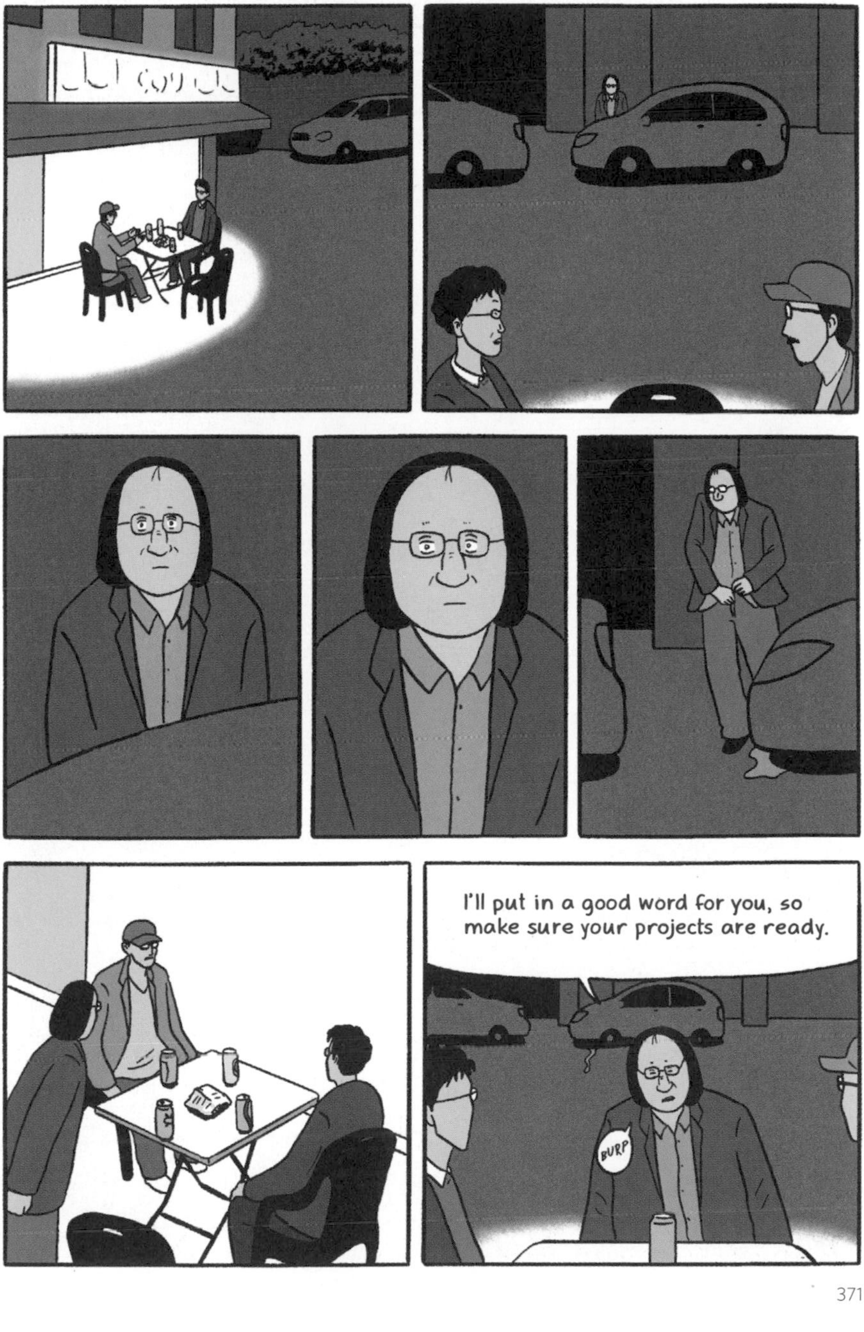
I'll put in a good word for you, so make sure your projects are ready.
BURP

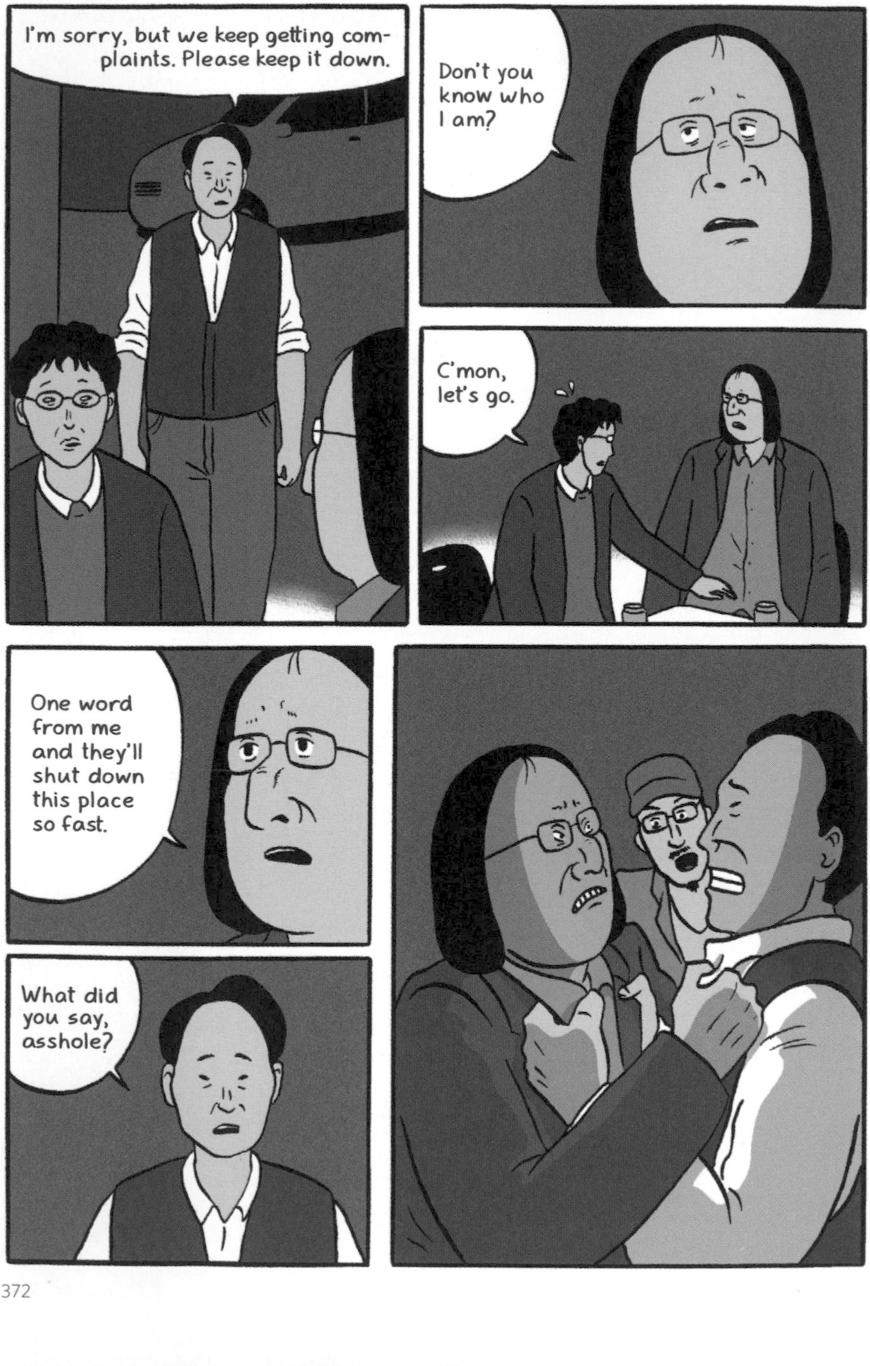
I'm sorry, but we keep getting complaints. Please keep it down.
Don't you know who I am?
C'mon, let's go.
One word from me and they'll shut down this place so fast.
What did you say, asshole?

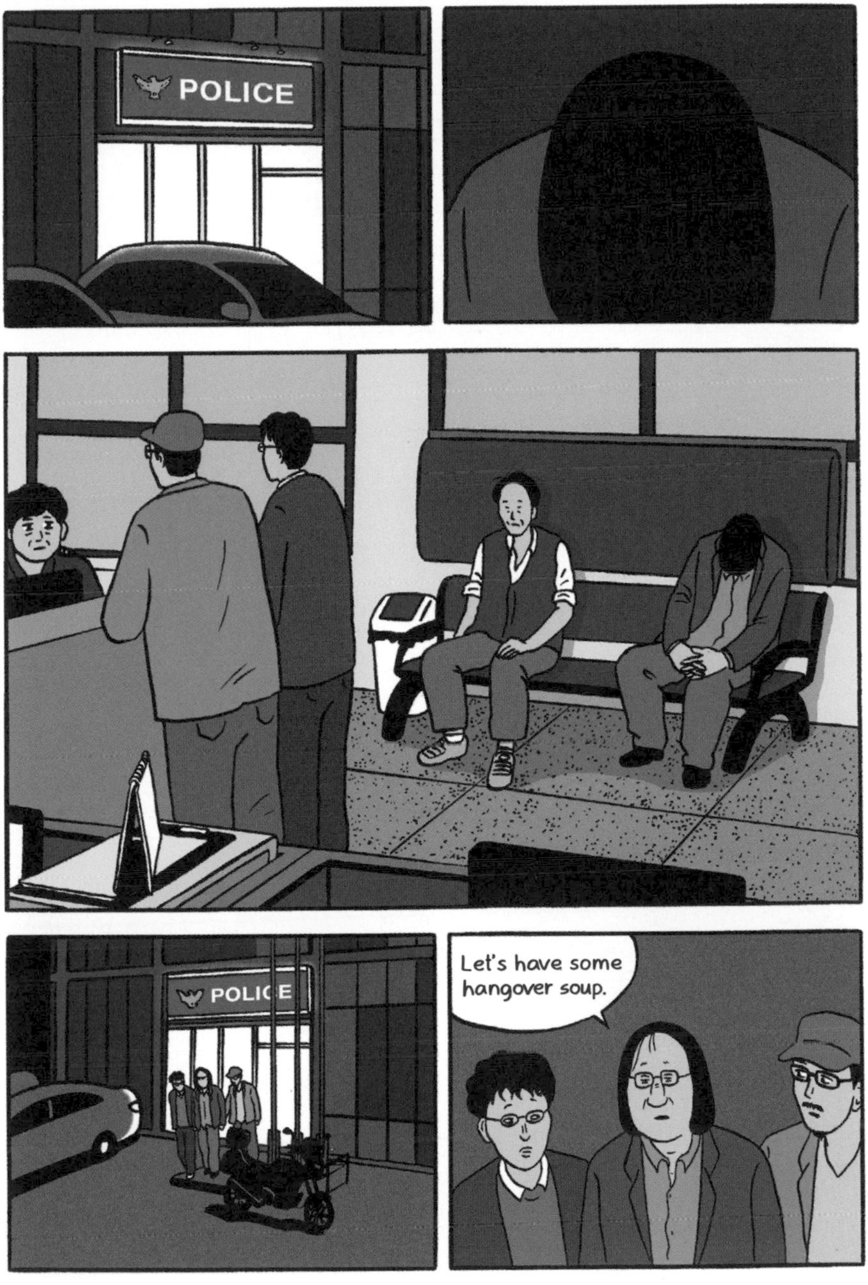
POLICE
POLICE
Let's have some hangover soup.

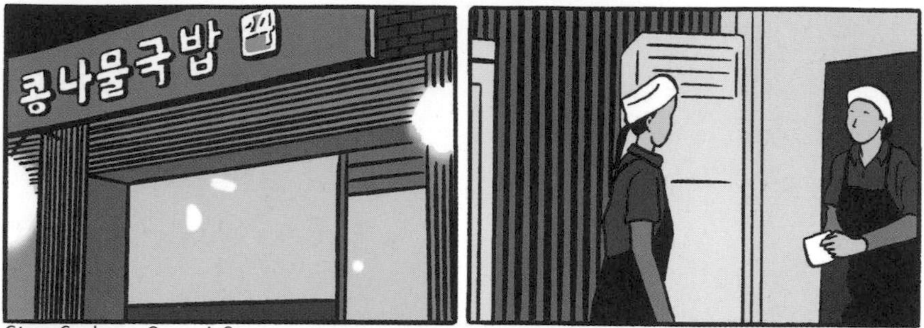
콩나물국밥
Sign: Soybean Sprout Soup

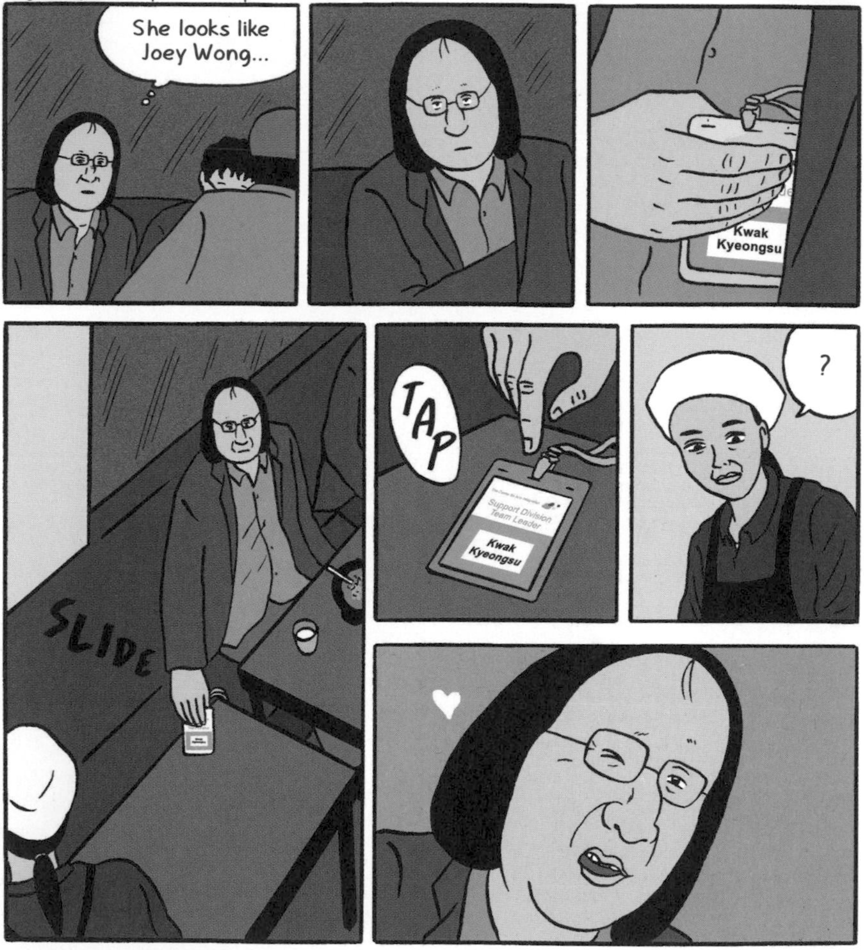
She looks like Joey Wong...
Kwak Kyeongsu
SLIDE
TAP
Support Division Team Leader
Kwak Kyeongsu
?

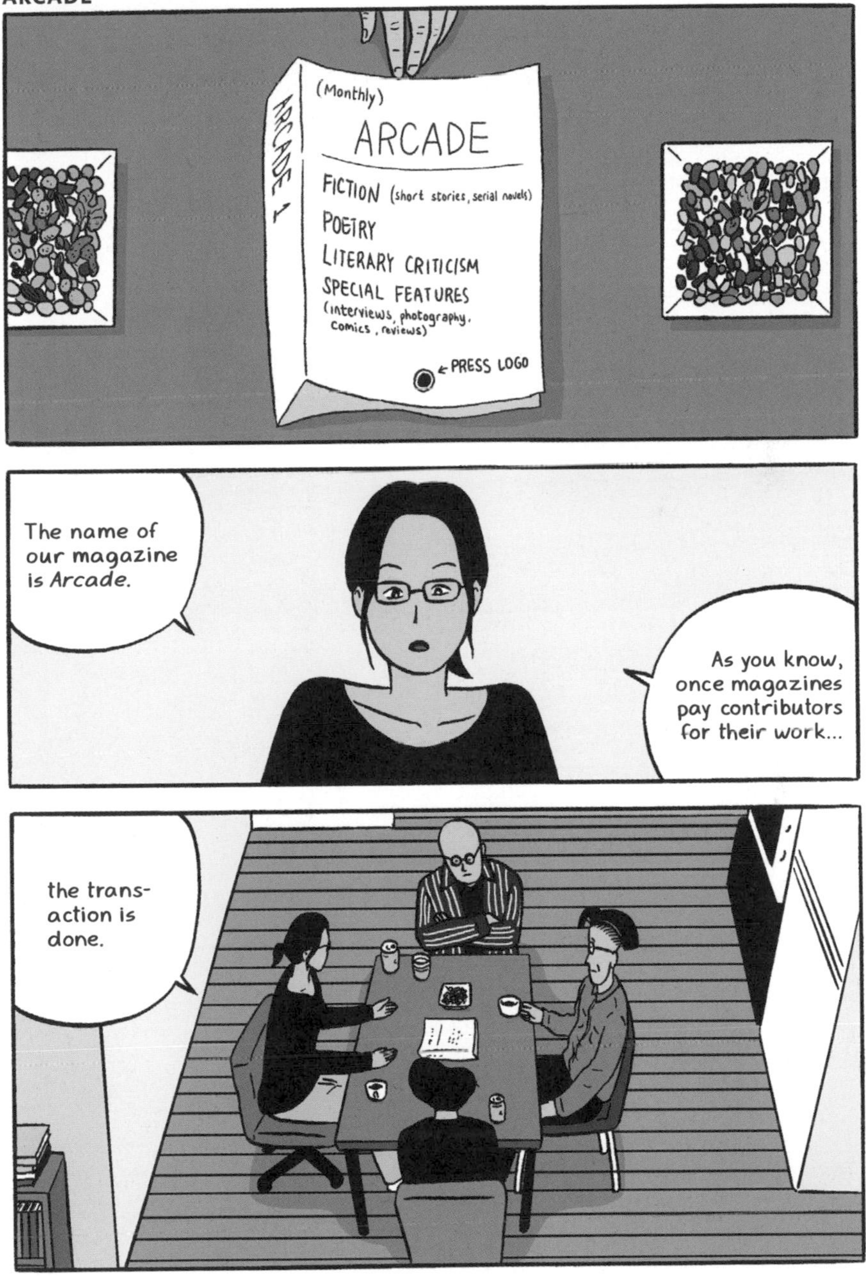
(Monthly)
ARCADE
ARCADE 1
FICTION (short stories, serial novels)
POETRY
LITERARY CRITICISM
SPECIAL FEATURES
(interviews, photography, comics, reviews)
← PRESS LOGO
The name of our magazine is *Arcade*.
As you know, once magazines pay contributors for their work...
the trans-action is done.

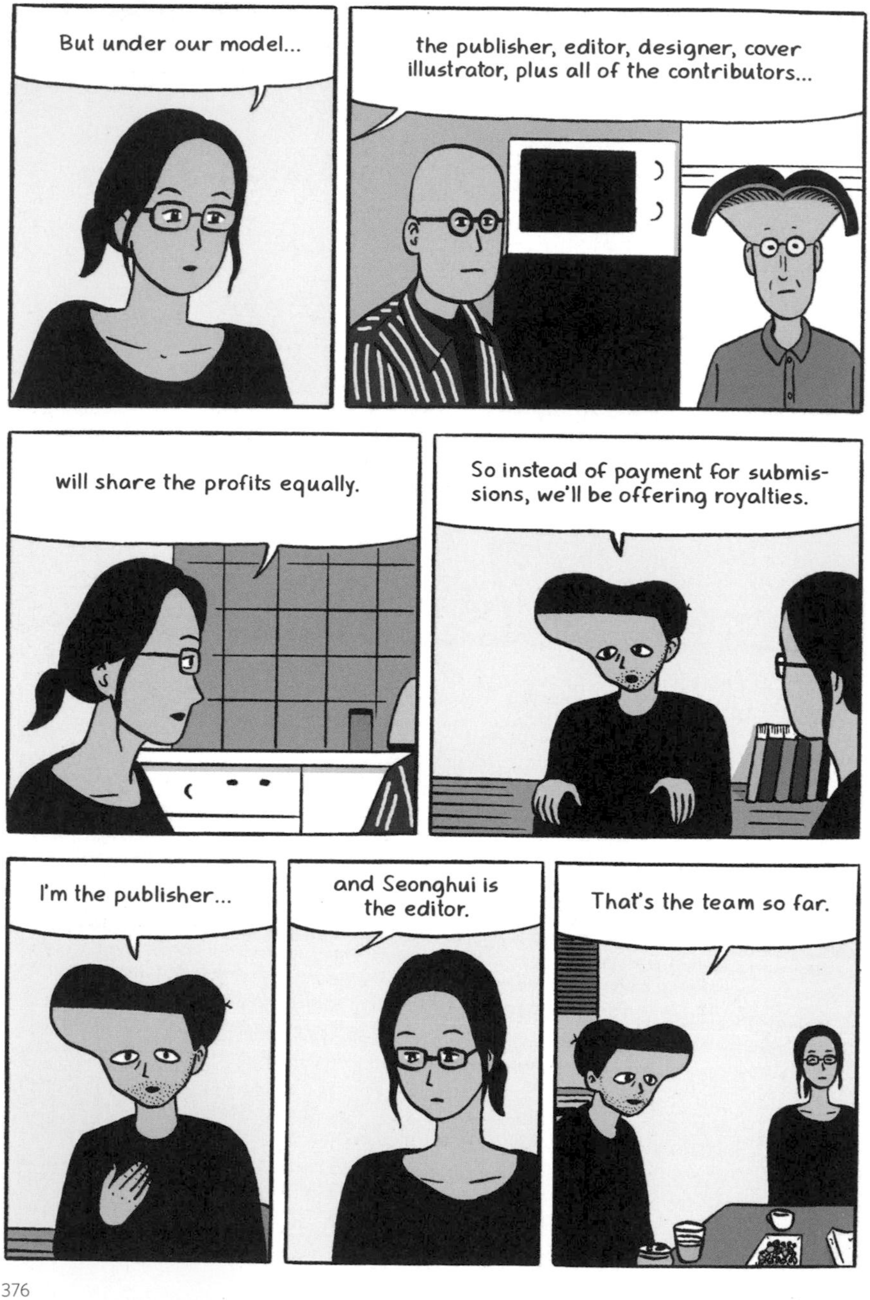
But under our model...
the publisher, editor, designer, cover illustrator, plus all of the contributors...
will share the profits equally.
So instead of payment for submissions, we'll be offering royalties.
I'm the publisher...
and Seonghui is the editor.
That's the team so far.

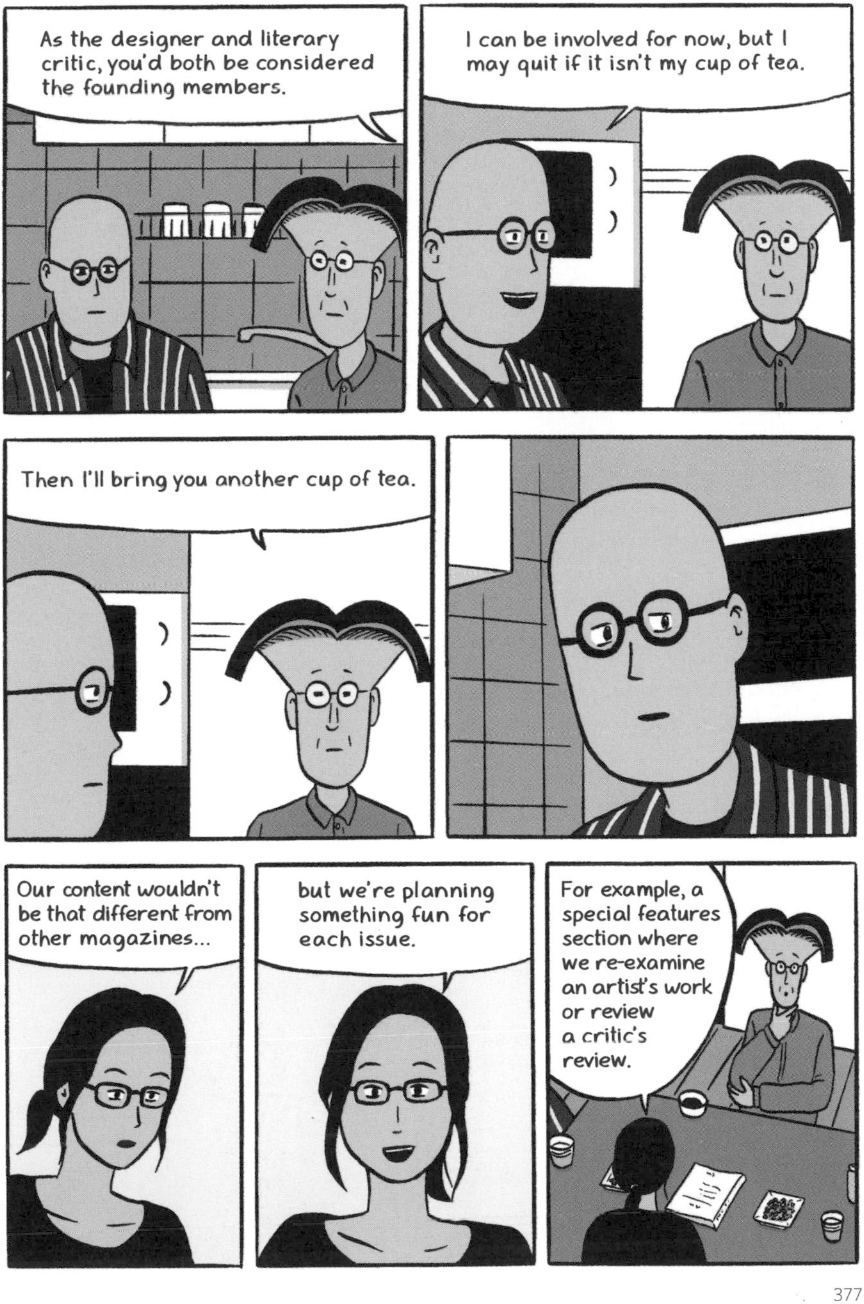
As the designer and literary critic, you'd both be considered the founding members.
I can be involved for now, but I may quit if it isn't my cup of tea.
Then I'll bring you another cup of tea.
Our content wouldn't be that different from other magazines...
but we're planning something fun for each issue.
For example, a special features section where we re-examine an artist's work or review a critic's review.

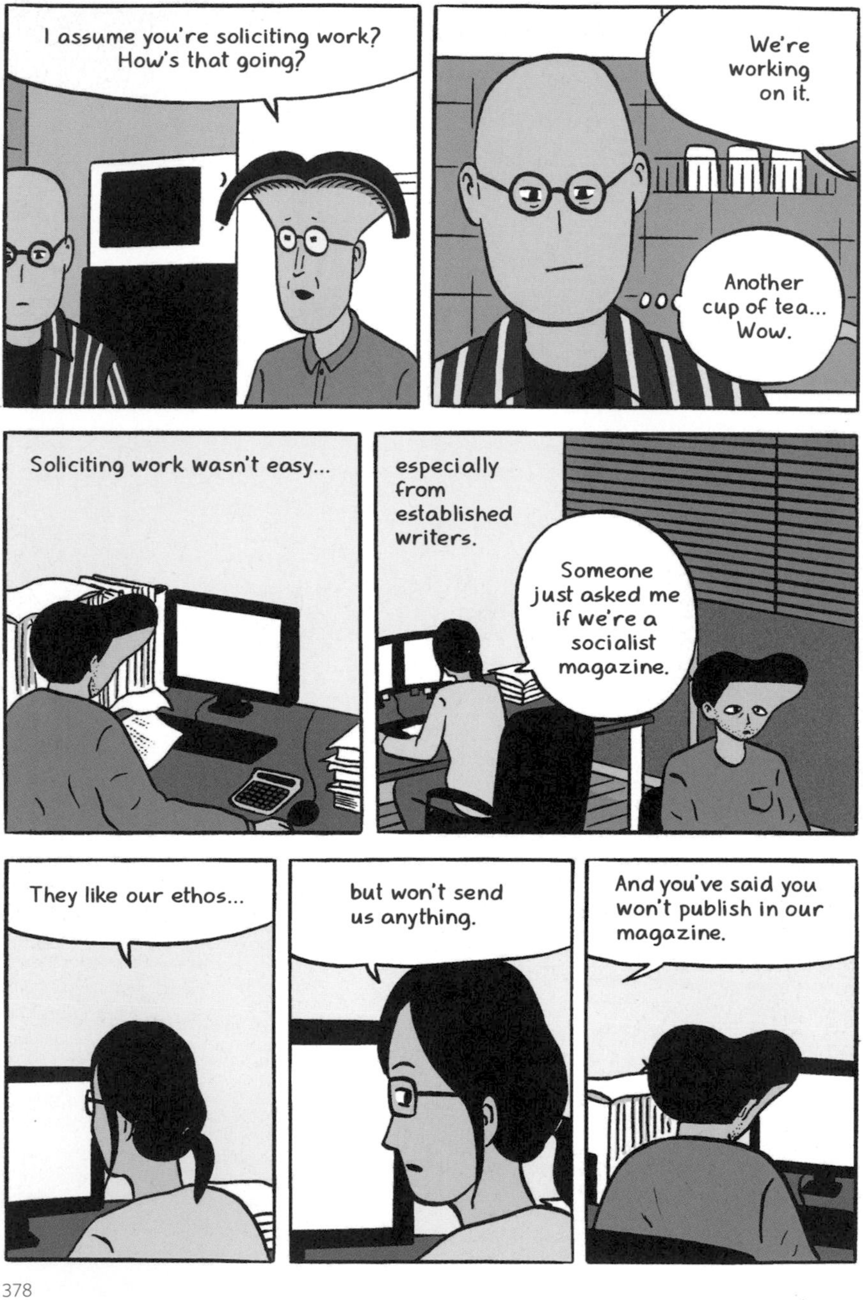
I assume you're soliciting work? How's that going?
We're working on it.
Another cup of tea... Wow.
Soliciting work wasn't easy...
especially from established writers.
Someone just asked me if we're a socialist magazine.
They like our ethos...
but won't send us anything.
And you've said you won't publish in our magazine.

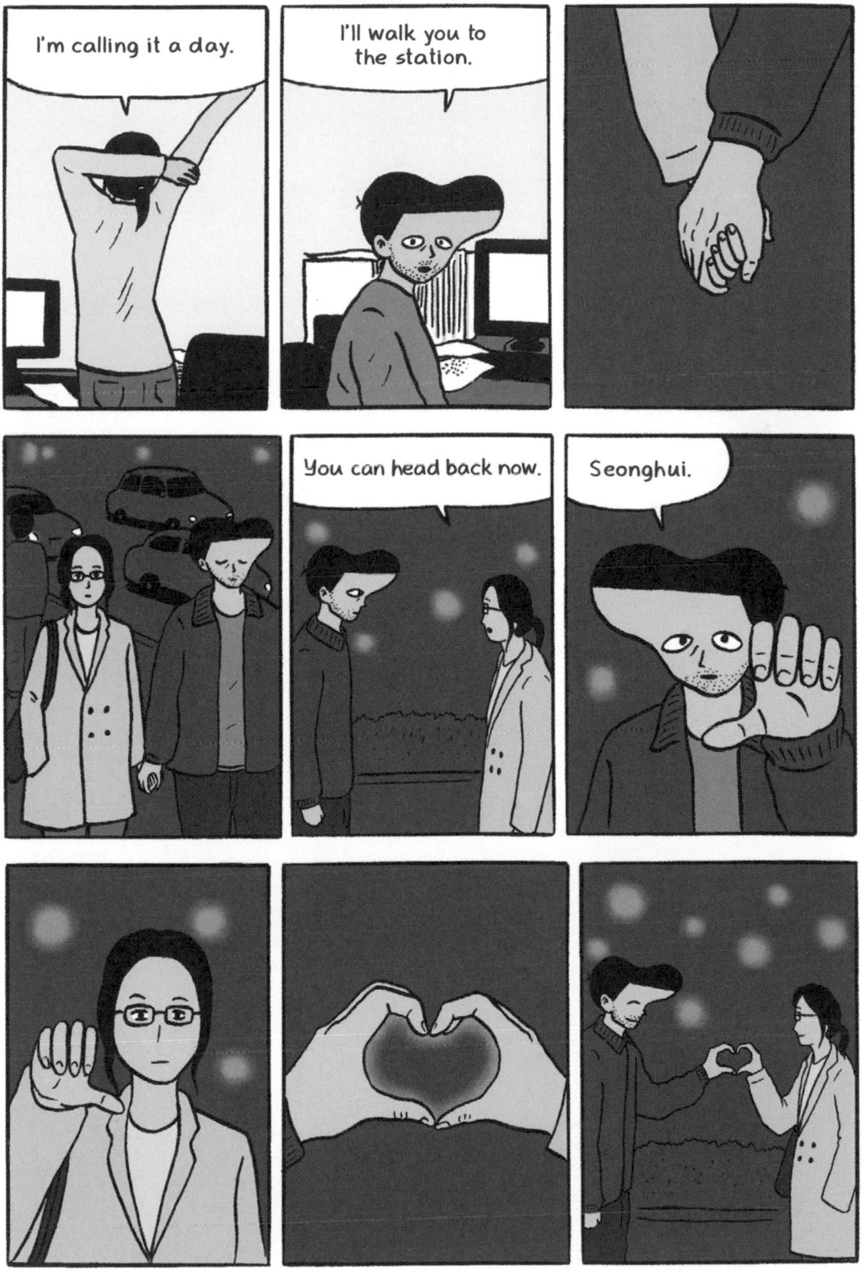
I'm calling it a day.
I'll walk you to the station.
You can head back now.
Seonghui.

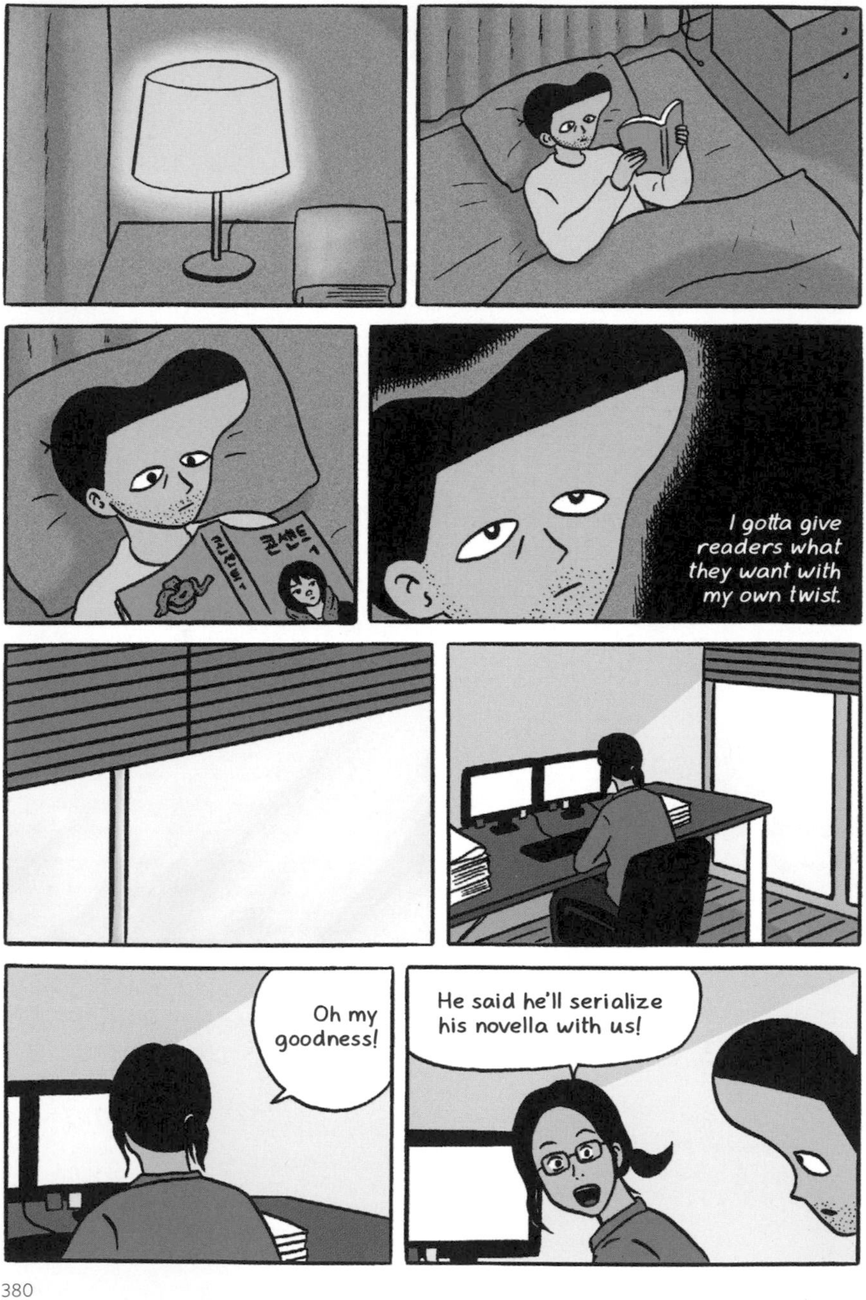
I gotta give readers what they want with my own twist.
Oh my goodness!
He said he'll serialize his novella with us!

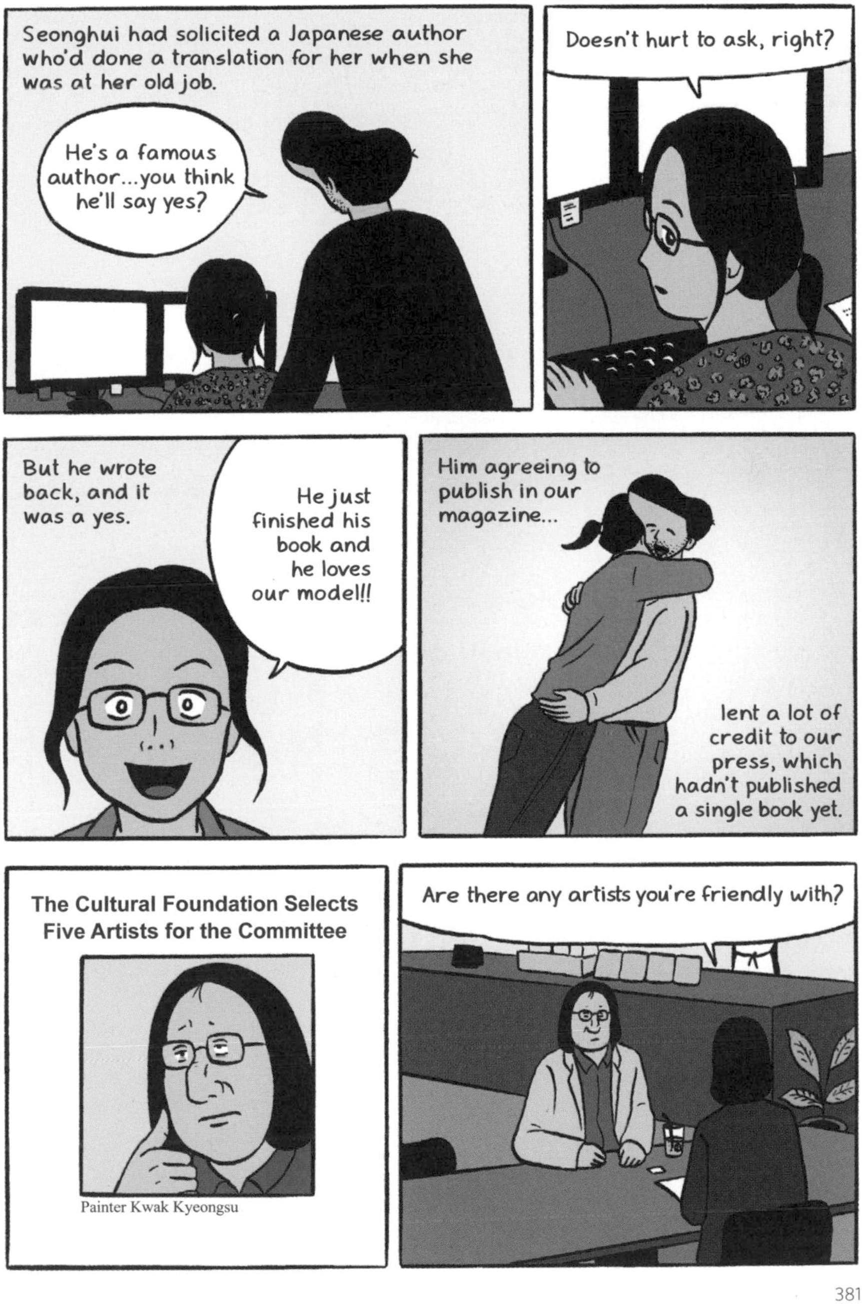
Seonghui had solicited a Japanese author who'd done a translation for her when she was at her old job.
He's a famous author...you think he'll say yes?
Doesn't hurt to ask, right?
But he wrote back, and it was a yes.
He just finished his book and he loves our model!!
Him agreeing to publish in our magazine...
lent a lot of credit to our press, which hadn't published a single book yet.
The Cultural Foundation Selects Five Artists for the Committee
Painter Kwak Kyeongsu
Are there any artists you're friendly with?

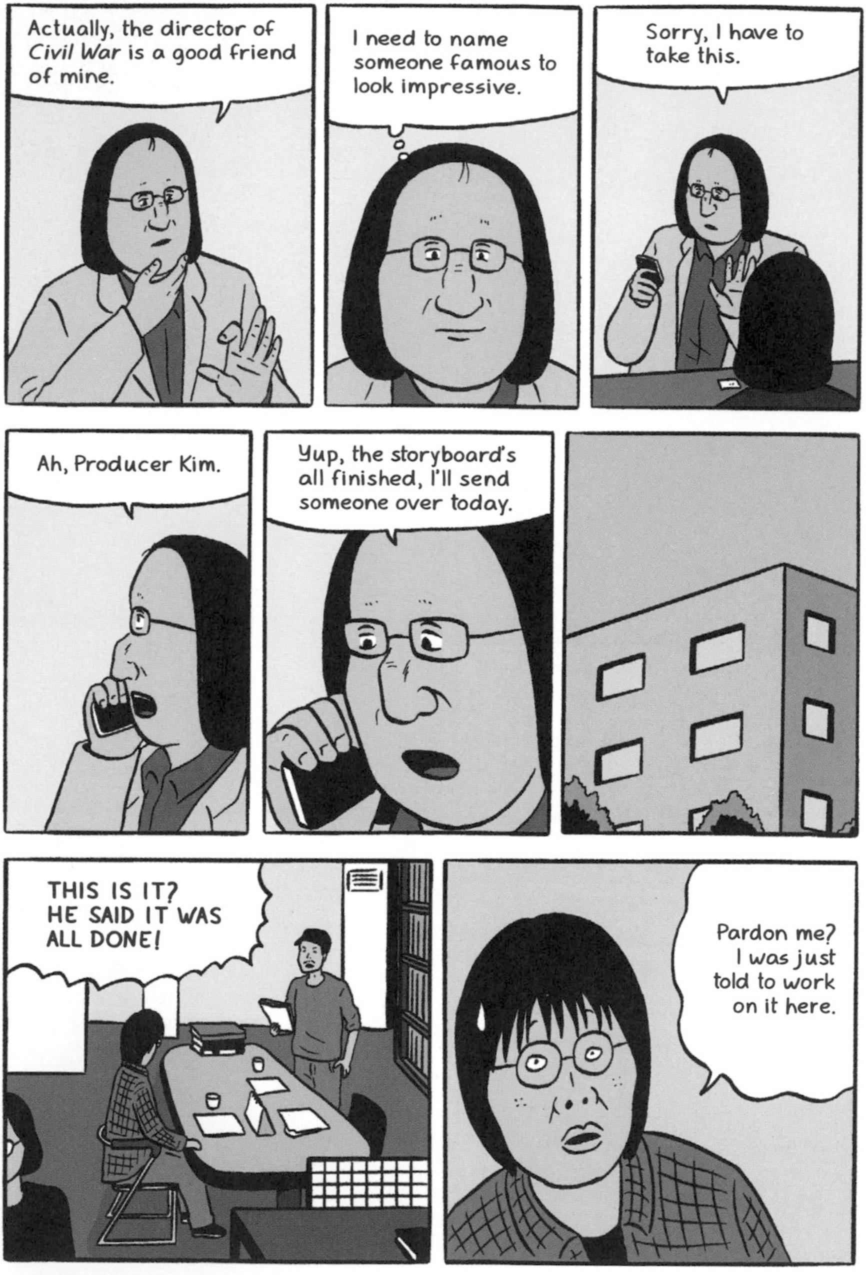
Actually, the director of *Civil War* is a good friend of mine.
I need to name someone famous to look impressive.
Sorry, I have to take this.
Ah, Producer Kim.
Yup, the storyboard's all finished, I'll send someone over today.
THIS IS IT? HE SAID IT WAS ALL DONE!
Pardon me? I was just told to work on it here.

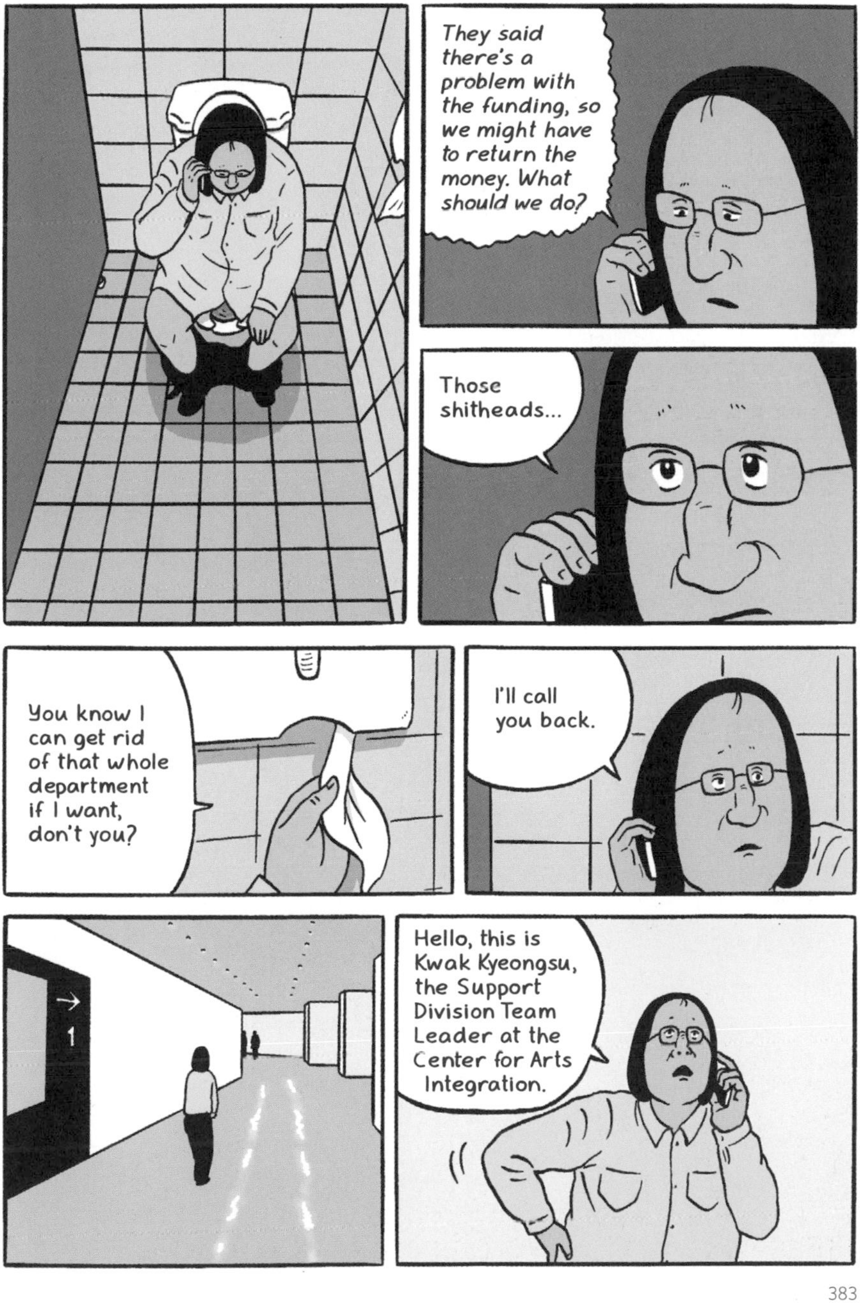
They said there's a problem with the funding, so we might have to return the money. What should we do?
Those shitheads...
You know I can get rid of that whole department if I want, don't you?
I'll call you back.
1
Hello, this is Kwak Kyeongsu, the Support Division Team Leader at the Center for Arts Integration.

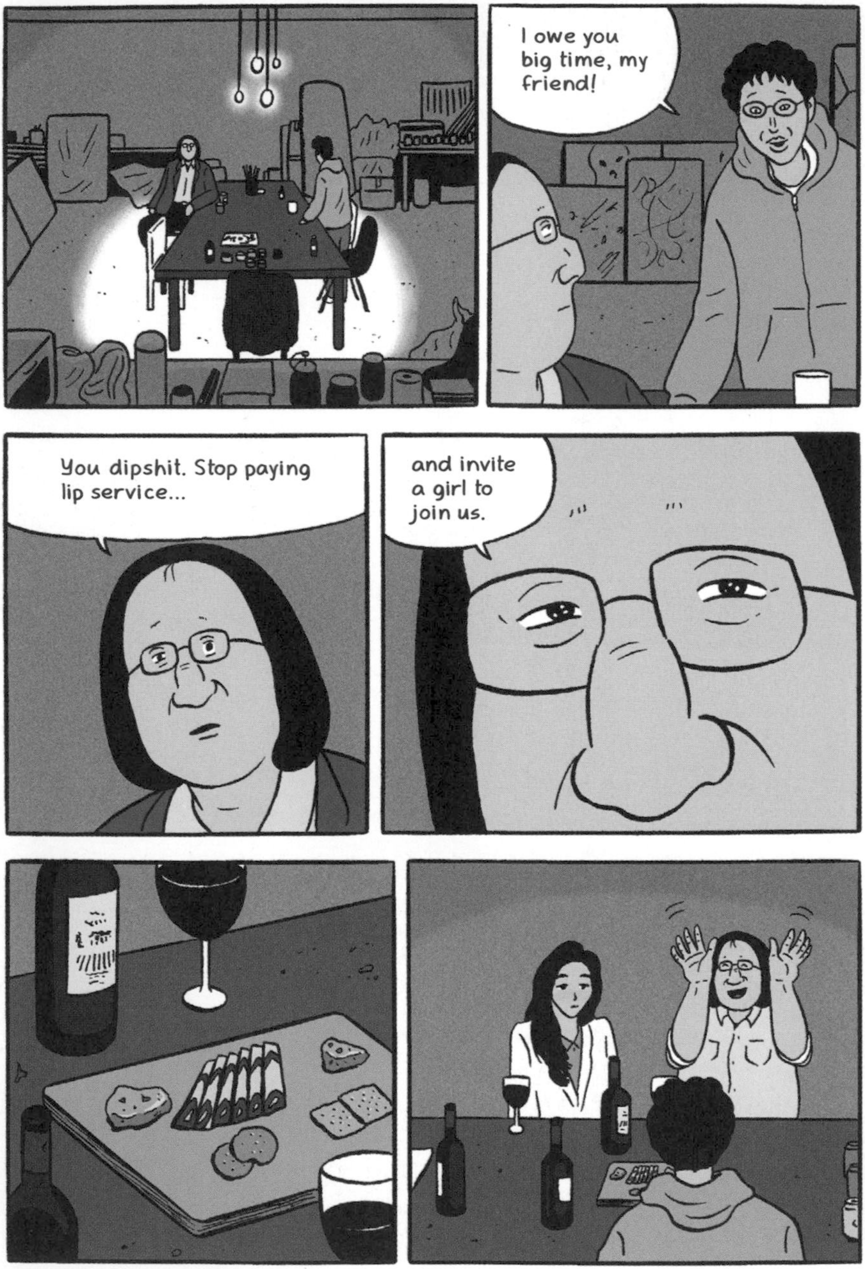
I owe you big time, my friend!
You dipshit. Stop paying lip service...
and invite a girl to join us.

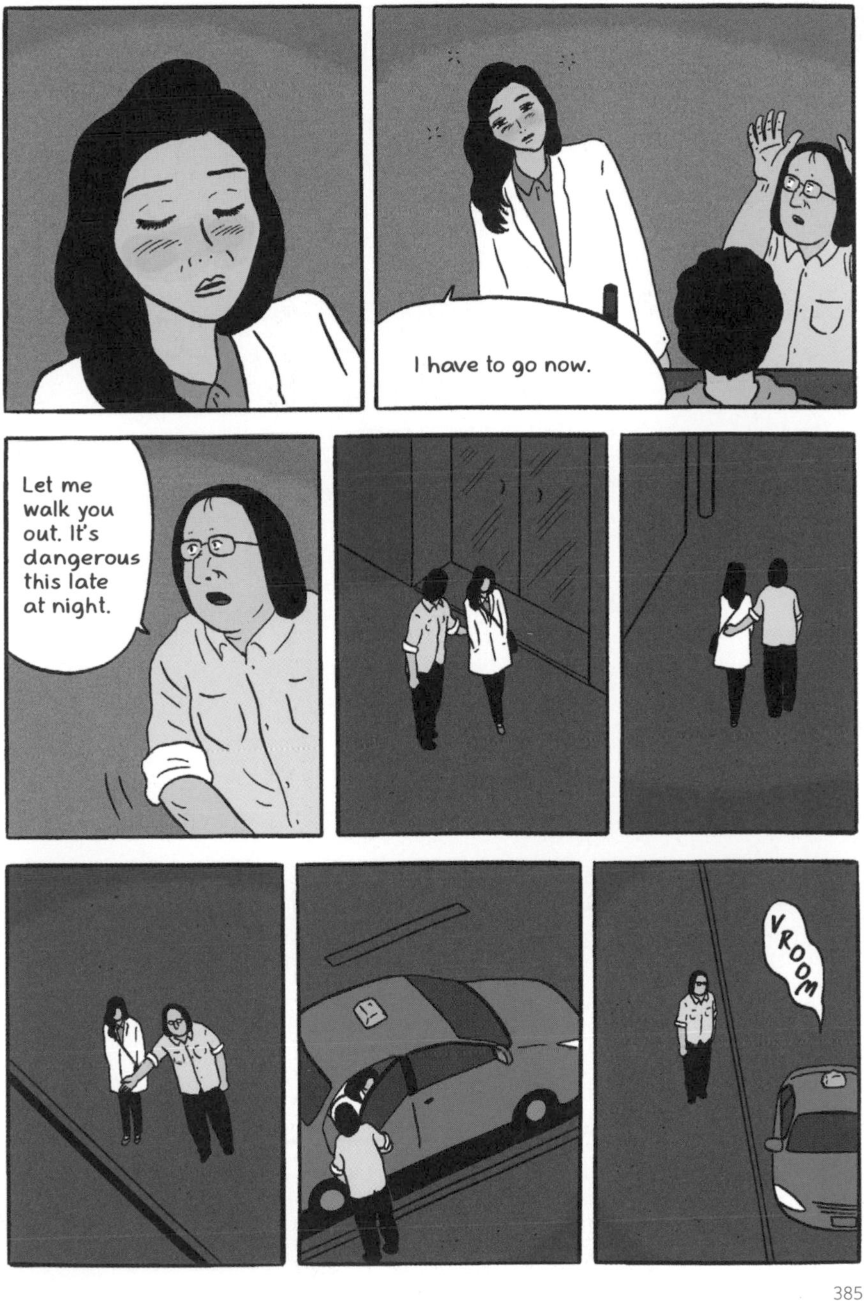
I have to go now.
Let me walk you out. It's dangerous this late at night.
VROOM

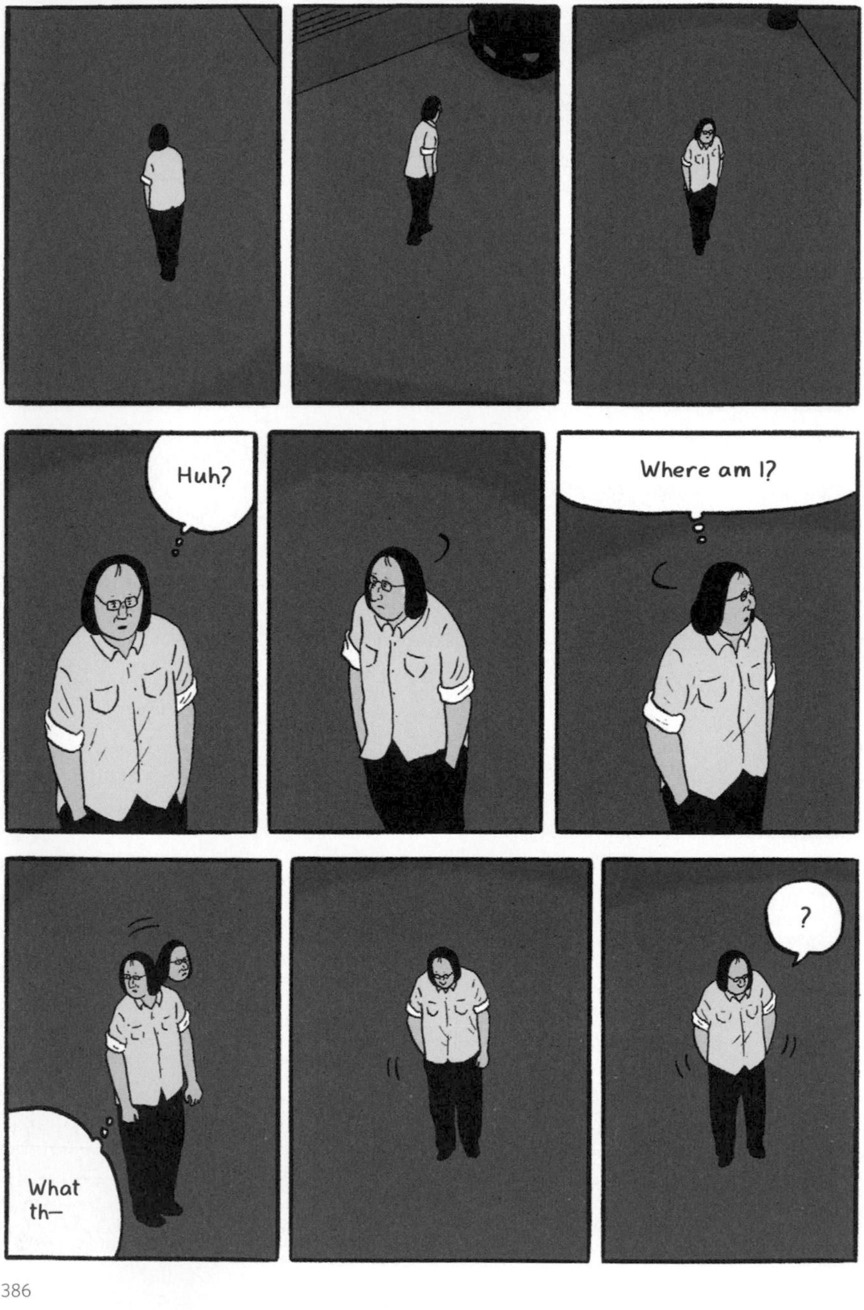
Huh?
Where am I?
What th—
?

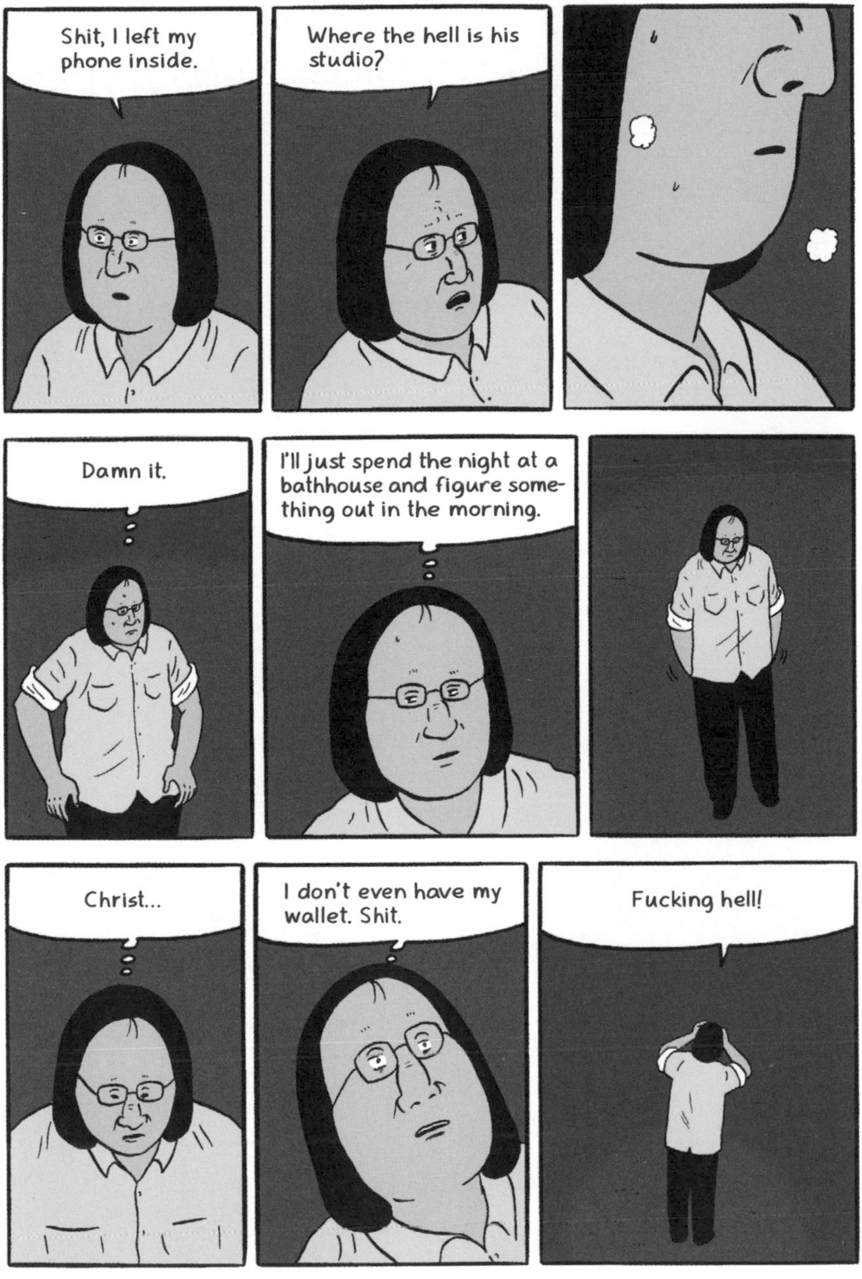
Shit, I left my phone inside.
Where the hell is his studio?
Damn it.
I'll just spend the night at a bathhouse and figure something out in the morning.
Christ...
I don't even have my wallet. Shit.
Fucking hell!

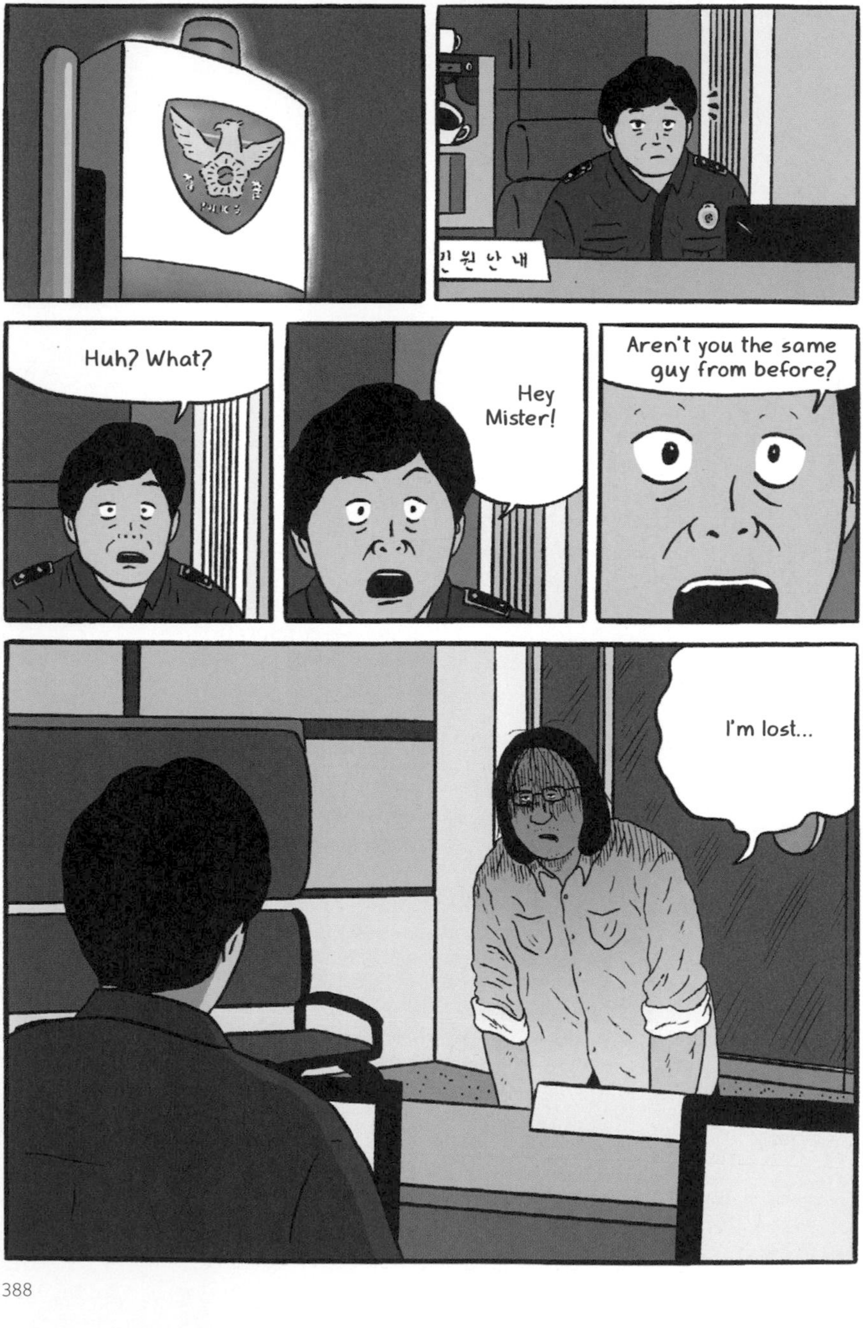
Huh? What?
Hey Mister!
Aren't you the same guy from before?
I'm lost...

A SECRET PARTNERSHIP

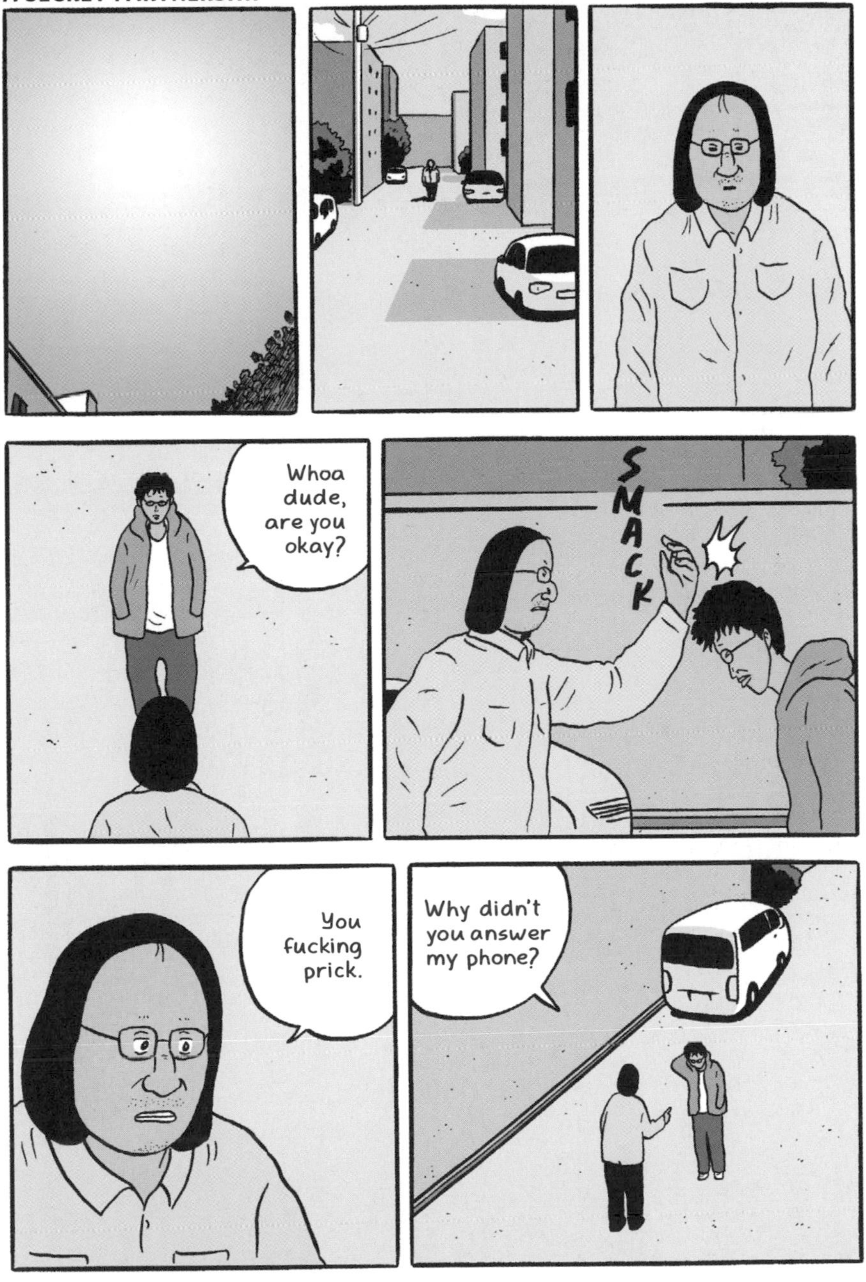
Whoa dude, are you okay?
SMACK
You fucking prick.
Why didn't you answer my phone?

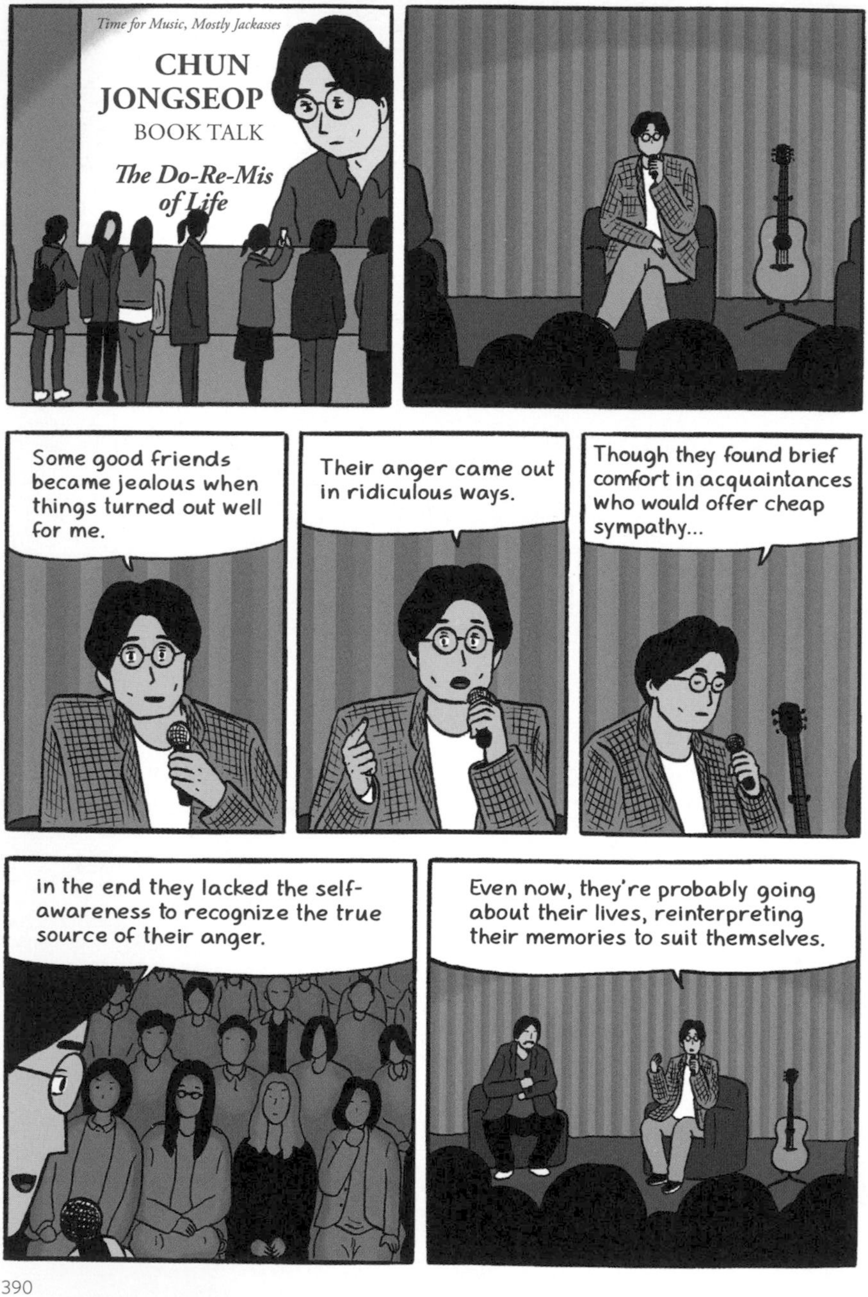
Time for Music, Mostly Jackasses
CHUN JONGSEOP BOOK TALK
The Do-Re-Mis of Life
Some good friends became jealous when things turned out well for me.
Their anger came out in ridiculous ways.
Though they found brief comfort in acquaintances who would offer cheap sympathy...
in the end they lacked the self-awareness to recognize the true source of their anger.
Even now, they're probably going about their lives, reinterpreting their memories to suit themselves.

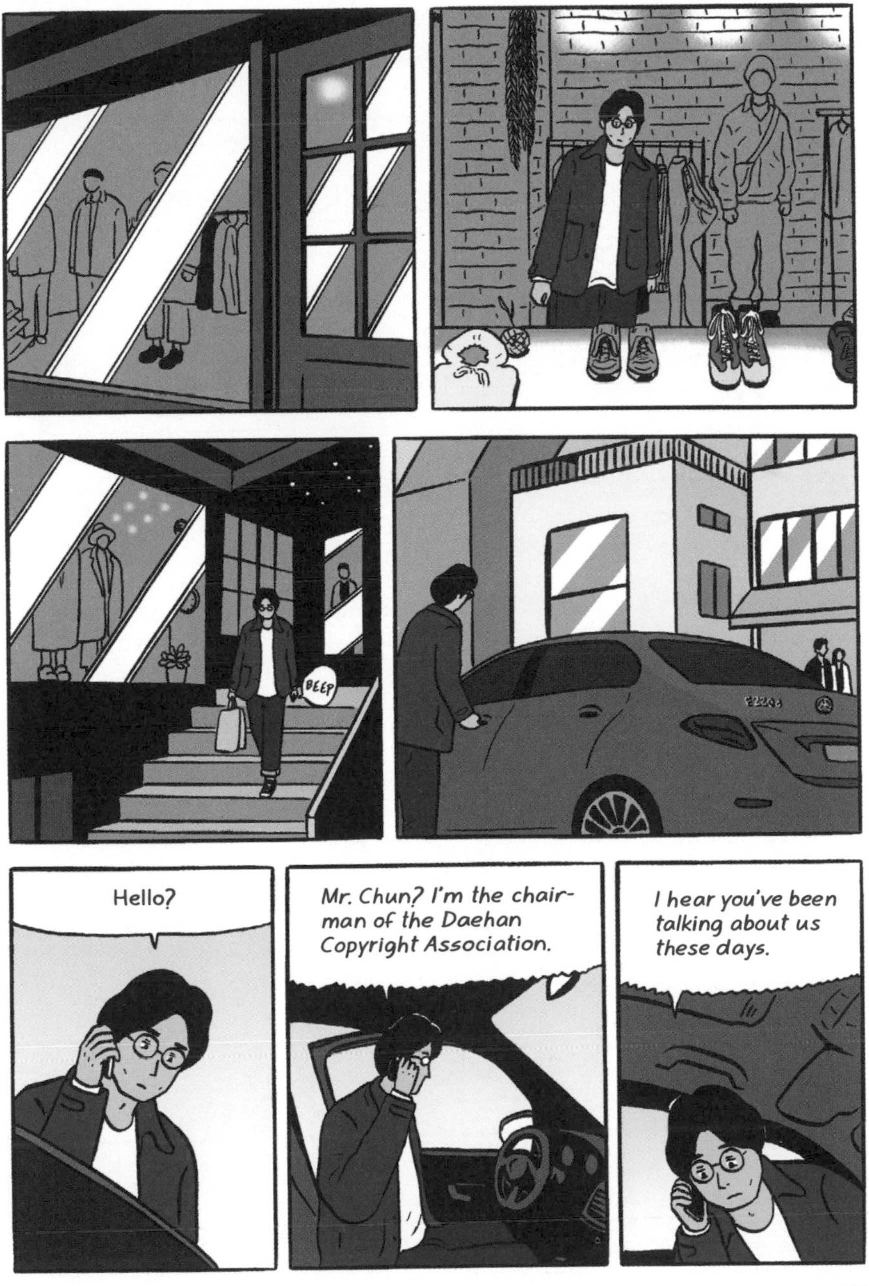
BEEP
Hello?
Mr. Chun? I'm the chairman of the Daehan Copyright Association.
I hear you've been talking about us these days.

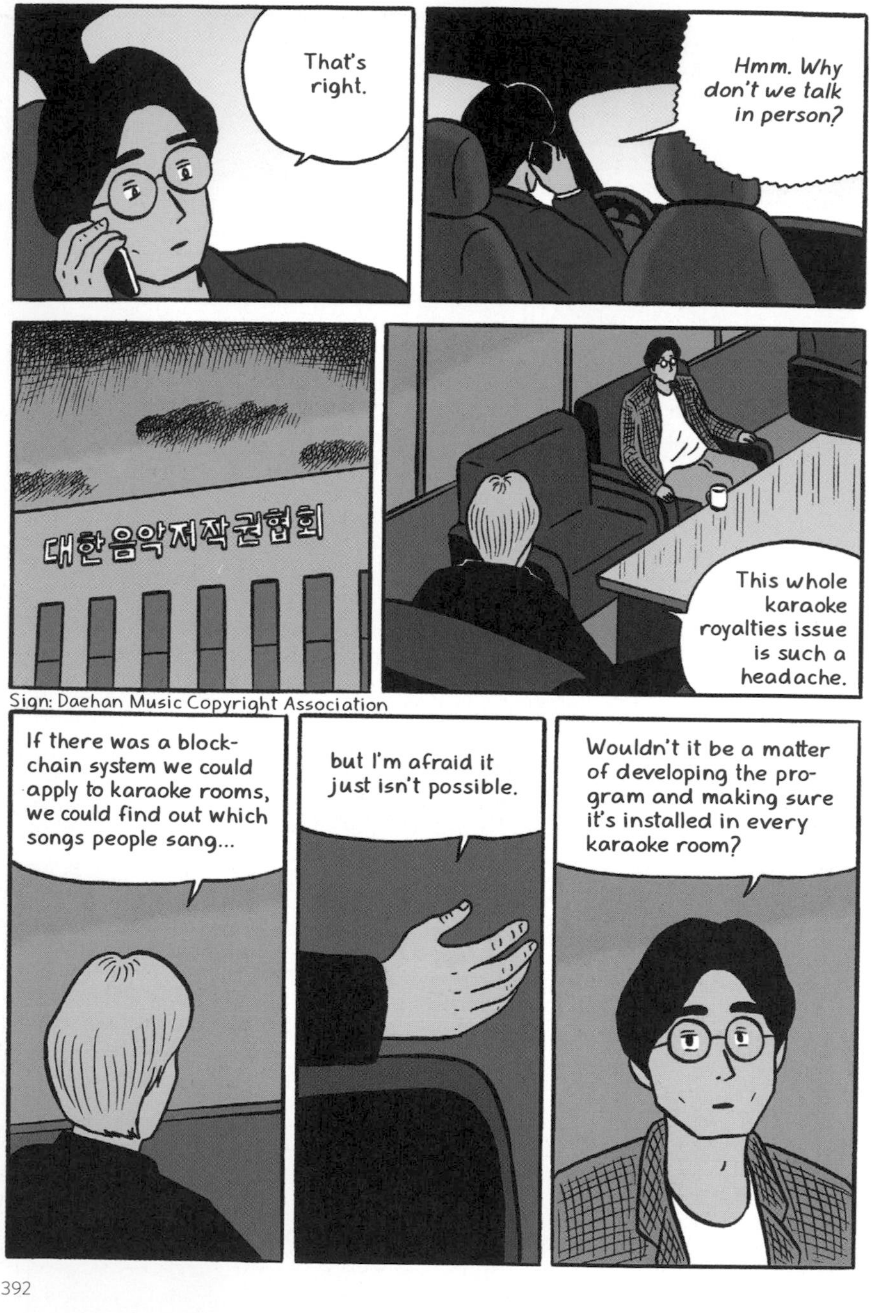
That's right.
Hmm. Why don't we talk in person?
대한음악저작권협회
This whole karaoke royalties issue is such a headache.
Sign: Daehan Music Copyright Association
If there was a block-chain system we could apply to karaoke rooms, we could find out which songs people sang...
but I'm afraid it just isn't possible.
Wouldn't it be a matter of developing the pro-gram and making sure it's installed in every karaoke room?

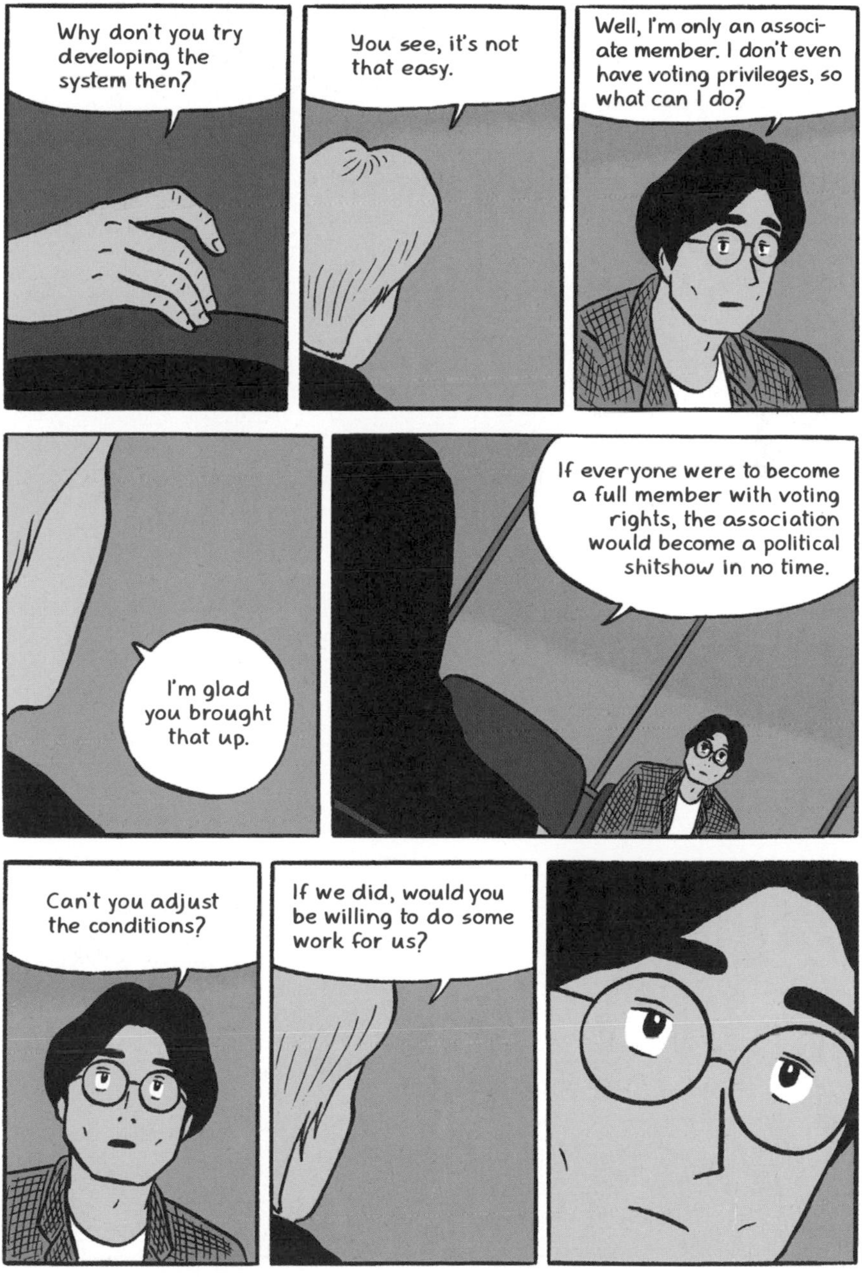
Why don't you try developing the system then?
You see, it's not that easy.
Well, I'm only an associate member. I don't even have voting privileges, so what can I do?
I'm glad you brought that up.
If everyone were to become a full member with voting rights, the association would become a political shitshow in no time.
Can't you adjust the conditions?
If we did, would you be willing to do some work for us?

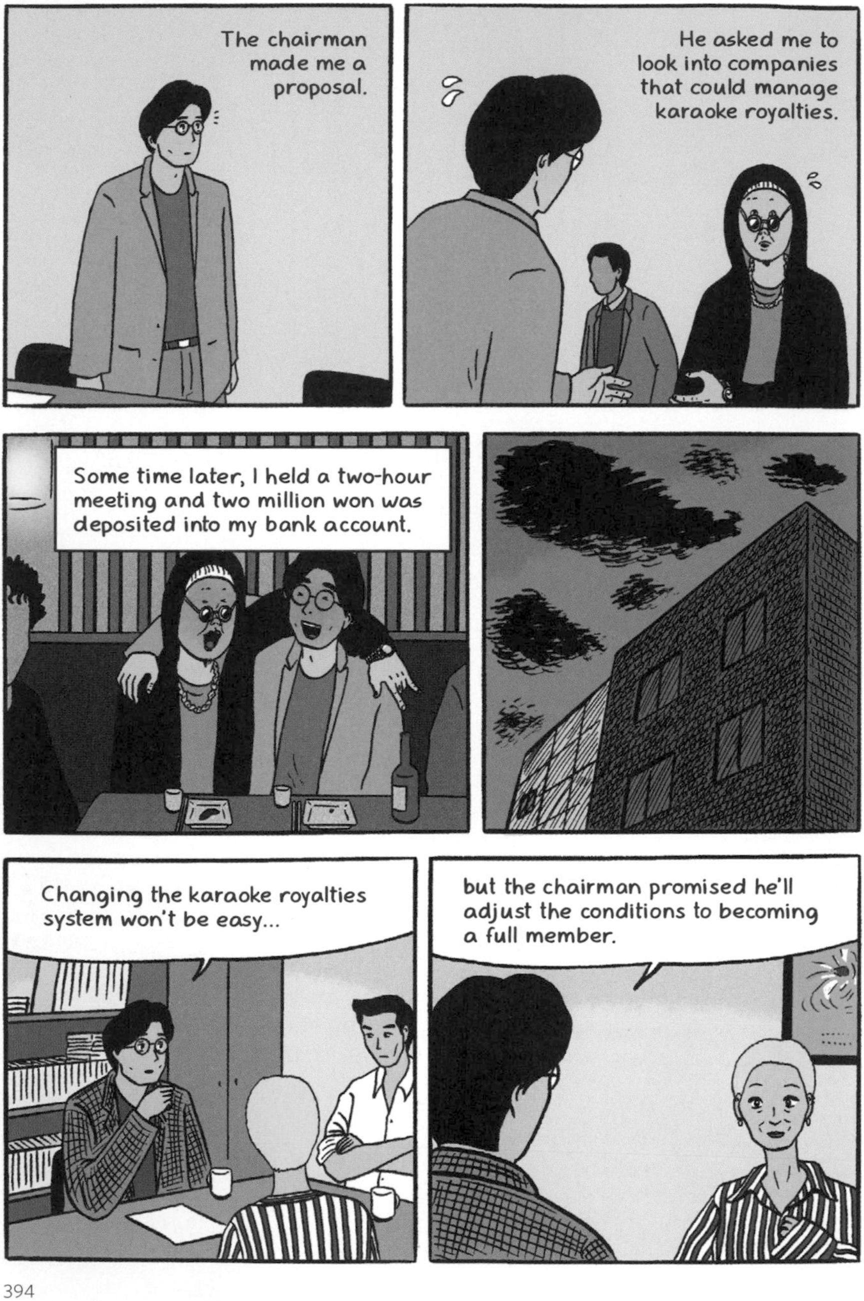
The chairman made me a proposal.
He asked me to look into companies that could manage karaoke royalties.
Some time later, I held a two-hour meeting and two million won was deposited into my bank account.
Changing the karaoke royalties system won't be easy...
but the chairman promised he'll adjust the conditions to becoming a full member.

Jongseop, I don't know how you pulled this off on your own!

Hey, if something like this comes up again, make sure you run it by us first.

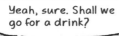

Yeah, sure. Shall we go for a drink?

Jongseop, say hi. Her music's really blowing up these days.

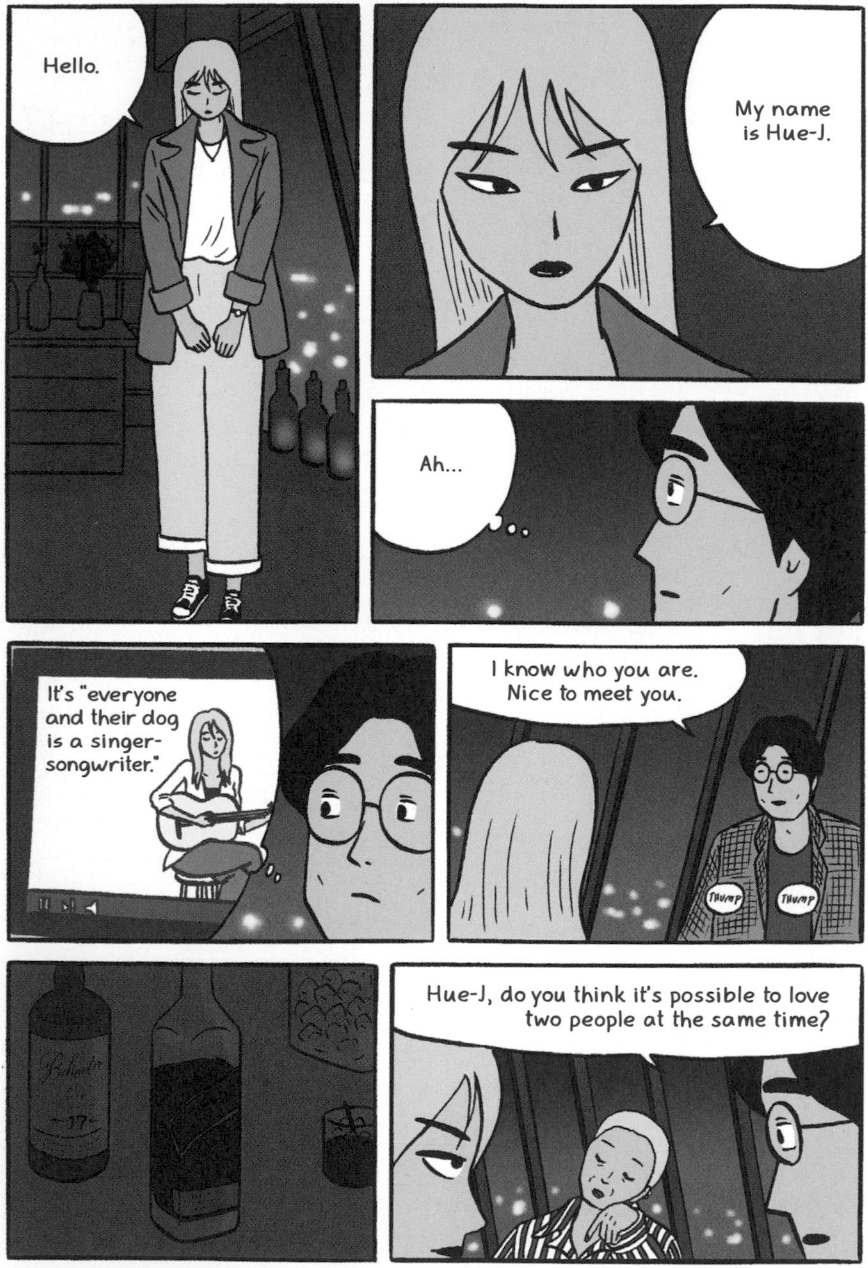
Hello.
My name is Hue-J.
Ah...
It's "everyone and their dog is a singer-songwriter."
I know who you are. Nice to meet you.
THUMP
THUMP
Hue-J, do you think it's possible to love two people at the same time?

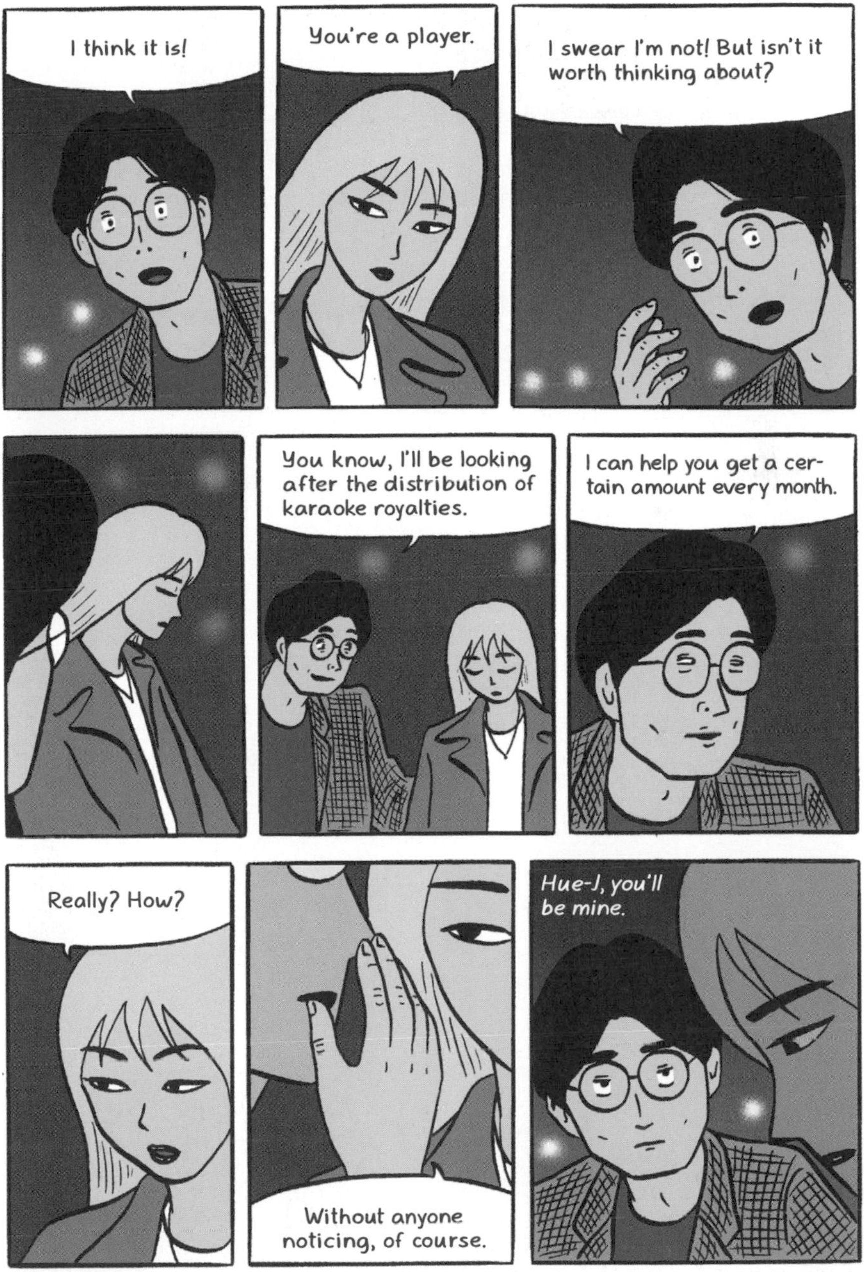
I think it is!
You're a player.
I swear I'm not! But isn't it worth thinking about?
You know, I'll be looking after the distribution of karaoke royalties.
I can help you get a certain amount every month.
Really? How?
Without anyone noticing, of course.
Hue-J, you'll be mine.

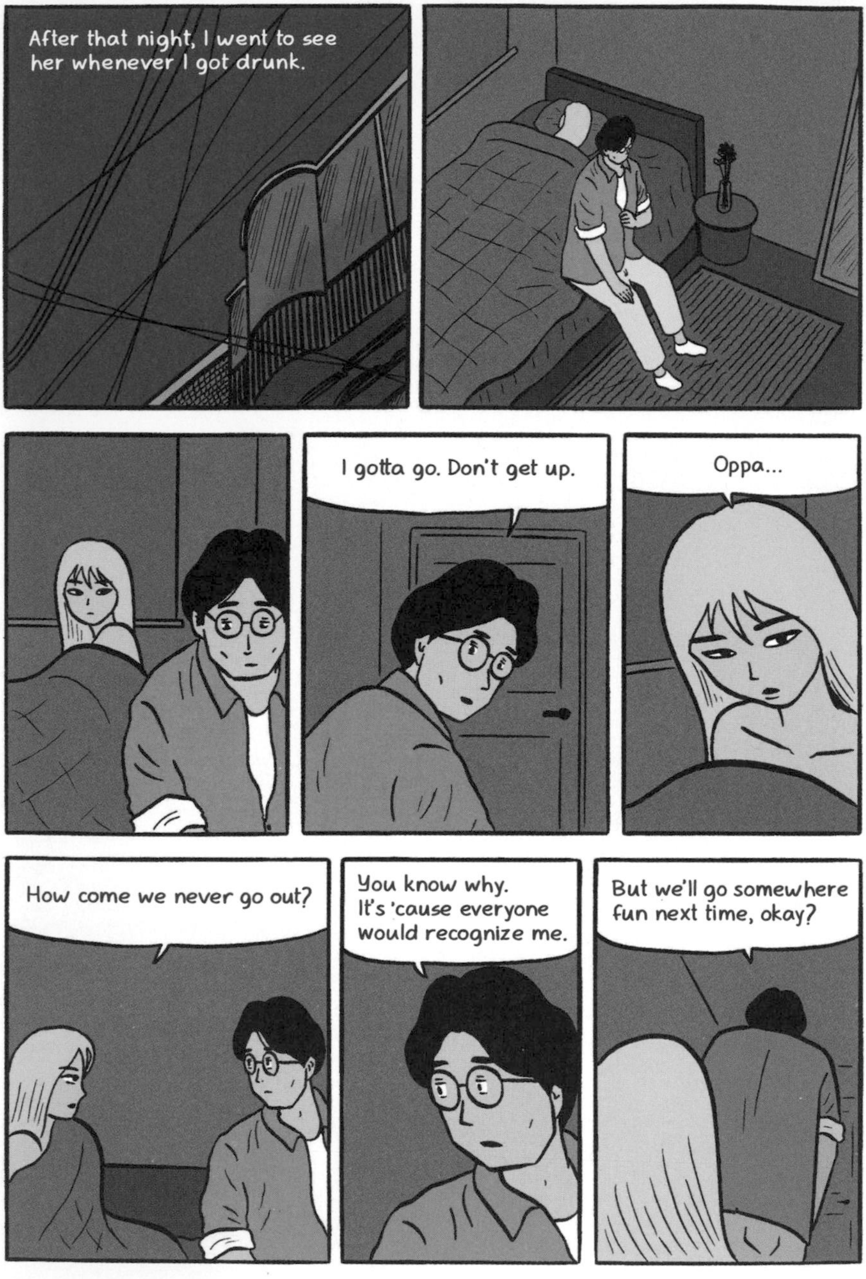
After that night, I went to see her whenever I got drunk.
I gotta go. Don't get up.
Oppa...
How come we never go out?
You know why. It's 'cause everyone would recognize me.
But we'll go somewhere fun next time, okay?

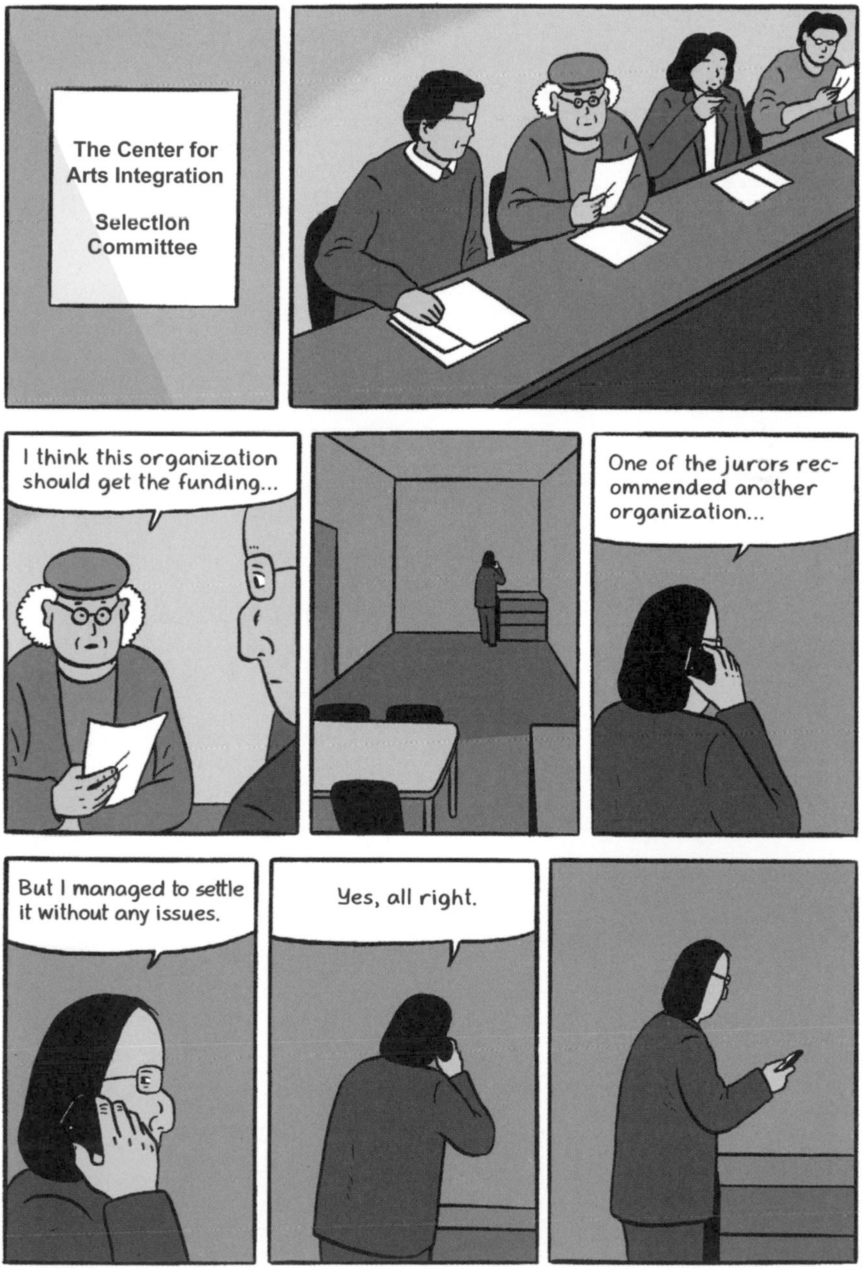
The Center for Arts Integration
Selection Committee
I think this organization should get the funding...
One of the jurors recommended another organization...
But I managed to settle it without any issues.
Yes, all right.

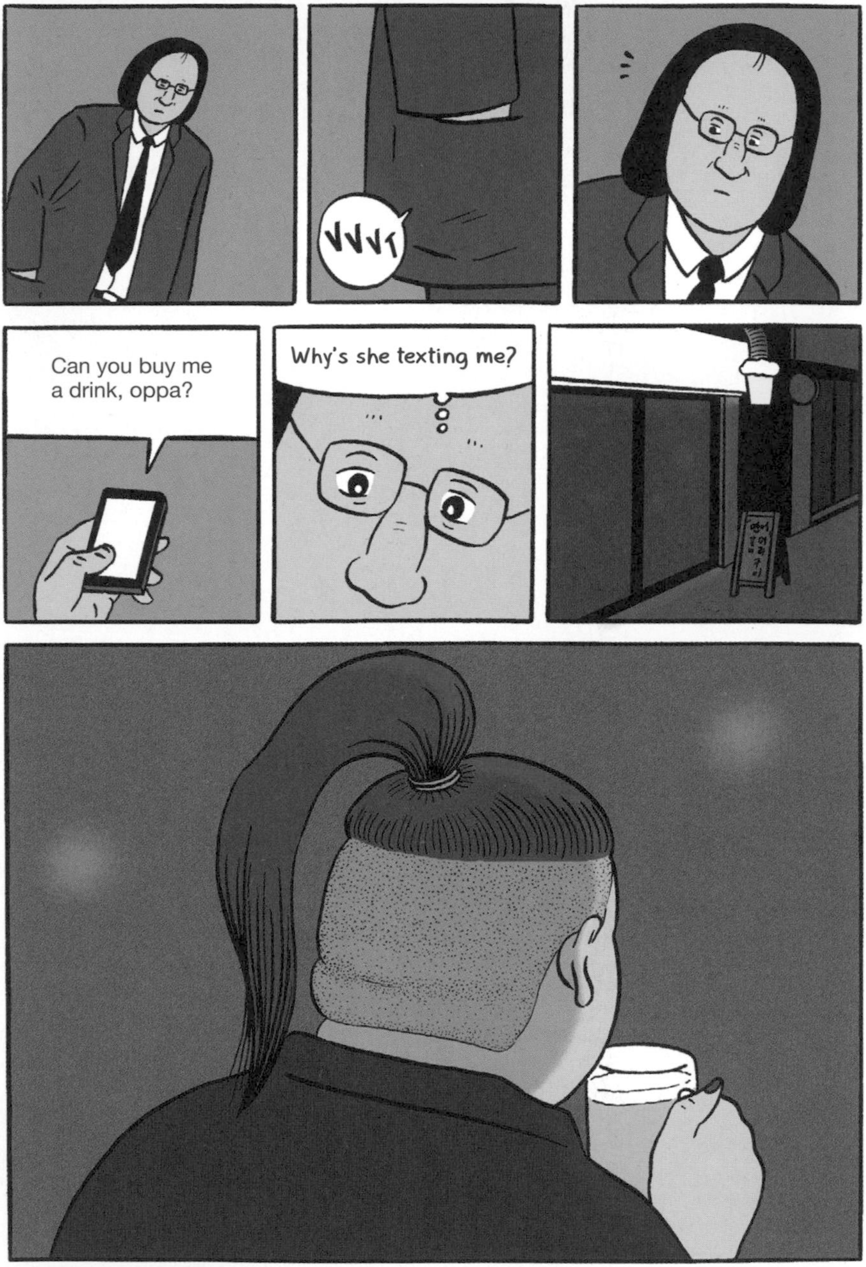
VVVT
Can you buy me a drink, oppa?
Why's she texting me?

THWARTED FEELINGS

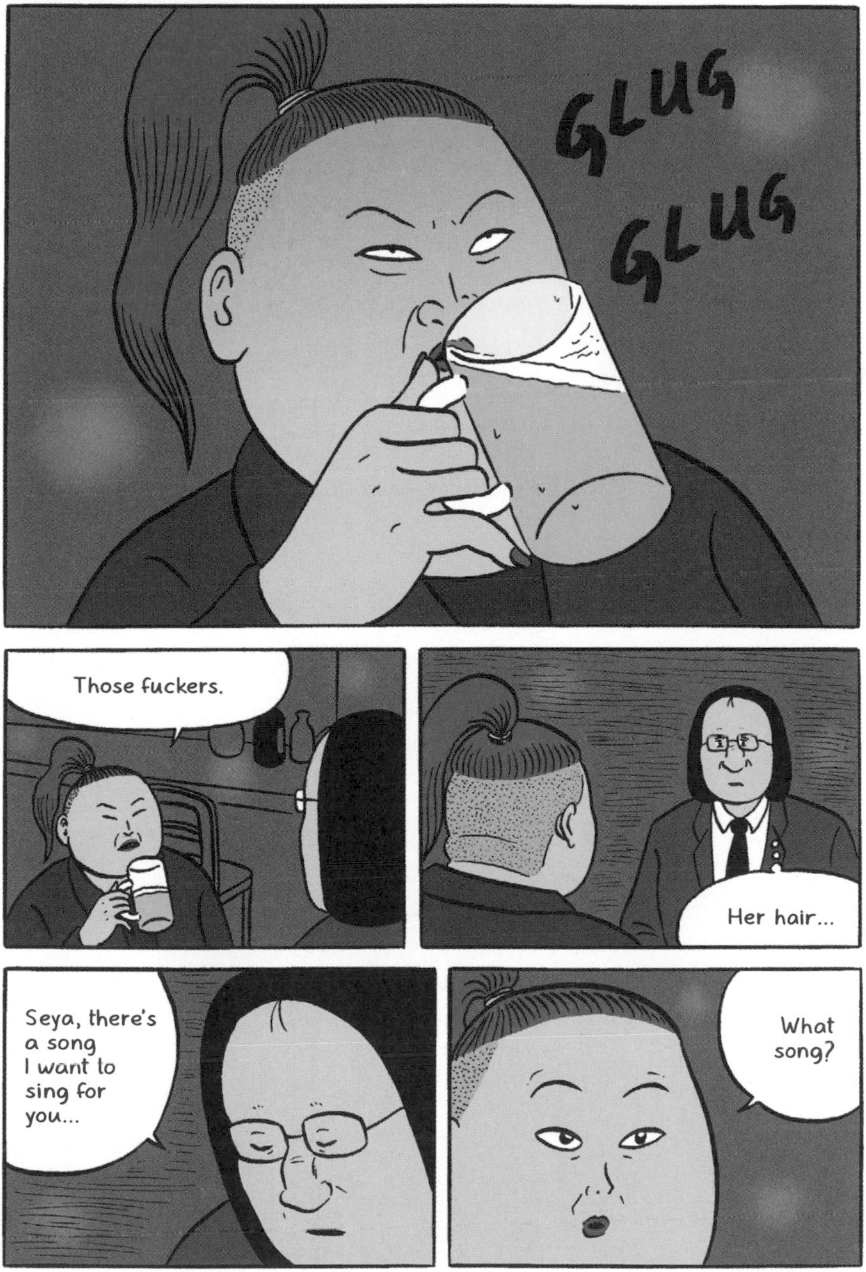
GLUG
GLUG
Those fuckers.
Her hair...
Seya, there's a song I want to sing for you...
What song?

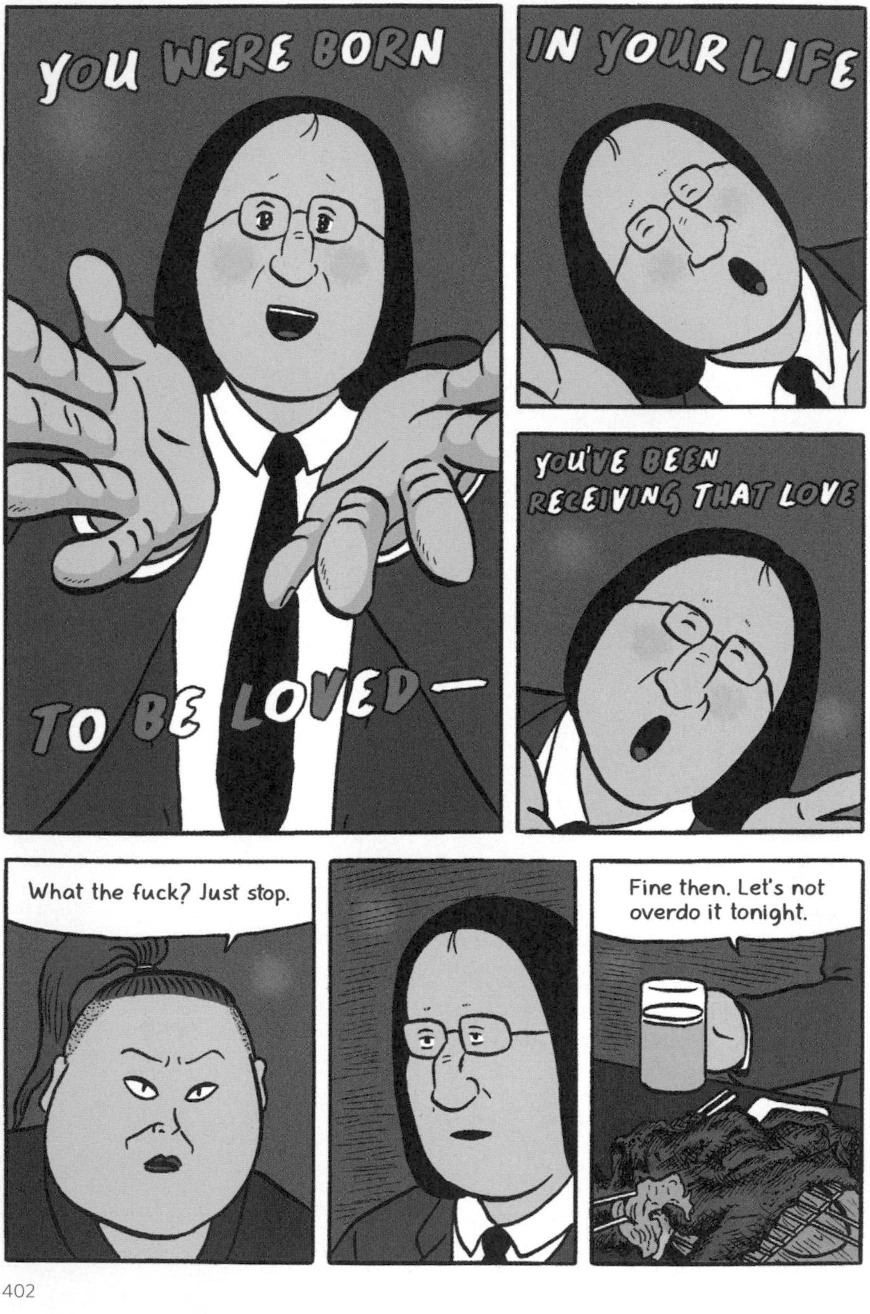
YOU WERE BORN
TO BE LOVED—
IN YOUR LIFE
YOU'VE BEEN RECEIVING THAT LOVE
What the fuck? Just stop.
Fine then. Let's not overdo it tonight.

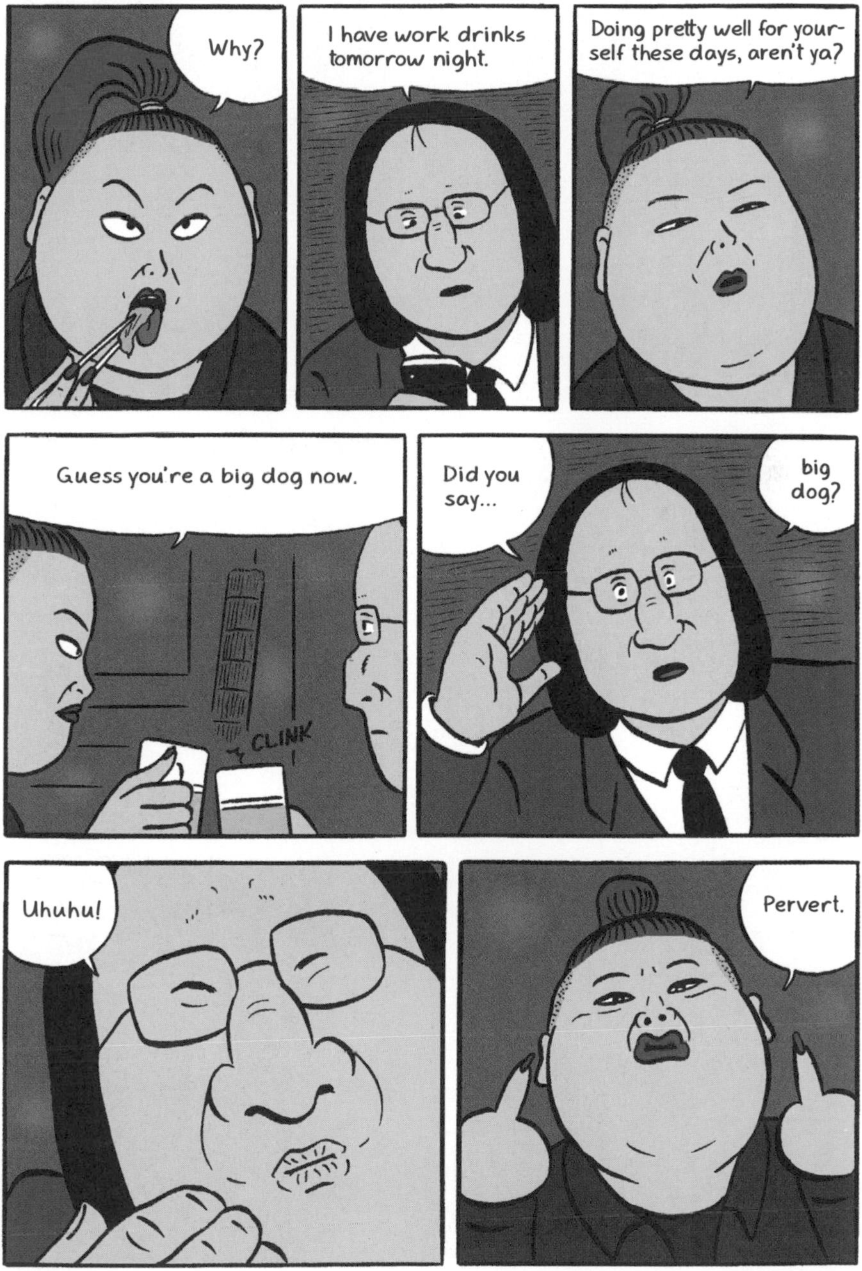
Why?
I have work drinks tomorrow night.
Doing pretty well for your-self these days, aren't ya?
Guess you're a big dog now.
CLINK
Did you say...
big dog?
Uhuhu!
Pervert.

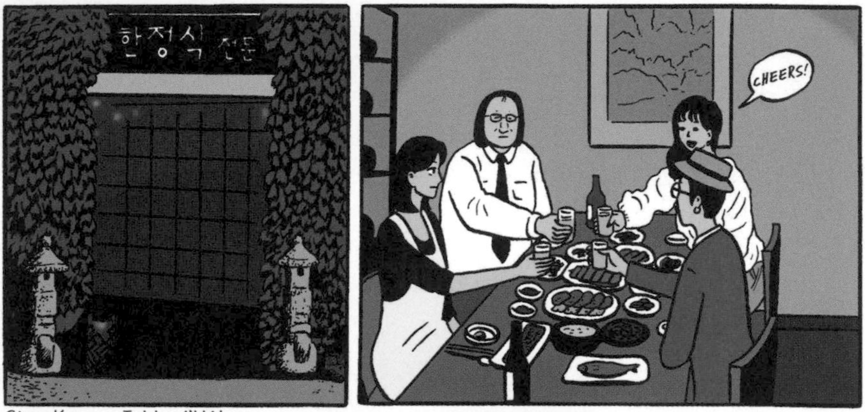
한정식 전문
CHEERS!

Sign: Korean Table d'Hôte

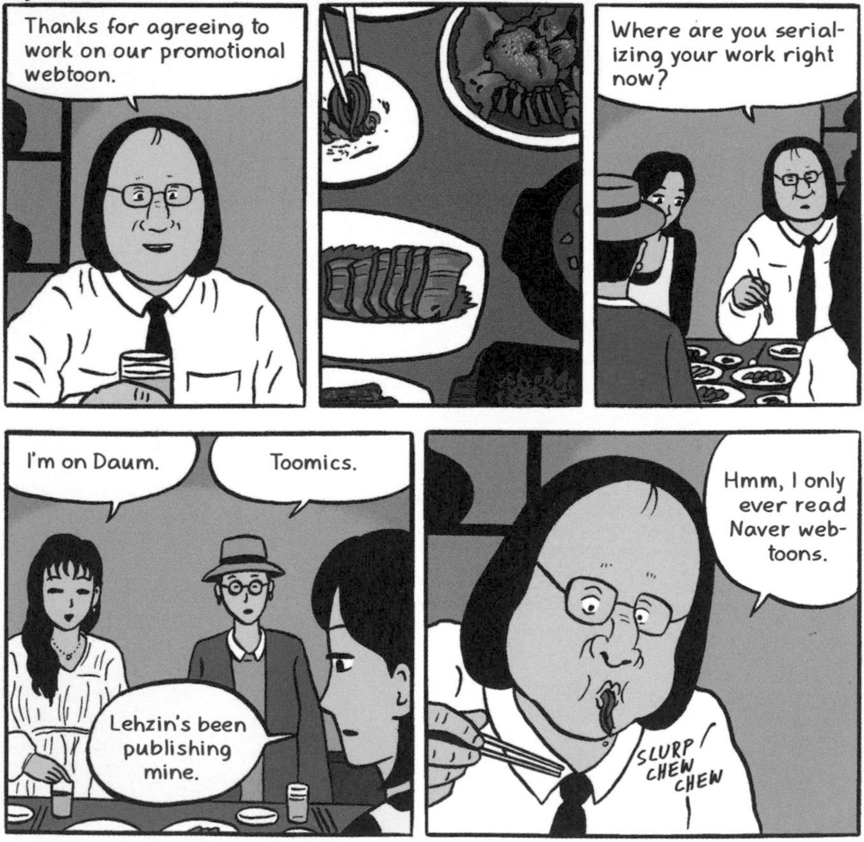
Thanks for agreeing to work on our promotional webtoon.
Where are you serializing your work right now?
I'm on Daum.
Toomics.
Lehzin's been publishing mine.
Hmm, I only ever read Naver webtoons.
SLURP CHEW CHEW

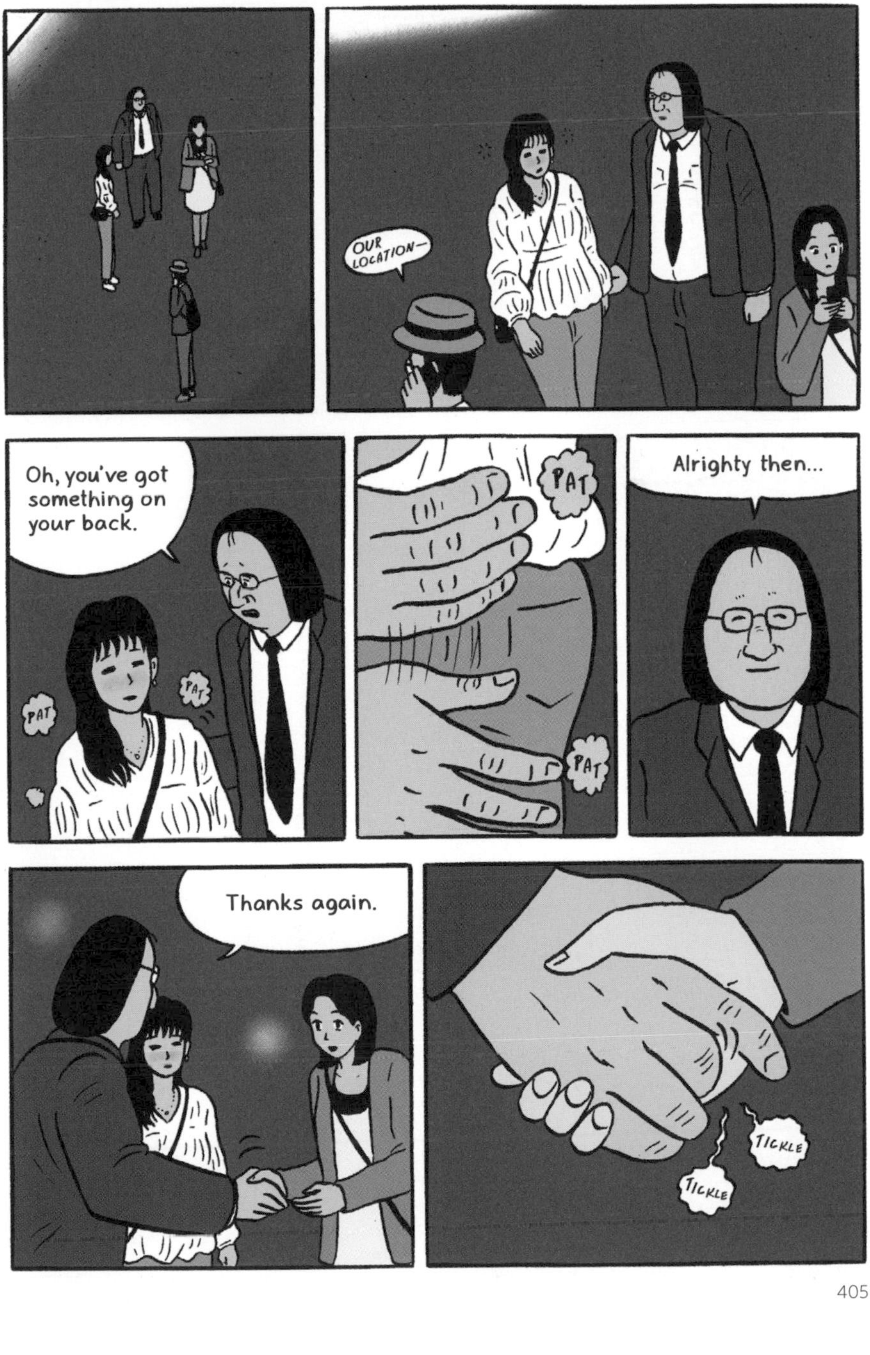
OUR LOCATION—
Oh, you've got something on your back.
PAT
PAT
PAT
PAT
Alrighty then...
Thanks again.
TICKLE
TICKLE

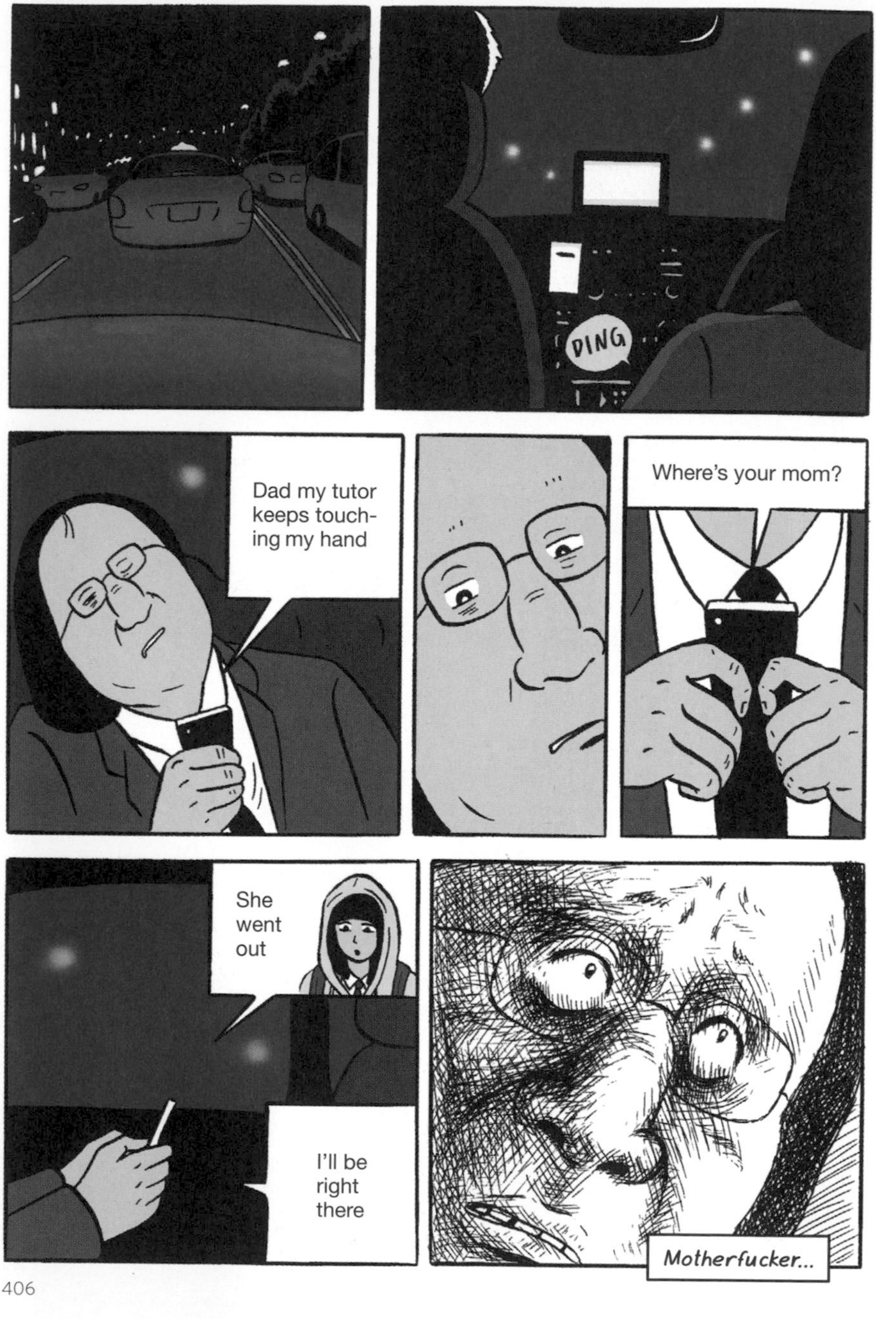
DING
Dad my tutor keeps touching my hand
Where's your mom?
She went out
I'll be right there
Motherfucker...

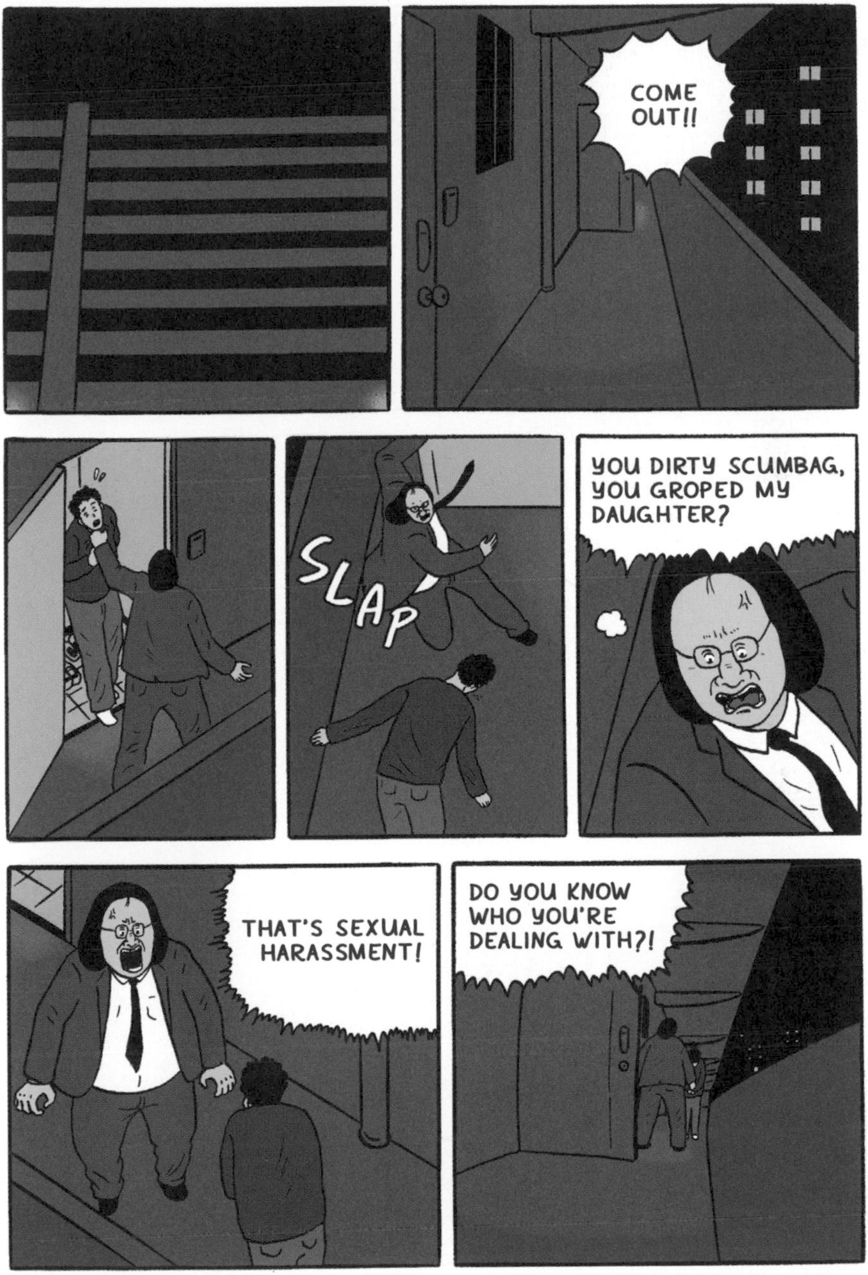
COME OUT!!
SLAP
YOU DIRTY SCUMBAG, YOU GROPED MY DAUGHTER?
THAT'S SEXUAL HARASSMENT!
DO YOU KNOW WHO YOU'RE DEALING WITH?!

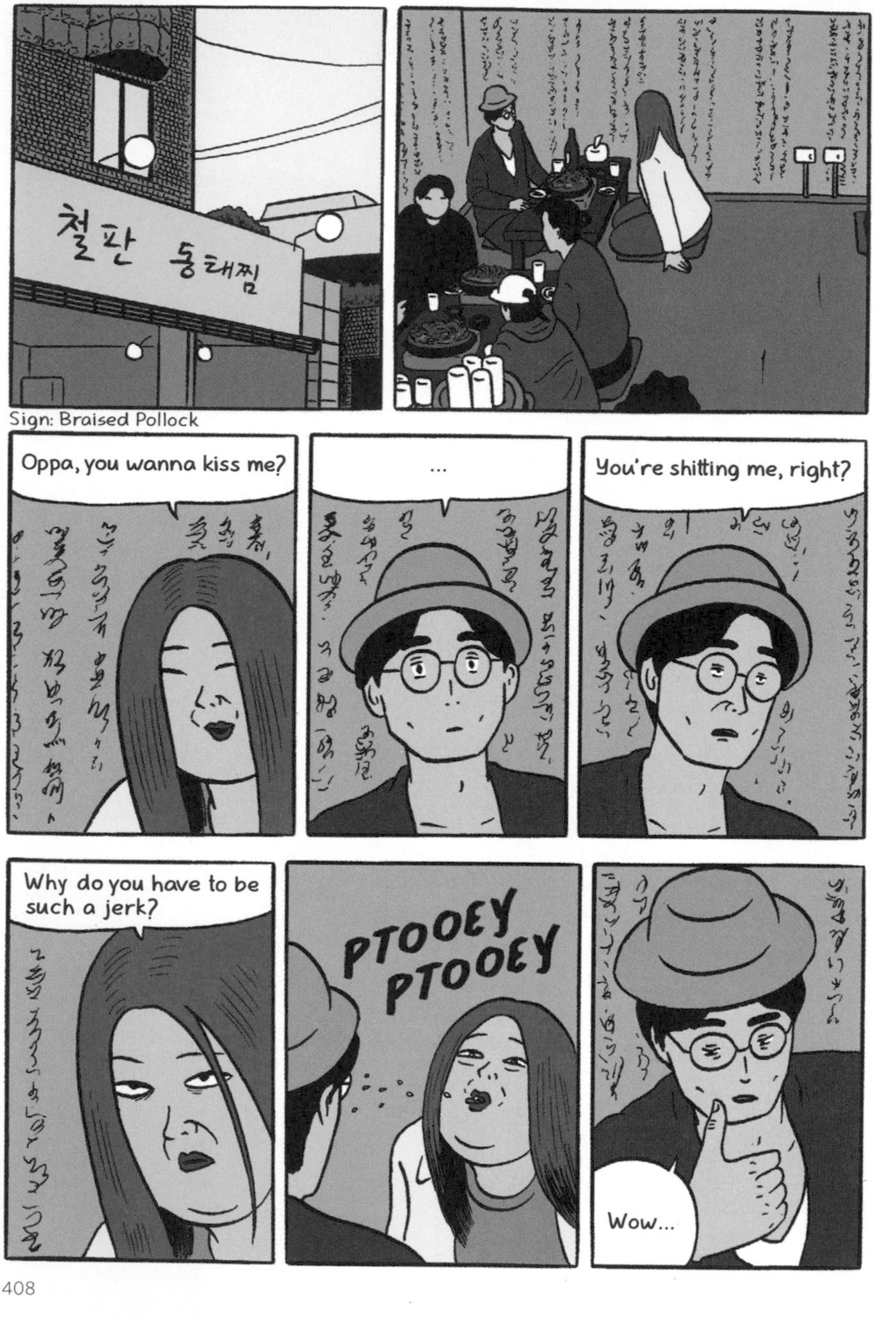
철판 동태찜
Sign: Braised Pollock
Oppa, you wanna kiss me?
...
You're shitting me, right?
Why do you have to be such a jerk?
PTOOEY PTOOEY
Wow...

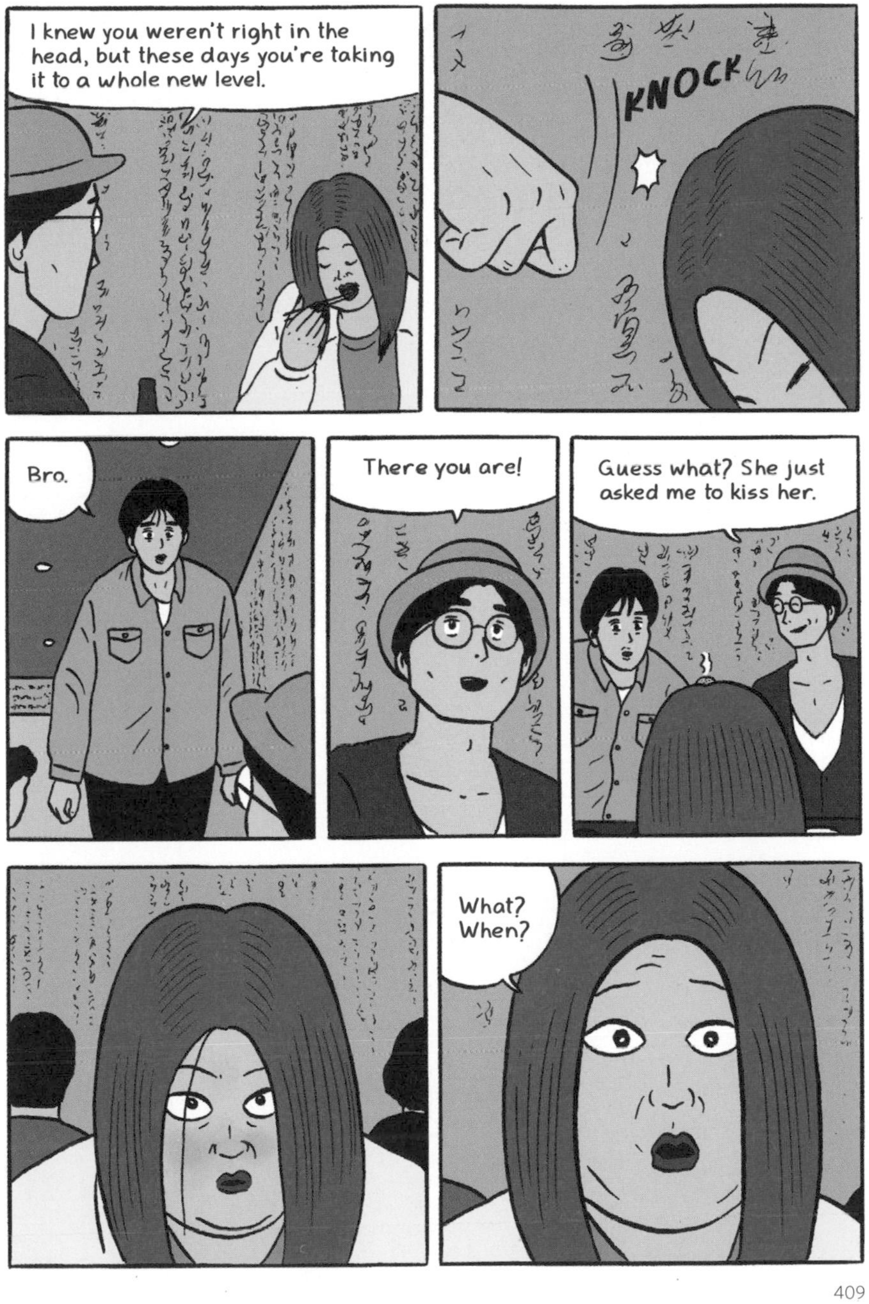
I knew you weren't right in the head, but these days you're taking it to a whole new level.
KNOCK
Bro.
There you are!
Guess what? She just asked me to kiss her.
What? When?

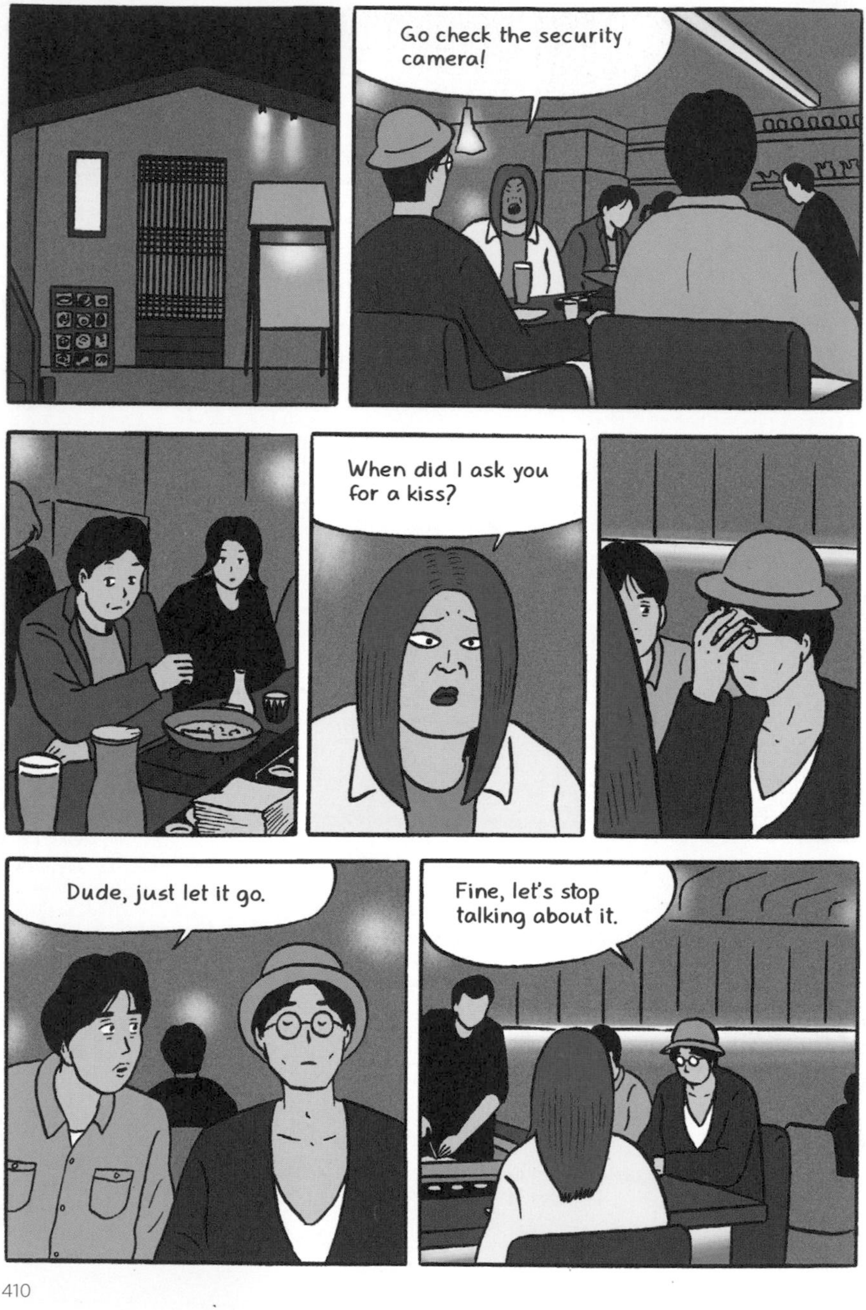
Go check the security camera!
When did I ask you for a kiss?
Dude, just let it go.
Fine, let's stop talking about it.

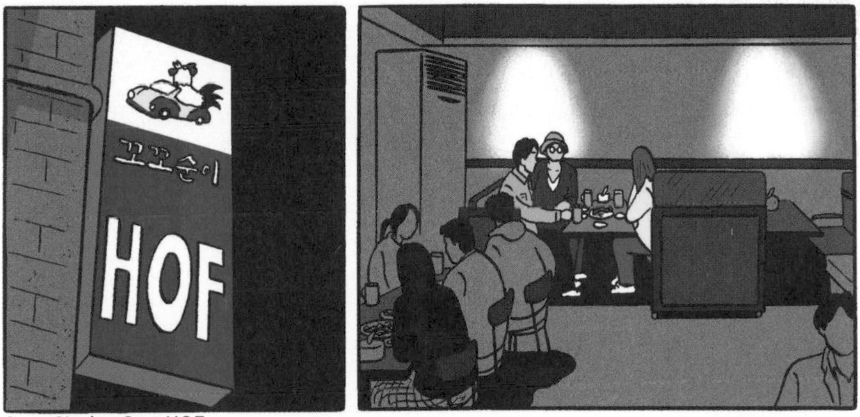
꼬꼬순이
HOF
Sign: Chickie Suni HOF

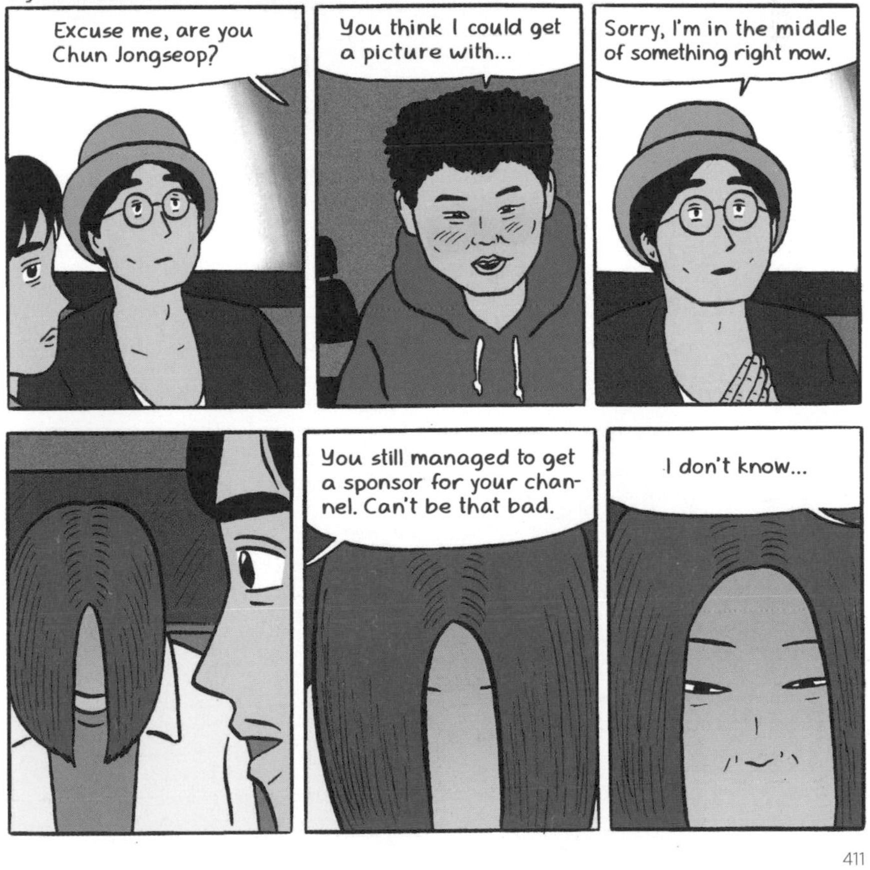
Excuse me, are you Chun Jongseop?
You think I could get a picture with...
Sorry, I'm in the middle of something right now.
You still managed to get a sponsor for your chan-nel. Can't be that bad.
I don't know...

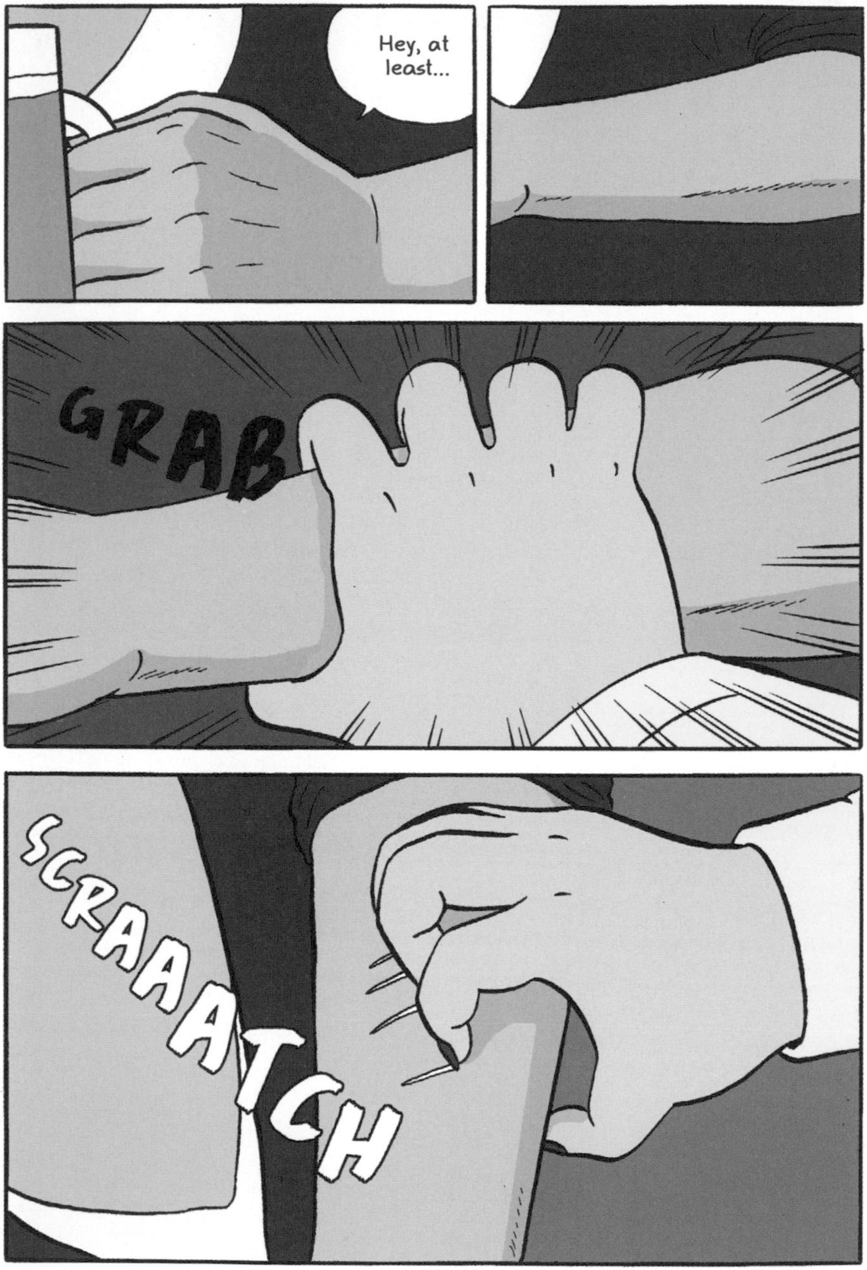
Hey, at least...
GRAB
SCRAAATCH

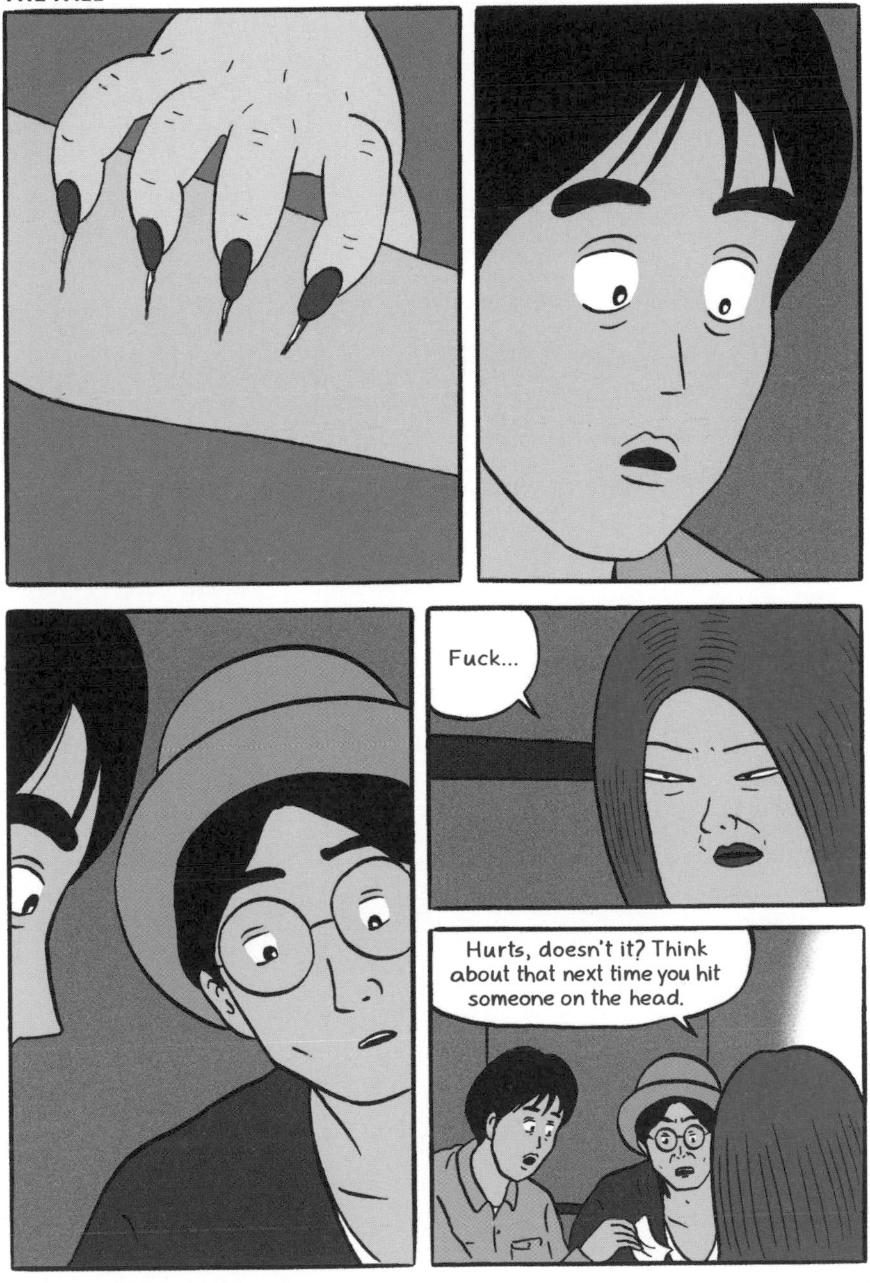
Fuck...
Hurts, doesn't it? Think about that next time you hit someone on the head.

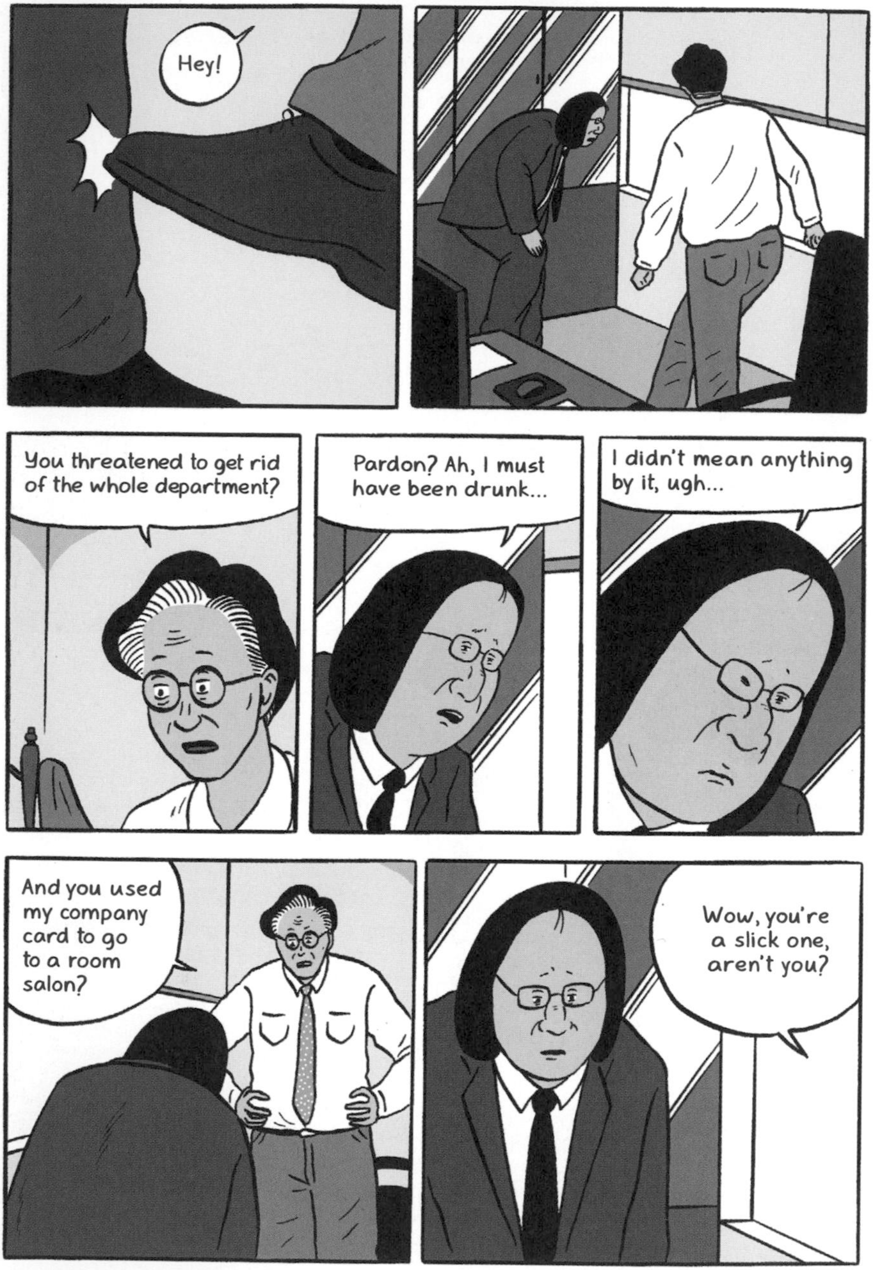

Hey!
You threatened to get rid of the whole department?
Pardon? Ah, I must have been drunk...
I didn't mean anything by it, ugh...
And you used my company card to go to a room salon?
Wow, you're a slick one, aren't you?

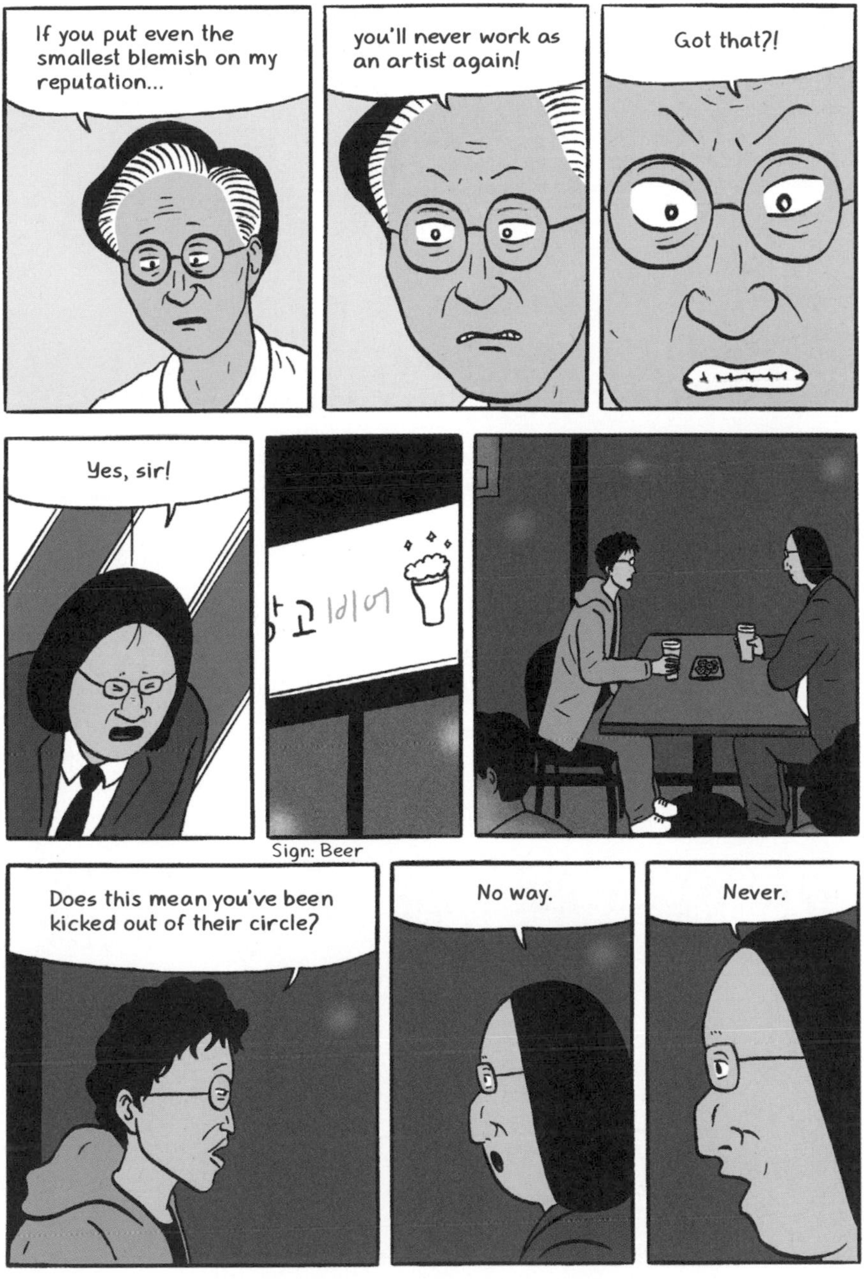
If you put even the smallest blemish on my reputation...
you'll never work as an artist again!
Got that?!
Yes, sir!
Does this mean you've been kicked out of their circle?
No way.
Never.

Sign: Beer

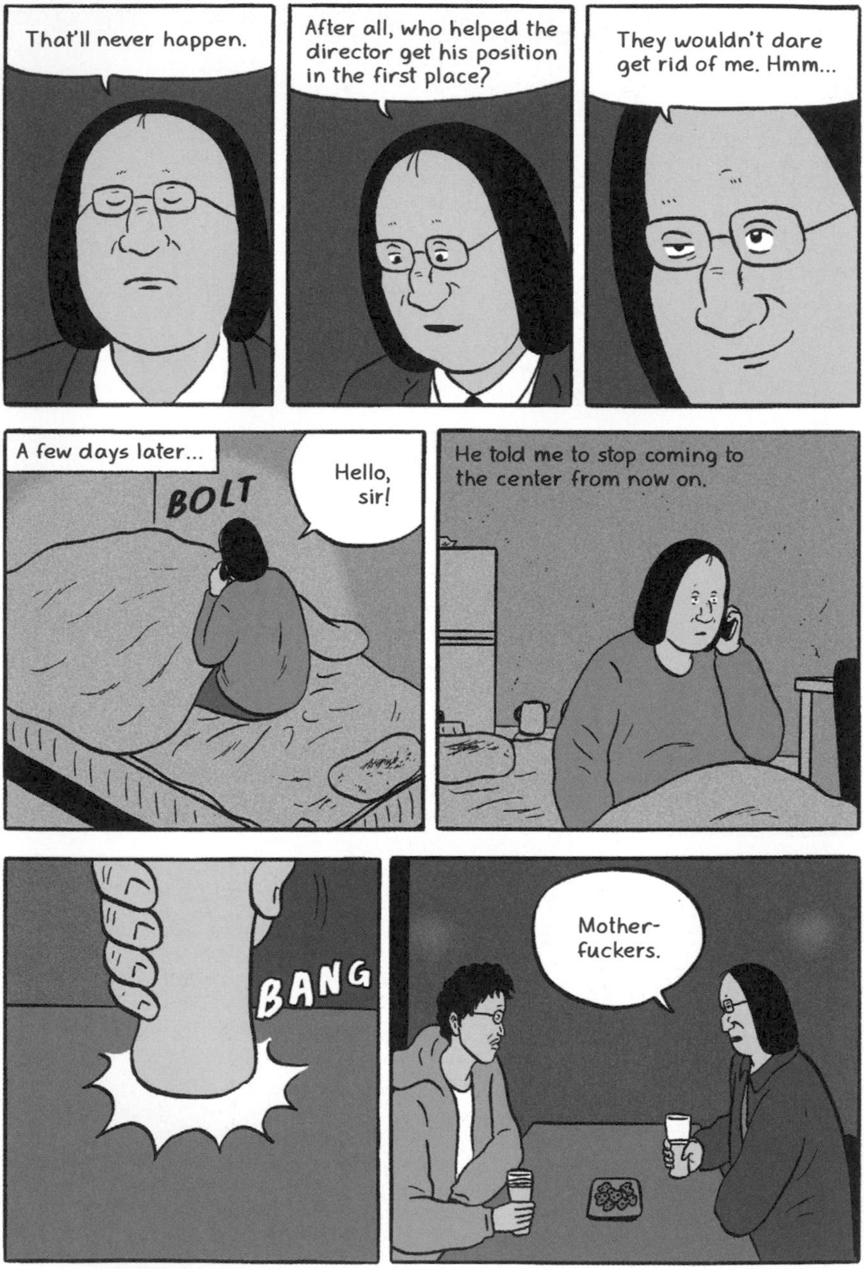
That'll never happen.
After all, who helped the director get his position in the first place?
They wouldn't dare get rid of me. Hmm...
A few days later...
BOLT
Hello, sir!
He told me to stop coming to the center from now on.
BANG
Mother-fuckers.

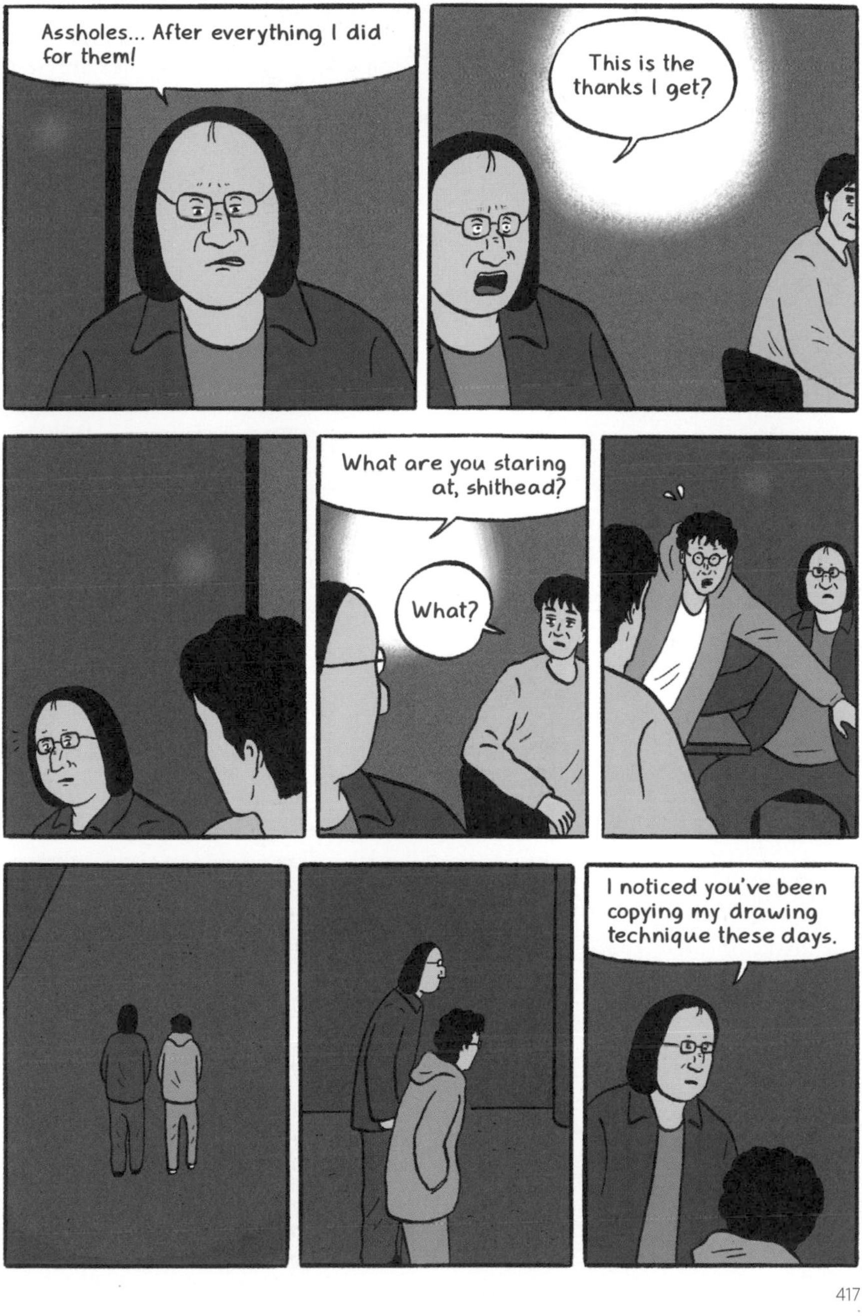
Assholes... After everything I did for them!
This is the thanks I get?
What are you staring at, shithead?
What?
I noticed you've been copying my drawing technique these days.

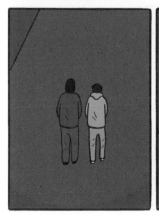

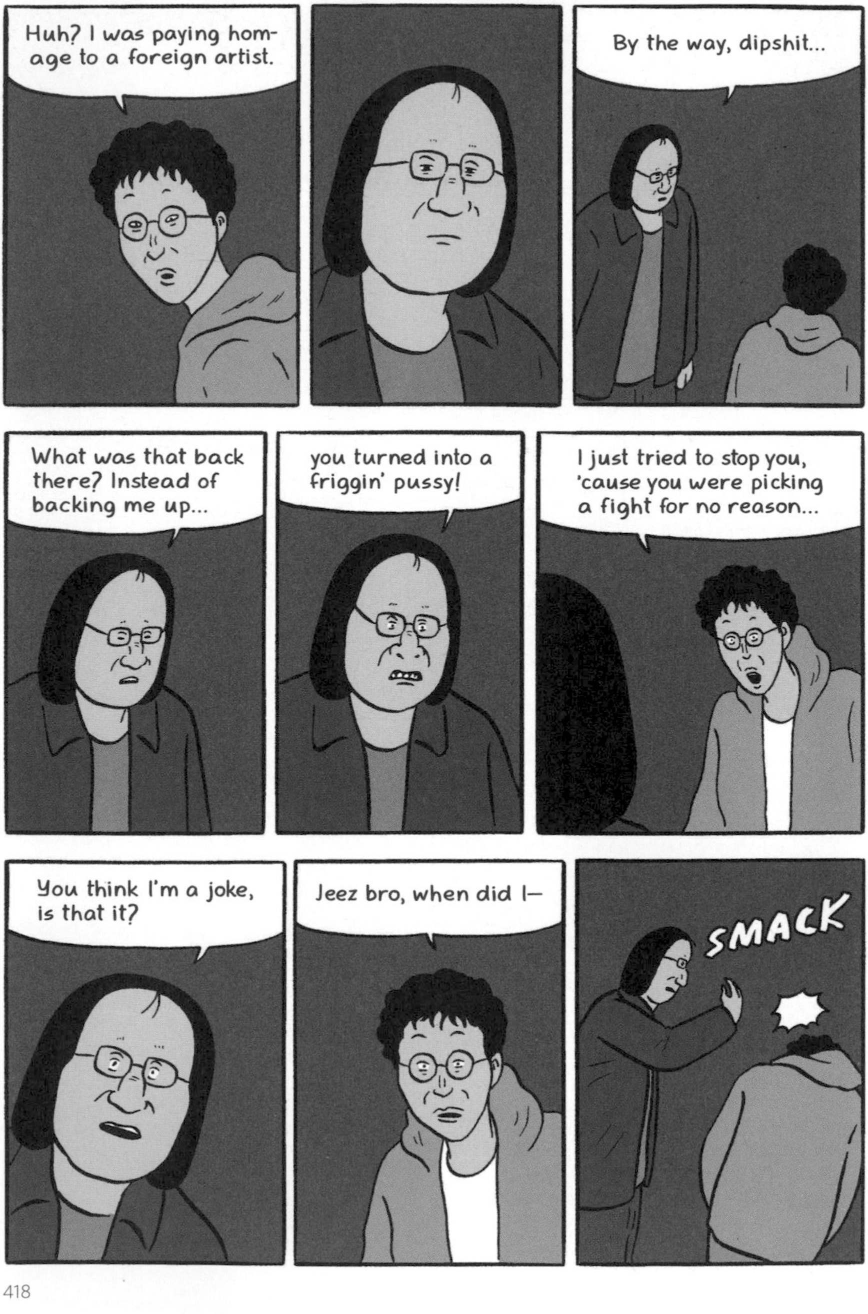
Huh? I was paying hom-age to a foreign artist.
By the way, dipshit...
What was that back there? Instead of backing me up...
you turned into a friggin' pussy!
I just tried to stop you, 'cause you were picking a fight for no reason...
You think I'm a joke, is that it?
Jeez bro, when did I—
SMACK

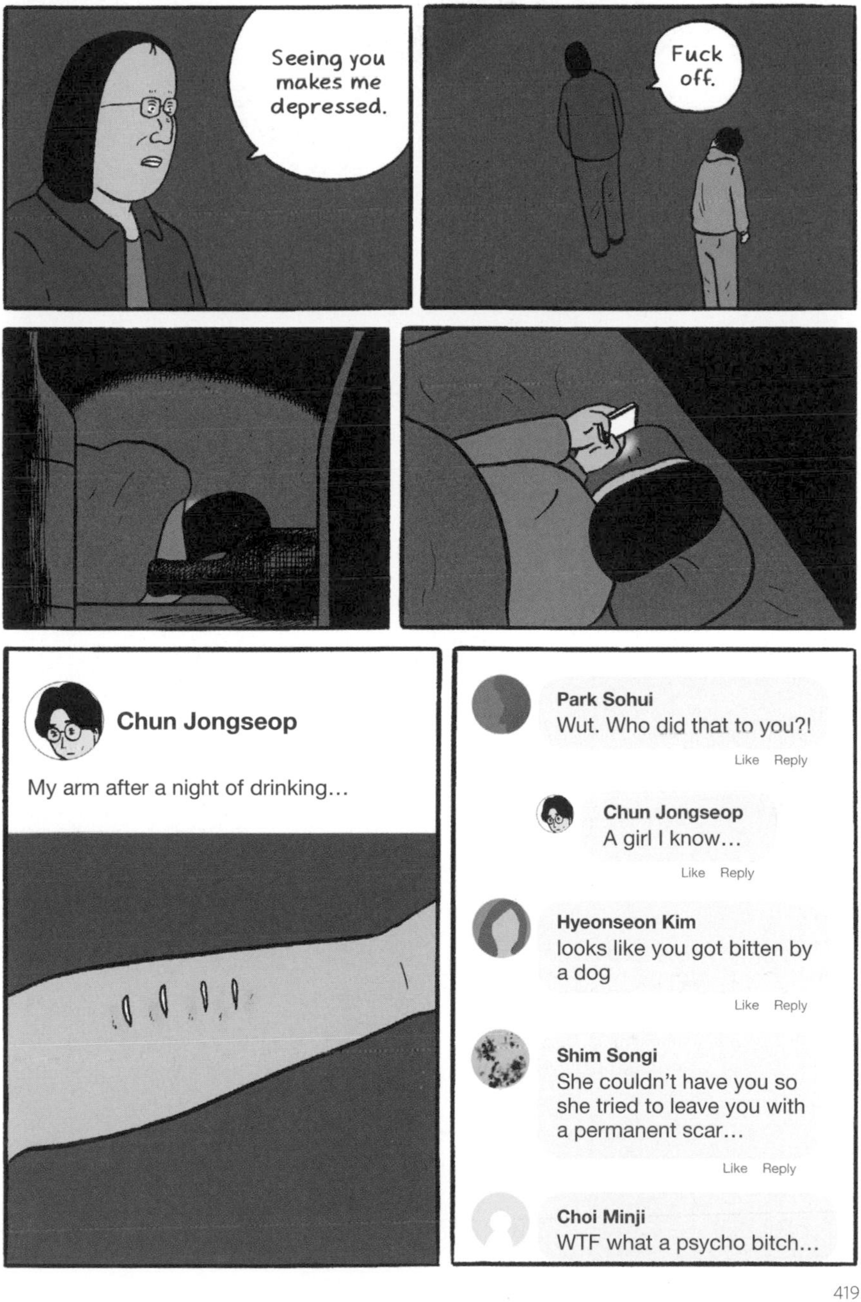
Seeing you makes me depressed.
Fuck off.
Chun Jongseop
My arm after a night of drinking...
Park Sohui
Wut. Who did that to you?!
Like Reply
Chun Jongseop
A girl I know...
Like Reply
Hyeonseon Kim
looks like you got bitten by a dog
Like Reply
Shim Songi
She couldn't have you so she tried to leave you with a permanent scar...
Like Reply
Choi Minji
WTF what a psycho bitch...

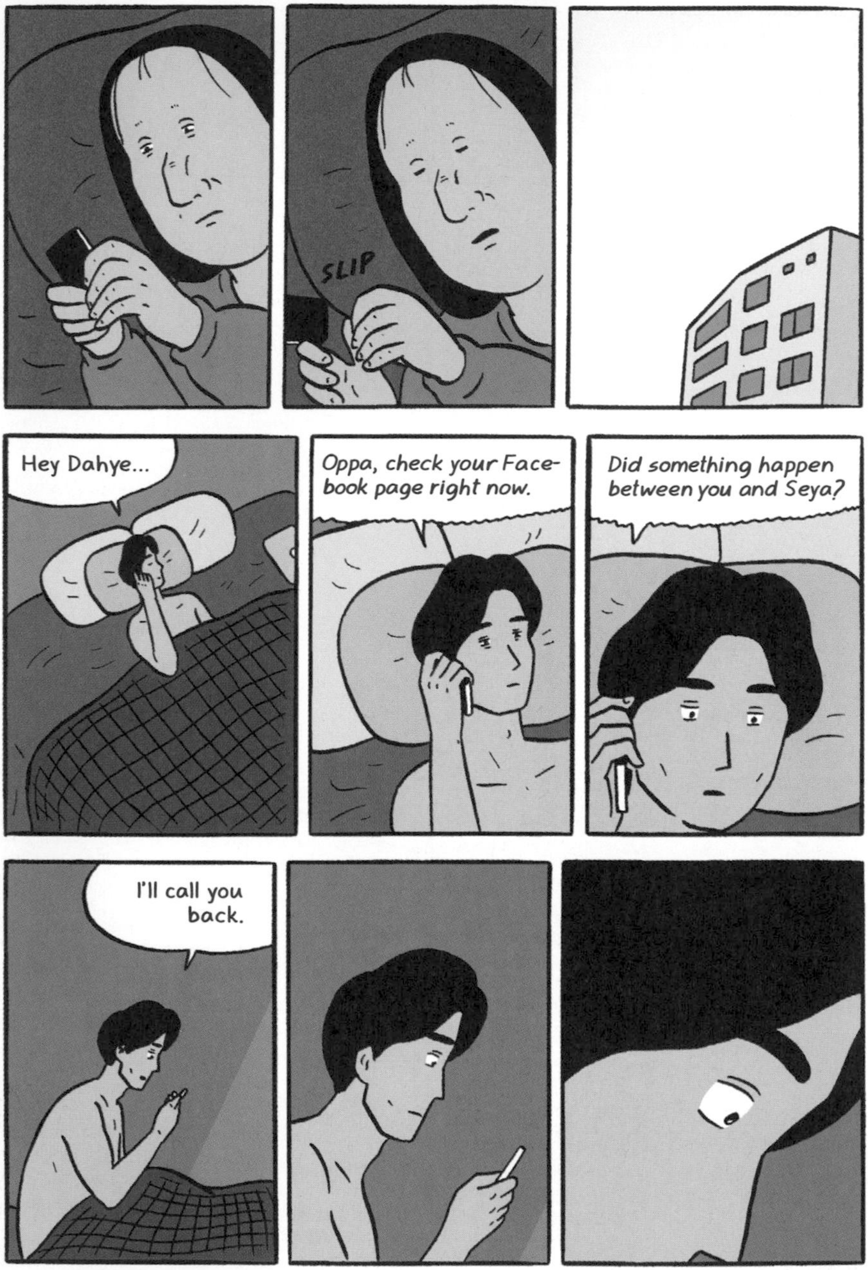
SLIP
Hey Dahye...
Oppa, check your Facebook page right now.
Did something happen between you and Seya?
I'll call you back.

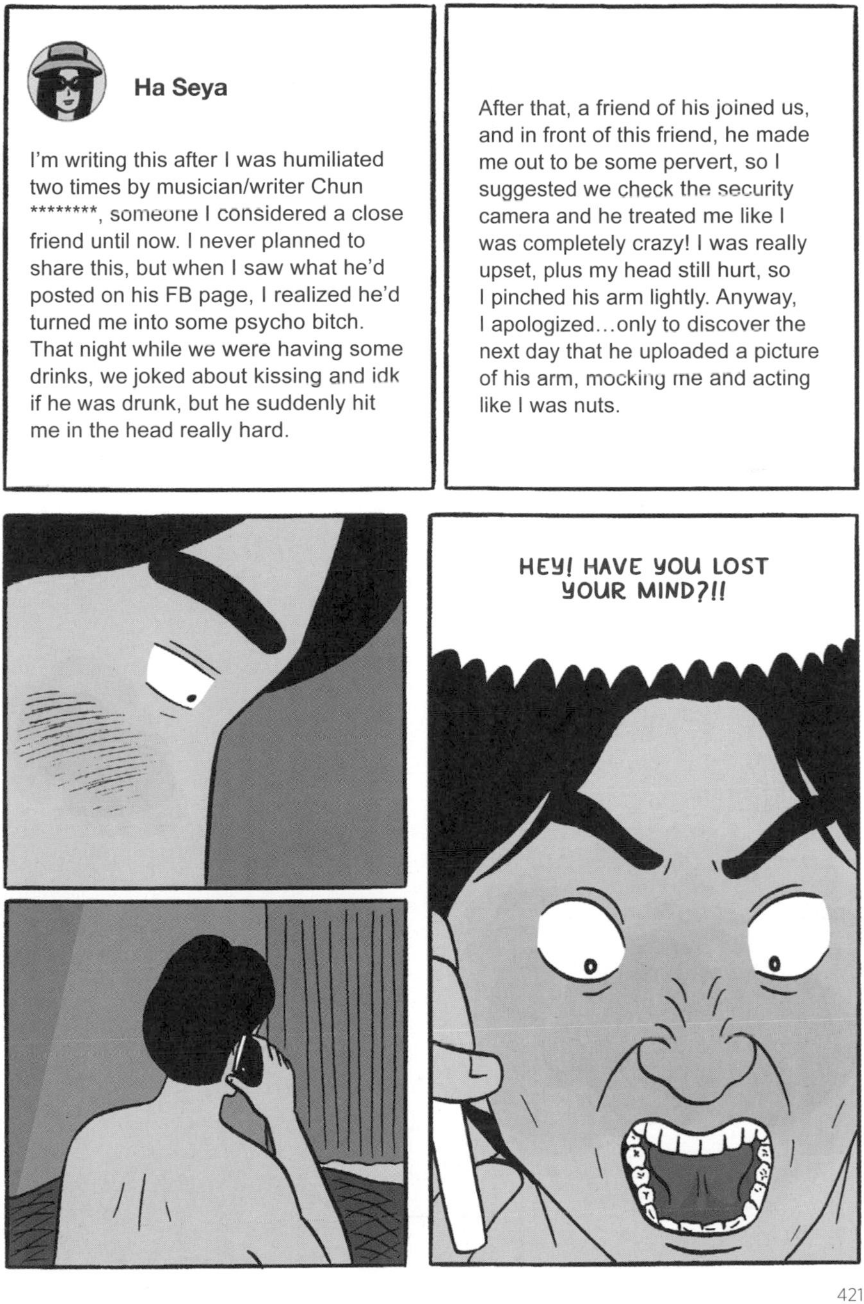
Ha Seya
I'm writing this after I was humiliated two times by musician/writer Chun ********, someone I considered a close friend until now. I never planned to share this, but when I saw what he'd posted on his FB page, I realized he'd turned me into some psycho bitch. That night while we were having some drinks, we joked about kissing and idk if he was drunk, but he suddenly hit me in the head really hard.
After that, a friend of his joined us, and in front of this friend, he made me out to be some pervert, so I suggested we check the security camera and he treated me like I was completely crazy! I was really upset, plus my head still hurt, so I pinched his arm lightly. Anyway, I apologized…only to discover the next day that he uploaded a picture of his arm, mocking me and acting like I was nuts.
HEY! HAVE YOU LOST YOUR MIND?!!

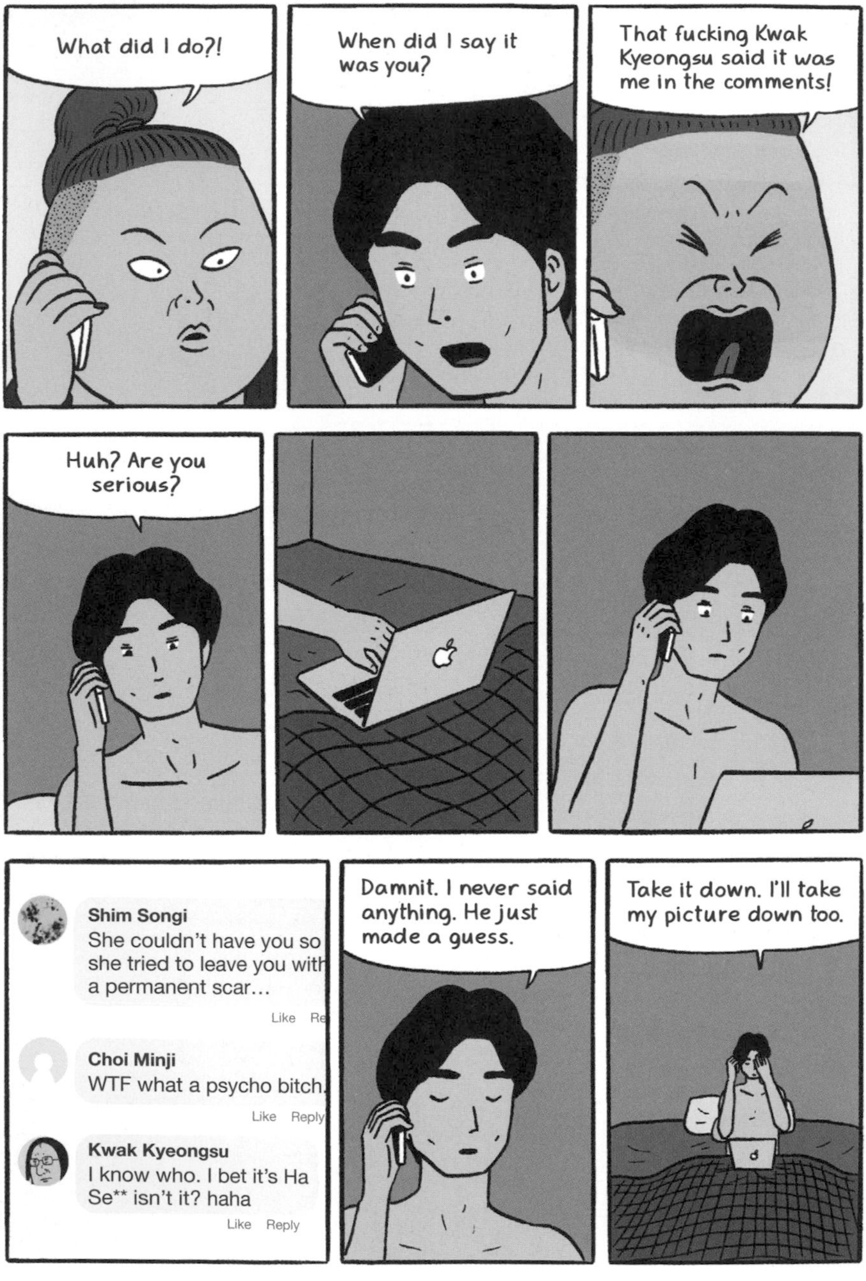
What did I do?!
When did I say it was you?
That fucking Kwak Kyeongsu said it was me in the comments!
Huh? Are you serious?
Shim Songi
She couldn't have you so she tried to leave you wit
a permanent scar...
Like
Choi Minji
WTF what a psycho bitch
Like Reply
Kwak Kyeongsu
I know who. I bet it's Ha Se** isn't it? haha
Like Reply
Damnit. I never said anything. He just made a guess.
Take it down. I'll take my picture down too.

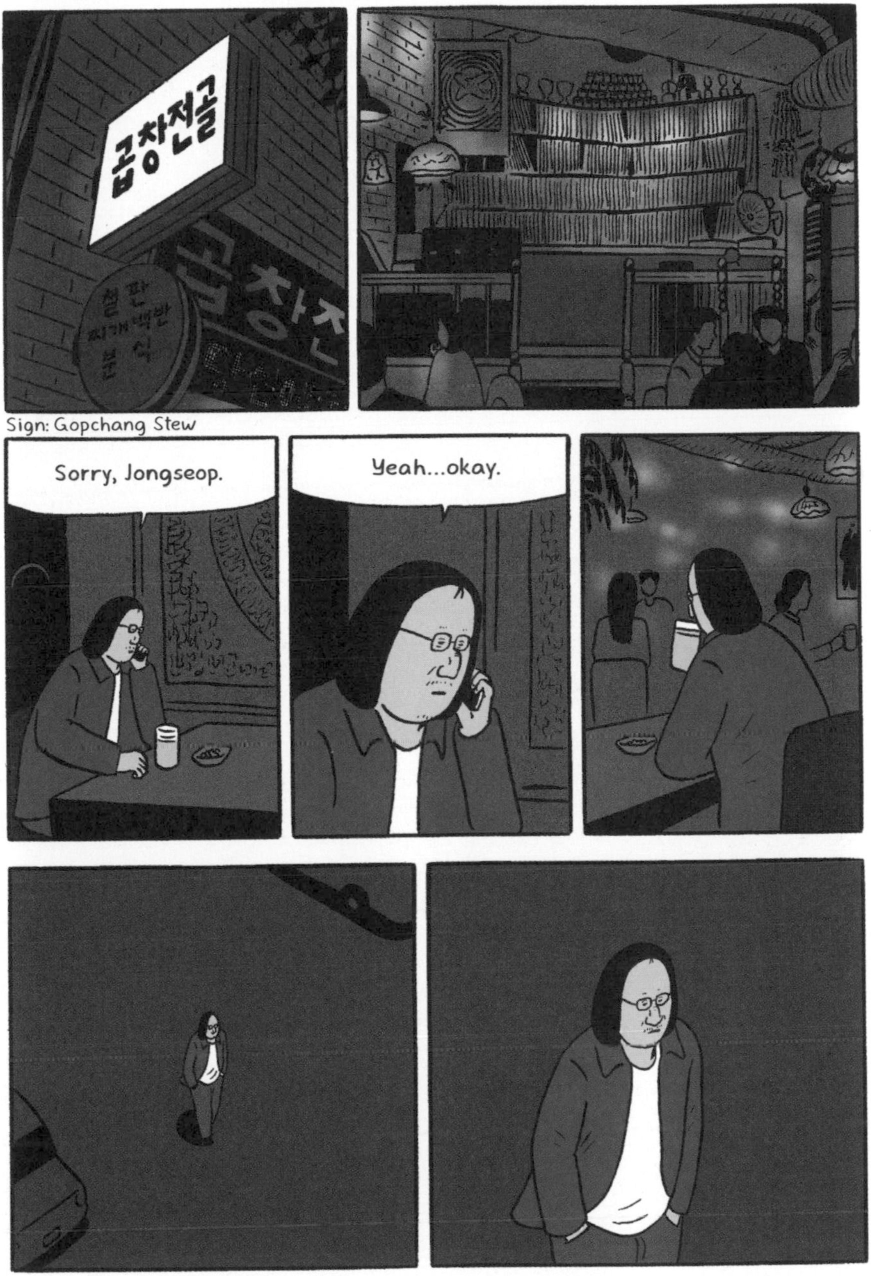
곱창전골
Sign: Gopchang Stew
Sorry, Jongseop.
Yeah...okay.

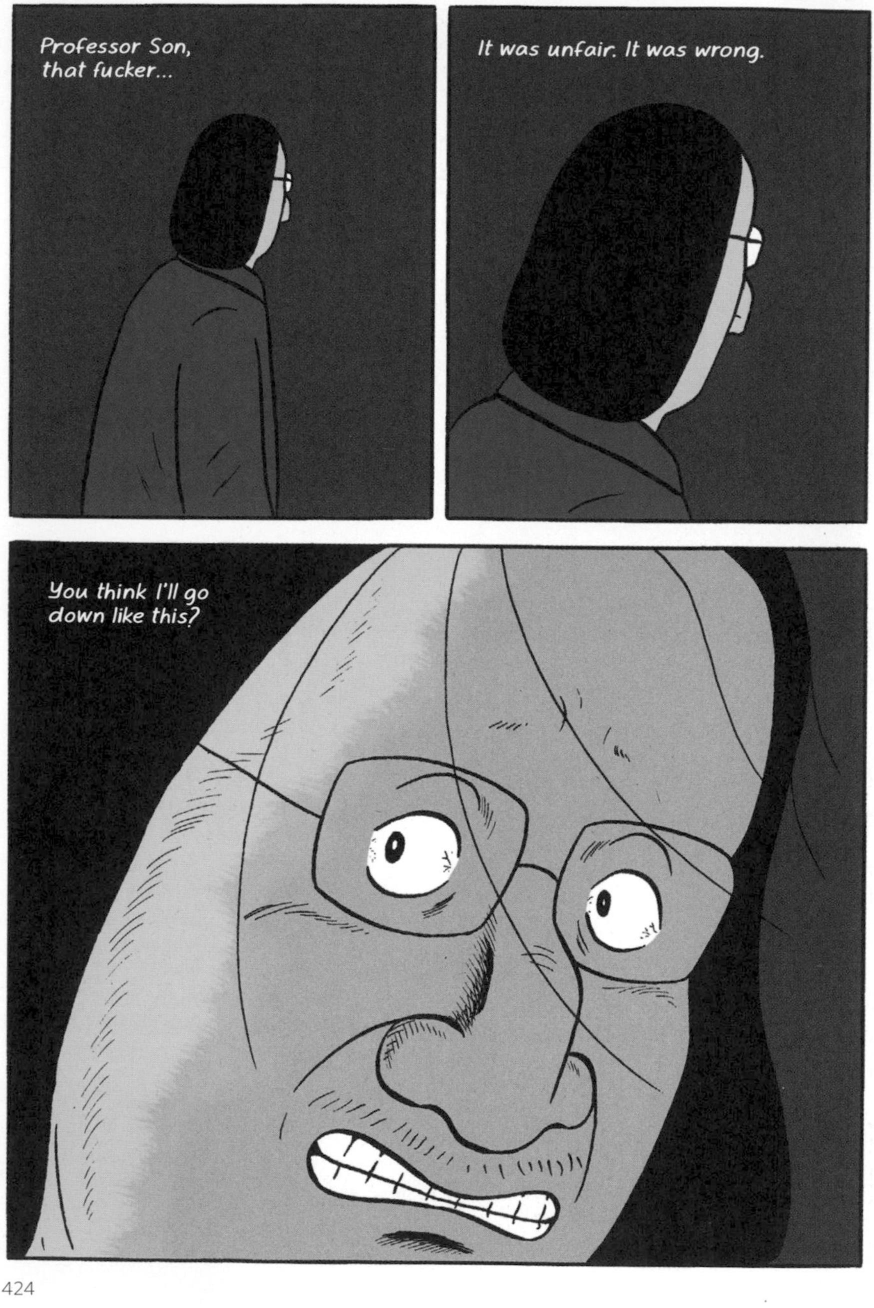
Professor Son, that fucker...
It was unfair. It was wrong.
You think I'll go down like this?

AUTHORITY

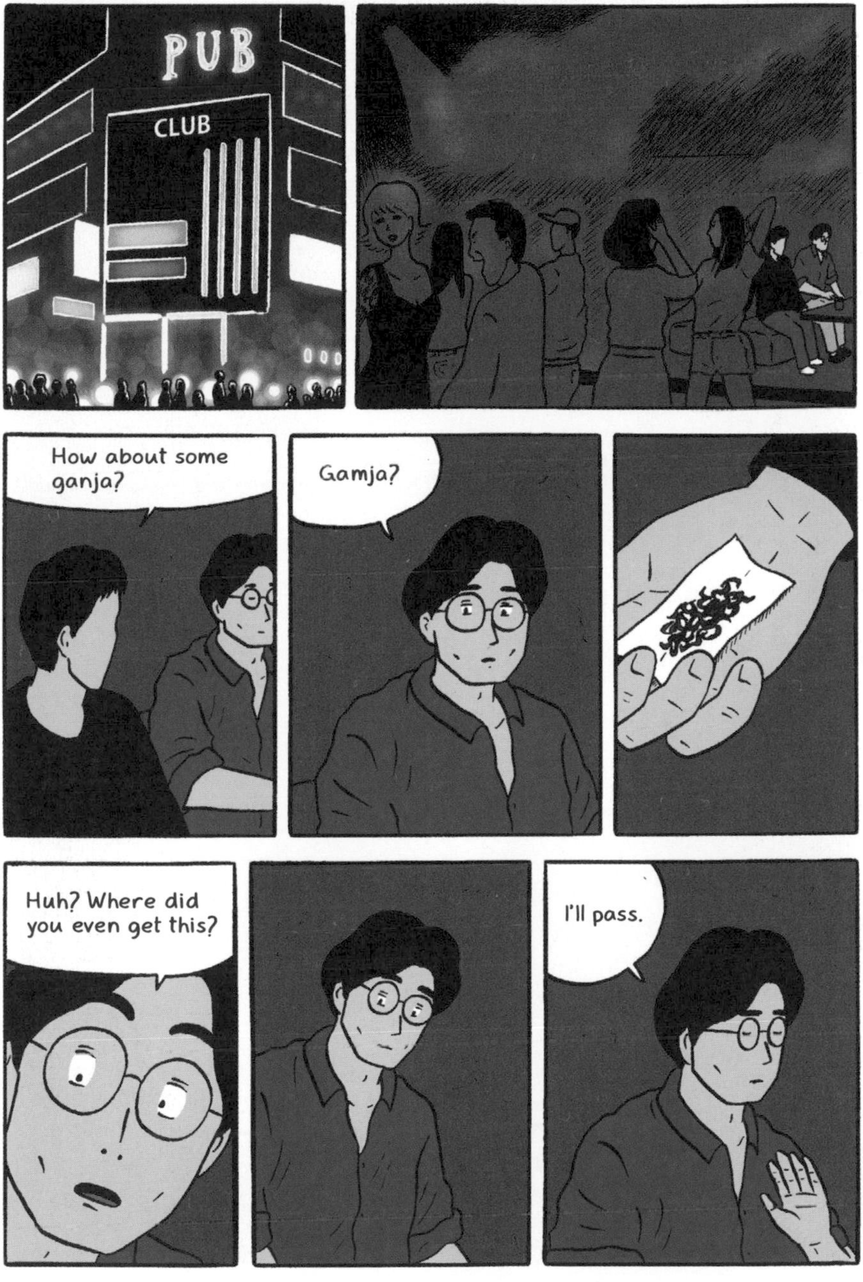
PUB
CLUB
How about some ganja?
Gamja?
Huh? Where did you even get this?
I'll pass.

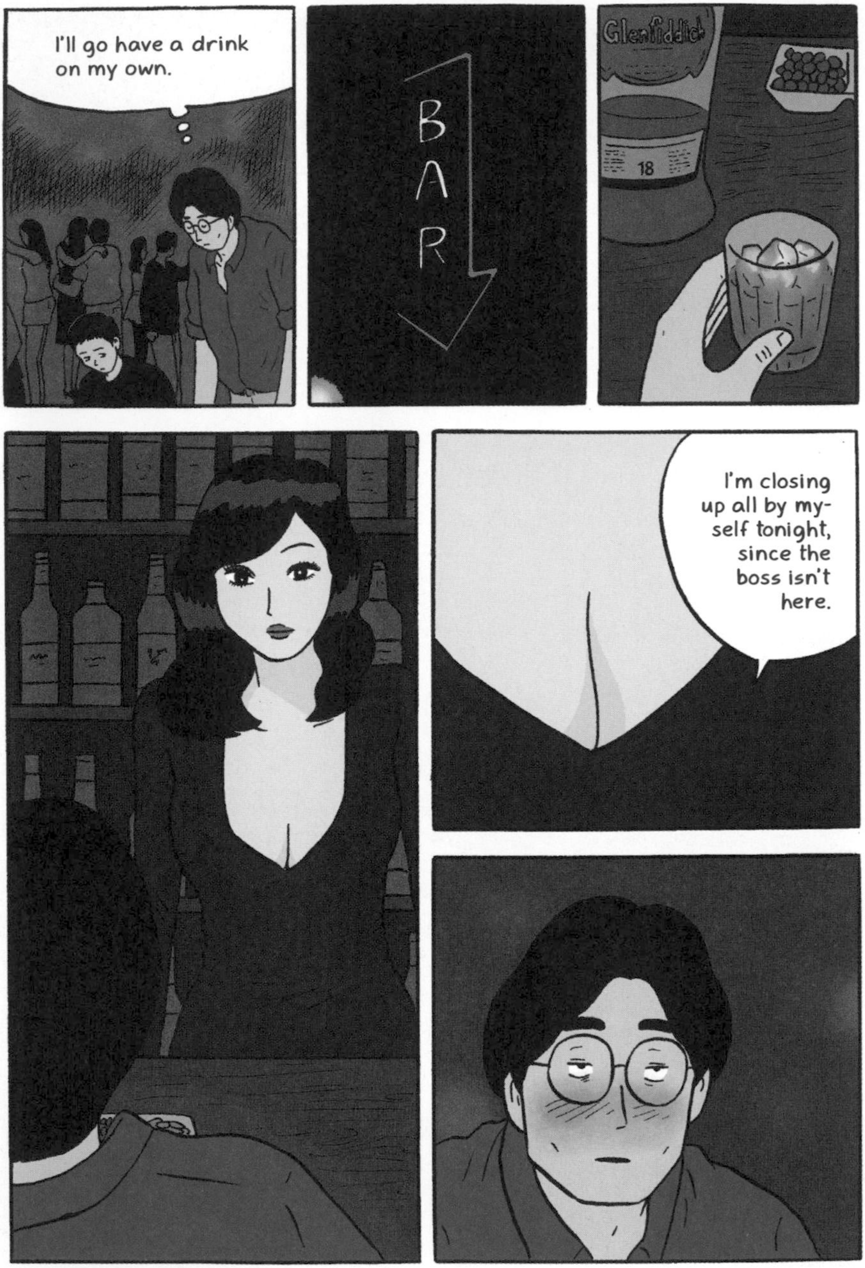

I'll go have a drink on my own.
BAR
Glenfiddich
18
I'm closing up all by myself tonight, since the boss isn't here.

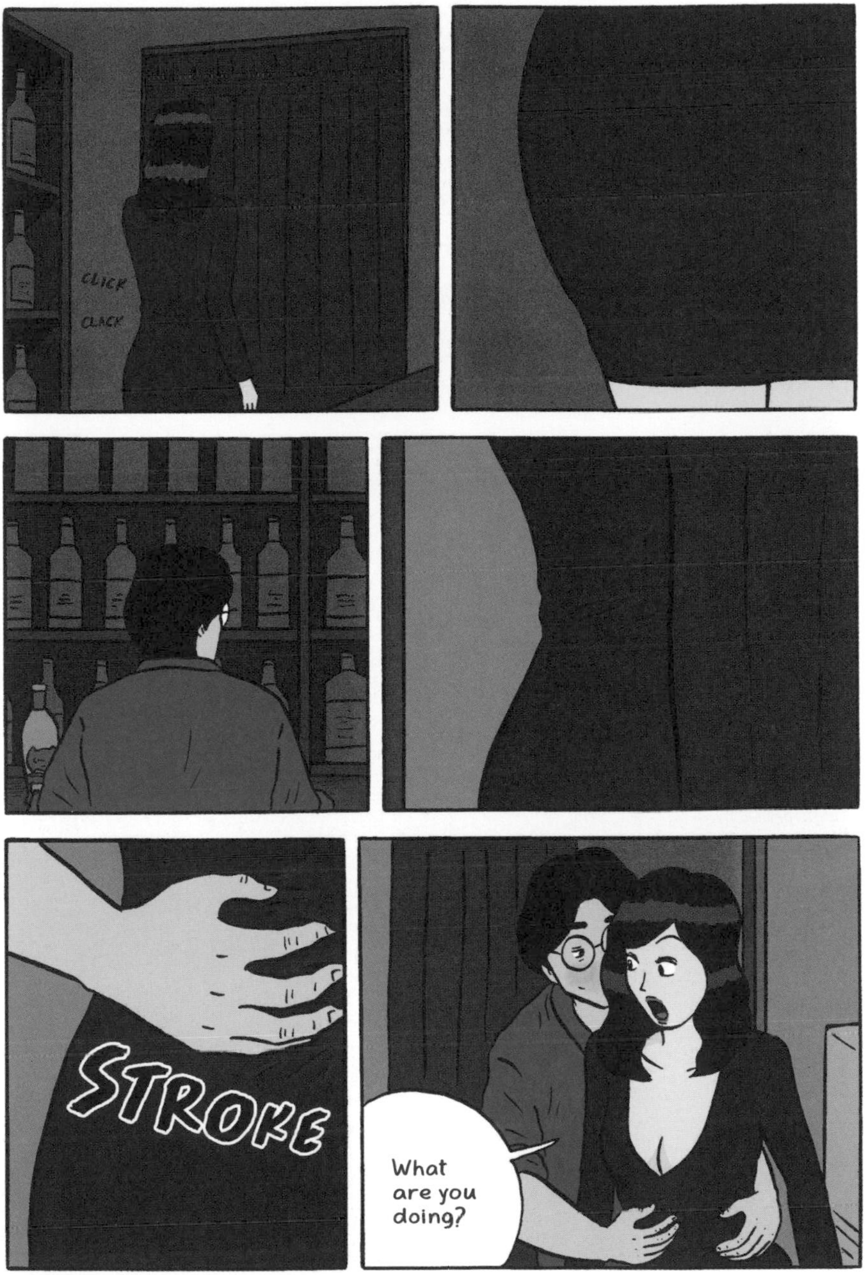
CLICK
CLACK
STROKE
What are you doing?

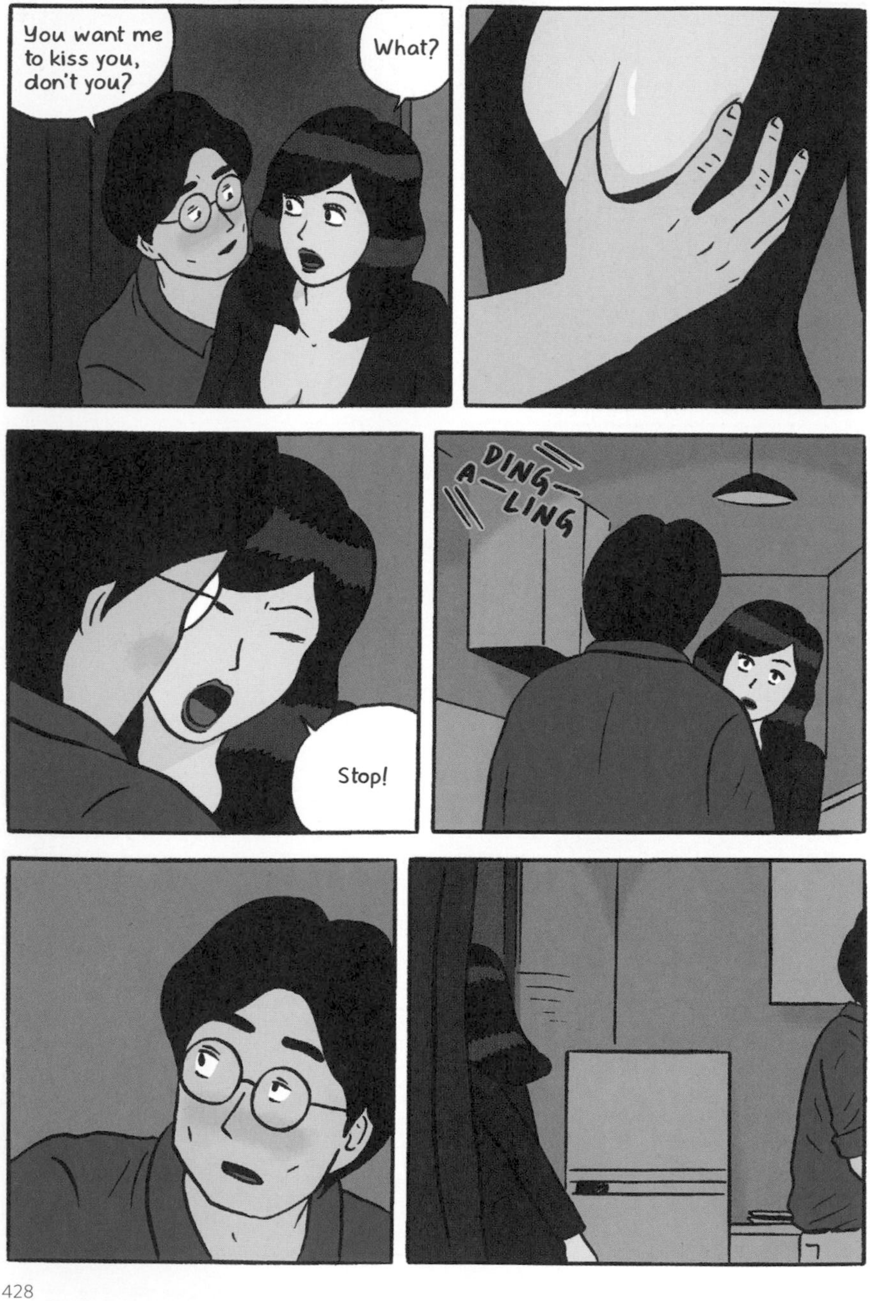
You want me to kiss you, don't you?
What?
Stop!
DING-A-LING

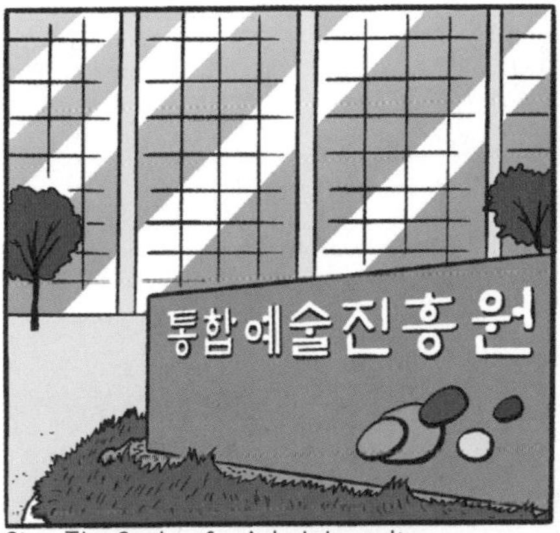
통합예술진흥원

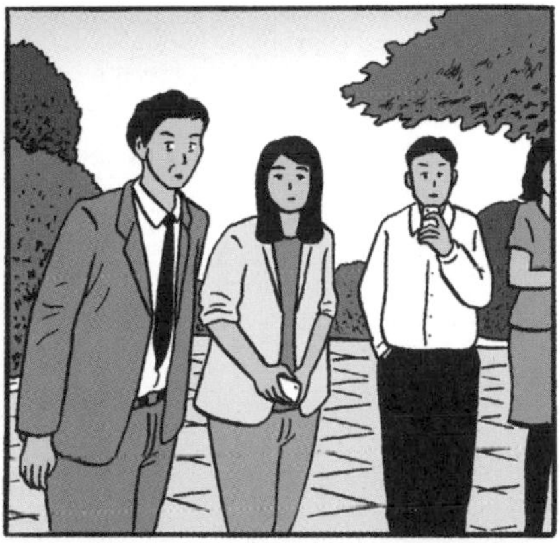

Sign: The Center for Arts Integration

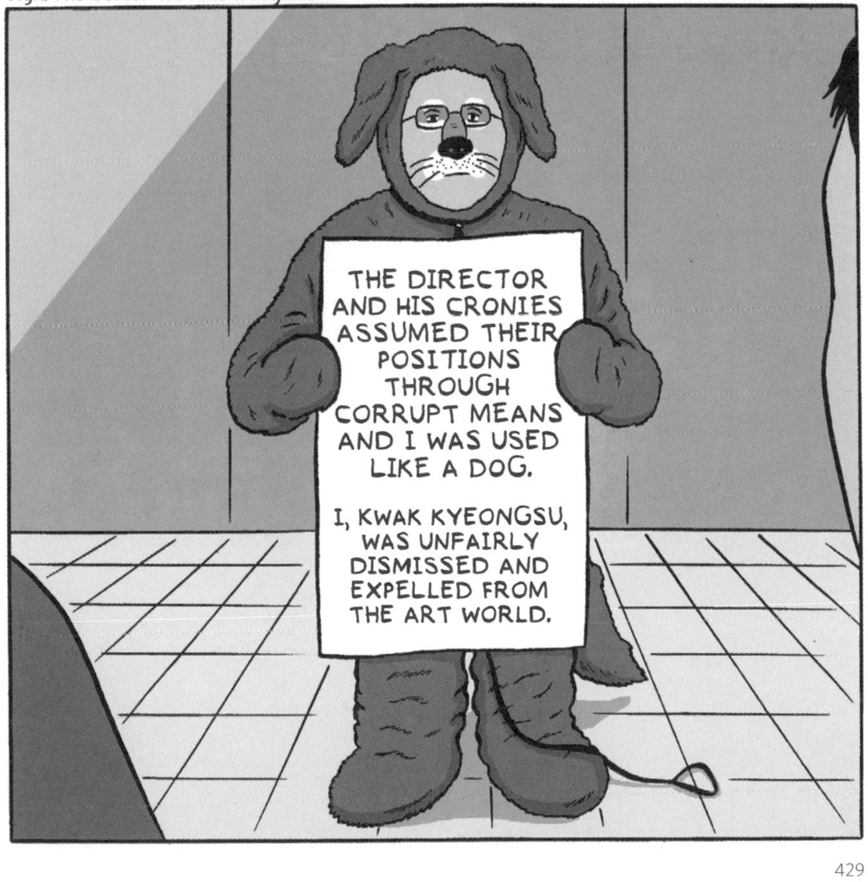
THE DIRECTOR AND HIS CRONIES ASSUMED THEIR POSITIONS THROUGH CORRUPT MEANS AND I WAS USED LIKE A DOG.
I, KWAK KYEONGSU, WAS UNFAIRLY DISMISSED AND EXPELLED FROM THE ART WORLD.

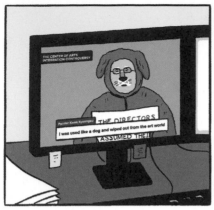

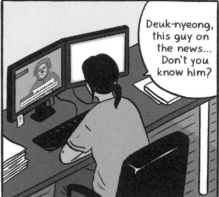

THE CENTER OF ARTS INTEGRATION CONTROVERSY
Painter Kwak Kyeongsu
THE DIRECTORS
I was used like a dog and wiped out from the art world
ASSUMED THEI
Deuk-nyeong, this guy on the news... Don't you know him?
Professor Son used me to oversee the Seoul Public Art project and took all the credit.
And then in a column, he forced me to expose the ugly past of Cartoonist Kim who'd been a candidate for the director position.
Through these means, Elder Gu was appointed Director and Professor Son was made Associate Director.
I simply became their dog, doing their bidding, only to be dismissed when I was of no use to them.

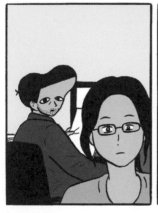

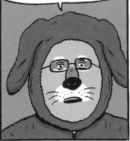

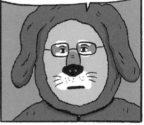

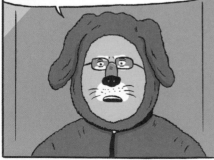

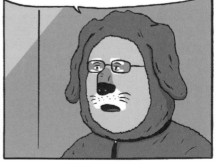

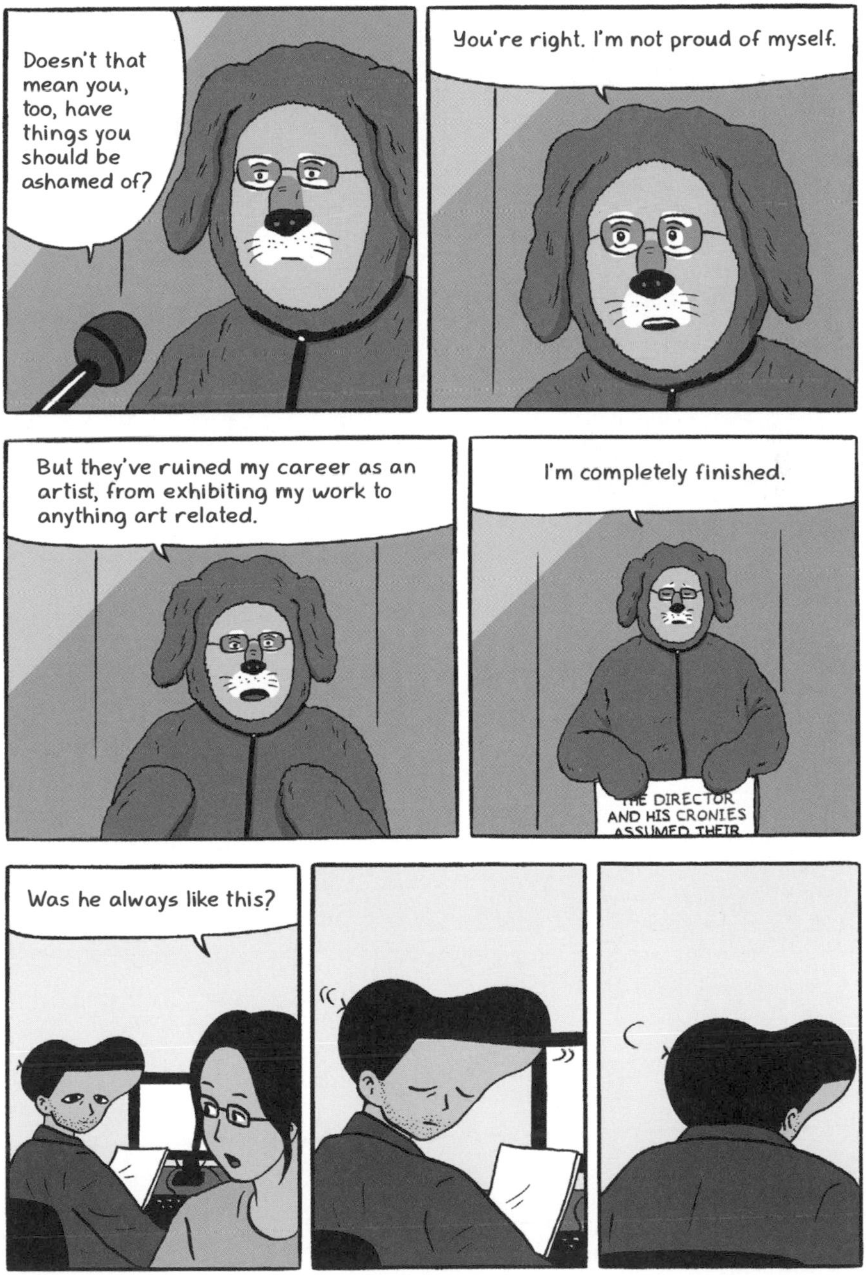
Doesn't that mean you, too, have things you should be ashamed of?
You're right. I'm not proud of myself.
But they've ruined my career as an artist, from exhibiting my work to anything art related.
I'm completely finished.
THE DIRECTOR AND HIS CRONIES ASSUMED THEIR
Was he always like this?

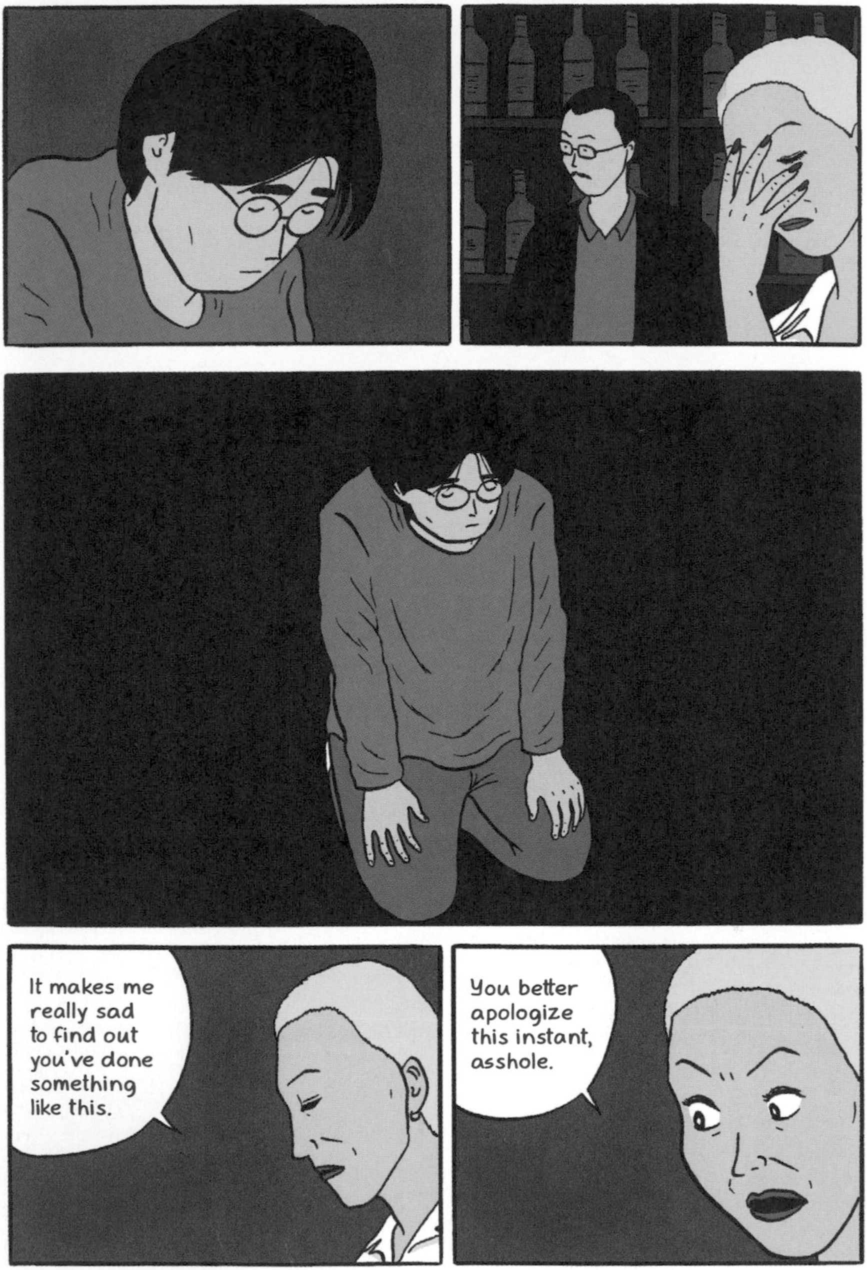
It makes me really sad to find out you've done something like this.
You better apologize this instant, asshole.

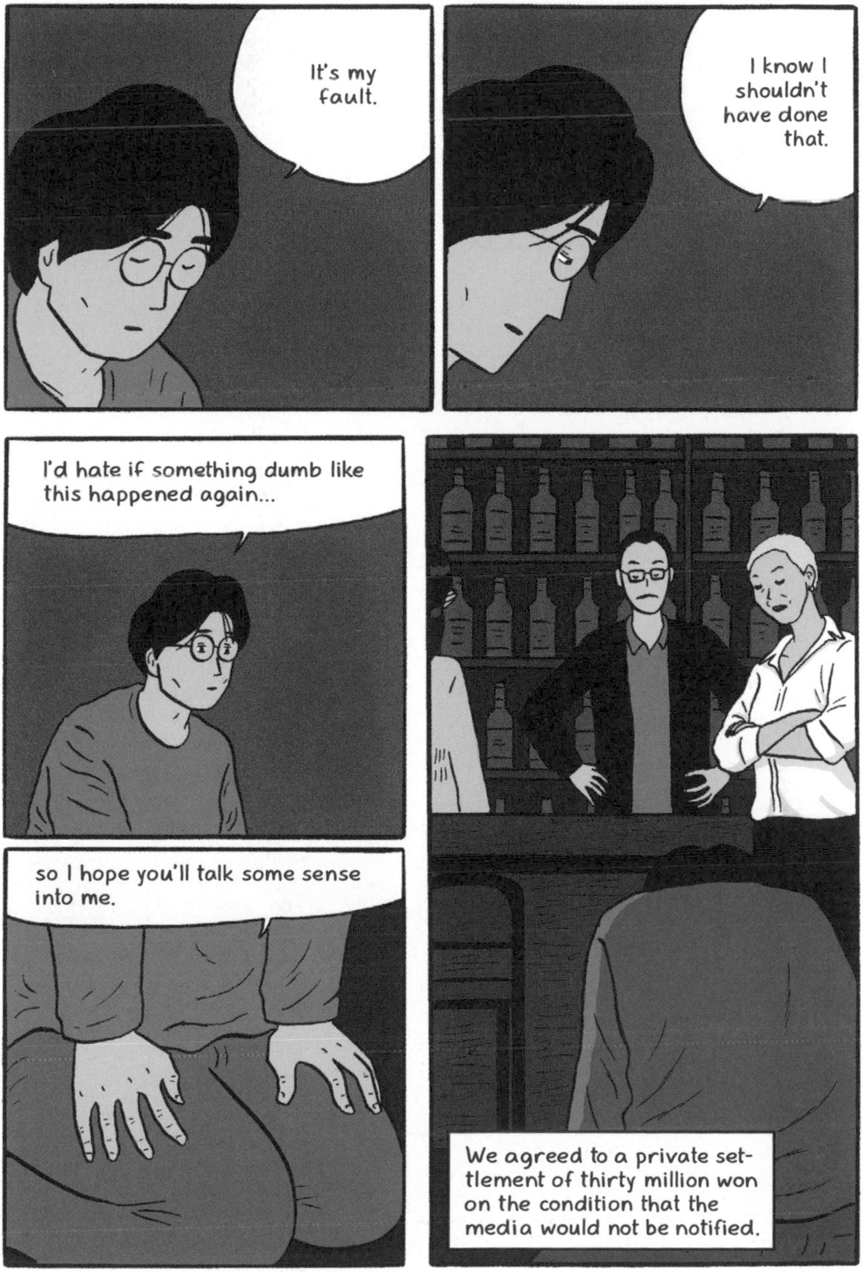
It's my fault.
I know I shouldn't have done that.
I'd hate if something dumb like this happened again...
so I hope you'll talk some sense into me.
We agreed to a private settlement of thirty million won on the condition that the media would not be notified.

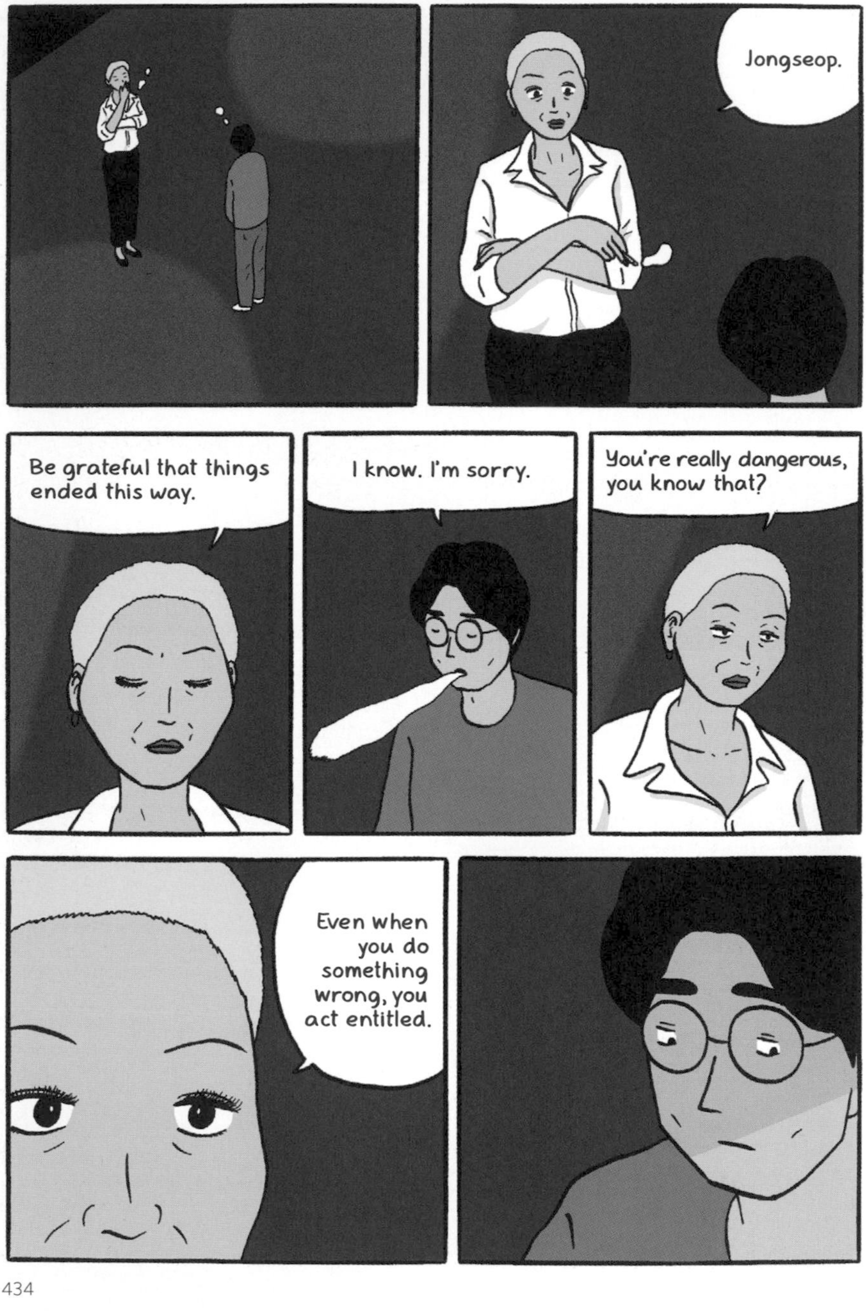
Jongseop.
Be grateful that things ended this way.
I know. I'm sorry.
You're really dangerous, you know that?
Even when you do something wrong, you act entitled.

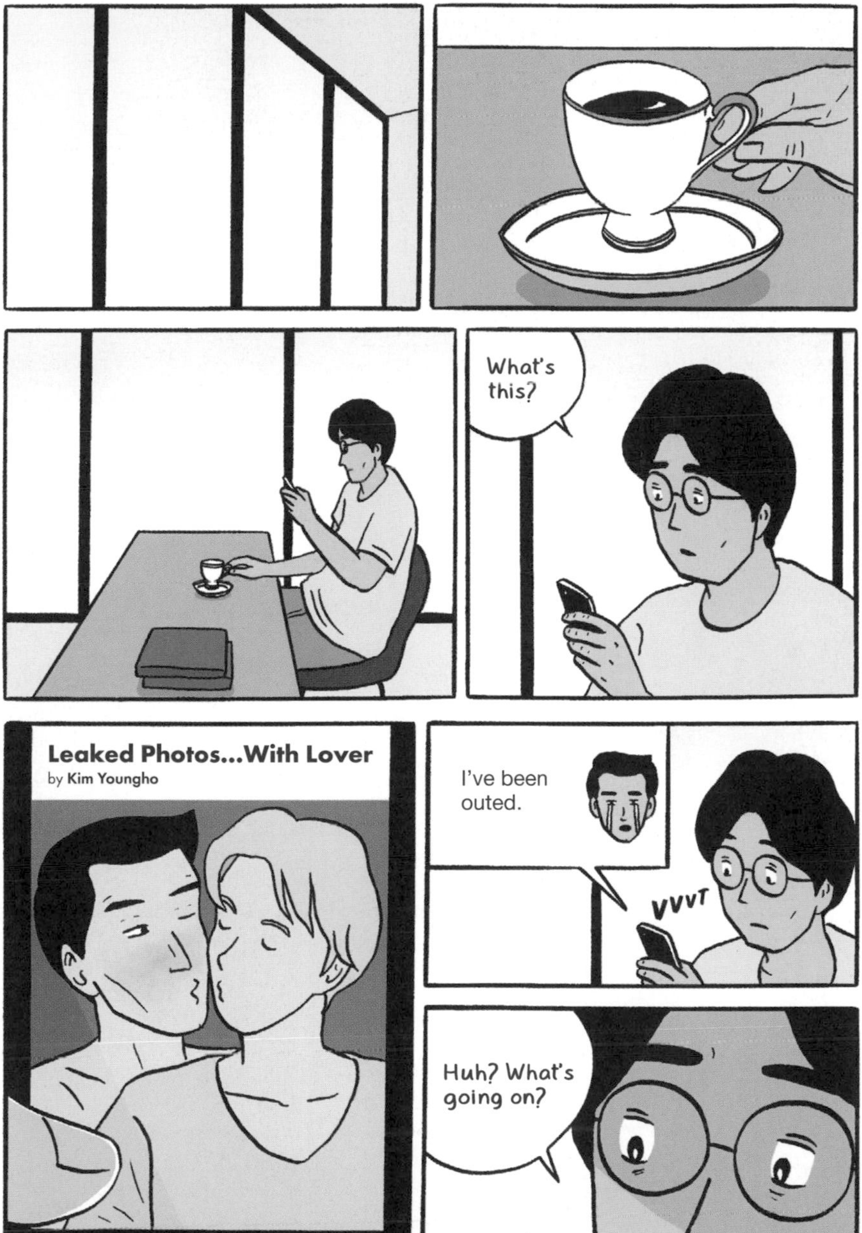
What's this?
Leaked Photos...With Lover
by Kim Youngho
I've been outed.
VVVT
Huh? What's going on?

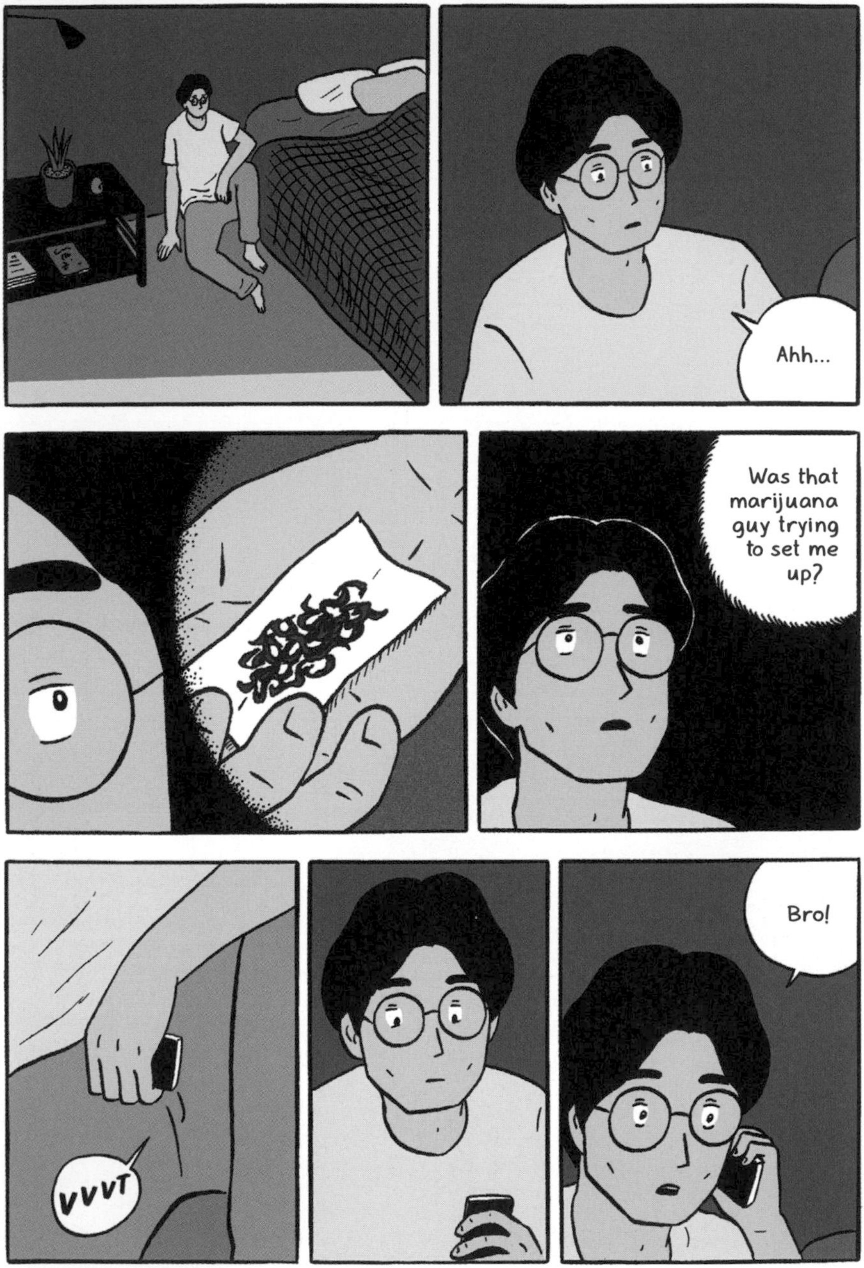
Ahh...
Was that marijuana guy trying to set me up?
VVVT
Bro!

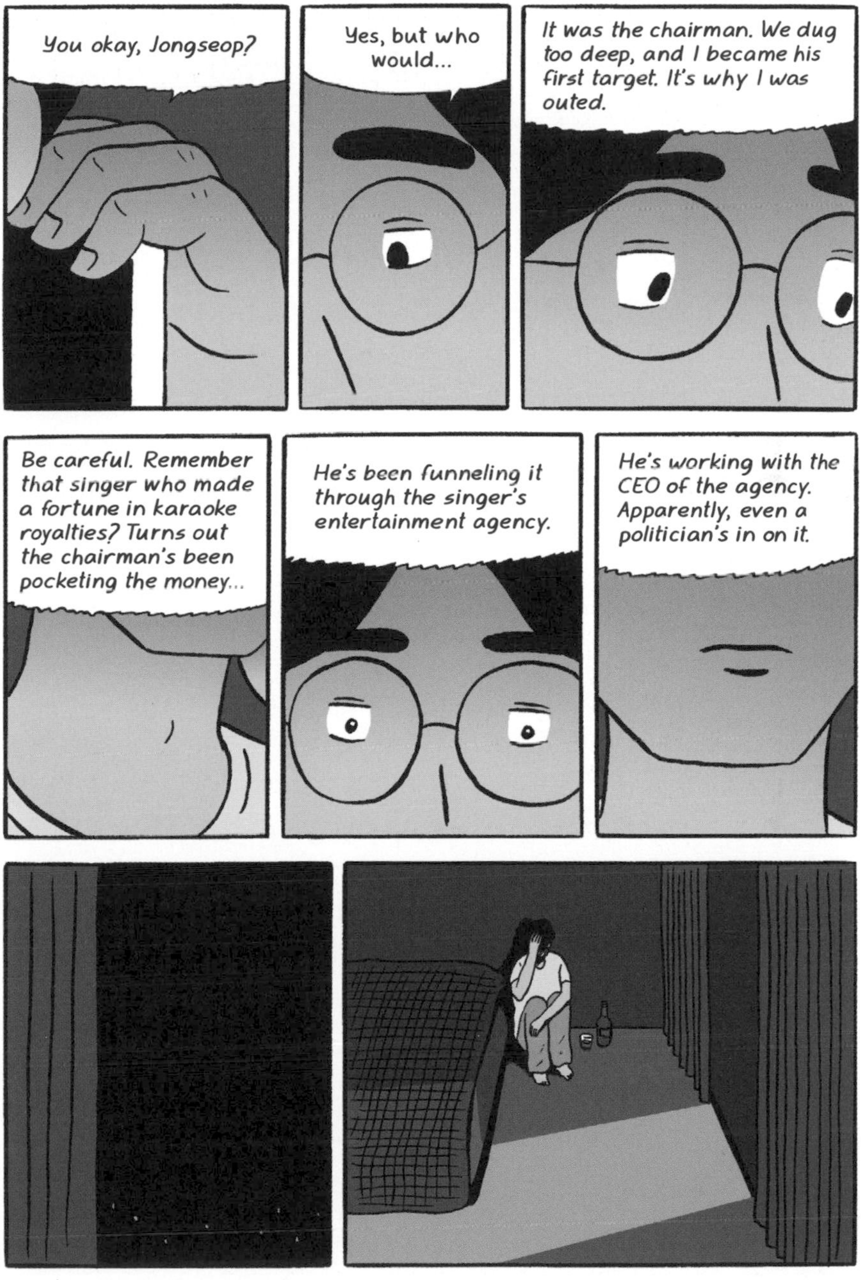
You okay, Jongseop?
Yes, but who would...
It was the chairman. We dug too deep, and I became his first target. It's why I was outed.
Be careful. Remember that singer who made a fortune in karaoke royalties? Turns out the chairman's been pocketing the money...
He's been funneling it through the singer's entertainment agency.
He's working with the CEO of the agency. Apparently, even a politician's in on it.

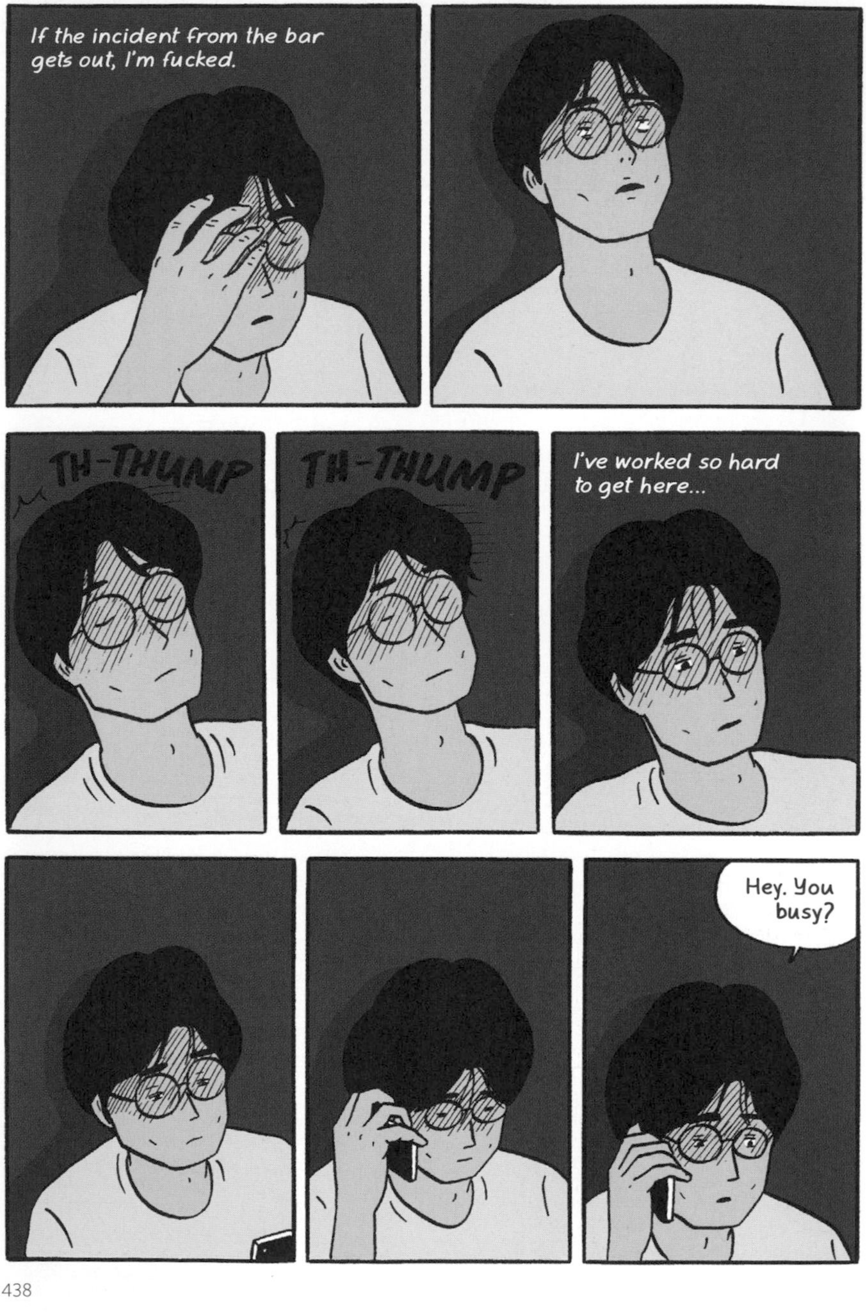
If the incident from the bar gets out, I'm fucked.
TH-THUMP
TH-THUMP
I've worked so hard to get here...
Hey. You busy?

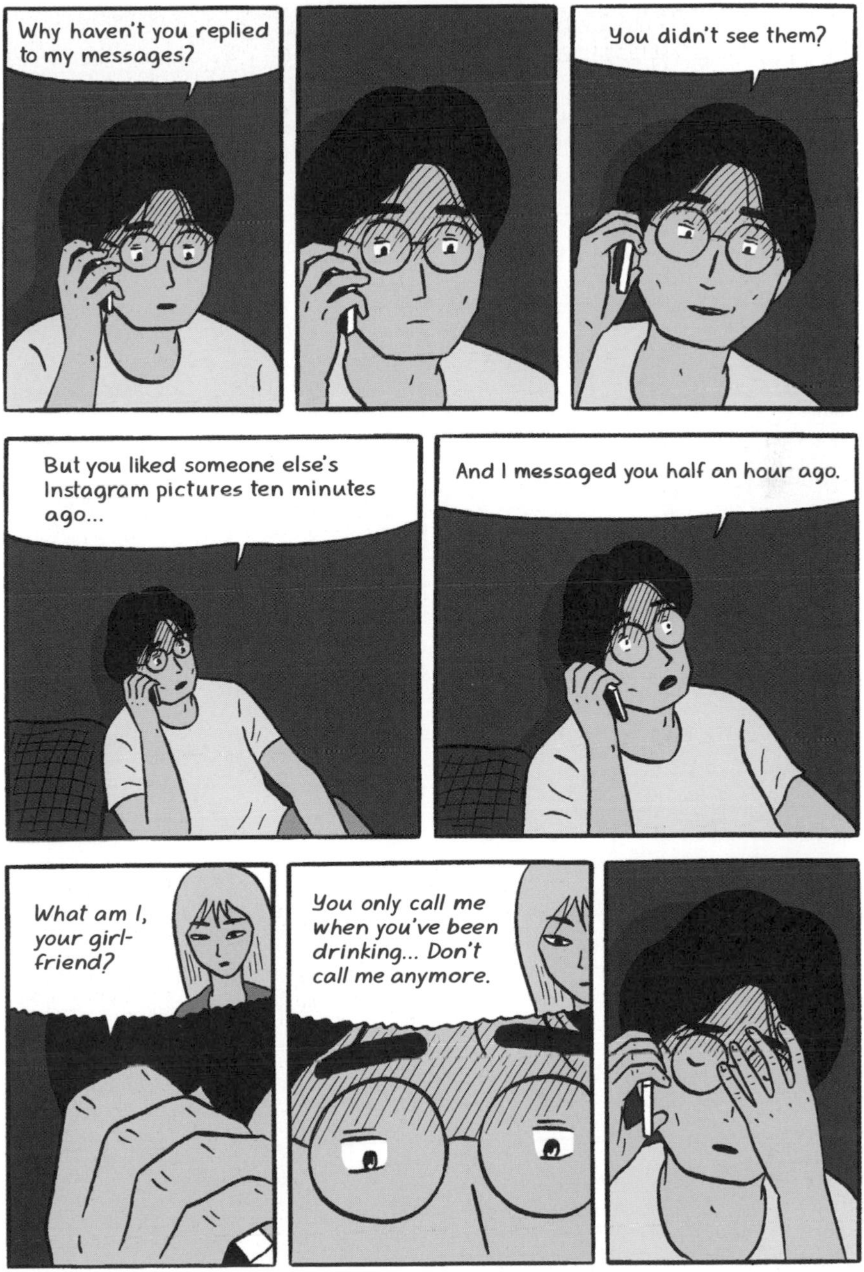
Why haven't you replied to my messages?
You didn't see them?
But you liked someone else's Instagram pictures ten minutes ago...
And I messaged you half an hour ago.
What am I, your girl-friend?
You only call me when you've been drinking... Don't call me anymore.

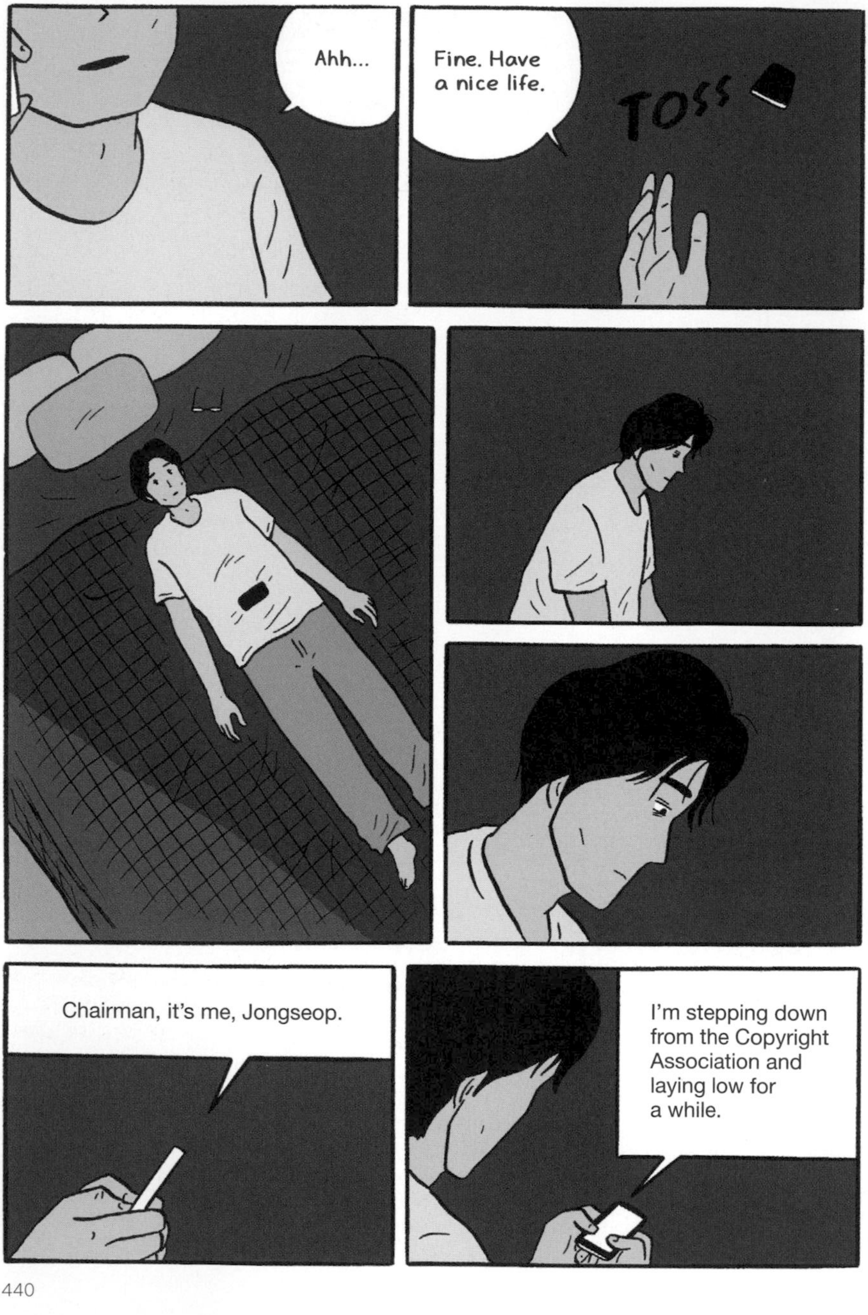
Ahh...
Fine. Have a nice life.
TOSS
Chairman, it's me, Jongseop.
I'm stepping down from the Copyright Association and laying low for a while.

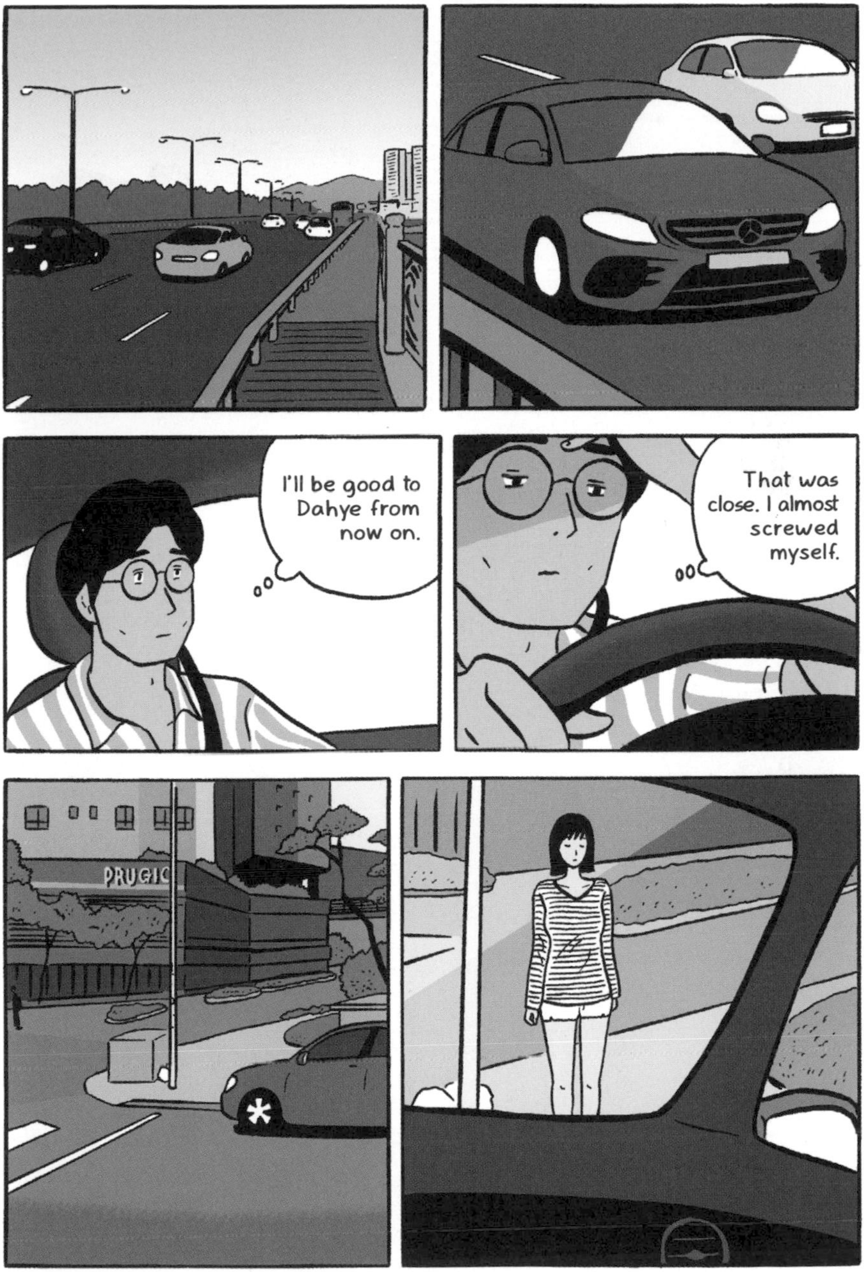
I'll be good to Dahye from now on.
That was close. I almost screwed myself.
PRUGIC

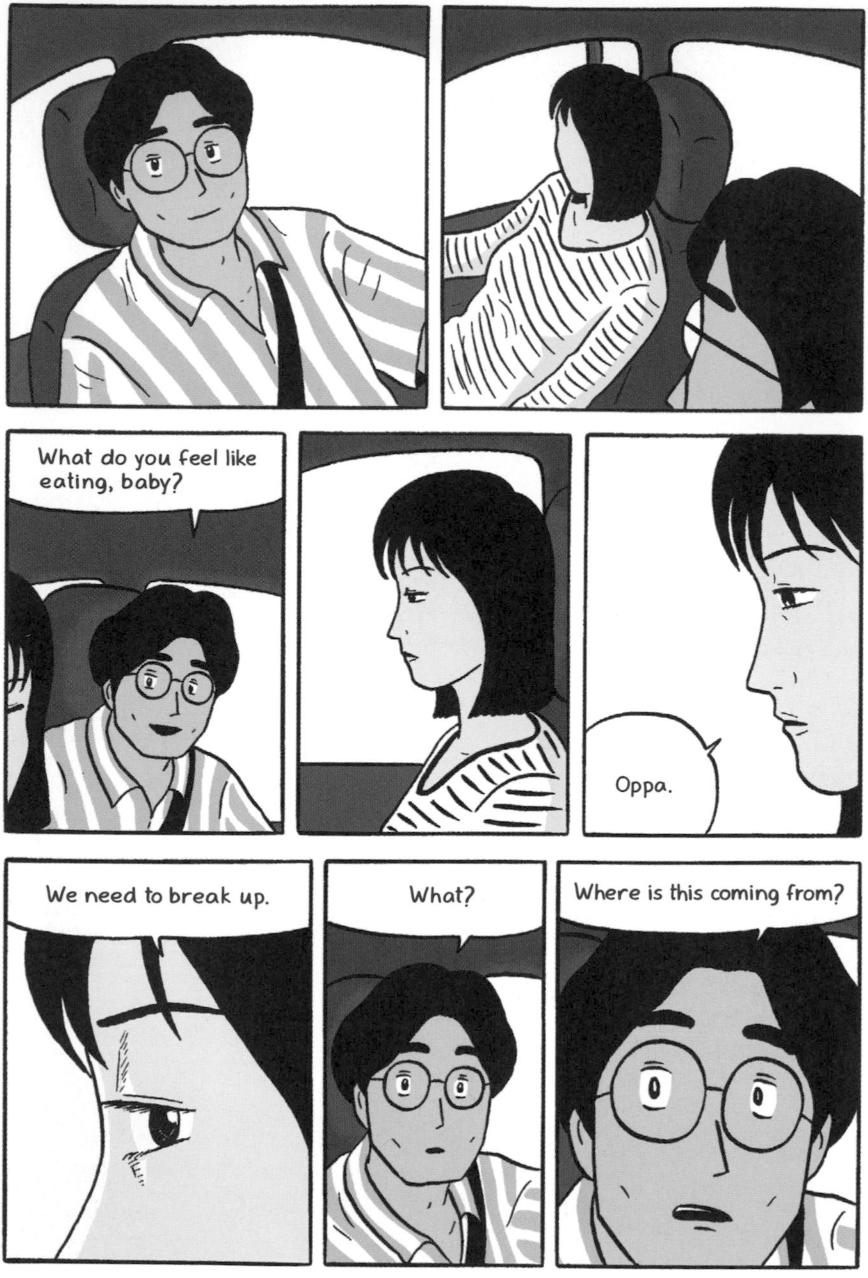
What do you feel like eating, baby?
Oppa.
We need to break up.
What?
Where is this coming from?

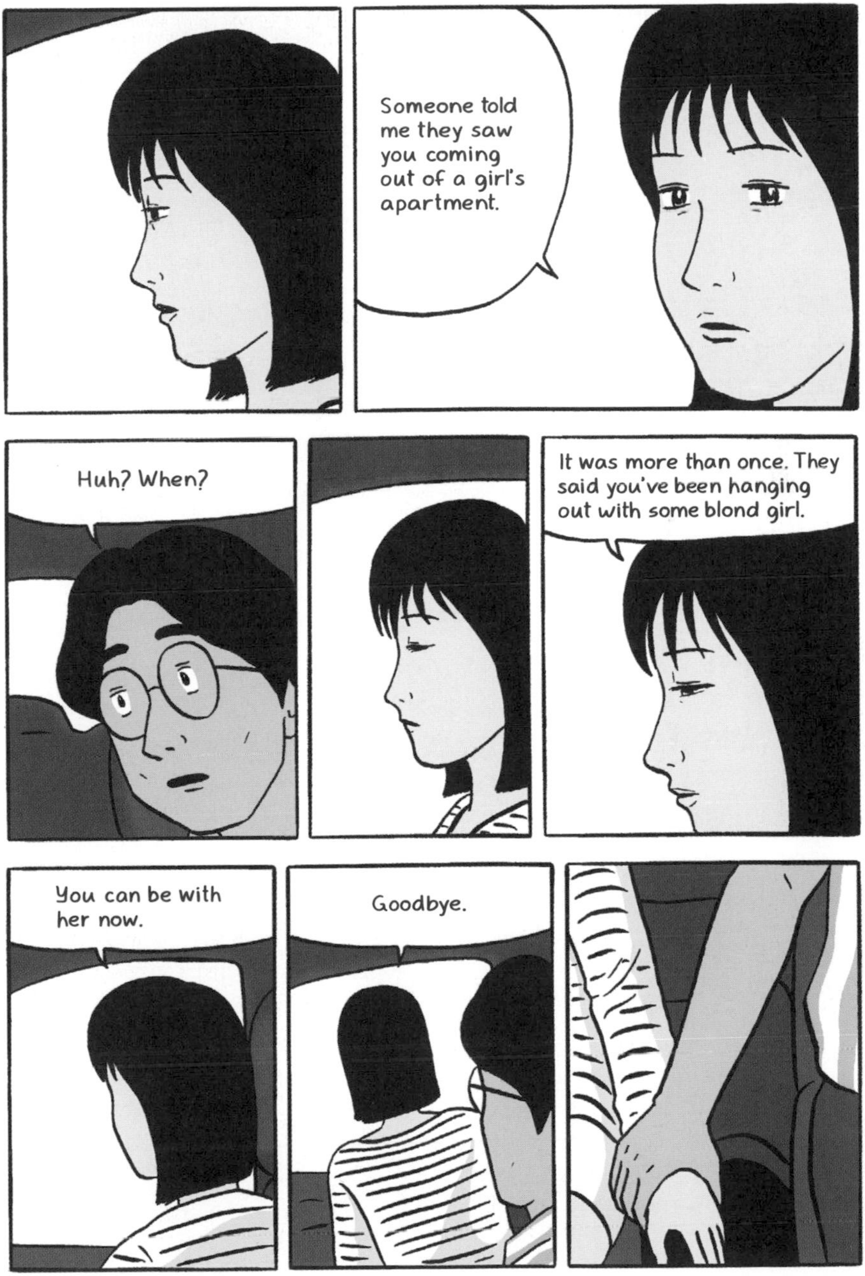
Someone told me they saw you coming out of a girl's apartment.
Huh? When?
It was more than once. They said you've been hanging out with some blond girl.
You can be with her now.
Goodbye.

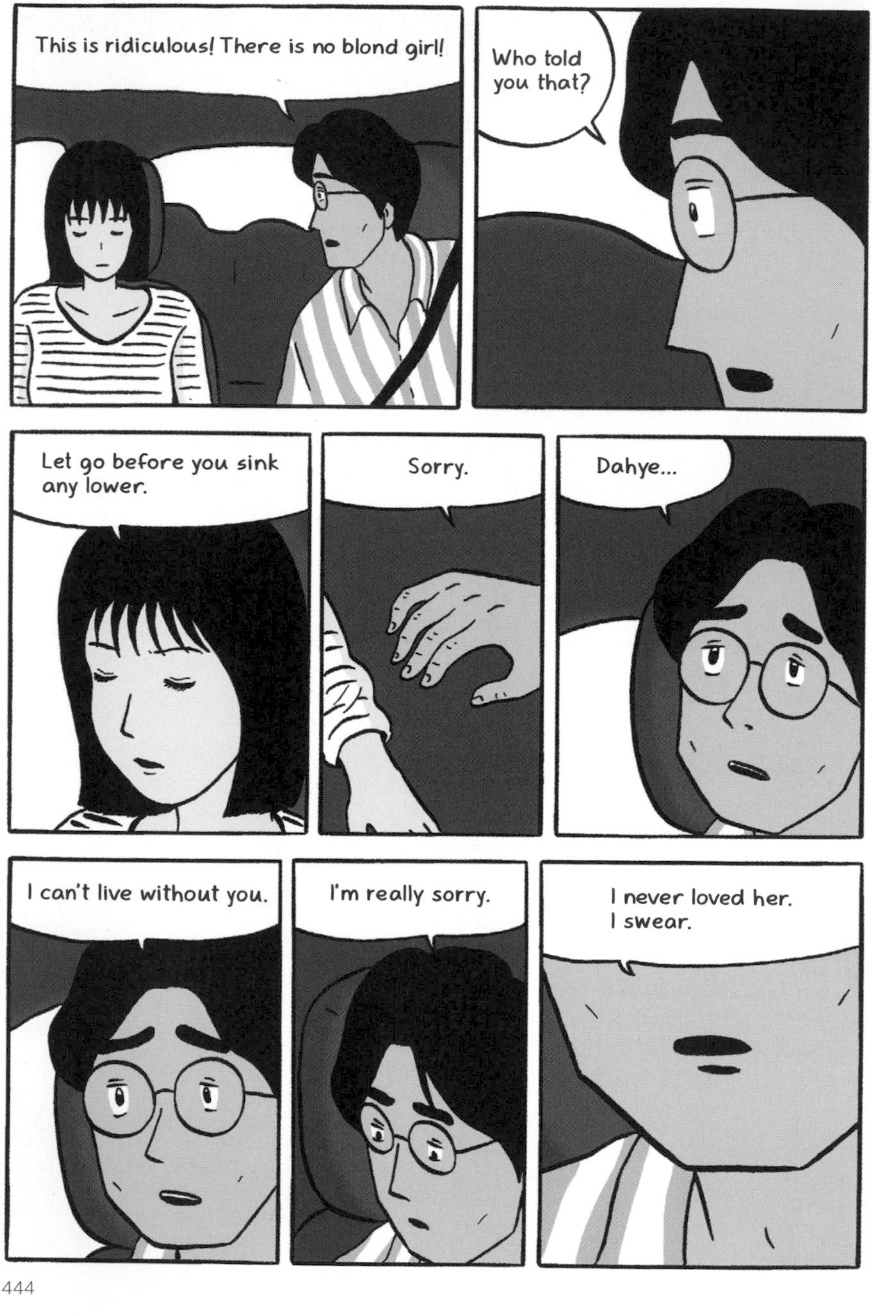
This is ridiculous! There is no blond girl!
Who told you that?
Let go before you sink any lower.
Sorry.
Dahye...
I can't live without you.
I'm really sorry.
I never loved her.
I swear.

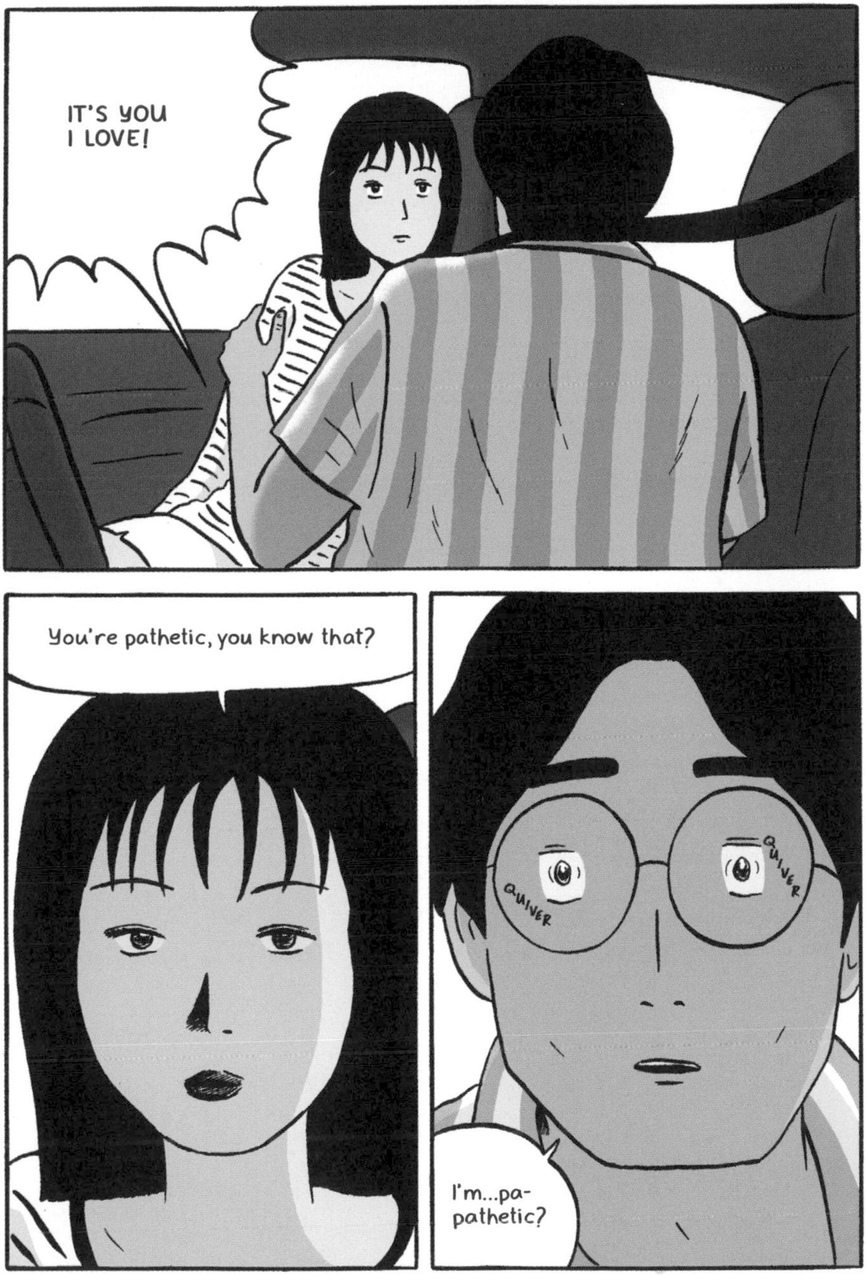
IT'S YOU
I LOVE!
You're pathetic, you know that?
QUIVER
QUIVER
I'm...pa-
pathetic?

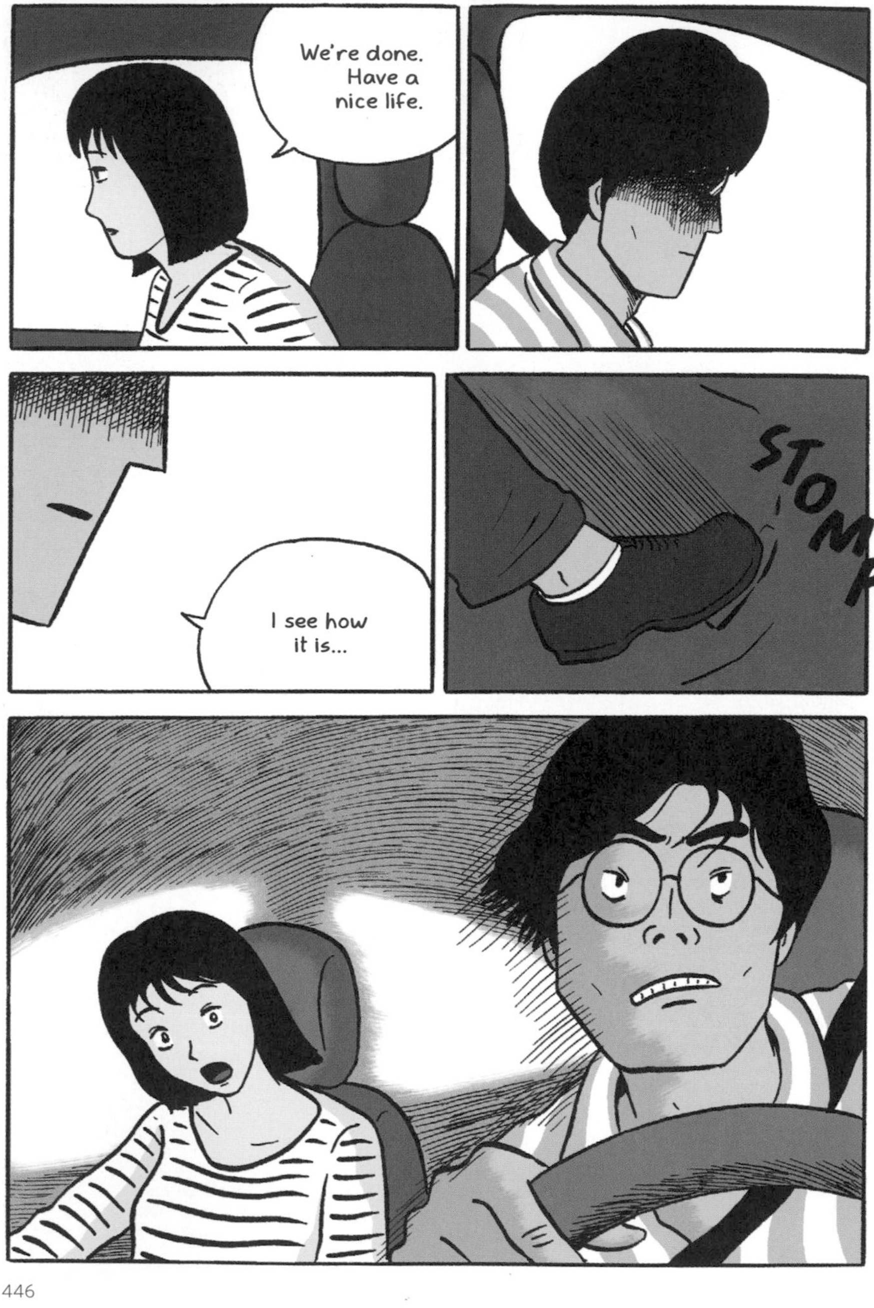
We're done. Have a nice life.
I see how it is...
STOMP

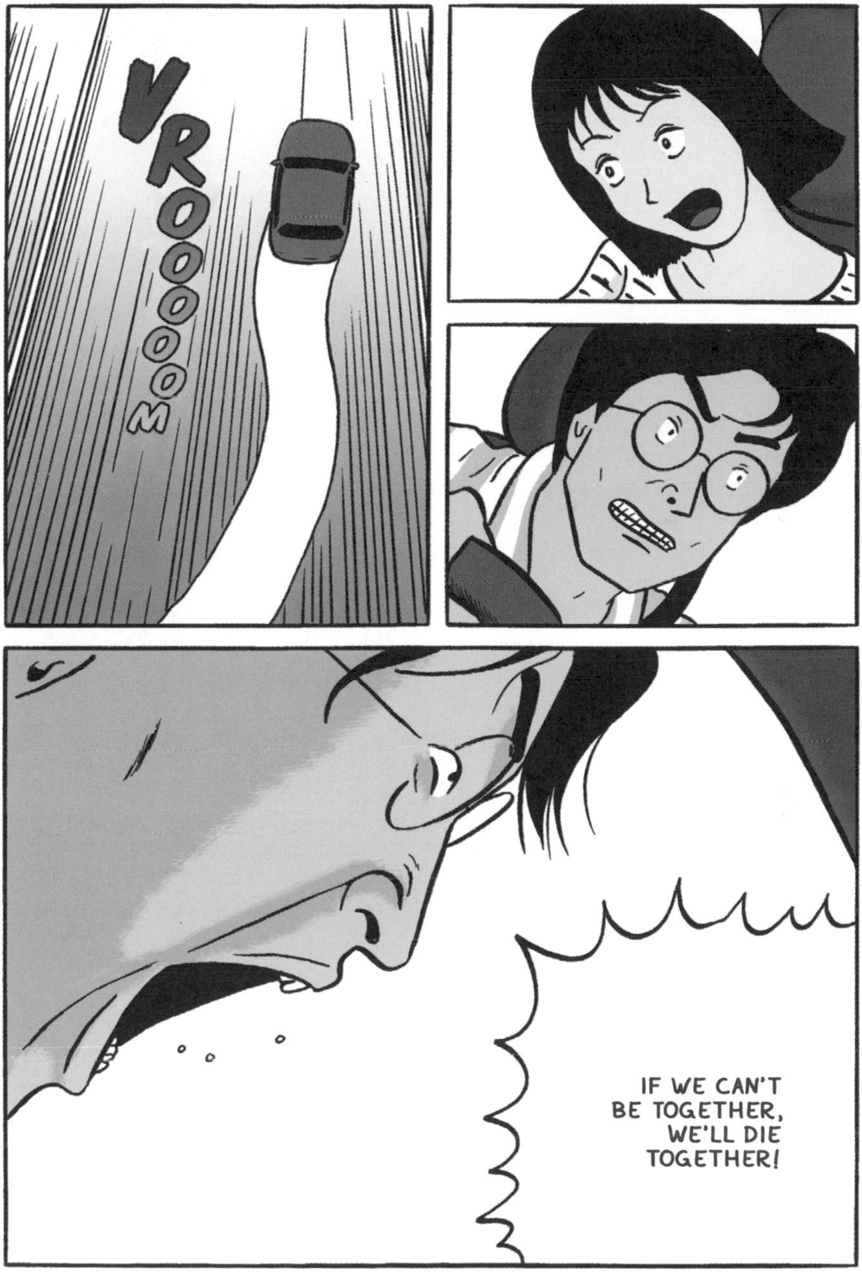
VROOOOOOOM
IF WE CAN'T BE TOGETHER, WE'LL DIE TOGETHER!

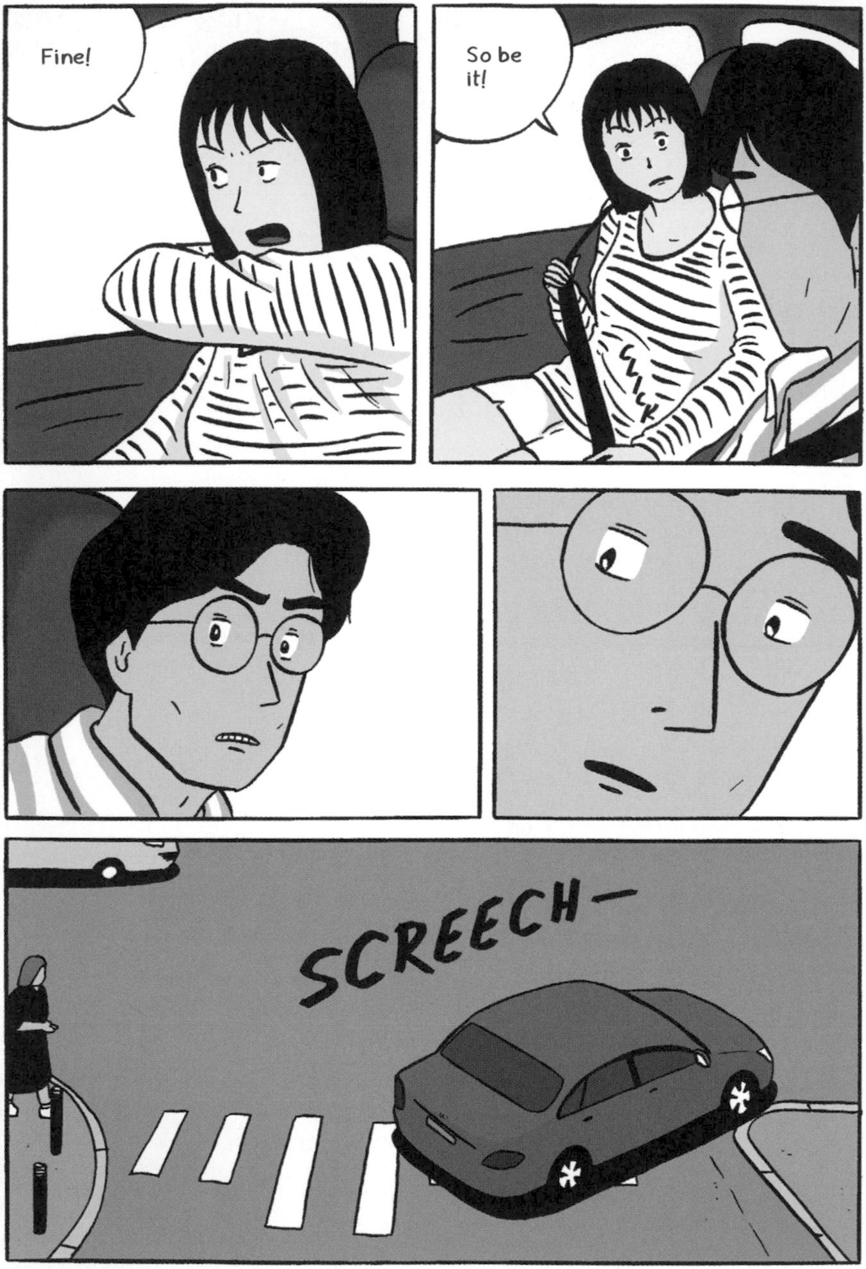
Fine!
So be it!
CLICK
SCREECH—

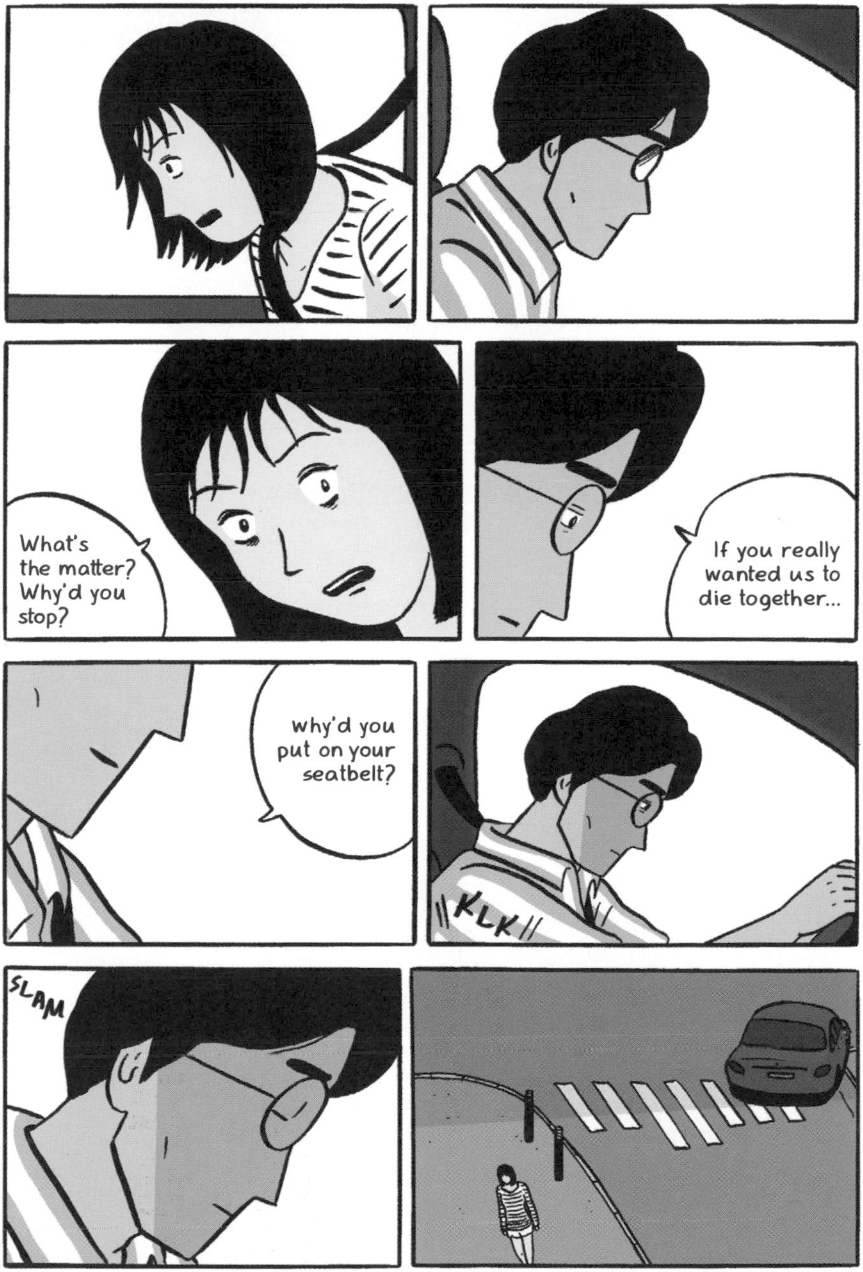
What's the matter? Why'd you stop?
If you really wanted us to die together...
why'd you put on your seatbelt?
KLK
SLAM

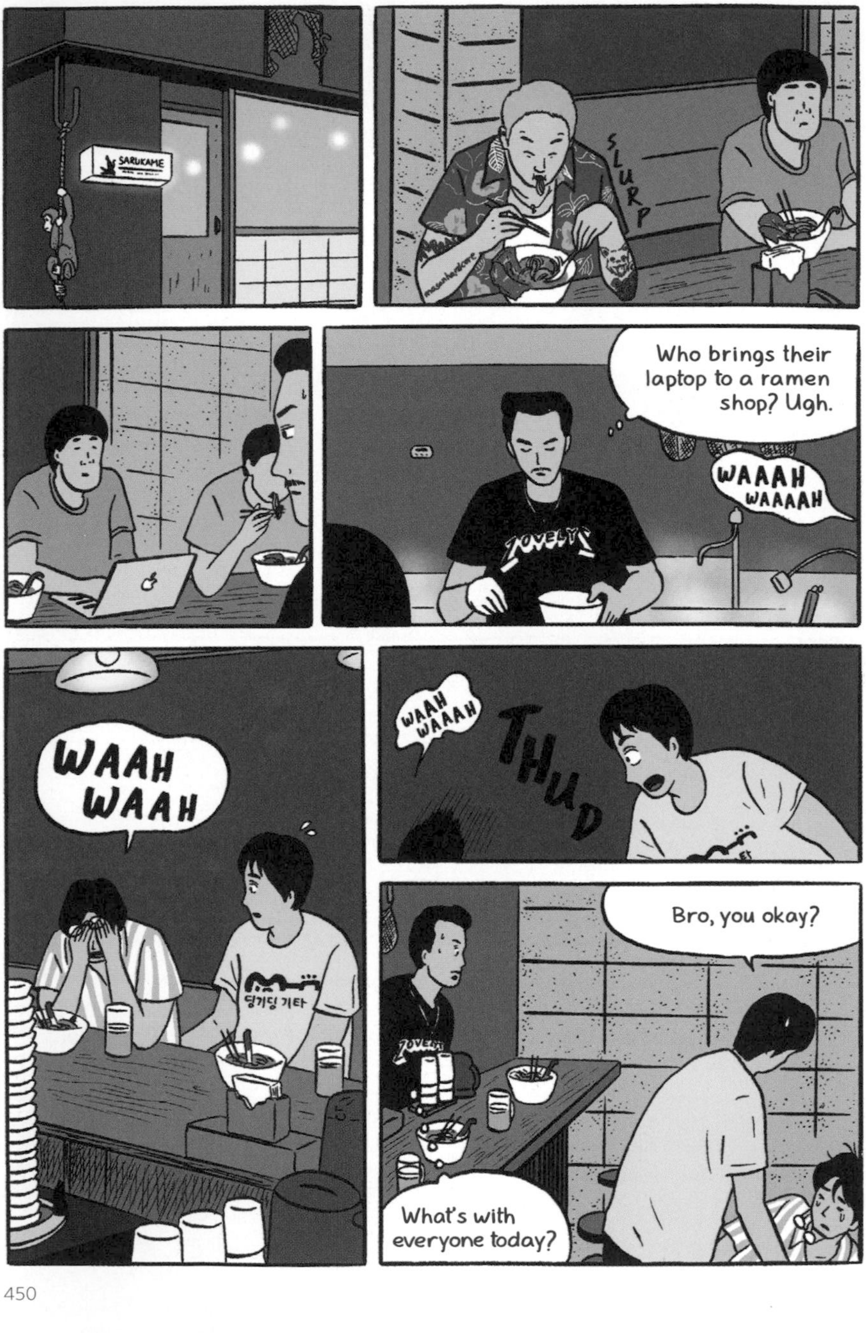
SARUKAME
SLURP
Who brings their laptop to a ramen shop? Ugh.
WAAAH WAAAAH
WAAH WAAH
딩기딩 기타
WAAH WAAAH
THUD
Bro, you okay?
What's with everyone today?

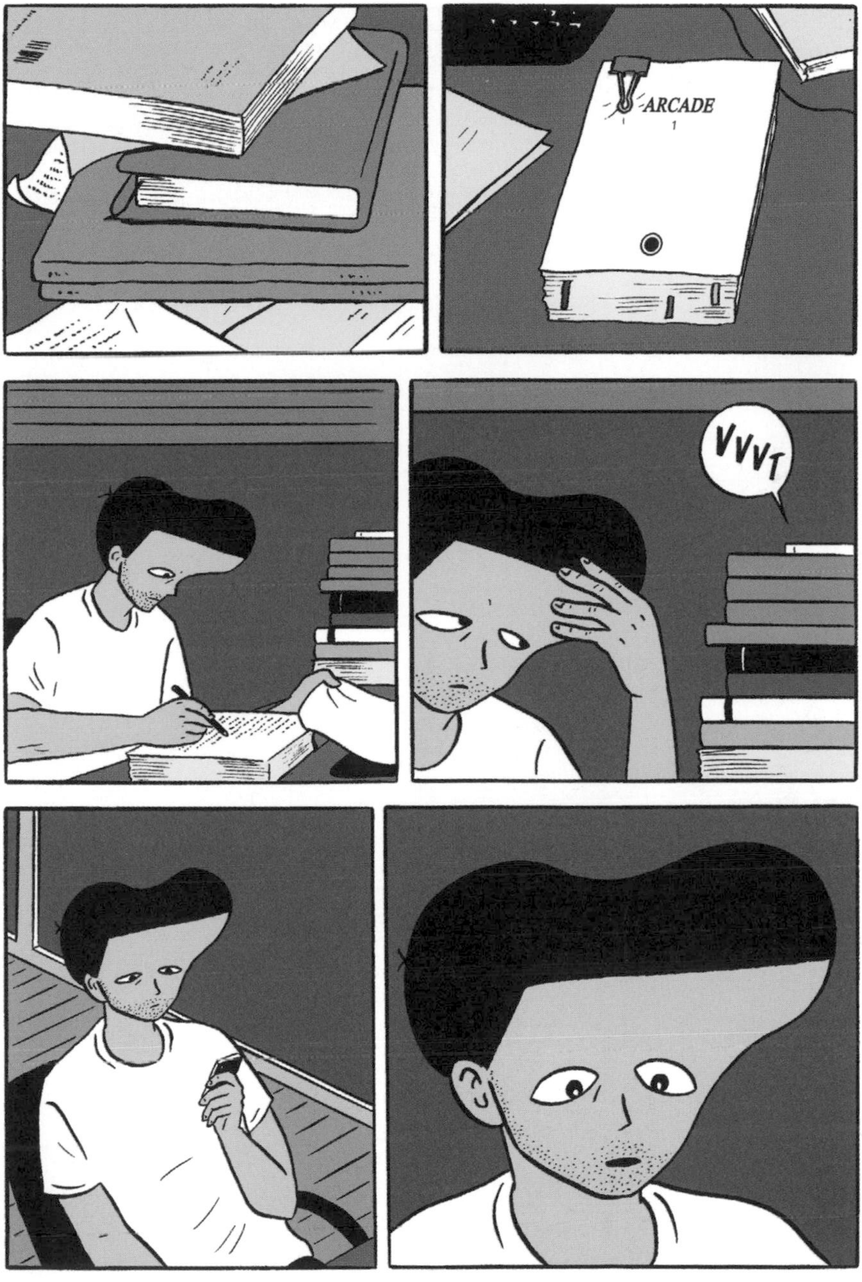
ARCADE
1
VVVT

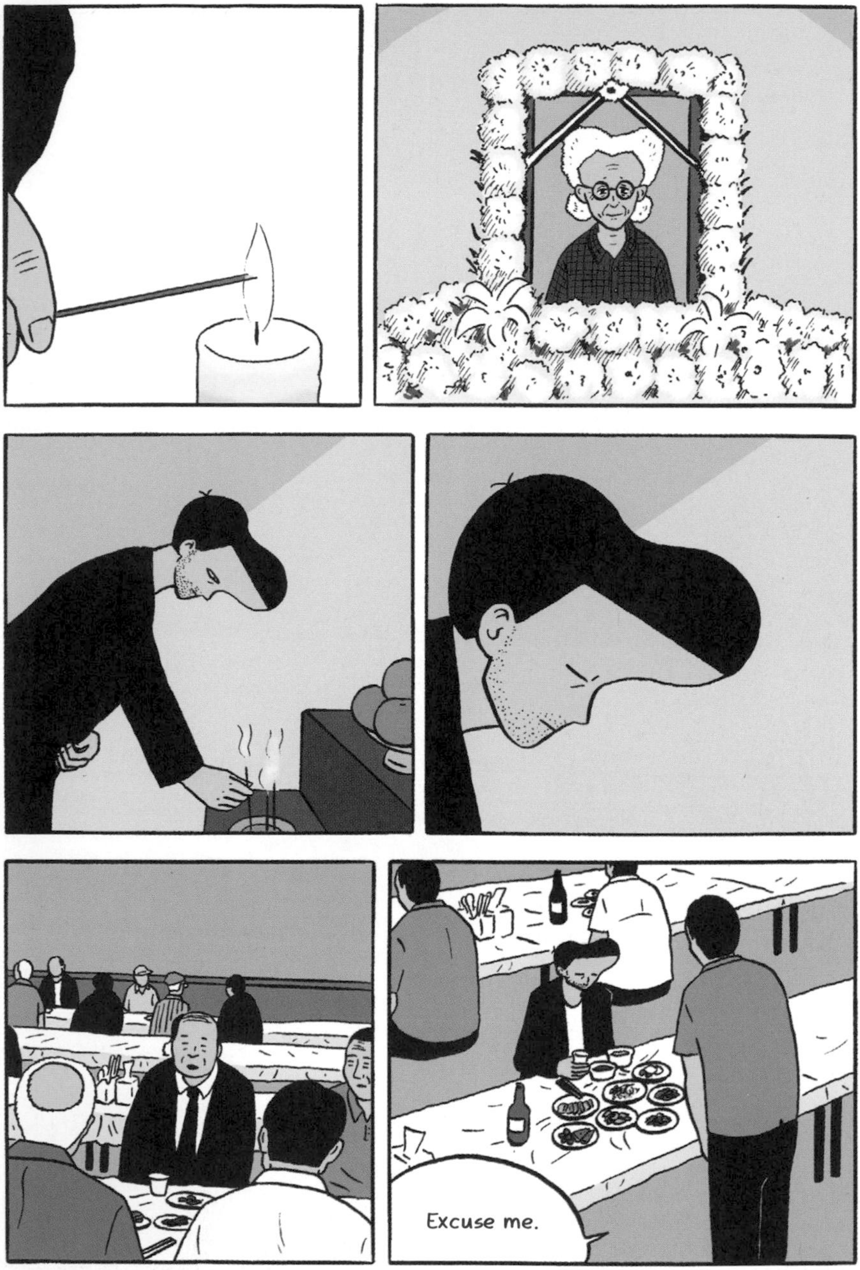
Excuse me.

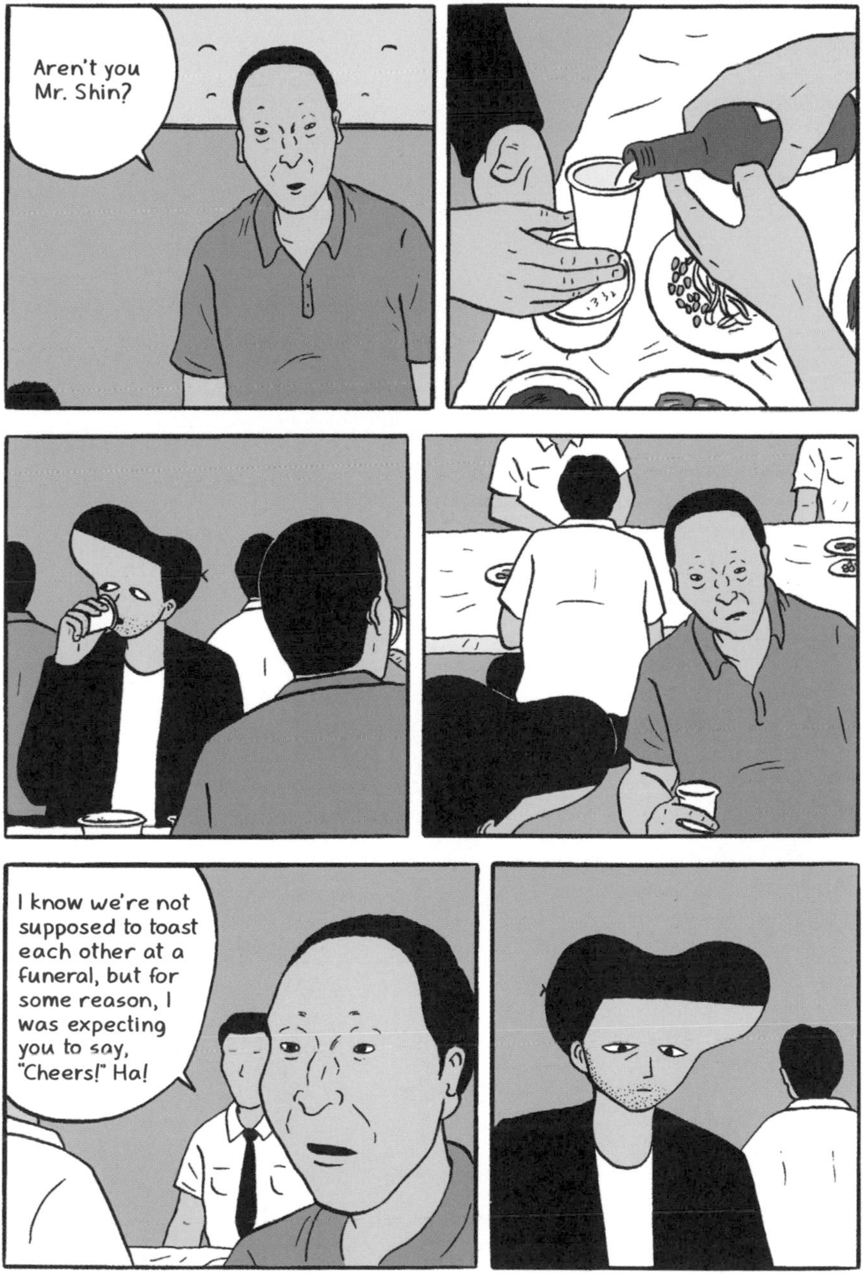
Aren't you Mr. Shin?
I know we're not supposed to toast each other at a funeral, but for some reason, I was expecting you to say, "Cheers!" Ha!

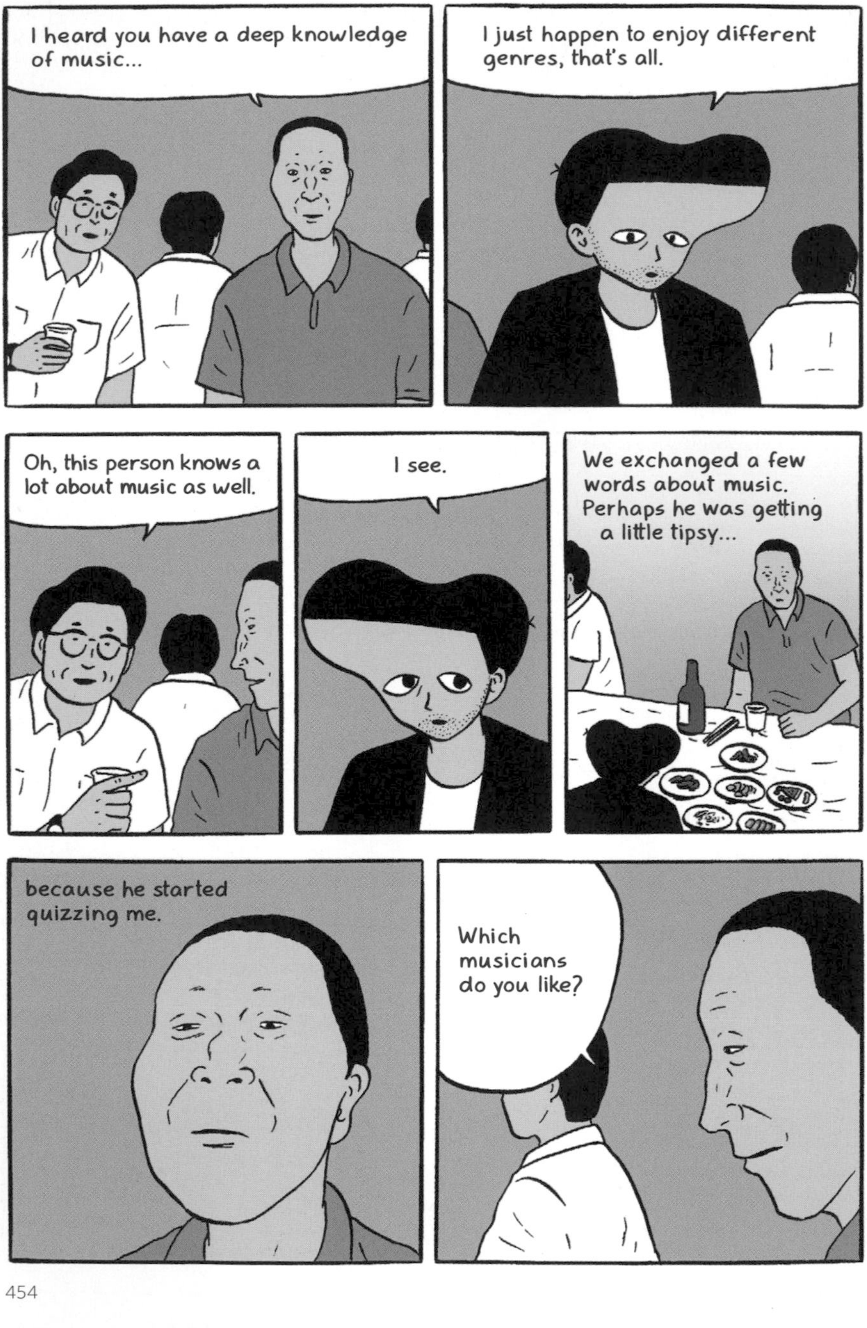
I heard you have a deep knowledge of music...
I just happen to enjoy different genres, that's all.
Oh, this person knows a lot about music as well.
I see.
We exchanged a few words about music. Perhaps he was getting a little tipsy...
because he started quizzing me.
Which musicians do you like?

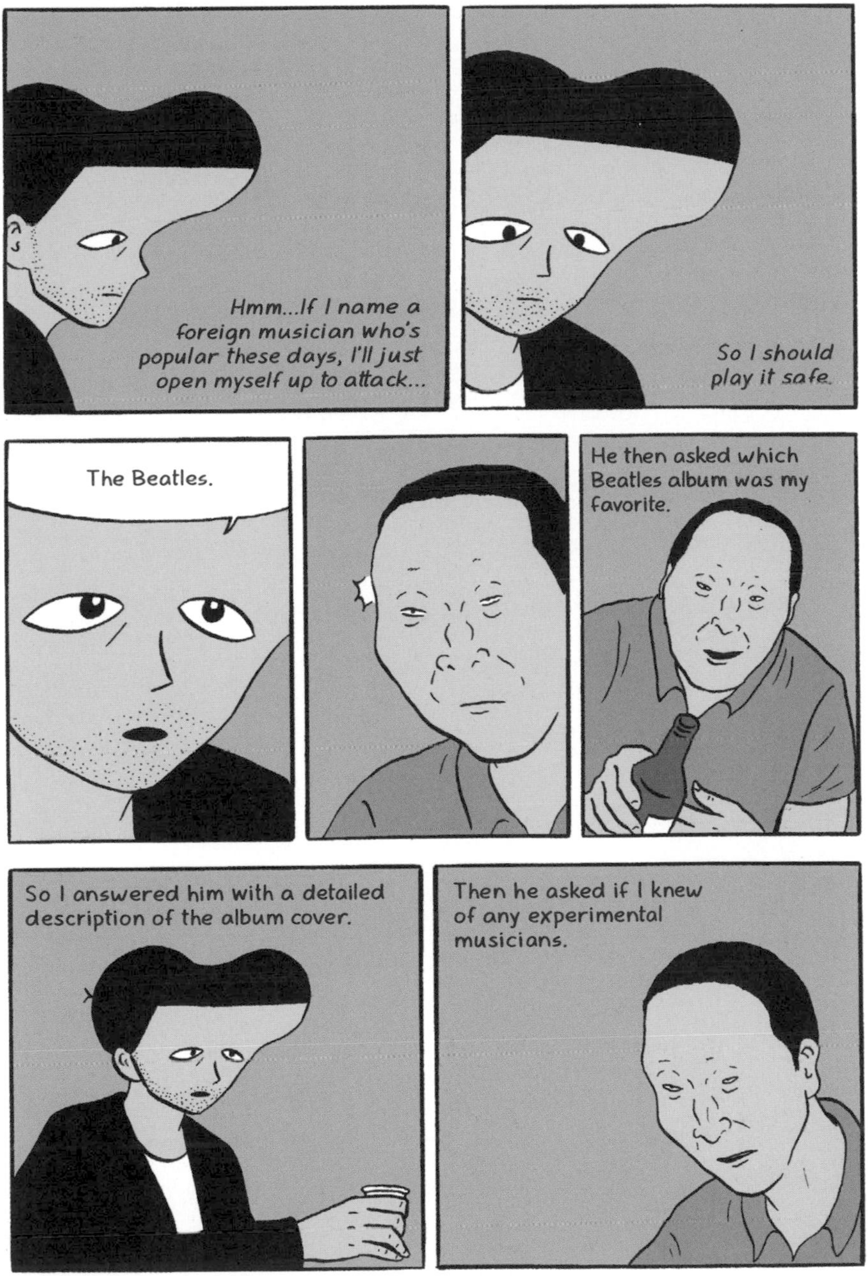

Hmm...If I name a foreign musician who's popular these days, I'll just open myself up to attack...
So I should play it safe.
The Beatles.
He then asked which Beatles album was my favorite.
So I answered him with a detailed description of the album cover.
Then he asked if I knew of any experimental musicians.

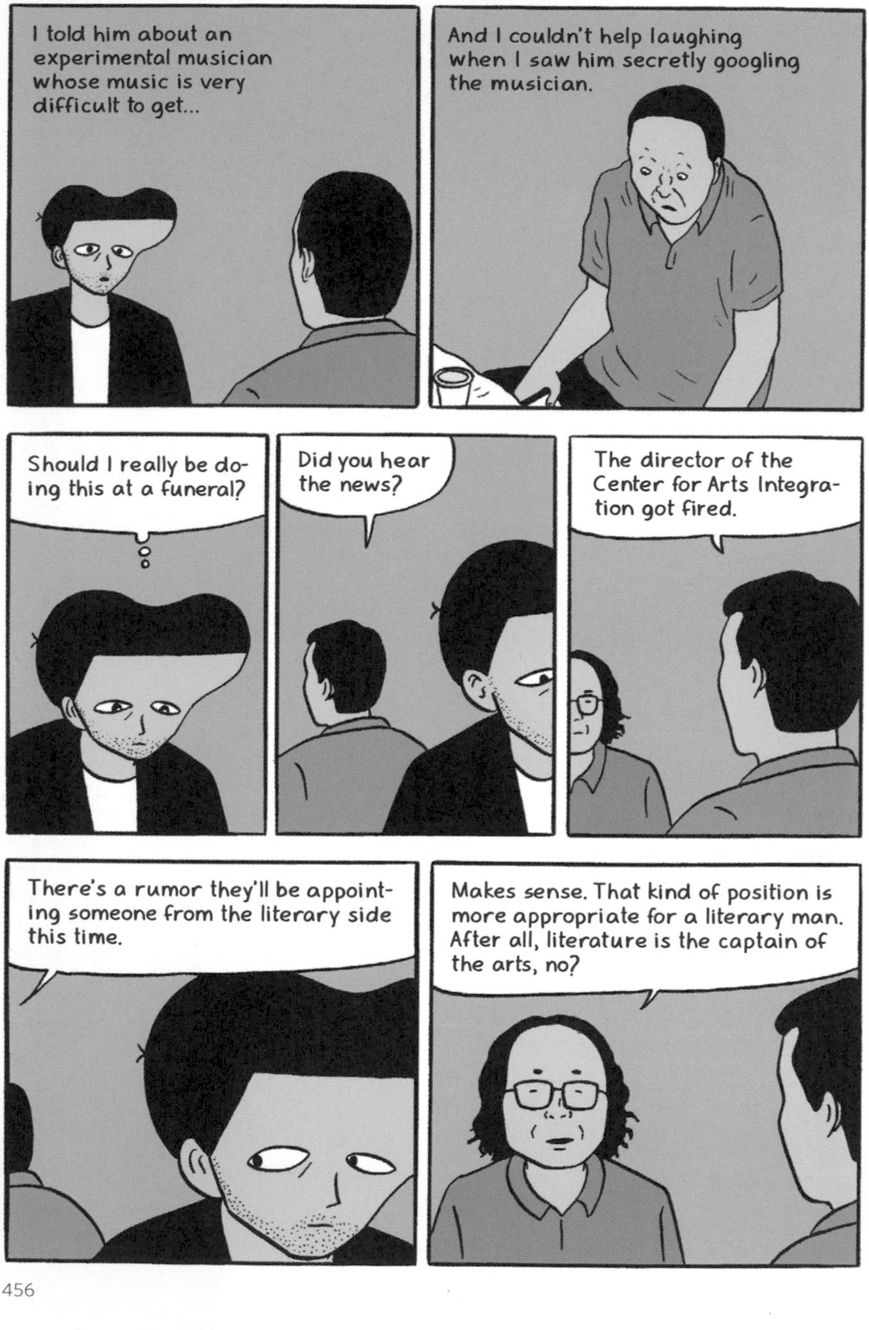
I told him about an experimental musician whose music is very difficult to get...
And I couldn't help laughing when I saw him secretly googling the musician.
Should I really be doing this at a funeral?
Did you hear the news?
The director of the Center for Arts Integration got fired.
There's a rumor they'll be appointing someone from the literary side this time.
Makes sense. That kind of position is more appropriate for a literary man. After all, literature is the captain of the arts, no?

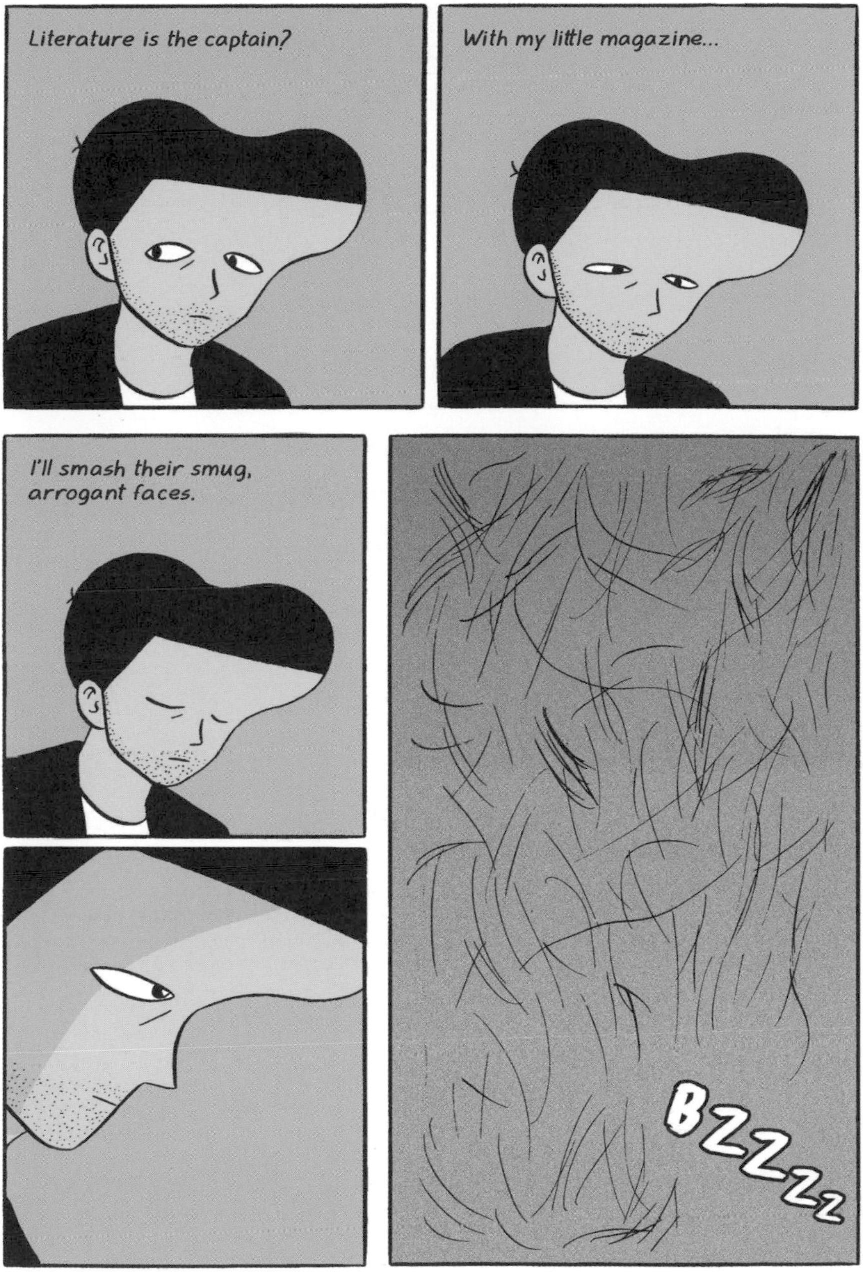
Literature is the captain?
With my little magazine...
I'll smash their smug, arrogant faces.
BZZZZZ

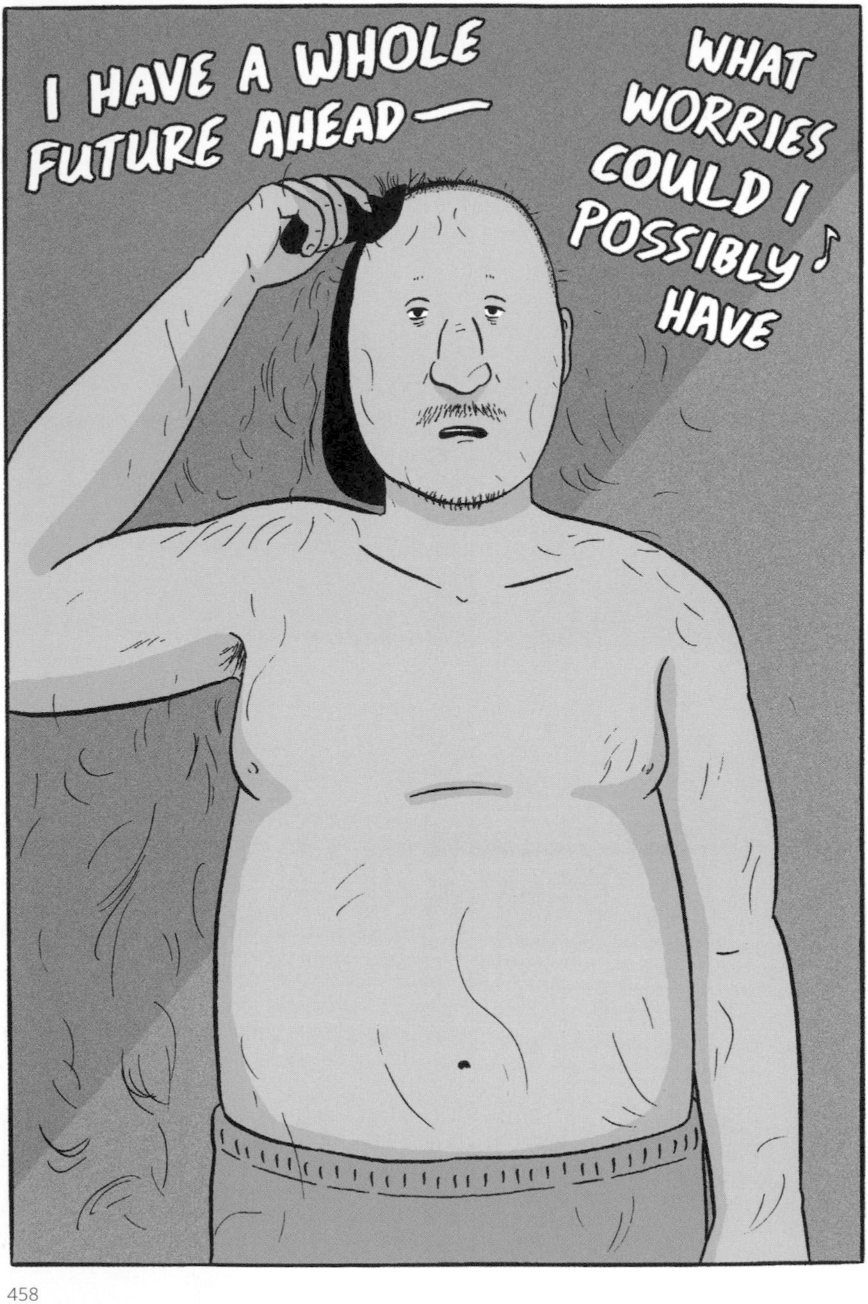
I HAVE A WHOLE FUTURE AHEAD—
WHAT WORRIES COULD I POSSIBLY HAVE ♪

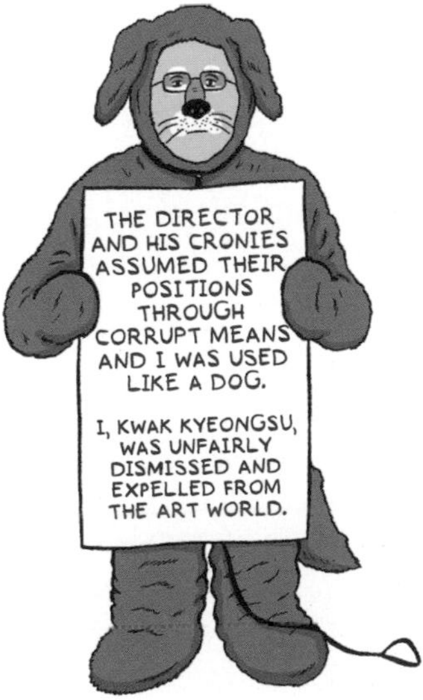
THE DIRECTOR AND HIS CRONIES ASSUMED THEIR POSITIONS THROUGH CORRUPT MEANS AND I WAS USED LIKE A DOG.
I, KWAK KYEONGSU, WAS UNFAIRLY DISMISSED AND EXPELLED FROM THE ART WORLD.

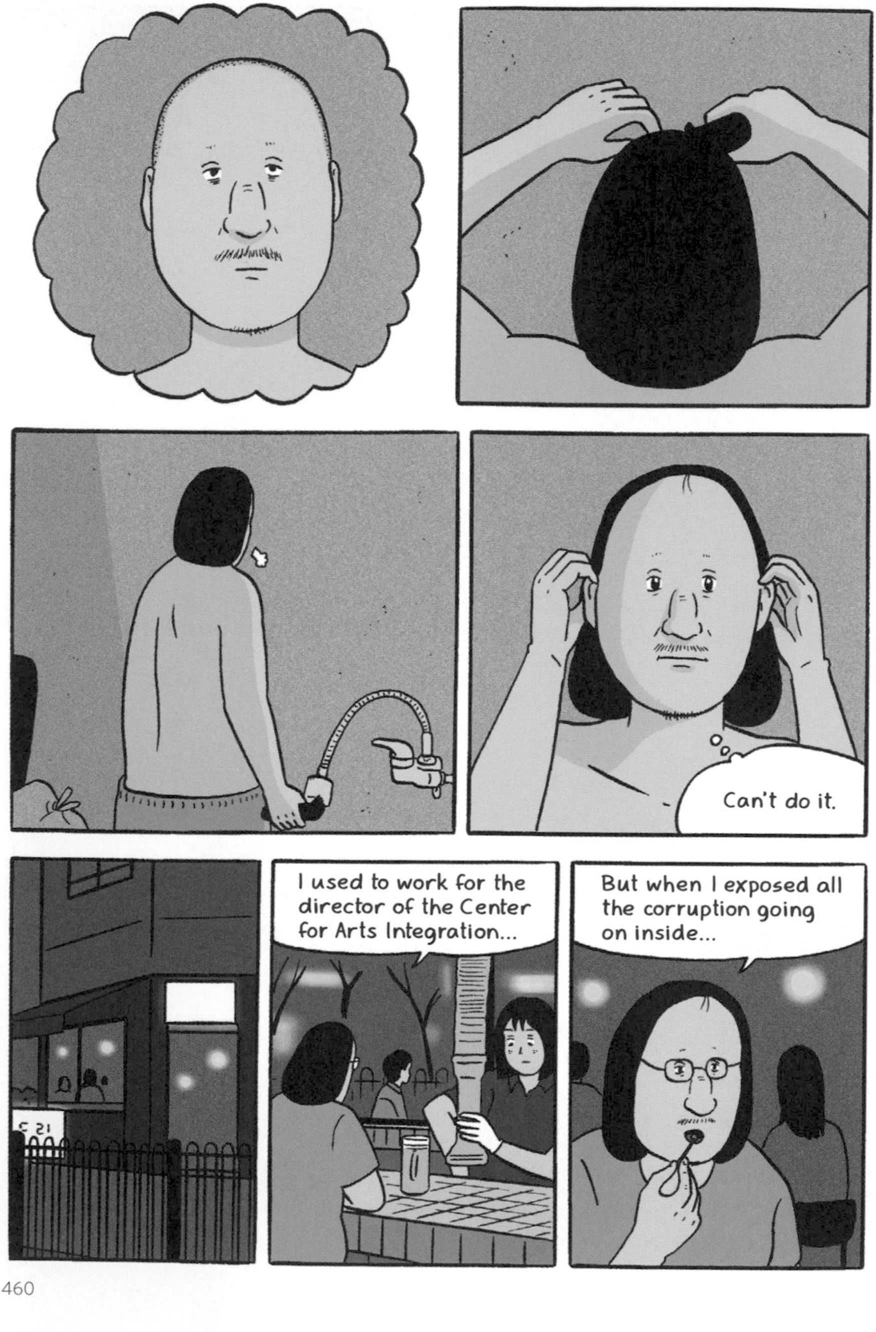
Can't do it.
I used to work for the director of the Center for Arts Integration...
But when I exposed all the corruption going on inside...

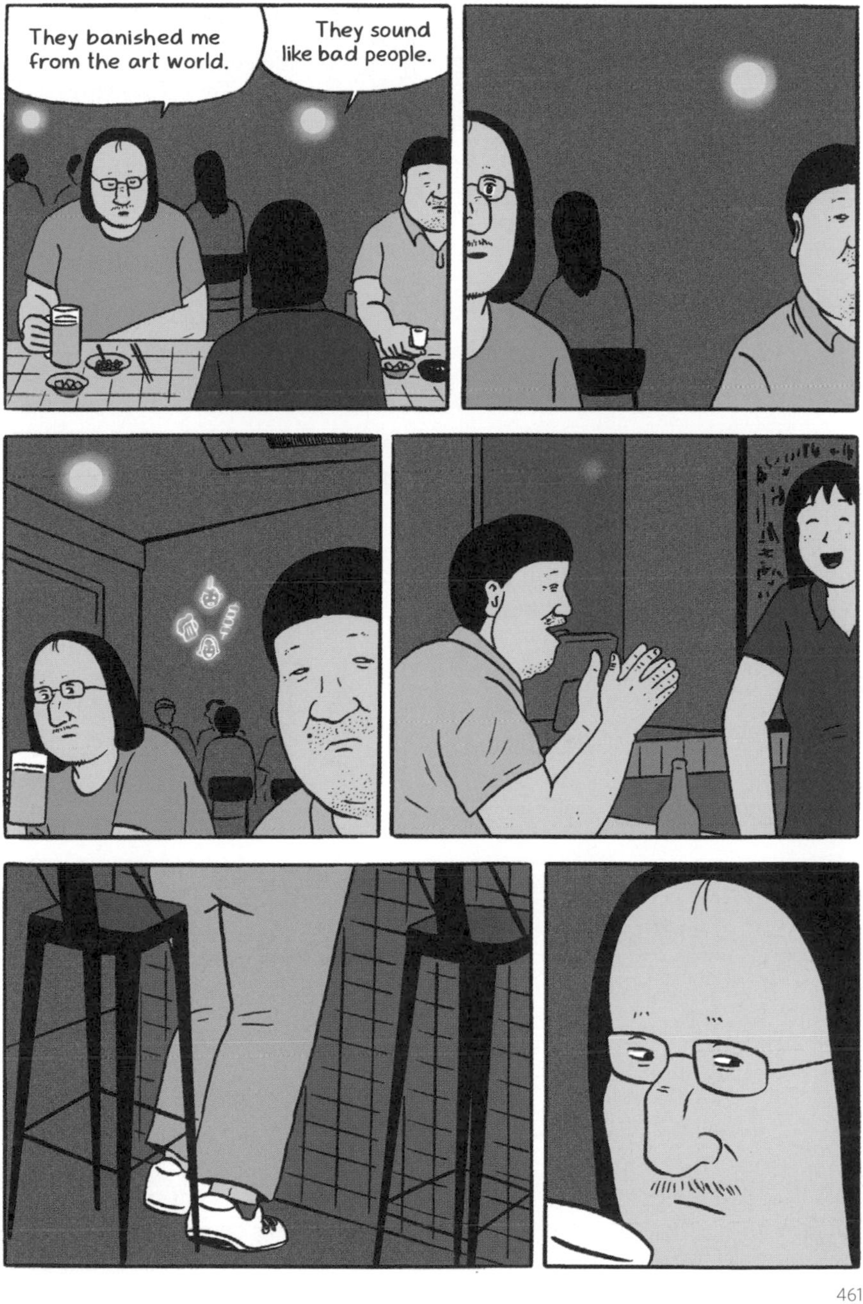
They banished me from the art world.
They sound like bad people.

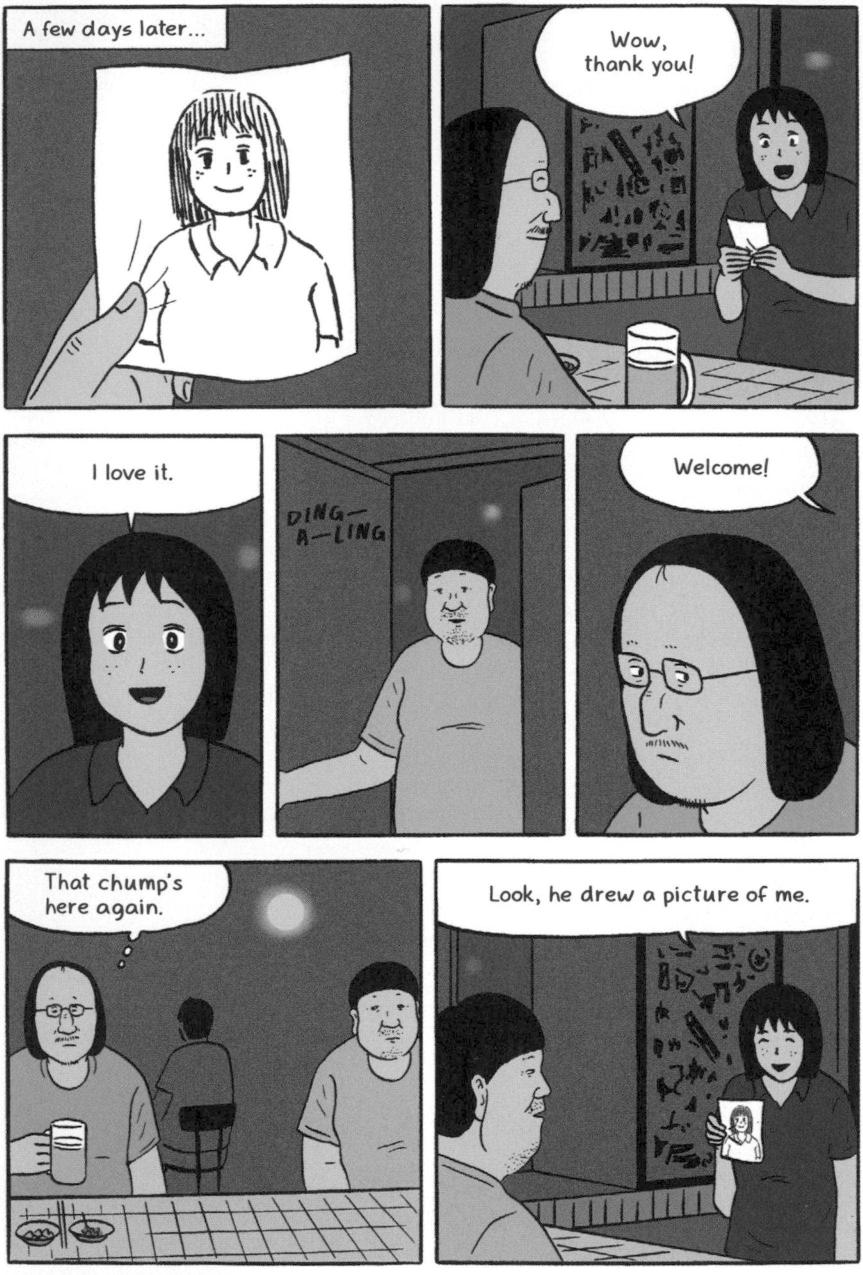
A few days later...
Wow, thank you!
I love it.
DING—A—LING
Welcome!
That chump's here again.
Look, he drew a picture of me.

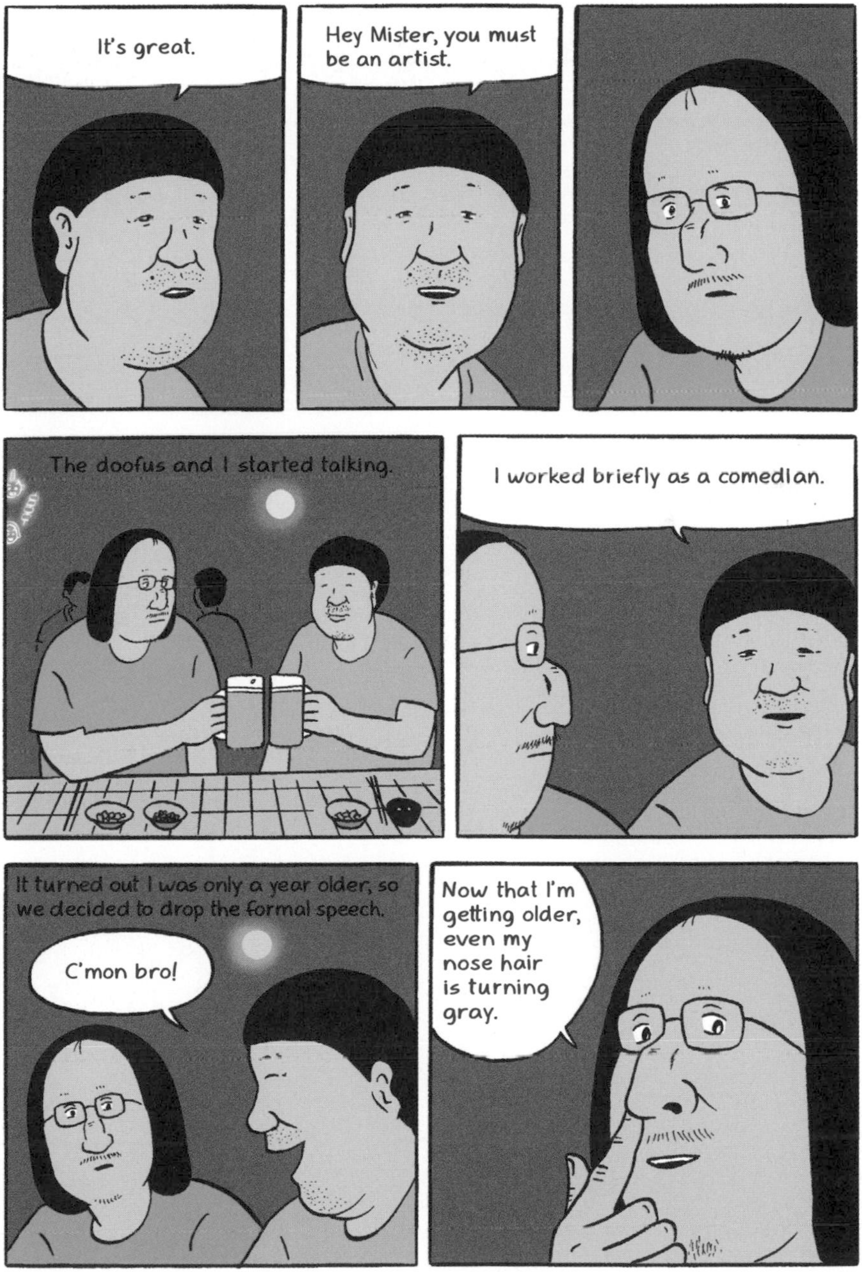
It's great.
Hey Mister, you must be an artist.
The doofus and I started talking.
I worked briefly as a comedian.
It turned out I was only a year older, so we decided to drop the formal speech.
C'mon bro!
Now that I'm getting older, even my nose hair is turning gray.

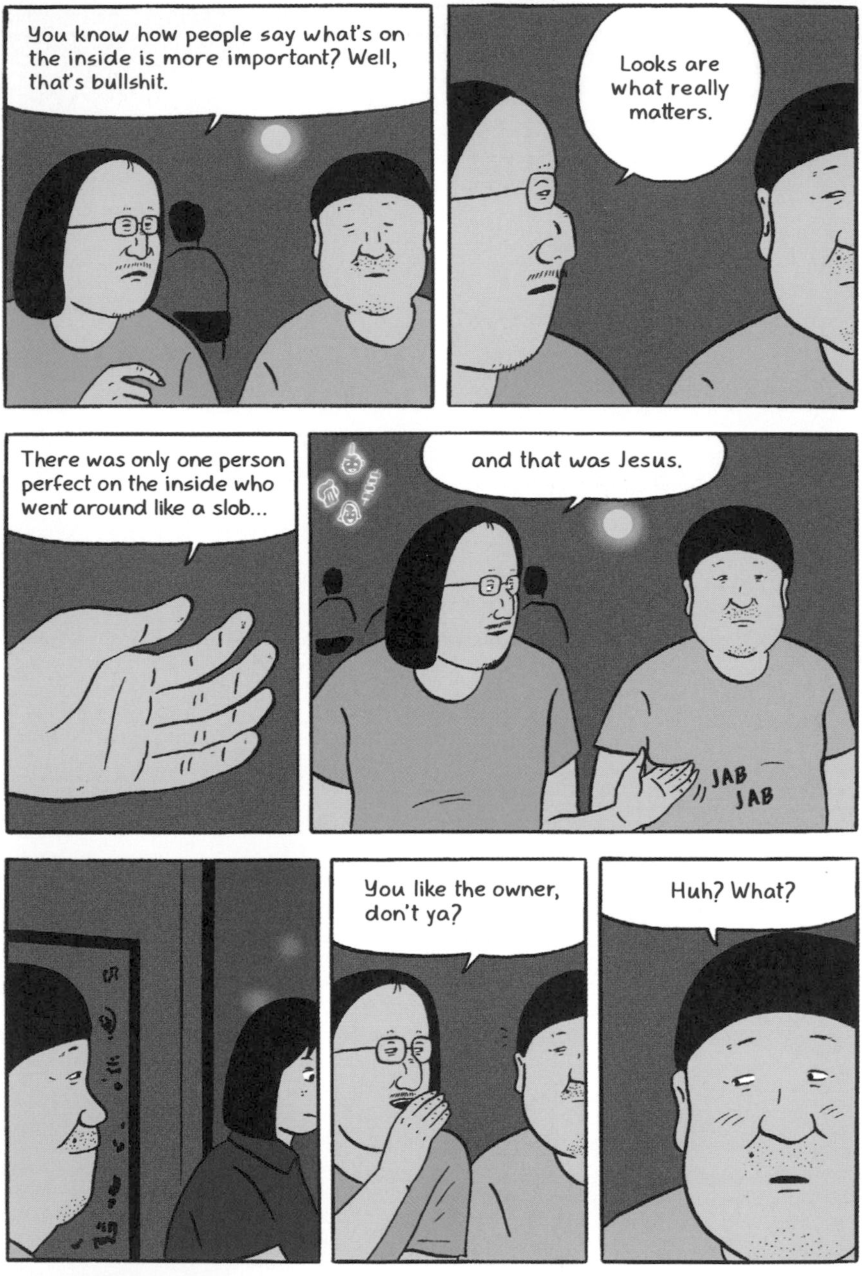
You know how people say what's on the inside is more important? Well, that's bullshit.
Looks are what really matters.
There was only one person perfect on the inside who went around like a slob...
and that was Jesus.
JAB
JAB
You like the owner, don't ya?
Huh? What?

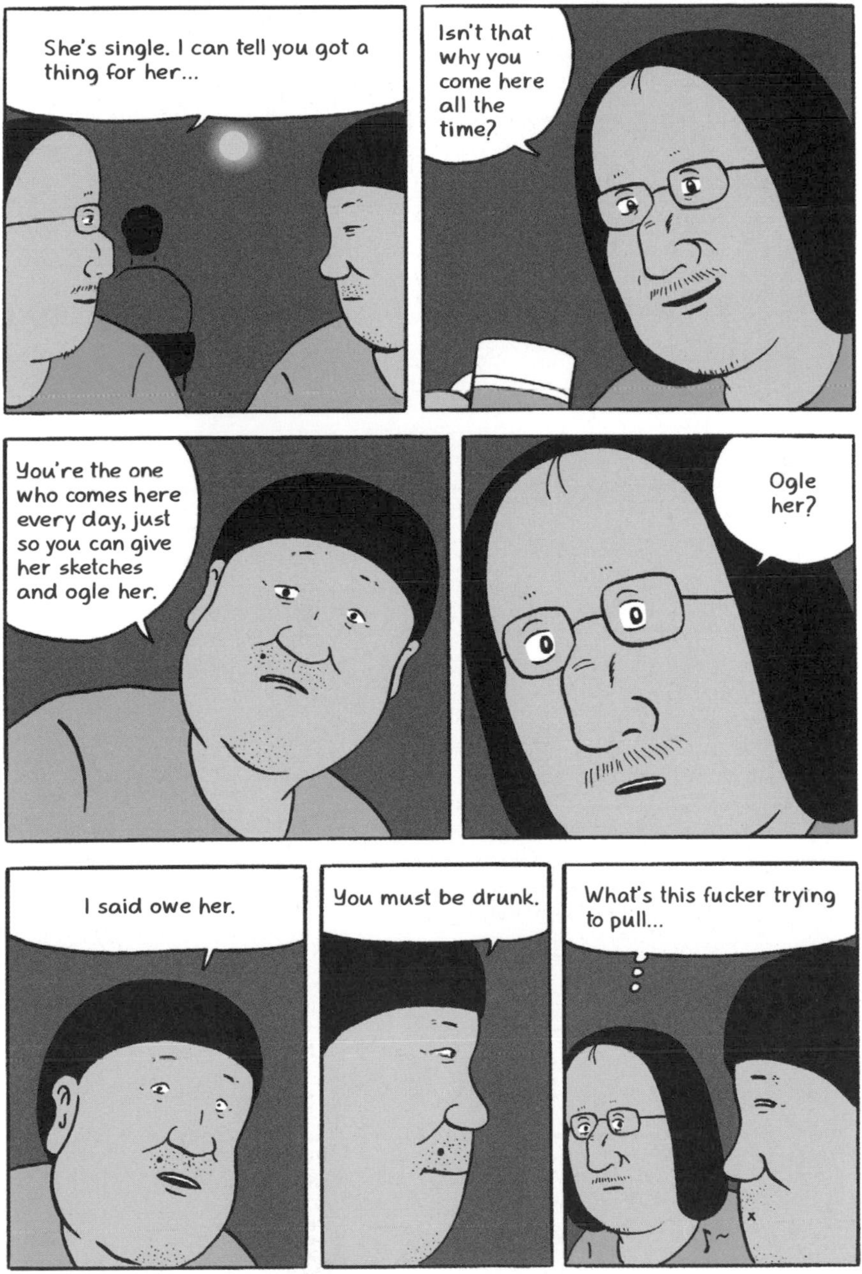
She's single. I can tell you got a thing for her...
Isn't that why you come here all the time?
You're the one who comes here every day, just so you can give her sketches and ogle her.
Ogle her?
I said owe her.
You must be drunk.
What's this fucker trying to pull...

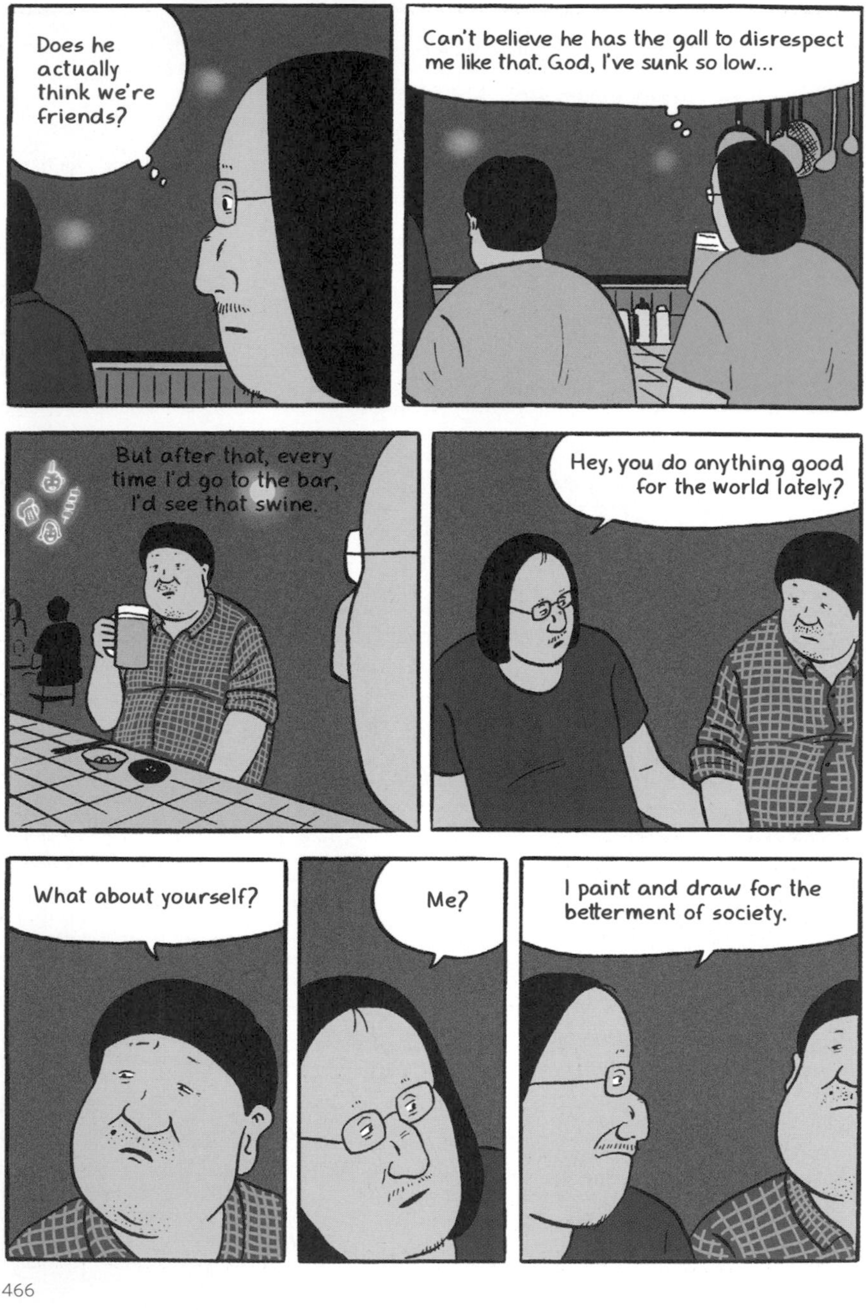
Does he actually think we're friends?
Can't believe he has the gall to disrespect me like that. God, I've sunk so low...
But after that, every time I'd go to the bar, I'd see that swine.
Hey, you do anything good for the world lately?
What about yourself?
Me?
I paint and draw for the betterment of society.

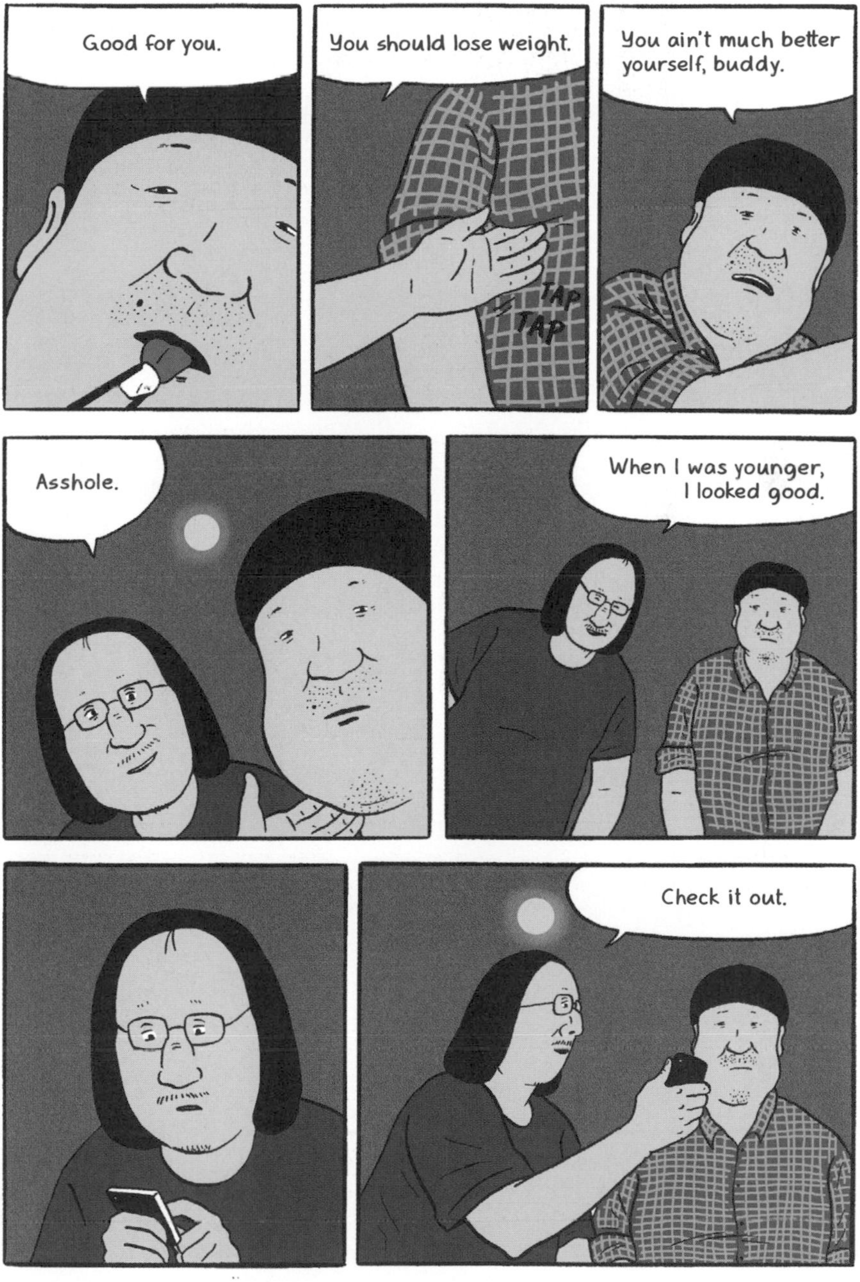
Good for you.
You should lose weight.
TAP TAP
You ain't much better yourself, buddy.
Asshole.
When I was younger, I looked good.
Check it out.

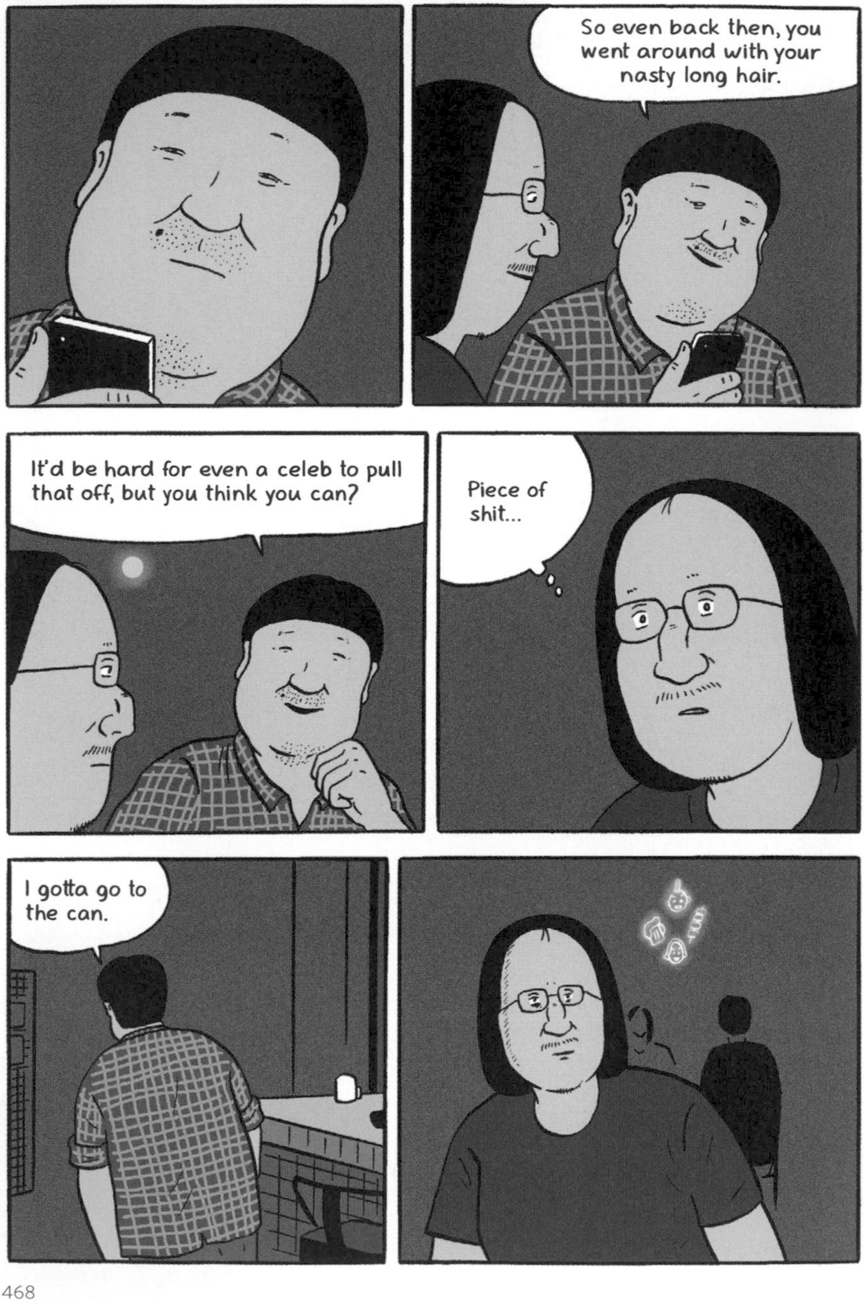
So even back then, you went around with your nasty long hair.
It'd be hard for even a celeb to pull that off, but you think you can?
Piece of shit...
I gotta go to the can.

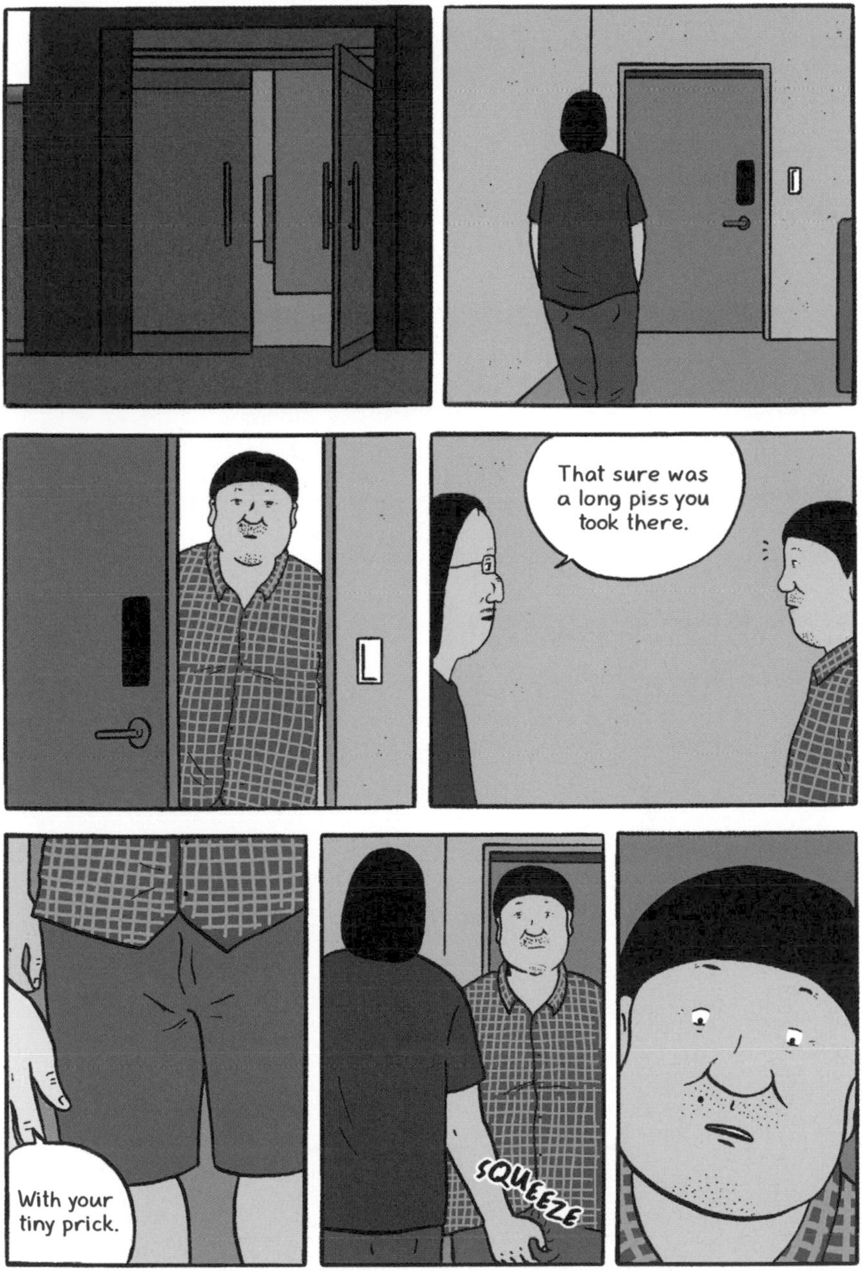
That sure was a long piss you took there.
With your tiny prick.
SQUEEZE

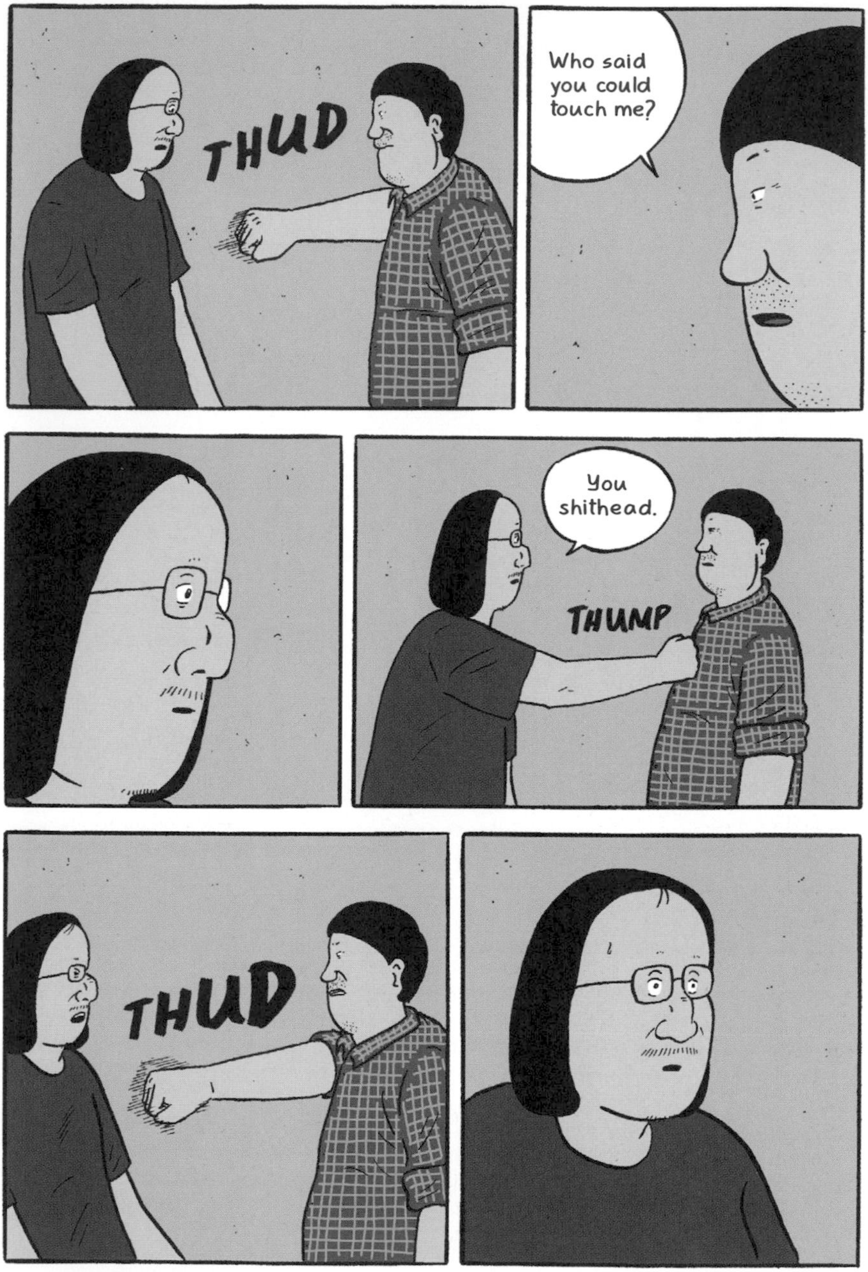
THUD
Who said you could touch me?
You shithead.
THUMP
THUD

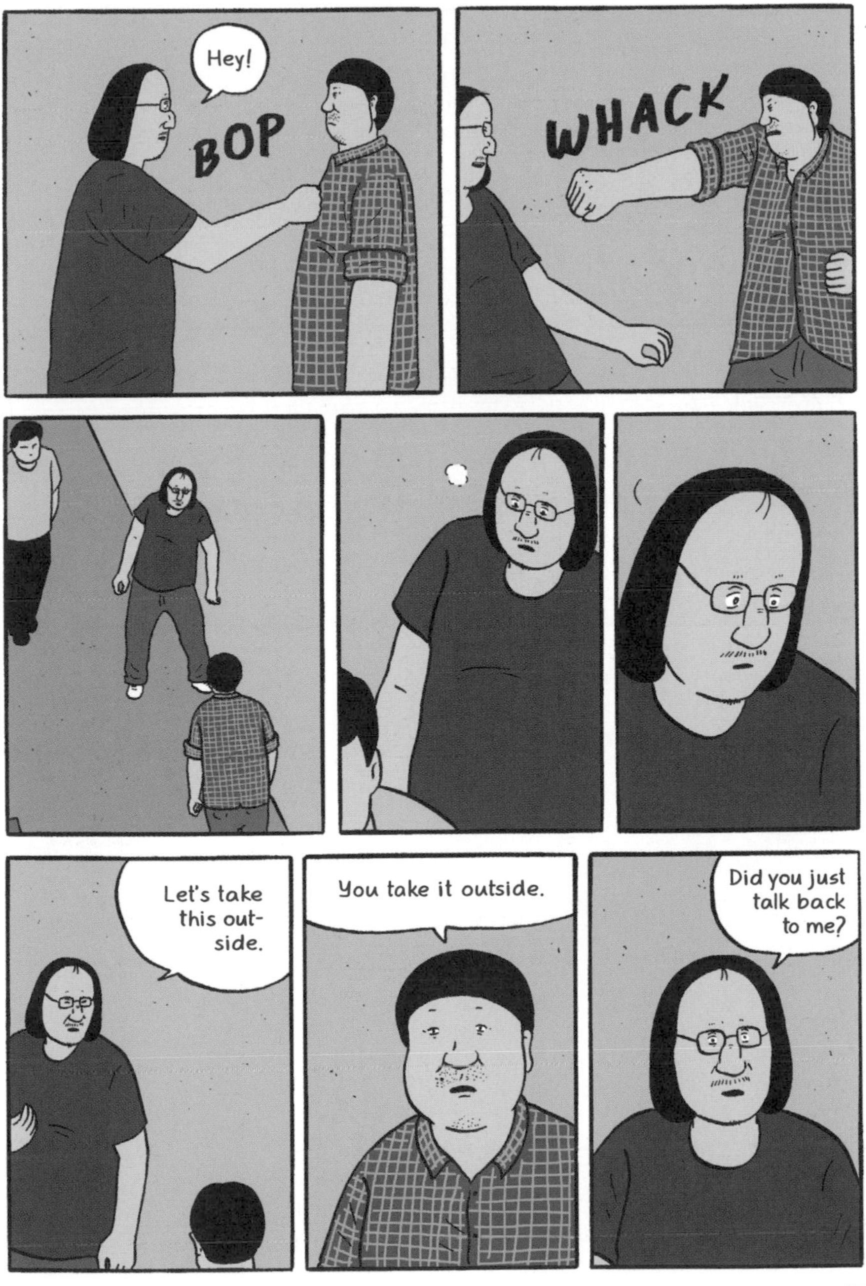
Hey!
BOP
WHACK
Let's take this out-side.
You take it outside.
Did you just talk back to me?

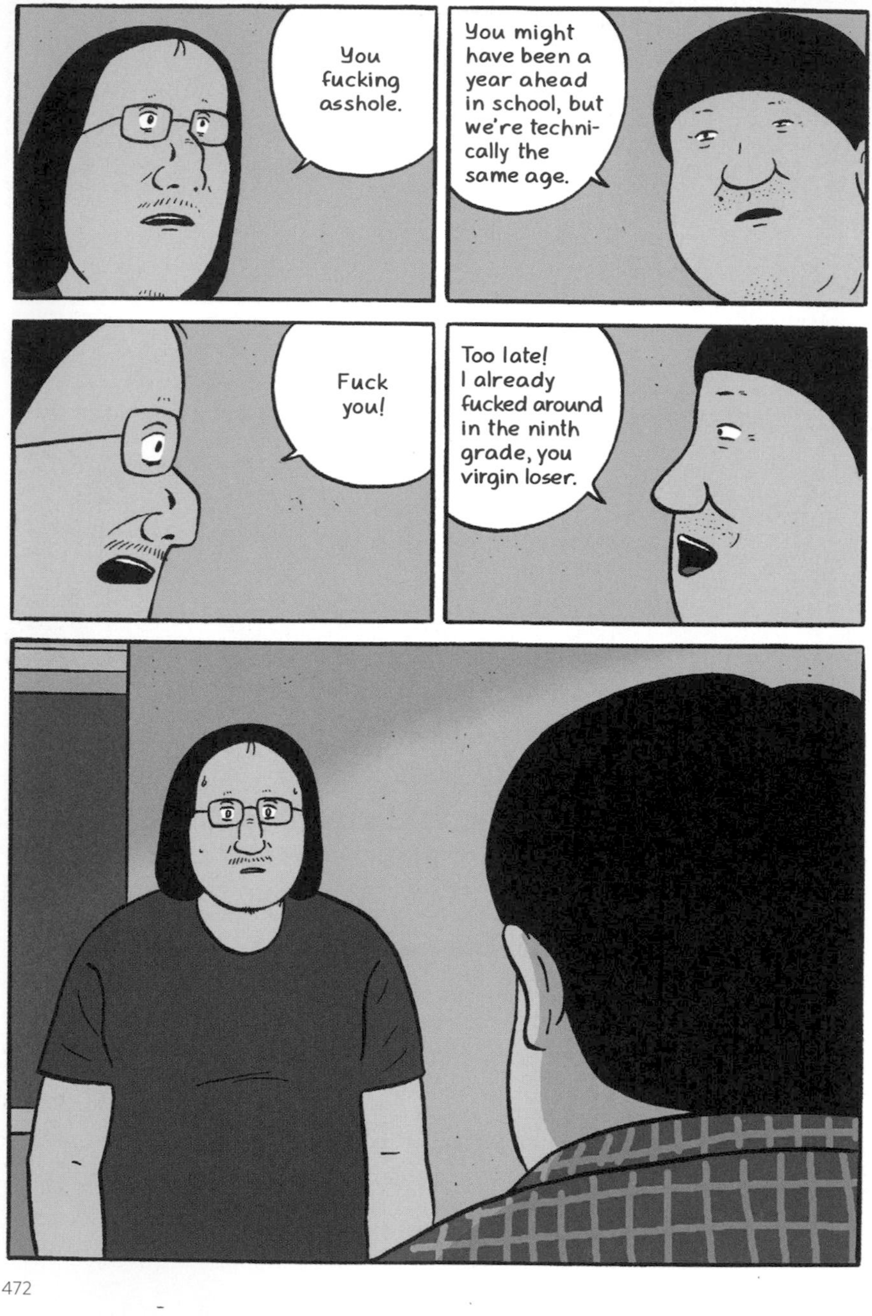
You fucking asshole.
You might have been a year ahead in school, but we're technically the same age.
Fuck you!
Too late! I already fucked around in the ninth grade, you virgin loser.

RIDICULOUS FIGHTS

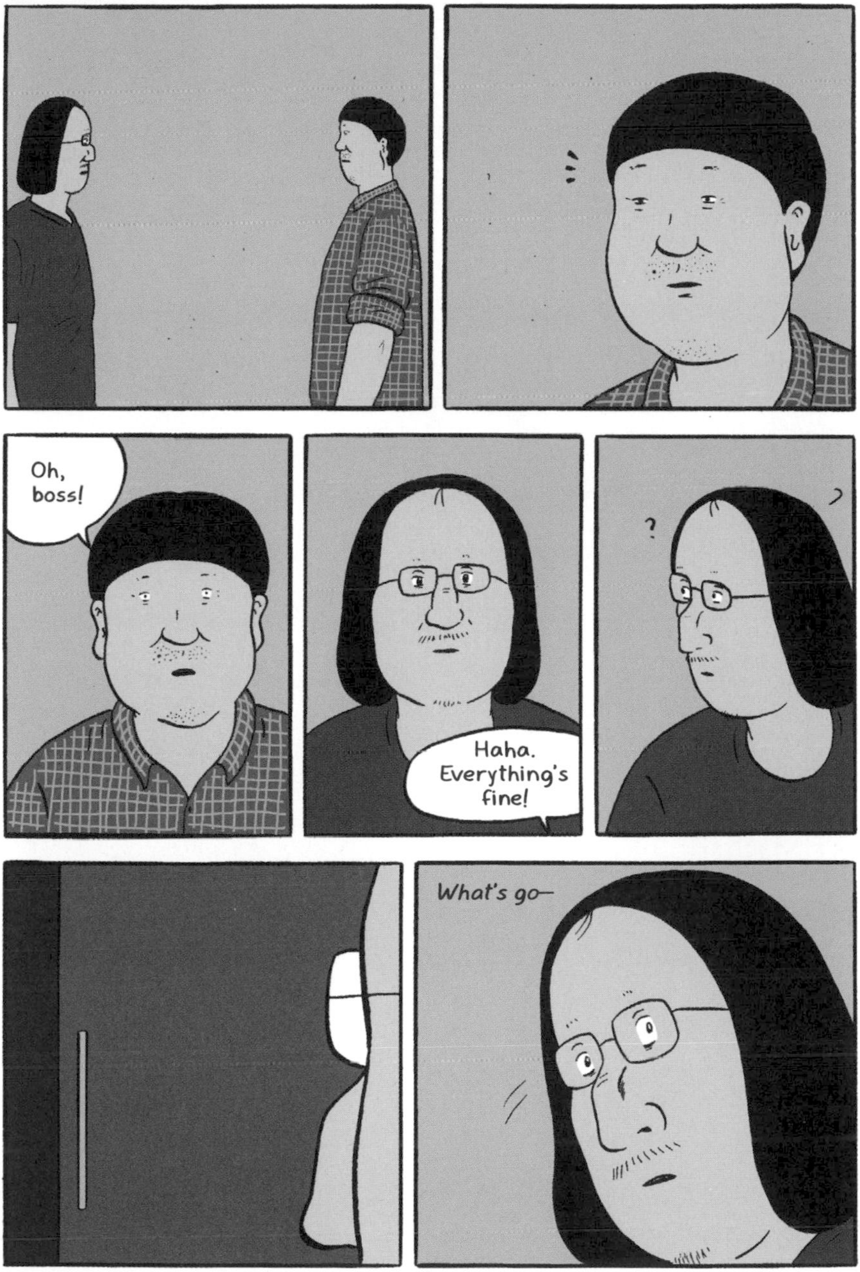
Oh, boss!
Haha. Everything's fine!
What's go—

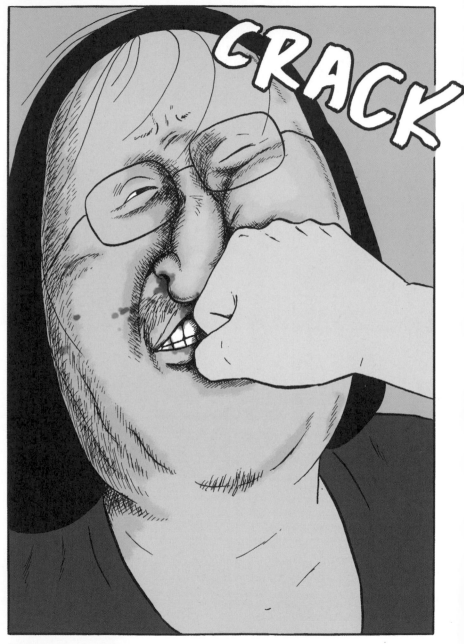

CRACK

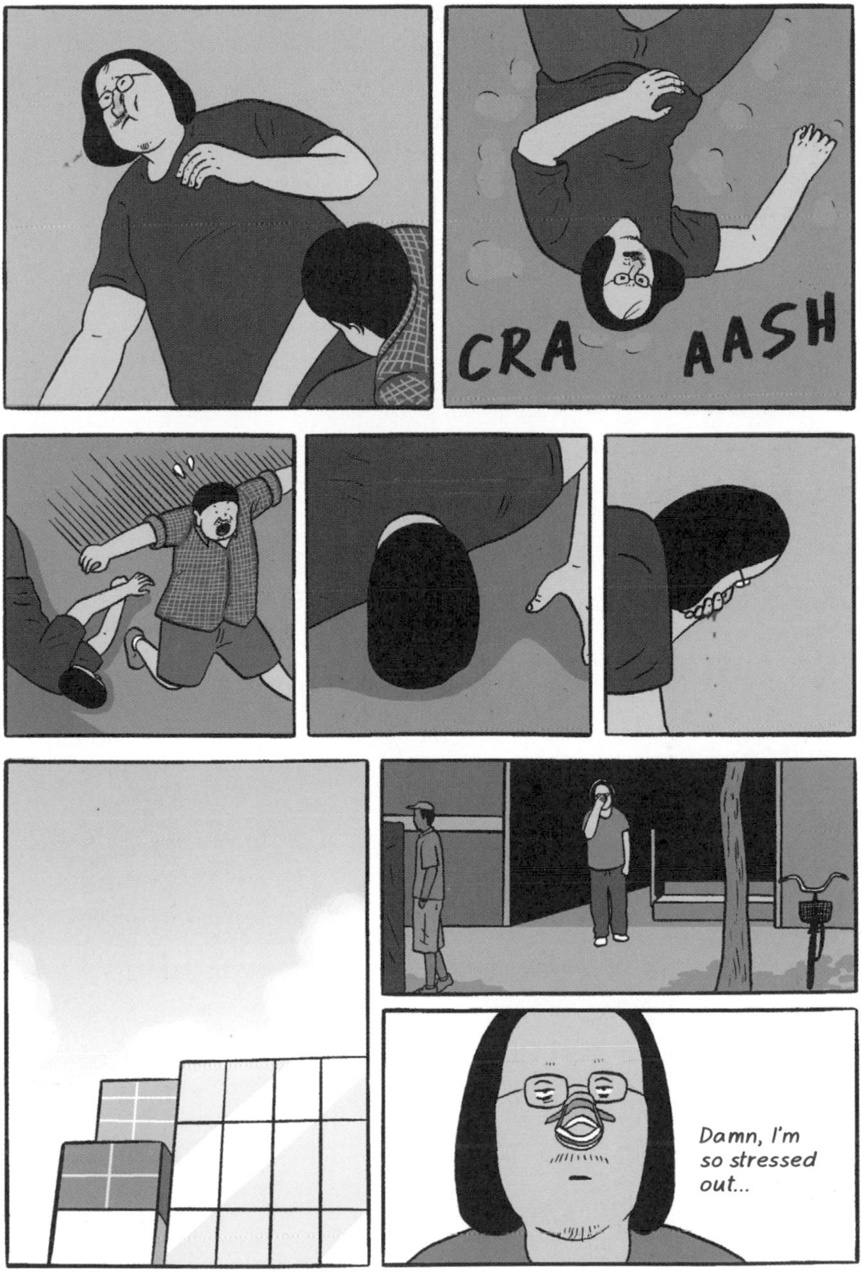
CRA AASH
Damn, I'm so stressed out...

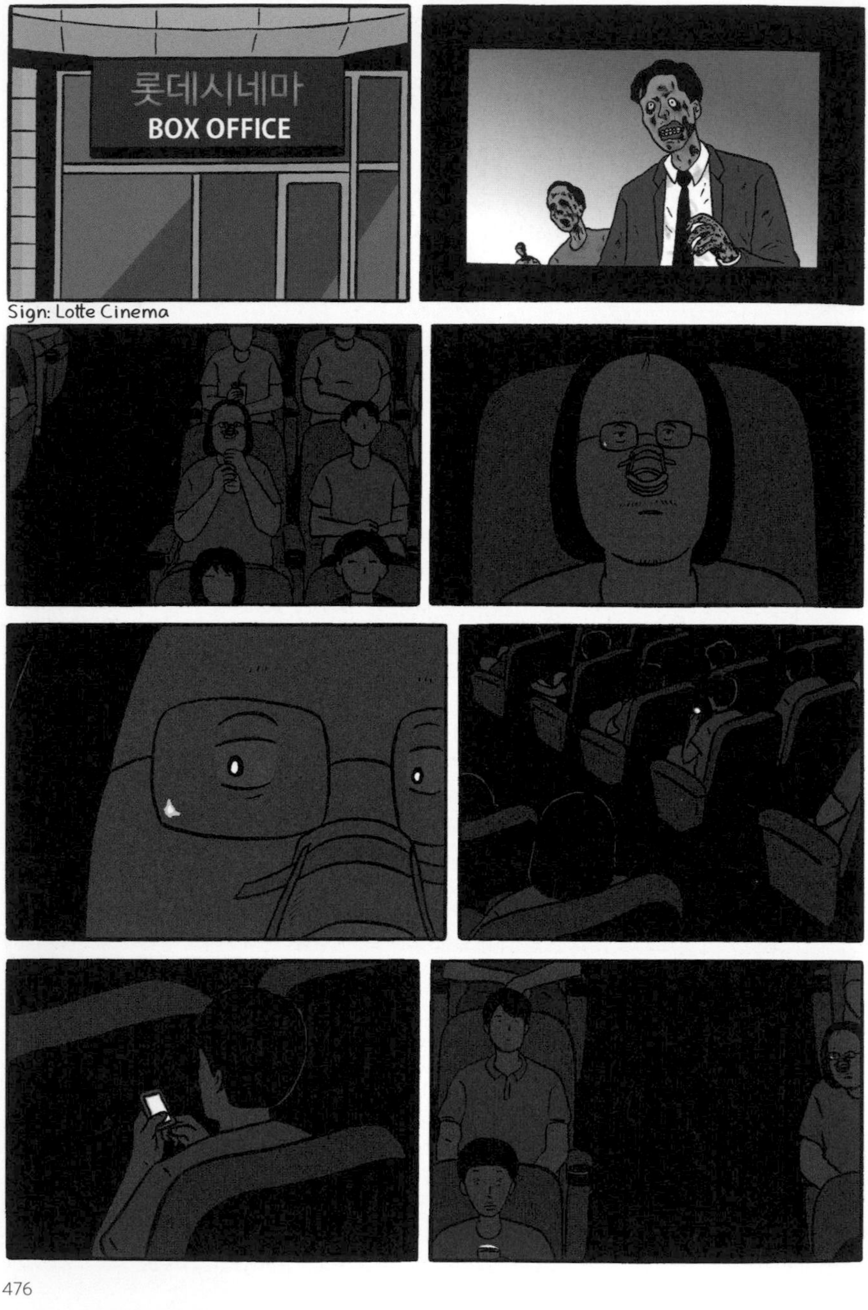
롯데시네마
BOX OFFICE

Sign: Lotte Cinema

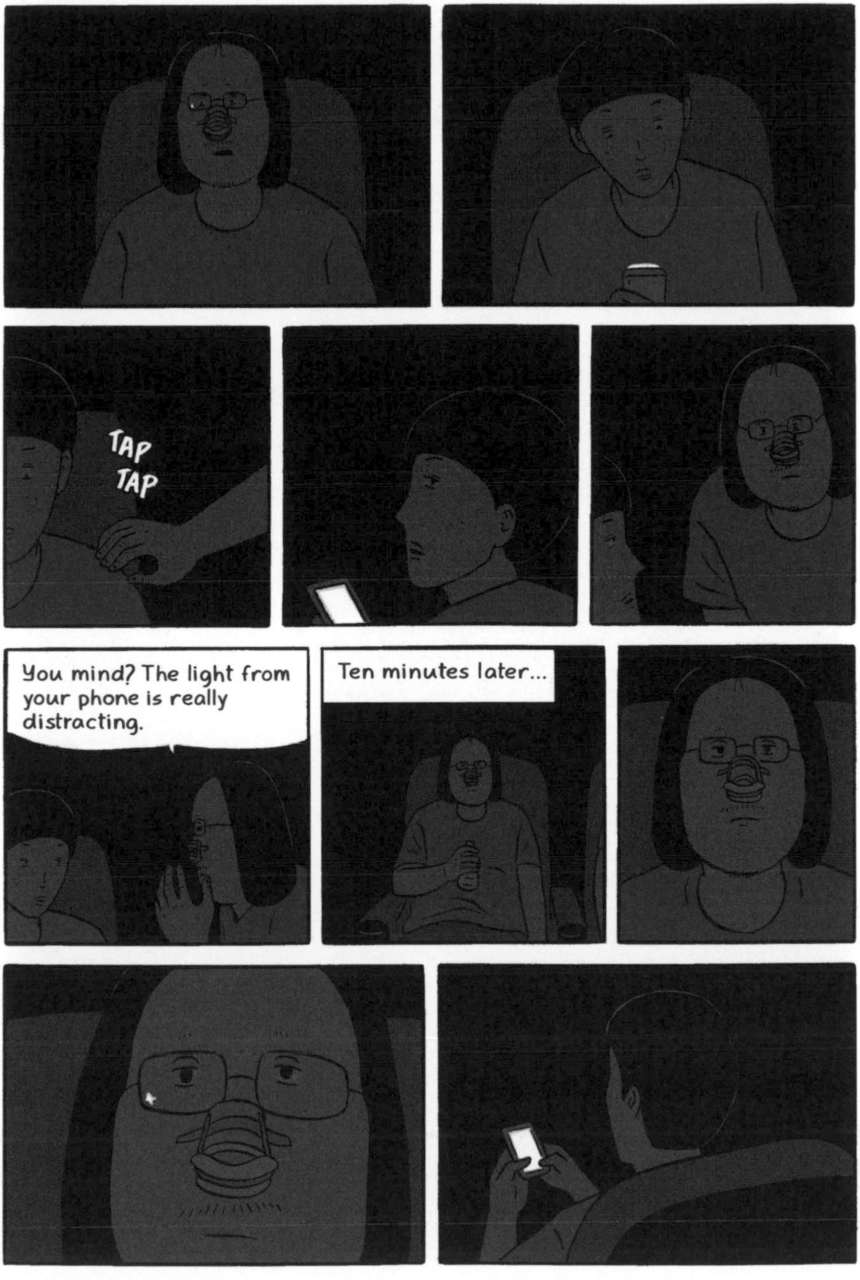
TAP
TAP
You mind? The light from your phone is really distracting.
Ten minutes later...

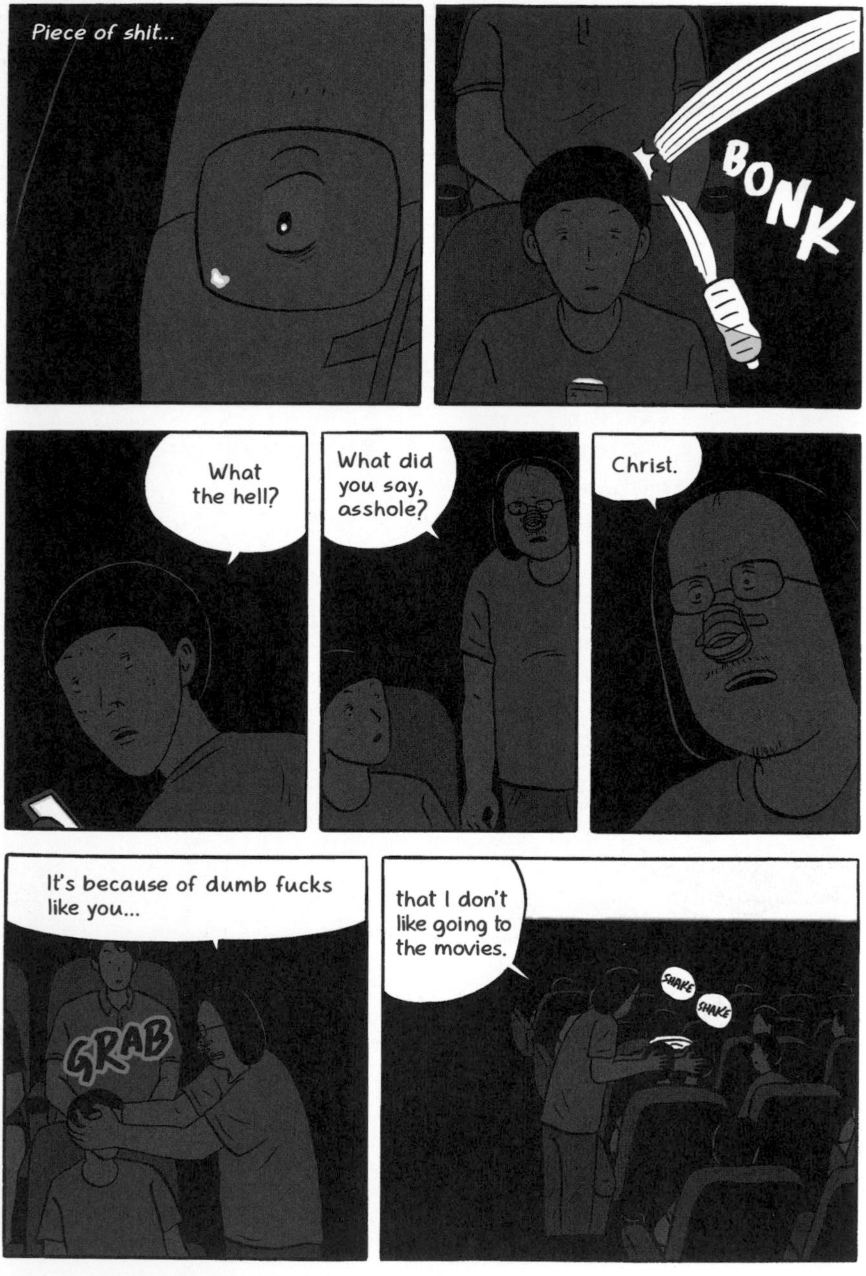
Piece of shit...
BONK
What the hell?
What did you say, asshole?
Christ.
It's because of dumb fucks like you...
GRAB
that I don't like going to the movies.
SHAKE
SHAKE

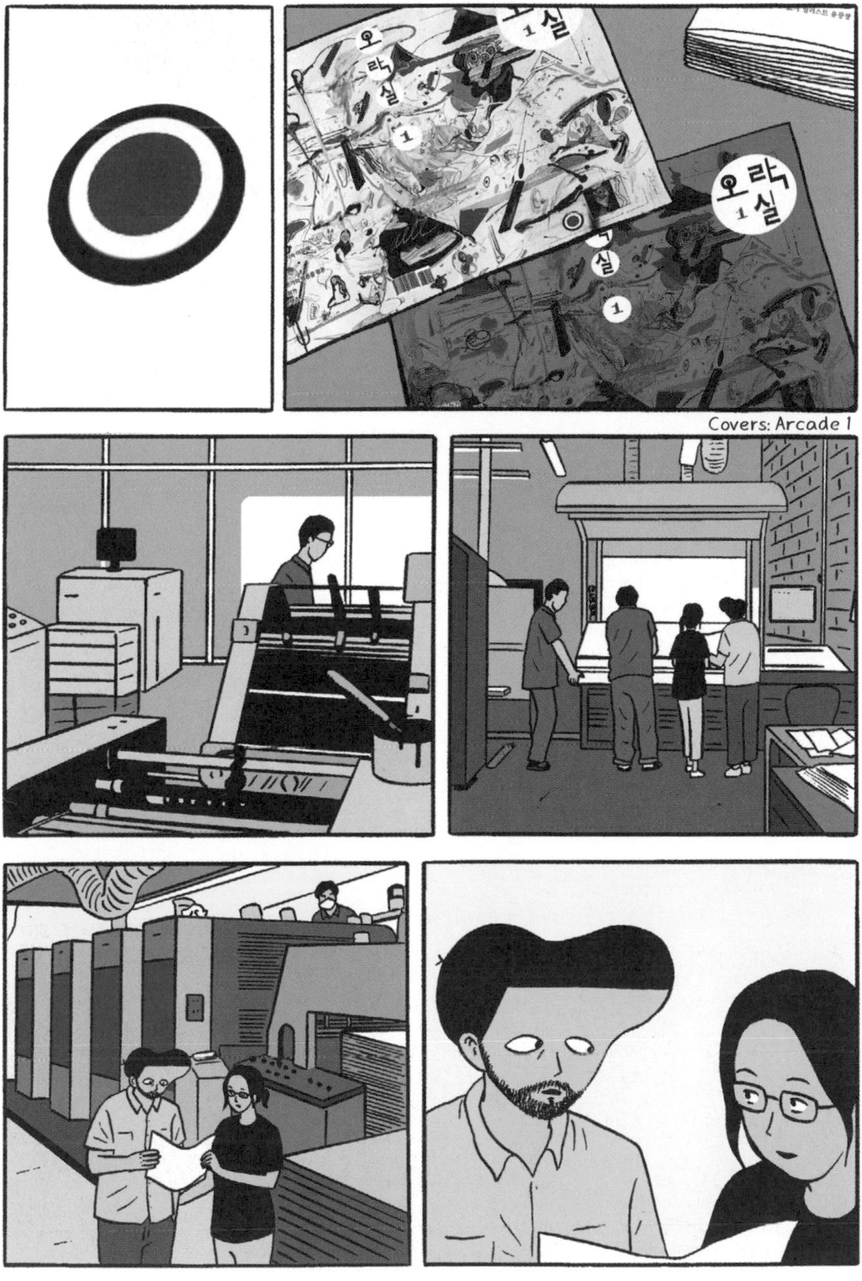
오락실 1
Covers: Arcade 1

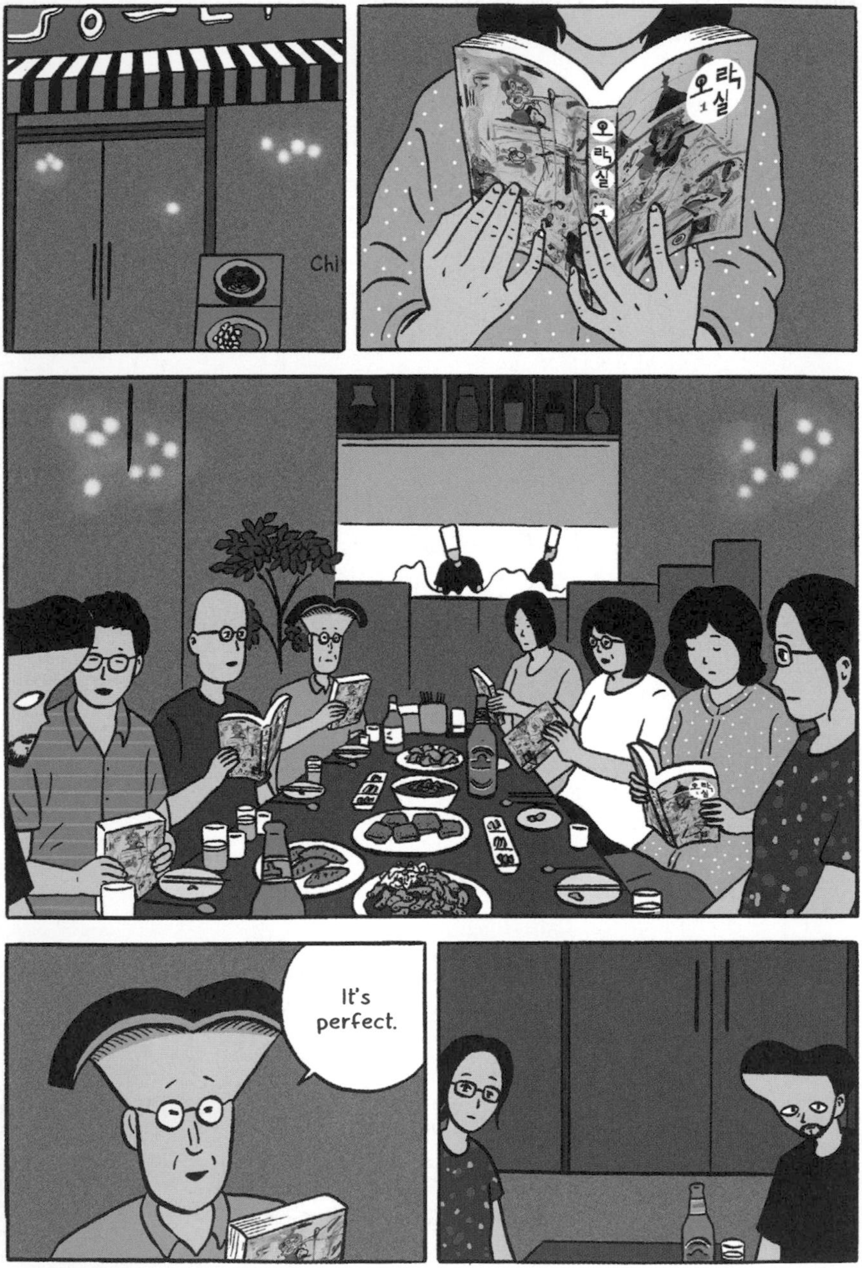
Chi
오락실 1
It's perfect.

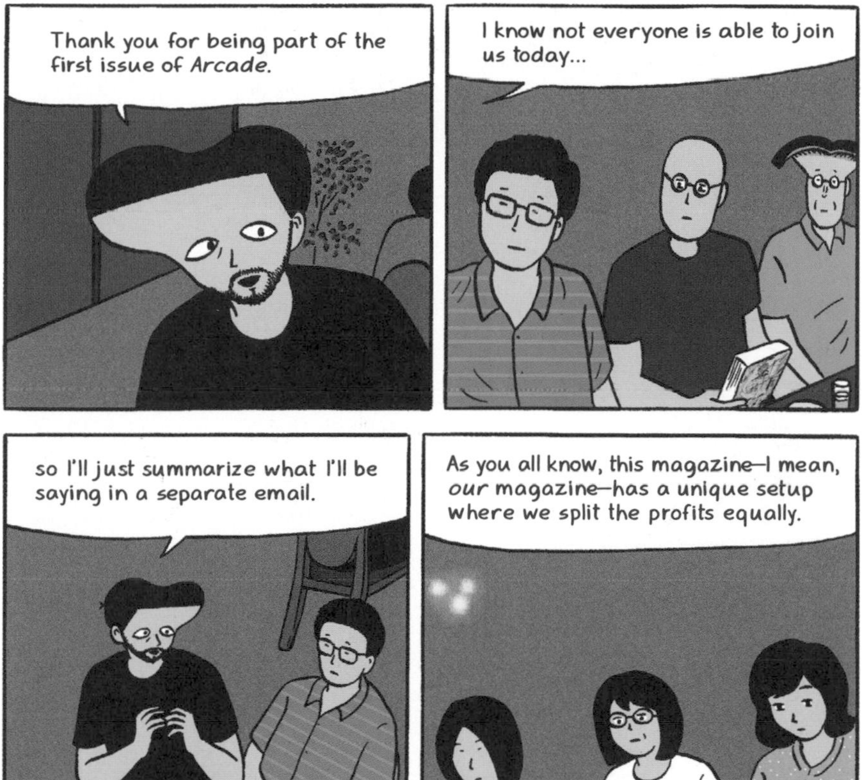
Thank you for being part of the first issue of *Arcade*.
I know not everyone is able to join us today...
so I'll just summarize what I'll be saying in a separate email.
As you all know, this magazine—I mean, *our* magazine—has a unique setup where we split the profits equally.
Our print run was two thousand copies.
The issue will be sold for 12,000 won apiece...
오락실
and the publisher gets about sixty percent of the list price.

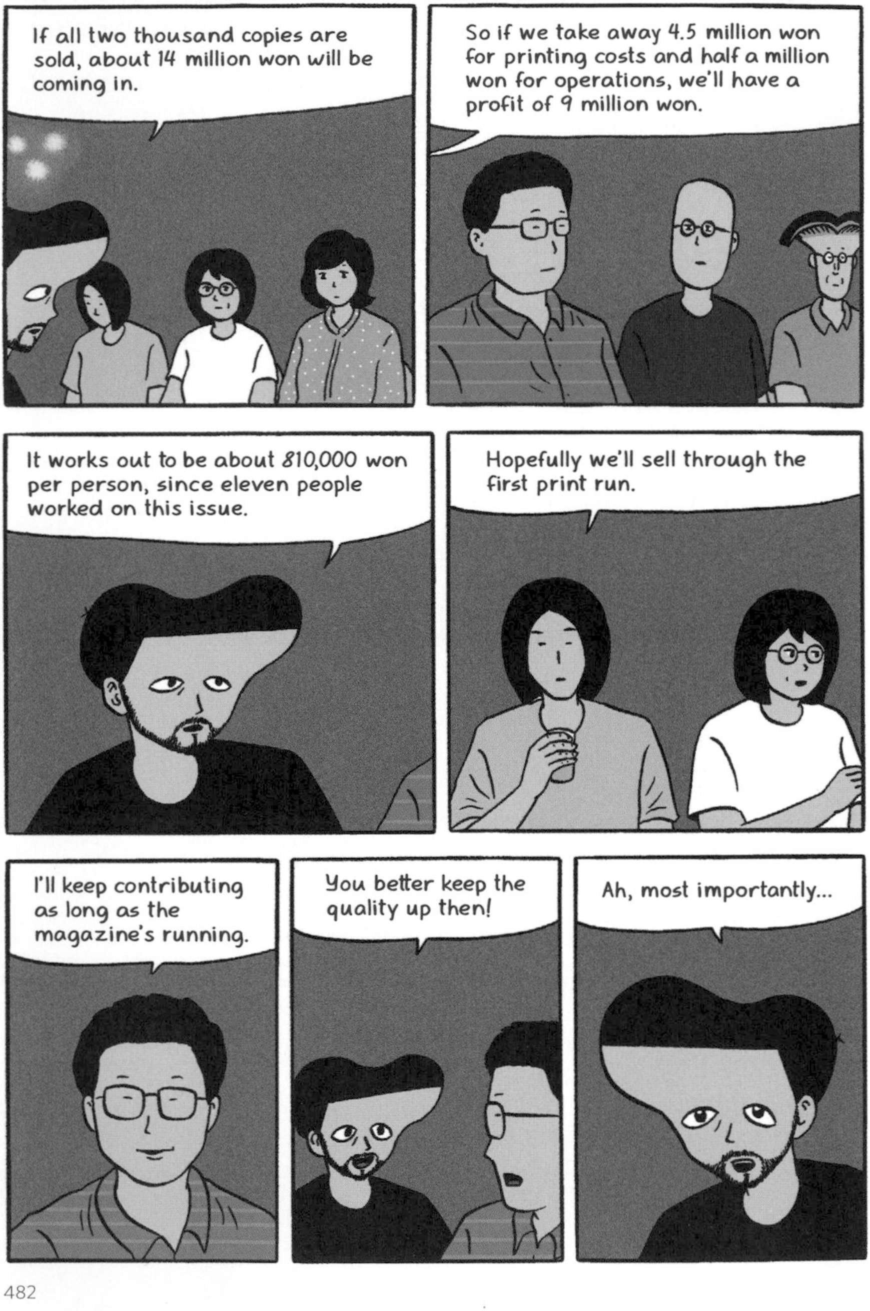
If all two thousand copies are sold, about 14 million won will be coming in.
So if we take away 4.5 million won for printing costs and half a million won for operations, we'll have a profit of 9 million won.
It works out to be about 810,000 won per person, since eleven people worked on this issue.
Hopefully we'll sell through the first print run.
I'll keep contributing as long as the magazine's running.
You better keep the quality up then!
Ah, most importantly...

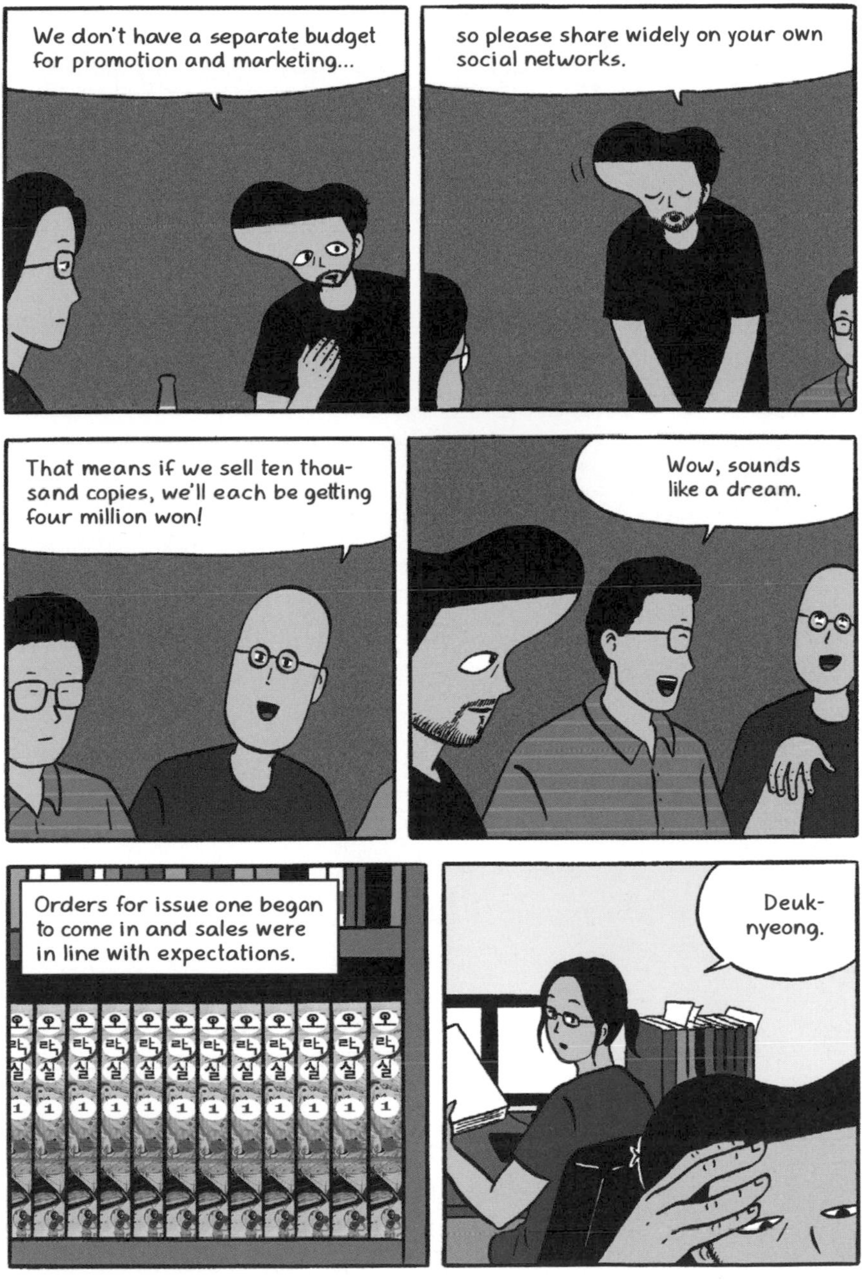
We don't have a separate budget for promotion and marketing...
so please share widely on your own social networks.
That means if we sell ten thousand copies, we'll each be getting four million won!
Wow, sounds like a dream.
Orders for issue one began to come in and sales were in line with expectations.
오락실
1
Deuk-nyeong.

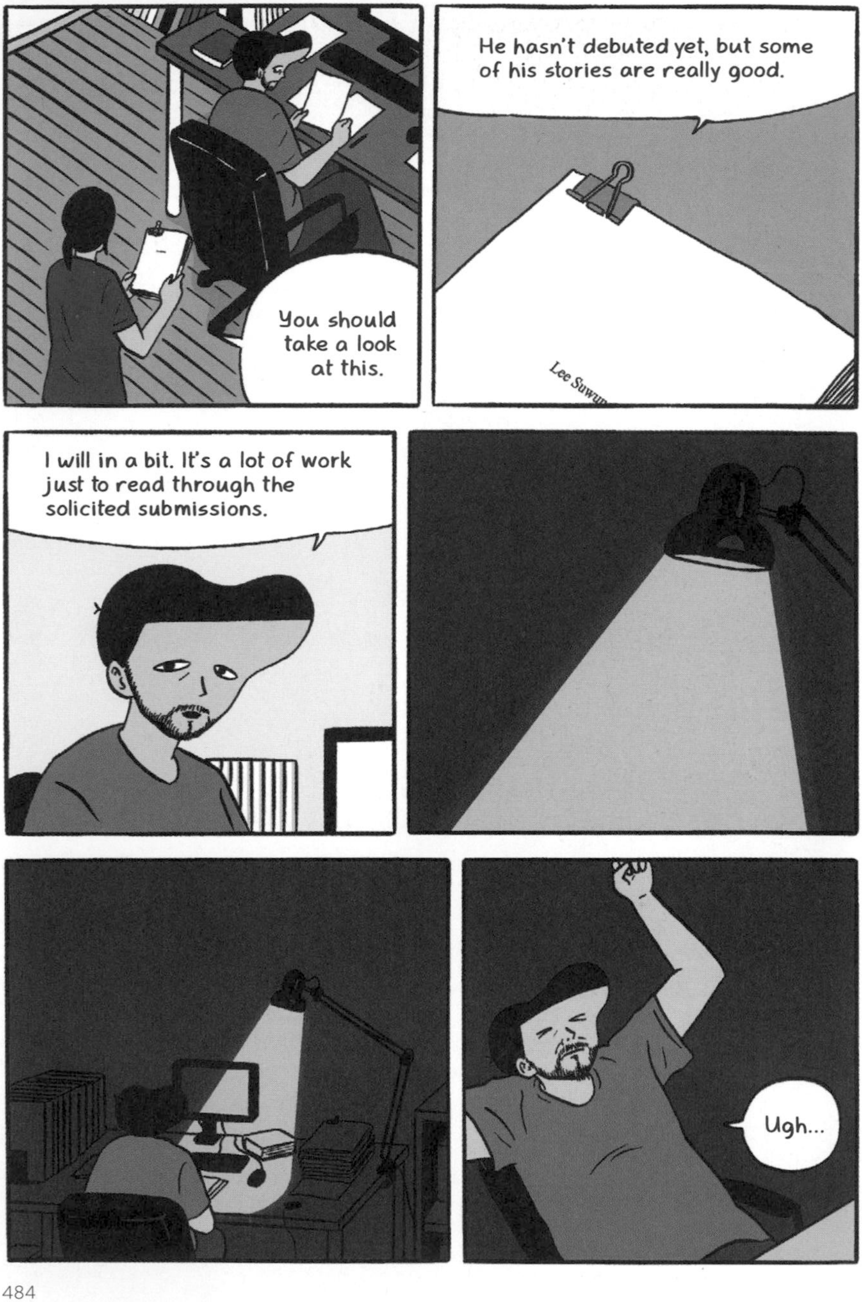
You should take a look at this.
He hasn't debuted yet, but some of his stories are really good.
I will in a bit. It's a lot of work just to read through the solicited submissions.
Ugh...

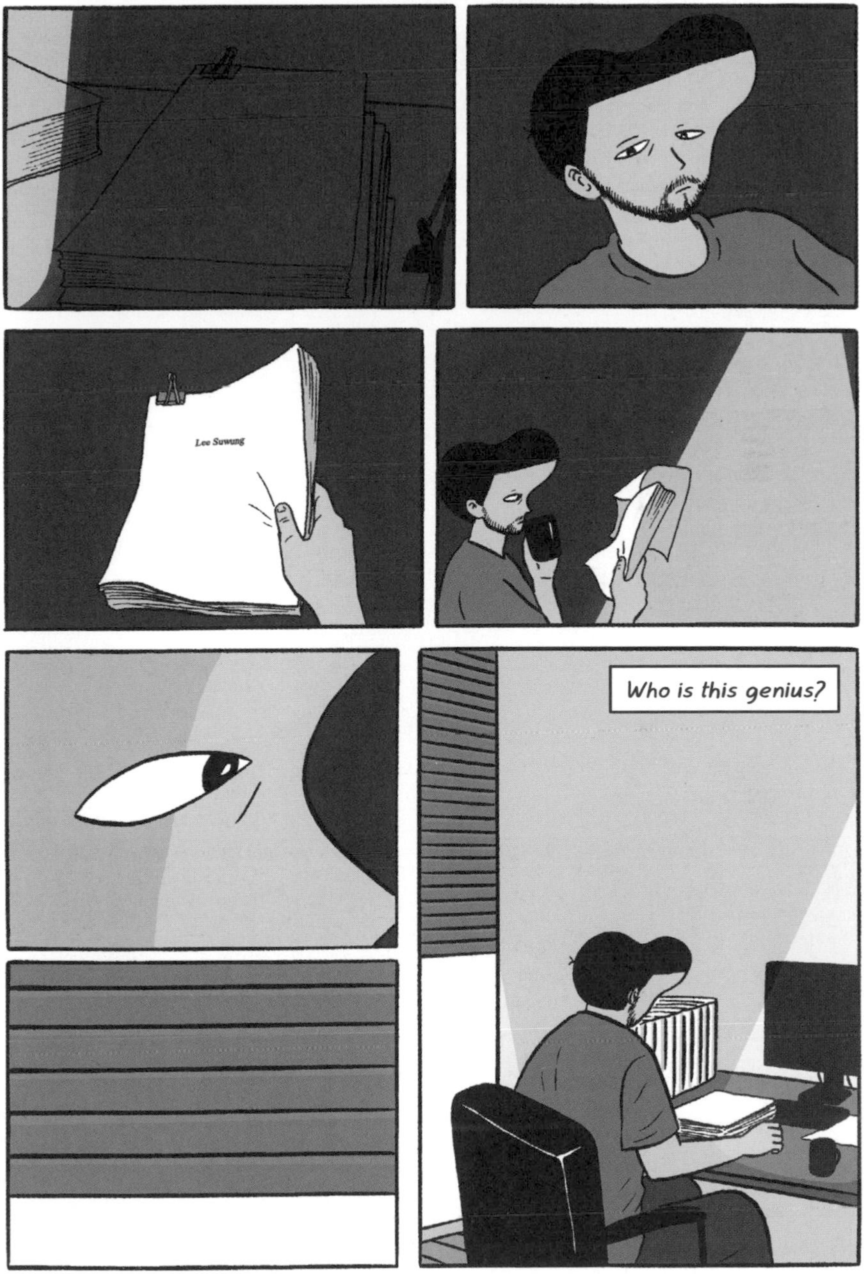
Lee Suwung
Who is this genius?

HANDSOME GENIUS WRITER

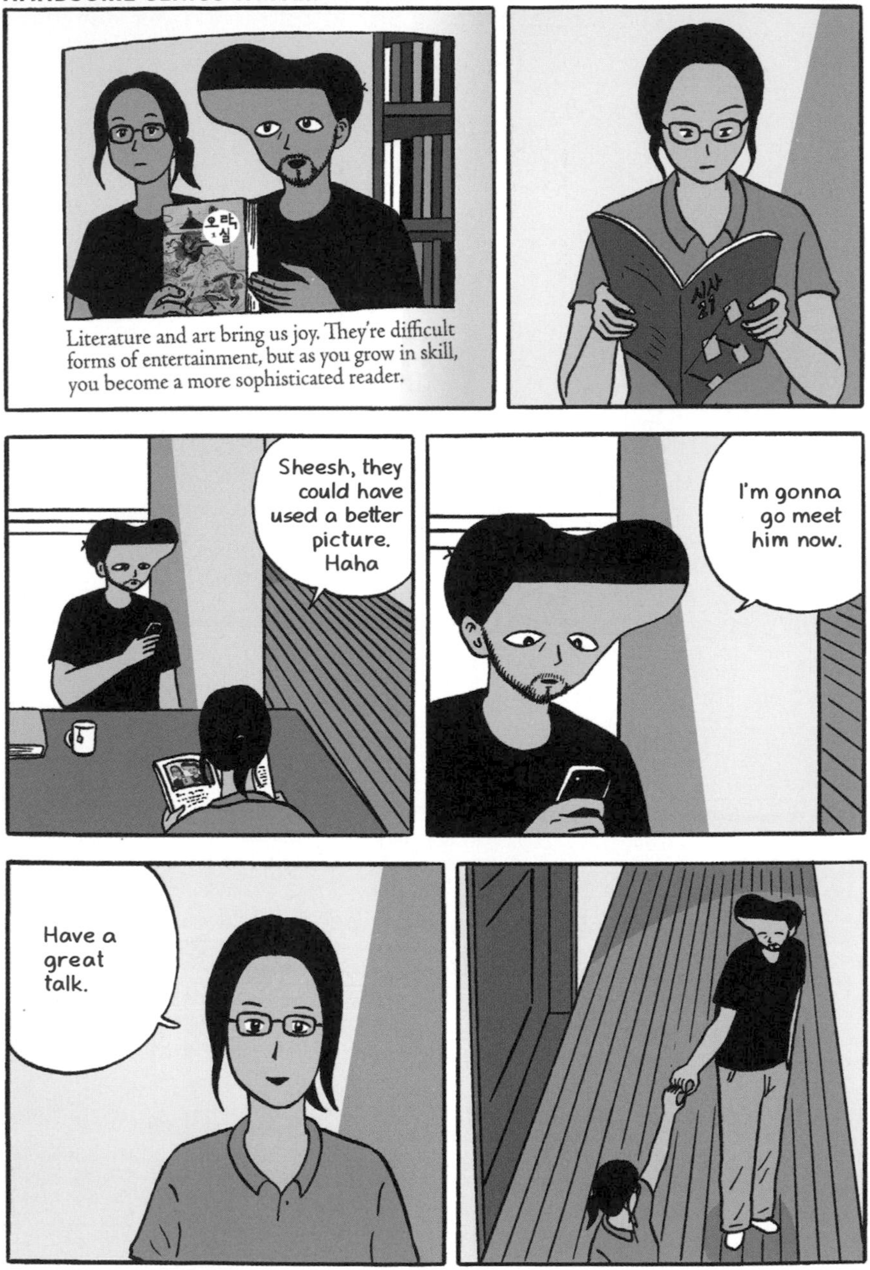
Literature and art bring us joy. They're difficult forms of entertainment, but as you grow in skill, you become a more sophisticated reader.
Sheesh, they could have used a better picture. Haha
I'm gonna go meet him now.
Have a great talk.

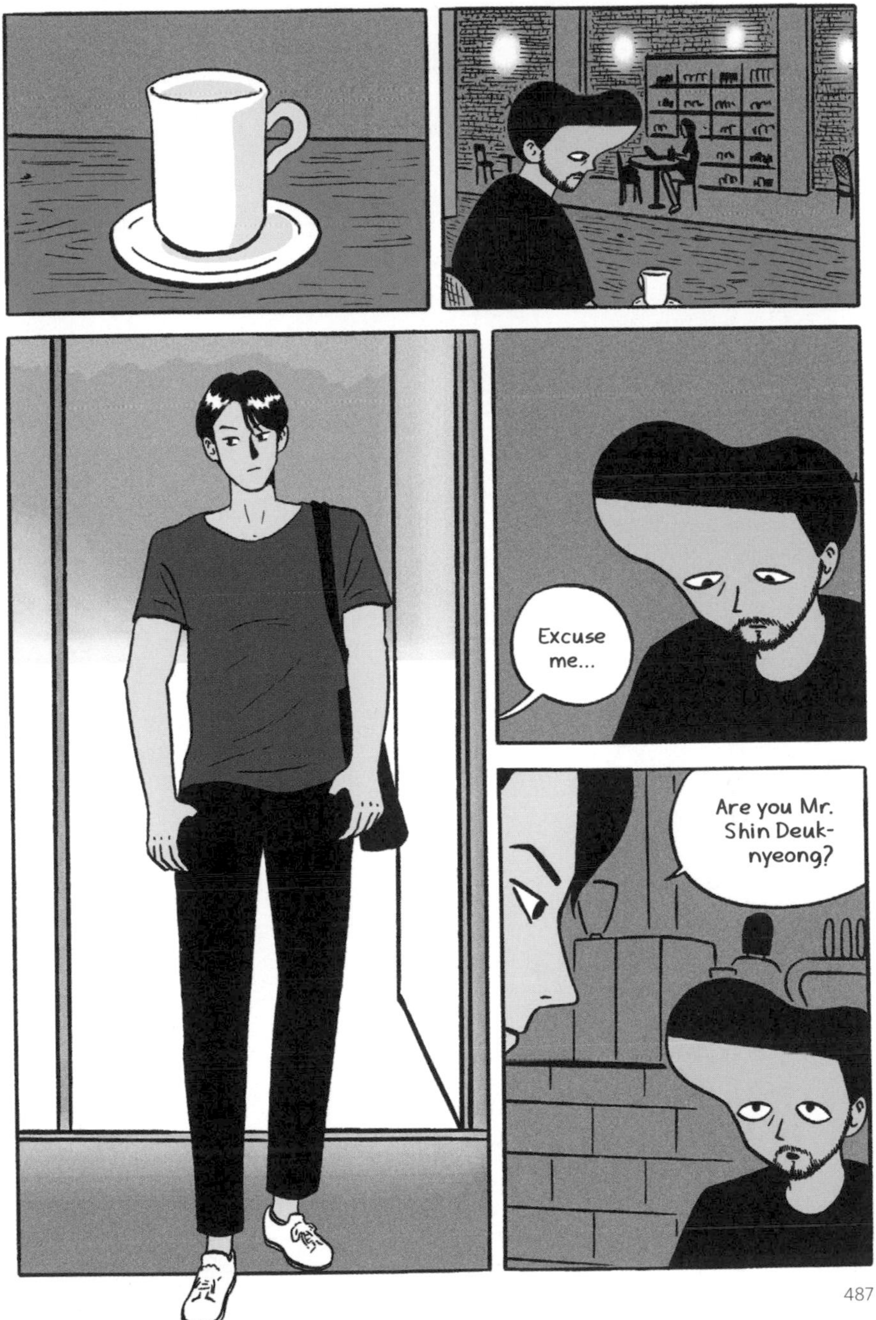
Excuse me...
Are you Mr. Shin Deuk-nyeong?

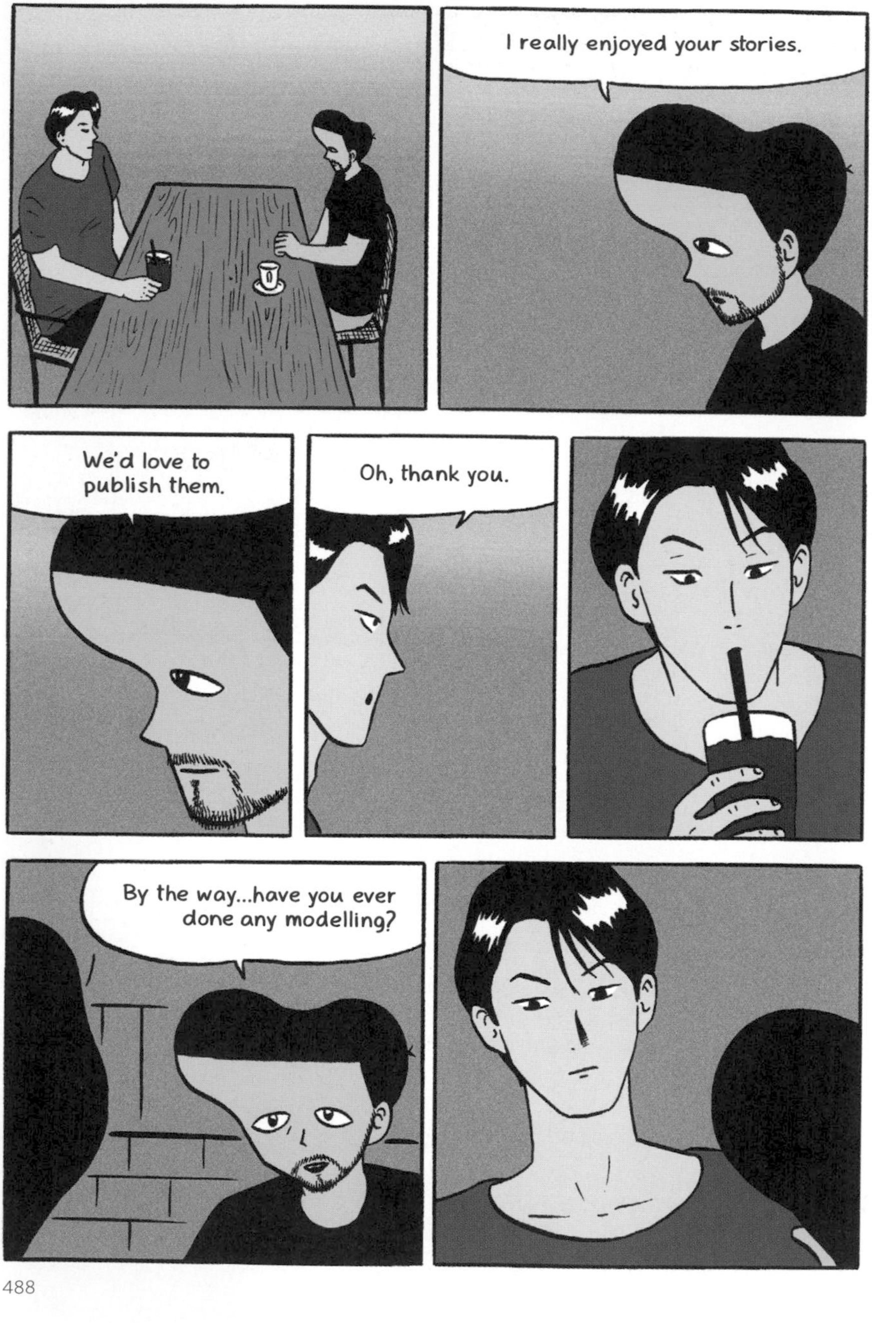
I really enjoyed your stories.
We'd love to publish them.
Oh, thank you.
By the way...have you ever done any modelling?

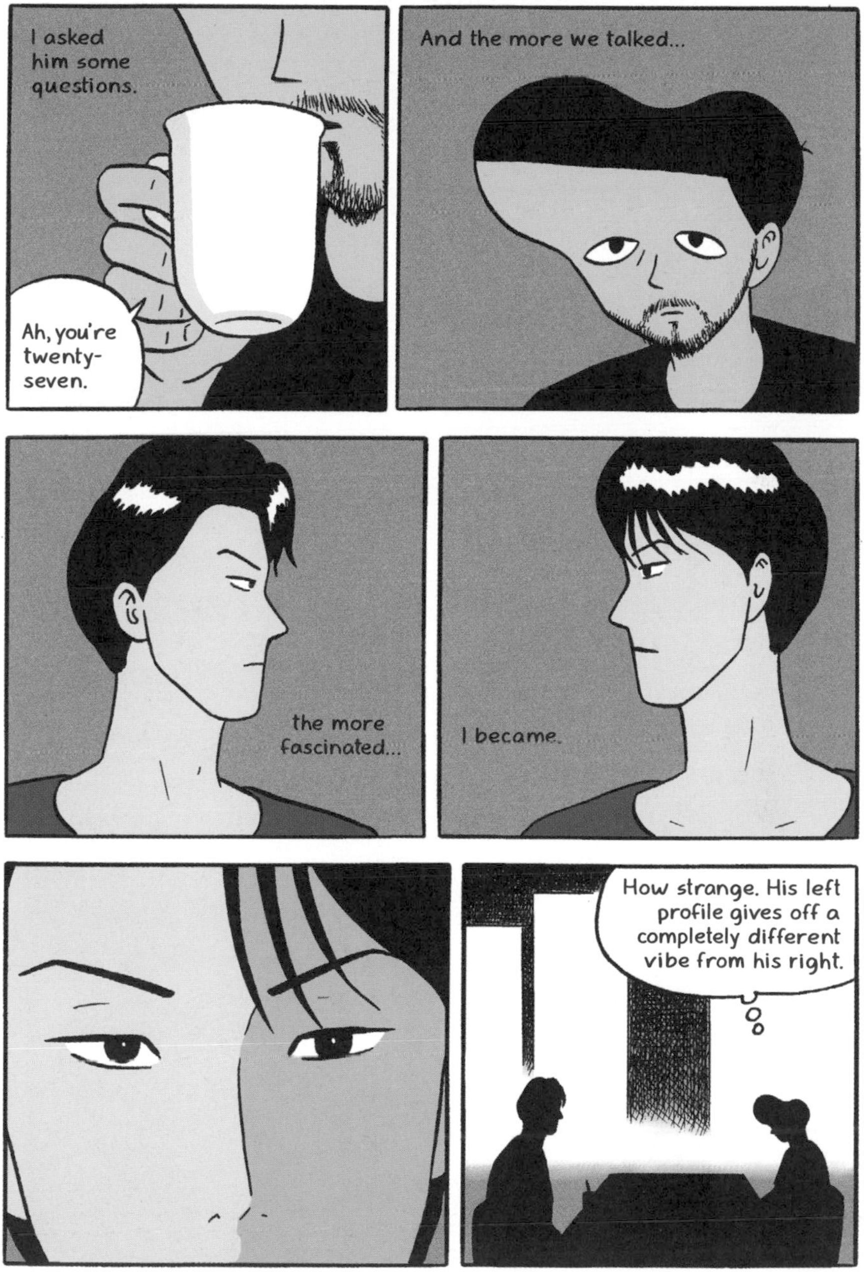
I asked him some questions.
Ah, you're twenty-seven.
And the more we talked...
the more fascinated...
I became.
How strange. His left profile gives off a completely different vibe from his right.

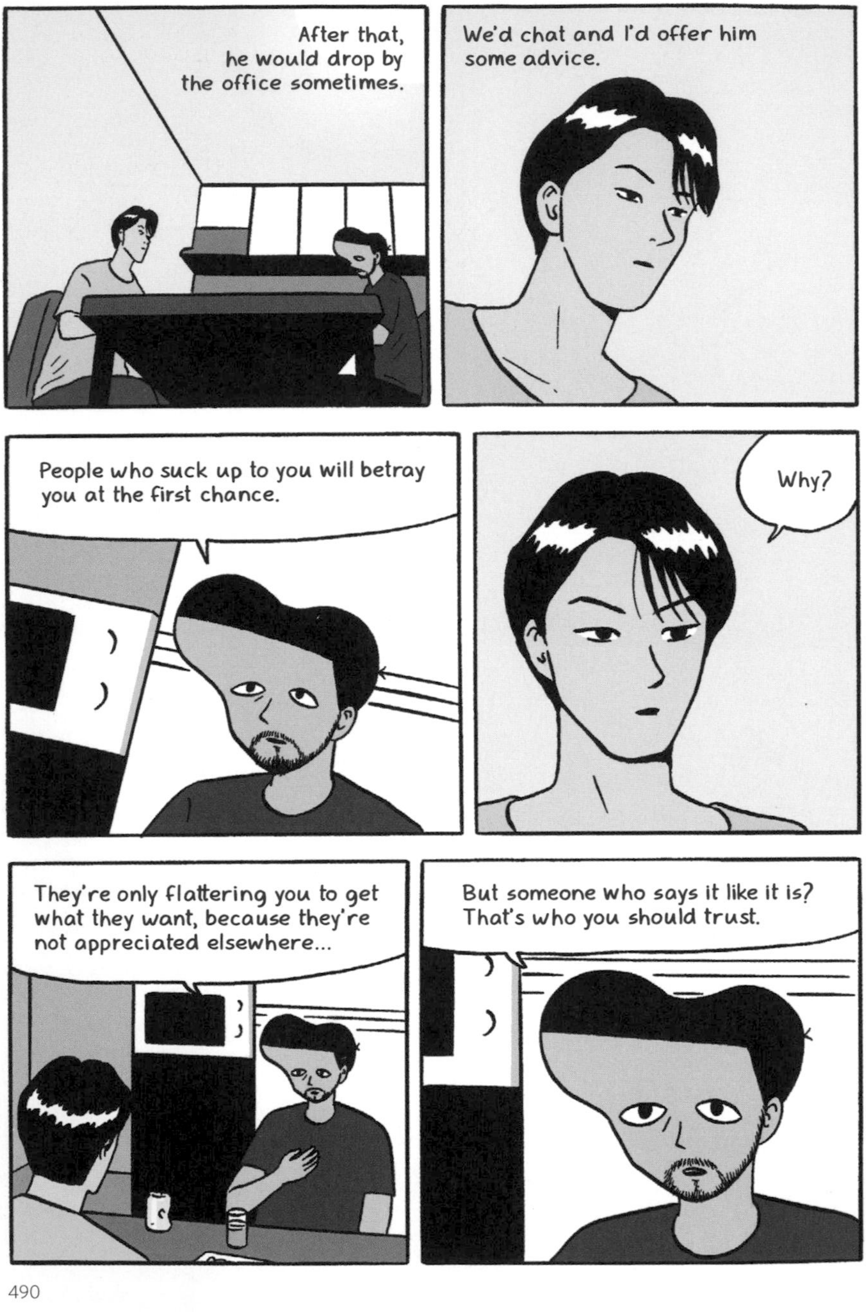
After that, he would drop by the office sometimes.
We'd chat and I'd offer him some advice.
People who suck up to you will betray you at the first chance.
Why?
They're only flattering you to get what they want, because they're not appreciated elsewhere...
But someone who says it like it is? That's who you should trust.

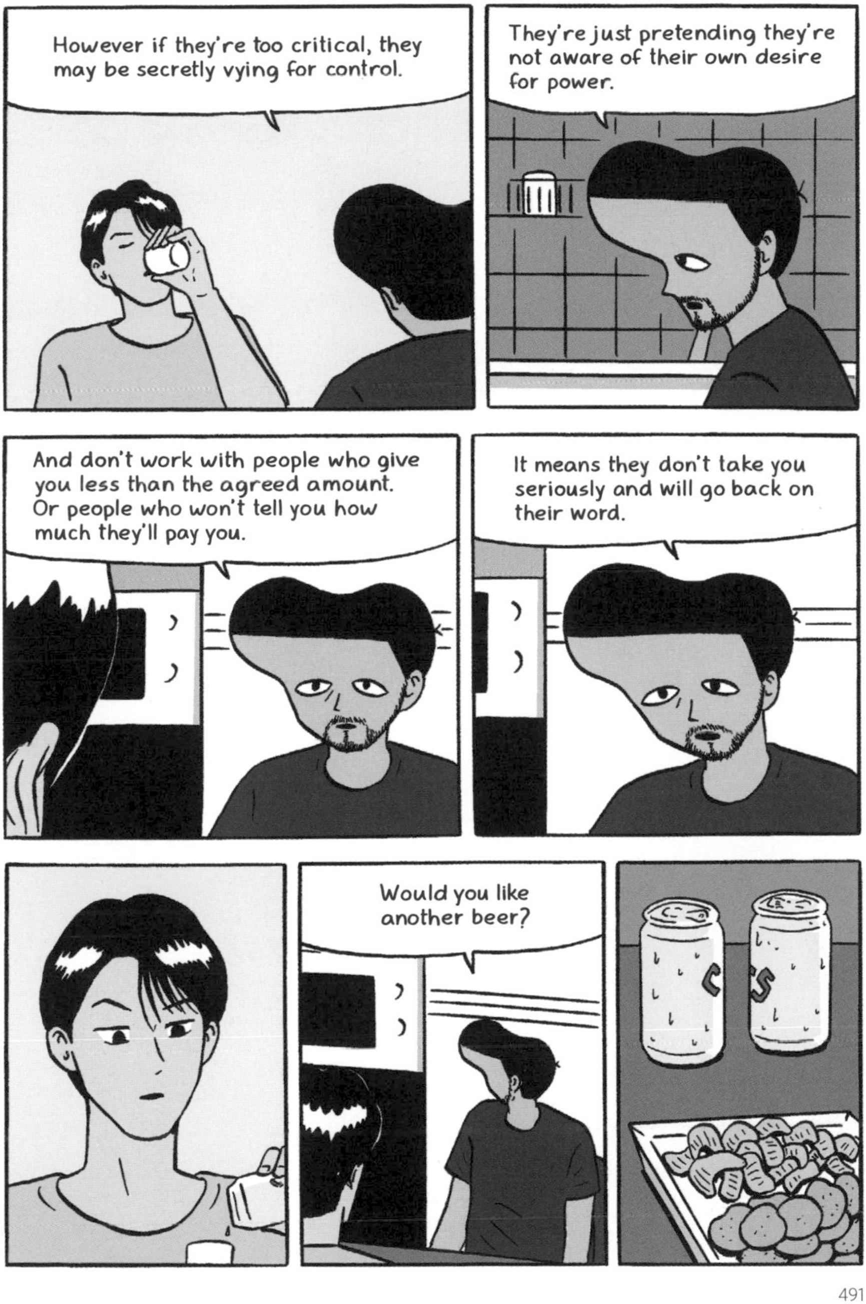
However if they're too critical, they may be secretly vying for control.
They're just pretending they're not aware of their own desire for power.
And don't work with people who give you less than the agreed amount. Or people who won't tell you how much they'll pay you.
It means they don't take you seriously and will go back on their word.
Would you like another beer?

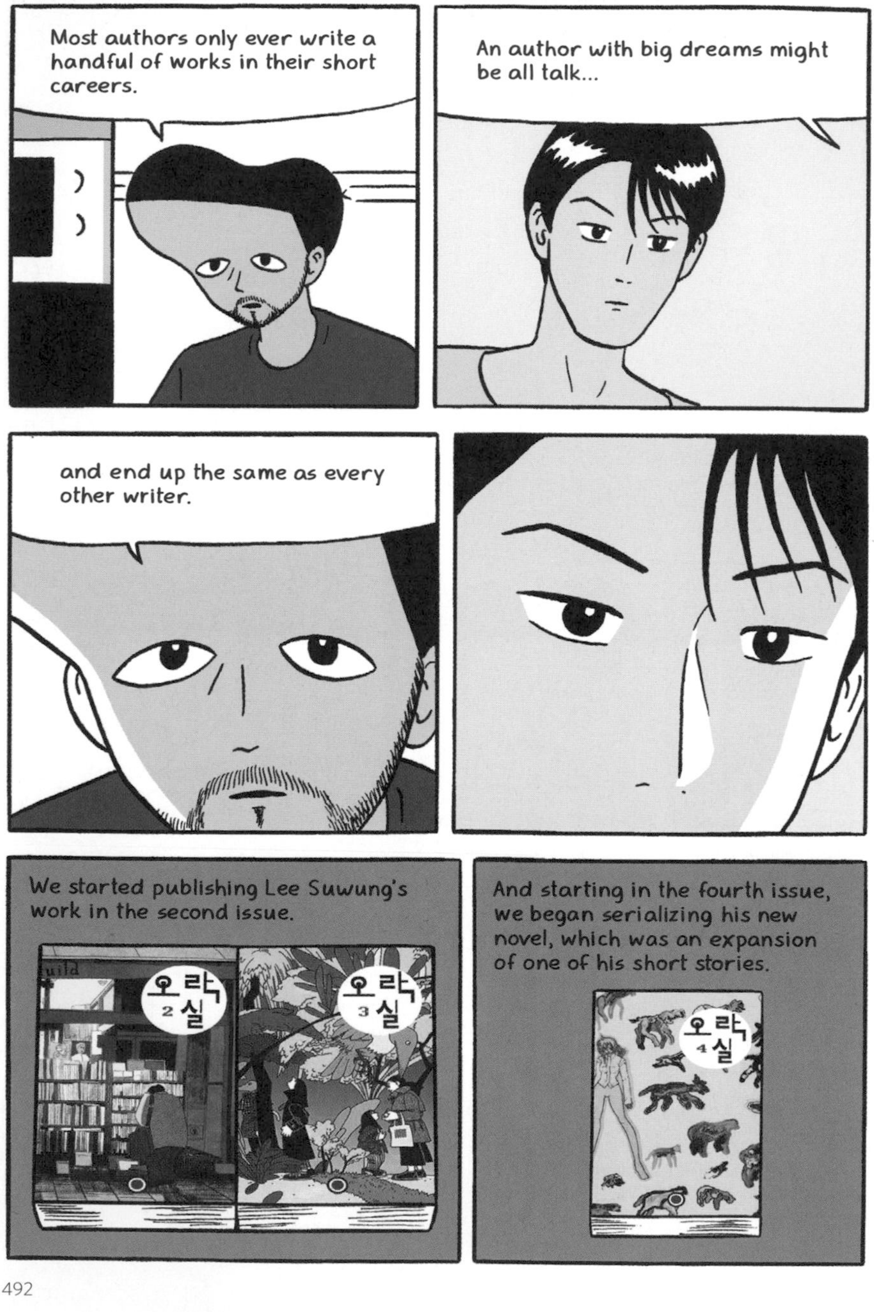
Most authors only ever write a handful of works in their short careers.
An author with big dreams might be all talk...
and end up the same as every other writer.
We started publishing Lee Suwung's work in the second issue.
오락실 2
오락실 3
And starting in the fourth issue, we began serializing his new novel, which was an expansion of one of his short stories.
오락실 4

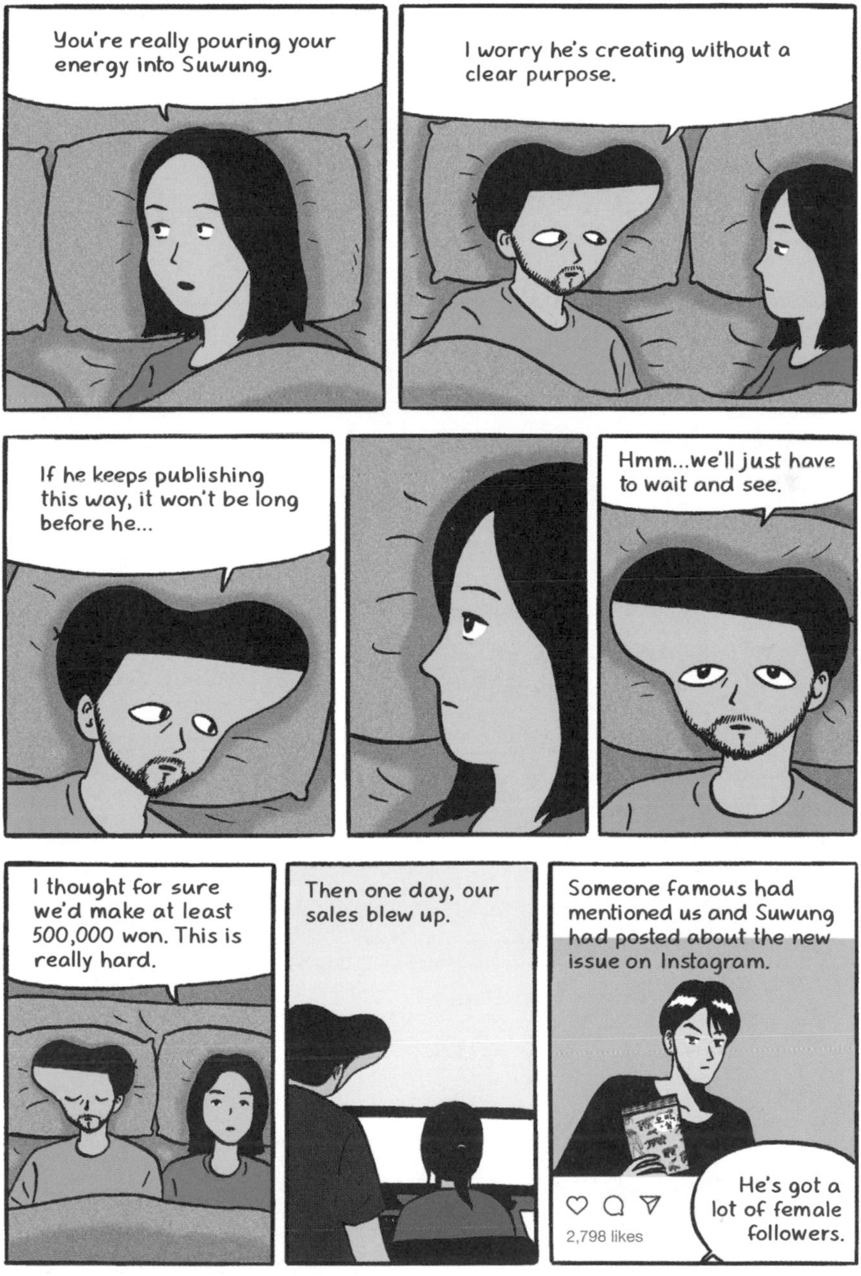
You're really pouring your energy into Suwung.
I worry he's creating without a clear purpose.
If he keeps publishing this way, it won't be long before he...
Hmm...we'll just have to wait and see.
I thought for sure we'd make at least 500,000 won. This is really hard.
Then one day, our sales blew up.
Someone famous had mentioned us and Suwung had posted about the new issue on Instagram.
2,798 likes
He's got a lot of female followers.

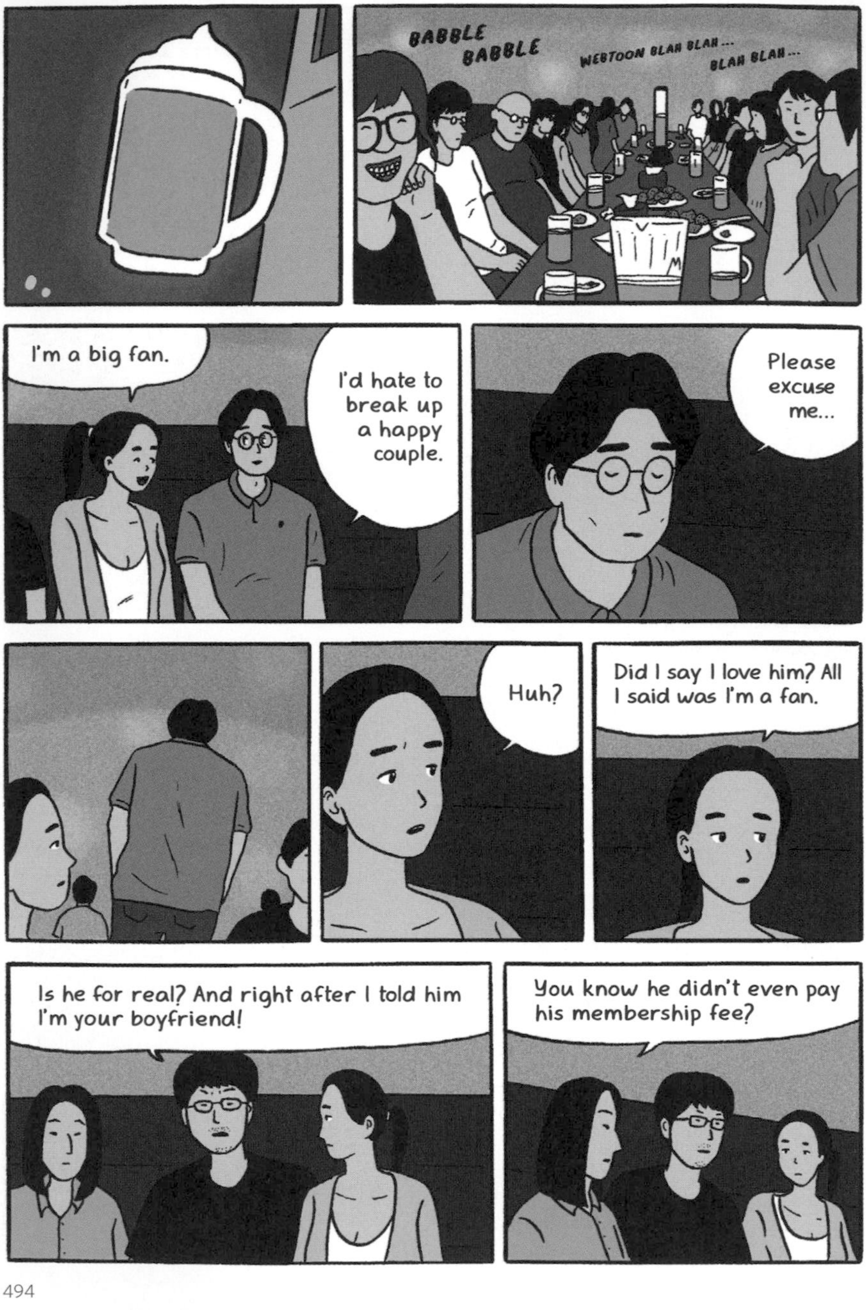
BABBLE
BABBLE
WEBTOON BLAH BLAH...
BLAH BLAH...
I'm a big fan.
I'd hate to break up a happy couple.
Please excuse me...
Huh?
Did I say I love him? All I said was I'm a fan.
Is he for real? And right after I told him I'm your boyfriend!
You know he didn't even pay his membership fee?

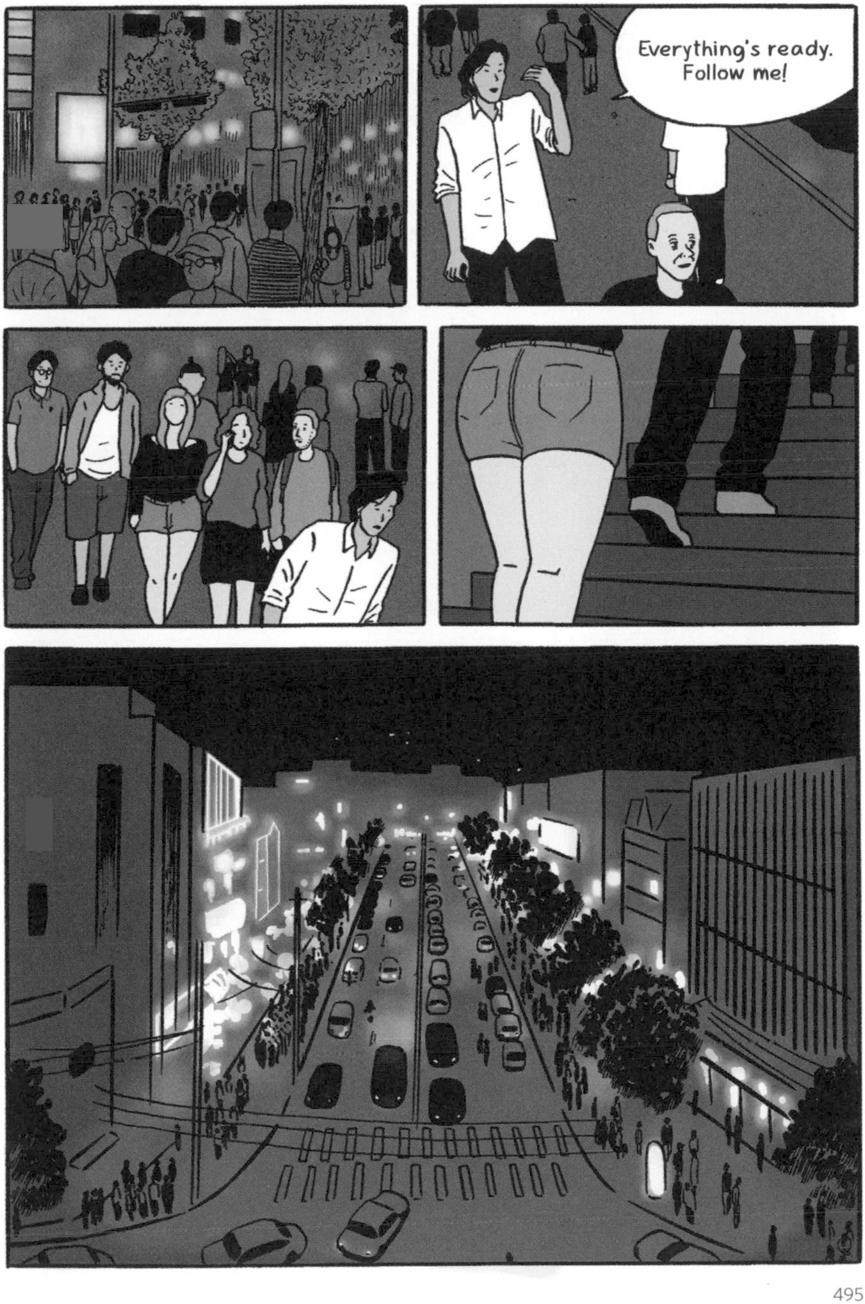
Everything's ready.
Follow me!

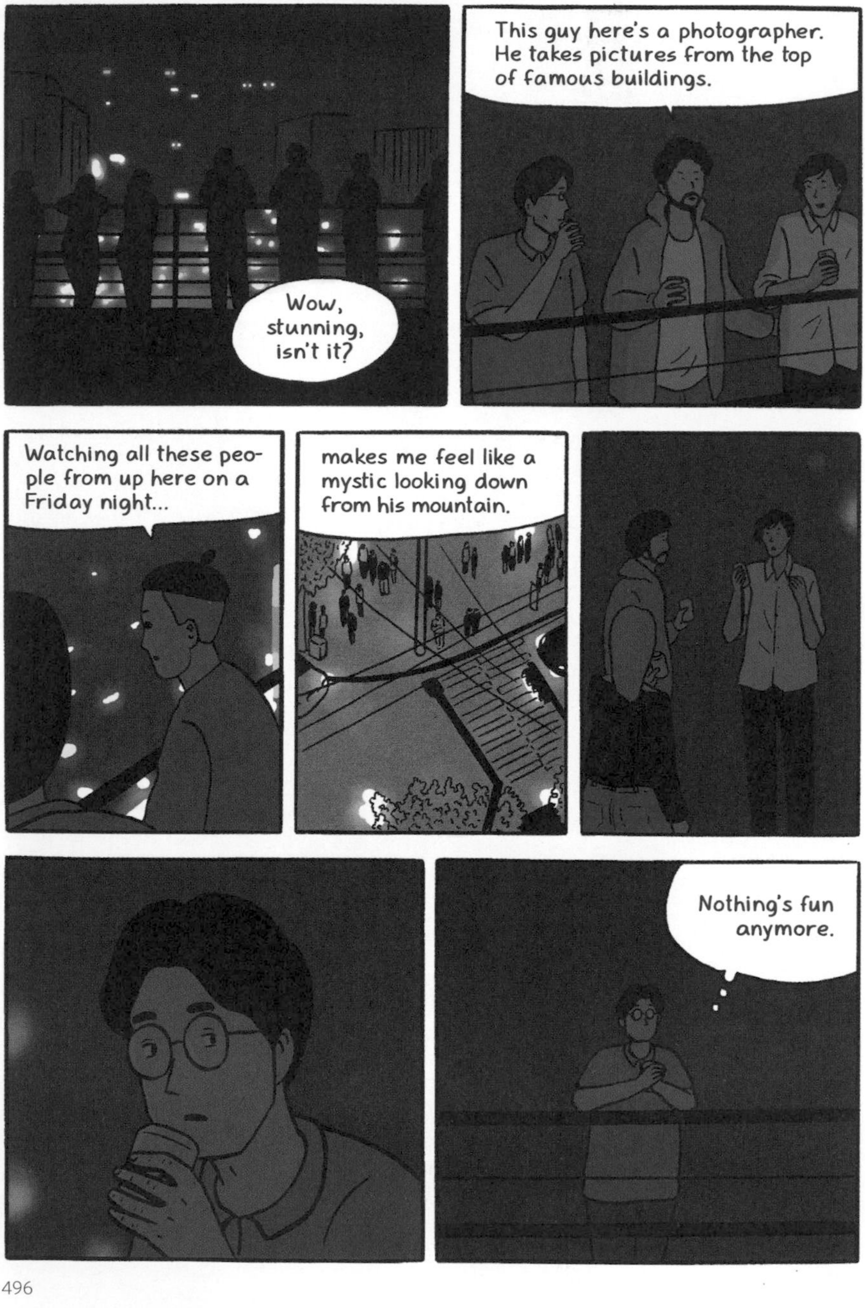
Wow, stunning, isn't it?
This guy here's a photographer. He takes pictures from the top of famous buildings.
Watching all these people from up here on a Friday night...
makes me feel like a mystic looking down from his mountain.
Nothing's fun anymore.

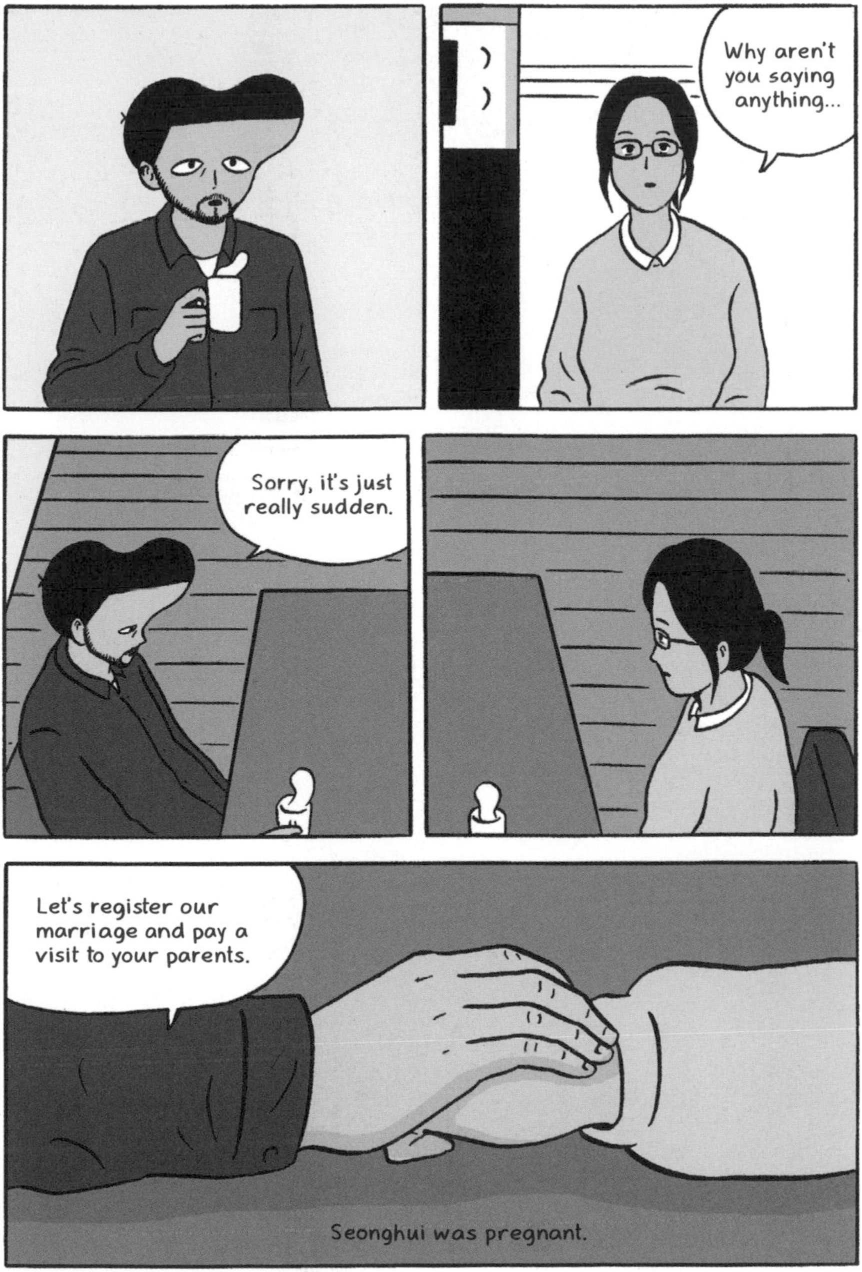
Why aren't you saying anything...
Sorry, it's just really sudden.
Let's register our marriage and pay a visit to your parents.
Seonghui was pregnant.

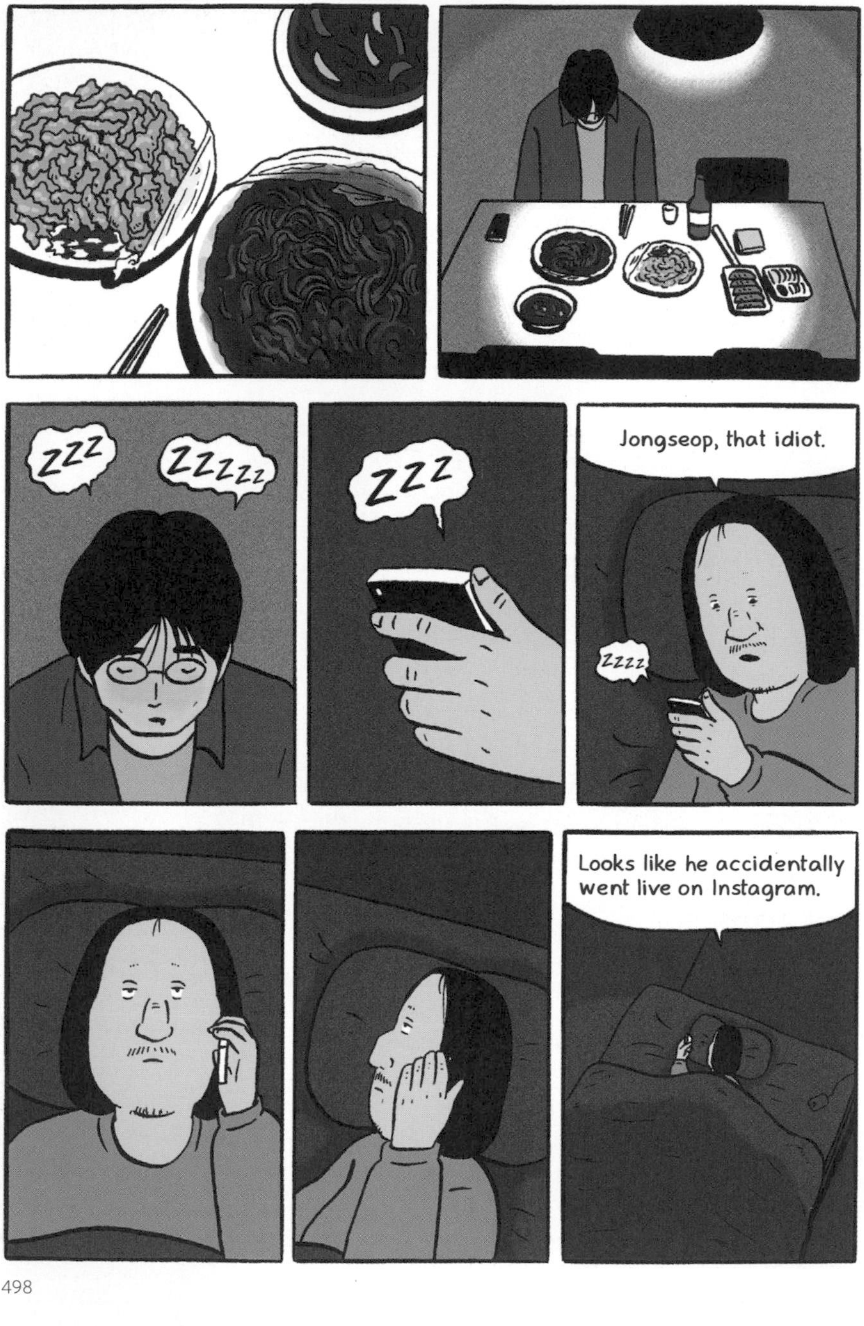
ZZZ
ZZZZZ
ZZZ
Jongseop, that idiot.
ZZZZ
Looks like he accidentally went live on Instagram.

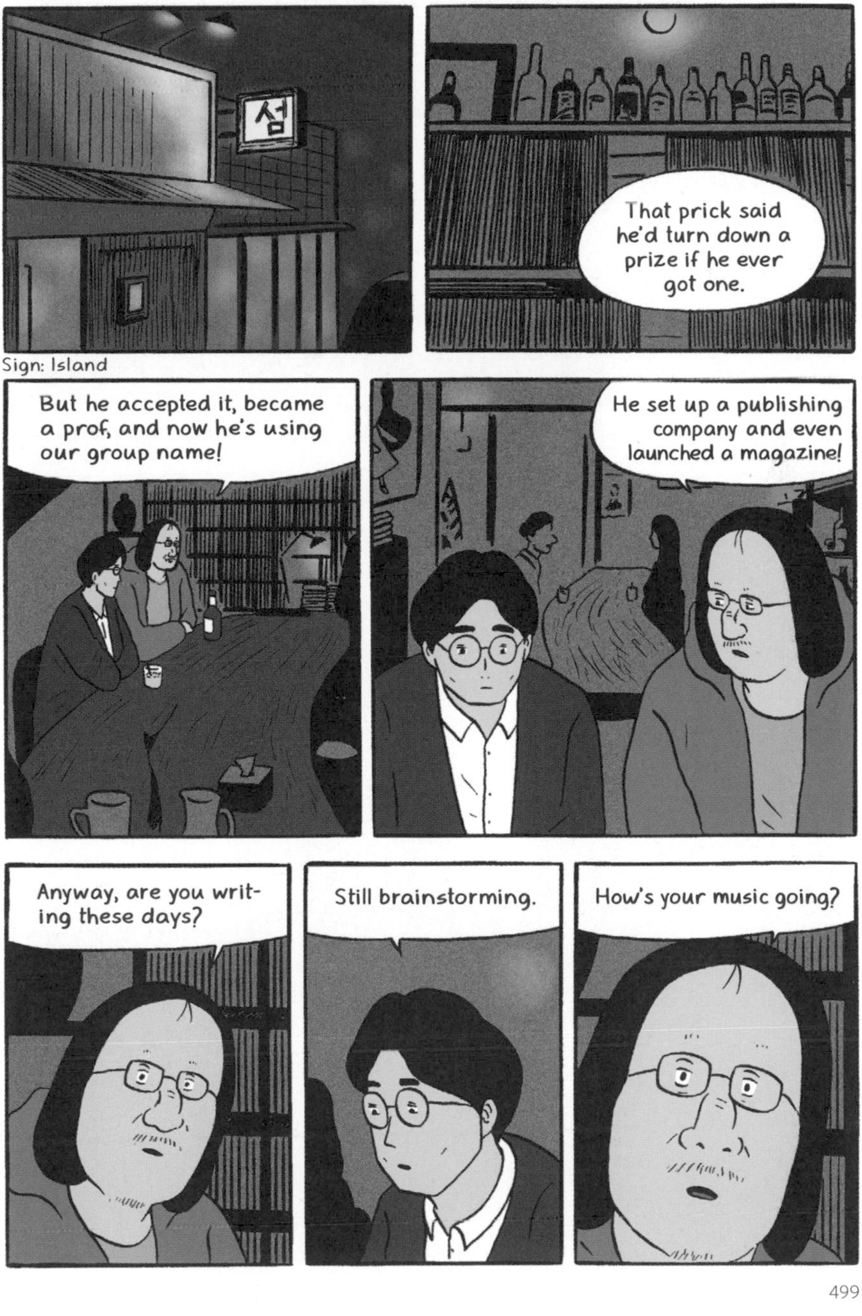
섬
That prick said he'd turn down a prize if he ever got one.
Sign: Island
But he accepted it, became a prof, and now he's using our group name!
He set up a publishing company and even launched a magazine!
Anyway, are you writ-ing these days?
Still brainstorming.
How's your music going?

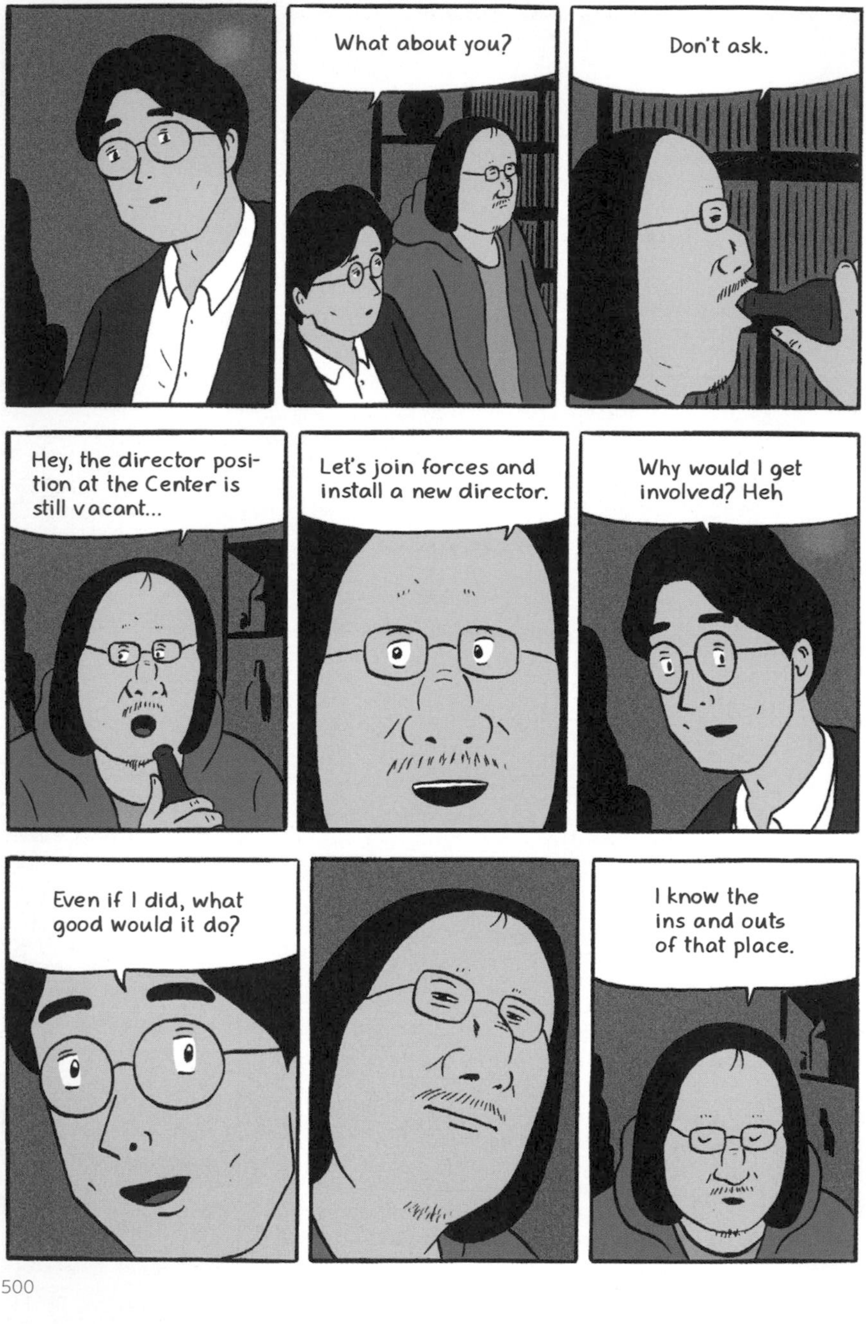
What about you?
Don't ask.
Hey, the director position at the Center is still vacant...
Let's join forces and install a new director.
Why would I get involved? Heh
Even if I did, what good would it do?
I know the ins and outs of that place.

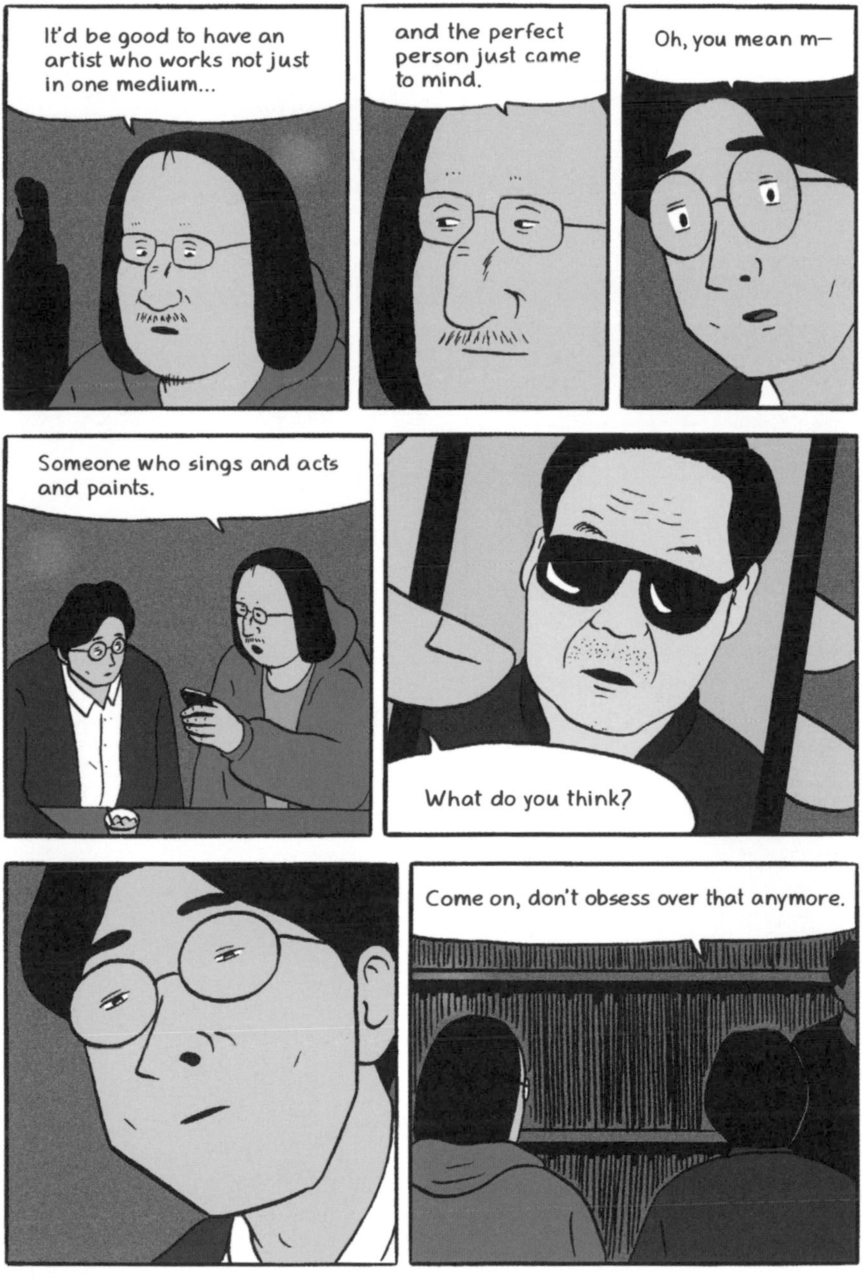
It'd be good to have an artist who works not just in one medium...
and the perfect person just came to mind.
Oh, you mean m—
Someone who sings and acts and paints.
What do you think?
Come on, don't obsess over that anymore.

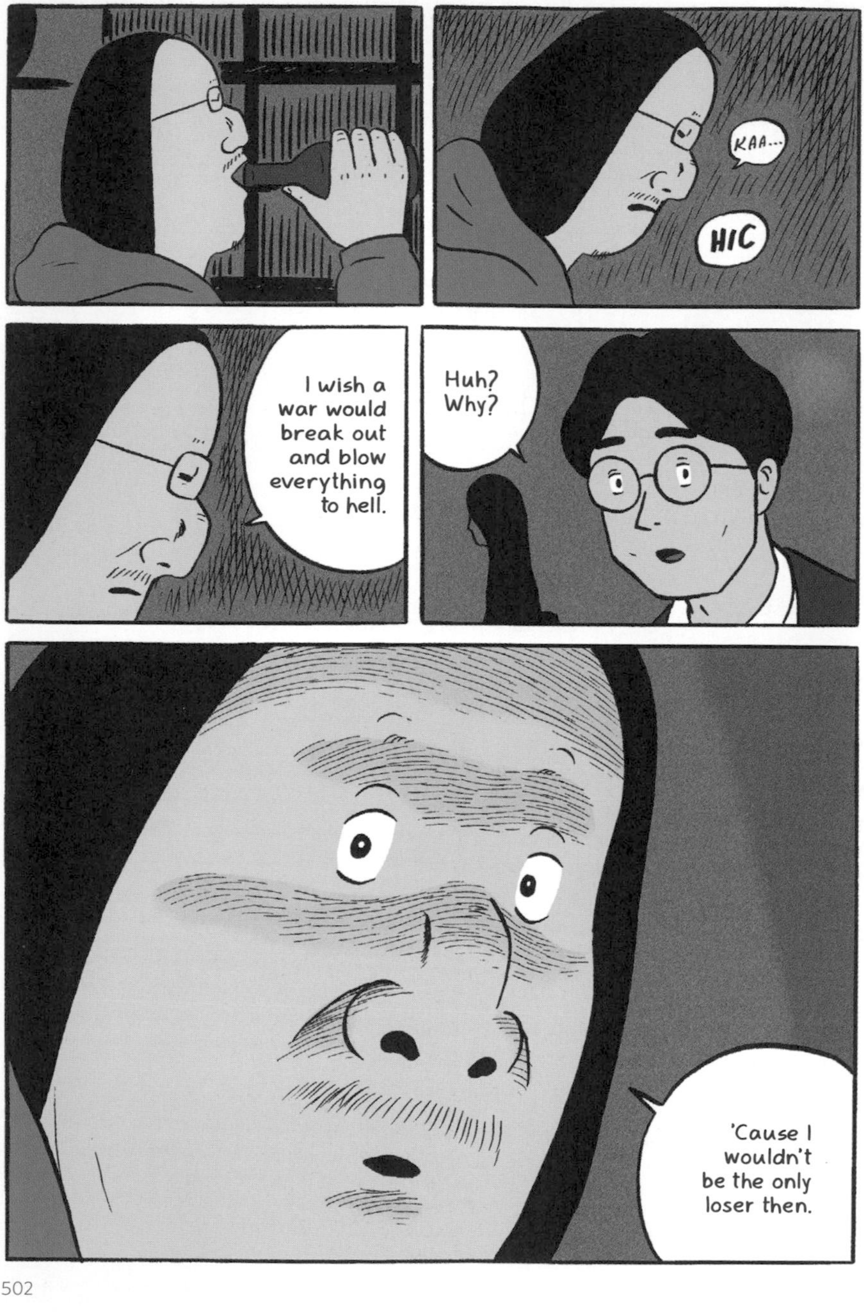
KAA...
HIC
I wish a war would break out and blow everything to hell.
Huh? Why?
'Cause I wouldn't be the only loser then.

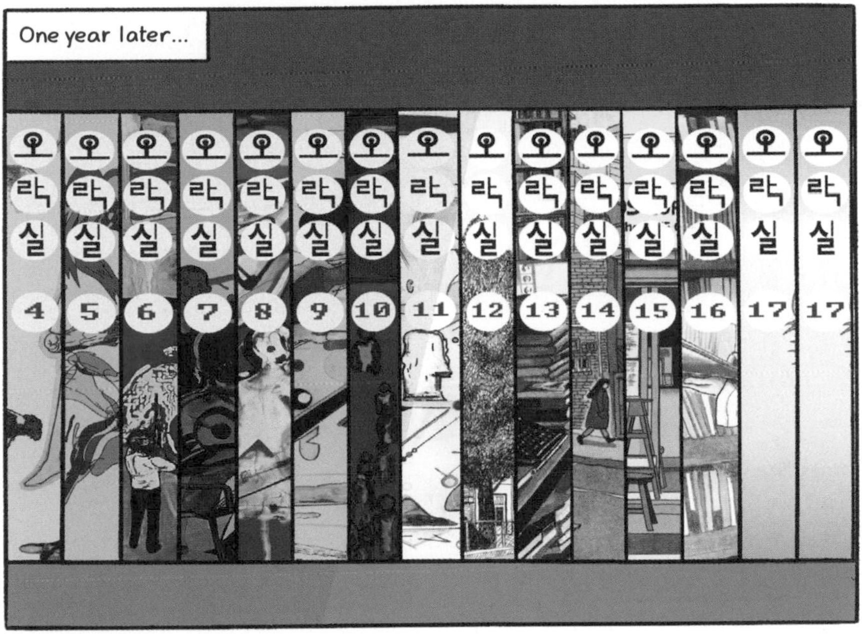
One year later...
오락실 4
오락실 5
오락실 6
오락실 7
오락실 8
오락실 9
오락실 10
오락실 11
오락실 12
오락실 13
오락실 14
오락실 15
오락실 16
오락실 17
오락실 17

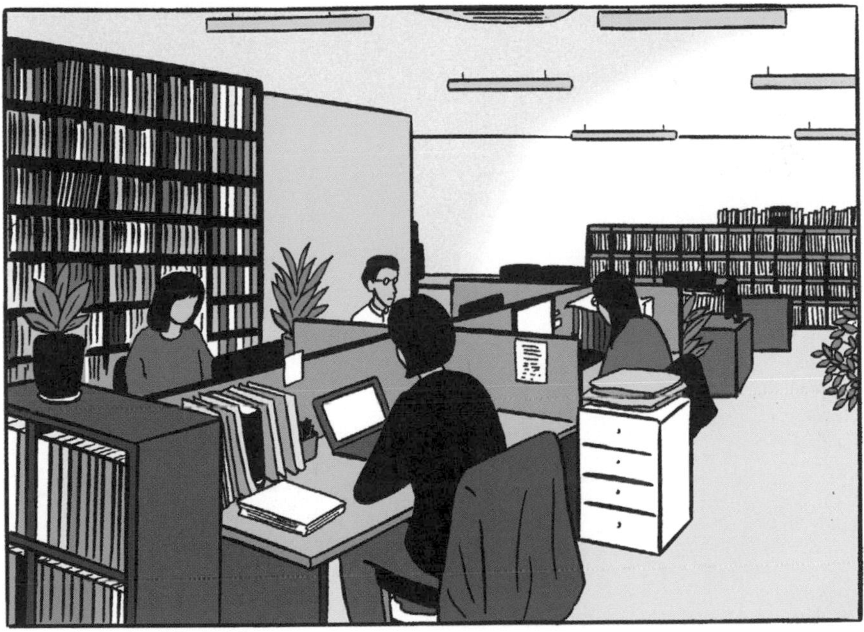

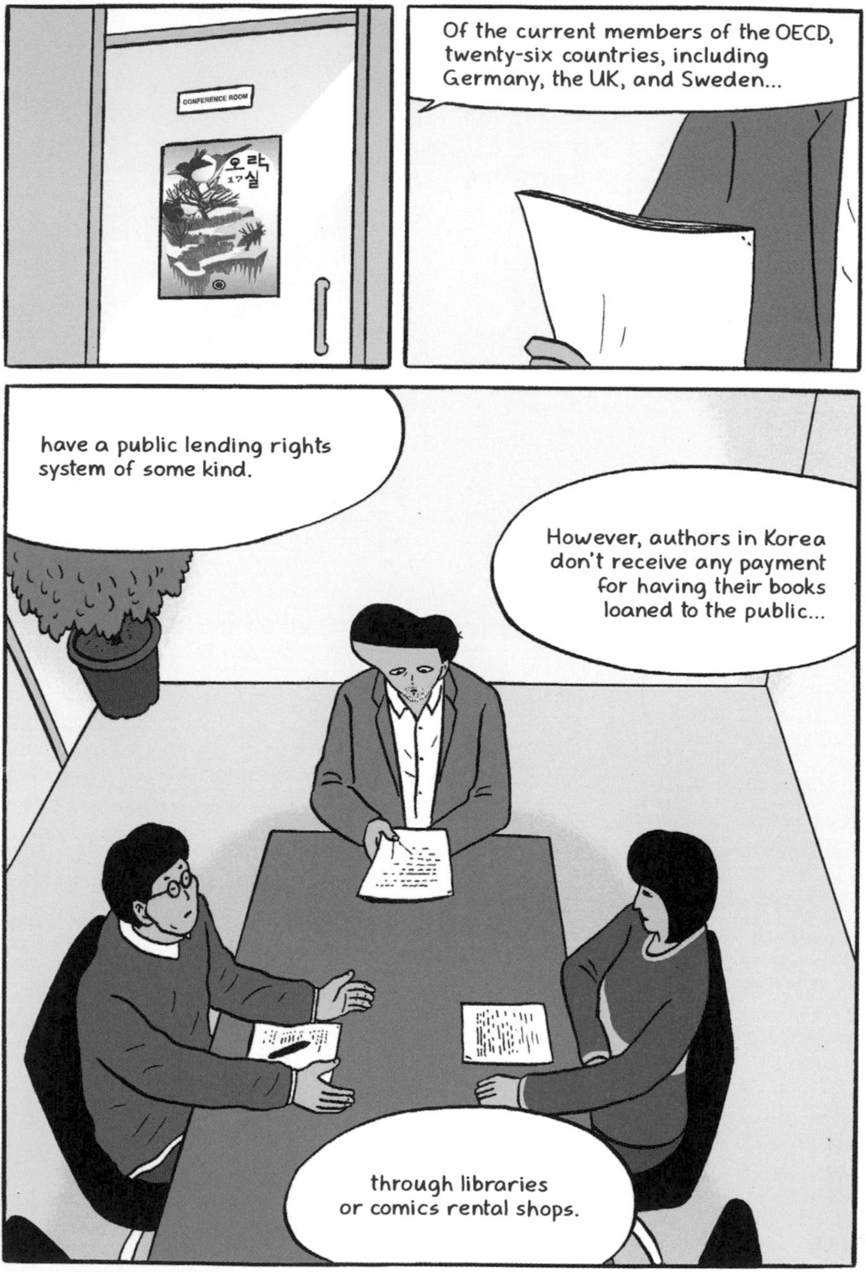
CONFERENCE ROOM
Of the current members of the OECD, twenty-six countries, including Germany, the UK, and Sweden...
have a public lending rights system of some kind.
However, authors in Korea don't receive any payment for having their books loaned to the public...
through libraries or comics rental shops.

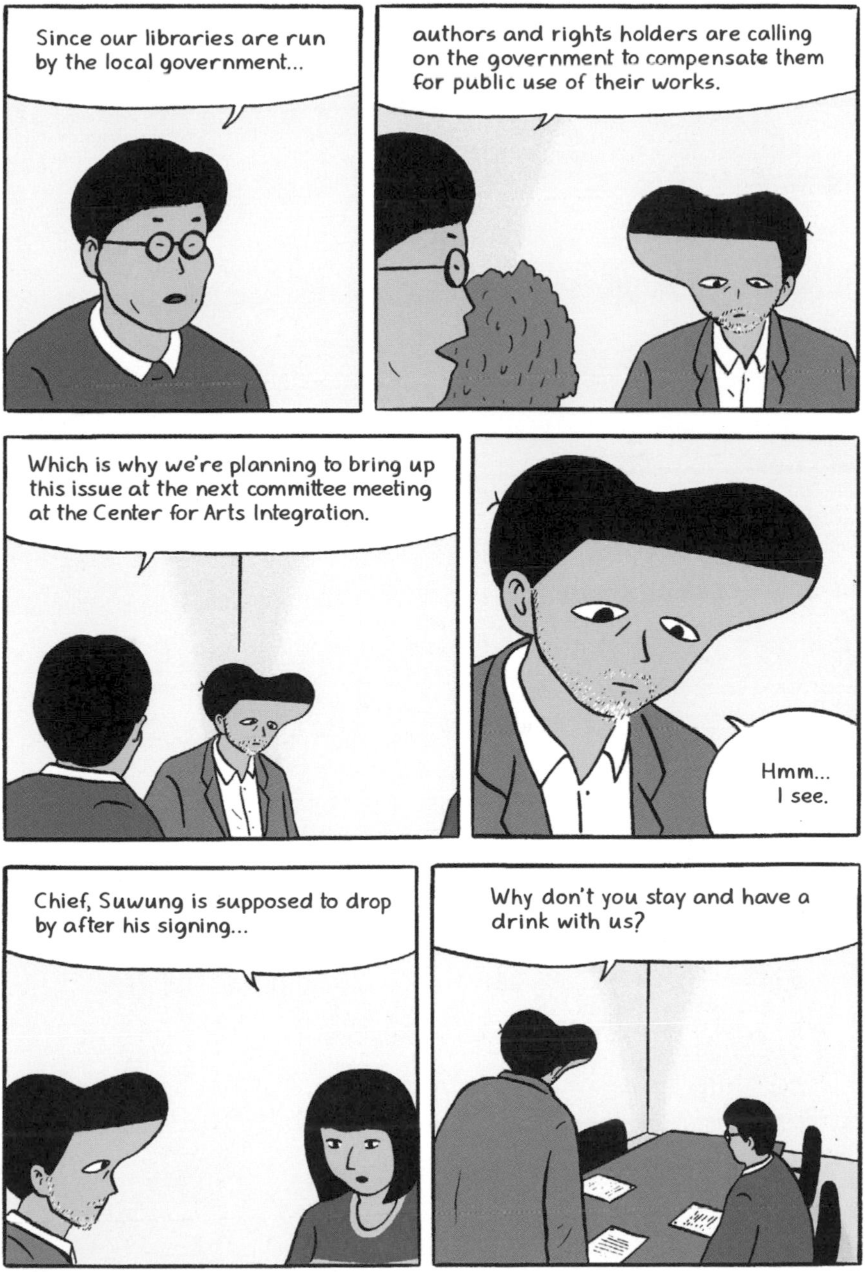
Since our libraries are run by the local government...
authors and rights holders are calling on the government to compensate them for public use of their works.
Which is why we're planning to bring up this issue at the next committee meeting at the Center for Arts Integration.
Hmm... I see.
Chief, Suwung is supposed to drop by after his signing...
Why don't you stay and have a drink with us?

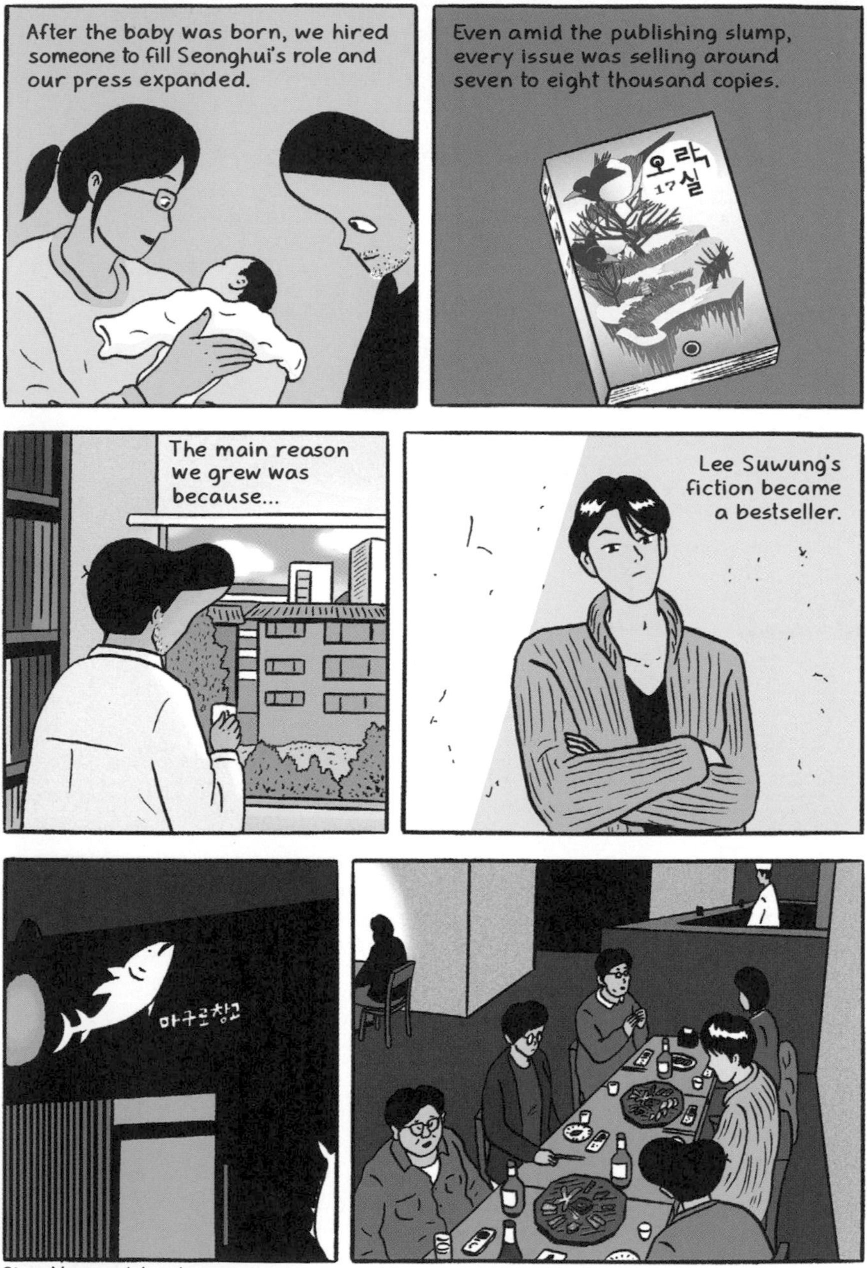
After the baby was born, we hired someone to fill Seonghui's role and our press expanded.
Even amid the publishing slump, every issue was selling around seven to eight thousand copies.
오락실
17
The main reason we grew was because...
Lee Suwung's fiction became a bestseller.
마구로창고

Sign: Maguro Warehouse

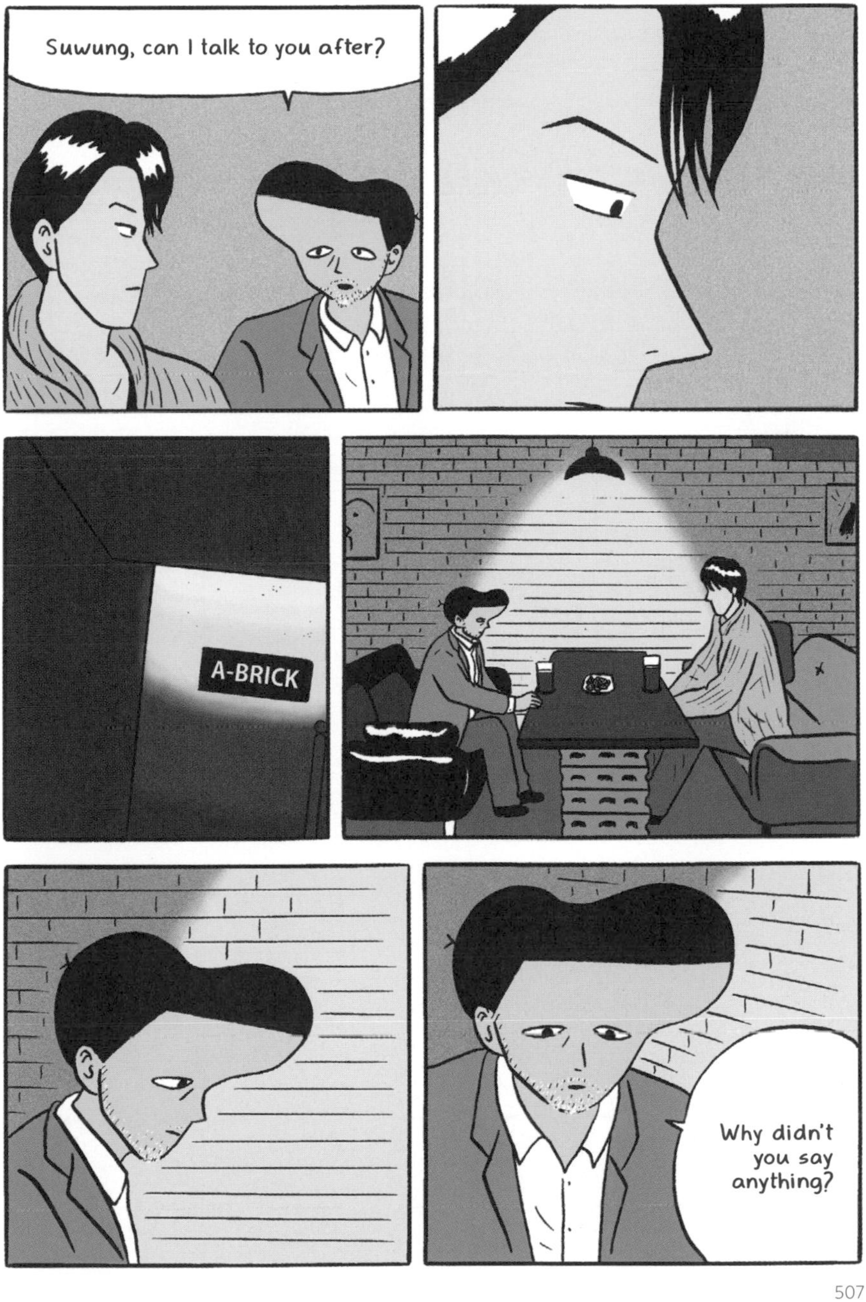
Suwung, can I talk to you after?
A-BRICK
Why didn't you say anything?

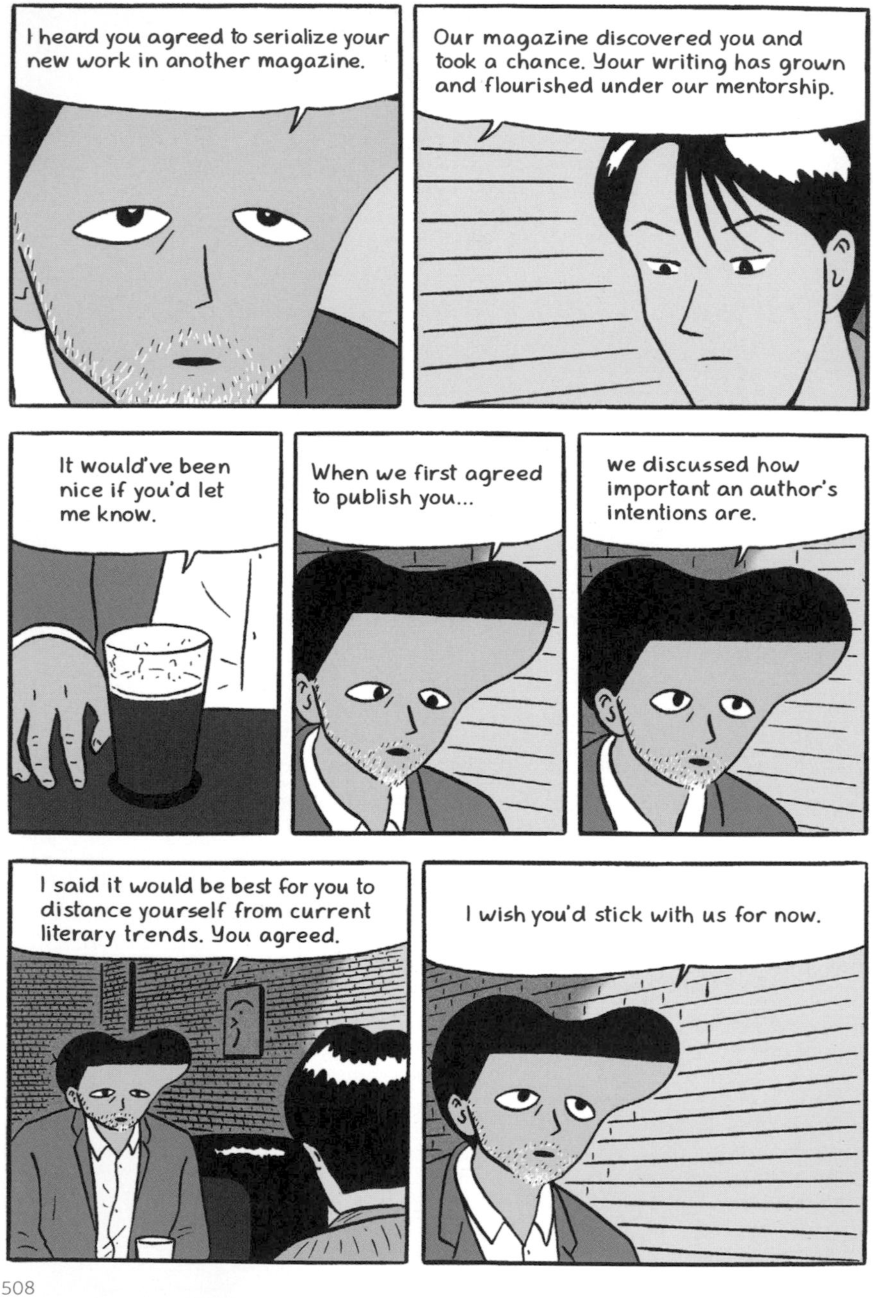
I heard you agreed to serialize your new work in another magazine.
Our magazine discovered you and took a chance. Your writing has grown and flourished under our mentorship.
It would've been nice if you'd let me know.
When we first agreed to publish you...
we discussed how important an author's intentions are.
I said it would be best for you to distance yourself from current literary trends. You agreed.
I wish you'd stick with us for now.

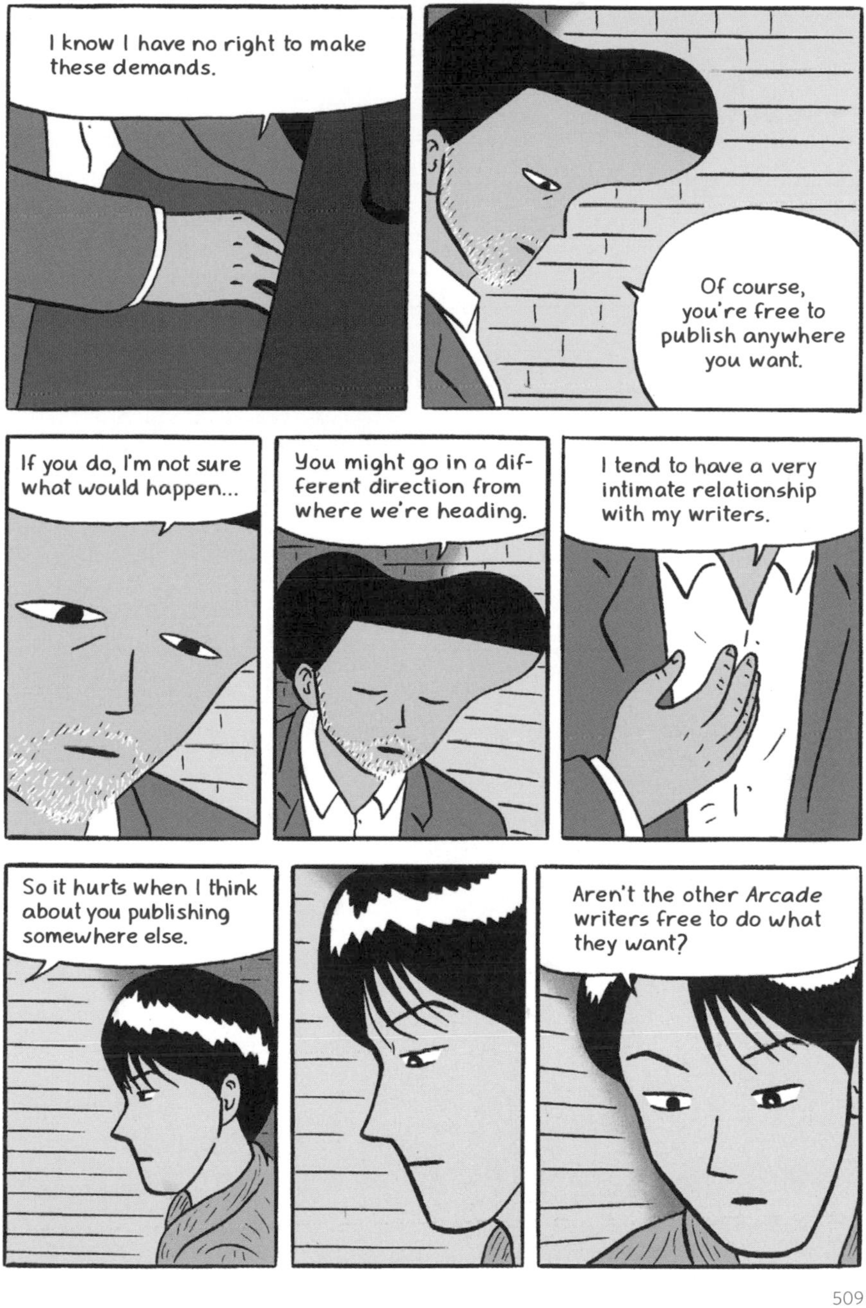
I know I have no right to make these demands.
Of course, you're free to publish anywhere you want.
If you do, I'm not sure what would happen...
You might go in a different direction from where we're heading.
I tend to have a very intimate relationship with my writers.
So it hurts when I think about you publishing somewhere else.
Aren't the other *Arcade* writers free to do what they want?

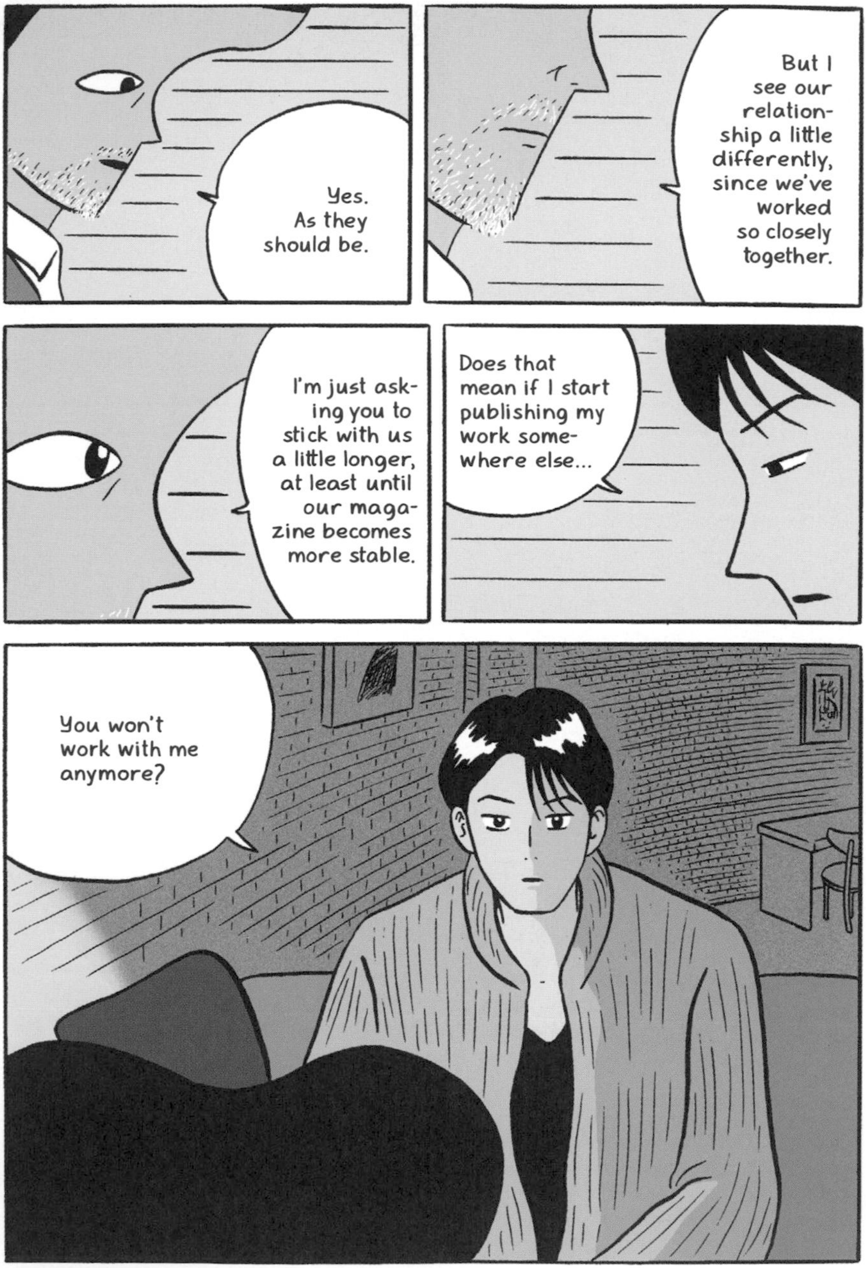
Yes.
As they should be.
But I see our relationship a little differently, since we've worked so closely together.
I'm just asking you to stick with us a little longer, at least until our magazine becomes more stable.
Does that mean if I start publishing my work somewhere else...
You won't work with me anymore?

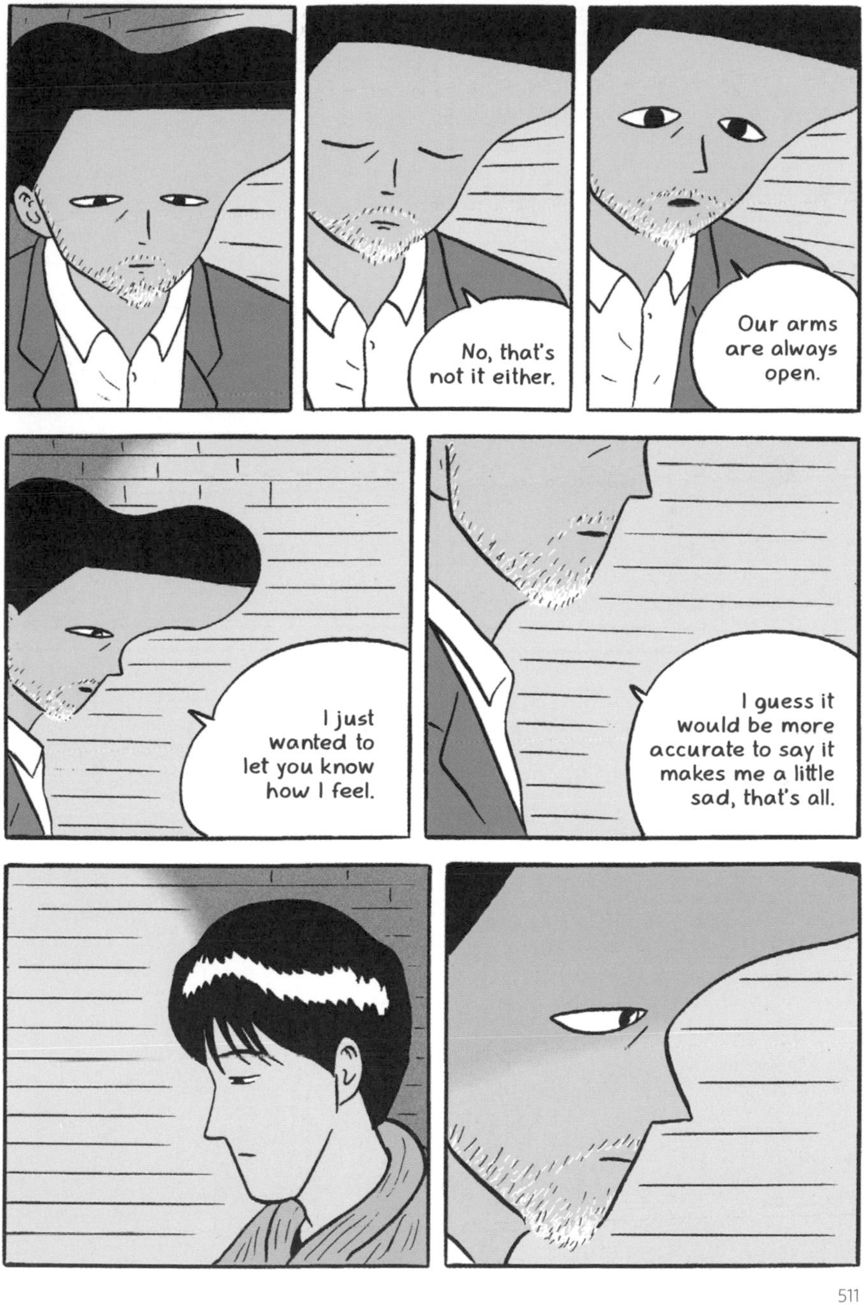
No, that's not it either.
Our arms are always open.
I just wanted to let you know how I feel.
I guess it would be more accurate to say it makes me a little sad, that's all.

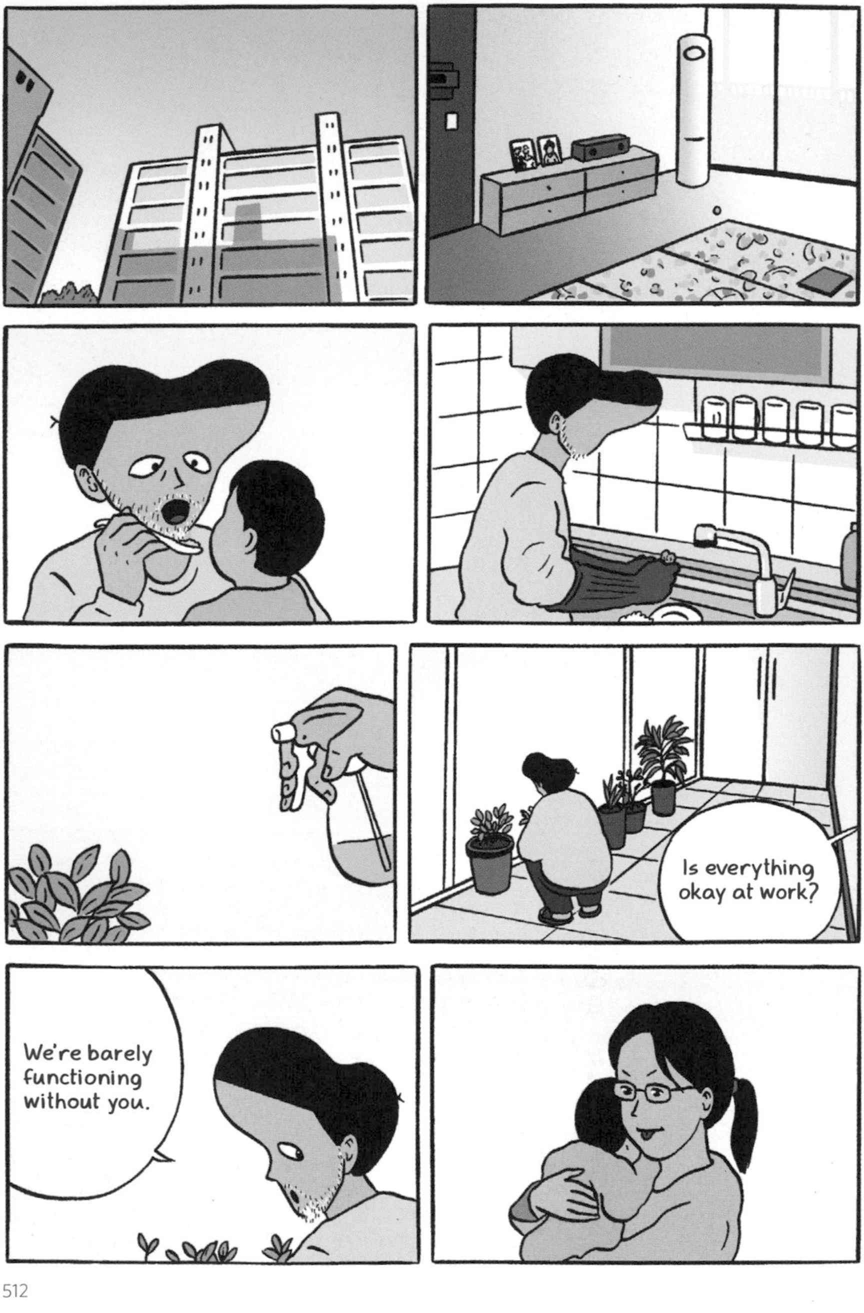
Is everything okay at work?
We're barely functioning without you.

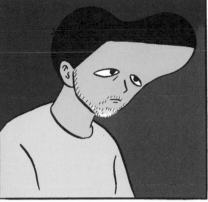

What's he doing these days...

m Chun

TAP TAP TAP

He hasn't released anything for more than a year.

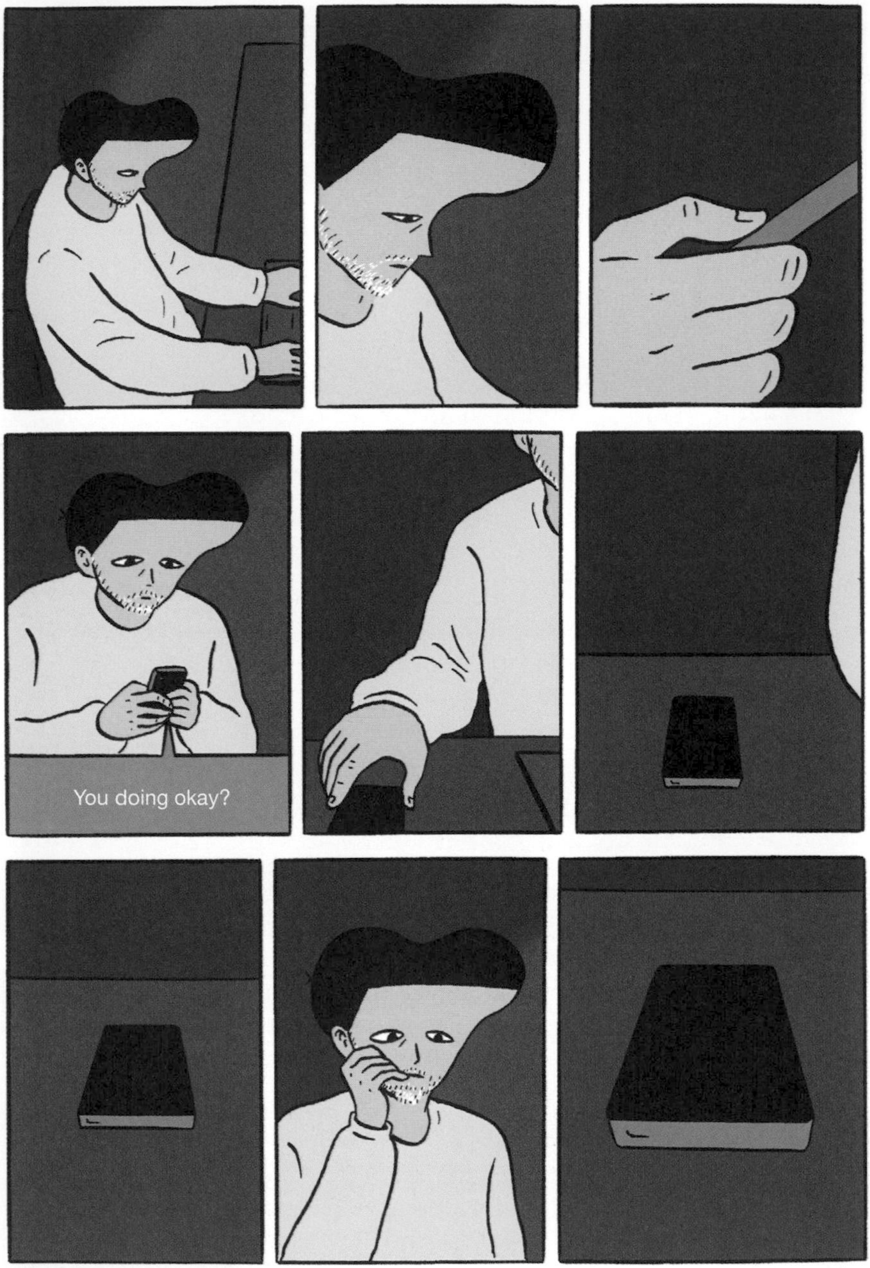
You doing okay?

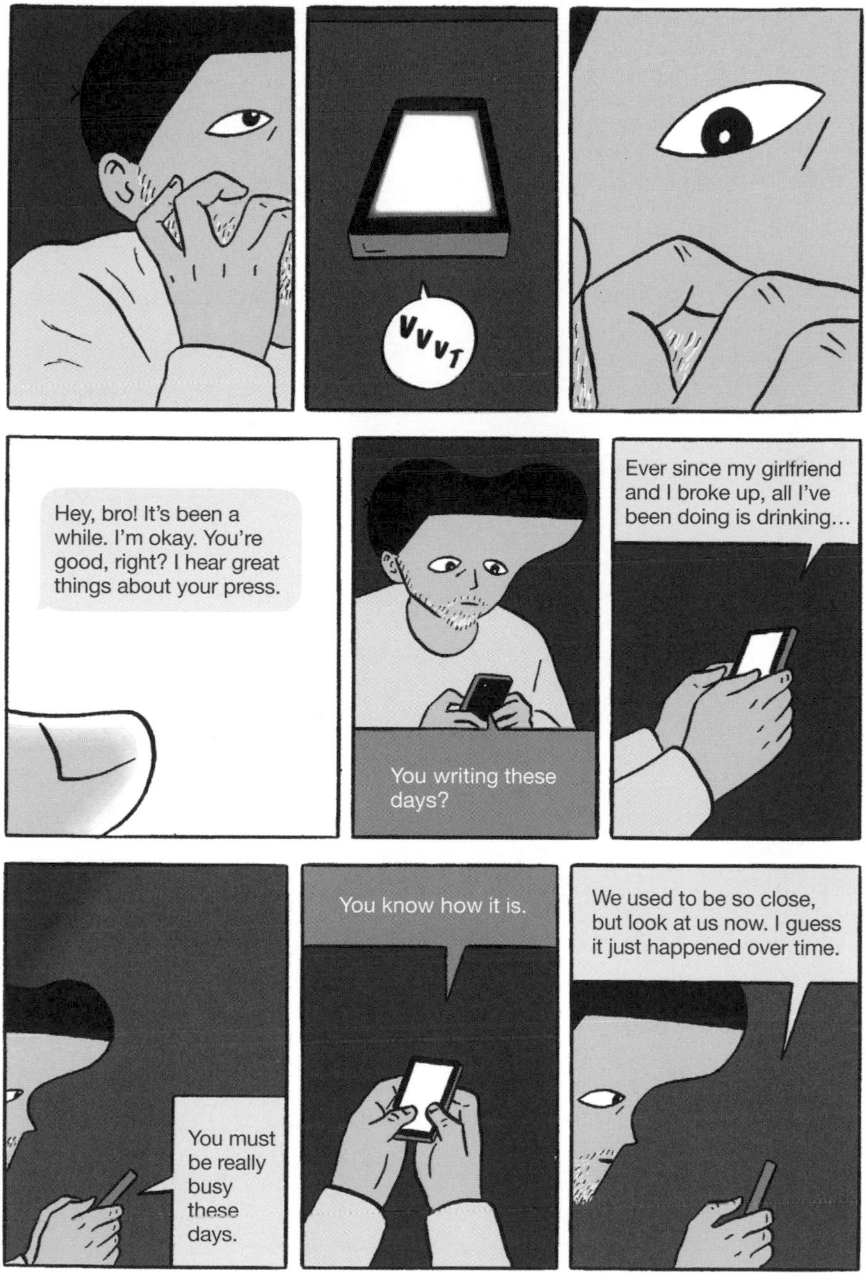
VVVT
Hey, bro! It's been a while. I'm okay. You're good, right? I hear great things about your press.
You writing these days?
Ever since my girlfriend and I broke up, all I've been doing is drinking…
You must be really busy these days.
You know how it is.
We used to be so close, but look at us now. I guess it just happened over time.

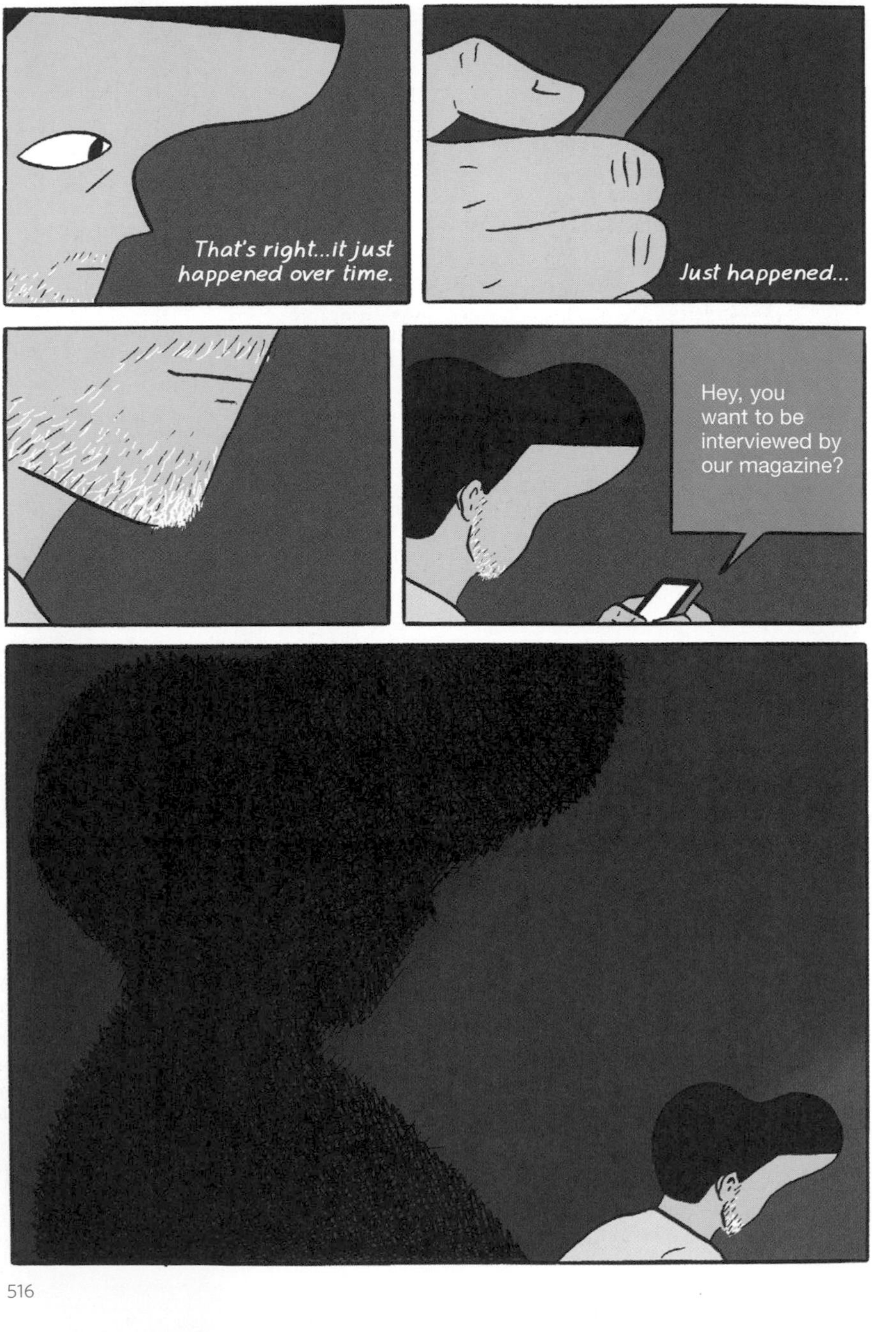
That's right...it just happened over time.
Just happened...
Hey, you want to be interviewed by our magazine?

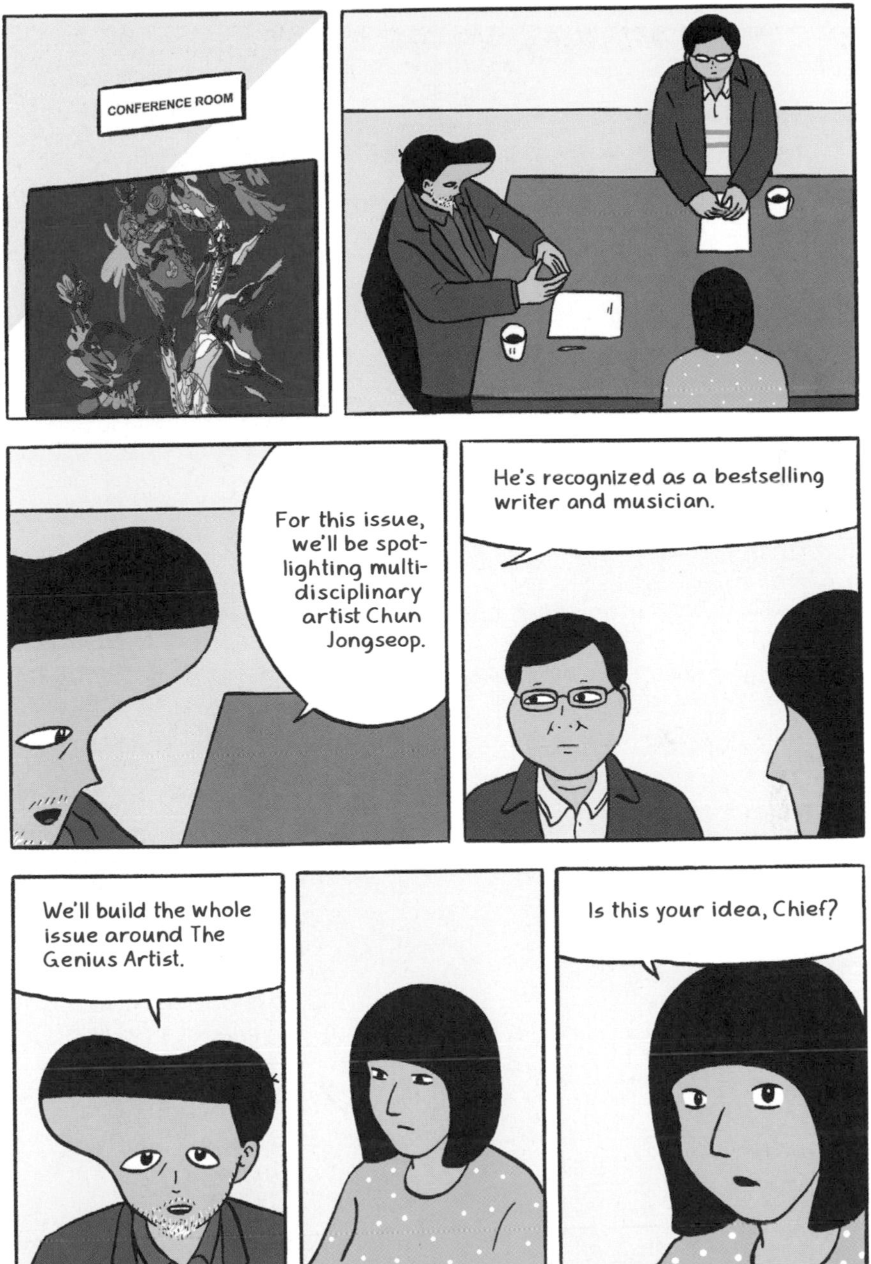
CONFERENCE ROOM
For this issue, we'll be spot-lighting multi-disciplinary artist Chun Jongseop.
He's recognized as a bestselling writer and musician.
We'll build the whole issue around The Genius Artist.
Is this your idea, Chief?

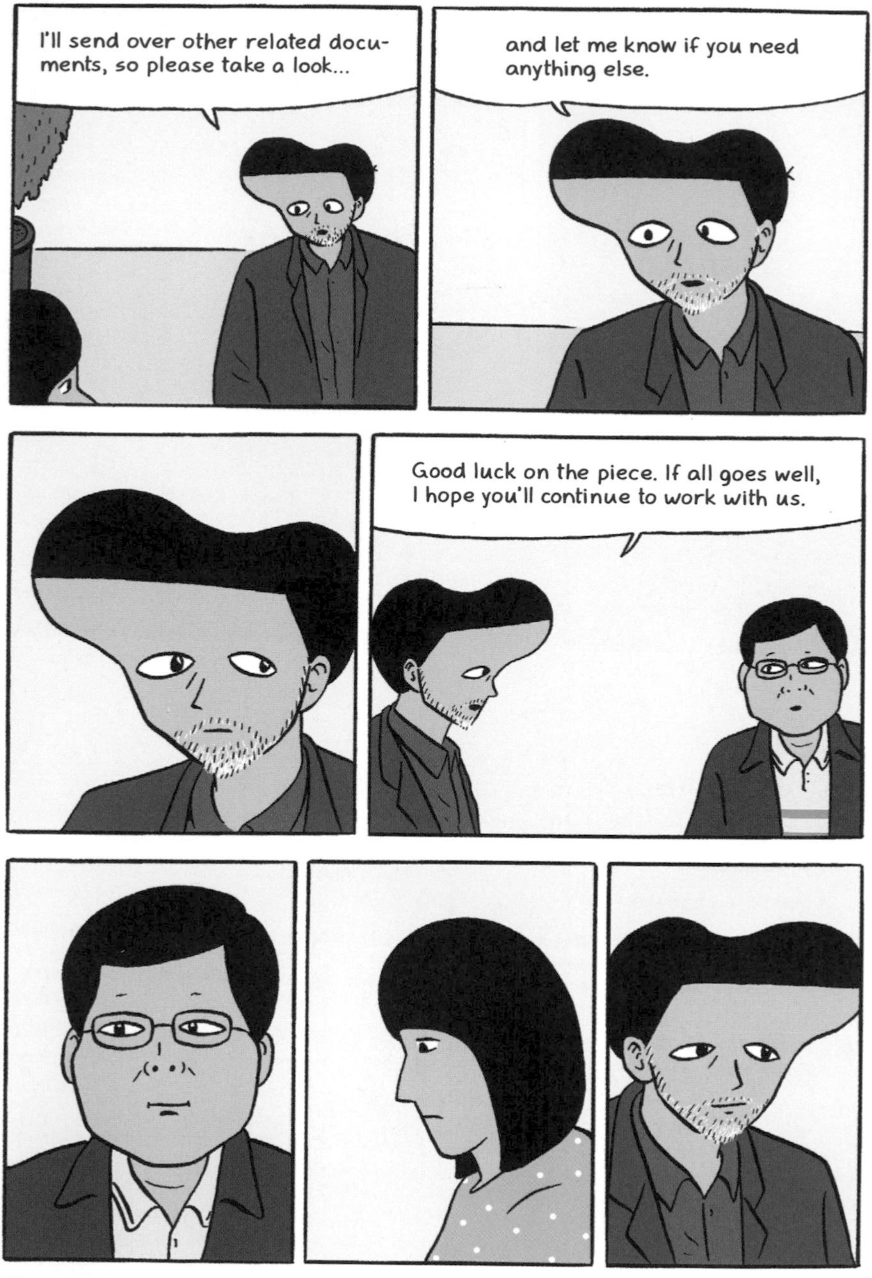
I'll send over other related documents, so please take a look...
and let me know if you need anything else.
Good luck on the piece. If all goes well, I hope you'll continue to work with us.

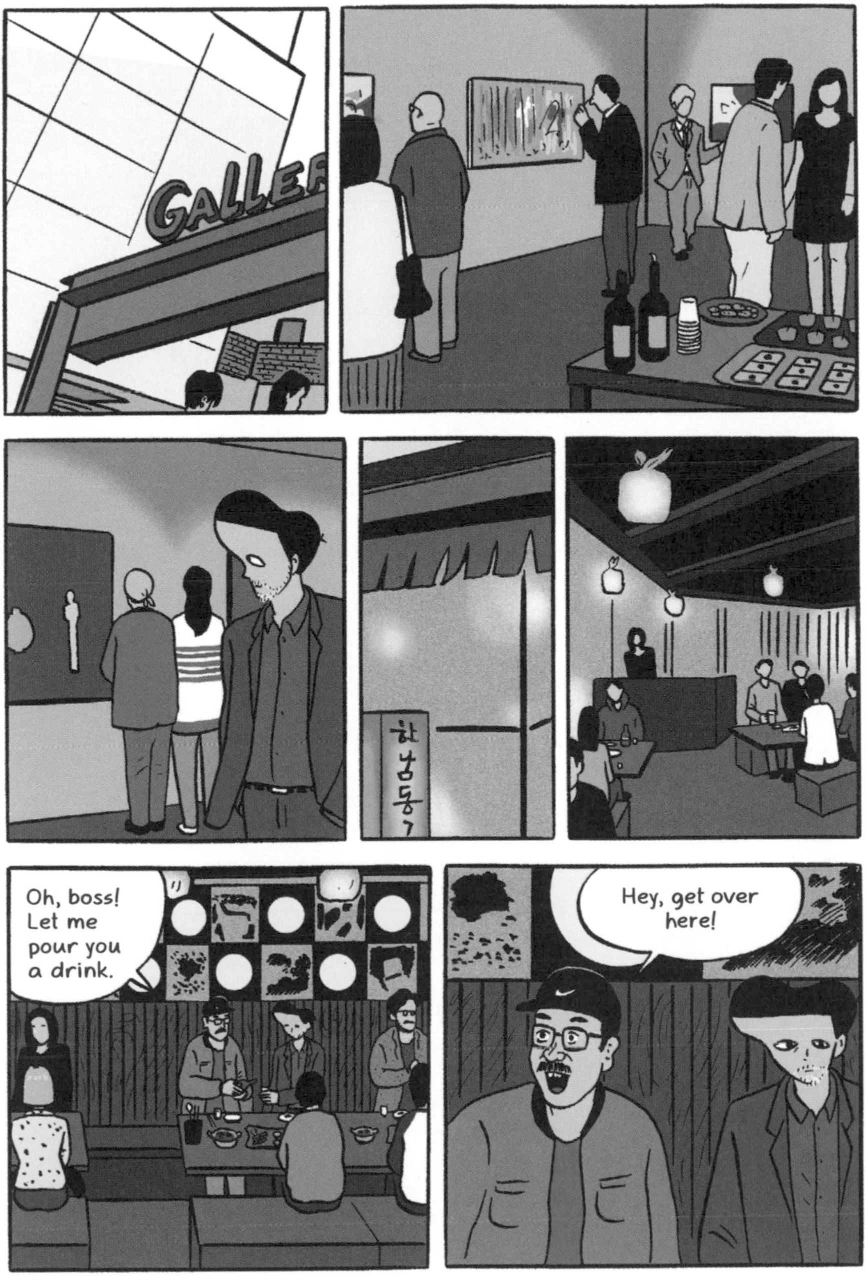
GALLER
Oh, boss! Let me pour you a drink.
Hey, get over here!

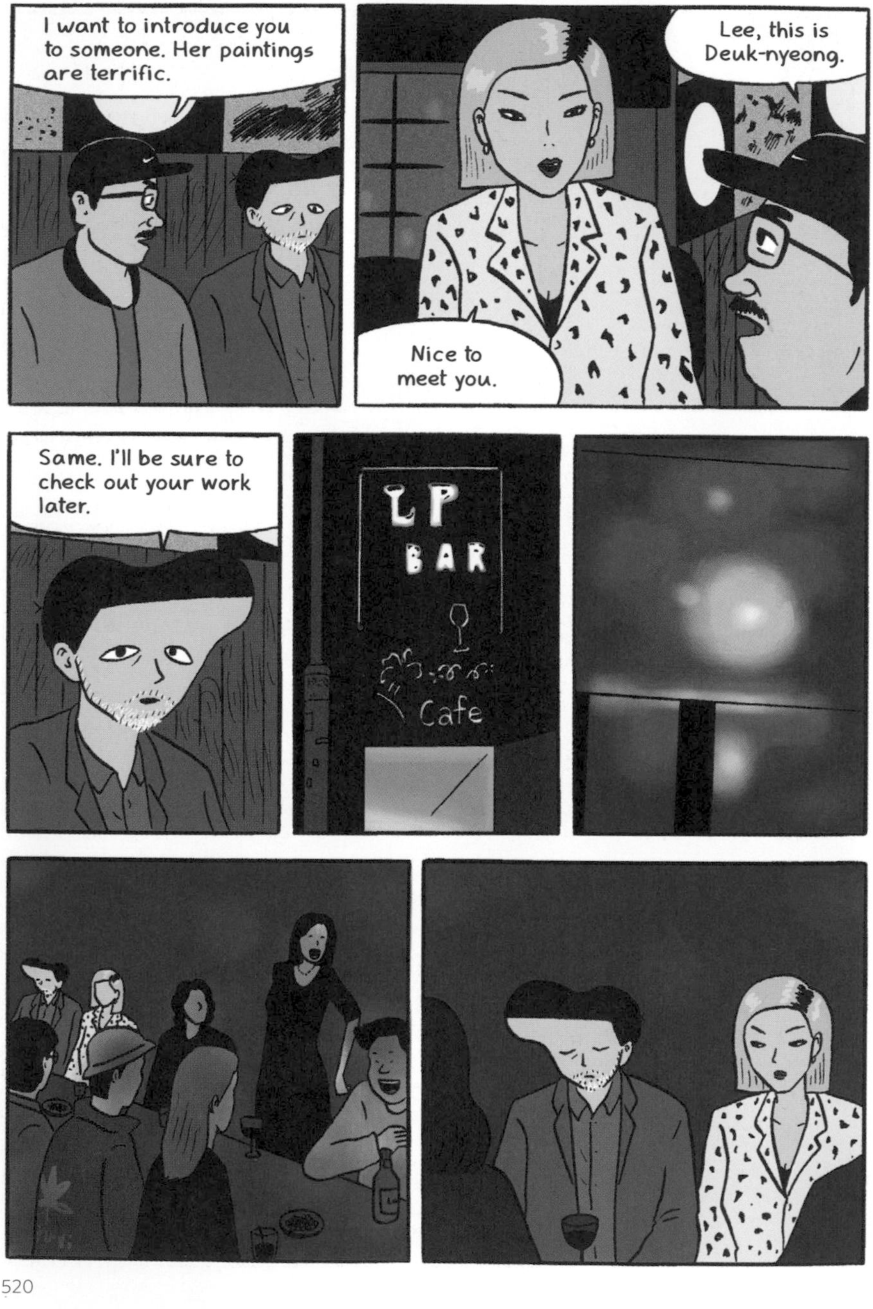
I want to introduce you to someone. Her paintings are terrific.
Lee, this is Deuk-nyeong.
Nice to meet you.
Same. I'll be sure to check out your work later.
LP BAR
Cafe

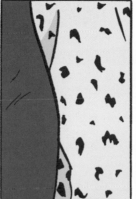

I'm getting ready for my solo exhibition...

Are you hitting on me?

So an interview would be greatly appreciated...

Hmm...

If I get mixed up with you and something goes wrong...

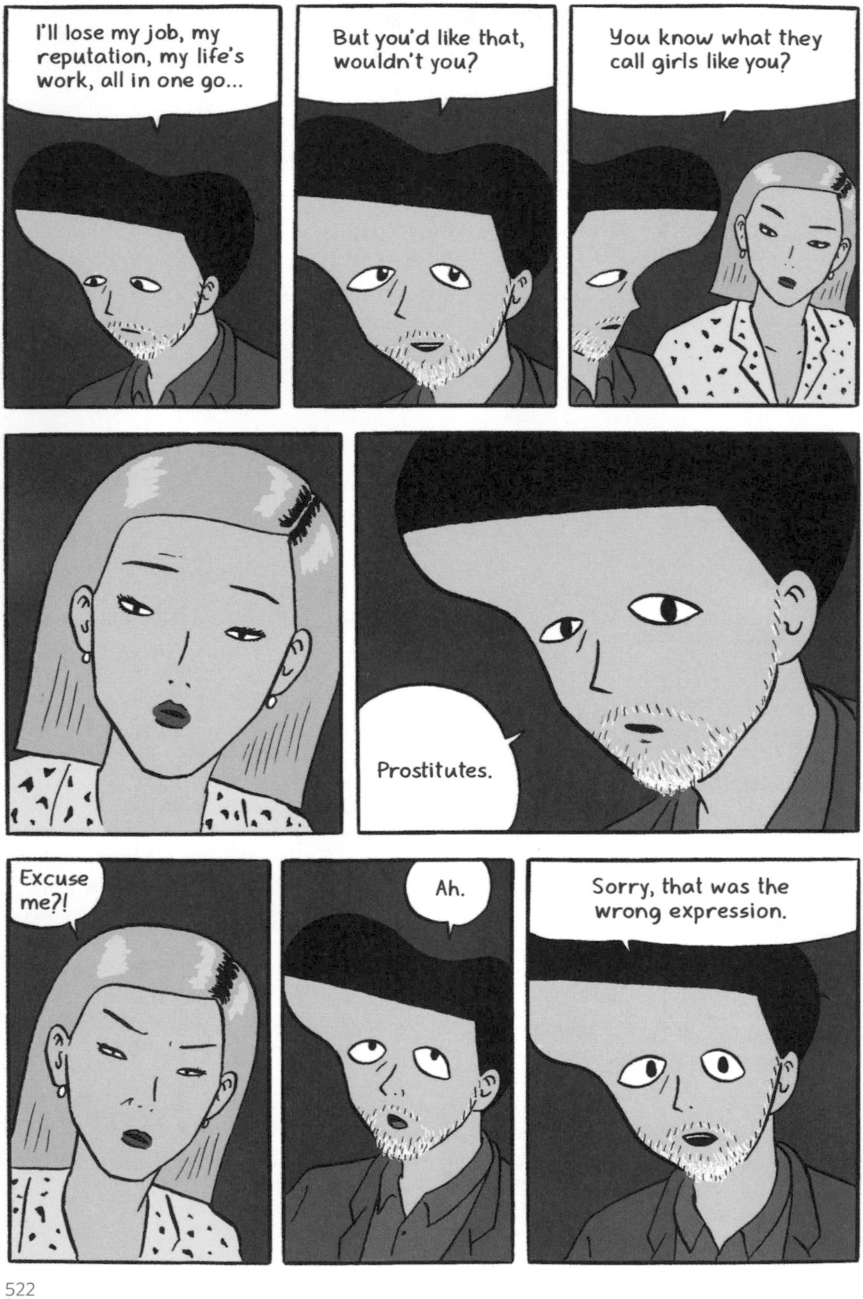
I'll lose my job, my reputation, my life's work, all in one go...
But you'd like that, wouldn't you?
You know what they call girls like you?
Prostitutes.
Excuse me?!
Ah.
Sorry, that was the wrong expression.

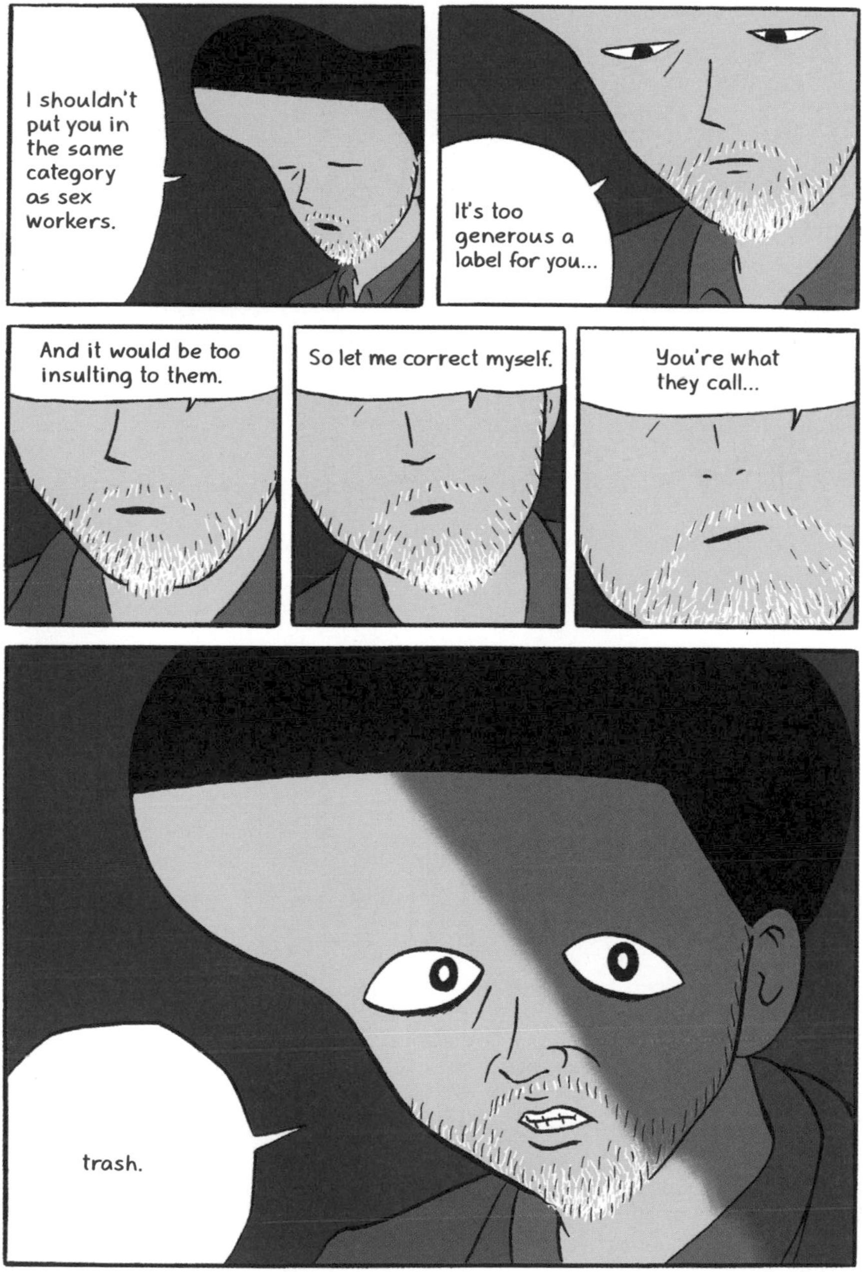
I shouldn't put you in the same category as sex workers.
It's too generous a label for you...
And it would be too insulting to them.
So let me correct myself.
You're what they call...
trash.

Finding Success as Both Musician and Writer

GENIUS ARTIST CHUN JONGSEOP

Chun Jongseop has been busy at work on his new book and music. I visited him in his home, a space simple yet accented with striking features, and spoke about his sensitive artist's eye.

While very few people manage to succeed in even one field, Chun has risen to the top in two fields, proving his genius. To gain insight into what inspires him, we held this interview in his home.

What have you been doing for the past year?
Not much. Just making music, writing, and drinking.

Do you work when inspiration strikes or do you set aside time regularly to work?
It depends. There have been times when all I've done was write for several weeks. There have also been times when I've separated my day, writing in the morning and working on my music in the evening and late at night. I don't follow rules when I'm creating, but I do try to be diligent.

What is your next book about?
I haven't decided yet if it should take the form of a web novel or webtoon. If my story ever gets adapted into a TV series, I sometimes fantasize about writing the script or composing the music myself.

What inspires you these days?
Hmm... People with charisma. When I meet beautiful people who have a lot of charm, something stirs within me.

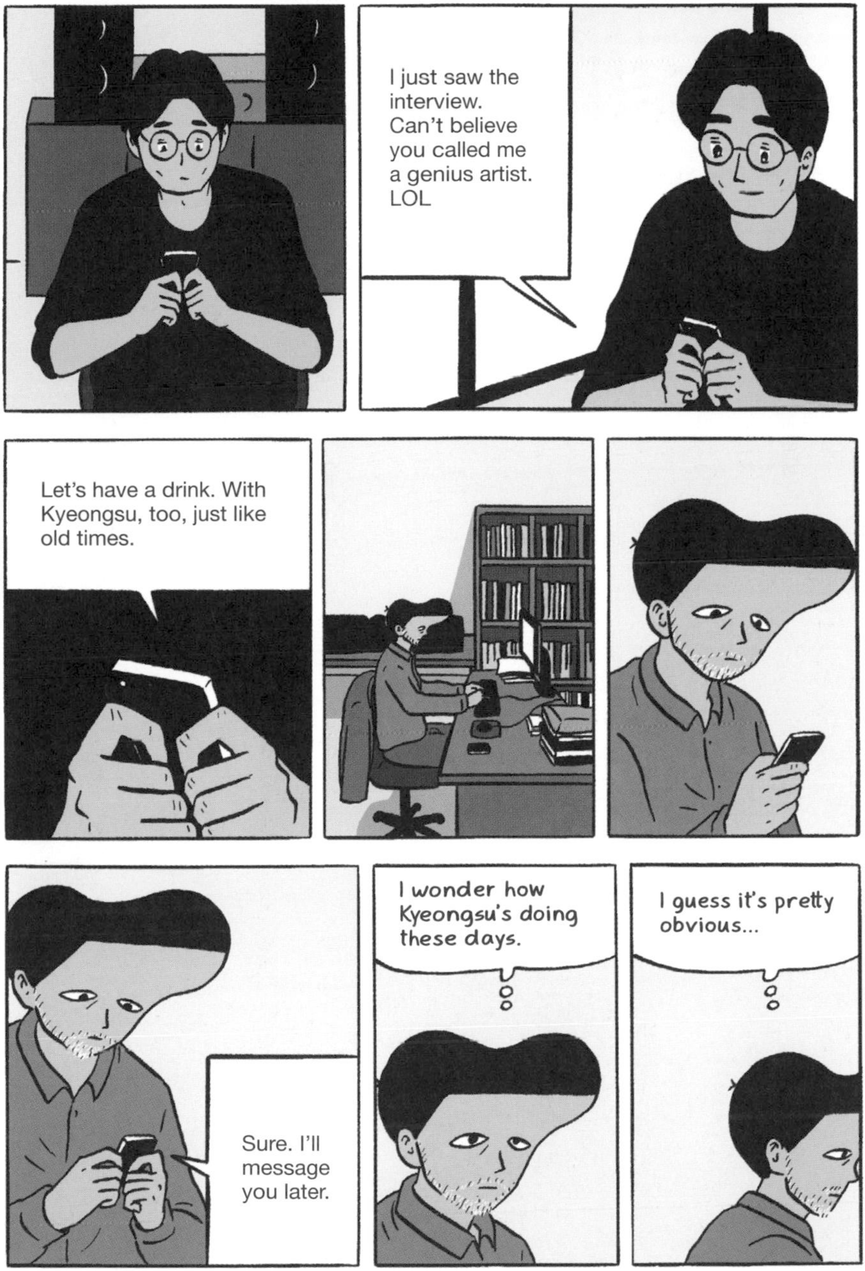
I just saw the interview. Can't believe you called me a genius artist. LOL
Let's have a drink. With Kyeongsu, too, just like old times.
Sure. I'll message you later.
I wonder how Kyeongsu's doing these days.
I guess it's pretty obvious...

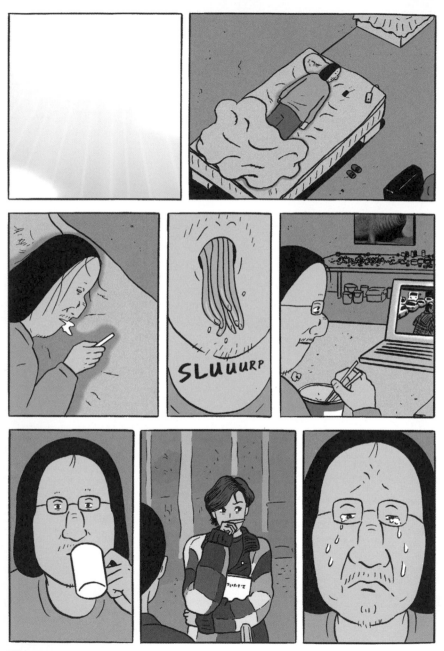

SLUUURP

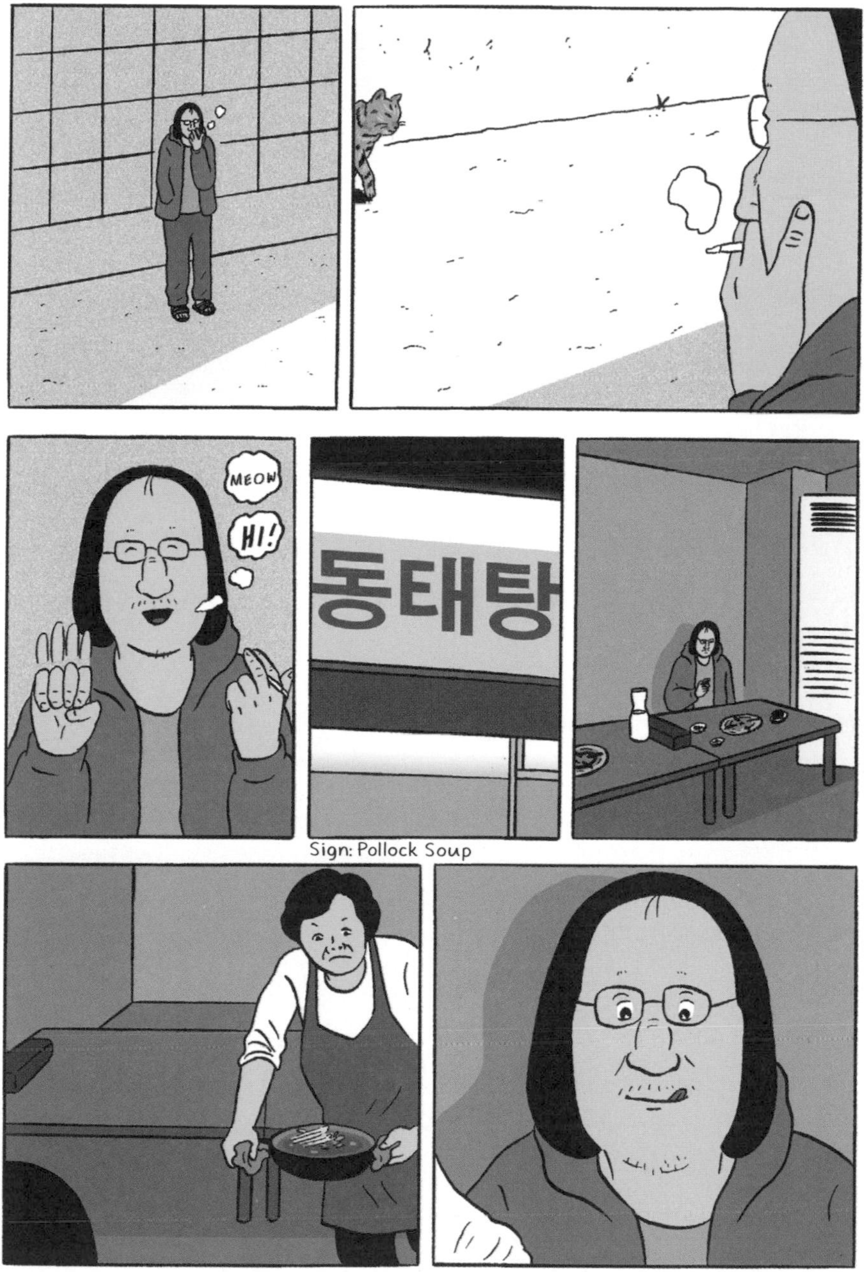
MEOW
HI!
동태탕
Sign: Pollock Soup

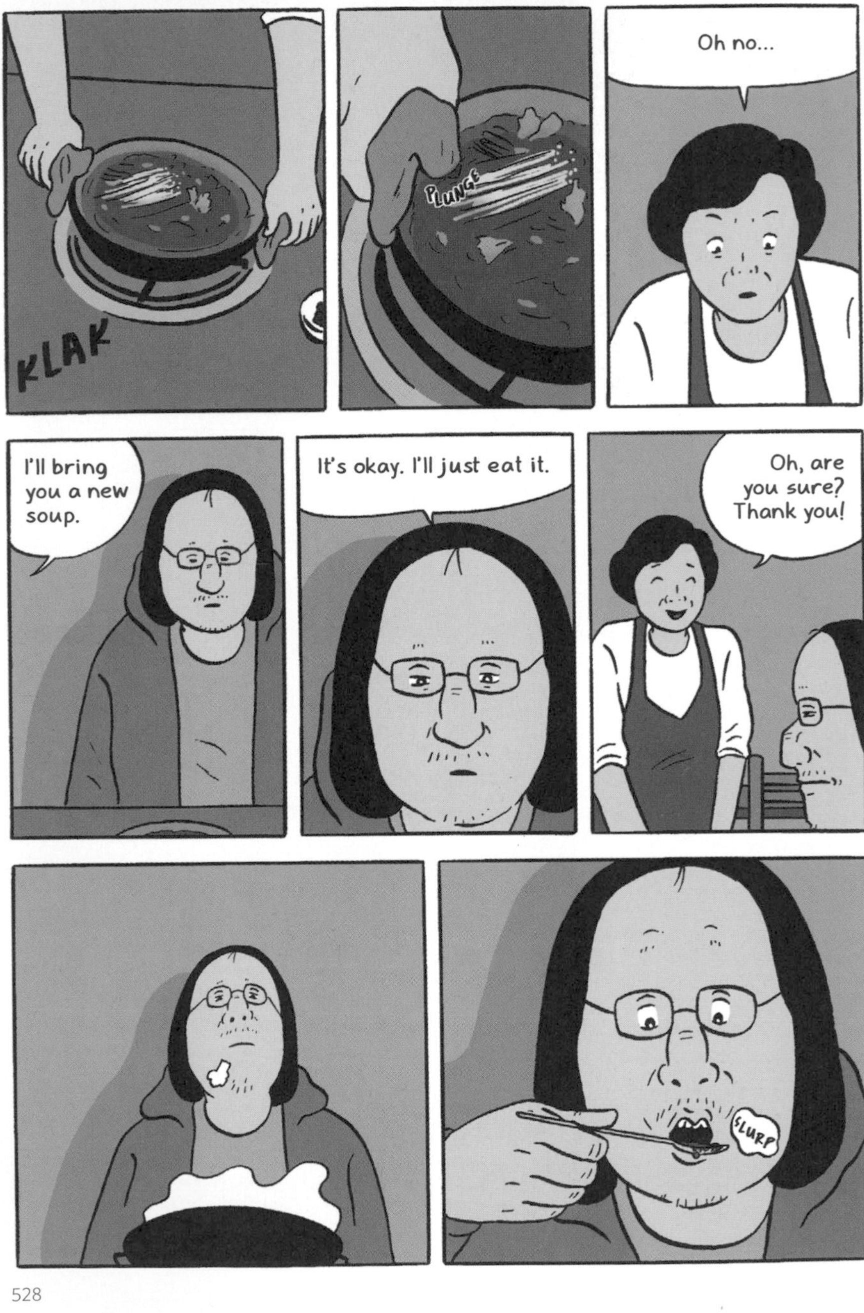
KLAK
PLUNGE
Oh no...
I'll bring you a new soup.
It's okay. I'll just eat it.
Oh, are you sure? Thank you!
SLURP

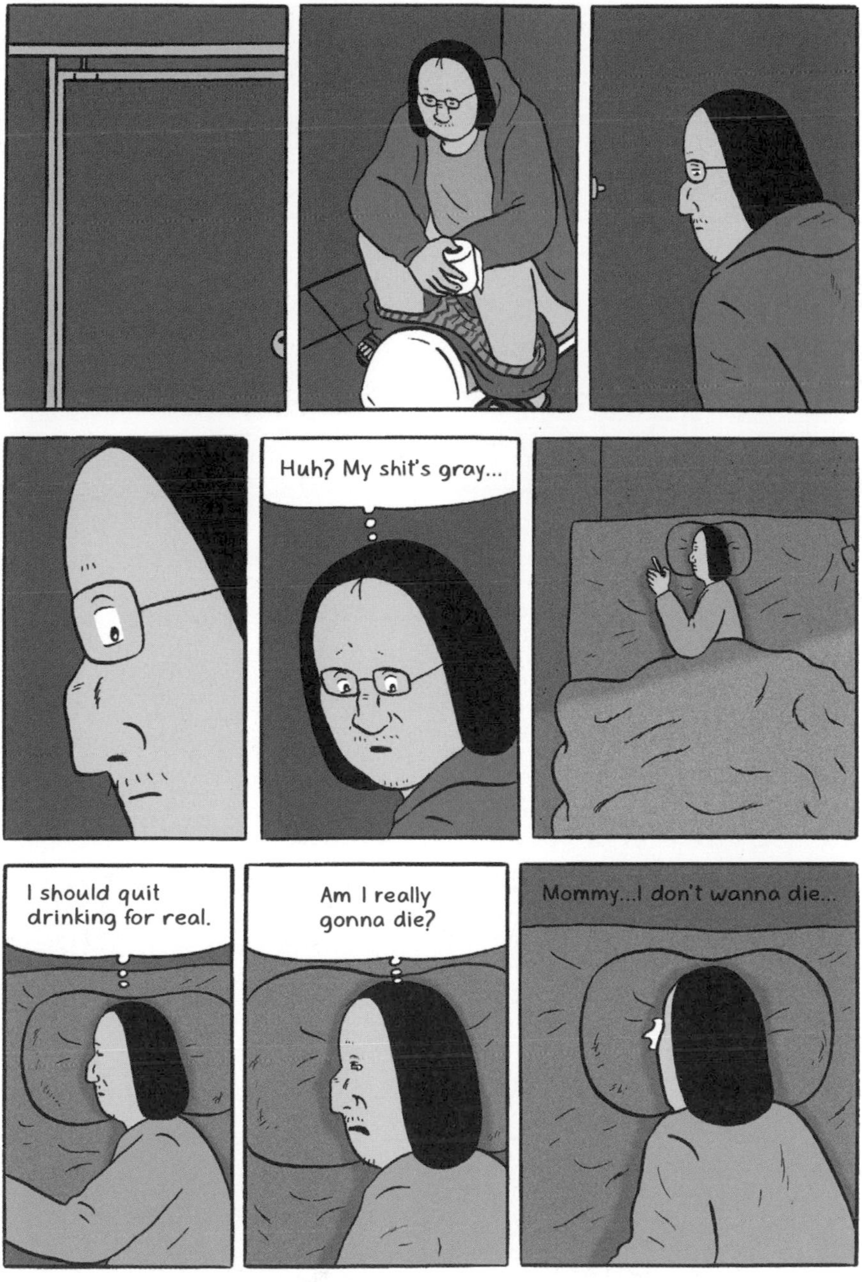
Huh? My shit's gray...
I should quit drinking for real.
Am I really gonna die?
Mommy...I don't wanna die...

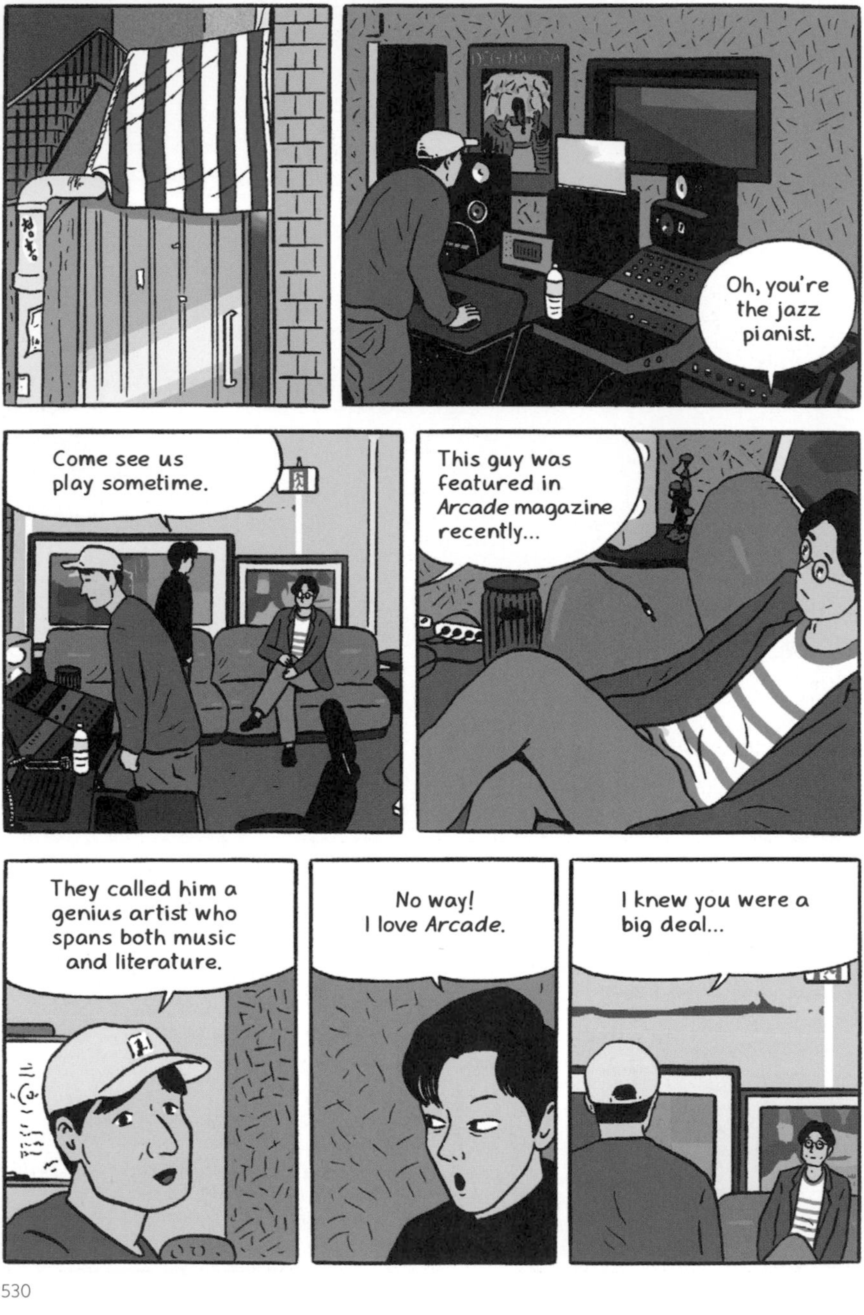
Oh, you're the jazz pianist.
Come see us play sometime.
This guy was featured in *Arcade* magazine recently...
They called him a genius artist who spans both music and literature.
No way! I love *Arcade*.
I knew you were a big deal...

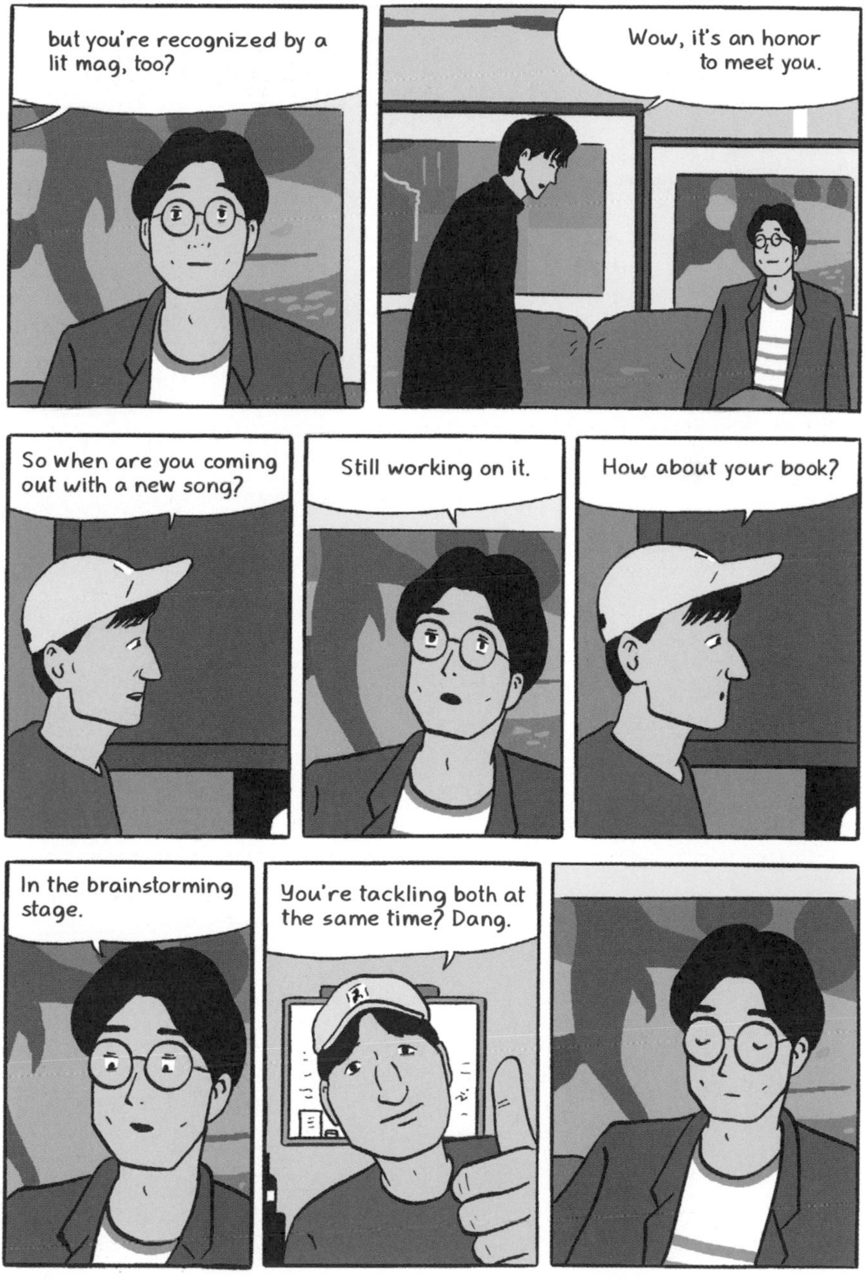
but you're recognized by a lit mag, too?
Wow, it's an honor to meet you.
So when are you coming out with a new song?
Still working on it.
How about your book?
In the brainstorming stage.
You're tackling both at the same time? Dang.

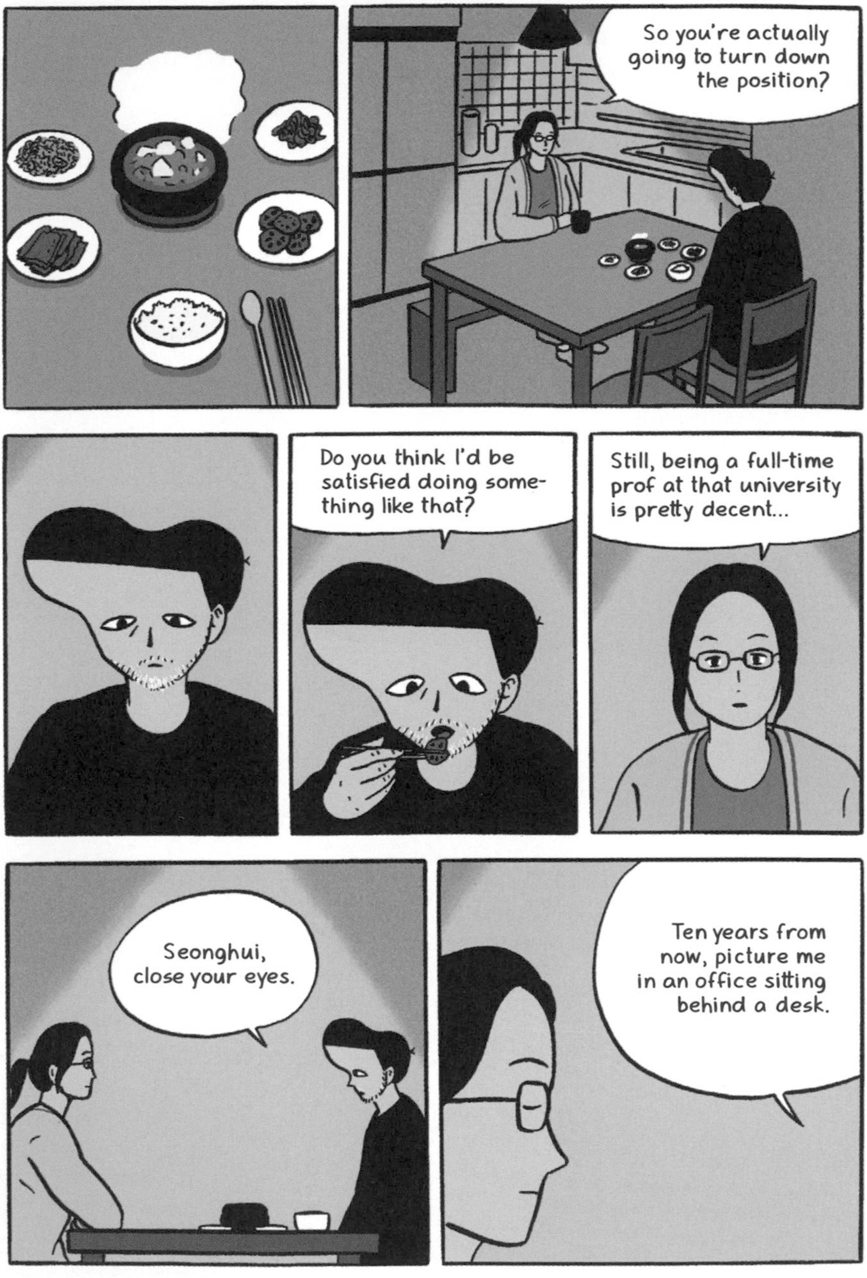
So you're actually going to turn down the position?
Do you think I'd be satisfied doing some-thing like that?
Still, being a full-time prof at that university is pretty decent...
Seonghui, close your eyes.
Ten years from now, picture me in an office sitting behind a desk.

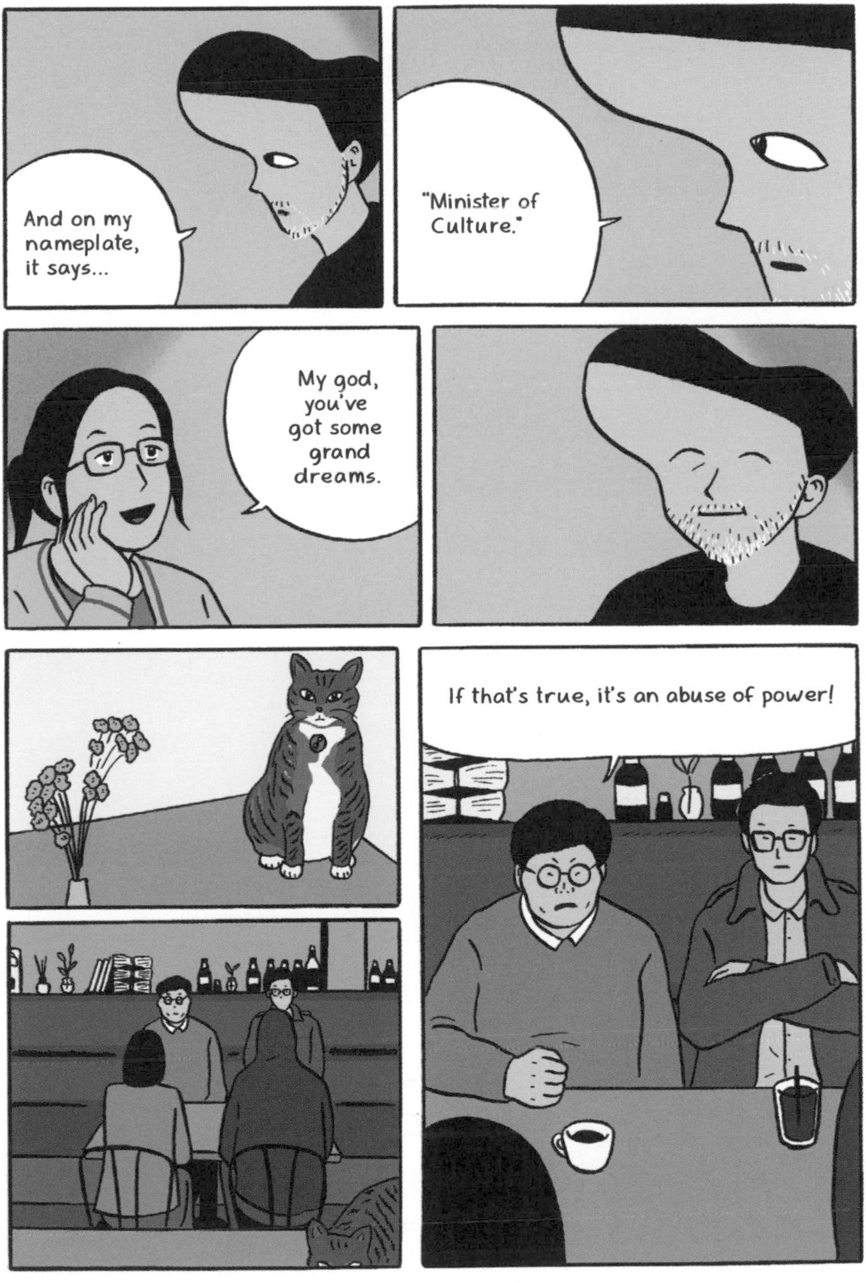
And on my nameplate, it says...
"Minister of Culture."
My god, you've got some grand dreams.
If that's true, it's an abuse of power!

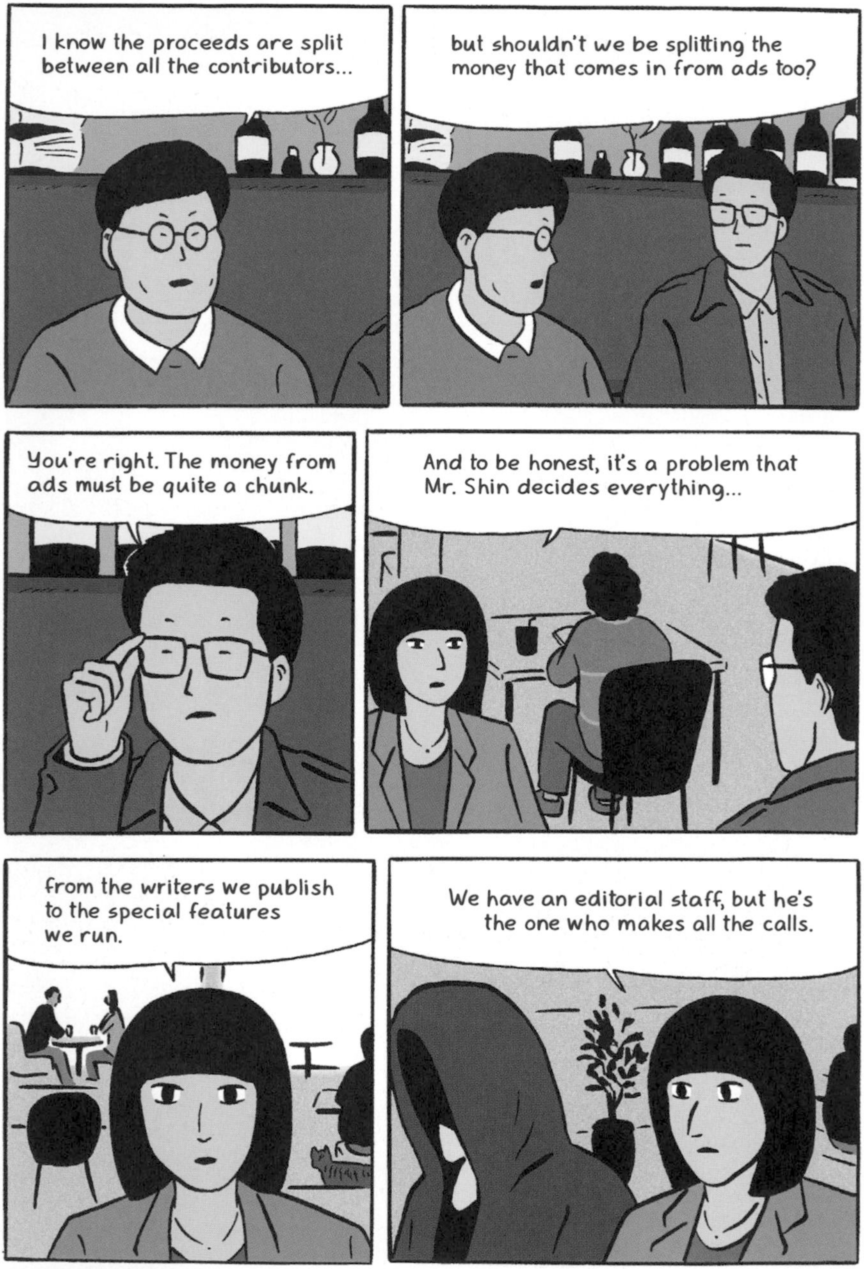
I know the proceeds are split between all the contributors...
but shouldn't we be splitting the money that comes in from ads too?
You're right. The money from ads must be quite a chunk.
And to be honest, it's a problem that Mr. Shin decides everything...
from the writers we publish to the special features we run.
We have an editorial staff, but he's the one who makes all the calls.

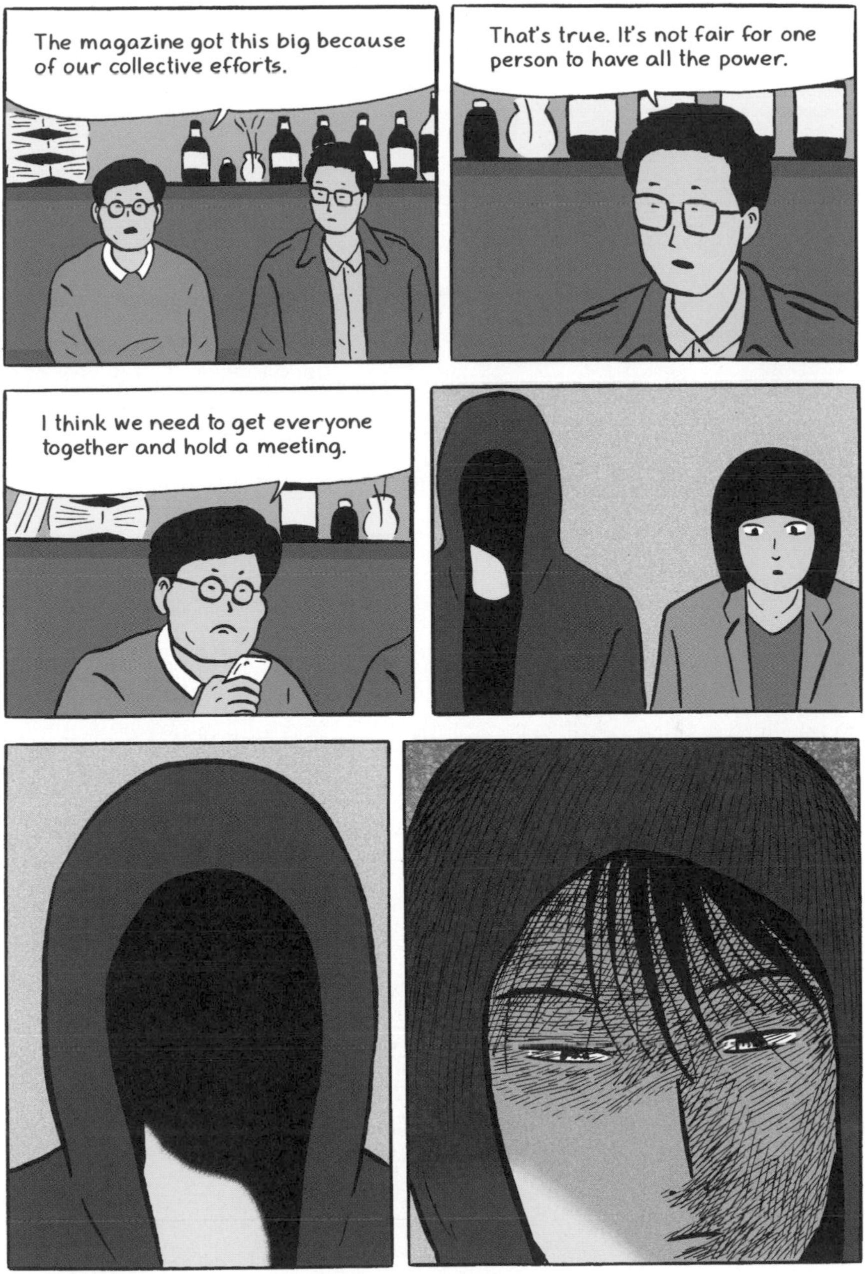
The magazine got this big because of our collective efforts.
That's true. It's not fair for one person to have all the power.
I think we need to get everyone together and hold a meeting.

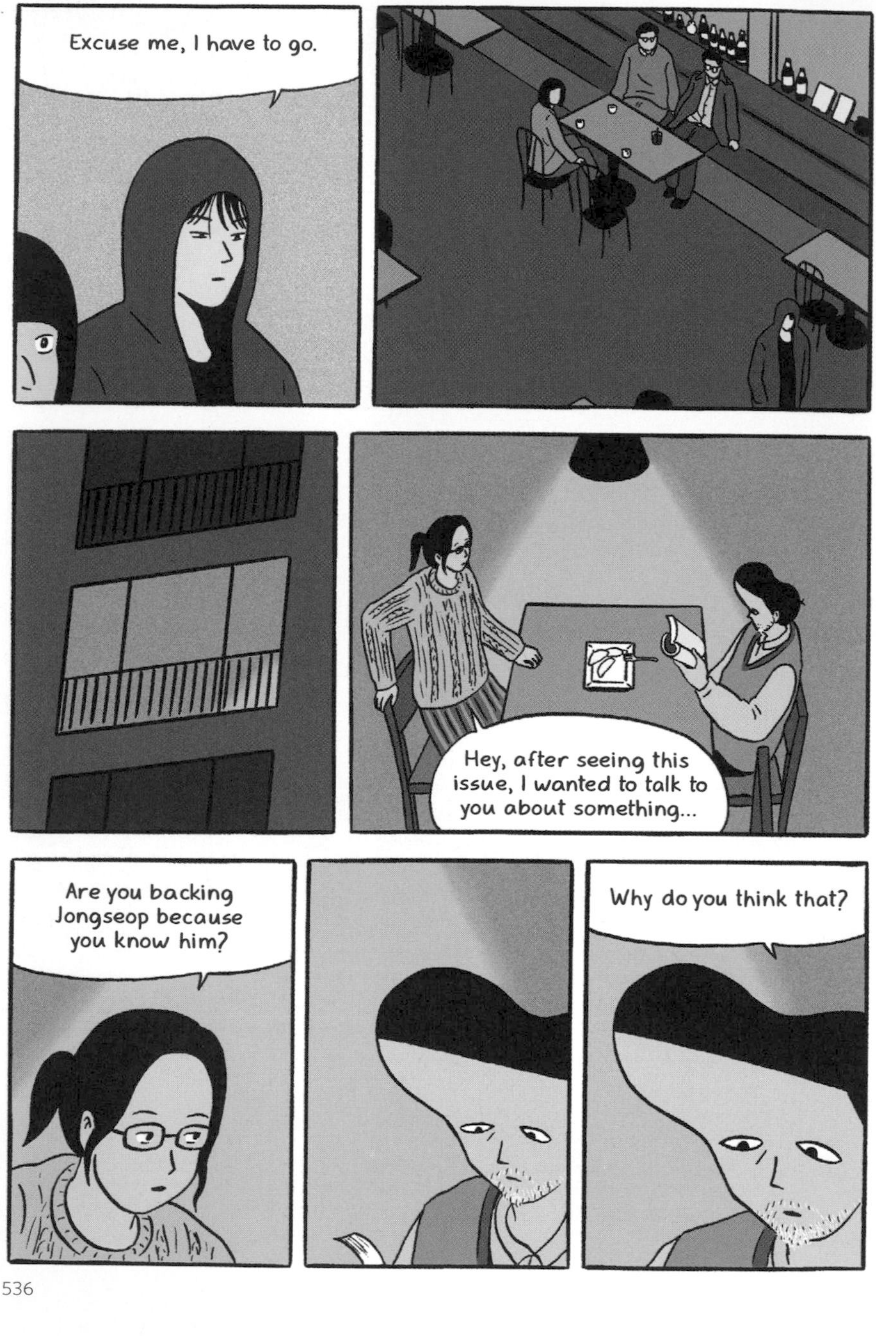
Excuse me, I have to go.
Hey, after seeing this issue, I wanted to talk to you about something...
Are you backing Jongseop because you know him?
Why do you think that?

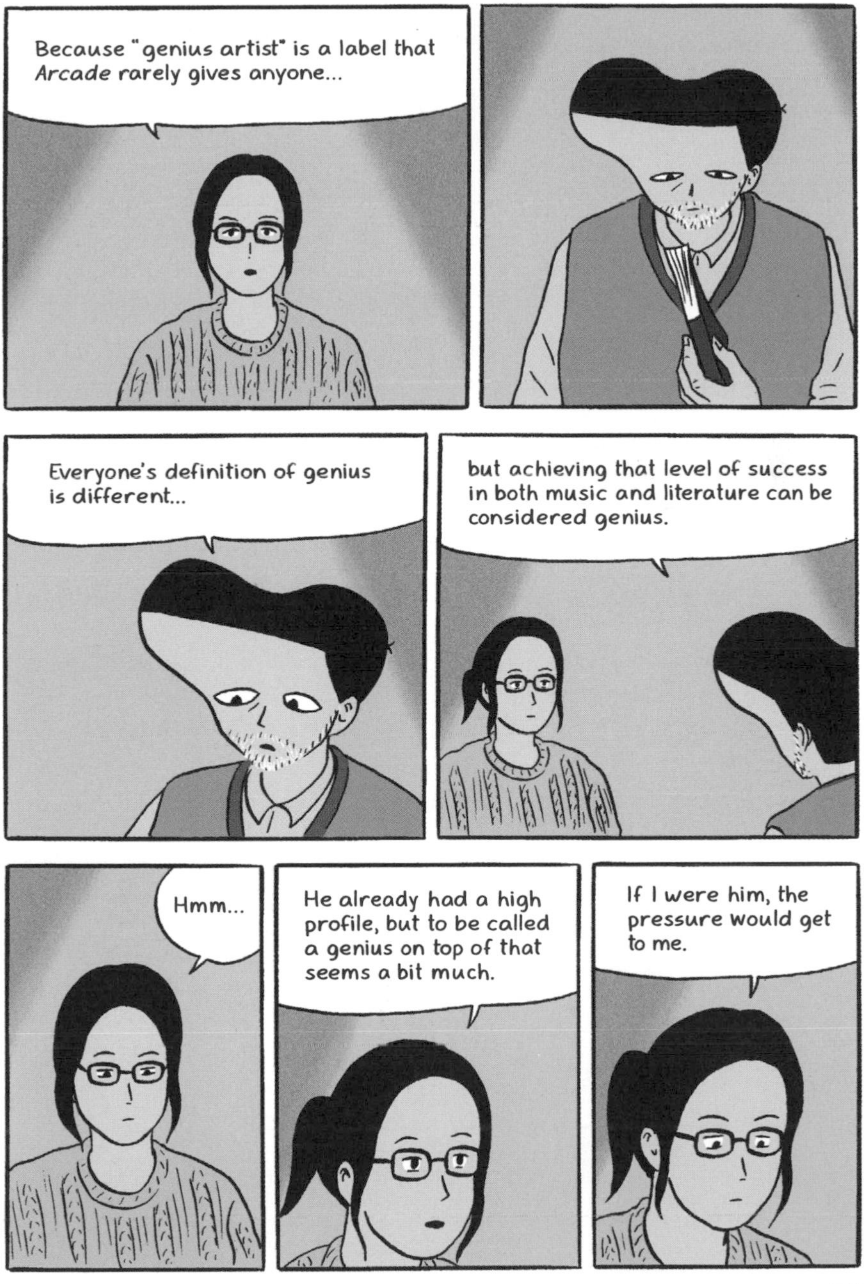
Because "genius artist" is a label that *Arcade* rarely gives anyone...
Everyone's definition of genius is different...
but achieving that level of success in both music and literature can be considered genius.
Hmm...
He already had a high profile, but to be called a genius on top of that seems a bit much.
If I were him, the pressure would get to me.

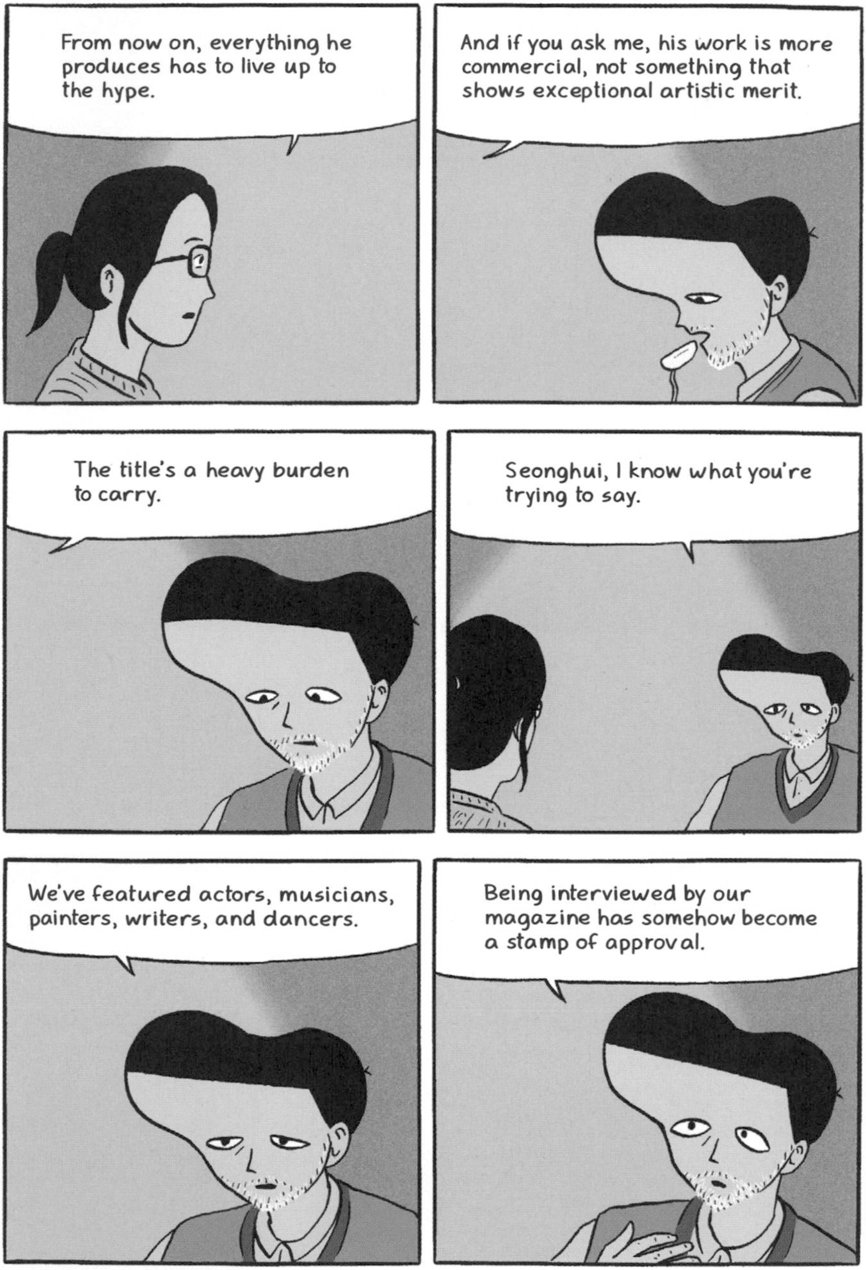
From now on, everything he produces has to live up to the hype.
And if you ask me, his work is more commercial, not something that shows exceptional artistic merit.
The title's a heavy burden to carry.
Seonghui, I know what you're trying to say.
We've featured actors, musicians, painters, writers, and dancers.
Being interviewed by our magazine has somehow become a stamp of approval.

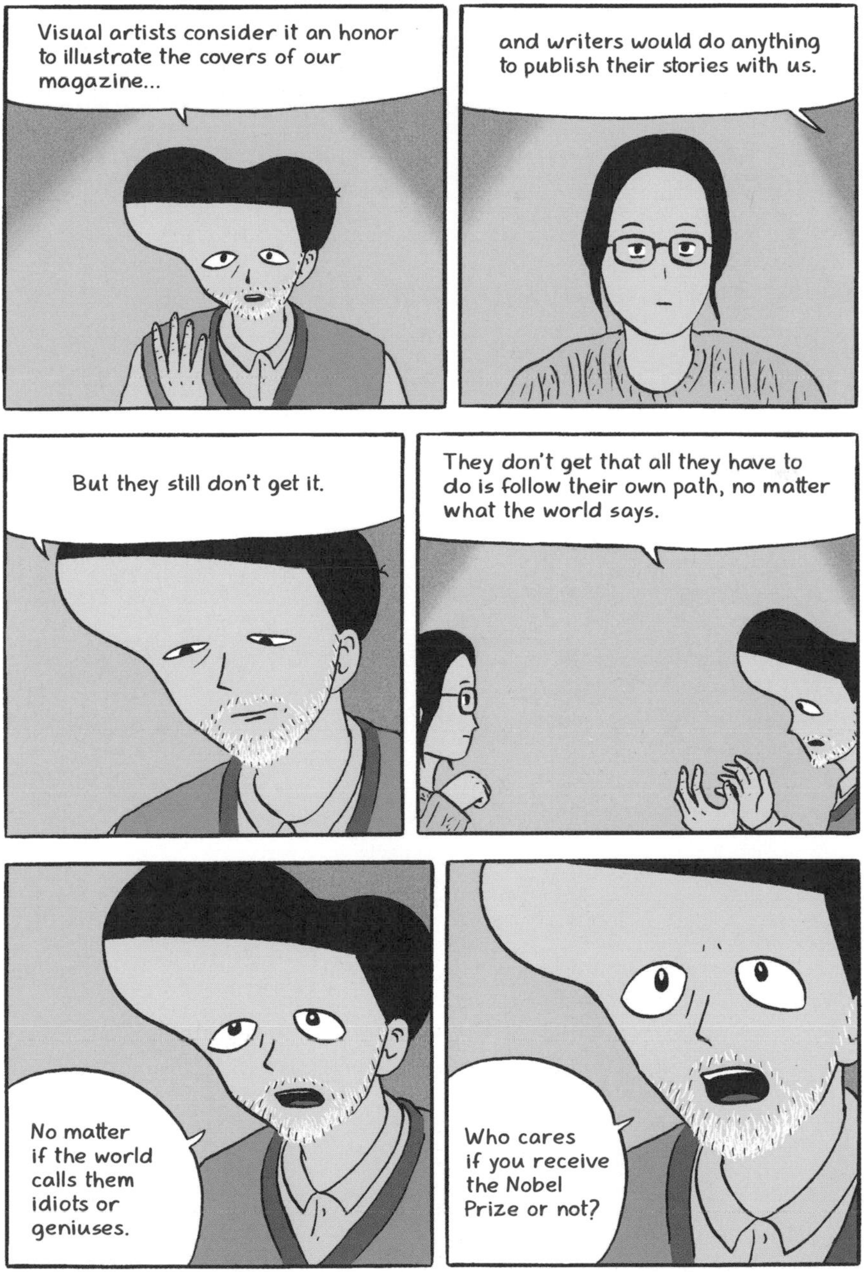
Visual artists consider it an honor to illustrate the covers of our magazine...
and writers would do anything to publish their stories with us.
But they still don't get it.
They don't get that all they have to do is follow their own path, no matter what the world says.
No matter if the world calls them idiots or geniuses.
Who cares if you receive the Nobel Prize or not?

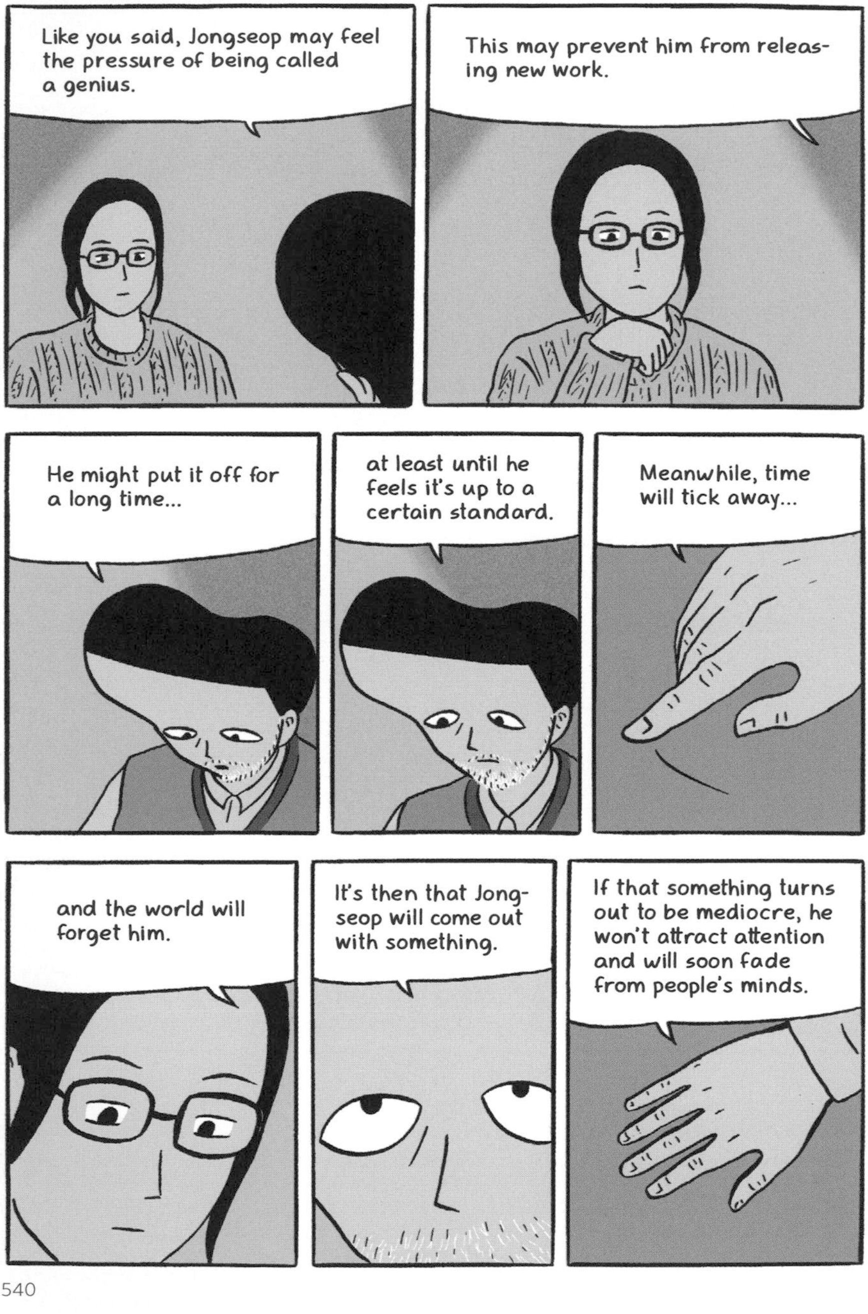
Like you said, Jongseop may feel the pressure of being called a genius.
This may prevent him from releas-ing new work.
He might put it off for a long time...
at least until he feels it's up to a certain standard.
Meanwhile, time will tick away...
and the world will forget him.
It's then that Jong-seop will come out with something.
If that something turns out to be mediocre, he won't attract attention and will soon fade from people's minds.

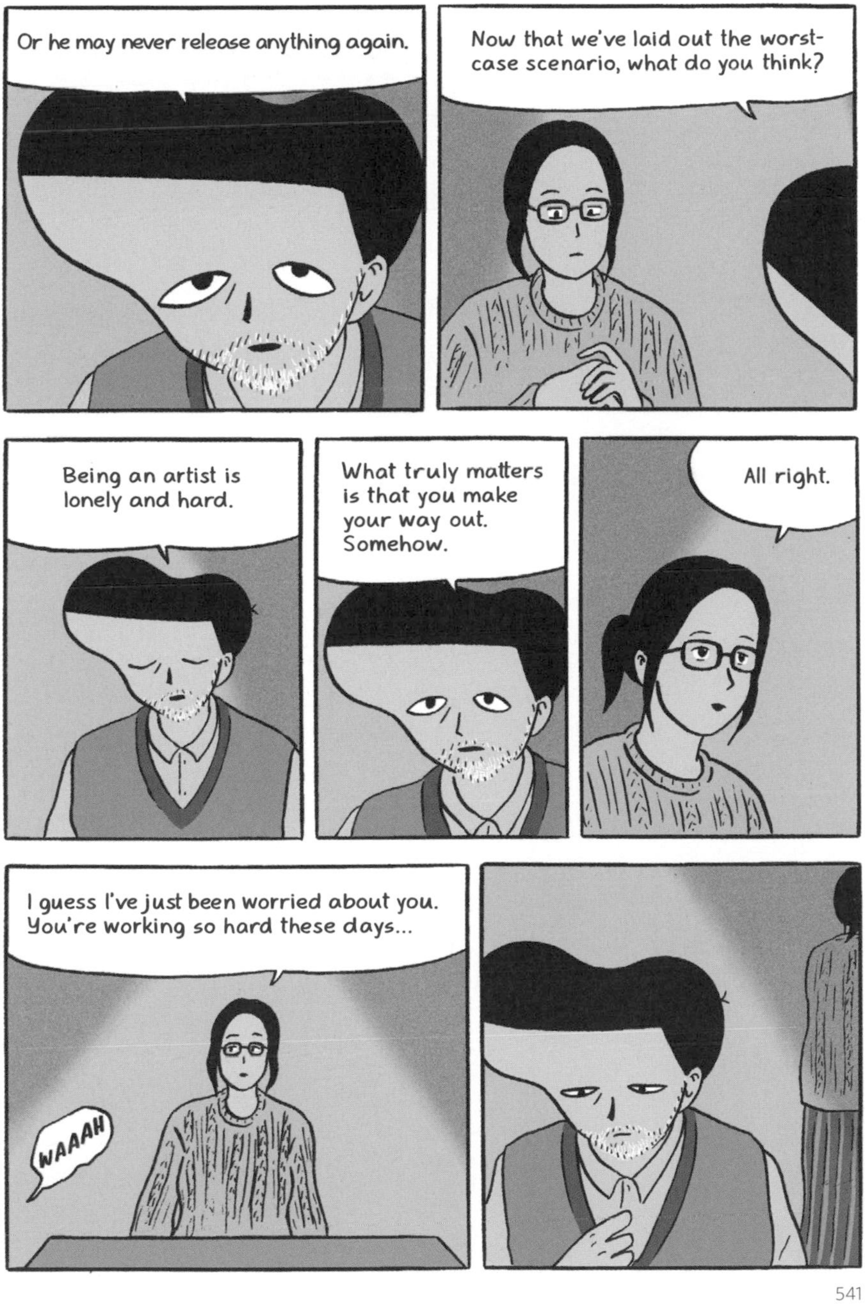
Or he may never release anything again.
Now that we've laid out the worst-case scenario, what do you think?
Being an artist is lonely and hard.
What truly matters is that you make your way out. Somehow.
All right.
I guess I've just been worried about you. You're working so hard these days...
WAAAH

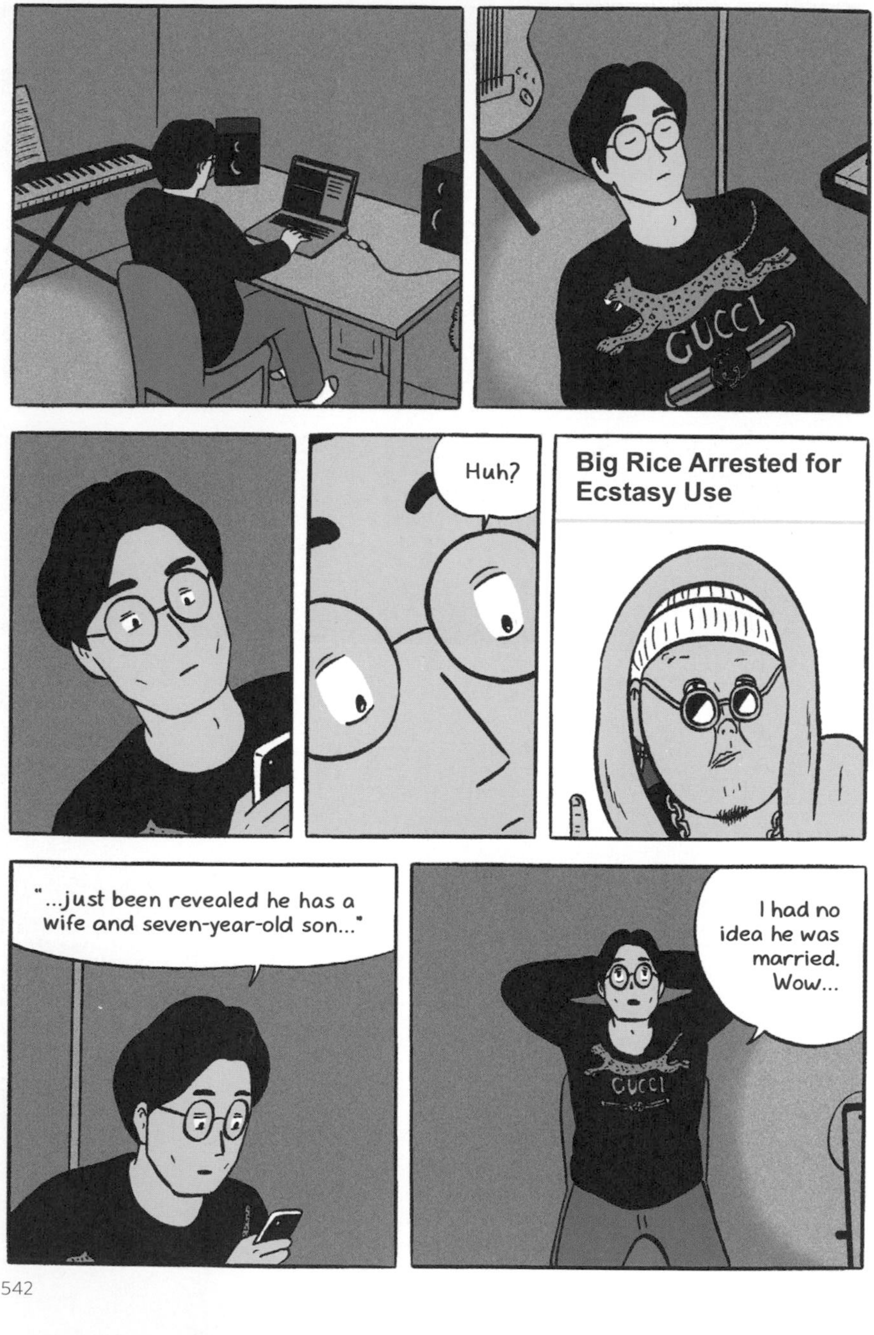
GUCCI
Huh?
Big Rice Arrested for Ecstasy Use
"...just been revealed he has a wife and seven-year-old son..."
I had no idea he was married. Wow...
GUCCI

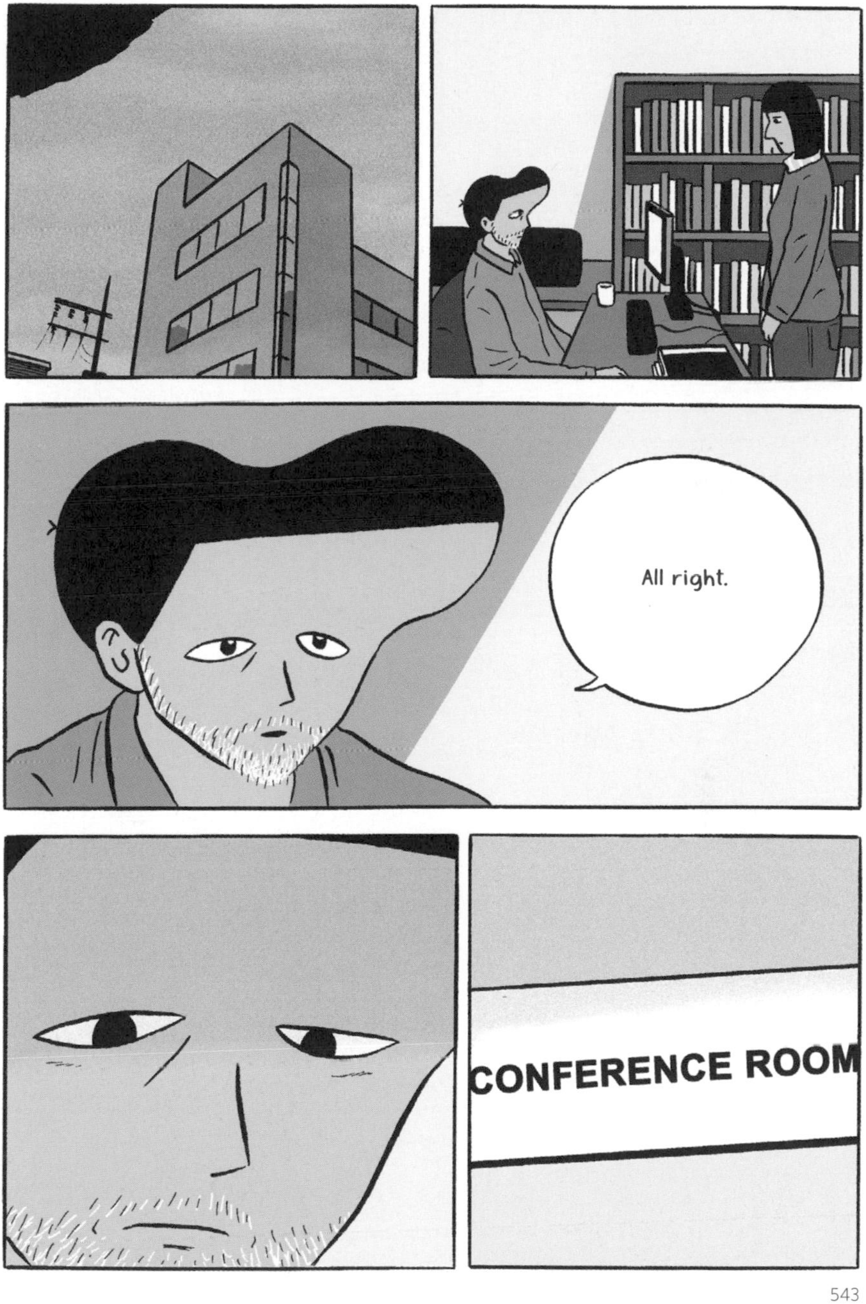
All right.
CONFERENCE ROOM

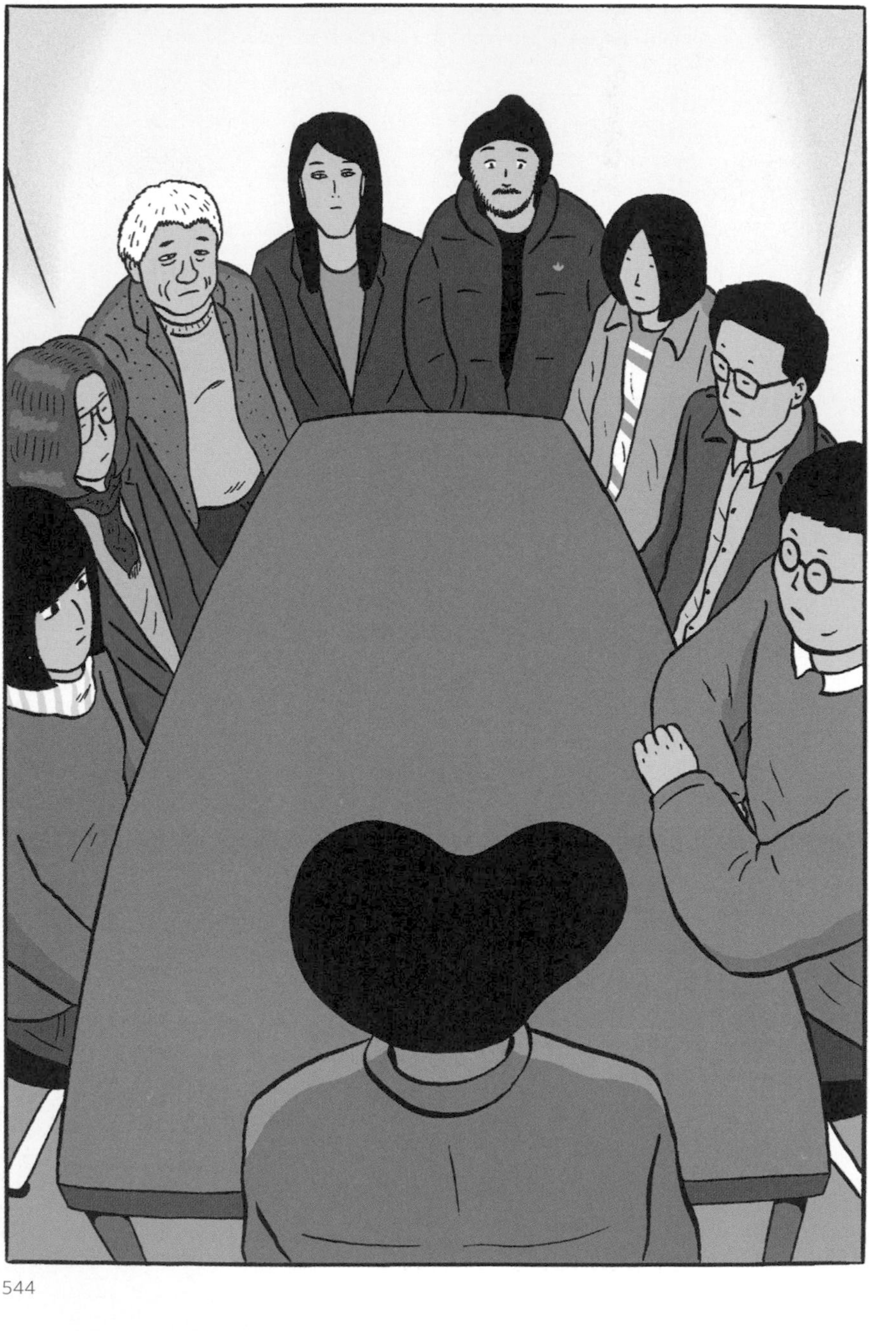

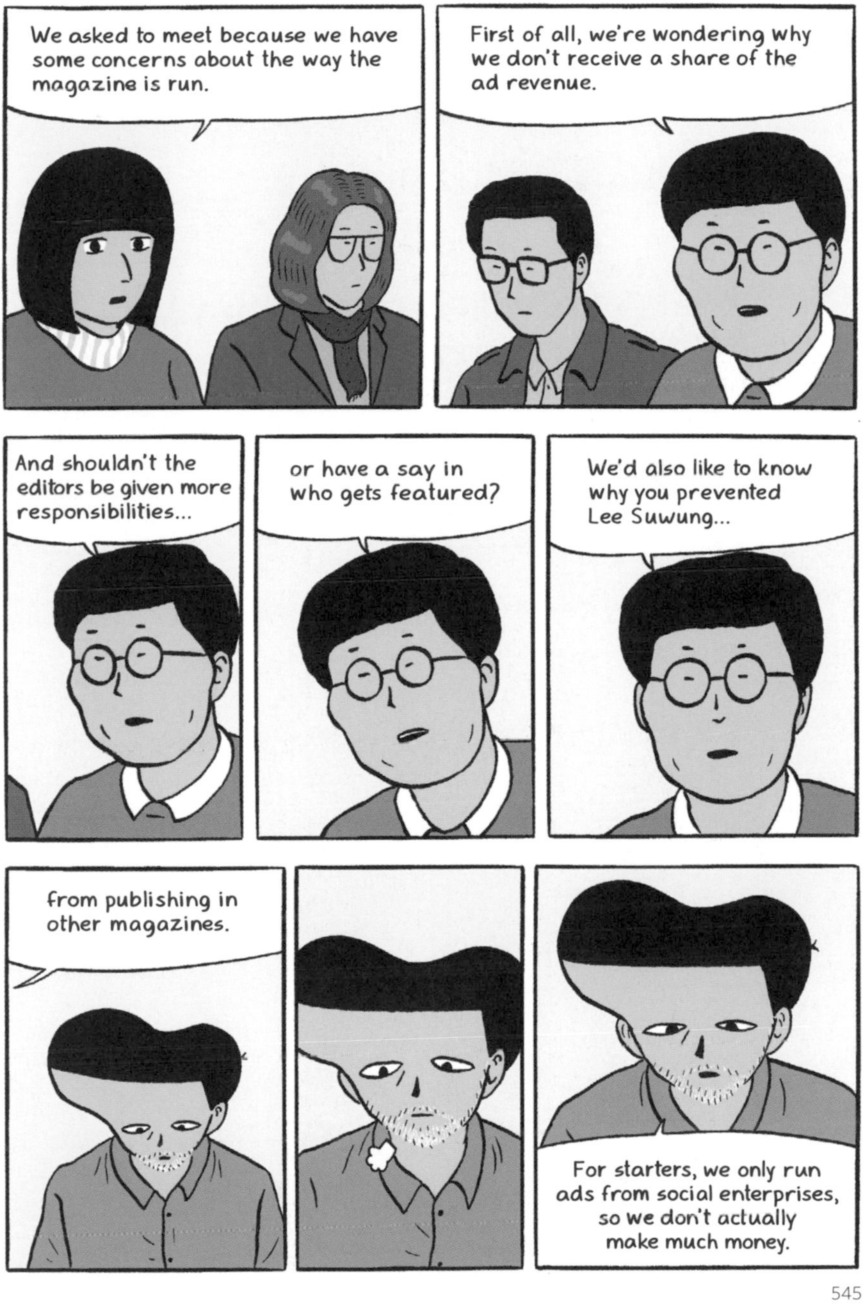
We asked to meet because we have some concerns about the way the magazine is run.
First of all, we're wondering why we don't receive a share of the ad revenue.
And shouldn't the editors be given more responsibilities...
or have a say in who gets featured?
We'd also like to know why you prevented Lee Suwung...
from publishing in other magazines.
For starters, we only run ads from social enterprises, so we don't actually make much money.

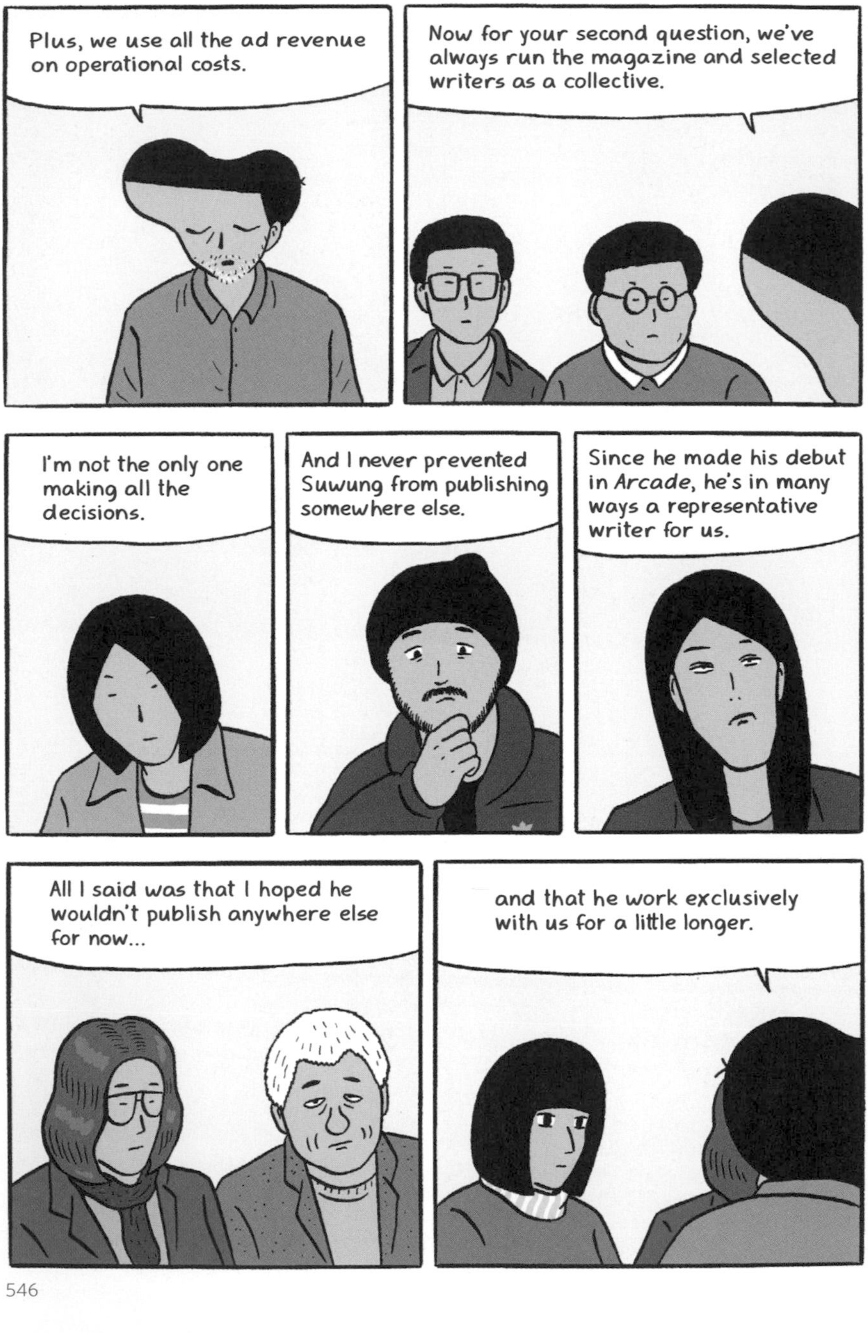
Plus, we use all the ad revenue on operational costs.
Now for your second question, we've always run the magazine and selected writers as a collective.
I'm not the only one making all the decisions.
And I never prevented Suwung from publishing somewhere else.
Since he made his debut in *Arcade*, he's in many ways a representative writer for us.
All I said was that I hoped he wouldn't publish anywhere else for now...
and that he work exclusively with us for a little longer.

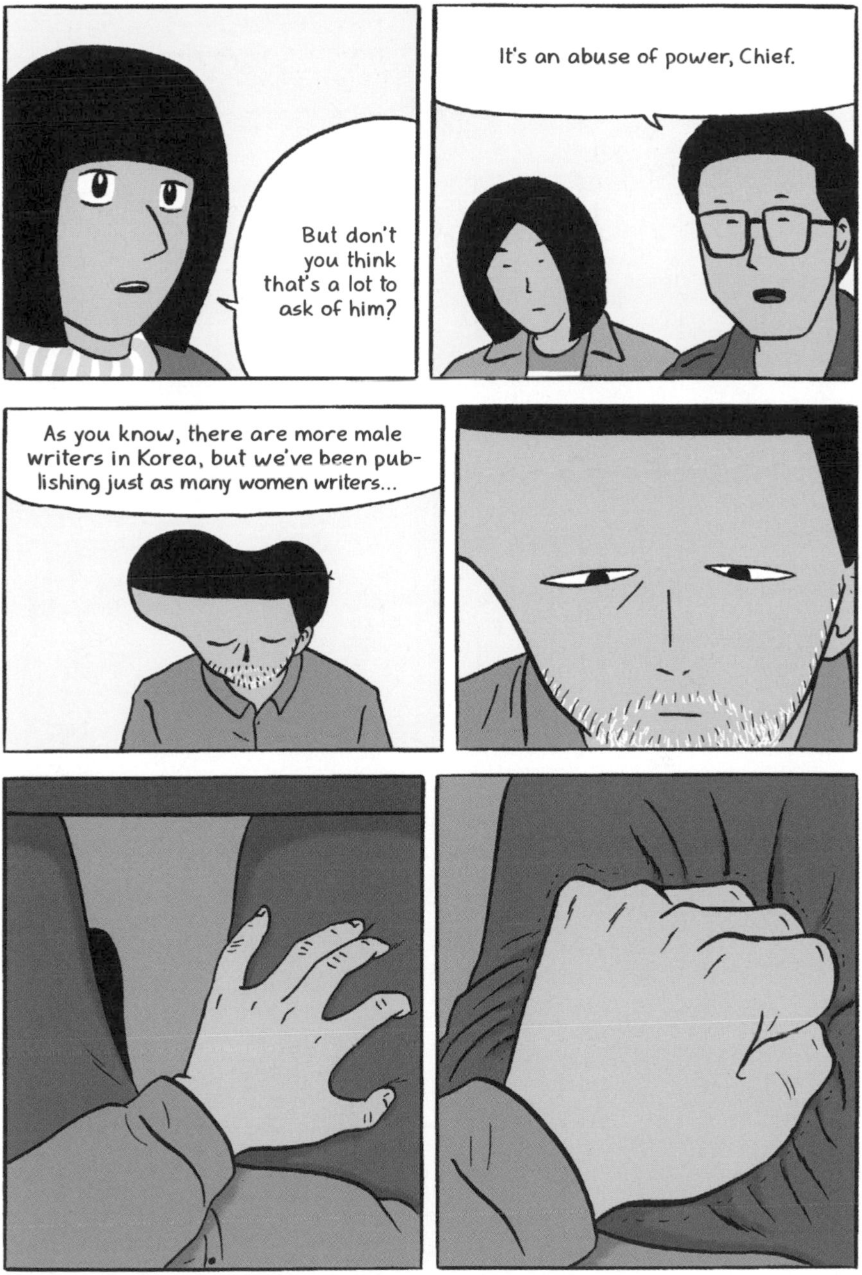
But don't you think that's a lot to ask of him?
It's an abuse of power, Chief.
As you know, there are more male writers in Korea, but we've been pub-lishing just as many women writers...

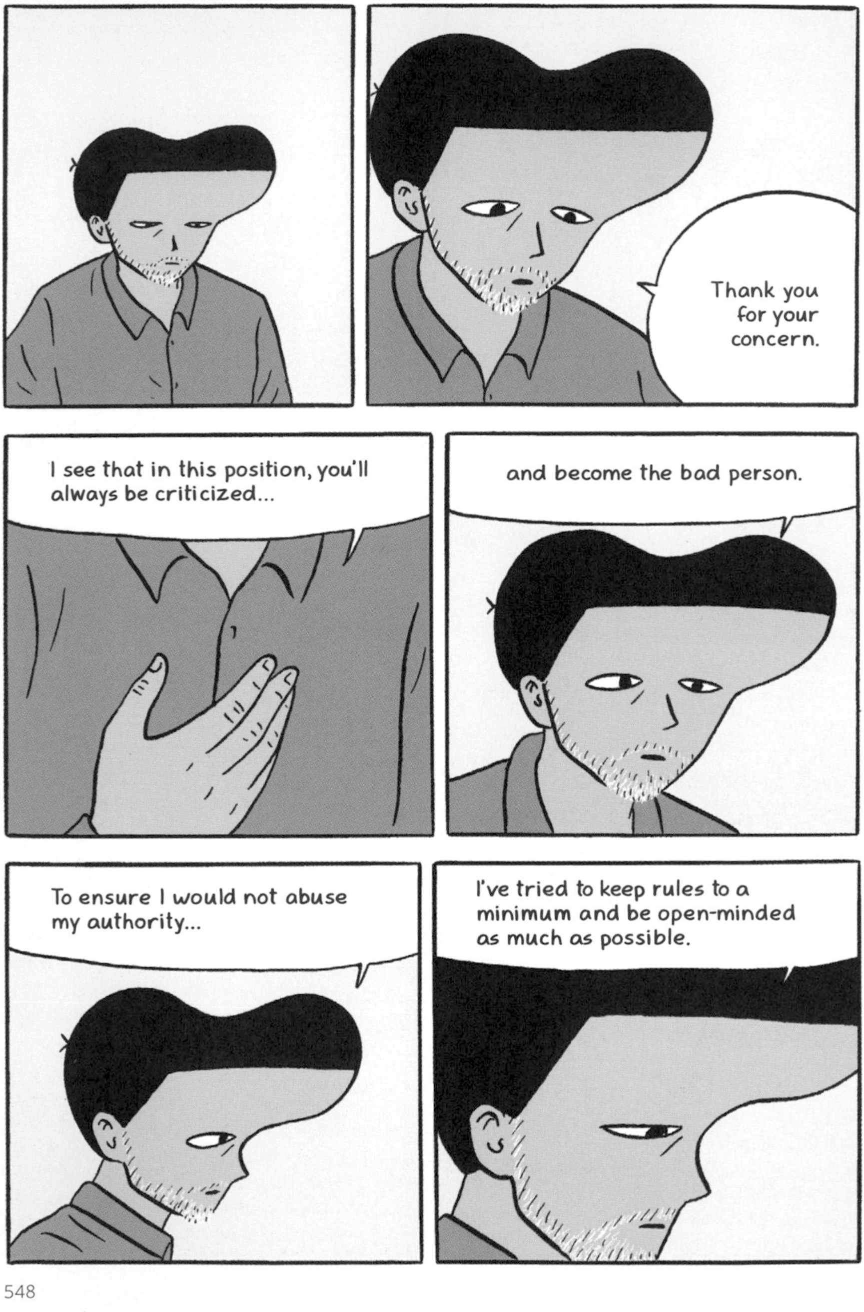
Thank you for your concern.
I see that in this position, you'll always be criticized...
and become the bad person.
To ensure I would not abuse my authority...
I've tried to keep rules to a minimum and be open-minded as much as possible.

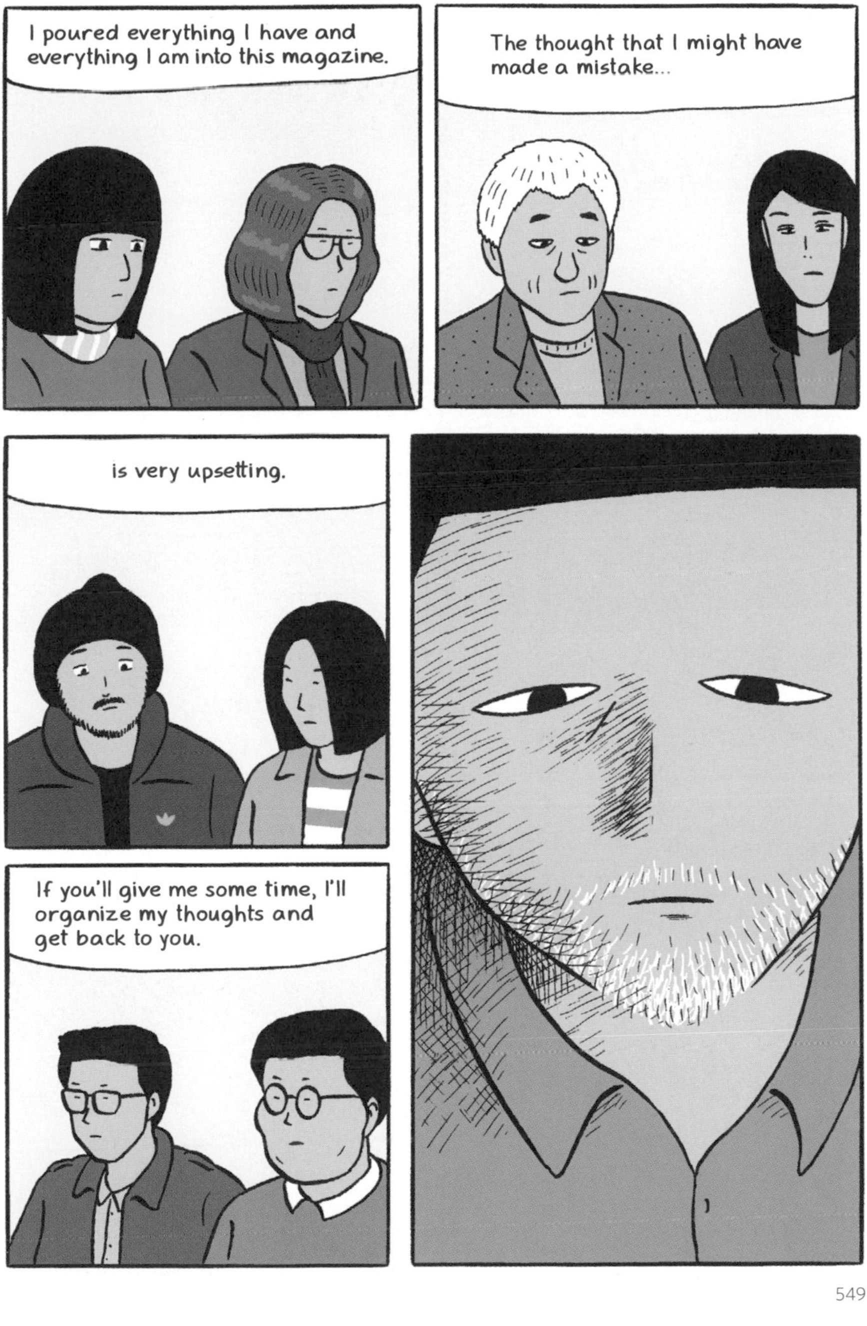
I poured everything I have and everything I am into this magazine.
The thought that I might have made a mistake...
is very upsetting.
If you'll give me some time, I'll organize my thoughts and get back to you.

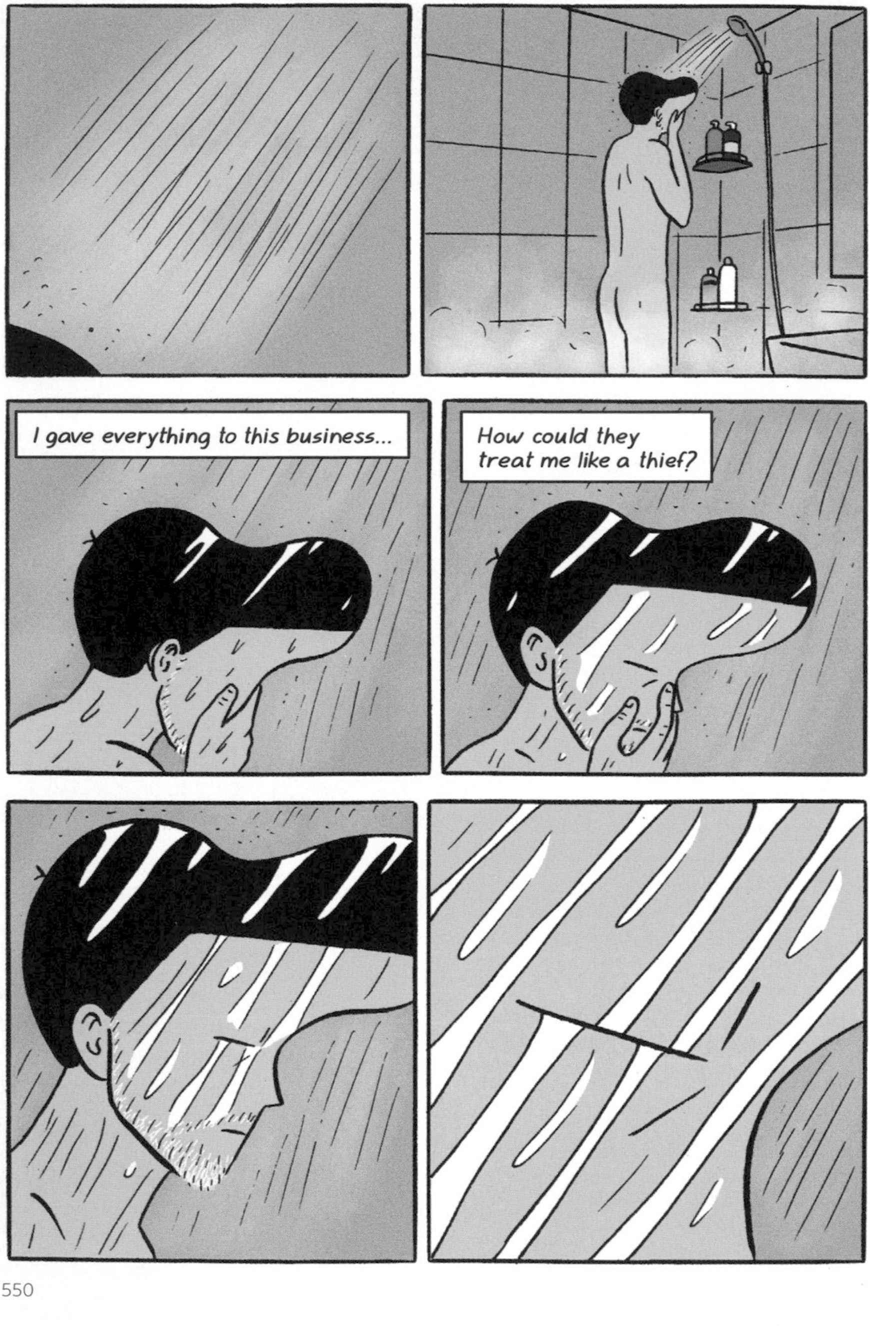
I gave everything to this business...
How could they treat me like a thief?

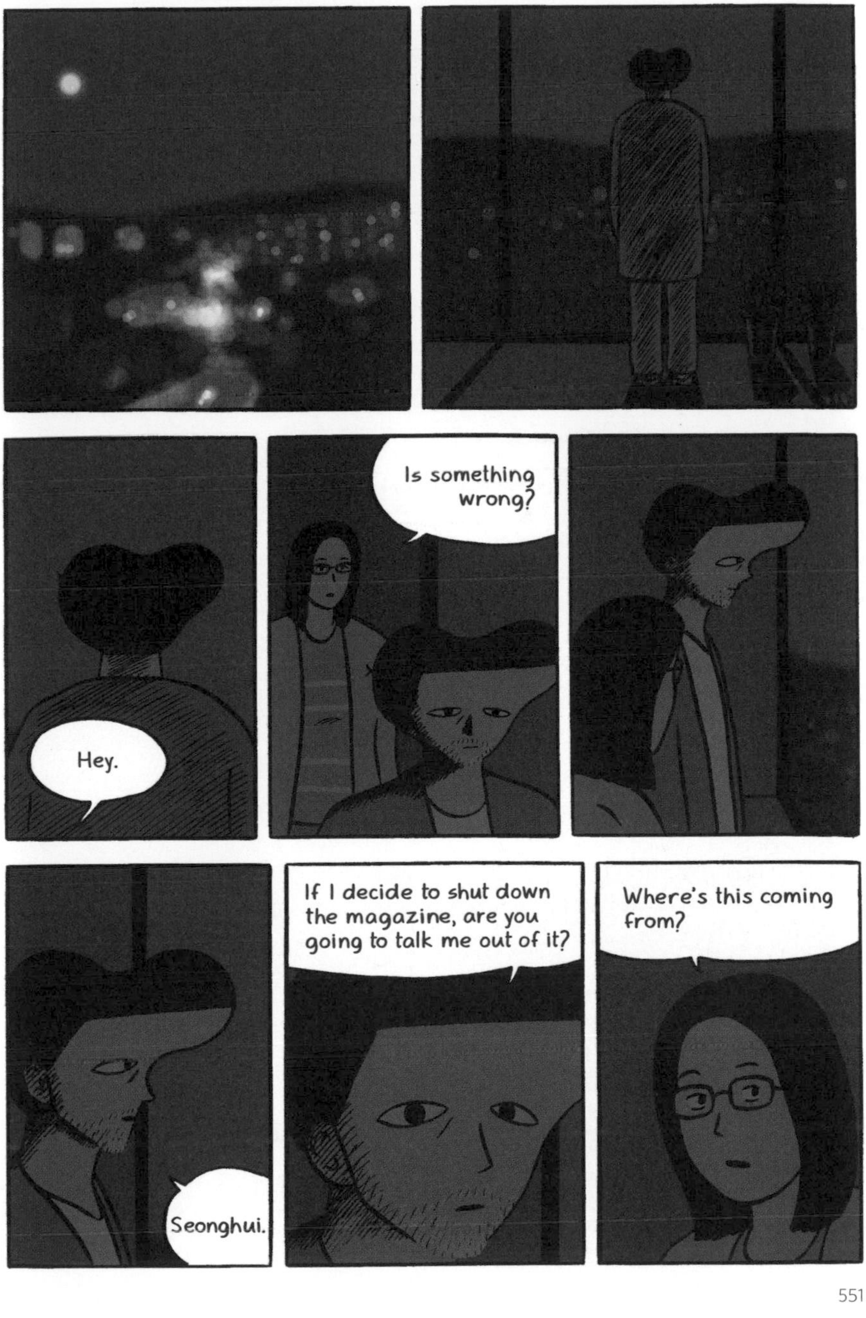
Hey.
Is something wrong?
Seonghui.
If I decide to shut down the magazine, are you going to talk me out of it?
Where's this coming from?

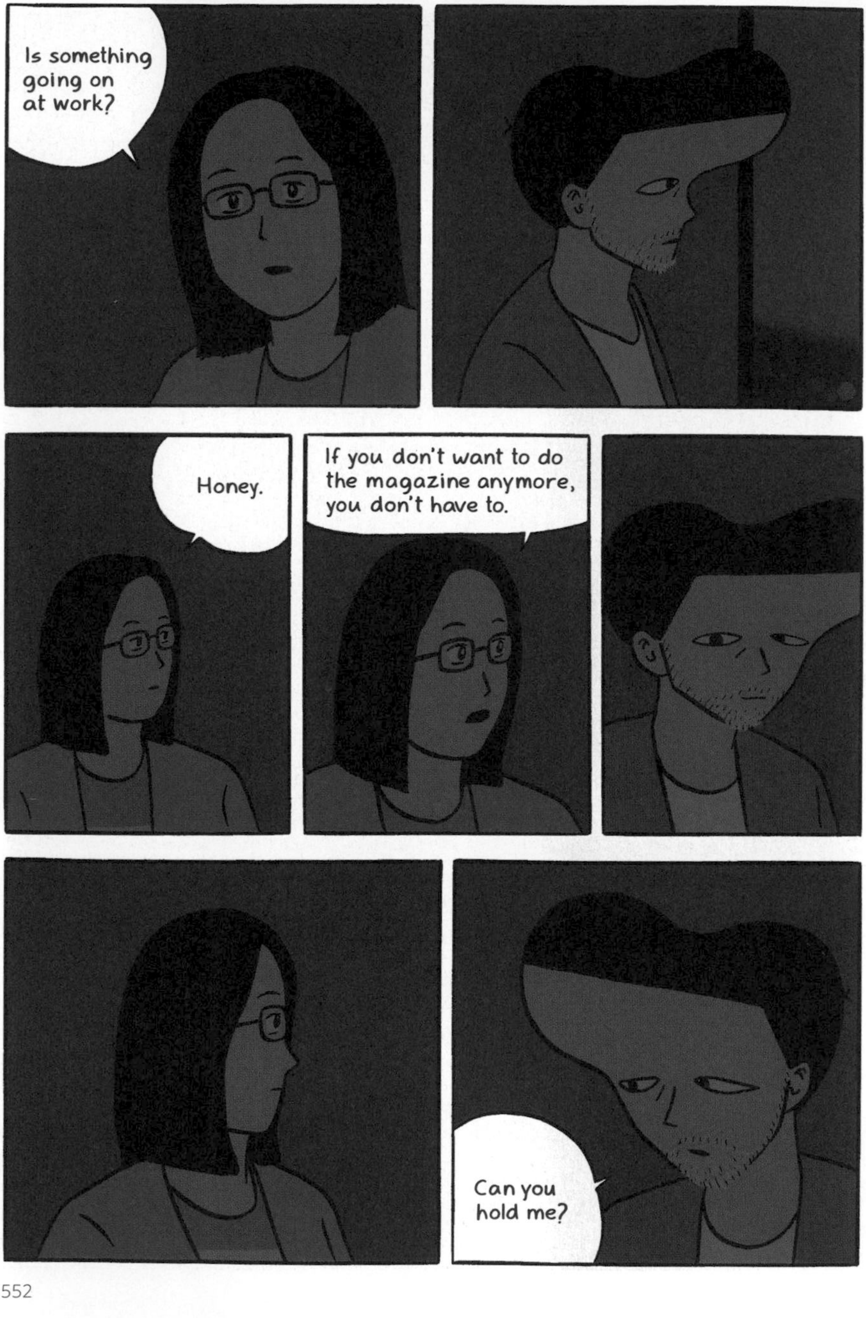
Is something going on at work?
Honey.
If you don't want to do the magazine anymore, you don't have to.
Can you hold me?

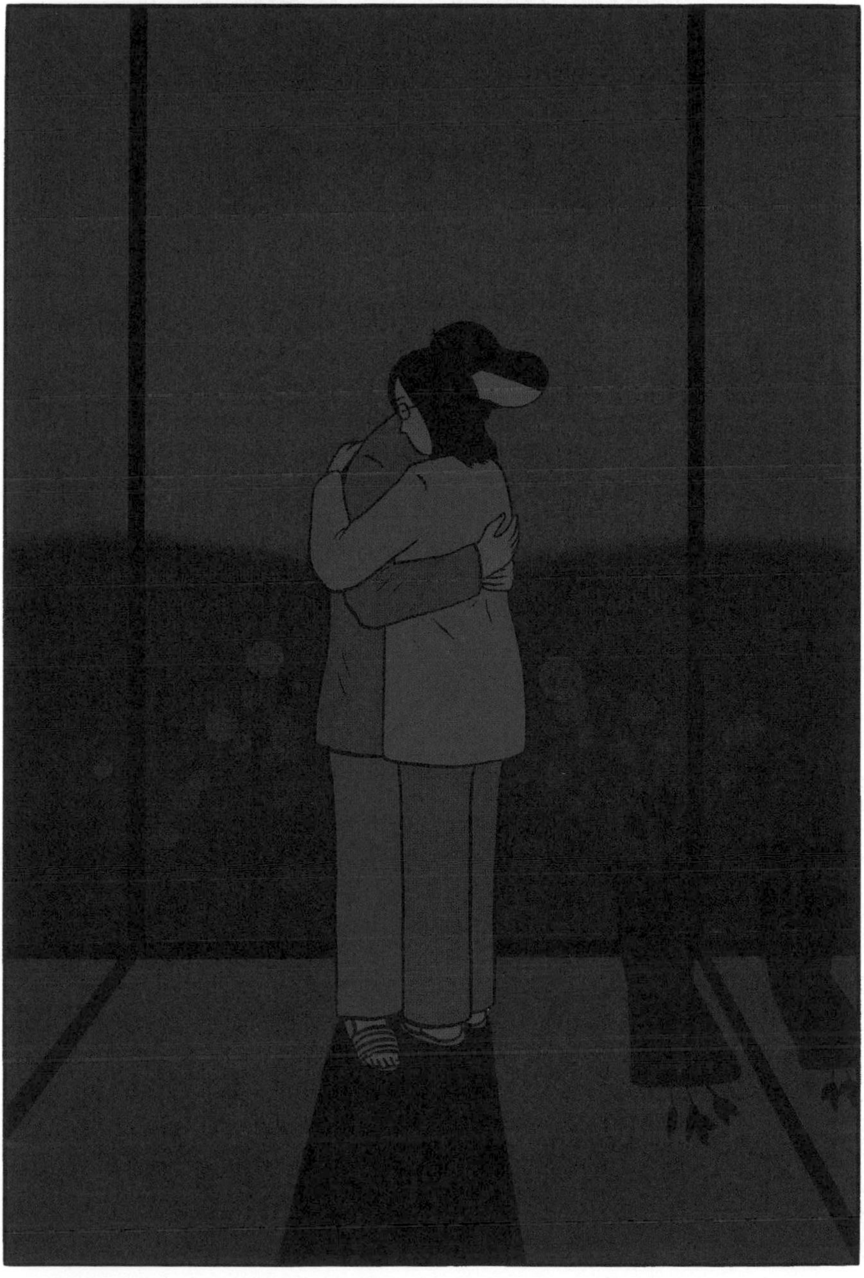

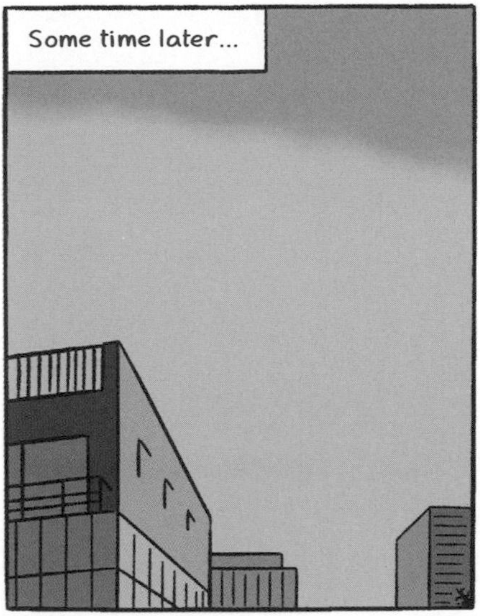
Some time later...

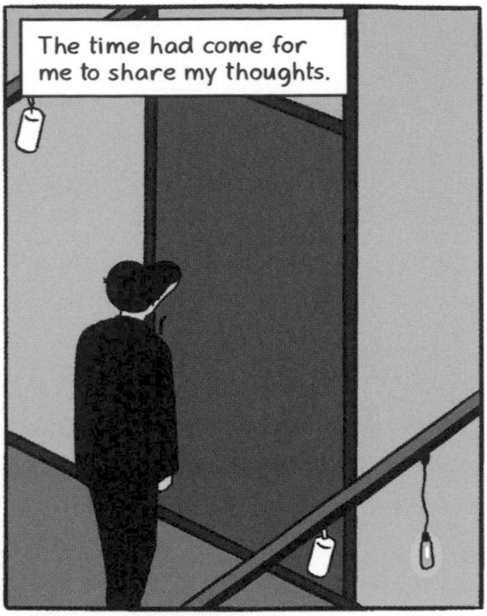
The time had come for me to share my thoughts.

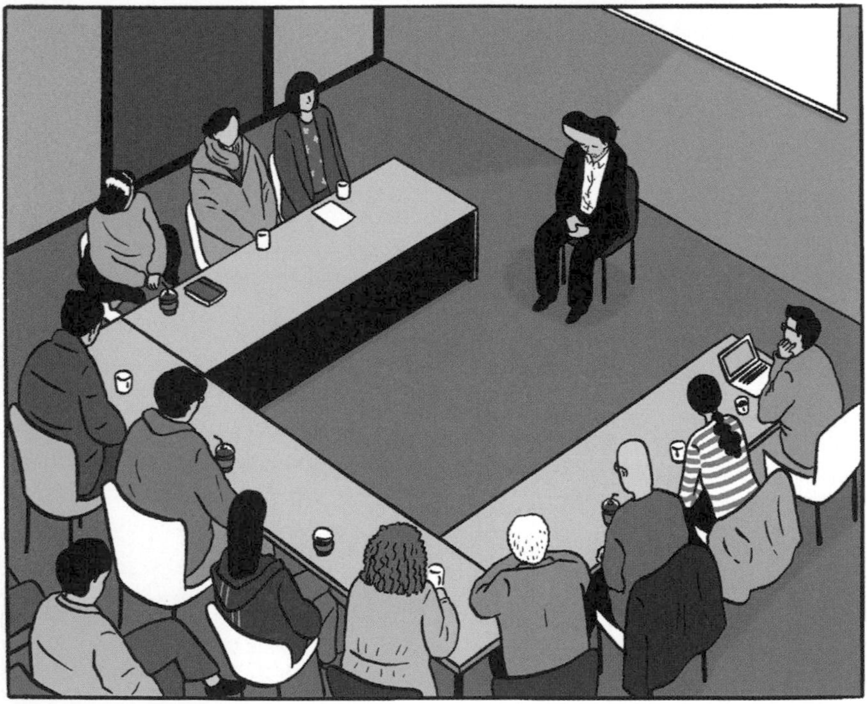

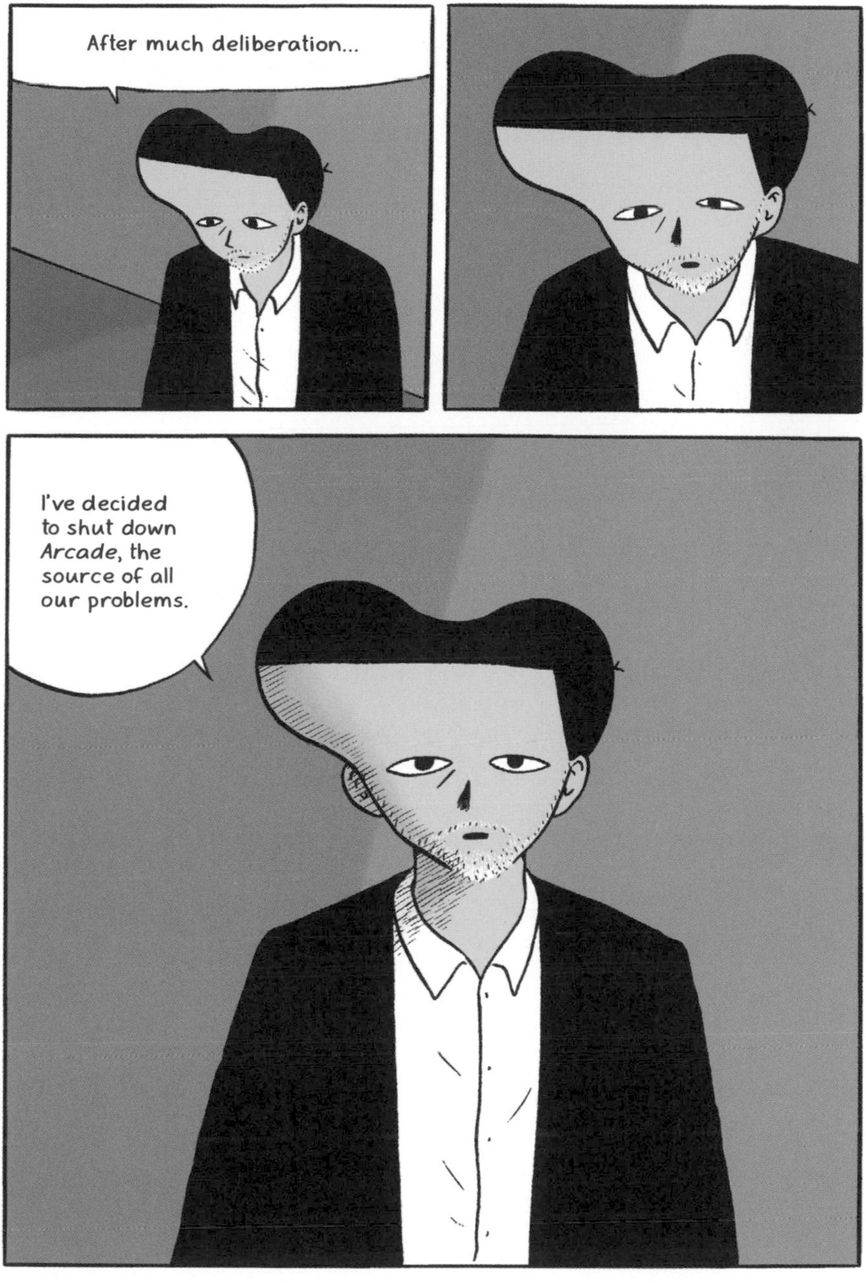
After much deliberation...
I've decided to shut down *Arcade*, the source of all our problems.

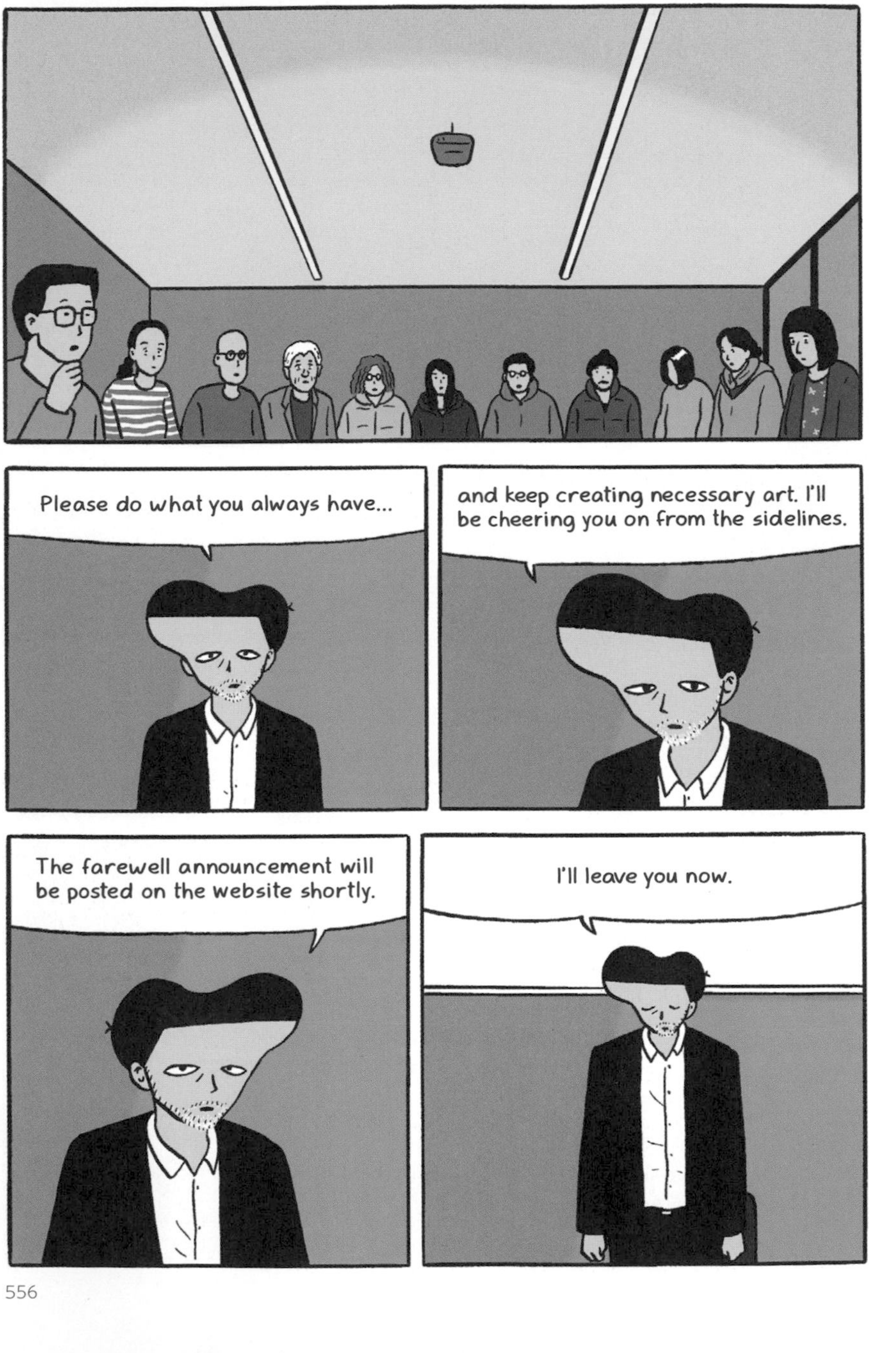
Please do what you always have...
and keep creating necessary art. I'll be cheering you on from the sidelines.
The farewell announcement will be posted on the website shortly.
I'll leave you now.

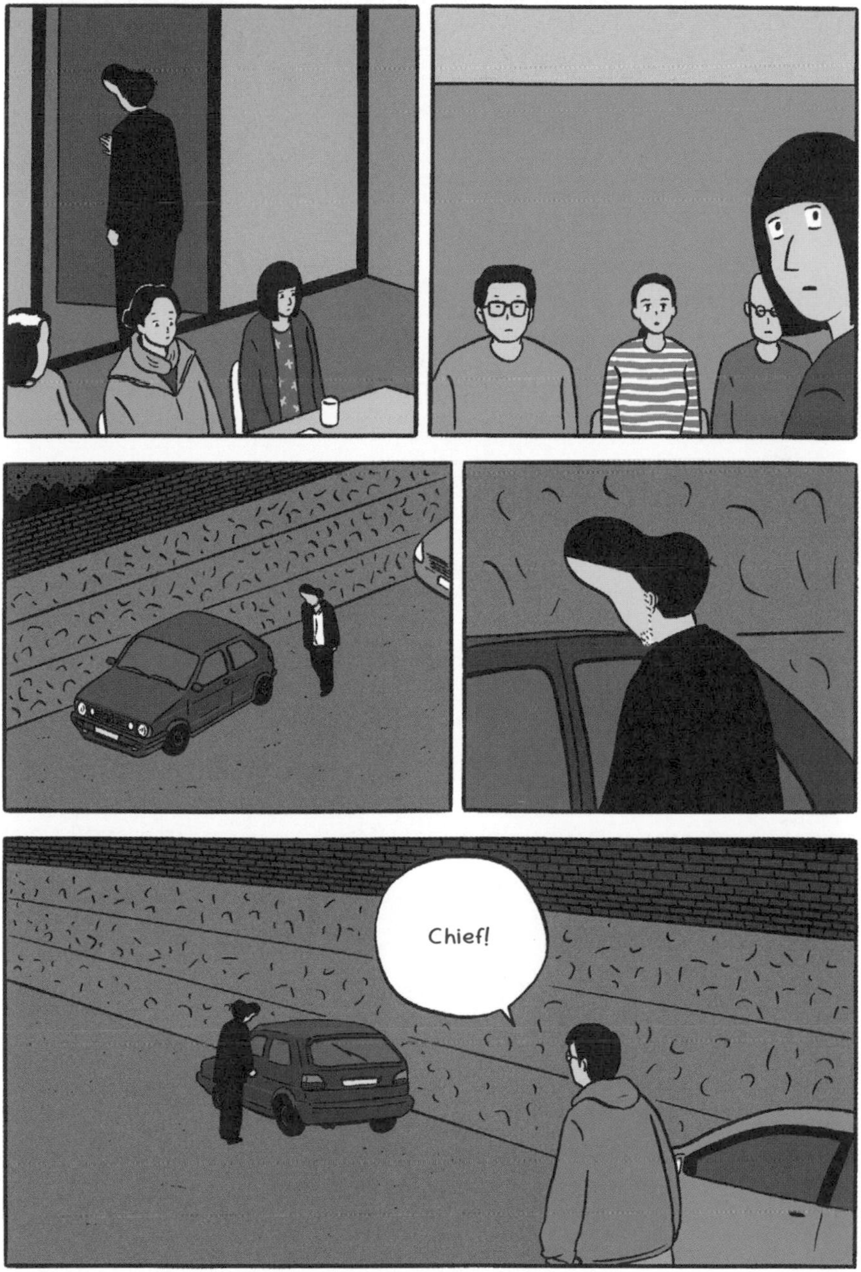
Chief!

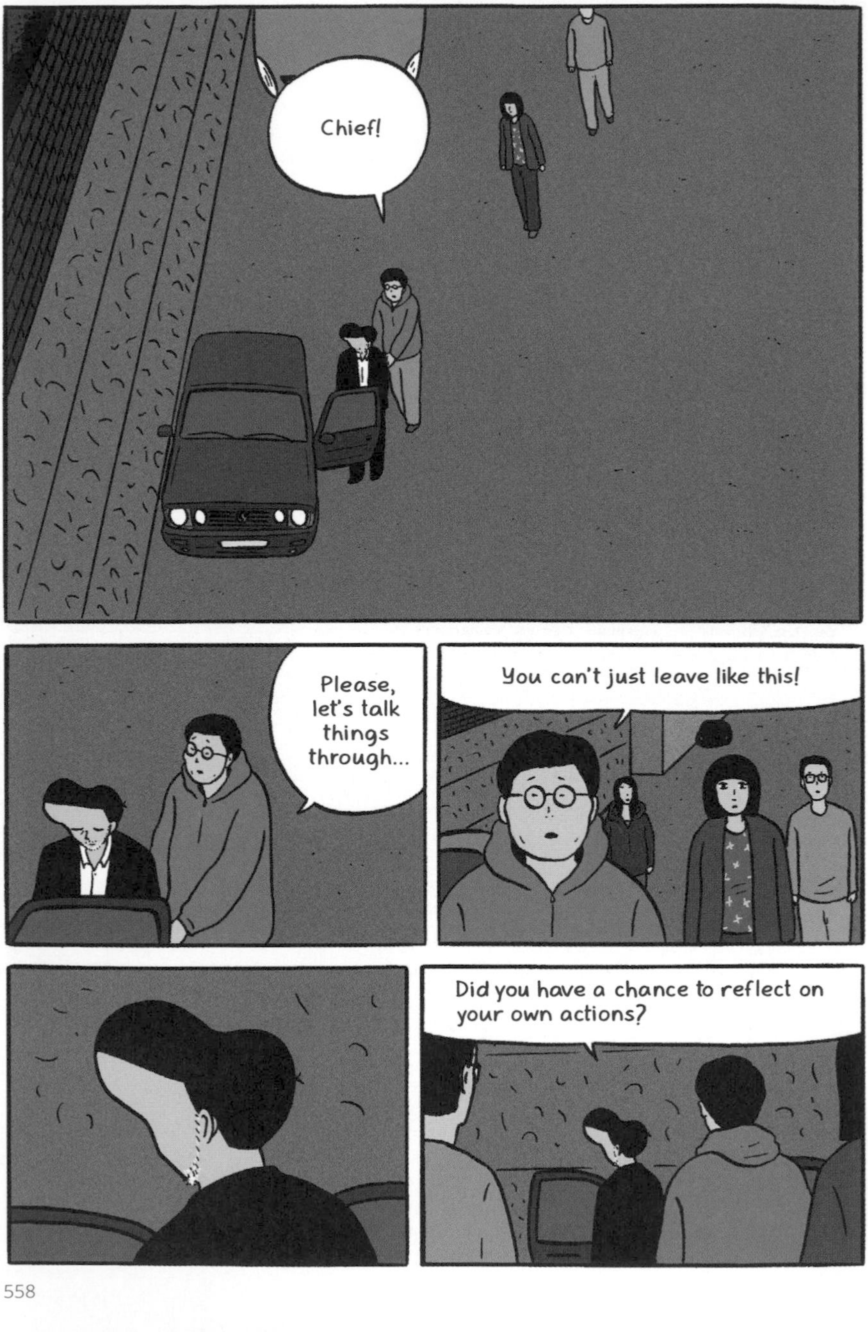
Chief!
Please, let's talk things through...
You can't just leave like this!
Did you have a chance to reflect on your own actions?

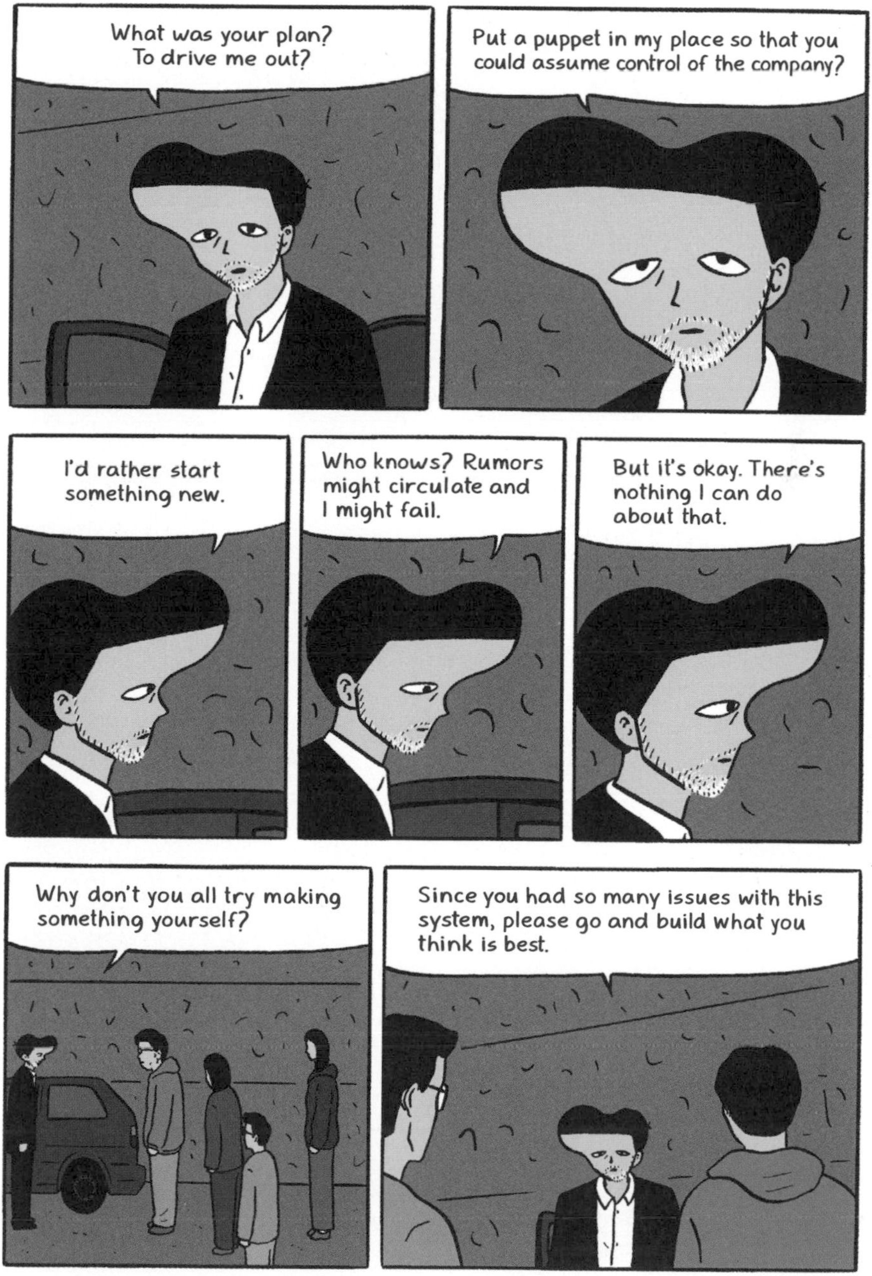
What was your plan? To drive me out?
Put a puppet in my place so that you could assume control of the company?
I'd rather start something new.
Who knows? Rumors might circulate and I might fail.
But it's okay. There's nothing I can do about that.
Why don't you all try making something yourself?
Since you had so many issues with this system, please go and build what you think is best.

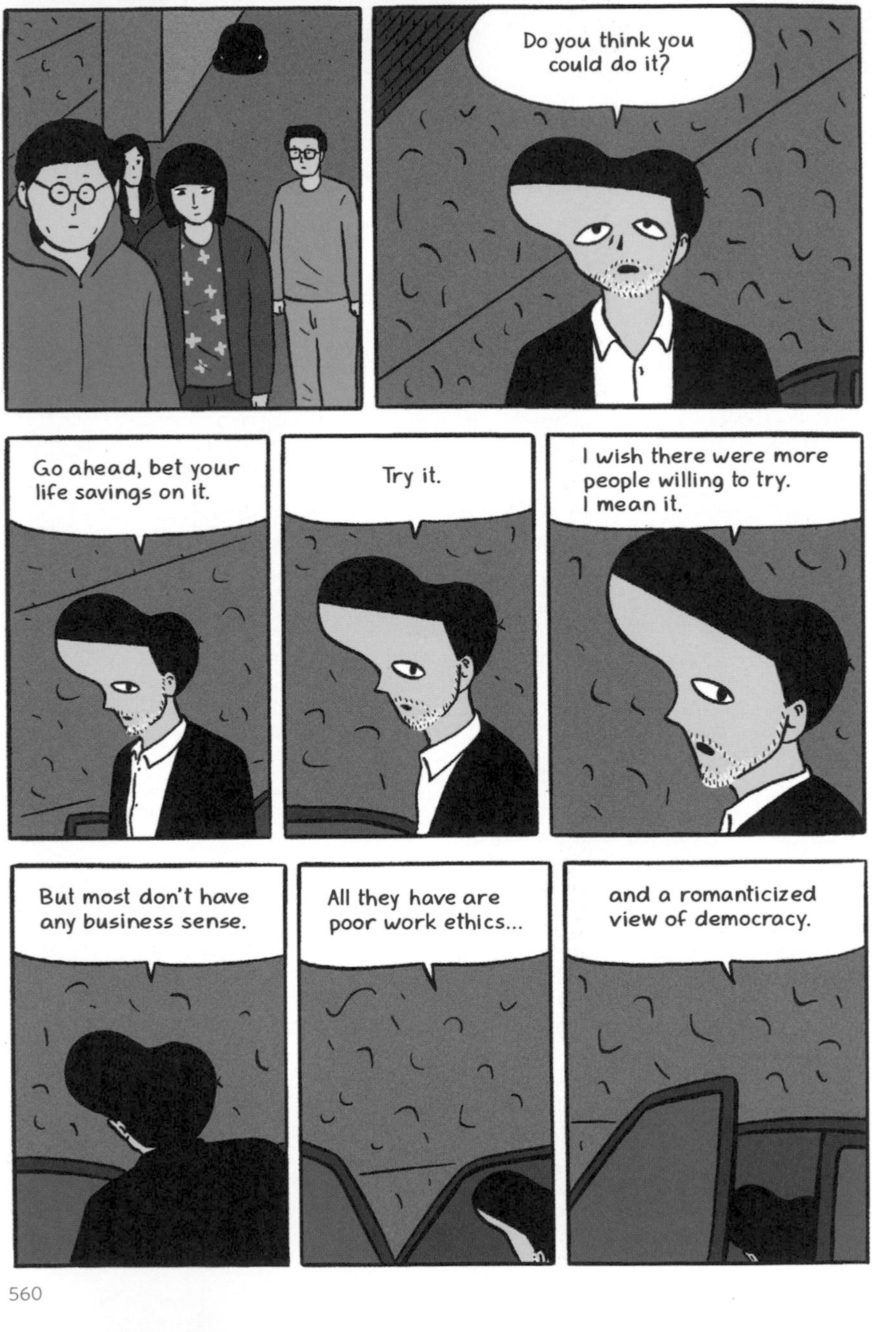
Do you think you could do it?
Go ahead, bet your life savings on it.
Try it.
I wish there were more people willing to try. I mean it.
But most don't have any business sense.
All they have are poor work ethics...
and a romanticized view of democracy.

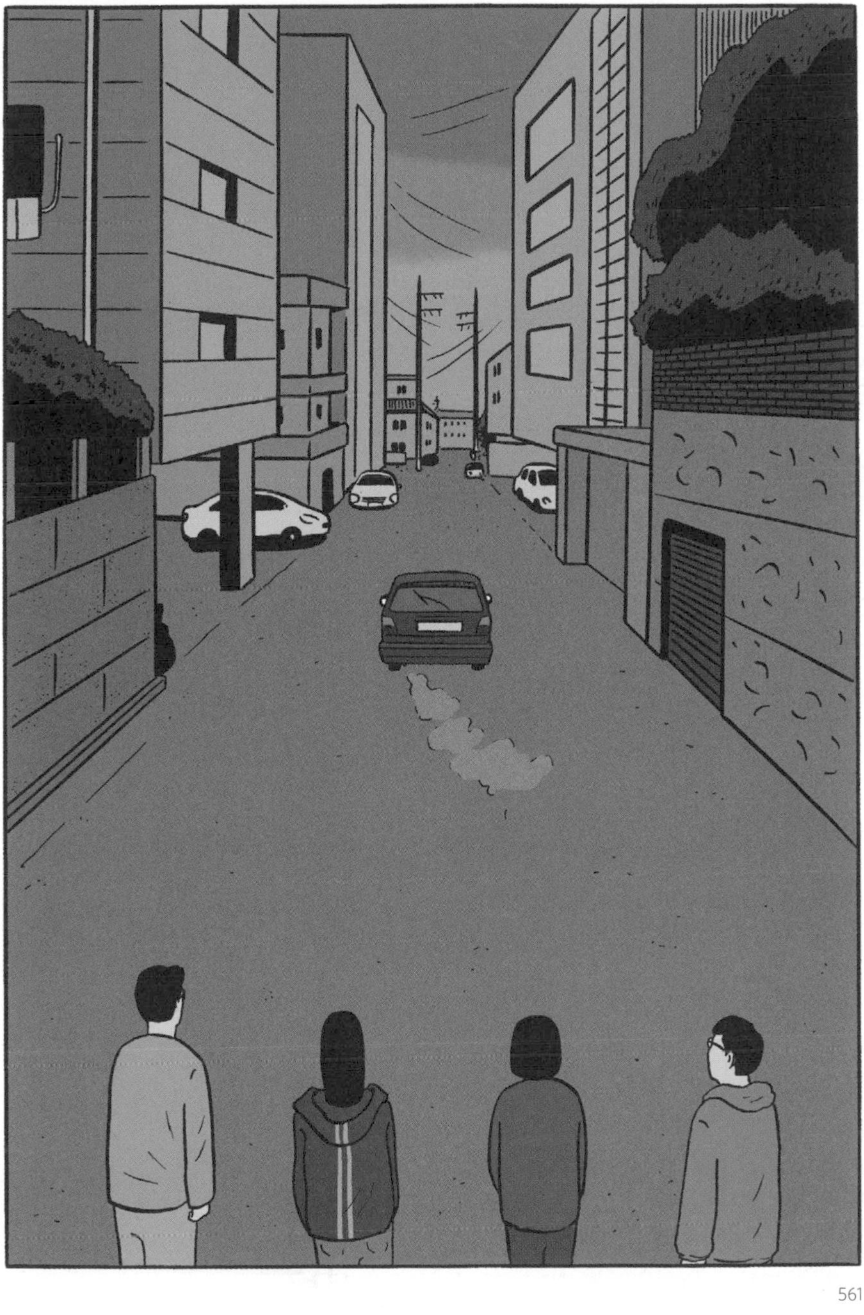

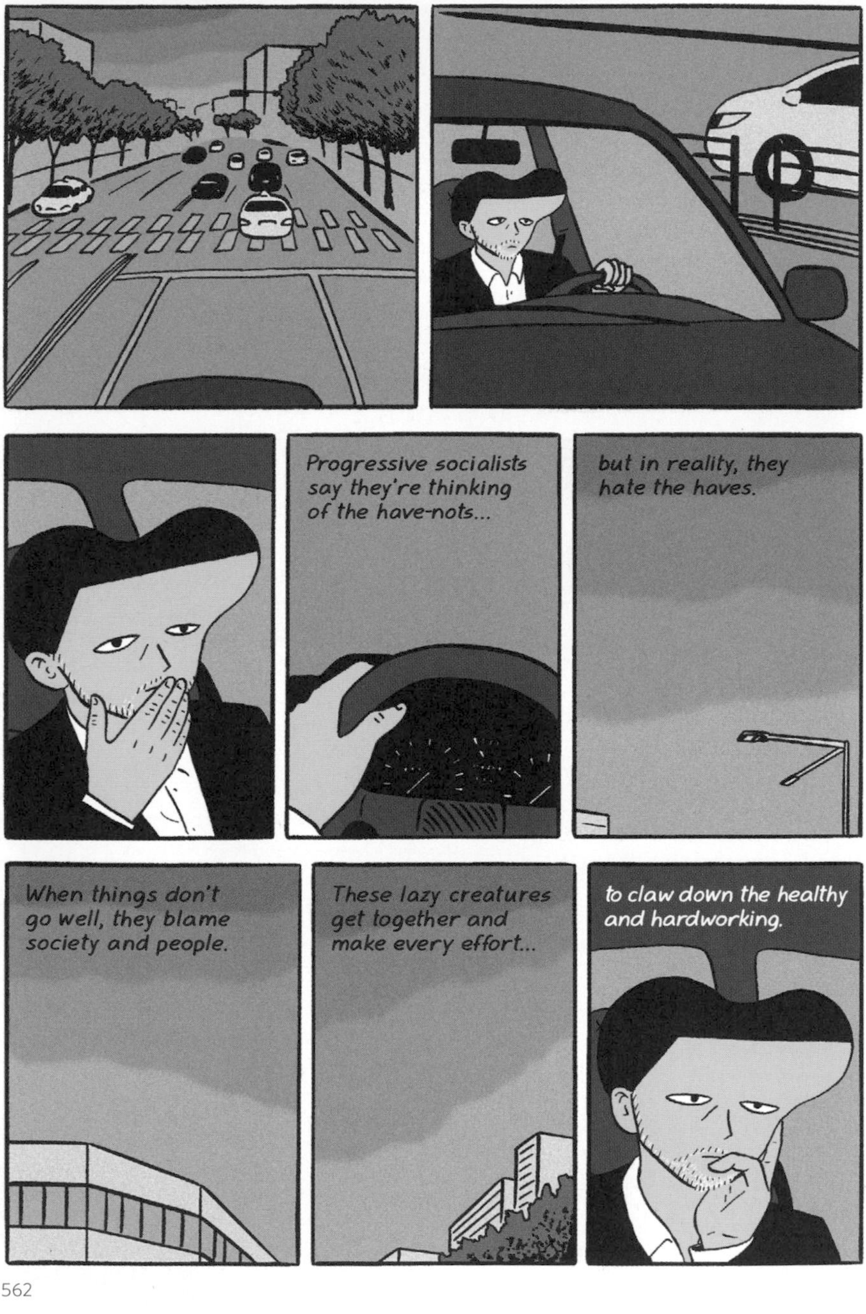
Progressive socialists say they're thinking of the have-nots...
but in reality, they hate the haves.
When things don't go well, they blame society and people.
These lazy creatures get together and make every effort...
to claw down the healthy and hardworking.

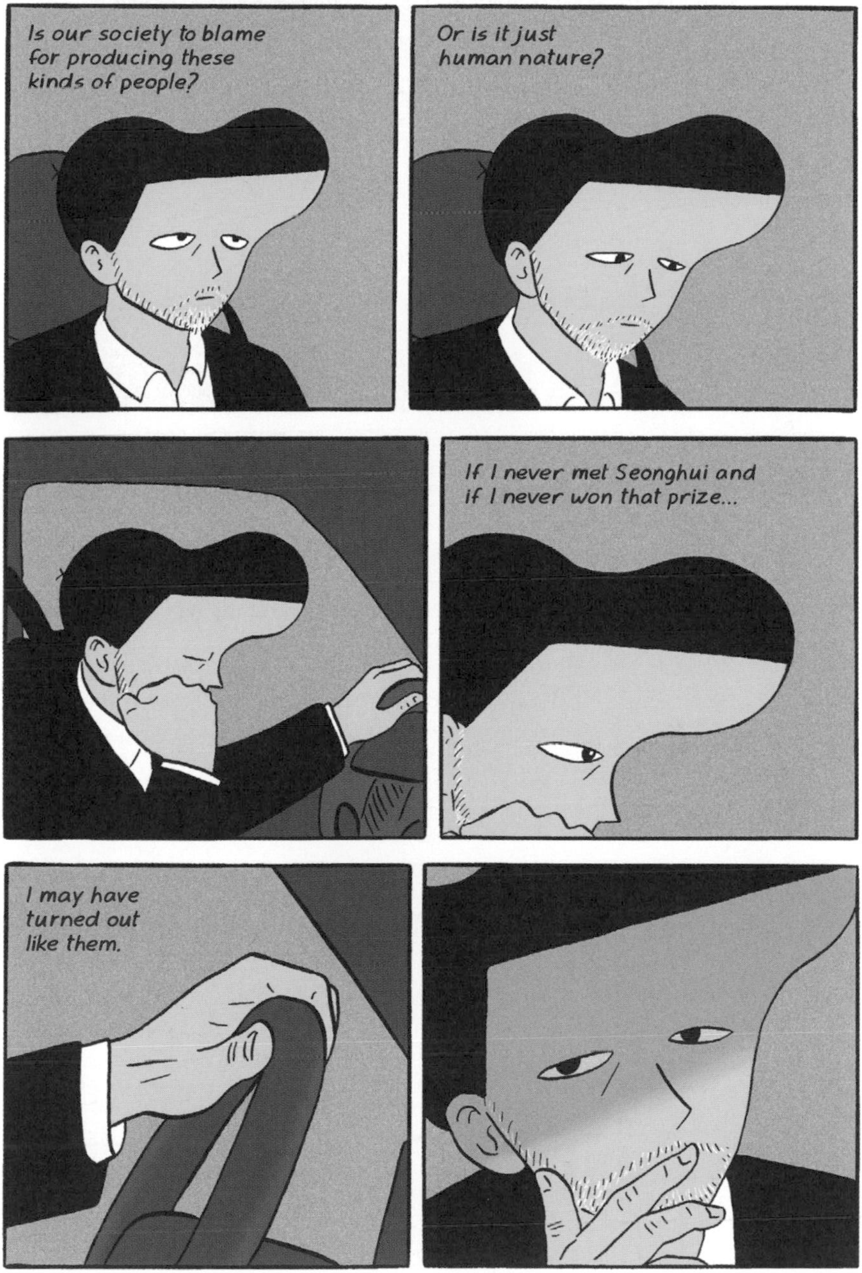
Is our society to blame for producing these kinds of people?
Or is it just human nature?
If I never met Seonghui and if I never won that prize...
I may have turned out like them.

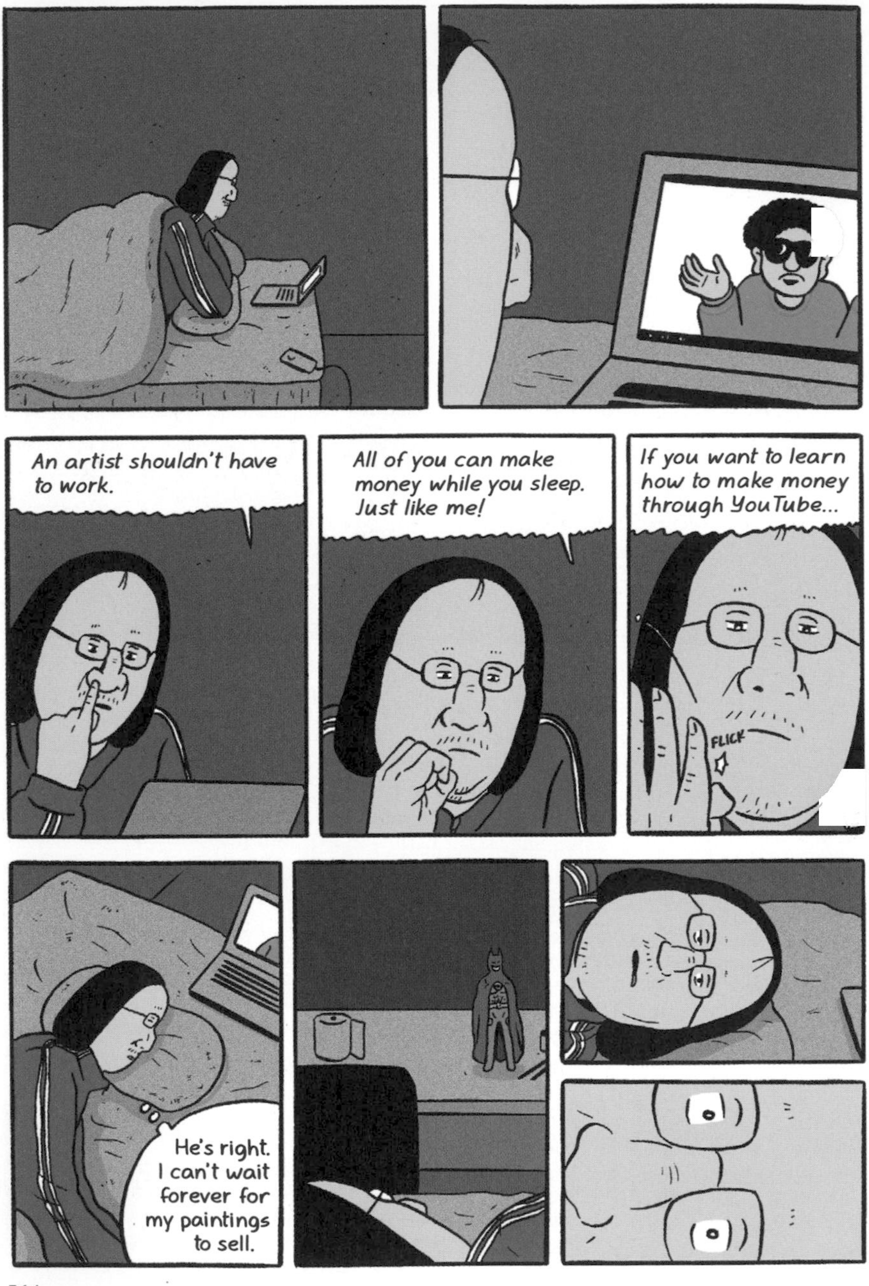
An artist shouldn't have to work.
All of you can make money while you sleep. Just like me!
If you want to learn how to make money through YouTube...
FLICK
He's right. I can't wait forever for my paintings to sell.

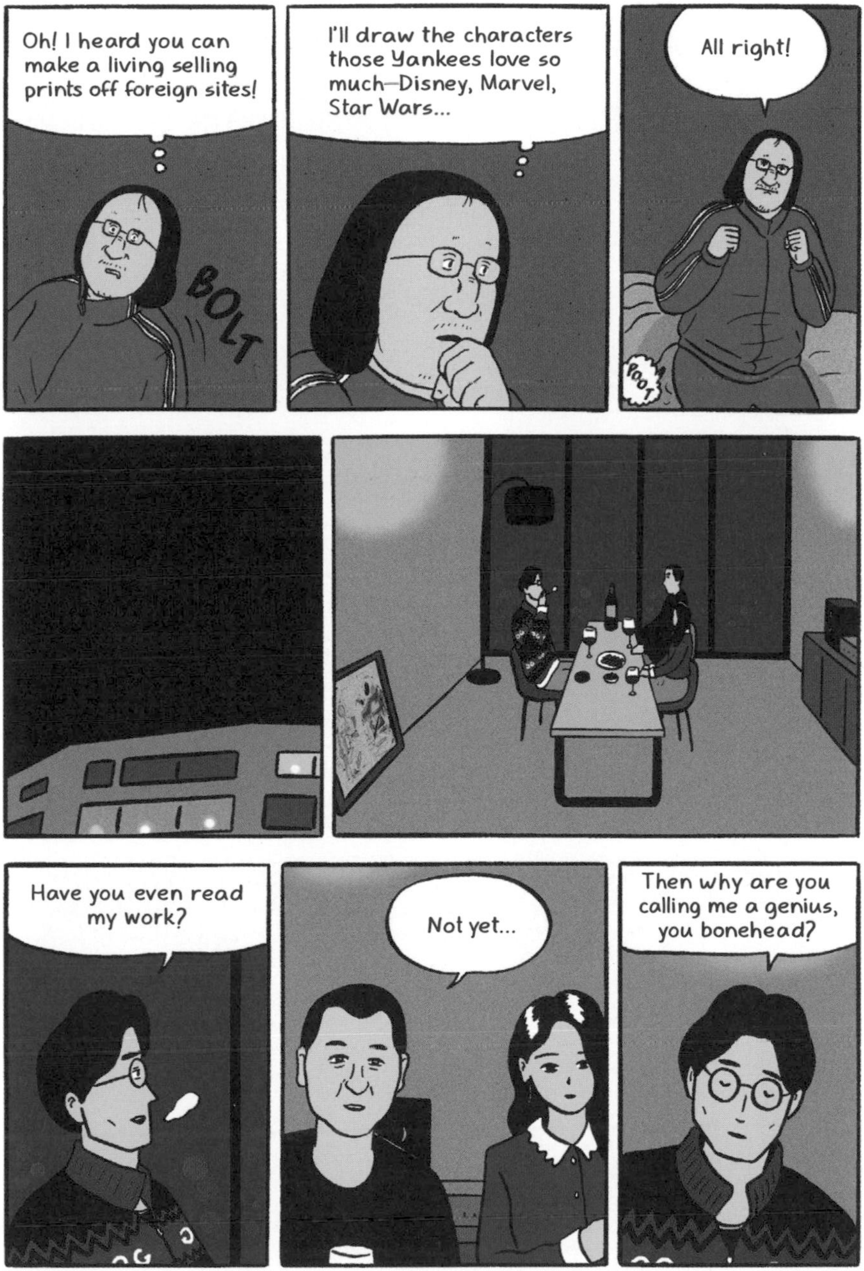
Oh! I heard you can make a living selling prints off foreign sites!
BOLT
I'll draw the characters those Yankees love so much—Disney, Marvel, Star Wars...
All right!
POOT
Have you even read my work?
Not yet...
Then why are you calling me a genius, you bonehead?

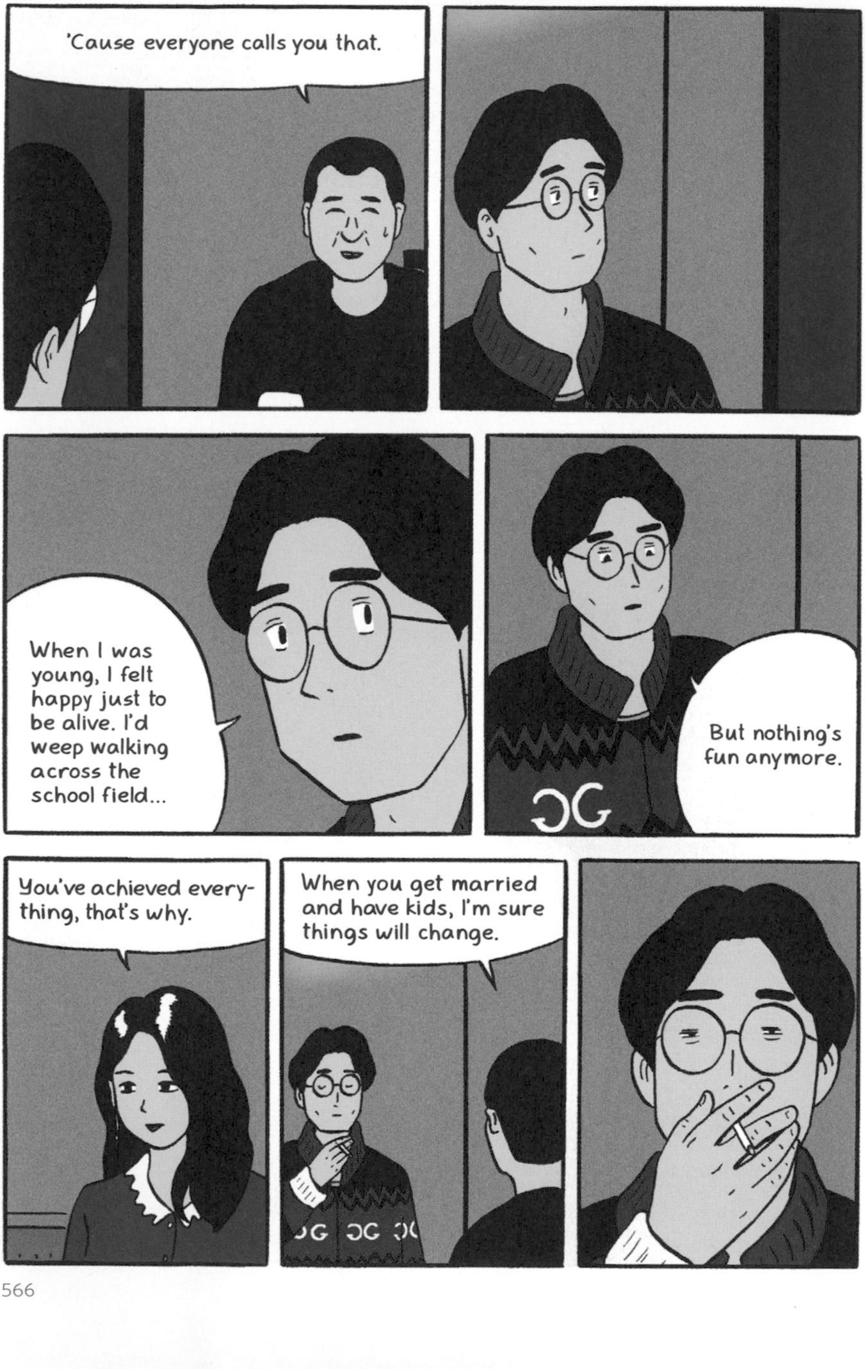
'Cause everyone calls you that.
When I was young, I felt happy just to be alive. I'd weep walking across the school field...
But nothing's fun anymore.
You've achieved everything, that's why.
When you get married and have kids, I'm sure things will change.

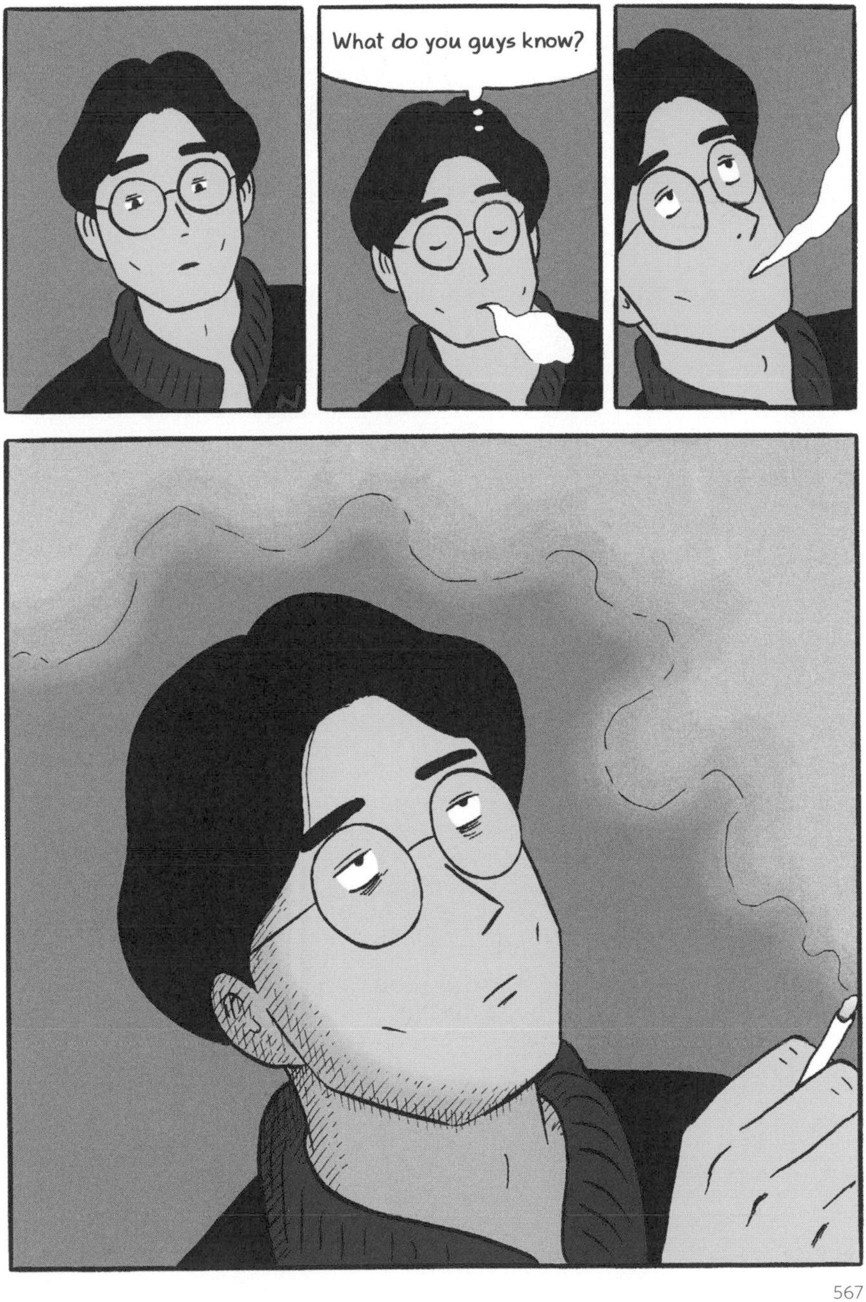
What do you guys know?

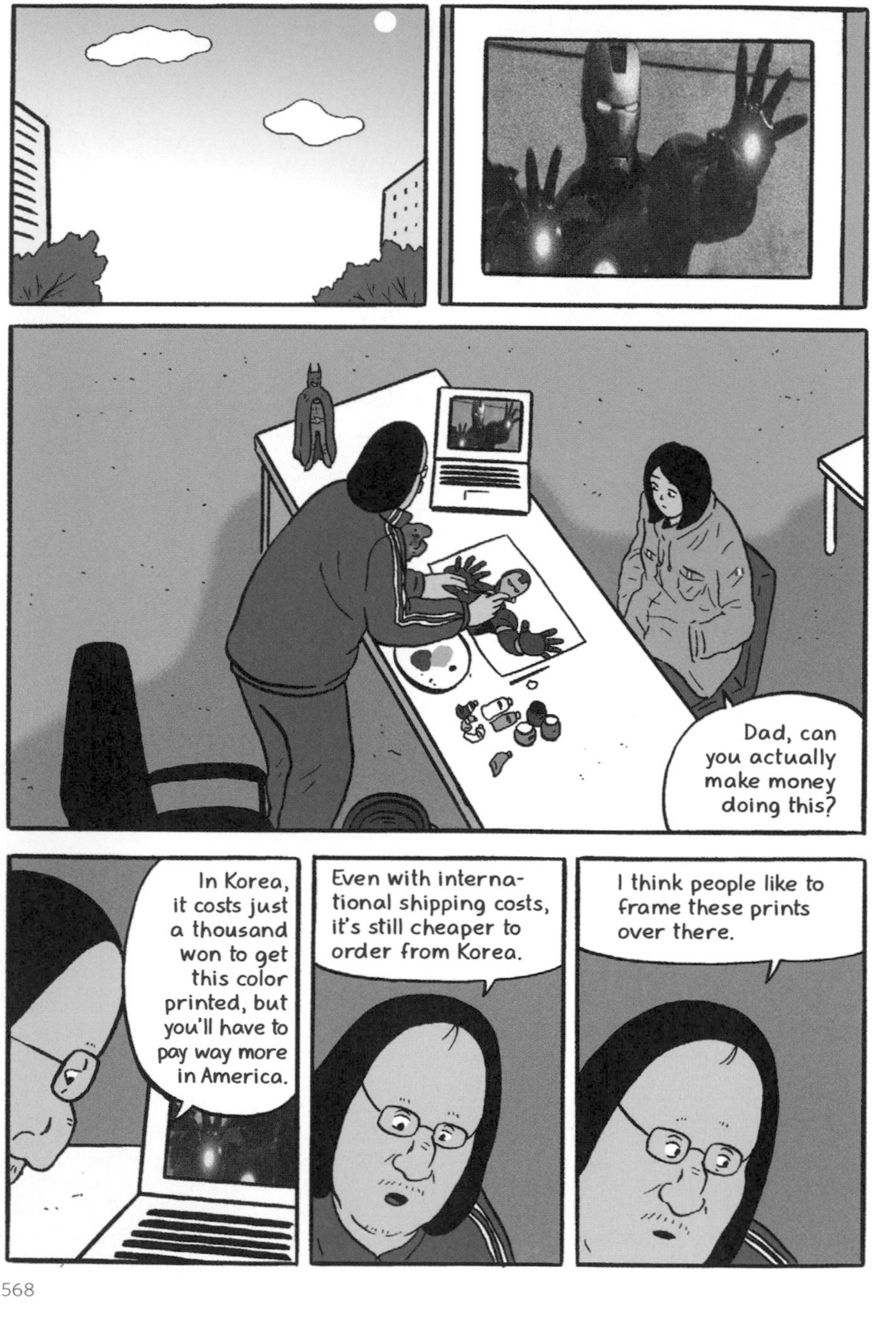
Dad, can you actually make money doing this?
In Korea, it costs just a thousand won to get this color printed, but you'll have to pay way more in America.
Even with interna-tional shipping costs, it's still cheaper to order from Korea.
I think people like to frame these prints over there.

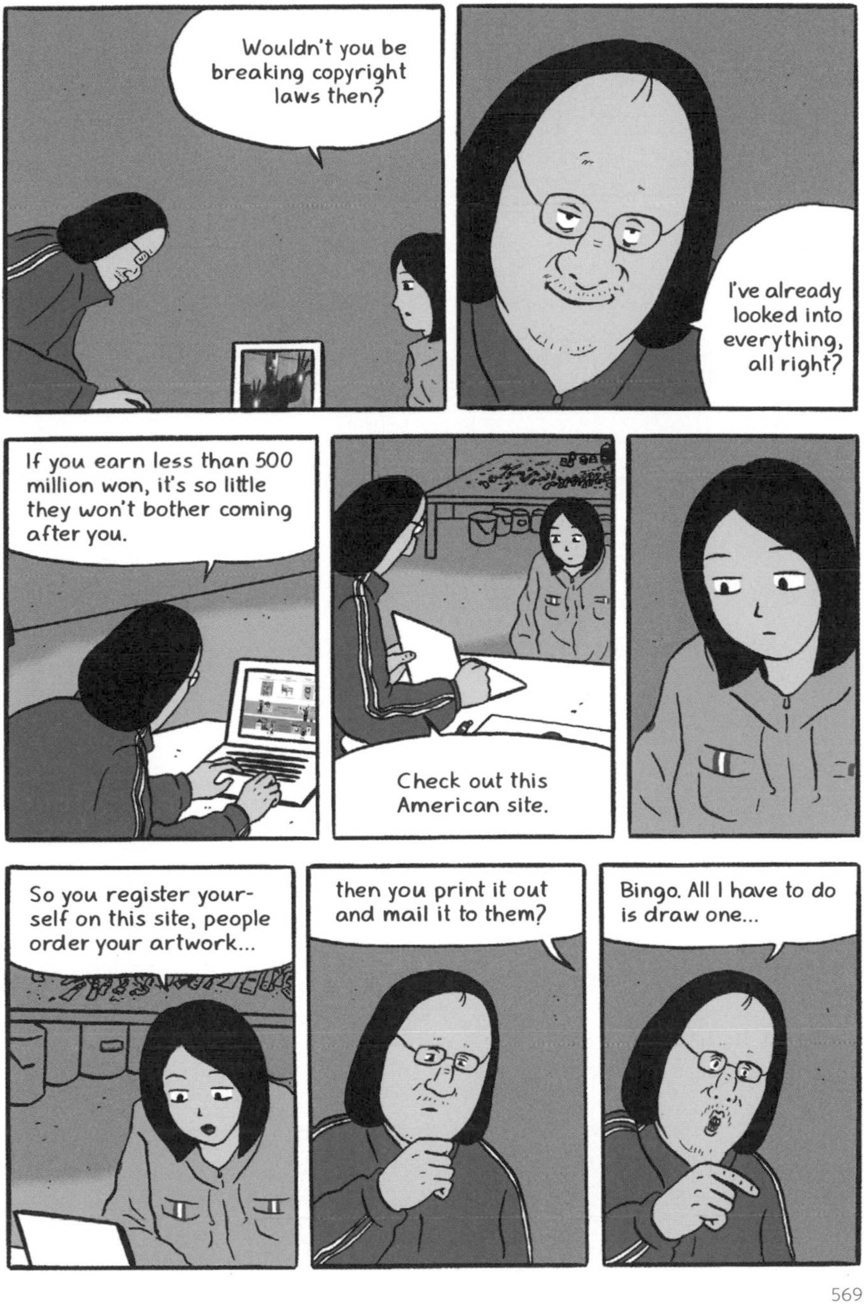
Wouldn't you be breaking copyright laws then?
I've already looked into everything, all right?
If you earn less than 500 million won, it's so little they won't bother coming after you.
Check out this American site.
So you register your-self on this site, people order your artwork...
then you print it out and mail it to them?
Bingo. All I have to do is draw one...

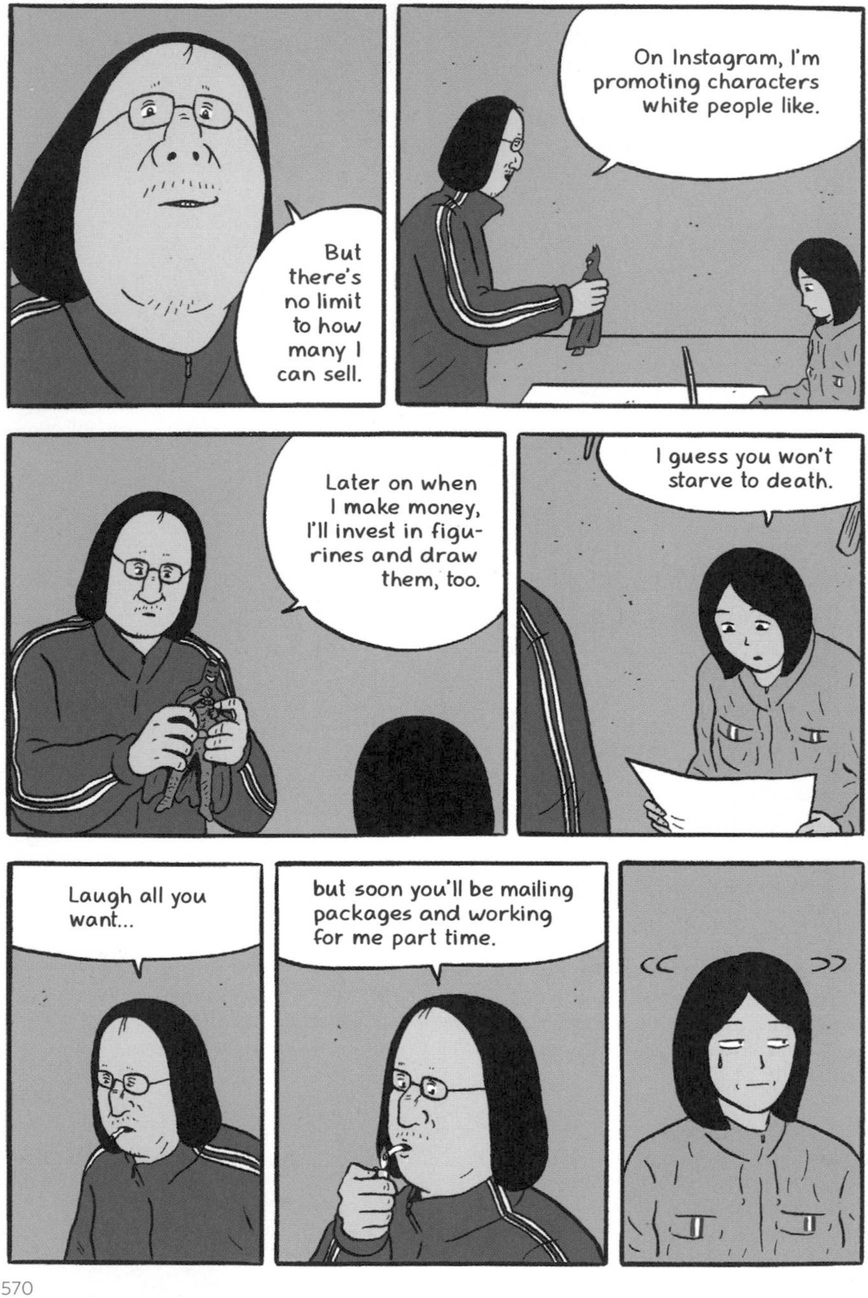
But there's no limit to how many I can sell.
On Instagram, I'm promoting characters white people like.
Later on when I make money, I'll invest in figurines and draw them, too.
I guess you won't starve to death.
Laugh all you want...
but soon you'll be mailing packages and working for me part time.

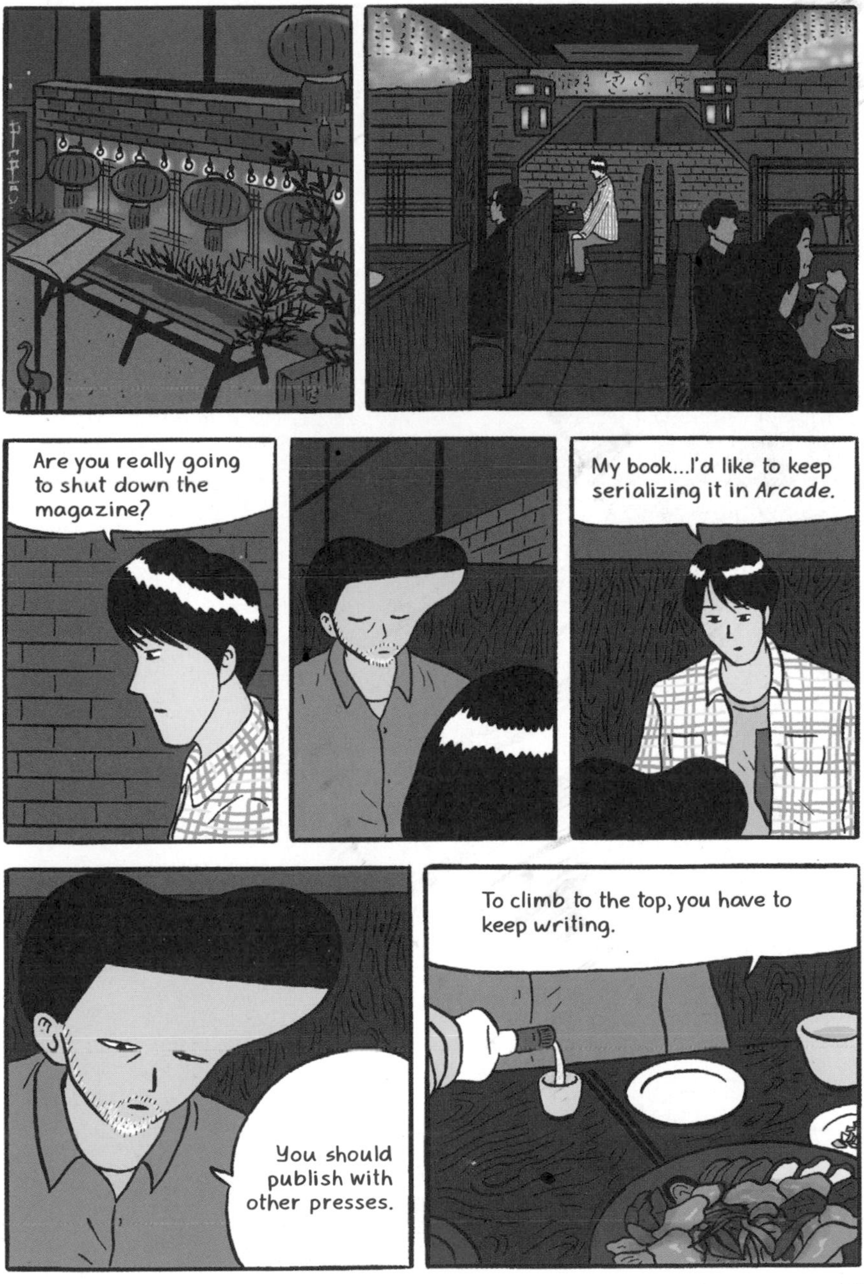
Are you really going to shut down the magazine?
My book...I'd like to keep serializing it in *Arcade*.
You should publish with other presses.
To climb to the top, you have to keep writing.

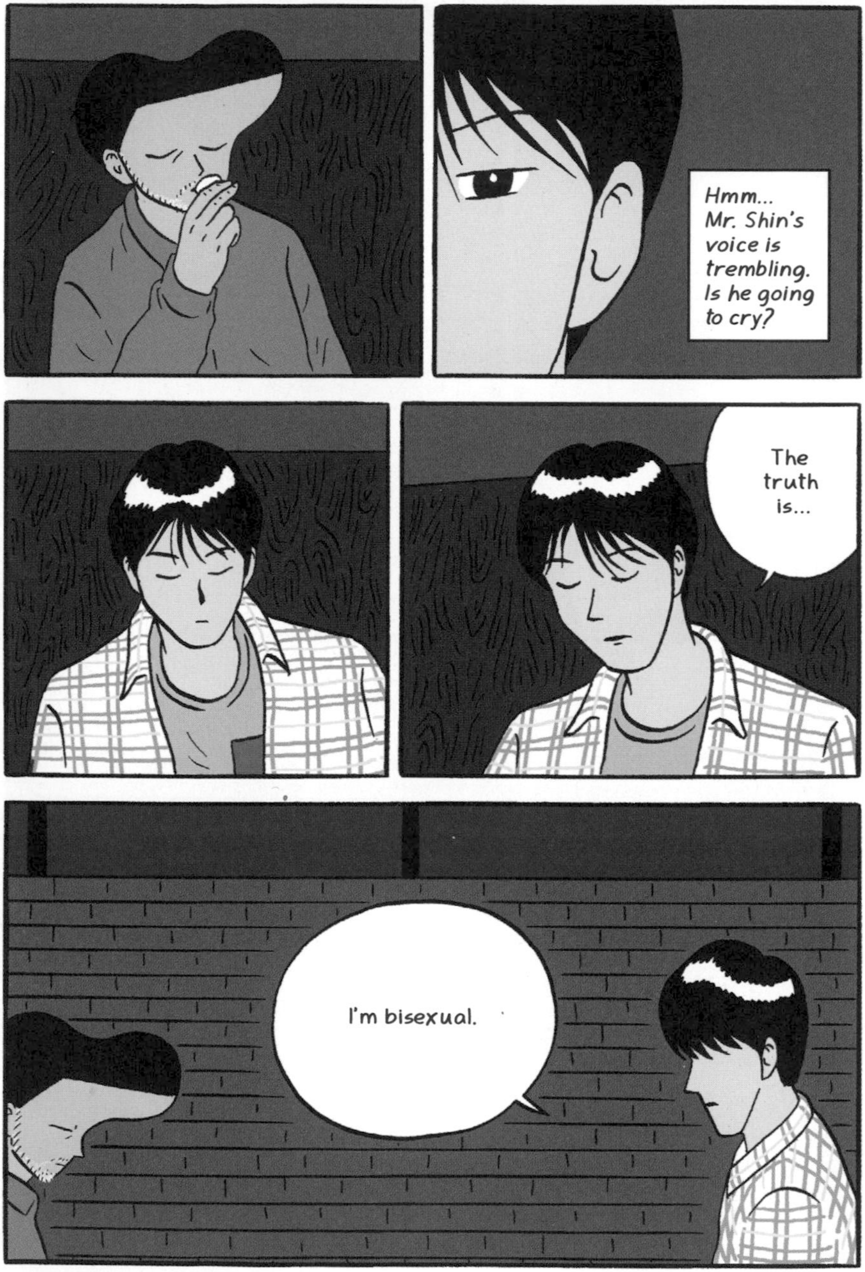
Hmm... Mr. Shin's voice is trembling. Is he going to cry?
The truth is...
I'm bisexual.

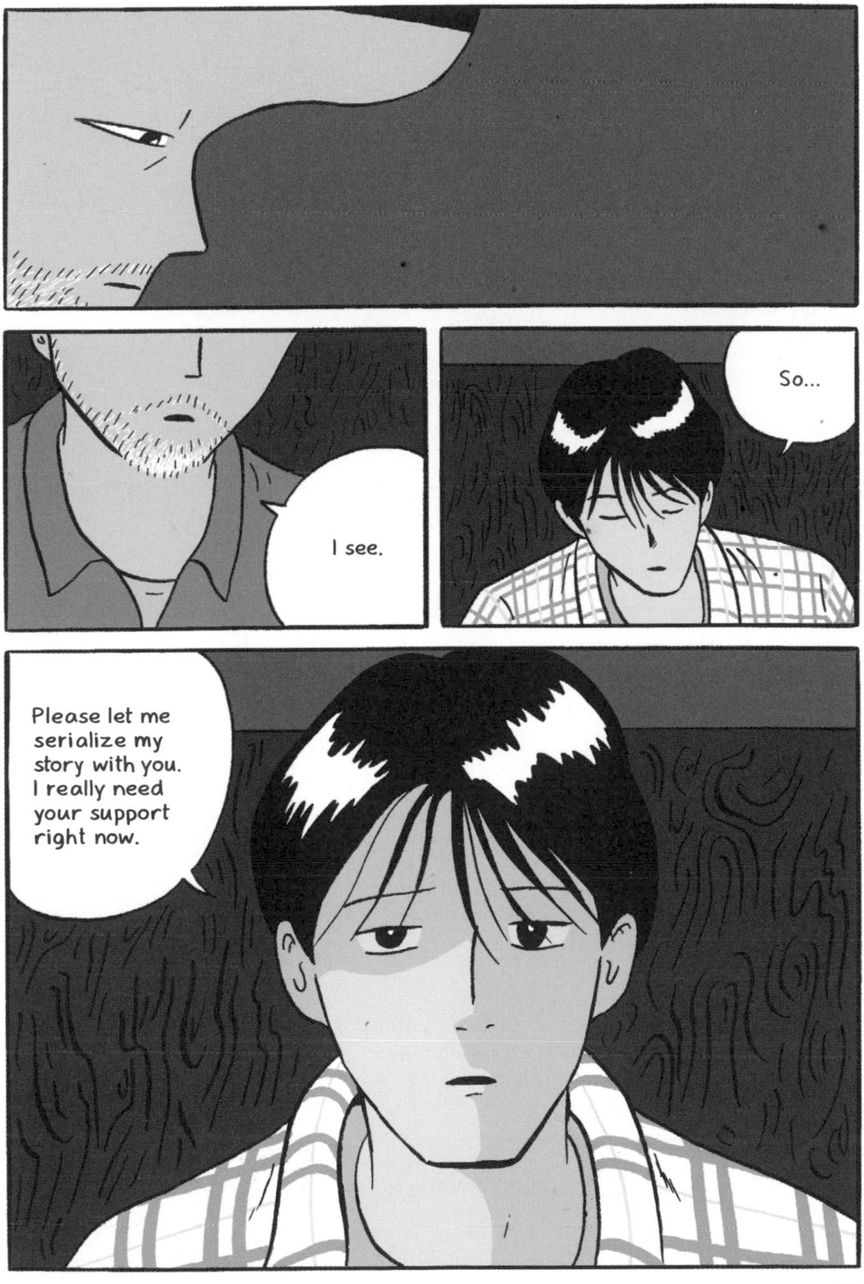
I see.
So...
Please let me serialize my story with you. I really need your support right now.

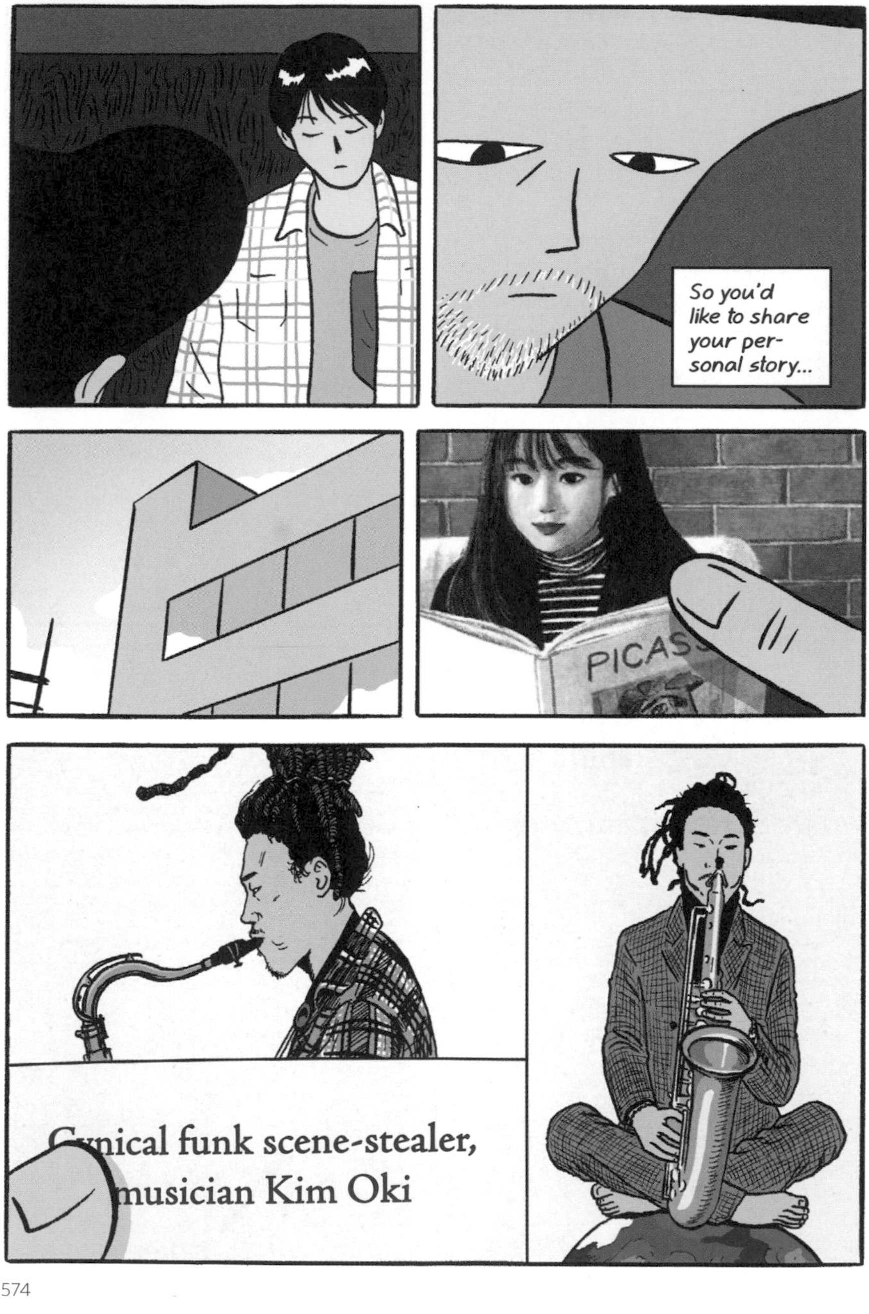
So you'd like to share your per- sonal story...
PICASS
Cynical funk scene-stealer, musician Kim Oki

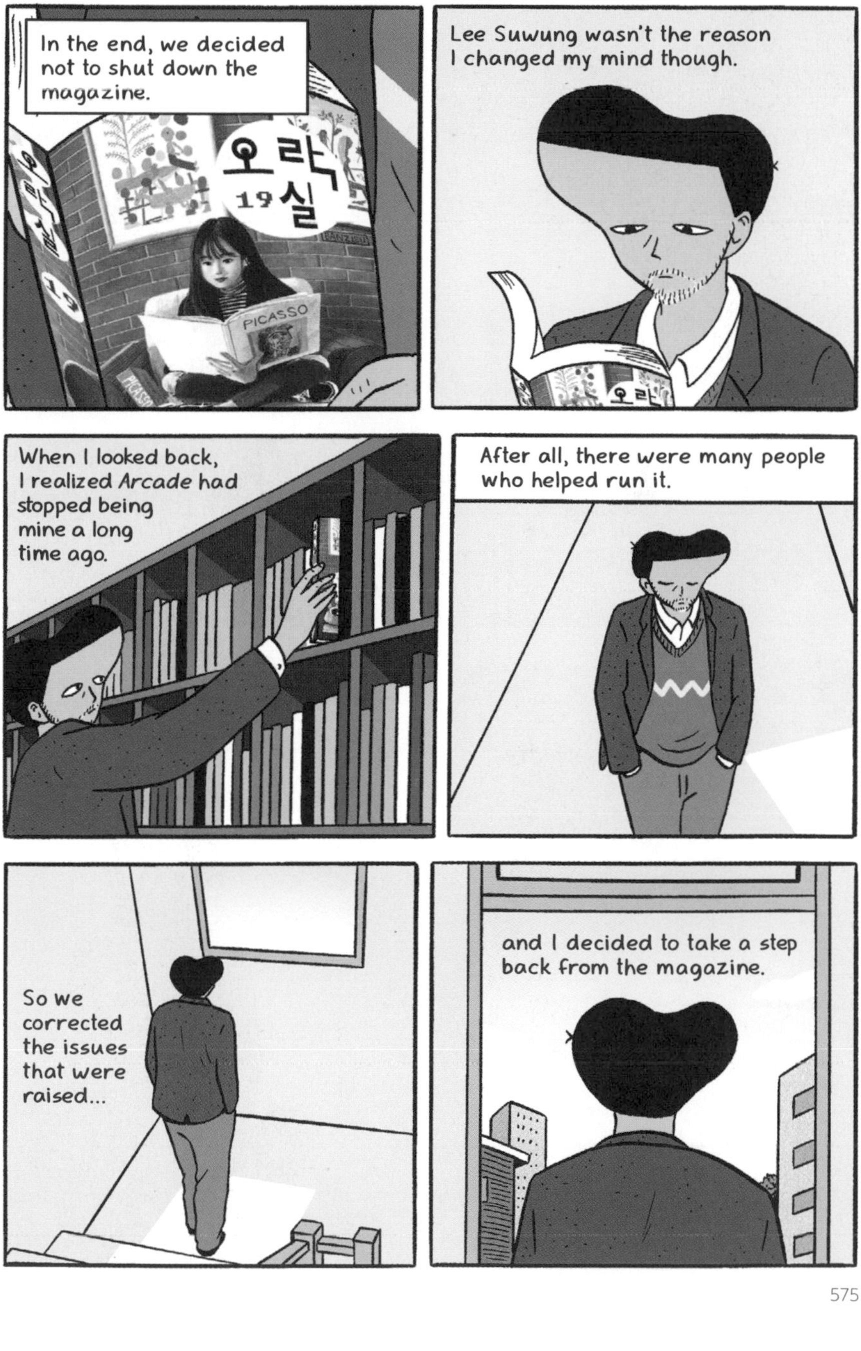
In the end, we decided not to shut down the magazine.
오락
19 실
PICASSO
Lee Suwung wasn't the reason I changed my mind though.
When I looked back, I realized *Arcade* had stopped being mine a long time ago.
After all, there were many people who helped run it.
So we corrected the issues that were raised...
and I decided to take a step back from the magazine.

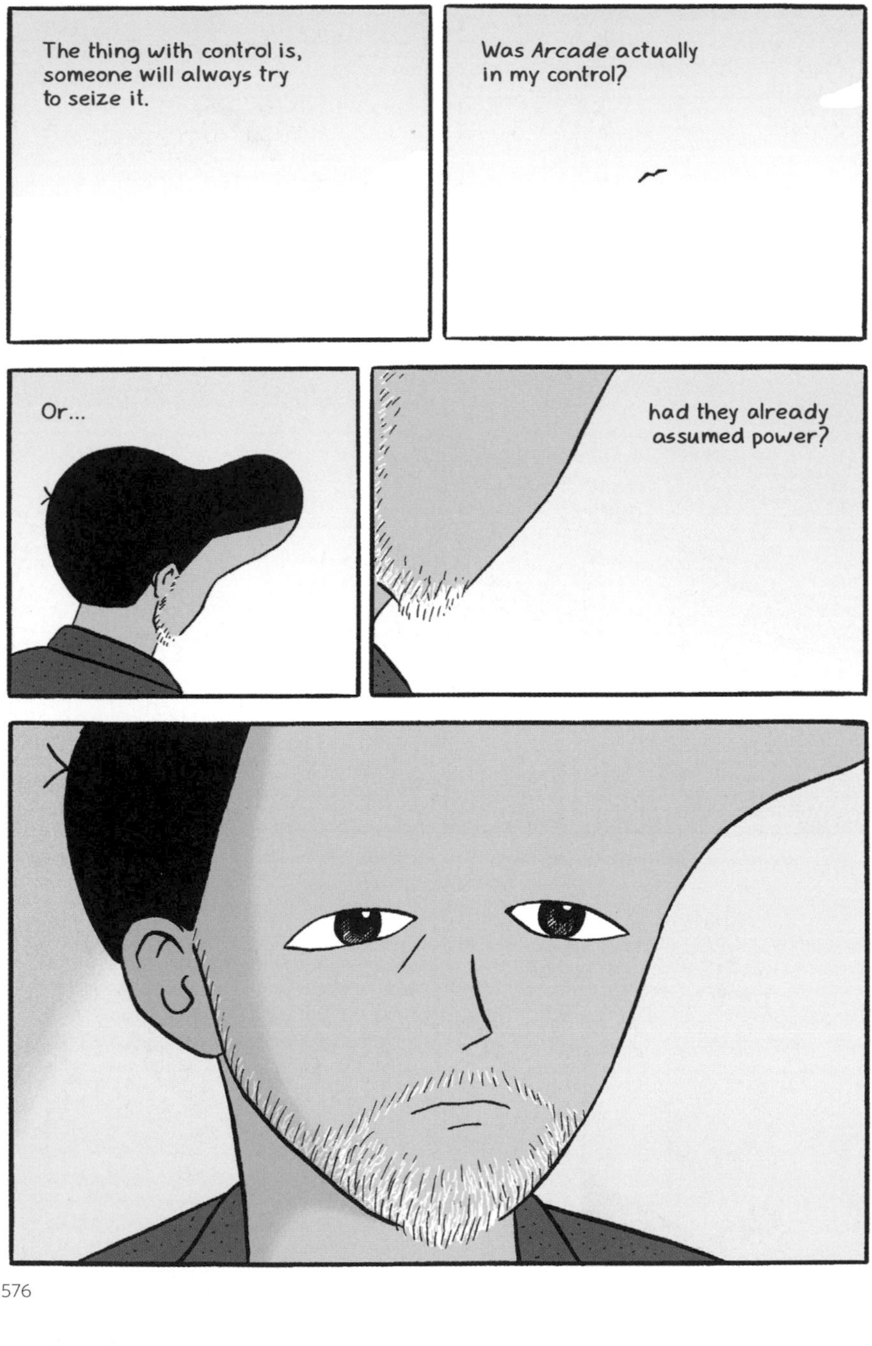
The thing with control is, someone will always try to seize it.
Was *Arcade* actually in my control?
Or...
had they already assumed power?

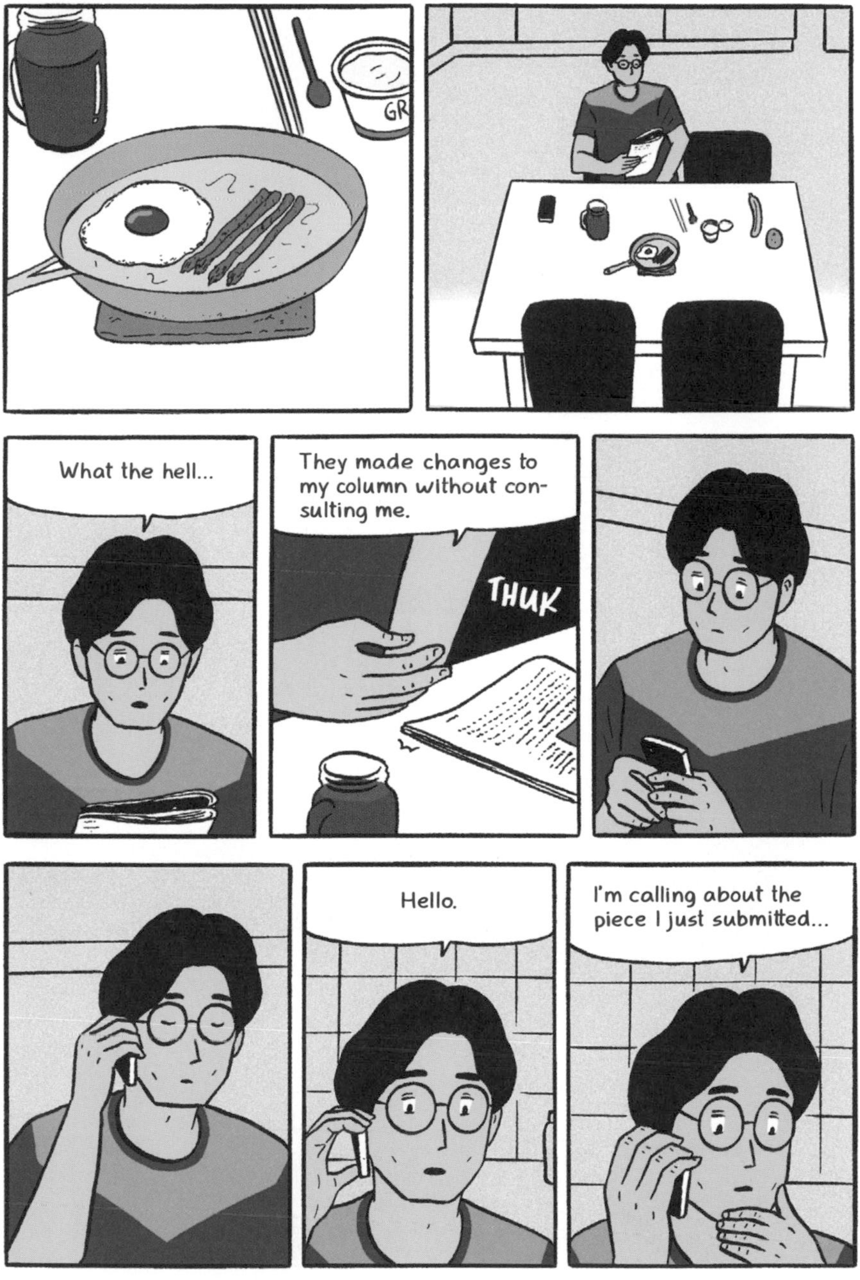
GR
What the hell...
They made changes to my column without consulting me.
THUK
Hello.
I'm calling about the piece I just submitted...

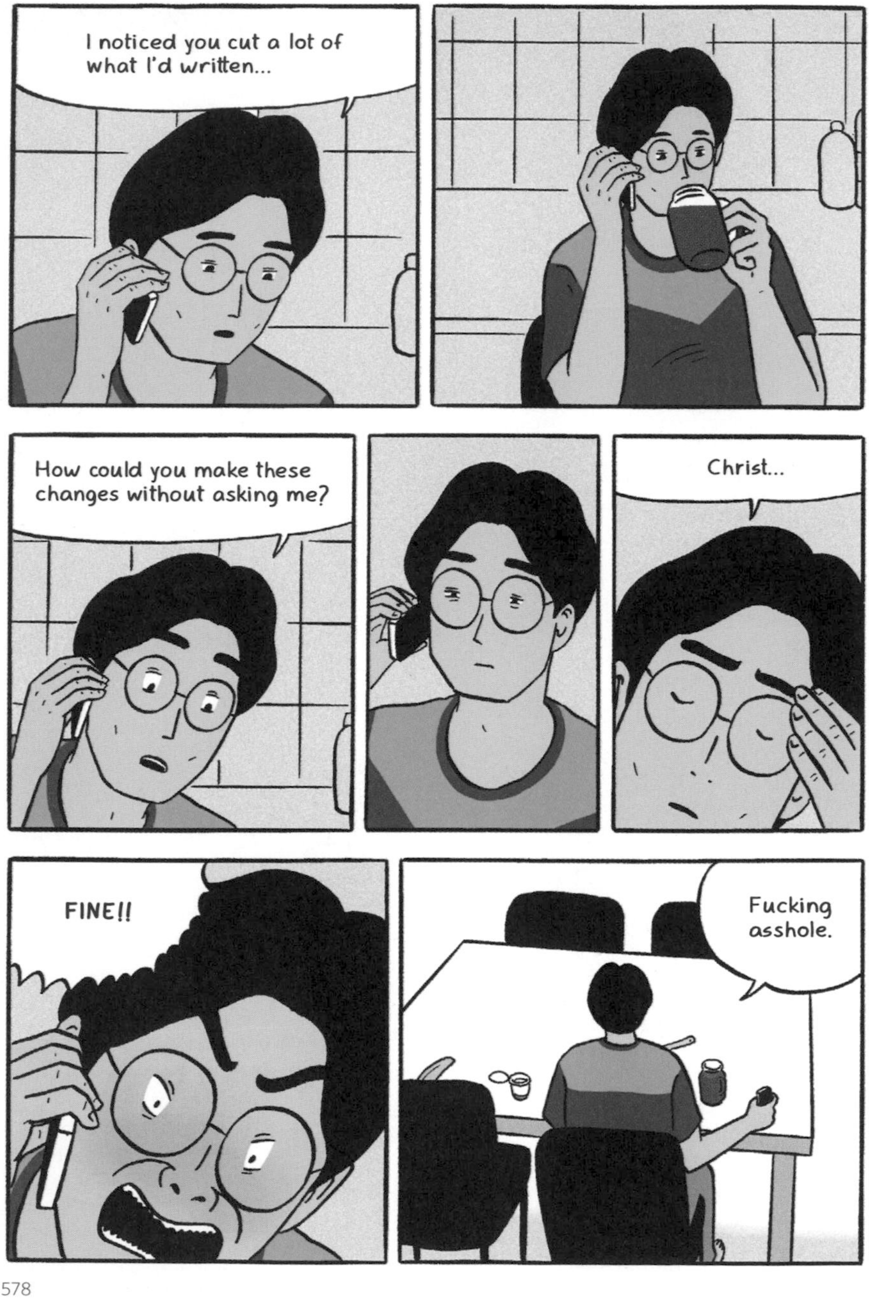
I noticed you cut a lot of what I'd written...
How could you make these changes without asking me?
Christ...
FINE!!
Fucking asshole.

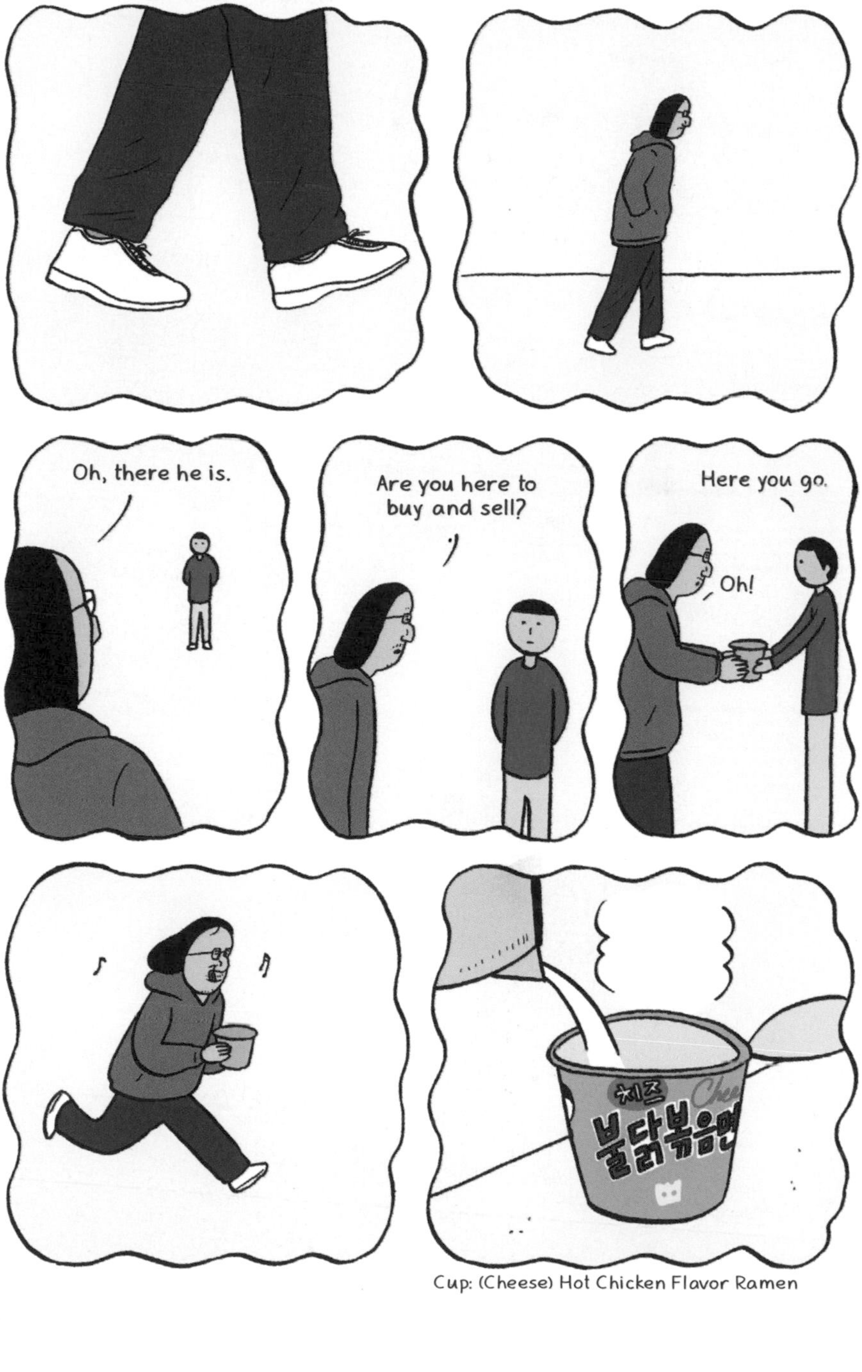
Oh, there he is.
Are you here to buy and sell?
Here you go.
Oh!
치즈
Chees
불닭볶음면

Cup: (Cheese) Hot Chicken Flavor Ramen

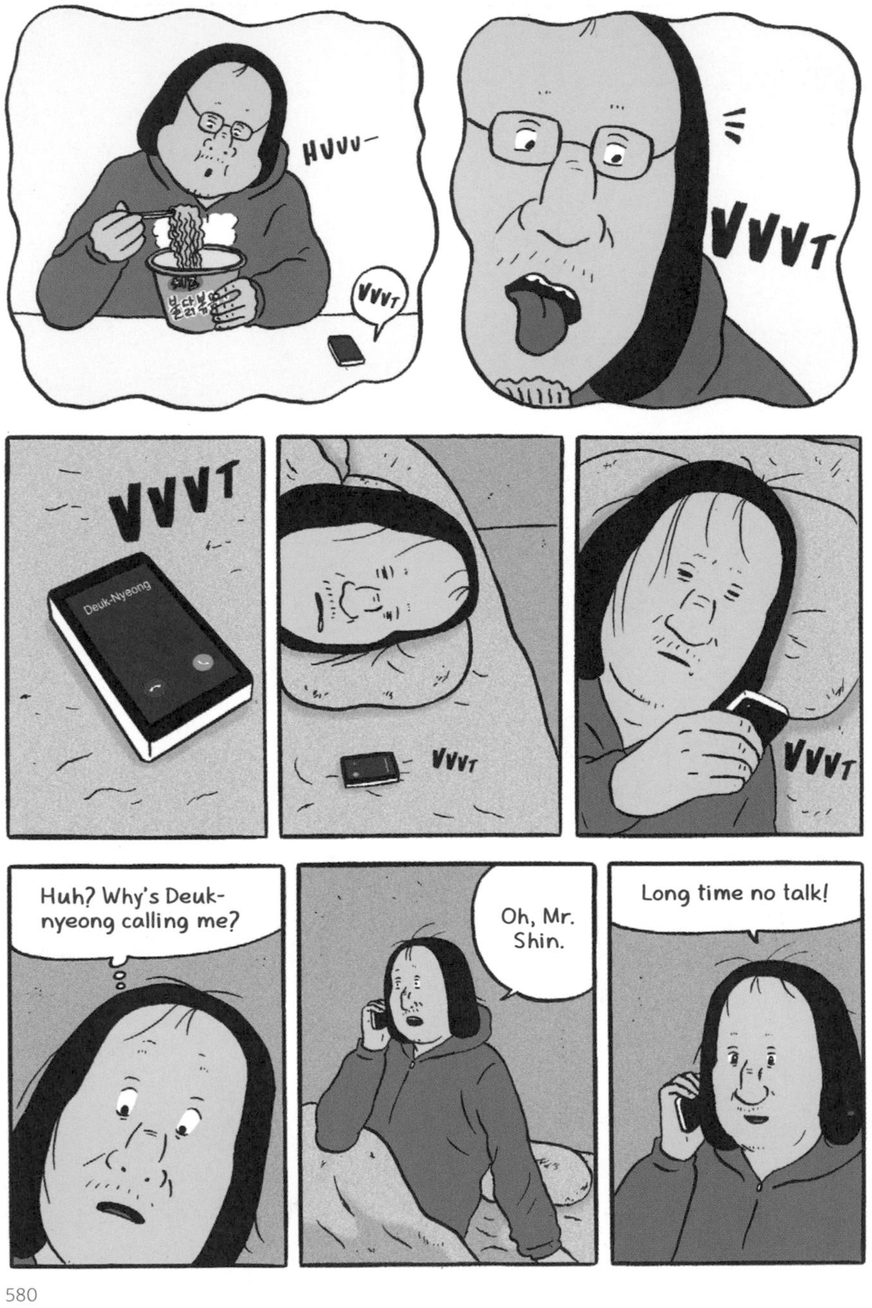
HUUU-
VVVT
VVVT
VVVT
Deuk-Nyeong
VVVT
VVVT
Huh? Why's Deuk-nyeong calling me?
Oh, Mr. Shin.
Long time no talk!

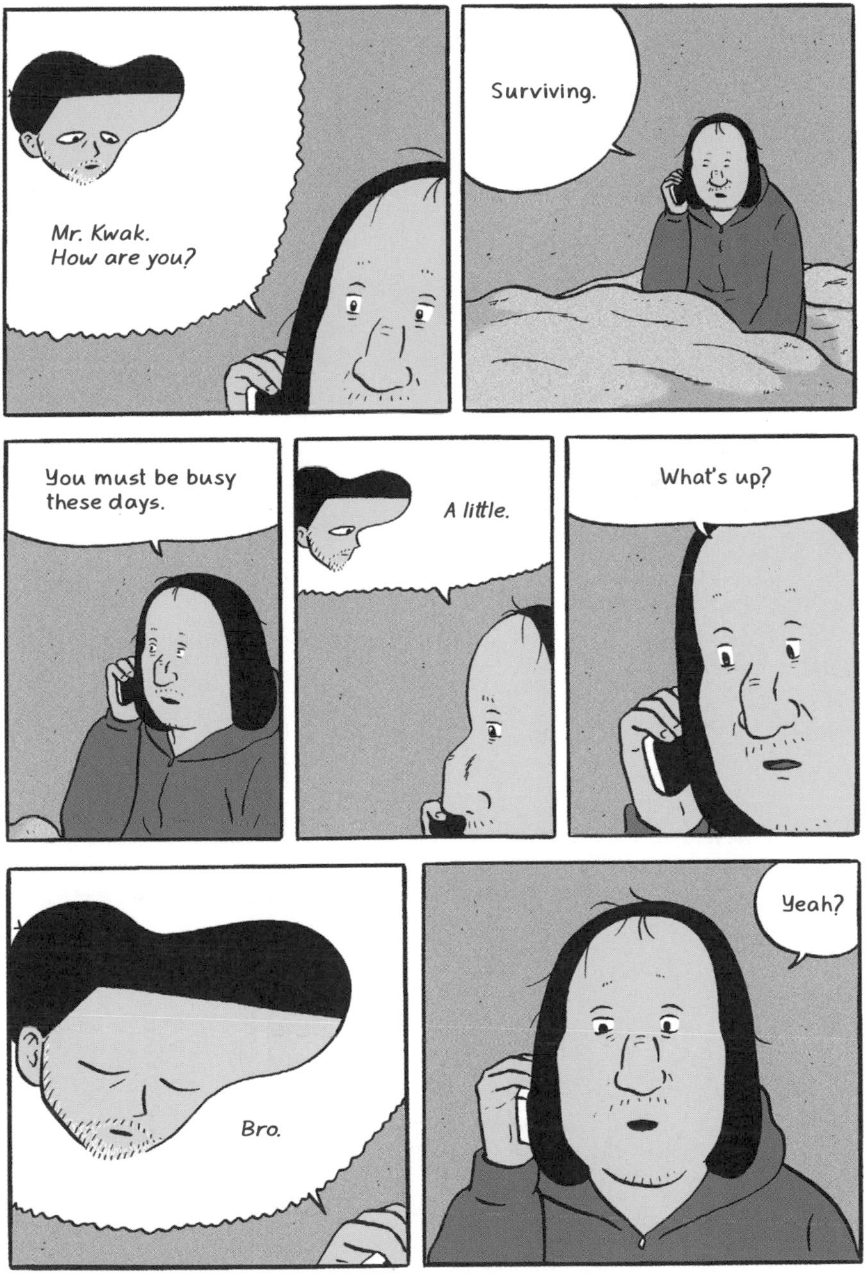
Mr. Kwak.
How are you?
Surviving.
You must be busy these days.
A little.
What's up?
Bro.
Yeah?

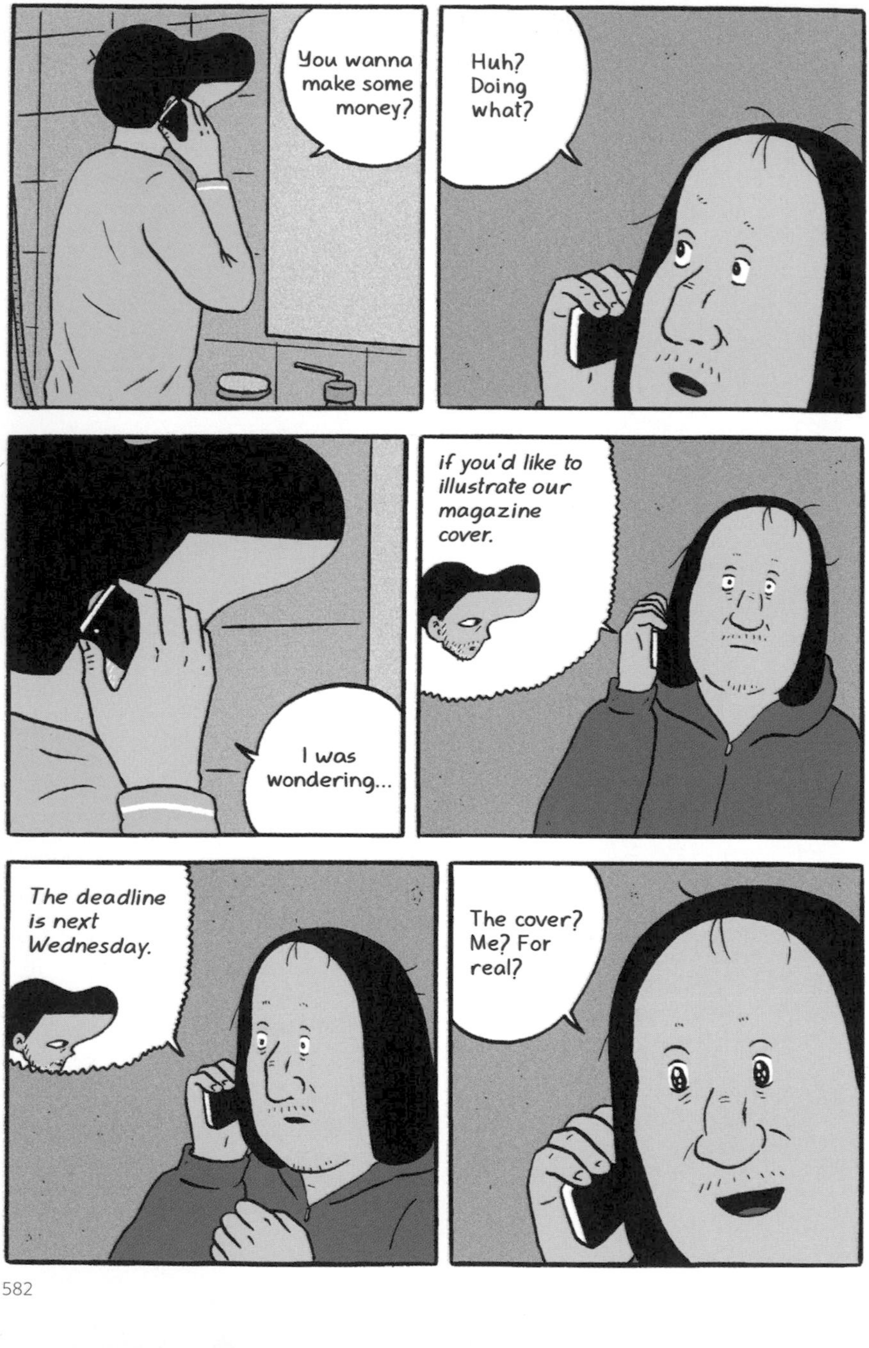
You wanna make some money?
Huh? Doing what?
I was wondering...
if you'd like to illustrate our magazine cover.
The deadline is next Wednesday.
The cover? Me? For real?

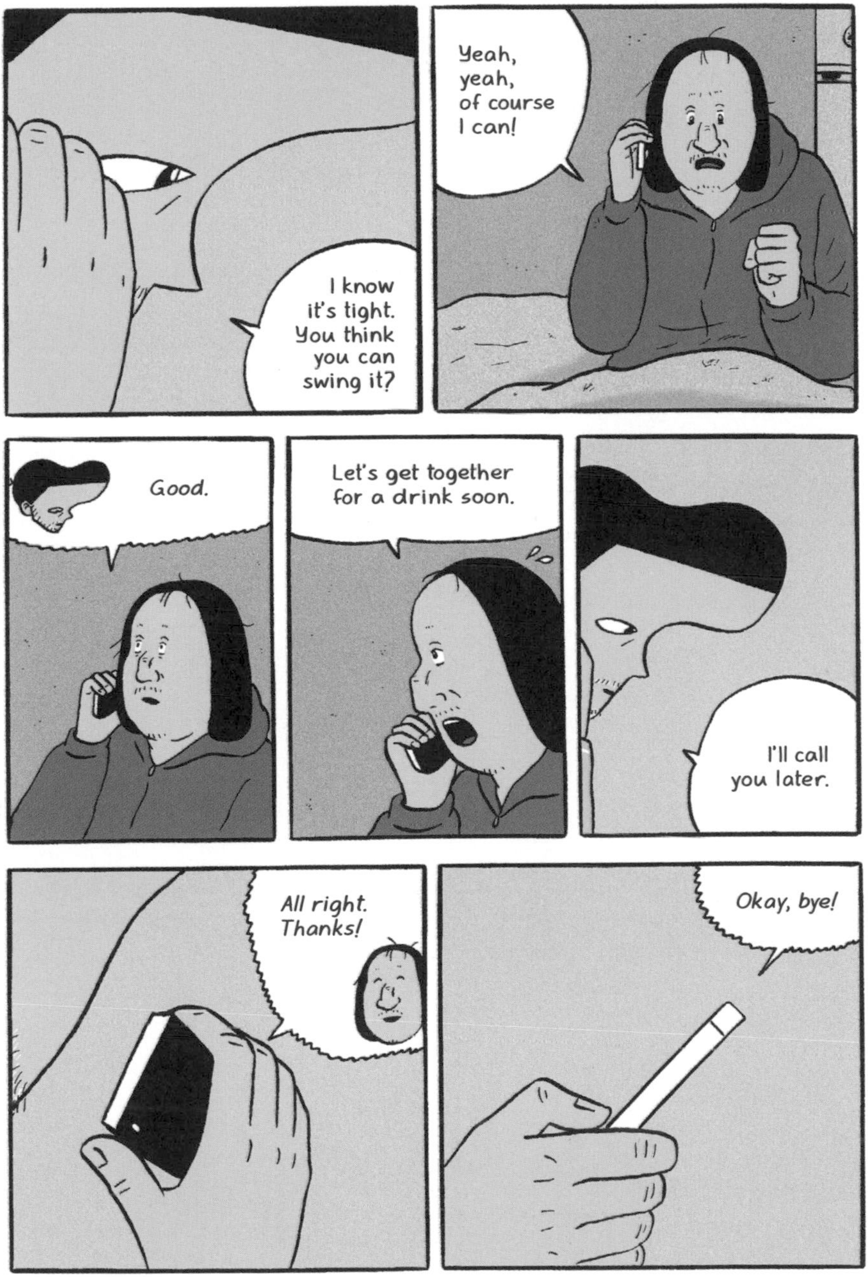
I know it's tight. You think you can swing it?
Yeah, yeah, of course I can!
Good.
Let's get together for a drink soon.
I'll call you later.
All right. Thanks!
Okay, bye!

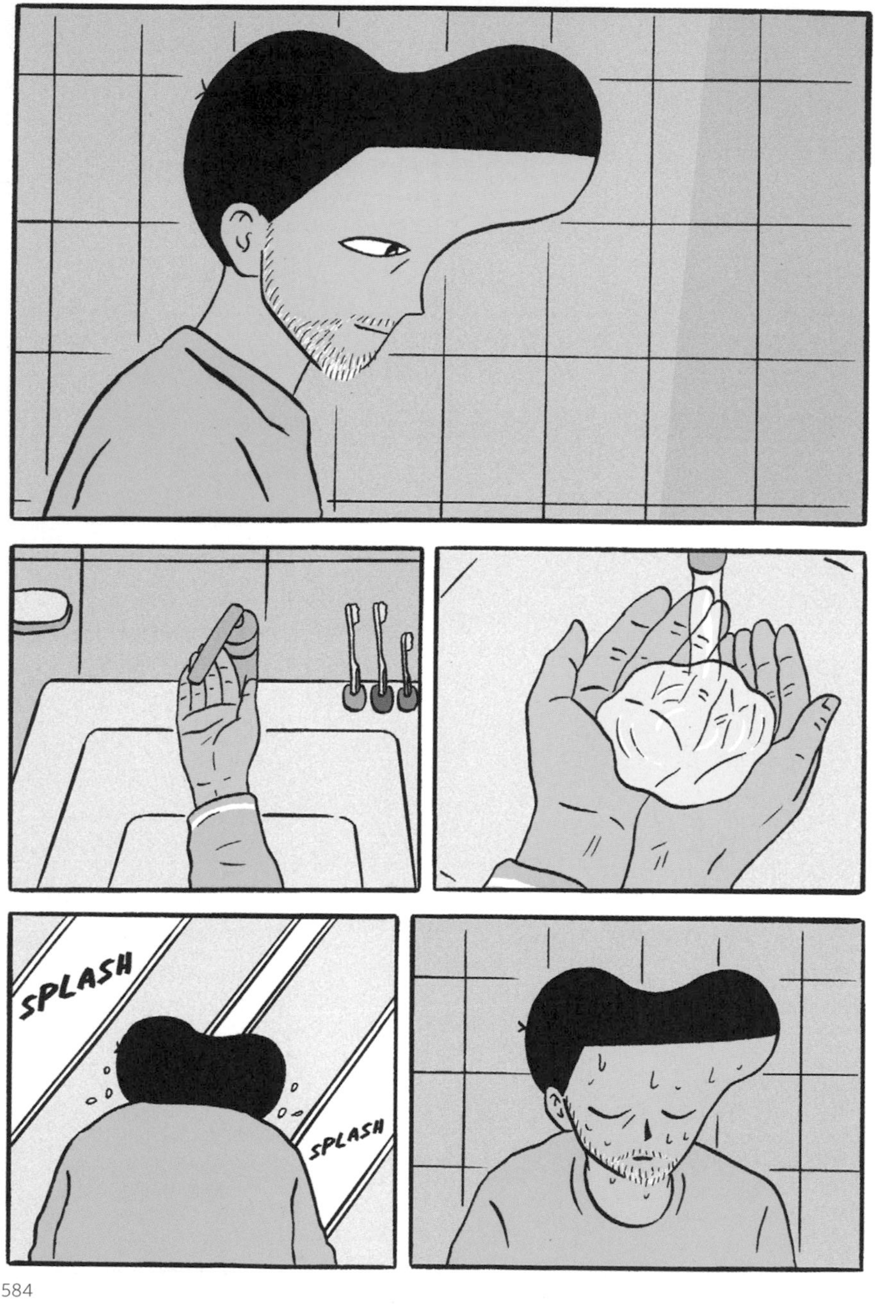
SPLASH
SPLASH

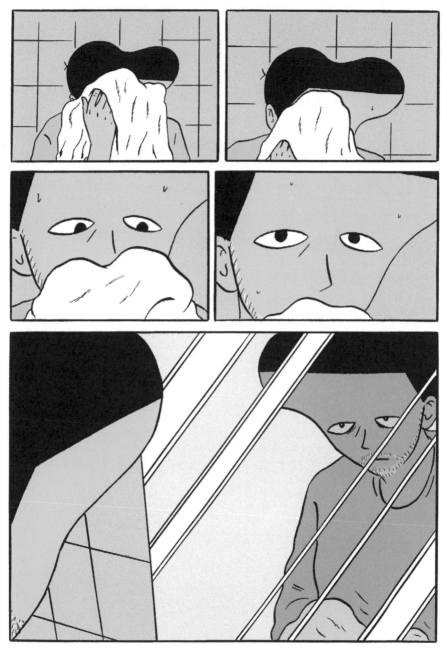

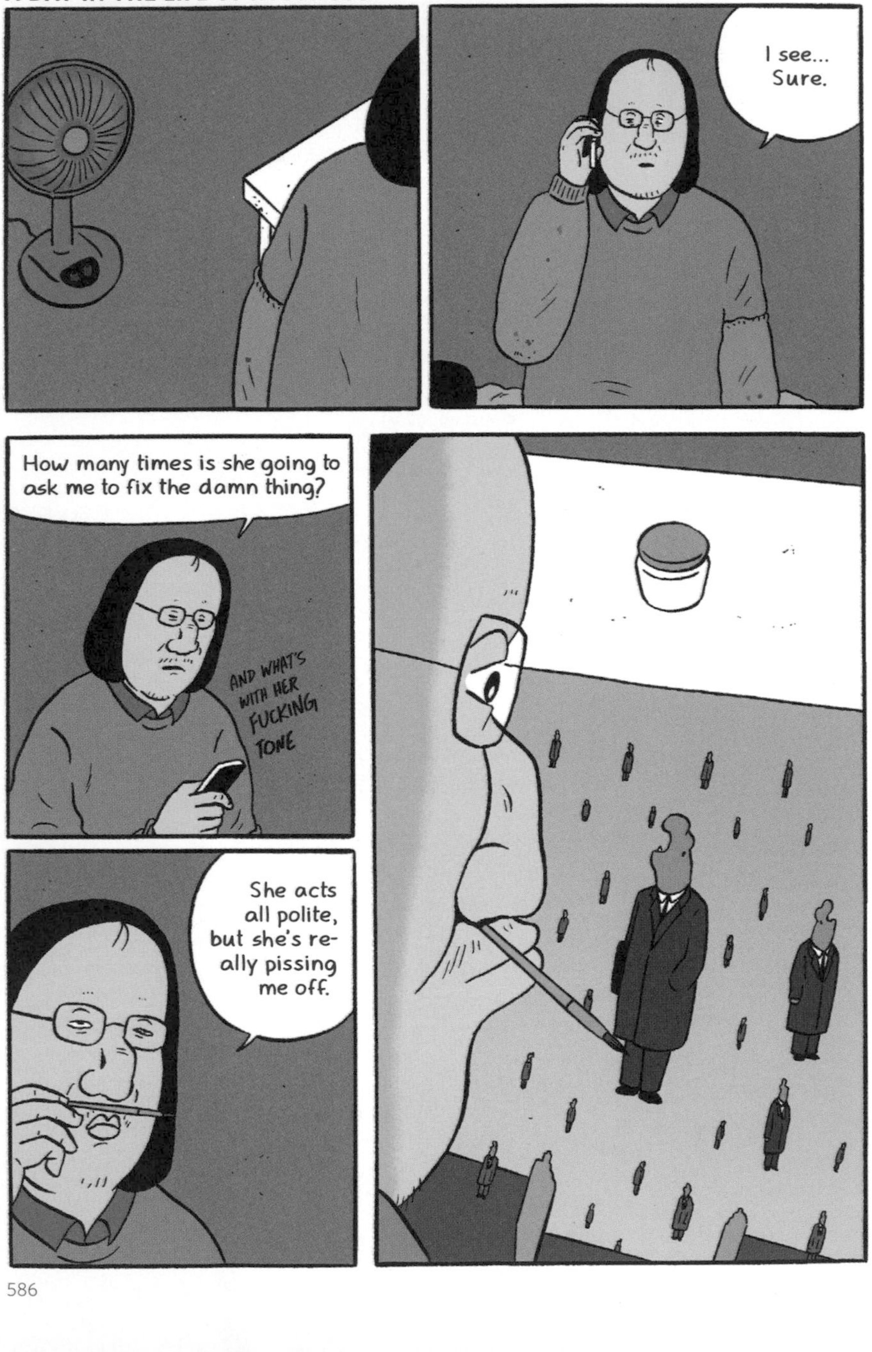
I see... Sure.
How many times is she going to ask me to fix the damn thing?
AND WHAT'S WITH HER FUCKING TONE
She acts all polite, but she's re-ally pissing me off.

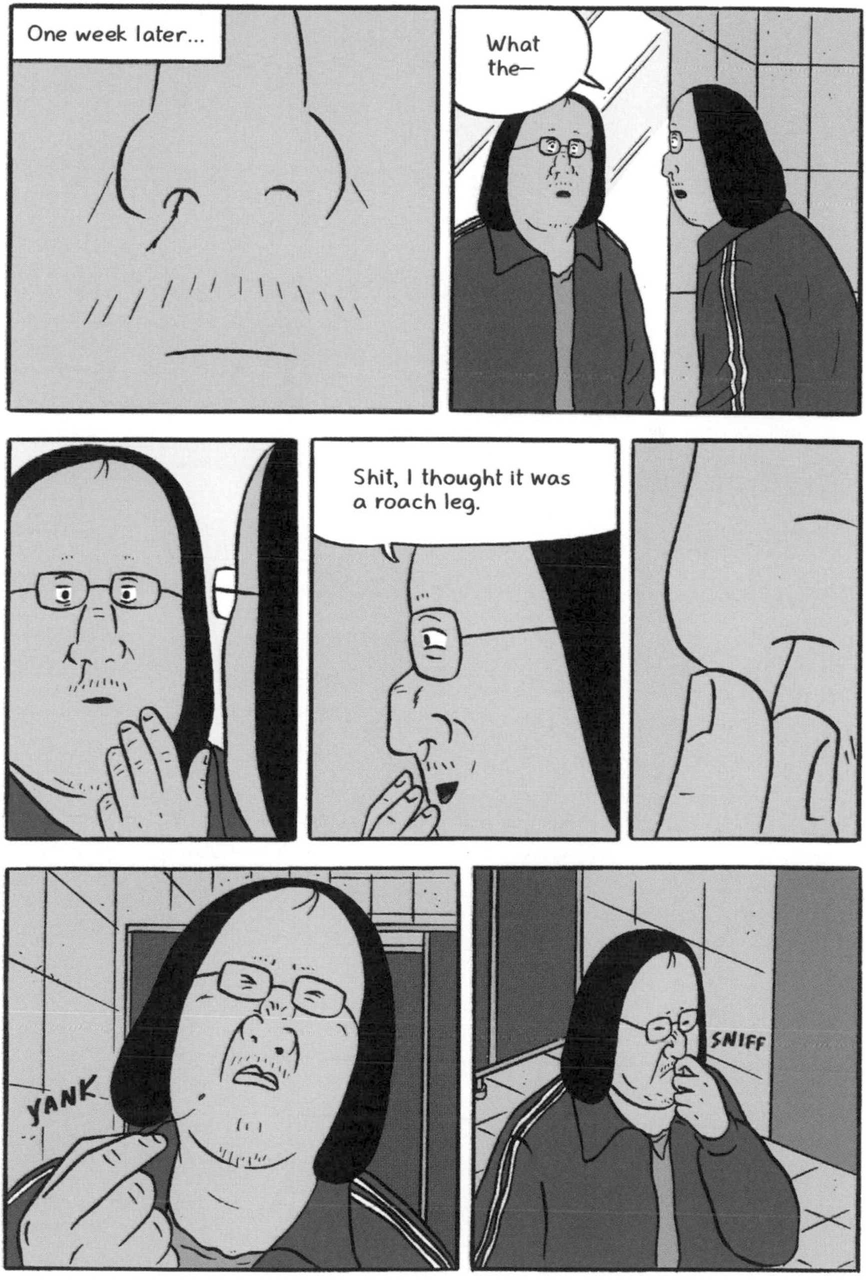

One week later...
What the—
Shit, I thought it was a roach leg.
YANK
SNIFF

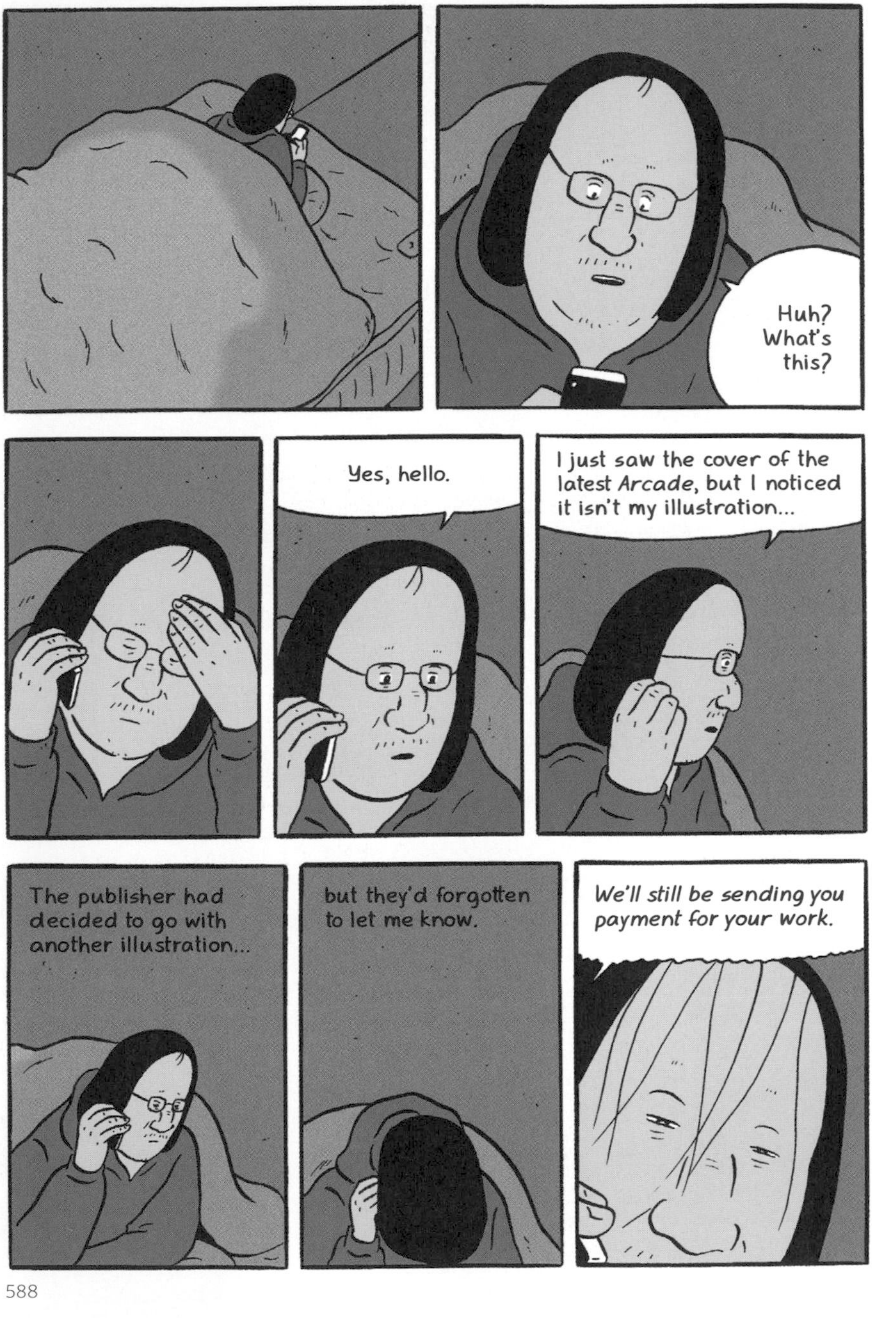
Huh? What's this?
Yes, hello.
I just saw the cover of the latest *Arcade*, but I noticed it isn't my illustration...
The publisher had decided to go with another illustration...
but they'd forgotten to let me know.
We'll still be sending you payment for your work.

1969
You think BTS are artists?
They're musicians, but they sure as hell aren't artists!
I like them, not just because they're a boy band.
It's because they give off such whole-some energy...
But my question is, are they *artists*?

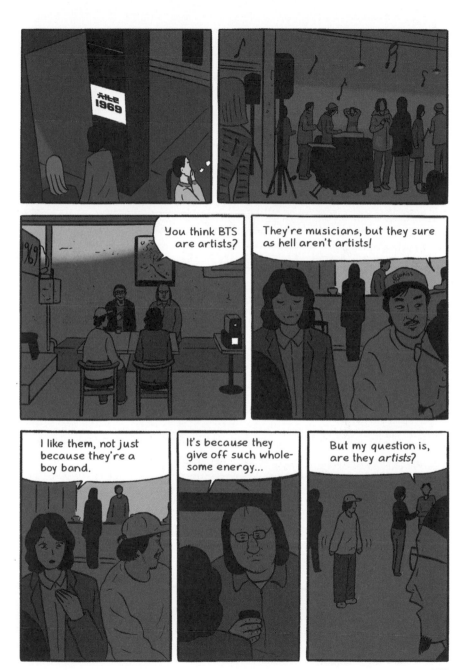

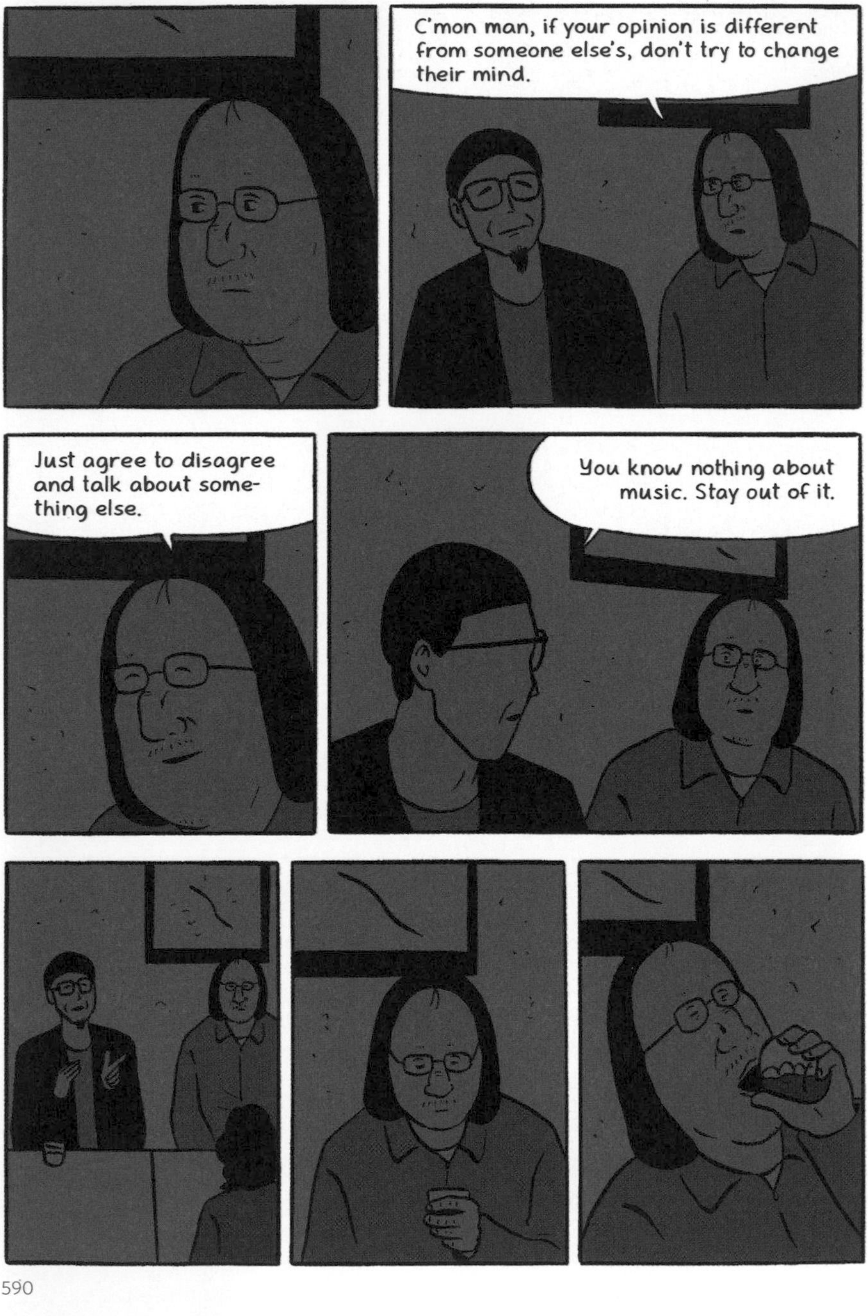
C'mon man, if your opinion is different from someone else's, don't try to change their mind.
Just agree to disagree and talk about something else.
You know nothing about music. Stay out of it.

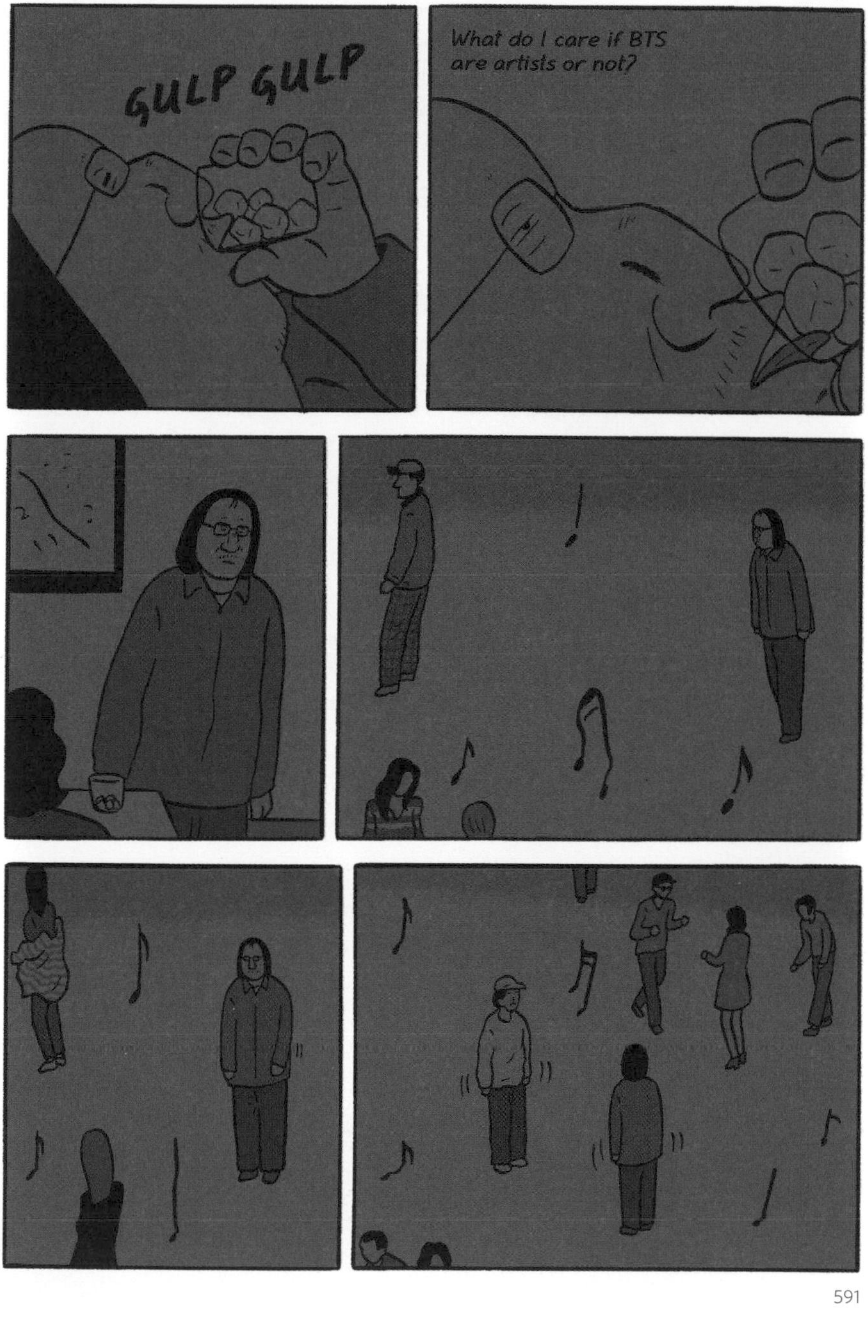
GULP GULP
What do I care if BTS are artists or not?

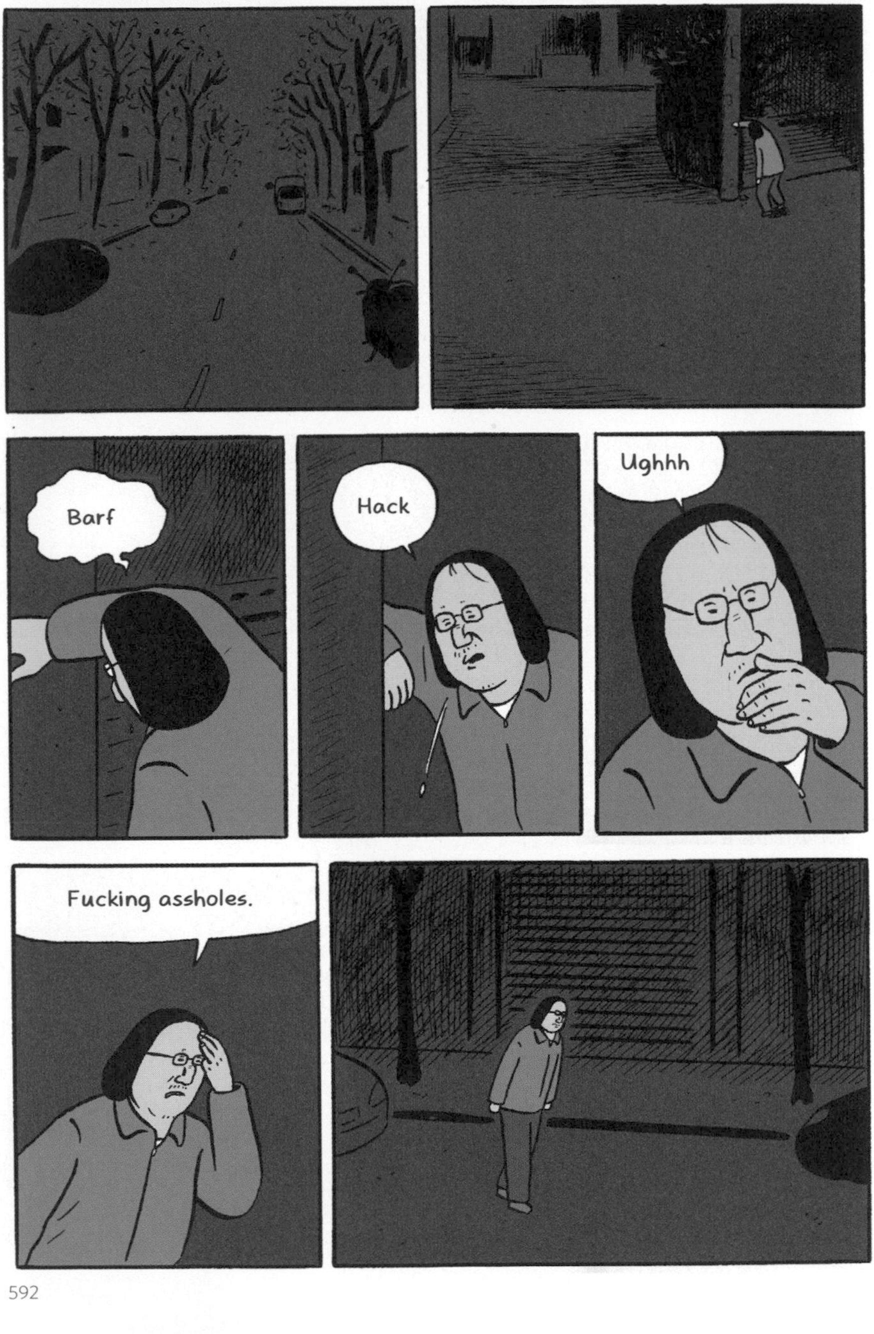
Barf
Hack
Ughhh
Fucking assholes.

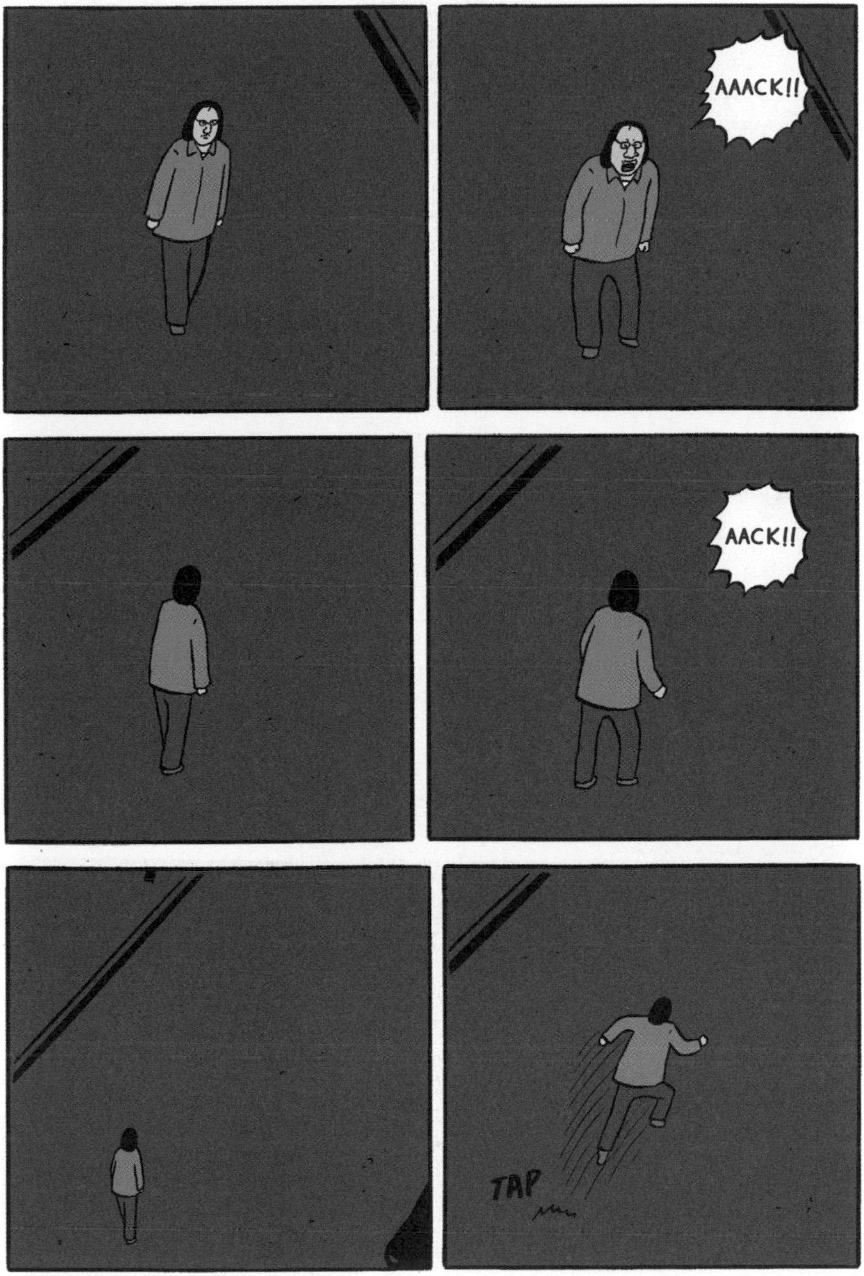
AAACK!!
AACK!!
TAP

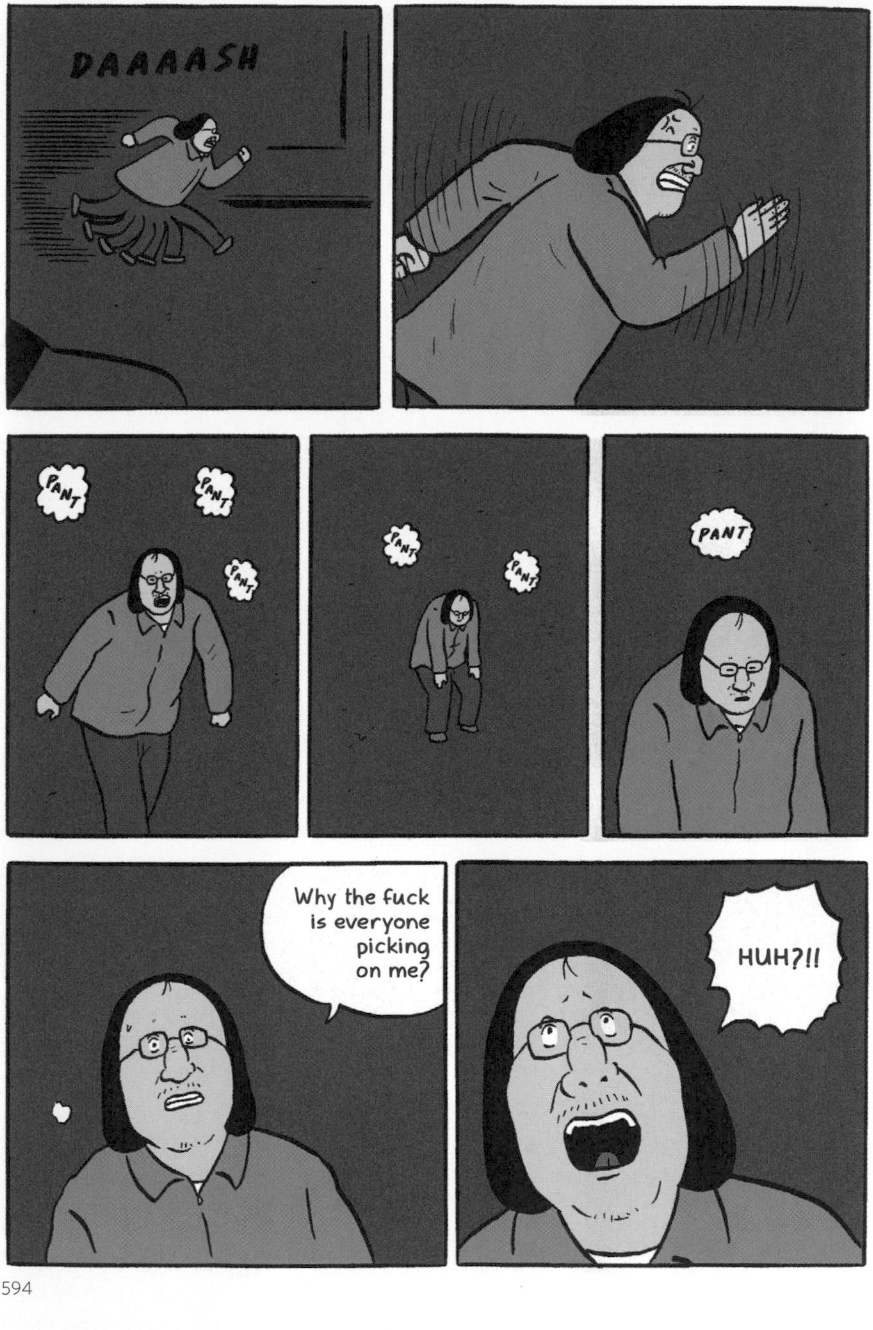
DAAAASH
PANT
PANT
PANT
PANT
PANT
PANT
Why the fuck is everyone picking on me?
HUH?!!

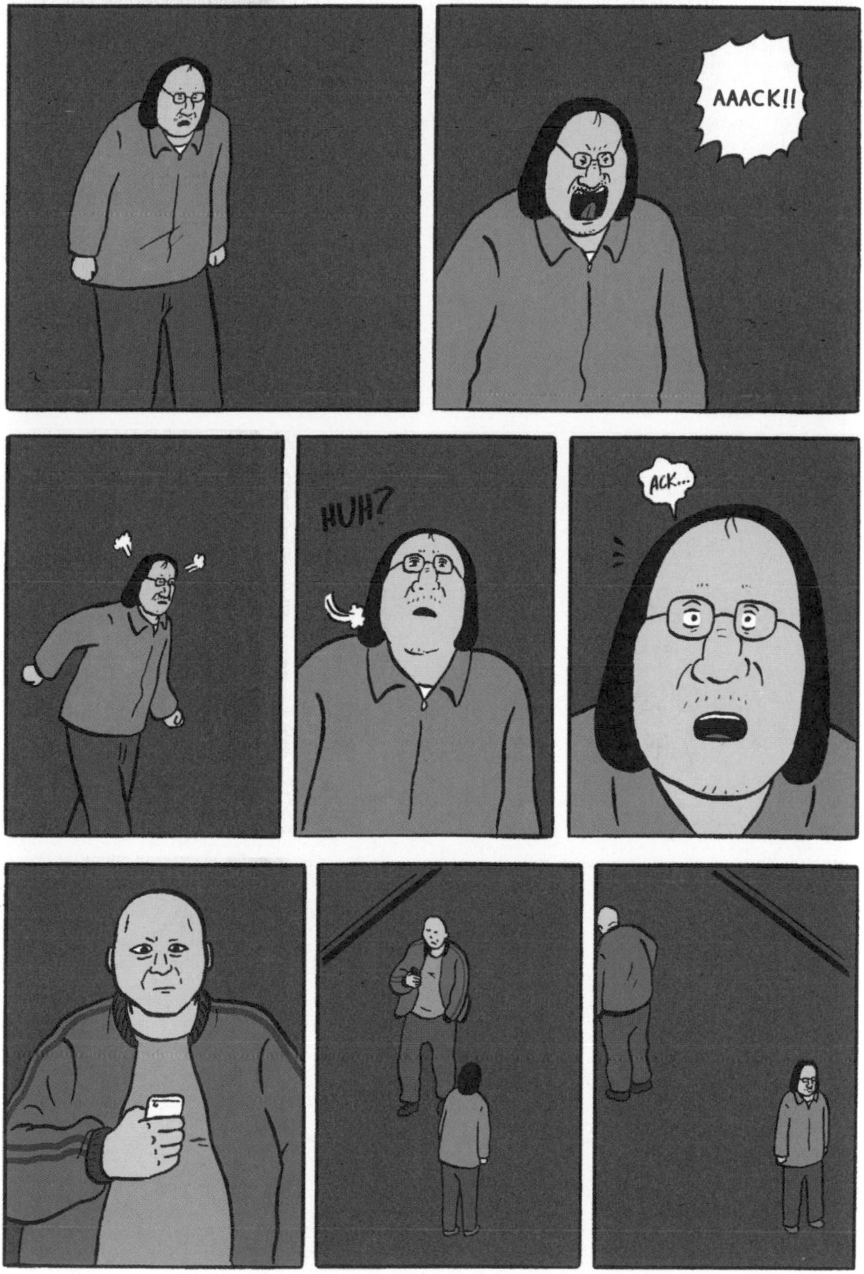
AAACK!!
HUH?
ACK...

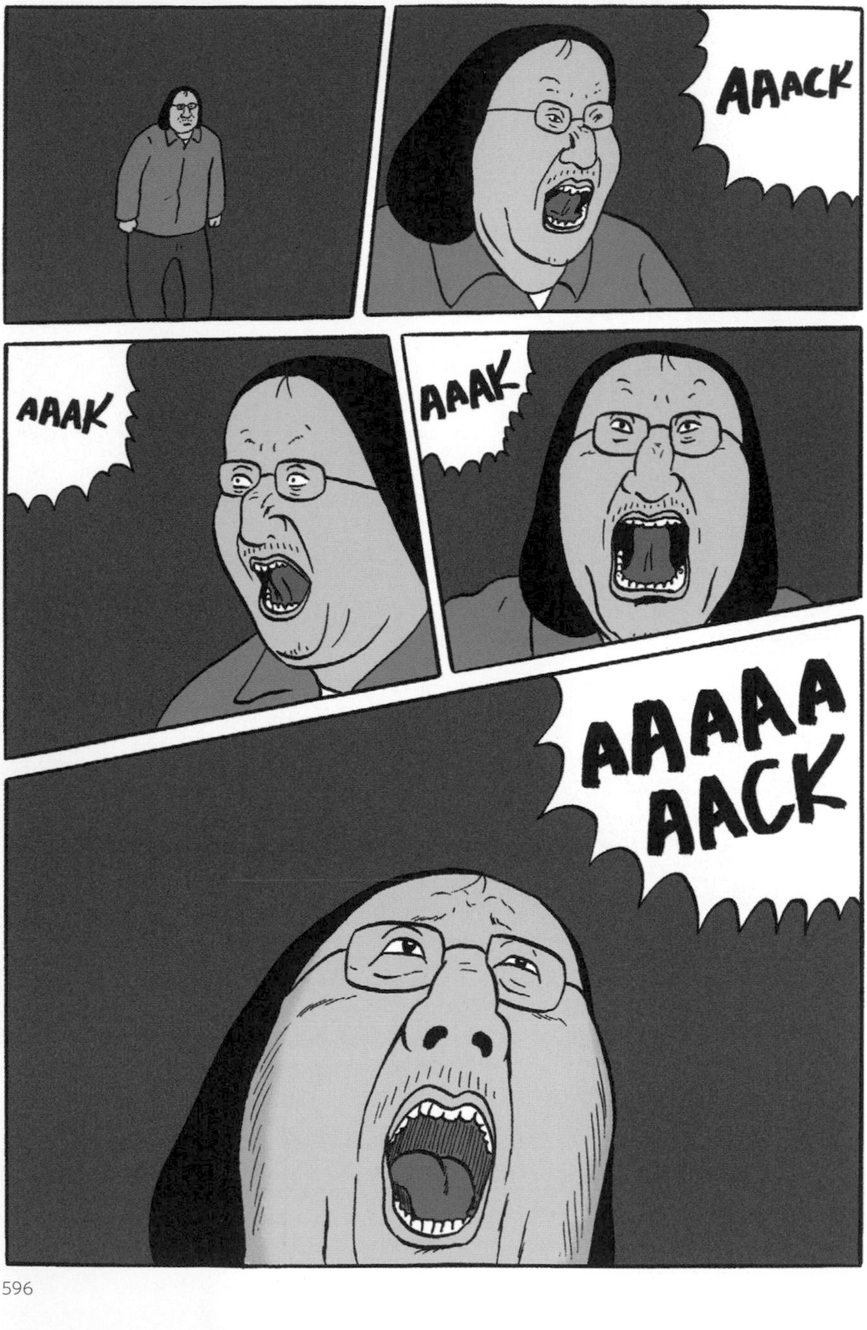
AAACK
AAAK
AAAK
AAAAA AACK

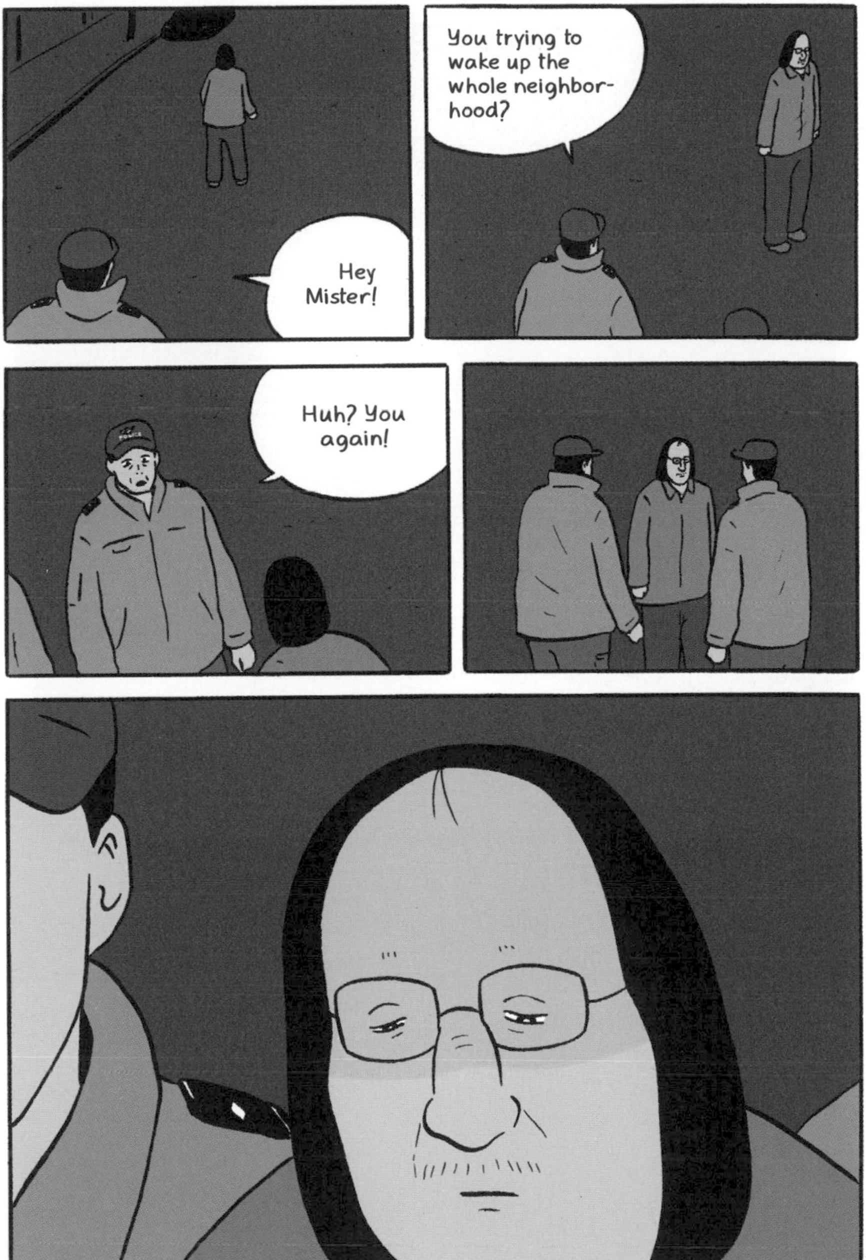
Hey Mister!
You trying to wake up the whole neighbor-hood?
Huh? You again!

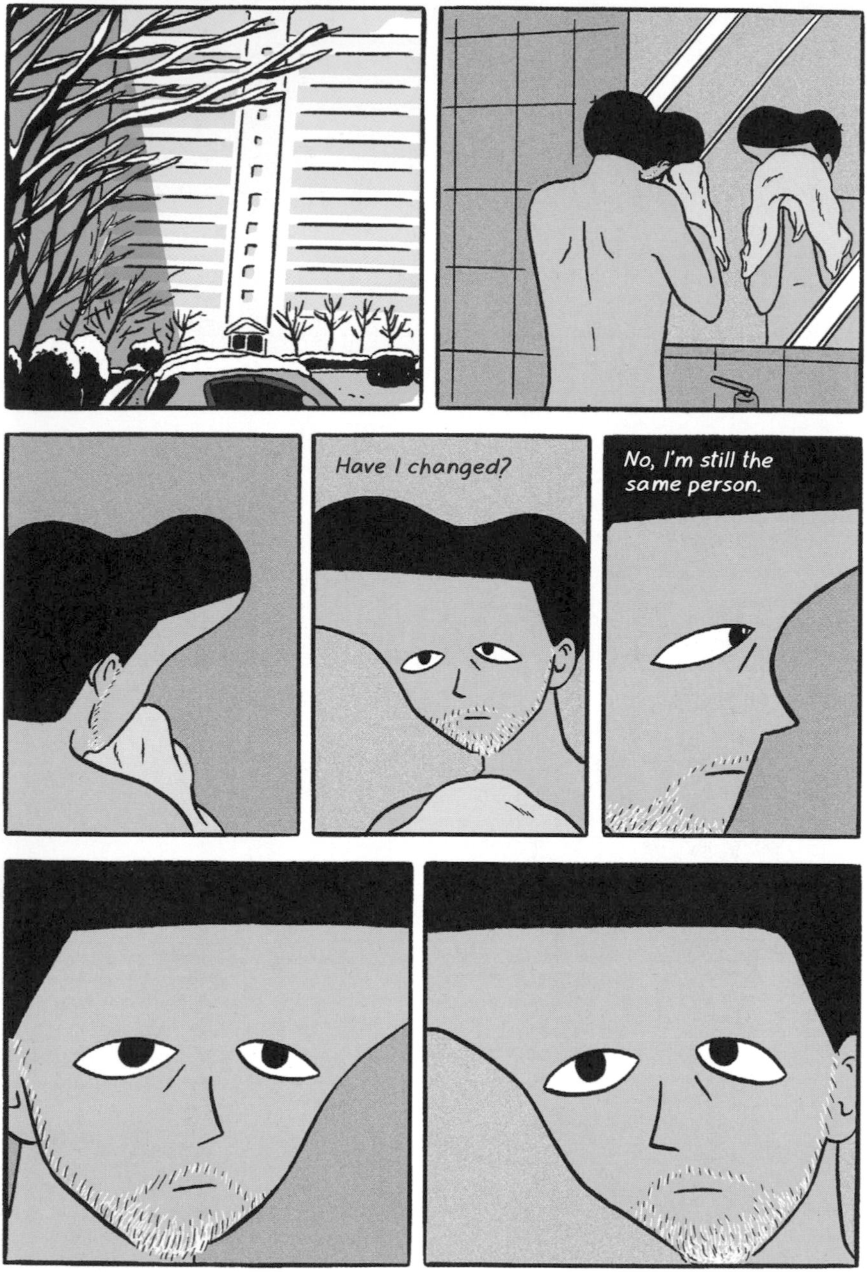
Have I changed?
No, I'm still the same person.

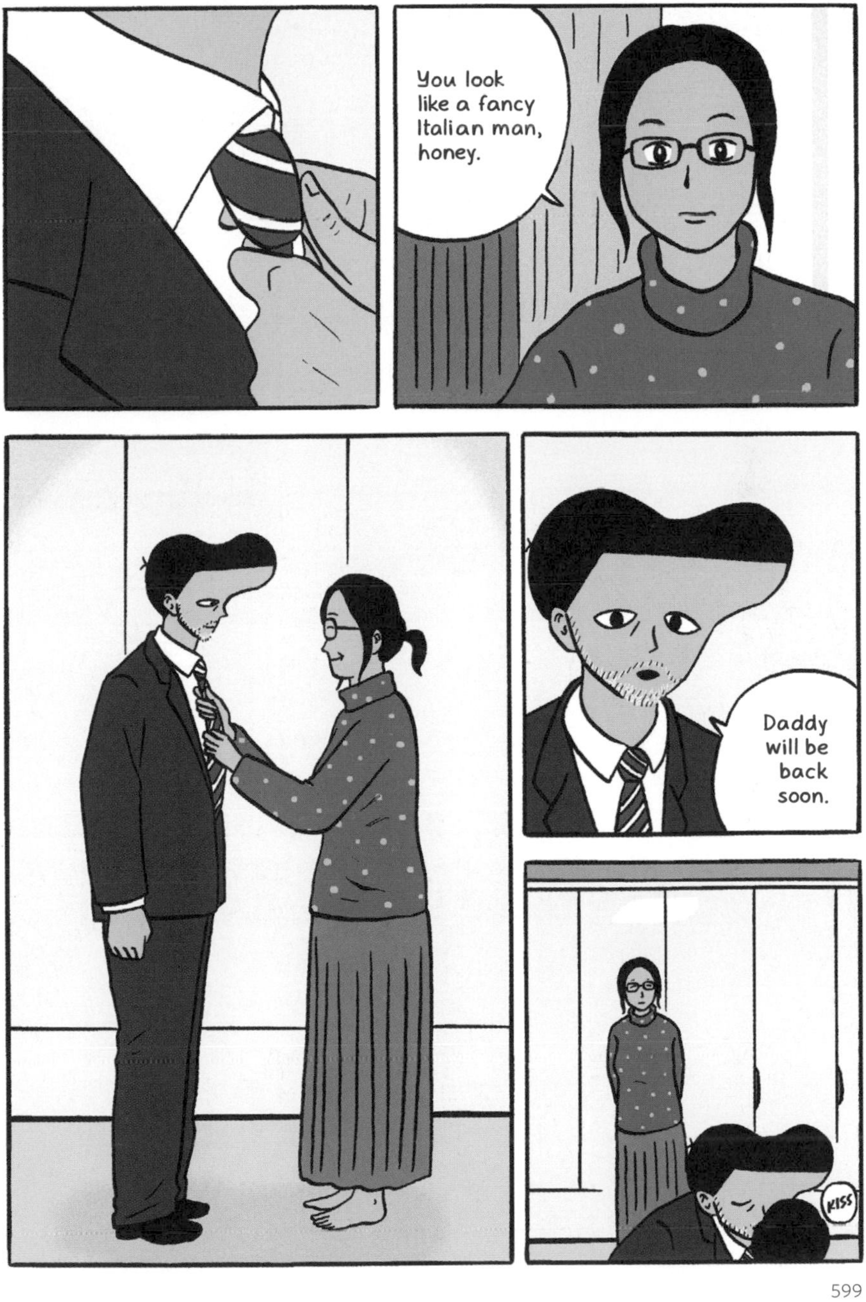
You look like a fancy Italian man, honey.
Daddy will be back soon.
KISS

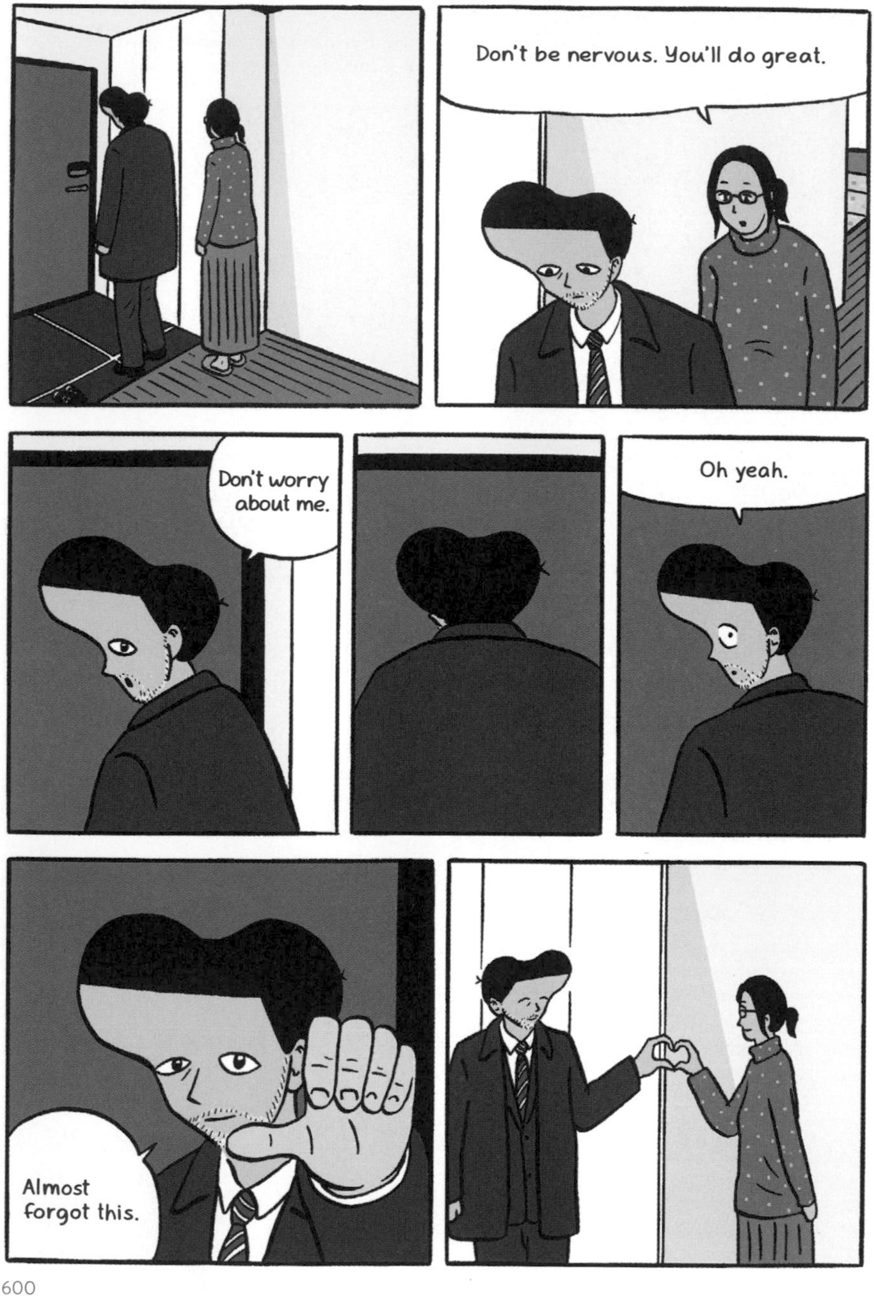
Don't be nervous. You'll do great.
Don't worry about me.
Oh yeah.
Almost forgot this.

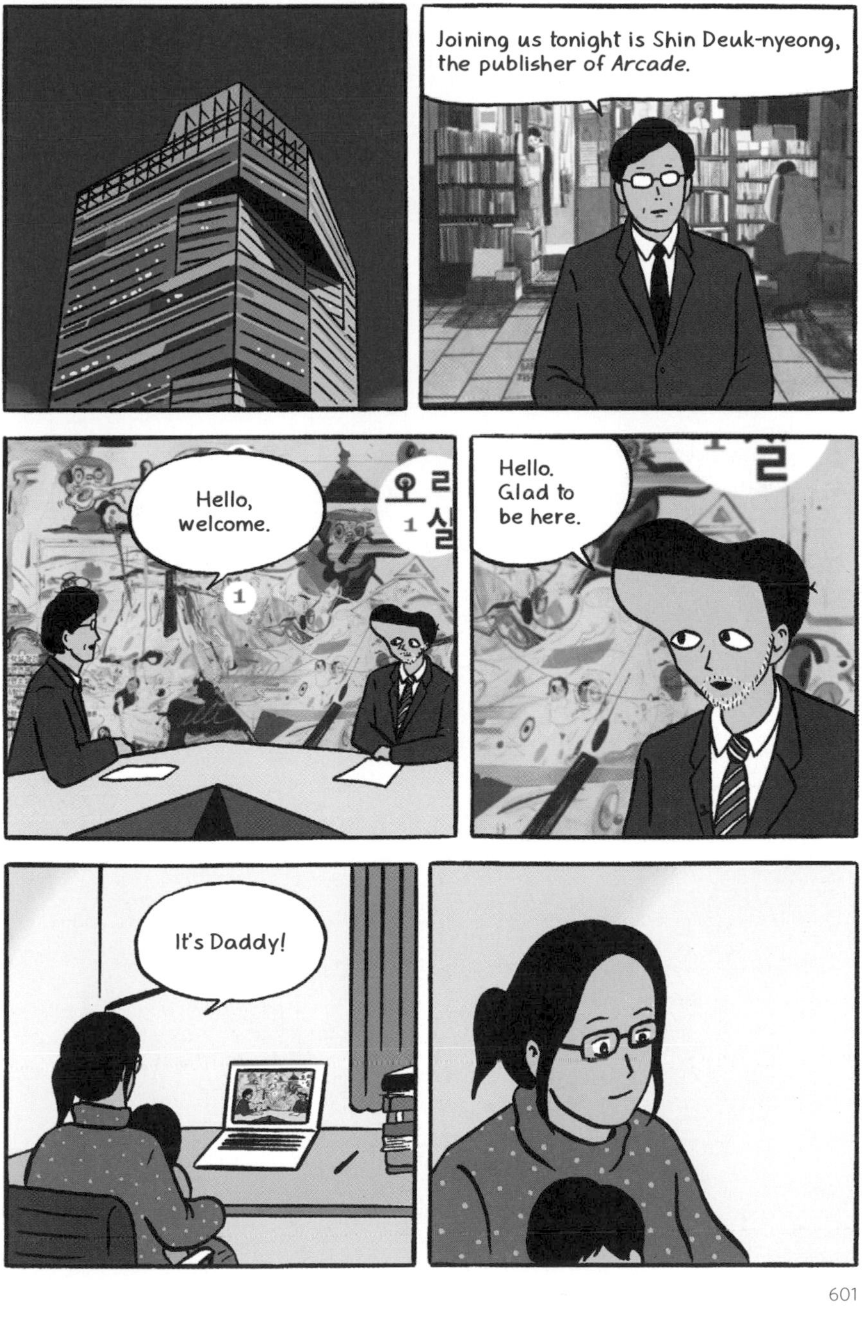
Joining us tonight is Shin Deuk-nyeong, the publisher of *Arcade*.
Hello, welcome.
Hello. Glad to be here.
It's Daddy!

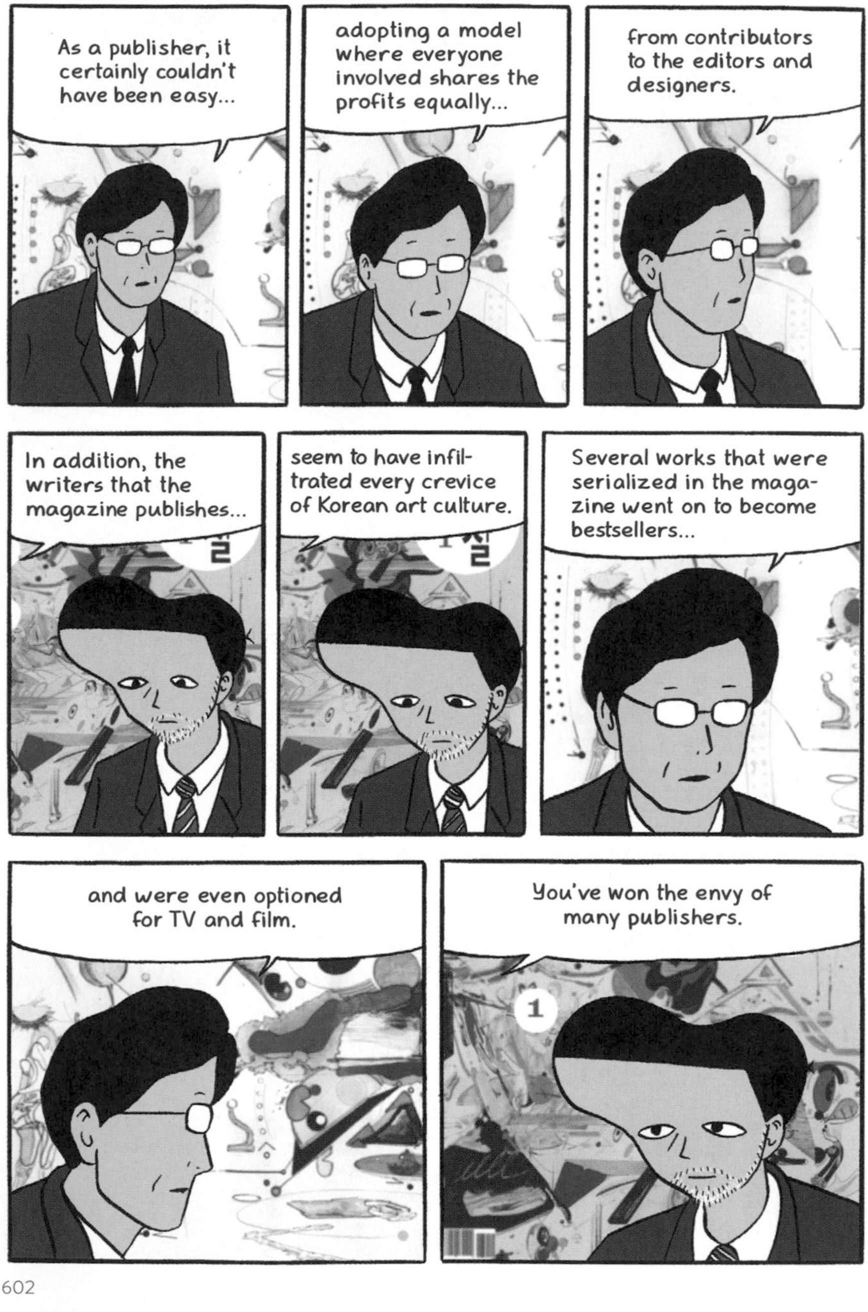
As a publisher, it certainly couldn't have been easy...
adopting a model where everyone involved shares the profits equally...
from contributors to the editors and designers.
In addition, the writers that the magazine publishes...
seem to have infil-trated every crevice of Korean art culture.
Several works that were serialized in the maga-zine went on to become bestsellers...
and were even optioned for TV and film.
You've won the envy of many publishers.

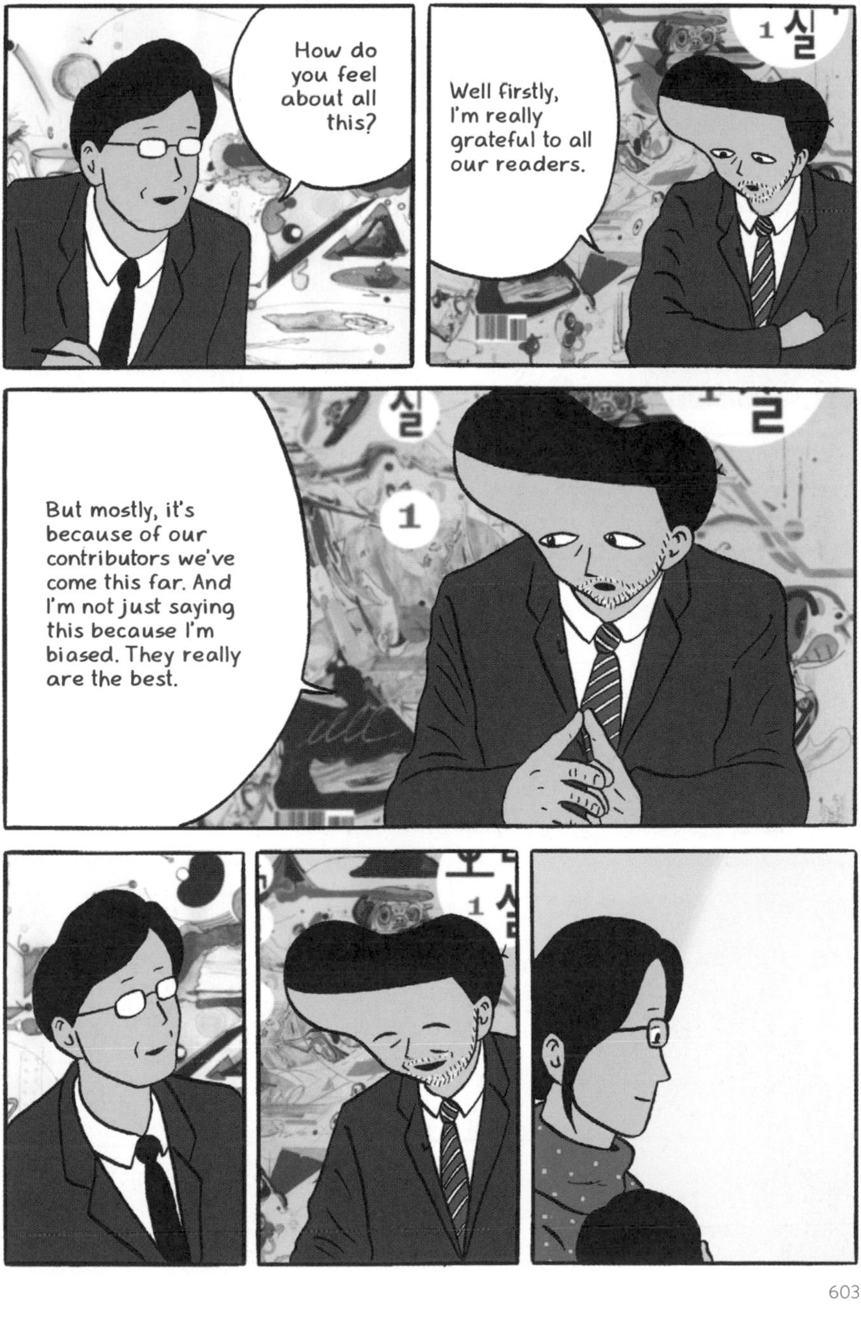
How do you feel about all this?
Well firstly, I'm really grateful to all our readers.
But mostly, it's because of our contributors we've come this far. And I'm not just saying this because I'm biased. They really are the best.

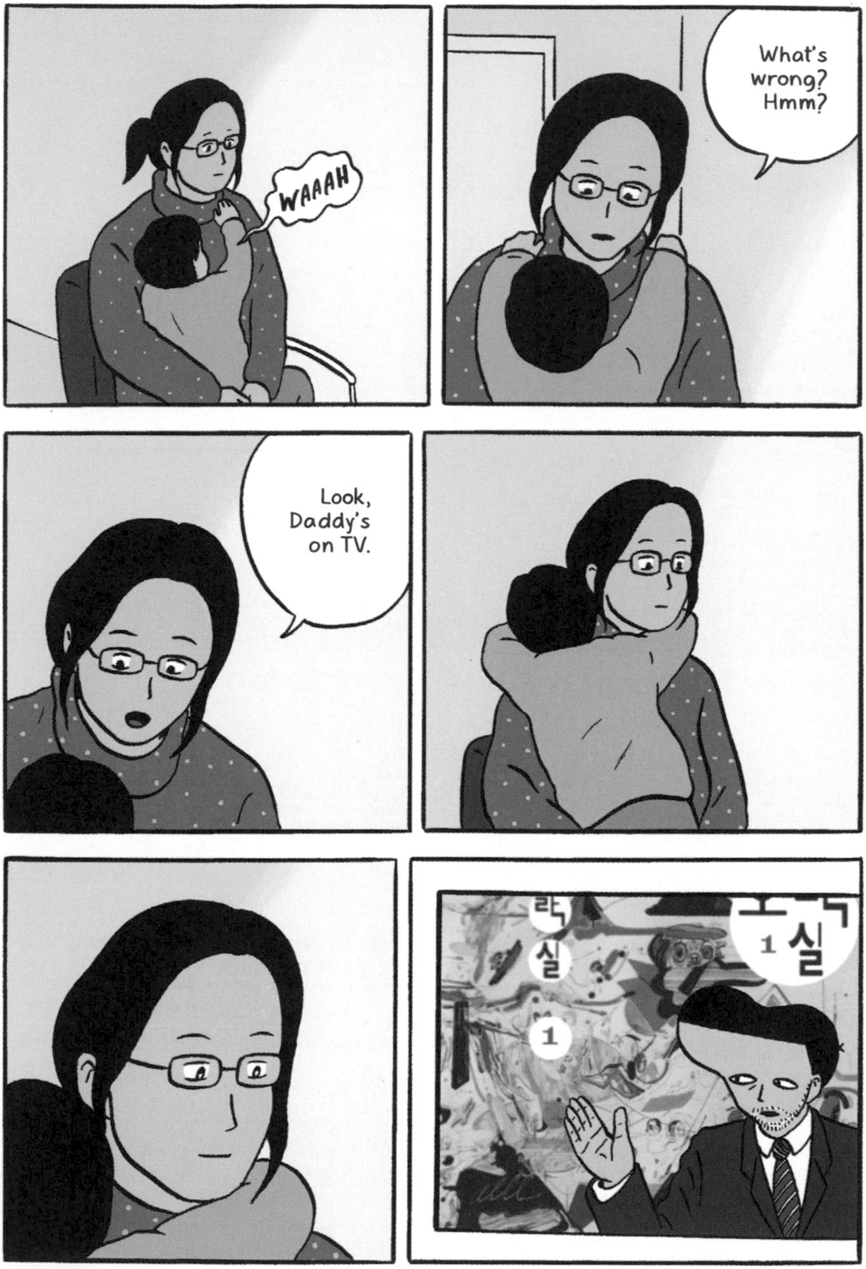
WAAAH
What's wrong? Hmm?
Look, Daddy's on TV.

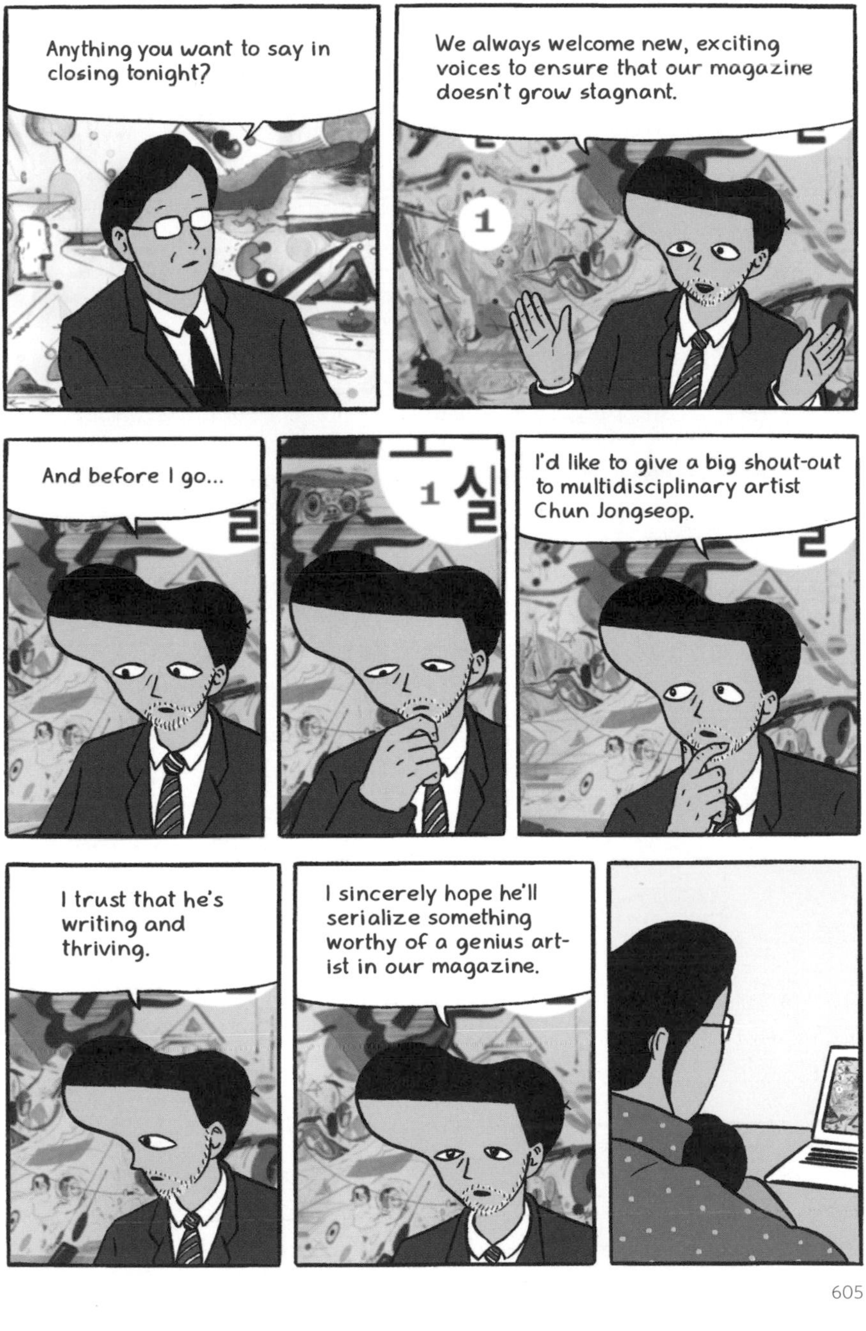
Anything you want to say in closing tonight?
We always welcome new, exciting voices to ensure that our magazine doesn't grow stagnant.
And before I go...
1 실
I'd like to give a big shout-out to multidisciplinary artist Chun Jongseop.
I trust that he's writing and thriving.
I sincerely hope he'll serialize something worthy of a genius art-ist in our magazine.

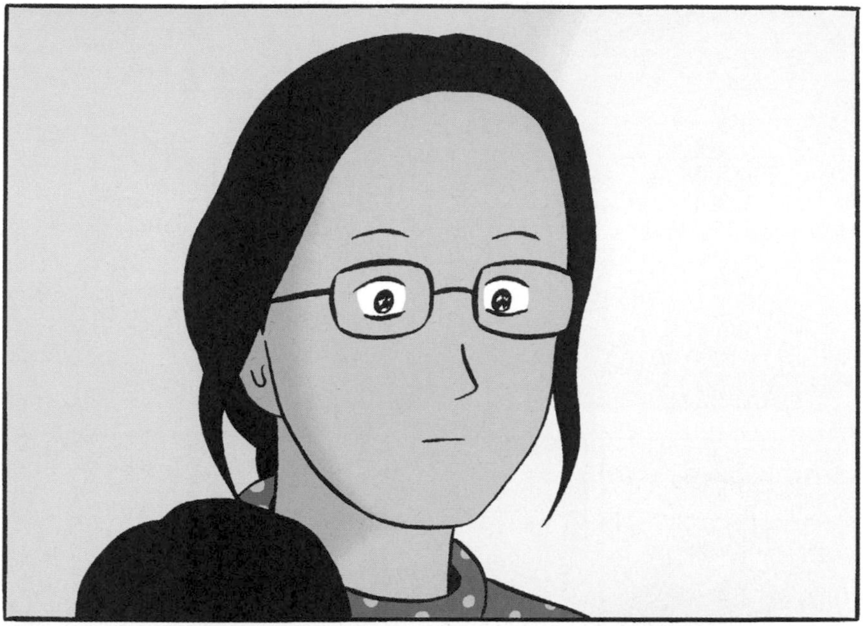

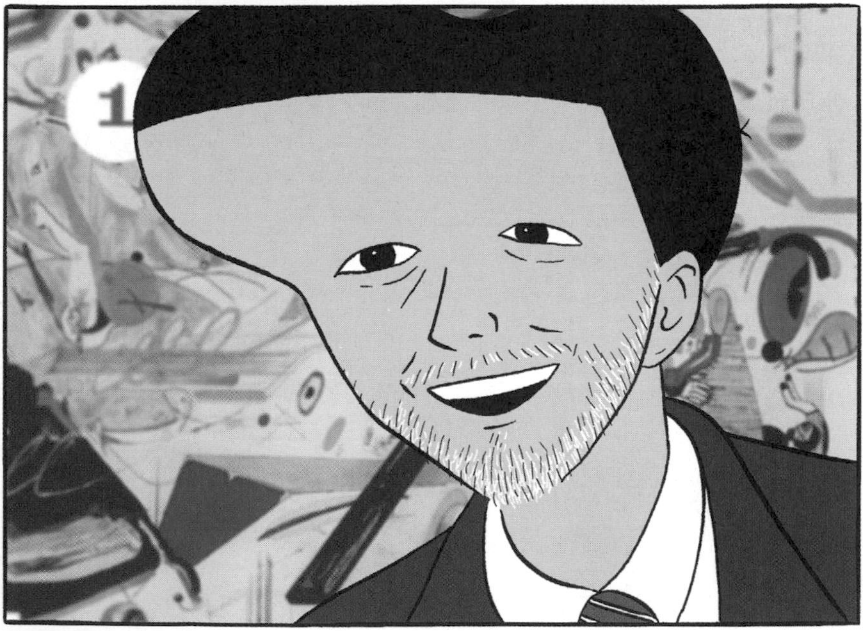

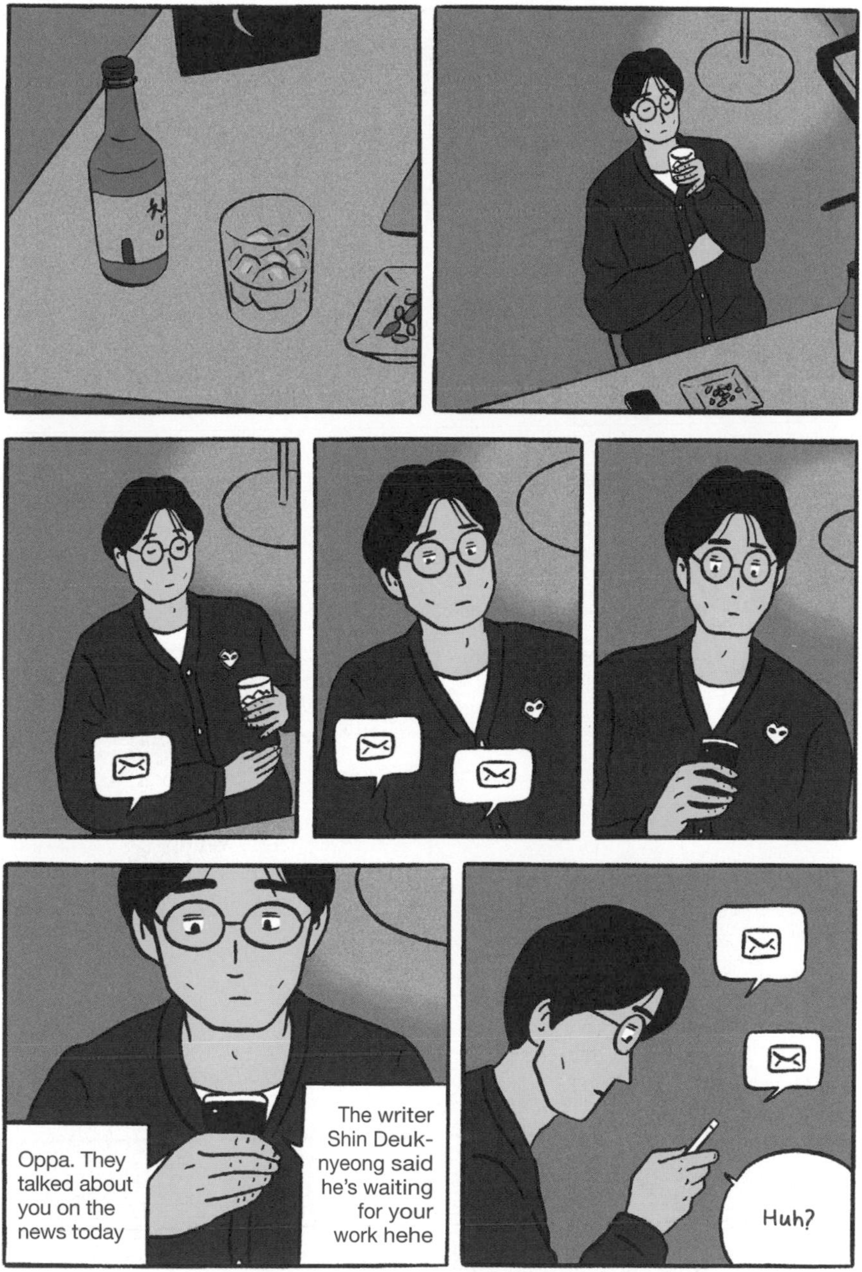
Oppa. They talked about you on the news today
The writer Shin Deuk-nyeong said he's waiting for your work hehe
Huh?

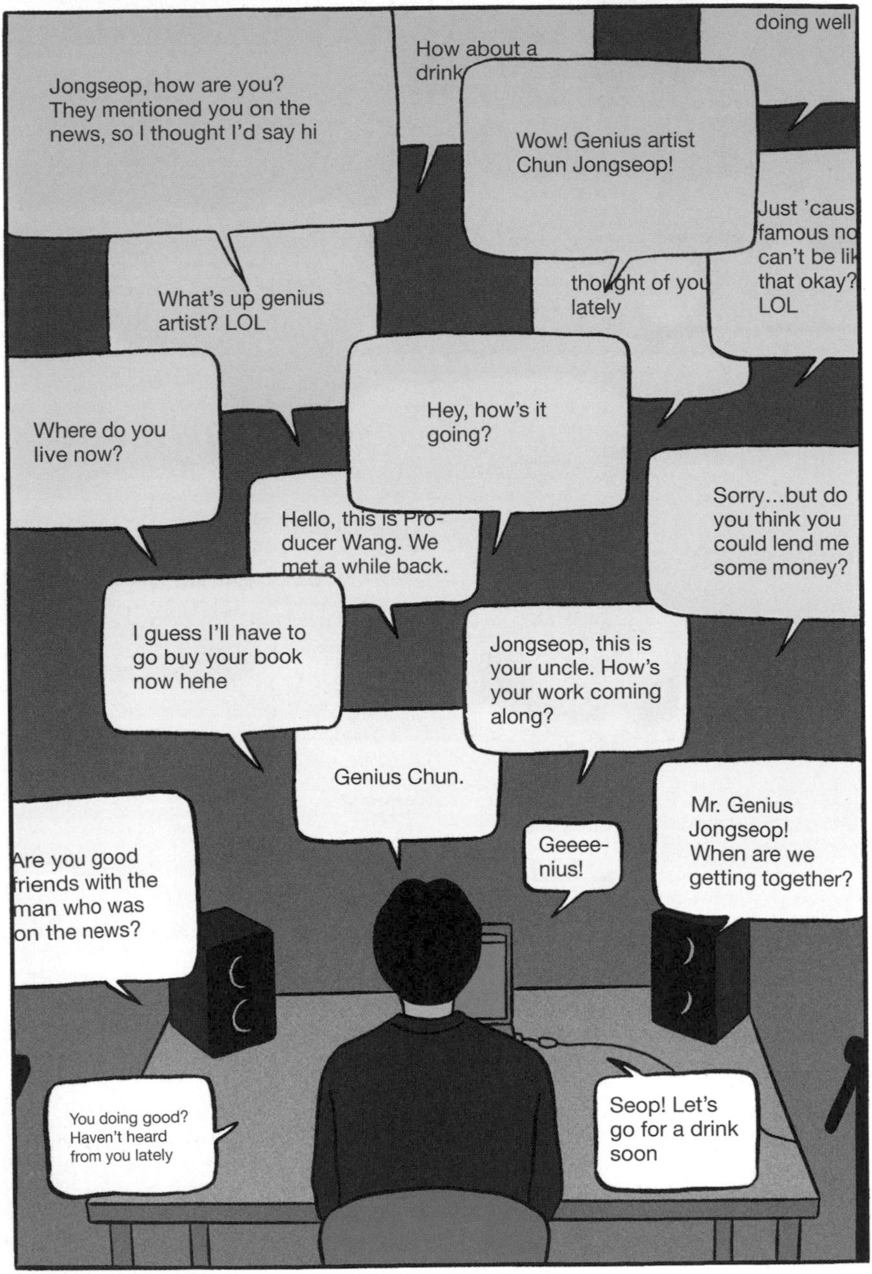
Jongseop, how are you? They mentioned you on the news, so I thought I'd say hi
How about a drink
doing well
Wow! Genius artist Chun Jongseop!
Just 'caus famous no can't be lik that okay? LOL
What's up genius artist? LOL
thought of you lately
Where do you live now?
Hey, how's it going?
Hello, this is Producer Wang. We met a while back.
Sorry…but do you think you could lend me some money?
I guess I'll have to go buy your book now hehe
Jongseop, this is your uncle. How's your work coming along?
Genius Chun.
Are you good friends with the man who was on the news?
Geeee-nius!
Mr. Genius Jongseop! When are we getting together?
You doing good? Haven't heard from you lately
Seop! Let's go for a drink soon

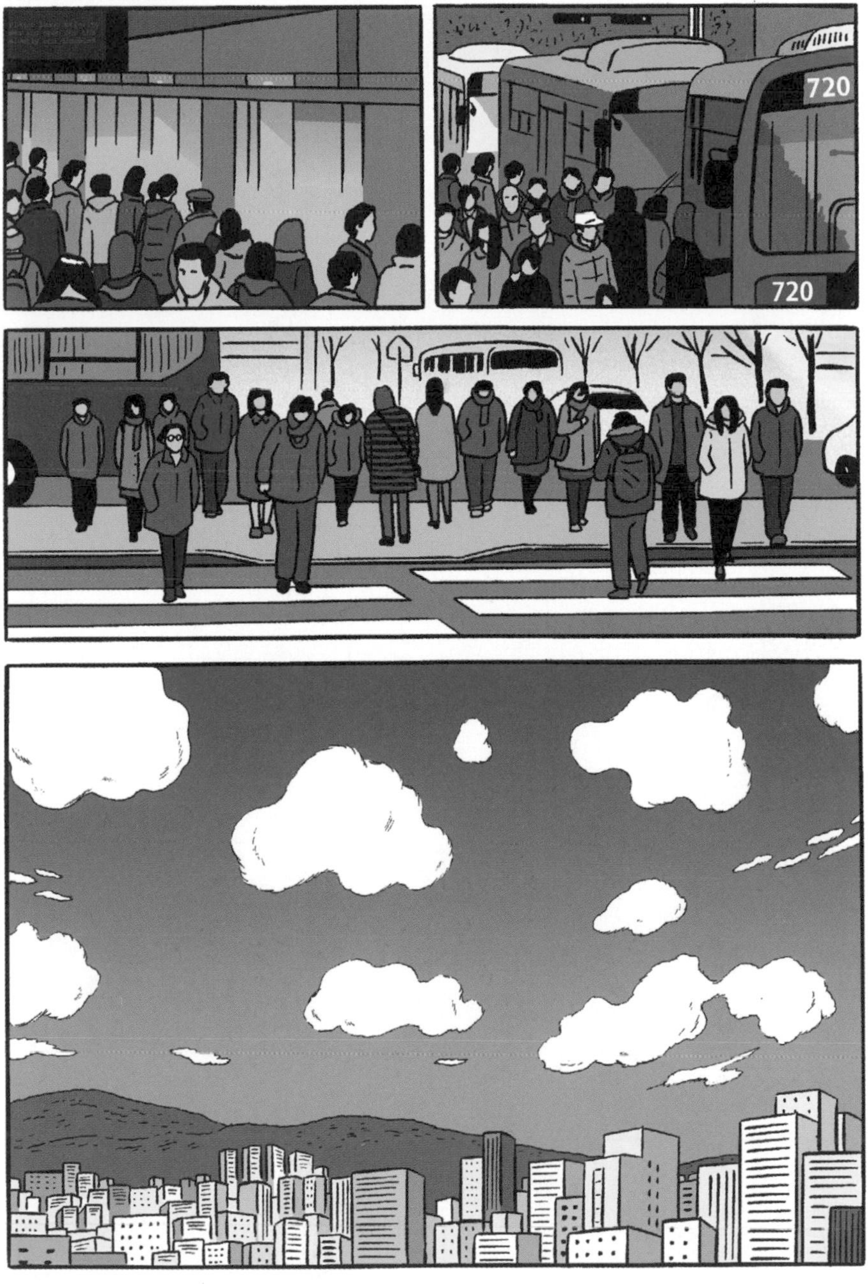
720
720

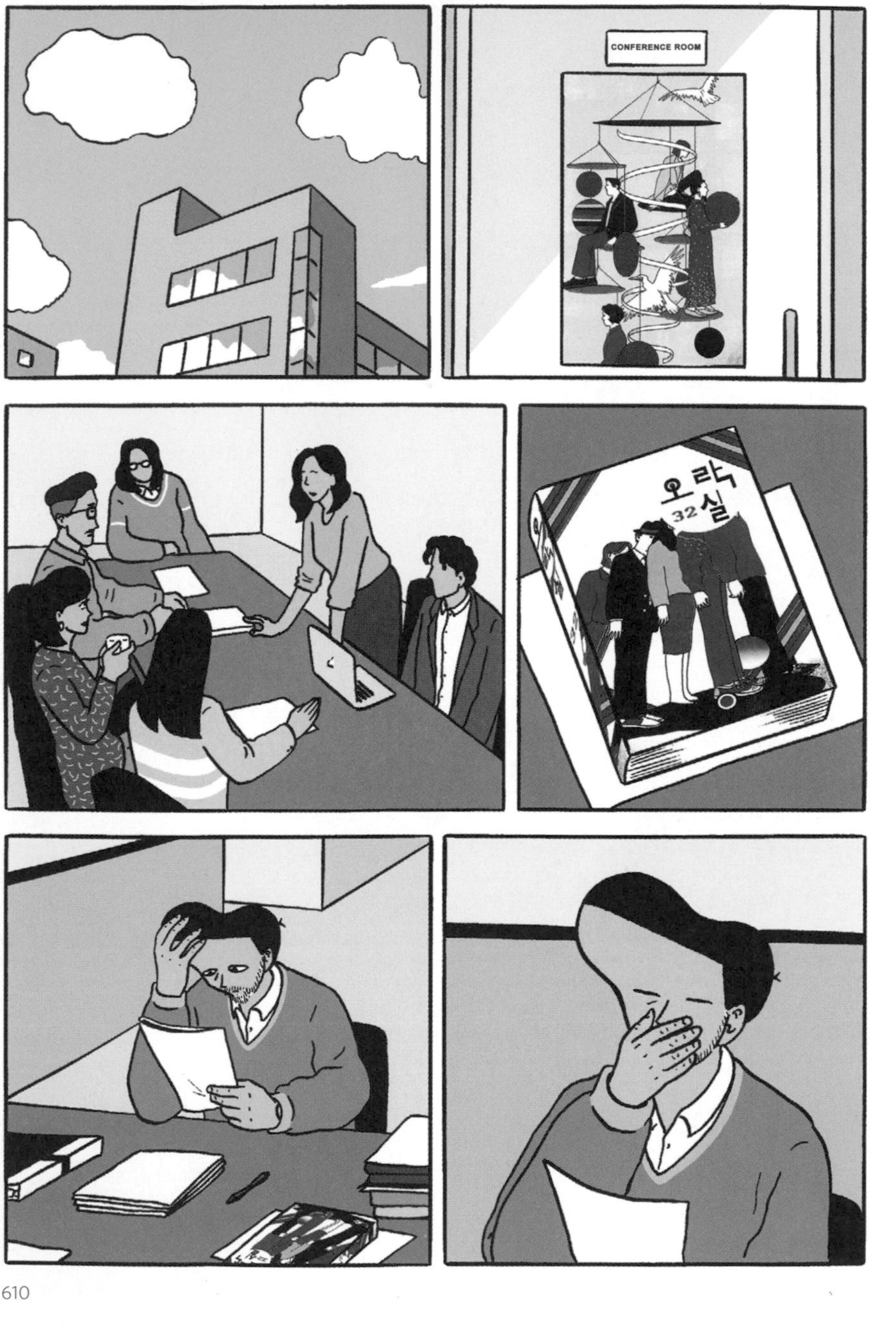
CONFERENCE ROOM
오락실
32

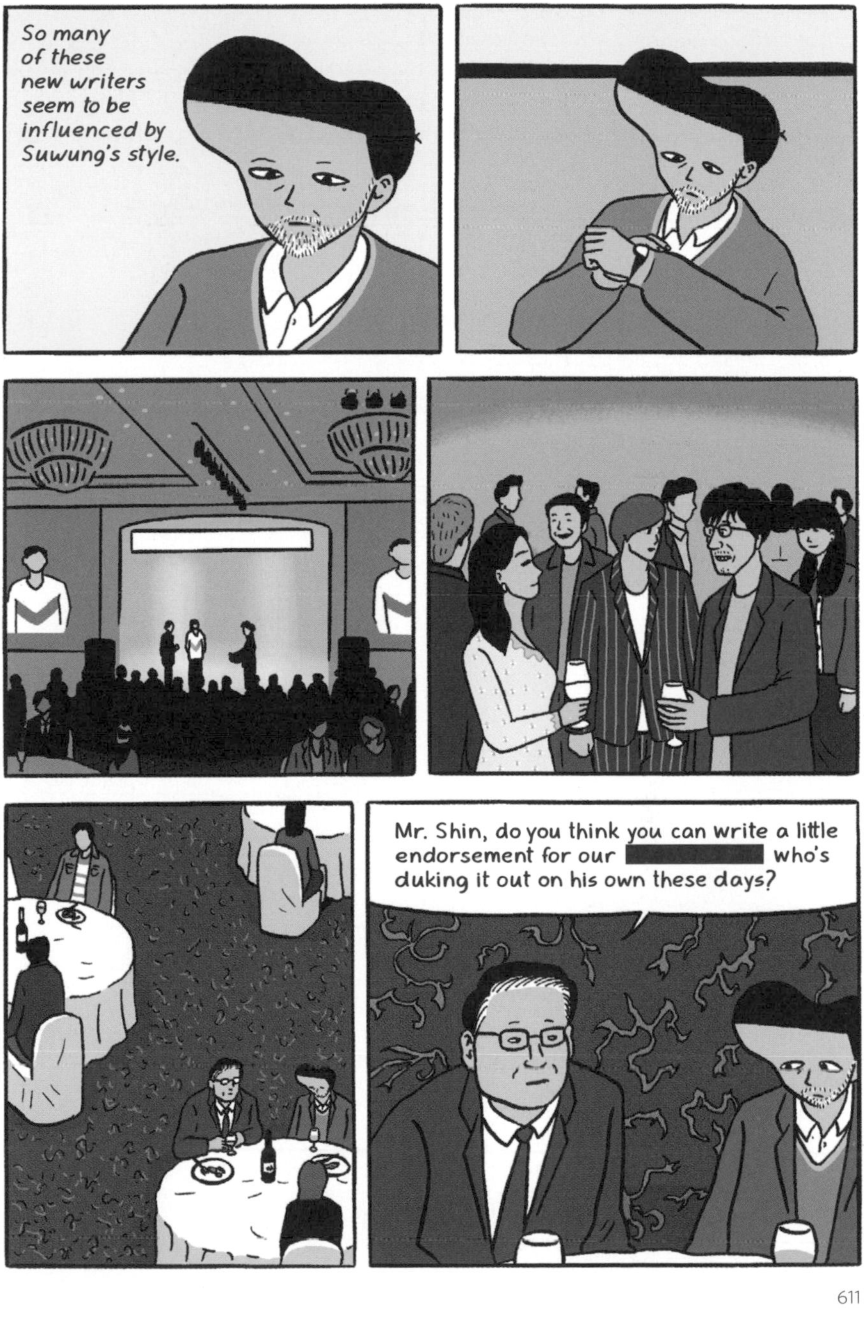
So many of these new writers seem to be influenced by Suwung's style.
Mr. Shin, do you think you can write a little endorsement for our [redacted] who's duking it out on his own these days?

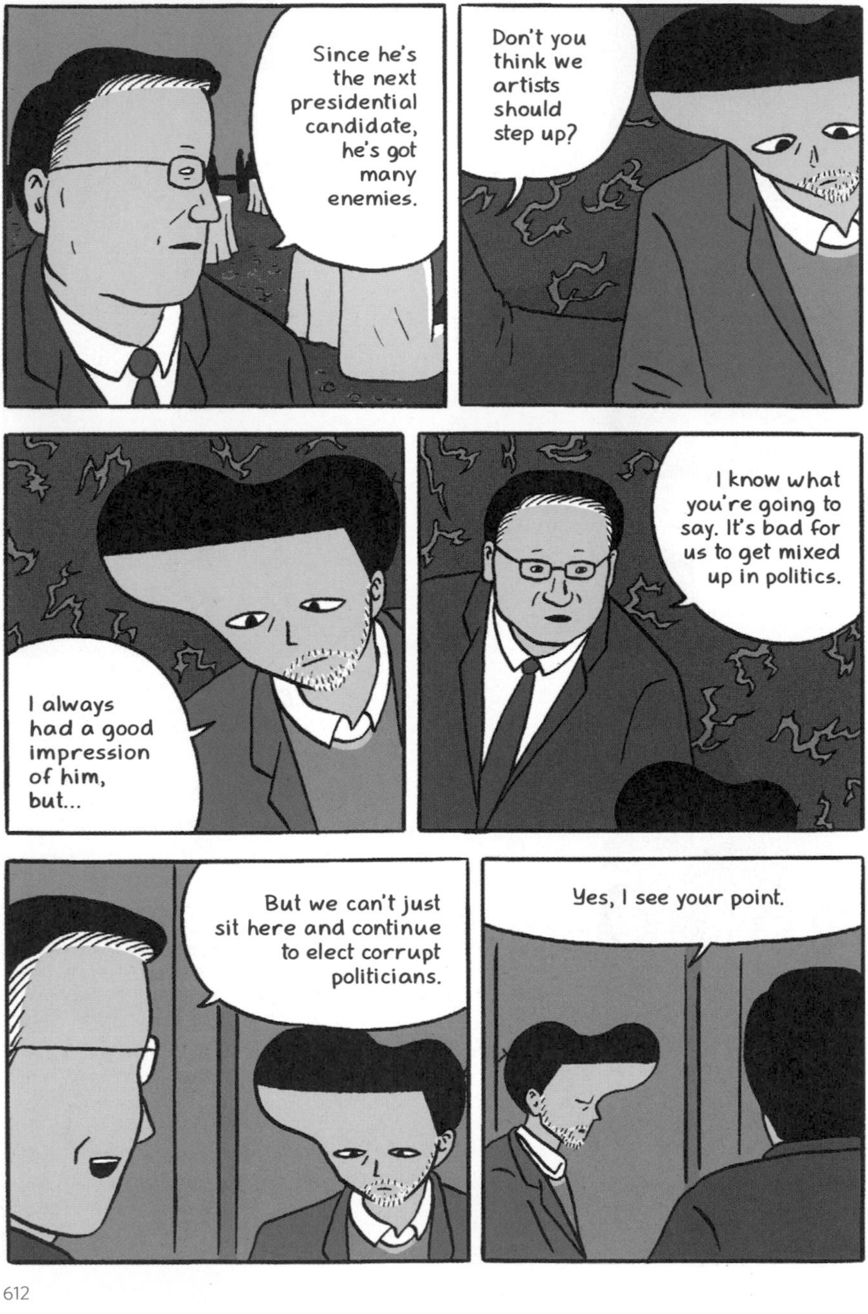

Since he's the next presidential candidate, he's got many enemies.
Don't you think we artists should step up?
I always had a good impression of him, but...
I know what you're going to say. It's bad for us to get mixed up in politics.
But we can't just sit here and continue to elect corrupt politicians.
Yes, I see your point.

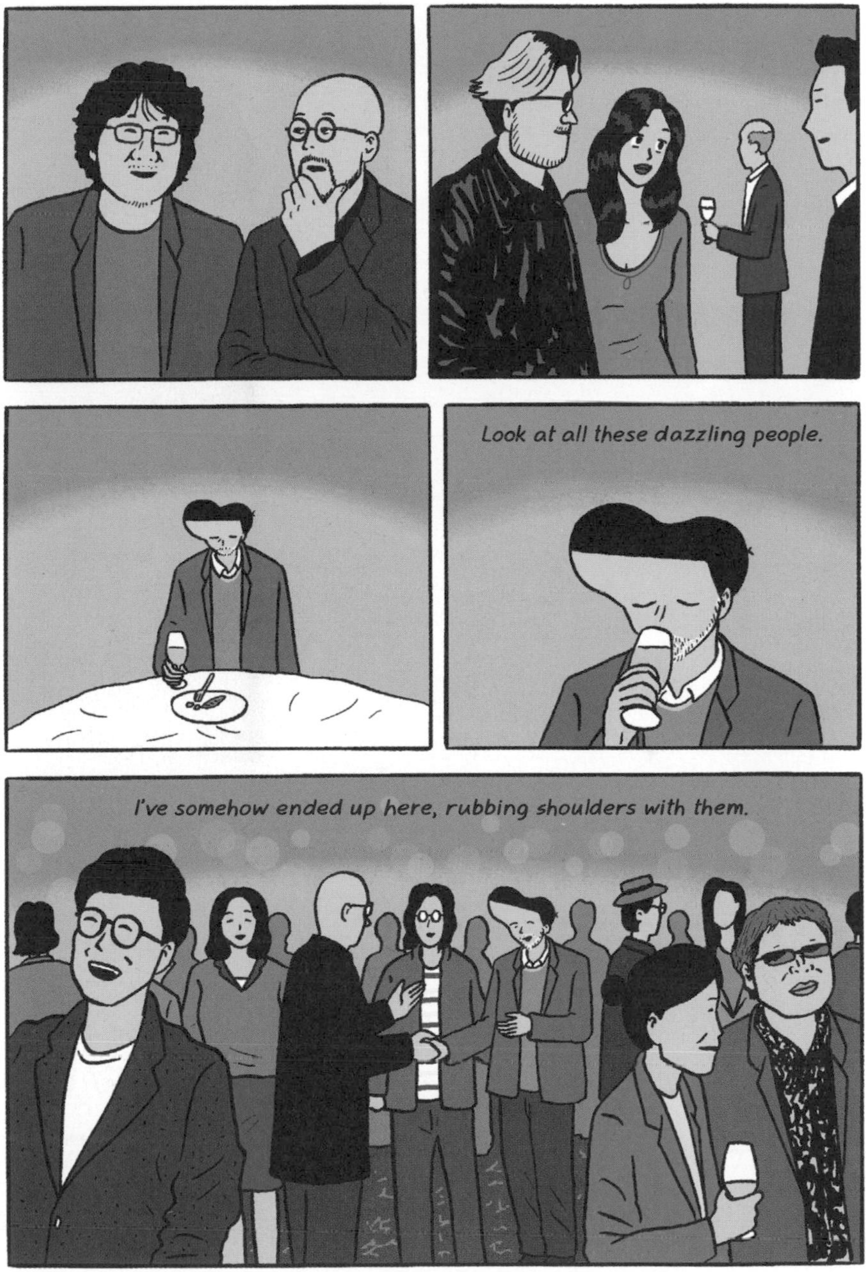
Look at all these dazzling people.
I've somehow ended up here, rubbing shoulders with them.

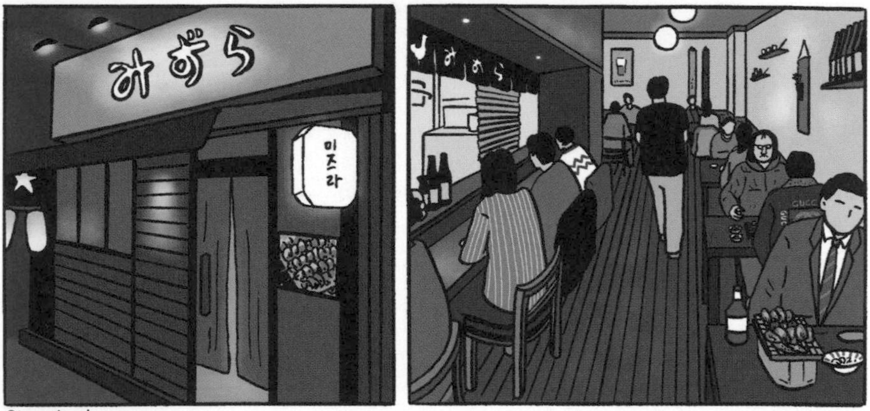
みずら
미즈라
Sign: Izakaya

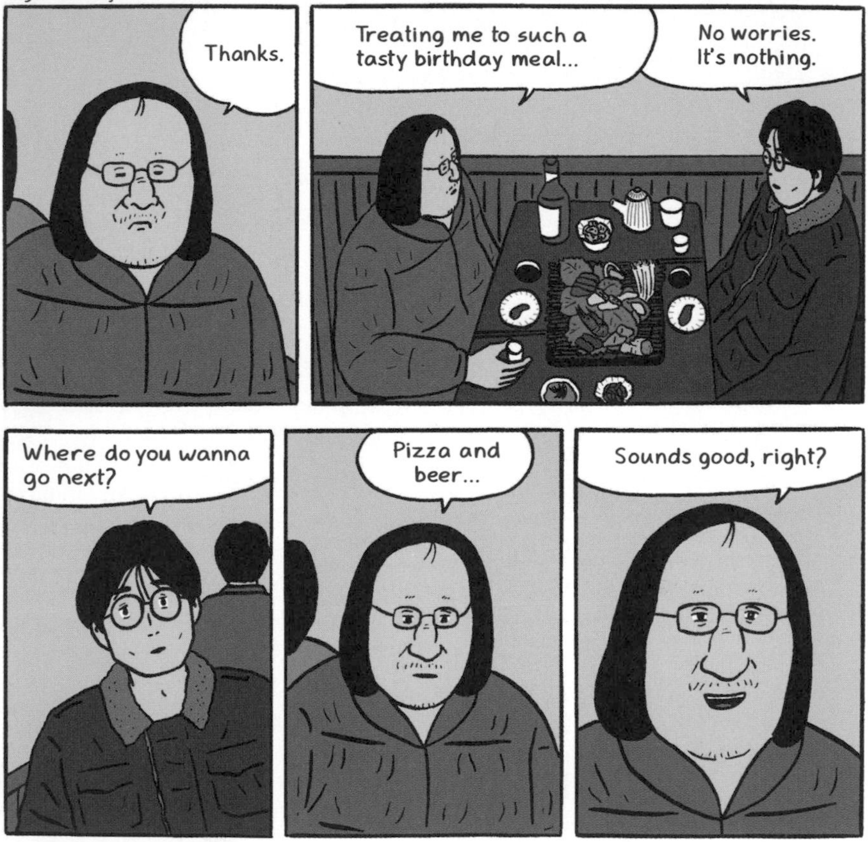
Thanks.
Treating me to such a tasty birthday meal...
No worries. It's nothing.
Where do you wanna go next?
Pizza and beer...
Sounds good, right?

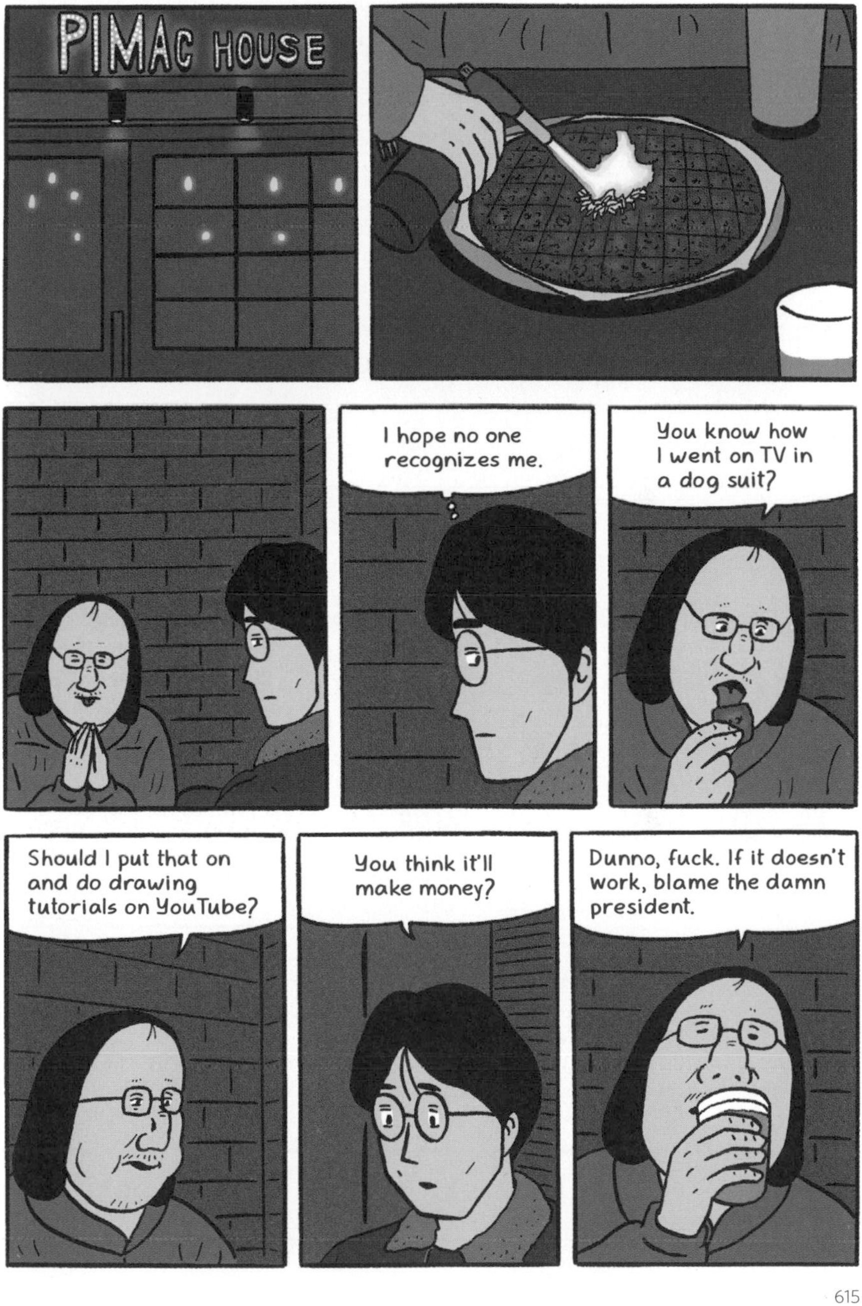
PIMAC HOUSE
I hope no one recognizes me.
You know how I went on TV in a dog suit?
Should I put that on and do drawing tutorials on YouTube?
You think it'll make money?
Dunno, fuck. If it doesn't work, blame the damn president.

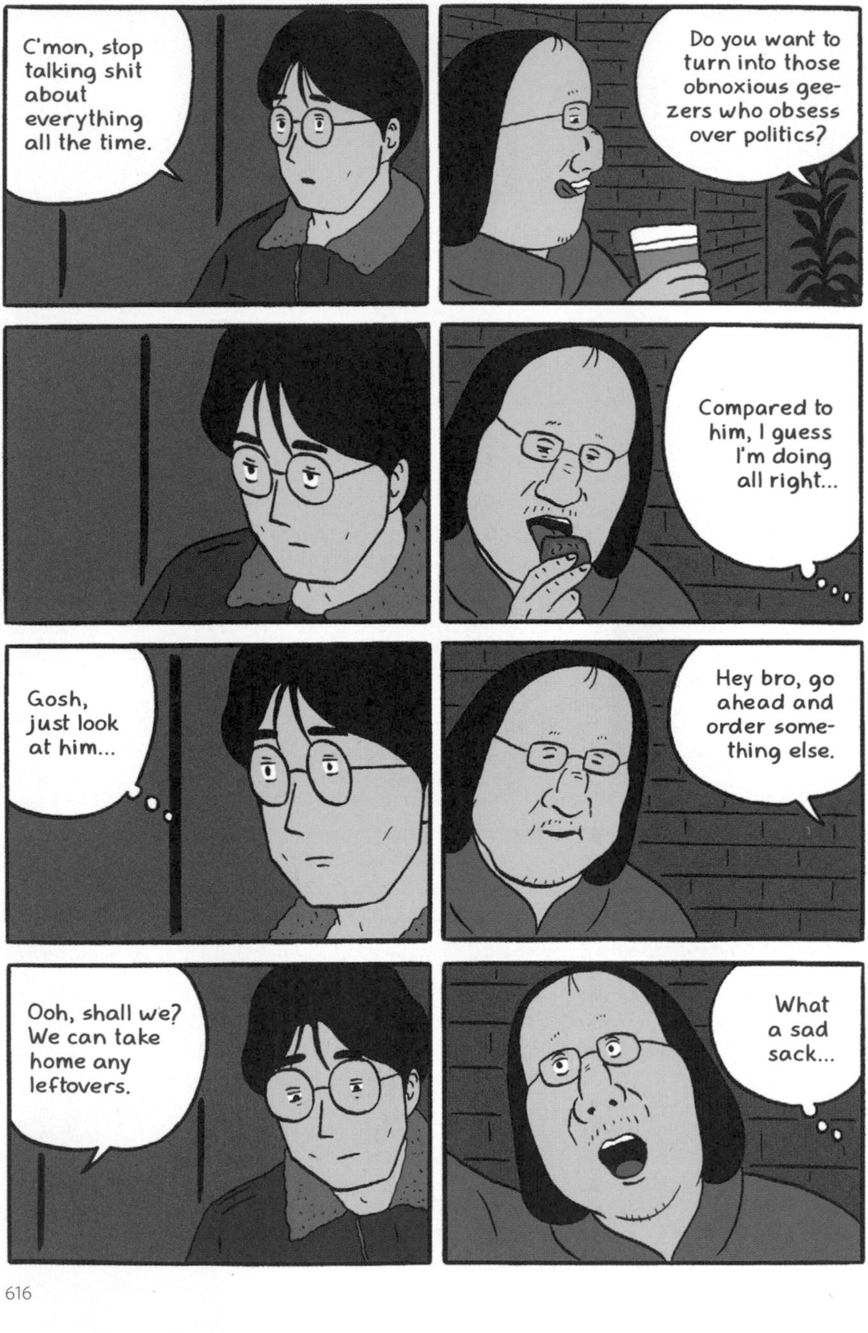
C'mon, stop talking shit about everything all the time.
Do you want to turn into those obnoxious geezers who obsess over politics?
Compared to him, I guess I'm doing all right...
Gosh, just look at him...
Hey bro, go ahead and order something else.
Ooh, shall we? We can take home any leftovers.
What a sad sack...

Sign: Kyobo Book Center

Excuse me...

Aren't you Shin Deuk-nyeong, the writer?

Ah, yes.

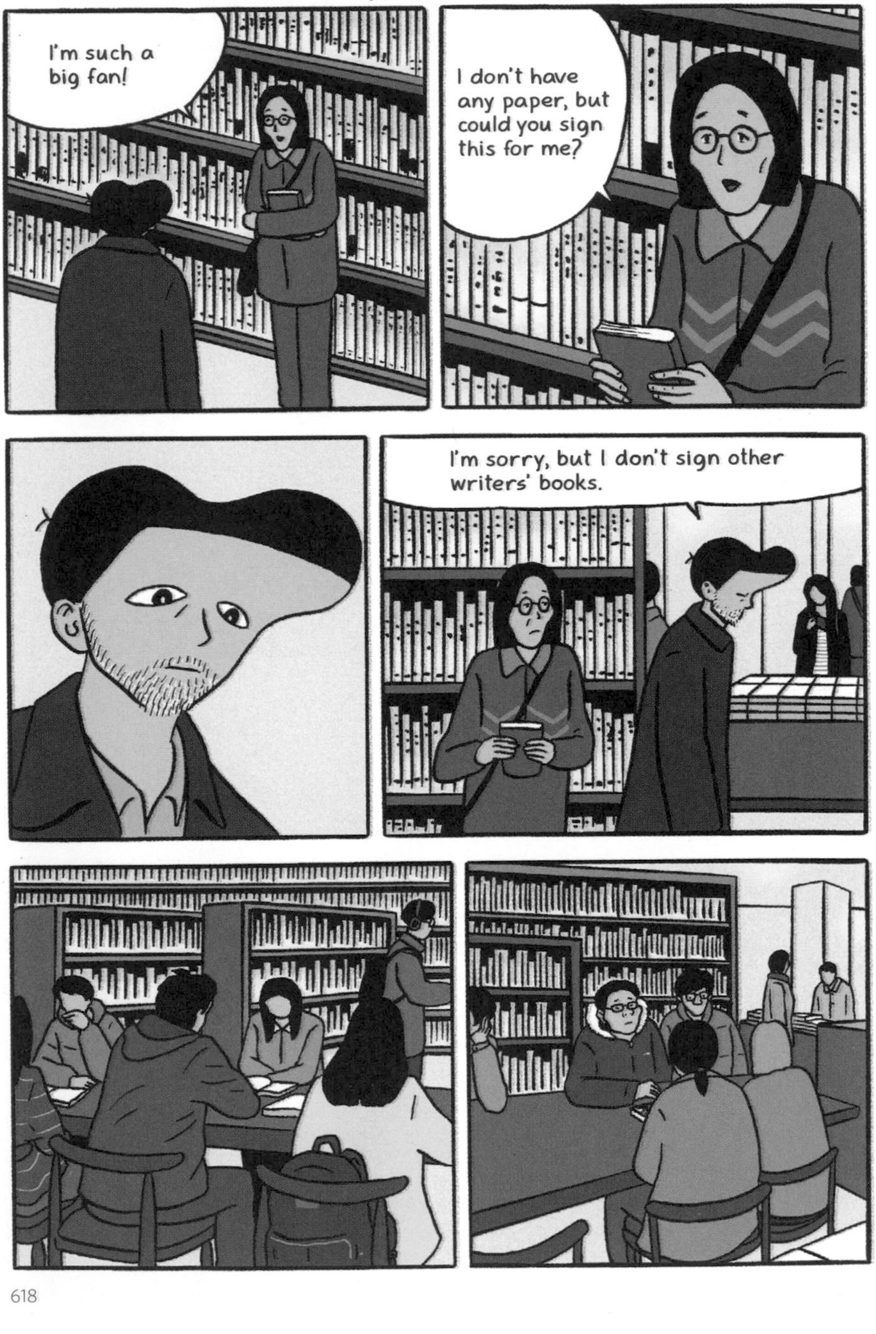
I'm such a big fan!
I don't have any paper, but could you sign this for me?
I'm sorry, but I don't sign other writers' books.

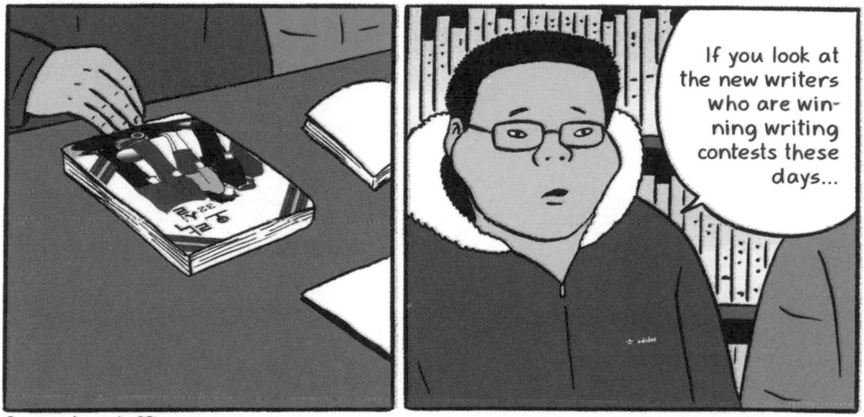
If you look at the new writers who are win-ning writing contests these days...

Cover: *Arcade* 32

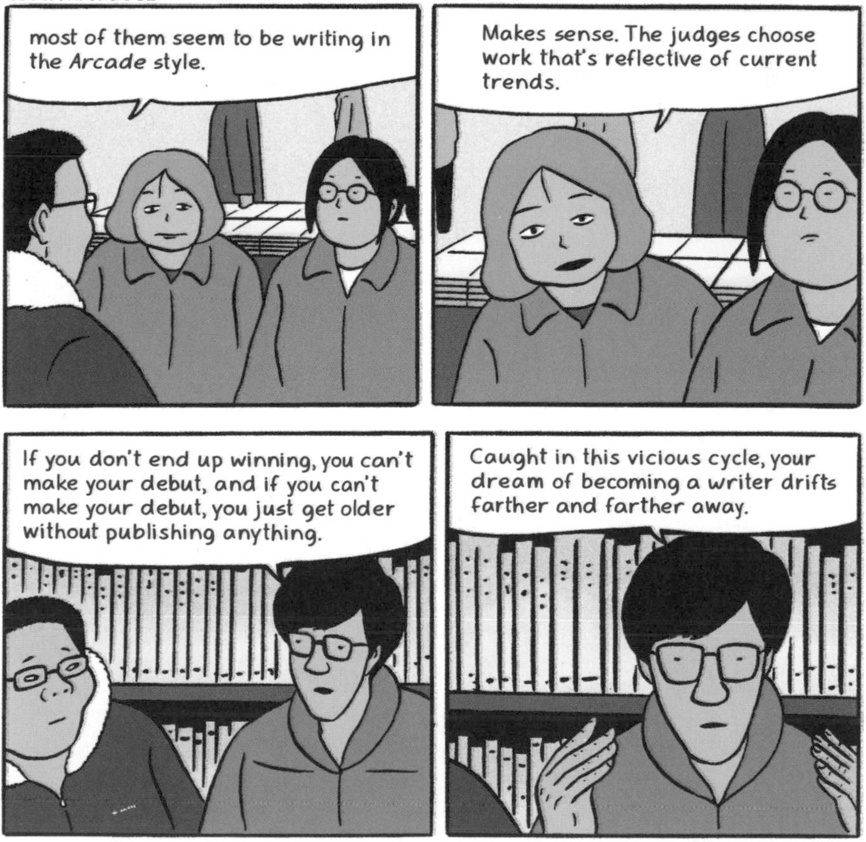
most of them seem to be writing in the *Arcade* style.
Makes sense. The judges choose work that's reflective of current trends.
If you don't end up winning, you can't make your debut, and if you can't make your debut, you just get older without publishing anything.
Caught in this vicious cycle, your dream of becoming a writer drifts farther and farther away.

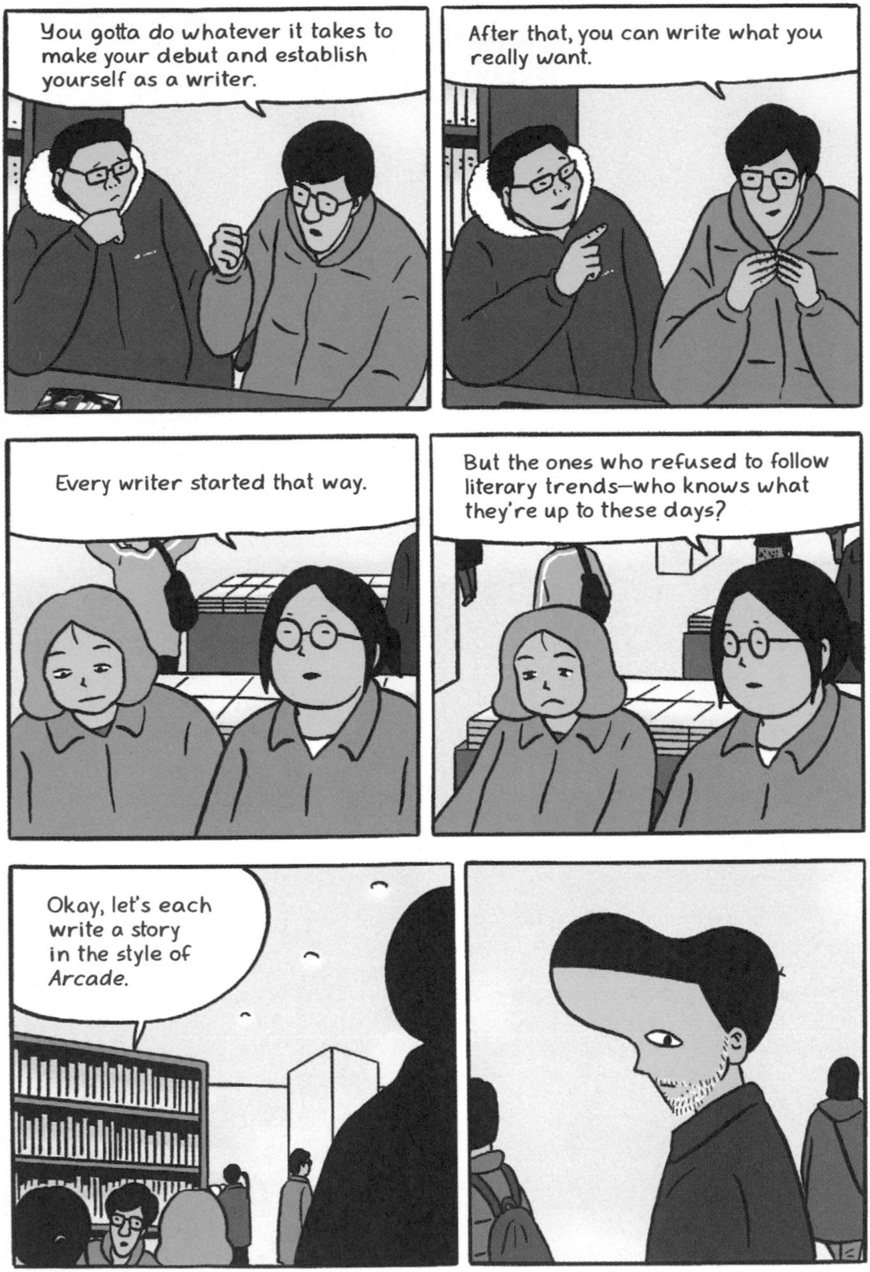
You gotta do whatever it takes to make your debut and establish yourself as a writer.
After that, you can write what you really want.
Every writer started that way.
But the ones who refused to follow literary trends—who knows what they're up to these days?
Okay, let's each write a story in the style of *Arcade*.

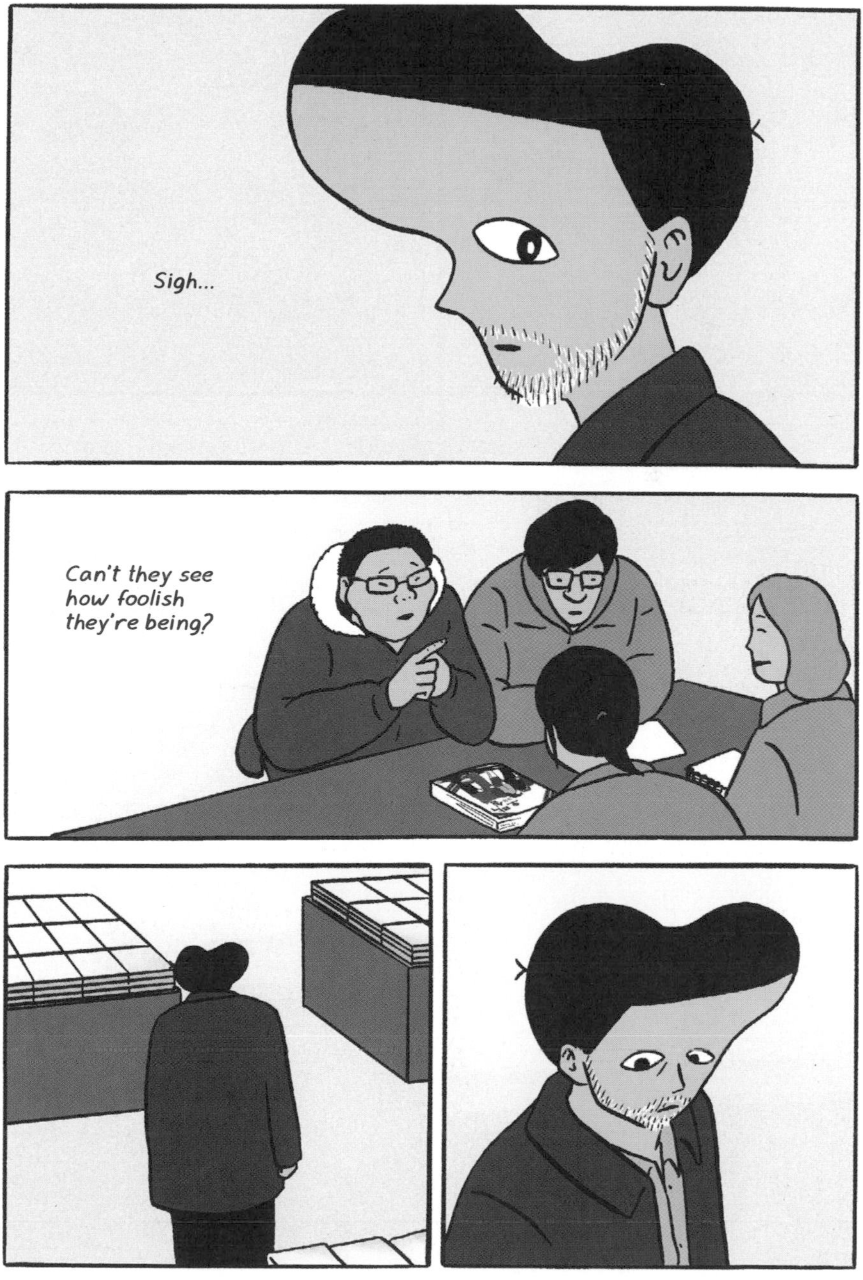
Sigh...
Can't they see how foolish they're being?

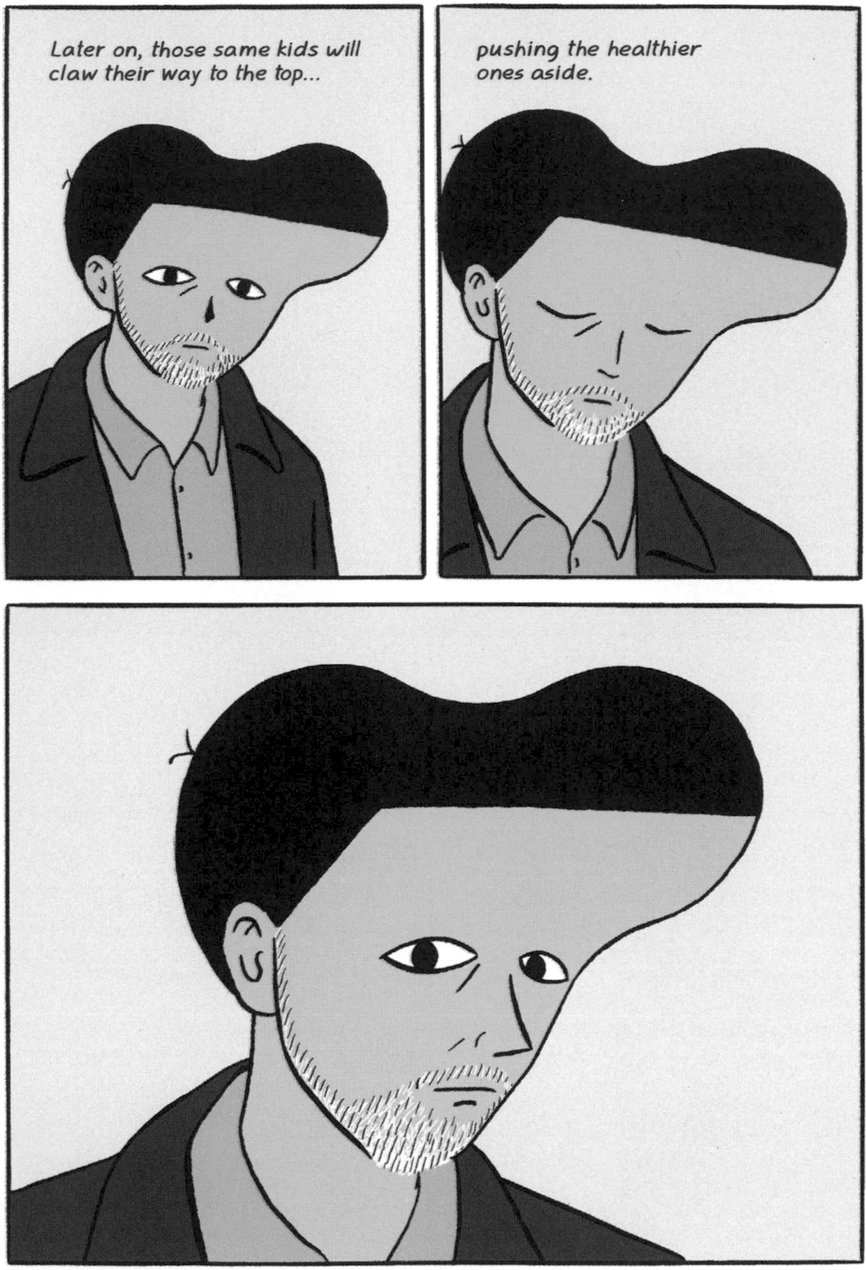
Later on, those same kids will claw their way to the top...
pushing the healthier ones aside.

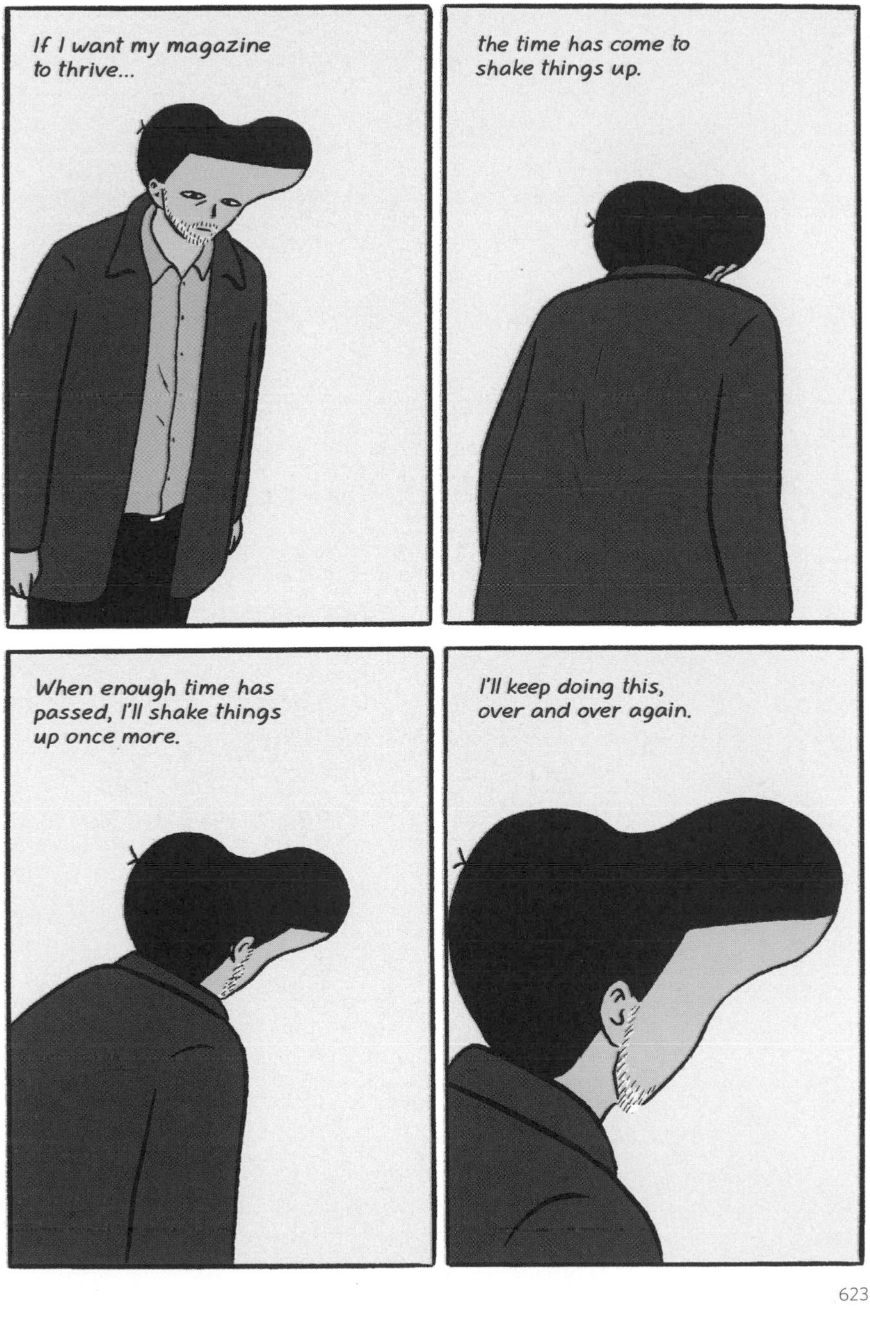
If I want my magazine to thrive...
the time has come to shake things up.
When enough time has passed, I'll shake things up once more.
I'll keep doing this, over and over again.

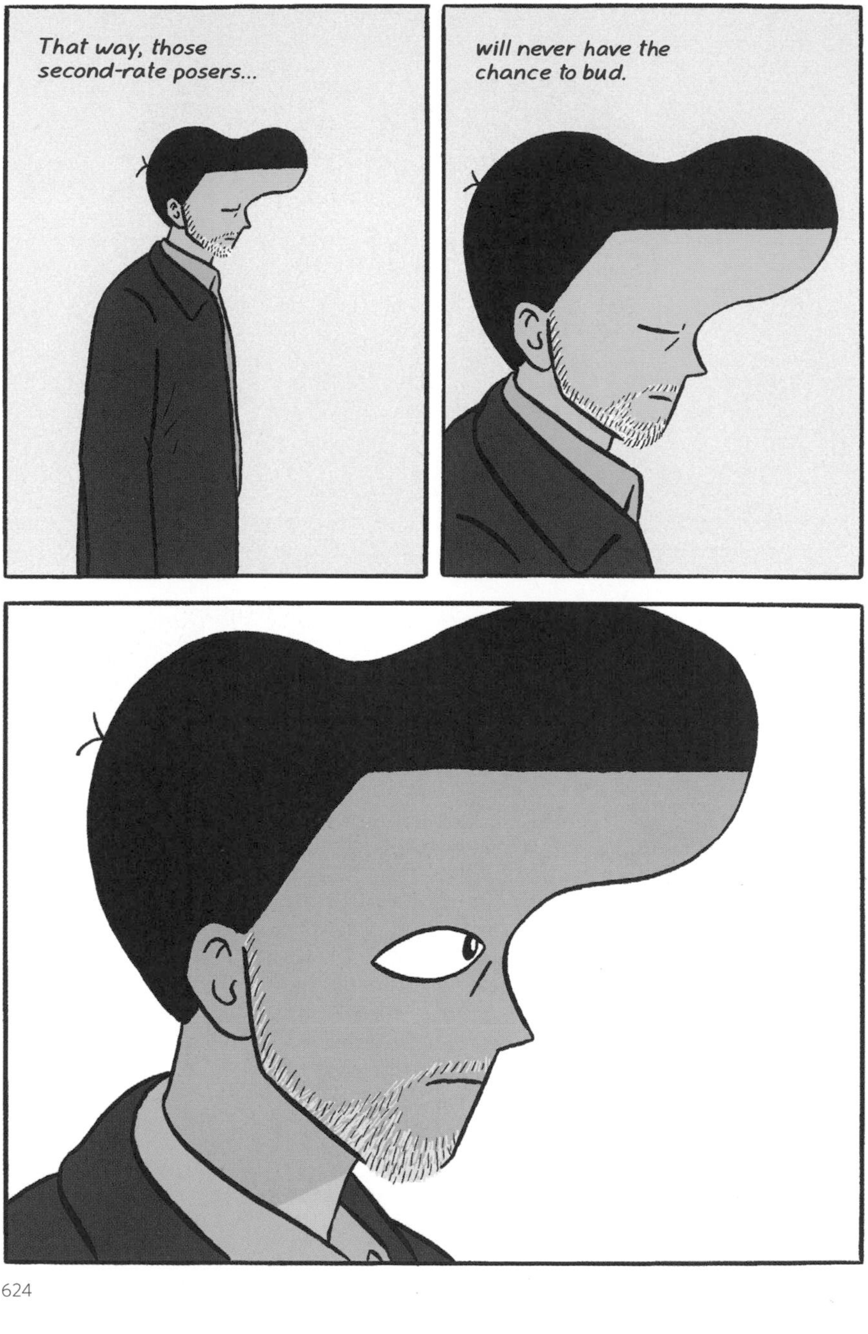
That way, those second-rate posers...
will never have the chance to bud.

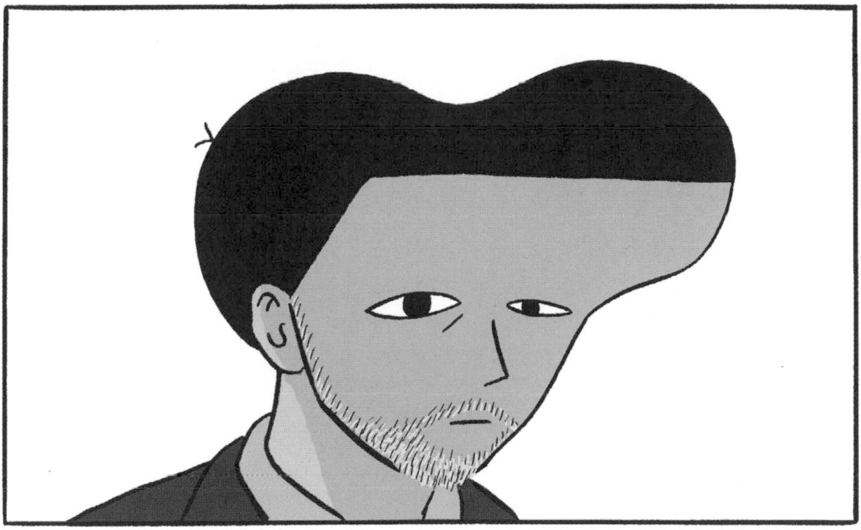
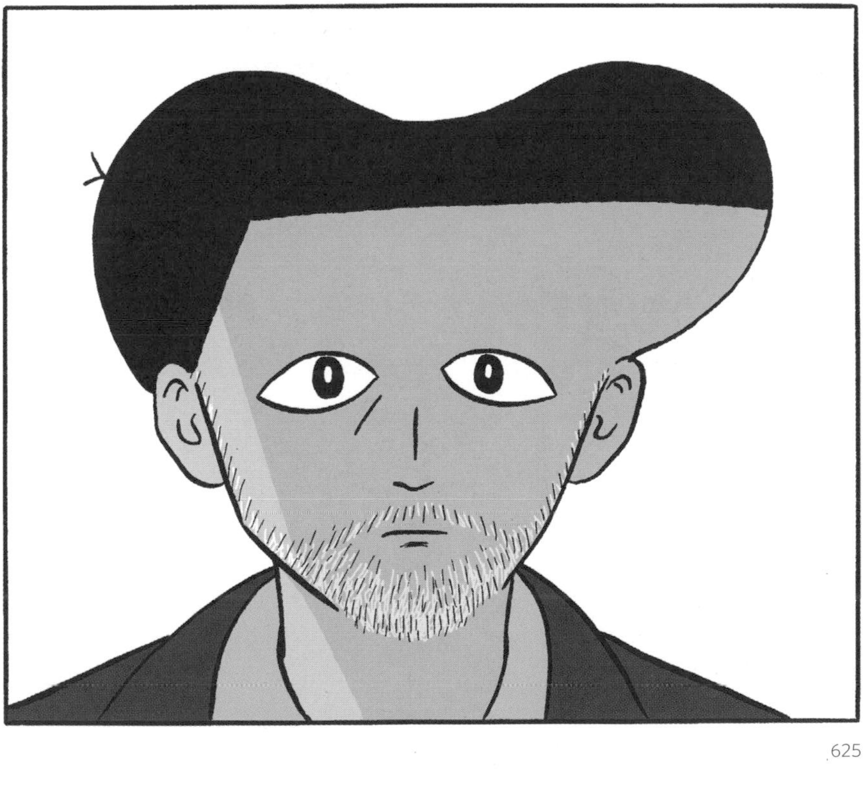

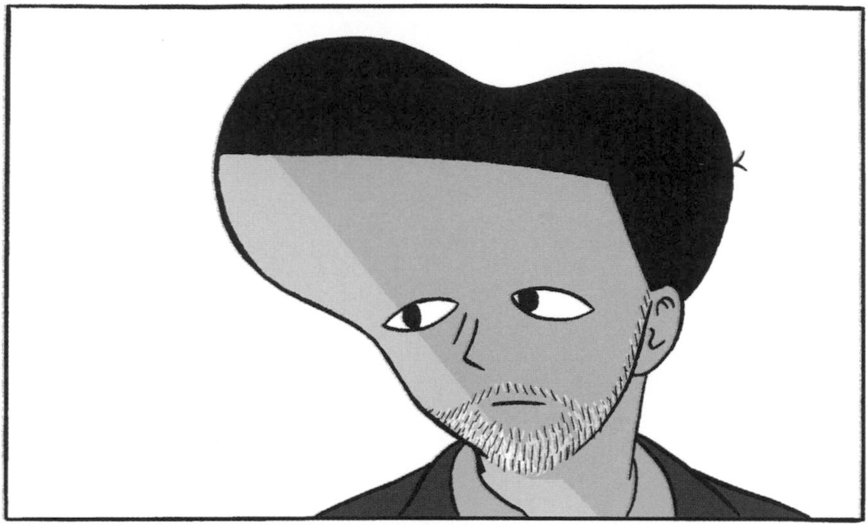

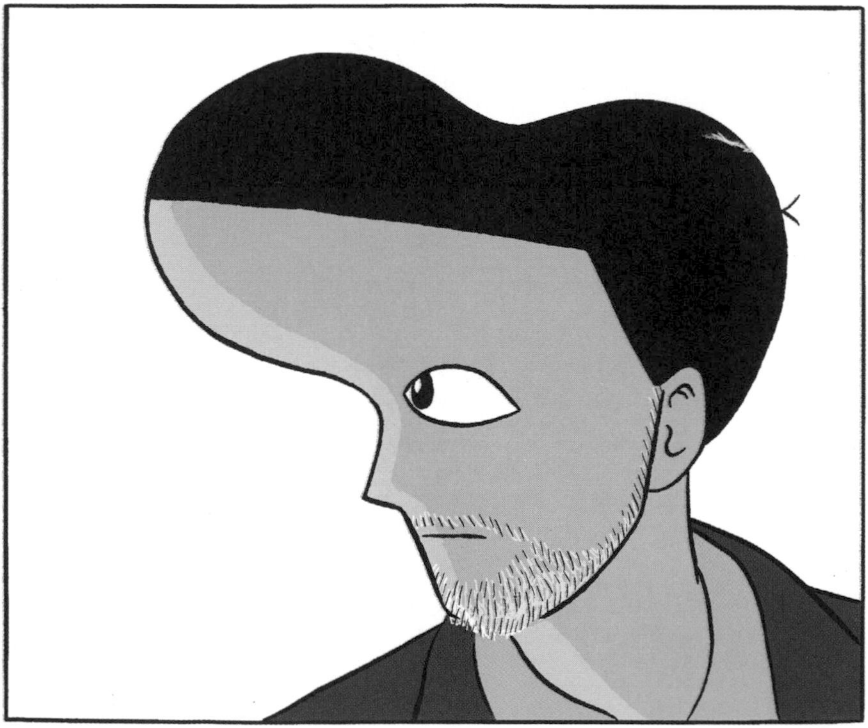